IMMIGRATION AND NATIONALITY LAWS OF THE UNITED STATES

SELECTED STATUTES, REGULATIONS AND FORMS

As Amended to May 15, 2020

Selected by

T. Alexander Aleinikoff
University Professor
Director, Zolberg Institute on Migration and Mobility
The New School

David A. Martin
Warner-Booker Distinguished Professor of International Law Emeritus
University of Virginia

Hiroshi Motomura
Susan Westerberg Prager Distinguished Professor of Law
University of California, Los Angeles, School of Law

Maryellen Fullerton
Suzanne J. and Norman Miles Professor of Law
Brooklyn Law School

Juliet P. Stumpf
Robert E. Jones Professor of Advocacy and Ethics
Lewis & Clark Law School

Pratheepan Gulasekaram
Professor of Law
Santa Clara University School of Law

WEST
ACADEMIC
PUBLISHING

The publisher is not engaged in rendering legal or other professional advice, and this publication is not a substitute for the advice of an attorney. If you require legal or other expert advice, you should seek the services of a competent attorney or other professional.

COPYRIGHT © 1982, 1985, 1987, 1990, 1992–1998 WEST PUBLISHING CO.
© West, a Thomson business, 1999–2008
© 2009–2012 Thomson Reuters
© 2014, 2016, 2018 LEG, Inc. d/b/a West Academic
© 2020 LEG, Inc. d/b/a West Academic
    444 Cedar Street, Suite 700
    St. Paul, MN 55101
    1-877-888-1330

Printed in the United States of America

ISBN: 978-1-68467-969-0

[No claim of copyright is made for official U.S. government statutes, rules or regulations.]

TABLE OF CONTENTS

Page

IV OTHER FEDERAL MATERIALS

DEFERRED ACTION

ENFORCEMENT AND REMOVAL

REFUGEES AND ASYLUM

TABLE OF CONTENTS

Page

INADMISSIBILITY

SUSPENSION OF ENTRY

V. TREATIES AND RELATED MATERIALS

VI. SELECTED IMMIGRATION FORMS

BASIC DOCUMENTS

TABLE OF CONTENTS

TABLE OF
IMMIGRATION AND NATIONALITY ACT SECTION
CLASSIFICATION TO U.S.C.A.

TABLE OF IMMIGRATION AND NATIONALITY ACT
SECTION CLASSIFICATION TO U.S.C.A.

TABLE OF IMMIGRATION AND NATIONALITY ACT
SECTION CLASSIFICATION TO U.S.C.A.

TABLE OF IMMIGRATION AND NATIONALITY ACT
SECTION CLASSIFICATION TO U.S.C.A.

IMMIGRATION AND NATIONALITY LAWS OF THE UNITED STATES

SELECTED STATUTES, REGULATIONS AND FORMS

I. IMMIGRATION AND NATIONALITY ACT [INA § ___]

TITLE I—GENERAL PROVISIONS

TITLE II—IMMIGRATION

Chapter I—Selection System

CHAPTER III—ISSUANCE OF ENTRY DOCUMENTS

IMMIGRATION AND NATIONALITY ACT

IMMIGRATION AND NATIONALITY ACT

TITLE III—NATIONALITY AND NATURALIZATION

CHAPTER I—NATIONALITY AT BIRTH AND COLLECTIVE NATURALIZATION

CHAPTER III—LOSS OF NATIONALITY

CHAPTER IV—MISCELLANEOUS

TITLE IV—MISCELLANEOUS AND REFUGEE ASSISTANCE

TITLE I

GENERAL PROVISIONS

§ 101. Definitions [8 U.S.C.A. § 1101]

(a) As used in this Act—

(1) The term "administrator" means the official designated by the Secretary of State pursuant to section 104(b) of this Act [8 U.S.C.A. § 1104(b)]. INA § 101(a)

(2) The term "advocates" includes, but is not limited to, advises, recommends, furthers by overt act, and admits belief in.

(3) The term "alien" means any person not a citizen or national of the United States.

(4) The term "application for admission" has reference to the application for admission into the United States and not to the application for the issuance of an immigrant or nonimmigrant visa.

(5) The term "Attorney General" means the Attorney General of the United States.

(6) The term "border crossing identification card" means a document of identity bearing that designation issued to an alien who is lawfully admitted for permanent residence, or to an alien who is a resident in foreign contiguous territory, by a consular officer or an immigration officer for the purpose of crossing over the borders between the United States and foreign contiguous territory in accordance with such conditions for its issuance and use as may be prescribed by regulations. Such regulations shall provide that **(A)** each such document include a biometric identifier (such as the fingerprint or handprint of the alien) that is machine readable and **(B)** an alien presenting a border crossing identification card is not permitted to cross over the border into the United States unless the biometric identifier contained on the card matches the appropriate biometric characteristic of the alien.

(7) The term "clerk of court" means a clerk of a naturalization court.

(8) The terms "Commissioner" and "Deputy Commissioner" mean the Commissioner of Immigration and Naturalization and a Deputy Commissioner of Immigration and Naturalization, respectively.

(9) The term "consular officer" means any consular, diplomatic, or other officer or employee of the United States designated under regulations prescribed under authority contained in this chapter, for the purpose of issuing immigrant or nonimmigrant visas or, when used in title III [8 U.S.C.A. § 1401 et seq.], for the purpose of adjudicating nationality.

(10) The term "crewman" means a person serving in any capacity on board a vessel or aircraft.

(11) The term "diplomatic visa" means a nonimmigrant visa bearing that title and issued to a nonimmigrant in accordance with such regulations as the Secretary of State may prescribe.

(12) The term "doctrine" includes, but is not limited to, policies, practices, purposes, aims, or procedures.

(13)(A) The terms "admission" and "admitted" mean, with respect to an alien, the lawful entry of the alien into the United States after inspection and authorization by an immigration officer.

(B) An alien who is paroled under section 212(d)(5) [8 U.S.C.A. § 1182(d)(5)] or permitted to land temporarily as an alien crewman shall not be considered to have been admitted.

(C) An alien lawfully admitted for permanent residence in the United States shall not be regarded as seeking an admission into the United States for purposes of the immigration laws unless the alien—

(i) has abandoned or relinquished that status,

(ii) has been absent from the United States for a continuous period in excess of 180 days,

(iii) has engaged in illegal activity after having departed the United States,

(iv) has departed from the United States while under legal process seeking removal of the alien from the United States, including removal proceedings under this Act and extradition proceedings,

(v) has committed an offense identified in section 212(a)(2) [8 U.S.C.A. § 1182(a)(2)], unless since such offense the alien has been granted relief under section 212(h) [8 U.S.C.A. § 1182(h)] or 240A(a) [8 U.S.C.A. § 1229b(a)], or

(vi) is attempting to enter at a time or place other than as designated by immigration officers or has not been admitted to the United States after inspection and authorization by an immigration officer.

(14) The term "foreign state" includes outlying possessions of a foreign state, but self-governing dominions or territories under mandate or trusteeship shall be regarded as separate foreign states.

(15) The term "immigrant" means every alien except an alien who is within one of the following classes of nonimmigrant aliens—

(A)(i) an ambassador, public minister, or career diplomatic or consular officer who has been accredited by a foreign government recognized de jure by the United States and who is accepted by the President or by the Secretary of State, and the members of the alien's immediate family;

(ii) upon a basis of reciprocity, other officials and employees who have been accredited by a foreign government recognized de jure by the United States, who are accepted by the Secretary of State, and the members of their immediate families; and

(iii) upon a basis of reciprocity, attendants, servants, personal employees, and members of their immediate families, of the officials and employees who have a nonimmigrant status under (i) and (ii) above;

(B) an alien (other than one coming for the purpose of study or of performing skilled or unskilled labor or as a representative of foreign press, radio, film, or other foreign information media coming to engage in such vocation) having a residence in a foreign country which he has no intention of abandoning and who is visiting the United States temporarily for business or temporarily for pleasure;

(C) an alien in immediate and continuous transit through the United States, or an alien who qualifies as a person entitled to pass in transit to and from the United Nations Headquarters District and foreign countries, under the provisions of paragraphs (3), (4), and (5) of section 11 of the Headquarters Agreement with the United Nations (61 Stat. 758);

(D)(i) an alien crewman serving in good faith as such in a capacity required for normal operation and service on board a vessel, as defined in section 258(a) [8 U.S.C.A. § 1288(a)] (other than a fishing vessel having its home port or an operating base in the United States), or aircraft, who intends to land temporarily and solely in pursuit of his calling as a crewman and to depart from the United States with the vessel or aircraft on which he arrived or some other vessel or aircraft;

(ii) an alien crewman serving in good faith as such in any capacity required for normal operations and service aboard a fishing vessel having its home port or an operating base in the United States who intends to land temporarily in Guam or the Commonwealth of the Northern Mariana Islands and solely in pursuit of his calling as a crewman and to depart from Guam or the Commonwealth of the Northern Mariana Islands with the vessel on which he arrived;

(E) an alien entitled to enter the United States under and in pursuance of the provisions of a treaty of commerce and navigation between the United States and the foreign state of which he is a national, and the spouse and children of any such alien if accompanying or following to join him; **(i)** solely to carry on substantial trade, including trade in services or trade in technology, principally between the United States and the foreign state of which he is a national; **(ii)** solely to develop and direct the operations of an enterprise in which he has invested, or of an enterprise in which he is actively in the process of investing, a substantial amount of capital; or **(iii)** solely to perform services in a specialty occupation in the United States if the alien is a national of the Commonwealth of Australia and with respect to whom the Secretary of Labor determines and certifies to the Secretary of Homeland Security and the Secretary of State that the intending employer has filed with the Secretary of Labor an attestation under section 212(t)(1) [8 U.S.C.A. § 1182(t)(1)];

(F)(i) an alien having a residence in a foreign country which he has no intention of abandoning, who is a bona fide student qualified to pursue a full course of study and who seeks to enter the United States temporarily and solely for the purpose of pursuing such a course of study consistent with section 214(*l*) [8 U.S.C.A. § 1184(*l*)] at an established college, university, seminary, conservatory, academic high school, elementary school, or other academic institution or in an accredited language training program in the United States, particularly designated by him and approved by the Attorney General after consultation with the Secretary of Education, which institution or place of study shall have agreed to report to the Attorney General the termination of attendance of each nonimmigrant student, and if any such institution of learning or place of study fails to make reports promptly the approval shall be withdrawn, **(ii)** the alien spouse and minor children of any alien described in clause (i) if accompanying or following to join such an alien, and **(iii)** an alien who is a national of Canada or Mexico, who maintains actual residence and place of abode in the country of nationality, who is described in clause (i) except that the alien's qualifications for and actual course of study may be full or part-time, and who commutes to the United States institution or place of study from Canada or Mexico;

(G)(i) a designated principal resident representative of a foreign government recognized de jure by the United States, which foreign government is a member of an international organization entitled to enjoy privileges, exemptions, and immunities as an international organization under the International Organizations Immunities Act (59 Stat. 669), accredited resident members of the staff of such representatives, and members of his or their immediate family;

(ii) other accredited representatives of such a foreign government to such international organizations, and the members of their immediate families;

(iii) an alien able to qualify under (i) or (ii) above except for the fact that the government of which such alien is an accredited representative is not recognized de jure by the United States, or that the government of which he is an accredited representative is not a member of such international organization; and the members of his immediate family;

(iv) officers, or employees of such international organizations, and the members of their immediate families;

(v) attendants, servants, and personal employees of any such representative, officer, or employee, and the members of the immediate families of such attendants, servants, and personal employees;

(H) an alien

(i)(a) Repealed. Pub.L. 106–95, § 2(c), Nov. 12, 1999, 113 Stat. 1316.

(b) subject to section 212(j)(2) [8 U.S.C.A. § 1182(j)(2)], who is coming temporarily to the United States to perform services (other than services described in subclause (a) during the period in which such subclause applies and other than services described in subclause (ii)(a) or in subparagraph (O) or (P)) in a specialty occupation described in section 214(i)(1) [8 U.S.C.A. § 1184(i)(1)] or as a fashion model, who meets the requirements for the occupation specified in section 214(i)(2) [8 U.S.C.A. § 1184(i)(2)] or, in the case of a fashion model, is of distinguished merit and ability, and with respect to whom the Secretary of Labor determines and certifies to the Attorney General that the intending employer has filed with the Secretary an application under section 212(n)(1) [8 U.S.C.A. § 1182(n)(1)], or (b1) who is entitled to enter the United States under and in pursuance of the provisions of an agreement listed in section 214(g)(8)(A) [8 U.S.C.A. § 1184(g)(8)(A)], who is engaged in a specialty occupation described in section 214(i)(3) [8 U.S.C.A. § 1184(i)(3)], and with respect to whom the Secretary of Labor determines and certifies to the Secretary of Homeland Security and the Secretary of State that the intending employer has filed with the Secretary of Labor an attestation under section 212(t)(1) [8 U.S.C.A. § 1182(t)(1)], or

(c) who is coming temporarily to the United States to perform services as a registered nurse, who meets the qualifications described in section 212(m)(1) [8 U.S.C.A. § 1182(m)(1)], and with respect to whom the Secretary of Labor determines and certifies to the Attorney General that an unexpired attestation is on file and in effect under section 212(m)(2) [8 U.S.C.A. § 1182(m)(2)] for the facility (as defined in section 212(m)(6) [8 U.S.C.A. § 1182(m)(6)]) for which the alien will perform the services; or

(ii)(a) having a residence in a foreign country which he has no intention of abandoning who is coming temporarily to the United States to perform agricultural labor or services, as defined by the Secretary of Labor in regulations and including agricultural labor defined in section 3121(g) of the Internal Revenue Code of 1986, agriculture as defined in section 3(f) of the Fair Labor Standards Act of 1938 (29 U.S.C. § 203(f)), and the pressing of apples for cider on a farm, of a temporary or seasonal nature, or

(b) having a residence in a foreign country which he has no intention of abandoning who is coming temporarily to the United States to perform other temporary service or labor if unemployed persons capable of performing such service or labor cannot be found in this country, but this clause shall not apply to graduates of medical schools coming to the United States to perform services as members of the medical profession; or

(iii) having a residence in a foreign country which he has no intention of abandoning who is coming temporarily to the United States as a trainee, other than to receive graduate medical education or training, in a training program that is not designed primarily to provide productive employment; and the alien spouse and minor children of any such alien specified in this paragraph if accompanying him or following to join him;

(I) upon a basis of reciprocity, an alien who is a bona fide representative of foreign press, radio, film, or other foreign information media, who seeks to enter the United States solely to engage in such vocation, and the spouse and children of such a representative, if accompanying or following to join him;

(J) an alien having a residence in a foreign country which he has no intention of abandoning who is a bona fide student, scholar, trainee, teacher, professor, research assistant, specialist, or leader in a field of specialized knowledge or skill, or other person of similar description, who is coming temporarily to the United States as a participant in a program designated by the Director of the United States Information Agency, for the purpose of teaching, instructing or lecturing, studying, observing, conducting research, consulting, demonstrating special skills, or receiving training and who, if he is coming to the United States to participate in a program under which he will receive graduate medical education or training, also meets the requirements of section 212(j) [8 U.S.C.A. § 1182(j)], and the alien spouse and minor children of any such alien if accompanying him or following to join him;

(K) subject to subsections (d) and (p) of section 214 [8 U.S.C.A. § 1184], an alien who—

(i) is the fiancée or fiancé of a citizen of the United States (other than a citizen described in section 204(a)(1)(A)(viii)(I) [8 U.S.C.A. § 1154(a)(1)(A)(viii)(I)]) and who seeks to enter the United States solely to conclude a valid marriage with the petitioner within ninety days after admission;

(ii) has concluded a valid marriage with a citizen of the United States (other than a citizen described in section 204(a)(1)(A)(viii)(I) [8 U.S.C.A. § 1154(a)(1)(A)(viii)(I)]) who is the petitioner, is the beneficiary of a petition to accord a status under section 201(b)(2)(A)(i) [8 U.S.C.A. § 1151(b)(2)(A)(i)] that was filed under section 204 [8 U.S.C.A. § 1154] by the petitioner, and seeks to enter the United States to await the approval of such petition and the availability to the alien of an immigrant visa; or

(iii) is the minor child of an alien described in clause (i) or (ii) and is accompanying, or following to join, the alien;

(L) subject to section 214(c)(2) [8 U.S.C.A. § 1184(c)(2)], an alien who, within 3 years preceding the time of his application for admission into the United States, has been employed continuously for one year by a firm or corporation or other legal entity or an affiliate or subsidiary thereof and who seeks to enter the United States temporarily in order to continue to render his services to the same employer or a subsidiary or affiliate thereof in a capacity that is managerial, executive, or involves specialized knowledge, and the alien spouse and minor children of any such alien if accompanying him or following to join him;

(M)(i) an alien having a residence in a foreign country which he has no intention of abandoning who seeks to enter the United States temporarily and solely for the purpose of pursuing a full course of study at an established vocational or other recognized nonacademic institution (other than in a language training program) in the United States particularly designated by him and approved by the Attorney General, after consultation with the Secretary of Education, which institution shall have agreed to report to the Attorney General the termination of attendance of each nonimmigrant nonacademic student and if any such institution fails to make reports promptly the approval shall be withdrawn, and (ii) the alien spouse and minor children of any alien described in clause (i) if accompanying or following to join such an alien, and (iii) an alien who is a national of Canada or Mexico, who maintains actual residence and place of abode in the country of nationality, who is described in clause (i) except that the alien's course of study may be full or part-time, and who commutes to the United States institution or place of study from Canada or Mexico;

(N)(i) the parent of an alien accorded the status of special immigrant under paragraph (27)(I)(i) (or under analogous authority under paragraph (27)(L)), but only if and while the alien is a child, or

(ii) a child of such parent or of an alien accorded the status of a special immigrant under clause (ii), (iii), or (iv) of paragraph (27)(I) (or under analogous authority under paragraph (27)(L));

(O) an alien who—

(i) has extraordinary ability in the sciences, arts, education, business, or athletics which has been demonstrated by sustained national or international acclaim or, with regard to motion picture and television productions a demonstrated record of extraordinary achievement, and whose achievements have been recognized in the field through extensive documentation, and seeks to enter the United States to continue work in the area of extraordinary ability; or

(ii)(I) seeks to enter the United States temporarily and solely for the purpose of accompanying and assisting in the artistic or athletic performance by an alien who is admitted under clause (i) for a specific event or events,

(II) is an integral part of such actual performance,

(III)(a) has critical skills and experience with such alien which are not of a general nature and which cannot be performed by other individuals, or **(b)** in the case of a motion picture or television production, has skills and experience with such alien which are not of a general nature and which are critical either based on a pre-existing longstanding working relationship or, with respect to the specific production, because significant production (including pre-and post-production work) will take place both inside and outside the United States and the continuing participation of the alien is essential to the successful completion of the production, and

(IV) has a foreign residence which the alien has no intention of abandoning; or

(iii) is the alien spouse or child of an alien described in clause (i) or (ii) and is accompanying, or following to join, the alien;

(P) an alien having a foreign residence which the alien has no intention of abandoning who—

(i)(a) is described in section 214(c)(4)(A) [8 U.S.C.A. § 1184(c)(4)(A)] (relating to athletes), or, **(b)** is described in section 214(c)(4)(B) [8 U.S.C.A. § 1184(c)(4)(B)] (relating to entertainment groups);

(ii)(I) performs as an artist or entertainer, individually or as part of a group, or is an integral part of the performance of such a group, and

(II) seeks to enter the United States temporarily and solely for the purpose of performing as such an artist or entertainer or with such a group under a reciprocal exchange program which is between an organization or organizations in the United States and an organization or organizations in one or more foreign states and which provides for the temporary exchange of artists and entertainers, or groups of artists and entertainers;

(iii)(I) performs as an artist or entertainer, individually or as part of a group, or is an integral part of the performance of such a group, and

(II) seeks to enter the United States temporarily and solely to perform, teach, or coach as such an artist or entertainer or with such a group under a commercial or noncommercial program that is culturally unique; or

(iv) is the spouse or child of an alien described in clause (i), (ii), or (iii) and is accompanying, or following to join, the alien;

(Q) an alien having a residence in a foreign country which he has no intention of abandoning who is coming temporarily (for a period not to exceed 15 months) to the United States as a participant in an international cultural exchange program approved by the Secretary of Homeland Security for the purpose of providing practical training, employment, and the sharing of the history, culture, and traditions of the country of the alien's nationality and who will be employed under the same wages and working conditions as domestic workers;

(R) an alien, and the spouse and children of the alien if accompanying or following to join the alien, who—

(i) for the 2 years immediately preceding the time of application for admission, has been a member of a religious denomination having a bona fide nonprofit, religious organization in the United States; and

(ii) seeks to enter the United States for a period not to exceed 5 years to perform the work described in subclause (I), (II), or (III) of paragraph (27)(C)(ii);

(S) subject to section 214(k) [8 U.S.C.A. § 1184(k)], an alien—

(i) who the Attorney General determines—

(I) is in possession of critical reliable information concerning a criminal organization or enterprise;

(II) is willing to supply or has supplied such information to Federal or State law enforcement authorities or a Federal or State court; and

(III) whose presence in the United States the Attorney General determines is essential to the success of an authorized criminal investigation or the successful prosecution of an individual involved in the criminal organization or enterprise; or

(ii) who the Secretary of State and the Attorney General jointly determine—

(I) is in possession of critical reliable information concerning a terrorist organization, enterprise, or operation;

(II) is willing to supply or has supplied such information to Federal law enforcement authorities or a Federal court;

(III) will be or has been placed in danger as a result of providing such information; and

(IV) is eligible to receive a reward under section 2708(a) of Title 22,

and, if the Attorney General (or with respect to clause (ii), the Secretary of State and the Attorney General jointly) considers it to be appropriate, the spouse, married and unmarried sons and daughters, and parents of an alien described in clause (i) or (ii) if accompanying, or following to join, the alien;

(T)(i) subject to section 214(*o*) [8 U.S.C.A. § 1184(*o*)], an alien who the Secretary of Homeland Security, or in the case of subclause (III)(aa) the Secretary of Homeland Security, in consultation with the Attorney General, determines—

(I) is or has been a victim of a severe form of trafficking in persons, as defined in section 7102 of Title 22;

(II) is physically present in the United States, American Samoa, or the Commonwealth of the Northern Mariana Islands, or at a port of entry thereto, on account of such trafficking, including physical presence on account of the alien having been allowed entry into the United States for participation in investigative or judicial processes associated with an act or a perpetrator of trafficking;

(III)(aa) has complied with any reasonable request for assistance in the Federal, State, or local investigation or prosecution of acts of trafficking or the investigation of crime where acts of trafficking are at least one central reason for the commission of that crime;

(bb) in consultation with the Attorney General, as appropriate, is unable to cooperate with a request described in item (aa) due to physical or psychological trauma; or

(cc) has not attained 18 years of age; and

(IV) the alien would suffer extreme hardship involving unusual and severe harm upon removal; and

(ii) if accompanying, or following to join, the alien described in clause (i)—

(I) in the case of an alien described in clause (i) who is under 21 years of age, the spouse, children, unmarried siblings under 18 years of age on the date on which such alien applied for status under such clause, and parents of such alien;

(II) in the case of an alien described in clause (i) who is 21 years of age or older, the spouse and children of such alien; or

(III) any parent or unmarried sibling under 18 years of age, or any adult or minor children of a derivative beneficiary of the alien, as of an alien described in subclause (I) or (II) who the Secretary of Homeland Security, in consultation with the law enforcement officer investigating a severe form of trafficking, determines faces a present danger of retaliation as a result of the alien's escape from the severe form of trafficking or cooperation with law enforcement.

(iii) Repealed. Pub.L. 110–457, Title II, § 201(a)(3), Dec. 23, 2008, 122 Stat. 5053.

(U)(i) subject to section 214(p) [8 U.S.C.A § 1184(p)], an alien who files a petition for status under this subparagraph, if the Secretary of Homeland Security determines that—

(I) the alien has suffered substantial physical or mental abuse as a result of having been a victim of criminal activity described in clause (iii);

(II) the alien (or in the case of an alien child under the age of 16, the parent, guardian, or next friend of the alien) possesses information concerning criminal activity described in clause (iii);

(III) the alien (or in the case of an alien child under the age of 16, the parent, guardian, or next friend of the alien) has been helpful, is being helpful, or is likely to be helpful to a Federal, State, or local law enforcement official, to a Federal, State, or local prosecutor, to a Federal or State judge, to the Service, or to other Federal, State, or local authorities investigating or prosecuting criminal activity described in clause (iii); and

(IV) the criminal activity described in clause (iii) violated the laws of the United States or occurred in the United States (including in Indian country and military installations) or the territories and possessions of the United States;

(ii) if accompanying, or following to join, the alien described in clause (i)—

(I) in the case of an alien described in clause (i) who is under 21 years of age, the spouse, children, unmarried siblings under 18 years of age on the date on which such alien applied for status under such clause, and parents of such alien; or

(II) in the case of an alien described in clause (i) who is 21 years of age or older, the spouse and children of such alien; and

(iii) the criminal activity referred to in this clause is that involving one or more of the following or any similar activity in violation of Federal, State, or local criminal law: rape; torture; trafficking; incest; domestic violence; sexual assault; abusive sexual contact; prostitution; sexual exploitation; stalking; female genital mutilation; being held hostage; peonage; involuntary servitude; slave trade; kidnapping; abduction; unlawful criminal restraint; false imprisonment; blackmail; extortion; manslaughter; murder; felonious assault; witness tampering; obstruction of justice; perjury; fraud in foreign labor contracting (as defined in section 1351 of Title 18);

or attempt, conspiracy, or solicitation to commit any of the above mentioned crimes; or

(V) subject to section 214(q) [8 U.S.C.A. § 1184(q)], an alien who is the beneficiary (including a child of the principal alien, if eligible to receive a visa under section 203(d) [8 U.S.C.A. § 1153(d)]) of a petition to accord a status under section 203(a)(2)(A) [8 U.S.C.A. § 1153(a)(2)(A)] that was filed with the Attorney General under section 204 [8 U.S.C.A. § 1154] on or before the date of the enactment of the Legal Immigration Family Equity Act [December 21, 2000], if—

(i) such petition has been pending for 3 years or more; or

(ii) such petition has been approved, 3 years or more have elapsed since such filing date, and—

(I) an immigrant visa is not immediately available to the alien because of a waiting list of applicants for visas under section 203(a)(2)(A) [8 U.S.C.A. § 1153(a)(2)(A)]; or

(II) the alien's application for an immigrant visa, or the alien's application for adjustment of status under section 245 [8 U.S.C.A. § 1255], pursuant to the approval of such petition, remains pending.

(16) The term "immigrant visa" means an immigrant visa required by this Act and properly issued by a consular officer at his office outside of the United States to an eligible immigrant under the provisions of this Act.

(17) The term "immigration laws" includes this Act and all laws, conventions, and treaties of the United States relating to the immigration, exclusion, deportation, expulsion, or removal of aliens.

(18) The term "immigration officer" means any employee or class of employees of the Service or of the United States designated by the Attorney General, individually or by regulation, to perform the functions of an immigration officer specified by this Act or any section thereof.

(19) The term "ineligible to citizenship," when used in reference to any individual, means, notwithstanding the provisions of any treaty relating to military service, an individual who is, or was at any time, permanently debarred from becoming a citizen of the United States under section 3(a) of the Selective Training and Service Act of 1940, as amended (54 Stat. 885; 55 Stat. 844), or under section 454(a) of Appendix to Title 50, or under any section of this title, or any other Act, or under any law amendatory of, supplementary to, or in substitution for, any of such sections or Acts.

(20) The term "lawfully admitted for permanent residence" means the status of having been lawfully accorded the privilege of residing permanently in the United States as an immigrant in accordance with the immigration laws, such status not having changed.

(21) The term "national" means a person owing permanent allegiance to a state.

(22) The term "national of the United States" means **(A)** a citizen of the United States, or **(B)** a person who, though not a citizen of the United States, owes permanent allegiance to the United States.

(23) The term "naturalization" means the conferring of nationality of a state upon a person after birth, by any means whatsoever.

(24) Repealed. Pub.L. 102–232, Title III, § 305(m)(1), Dec. 12, 1991, 105 Stat. 1750.

(25) The term "noncombatant service" shall not include service in which the individual is not subject to military discipline, court martial, or does not wear the uniform of any branch of the armed forces.

(26) The term "nonimmigrant visa" means a visa properly issued to an alien as an eligible nonimmigrant by a competent officer as provided in this Act.

(27) The term "special immigrant" means—

  (A) an immigrant, lawfully admitted for permanent residence, who is returning from a temporary visit abroad;

  (B) an immigrant who was a citizen of the United States and may, under section 324(a) [8 U.S.C.A. § 1435(a)] or 327 [8 U.S.C.A. § 1438], apply for reacquisition of citizenship;

  (C) an immigrant and the immigrant's spouse and children if accompanying or following to join the immigrant, who—

    (i) for at least 2 years immediately preceding the time of application for admission, has been a member of a religious denomination having a bona fide nonprofit, religious organization in the United States;

    (ii) seeks to enter the United States—

      (I) solely for the purpose of carrying on the vocation of a minister of that religious denomination,

      (II) before September 30, 2018, in order to work for the organization at the request of the organization in a professional capacity in a religious vocation or occupation, or

      (III) before September 30, 2018, in order to work for the organization (or for a bona fide organization which is affiliated with the religious denomination and is exempt from taxation as an organization described in section 501(c)(3) of Title 26) at the request of the organization in a religious vocation or occupation; and

    (iii) has been carrying on such vocation, professional work, or other work continuously for at least the 2-year period described in clause (i);

(D) an immigrant who is an employee, or an honorably retired former employee, of the United States Government abroad, or of the American Institute in Taiwan, and who has performed faithful service for a total of fifteen years, or more, and his accompanying spouse and children: Provided, That the principal officer of a Foreign Service establishment (or, in the case of the American Institute in Taiwan, the Director thereof), in his discretion, shall have recommended the granting of special immigrant status to such alien in exceptional circumstances and the Secretary of State approves such recommendation and finds that it is in the national interest to grant such status;

(E) an immigrant, and his accompanying spouse and children, who is or has been an employee of the Panama Canal Company or Canal Zone Government before the date on which the Panama Canal Treaty of 1977 (as described in section 3602(a)(1) of Title 22) enters into force [October 1, 1979], who was resident in the Canal Zone on the effective date of the exchange of instruments of ratification of such Treaty [April 1, 1979], and who has performed faithful service as such an employee for one year or more;

(F) an immigrant, and his accompanying spouse and children, who is a Panamanian national and (i) who, before the date on which such Panama Canal Treaty of 1977 enters into force [October 1, 1979], has been honorably retired from United States Government employment in the Canal Zone with a total of 15 years or more of faithful service, or (ii) who, on the date on which such Treaty enters into force, has been employed by the United States Government in the Canal Zone with a total of 15 years or more of faithful service and who subsequently is honorably retired from such employment or continues to be employed by the United States Government in an area of the former Canal Zone;

(G) an immigrant, and his accompanying spouse and children, who was an employee of the Panama Canal Company or Canal Zone Government on the effective date of the exchange of instruments of ratification of such Panama Canal Treaty of 1977 [April 1, 1979], who has performed faithful service for five years or more as such an employee, and whose personal safety, or the personal safety of whose spouse or children, as a direct result of such Treaty, is reasonably placed in danger because of the special nature of any of that employment;

(H) an immigrant, and his accompanying spouse and children, who—

(i) has graduated from a medical school or has qualified to practice medicine in a foreign state,

(ii) was fully and permanently licensed to practice medicine in a State on January 9, 1978, and was practicing medicine in a State on that date,

(iii) entered the United States as a nonimmigrant under subsection (a)(15)(H) or (a)(15)(J) before January 10, 1978, and

(iv) has been continuously present in the United States in the practice or study of medicine since the date of such entry;

(I)(i) an immigrant who is the unmarried son or daughter of an officer or employee, or of a former officer or employee, of an international organization described in paragraph (15)(G)(i), and who **(I)** while maintaining the status of a nonimmigrant under paragraph (15)(G)(iv) or paragraph (15)(N), has resided and been physically present in the United States for periods totaling at least one-half of the seven years before the date of application for a visa or for adjustment of status to a status under this subparagraph and for a period or periods aggregating at least seven years between the ages of five and 21 years, and **(II)** applies for a visa or adjustment of status under this subparagraph no later than his twenty-fifth birthday or six months after October 24, 1988, whichever is later;

(ii) an immigrant who is the surviving spouse of a deceased officer or employee of such an international organization, and who **(I)** while maintaining the status of a nonimmigrant under paragraph (15)(G)(iv) or paragraph (15)(N), has resided and been physically present in the United States for periods totaling at least one-half of the seven years before the date of application for a visa or for adjustment of status to a status under this subparagraph and for a period or periods aggregating at least 15 years before the date of the death of such officer or employee, and **(II)** files a petition for status under this subparagraph no later than six months after the date of such death or six months after October 24, 1988, whichever is later;

(iii) an immigrant who is a retired officer or employee of such an international organization, and who **(I)** while maintaining the status of a nonimmigrant under paragraph (15)(G)(iv), has resided and been physically present in the United States for periods totaling at least one-half of the seven years before the date of application for a visa or for adjustment of status to a status under this subparagraph and for a period or periods aggregating at least 15 years before the date of the officer or employee's retirement from any such international organization, and **(II)** files a petition for status under this subparagraph no later than six months after the date of such retirement or six months after October 25, 1994, whichever is later; or

(iv) an immigrant who is the spouse of a retired officer or employee accorded the status of special immigrant under clause (iii), accompanying or following to join such retired officer or employee as a member of his immediate family;

34

(J) an immigrant who is present in the United States—

(i) who has been declared dependent on a juvenile court located in the United States or whom such a court has legally committed to, or placed under the custody of, an agency or department of a State, or an individual or entity appointed by a State or juvenile court located in the United States, and whose reunification with 1 or both of the immigrant's parents is not viable due to abuse, neglect, abandonment, or a similar basis found under State law;

(ii) for whom it has been determined in administrative or judicial proceedings that it would not be in the alien's best interest to be returned to the alien's or parent's previous country of nationality or country of last habitual residence; and

(iii) in whose case the Secretary of Homeland Security consents to the grant of special immigrant juvenile status, except that—

(I) no juvenile court has jurisdiction to determine the custody status or placement of an alien in the custody of the Secretary of Health and Human Services unless the Secretary of Health and Human Services specifically consents to such jurisdiction; and

(II) no natural parent or prior adoptive parent of any alien provided special immigrant status under this subparagraph shall thereafter, by virtue of such parentage, be accorded any right, privilege, or status under this chapter; or

(K) an immigrant who has served honorably on active duty in the Armed Forces of the United States after October 15, 1978, and after original lawful enlistment outside the United States (under a treaty or agreement in effect on October 1, 1991) for a period or periods aggregating—

(i) 12 years and who, if separated from such service, was never separated except under honorable conditions, or

(ii) 6 years, in the case of an immigrant who is on active duty at the time of seeking special immigrant status under this subparagraph and who has reenlisted to incur a total active duty service obligation of at least 12 years,

and the spouse or child of any such immigrant if accompanying or following to join the immigrant, but only if the executive department under which the immigrant serves or served recommends the granting of special immigrant status to the immigrant;

(L) an immigrant who would be described in clause (i), (ii), (iii), or (iv) of subparagraph (I) if any reference in such a clause—

(i) to an international organization described in paragraph (15)(G)(i) were treated as a reference to the North Atlantic Treaty Organization (NATO);

(ii) to a nonimmigrant under paragraph (15)(G)(iv) were treated as a reference to a nonimmigrant classifiable under NATO–6 (as a member of a civilian component accompanying a force entering in accordance with the provisions of the NATO Status-of-Forces Agreement, a member of a civilian component attached to or employed by an Allied Headquarters under the "Protocol on the Status of International Military Headquarters" set up pursuant to the North Atlantic Treaty, or as a dependent); and

(iii) to the Immigration Technical Corrections Act of 1988 or to the Immigration and Nationality Technical Corrections Act of 1994 were a reference to the American Competitiveness and Workforce Improvement Act of 1998 [Pub.L. 105–277, Div. C, Title IV, Oct. 21, 1998, 112 Stat. 2681–641]

(M) subject to the numerical limitations of section 203(b)(4) [8 U.S.C.A. § 1153(b)(4)], an immigrant who seeks to enter the United States to work as a broadcaster in the United States for the International Broadcasting Bureau of the Broadcasting Board of Governors, or for a grantee of the Broadcasting Board of Governors, and the immigrant's accompanying spouse and children.

(28) The term "organization" means, but is not limited to, an organization, corporation, company, partnership, association, trust, foundation or fund; and includes a group of persons, whether or not incorporated, permanently or temporarily associated together with joint action on any subject or subjects.

(29) The term "outlying possessions of the United States" means American Samoa and Swains Island.

(30) The term "passport" means any travel document issued by competent authority showing the bearer's origin, identity, and nationality if any, which is valid for the admission of the bearer into a foreign country.

(31) The term "permanent" means a relationship of continuing or lasting nature, as distinguished from temporary, but a relationship may be permanent even though it is one that may be dissolved eventually at the instance either of the United States or of the individual, in accordance with law.

(32) The term "profession" shall include but not be limited to architects, engineers, lawyers, physicians, surgeons, and teachers in elementary or secondary schools, colleges, academies, or seminaries.

(33) The term "residence" means the place of general abode; the place of general abode of a person means his principal, actual dwelling place in fact, without regard to intent.

(34) The term "Service" means the Immigration and Naturalization Service of the Department of Justice.

(35) The term "spouse", "wife", or "husband" do not include a spouse, wife, or husband by reason of any marriage ceremony where the contracting parties thereto are not physically present in the presence of each other, unless the marriage shall have been consummated.

(36) The term "State" includes the District of Columbia, Puerto Rico, Guam, the Virgin Islands of the United States, and the Commonwealth of the Northern Mariana Islands.

(37) The term "totalitarian party" means an organization which advocates the establishment in the United States of a totalitarian dictatorship or totalitarianism. The terms "totalitarian dictatorship" and "totalitarianism" mean and refer to systems of government not representative in fact, characterized by (A) the existence of a single political party, organized on a dictatorial basis, with so close an identity between such party and its policies and the governmental policies of the country in which it exists, that the party and the government constitute an indistinguishable unit, and (B) the forcible suppression of opposition to such party.

(38) The term "United States", except as otherwise specifically herein provided, when used in a geographical sense, means the continental United States, Alaska, Hawaii, Puerto Rico, Guam, the Virgin Islands of the United States, and the Commonwealth of the Northern Mariana Islands.

(39) The term "unmarried", when used in reference to any individual as of any time, means an individual who at such time is not married, whether or not previously married.

(40) The term "world communism" means a revolutionary movement, the purpose of which is to establish eventually a Communist totalitarian dictatorship in any or all the countries of the world through the medium of an internationally coordinated Communist political movement.

(41) The term "graduates of a medical school" means aliens who have graduated from a medical school or who have qualified to practice medicine in a foreign state, other than such aliens who are of national or international renown in the field of medicine.

(42) The term "refugee" means **(A)** any person who is outside any country of such person's nationality or, in the case of a person having no nationality, is outside any country in which such person last habitually resided, and who is unable or unwilling to return to, and is unable or unwilling to avail himself or herself of the protection of, that country because of persecution or a well-founded fear of persecution on account of race, religion, nationality, membership in a particular social group, or political opinion, or **(B)** in such special circumstances as the President after appropriate consultation (as defined in section 207(e) of this Act [8 U.S.C.A. § 1157(e)]) may specify, any person who is within the country of such person's nationality or, in the case of a person having no nationality, within the country in which such person is habitually residing, and who is persecuted or who has a well-founded fear of persecution on account of race, religion, nationality, membership in a particular social group, or political opinion. The term "refugee" does not include any person who ordered, incited, assisted, or otherwise participated in the persecution of any person on account of race, religion, nationality, membership in a particular social group, or political opinion. For purposes of determinations under this Act, a person who has been forced to abort a pregnancy or to undergo involuntary sterilization, or who has been persecuted for failure or refusal to undergo such a procedure or for other resistance to a coercive population control program, shall be deemed to have been persecuted on account of political opinion, and a person who has a well founded fear that he or she will be forced to undergo such a procedure or subject to persecution for such failure, refusal, or resistance shall be deemed to have a well founded fear of persecution on account of political opinion.

(43) The term "aggravated felony" means—

(A) murder, rape, or sexual abuse of a minor;

(B) illicit trafficking in a controlled substance (as defined in section 802 of Title 21), including a drug trafficking crime (as defined in section 924(c) of Title 18);

(C) illicit trafficking in firearms or destructive devices (as defined in section 921 of Title 18) or in explosive materials (as defined in section 841(c) of that title);

(D) an offense described in section 1956 of Title 18 (relating to laundering of monetary instruments) or section 1957 of that title (relating to engaging in monetary transactions in property derived from specific unlawful activity) if the amount of the funds exceeded $10,000;

(E) an offense described in—

(i) section 842(h) or (i) of Title 18, or section 844(d), (e), (f), (g), (h), or (i) of that title (relating to explosive materials offenses);

(ii) section 922(g)(1), (2), (3), (4), or (5), (j), (n), (o), (p), or (r) or 924(b) or (h) of Title 18 (relating to firearms offenses); or

(iii) section 5861 of Title 26 (relating to firearms offenses);

(F) a crime of violence (as defined in section 16 of Title 18, but not including a purely political offense) for which the term of imprisonment at least one year [sic];

(G) a theft offense (including receipt of stolen property) or burglary offense for which the term of imprisonment at least one year [sic];

(H) an offense described in section 875, 876, 877, or 1202 of Title 18 (relating to the demand for or receipt of ransom);

(I) an offense described in section 2251, 2251A, or 2252 of Title 18 (relating to child pornography);

(J) an offense described in section 1962 of Title 18 (relating to racketeer influenced corrupt organizations), or an offense described in section 1084 (if it is a second or subsequent offense) or 1955 of that title (relating to gambling offenses), for which a sentence of one year imprisonment or more may be imposed;

(K) an offense that—

    (i) relates to the owning, controlling, managing, or supervising of a prostitution business;

    (ii) is described in section 2421, 2422, or 2423 of Title 18 (relating to transportation for the purpose of prostitution) if committed for commercial advantage; or

    (iii) is described in any of sections 1581–1585 or 1588–1591 of Title 18 (relating to peonage, slavery, involuntary servitude, and trafficking in persons);

(L) an offense described in—

    (i) section 793 (relating to gathering or transmitting national defense information), 798 (relating to disclosure of classified information), 2153 (relating to sabotage) or 2381 or 2382 (relating to treason) of Title 18;

    (ii) section 421 of Title 50 (relating to protecting the identity of undercover intelligence agents); or

    (iii) section 421 of Title 50 (relating to protecting the identity of undercover agents);

(M) an offense that—

    (i) involves fraud or deceit in which the loss to the victim or victims exceeds $10,000; or

    (ii) is described in section 7201 of Title 26 (relating to tax evasion) in which the revenue loss to the Government exceeds $10,000;

(N) an offense described in paragraph (1)(A) or (2) of section 274(a) [8 U.S.C.A. § 1324(a)] (relating to alien smuggling), except in the case of a first offense for which the alien has affirmatively shown that the alien committed the offense for the purpose of assisting, abetting, or aiding only the alien's spouse, child, or parent (and no other individual) to violate a provision of this Act;

(O) an offense described in section 275(a) [8 U.S.C.A. § 1325(a)] or 276 [8 U.S.C.A. § 1326] committed by an alien who was previously deported on the basis of a conviction for an offense described in another subparagraph of this paragraph;

(P) an offense **(i)** which either is falsely making, forging, counterfeiting, mutilating, or altering a passport or instrument in violation of section 1543 of Title 18, or is described in section 1546(a) of such title (relating to document fraud) and **(ii)** for which the term of imprisonment is at least 12 months, except in the case of a first offense for which the alien has affirmatively shown that the alien committed the offense for the purpose of assisting, abetting, or aiding only the alien's spouse, child, or parent (and no other individual) to violate a provision of this Act;

(Q) an offense relating to a failure to appear by a defendant for service of sentence if the underlying offense is punishable by imprisonment for a term of 5 years or more;

(R) an offense relating to commercial bribery, counterfeiting, forgery, or trafficking in vehicles the identification numbers of which have been altered for which the term of imprisonment is at least one year;

(S) an offense relating to obstruction of justice, perjury or subornation of perjury, or bribery of a witness, for which the term of imprisonment is at least one year;

(T) an offense relating to a failure to appear before a court pursuant to a court order to answer to or dispose of a charge of a felony for which a sentence of 2 years' imprisonment or more may be imposed; and

(U) an attempt or conspiracy to commit an offense described in this paragraph.

The term applies to an offense described in this paragraph whether in violation of Federal or State law and applies to such an offense in violation of the law of a foreign country for which the term of imprisonment was completed within the previous 15 years. Notwithstanding any other provision of law (including any effective date), the term applies regardless of whether the conviction was entered before, on, or after the date of enactment of this paragraph [September 30, 1996].

(44)(A) The term "managerial capacity" means an assignment within an organization in which the employee primarily—

(i) manages the organization, or a department, subdivision, function, or component of the organization;

(ii) supervises and controls the work of other supervisory, professional, or managerial employees, or manages an essential function within the organization, or a department or subdivision of the organization;

(iii) if another employee or other employees are directly supervised, has the authority to hire and fire or recommend those as well as other personnel actions (such as promotion and leave authorization) or, if no other employee is directly supervised, functions at a senior level within the organizational hierarchy or with respect to the function managed; and

(iv) exercises discretion over the day-to-day operations of the activity or function for which the employee has authority.

A first-line supervisor is not considered to be acting in a managerial capacity merely by virtue of the supervisor's supervisory duties unless the employees supervised are professional.

(B) The term "executive capacity" means an assignment within an organization in which the employee primarily—

(i) directs the management of the organization or a major component or function of the organization;

(ii) establishes the goals and policies of the organization, component, or function;

(iii) exercises wide latitude in discretionary decision-making; and

(iv) receives only general supervision or direction from higher level executives, the board of directors, or stockholders of the organization.

(C) If staffing levels are used as a factor in determining whether an individual is acting in a managerial or executive capacity, the Attorney General shall take into account the reasonable needs of the organization, component, or function in light of the overall purpose and stage of development of the organization, component, or function. An individual shall not be considered to be acting in a managerial or executive capacity (as previously defined) merely on the basis of the number of employees that the individual supervises or has supervised or directs or has directed.

(45) The term "substantial" means, for purposes of paragraph (15) (E) with reference to trade or capital, such an amount of trade or capital as is established by the Secretary of State, after consultation with appropriate agencies of Government.

(46) The term "extraordinary ability" means, for purposes of § 101(a)(15)(O)(i), in the case of the arts, distinction.

(47)(A) The term "order of deportation" means the order of the special inquiry officer, or other such administrative officer to whom the Attorney General has delegated the responsibility for determining whether an alien is deportable, concluding that the alien is deportable or ordering deportation.

(B) The order described under subparagraph (A) shall become final upon the earlier of—

(i) a determination by the Board of Immigration Appeals affirming such order; or

(ii) the expiration of the period in which the alien is permitted to seek review of such order by the Board of Immigration Appeals.

(48)(A) The term "conviction" means, with respect to an alien, a formal judgment of guilt of the alien entered by a court or, if adjudication of guilt has been withheld, where—

(i) a judge or jury has found the alien guilty or the alien has entered a plea of guilty or nolo contendere or has admitted sufficient facts to warrant a finding of guilt, and

(ii) the judge has ordered some form of punishment, penalty, or restraint on the alien's liberty to be imposed.

(B) Any reference to a term of imprisonment or a sentence with respect to an offense is deemed to include the period of incarceration or confinement ordered by a court of law regardless of any suspension of the imposition or execution of that imprisonment or sentence in whole or in part.

(49) The term "stowaway" means any alien who obtains transportation without the consent of the owner, charterer, master or person in command of any vessel or aircraft through concealment aboard such vessel or aircraft. A passenger who boards with a valid ticket is not to be considered a stowaway.

(50) The term "intended spouse" means any alien who meets the criteria set forth in section 204(a)(1)(A)(iii)(II)(aa)(BB) [8 U.S.C.A. § 1154(a)(1)(A)(iii)(II)(aa)(BB)], 204(a)(1)(B)(ii)(II)(aa)(BB) [8 U.S.C.A. § 1154(a)(1)(B)(ii)(II)(aa)(BB)], or 240A(b)(2)(A)(i)(III) [8 U.S.C.A. § 1229b(b)(2)(A)(i)(III)].

(51) The term "VAWA self-petitioner" means an alien, or a child of the alien, who qualifies for relief under—

(A) clause (iii), (iv), or (vii) of section 204(a)(1)(A) [8 U.S.C.A § 1154(a)(1)(A)];

(B) clause (ii) or (iii) of section 204(a)(1)(B) [8 U.S.C.A § 1154(a)(1)(B)];

(C) section 216(c)(4)(C) [8 U.S.C.A § 1186a(c)(4)(C)];

(D) the first section of Public Law 89–732 [8 U.S.C.A. § 1255 note] (commonly known as the Cuban Adjustment Act) as a child or spouse who has been battered or subjected to extreme cruelty;

(E) section 902(d)(1)(B) of the Haitian Refugee Immigration Fairness Act of 1998 [8 U.S.C.A. § 1255 note];

(F) section 202(d)(1) of the Nicaraguan Adjustment and Central American Relief Act; or

(G) section 309 of the Illegal Immigration Reform and Immigrant Responsibility Act of 1996 (division C of Public Law 104–208).

(52) The term "accredited language training program" means a language training program that is accredited by an accrediting agency recognized by the Secretary of Education.

(b) As used in titles I and II—

(1) The term "child" means an unmarried person under twenty-one years of age who is—

(A) a child born in wedlock;

(B) a stepchild, whether or not born out of wedlock, provided the child had not reached the age of eighteen years at the time the marriage creating the status of stepchild occurred;

(C) a child legitimated under the law of the child's residence or domicile, or under the law of the father's residence or domicile, whether in or outside the United States, if such legitimation takes place before the child reaches the age of eighteen years and the child is in the legal custody of the legitimating parent or parents at the time of such legitimation;

(D) a child born out of wedlock, by, through whom, or on whose behalf a status, privilege, or benefit is sought by virtue of the relationship of the child to its natural mother or to its natural father if the father has or had a bona fide parent-child relationship with the person;

(E)(i) a child adopted while under the age of sixteen years if the child has been in the legal custody of, and has resided with, the adopting parent or parents for at least two years or if the child has been battered or subject to extreme cruelty by the adopting parent or by a family member of the adopting parent residing in the same household: *Provided*, That no natural parent of any such adopted child shall thereafter, by virtue of such parentage, be accorded any right, privilege, or status under this Act; or

(ii) subject to the same proviso as in clause (i), a child who: **(I)** is a natural sibling of a child described in clause (i) or subparagraph (F)(i); **(II)** was adopted by the adoptive parent or parents of the sibling described in such clause or subparagraph; and **(III)** is otherwise described in clause (i), except that the child was adopted while under the age of 18 years; or

(F)(i) a child, under the age of sixteen at the time a petition is filed in his behalf to accord a classification as an immediate relative under section 201(b) [8 U.S.C.A. § 1151(b)], who is an orphan because of the death or disappearance of, abandonment or desertion by, or separation or loss from, both parents, or for whom the sole or surviving parent is incapable of providing the proper care and has in writing irrevocably released the child for emigration and adoption; who has been adopted abroad by a United States citizen and spouse jointly, or by an unmarried United States citizen who is at least 25 years of age, at least 1 of whom personally saw and observed the child before or during the adoption proceedings; or who is coming to the United States for adoption by a United States citizen and spouse jointly, or by an unmarried United States citizen at least twenty-five years of age, who have or has complied with the preadoption requirements, if any, of the child's proposed residence; *Provided*, That the Attorney General is satisfied that proper care will be furnished the child if admitted to the United States: *Provided further*, That no natural parent or prior adoptive parent of any such child shall thereafter, by virtue of such parentage, be accorded any right, privilege, or status under this Act; or

(ii) subject to the same provisos as in clause (i), a child who: (I) is a natural sibling of a child described in clause (i) or subparagraph (E)(i); (II) has been adopted abroad, or is coming to the United States for adoption, by the adoptive parent (or prospective adoptive parent) or parents of the sibling described in such clause or subparagraph; and (III) is otherwise described in clause (i), except that the child is under the age of 18 at the time a petition is filed in his or her behalf to accord a classification as an immediate relative under section 201(b) [8 U.S.C.A. § 1151(b)]; or

(G)(i) a child, younger than 16 years of age at the time a petition is filed on the child's behalf to accord a classification as an immediate relative under section 201(b) [8 U.S.C.A. § 1151(b)], who has been adopted in a foreign state that is a party to the Convention on Protection of Children and Co-operation in Respect of Intercountry Adoption, done at The Hague on May 29, 1993, or who is emigrating from such a foreign state to be adopted in the United States by a United States citizen and spouse jointly or by an unmarried United States citizen who is at least 25 years of age, Provided, That—

(I) the Secretary of Homeland Security is satisfied that proper care will be furnished the child if admitted to the United States;

(II) the child's natural parents (or parent, in the case of a child who has one sole or surviving parent because of the death or disappearance of, abandonment or desertion by, the other parent), or other persons or institutions that retain legal custody of the child, have freely given their written irrevocable consent to the termination of their legal relationship with the child, and to the child's emigration and adoption;

(III) in the case of a child having two living natural parents, the natural parents are incapable of providing proper care for the child;

(IV) the Secretary of Homeland Security is satisfied that the purpose of the adoption is to form a bona fide parent-child relationship, and the parent-child relationship of the child and the natural parents has been terminated (and in carrying out both obligations under this subclause the Secretary of Homeland Security may consider whether there is a petition pending to confer immigrant status on one or both of such natural parents); and

(V) in the case of a child who has not been adopted—

(aa) the competent authority of the foreign state has approved the child's emigration to the United States for the purpose of adoption by the prospective adoptive parent or parents; and

(bb) the prospective adoptive parent or parents has or have complied with any pre-adoption requirements of the child's proposed residence; and

(ii) except that no natural parent or prior adoptive parent of any such child shall thereafter, by virtue of such parentage, be accorded any right, privilege, or status under this chapter; or

(iii) subject to the same provisos as in clauses (i) and (ii), a child who—

(I) is a natural sibling of a child described in clause (i), subparagraph (E)(i), or subparagraph (F)(i);

(II) was adopted abroad, or is coming to the United States for adoption, by the adoptive parent (or prospective adoptive parent) or parents of the sibling described in clause (i), subparagraph (E)(i), or subparagraph (F)(i); and

(III) is otherwise described in clause (i), except that the child is younger than 18 years of age at the time a petition is filed on his or her behalf for classification as an immediate relative under section 201(b) [8 U.S.C.A. § 1151(b)].

(2) The terms "parent", "father", or "mother" mean a parent, father, or mother only where the relationship exists by reason of any of the circumstances set forth in subdivision (1) of this subsection, except that, for purposes of paragraph (1)(F) (other than the second proviso therein) and paragraph (1)(G)(i) in the case of a child born out of wedlock described in paragraph (1)(D) (and not described in paragraph (1)(C)), the term "parent" does not include the natural father of the child if the father has disappeared or abandoned or deserted the child or if the father has in writing irrevocably released the child for emigration and adoption.

(3) The term "person" means an individual or an organization.

(4) The term "immigration judge" means an attorney whom the Attorney General appoints as an administrative judge within the Executive Office for Immigration Review, qualified to conduct specified classes of proceedings, including a hearing under section 240 [8 U.S.C.A. § 1229a]. An immigration judge shall be subject to such supervision and shall perform such duties as the Attorney General shall prescribe, but shall not be employed by the Immigration and Naturalization Service.

(5) The term "adjacent islands" includes Saint Pierre, Miquelon, Cuba, the Dominican Republic, Haiti, Bermuda, the Bahamas, Barbados, Jamaica, the Windward and Leeward Islands, Trinidad, Martinique, and other British, French, and Netherlands territory or possessions in or bordering on the Caribbean Sea.

(c) As used in title III—

(1) The term "child" means an unmarried person under twenty-one years of age and includes a child legitimated under the law of the child's residence or domicile, or under the law of the father's residence or domicile, whether in the United States or elsewhere, and, except as otherwise provided in sections 320 [8 U.S.C.A. § 1431] and 321 [8 U.S.C.A. § 1432], a child adopted in the United States, if such legitimation or adoption takes place before the child reaches the age of 16 years (except to the extent that the child is described in subparagraph (E) (ii) or (F)(ii) of subsection (b)(1)), and the child is in the legal custody of the legitimating or adopting parent or parents at the time of such legitimation or adoption.

(2) The terms "parent", "father", and "mother" include in the case of a posthumous child a deceased parent, father, and mother.

(d) Repealed. Pub.L. 100–525, § 9(a)(3), Oct. 24, 1988, 102 Stat. 2619.

(e) For the purposes of this Act—

(1) The giving, loaning, or promising of support or of money or any other thing of value to be used for advocating any doctrine shall constitute the advocating of such doctrine; but nothing in this paragraph shall be construed as an exclusive definition of advocating.

(2) The giving, loaning, or promising of support or of money or any other thing of value for any purpose to any organization shall be presumed to constitute affiliation therewith; but nothing in this paragraph shall be construed as an exclusive definition of affiliation.

(3) Advocating the economic, international, and governmental doctrines of world communism means advocating the establishment of a totalitarian Communist dictatorship in any or all of the countries of the world through the medium of an internationally coordinated Communist movement.

(f) For the purposes of this Act—

No person shall be regarded as, or found to be, a person of good moral character who, during the period for which good moral character is required to be established, is, or was—

(1) a habitual drunkard;

(2) Repealed. Pub.L. 97–116, § 2(c)(1), Dec. 29, 1981, 95 Stat. 1611

(3) a member of one or more of the classes of persons, whether inadmissible or not, described in paragraphs (2)(D), (6)(E), and (10)(A) of section 212(a) [8 U.S.C.A § 1182(a)]; or subparagraphs (A) and (B) of section 212(a)(2) [8 U.S.C.A § 1182(a)(2)] and subparagraph (C) thereof of such section[*] (except as such paragraph relates to a single offense of simple possession of 30 grams or less of marihuana), if the offense described therein, for which such person was convicted or of which he admits the commission, was committed during such period;

(4) one whose income is derived principally from illegal gambling activities;

(5) one who has been convicted of two or more gambling offenses committed during such period;

(6) one who has given false testimony for the purpose of obtaining any benefits under this Act;

(7) one who during such period has been confined, as a result of conviction, to a penal institution for an aggregate period of one hundred and eighty days or more, regardless of whether the offense, or offenses, for which he has been confined were committed within or without such period;

(8) one who at any time has been convicted of an aggravated felony (as defined in subsection (a)(43));

(9) one who at any time has engaged in conduct described in section 212(a)(3)(E) [8 U.S.C.A. § 1182(a)(3)(E)] (relating to assistance in Nazi persecution, participation in genocide, or commission of acts of torture or extrajudicial killings) or 212(a)(2)(G) [8 U.S.C.A § 1182(a)(2)(G)] (relating to severe violations of religious freedom).

The fact that any person is not within any of the foregoing classes shall not preclude a finding that for other reasons such person is or was not of good moral character.

In the case of an alien who makes a false statement or claim of citizenship, or who registers to vote or votes in a Federal, State, or local election (including an initiative, recall, or referendum) in violation of a lawful restriction of such registration or voting to citizens, if each natural parent of the alien (or, in the case of an adopted alien, each adoptive parent of the alien) is or was a citizen (whether by birth or naturalization), the alien permanently resided in the United States prior to attaining the age of 16, and the alien reasonably believed at the time of such statement, claim, or violation that he or she was a citizen, no finding that the alien is, or was, not of good moral character may be made based on it.

(g) For the purposes of this Act any alien ordered deported or removed (whether before or after the enactment of this Act) who has left the United States, shall be considered to have been deported or removed in pur-

---

[*]So in original. The phrase "of such section" probably should not appear.

suance of law, irrespective of the source from which the expenses of his transportation were defrayed or of the place to which he departed.

(h) For purposes of section 212(a)(2)(E) [8 U.S.C.A. § 1182(a)(2)(E)], the term "serious criminal offense" means—

(1) any felony;

(2) any crime of violence, as defined in section 16 of Title 18; or

(3) any crime of reckless driving or of driving while intoxicated or under the influence of alcohol or of prohibited substances if such crime involves personal injury to another.

(i) With respect to each nonimmigrant alien described in subsection (a)(15)(T)(i) of this section—

(1) the Secretary of Homeland Security, the Attorney General, and other Government officials, where appropriate, shall provide the alien with a referral to a nongovernmental organization that would advise the alien regarding the alien's options while in the United States and the resources available to the alien; and

(2) the Secretary of Homeland Security shall, during the period the alien is in lawful temporary resident status under that subsection, grant the alien authorization to engage in employment in the United States and provide the alien with an "employment authorized" endorsement or other appropriate work permit.

(June 27, 1952, c. 477, Title I, § 101, 66 Stat. 166; Sept. 11, 1957, Pub.L. 85–316, §§ 1, 2, 71 Stat. 639; July 7, 1958, Pub.L. 85–508, § 22, 72 Stat. 351; Mar. 18, 1959, Pub.L. 86–3, § 20(a), 73 Stat. 13; Sept. 21, 1961, Pub.L. 87–256, § 109(a), (b), 75 Stat. 534; Sept. 26, 1961, Pub.L. 87–301, §§ 1, 2, 7, 75 Stat. 650, 653; Oct. 3, 1965, Pub.L. 89–236, §§ 8, 24, 79 Stat. 916, 922; Nov. 2, 1966, Pub.L. 89–710, 80 Stat. 1104; Apr. 7, 1970, Pub.L. 91–225, § 1, 84 Stat. 116; Dec. 16, 1975, Pub.L. 94–155, 89 Stat. 824; Oct. 12, 1976, Pub.L. 94–484, Title VI, § 601(b), (e), 90 Stat. 2301, 2302; Oct. 20, 1976, Pub.L. 94–571, § 7(a), 90 Stat. 2706; Oct. 12, 1976, Pub.L. 94–484, Title VI, § 602(c), as added Aug. 1, 1977, Pub.L. 95–83, Title III, § 307(q)(3), 91 Stat. 395; Aug. 17, 1977, Pub.L. 95–105, Title I, § 109(b)(3), 91 Stat. 847; 1977 Reorg. Plan No. 2, § 7(a)(8), 42 F.R. 62461, 91 Stat. 1637; Sept. 27, 1979, Pub.L. 96–70, Title III, § 3201(a), 93 Stat. 496; Mar. 17, 1980, Pub.L. 96–212, Title II, § 201(a), 94 Stat. 102; Dec. 29, 1981, Pub.L. 97–116, §§ 2, 5(d)(1), 18(a), 95 Stat. 1611, 1614, 1619; Oct. 30, 1984, Priv.Law 98–47, § 3, 98 Stat. 3435; Oct. 21,1986, Pub.L. 99–505, § 1, 100 Stat. 1806; Nov. 6, 1986, Pub.L. 99–603, Title III, §§ 301(a), 312, 315(a), 100 Stat. 3411, 3434, 3439; Nov. 14, 1986, Pub.L. 99–653, §§ 2, 3, 100 Stat. 3655; Oct. 1, 1988, Pub.L. 100–459, Title II, § 210(a), 102 Stat. 2203; Oct. 24, 1988, Pub.L. 100–525, §§ 2(O)(1), 8(b), 9(a), 102 Stat. 2613, 2617, 2619; Nov. 18, 1988, Pub.L. 100–690, Title VII, § 7342, 102 Stat. 4469; Nov. 21, 1989, Pub.L. 101–162, Title VI, § 611(a), 103 Stat. 1038; Dec. 18, 1989, Pub.L. 101–238, § 3(a), 103 Stat. 2100; Feb. 16, 1990, Pub.L. 101–246, Title 1, § 131(b), 104 Stat. 31; Nov. 29, 1990, Pub.L. 101–649, Title I, §§ 123, 151(a), 153(a), 162(f)(2)(A), Title II, §§ 203(c), 204(a), (c), 205(c)(1), (d), (e), 206(c), 207(a), 208, 209(a), Title IV, § 407(a)(2), Title V, §§ 501(a), 509(a), Title VI, § 603(a)(1), 104 Stat. 4995, 5004, 5005, 5012, 5018, 5019, 5020, 5022, 5023, 5024, 5026, 5027, 5040, 5048, 5051, 5082; Oct. 1, 1991, Pub.L. 102–110, § 2(a), 105 Stat. 555; Dec. 12, 1991, Pub.L. 102–232, Title II, §§ 203(a), 205(a) to (c), 206(b), (c)(1), (d), 207(b), Title III, §§ 302(e)(8)(A), 303(a)(5)(A), (7)(A), (14), 305(m)(1), 306(a)(1), 309(b)(1), (4), 105 Stat. 1737, 1740, 1741, 1746 to 1748, 1750, 1751, 1758; Apr. 30, 1994, Pub.L. 103–236, Title I, § 162(h)(1), 108 Stat. 407; Sept. 13, 1994, Pub.L. 103–322, Title XIII, § 130003(a), 108 Stat. 2024; Oct. 5, 1994, Pub.L. 103–337, Div. C, Title XXXVI, § 3605, 108 Stat. 3113; Oct. 25, 1994, Pub.L. 103–416, Title II, §§ 201, 202, 214, 219(a), 222(a), 108 Stat. 4310, 4311, 4314, 4316,

4320; Nov. 15, 1995, Pub.L. 104–51, § 1, 109 Stat. 467; Apr. 24, 1996, Pub.L. 104–132, Title IV, § 440(b), (e), 110 Stat. 1277; Sept. 30, 1996, Pub.L. 104–208, Div. C, Title I, § 104(a), Title III, §§ 301(a), 308(d)(3)(A), (4)(A), (e)(3), (f)(1)(A), (B), 321(a), (b), 322(a)(1), (2)(A), 361(a), 371(a), Title VI, §§ 601(a)(1), 625(a)(2), 671(a)(3)(B), (b)(5), (e)(2), 110 Stat. 3009–555, 3009–575, 3009–617, 3009–620, 3009–621, 3009–627, 3009–628, 3009–629, 3009–644, 3009–645, 3009–689, 3009–700, 3009–721 to 3009–723; Oct. 6, 1997, Pub.L. 105–54, § 1(a), 111 Stat. 1175; Nov. 26, 1997, Pub.L. 105–119, Title I, § 113, 111 Stat. 2460; Oct. 21, 1998, Pub.L. 105–277, Div. C, Title IV, § 421, Div. G, Title XXII, § 2222(e), 112 Stat. 2681–657, 2681–819; Oct. 30, 1998, Pub.L. 105–319, § 2(b)(1), (e)(2), 112 Stat. 3014, 3015; Nov. 12, 1999, Pub.L. 106–95, § 2(a), (c), 113 Stat. 1312; Dec. 7, 1999, Pub.L. 106–139, § (1)(a), (b)(1), 113 Stat. 1696; Oct. 6, 2000, Pub.L. 106–279, Title III, § 302(a), (c), 114 Stat. 838, 839; Oct. 28, 2000, Pub.L. 106–386, Div. A, § 107(e)(1), (4), Div. B, Title V, §§ 1503(a), 1513(b), 114 Stat. 1477, 1479, 1518, 1534; Oct. 30, 2000, Pub.L. 106–395, Title II, § 201(a)(1), 114 Stat. 1633; Nov. 1, 2000, Pub.L. 106–409, § 2(a), 114 Stat. 1787; Nov. 22, 2000, Pub.L. 106–536, § 1(a), 114 Stat. 2560; Dec. 21, 2000, Pub.L. 106–553, § 1(a)(2) [Title XI, § 1102(a), 1103(a)], 114 Stat. 2762; Jan. 16, 2002, Pub.L. 107–125, § 2(b), 115 Stat. 2403; Oct. 4, 2002, Pub.L. 107–234, § 1(4), 116 Stat. 1481; Nov. 2, 2002, Pub.L. 107–274, § 2(a), (b), 116 Stat. 1923; Sept. 3, 2003, Pub.L. 108–77, Title IV, § 402(a)(1), 117 Stat. 939; Oct. 15, 2003, Pub.L. 108–99, § 1, 117 Stat. 1176; Dec. 19, 2003, Pub.L. 108–193, §§ 4(b)(1), (5), 8(a)(1), 117 Stat. 2878, 2879, 2886; Dec. 10, 2004, Pub.L. 108–449, § 1(a)(2)(B), (b)(1), 118 Stat. 3469, 3470; Dec. 17, 2004, Pub.L. 108–458, Title V, § 5504, 118 Stat. 3741; May 11, 2005, Pub.L. 109–13, Div. B, § 501, 119 Stat. 231, 321; Oct. 18, 2005, Pub.L. 109–90, § 536, 119 Stat. 2087; Jan. 5, 2006, Pub.L. 109–162, Title VIII, §§ 801, 805(d), 811, 822(c)(1), 119 Stat. 3053, 3056, 3057, 3063; July 27, 2006, Pub.L. 109–248, Title IV, § 402(b), 120 Stat. 623; May 8, 2008, Pub.L. 110–229, Title VII, Subtitle A, § 702(j)(1)–(3), 122 Stat. 866; October 10, 2008, Pub. L. 110–391, § 2(a), 122 Stat. 4193; Dec. 23, 2008, Pub.L. 110–457, Title II, §§ 201(a), 235(d)(1), 122 Stat. 5052, 5079; Mar. 20, 2009, Pub.L. 111–9, § 1, 123 Stat. 989; Oct. 28, 2009, Pub.L. 111–83, Title V, § 568(a)(1), 123 Stat. 2186; Nov. 30, 2010, Pub.L. 111–287, § 3, 124 Stat. 3058; Pub.L. 111–306, § 1(a), (b), Dec. 14, 2010, 124 Stat. 3280; Pub.L. 112–176, § 3, Sept. 28, 2012, 126 Stat. 1325; Pub.L. 113–4, Title VIII, § 801, Title XII, §§ 1221, 1222, Mar. 7, 2013, 127 Stat. 110, 144; Pub.L. 113–76, Div. K, Title VII, § 7083, Jan. 17, 2014, 128 Stat. 567; Pub.L. 115–141, Div. M, Title II, § 202, Mar. 23, 2018, 132 Stat. 1049)

§ 102. Diplomatic and semidiplomatic immunities [8 U.S.C.A. § 1102]

Except as otherwise provided in this Act, for so long as they continue in the nonimmigrant classes enumerated in this section, the provisions of this Act relating to ineligibility to receive visas and the removal of aliens shall not be construed to apply to nonimmigrants—

(1) within the class described in paragraph (15)(A)(i) of section 101(a) [8 U.S.C.A. § 1101(a)], except those provisions relating to reasonable requirements of passports and visas as a means of identification and documentation necessary to establish their qualifications under such paragraph (15)(A)(i), and, under such rules and regulations as the President may deem to be necessary, the provisions of subparagraphs (A) through (C) of section 212(a)(3) [8 U.S.C.A. § 1182(a)(3)];

(2) within the class described in paragraph (15)(G)(i) of section 101(a) [8 U.S.C.A. § 1101(a)], except those provisions relating to reasonable requirements of passports and visas as a means of identification and documentation necessary to establish their qualifications under such paragraph (15)(G)(i), and the provisions of subparagraphs (A) through (C) of section 212(a)(3) [8 U.S.C.A. § 1182(a)(3)]; and

(3) within the classes described in paragraphs (15)(A)(ii), (15)(G) (ii), (15)(G)(iii), or (15)(G)(iv) of section 101(a) [8 U.S.C.A. § 1101(a)], except those provisions relating to reasonable requirements of passports and visas as a means of identification and documentation necessary to establish their qualifications under such paragraphs, and the provisions of subparagraphs (A) through (C) of section 212(a)(3) [8 U.S.C.A. § 1182(a)(3)].

(June 27, 1952, c. 477, Title I, § 102, 66 Stat. 173; Oct. 24, 1988, Pub.L. 100–525, § 9(b), 102 Stat. 2619; Nov. 29, 1990, Pub.L. 101–649, Title VI, § 603(a)(2), 104 Stat. 5082; Dec. 12, 1991, Pub.L. 102–232, Title III, § 307(i), 105 Stat. 1756; Sept. 30, 1996, Pub.L. 104–208, Div. C, Title III, § 308(d)(4)(B), 110 Stat. 3009–617.)

§ 103. Powers and duties of the Secretary, the Under Secretary, and the Attorney General [8 U.S.C.A. § 1103]

(a) Secretary of Homeland Security

(1) The Secretary of Homeland Security shall be charged with the administration and enforcement of this chapter and all other laws relating to the immigration and naturalization of aliens, except insofar as this chapter or such laws relate to the powers, functions, and duties conferred upon the President, Attorney General, the Secretary of State, the officers of the Department of State, or diplomatic or consular officers: *Provided, however,* That determination and ruling by the Attorney General with respect to all questions of law shall be controlling.

(2) He shall have control, direction, and supervision of all employees and of all the files and records of the Service.

(3) He shall establish such regulations; prescribe such forms of bond, reports, entries, and other papers; issue such instructions; and perform such other acts as he deems necessary for carrying out his authority under the provisions of this Act.

(4) He may require or authorize any employee of the Service or the Department of Justice to perform or exercise any of the powers, privileges, or duties conferred or imposed by this Act or regulations issued thereunder upon any other employee of the Service.

(5) He shall have the power and duty to control and guard the boundaries and borders of the United States against the illegal entry of aliens and shall, in his discretion, appoint for that purpose such number of employees of the Service as to him shall appear necessary and proper.

(6) He is authorized to confer or impose upon any employee of the United States, with the consent of the head of the Department or other independent establishment under whose jurisdiction the employee is serving, any of the powers, privileges, or duties conferred or imposed by this Act or regulations issued thereunder upon officers or employees of the Service.

(7) He may, with the concurrence of the Secretary of State, establish offices of the Service in foreign countries; and, after consultation with the Secretary of State, he may, whenever in his judgment such action may be necessary to accomplish the purposes of this chapter, detail employees of the Service for duty in foreign countries.

(8) After consultation with the Secretary of State, the Attorney General may authorize officers of a foreign country to be stationed at preclearance facilities in the United States for the purpose of ensuring that persons traveling from or through the United States to that foreign country comply with that country's immigration and related laws.

(9) Those officers may exercise such authority and perform such duties as United States immigration officers are authorized to exercise and perform in that foreign country under reciprocal agreement, and they shall enjoy such reasonable privileges and immunities necessary for the performance of their duties as the government of their country extends to United States immigration officers.

(10) In the event the Attorney General determines that an actual or imminent mass influx of aliens arriving off the coast of the United States, or near a land border, presents urgent circumstances requiring an immediate Federal response, the Attorney General may authorize any State or local law enforcement officer, with the consent of the head of the department, agency, or establishment under whose jurisdiction the individual is serving, to perform or exercise any of the powers, privileges, or duties conferred or imposed by this chapter or regulations issued thereunder upon officers or employees of the Service.

(11) The Attorney General, in support of persons in administrative detention in non-Federal institutions, is authorized—

(A) to make payments from funds appropriated for the administration and enforcement of the laws relating to immigration, naturalization, and alien registration for necessary clothing, medical care, necessary guard hire, and the housing, care, and security of persons detained by the Service pursuant to Federal law under an agreement with a State or political subdivision of a State; and

(B) to enter into a cooperative agreement with any State, territory, or political subdivision thereof, for the necessary construction, physical renovation, acquisition of equipment, supplies or materials required to establish acceptable conditions of confinement and detention services in any State or unit of local government which agrees to provide guaranteed bed space for persons detained by the Service.

(b) Land acquisition authority

(1) The Attorney General may contract for or buy any interest in land, including temporary use rights, adjacent to or in the vicinity of an international land border when the Attorney General deems the land essential to control and guard the boundaries and borders of the United States against any violation of this Act.

(2) The Attorney General may contract for or buy any interest in land identified pursuant to paragraph (1) as soon as the lawful owner of that interest fixes a price for it and the Attorney General considers that price to be reasonable.

(3) When the Attorney General and the lawful owner of an interest identified pursuant to paragraph (1) are unable to agree upon a reasonable price, the Attorney General may commence condemnation proceedings pursuant to the Act of August 1, 1888 (Chapter 728; 25 Stat. 357).

(4) The Attorney General may accept for the United States a gift of any interest in land identified pursuant to paragraph (1).

(c) Commissioner; appointment

The Commissioner shall be a citizen of the United States and shall be appointed by the President, by and with the advice and consent of the Senate. He shall be charged with any and all responsibilities and authority in the administration of the Service and of this Act which are conferred upon the Attorney General as may be delegated to him by the Attorney General or which may be prescribed by the Attorney General. The Commissioner may enter into cooperative agreements with State and local law enforcement agencies for the purpose of assisting in the enforcement of the immigration laws.

(d) Statistical information system

(1) The Commissioner, in consultation with interested academicians, government agencies, and other parties, shall provide for a system for collection and dissemination, to Congress and the public, of information (not in individually identifiable form) useful in evaluating the social, economic, environmental, and demographic impact of immigration laws.

(2) Such information shall include information on the alien population in the United States, on the rates of naturalization and emigration of resident aliens, on aliens who have been admitted, paroled, or granted asylum, on nonimmigrants in the United States (by occupation, basis for admission, and duration of stay), on aliens who have not been admitted or have been removed from the United States, on the number of applications filed and granted for cancellation of removal, and on the number of aliens estimated to be present unlawfully in the United States in each fiscal year.

(3) Such system shall provide for the collection and dissemination of such information not less often than annually.

(e) Annual report

(1) The Commissioner shall submit to Congress annually a report which contains a summary of the information collected under subsection (d) and an analysis of trends in immigration and naturalization.

(2) Each annual report shall include information on the number, and rate of denial administratively, of applications for naturalization, for each district office of the Service and by national origin group.

(f) Minimum number of agents in States

The Attorney General shall allocate to each State not fewer than 10 full-time active duty agents of the Immigration and Naturalization Service to carry out the functions of the Service, in order to ensure the effective enforcement of this Act.

(g) Attorney General

(1) In general

The Attorney General shall have such authorities and functions under this chapter and all other laws relating to the immigration and naturalization of aliens as were exercised by the Executive Office for Immigration Review, or by the Attorney General with respect to the Executive Office for Immigration Review, on the day before the effective date of the Immigration Reform, Accountability and Security Enhancement Act of 2002.

(2) Powers

The Attorney General shall establish such regulations, prescribe such forms of bond, reports, entries, and other papers, issue such instructions, review such administrative determinations in immigration proceedings, delegate such authority, and perform such other acts as the Attorney General determines to be necessary for carrying out this section.

(h) Repealed. Pub.L. 111–122, § 2(a), Dec. 22, 2009, 123 Stat. 3480.

(June 27, 1952, c. 477, Title I, § 103, 66 Stat. 173; Oct. 24, 1988, Pub.L. 100–525, § 9(c), 102 Stat. 2619, 2620; Nov. 29, 1990, Pub.L. 101–649, Title I, § 142, 104 Stat. 5004; Sept. 30, 1996, Pub.L 104–208, Div. C, Title I, §§ 102(d), 125, 134(a), Title III, §§ 308(d)(4)(C), (e)(4), 372, 373, 110 Stat. 3009–555, 3009–562, 3009–564, 3009–618, 3009–620, 3009–646, 3009–647; Nov. 25, 2002, Pub.L. 107–296, Title XI, § 1102, 116 Stat. 2273; Feb. 20, 2003, Pub.L. 108–7, Div. L, § 105(a)(1), (2), 117 Stat. 531; Dec. 17, 2004, Pub.L. 108–458, Title V, § 5505(a), 118 Stat. 3741; Dec. 22, 2009, Pub.L. 111–122, § 2(a), 123 Stat. 3480.)

§ 104.   Powers and duties of Secretary of State; Bureau of Consular Affairs [8 U.S.C.A. § 1104]

(a) Powers and duties

The Secretary of State shall be charged with the administration and the enforcement of the provisions of this Act and all other immigration and nationality laws relating to **(1)** the powers, duties, and functions of diplomatic and consular officers of the United States, except those powers, duties, and functions conferred upon the consular officers relating to the granting or refusal of visas; **(2)** the powers, duties, and functions of the Administrator; and **(3)** the determination of nationality of a person not in the United States. He shall establish such regulations; prescribe such forms of reports, entries and other papers; issue such instructions; and perform such other acts as he deems necessary for carrying out such provisions. He is authorized to confer or impose upon any employee of the United States, with the consent of the head of the department or independent establishment under whose jurisdiction the employee is serving, any of the powers, functions, or duties conferred or imposed by this Act or regulations issued thereunder upon officers or employees of the Department of State or of the American Foreign Service.

(b) Designation and duties of Administrator

The Secretary of State shall designate an Administrator who shall be a citizen of the United States, qualified by experience. The Administrator shall maintain close liaison with the appropriate committees of Congress in order that they may be advised regarding the administration of this Act by consular officers. The Administrator shall be charged with any and all responsibility and authority in the administration of this Act which are conferred on the Secretary of State as may be delegated to the Administrator by the Secretary of State or which may be prescribed by the Secretary of State, and shall perform such other duties as the Secretary of State may prescribe.

(c) Passport Office, Visa Office, and other offices; Directors

Within the Department of State there shall be a Passport Office, a Visa Office, and such other offices as the Secretary of State may deem to be appropriate, each office to be headed by a director. The Directors of the Passport Office and the Visa Office shall be experienced in the administration of the nationality and immigration laws.

(d) Transfer of duties

The functions heretofore performed by the Passport Division and the Visa Division of the Department of State shall hereafter be performed by the Passport Office and the Visa Office, respectively.

(e) General Counsel of Visa Office; appointment and duties

There shall be a General Counsel of the Visa Office, who shall be appointed by the Secretary of State and who shall serve under the general direction of the Legal Advisor of the Department of State. The General Counsel shall have authority to maintain liaison with the appropriate officers of the Service with a view to securing uniform interpretations of the provisions of this Act.

(June 27, 1952, c. 477, Title I, § 104, 66 Stat. 174; June 28, 1962, Pub.L. 87–510, § 4(a)(2), 76 Stat. 123; Aug. 14, 1964, Pub.L. 88–426, Title III, § 305(43), 78 Stat. 428; Aug. 17, 1977, Pub.L. 95–105, Title I, § 109(b)(1), 91 Stat. 847; Oct. 24, 1988, Pub.L. 100–525, § 9(d), 102 Stat. 2620; Apr. 30, 1994, Pub.L. 103–236, Title I, § 162(h)(2), 108 Stat. 407.)

§ 105.   Liaison with internal security officers data exchange [8 U.S.C.A. § 1105]

(a) The Commissioner and the Administrator shall have authority to maintain direct and continuous liaison with the Directors of the Federal Bureau of Investigation and the Central Intelligence Agency and with other internal security officers of the Government for the purpose of obtaining and exchanging information for use in enforcing the provisions of this Act in the interest of the internal and border security of the United States. The Commissioner and the Administrator shall maintain direct and continuous liaison with each other with a view to a coordinated, uniform, and efficient administration of this Act, and all other immigration and nationality laws.

(b)(1) The Attorney General and the Director of the Federal Bureau of Investigation shall provide the Department of State and the Service access to the criminal history record information contained in the National Crime Information Center's Interstate Identification Index (NCIC–III), Wanted Persons File, and to any other files maintained by the National Crime Information Center that may be mutually agreed upon by the Attorney General and the agency receiving the access, for the purpose of determining whether or not a visa applicant or applicant for admission has a criminal history record indexed in any such file.

(2) Such access shall be provided by means of extracts of the records for placement in the automated visa lookout or other appropriate database, and shall be provided without any fee or charge.

(3) The Federal Bureau of Investigation shall provide periodic updates of the extracts at intervals mutually agreed upon with the agency receiving the access. Upon receipt of such updated extracts, the receiving agency shall make corresponding updates to its database and destroy previously provided extracts.

(4) Access to an extract does not entitle the Department of State to obtain the full content of the corresponding automated criminal history record. To obtain the full content of a criminal history record, the Department of State shall submit the applicant's fingerprints and any appropriate fingerprint processing fee authorized by law to the Criminal Justice Information Services Division of the Federal Bureau of Investigation.

(c) The provision of the extracts described in subsection (b) may be reconsidered by the Attorney General and the receiving agency upon the development and deployment of a more cost-effective and efficient means of sharing the information.

(d) For purposes of administering this section, the Department of State shall, prior to receiving access to NCIC data but not later than 4 months after the date of enactment of this subsection, promulgate final regulations—

(1) to implement procedures for the taking of fingerprints; and

(2) to establish the conditions for the use of the information received from the Federal Bureau of Investigation, in order—

(A) to limit the redissemination of such information;

(B) to ensure that such information is used solely to determine whether or not to issue a visa to an alien or to admit an alien to the United States;

(C) to ensure the security, confidentiality, and destruction of such information; and

(D) to protect any privacy rights of individuals who are subjects of such information.

(As amended Oct. 26, 2001, Pub.L. 107–56, Title IV, § 403(a), 115 Stat. 343.)

§ 106. Employment authorization for battered spouses of certain nonimmigrants [8 U.S.C.A. § 1105a]

(a) In general

In the case of an alien spouse admitted under subparagraph (A), (E)(iii), (G), or (H) of section 101(a)(15) [8 U.S.C.A § 1101(a)(15)] who is accompanying or following to join a principal alien admitted under subparagraph (A), (E)(iii), (G), or (H) of such section, respectively, the Secretary of Homeland Security may authorize the alien spouse to engage in employment in the United States and provide the spouse with an "employment authorized" endorsement or other appropriate work permit if the alien spouse demonstrates that during the marriage the alien spouse or a child of the alien spouse has been battered or has been the subject of extreme cruelty perpetrated by the spouse of the alien spouse. Requests for relief under this section shall be handled under the procedures that apply to aliens seeking relief under section 204(a)(1)(A)(iii) [8 U.S.C.A § 1154(a)(1)(A)(iii)].

(b) Construction

The grant of employment authorization pursuant to this section shall not confer upon the alien any other form of relief.

(June 27, 1952, c. 477, Title I, § 106, as added Jan. 5, 2006, Pub.L. 109–162, Title VIII, § 814(c), 119 Stat. 3059.)

TITLE II

IMMIGRATION

CHAPTER I—SELECTION SYSTEM

§ 201. Worldwide level of immigration [8 U.S.C.A. § 1151]

(a) In general

Exclusive of aliens described in subsection (b), aliens born in a foreign state or dependent area who may be issued immigrant visas or who may otherwise acquire the status of an alien lawfully admitted to the United States for permanent residence are limited to—

(1) family-sponsored immigrants described in section 203(a) [8 U.S.C.A. § 1153(a)] (or who are admitted under section 211(a) [8 U.S.C.A. § 1181(a)] on the basis of a prior issuance of a visa to their accompanying parent under section 203(a) [8 U.S.C.A. § 1153(a)]) in a number not to exceed in any fiscal year the number specified in subsection (c) for that year, and not to exceed in any of the first 3 quarters of any fiscal year 27 percent of the worldwide level under such subsection for all of such fiscal year;

(2) employment-based immigrants described in section 203(b) [8 U.S.C.A. § 1153(b)] (or who are admitted under section 211(a) [8 U.S.C.A. § 1181(a)] on the basis of a prior issuance of a visa to their accompanying parent under section 203(b) [8 U.S.C.A. § 1153(b)]), in a number not to exceed in any fiscal year the number specified in subsection (d) for that year, and not to exceed in any of the first 3 quarters of any fiscal year 27 percent of the worldwide level under such subsection for all of such fiscal year; and

(3) for fiscal years beginning with fiscal year 1995, diversity immigrants described in section 203(c) [8 U.S.C.A. § 1153(c)] (or who are admitted under section 211(a) [8 U.S.C.A. § 1181(a)] on the basis of a prior issuance of a visa to their accompanying parent under section 203(c) [8 U.S.C.A. § 1153(c)]) in a number not to exceed in any fiscal year the number specified in subsection (e) for that year, and not to exceed in any of the first 3 quarters of any fiscal year 27 percent of the worldwide level under such subsection for all of such fiscal year.

(b) Aliens not subject to direct numerical limitations

Aliens described in this subsection, who are not subject to the worldwide levels or numerical limitations of subsection (a), are as follows:

(1)(A) Special immigrants described in subparagraph (A) or (B) of section 101(a)(27) [8 U.S.C.A. § 1101(a)(27)].

(B) Aliens who are admitted under section 207 [8 U.S.C.A. § 1157] or whose status is adjusted under section 209 [8 U.S.C.A. § 1159].

(C) Aliens whose status is adjusted to permanent residence under section 210 [8 U.S.C.A. § 1160] or 245A [8 U.S.C.A. § 1255a].

(D) Aliens whose removal is cancelled under section 240A(a) [8 U.S.C.A. § 1229b(a)].

(E) Aliens provided permanent resident status under section 249 [8 U.S.C.A. § 1259].

(2)(A)(i) Immediate relatives.

For purposes of this subsection, the term "immediate relatives" means the children, spouses, and parents of a citizen of the United States, except that, in the case of parents, such citizens shall be at least 21 years of age. In the case of an alien who was the spouse of a citizen of the United States and was not legally separated from the citizen at the time of the citizen's death, the alien (and each child of the alien) shall be considered, for purposes of this subsection, to remain an immediate relative after the date of the citizen's death but only if the spouse files a petition under section § 204(a)(1)(A)(ii) [8 U.S.C.A. § 1154(a)(1)(A)(ii)] within 2 years after such date and only until the date the spouse remarries. For purposes of this clause, an alien who has filed a petition under clause (iii) or (iv) of section § 204(a)(1)(A) [8 U.S.C.A. § 1154(a)(1)(A)] remains an immediate relative in the event that the United States citizen spouse or parent loses United States citizenship on account of the abuse.

(ii) Aliens admitted under section 211(a) [8 U.S.C.A. § 1181(a)] on the basis of a prior issuance of a visa to their accompanying parent who is such an immediate relative.

(B) Aliens born to an alien lawfully admitted for permanent residence during a temporary visit abroad.

(c) Worldwide level of family-sponsored immigrants

(1)(A) The worldwide level of family-sponsored immigrants under this subsection for a fiscal year is, subject to subparagraph (B), equal to—

(i) 480,000, minus

(ii) the sum of the number computed under paragraph (2) and the number computed under paragraph (4), plus

(iii) the number (if any) computed under paragraph (3).

(B)(i) For each of fiscal years 1992, 1993, and 1994, 465,000 shall be substituted for 480,000 in subparagraph (A)(i).

(ii) In no case shall the number computed under subparagraph (A) be less than 226,000.

(2) The number computed under this paragraph for a fiscal year is the sum of the number of aliens described in subparagraphs (A) and

(B) of subsection (b)(2) who were issued immigrant visas or who otherwise acquired the status of aliens lawfully admitted to the United States for permanent residence in the previous fiscal year.

(3)(A) The number computed under this paragraph for fiscal year 1992 is zero.

(B) The number computed under this paragraph for fiscal year 1993 is the difference (if any) between the worldwide level established under paragraph (1) for the previous fiscal year and the number of visas issued under section 203(a) [8 U.S.C.A. § 1153(a)] during that fiscal year.

(C) The number computed under this paragraph for a subsequent fiscal year is the difference (if any) between the maximum number of visas which may be issued under section 203(b) [8 U.S.C.A. § 1153(b)] (relating to employment-based immigrants) during the previous fiscal year and the number of visas issued under that section during that year.

(4) The number computed under this paragraph for a fiscal year (beginning with fiscal year 1999) is the number of aliens who were paroled into the United States under section 212(d)(5) [8 U.S.C.A. § 1182(d)(5)] in the second preceding fiscal year—

(A) who did not depart from the United States (without advance parole) within 365 days; and

(B) who (i) did not acquire the status of aliens lawfully admitted to the United States for permanent residence in the two preceding fiscal years, or (ii) acquired such status in such years under a provision of law (other than § 201(b)) which exempts such adjustment from the numerical limitation on the worldwide level of immigration under this section.

(5) If any alien described in paragraph (4) (other than an alien described in paragraph (4)(B)(ii)) is subsequently admitted as an alien lawfully admitted for permanent residence, such alien shall not again be considered for purposes of paragraph (1).

(d) Worldwide level of employment-based immigrants

(1) The worldwide level of employment-based immigrants under this subsection for a fiscal year is equal to—

(A) 140,000, plus

(B) the number computed under paragraph (2).

(2)(A) The number computed under this paragraph for fiscal year 1992 is zero.

(B) The number computed under this paragraph for fiscal year 1993 is the difference (if any) between the worldwide level established under paragraph (1) for the previous fiscal year and the number of visas issued under section 203(b) [8 U.S.C.A. § 1153(b)] during that fiscal year.

(C) The number computed under this paragraph for a subsequent fiscal year is the difference (if any) between the maximum number of visas which may be issued under section 203(a) [8 U.S.C.A. § 1153(a)] (relating to family-sponsored immigrants) during the previous fiscal year and the number of visas issued under that section during that year.

(e) Worldwide level of diversity immigrants

The worldwide level of diversity immigrants is equal to 55,000 for each fiscal year.

(f) Rules for determining whether certain aliens are immediate relatives

(1) Age on petition filing date

Except as provided in paragraphs (2) and (3), for purposes of subsection (b)(2)(A)(i) of this section, a determination of whether an alien satisfies the age requirement in the matter preceding subparagraph (A) of section 101(b)(1) [8 U.S.C.A. § 1101(b)(1)] shall be made using the age of the alien on the date on which the petition is filed with the Attorney General under section 204 [8 U.S.C.A. § 1154] to classify the alien as an immediate relative under subsection (b)(2)(A)(i) of this section.

(2) Age on parent's naturalization date

In the case of a petition under section 204 [8 U.S.C.A. § 1154] initially filed for an alien child's classification as a family-sponsored immigrant under section 203(a)(2)(A) [8 U.S.C.A. § 1153(a)(2)(A)], based on the child's parent being lawfully admitted for permanent residence, if the petition is later converted, due to the naturalization of the parent, to a petition to classify the alien as an immediate relative under subsection (b)(2)(A)(i) of this section, the determination described in paragraph (1) shall be made using the age of the alien on the date of the parent's naturalization.

(3) Age on marriage termination date

In the case of a petition under section 204 [8 U.S.C.A. § 1154] initially filed for an alien's classification as a family-sponsored immigrant under section 203(a)(3), based on the alien's being a married son or daughter of a citizen, if the petition is later converted, due to the legal termination of the alien's marriage, to a petition to classify the alien as an immediate relative under subsection (b)(2)(A)(i) of this section or as an unmarried son or daughter of a citizen under section 203(a)(1), the determination described in paragraph (1) shall be made using the age of the alien on the date of the termination of the marriage.

(4) Application to self-petitions

Paragraphs (1) through (3) shall apply to self-petitioners and derivatives of self-petitioners.

(June 27, 1952, c. 477, Title II, ch. 1, § 201, 66 Stat. 175; Oct. 3, 1965, Pub.L. 89–236, § 1, 79 Stat. 911; Oct. 20, 1976, Pub.L. 94–571, § 2, 90 Stat. 2703; Oct. 5, 1978, Pub.L. 95–412, § 1, 92 Stat. 907; Mar. 17, 1980, Pub.L. 96–212, Title II, § 203(a), 94 Stat. 106; Dec. 29, 1981, Pub.L. 97–116, § 20[(a)], 95 Stat. 1621; Nov. 29, 1990, Pub.L. 101–649, Title I, § 101(a), 104 Stat. 4980; Dec. 12, 1991, Pub.L. 102–232, Title III, § 302(a)(1), 105 Stat. 1742; Sept. 13, 1994, Pub.L. 103–322, Title IV, § 40701(b)(2), 108 Stat. 1954; Oct. 25, 1994, Pub.L. 103–416, Title II, § 219(b)(1), 108 Stat. 4316; Sept. 30, 1996, Pub.L. 104–208, Div. C, Title III, § 308(e)(5), (g)(8)(A)(i), Title VI, §§ 603, 671(d)(1)(A), 110 Stat. 3009–620, 3009–624, 3009–690, 3009–723; Oct. 28, 2000, Pub.L. 106–386, Div. B, Title V, § 1507(a)(3), 114 Stat. 1530; Aug. 6, 2002, Pub.L. 107–208, § 2, 116 Stat. 927; Jan. 5, 2006, Pub.L. 109–162, Title VIII, § 805(b)(1), 119 Stat. 3056; Oct. 28, 2009, Pub.L. 111–83, Title V, § 568(c)(1), 123 Stat. 2186.)

§ 202.   Numerical limitations on individual foreign states [8 U.S.C.A. § 1152]

(a) Per country level

(1) Nondiscrimination

(A) Except as specifically provided in paragraph (2) and in sections 101(a)(27) [8 U.S.C.A. § 1101(a)(27)], 201(b)(2)(A)(i) [8 U.S.C.A. § 1151(b)(2)(A)(i)], and 203 [8 U.S.C.A. § 1153], no person shall receive any preference or priority or be discriminated against in the issuance of an immigrant visa because of the person's race, sex, nationality, place of birth, or place of residence.

(B) Nothing in this paragraph shall be construed to limit the authority of the Secretary of State to determine the procedures for the processing of immigrant visa applications or the locations where such applications will be processed.

(2) Per country levels for family-sponsored and employment-based immigrants

Subject to paragraphs (3), (4), and (5), the total number of immigrant visas made available to natives of any single foreign state or dependent area under subsections (a) and (b) of section 203 [8 U.S.C.A. § 1153] in any fiscal year may not exceed 7 percent (in the case of a single foreign state) or 2 percent (in the case of a dependent area) of the total number of such visas made available under such subsections in that fiscal year.

(3) Exception if additional visas available

If because of the application of paragraph (2) with respect to one or more foreign states or dependent areas, the total number of visas available under both subsections (a) and (b) of section 203 [8 U.S.C.A. § 1153] for a calendar quarter exceeds the number of qualified immigrants who otherwise may be issued such a visa, paragraph (2) shall not apply to visas made available to such states or areas during the remainder of such calendar quarter.

(4) Special rules for spouses and children of lawful permanent resident aliens

(A) 75 percent of 2nd preference set-aside for spouses and children not subject to per country limitation

(i) In general

Of the visa numbers made available under section 203(a) [8 U.S.C.A. § 1153(a)] to immigrants described in section 203(a)(2) (A) [8 U.S.C.A. § 1153(a)(2)(A)] in any fiscal year, 75 percent of the 2–A floor (as defined in clause (ii)) shall be issued without regard to the numerical limitation under paragraph (2).

(ii) 2–A floor defined

In this paragraph, the term "2–A floor" means, for a fiscal year, 77 percent of the total number of visas made available under section 203(a) [8 U.S.C.A. § 1153(a)] to immigrants described in section 203(a)(2) [8 U.S.C.A. § 1153(a)(2)] in the fiscal year.

(B) Treatment of remaining 25 percent for countries subject to subsection (e)

(i) In general

Of the visa numbers made available under section 203(a) [8 U.S.C.A. § 1153(a)] to immigrants described in section 203(a)(2) (A) [8 U.S.C.A. § 1153(a)(2)(A)] in any fiscal year, the remaining 25 percent of the 2–A floor shall be available in the case of a state or area that is subject to subsection (e) only to the extent that the total number of visas issued in accordance with subparagraph (A) to natives of the foreign state or area is less than the subsection (e) ceiling (as defined in clause (ii)).

(ii) Subsection (e) ceiling defined

In clause (i), the term "subsection (e) ceiling" means, for a foreign state or dependent area, 77 percent of the maximum number of visas that may be made available under section 203(a) [8 U.S.C.A. § 1153(a)] to immigrants who are natives of the state or area under section 203(a)(2) [8 U.S.C.A. § 1153(a)(2)] consistent with subsection (e).

(C) Treatment of unmarried sons and daughters in countries subject to subsection (e)

In the case of a foreign state or dependent area to which subsection (e) applies, the number of immigrant visas that may be made available to natives of the state or area under section 203(a)(2)(B) [8 U.S.C.A. § 1153(a)(2)(B)] may not exceed—

(i) 23 percent of the maximum number of visas that may be made available under section 203(a) [8 U.S.C.A. § 1153(a)] to immigrants of the state or area described in section 203(a)(2) [8 U.S.C.A. § 1153(a)(2)] consistent with subsection (e), or

(ii) the number (if any) by which the maximum number of visas that may be made available under section 203(a) [8 U.S.C.A. § 1153(a)] to immigrants of the state or area described in section 203(a)(2) [8 U.S.C.A. § 1153(a)(2)] consistent with subsection (e) exceeds the number of visas issued under section 203(a)(2)(A) [8 U.S.C.A. § 1153(a)(2)(A)],

whichever is greater.

(D) Limiting pass down for certain countries subject to subsection (e)

In the case of a foreign state or dependent area to which subsection (e) applies, if the total number of visas issued under section 203(a)(2) [8 U.S.C.A. § 1153(a)(2)] exceeds the maximum number of visas that may be made available to immigrants of the state or area under section 203(a)(2) [8 U.S.C.A. § 1153(a)(2)] consistent with subsection (e) (determined without regard to this paragraph), in applying paragraphs (3) and (4) of section 203(a) [8 U.S.C.A. § 1153(a)] under subsection (e)(2) all visas shall be deemed to have been required for the classes specified in paragraphs (1) and (2) of such section.

(5) Rules for employment-based immigrants

(A) Employment-based immigrants not subject to per country limitation if additional visas available

If the total number of visas available under paragraph (1), (2), (3), (4), or (5) of section 203(b) [8 U.S.C.A. § 1153(b)] for a calendar quarter exceeds the number of qualified immigrants who may otherwise be issued such visas, the visas made available under that paragraph shall be issued without regard to the numerical limitation under paragraph (2) of this subsection during the remainder of the calendar quarter.

(B) Limiting fall across for certain countries subject to subsection (e)

In the case of a foreign state or dependent area to which subsection (e) applies, if the total number of visas issued under section 203(b) [8 U.S.C.A. § 1153(b)] exceeds the maximum number of visas that may be made available to immigrants of the state or area under section 203(b) [8 U.S.C.A. § 1153(b)] consistent with subsection (e) (determined without regard to this paragraph), in applying subsection (e) all visas shall be deemed to have been required for the classes of aliens specified in section 203(b) [8 U.S.C.A. § 1153(b)].

(b) Rules for chargeability

Each independent country, self-governing dominion, mandated territory, and territory under the international trusteeship system of the United Nations, other than the United States and its outlying possessions, shall be treated as a separate foreign state for the purposes of a numerical level established under subsection (a)(2) when approved by the Secretary of State. All other inhabited lands shall be attributed to a foreign state specified by the Secretary of State. For the purposes of this Act the foreign state to which an immigrant is chargeable shall be determined by birth within such foreign state except that **(1)** an alien child, when accompanied by or following to join his alien parent or parents, may be charged to the foreign state of either parent if such parent has received or would be qualified for an immigrant visa, if necessary to prevent the separation of the child from the parent or parents, and if immigration charged to the foreign state to which such parent has been or would be chargeable has not reached a numerical level established under subsection (a)(2) for that fiscal year; **(2)** if an alien is chargeable to a different foreign state from that of his spouse, the foreign state to which such alien is chargeable may, if necessary to prevent the separation of husband and wife, be determined by the foreign state of the spouse he is accompanying or following to join, if such spouse has received or would be qualified for an immigrant visa and if immigration charged to the foreign state to which such spouse has been or would be chargeable has not reached a numerical level established under subsection (a)(2) for that fiscal year; **(3)** an alien born in the United States shall be considered as having been born in the country of which he is a citizen or subject, or, if he is not a citizen or subject of any country, in the last foreign country in which he had his residence as determined by the consular officer; and **(4)** an alien born within any foreign state in which neither of his parents was born and in which neither of his parents had a residence at the time of such alien's birth may be charged to the foreign state of either parent.

(c) Chargeability for dependent areas

Any immigrant born in a colony or other component or dependent area of a foreign state overseas from the foreign state, other than an alien described in section 201(b) [8 U.S.C.A. § 1151(b)], shall be chargeable for the purpose of the limitation set forth in subsection (a), to the foreign state.

(d) Changes in territory

In the case of any change in the territorial limits of foreign states, the Secretary of State shall, upon recognition of such change, issue appropriate instructions to all diplomatic and consular offices.

(e) Special rules for countries at ceiling

If it is determined that the total number of immigrant visas made available under subsections (a) and (b) of section 203 [8 U.S.C.A. § 1153] to natives of any single foreign state or dependent area will exceed the numerical limitation specified in subsection (a)(2) in any fiscal year, in determining the allotment of immigrant visa numbers to natives under subsections (a) and (b) of section 203 [8 U.S.C.A. § 1153], visa numbers with respect to natives of that state or area shall be allocated (to the extent practicable and otherwise consistent with this section and section 203 [8 U.S.C.A. § 1153]) in a manner so that—

(1) the ratio of the visa numbers made available under section 203(a) [8 U.S.C.A. § 1153(a)] to the visa numbers made available under section 203(b) [8 U.S.C.A. § 1153(b)] is equal to the ratio of the worldwide level of immigration under section 201(c) [8 U.S.C.A. § 1151(c)] to such level under section 201(d) [8 U.S.C.A. § 1151(d)];

(2) except as provided in subsection (a)(4), the proportion of the visa numbers made available under each of paragraphs (1) through (4) of section 203(a) [8 U.S.C.A. § 1153(a)] is equal to the ratio of the total number of visas made available under the respective paragraph to the total number of visas made available under section 203(a) [8 U.S.C.A. § 1153(a)], and

(3) except as provided in subsection (a)(5), the proportion of the visa numbers made available under each of paragraphs (1) through (5) of section 203(b) [8 U.S.C.A. § 1153(b)] is equal to the ratio of the total number of visas made available under the respective paragraph to the total number of visas made available under section 203(b) [8 U.S.C.A. § 1153(b)].

Nothing in this subsection shall be construed as limiting the number of visas that may be issued to natives of a foreign state or dependent area under section 203(a) [8 U.S.C.A. § 1153(a)] or 203(b) [8 U.S.C.A. § 1153(b)] if there is insufficient demand for visas for such natives under section 203(b) [8 U.S.C.A. § 1153(b)],or 203(a) [8 U.S.C.A. § 1153(a)], respectively, or as limiting the number of visas that may be issued under section 203(a)(2)(A) [8 U.S.C.A. § 1153(a)(2)(A)] pursuant to subsection (a)(4)(A).

(June 27, 1952, c. 477, Title II, ch. 1, § 202, 66 Stat. 176; Sept. 26, 1961, Pub.L. 87–301, § 9, 75 Stat. 654; Oct. 3, 1965, Pub.L. 89–236, § 2, 79 Stat. 911; Oct. 20, 1976, Pub.L. 94–571, § 3, 90 Stat. 2703; Oct. 5, 1978, Pub.L. 95–412, § 2, 92 Stat. 907; Mar. 17, 1980, Pub.L. 96–212, Title II, § 203(b), 94 Stat. 107; Dec. 29, 1981, Pub.L. 97–116, §§ 18(c), 20(b), 95 Stat. 1620, 1622; Nov. 6, 1986, Pub.L. 99–603, Title III, § 311(a), 100 Stat. 3434; Nov. 14, 1986, Pub.L. 99–653, § 4, 100 Stat. 3655; Oct. 24, 1988, Pub. L. 100–525, §§ 8(c), 9(f), 102 Stat. 2617, 2620; Nov. 29, 1990, Pub.L. 101–649, Title I, § 102, 104 Stat. 4982; Dec. 12, 1991, Pub.L. 102–232, Title III, § 302(a)(3), 105 Stat. 1742; Sept. 30, 1996, Pub.L. 104–208, Div. C, Title VI, § 633, 110 Stat. 3009–701; Oct. 17, 2000, Pub.L. 106–313, Title I, § 104(a), (b), 114 Stat. 1252, 1253.)

§ 203.   Allocation of immigrant visas [8 U.S.C.A. § 1153]

(a) Preference allocation for family-sponsored immigrants

Aliens subject to the worldwide level specified in section 201(c) [8 U.S.C.A. § 1151(c)] for family-sponsored immigrants shall be allotted visas as follows:

(1) Unmarried sons and daughters of citizens

Qualified immigrants who are the unmarried sons or daughters of citizens of the United States shall be allocated visas in a number not to exceed 23,400, plus any visas not required for the class specified in paragraph (4).

(2) Spouses and unmarried sons and unmarried daughters of permanent resident aliens

Qualified immigrants—

(A) who are the spouses or children of an alien lawfully admitted for permanent residence, or

(B) who are the unmarried sons or unmarried daughters (but are not the children) of an alien lawfully admitted for permanent residence,

shall be allocated visas in a number not to exceed 114,200, plus the number (if any) by which such worldwide level exceeds 226,000, plus any visas not required for the class specified in paragraph (1); except that not less than 77 percent of such visa numbers shall be allocated to aliens described in subparagraph (A).

(3) Married sons and married daughters of citizens

Qualified immigrants who are the married sons or married daughters of citizens of the United States shall be allocated visas in a number not to exceed 23,400, plus any visas not required for the classes specified in paragraphs (1) and (2).

(4) Brothers and sisters of citizens

Qualified immigrants who are the brothers or sisters of citizens of the United States, if such citizens are at least 21 years of age, shall be allocated visas in a number not to exceed 65,000, plus any visas not required for the classes specified in paragraphs (1) through (3).

(b) Preference allocation for employment-based immigrants

Aliens subject to the worldwide level specified in section 201(d) [8 U.S.C.A. § 1151(d)] for employment-based immigrants in a fiscal year shall be allotted visas as follows:

(1) Priority workers

Visas shall first be made available in a number not to exceed 28.6 percent of such worldwide level, plus any visas not required for the classes specified in paragraphs (4) and (5), to qualified immigrants who are aliens described in any of the following subparagraphs (A) through (C):

(A) Aliens with extraordinary ability

An alien is described in this subparagraph if—

(i) the alien has extraordinary ability in the sciences, arts, education, business, or athletics which has been demonstrated by sustained national or international acclaim and whose achievements have been recognized in the field through extensive documentation,

(ii) the alien seeks to enter the United States to continue work in the area of extraordinary ability, and

(iii) the alien's entry into the United States will substantially benefit prospectively the United States.

(B) Outstanding professors and researchers

An alien is described in this subparagraph if—

(i) the alien is recognized internationally as outstanding in a specific academic area,

(ii) the alien has at least 3 years of experience in teaching or research in the academic area, and

(iii) the alien seeks to enter the United States—

(I) for a tenured position (or tenure-track position) within a university or institution of higher education to teach in the academic area,

(II) for a comparable position with a university or institution of higher education to conduct research in the area, or

(III) for a comparable position to conduct research in the area with a department, division, or institute of a private employer, if the department, division, or institute employs at least 3 persons full-time in research activities and has achieved documented accomplishments in an academic field.

(C) Certain multinational executives and managers

An alien is described in this subparagraph if the alien, in the 3 years preceding the time of the alien's application for classification and admission into the United States under this subparagraph, has been employed for at least 1 year by a firm or corporation or other legal entity or an affiliate or subsidiary thereof and the alien seeks to enter the United States in order to continue to render services to the same employer or to a subsidiary or affiliate thereof in a capacity that is managerial or executive.

(2) Aliens who are members of the professions holding advanced degrees or aliens of exceptional ability

(A) In general

Visas shall be made available, in a number not to exceed 28.6 percent of such worldwide level, plus any visas not required for the classes specified in paragraph (1), to qualified immigrants who are members of the professions holding advanced degrees or their equivalent or who because of their exceptional ability in the sciences, arts, or business, will substantially benefit prospectively the national economy, cultural or educational interests, or welfare of the United States, and whose services in the sciences, arts, professions, or business are sought by an employer in the United States.

(B) Waiver of job offer

(i) National interest waiver

Subject to clause (ii), the Attorney General may, when the Attorney General deems it to be in the national interest, waive the requirements of subparagraph (A) that an alien's services in the sciences, arts, professions, or business be sought by an employer in the United States.

(ii) Physicians working in shortage areas or veterans facilities

(I) In general

The Attorney General shall grant a national interest waiver pursuant to clause (i) on behalf of any alien physician with respect to whom a petition for preference classification has been filed under subparagraph (A) if—

(aa) the alien physician agrees to work full time as a physician in an area or areas designated by the Secretary of Health and Human Services as having a shortage of health care professionals or at a health care facility under the jurisdiction of the Secretary of Veterans Affairs; and

(bb) a Federal agency or a department of public health in any State has previously determined that the alien physician's work in such an area or at such facility was in the public interest.

(II) Prohibition

No permanent resident visa may be issued to an alien physician described in subclause (I) by the Secretary of State under section 204(b) [8 U.S.C.A. § 1154(b)], and the Attorney General may not adjust the status of such an alien physician from that of a nonimmigrant alien to that of a permanent resident alien under section 245 [8 U.S.C.A. § 1255], until such time as the alien has worked full time as a physician for an aggregate of 5 years (not including the time served in the status of an alien described in section 101(a)(15)(J) [8 U.S.C.A. § 1101(a)(15)(J)]), in an area or areas designated by the Secretary of Health and Human Services as having a shortage of health care professionals or at a health care facility under the jurisdiction of the Secretary of Veterans Affairs.

(III) Statutory construction

Nothing in this subparagraph may be construed to prevent the filing of a petition with the Attorney General for classification under section 204(a) [8 U.S.C.A. § 1154(a)], or the filing of an application for adjustment of status under section 245 [8 U.S.C.A. § 1255], by an alien physician described in subclause (I) prior to the date by which such alien physician has completed the service described in subclause (II).

(IV) Effective date

The requirements of this subsection do not affect waivers on behalf of alien physicians approved under subsection (b)(2)(B) of this section before the enactment date of this subsection. In the case of a physician for whom an application for a waiver was filed under subsection (b)(2)(B) of this section prior to November 1, 1998, the Attorney General shall grant a national interest waiver pursuant to subsection (b)(2)(B) of this section except that the alien is required to have worked full time as a physician for an aggregate of 3 years (not including time served in the status of an alien described in section 101(a)(15)(J) [8 U.S.C.A. § 1101(a)(15)(J)]) before a visa can be issued to the alien under section 204(b) [8 U.S.C.A. § 1154(b)] or the status of the alien is adjusted to permanent resident under section 245 [8 U.S.C.A. § 1255].

(C) Determination of exceptional ability

In determining under subparagraph (A) whether an immigrant has exceptional ability, the possession of a degree, diploma, certificate, or similar award from a college, university, school, or other institution of learning or a license to practice or certification for a particular profession or occupation shall not by itself be considered sufficient evidence of such exceptional ability.

(3) Skilled workers, professionals, and other workers

(A) In general

Visas shall be made available, in a number not to exceed 28.6 percent of such worldwide level, plus any visas not required for the classes specified in paragraphs (1) and (2), to the following classes of aliens who are not described in paragraph (2):

(i) Skilled workers

Qualified immigrants who are capable, at the time of petitioning for classification under this paragraph, of performing skilled labor (requiring at least 2 years training or experience), not of a temporary or seasonal nature, for which qualified workers are not available in the United States.

(ii) Professionals

Qualified immigrants who hold baccalaureate degrees and who are members of the professions.

(iii) Other workers

Other qualified immigrants who are capable, at the time of petitioning for classification under this paragraph, of performing unskilled labor, not of a temporary or seasonal nature, for which qualified workers are not available in the United States.

(B) Limitation on other workers

Not more than 10,000 of the visas made available under this paragraph in any fiscal year may be available for qualified immigrants described in subparagragh (A)(iii).

(C) Labor certification required

An immigrant visa may not be issued to an immigrant under subparagraph (A) until the consular officer is in receipt of a determination made by the Secretary of Labor pursuant to the provisions of section 212(a)(5)(A) [8 U.S.C.A. § 1182(a)(5)(A)].

(4) Certain special immigrants

Visas shall be made available, in a number not to exceed 7.1 percent of such worldwide level, to qualified special immigrants described in section 101(a)(27) [8 U.S.C.A. § 1101(a)(27)] (other than those described in subparagraph (A) or (B) thereof), of which not more than 5,000 may be made available in any fiscal year to special immigrants described in subclause (II) or (III) of section 101(a)(27)(C)(ii) [8 U.S.C.A. § 1101(a)(27)(C)(ii)], and not more than 100 may be made available in any fiscal year to special immigrants, excluding spouses and children, who are described in section 101(a)(27)(M) [8 U.S.C.A. § 1101(a)(27)(M)].

(5) Employment creation

(A) In general

Visas shall be made available, in a number not to exceed 7.1 percent of such worldwide level, to qualified immigrants seeking to enter the United States for the purpose of engaging in a new commercial enterprise (including a limited partnership)—

(i) in which such alien has invested (after November 29, 1990) or, is actively in the process of investing, capital in an amount not less than the amount specified in subparagraph (C), and

(ii) which will benefit the United States economy and create full-time employment for not fewer than 10 United States citizens or aliens lawfully admitted for permanent residence or other immigrants lawfully authorized to be employed in the United States (other than the immigrant and the immigrant's spouse, sons, or daughters).

(iii) Redesignated (ii)

(B) Set-aside for targeted employment areas

(i) In general

Not less than 3,000 of the visas made available under this paragraph in each fiscal year shall be reserved for qualified immigrants who invest in a new commercial enterprise described in subparagraph (A) which will create employment in a targeted employment area.

(ii) Targeted employment area defined

In this paragraph, the term "targeted employment area" means, at the time of the investment, a rural area or an area which has experienced high unemployment (of at least 150 percent of the national average rate).

(iii) Rural area defined

In this paragraph, the term "rural area" means any area other than an area within a metropolitan statistical area or within the outer boundary of any city or town having a population of 20,000 or more (based on the most recent decennial census of the United States).

(C) Amount of capital required

(i) In general

Except as otherwise provided in this subparagraph, the amount of capital required under subparagraph (A) shall be $1,000,000. The Attorney General, in consultation with the Secretary of Labor and the Secretary of State, may from time to time prescribe regulations increasing the dollar amount specified under the previous sentence.

(ii) Adjustment for targeted employment areas

The Attorney General may, in the case of investment made in a targeted employment area, specify an amount of capital required under subparagraph (A) that is less than (but not less than $1/2$ of) the amount specified in clause (i).

(iii) Adjustment for high employment areas

In the case of an investment made in a part of a metropolitan statistical area that at the time of the investment—

(I) is not a targeted employment area, and

(II) is an area with an unemployment rate significantly below the national average unemployment rate,

the Attorney General may specify an amount of capital required under subparagraph (A) that is greater than (but not greater than 3 times) the amount specified in clause (i).

(D) Full-time employment defined

In this paragraph, the term "full-time employment" means employment in a position that requires at least 35 hours of service per week at any time, regardless of who fills the position.

(6) Special rules for "K" special immigrants

(A) Not counted against numerical limitation in year involved

Subject to subparagraph (B), the number of immigrant visas made available to special immigrants under section 101(a)(27)(K) [8 U.S.C.A. § 1101(a)(27)(K)] in a fiscal year shall not be subject to the numerical limitations of this subsection or of section 202(a) [8 U.S.C.A. § 1152(a)].

(B) Counted against numerical limitations in following year

(i) Reduction in employment-based immigrant classifications

The number of visas made available in any fiscal year under paragraphs (1), (2), and (3) shall each be reduced by ⅓ of the number of visas made available in the previous fiscal year to special immigrants described in section 101(a)(27)(K) [8 U.S.C.A. § 1101(a)(27)(K)].

(ii) Reduction in per country level

The number of visas made available in each fiscal year to natives of a foreign state under section 202(a) [8 U.S.C.A. § 1152(a)] shall be reduced by the number of visas made available in the previous fiscal year to special immigrants described in section 101(a)(27)(K) [8 U.S.C.A. § 1101(a)(27)(K)] who are natives of the foreign state.

(iii) Reduction in employment-based immigrant classifications within per country ceiling

In the case of a foreign state subject to section 202(e) [8 U.S.C.A. § 1152(e)] in a fiscal year (and in the previous fiscal year), the number of visas made available and allocated to each of paragraphs (1) through (3) of this subsection in the fiscal year shall be reduced by ⅓ of the number of visas made available in the previous fiscal year to special immigrants described in section 101(a)(27)(K) [8 U.S.C.A. § 1101(a)(27)(K)] who are natives of the foreign state.

(c) Diversity immigrants

(1) In general

Except as provided in paragraph (2), aliens subject to the worldwide level specified in section 201(e) [8 U.S.C.A. § 1151(e)] for diversity immigrants shall be allotted visas each fiscal year as follows:

(A) Determination of preference immigration

The Attorney General shall determine for the most recent previous 5–fiscal-year period for which data are available, the total number of aliens who are natives of each foreign state and who (i) were admitted or otherwise provided lawful permanent resident status (other than under this subsection) and (ii) were subject to the numerical limitations of section 201(a) [8 U.S.C.A. § 1151(a)] (other than paragraph (3) thereof) or who were admitted or otherwise provided lawful permanent resident status as an immediate relative or other alien described in section 201(b)(2) [8 U.S.C.A. § 1151(b)(2)].

(B) Identification of high-admission and low-admission regions and high-admission and low-admission states

The Attorney General—

(i) shall identify—

(I) each region (each in this paragraph referred to as a "high-admission region") for which the total of the numbers determined under subparagraph (A) for states in the region is greater than $1/6$ of the total of all such numbers, and

(II) each other region (each in this paragraph referred to as a "low-admission region"); and

(ii) shall identify—

(I) each foreign state for which the number determined under subparagraph (A) is greater than 50,000 (each such state in this paragraph referred to as a "high-admission state"), and

(II) each other foreign state (each such state in this paragraph referred to as a "low-admission state").

(C) Determination of percentage of worldwide immigration attributable to high-admission regions

The Attorney General shall determine the percentage of the total of the numbers determined under subparagraph (A) that are numbers for foreign states in high-admission regions.

(D) Determination of regional populations excluding high-admission states and ratios of populations of regions within low-admission regions and high-admission regions

The Attorney General shall determine—

(i) based on available estimates for each region, the total population of each region not including the population of any high-admission state;

(ii) for each low-admission region, the ratio of the population of the region determined under clause (i) to the total of the populations determined under such clause for all the low-admission regions; and

(iii) for each high-admission region, the ratio of the population of the region determined under clause (i) to the total of the populations determined under such clause for all the high-admission regions.

(E) Distribution of visas

(i) No visas for natives of high-admission states

The percentage of visas made available under this paragraph to natives of a high-admission state is 0.

(ii) For low-admission states in low-admission regions

Subject to clauses (iv) and (v), the percentage of visas made available under this paragraph to natives (other than natives of a high-admission state) in a low-admission region is the product of—

  (I) the percentage determined under subparagraph (C), and

  (II) the population ratio for that region determined under subparagraph (D)(ii).

(iii) For low-admission states in high-admission regions

Subject to clauses (iv) and (v), the percentage of visas made available under this paragraph to natives (other than natives of a high-admission state) in a high-admission region is the product of—

  (I) 100 percent minus the percentage determined under subparagraph (C), and

  (II) the population ratio for that region determined under subparagraph (D)(iii).

(iv) Redistribution of unused visa numbers

If the Secretary of State estimates that the number of immigrant visas to be issued to natives in any region for a fiscal year under this paragraph is less than the number of immigrant visas made available to such natives under this paragraph for the fiscal year, subject to clause (v), the excess visa numbers shall be made available to natives (other than natives of a high-admission state) of the other regions in proportion to the percentages otherwise specified in clauses (ii) and (iii).

(v) Limitation on visas for natives of a single foreign state

The percentage of visas made available under this paragraph to natives of any single foreign state for any fiscal year shall not exceed 7 percent.

(F) Region defined

Only for purposes of administering the diversity program under this subsection, Northern Ireland shall be treated as a separate foreign state, each colony or other component or dependent area of a foreign state overseas from the foreign state shall be treated as part of the foreign state, and the areas described in each of the following clauses shall be considered to be a separate region:

  (i) Africa.

  (ii) Asia.

  (iii) Europe.

(iv) North America (other than Mexico).

(v) Oceania.

(vi) South America, Mexico, Central America, and the Caribbean.

(2) Requirement of education or work experience

An alien is not eligible for a visa under this subsection unless the alien—

(A) has at least a high school education or its equivalent, or

(B) has, within 5 years of the date of application for a visa under this subsection, at least 2 years of work experience in an occupation which requires at least 2 years of training or experience.

(3) Maintenance of information

The Secretary of State shall maintain information on the age, occupation, education level, and other relevant characteristics of immigrants issued visas under this subsection.

(d) Treatment of family members

A spouse or child as defined in subparagraph (A), (B), (C), (D), or (E) of section 101(b)(1) [8 U.S.C.A. § 1101(b)(1)] shall, if not otherwise entitled to an immigrant status and the immediate issuance of a visa under subsection (a), (b), or (c), be entitled to the same status, and the same order of consideration provided in the respective subsection, if accompanying or following to join, the spouse or parent.

(e) Order of consideration

(1) Immigrant visas made available under subsection (a) or (b) shall be issued to eligible immigrants in the order in which a petition in behalf of each such immigrant is filed with the Attorney General (or in the case of special immigrants under section 101(a)(27)(D) [8 U.S.C.A. § 1101(a)(27)(D)], with the Secretary of State) as provided in section 204(a) [8 U.S.C.A. § 1154(a)].

(2) Immigrant visa numbers made available under subsection (c) (relating to diversity immigrants) shall be issued to eligible qualified immigrants strictly in a random order established by the Secretary of State for the fiscal year involved.

(3) Waiting lists of applicants for visas under this section shall be maintained in accordance with regulations prescribed by the Secretary of State.

(f) Authorization for issuance

In the case of any alien claiming in his application for an immigrant visa to be described in section 201(b)(2) [8 U.S.C.A. § 1151(b)(2)] or in subsection (a), (b), or (c) of this section, the consular officer shall not grant such status until he has been authorized to do so as provided by section 204 [8 U.S.C.A. § 1154].

(g) Lists

For purposes of carrying out the Secretary's responsibilities in the orderly administration of this section, the Secretary of State may make reasonable estimates of the anticipated numbers of visas to be issued during any quarter of any fiscal year within each of the categories under subsections (a), (b), and (c) and to rely upon such estimates in authorizing the issuance of visas. The Secretary of State shall terminate the registration of any alien who fails to apply for an immigrant visa within one year following notification to the alien of the availability of such visa, but the Secretary shall reinstate the registration of any such alien who establishes within 2 years following the date of notification of the availability of such visa that such failure to apply was due to circumstances beyond the alien's control.

(h) Rules for determining whether certain aliens are children

(1) In general

For purposes of subsections (a)(2)(A) and (d) of this section, a determination of whether an alien satisfies the age requirement in the matter preceding subparagraph (A) of section 101(b)(1) [8 U.S.C.A. § 1101(b)(1)] shall be made using—

(A) the age of the alien on the date on which an immigrant visa number becomes available for such alien (or, in the case of subsection (d) of this section, the date on which an immigrant visa number became available for the alien's parent), but only if the alien has sought to acquire the status of an alien lawfully admitted for permanent residence within one year of such availability; reduced by

(B) the number of days in the period during which the applicable petition described in paragraph (2) was pending.

(2) Petitions described

The petition described in this paragraph is—

(A) with respect to a relationship described in subsection (a)(2)(A) of this section, a petition filed under section 204 [8 U.S.C.A. § 1154] for classification of an alien child under subsection (a)(2)(A) of this section; or

(B) with respect to an alien child who is a derivative beneficiary under subsection (d) of this section, a petition filed under section 204 [8 U.S.C.A. § 1154] for classification of the alien's parent under subsection (a), (b), or (c) of this section.

(3) Retention of priority date

If the age of an alien is determined under paragraph (1) to be 21 years of age or older for the purposes of subsections (a)(2)(A) and (d) of this section, the alien's petition shall automatically be converted to the appropriate category and the alien shall retain the original priority date issued upon receipt of the original petition.

(4) Application to self-petitions

Paragraphs (1) through (3) shall apply to self-petitioners and derivatives of self-petitioners.

(June 27, 1952, c. 477, Title II, ch. 1, § 203, 66 Stat. 178; Sept. 11, 1957, Pub.L. 85–316, § 3, 71 Stat. 639; Sept. 22, 1959, Pub.L. 86–363, §§ 1–3, 73 Stat. 644; Oct. 3, 1965, Pub.L. 89–236, § 3, 79 Stat. 912; Oct. 20, 1976, Pub.L. 94–571, § 4, 90 Stat. 2705; Oct. 5, 1978, Pub.L. 95–412, § 3, 92 Stat. 907; Oct. 5, 1978, Pub.L. 95–417, § 1, 92 Stat. 917; Mar. 17, 1980, Pub.L. 96–212, Title II, § 203(c), (i), 94 Stat. 107, 108; Nov. 29, 1990, Pub.L. 101–649, Title I, §§ 111, 121(a), 131, 162(a)(1), Title VI, § 603(a)(3), 104 Stat. 4986, 4987, 4997, 5009, 5082; Oct. 1, 1991, Pub.L. 102–110, § 2(b), 105 Stat. 555; Dec. 12, 1991, Pub.L. 102–232, Title III, § 302(b)(2), (e)(3), 105 Stat. 1743, 1745; Oct. 25, 1994, Pub.L. 103–416, Title II, §§ 212(b), 219(c), 108 Stat. 4314, 4316; Nov. 12, 1999, Pub.L. 106–95, § 5, 113 Stat. 1318; Nov. 29, 1999, Pub.L. 106–113, Div. B, § 1000(a)(1) [H.R. 3421, Title I, § 117], 113 Stat. 1535, 1537; Nov. 22, 2000, Pub.L. 106–536, § 1(b)(1), 114 Stat. 2560; Aug. 6, 2002, Pub.L. 107–208, § 3, 116 Stat. 928; Nov. 2, 2002, Pub.L. 107–273, Div. C, Title I, §§ 11035, 11036(a), 116 Stat. 1846; Jan. 5, 2006, Pub.L. 109–162, Title VIII, § 805(b)(2), 119 Stat. 3056.)

§ 204.   Procedure for granting immigrant status [8 U.S.C.A. § 1154]

(a) Petitioning procedure

(1)(A)(i) Except as provided in clause (viii), any citizen of the United States claiming that an alien is entitled to classification by reason of a relationship described in paragraph (1), (3), or (4) of section 203(a) [8 U.S.C.A. § 1153(a)] or to an immediate relative status under section 201(b)(2)(A)(i) [8 U.S.C.A. § 1151(b)(2)(A)(i)] may file a petition with the Attorney General for such classification.

(ii) An alien spouse described in the second sentence of section 201(b)(2)(A)(i) [8 U.S.C.A. § 1151(b)(2)(A)(i)] also may file a petition with the Attorney General under this subparagraph for classification of the alien (and the alien's children) under such section.

(iii)(I) An alien who is described in subclause (II) may file a petition with the Attorney General under this clause for classification of the alien (and any child of the alien) if the alien demonstrates to the attorney general that

    (aa) the marriage or the intent to marry the United States citizen was entered into in good faith by the alien; and

    (bb) during the marriage or relationship intended by the alien to be legally a marriage, the alien or a child of the alien has been battered or has been the subject of extreme cruelty perpetrated by the alien's spouse or intended spouse.

(II) For purposes of subclause (I), an alien described in this subclause is an alien

    (aa)(AA) who is the spouse of a citizen of the United States;

    (BB) who believed that he or she had married a citizen of the United States and with whom a marriage ceremony was actually performed and who otherwise meets any applicable requirements under this Act to establish the existence of and bona fides of a marriage, but whose marriage is not legitimate solely because of the bigamy of such citizen of the United States; or

(CC) who was a bona fide spouse of a United States citizen within the past 2 years and—

(aaa) whose spouse died within the past 2 years;

(bbb) whose spouse lost or renounced citizenship status within the past 2 years related to an incident of domestic violence; or

(ccc) who demonstrates a connection between the legal termination of the marriage within the past 2 years and battering or extreme cruelty by the United States citizen spouse;

(bb) who is a person of good moral character;

(cc) who is eligible to be classified as an immediate relative under section 201(b)(2)(A)(i) [8 U.S.C.A. § 1151(b)(2)(A)(i)] or who would have been so classified but for the bigamy of the citizen of the United States that the alien intended to marry; and

(dd) who has resided with the alien's spouse or intended spouse.

(iv) An alien who is the child of a citizen of the United States, or who was a child of a United States citizen parent who within the past 2 years lost or renounced citizenship status related to an incident of domestic violence, and who is a person of good moral character, who is eligible to be classified as an immediate relative under section 201(b)(2)(A)(i) [8 U.S.C.A. § 1151(b)(2)(A)(i)], and who resides, or has resided in the past, with the citizen parent may file a petition with the Attorney General under this subparagraph for classification of the alien (and any child of the alien) under such section if the alien demonstrates to the Attorney General that the alien has been battered by or has been the subject of extreme cruelty perpetrated by the alien's citizen parent. For purposes of this clause, residence includes any period of visitation.

(v) An alien who—

(I) is the spouse, intended spouse, or child living abroad of a citizen who—

(aa) is an employee of the United States Government;

(bb) is a member of the uniformed services (as defined in section 101(a) of Title 10); or

(cc) has subjected the alien or the alien's child to battery or extreme cruelty in the United States; and

(II) is eligible to file a petition under clause (iii) or (iv), shall file such petition with the Attorney General under the procedures that apply to self-petitioners under clause (iii) or (iv), as applicable.

(vi) For the purposes of any petition filed under clause (iii) or (iv), the denaturalization, loss or renunciation of citizenship, death of the abuser, divorce, or changes to the abuser's citizenship status after filing of the petition shall not adversely affect the approval of the petition, and for approved petitions shall not preclude the classification of the eligible self-petitioning spouse or child as an immediate relative or affect the alien's ability to adjust status under subsections (a) and (c) of section 245 [8 U.S.C.A. § 1255] or obtain status as a lawful permanent resident based on the approved self-petition under such clauses.

(vii) An alien may file a petition with the Secretary of Homeland Security under this subparagraph for classification of the alien under section 201(b)(2)(a)(i) [8 U.S.C.A § 1151(b)(2)(a)(i)] if the alien—

(I) is the parent of a citizen of the United States or was a parent of a citizen of the United States who, within the past 2 years, lost or renounced citizenship status related to an incident of domestic violence or died;

(II) is a person of good moral character;

(III) is eligible to be classified as an immediate relative under section 201(b)(2)(A)(i) [8 U.S.C.A § 1151(b)(2)(A)(i)];

(IV) resides, or has resided, with the citizen daughter or son; and

(V) demonstrates that the alien has been battered or subject to extreme cruelty by the citizen daughter or son.

(viii)(I) Clause (i) shall not apply to a citizen of the United States who has been convicted of a specified offense against a minor, unless the Secretary of Homeland Security, in the Secretary's sole and unreviewable discretion, determines that the citizen poses no risk to the alien with respect to whom a petition described in clause (i) is filed.

(II) For purposes of subclause (I), the term "specified offense against a minor" is defined as in section 111 of the Adam Walsh Child Protection and Safety Act of 2006 [Pub. L. 109–248, 120 Stat. 587].

(B)(i)(I) Except as provided in subclause (II), any alien lawfully admitted for permanent residence claiming that an alien is entitled to a classification by reason of the relationship described in section 203(a)(2) [8 U.S.C.A. § 1153(a)(2)] may file a petition with the Attorney General for such classification.

(II) Subclause (I) shall not apply in the case of an alien lawfully admitted for permanent residence who has been convicted of a specified offense against a minor (as defined in subparagraph (A)(viii) (II)), unless the Secretary of Homeland Security, in the Secretary's sole and unreviewable discretion, determines that such person poses no risk to the alien with respect to whom a petition described in subclause (I) is filed.

(ii)(I) An alien who is described in subclause (II) may file a petition with the Attorney General under this clause for classification of the alien (and any child of the alien) if such a child has not been classified under clause (iii) of section 203(a)(2)(A) [8 U.S.C.A. § 1153(a)(2)(A)] and if the alien demonstrates to the attorney general that

(aa) the marriage or the intent to marry the lawful permanent resident was entered into in good faith by the alien; and

(bb) during the marriage or relationship intended by the alien to be legally a marriage, the alien or a child of the alien has been battered or has been the subject of extreme cruelty perpetrated by the alien's spouse or intended spouse.

(II) For purposes of subclause (I), an alien described in this paragraph is an alien

(aa)(AA) who is the spouse of a lawful permanent resident of the United States; or

(BB) who believed that he or she had married a lawful permanent resident of the United States and with whom a marriage ceremony was actually performed and who otherwise meets any applicable requirements under this Act to establish the existence of and bona fides of a marriage, but whose marriage is not legitimate solely because of the bigamy of such lawful permanent resident of the United States; or

(CC) who was a bona fide spouse of a lawful permanent resident within the past 2 years and—

(aaa) whose spouse lost status within the past 2 years due to an incident of domestic violence; or

(bbb) who demonstrates a connection between the legal termination of the marriage within the past 2 years and battering or extreme cruelty by the lawful permanent resident spouse;

(bb) who is a person of good moral character;

(cc) who is eligible to be classified as a spouse of an alien lawfully admitted for permanent residence under section 203(a)(2)(A) [8 U.S.C.A. § 1153(a)(2)(A)] or who would have been so classified but for the bigamy of the lawful permanent resident of the United States that the alien intended to marry; and

(dd) who has resided with the alien's spouse or intended spouse.

(iii) An alien who is the child of an alien lawfully admitted for permanent residence, or who was the child of a lawful permanent resident who within the past 2 years lost lawful permanent resident status due to an incident of domestic violence, and who is a person of good moral character, who is eligible for classification under section 203(a)(2)(A) [8 U.S.C.A. § 1153(a)(2)(A)], and who resides, or has resided in the past, with the alien's permanent resident alien parent may file a petition with the Attorney General under this subparagraph for classification of the alien (and any child of the alien) under such section if the alien demonstrates to the Attorney General that the alien has been battered by or has been the subject of extreme cruelty perpetrated by the alien's permanent resident parent.

(iv) An alien who

(I) is the spouse, intended spouse, or child living abroad of a lawful permanent resident who—

(aa) is an employee of the United States Government;

(bb) is a member of the uniformed services (as defined in section 101(a) of Title 10); or

(cc) has subjected the alien or the alien's child to battery or extreme cruelty in the United States; and

(II) is eligible to file a petition under clause (ii) or (iii), shall file such petition with the Attorney General under the procedures that apply to self-petitioners under clause (ii) or (iii), as applicable.

(v)(I) For the purposes of any petition filed or approved under clause (ii) or (iii), divorce, or the loss of lawful permanent resident status by a spouse or parent after the filing of a petition under that clause shall not adversely affect approval of the petition, and, for an approved petition, shall not affect the alien's ability to adjust status under subsections (a) and (c) of section 245 [8 U.S.C.A. § 1255] or obtain status as a lawful permanent resident based on an approved self-petition under clause (ii) or (iii).

(II) Upon the lawful permanent resident spouse or parent becoming or establishing the existence of United States citizenship through naturalization, acquisition of citizenship, or other means, any petition filed with the Immigration and Naturalization Service and pending or approved under clause (ii) or (iii) on behalf of an alien who has been battered or subjected to extreme cruelty shall be deemed reclassified as a petition filed under subparagraph (A) even if the acquisition of citizenship occurs after divorce or termination of parental rights.

(C) Notwithstanding section 101(f) [8 U.S.C.A. § 1101(f)], an act or conviction that is waivable with respect to the petitioner for purposes of a determination of the petitioner's admissibility under section 212(a) [8 U.S.C.A. § 1182(a)] or deportability under section

237(a) [8 U.S.C.A. § 1227(a)] shall not bar the Attorney General from finding the petitioner to be of good moral character under subparagraph (A)(iii), (A)(iv), (B)(ii), or (B)(iii) if the Attorney General finds that the act or conviction was connected to the alien's having been battered or subjected to extreme cruelty.

(D)(i)(I) Any child who attains 21 years of age who has filed a petition under clause (iv) of section 204(a)(1)(A) [8 U.S.C.A § 1154(a)(1)(A)] or section 204(a)(1)(B)(iii) [8 U.S.C.A. § 1154(a)(1)(B)(iii)] that was filed or approved before the date on which the child attained 21 years of age shall be considered (if the child has not been admitted or approved for lawful permanent residence by the date the child attained 21 years of age) a petitioner for preference status under paragraph (1), (2), or (3) of section 203(a) [8 U.S.C.A § 1153(a)], whichever paragraph is applicable, with the same priority date assigned to the self-petition filed under clause (iv) of section 204(a)(1)(A) [8 U.S.C.A § 1154(a)(1)(A)] or section 204(a)(1)(B)(iii) [8 U.S.C.A. § 1154(a)(1)(B)(iii)]. No new petition shall be required to be filed.

(II) Any individual described in subclause (I) is eligible for deferred action and work authorization.

(III) Any derivative child who attains 21 years of age who is included in a petition described in clause (ii) that was filed or approved before the date on which the child attained 21 years of age shall be considered (if the child has not been admitted or approved for lawful permanent residence by the date the child attained 21 years of age) a VAWA self-petitioner with the same priority date as that assigned to the petitioner in any petition described in clause (ii). No new petition shall be required to be filed.

(IV) Any individual described in subclause (III) and any derivative child of a petition described in clause (ii) is eligible for deferred action and work authorization.

(ii) The petition referred to in clause (i)(III) is a petition filed by an alien under subparagraph (A)(iii), (A)(iv), (B)(ii) or (B)(iii) in which the child is included as a derivative beneficiary.

(iii) Nothing in the amendments made by the Child Status Protection Act shall be construed to limit or deny any right or benefit provided under this subparagraph.

(iv) Any alien who benefits from this subparagraph may adjust status in accordance with subsections (a) and (c) of section 245 [8 U.S.C.A § 1255] as an alien having an approved petition for classification under subparagraph (A)(iii), (A)(iv), (B)(ii), or (B)(iii).

(v) For purposes of this paragraph, an individual who is not less than 21 years of age, who qualified to file a petition under subparagraph (A)(iv) or (B)(iii) as of the day before the date on which the individual attained 21 years of age, and who did not file such a petition before such day, shall be treated as having filed a petition under such subparagraph as of such day if a petition is filed for the status described in such subparagraph before the individual attains 25 years of age and the individual shows that the abuse was at least one central reason for the filing delay. Clauses (i) through (iv) of this subparagraph shall apply to an individual described in this clause in the same manner as an individual filing a petition under subparagraph (A)(iv) or (B)(iii).

(E) Any alien desiring to be classified under section 203(b)(1) (A) [8 U.S.C.A. § 1153(b)(1)(A)], or any person on behalf of such an alien, may file a petition with the Attorney General for such classification.

(F) Any employer desiring and intending to employ within the United States an alien entitled to classification under section 203(b)(1)(B) [8 U.S.C.A. § 1153(b)(1)(B)], 203(b)(1)(C) [8 U.S.C.A. § 1153(b)(1)(C)], 203(b)(2) [8 U.S.C.A. § 1153(b)(2)], or 203(b)(3) [8 U.S.C.A. § 1153(b)(3)] may file a petition with the Attorney General for such classification.

(G)(i) Any alien (other than a special immigrant under section 101(a)(27)(D) [8 U.S.C.A. § 1101(a)(27)(D)]) desiring to be classified under section 203(b)(4) [8 U.S.C.A. § 1153(b)(4)], or any person on behalf of such an alien, may file a petition with the Attorney General for such classification.

(ii) Aliens claiming status as a special immigrant under section 101(a)(27)(D) [8 U.S.C.A. § 1101(a)(27)(D)] may file a petition only with the Secretary of State and only after notification by the Secretary that such status has been recommended and approved pursuant to such section.

(H) Any alien desiring to be classified under section 203(b)(5) [8 U.S.C.A. § 1153(b)(5)] may file a petition with the Attorney General for such classification.

(I)(i) Any alien desiring to be provided an immigrant visa under section 203(c) [8 U.S.C.A. § 1153(c)] may file a petition at the place and time determined by the Secretary of State by regulation. Only one such petition may be filed by an alien with respect to any petitioning period established. If more than one petition is submitted all such petitions submitted for such period by the alien shall be voided.

(ii)(I) The Secretary of State shall designate a period for the filing of petitions with respect to visas which may be issued under section 203(c) [8 U.S.C.A. § 1153(c)] for the fiscal year beginning after the end of the period.

(II) Aliens who qualify, through random selection, for a visa under section 203(c) [8 U.S.C.A. § 1153(c)] shall remain eligible to receive such visa only through the end of the specific fiscal year for which they were selected.

(III) The Secretary of State shall prescribe such regulations as may be necessary to carry out this clause.

(iii) A petition under this subparagraph shall be in such form as the Secretary of State may by regulation prescribe and shall contain such information and be supported by such documentary evidence as the Secretary of State may require.

(iv) Repealed. Pub.L. 113–6, Div. D, Title V, § 563, Mar. 26, 2013, 127 Stat. 380.

(J) In acting on petitions filed under clause (iii) or (iv) of subparagraph (A) or clause (ii) or (iii) of subparagraph (B), or in making determinations under subparagraphs (C) and (D), the Attorney General shall consider any credible evidence relevant to the petition. The determination of what evidence is credible and the weight to be given that evidence shall be within the sole discretion of the Attorney General.

(K) Upon the approval of a petition as a VAWA self-petitioner, the alien—

(i) is eligible for work authorization; and

(ii) may be provided an "employment authorized" endorsement or appropriate work permit incidental to such approval.

(L) Notwithstanding the previous provisions of this paragraph, an individual who was a VAWA petitioner or who had the status of a nonimmigrant under subparagraph (T) or (U) of section 101(a)(15) [8 U.S.C.A § 1101(a)(15)] may not file a petition for classification under this section or section 214 [8 U.S.C.A § 1184] to classify any person who committed the battery or extreme cruelty or trafficking against the individual (or the individual's child) which established the individual's (or individual's child) eligibility as a VAWA petitioner or for such nonimmigrant status.

(2)(A) The Attorney General may not approve a spousal second preference petition for the classification of the spouse of an alien if the alien, by virtue of a prior marriage, has been accorded the status of an alien lawfully admitted for permanent residence as the spouse of a citizen of the United States or as the spouse of an alien lawfully admitted for permanent residence, unless—

(i) a period of 5 years has elapsed after the date the alien acquired the status of an alien lawfully admitted for permanent residence, or

(ii) the alien establishes to the satisfaction of the Attorney General by clear and convincing evidence that the prior marriage (on the basis of which the alien obtained the status of an alien lawfully admitted for permanent residence) was not entered into for the purpose of evading any provision of the immigration laws.

In this subparagraph, the term "spousal second preference petition" refers to a petition, seeking preference status under section 203(a)(2) [8 U.S.C.A. § 1153(a)(2)], for an alien as a spouse of an alien lawfully admitted for permanent residence.

(B) Subparagraph (A) shall not apply to a petition filed for the classification of the spouse of an alien if the prior marriage of the alien was terminated by the death of his or her spouse.

(b) Investigation; consultation; approval; authorization to grant preference status

After an investigation of the facts in each case, and after consultation with the Secretary of Labor with respect to petitions to accord a status under section 203(b)(2) [8 U.S.C.A. § 1153(b)(2)] or 203(b)(3) [8 U.S.C.A. § 1153(b)(3)], the Attorney General shall, if he determines that the facts stated in the petition are true and that the alien in behalf of whom the petition is made is an immediate relative specified in section 201(b) [8 U.S.C.A. § 1151(b)] or is eligible for preference under subsection (a) or (b) of section 203 [8 U.S.C.A. § 1153], approve the petition and forward one copy thereof to the Department of State. The Secretary of State shall then authorize the consular officer concerned to grant the preference status.

(c) Prohibition against approval in cases of marriages entered into in order to evade immigration laws

Notwithstanding the provisions of subsection (b) no petition shall be approved if **(1)** the alien has previously been accorded, or has sought to be accorded, an immediate relative or preference status as the spouse of a citizen of the United States or the spouse of an alien lawfully admitted for permanent residence, by reason of a marriage determined by the Attorney General to have been entered into for the purpose of evading the immigration laws, or **(2)** the Attorney General has determined that the alien has attempted or conspired to enter into a marriage for the purpose of evading the immigration laws.

(d) Recommendation of valid home-study

(1) Notwithstanding the provisions of subsections (a) and (b) no petition may be approved on behalf of a child defined in subparagraph (F) or (G) of section 101(b)(1) [8 U.S.C.A. § 1101(b)(1)] unless a valid home-study has been favorably recommended by an agency of the State of the child's proposed residence, or by an agency authorized by that State to conduct such a study, or, in the case of a child adopted abroad, by an appropriate public or private adoption agency which is licensed in the United States.

(2) Notwithstanding the provisions of subsections (a) and (b), no petition may be approved on behalf of a child defined in section 101(b)(1)(G) [8 U.S.C.A. § 1101(b)(1)(G)] unless the Secretary of State has certified that the central authority of the child's country of origin has notified the United States central authority under the convention referred to in such section 101(b)(1)(G) [8 U.S.C.A. § 1101(b)(1)(G)] that a United States citizen habitually resident in the United States has effected final adoption of the child, or has been granted custody of the child for the purpose of emigration and adoption, in accordance with such convention and the Intercountry Adoption Act of 2000.

(e) Subsequent finding of non-entitlement to preference classification

Nothing in this section shall be construed to entitle an immigrant, in behalf of whom a petition under this section is approved, to be admitted [sic] the United States as an immigrant under subsection (a), (b), or (c) of section 203 [8 U.S.C.A. § 1153] or as an immediate relative under section 201(b) [8 U.S.C.A. § 1151(b)] if upon his arrival at a port of entry in the United States he is found not to be entitled to such classification.

(f) Preferential treatment for children fathered by United States citizens and born in Korea, Vietnam, Laos, Kampuchea, or Thailand after 1950 and before October 22, 1982

(1) Any alien claiming to be an alien described in paragraph (2)(A) of this subsection (or any person on behalf of such an alien) may file a petition with the Attorney General for classification under section 201(b) [8 U.S.C.A. § 1151(b)], 203(a)(1) [8 U.S.C.A. § 1153(a)(1)], or 203(a)(3) [8 U.S.C.A. § 1153(a)(3)], as appropriate. After an investigation of the facts of each case the Attorney General shall, if the conditions described in paragraph (2) are met, approve the petition and forward one copy to the Secretary of State.

(2) The Attorney General may approve a petition for an alien under paragraph (1) if—

(A) he has reason to believe that the alien (i) was born in Korea, Vietnam, Laos, Kampuchea, or Thailand after 1950 and before October 22, 1982, and (ii) was fathered by a United States citizen;

(B) he has received an acceptable guarantee of legal custody and financial responsibility described in paragraph (4); and

(C) in the case of an alien under eighteen years of age, (i) the alien's placement with a sponsor in the United States has been arranged by an appropriate public, private, or State child welfare agency licensed in the United States and actively involved in the intercountry placement of children and (ii) the alien's mother or guardian has in writing irrevocably released the alien for emigration.

(3) In considering petitions filed under paragraph (1), the Attorney General shall—

(A) consult with appropriate governmental officials and officials of private voluntary organizations in the country of the alien's birth in order to make the determinations described in subparagraphs (A) and (C)(ii) of paragraph 2; and

(B) consider the physical appearance of the alien and any evidence provided by the petitioner, including birth and baptismal certificates, local civil records, photographs of, and letters or proof of financial support from, a putative father who is a citizen of the United States, and the testimony of witnesses, to the extent it is relevant or probative.

(4)(A) A guarantee of legal custody and financial responsibility for an alien described in paragraph (2) must—

(i) be signed in the presence of an immigration officer or consular officer by an individual (hereinafter in this paragraph referred to as the "sponsor") who is twenty-one years of age or older, is of good moral character, and is a citizen of the United States or alien lawfully admitted for permanent residence, and

(ii) provide that the sponsor agrees **(I)** in the case of an alien under eighteen years of age, to assume legal custody for the alien after the alien's departure to the United States and until the alien becomes eighteen years of age, in accordance with the laws of the State where the alien and the sponsor will reside, and **(II)** to furnish, during the five-year period beginning on the date of the alien's acquiring the status of an alien lawfully admitted for permanent residence, or during the period beginning on the date of the alien's acquiring the status of an alien lawfully admitted for permanent residence and ending on the date on which the alien becomes twenty-one years of age, whichever period is longer, such financial support as is necessary to maintain the family in the United States of which the alien is a member at a level equal to at least 125 per centum of the current official poverty line (as established by the Director of the Office of Management and Budget, under section 9902(2) of Title 42 and as revised by the Secretary of Health and Human Services under the second and third sentences of such section) for a family of the same size as the size of the alien's family.

(B) A guarantee of legal custody and financial responsibility described in subparagraph (A) may be enforced with respect to an alien against his sponsor in a civil suit brought by the Attorney General in the United States district court for the district in which the sponsor resides, except that a sponsor or his estate shall not be liable under such a guarantee if the sponsor dies or is adjudicated a bankrupt under Title 11.

(g) Restrictions on petitions based on marriages entered while in exclusion or deportation proceedings

Notwithstanding subsection (a), except as provided in section 245(e)(3) [8 U.S.C.A. § 1255(e)(3)], a petition may not be approved to grant an alien immediate relative status or preference status by reason of a marriage which was entered into during the period described in section 245(e)(2) [8 U.S.C.A. § 1255(e)(2)], until the alien has resided outside the United States for a 2-year period beginning after the date of the marriage.

(h) Survival of rights to petition

The legal termination of a marriage may not be the sole basis for revocation under section 205 [8 U.S.C.A. § 1155] of a petition filed under subsection (a)(1)(A)(iii) or a petition filed under subsection (a)(1)(B)(ii) pursuant to conditions described in subsection (a)(1)(A)(iii)(I). Remarriage of an alien whose petition was approved under section 204(a)(1)(B) (ii) [8 U.S.C.A. § 1154(a)(1)(B)(ii)] or section 204(a)(1)(A)(iii) [8 U.S.C.A. § 1154(a)(1)(A)(iii)] or marriage of an alien described in clause (iv) or (vi) of section 204(a)(1)(A) [8 U.S.C.A. § 1154(a)(1)(A)] or in section 204(a)(1) (B)(iii) [8 U.S.C.A. § 1154(a)(1)(B)(iii)] shall not be the basis for revocation of a petition approval under section 205 [8 U.S.C.A. § 1155].

(i) Professional athletes

(1) In general

A petition under subsection (a)(4)(D) for classification of a professional athlete shall remain valid for the athlete after the athlete changes employers, if the new employer is a team in the same sport as the team which was the employer who filed the petition.

(2) Definition

For purposes of paragraph (1), the term "professional athlete" means an individual who is employed as an athlete by—

(A) a team that is a member of an association of 6 or more professional sports teams whose total combined revenues exceed $10,000,000 per year, if the association governs the conduct of its members and regulates the contests and exhibitions in which its member teams regularly engage; or

(B) any minor league team that is affiliated with such an association.

(j) Job flexibility for long delayed applicants for adjustment of status to permanent residence

A petition under subsection (a)(1)(D)* of this section for an individual whose application for adjustment of status pursuant to section 245 [8 U.S.C.A. § 1255] has been filed and remained unadjudicated for 180 days or more shall remain valid with respect to a new job if the individual changes jobs or employers if the new job is in the same or a similar occupational classification as the job for which the petition was filed.

(k) Procedures for unmarried sons and daughters of citizens

(1) In general

---

*Probably should refer to subsection (a)(1)(F)—eds.

Except as provided in paragraph (2), in the case of a petition under this section initially filed for an alien unmarried son or daughter's classification as a family-sponsored immigrant under section 203(a)(2)(B) [8 U.S.C.A. § 1153(a)(2)(B)], based on a parent of the son or daughter being an alien lawfully admitted for permanent residence, if such parent subsequently becomes a naturalized citizen of the United States, such petition shall be converted to a petition to classify the unmarried son or daughter as a family-sponsored immigrant under section 203(a) (1) [8 U.S.C.A. § 1153(a)(1)].

(2) Exception

Paragraph (1) does not apply if the son or daughter files with the Attorney General a written statement that he or she elects not to have such conversion occur (or if it has occurred, to have such conversion revoked). Where such an election has been made, any determination with respect to the son or daughter's eligibility for admission as a family-sponsored immigrant shall be made as if such naturalization had not taken place.

(3) Priority date

Regardless of whether a petition is converted under this subsection or not, if an unmarried son or daughter described in this subsection was assigned a priority date with respect to such petition before such naturalization, he or she may maintain that priority date.

(4) Clarification

This subsection shall apply to a petition if it is properly filed, regardless of whether it was approved or not before such naturalization.

(*l*) Surviving relative consideration for certain petitions and applications

(1) In general

An alien described in paragraph (2) who resided in the United States at the time of the death of the qualifying relative and who continues to reside in the United States shall have such petition described in paragraph (2), or an application for adjustment of status to that of a person admitted for lawful permanent residence based upon the family relationship described in paragraph (2), and any related applications, adjudicated notwithstanding the death of the qualifying relative, unless the Secretary of Homeland Security determines, in the unreviewable discretion of the Secretary, that approval would not be in the public interest.

(2) Alien described

An alien described in this paragraph is an alien who, immediately prior to the death of his or her qualifying relative, was—

(A) the beneficiary of a pending or approved petition for classification as an immediate relative (as described in section 201(b)(2)(A) (i) [8 U.S.C.A. § 1151(b)(2)(A)(i)]);

(B) the beneficiary of a pending or approved petition for classification under section 203(a) or (d) [8 U.S.C.A. § 1153(a) or (d)];

(C) a derivative beneficiary of a pending or approved petition for classification under section 203(b) [8 U.S.C.A. § 1153(b)] (as described in section 203(d) [8 U.S.C.A. § 1153(d)]);

(D) the beneficiary of a pending or approved refugee/asylee relative petition under section 207 or 208 [8 U.S.C.A. § 1157 or 1158];

(E) an alien admitted in "T" nonimmigrant status as described in section 101(a)(15)(T)(ii) [8 U.S.C.A. § 1101(a)(15)(T)(ii)] or in "U" nonimmigrant status as described in section 101(a)(15)(U)(ii) [8 U.S.C.A. § 1101(a)(15)(U)(ii)];

(F) a child of an alien who filed a pending or approved petition for classification or application for adjustment of status or other benefit specified in section 101(a)(51) [8 U.S.C.A. § 1101(a)(51)] as a VAWA self-petitioner; or

(G) an asylee (as described in section 208(b)(3) [8 U.S.C.A. § 1158(b)(3)]).

(June 27, 1952, c. 477, Title II, ch. 1, § 204, 66 Stat. 179; Oct. 24, 1962, Pub.L. 87–885, § 3, 76 Stat. 1247; Oct. 3, 1965, Pub.L. 89–236, § 4, 79 Stat. 915; Oct. 20, 1976, Pub.L. 94–571, § 7(b), 90 Stat. 2706; Oct. 5, 1978, Pub.L. 95–417, §§ 2, 3, 92 Stat. 917; Oct. 19, 1980, Pub.L. 96–470, Title II, § 207, 94 Stat. 2245; Dec. 29, 1981, Pub.L. 97–116, §§ 3, 18(d), 95 Stat. 1611, 1620; Oct. 22, 1982, Pub.L. 97–359, 96 Stat. 1716; Nov. 10, 1986, Pub.L. 99–639, §§ 2(c), 4(a), 5(b), 100 Stat. 3541, 3543; Oct. 24, 1988, Pub. L. 100–525, § 9(g), 102 Stat. 2620; Nov. 29, 1990, Pub.L. 101–649, Title I, § 162(b), Title VII, § 702(b), 104 Stat. 5010, 5086; Dec. 12, 1991, Pub.L. 102–232, Title III, §§ 302(e)(4),(5), 308(b), 309(b)(5), 105 Stat. 1745, 1746, 1757, 1758; Sept. 13, 1994, Pub.L. 103–322, Title IV, § 40701(a), (b)(1), (c), 108 Stat. 1953, 1954; Oct. 25, 1994, Pub.L. 103–416, Title II, § 219(b)(2), 108 Stat. 4316; Sept. 30, 1996, Pub.L. 104–208, Div. C, Title III, § 308(e)(1)(A), (f)(2)(A), Title VI, § 624(b), 110 Stat. 3009–619, 3009–621, 3009–699; Oct. 6, 2000, Pub.L. 106–279, Title III, § 302(b), 114 Stat. 839; Oct. 17, 2000, Pub.L. 106–313, Title I, § 106(c)(1), 114 Stat. 1254; Oct. 28, 2000, Pub.L. 106–386, Div. B, Title V, §§ 1503(b), (c), (d), 1507(a)(1), (2), (b), 114 Stat. 1518, 1520, 1521, 1529, 1530; Aug. 6, 2002, Pub.L. 107–208, §§ 6, 7, 116 Stat. 929; Jan. 5, 2006, Pub.L. 109–162, Title VIII, §§ 805(a), (c), 814(b), (e), 816, 119 Stat. 3056, 3059, 3060; July 27, 2006, Pub.L. 109–248, Title IV, § 402(a), 120 Stat. 622; Aug. 12, 2006, Pub.L. 109–271, § 6(a), 120 Stat. 762; Oct. 28, 2009, Pub.L. 111–83, Title V, § 568(d)(1), 123 Stat. 2187; Pub.L. 113–4, Title VIII, § 803, Mar. 7, 2013, 127 Stat. 111; Pub.L. 113–6, Div. D, Title V, § 563, Mar. 26, 2013, 127 Stat. 380.)

§ 205.   Revocation of approval of petitions; notice of revocation; effective date [8 U.S.C.A. § 1155]

The Secretary of Homeland Security may, at any time, for what he deems to be good and sufficient cause, revoke the approval of any petition approved by him under section 204 [8 U.S.C.A. § 1154]. Such revocation shall be effective as of the date of approval of any such petition.

(June 27, 1952, c. 477, Title II, ch. 1, § 205, 66 Stat. 180; Sept. 22, 1959, Pub.L. 86–363, § 5(a), (b), 73 Stat. 644; Sept. 26, 1961, Pub.L. 87–301, §§ 3, 10, 75 Stat. 650, 654; Oct. 3, 1965, Pub.L. 89–236, § 5, 79 Stat. 916; Sept. 30, 1996, Pub.L. 104–208, Div. C, Title III, § 308(g)(3)(A), 110 Stat. 3009–622; Dec. 17, 2004, Pub.L. 108–458, Title V, § 5304(c), 118 Stat. 3736.)

§ 206.   Unused immigrant visas [8 U.S.C.A. § 1156]

If an immigrant having an immigrant visa is denied admission to the United States and removed, or does not apply for admission before the expiration of the validity of his visa, or if an alien having an immigrant visa issued to him as a preference immigrant is found not to be a preference immigrant, an immigrant visa or a preference immigrant visa, as the case may be, may be issued in lieu thereof to another qualified alien.

(June 27, 1952, c. 477, Title II, ch. 1, § 206, 66 Stat. 181; Oct. 3, 1965, Pub.L. 89–236, § 6, 79 Stat. 916; Sept. 30, 1996, Pub.L. 104–208, Div. C, Title III, § 308(d)(4)(D), 110 Stat. 3009–618.)

§ 207.   Annual admission of refugees and admission of emergency situation refugees [8 U.S.C.A. § 1157]

(a) Maximum number of admissions; increases for humanitarian concerns; allocations

(1) Except as provided in subsection (b), the number of refugees who may be admitted under this section in fiscal year 1980, 1981, or 1982, may not exceed fifty thousand unless the President determines, before the beginning of the fiscal year and after appropriate consultation (as defined in subsection (e)), that admission of a specific number of refugees in excess of such number is justified by humanitarian concerns or is otherwise in the national interest.

(2) Except as provided in subsection (b), the number of refugees who may be admitted under this section in any fiscal year after fiscal year 1982 shall be such number as the President determines, before the beginning of the fiscal year and after appropriate consultation, is justified by humanitarian concerns or is otherwise in the national interest.

(3) Admissions under this subsection shall be allocated among refugees of special humanitarian concern to the United States in accordance with a determination made by the President after appropriate consultation.

(4) In the determination made under this subsection for each fiscal year (beginning with fiscal year 1992), the President shall enumerate, with the respective number of refugees so determined, the number of aliens who were granted asylum in the previous year.

(b) Determinations by President respecting number of admissions for humanitarian concerns

If the President determines, after appropriate consultation, that (1) an unforeseen emergency refugee situation exists, (2) the admission of certain refugees in response to the emergency refugee situation is justified by grave humanitarian concerns or is otherwise in the national interest, and (3) the admission to the United States of these refugees cannot be accomplished under subsection (a), the President may fix a number of refugees to be admitted to the United States during the succeeding period (not to exceed twelve months) in response to the emergency refugee situation and such admissions shall be allocated among refugees of special humanitarian concern to the United States in accordance with a determination made by the President after the appropriate consultation provided under this subsection.

(c) Admission by Attorney General of refugees; criteria; admission status of spouse or child; applicability of other statutory requirements; termination of refugee status of alien, spouse or child

(1) Subject to the numerical limitations established pursuant to subsections (a) and (b), the Attorney General may, in the Attorney General's discretion and pursuant to such regulations as the Attorney General may prescribe, admit any refugee who is not firmly resettled in any foreign country, is determined to be of special humanitarian concern to the United States, and is admissible except as otherwise provided under paragraph (3) as an immigrant under this Act.

(2)(A) A spouse or child (as defined in section 101(b)(1)(A), (B), (C), (D), or (E) [8 U.S.C.A. § 1101(b)(1)(A), (B), (C), (D), or (E)]) of any refugee who qualifies for admission under paragraph (1) shall, if not otherwise entitled to admission under paragraph (1) and if not a person described in the second sentence of section 101(a)(42) [8 U.S.C.A. § 1101(a)(42)], be entitled to the same admission status as such refugee if accompanying, or following to join, such refugee and if the spouse or child is admissible (except as otherwise provided under paragraph (3)) as an immigrant under this chapter. Upon the spouse's or child's admission to the United States, such admission shall be charged against the numerical limitation established in accordance with the appropriate subsection under which the refugee's admission is charged.

(B) An unmarried alien who seeks to accompany, or follow to join, a parent granted admission as a refugee under this subsection, and who was under 21 years of age on the date on which such parent applied for refugee status under this section, shall continue to be classified as a child for purposes of this paragraph, if the alien attained 21 years of age after such application was filed but while it was pending.

(3) The provisions of paragraphs (4), (5), and (7)(A) of section 212(a) [8 U.S.C.A. § 1182(a)] shall not be applicable to any alien seeking admission to the United States under this subsection, and the Attorney General may waive any other provision of such section (other than paragraph (2)(C) or subparagraph (A), (B), (C), or (E) of paragraph (3)) with respect to such an alien for humanitarian purposes, to assure family unity, or when it is otherwise in the public interest. Any such waiver by the Attorney General shall be in writing and shall be granted only on an individual basis following an investigation. The Attorney General shall provide for the annual reporting to Congress of the number of waivers granted under this paragraph in the previous fiscal year and a summary of the reasons for granting such waivers.

(4) The refugee status of any alien (and of the spouse or child of the alien) may be terminated by the Attorney General pursuant to such regulations as the Attorney General may prescribe if the Attorney General determines that the alien was not in fact a refugee within the meaning of section 101(a)(42) [8 U.S.C.A. § 1101(a)(42)] at the time of the alien's admission.

(d) Oversight reporting and consultation requirements

(1) Before the start of each fiscal year the President shall report to the Committees on the Judiciary of the House of Representatives and of the Senate regarding the foreseeable number of refugees who will be in need of resettlement during the fiscal year and the anticipated allocation of refugee admissions during the fiscal year. The President shall provide for periodic discussions between designated representatives of the President and members of such committees regarding changes in the worldwide refugee situation, the progress of refugee admissions, and the possible need for adjustments in the allocation of admissions among refugees.

(2) As soon as possible after representatives of the President initiate appropriate consultation with respect to the number of refugee admissions under subsection (a) or with respect to the admission of refugees in response to an emergency refugee situation under subsection (b), the Committees on the Judiciary of the House of Representatives and of the Senate shall cause to have printed in the Congressional Record the substance of such consultation.

(3)(A) After the President initiates appropriate consultation prior to making a determination under subsection (a), a hearing to review the proposed determination shall be held unless public disclosure of the details of the proposal would jeopardize the lives or safety of individuals.

(B) After the President initiates appropriate consultation prior to making a determination, under subsection (b), that the number of refugee admissions should be increased because of an unforeseen emergency refugee situation, to the extent that time and the nature of the emergency refugee situation permit, a hearing to review the proposal to increase refugee admissions shall be held unless public disclosure of the details of the proposal would jeopardize the lives or safety of individuals.

(e) "Appropriate consultation" defined

For purposes of this section, the term "appropriate consultation" means, with respect to the admission of refugees and allocation of refugee admissions, discussions in person by designated Cabinet-level representatives of the President with members of the Committees on the Judiciary of the Senate and of the House of Representatives to review the refugee situation or emergency refugee situation, to project the extent of possible participation of the United States therein, to discuss the reasons for believing that the proposed admission of refugees is justified by humanitarian concerns or grave humanitarian concerns or is otherwise in the national interest, and to provide such members with the following information:

(1) A description of the nature of the refugee situation.

(2) A description of the number and allocation of the refugees to be admitted and an analysis of conditions within the countries from which they came.

(3) A description of the proposed plans for their movement and resettlement and the estimated cost of their movement and resettlement.

(4) An analysis of the anticipated social, economic, and demographic impact of their admission to the United States.

(5) A description of the extent to which other countries will admit and assist in the resettlement of such refugees.

(6) An analysis of the impact of the participation of the United States in the resettlement of such refugees on the foreign policy interests of the United States.

(7) Such additional information as may be appropriate or requested by such members.

To the extent possible, information described in this subsection shall be provided at least two weeks in advance of discussions in person by designated representatives of the President with such members.

(f) Training United States officials adjudicating refugee cases

(1) The Attorney General, in consultation with the Secretary of State, shall provide all United States officials adjudicating refugee cases under this section with the same training as that provided to officers adjudicating asylum cases under section 208 [8 U.S.C.A. § 1158].

(2) Such training shall include country-specific conditions, instruction on the internationally recognized right to freedom of religion, instruction on methods of religious persecution practiced in foreign countries, and applicable distinctions within a country between the nature of and treatment of various religious practices and believers.

(June 27, 1952, c. 477, Title II, ch. 1, § 207, as added Mar. 17, 1980, Pub.L. 96–212, Title II, § 201(b), 94 Stat. 103, and amended Oct. 24, 1988, Pub.L. 100–525, § 9(h), 102 Stat. 2620; Nov. 29, 1990, Pub.L. 101–649, Title I, § 104(b), Title VI, § 603(a)(4), 104 Stat. 4985, 5082; Dec. 12, 1991, Pub.L. 102–232, Title III, § 307(*l*)(1), 105 Stat. 1756; Sept. 30, 1996, Pub.L. 104–208, Div. C, Title VI, § 601(b), 110 Stat. 3009–689; Oct. 27, 1998, Pub.L. 105–292, Title VI, § 602(a), 112 Stat. 2812; Aug. 6, 2002, Pub.L. 107–208, § 5, 116 Stat. 929; May 11, 2005, Pub.L. 109–13, Div. B, § 101(g), 119 Stat. 231, 305.)

§ 208.   Asylum procedure [8 U.S.C.A. § 1158]

(a) Authority to apply for asylum

(1) In general

Any alien who is physically present in the United States or who arrives in the United States (whether or not at a designated port of arrival and including an alien who is brought to the United States after having been interdicted in international or United States waters), irrespective of such alien's status, may apply for asylum in accordance with this section or, where applicable, section 235(b) [8 U.S.C.A. § 1225(b)].

(2) Exceptions

(A) Safe third country

Paragraph (1) shall not apply to an alien if the Attorney General determines that the alien may be removed, pursuant to a bilateral or multilateral agreement, to a country (other than the country of the alien's nationality or, in the case of an alien having no nationality, the country of the alien's last habitual residence) in which the alien's life or freedom would not be threatened on account of race, religion, nationality, membership in a particular social group, or political opinion, and where the alien would have access to a full and fair procedure for determining a claim to asylum or equivalent temporary protection, unless the Attorney General finds that it is in the public interest for the alien to receive asylum in the United States.

(B) Time limit

Subject to subparagraph (D), paragraph (1) shall not apply to an alien unless the alien demonstrates by clear and convincing evidence that the application has been filed within 1 year after the date of the alien's arrival in the United States.

(C) Previous asylum applications

Subject to subparagraph (D), paragraph (1) shall not apply to an alien if the alien has previously applied for asylum and had such application denied.

(D) Changed circumstances

An application for asylum of an alien may be considered, notwithstanding subparagraphs (B) and (C), if the alien demonstrates to the satisfaction of the Attorney General either the existence of changed circumstances which materially affect the applicant's eligibility for asylum or extraordinary circumstances relating to the delay in filing an application within the period specified in subparagraph (B).

(E) Applicability

Subparagraphs (A) and (B) shall not apply to an unaccompanied alien child (as defined in section 462(g) of the Homeland Security Act of 2002 [6 U.S.C.A. § 279(g)]).

(3) Limitation on judicial review

No court shall have jurisdiction to review any determination of the Attorney General under paragraph (2).

(b) Conditions for granting asylum

(1) In general

(A) Eligibility

The Secretary of Homeland Security or the Attorney General may grant asylum to an alien who has applied for asylum in accordance with the requirements and procedures established by the Secretary of Homeland Security or the Attorney General under this section if the Secretary of Homeland Security or the Attorney General determines that such alien is a refugee within the meaning of section 101(a)(42)(A) [8 U.S.C.A. § 1101(a)(42)(A)].

(B) Burden of proof

(i) In general

The burden of proof is on the applicant to establish that the applicant is a refugee, within the meaning of section 101(a)(42)(A) [8 U.S.C.A. § 1101(a)(42)(A)]. To establish that the applicant is a refugee within the meaning of such section, the applicant must establish that race, religion, nationality, membership in a particular social group, or political opinion was or will be at least one central reason for persecuting the applicant.

(ii) Sustaining burden

The testimony of the applicant may be sufficient to sustain the applicant's burden without corroboration, but only if the applicant satisfies the trier of fact that the applicant's testimony is credible, is persuasive, and refers to specific facts sufficient to demonstrate that the applicant is a refugee. In determining whether the applicant has met the applicant's burden, the trier of fact may weigh the credible testimony along with other evidence of record. Where the trier of fact determines that the applicant should provide evidence that corroborates otherwise credible testimony, such evidence must be provided unless the applicant does not have the evidence and cannot reasonably obtain the evidence.

(iii) Credibility determination

Considering the totality of the circumstances, and all relevant factors, a trier of fact may base a credibility determination on the demeanor, candor, or responsiveness of the applicant or witness, the inherent plausibility of the applicant's or witness's account, the consistency between the applicant's or witness's written and oral statements (whenever made and whether or not under oath, and considering the circumstances under which the statements were made), the internal consistency of each such statement, the consistency of such statements with other evidence of record (including the reports of the Department of State on country conditions), and any inaccuracies or falsehoods in such statements, without regard to whether an inconsistency, inaccuracy, or falsehood goes to the heart of the applicant's claim, or any other relevant factor. There is no presumption of credibility, however, if no adverse credibility determination is explicitly made, the applicant or witness shall have a rebuttable presumption of credibility on appeal.

(2) Exceptions

(A) In general

Paragraph (1) shall not apply to an alien if the Attorney General determines that—

(i) the alien ordered, incited, assisted, or otherwise participated in the persecution of any person on account of race, religion, nationality, membership in a particular social group, or political opinion;

(ii) the alien, having been convicted by a final judgment of a particularly serious crime, constitutes a danger to the community of the United States;

(iii) there are serious reasons for believing that the alien has committed a serious nonpolitical crime outside the United States prior to the arrival of the alien in the United States;

(iv) there are reasonable grounds for regarding the alien as a danger to the security of the United States;

(v) the alien is described in subclause (I), (II), (III), (IV), or (VI) of section 212(a)(3)(B)(i) [8 U.S.C.A. § 1182(a)(3)(B)(i)] or section 237(a)(4)(B) [8 U.S.C.A. § 1227(a)(4)(B)] (relating to terrorist activity), unless, in the case only of an alien described in subclause (IV) of section 212(a)(3)(B)(i) [8 U.S.C.A. § 1182(a)(3)(B)(i)], the Attorney General determines, in the Attorney General's discretion, that there are not reasonable grounds for regarding the alien as a danger to the security of the United States; or

(vi) the alien was firmly resettled in another country prior to arriving in the United States.

(B) Special rules

(i) Conviction of aggravated felony

For purposes of clause (ii) of subparagraph (A), an alien who has been convicted of an aggravated felony shall be considered to have been convicted of a particularly serious crime.

(ii) Offenses

The Attorney General may designate by regulation offenses that will be considered to be a crime described in clause (ii) or (iii) of subparagraph (A).

(C) Additional limitations

The Attorney General may by regulation establish additional limitations and conditions, consistent with this section, under which an alien shall be ineligible for asylum under paragraph (1).

(D) No judicial review

There shall be no judicial review of a determination of the Attorney General under subparagraph (A)(v).

(3) Treatment of spouse and children

(A) In general

A spouse or child (as defined in section 101(b)(1)(A), (B), (C), (D), or (E)) [8 U.S.C.A. § 1101(b)(1)(A), (B), (C), (D), or (E)] of an alien who is granted asylum under this subsection may, if not otherwise eligible for asylum under this section, be granted the same status as the alien if accompanying, or following to join, such alien.

(B) Continued classification of certain aliens as children

An unmarried alien who seeks to accompany, or follow to join, a parent granted asylum under this subsection, and who was under 21 years of age on the date on which such parent applied for asylum under this section, shall continue to be classified as a child for purposes of this paragraph and section 209(b)(3) [8 U.S.C.A. § 1159(b)(3)], if the alien attained 21 years of age after such application was filed but while it was pending.

(C) Initial jurisdiction

An asylum officer (as defined in section 235(b)(1)(E) [8 U.S.C.A. § 1225(b)(1)(E)]) shall have initial jurisdiction over any asylum application filed by an unaccompanied alien child (as defined in section 462(g) of the Homeland Security Act of 2002 [6 U.S.C.A. § 279(g)]), regardless of whether filed in accordance with this section or section 235(b) [8 U.S.C.A. § 1225(b)].

(c) Asylum status

(1) In general

In the case of an alien granted asylum under subsection (b), the Attorney General—

(A) shall not remove or return the alien to the alien's country of nationality or, in the case of a person having no nationality, the country of the alien's last habitual residence;

(B) shall authorize the alien to engage in employment in the United States and provide the alien with appropriate endorsement of that authorization; and

(C) may allow the alien to travel abroad with the prior consent of the Attorney General.

(2) Termination of asylum

Asylum granted under subsection (b) does not convey a right to remain permanently in the United States, and may be terminated if the Attorney General determines that—

(A) the alien no longer meets the conditions described in subsection (b)(1) owing to a fundamental change in circumstances;

(B) the alien meets a condition described in subsection (b)(2);

(C) the alien may be removed, pursuant to a bilateral or multilateral agreement, to a country (other than the country of the alien's nationality or, in the case of an alien having no nationality, the country of the alien's last habitual residence) in which the alien's life or freedom would not be threatened on account of race, religion, nationality, membership in a particular social group, or political opinion, and where the alien is eligible to receive asylum or equivalent temporary protection;

(D) the alien has voluntarily availed himself or herself of the protection of the alien's country of nationality or, in the case of an alien having no nationality, the alien's country of last habitual residence, by returning to such country with permanent resident status or the reasonable possibility of obtaining such status with the same rights and obligations pertaining to other permanent residents of that country; or

(E) the alien has acquired a new nationality and enjoys the protection of the country of his or her new nationality.

(3) Removal when asylum is terminated

An alien described in paragraph (2) is subject to any applicable grounds of inadmissibility or deportability under section [sic] 212(a) [8 U.S.C.A. § 1182(a)] and 237(a) [8 U.S.C.A. § 1227(a)], and the alien's removal or return shall be directed by the Attorney General in accordance with sections 240 [8 U.S.C.A. § 1229a] and 241 [8 U.S.C.A. § 1231].

(d) Asylum procedure

(1) Applications

The Attorney General shall establish a procedure for the consideration of asylum applications filed under subsection (a). The Attorney General may require applicants to submit fingerprints and a photograph at such time and in such manner to be determined by regulation by the Attorney General.

(2) Employment

An applicant for asylum is not entitled to employment authorization, but such authorization may be provided under regulation by the Attorney General. An applicant who is not otherwise eligible for employment authorization shall not be granted such authorization prior to 180 days after the date of filing of the application for asylum.

(3) Fees

The Attorney General may impose fees for the consideration of an application for asylum, for employment authorization under this section, and for adjustment of status under section 209(b) [8 U.S.C.A. § 1159(b)]. Such fees shall not exceed the Attorney General's costs in adjudicating the applications. The Attorney General may provide for the assessment and payment of such fees over a period of time or by installments. Nothing in this paragraph shall be construed to require the Attorney General to charge fees for adjudication services provided to asylum applicants, or to limit the authority of the Attorney General to set adjudication and naturalization fees in accordance with section 286(m) [8 U.S.C.A. § 1356(m)].

(4) Notice of privilege of counsel and consequences of frivolous application

At the time of filing an application for asylum, the Attorney General shall—

(A) advise the alien of the privilege of being represented by counsel and of the consequences, under paragraph (6), of knowingly filing a frivolous application for asylum; and

(B) provide the alien a list of persons (updated not less often than quarterly) who have indicated their availability to represent aliens in asylum proceedings on a pro bono basis.

(5) Consideration of asylum applications

(A) Procedures

The procedure established under paragraph (1) shall provide that—

(i) asylum cannot be granted until the identity of the applicant has been checked against all appropriate records or databases maintained by the Attorney General and by the Secretary of State, including the Automated Visa Lookout System, to determine any grounds on which the alien may be inadmissible to or deportable from the United States, or ineligible to apply for or be granted asylum;

(ii) in the absence of exceptional circumstances, the initial interview or hearing on the asylum application shall commence not later than 45 days after the date an application is filed;

(iii) in the absence of exceptional circumstances, final administrative adjudication of the asylum application, not including administrative appeal, shall be completed within 180 days after the date an application is filed;

(iv) any administrative appeal shall be filed within 30 days of a decision granting or denying asylum, or within 30 days of the completion of removal proceedings before an immigration judge under section 240 [8 U.S.C.A. § 1229a], whichever is later; and

(v) in the case of an applicant for asylum who fails without prior authorization or in the absence of exceptional circumstances to appear for an interview or hearing, including a hearing under section 240 [8 U.S.C.A. § 1229a], the application may be dismissed or the applicant may be otherwise sanctioned for such failure.

(B) Additional regulatory conditions

The Attorney General may provide by regulation for any other conditions or limitations on the consideration of an application for asylum not inconsistent with this Act.

(6) Frivolous applications

If the Attorney General determines that an alien has knowingly made a frivolous application for asylum and the alien has received the notice under paragraph (4)(A), the alien shall be permanently ineligible for any benefits under this Act, effective as of the date of a final determination on such application.

(7) No private right of action

Nothing in this subsection shall be construed to create any substantive or procedural right or benefit that is legally enforceable by any party against the United States or its agencies or officers or any other person.

(e) Commonwealth of the Northern Mariana Islands

The provisions of this section and section 209(b) [8 U.S.C.A. § 1159(b)] shall apply to persons physically present in the Commonwealth of the Northern Mariana Islands or arriving in the Commonwealth (whether or not at a designated port of arrival and including persons who are brought to the Commonwealth after having been interdicted in international or United States waters) only on or after January 1, 2014.

(June 27, 1952, c. 477, Title II, ch. 1, § 208, as added Mar. 17, 1980, Pub.L. 96–212, Title II, § 201(b), 94 Stat. 105, and amended Nov. 29, 1990, Pub.L. 101–649, Title V, § 515(a) (1), 104 Stat. 5053; Sept. 13, 1994, Pub.L. 103–322, Title XIII, § 130005(b), 108 Stat. 2028; Apr. 24, 1996, Pub.L. 104–132, Title IV, § 421(a), 110 Stat. 1270; Sept. 30, 1996, Pub.L. 104–208, Div. C, Title VI, § 604(a), 110 Stat. 3009–690; Oct. 26, 2001, Pub.L. 107–56, Title IV, § 411(b)(2), 115 Stat. 348; Aug. 6, 2002, Pub.L. 107–208, § 4, 116 Stat. 928; May 11, 2005, Pub.L. 109–13, Div. B, §§ 101(a), (b), 119 Stat. 231, 302–03; May 8, 2008, Pub.L. 110–229, Title VII, § 702(j)(4), 122 Stat. 866; Dec. 23, 2008, Pub.L. 110–457, Title II, § 235(d)(7), 122 Stat. 5071, 5080.)

§ 209. Adjustment of status of refugees [8 U.S.C.A. § 1159]

(a) Criteria and procedures applicable for admission as immigrant; effect of adjustment

(1) Any alien who has been admitted to the United States under section 207 [8 U.S.C.A. § 1157]—

(A) whose admission has not been terminated by the Secretary of Homeland Security or the Attorney General pursuant to such regulations as the Secretary of Homeland Security or the Attorney General may prescribe,

(B) who has been physically present in the United States for at least one year, and

(C) who has not acquired permanent resident status,

shall, at the end of such year period, return or be returned to the custody of the Department of Homeland Security for inspection and examination for admission to the United States as an immigrant in accordance with the provisions of sections 235 [8 U.S.C.A. § 1225], 240 [8 U.S.C.A. § 1229a], and 241 [8 U.S.C.A. § 1231].

(2) Any alien who is found upon inspection and examination by an immigration officer pursuant to paragraph (1) or after a hearing before an immigration judge to be admissible (except as otherwise provided under subsection (c)) as an immigrant under this Act at the time of the alien's inspection and examination shall, notwithstanding any numerical limitation specified in this Act, be regarded as lawfully admitted to the United States for permanent residence as of the date of such alien's arrival into the United States.

(b) Maximum number of adjustments; recordkeeping

The Secretary of Homeland Security or the Attorney General, in the Secretary's or the Attorney General's discretion and under such regulations as the Secretary or the Attorney General may prescribe, may adjust to the status of an alien lawfully admitted for permanent residence the status of any alien granted asylum who—

(1) applies for such adjustment,

(2) has been physically present in the United States for at least one year after being granted asylum,

(3) continues to be a refugee within the meaning of section 101(a) (42)(A) [8 U.S.C.A. § 1101(a)(42)(A)] or a spouse or child of such a refugee,

(4) is not firmly resettled in any foreign country, and

(5) is admissible (except as otherwise provided under subsection (c)) as an immigrant under this Act at the time of examination for adjustment of such alien.

Upon approval of an application under this subsection, the Secretary of Homeland Security or the Attorney General shall establish a record of the alien's admission for lawful permanent residence as of the date one year before the date of the approval of the application.

(c) Applicability of other Federal statutory requirements

The provisions of paragraphs (4), (5), and (7)(A) of section 212(a) [8 U.S.C.A. § 1182(a)] shall not be applicable to any alien seeking adjustment of status under this section, and the Secretary of Homeland Security or the Attorney General may waive any other provision of such section (other than paragraph (2)(C) or subparagraph (A), (B), (C), or (E) of paragraph (3)) with respect to such an alien for humanitarian purposes, to assure family unity, or when it is otherwise in the public interest.

(June 27, 1952, c. 477, Title II, ch. 1, § 209, as added Mar. 17, 1980, Pub.L. 96–212, Title II, § 201(b), 94 Stat. 105, and amended Nov. 29, 1990, Pub.L. 101–649, Title I, § 104(a)(1), Title VI, § 603(a)(4), 104 Stat. 4985, 5082; Dec. 12, 1991, Pub.L. 102–232, Title III, § 307(*l*) (1), 105 Stat. 1756; Sept. 30, 1996, Pub.L. 104–208, Div. C, Title III, §§ 308(g)(3)(A), (4)(A), 371(b)(2), 110 Stat. 3009–622, 3009–645; May 11, 2005, Pub.L. 109–13, Div. B, § 101(g), 119 Stat. 231, 305.)

§ 210. Special agricultural workers [8 U.S.C.A. § 1160]

(a) Lawful residence

(1) In general

The Attorney General shall adjust the status of an alien to that of an alien lawfully admitted for temporary residence if the Attorney General determines that the alien meets the following requirements:

(A) Application period

The alien must apply for such adjustment during the 18-month period beginning on the first day of the seventh month that begins after November 6, 1986.

(B) Performance of Seasonal Agricultural Services and residence in the United States

The alien must establish that he has—

(i) resided in the United States, and

(ii) performed seasonal agricultural services in the United States for at least 90 man-days,

during the 12-month period ending on May 1, 1986. For purposes of the previous sentence, performance of seasonal agricultural services in the United States for more than one employer on any one day shall be counted as performance of services for only 1 man-day.

(C) Admissible as immigrant

The alien must establish that he is admissible to the United States as an immigrant, except as otherwise provided under subsection (c)(2).

(2) Adjustment to permanent residence

The Attorney General shall adjust the status of any alien provided lawful temporary resident status under paragraph (1) to that of an alien lawfully admitted for permanent residence on the following date:

(A) Group 1

Subject to the numerical limitation established under subparagraph (C), in the case of an alien who has established, at the time of application for temporary residence under paragraph (1), that the alien performed seasonal agricultural services in the United States for at least 90 man-days during each of the 12-month periods ending on May 1, 1984, 1985, and 1986, the adjustment shall occur on the first day after the end of the one-year period that begins on the later of **(I)** the date the alien was granted such temporary resident status, or **(II)** the day after the last day of the application period described in paragraph (1)(A).

(B) Group 2

In the case of aliens to which subparagraph (A) does not apply, the adjustment shall occur on the day after the last day of the two-year period that begins on the later of **(I)** the date the alien was granted such temporary resident status, or **(II)** the day after the last day of the application period described in paragraph (1)(A).

(C) Numerical limitation

Subparagraph (A) shall not apply to more than 350,000 aliens. If more than 350,000 aliens meet the requirements of such subparagraph, such subparagraph shall apply to the 350,000 aliens whose applications for adjustment were first filed under paragraph (1) and subparagraph (B) shall apply to the remaining aliens.

(3) Termination of temporary residence

(A) During the period of temporary resident status granted an alien under paragraph (1), the Attorney General may terminate such status only upon a determination under this Act that the alien is deportable.

(B) Before any alien becomes eligible for adjustment of status under paragraph (2), the Attorney General may deny adjustment to permanent status and provide for termination of the temporary resident status granted such alien under paragraph (1) if—

    (i) the Attorney General finds by a preponderance of the evidence that the adjustment to temporary resident status was the result of fraud or willful misrepresentation as set out in section 212(a)(6)(C)(i) [8 U.S.C.A. § 1182(a)(6)(C)(i)], or

    (ii) the alien commits an act that (I) makes the alien inadmissible to the United States as an immigrant, except as provided under subsection (c)(2), or (II) is convicted of a felony or 3 or more misdemeanors committed in the United States.

(4) Authorized travel and employment during temporary residence

During the period an alien is in lawful temporary resident status granted under this subsection, the alien has the right to travel abroad (including commutation from a residence abroad) and shall be granted authorization to engage in employment in the United States and shall be provided an "employment authorized" endorsement or other appropriate work permit, in the same manner as for aliens lawfully admitted for permanent residence.

(5) In general

Except as otherwise provided in this subsection, an alien who acquires the status of an alien lawfully admitted for temporary residence under paragraph (1), such status not having changed, is considered to be an alien lawfully admitted for permanent residence (as described in section 101(a)(20) [8 U.S.C.A. § 1101(a)(20)]), other than under any provision of the immigration laws.

(b) Applications for adjustment of status

    (1) To whom may be made

    (A) Within the United States

The Attorney General shall provide that applications for adjustment of status under subsection (a) may be filed—

    (i) with the Attorney General, or

    (ii) with a designated entity (designated under paragraph (2)), but only if the applicant consents to the forwarding of the application to the Attorney General.

    (B) Outside the United States

The Attorney General, in cooperation with the Secretary of State, shall provide a procedure whereby an alien may apply for adjustment of status under subsection (a)(1) at an appropriate consular office outside the United States. If the alien otherwise qualifies for such adjustment, the Attorney General shall provide such documentation of authorization to enter the United States and to have the alien's status adjusted upon entry as may be necessary to carry out the provisions of this section.

(2) Designation of entities to receive applications

For purposes of receiving applications under this section, the Attorney General—

(A) shall designate qualified voluntary organizations and other qualified State, local community, farm labor organizations, and associations of agricultural employers, and

(B) may designate such other persons as the Attorney General determines are qualified and have substantial experience, demonstrated competence, and traditional long-term involvement in the preparation and submittal of applications for adjustment of status under section 209 [8 U.S.C.A. § 1159] or 245 [8 U.S.C.A. § 1255], Public Law 89–732 [8 U.S.C.A. § 1255 note], or Public Law 95–145.

(3) Proof of eligibility

(A) In general

An alien may establish that he meets the requirement of subsection (a)(1)(B)(ii) through government employment records, records supplied by employers or collective bargaining organizations, and such other reliable documentation as the alien may provide. The Attorney General shall establish special procedures to credit properly work in cases in which an alien was employed under an assumed name.

(B) Documentation of work history

(i) An alien applying for adjustment of status under subsection (a)(1) has the burden of proving by a preponderance of the evidence that the alien has worked the requisite number of man-days (as required under subsection (a)(1)(B)(ii)).

(ii) If an employer or farm labor contractor employing such an alien has kept proper and adequate records respecting such employment, the alien's burden of proof under clause (i) may be met by securing timely production of those records under regulations to be promulgated by the Attorney General.

(iii) An alien can meet such burden of proof if the alien establishes that the alien has in fact performed the work described in subsection (a)(1)(B)(ii) by producing sufficient evidence to show the extent of that employment as a matter of just and reasonable inference. In such a case, the burden then shifts to the Attorney

General to disprove the alien's evidence with a showing which negates the reasonableness of the inference to be drawn from the evidence.

(4) Treatment of applications by designated entities

Each designated entity must agree to forward to the Attorney General applications filed with it in accordance with paragraph (1)(A)(ii) but not to forward to the Attorney General applications filed with it unless the applicant has consented to such forwarding. No such entity may make a determination required by this section to be made by the Attorney General.

(5) Limitation on access to information

Files and records prepared for purposes of this section by designated entities operating under this section are confidential and the Attorney General and the Service shall not have access to such files or records relating to an alien without the consent of the alien, except as allowed by a court order issued pursuant to paragraph (6) of this subsection.

(6) Confidentiality of information

(A) In general

Except as provided in this paragraph, neither the Attorney General, nor any other official or employee of the Department of Justice, or bureau or agency thereof, may—

(i) use the information furnished by the applicant pursuant to an application filed under this section for any purpose other than to make a determination on the application, including a determination under subsection (a)(3)(B), or for enforcement of paragraph (7);

(ii) make any publication whereby the information furnished by any particular individual can be identified; or

(iii) permit anyone other than the sworn officers and employees of the Department or bureau or agency or, with respect to applications filed with a designated entity, that designated entity, to examine individual applications.

(B) Required disclosures

The Attorney General shall provide information furnished under this section, and any other information derived from such furnished information, to a duly recognized law enforcement entity in connection with a criminal investigation or prosecution, when such information is requested in writing by such entity, or to an official coroner for purposes of affirmatively identifying a deceased individual (whether or not such individual is deceased as a result of a crime).

(C) Construction

(i) In general

Nothing in this paragraph shall be construed to limit the use, or release, for immigration enforcement purposes or law enforcement purposes of information contained in files or records of the Service pertaining to an application filed under this section, other than information furnished by an applicant pursuant to the application, or any other information derived from the application, that is not available from any other source.

(ii) Criminal convictions

Information concerning whether the applicant has at any time been convicted of a crime may be used or released for immigration enforcement or law enforcement purposes.

(D) Crime

Whoever knowingly uses, publishes, or permits information to be examined in violation of this paragraph shall be fined not more than $10,000.

(7) Penalties for false statements in applications

(A) Criminal penalty

Whoever—

(i) files an application for adjustment of status under this section and knowingly and willfully falsifies, conceals, or covers up a material fact or makes any false, fictitious, or fraudulent statements or representations, or makes or uses any false writing or document knowing the same to contain any false, fictitious, or fraudulent statement or entry, or

(ii) creates or supplies a false writing or document for use in making such an application,

shall be fined in accordance with Title 18, or imprisoned not more than five years, or both.

(B) Exclusion

An alien who is convicted of a crime under subparagraph (A) shall be considered to be inadmissible to the United States on the ground described in section 212(a)(6)(C)(i) [8 U.S.C.A. § 1182(a)(6)(C)(i)].

(c) Waiver of numerical limitations and certain grounds for exclusion

(1) Numerical limitations do not apply

The numerical limitations of sections 201 [8 U.S.C.A. § 1151] and 202 [8 U.S.C.A. § 1152] shall not apply to the adjustment of aliens to lawful permanent resident status under this section.

(2) Waiver of grounds for exclusion

In the determination of an alien's admissibility under subsection (a)(1)(C)—

(A) Grounds of exclusion not applicable

The provisions of paragraphs (5) and (7)(A) of section 212(a) [8 U.S.C.A. § 1182(a)] shall not apply.

(B) Waiver of other grounds

(i) In general

Except as provided in clause (ii), the Attorney General may waive any other provision of section 212(a) [8 U.S.C.A. § 1182(a)] in the case of individual aliens for humanitarian purposes, to assure family unity, or when it is otherwise in the public interest.

(ii) Grounds that may not be waived

The following provisions of section 212(a) [8 U.S.C.A. § 1182(a)] may not be waived by the Attorney General under clause (i):

(I) Paragraphs (2)(A) and (2)(B) (relating to criminals).

(II) Paragraph (4) (relating to aliens likely to become public charges).

(III) Paragraph (2)(C) (relating to drug offenses), except for so much of such paragraph as relates to a single offense of simple possession of 30 grams or less of marihuana.

(IV) Paragraph (3) (relating to security and related grounds), other than subparagraph (E) thereof.

(V) Omitted

(C) Special rule for determination of public charge

An alien is not ineligible for adjustment of status under this section due to being inadmissible under section 212(a)(4) [8 U.S.C.A. § 1182(a)(4)] if the alien demonstrates a history of employment in the United States evidencing self-support without reliance on public cash assistance.

(d) Temporary stay of exclusion or deportation and work authorization for certain applicants

(1) Before application period

The Attorney General shall provide that in the case of an alien who is apprehended before the beginning of the application period described in subsection (a)(1) and who can establish a nonfrivolous case of eligibility to have his status adjusted under subsection (a) (but for the fact that he may not apply for such adjustment until the beginning of such period), until the alien has had the opportunity during the first 30 days of the application period to complete the filing of an application for adjustment, the alien—

(A) may not be excluded or deported, and

(B) shall be granted authorization to engage in employment in the United States and be provided an "employment authorized" endorsement or other appropriate work permit.

(2) During application period

The Attorney General shall provide that in the case of an alien who presents a nonfrivolous application for adjustment of status under subsection (a) during the application period, and until a final determination on the application has been made in accordance with this section, the alien—

(A) may not be excluded or deported, and

(B) shall be granted authorization to engage in employment in the United States and be provided an "employment authorized" endorsement or other appropriate work permit.

(3) Use of application fees to offset program costs

No application fees collected by the Service pursuant to this subsection may be used by the Service to offset the costs of the special agricultural worker legalization program until the Service implements the program consistent with the statutory mandate as follows:

(A) During the application period described in subsection (a)(1)(A) the Service may grant temporary admission to the United States, work authorization, and provide an "employment authorized" endorsement or other appropriate work permit to any alien who presents a preliminary application for adjustment of status under subsection (a) at a designated port of entry on the southern land border. An alien who does not enter through a port of entry is subject to deportation and removal as otherwise provided in this Act.

(B) During the application period described in subsection (a)(1)(A) any alien who has filed an application for adjustment of status within the United States as provided in subsection (b)(1)(A) pursuant to the provision of 8 CFR section 210.1(j) is subject to paragraph (2) of this subsection.

(C) A preliminary application is defined as a fully completed and signed application with fee and photographs which contains specific information concerning the performance of qualifying employment in the United States and the documentary evidence which the applicant intends to submit as proof of such employment. The applicant must be otherwise admissible to the United States and must establish to the satisfaction of the examining officer during an interview that his or her claim to eligibility for special agriculture worker status is credible.

(e) Administrative and judicial review

(1) Administrative and judicial review

There shall be no administrative or judicial review of a determination respecting an application for adjustment of status under this section except in accordance with this subsection.

(2) Administrative review

(A) Single level of administrative appellate review

The Attorney General shall establish an appellate authority to provide for a single level of administrative appellate review of such a determination.

(B) Standard for review

Such administrative appellate review shall be based solely upon the administrative record established at the time of the determination on the application and upon such additional or newly discovered evidence as may not have been available at the time of the determination.

(3) Judicial review

(A) Limitation to review of exclusion or deportation

There shall be judicial review of such a denial only in the judicial review of an order of exclusion or deportation under section 106 [8 U.S.C.A. § 1105a] (as in effect before October 1, 1996).

(B) Standard for judicial review

Such judicial review shall be based solely upon the administrative record established at the time of the review by the appellate authority and the findings of fact and determinations contained in such record shall be conclusive unless the applicant can establish abuse of discretion or that the findings are directly contrary to clear and convincing facts contained in the record considered as a whole.

(f) Temporary disqualification of newly legalized aliens from receiving aid to families with dependent children

During the five-year period beginning on the date an alien was granted lawful temporary resident status under subsection (a), and notwithstanding any other provision of law, the alien is not eligible for aid under a State plan approved under part A of title IV of the Social Security Act [42 U.S.C.A. § 601 et seq.]. Notwithstanding the previous sentence, in the case of an alien who would be eligible for aid under a State plan approved under part A of title IV of the Social Security Act but for the previous sentence, the provisions of paragraph (3) of section 245A(h) [8 U.S.C.A. § 1255a(h)] shall apply in the same manner as they apply with respect to paragraph (1) of such section and, for this purpose, any reference in section 245A(h) [8 U.S.C.A. § 1255a(h)] to paragraph (1) is deemed a reference to the previous sentence.

(g) Treatment of special agricultural workers

For all purposes (subject to subsections (a)(5) and (f)) an alien whose status is adjusted under this section to that of an alien lawfully admitted for permanent residence, such status not having changed, shall be considered to be an alien lawfully admitted for permanent residence (within the meaning of section 101(a)(20) [8 U.S.C.A. § 1101(a)(20)]).

(h) "Seasonal agricultural services" defined

In this section, the term "seasonal agricultural services" means the performance of field work related to planting, cultural practices, cultivating, growing and harvesting of fruits and vegetables of every kind and other perishable commodities, as defined in regulations by the Secretary of Agriculture.

(June 27, 1952, c. 477, Title II, ch. 1, § 210, as added Nov. 6, 1986, Pub.L. 99–603, Title III, § 302(a)(1), 100 Stat. 3417, and amended Dec. 22, 1987, Pub.L. 100–202, § 101(a) [Title II, § 211], 101 Stat. 1329–18; Oct. 24, 1988, Pub. L. 100–525, § 2(m), 102 Stat. 2613; Dec. 18, 1989, Pub.L. 101–238, § 4, 103 Stat. 2103; Nov. 29, 1990, Pub.L. 101–649, Title VI, § 603(a) (5), 104 Stat. 5082; Dec. 12, 1991, Pub.L. 102–232, Title III, §§ 307(j), 309(b)(6), 105 Stat. 1756, 1758; Oct. 25, 1994, Pub.L. 103–416, Title II, § 219(d), (z)(7), 108 Stat. 4316, 4318; Apr. 24, 1996, Pub.L. 104–132, Title IV, § 431(b), 110 Stat. 1273; Aug. 22, 1996, Pub.L. 104–193, Title I, § 110(s)(1), 110 Stat. 2175; Sept. 30, 1996, Pub.L. 104–208, Div. C, Title III, §§ 308(g)(2)(B), 384(d)(1), Title VI, § 623(b), 110 Stat. 3009–622, 3009–653, 3009–697.)

CHAPTER II—ADMISSION QUALIFICATIONS FOR ALIENS; TRAVEL CONTROL OF CITIZENS AND ALIENS

§ 211. Admission of immigrants into the United States [8 U.S.C.A. § 1181]

(a) Documents required; admission under quotas before June 30, 1968

Except as provided in subsection (b) and subsection (c) no immigrant shall be admitted into the United States unless at the time of application for admission he **(1)** has a valid unexpired immigrant visa or was born subsequent to the issuance of such visa of the accompanying parent, and **(2)** presents a valid unexpired passport or other suitable travel document, or document of identity and nationality, if such document is required under the regulations issued by the Attorney General. With respect to immigrants to be admitted under quotas of quota areas prior to June 30, 1968, no immigrant visa shall be deemed valid unless the immigrant is properly chargeable to the quota area under the quota of which the visa is issued.

(b) Readmission without required documents; Attorney General's discretion

Notwithstanding the provisions of section 212(a)(7)(A) [8 U.S.C.A. § 1182(a)(7)(A)] in such cases or in such classes of cases and under such conditions as may be by regulations prescribed, returning resident immigrants, defined in section 101(a)(27)(A) [8 U.S.C.A. § 1101(a)(27)(A)], who are otherwise admissible may be readmitted to the United States by the Attorney General in his discretion without being required to obtain a passport, immigrant visa, reentry permit or other documentation.

(c) Nonapplicability to aliens admitted as refugees

The provisions of subsection (a) shall not apply to an alien whom the Attorney General admits to the United States under section 207 [8 U.S.C.A. § 1157].

(June 27, 1952, c. 477, Title II, ch. 2, § 211, 66 Stat. 181; Pub. L. 89–236, § 9, Oct. 3, 1965, 79 Stat. 917; Pub. L. 94–571, § 7(c), Oct. 20, 1976, 90 Stat. 2706; Pub. L. 96–212, Title II, § 202, Mar. 17, 1980, 94 Stat. 106; Pub.L. 101–649, Title VI, § 603(a)(7), Nov. 29, 1990, 104 Stat. 5083.)

§ 212.   Excludable aliens [8 U.S.C.A. § 1182]

(a) Classes of aliens ineligible for visas or admission

Except as otherwise provided in this Act, aliens who are inadmissible under the following paragraphs are ineligible to receive visas and ineligible to be admitted to the United States:

(1) Health-related grounds

(A) In general

Any alien—

(i) who is determined (in accordance with regulations prescribed by the Secretary of Health and Human Services) to have a communicable disease of public health significance;

(ii) except as provided in subparagraph (C), who seeks admission as an immigrant, or who seeks adjustment of status to the status of an alien lawfully admitted for permanent residence, and who has failed to present documentation of having received vaccination against vaccine-preventable diseases, which shall include at least the following diseases: mumps, measles, rubella, polio, tetanus and diphtheria toxoids, pertussis, influenza type B and hepatitis B, and any other vaccinations against vaccine-preventable diseases recommended by the Advisory Committee for Immunization Practices,

(iii) who is determined (in accordance with regulations prescribed by the Secretary of Health and Human Services in consultation with the Attorney General)—

(I) to have a physical or mental disorder and behavior associated with the disorder that may pose, or has posed, a threat to the property, safety, or welfare of the alien or others, or

(II) to have had a physical or mental disorder and a history of behavior associated with the disorder, which behavior has posed a threat to the property, safety, or welfare of the alien or others and which behavior is likely to recur or to lead to other harmful behavior, or

(iv) who is determined (in accordance with regulations prescribed by the Secretary of Health and Human Services) to be a drug abuser or addict,

is inadmissible.

(B) Waiver authorized

For provision authorizing waiver of certain clauses of subparagraph (A), see subsection (g).

(C) Exception from immunization requirement for adopted children 10 years of age or younger

Clause (ii) of subparagraph (A) shall not apply to a child who—

(i) is 10 years of age or younger,

(ii) is described in subparagraph (F) or (G) of section 101(b)(1) [8 U.S.C.A. § 1101(b)(1)]; and

(iii) is seeking an immigrant visa as an immediate relative under section 201(b) [8 U.S.C.A. § 1151(b)],

if, prior to the admission of the child, an adoptive parent or prospective adoptive parent of the child, who has sponsored the child for admission as an immediate relative, has executed an affidavit stating that the parent is aware of the provisions of subparagraph (A)(ii) and will ensure that, within 30 days of the child's admission, or at the earliest time that is medically appropriate, the child will receive the vaccinations identified in such subparagraph.

(2) Criminal and related grounds

(A) Conviction of certain crimes

(i) In general

Except as provided in clause (ii), any alien convicted of, or who admits having committed, or who admits committing acts which constitute the essential elements of—

(I) a crime involving moral turpitude (other than a purely political offense) or an attempt or conspiracy to commit such a crime, or

(II) a violation of (or a conspiracy or attempt to violate) any law or regulation of a State, the United States, or a foreign country relating to a controlled substance (as defined in section 802 of Title 21),

is inadmissible.

(ii) Exception

Clause (i)(I) shall not apply to an alien who committed only one crime if—

(I) the crime was committed when the alien was under 18 years of age, and the crime was committed (and the alien released from any confinement to a prison or correctional institution imposed for the crime) more than 5 years before the date of application for a visa or other documentation and the date of application for admission to the United States, or

(II) the maximum penalty possible for the crime of which the alien was convicted (or which the alien admits having committed or of which the acts that the alien admits having committed constituted the essential elements) did not exceed imprisonment for one year and, if the alien was convicted of such crime, the alien was not sentenced to a term of imprisonment in excess of 6 months (regardless of the extent to which the sentence was ultimately executed).

(B) Multiple criminal convictions

Any alien convicted of 2 or more offenses (other than purely political offenses), regardless of whether the conviction was in a single trial or whether the offenses arose from a single scheme of misconduct and regardless of whether the offenses involved moral turpitude, for which the aggregate sentences to confinement were 5 years or more is inadmissible.

(C) Controlled substance traffickers

Any alien who the consular officer or the Attorney General knows or has reason to believe—

(i) is or has been an illicit trafficker in any controlled substance or in any listed chemical (as defined in section 102 of the Controlled Substances Act (21 U.S.C. 802)), or is or has been a knowing aider, abettor, assister, conspirator, or colluder with others in the illicit trafficking in any such controlled or listed substance or chemical, or endeavored to do so; or

(ii) is the spouse, son, or daughter of an alien inadmissible under clause (i), has, within the previous 5 years, obtained any financial or other benefit from the illicit activity of that alien, and knew or reasonably should have known that the financial or other benefit was the product of such illicit activity,

is inadmissible.

(D) Prostitution and commercialized vice

Any alien who—

(i) is coming to the United States solely, principally, or incidentally to engage in prostitution, or has engaged in prostitution within 10 years of the date of application for a visa, admission, or adjustment of status,

(ii) directly or indirectly procures or attempts to procure, or (within 10 years of the date of application for a visa, admission, or adjustment of status) procured or attempted to procure or to import, prostitutes or persons for the purpose of prostitution, or receives or (within such 10-year period) received, in whole or in part, the proceeds of prostitution, or

   (iii) is coming to the United States to engage in any other unlawful commercialized vice, whether or not related to prostitution,

is inadmissible.

(E) Certain aliens involved in serious criminal activity who have asserted immunity from prosecution

Any alien—

   (i) who has committed in the United States at any time a serious criminal offense (as defined in section 101(h) [8 U.S.C.A. § 1101(h)]),

   (ii) for whom immunity from criminal jurisdiction was exercised with respect to that offense,

   (iii) who as a consequence of the offense and exercise of immunity has departed from the United States, and

   (iv) who has not subsequently submitted fully to the jurisdiction of the court in the United States having jurisdiction with respect to that offense,

is inadmissible.

(F) Waiver authorized

For provision authorizing waiver of certain subparagraphs of this paragraph, see subsection (h).

(G) Foreign government officials who have committed particularly severe violations of religious freedom

Any alien who, while serving as a foreign government official, was responsible for or directly carried out, at any time, particularly severe violations of religious freedom, as defined in section 3 of the International Religious Freedom Act of 1998 (22 U.S.C. 6402), is inadmissible.

(H) Significant traffickers in persons

(i) In general

Any alien who commits or conspires to commit human trafficking offenses in the United States or outside the United States, or who the consular officer, the Secretary of Homeland Security, the Secretary of State, or the Attorney General knows or has reason to believe is or has been a knowing aider, abettor, assister, conspirator, or colluder with such a trafficker in severe forms of trafficking in persons, as defined in the [sic] section 7102 of Title 22, is inadmissible.

(ii) Beneficiaries of trafficking

Except as provided in clause (iii), any alien who the consular officer or the Attorney General knows or has reason to believe is the spouse, son, or daughter of an alien inadmissible under clause (i), has, within the previous 5 years, obtained any financial or other benefit from the illicit activity of that alien, and knew or reasonably should have known that the financial or other benefit was the product of such illicit activity, is inadmissible.

(iii) Exception for certain sons and daughters

Clause (ii) shall not apply to a son or daughter who was a child at the time he or she received the benefit described in such clause.

(I) Money laundering

Any alien—

(i) who a consular officer or the Attorney General knows, or has reason to believe, has engaged, is engaging, or seeks to enter the United States to engage, in an offense which is described in section 1956 or 1957 of Title 18 (relating to laundering of monetary instruments); or

(ii) who a consular officer or the Attorney General knows is, or has been, a knowing aider, abettor, assister, conspirator, or colluder with others in an offense which is described in such section;

is inadmissible.

(3) Security and related grounds

(A) In general

Any alien who a consular officer or the Attorney General knows, or has reasonable ground to believe, seeks to enter the United States to engage solely, principally, or incidentally in—

(i) any activity (I) to violate any law of the United States relating to espionage or sabotage or (II) to violate or evade any law prohibiting the export from the United States of goods, technology, or sensitive information,

(ii) any other unlawful activity, or

(iii) any activity a purpose of which is the opposition to, or the control or overthrow of, the Government of the United States by force, violence, or other unlawful means,

is inadmissible.

(B) Terrorist activities

(i) In general

Any alien who—

(I) has engaged in a terrorist activity;

(II) a consular officer, the Attorney General, or the Secretary of Homeland Security knows, or has reasonable ground to believe, is engaged in or is likely to engage after entry in any terrorist activity (as defined in clause (iv));

(III) has, under circumstances indicating an intention to cause death or serious bodily harm, incited terrorist activity;

(IV) is a representative (as defined in clause (v)) of—

(aa) a terrorist organization (as defined in clause (vi)); or

(bb) a political, social, or other group that endorses or espouses terrorist activity;

(V) is a member of a terrorist organization described in subclause (I) or (II) of clause (vi);

(VI) is a member of a terrorist organization described in clause (vi)(III), unless the alien can demonstrate by clear and convincing evidence that the alien did not know, and should not reasonably have known, that the organization was a terrorist organization;

(VII) endorses or espouses terrorist activity or persuades others to endorse or espouse terrorist activity or support a terrorist organization;

(VIII) has received military-type training (as defined in section 2339D(c)(1) of title 18, United States Code) from or on behalf of any organization that, at the time the training was received, was a terrorist organization (as defined in clause (vi)); or

(IX) is the spouse or child of an alien who is inadmissible under this subparagraph, if the activity causing the alien to be found inadmissible occurred within the last 5 years,

is inadmissible. An alien who is an officer, official, representative, or spokesman of the Palestine Liberation Organization is considered, for purposes of this Act, to be engaged in a terrorist activity.

(ii) Exception

Subclause (IX) of clause (i) does not apply to a spouse or child—

(I) who did not know or should not reasonably have known of the activity causing the alien to be found inadmissible under this section; or

(II) whom the consular officer or Attorney General has reasonable grounds to believe has renounced the activity causing the alien to be found inadmissible under this section.

(iii) "Terrorist activity" defined

As used in this Act, the term "terrorist activity" means any activity which is unlawful under the laws of the place where it is committed (or which, if it had been committed in the United States, would be unlawful under the laws of the United States or any State) and which involves any of the following:

(I) The highjacking [sic] or sabotage of any conveyance (including an aircraft, vessel, or vehicle).

(II) The seizing or detaining, and threatening to kill, injure, or continue to detain, another individual in order to compel a third person (including a governmental organization) to do or abstain from doing any act as an explicit or implicit condition for the release of the individual seized or detained.

(III) A violent attack upon an internationally protected person (as defined in section 1116(b)(4) of Title 18) or upon the liberty of such a person.

(IV) An assassination.

(V) The use of any—

(a) biological agent, chemical agent, or nuclear weapon or device, or

(b) explosive, firearm, or other weapon or dangerous device (other than for mere personal monetary gain),

with intent to endanger, directly or indirectly, the safety of one or more individuals or to cause substantial damage to property.

(VI) A threat, attempt, or conspiracy to do any of the foregoing.

(iv) Engage in terrorist activity defined

As used in this Act, the term "engage in terrorist activity" means, in an individual capacity or as a member of an organization—

(I) to commit or to incite to commit, under circumstances indicating an intention to cause death or serious bodily injury, a terrorist activity;

(II) to prepare or plan a terrorist activity;

(III) to gather information on potential targets for terrorist activity;

(IV) to solicit funds or other things of value for—

(aa) a terrorist activity;

(bb) a terrorist organization described in clause (vi)(I) or (vi)(II); or

(cc) a terrorist organization described in clause (vi)(III), unless the solicitor can demonstrate by clear and convincing evidence that he did not know, and should not reasonably have known, that the organization was a terrorist organization;

(V) to solicit any individual—

(aa) to engage in conduct otherwise described in this subsection;

(bb) for membership in a terrorist organization described in clause (vi)(I) or (vi)(II); or

(cc) for membership in a terrorist organization described in clause (vi)(III) unless the solicitor can demonstrate by clear and convincing evidence that he did not know, and should not reasonably have known, that the organization was a terrorist organization; or

(VI) to commit an act that the actor knows, or reasonably should know, affords material support, including a safe house, transportation, communications, funds, transfer of funds or other material financial benefit, false documentation or identification, weapons (including chemical, biological, or radiological weapons), explosives, or training—

(aa) for the commission of a terrorist activity;

(bb) to any individual who the actor knows, or reasonably should know, has committed or plans to commit a terrorist activity;

(cc) to a terrorist organization described in subclause (I) or (II) of clause (vi) or to any member of such an organization; or

(dd) to a terrorist organization described in clause (vi)(III), or to any member of such an organization, unless the actor can demonstrate by clear and convincing evidence that the actor did not know, and should not reasonably have known, that the organization was a terrorist organization.

(v) "Representative" defined

As used in this paragraph, the term "representative" includes an officer, official, or spokesman of an organization, and any person who directs, counsels, commands, or induces an organization or its members to engage in terrorist activity.

(vi) Terrorist organization defined

As used in this section, the term "terrorist organization" means an organization—

(I) designated under section 219 [8 U.S.C.A. § 1189];

(II) otherwise designated, upon publication in the Federal Register, by the Secretary of State in consultation with or upon the request of the Attorney General or the Secretary of Homeland Security, as a terrorist organization, after finding that the organization engages in the activities described in subclauses (I) through (VI) of clause (iv); or

(III) that is a group of two or more individuals, whether organized or not, which engages in, or has a subgroup which engages in, the activities described in subclauses (I) through (VI) of clause (iv).

(C) Foreign policy

(i) In general

An alien whose entry or proposed activities in the United States the Secretary of State has reasonable ground to believe would have potentially serious adverse foreign policy consequences for the United States is inadmissible.

(ii) Exception for officials

An alien who is an official of a foreign government or a purported government, or who is a candidate for election to a foreign government office during the period immediately preceding the election for that office, shall not be excludable or subject to restrictions or conditions on entry into the United States under clause (i) solely because of the alien's past, current, or expected beliefs, statements, or associations, if such beliefs, statements, or associations would be lawful within the United States.

(iii) Exception for other aliens

An alien, not described in clause (ii), shall not be excludable or subject to restrictions or conditions on entry into the United States under clause (i) because of the alien's past, current, or expected beliefs, statements, or associations, if such beliefs, statements, or associations would be lawful within the United States, unless the Secretary of State personally determines that the alien's admission would compromise a compelling United States foreign policy interest.

(iv) Notification of determinations

If a determination is made under clause (iii) with respect to an alien, the Secretary of State must notify on a timely basis the chairmen of the Committees on the Judiciary and Foreign Affairs of the House of Representatives and of the Committees on the Judiciary and Foreign Relations of the Senate of the identity of the alien and the reasons for the determination.

(D) Immigrant membership in totalitarian party

(i) In general

Any immigrant who is or has been a member of or affiliated with the Communist or any other totalitarian party (or subdivision or affiliate thereof), domestic or foreign, is inadmissible.

(ii) Exception for involuntary membership

Clause (i) shall not apply to an alien because of membership or affiliation if the alien establishes to the satisfaction of the consular officer when applying for a visa (or to the satisfaction of the Attorney General when applying for admission) that the membership or affiliation is or was involuntary, or is or was solely when under 16 years of age, by operation of law, or for purposes of obtaining employment, food rations, or other essentials of living and whether necessary for such purposes.

(iii) Exception for past membership

Clause (i) shall not apply to an alien because of membership or affiliation if the alien establishes to the satisfaction of the consular officer when applying for a visa (or to the satisfaction of the Attorney General when applying for admission) that—

> **(I)** the membership or affiliation terminated at least—

> > **(a)** 2 years before the date of such application, or

> > **(b)** 5 years before the date of such application, in the case of an alien whose membership or affiliation was with the party controlling the government of a foreign state that is a totalitarian dictatorship as of such date, and

> **(II)** the alien is not a threat to the security of the United States.

(iv) Exception for close family members

The Attorney General may, in the Attorney General's discretion, waive the application of clause (i) in the case of an immigrant who is the parent, spouse, son, daughter, brother, or sister of a citizen of the United States or a spouse, son, or daughter of an alien lawfully admitted for permanent residence for humanitarian purposes, to assure family unity, or when it is otherwise in the public interest if the immigrant is not a threat to the security of the United States.

(E) Participants in Nazi persecution, genocide, or the commission of any act of torture or extrajudicial killing

(i) Participation in Nazi persecutions

Any alien who, during the period beginning on March 23, 1933, and ending on May 8, 1945, under the direction of, or in association with—

> **(I)** the Nazi government of Germany,

(II) any government in any area occupied by the military forces of the Nazi government of Germany,

(III) any government established with the assistance or cooperation of the Nazi government of Germany, or

(IV) any government which was an ally of the Nazi government of Germany,

ordered, incited, assisted, or otherwise participated in the persecution of any person because of race, religion, national origin, or political opinion is inadmissible.

(ii) Participation in genocide

Any alien who ordered, incited, assisted, or otherwise participated in genocide, as defined in section 1091(a) of Title 18, is inadmissible.

(iii) Commission of acts of torture or extrajudicial killings

Any alien who, outside the United States, has committed, ordered, incited, assisted, or otherwise participated in the commission of—

(I) any act of torture, as defined in section 2340 of Title 18; or

(II) under color of law of any foreign nation, any extrajudicial killing, as defined in section 3(a) of the Torture Victim Protection Act of 1991 (28 U.S.C. 1350 note),

is inadmissible.

(F) Association with terrorist organizations

Any alien who the Secretary of State, after consultation with the Attorney General, or the Attorney General, after consultation with the Secretary of State, determines has been associated with a terrorist organization and intends while in the United States to engage solely, principally, or incidentally in activities that could endanger the welfare, safety, or security of the United States is inadmissible.

(G) Recruitment or use of child soldiers

Any alien who has engaged in the recruitment or use of child soldiers in violation of section 2442 of Title 18, United States Code, is inadmissible.

(4) Public charge

(A) In general

Any alien who, in the opinion of the consular officer at the time of application for a visa, or in the opinion of the Attorney General at the time of application for admission or adjustment of status, is likely at any time to become a public charge is inadmissible.

(B) Factors to be taken into account

(i) In determining whether an alien is inadmissible under this paragraph, the consular officer or the Attorney General shall at a minimum consider the alien's—

(I) age;

(II) health;

(III) family status;

(IV) assets, resources, and financial status; and

(V) education and skills.

(ii) In addition to the factors under clause (i), the consular officer or the Attorney General may also consider any affidavit of support under section 213A [8 U.S.C.A. § 1183a] for purposes of exclusion under this paragraph.

(C) Family-sponsored immigrants

Any alien who seeks admission or adjustment of status under a visa number issued under section 201(b)(2) [8 U.S.C.A. § 1151(b)(2)] or 203(a) [8 U.S.C.A. § 1153(a)] is inadmissible under this paragraph unless—

(i) the alien has obtained—

(I) status as a spouse or a child of a United States citizen pursuant to clause (ii), (iii), or (iv) of section 204(a)(1)(A) [8 U.S.C.A. § 1154(a)(1)(A)] or

(II) classification pursuant to clause (ii) or (iii) of section 204(a)(1)(B) [8 U.S.C.A. § 1154(a)(1)(B)];

(III) classification or status as a VAWA self-petitioner; or

(ii) the person petitioning for the alien's admission (and any additional sponsor required under section 213A(f) [8 U.S.C.A. § 1183a(f)] or any alternative sponsor permitted under paragraph (5)(B) of such section) has executed an affidavit of support described in section 213A [8 U.S.C.A. § 1183a] with respect to such alien.

(D) Certain employment-based immigrants

Any alien who seeks admission or adjustment of status under a visa number issued under section 203(b) [8 U.S.C.A. § 1153(b)] by virtue of a classification petition filed by a relative of the alien (or by an entity in which such relative has a significant ownership interest) is inadmissible under this paragraph unless such relative has executed an affidavit of support described in section 213A [8 U.S.C.A. § 1183a] with respect to such alien.

(E) Special rule for qualified alien victims

Subparagraphs (A), (B), and (C) shall not apply to an alien who—

(i) is a VAWA self-petitioner;

(ii) is an applicant for, or is granted, nonimmigrant status under section 101(a)(15)(U) [8 U.S.C.A. § 1101(a)(15)(U)]; or

(iii) is a qualified alien described in section 431(c) of the Personal Responsibility and Work Opportunity Reconciliation Act of 1996 [8 U.S.C.A. § 1641(c)].

(5) Labor certification and qualifications for certain immigrants

(A) Labor certification

(i) In general

Any alien who seeks to enter the United States for the purpose of performing skilled or unskilled labor is inadmissible, unless the Secretary of Labor has determined and certified to the Secretary of State and the Attorney General that—

(I) there are not sufficient workers who are able, willing, qualified (or equally qualified in the case of an alien described in clause (ii)) and available at the time of application for a visa and admission to the United States and at the place where the alien is to perform such skilled or unskilled labor, and

(II) the employment of such alien will not adversely affect the wages and working conditions of workers in the United States similarly employed.

(ii) Certain aliens subject to special rule

For purposes of clause (i)(I), an alien described in this clause is an alien who—

(I) is a member of the teaching profession, or

(II) has exceptional ability in the sciences or the arts.

(iii) Professional athletes

(I) In general

A certification made under clause (i) with respect to a professional athlete shall remain valid with respect to the athlete after the athlete changes employer, if the new employer is a team in the same sport as the team which employed the athlete when the athlete first applied for the certification.

(II) Definition

For purposes of subclause (I), the term "professional athlete" means an individual who is employed as an athlete by—

(aa) a team that is a member of an association of 6 or more professional sports teams whose total combined revenues exceed $10,000,000 per year, if the association governs the conduct of its members and regulates the contests and exhibitions in which its member teams regularly engage; or

(bb) any minor league team that is affiliated with such an association.

(iv) Long delayed adjustment applicants

A certification made under clause (i) with respect to an individual whose petition is covered by section 204(j) [8 U.S.C.A. § 1154(j)] shall remain valid with respect to a new job accepted by the individual after the individual changes jobs or employers if the new job is in the same or a similar occupational classification as the job for which the certification was issued.

(B) Unqualified physicians

An alien who is a graduate of a medical school not accredited by a body or bodies approved for the purpose by the Secretary of Education (regardless of whether such school of medicine is in the United States) and who is coming to the United States principally to perform services as a member of the medical profession is inadmissible, unless the alien (i) has passed parts I and II of the National Board of Medical Examiners Examination (or an equivalent examination as determined by the Secretary of Health and Human Services) and (ii) is competent in oral and written English. For purposes of the previous sentence, an alien who is a graduate of a medical school shall be considered to have passed parts I and II of the National Board of Medical Examiners if the alien was fully and permanently licensed to practice medicine in a State on January 9, 1978, and was practicing medicine in a State on that date.

(C) Uncertified foreign health-care workers

Subject to subsection (r), any alien who seeks to enter the United States for the purpose of performing labor as a health-care worker, other than a physician, is inadmissible unless the alien presents to the consular officer, or, in the case of an adjustment of status, the Attorney General, a certificate from the Commission on Graduates of Foreign Nursing Schools, or a certificate from an equivalent independent credentialing organization approved by the Attorney General in consultation with the Secretary of Health and Human Services, verifying that—

(i) the alien's education, training, license, and experience—

(I) meet all applicable statutory and regulatory requirements for entry into the United States under the classification specified in the application;

(II) are comparable with that required for an American health-care worker of the same type; and

(III) are authentic and, in the case of a license, unencumbered;

(ii) the alien has the level of competence in oral and written English considered by the Secretary of Health and Human Services, in consultation with the Secretary of Education, to be appropriate for health care work of the kind in which the alien will be engaged, as shown by an appropriate score on one or more nationally recognized, commercially available, standardized assessments of the applicant's ability to speak and write; and

(iii) if a majority of States licensing the profession in which the alien intends to work recognize a test predicting the success on the profession's licensing or certification examination, the alien has passed such a test or has passed such an examination.

For purposes of clause (ii), determination of the standardized tests required and of the minimum scores that are appropriate are within the sole discretion of the Secretary of Health and Human Services and are not subject to further administrative or judicial review.

(D) Application of grounds

The grounds for inadmissibility of aliens under subparagraphs (A) and (B) shall apply to immigrants seeking admission or adjustment of status under paragraph (2) or (3) of section 203(b) [8 U.S.C.A. § 1153(b)].

(6) Illegal entrants and immigration violators

(A) Aliens present without admission or parole

(i) In general

An alien present in the United States without being admitted or paroled, or who arrives in the United States at any time or place other than as designated by the Attorney General, is inadmissible.

(ii) Exception for certain battered women and children

Clause (i) shall not apply to an alien who demonstrates that—

(I) the alien is a VAWA self-petitioner;

(II) (a) the alien has been battered or subjected to extreme cruelty by a spouse or parent, or by a member of the spouse's or parent's family residing in the same household as the alien and the spouse or parent consented or acquiesced to such battery or cruelty, or **(b)** the alien's child has been battered or subjected to extreme cruelty by a spouse or parent of the alien (without the active participation of the alien in the battery or cruelty) or by a member of the spouse's or parent's family residing in the same household as the alien when the spouse or parent consented to or acquiesced in such battery or cruelty and the alien did not actively participate in such battery or cruelty, and

(III) there was a substantial connection between the battery or cruelty described in subclause (I) or (II) and the alien's unlawful entry into the United States.

(B) Failure to attend removal proceeding

Any alien who without reasonable cause fails or refuses to attend or remain in attendance at a proceeding to determine the alien's inadmissibility or deportability and who seeks admission to the United States within 5 years of such alien's subsequent departure or removal is inadmissible.

(C) Misrepresentation

(i) In general

Any alien who, by fraud or willfully misrepresenting a material fact, seeks to procure (or has sought to procure or has procured) a visa, other documentation, or admission into the United States or other benefit provided under this Act is inadmissible.

(ii) Falsely claiming citizenship

(I) In general

Any alien who falsely represents, or has falsely represented, himself or herself to be a citizen of the United States for any purpose or benefit under this Act (including section 274A [8 U.S.C.A. § 1324a]) or any other Federal or State law is inadmissible.

(II) Exception

In the case of an alien making a representation described in subclause (I), if each natural parent of the alien (or, in the case of an adopted alien, each adoptive parent of the alien) is or was a citizen (whether by birth or naturalization), the alien permanently resided in the United States prior to attaining the age of 16, and the alien reasonably believed at the time of making such representation that he or she was a citizen, the alien shall not be considered to be inadmissible under any provision of this subsection based on such representation.

(iii) Waiver authorized

For provision authorizing waiver of clause (i), see subsection (i).

(D) Stowaways

Any alien who is a stowaway is inadmissible.

(E) Smugglers

(i) In general

Any alien who at any time knowingly has encouraged, induced, assisted, abetted, or aided any other alien to enter or to try to enter the United States in violation of law is inadmissible.

(ii) Special rule in the case of family reunification

Clause (i) shall not apply in the case of alien who is an eligible immigrant (as defined in section 301(b)(1) of the Immigration Act of 1990), was physically present in the United States on May 5, 1988, and is seeking admission as an immediate relative or under section 203(a)(2) [8 U.S.C.A. § 1153(a)(2)] (including under section 112 of the Immigration Act of 1990) or benefits under section 301(a) of the Immigration Act of 1990 if the alien, before May 5, 1988, has encouraged, induced, assisted, abetted, or aided only the alien's spouse, parent, son, or daughter (and no other individual) to enter the United States in violation of law.

(iii) Waiver authorized

For provision authorizing waiver of clause (i), see subsection (d)(11).

(F) Subject of civil penalty

(i) In general

An alien who is the subject of a final order for violation of section 274C [8 U.S.C.A. § 1324c] is inadmissible.

(ii) Waiver authorized

For provision authorizing waiver of clause (i), see subsection (d)(12).

(G) Student visa abusers

An alien who obtains the status of a nonimmigrant under section 101(a)(15)(F)(i) [8 U.S.C.A. § 1101(a)(15)(F)(i)] and who violates a term or condition of such status under section 214(*l*) [8 U.S.C.A. § 1184(*l*)]* is inadmissible until the alien has been outside the United States for a continuous period of 5 years after the date of the violation.

(7) Documentation requirements

(A) Immigrants

(i) In general

Except as otherwise specifically provided in this Act, any immigrant at the time of application for admission—

(I) who is not in possession of a valid unexpired immigrant visa, reentry permit, border crossing identification card, or other valid entry document required by this Act, and a valid unexpired passport, or other suitable travel document, or document of identity and nationality if such document is required under the regulations issued by the Attorney General under section 211(a) [8 U.S.C.A. § 1181(a)], or

---

* So in original; probably should refer to section 214(m).

(II) whose visa has been issued without compliance with the provisions of section 203 [8 U.S.C.A. § 1153],

is inadmissible.

(ii) Waiver authorized

For provision authorizing waiver of clause (i), see subsection (k).

(B) Nonimmigrants

(i) In general

Any nonimmigrant who—

(I) is not in possession of a passport valid for a minimum of six months from the date of the expiration of the initial period of the alien's admission or contemplated initial period of stay authorizing the alien to return to the country from which the alien came or to proceed to and enter some other country during such period, or

(II) is not in possession of a valid nonimmigrant visa or border crossing identification card at the time of application for admission,

is inadmissible.

(ii) General waiver authorized

For provision authorizing waiver of clause (i), see subsection (d)(4).

(iii) Guam and Northern Mariana Islands visa waiver

For provision authorizing waiver of clause (i) in the case of visitors to Guam or the Commonwealth of the Northern Mariana Islands, see subsection (*l*).

(iv) Visa waiver program

For authority to waive the requirement of clause (i) under a program, see section 217 [8 U.S.C.A. § 1187].

(8) Ineligible for citizenship

(A) In general

Any immigrant who is permanently ineligible to citizenship is inadmissible.

(B) Draft evaders

Any person who has departed from or who has remained outside the United States to avoid or evade training or service in the armed forces in time of war or a period declared by the President to be a national emergency is inadmissible, except that this subparagraph shall not apply to an alien who at the time of such departure was a nonimmigrant and who is seeking to reenter the United States as a nonimmigrant.

(9) Aliens previously removed

(A) Certain aliens previously removed

(i) Arriving aliens

Any alien who has been ordered removed under section 235(b)(1) [8 U.S.C.A. § 1225(b)(1)] or at the end of proceedings under section 240 [8 U.S.C.A. § 1229a] initiated upon the alien's arrival in the United States and who again seeks admission within 5 years of the date of such removal (or within 20 years in the case of a second or subsequent removal or at any time in the case of an alien convicted of an aggravated felony) is inadmissible.

(ii) Other aliens

Any alien not described in clause (i) who—

(I) has been ordered removed under section 240 or any other provision of law, or

(II) departed the United States while an order of removal was outstanding,

and who seeks admission within 10 years of the date of such alien's departure or removal (or within 20 years of such date in the case of a second or subsequent removal or at any time in the case of an alien convicted of an aggravated felony) is inadmissible.

(iii) Exception

Clauses (i) and (ii) shall not apply to an alien seeking admission within a period if, prior to the date of the alien's reembarkation at a place outside the United States or attempt to be admitted from foreign contiguous territory, the Attorney General has consented to the alien's reapplying for admission.

(B) Aliens unlawfully present

(i) In general

Any alien (other than an alien lawfully admitted for permanent residence) who—

(I) was unlawfully present in the United States for a period of more than 180 days but less than 1 year, voluntarily departed the United States (whether or not pursuant to section 244(e) [8 U.S.C.A. § 1254(e)])* prior to the commencement of proceedings under section 235(b)(1) [8 U.S.C.A. § 1225(b)(1)]or section 239(a) [8 U.S.C.A. § 1229(a)], and again seeks admission within 3 years of the date of such alien's departure or removal, or

---

* So in original. Probably should refer to the voluntary departure provisions, now in § 240B.

(II) has been unlawfully present in the United States for one year or more, and who again seeks admission within 10 years of the date of such alien's departure or removal from the United States,

is inadmissible.

(ii) Construction of unlawful presence

For purposes of this paragraph, an alien is deemed to be unlawfully present in the United States if the alien is present in the United States after the expiration of the period of stay authorized by the Attorney General or is present in the United States without being admitted or paroled.

(iii) Exceptions

(I) Minors

No period of time in which an alien is under 18 years of age shall be taken into account in determining the period of unlawful presence in the United States under clause (i).

(II) Asylees

No period of time in which an alien has a bona fide application for asylum pending under section 208 [8 U.S.C.A. § 1158] shall be taken into account in determining the period of unlawful presence in the United States under clause (i) unless the alien during such period was employed without authorization in the United States.

(III) Family unity

No period of time in which the alien is a beneficiary of family unity protection pursuant to section 301 of the Immigration Act of 1990 shall be taken into account in determining the period of unlawful presence in the United States under clause (i).

(IV) Battered women and children

Clause (i) shall not apply to an alien who would be described in paragraph (6)(A)(ii) if "violation of the terms of the alien's nonimmigrant visa" were substituted for "unlawful entry into the United States" in subclause (III) of that paragraph.

(V) Victims of a severe form of trafficking in persons

Clause (i) shall not apply to an alien who demonstrates that the severe form of trafficking (as that term is defined in section 103 of the Trafficking Victims Protection Act of 2000 (22 U.S.C. 7102)) was at least one central reason for the alien's unlawful presence in the United States.

(iv) Tolling for good cause

In the case of an alien who—

(I) has been lawfully admitted or paroled into the United States,

(II) has filed a nonfrivolous application for a change or extension of status before the date of expiration of the period of stay authorized by the Attorney General, and

(III) has not been employed without authorization in the United States before or during the pendency of such application,

the calculation of the period of time specified in clause (i)(I) shall be tolled during the pendency of such application, but not to exceed 120 days.

(v) Waiver

The Attorney General has sole discretion to waive clause (i) in the case of an immigrant who is the spouse or son or daughter of a United States citizen or of an alien lawfully admitted for permanent residence, if it is established to the satisfaction of the Attorney General that the refusal of admission to such immigrant alien would result in extreme hardship to the citizen or lawfully resident spouse or parent of such alien. No court shall have jurisdiction to review a decision or action by the Attorney General regarding a waiver under this clause.

(C) Aliens unlawfully present after previous immigration violations

(i) In general

Any alien who—

(I) has been unlawfully present in the United States for an aggregate period of more than 1 year, or

(II) has been ordered removed under section 235(b)(1) [8 U.S.C.A. § 1225(b)(1)], section 240 [8 U.S.C.A. § 1229a], or any other provision of law,

and who enters or attempts to reenter the United States without being admitted is inadmissible.

(ii) Exception

Clause (i) shall not apply to an alien seeking admission more than 10 years after the date of the alien's last departure from the United States if, prior to the alien's reembarkation at a place outside the United States or attempt to be readmitted from a foreign contiguous territory, the Secretary of Homeland Security has consented to the alien's reapplying for admission.

(iii) Waiver

The Secretary of Homeland Security may waive the application of clause (i) in the case of an alien who is a VAWA self-petitioner if there is a connection between—

(I) the alien's battering or subjection to extreme cruelty; and

(II) the alien's removal, departure from the United States, reentry or reentries into the United States; or attempted reentry into the United States.

(10) Miscellaneous

(A) Practicing polygamists

Any immigrant who is coming to the United States to practice polygamy is inadmissible.

(B) Guardian required to accompany helpless alien

Any alien—

(i) who is accompanying another alien who is inadmissible and who is certified to be helpless from sickness, mental or physical disability, or infancy pursuant to section 232(c) [8 U.S.C.A. § 1222(c)], and

(ii) whose protection or guardianship is determined to be required by the alien described in clause (i),

is inadmissible.

(C) International child abduction

(i) In general

Except as provided in clause (ii), any alien who, after entry of an order by a court in the United States granting custody to a person of a United States citizen child who detains or retains the child, or withholds custody of the child, outside the United States from the person granted custody by that order, is inadmissible until the child is surrendered to the person granted custody by that order.

(ii) Aliens supporting abductors and relatives of abductors

Any alien who—

(I) is known by the Secretary of State to have intentionally assisted an alien in the conduct described in clause (i),

(II) is known by the Secretary of State to be intentionally providing material support or safe haven to an alien described in clause (i), or

(III) is a spouse (other than the spouse who is the parent of the abducted child), child (other than the abducted child), parent, sibling, or agent of an alien described in clause (i), if such person has been designated by the Secretary of State at the Secretary's sole and unreviewable discretion, is inadmissible until the child described in clause (i) is surrendered to the person granted custody by the order described in that clause, and such person and child are permitted to return to the United States or such person's place of residence.

(iii) Exceptions

Clauses (i) and (ii) shall not apply—

(I) to a government official of the United States who is acting within the scope of his or her official duties;

(II) to a government official of any foreign government if the official has been designated by the Secretary of State at the Secretary's sole and unreviewable discretion; or

(III) so long as the child is located in a foreign state that is a party to the Convention on the Civil Aspects of International Child Abduction, done at The Hague on October 25, 1980.

(D) Unlawful voters

(i) In general

Any alien who has voted in violation of any Federal, State, or local constitutional provision, statute, ordinance, or regulation is inadmissible.

(ii) Exception

In the case of an alien who voted in a Federal, State, or local election (including an initiative, recall, or referendum) in violation of a lawful restriction of voting to citizens, if each natural parent of the alien (or, in the case of an adopted alien, each adoptive parent of the alien) is or was a citizen (whether by birth or naturalization), the alien permanently resided in the United States prior to attaining the age of 16, and the alien reasonably believed at the time of such violation that he or she was a citizen, the alien shall not be considered to be inadmissible under any provision of this subsection based on such violation.

(E) Former citizens who renounced citizenship to avoid taxation

Any alien who is a former citizen of the United States who officially renounces United States citizenship and who is determined by the Attorney General to have renounced United States citizenship for the purpose of avoiding taxation by the United States is inadmissible.

(b) Notices of denials

(1) Subject to paragraphs (2) and (3), if an alien's application for a visa, for admission to the United States, or for adjustment of status is denied by an immigration or consular officer because the officer determines the alien to be inadmissible under subsection (a), the officer shall provide the alien with a timely written notice that—

(A) states the determination, and

(B) lists the specific provision or provisions of law under which the alien is inadmissible or ineligible for entry or adjustment of status.

(2) The Secretary of State may waive the requirements of paragraph (1) with respect to a particular alien or any class or classes of inadmissible aliens.

(3) Paragraph (1) does not apply to any alien inadmissible under paragraph (2) or (3) of subsection (a).

(c) Repealed. Pub.L. 104–208, Div. C, Title III, § 304(b), Sept. 30, 1996, 110 Stat. 3009–597.

(d) Temporary admission of nonimmigrants

(1) The Attorney General shall determine whether a ground for inadmissibility exists with respect to a nonimmigrant described in section 101(a)(15)(S) [8 U.S.C.A. § 1101(a)(15)(S)]. The Attorney General, in the Attorney General's discretion, may waive the application of subsection (a) (other than paragraph (3)(E)) in the case of a nonimmigrant described in section 101(a)(15)(S) [8 U.S.C.A. § 1101(a)(15)(S)], if the Attorney General considers it to be in the national interest to do so. Nothing in this section shall be regarded as prohibiting the Immigration and Naturalization Service from instituting removal proceedings against an alien admitted as a nonimmigrant under section 101(a)(15)(S) [8 U.S.C.A. § 1101(a)(15)(S)] for conduct committed after the alien's admission into the United States, or for conduct or a condition that was not disclosed to the Attorney General prior to the alien's admission as a nonimmigrant under section 101(a)(15)(S) [8 U.S.C.A. § 1101(a)(15)(S)].

(2) Repealed. Pub.L. 101–649, Title VI, § 601(d)(2)(A), Nov. 29, 1990, 104 Stat. 5076.

(3)(A) Except as provided in this subsection, an alien (i) who is applying for a nonimmigrant visa and is known or believed by the consular officer to be ineligible for such visa under subsection (a) of this section (other than paragraphs (3)(A)(i)(I), (3)(A)(ii), (3)(A)(iii), (3)(C), and clauses (i) and (ii) of paragraph (3)(E) of such subsection), may, after approval by the Attorney General of a recommendation by the Secretary of State or by the consular officer that the alien be admitted temporarily despite his inadmissibility, be granted such a visa and may be admitted into the United States temporarily as a nonimmigrant in the discretion of the Attorney General, or (ii) who is inadmissible under subsection (a) of this section (other than paragraphs (3)(A)(i)(I), (3)(A)(ii), (3)(A)(iii), (3)(C), and clauses (i) and (ii) of paragraph (3)(E) of such subsection), but who is in possession of appropriate documents or is granted a waiver thereof and is seeking admission, may be admitted into the United States temporarily as a nonimmigrant in the discretion of the Attorney General. The Attorney General shall prescribe conditions, including exaction of such bonds as may be necessary, to control and regulate the admission and return of inadmissible aliens applying for temporary admission under this paragraph.

(B)(i) The Secretary of State, after consultation with the Attorney General and the Secretary of Homeland Security, or the Secretary of Homeland Security, after consultation with the Secretary of State and the Attorney General, may determine in such Secretary's sole unreviewable discretion that subsection (a)(3)(B) shall not apply with respect to an alien within the scope of that subsection or that subsection (a)(3)(B)(vi)(III) shall not apply to a group within the scope of that subsection, except that no such waiver may be extended to an alien who is within the scope of subsection (a)(3)(B)(i)(II), no such waiver may be extended to an alien who is a member or representative of, has voluntarily and knowingly engaged in or endorsed or espoused or persuaded others to endorse or espouse or support terrorist activity on behalf of, or has voluntarily and knowingly received military-type training from a terrorist organization that is described in subclause (I) or (II) of subsection (a)(3)(B)(vi), and no such waiver may be extended to a group that has engaged terrorist activity against the United States or another democratic country or that has purposefully engaged in a pattern or practice of terrorist activity that is directed at civilians. Such a determination shall neither prejudice the ability of the United States Government to commence criminal or civil proceedings involving a beneficiary of such a determination or any other person, nor create any substantive or procedural right or benefit for a beneficiary of such a determination or any other person. Notwithstanding any other provision of law (statutory or nonstatutory), including section 2241 of title 28, or any other habeas corpus provision, and sections 1361 and 1651 of such title, no court shall have jurisdiction to review such a determination or revocation except in a proceeding for review of a final order of removal pursuant to section 242 [8 U.S.C.A. § 1252], and review shall be limited to the extent provided in section 242(a)(2)(D) [8 U.S.C.A. § 1252(a)(2)(D)]. The Secretary of State may not exercise the discretion provided in this clause with respect to an alien at any time during which the alien is the subject of pending removal proceedings under section 240 [8 U.S.C.A. § 1229a].

(ii) Not later than 90 days after the end of each fiscal year, the Secretary of State and the Secretary of Homeland Security shall each provide to the Committees on the Judiciary of the House of Representatives and of the Senate, the Committee on International Relations of the House of Representatives, the Committee on Foreign Relations of the Senate, and the Committee on Homeland Security of the House of Representatives a report on the aliens to whom such Secretary has applied clause (i). Within one week of applying clause (i) to a group, the

Secretary of State or the Secretary of Homeland Security shall provide a report to such Committees.

(4) Either or both of the requirements of paragraph (7)(B)(i) of subsection (a) may be waived by the Attorney General and the Secretary of State acting jointly **(A)** on the basis of unforeseen emergency in individual cases, or **(B)** on the basis of reciprocity with respect to nationals of foreign contiguous territory or of adjacent islands and residents thereof having a common nationality with such nationals, or **(C)** in the case of aliens proceeding in immediate and continuous transit through the United States under contracts authorized in section 233(c) [8 U.S.C.A. § 1223(c)].

(5)(A) The Attorney General may, except as provided in subparagraph (B) or in section 214(f) [8 U.S.C.A. § 1184(f)], in his discretion parole into the United States temporarily under such conditions as he may prescribe only on a case-by-case basis for urgent humanitarian reasons or significant public benefit any alien applying for admission to the United States, but such parole of such alien shall not be regarded as an admission of the alien and when the purposes of such parole shall, in the opinion of the Attorney General, have been served the alien shall forthwith return or be returned to the custody from which he was paroled and thereafter his case shall continue to be dealt with in the same manner as that of any other applicant for admission to the United States.

(B) The Attorney General may not parole into the United States an alien who is a refugee unless the Attorney General determines that compelling reasons in the public interest with respect to that particular alien require that the alien be paroled into the United States rather than be admitted as a refugee under section 207 [8 U.S.C.A. § 1157].

(6) Repealed. Pub.L. 101–649, Title VI, § 601(d)(2)(A), Nov. 29, 1990, 104 Stat. 5076.

(7) The provisions of subsection (a) (other than paragraph (7)) shall be applicable to any alien who shall leave Guam, the Commonwealth of the Northern Mariana Islands, Puerto Rico, or the Virgin Islands of the United States, and who seeks to enter the continental United States or any other place under the jurisdiction of the United States. The Attorney General shall by regulations provide a method and procedure for the temporary admission to the United States of the aliens described in this proviso. Any alien described in this paragraph, who is denied admission to the United States, shall be immediately removed in the manner provided by section 241(c) [8 U.S.C.A. § 1231(c)].

(8) Upon a basis of reciprocity accredited officials of foreign governments, their immediate families, attendants, servants, and personal employees may be admitted in immediate and continuous transit through the United States without regard to the provisions of this section except paragraphs (3)(A), (3)(B), (3)(C), and (7)(B) of subsection (a) of this section.

(9), (10) Repealed. Pub.L. 101–649, Title VI, § 601(d)(2)(A), Nov. 29, 1990, 104 Stat. 5076.

(11) The Attorney General may, in his discretion for humanitarian purposes, to assure family unity, or when it is otherwise in the public interest, waive application of clause (i) of subsection (a)(6)(E) in the case of any alien lawfully admitted for permanent residence who temporarily proceeded abroad voluntarily and not under an order of removal, and who is otherwise admissible to the United States as a returning resident under section 211(b) [8 U.S.C.A. § 1181(b)] and in the case of an alien seeking admission or adjustment of status as an immediate relative or immigrant under section 203(a) [8 U.S.C.A. § 1153(a)] (other than paragraph (4) thereof), if the alien has encouraged, induced, assisted, abetted, or aided only an individual who at the time of such action was the alien's spouse, parent, son, or daughter (and no other individual) to enter the United States in violation of law.

(12) The Attorney General may, in the discretion of the Attorney General for humanitarian purposes or to assure family unity, waive application of clause (i) of subsection (a)(6)(F)—

(A) in the case of an alien lawfully admitted for permanent residence who temporarily proceeded abroad voluntarily and not under an order of deportation or removal and who is otherwise admissible to the United States as a returning resident under section 211(b) [8 U.S.C.A. § 1181(b)], and

(B) in the case of an alien seeking admission or adjustment of status under section 201(b)(2)(A) [8 U.S.C.A. § 1151(b)(2)(A)] or under section 203(a) [8 U.S.C.A. § 1153(a)],

if no previous civil money penalty was imposed against the alien under section 274C [8 U.S.C.A. § 1324c] and the offense was committed solely to assist, aid, or support the alien's spouse or child (and not another individual). No court shall have jurisdiction to review a decision of the Attorney General to grant or deny a waiver under this paragraph.

(13)(A) The Secretary of Homeland Security shall determine whether a ground for inadmissibility exists with respect to a nonimmigrant described in section 101(a)(15)(T) [8 U.S.C.A § 1101(a)(15)(T)], except that the ground for inadmissibility described in subsection (a)(4) of this section shall not apply with respect to such a nonimmigrant.

(B) In addition to any other waiver that may be available under this section, in the case of a nonimmigrant described in section 101(a)(15)(T) [8 U.S.C.A § 1101(a)(15)(T)], if the Secretary of Homeland Security considers it to be in the National interest to do so, the Secretary of Homeland Security, in the Secretary of Homeland Security's discretion, may waive the application of

(i) subsection (a)(1) of this section; and

(ii) any other provision of subsection (a) of this section (excluding paragraphs (3), (4), (10)(C), and (10)(E)) if the activities rendering the alien inadmissible under the provision were caused by, or were incident to, the victimization described in section 101(a)(15) (T)(i)(I) [8 U.S.C.A § 1101(a)(15)(T)(i)(I)].

(14) The Secretary of Homeland Security shall determine whether a ground of inadmissibility exists with respect to a nonimmigrant described in section 101(a)(15)(U) [8 U.S.C.A § 1101(a)(15)(U)]. The Secretary of Homeland Security, in the Secretary of Homeland Security's discretion, may waive the application of subsection (a) (other than paragraph (3)(E)) in the case of a nonimmigrant described in section 101(a)(15)(U) [8 U.S.C.A § 1101(a)(15)(U)], if the Secretary of Homeland Security considers it to be in the public or national interest to do so.

(e) Educational visitor status; foreign residence requirement; waiver

No person admitted under section 101(a)(15)(J) [8 U.S.C.A. § 1101(a) (15)(J)] or acquiring such status after admission (i) whose participation in the program for which he came to the United States was financed in whole or in part, directly or indirectly, by an agency of the Government of the United States or by the government of the country of his nationality or his last residence, (ii) who at the time of admission or acquisition of status under section 101(a)(15)(J) [8 U.S.C.A. § 1101(a)(15)(J)] was a national or resident of a country which the Director of the United States Information Agency, pursuant to regulations prescribed by him, had designated as clearly requiring the services of persons engaged in the field of specialized knowledge or skill in which the alien was engaged, or (iii) who came to the United States or acquired such status in order to receive graduate medical education or training, shall be eligible to apply for an immigrant visa, or for permanent residence, or for a nonimmigrant visa under section 101(a) (15)(H) [8 U.S.C.A. § 1101(a)(15)(H)] or section 101(a)(15)(L) [8 U.S.C.A. § 1101(a)(15)(L)] until it is established that such person has resided and been physically present in the country of his nationality or his last residence for an aggregate of at least two years following departure from the United States: *Provided*, That upon the favorable recommendation of the Director, pursuant to the request of an interested United States Government agency (or, in the case of an alien described in clause (iii), pursuant to the request of a State Department of Public Health, or its equivalent), or of the Commissioner of Immigration and Naturalization after he has determined that departure from the United States would impose exceptional hardship upon the alien's spouse or child (if such spouse or child is a citizen of the United States or a lawfully resident alien), or that the alien cannot return to the country of his nationality or last residence because he would be subject to persecution on account of race, religion, or political opinion, the Attorney General may waive the requirement of such two-year foreign residence abroad in the case of any alien whose admission to the United States is found by the Attorney General to be in the public interest except that in the case of a waiver requested by a State Department of Public Health, or its equivalent, or in the case of a waiver requested by an interested United States Government agency on behalf of an alien described in clause (iii), the waiver shall be subject to the requirements of section 214(*l*) [8 U.S.C.A. § 1184(*l*)]: And *provided further*, That, except in the case of an alien described in clause (iii), the Attorney General may, upon the favorable recommendation of the Director, waive such two-year foreign residence requirement in any case in which the foreign country of the alien's nationality or last residence has furnished the Director a statement in writing that it has no objection to such waiver in the case of such alien.

(f) Suspension of entry or imposition of restrictions by President

Whenever the President finds that the entry of any aliens or of any class of aliens into the United States would be detrimental to the interests of the United States, he may by proclamation, and for such period as he shall deem necessary, suspend the entry of all aliens or any class of aliens as immigrants or nonimmigrants, or impose on the entry of aliens any restrictions he may deem to be appropriate. Whenever the Attorney General finds that a commercial airline has failed to comply with regulations of the Attorney General relating to requirements of airlines for the detection of fraudulent documents used by passengers traveling to the United States (including the training of personnel in such detection), the Attorney General may suspend the entry of some or all aliens transported to the United States by such airline.

(g) Bond and conditions for admission of alien excludable on health-related grounds

The Attorney General may waive the application of—

(1) subsection (a)(1)(A)(i) in the case of any alien who—

(A) is the spouse or the unmarried son or daughter, or the minor unmarried lawfully adopted child, of a United States citizen, or of an alien lawfully admitted for permanent residence, or of an alien who has been issued an immigrant visa,

(B) has a son or daughter who is a United States citizen, or an alien lawfully admitted for permanent residence, or an alien who has been issued an immigrant visa; or

(C) is a VAWA self-petitioner,

in accordance with such terms, conditions, and controls, if any, including the giving of bond, as the Attorney General, in the discretion of the Attorney General after consultation with the Secretary of Health and Human Services, may by regulation prescribe;

(2) subsection (a)(1)(A)(ii) in the case of any alien—

(A) who receives vaccination against the vaccine-preventable disease or diseases for which the alien has failed to present documentation of previous vaccination,

(B) for whom a civil surgeon, medical officer, or panel physician (as those terms are defined by section 34.2 of title 42 of the Code of Federal Regulations) certifies, according to such regulations as the Secretary of Health and Human Services may prescribe, that such vaccination would not be medically appropriate, or

(C) under such circumstances as the Attorney General provides by regulation, with respect to whom the requirement of such a vaccination would be contrary to the alien's religious beliefs or moral convictions; or

(3) subsection (a)(1)(A)(iii) in the case of any alien, in accordance with such terms, conditions, and controls, if any, including the giving of bond, as the Attorney General, in the discretion of the Attorney General after consultation with the Secretary of Health and Human Services, may by regulation prescribe.

(h) Waiver of subsection (a)(2)(A)(i)(I), (II), (B), (D), and (E)

The Attorney General may, in his discretion, waive the application of subparagraphs (A)(i)(I), (B), (D), and (E) of subsection (a)(2) and subparagraph (A)(i)(II) of such subsection insofar as it relates to a single offense of simple possession of 30 grams or less of marijuana if—

(1)(A) in the case of any immigrant it is established to the satisfaction of the Attorney General that—

(i) the alien is inadmissible only under subparagraph (D)(i) or (D)(ii) of such subsection or the activities for which the alien is inadmissible occurred more than 15 years before the date of the alien's application for a visa, admission, or adjustment of status,

(ii) the admission to the United States of such alien would not be contrary to the national welfare, safety, or security of the United States, and

(iii) the alien has been rehabilitated; or

(B) in the case of an immigrant who is the spouse, parent, son, or daughter of a citizen of the United States or an alien lawfully admitted for permanent residence if it is established to the satisfaction of the Attorney General that the alien's denial of admission would result in extreme hardship to the United States citizen or lawfully resident spouse, parent, son, or daughter of such alien; or

(C) the alien is a VAWA self-petitioner; and

(2) the Attorney General, in his discretion, and pursuant to such terms, conditions and procedures as he may by regulations prescribe, has consented to the alien's applying or reapplying for a visa, for admission to the United States, or adjustment of status.

No waiver shall be provided under this subsection in the case of an alien who has been convicted of (or who has admitted committing acts that constitute) murder or criminal acts involving torture, or an attempt or conspiracy to commit murder or a criminal act involving torture. No waiver shall be granted under this subsection in the case of an alien who has previously been admitted to the United States as an alien lawfully admitted for permanent residence if either since the date of such admission the alien has been convicted of an aggravated felony or the alien has not lawfully resided continuously in the United States for a period of not less than 7 years immediately preceding the date of initiation of proceedings to remove the alien from the United States. No court shall have jurisdiction to review a decision of the Attorney General to grant or deny a waiver under this subsection.

(i) Admission of immigrant excludable for fraud or willful misrepresentation of material fact

(1) The Attorney General may, in the discretion of the Attorney General, waive the application of clause (i) of subsection (a)(6)(C) of this section in the case of an immigrant who is the spouse, son, or daughter of a United States citizen or of an alien lawfully admitted for permanent residence if it is established to the satisfaction of the Attorney General that the refusal of admission to the United States of such immigrant alien would result in extreme hardship to the citizen or lawfully resident spouse or parent of such an alien or, in the case of a VAWA self-petitioner, the alien demonstrates extreme hardship to the alien or the alien's United States citizen, lawful permanent resident, or qualified alien parent or child.

(2) No court shall have jurisdiction to review a decision or action of the Attorney General regarding a waiver under paragraph (1).

(j) Limitation on immigration of foreign medical graduates

(1) The additional requirements referred to in section 101(a)(15)(J) [8 U.S.C.A. § 1101(a)(15)(J)] for an alien who is coming to the United States under a program under which he will receive graduate medical education or training are as follows:

(A) A school of medicine or of one of the other health professions, which is accredited by a body or bodies approved for the purpose by the Secretary of Education, has agreed in writing to provide the graduate medical education or training under the program for which the alien is coming to the United States or to assume responsibility for arranging for the provision thereof by an appropriate public or nonprofit private institution or agency, except that, in the case of such an agreement by a school of medicine, any one or more of its affiliated hospitals which are to participate in the provision of the graduate medical education or training must join in the agreement.

(B) Before making such agreement, the accredited school has been satisfied that the alien **(i)** is a graduate of a school of medicine which is accredited by a body or bodies approved for the purpose by the Secretary of Education (regardless of whether such school of medicine is in the United States); or **(ii)(I)** has passed parts I and II of the National Board of Medical Examiners Examination (or an equivalent examination as determined by the Secretary of Health and Human Services), **(II)** has competency in oral and written English, **(III)** will be able to adapt to the educational and cultural environment in which he will be receiving his education or training, and **(IV)** has adequate prior education and training to participate satisfactorily in the program for which he is coming to the United States. For the purposes of this subparagraph, an alien who is a graduate of a medical school shall be considered to have passed parts I and II of the National Board of Medical Examiners Examination if the alien was fully and permanently licensed to practice medicine in a State on January 9, 1978, and was practicing medicine in a State on that date.

(C) The alien has made a commitment to return to the country of his nationality or last residence upon completion of the education or training for which he is coming to the United States, and the government of the country of his nationality or last residence has provided a written assurance, satisfactory to the Secretary of Health and Human Services, that there is a need in that country for persons with the skills the alien will acquire in such education or training.

(D) The duration of the alien's participation in the program of graduate medical education or training for which the alien is coming to the United States is limited to the time typically required to complete such program, as determined by the Director of the United States Information Agency at the time of the alien's admission into the United States, based on criteria which are established in coordination with the Secretary of Health and Human Services and which take into consideration the published requirements of the medical specialty board which administers such education or training program; except that—

(i) such duration is further limited to seven years unless the alien has demonstrated to the satisfaction of the Director that the country to which the alien will return at the end of such specialty education or training has an exceptional need for an individual trained in such specialty, and

(ii) the alien may, once and not later than two years after the date the alien is admitted to the United States as an exchange visitor or acquires exchange visitor status, change the alien's designated program of graduate medical education or training if the Director approves the change and if a commitment and written assurance with respect to the alien's new program have been provided in accordance with subparagraph (C).

(E) The alien furnishes the Attorney General each year with an affidavit (in such form as the Attorney General shall prescribe) that attests that the alien **(i)** is in good standing in the program of graduate medical education or training in which the alien is participating, and **(ii)** will return to the country of his nationality or last residence upon completion of the education or training for which he came to the United States.

(2) An alien who is a graduate of a medical school and who is coming to the United States to perform services as a member of the medical profession may not be admitted as a nonimmigrant under section 101(a)(15)(H)(i)(b) [8 U.S.C.A. § 1101(a)(15)(H)(i)(b)] unless—

(A) the alien is coming pursuant to an invitation from a public or nonprofit private educational or research institution or agency in the United States to teach or conduct research, or both, at or for such institution or agency, or

(B)(i) the alien has passed the Federation licensing examination (administered by the Federation of State Medical Boards of the United States) or an equivalent examination as determined by the Secretary of Health and Human Services, and

(ii) (I) has competency in oral and written English or **(II)** is a graduate of a school of medicine which is accredited by a body or bodies approved for the purpose by the Secretary of Education (regardless of whether such school of medicine is in the United States).

(3) The Director of the United States Information Agency annually shall transmit to the Congress a report on aliens who have submitted affidavits described in paragraph (1)(E), and shall include in such report the name and address of each such alien, the medical education or training program in which such alien is participating, and the status of such alien in that program.

(k) Attorney General's discretion to admit otherwise inadmissible aliens who possess immigrant visas

Any alien, inadmissible from the United States under paragraph (5)(A) or (7)(A)(i) of subsection (a), who is in possession of an immigrant visa may, if otherwise admissible, be admitted in the discretion of the Attorney General if the Attorney General is satisfied that inadmissibility was not known to, and could not have been ascertained by the exercise of reasonable diligence by, the immigrant before the time of departure of the vessel or aircraft from the last port outside the United States and outside foreign contiguous territory or, in the case of an immigrant coming from foreign contiguous territory, before the time of the immigrant's application for admission.

(*l*) Guam and Northern Mariana Islands Visa Waiver Program

(1) In general

The requirement of subsection (a)(7)(B)(i) may be waived by the Secretary of Homeland Security, in the case of an alien applying for admission as a nonimmigrant visitor for business or pleasure and solely for entry into and stay in Guam or the Commonwealth of the Northern Mariana Islands for a period not to exceed 45 days, if the Secretary of Homeland Security, after consultation with the Secretary of the Interior, the Secretary of State, the Governor of Guam and the Governor of the Commonwealth of the Northern Mariana Islands, determines that—

(A) an adequate arrival and departure control system has been developed in Guam and the Commonwealth of the Northern Mariana Islands; and

(B) such a waiver does not represent a threat to the welfare, safety, or security of the United States or its territories and commonwealths.

(2) Alien waiver of rights

An alien may not be provided a waiver under this subsection unless the alien has waived any right—

(A) to review or appeal under this Act an immigration officer's determination as to the admissibility of the alien at the port of entry into Guam or the Commonwealth of the Northern Mariana Islands; or

(B) to contest, other than on the basis of an application for withholding of removal under section 241(b)(3) [8 U.S.C.A. § 1231(b)(3)] or under the Convention Against Torture, or an application for asylum if permitted under section 208 [8 U.S.C.A. § 1158], any action for removal of the alien.

(3) Regulations

All necessary regulations to implement this subsection shall be promulgated by the Secretary of Homeland Security, in consultation with the Secretary of the Interior and the Secretary of State, on or before the 180th day after the date of enactment of the Consolidated Natural Resources Act of 2008 [May 8, 2008]. The promulgation of such regulations shall be considered a foreign affairs function for purposes of section 553(a) of title 5, United States Code. At a minimum, such regulations should include, but not necessarily be limited to—

(A) a listing of all countries whose nationals may obtain the waiver also provided by this subsection, except that such regulations shall provide for a listing of any country from which the Commonwealth has received a significant economic benefit from the number of visitors for pleasure within the one-year period preceding the date of enactment of the Consolidated Natural Resources Act of 2008, [May 8, 2008] unless the Secretary of Homeland Security determines that such country's inclusion on such list would represent a threat to the welfare, safety, or security of the United States or its territories; and

(B) any bonding requirements for nationals of some or all of those countries who may present an increased risk of overstays or other potential problems, if different from such requirements otherwise provided by law for nonimmigrant visitors.

(4) Factors

In determining whether to grant or continue providing the waiver under this subsection to nationals of any country, the Secretary of Homeland Security, in consultation with the Secretary of the Interior and the Secretary of State, shall consider all factors that the Secretary deems relevant, including electronic travel authorizations, procedures for reporting lost and stolen passports, repatriation of aliens, rates of refusal for nonimmigrant visitor visas, overstays, exit systems, and information exchange.

(5) Suspension

The Secretary of Homeland Security shall monitor the admission of nonimmigrant visitors to Guam and the Commonwealth of the Northern Mariana Islands under this subsection. If the Secretary determines that such admissions have resulted in an unacceptable number of visitors from a country remaining unlawfully in Guam or the Commonwealth of the Northern Mariana Islands, unlawfully obtaining entry to other parts of the United States, or seeking withholding of removal or asylum, or that visitors from a country pose a risk to law enforcement or security interests of Guam or the Commonwealth of the Northern Mariana Islands or of the United States (including the interest in the enforcement of the immigration laws of the United States), the Secretary shall suspend the admission of nationals of such country under this subsection. The Secretary of Homeland Security may in the Secretary's discretion suspend the Guam and Northern Mariana Islands visa waiver program at any time, on a country-by-country basis, for other good cause.

(6) Addition of countries

The Governor of Guam and the Governor of the Commonwealth of the Northern Mariana Islands may request the Secretary of the Interior and the Secretary of Homeland Security to add a particular country to the list of countries whose nationals may obtain the waiver provided by this subsection, and the Secretary of Homeland Security may grant such request after consultation with the Secretary of the Interior and the Secretary of State, and may promulgate regulations with respect to the inclusion of that country and any special requirements the Secretary of Homeland Security, in the Secretary's sole discretion, may impose prior to allowing nationals of that country to obtain the waiver provided by this subsection.

(m) Requirements for admission of nonimmigrant nurses during five-year period

(1) The qualifications referred to in section 101(a)(15)(H)(i)(c) [8 U.S.C.A. § 1101(a)(15)(H)(i)(c)], with respect to an alien who is coming to the United States to perform nursing services for a facility, are that the alien—

(A) has obtained a full and unrestricted license to practice professional nursing in the country where the alien obtained nursing education or has received nursing education in the United States;

(B) has passed an appropriate examination (recognized in regulations promulgated in consultation with the Secretary of Health and Human Services) or has a full and unrestricted license under State law to practice professional nursing in the State of intended employment; and

(C) is fully qualified and eligible under the laws (including such temporary or interim licensing requirements which authorize the nurse to be employed) governing the place of intended employment to engage in the practice of professional nursing as a registered nurse immediately upon admission to the United States and is authorized under such laws to be employed by the facility.

(2)(A) The attestation referred to in section 101(a)(15)(H)(i)(c) [8 U.S.C.A. § 1101(a)(15)(H)(i)(c)], with respect to a facility for which an alien will perform services, is an attestation as to the following:

(i) The facility meets all the requirements of paragraph (6).

(ii) The employment of the alien will not adversely affect the wages and working conditions of registered nurses similarly employed.

(iii) The alien employed by the facility will be paid the wage rate for registered nurses similarly employed by the facility.

(iv) The facility has taken and is taking timely and significant steps designed to recruit and retain sufficient registered nurses who are United States citizens or immigrants who are authorized to perform nursing services, in order to remove as quickly as reasonably possible the dependence of the facility on nonimmigrant registered nurses.

(v) There is not a strike or lockout in the course of a labor dispute, the facility did not lay off and will not lay off a registered nurse employed by the facility within the period beginning 90 days before and ending 90 days after the date of filing of any visa petition, and the employment of such an alien is not intended or designed to influence an election for a bargaining representative for registered nurses of the facility.

(vi) At the time of the filing of the petition for registered nurses under section 101(a)(15)(H)(i)(c) [8 U.S.C.A. § 1101(a)(15)(H)(i)(c)], notice of the filing has been provided by the facility to the bargaining representative of the registered nurses at the facility or, where there is no such bargaining representative, notice of the filing has been provided to the registered nurses employed at the facility through posting in conspicuous locations.

(vii) The facility will not, at any time, employ a number of aliens issued visas or otherwise provided nonimmigrant status under section 101(a)(15)(H)(i)(c) [8 U.S.C.A. § 1101(a)(15)(H)(i)(c)] that exceeds 33 percent of the total number of registered nurses employed by the facility.

(viii) The facility will not, with respect to any alien issued a visa or otherwise provided nonimmigrant status under section 101(a)(15)(H)(i)(c) [8 U.S.C.A. § 1101(a)(15)(H)(i)(c)]—

(I) authorize the alien to perform nursing services at any worksite other than a worksite controlled by the facility; or

(II) transfer the place of employment of the alien from one worksite to another.

Nothing in clause (iv) shall be construed as requiring a facility to have taken significant steps described in such clause before the date of the enactment of the Nursing Relief for Disadvantaged Areas Act of 1999. A copy of the attestation shall be provided, within 30 days of the date of filing, to registered nurses employed at the facility on the date of filing.

(B) For purposes of subparagraph (A)(iv), each of the following shall be considered a significant step reasonably designed to recruit and retain registered nurses:

(i) Operating a training program for registered nurses at the facility or financing (or providing participation in) a training program for registered nurses elsewhere.

(ii) Providing career development programs and other methods of facilitating health care workers to become registered nurses.

(iii) Paying registered nurses wages at a rate higher than currently being paid to registered nurses similarly employed in the geographic area.

(iv) Providing reasonable opportunities for meaningful salary advancement by registered nurses.

The steps described in this subparagraph shall not be considered to be an exclusive list of the significant steps that may be taken to meet the conditions of subparagraph (A)(iv). Nothing in this subparagraph shall require a facility to take more than one step if the facility can demonstrate that taking a second step is not reasonable.

(C) Subject to subparagraph (E), an attestation under subparagraph (A)—

(i) shall expire on the date that is the later of—

(I) the end of the one-year period beginning on the date of its filing with the Secretary of Labor; or

(II) the end of the period of admission under section 101(a)(15)(H)(i)(c) [8 U.S.C.A. § 1101(a)(15)(H)(i)(c)] of the last alien with respect to whose admission it was applied (in accordance with clause (ii)); and

(ii) shall apply to petitions filed during the one-year period beginning on the date of its filing with the Secretary of Labor if the facility states in each such petition that it continues to comply with the conditions in the attestation.

(D) A facility may meet the requirements under this paragraph with respect to more than one registered nurse in a single petition.

(E)(i) The Secretary of Labor shall compile and make available for public examination in a timely manner in Washington, D.C., a list identifying facilities which have filed petitions for nonimmigrants under section 101(a)(15)(H)(i)(c) [8 U.S.C.A. § 1101(a)(15)(H)(i)(c)] and, for each such facility, a copy of the facility's attestation under subparagraph (A) (and accompanying documentation) and each such petition filed by the facility.

(ii) The Secretary of Labor shall establish a process, including reasonable time limits, for the receipt, investigation, and disposition of complaints respecting a facility's failure to meet conditions attested to or a facility's misrepresentation of a material fact in an attestation. Complaints may be filed by any aggrieved person or organization (including bargaining representatives, associations deemed appropriate by the Secretary, and other aggrieved parties as determined under regulations of the Secretary). The Secretary shall conduct an investigation under this clause if there is reasonable cause to believe that a facility fails to meet conditions attested to. Subject to the time limits established under this clause, this subparagraph shall apply regardless of whether an attestation is expired or unexpired at the time a complaint is filed.

(iii) Under such process, the Secretary shall provide, within 180 days after the date such a complaint is filed, for a determination as to whether or not a basis exists to make a finding described in clause (iv). If the Secretary determines that such a basis exists, the Secretary shall provide for notice of such determination to the interested parties and an opportunity for a hearing on the complaint within 60 days of the date of the determination.

(iv) If the Secretary of Labor finds, after notice and opportunity for a hearing, that a facility (for which an attestation is made) has failed to meet a condition attested to or that there was a misrepresentation of material fact in the attestation, the Secretary shall notify the Attorney General of such finding and may, in addition, impose such other administrative remedies (including civil monetary penalties in an amount not to exceed $1,000 per nurse per violation, with the total penalty not to exceed $10,000 per violation) as the Secretary determines to be appropriate. Upon receipt of such notice, the Attorney General shall not approve petitions filed with respect to a facility during a period of at least one year for nurses to be employed by the facility.

(v) In addition to the sanctions provided for under clause (iv), if the Secretary of Labor finds, after notice and an opportunity for a hearing, that a facility has violated the condition attested to under subparagraph (A)(iii) (relating to payment of registered nurses at the prevailing wage rate), the Secretary shall order the facility to provide for payment of such amounts of back pay as may be required to comply with such condition.

(F)(i) The Secretary of Labor shall impose on a facility filing an attestation under subparagraph (A) a filing fee, in an amount prescribed by the Secretary based on the costs of carrying out the Secretary's duties under this subsection, but not exceeding $250.

(ii) Fees collected under this subparagraph shall be deposited in a fund established for this purpose in the Treasury of the United States.

(iii) The collected fees in the fund shall be available to the Secretary of Labor, to the extent and in such amounts as may be provided in appropriations Acts, to cover the costs described in clause (i), in addition to any other funds that are available to the Secretary to cover such costs.

(3) The period of admission of an alien under section 101(a)(15)(H)(i)(c) [8 U.S.C.A. § 1101(a)(15)(H)(i)(c)] shall be 3 years.

(4) The total number of nonimmigrant visas issued pursuant to petitions granted under section 101(a)(15)(H)(i)(c) [8 U.S.C.A. § 1101(a)(15)(H)(i)(c)] in each fiscal year shall not exceed 500. The number of such visas issued for employment in each State in each fiscal year shall not exceed the following:

(A) For States with populations of less than 9,000,000, based upon the 1990 decennial census of population, 25 visas.

(B) For States with populations of 9,000,000 or more, based upon the 1990 decennial census of population, 50 visas.

(C) If the total number of visas available under this paragraph for a fiscal year quarter exceeds the number of qualified nonimmigrants who may be issued such visas during those quarters, the visas made available under this paragraph shall be issued without regard to the numerical limitation under subparagraph (A) or (B) of this paragraph during the last fiscal year quarter.

(5) A facility that has filed a petition under section 101(a)(15)(H)(i)(c) [8 U.S.C.A. § 1101(a)(15)(H)(i)(c)] to employ a nonimmigrant to perform nursing services for the facility—

(A) shall provide the nonimmigrant a wage rate and working conditions commensurate with those of nurses similarly employed by the facility;

(B) shall require the nonimmigrant to work hours commensurate with those of nurses similarly employed by the facility; and

(C) shall not interfere with the right of the nonimmigrant to join or organize a union.

(6) For purposes of this subsection and section 101(a)(15)(H)(i)(c) [8 U.S.C.A. § 1101(a)(15)(H)(i)(c)], the term "facility" means a subsection (d) hospital (as defined in section 1886(d)(1)(B) of the Social Security Act (42 U.S.C. 1395ww (d)(1)(B))) that meets the following requirements:

(A) As of March 31, 1997, the hospital was located in a health professional shortage area (as defined in section 332 of the Public Health Service Act (42 U.S.C. 254e)).

(B) Based on its settled cost report filed under title XVIII of the Social Security Act for its cost reporting period beginning during fiscal year 1994—

(i) the hospital has not less than 190 licensed acute care beds;

(ii) the number of the hospital's inpatient days for such period which were made up of patients who (for such days) were entitled to benefits under part A of such title is not less than 35 percent of the total number of such hospital's acute care inpatient days for such period; and

(iii) the number of the hospital's inpatient days for such period which were made up of patients who (for such days) were eligible for medical assistance under a State plan approved under title XIX of the Social Security Act, is not less than 28 percent of the total number of such hospital's acute care inpatient days for such period.

(7) For purposes of paragraph (2)(A)(v), the term "lay off", with respect to a worker—

(A) means to cause the worker's loss of employment, other than through a discharge for inadequate performance, violation of workplace rules, cause, voluntary departure, voluntary retirement, or the expiration of a grant or contract; but

(B) does not include any situation in which the worker is offered, as an alternative to such loss of employment, a similar employment opportunity with the same employer at equivalent or higher compensation and benefits than the position from which the employee was discharged, regardless of whether or not the employee accepts the offer.

Nothing in this paragraph is intended to limit an employee's or an employer's rights under a collective bargaining agreement or other employment contract.

(n) Labor condition application

(1) No alien may be admitted or provided status as an H–1B non-immigrant in an occupational classification unless the employer has filed with the Secretary of Labor an application stating the following:

(A) The employer—

(i) is offering and will offer during the period of authorized employment to aliens admitted or provided status as a non-immigrant described in section 101(a)(15)(H)(i)(b) [8 U.S.C.A. § 1101(a)(15)(H)(i)(b)] wages that are at least—

(I) the actual wage level paid by the employer to all other individuals with similar experience and qualifications for the specific employment in question, or

(II) the prevailing wage level for the occupational classification in the area of employment,

whichever is greater, based on the best information available as of the time of filing the application, and

(ii) will provide working conditions for such a nonimmigrant that will not adversely affect the working conditions of workers similarly employed.

(B) There is not a strike or lockout in the course of a labor dispute in the occupational classification at the place of employment.

(C) The employer, at the time of filing the application—

(i) has provided notice of the filing under this paragraph to the bargaining representative (if any) of the employer's employees in the occupational classification and area for which aliens are sought, or

(ii) if there is no such bargaining representative, has provided notice of filing in the occupational classification through such methods as physical posting in conspicuous locations at the place of employment or electronic notification to employees in the occupational classification for which H–1B nonimmigrants are sought.

(D) The application shall contain a specification of the number of workers sought, the occupational classification in which the workers will be employed, and wage rate and conditions under which they will be employed.

(E)(i) In the case of an application described in clause (ii), the employer did not displace and will not displace a United States worker (as defined in paragraph (4)) employed by the employer within the period beginning 90 days before and ending 90 days after the date of filing of any visa petition supported by the application.

(ii) An application described in this clause is an application filed on or after the date final regulations are first promulgated to carry out this subparagraph, and before, by an H–1B-dependent employer (as defined in paragraph (3)) or by an employer that has been found, on or after October 21, 1998, under paragraph (2)(C) or (5) to have committed a willful failure or misrepresentation during the 5-year period preceding the filing of the application. An application is not described in this clause if the only H–1B nonimmigrants sought in the application are exempt H–1B nonimmigrants.

(F) In the case of an application described in subparagraph (E)(ii), the employer will not place the nonimmigrant with another employer (regardless of whether or not such other employer is an H–1B-dependent employer) where—

(i) the nonimmigrant performs duties in whole or in part at one or more worksites owned, operated, or controlled by such other employer; and

(ii) there are indicia of an employment relationship between the nonimmigrant and such other employer;

unless the employer has inquired of the other employer as to whether, and has no knowledge that, within the period beginning 90 days before and ending 90 days after the date of the placement of the nonimmigrant with the other employer, the other employer has displaced or intends to displace a United States worker employed by the other employer.

(G)(i) In the case of an application described in subparagraph (E)(ii), subject to clause (ii), the employer, prior to filing the application—

(I) has taken good faith steps to recruit, in the United States using procedures that meet industry wide standards and offering compensation that is at least as great as that required to be offered to H–1B nonimmigrants under subparagraph (A), United States workers for the job for which the nonimmigrant or nonimmigrants is or are sought; and

(II) has offered the job to any United States worker who applies and is equally or better qualified for the job for which the nonimmigrant or nonimmigrants is or are sought.

(ii) The conditions described in clause (i) shall not apply to an application filed with respect to the employment of an H–1B nonimmigrant who is described in subparagraph (A), (B), or (C) of section 203(b)(1).

The employer shall make available for public examination, within one working day after the date on which an application under this paragraph is filed, at the employer's principal place of business or worksite, a copy of each such application (and such accompanying documents as are necessary). The Secretary shall compile, on a current basis, a list (by employer and by occupational classification) of the applications filed under this subsection. Such list shall include the wage rate, number of aliens sought, period of intended employment, and date of need. The Secretary shall make such list available for public examination in Washington, D.C. The Secretary of Labor shall review such an application only for completeness and obvious inaccuracies. Unless the Secretary finds that the application is incomplete or obviously inaccurate, the Secretary shall provide the certification described in section 101(a)(15)(H)(i)(b) [8 U.S.C.A. § 1101(a)(15)(H)(i)(b)] within 7 days of the date of the filing of the application. The application form shall include a clear statement explaining the liability under subparagraph (F) of a place employer if the other employer described in such subparagraph displaces a United States worker as described in such subparagraph. Nothing in subparagraph (G) shall be construed to prohibit an employer from using legitimate selection criteria relevant to the job that are normal or customary to the type of job involved, so long as such criteria are not applied in a discriminatory manner.

(2)(A) Subject to paragraph (5)(A), the Secretary shall establish a process for the receipt, investigation, and disposition of complaints respecting a petitioner's failure to meet a condition specified in an application submitted under paragraph (1) or a petitioner's misrepresentation of material facts in such an application. Complaints may be filed by any aggrieved person or organization (including bargaining representatives). No investigation or hearing shall be conducted on a complaint concerning such a failure or misrepresentation unless the complaint was filed not later than 12 months after the date of the failure or misrepresentation, respectively. The Secretary shall conduct an investigation under this paragraph if there is reasonable cause to believe that such a failure or misrepresentation has occurred.

(B) Under such process, the Secretary shall provide, within 30 days after the date such a complaint is filed, for a determination as to whether or not a reasonable basis exists to make a finding described in subparagraph (C). If the Secretary determines that such a reasonable basis exists, the Secretary shall provide for notice of such determination to the interested parties and an opportunity for a hearing on the complaint, in accordance with section 556 of Title 5, within 60 days after the date of the determination. If such a hearing is requested, the Secretary shall make a finding concerning the matter by not later than 60 days after the date of the hearing. In the case of similar complaints respecting the same applicant, the Secretary may consolidate the hearings under this subparagraph on such complaints.

(C)(i) If the Secretary finds, after notice and opportunity for a hearing, a failure to meet a condition of paragraph (1)(b), (1)(e), or (1)(f), a substantial failure to meet a condition of paragraph (1)(c), (1)(d), or (1)(g)(i)(i), or a misrepresentation of material fact in an application—

(I) the Secretary shall notify the Attorney General of such finding and may, in addition, impose such other administrative remedies (including civil monetary penalties in an amount not to exceed $1,000 per violation) as the Secretary determines to be appropriate; and

(II) the Attorney General shall not approve petitions filed with respect to that employer under section 204 [8 U.S.C.A. § 1154] or 214(c) [8 U.S.C.A. § 1184(c)] during a period of at least 1 year for aliens to be employed by the employer.

(ii) If the Secretary finds, after notice and opportunity for a hearing, a willful failure to meet a condition of paragraph (1), a willful misrepresentation of material fact in an application, or a violation of clause (iv)—

(I) the Secretary shall notify the Attorney General of such finding and may, in addition, impose such other administrative remedies (including civil monetary penalties in an amount not to exceed $5,000 per violation) as the Secretary determines to be appropriate; and

(II) the Attorney General shall not approve petitions filed with respect to that employer under section 204 [8 U.S.C.A. § 1154] or 214(c) [8 U.S.C.A. § 1184(c)] during a period of at least 2 years for aliens to be employed by the employer.

(iii) If the Secretary finds, after notice and opportunity for a hearing, a willful failure to meet a condition of paragraph (1) or a willful misrepresentation of material fact in an application, in the course of which failure or misrepresentation the employer displaced a United States worker employed by the employer within the period beginning 90 days before and ending 90 days after the date of filing of any visa petition supported by the application—

(I) the Secretary shall notify the Attorney General of such finding and may, in addition, impose such other administrative remedies (including civil monetary penalties in an amount not to exceed $35,000 per violation) as the Secretary determines to be appropriate; and

(II) the Attorney General shall not approve petitions filed with respect to that employer under section 204 [8 U.S.C.A. § 1154] or 214(c) [8 U.S.C.A. § 1184(c)] during a period of at least 3 years for aliens to be employed by the employer.

(iv) It is a violation of this clause for an employer who has filed an application under this subsection to intimidate, threaten, restrain, coerce, blacklist, discharge, or in any other manner discriminate against an employee (which term, for purposes of this clause, includes a former employee and an applicant for employment) because the employee has disclosed information to the employer, or to any other person, that the employee reasonably believes evidences a violation of this subsection, or any rule or regulation pertaining to this subsection, or because the employee cooperates or seeks to cooperate in an investigation or other proceeding concerning the employer's compliance with the requirements of this subsection or any rule or regulation pertaining to this subsection.

(v) The Secretary of Labor and the Attorney General shall devise a process under which an H–1B nonimmigrant who files a complaint regarding a violation of clause (iv) and is otherwise eligible to remain and work in the United States may be allowed to seek other appropriate employment in the United States for a period not to exceed the maximum period of stay authorized for such nonimmigrant classification.

(vi)(I) It is a violation of this clause for an employer who has filed an application under this subsection to require an H–1B nonimmigrant to pay a penalty for ceasing employment with the employer prior to a date agreed to by the nonimmigrant and the employer. The Secretary shall determine whether a required payment is a penalty (and not liquidated damages) pursuant to relevant State law.

(II) It is a violation of this clause for an employer who has filed an application under this subsection to require an alien who is the subject of a petition filed under section 214(c)(1) [8 U.S.C.A. § 1184(c)(1)], for which a fee is imposed under section 214(c)(9) [8 U.S.C.A. § 1184(c)(9)], to reimburse, or otherwise compensate, the employer for part or all of the cost of such fee. It is a violation of this clause for such an employer otherwise to accept such reimbursement or compensation from such an alien.

(III) If the Secretary finds, after notice and opportunity for a hearing, that an employer has committed a violation of this clause, the Secretary may impose a civil monetary penalty of $1,000 for each such violation and issue an administrative order requiring the return to the nonimmigrant of any amount paid in violation of this clause, or, if the nonimmigrant cannot be located, requiring payment of any such amount to the general fund of the Treasury.

(vii)(I) It is a failure to meet a condition of paragraph (1)(A) for an employer, who has filed an application under this subsection and who places an H–1B nonimmigrant designated as a full-time employee on the petition filed under section 214(c)(1) [8 U.S.C.A. § 1184(c)(1)] by the employer with respect to the nonimmigrant, after the nonimmigrant has entered into employment with the employer, in nonproductive status due to a decision by the employer (based on factors such as lack of work), or due to the nonimmigrant's lack of a permit or license, to fail to pay the nonimmigrant full-time wages in accordance with paragraph (1)(A) for all such nonproductive time.

(II) It is a failure to meet a condition of paragraph (1)(A) for an employer, who has filed an application under this subsection and who places an H–1B nonimmigrant designated as a part-time employee on the petition filed under section 214(c)(1) [8 U.S.C.A. § 1184(c)(1)] by the employer with respect to the nonimmigrant, after the nonimmigrant has entered into employment with the employer, in nonproductive status under circumstances described in subclause (I), to fail to pay such a nonimmigrant for such hours as are designated on such petition consistent with the rate of pay identified on such petition.

(III) In the case of an H–1B nonimmigrant who has not yet entered into employment with an employer who has had approved an application under this subsection, and a petition under section 214(c)(1) [8 U.S.C.A. § 1184(c)(1)], with respect to the nonimmigrant, the provisions of subclauses (I) and (II) shall apply to the employer beginning 30 days after the date the nonimmigrant first is admitted into the United States pursuant to the petition, or 60 days after the date the nonimmigrant becomes eligible to work for the employer (in the case of a nonimmigrant who is present in the United States on the date of the approval of the petition).

(IV) This clause does not apply to a failure to pay wages to an H–1B nonimmigrant for nonproductive time due to non-work-related factors, such as the voluntary request of the nonimmigrant for an absence or circumstances rendering the nonimmigrant unable to work.

(V) This clause shall not be construed as prohibiting an employer that is a school or other educational institution from applying to an H–1B nonimmigrant an established salary practice of the employer, under which the employer pays to H–1B nonimmigrants and United States workers in the same occupational classification an annual salary in disbursements over fewer than 12 months, if—

   (aa) the nonimmigrant agrees to the compressed annual salary payments prior to the commencement of the employment; and

   (bb) the application of the salary practice to the nonimmigrant does not otherwise cause the nonimmigrant to violate any condition of the nonimmigrant's authorization under this Act to remain in the United States.

(VI) This clause shall not be construed as superseding clause (viii).

(viii) It is a failure to meet a condition of paragraph (1)(A) for an employer who has filed an application under this subsection to fail to offer to an H–1B nonimmigrant, during the nonimmigrant's period of authorized employment, benefits and eligibility for benefits (including the opportunity to participate in health, life, disability, and other insurance plans; the opportunity to participate in retirement and savings plans; and cash bonuses and non-cash compensation, such as stock options (whether or not based on performance)) on the same basis, and in accordance with the same criteria, as the employer offers to United States workers.

(D) If the Secretary finds, after notice and opportunity for a hearing, that an employer has not paid wages at the wage level specified under the application and required under paragraph (1), the Secretary shall order the employer to provide for payment of such amounts of back pay as may be required to comply with the requirements of paragraph (1), whether or not a penalty under subparagraph (C) has been imposed.

(E) If an H–1B-dependent employer places a nonexempt H–1B nonimmigrant with another employer as provided under paragraph (1) (f) and the other employer has displaced or displaces a United States worker employed by such other employer during the period described in such paragraph, such displacement shall be considered for purposes of this paragraph a failure, by the placing employer, to meet a condition specified in an application submitted under paragraph (1); except that the attorney general may impose a sanction described in subclause (ii) of subparagraph (C)(i), (C)(ii), or (C)(iii) only if the Secretary of labor found that such placing employer

(i) knew or had reason to know of such displacement at the time of the placement of the nonimmigrant with the other employer; or

(ii) has been subject to a sanction under this subparagraph based upon a previous placement of an H–1B nonimmigrant with the same other employer.

(F) The Secretary may, on a case-by-case basis, subject an employer to random investigations for a period of up to 5 years, beginning on the date (on or after October 21, 1998) on which the employer is found by the Secretary to have committed a willful failure to meet a condition of paragraph (1) (or has been found under paragraph (5) to have committed a willful failure to meet the condition of paragraph (1) (G)(i)(II)) or to have made a willful misrepresentation of material fact in an application. The preceding sentence shall apply to an employer regardless of whether or not the employer is an H–1B-dependent employer. The authority of the Secretary under this subparagraph shall not be construed to be subject to, or limited by, the requirements of subparagraph (A).

(G)(i)[*] If the Secretary receives specific credible information from a source, who is likely to have knowledge of an employer's practices or employment conditions, or an employer's compliance with the employer's labor condition application under paragraph (1), and whose identity is known to the Secretary, and such information provides reasonable cause to believe that the employer has committed a willful failure

[*] So in original. Two subpars. (G) have been enacted.

to meet a condition of paragraph (1)(A), (1)(B), (1)(E), (1)(F), or (1)(G) (i)(I), has engaged in a pattern or practice of failures to meet such a condition, or has committed a substantial failure to meet such a condition that affects multiple employees, the Secretary may conduct a 30-day investigation into the alleged failure or failures. The Secretary (or the Acting Secretary in the case of the Secretary's absence or disability) shall personally certify that the requirements for conducting such an investigation have been met and shall approve commencement of the investigation. The Secretary may withhold the identity of the source from the employer, and the source's identity shall not be subject to disclosure under section 552 of Title 5.

(ii) The Secretary shall establish a procedure for any person, desiring to provide to the Secretary information described in clause (i) that may be used, in whole or in part, as the basis for commencement of an investigation described in such clause, to provide the information in writing on a form developed and provided by the Secretary and completed by or on behalf of the person. The person may not be an officer or employee of the Department of Labor, unless the information satisfies the requirement of clause (iii)(II) (although an officer or employee of the Department of Labor may complete the form on behalf of the person).

(iii) Any investigation initiated or approved by the Secretary under clause (i) shall be based on information that satisfies the requirements of such clause and that (I) originates from a source other than an officer or employee of the Department of Labor, or (II) was lawfully obtained by the Secretary of Labor in the course of lawfully conducting another Department of Labor investigation under this chapter or any other Act.

(iv) The receipt by the Secretary of information submitted by an employer to the Attorney General or the Secretary for purposes of securing the employment of an H–1B nonimmigrant shall not be considered a receipt of information for purposes of clause (i).

(v) No investigation described in clause (i) (or hearing described in clause (vii)) may be conducted with respect to information about a failure to meet a condition described in clause (i), unless the Secretary receives the information not later than 12 months after the date of the alleged failure.

(vi) The Secretary shall provide notice to an employer with respect to whom the Secretary has received information described in clause (i), prior to the commencement of an investigation under such clause, of the receipt of the information and of the potential for an investigation. The notice shall be provided in such a manner, and shall contain sufficient detail, to permit the employer to respond to the allegations before an investigation is commenced. The Secretary is not required to comply with this clause if the Secretary determines that to do so would interfere with an effort by the Secretary to secure compliance by the employer with the requirements of this subsection. There shall be no judicial review of a determination by the Secretary under this clause.

(vii) If the Secretary determines under this subparagraph that a reasonable basis exists to make a finding that a failure described in clause (i) has occurred, the Secretary shall provide for notice of such determination to the interested parties and an opportunity for a hearing, in accordance with section 556 of Title 5, within 60 days after the date of the determination. If such a hearing is requested, the Secretary shall make a finding concerning the matter by not later than 60 days after the date of the hearing.

(G)(i)* The Secretary of Labor may initiate an investigation of any employer that employs nonimmigrants described in section 101(a)(15) (H)(i)(b) [8 U.S.C.A. § 1101(a)(15)(H)(i)(b)] if the Secretary of Labor has reasonable cause to believe that the employer is not in compliance with this subsection. In the case of an investigation under this clause, the Secretary of Labor (or the acting Secretary in the case of the absence of disability of the Secretary of Labor) shall personally certify that reasonable cause exists and shall approve commencement of the investigation. The investigation may be initiated for reasons other than completeness and obvious inaccuracies by the employer in complying with this subsection.

(ii) If the Secretary of Labor receives specific credible information from a source who is likely to have knowledge of an employer's practices or employment conditions, or an employer's compliance with the employer's labor condition application under paragraph (1), and whose identity is known to the Secretary of Labor, and such information provides reasonable cause to believe that the employer has committed a willful failure to meet a condition of paragraph (1)(A), (1)(B), (1)(C), (1) (E), (1)(F), or (1)(G)(i)(I), has engaged in a pattern or practice of failures to meet such a condition, or has committed a substantial failure to meet such a condition that affects multiple employees, the Secretary of Labor may conduct an investigation into the alleged failure or failures. The Secretary of Labor may withhold the identity of the source from the employer, and the source's identity shall not be subject to disclosure under section 552 of Title 5.

(iii) The Secretary of Labor shall establish a procedure for any person desiring to provide to the Secretary of Labor information described in clause (ii) that may be used, in whole or in part, as the basis for the commencement of an investigation described in such clause, to provide the information in writing on a form developed and provided by the Secretary of Labor and completed by or on behalf of the person. The person may not be an officer or employee of the Department of Labor, unless the information satisfies the requirement of clause (iv)

*So in original. Two subpars. (G) have been enacted.

(II) (although an officer or employee of the Department of Labor may complete the form on behalf of the person).

(iv) Any investigation initiated or approved by the Secretary of labor under clause (ii) shall be based on information that satisfies the requirements of such clause and that

(I) originates from a source other than an officer or employee of the Department of Labor; or

(II) was lawfully obtained by the Secretary of Labor in the course of lawfully conducting another Department of Labor investigation under this Act of* any other Act.

(v) The receipt by the Secretary of Labor of information submitted by an employer to the Attorney General or the Secretary of Labor for purposes of securing the employment of a nonimmigrant described in section 101(a)(15)(H)(i)(b) [8 U.S.C.A. § 1101(a)(15)(H)(i)(b)] shall not be considered a receipt of information for purposes of clause (ii).

(vi) No investigation described in clause (ii) (or hearing described in clause (viii) based on such investigation) may be conducted with respect to information about a failure to meet a condition described in clause (ii), unless the Secretary of Labor receives the information not later than 12 months after the date of the alleged failure.

(vii) The Secretary of Labor shall provide notice to an employer with respect to whom there is reasonable cause to initiate an investigation described in clauses (i) or (ii), prior to the commencement of an investigation under such clauses, of the intent to conduct an investigation. The notice shall be provided in such a manner, and shall contain sufficient detail, to permit the employer to respond to the allegations before an investigation is commenced. The Secretary of Labor is not required to comply with this clause if the Secretary of Labor determines that to do so would interfere with an effort by the Secretary of Labor to secure compliance by the employer with the requirements of this subsection. There shall be no judicial review of a determination by the Secretary of Labor under this clause.

(viii) An investigation under clauses (i) or (ii) may be conducted for a period of up to 60 days. If the Secretary of Labor determines after such an investigation that a reasonable basis exists to make a finding that the employer has committed a willful failure to meet a condition of paragraph (1)(A), (1)(B), (1)(C), (1)(E), (1)(F), or (1)(G)(i)(I), has engaged in a pattern or practice of failures to meet such a condition, or has committed a substantial failure to meet such a condition that affects multiple employees, the Secretary of Labor shall provide for notice of such determination to the interested parties and an opportunity for a hearing in accordance with section 556 of Title 5, within 120 days after the date of the determination. If such a hearing is requested, the

---

* So in original; probably should be "or".

Secretary of Labor shall make a finding concerning the matter by not later than 120 days after the date of the hearing.

(H)(i) Except as provided in clauses (ii) and (iii), a person or entity is considered to have complied with the requirements of this subsection, notwithstanding a technical or procedural failure to meet such requirements, if there was a good faith attempt to comply with the requirements.

(ii) Clause (i) shall not apply if—

(I) the Department of Labor (or another enforcement agency) has explained to the person or entity the basis for the failure;

(II) the person or entity has been provided a period of not less than 10 business days (beginning after the date of the explanation) within which to correct the failure; and

(III) the person or entity has not corrected the failure voluntarily within such period.

(iii) A person or entity that, in the course of an investigation, is found to have violated the prevailing wage requirements set forth in paragraph (1)(A), shall not be assessed fines or other penalties for such violation if the person or entity can establish that the manner in which the prevailing wage was calculated was consistent with recognized industry standards and practices.

(iv) Clauses (i) and (iii) shall not apply to a person or entity that has engaged in or is engaging in a pattern or practice of willful violations of this subsection.

(I) Nothing in this subsection shall be construed as superseding or preempting any other enforcement-related authority under this Act (such as the authorities under section 274B [8 U.S.C.A. § 1324b]), or any other Act.

(3)(A) For purposes of this subsection, the term "H–1B-dependent employer" means an employer that

(i)(I) has 25 or fewer full-time equivalent employees who are employed in the United States; and **(II)** employs more than 7 H–1B nonimmigrants;

(ii)(I) has at least 26 but not more than 50 full-time equivalent employees who are employed in the United States; and **(II)** employs more than 12 H–1B nonimmigrants; or

(iii)(I) has at least 51 full-time equivalent employees who are employed in the United States; and **(II)** employs H–1B nonimmigrants in a number that is equal to at least 15 percent of the number of such full-time equivalent employees.

(B) For purposes of this subsection

(i) the term "exempt H–1B nonimmigrant" means an H–1B nonimmigrant who—

(I) receives wages (including cash bonuses and similar compensation) at an annual rate equal to at least $60,000; or

(II) has attained a master's or higher degree (or its equivalent) in a specialty related to the intended employment; and

(ii) the term "nonexempt H–1B nonimmigrant" means an H–1B nonimmigrant who is not an exempt H–1B nonimmigrant.

(C) For purposes of subparagraph (A)

(i) in computing the number of full-time equivalent employees and the number of H–1B nonimmigrants, exempt H–1B nonimmigrants shall not be taken into account during the longer of—

(I) the 6-month period beginning on October 21, 1998; or

(II) the period beginning on October 21, 1998 and ending on the date final regulations are issued to carry out this paragraph; and

(ii) any group treated as a single employer under subsection (b), (c), (m), or (o) of section 414 of the Internal Revenue Code of 1986 shall be treated as a single employer.

(4) For purposes of this subsection:

(A) The term "area of employment" means the area within normal commuting distance of the worksite or physical location where the work of the H–1B nonimmigrant is or will be performed. If such worksite or location is within a Metropolitan Statistical Area, any place within such area is deemed to be within the area of employment.

(B) In the case of an application with respect to one or more H–1B nonimmigrants by an employer, the employer is considered to "displace" a United States worker from a job if the employer lays off the worker from a job that is essentially the equivalent of the job for which the nonimmigrant or nonimmigrants is or are sought. A job shall not be considered to be essentially equivalent of another job unless it involves essentially the same responsibilities, was held by a United States worker with substantially equivalent qualifications and experience, and is located in the same area of employment as the other job.

(C) The term "H–1B nonimmigrant" means an alien admitted or provided status as a nonimmigrant described in section 101(a)(15) (H)(i)(b) [8 U.S.C.A. § 1101(a)(15)(H)(i)(b)].

(D)(i) The term "lays off", with respect to a worker—

(I) means to cause the worker's loss of employment, other than through a discharge for inadequate performance, violation of workplace rules, cause, voluntary departure, voluntary retirement, or the expiration of a grant or contract (other than a temporary employment contract entered into in order to evade a condition described in subparagraph (E) or (F) of paragraph (1)); but

(II) does not include any situation in which the worker is offered, as an alternative to such loss of employment, a similar employment opportunity with the same employer (or, in the case of a placement of a worker with another employer under paragraph (1)(F), with either employer described in such paragraph) at equivalent or higher compensation and benefits than the position from which the employee was discharged, regardless of whether or not the employee accepts the offer.

(ii) Nothing in this subparagraph is intended to limit an employee's rights under a collective bargaining agreement or other employment contract.

(E) The term "United States worker" means an employee who—

(i) is a citizen or national of the United States; or

(ii) is an alien who is lawfully admitted for permanent residence, is admitted as a refugee under section 207 [8 U.S.C.A. § 1157], is granted asylum under section 208 [8 U.S.C.A. § 1158], or is an immigrant otherwise authorized, by this chapter or by the Attorney General, to be employed.

(5)(A) This paragraph shall apply instead of subparagraphs (A) through (E) of paragraph (2) in the case of a violation described in subparagraph (B), but shall not be construed to limit or affect the authority of the Secretary or the Attorney General with respect to any other violation.

(B) The Attorney General shall establish a process for the receipt, initial review, and disposition in accordance with this paragraph of complaints respecting an employer's failure to meet the condition of paragraph (1)(G)(i)(II) or a petitioner's misrepresentation of material facts with respect to such condition. Complaints may be filed by an aggrieved individual who has submitted a resume or otherwise applied in a reasonable manner for the job that is the subject of the condition. No proceeding shall be conducted under this paragraph on a complaint concerning such a failure or misrepresentation unless the Attorney General determines that the complaint was filed not later than 12 months after the date of the failure or misrepresentation, respectively.

(C) If the Attorney General finds that a complaint has been filed in accordance with subparagraph (B) and there is reasonable cause to believe that such a failure or misrepresentation described in such complaint has occurred, the Attorney General shall initiate binding arbitration proceedings by requesting the Federal Mediation and Conciliation Service to appoint an arbitrator from the roster of arbitrators maintained by such Service. The procedure and rules of such Service shall be applicable to the selection of such arbitrator and to such arbitration proceedings. The Attorney General shall pay the fee and expenses of the arbitrator.

(D)(i) The arbitrator shall make findings respecting whether a failure or misrepresentation described in subparagraph (B) occurred. If the arbitrator concludes that failure or misrepresentation was willful, the arbitrator shall make a finding to that effect. The arbitrator may not find such a failure or misrepresentation (or that such a failure or misrepresentation was willful) unless the complainant demonstrates such a failure or misrepresentation (or its willful character) by clear and convincing evidence. The arbitrator shall transmit the findings in the form of a written opinion to the parties to the arbitration and the Attorney General. Such findings shall be final and conclusive, and, except as provided in this subparagraph, no official or court of the United States shall have power or jurisdiction to review any such findings.

(ii) The Attorney General may review and reverse or modify the findings of an arbitrator only on the same bases as an award of an arbitrator may be vacated or modified under section 10 or 11 of Title 9.

(iii) With respect to the findings of an arbitrator, a court may review only the actions of the Attorney General under clause (ii) and may set aside such actions only on the grounds described in subparagraph (A), (B), or (C) of section 706(a)(2) of Title 5. Notwithstanding any other provision of law, such judicial review may only be brought in an appropriate United States court of appeals.

(E) If the attorney general receives a finding of an arbitrator under this paragraph that an employer has failed to meet the condition of paragraph (1)(g)(i)(ii) or has misrepresented a material fact with respect to such condition, unless the attorney general reverses or modifies the finding under subparagraph (d)(ii)

(i) the Attorney General may impose administrative remedies (including civil monetary penalties in an amount not to exceed $1,000 per violation or $5,000 per violation in the case of a willful failure or misrepresentation) as the Attorney General determines to be appropriate; and

(ii) the Attorney General is authorized to not approve petitions filed, with respect to that employer and for aliens to be employed by the employer, under section 204 [8 U.S.C.A. § 1154] or 214(c) [8 U.S.C.A. § 1184(c)]—

(I) during a period of not more than 1 year; or

(II) in the case of a willful failure or willful misrepresentation, during a period of not more than 2 years.

(F) The Attorney General shall not delegate, to any other employee or official of the Department of Justice, any function of the Attorney General under this paragraph, until 60 days after the Attorney General has submitted a plan for such delegation to the Committees on the Judiciary of the United States House of Representatives and the Senate.

(*o*) Repealed.

(p) Computation of prevailing wage level

(1) In computing the prevailing wage level for an occupational classification in an area of employment for purposes of subsections (a)(5)(A), (n)(1)(A)(i)(II), and (t)(1)(A)(i)(II) in the case of an employee of

(A) an institution of higher education (as defined in section 1001(a) of Title 20), or a related or affiliated nonprofit entity; or

(B) a nonprofit research organization or a Governmental research organization,

the prevailing wage level shall only take into account employees at such institutions and organizations in the area of employment.

(2) With respect to a professional athlete (as defined in subsection (a)(5)(A)(iii)(II)) when the job opportunity is covered by professional sports league rules or regulations, the wage set forth in those rules or regulations shall be considered as not adversely affecting the wages of United States workers similarly employed and be considered the prevailing wage.

(3) The prevailing wage required to be paid pursuant to subsections (a)(5)(A), (n)(1)(A)(i)(II), and (t)(1)(A)(i)(II) shall be 100 percent of the wage determined pursuant to those sections.

(4) Where the Secretary of Labor uses, or makes available to employers, a governmental survey to determine the prevailing wage, such survey shall provide at least 4 levels of wages commensurate with experience, education, and the level of supervision. Where an existing government survey has only 2 levels, 2 intermediate levels may be created by dividing by 3, the difference between the 2 levels offered, adding the quotient thus obtained to the first level and subtracting that quotient from the second level.

(q) Any alien admitted under section 101(a)(15)(B) [8 U.S.C.A. § 1101(a)(15)(B)] may accept an honorarium payment and associated incidental expenses for a usual academic activity or activities (lasting not longer than 9 days at any single institution), as defined by the Attorney General in consultation with the Secretary of Education, if such payment is offered by an institution or organization described in subsection (p)(1) and is made for services conducted for the benefit of that institution or entity and if the alien has not accepted such payment or expenses from more than 5 institutions or organizations in the previous 6-month period.

(r) Certification for certain alien nurses

Subsection (a)(5)(C) shall not apply to an alien who seeks to enter the United States for the purpose of performing labor as a nurse who presents to the consular officer (or in the case of an adjustment of status, the Attorney General) a certified statement from the Commission on Graduates of

Foreign Nursing Schools (or an equivalent independent credentialing organization approved for the certification of nurses under subsection (a)(5)(C) by the Attorney General in consultation with the Secretary of Health and Human Services) that—

(1) the alien has a valid and unrestricted license as a nurse in a State where the alien intends to be employed and such State verifies that the foreign licenses of alien nurses are authentic and unencumbered;

(2) the alien has passed the National Council Licensure Examination (NCLEX);

(3) the alien is a graduate of a nursing program—

(A) in which the language of instruction was English;

(B) located in a country—

(i) designated by such commission not later than 30 days after the date of the enactment of the Nursing Relief for Disadvantaged Areas Act of 1999, based on such commission's assessment that the quality of nursing education in that country, and the English language proficiency of those who complete such programs in that country, justify the country's designation; or

(ii) designated on the basis of such an assessment by unanimous agreement of such commission and any equivalent credentialing organizations which have been approved under subsection (a)(5)(C) for the certification of nurses under this subsection; and

(C)(i) which was in operation on or before the date of the enactment of the Nursing Relief for Disadvantaged Areas Act of 1999; or

(ii) has been approved by unanimous agreement of such commission and any equivalent credentialing organizations which have been approved under subsection (a)(5)(C) for the certification of nurses under this subsection.

(s) Public charges

In determining whether an alien described in subsection (a)(4)(C)(i) is inadmissible under subsection (a)(4) or ineligible to receive an immigrant visa or otherwise to adjust to the status of permanent resident by reason of subsection (a)(4), the consular officer or the Attorney General shall not consider any benefits the alien may have received that were authorized under section 501 of the Illegal Immigration Reform and Immigrant Responsibility Act of 1996 [8 U.S.C.A. § 1641(c)].

(t)(1)* No alien may be admitted or provided status as a nonimmigrant under section 101(a)(15)(H)(i)(b1) [8 U.S.C.A. § 1101(a)(15)(H)(i)(b1)] or section 101(a)(15)(E)(iii) [8 U.S.C.A. § 1101(a)(15)(E)(iii)] in an occupa-

---

*So in original. Two subsecs. (t) have been enacted.

tional classification unless the employer has filed with the Secretary of Labor an attestation stating the following:

(A) The employer—

(i) is offering and will offer during the period of authorized employment to aliens admitted or provided status under section 101(a)(15)(H)(i)(b1) [8 U.S.C.A. § 1101(a)(15)(H)(i)(b1)] or section 101(a)(15)(E)(iii) [8 U.S.C.A. § 1101(a)(15)(E)(iii)] wages that are at least—

(I) the actual wage level paid by the employer to all other individuals with similar experience and qualifications for the specific employment in question; or

(II) the prevailing wage level for the occupational classification in the area of employment,

whichever is greater, based on the best information available as of the time of filing the attestation; and

(ii) will provide working conditions for such a nonimmigrant that will not adversely affect the working conditions of workers similarly employed.

(B) There is not a strike or lockout in the course of a labor dispute in the occupational classification at the place of employment.

(C) The employer, at the time of filing the attestation—

(i) has provided notice of the filing under this paragraph to the bargaining representative (if any) of the employer's employees in the occupational classification and area for which aliens are sought; or

(ii) if there is no such bargaining representative, has provided notice of filing in the occupational classification through such methods as physical posting in conspicuous locations at the place of employment or electronic notification to employees in the occupational classification for which nonimmigrants under section 101(a)(15)(H)(i)(b1) [8 U.S.C.A. § 1101(a)(15)(H)(i)(b1)] or section 101(a)(15)(E)(iii) [8 U.S.C.A. § 1101(a)(15)(E)(iii)] are sought.

(D) A specification of the number of workers sought, the occupational classification in which the workers will be employed, and wage rate and conditions under which they will be employed.

(2)(A) The employer shall make available for public examination, within one working day after the date on which an attestation under this subsection is filed, at the employer's principal place of business or worksite, a copy of each such attestation (and such accompanying documents as are necessary).

(B)(i) The Secretary of Labor shall compile, on a current basis, a list (by employer and by occupational classification) of the attestations filed under this subsection. Such list shall include, with respect to each attestation, the wage rate, number of aliens sought, period of intended employment, and date of need.

(ii) The Secretary of Labor shall make such list available for public examination in Washington, D.C.

(C) The Secretary of Labor shall review an attestation filed under this subsection only for completeness and obvious inaccuracies. Unless the Secretary of Labor finds that an attestation is incomplete or obviously inaccurate, the Secretary of Labor shall provide the certification described in section 101(a)(15)(H)(i)(b1) [8 U.S.C.A. § 1101(a)(15)(H)(i)(b1)] or section 101(a)(15)(E)(iii) [8 U.S.C.A. § 1101(a)(15)(E)(iii)] within 7 days of the date of the filing of the attestation.

(3)(A) The Secretary of Labor shall establish a process for the receipt, investigation, and disposition of complaints respecting the failure of an employer to meet a condition specified in an attestation submitted under this subsection or misrepresentation by the employer of material facts in such an attestation. Complaints may be filed by any aggrieved person or organization (including bargaining representatives). No investigation or hearing shall be conducted on a complaint concerning such a failure or misrepresentation unless the complaint was filed not later than 12 months after the date of the failure or misrepresentation, respectively. The Secretary of Labor shall conduct an investigation under this paragraph if there is reasonable cause to believe that such a failure or misrepresentation has occurred.

(B) Under the process described in subparagraph (A), the Secretary of Labor shall provide, within 30 days after the date a complaint is filed, for a determination as to whether or not a reasonable basis exists to make a finding described in subparagraph (C). If the Secretary of Labor determines that such a reasonable basis exists, the Secretary of Labor shall provide for notice of such determination to the interested parties and an opportunity for a hearing on the complaint, in accordance with section 556 of Title 5 within 60 days after the date of the determination. If such a hearing is requested, the Secretary of Labor shall make a finding concerning the matter by not later than 60 days after the date of the hearing. In the case of similar complaints respecting the same applicant, the Secretary of Labor may consolidate the hearings under this subparagraph on such complaints.

(C)(i) If the Secretary of Labor finds, after notice and opportunity for a hearing, a failure to meet a condition of paragraph (1)(b), a substantial failure to meet a condition of paragraph (1)(c) or (1)(d), or a misrepresentation of material fact in an attestation—

(I) the Secretary of Labor shall notify the Secretary of State and the Secretary of Homeland Security of such finding and may, in addition, impose such other administrative remedies (including civil monetary penalties in an amount not to exceed $1,000 per violation) as the Secretary of Labor determines to be appropriate; and

(II) the Secretary of State or the Secretary of Homeland Security, as appropriate, shall not approve petitions or applications filed with respect to that employer under section 204 [8 U.S.C.A. § 1154], 214(c) [8 U.S.C.A. § 1184(c)], 101(a)(15)(H)(i)(b1) [8 U.S.C.A. § 1101(a)(15) (H)(i)(b1)], or section 101(a)(15)(E)(iii) [8 U.S.C.A. § 1101(a)(15)(E)(iii)] during a period of at least 1 year for aliens to be employed by the employer.

(ii) If the Secretary of Labor finds, after notice and opportunity for a hearing, a willful failure to meet a condition of paragraph (1), a willful misrepresentation of material fact in an attestation, or a violation of clause (iv)—

(I) the Secretary of Labor shall notify the Secretary of State and the Secretary of Homeland Security of such finding and may, in addition, impose such other administrative remedies (including civil monetary penalties in an amount not to exceed $5,000 per violation) as the Secretary of Labor determines to be appropriate; and

(II) the Secretary of State or the Secretary of Homeland Security, as appropriate, shall not approve petitions or applications filed with respect to that employer under section 204 [8 U.S.C.A. § 1154], 214(c) [8 U.S.C.A. § 1184(c)], 101(a)(15)(H)(i)(b1) [8 U.S.C.A. § 1101(a)(15) (H)(i)(b1)], or section 101(a)(15)(E)(iii) [8 U.S.C.A. § 1101(a)(15)(E)(iii)] during a period of at least 2 years for aliens to be employed by the employer.

(iii) If the Secretary of Labor finds, after notice and opportunity for a hearing, a willful failure to meet a condition of paragraph (1) or a willful misrepresentation of material fact in an attestation, in the course of which failure or misrepresentation the employer displaced a United States worker employed by the employer within the period beginning 90 days before and ending 90 days after the date of filing of any visa petition or application supported by the attestation—

(I) the Secretary of Labor shall notify the Secretary of State and the Secretary of Homeland Security of such finding and may, in addition, impose such other administrative remedies (including civil monetary penalties in an amount not to exceed $35,000 per violation) as the Secretary of Labor determines to be appropriate; and

(II) the Secretary of State or the Secretary of Homeland Security, as appropriate, shall not approve petitions or applications filed with respect to that employer under section 204 [8 U.S.C.A. § 1154], 214(c) [8 U.S.C.A. § 1184(c)], 101(a)(15)(H)(i)(b1) [8 U.S.C.A. § 1101(a)(15) (H)(i)(b1)], or section 101(a)(15)(E)(iii) [8 U.S.C.A. § 1101(a)(15)(E)(iii)] during a period of at least 3 years for aliens to be employed by the employer.

(iv) It is a violation of this clause for an employer who has filed an attestation under this subsection to intimidate, threaten, restrain, coerce, blacklist, discharge, or in any other manner discriminate against an employee (which term, for purposes of this clause, includes a former employee and an applicant for employment) because the employee has disclosed information to the employer, or to any other person, that the employee reasonably believes evidences a violation of this subsection, or any rule or regulation pertaining to this subsection, or because the employee cooperates or seeks to cooperate in an investigation or other proceeding concerning the employer's compliance with the requirements of this subsection or any rule or regulation pertaining to this subsection.

(v) The Secretary of Labor and the Secretary of Homeland Security shall devise a process under which a nonimmigrant under section 101(a)(15)(H)(i)(b1) [8 U.S.C.A. § 1101(a)(15)(H)(i)(b1)] or section 101(a)(15)(E)(iii) [8 U.S.C.A. § 1101(a)(15)(E)(iii)] who files a complaint regarding a violation of clause (iv) and is otherwise eligible to remain and work in the United States may be allowed to seek other appropriate employment in the United States for a period not to exceed the maximum period of stay authorized for such nonimmigrant classification.

(vi)(I) It is a violation of this clause for an employer who has filed an attestation under this subsection to require a nonimmigrant under section 101(a)(15)(H)(i)(b1) [8 U.S.C.A. § 1101(a)(15)(H)(i)(b1)] or section 101(a)(15)(E)(iii) [8 U.S.C.A. § 1101(a)(15)(E)(iii)] to pay a penalty for ceasing employment with the employer prior to a date agreed to by the nonimmigrant and the employer. The Secretary of Labor shall determine whether a required payment is a penalty (and not liquidated damages) pursuant to relevant State law.

(II) If the Secretary of Labor finds, after notice and opportunity for a hearing, that an employer has committed a violation of this clause, the Secretary of Labor may impose a civil monetary penalty of $1,000 for each such violation and issue an administrative order requiring the return to the nonimmigrant of any amount paid in violation of this clause, or, if the nonimmigrant cannot be located, requiring payment of any such amount to the general fund of the Treasury.

(vii)(I) It is a failure to meet a condition of paragraph (1)(A) for an employer who has filed an attestation under this subsection and who places a nonimmigrant under section 101(a)(15)(H)(i)(b1) [8 U.S.C.A. § 1101(a)(15)(H)(i)(b1)] or section 101(a)(15)(E)(iii) [8 U.S.C.A. § 101(a)(15)(E)(iii)] designated as a full-time employee in the attestation, after the nonimmigrant has entered into employment with the employer, in nonproductive status due to a decision by the employer (based on factors such as lack of work), or due to the nonimmigrant's lack of a permit or license, to fail to pay the nonimmigrant full-time wages in accordance with paragraph (1)(A) for all such nonproductive time.

(II) It is a failure to meet a condition of paragraph (1)(A) for an employer who has filed an attestation under this subsection and who places a nonimmigrant under section 101(a)(15)(H)(i)(b1) [8 U.S.C.A. § 1101(a)(15)(H)(i)(b1)] or section 101(a)(15)(E)(iii) [8 U.S.C.A. § 1101(a)(15)(E)(iii)] designated as a part-time employee in the attestation, after the nonimmigrant has entered into employment with the employer, in nonproductive status under circumstances described in subclause (I), to fail to pay such a nonimmigrant for such hours as are designated on the attestation consistent with the rate of pay identified on the attestation.

(III) In the case of a nonimmigrant under section 101(a)(15)(H)(i)(b1) [8 U.S.C.A. § 1101(a)(15)(H)(i)(b1)] or section 101(a)(15)(E)(iii) [8 U.S.C.A. § 1101(a)(15)(E)(iii)] who has not yet entered into employment with an employer who has had approved an attestation under this subsection with respect to the nonimmigrant, the provisions of subclauses (I) and (II) shall apply to the employer beginning 30 days after the date the nonimmigrant first is admitted into the United States, or 60 days after the date the nonimmigrant becomes eligible to work for the employer in the case of a nonimmigrant who is present in the United States on the date of the approval of the attestation filed with the Secretary of Labor.

(IV) This clause does not apply to a failure to pay wages to a nonimmigrant under section 101(a)(15)(H)(i)(b1) [8 U.S.C.A. § 1101(a)(15)(H)(i)(b1)] or section 101(a)(15)(E)(iii) [8 U.S.C.A. § 1101(a)(15)(E)(iii)] for nonproductive time due to non-work-related factors, such as the voluntary request of the nonimmigrant for an absence or circumstances rendering the nonimmigrant unable to work.

(V) This clause shall not be construed as prohibiting an employer that is a school or other educational institution from applying to a nonimmigrant under section 101(a)(15)(H)(i)(b1) [8 U.S.C.A. § 1101(a)(15)(H)(i)(b1)] or section 101(a)(15)(E)(iii) [8 U.S.C.A. § 1101(a)(15)(E)(iii)] an established salary practice of the employer, under which the employer pays to nonimmigrants under section 101(a)(15)(H)(i)(b1) [8 U.S.C.A. § 1101(a)(15)(H)(i)(b1)] or section 101(a)(15)(E)(iii) [8 U.S.C.A. § 1101(a)(15)(E)(iii)] and United States workers in the same occupational classification an annual salary in disbursements over fewer than 12 months, if—

    (aa) the nonimmigrant agrees to the compressed annual salary payments prior to the commencement of the employment; and

    (bb) the application of the salary practice to the nonimmigrant does not otherwise cause the nonimmigrant to violate any condition of the nonimmigrant's authorization under this chapter to remain in the United States.

(VI) This clause shall not be construed as superseding clause (viii).

(viii) It is a failure to meet a condition of paragraph (1)(A) for an employer who has filed an attestation under this subsection to fail to offer to a nonimmigrant under section 101(a)(15)(H)(i)(b1) [8 U.S.C.A. § 1101(a)(15)(H)(i)(b1)] or section 101(a)(15)(E)(iii) [8 U.S.C.A. § 1101(a)(15)(E)(iii)], during the nonimmigrant's period of authorized employment, benefits and eligibility for benefits (including the opportunity to participate in health, life, disability, and other insurance plans; the opportunity to participate in retirement and savings plans; and cash bonuses and non-cash compensation, such as stock options (whether or not based on performance)) on the same basis, and in accordance with the same criteria, as the employer offers to United States workers.

(D) If the Secretary of Labor finds, after notice and opportunity for a hearing, that an employer has not paid wages at the wage level specified in the attestation and required under paragraph (1), the Secretary of Labor shall order the employer to provide for payment of such amounts of back pay as may be required to comply with the requirements of paragraph (1), whether or not a penalty under subparagraph (C) has been imposed.

(E) The Secretary of Labor may, on a case-by-case basis, subject an employer to random investigations for a period of up to 5 years, beginning on the date on which the employer is found by the Secretary of Labor to have committed a willful failure to meet a condition of paragraph (1) or to have made a willful misrepresentation of material fact in an attestation. The authority of the Secretary of Labor under this subparagraph shall not be construed to be subject to, or limited by, the requirements of subparagraph (A).

(F) Nothing in this subsection shall be construed as superseding or preempting any other enforcement-related authority under this chapter (such as the authorities under section 274B [8 U.S.C.A. § 1324b]), or any other Act.

(4) For purposes of this subsection:

(A) The term "area of employment" means the area within normal commuting distance of the worksite or physical location where the work of the nonimmigrant under section 101(a)(15)(H)(i)(b1) [8 U.S.C.A. § 1101(a)(15)(H)(i)(b1)] or section 101(a)(15)(E)(iii) [8 U.S.C.A. § 1101(a)(15)(E)(iii)] is or will be performed. If such worksite or location is within a Metropolitan Statistical Area, any place within such area is deemed to be within the area of employment.

(B) In the case of an attestation with respect to one or more nonimmigrants under section 101(a)(15)(H)(i)(b1) [8 U.S.C.A. § 1101(a)(15)(H)(i)(b1)] or section 101(a)(15)(E)(iii) [8 U.S.C.A. § 1101(a)(15)(E)(iii)] by an employer, the employer is considered to "displace" a United States worker from a job if the employer lays off the worker from a job that is essentially the equivalent of the job for which the nonimmigrant or nonimmigrants is or are sought. A job shall not be considered to be essentially equivalent of another job unless it involves essentially the same responsibilities, was held by a United States worker with substantially equivalent qualifications and experience, and is located in the same area of employment as the other job.

(C)(i) The term "lays off", with respect to a worker—

(I) means to cause the worker's loss of employment, other than through a discharge for inadequate performance, violation of workplace rules, cause, voluntary departure, voluntary retirement, or the expiration of a grant or contract; but

(II) does not include any situation in which the worker is offered, as an alternative to such loss of employment, a similar employment

174

opportunity with the same employer at equivalent or higher compensation and benefits than the position from which the employee was discharged, regardless of whether or not the employee accepts the offer.

(ii) Nothing in this subparagraph is intended to limit an employee's rights under a collective bargaining agreement or other employment contract.

(D) The term "United States worker" means an employee who—

(i) is a citizen or national of the United States; or

(ii) is an alien who is lawfully admitted for permanent residence, is admitted as a refugee under section 207 [8 U.S.C.A. § 1157], is granted asylum under section 208 [8 U.S.C.A. § 1158], or is an immigrant otherwise authorized, by this chapter or by the Secretary of Homeland Security, to be employed.

(t)(1)* Except as provided in paragraph (2), no person admitted under section 101(a)(15)(Q)(ii)(I) [8 U.S.C.A. § 1101(a)(15)(Q)(ii)(I)], or acquiring such status after admission, shall be eligible to apply for nonimmigrant status, an immigrant visa, or permanent residence under this Act until it is established that such person has resided and been physically present in the person's country of nationality or last residence for an aggregate of at least 2 years following departure from the United States.

(2) The Secretary of Homeland Security may waive the requirement of such 2-year foreign residence abroad if the Secretary determines that—

(A) departure from the United States would impose exceptional hardship upon the alien's spouse or child (if such spouse or child is a citizen of the United States or an alien lawfully admitted for permanent residence); or

(B) the admission of the alien is in the public interest or the national interest of the United States.

(June 27, 1952, c. 477, Title II, ch. 2, § 212, 66 Stat. 182; July 18, 1956, c. 629, Title III, § 301(a), 70 Stat. 575; July 7, 1958, Pub.L. 85–508, § 23, 72 Stat. 351; Mar. 18, 1959, Pub.L. 86–3, § 20(b), 73 Stat. 13; July 14, 1960, Pub.L. 86–648, § 8, 74 Stat. 505; Sept. 21, 1961, Pub.L. 87–256, § 109(c), 75 Stat. 535; Sept. 26, 1961, Pub.L. 87–301, §§ 11–15, 75 Stat. 654, 655; Oct. 3, 1965, Pub.L. 89–236, §§ 10, 15, 79 Stat. 917, 919; Apr. 7, 1970, Pub.L. 91–225, § 2, 84 Stat. 116; Oct. 12, 1976, Pub.L. 94–484, Title VI, § 601(a), (c), (d), 90 Stat. 2300, 2301; Oct. 20, 1976, Pub.L. 94–571, §§ 5, 7(d), 90 Stat. 2705, 2706; 1966 Reorg. Plan No. 3, §§ 1, 3, 31 F.R. 8855, 80 Stat. 1610; Aug. 1, 1977, Pub.L. 95–83, Title III, § 307(q)(1), (2), 91 Stat. 394; 1977 Reorg. Plan No. 2, § 7(a)(8), 42 F.R. 62461, 91 Stat. 1637; Oct. 30, 1978, Pub.L. 95–549, Title I, §§ 101, 102, 92 Stat. 2065; Sept. 27, 1979, Pub.L. 96–70, Title III, § 3201(b), 93 Stat. 497; Oct. 17, 1979, Pub.L. 96–88, Title III, § 301(a)(1), Title I, §§ 503, 509(b), 93 Stat. 677, 690, 695; Mar. 17, 1980, Pub.L. 96–212, Title II, § 203(d), (f), 94 Stat. 107; Dec. 17, 1980, Pub.L. 96–538, Title IV, § 404, 94 Stat. 3192; Dec. 29, 1981, Pub.L. 97–116, §§ 4, 5(a) (1), (2), (b), 18(e), 95 Stat. 1611, 1612, 1620; Oct. 5, 1984, Pub.L. 98–454, Title VI, § 602(a), 98 Stat. 1737; Oct. 12, 1984, Pub.L. 98–473, Title II, § 220(a), 98 Stat. 2028; Oct. 27, 1986, Pub.L. 99–396, § 14(a), 100 Stat. 842; Oct. 27, 1986, Pub.L. 99–570, Title I, § 1751(a), 100

* So in original. Two subsecs. (t) have been enacted.

Stat. 3207–47; Nov. 10, 1986, Pub.L. 99–639, § 6(a), 100 Stat. 3544; Oct. 24, 1988, Pub.L. 100–525, § 7(c)(1), 102 Stat. 2616; Nov. 10, 1986, Pub.L. 99–639, § 6(b), as added Oct. 24, 1988, Pub.L. 100–525, § 7(c)(3), 102 Stat. 2617; Nov. 14, 1986, Pub.L. 99–653, § 7(a), 100 Stat. 3657; Nov. 14, 1986, Pub. L. 99–653, § 7(d)(2), as added Oct. 24, 1988, Pub.L. 100–525, § 8(f), 102 Stat. 2617; Dec. 22, 1987, Pub.L. 100–204, § 806(c), 101 Stat. 1399; Oct. 24, 1988, Pub.L. 100–525, §§ 3(1)(A), 9(i), 102 Stat. 2614, 2620; Nov. 18, 1988, Pub.L. 100–690, Title VII, § 7349(a), 102 Stat. 4473; Dec. 18, 1989, Pub.L. 101–238, § 3(b), 103 Stat. 2100; Feb. 16, 1990, Pub.L. 101–246, Title I, § 131(a), (c), 104 Stat. 31; Nov. 29, 1990, Pub.L. 101–649, Title I, § 162(e)(1), (f)(2)(B), Title II, §§ 202(b), 205(c)(3), Title V, §§ 511(a), 514(a), Title VI, § 601(a), (b), (d), 104 Stat. 5011, 5012, 5014, 5020, 5052, 5053, 5067, 5075 to 5077; Dec. 12, 1991, Pub.L. 102–232, Title III, §§ 302(e)(6), (9), 303(a)(5)(B), (6), (7)(B), 306(a)(10), (12), 307(a) to (g), 309(b)(7), 105 Stat. 1746 to 1748, 1751, 1753 to 1755, 1759; June 10, 1993, Pub.L. 103–43, Title XX, § 2007(a), 107 Stat. 210; Aug. 26, 1994, Pub.L. 103–317, Title V, § 506(a), 108 Stat. 1765; Sept. 13, 1994, Pub.L. 103–322, Title XIII, § 130003(b)(1), 108 Stat. 2024; Oct. 25, 1994, Pub.L. 103–416, Title II, §§ 203(a), 219(e), (z)(1), (5), 220(a), 108 Stat. 4311, 4316, 4318, 4319; Apr. 24, 1996, Pub.L. 104–132, Title IV, §§ 411, 412, 440(d), 110 Stat. 1268, 1269, 1277; Sept. 30, 1996, Pub.L. 104–208, Div. C, Title I, § 124(b)(1), Title III, §§ 301(b)(1), (c)(1), 304(b), 305(c), 306(d), 308(c)(2)(B), (d)(1), (e)(1)(B), (C), (2)(A), (6), (f) (1)(C) to (F), (3)(A), (g)(1), (4)(B), (10)(A), (H), 322(a)(2)(B), 341(a), (b), 342(a), 343, 344(a), 345(a), 346(a), 347(a), 348(a), 349, 351(a), 352(a), 355, Title V, § 531(a), Title VI, §§ 602(a), 622(b), 624(a), 671(e)(3), 110 Stat. 3009–562, 3009–576, 3009–578, 3009–597, 3009–607, 3009–612, 3009–616, 3009–619, 3009–620, 3009–621, 3009–622, 3009–625, 3009–629, 3009–635 to 3009–641, 3009–644, 3009–674, 3009–689, 3009–695, 3009–698, 3009–723; Nov. 12, 1997, Pub.L. 105–73, § 1, 111 Stat. 1459; Oct. 21, 1998, Pub.L. 105–277, Div. C, Title IV, §§ 412, 413, 415(a), 431(a), Div. G, Title XXII, § 2226, 112 Stat. 2681–642, 2681–643, 2681–645, 2681–648, 2681–649, 2681–650, 2681–651, 2681–654, 2681–658, 2681–820; Oct. 27, 1998, Pub.L. 105–292, Title VI, § 604(a), 112 Stat. 2814; Nov. 12, 1999, Pub.L. 106–95, §§ 2(b), 4(a), 113 Stat. 1312, 1317; Dec. 3, 1999, Pub.L. 106–120, Title VIII, § 809, 113 Stat. 1632; Oct. 17, 2000, Pub.L. 106–313, Title I, §§ 106(c)(2), 107(a), 114 Stat. 1254, 1255; Oct. 28, 2000, Pub.L. 106–386, Div. A, §§ 107(e)(3), 111(d), Div. B, Title V, §§ 1505(a), (c)(1), (d), (e), (f), 1513(e), 114 Stat. 1478, 1485, 1525, 1526, 1536; Oct. 30, 2000, Pub.L. 106–395, Title II, § 201(b)(1), (2), 114 Stat. 1633, 1634; Oct. 30, 2000, Pub.L. 106–396, Title I, § 101(b)(1), 114 Stat. 1638; Oct. 26, 2001, Pub.L. 107–56, Title IV, § 411(a), Title X, § 1006(a), 115 Stat. 345, 394; Mar. 13, 2002, Pub.L. 107–150, § 2, 116 Stat. 74; Nov. 2, 2002, Pub.L. 107–273, Div. C, Title I, § 11018(c), 116 Stat. 1825; Sept. 3, 2003, Pub.L. 108–77, Title IV, § 402(b), (c), 117 Stat. 940, 946; Pub.L. 108–193, §§ 4(b)(4), 8(a)(2), Dec. 19, 2003, 117 Stat. 2879; Dec. 8, 2004, Pub.L. 108–447, Div. J, Title IV, §§ 422(a), 423, 424(a)(1), (b), 118 Stat. 3353, 3354, 3355; Dec. 10, 2004, Pub.L. 108–449, § 1(b)(2), 118 Stat. 3470; Dec. 17, 2004, Pub.L. 108–458, Title V, §§ 5501(a), 5502(a), 5503, 118 Stat. 3740; May 11, 2005, Pub.L. 109–13, Div. B, §§ 103, 104, 501(d), 119 Stat. 231, 306–09, 322; Jan. 5, 2006, Pub.L. 109–162, Title VIII, § 802, 119 Stat. 3054; Aug. 12, 2006, Pub.L. 109–271, § 6(b), 120 Stat. 762; Dec. 26, 2007, Pub.L. 110–161, Div. J, Title VI, § 691(a), (c), 121 Stat. 2364, 2365; May 8, 2008, Pub.L. 110–229, Title VII, Subtitle A, § 702(b)(2), (3), (d), 122 Stat. 860, 862; July 30, 2008, Pub.L. 110–293, Title III, § 305, 122 Stat. 2963; Oct. 3, 2008, Pub.L. 110–340, § 2(b), 122 Stat. 3736; Dec. 23, 2008, Pub.L. 110–457, Title II, §§ 222(f)(1), 234, 122 Stat. 5071, 5074; Dec. 22, 2009, Pub.L. 111–122, § 3(b), 123 Stat. 3481; Nov. 30, 2010, Pub.L. 111–287, § 2, 124 Stat. 3058; Pub.L. 113–4, Title VIII, § 804, Mar. 7, 2013, 127 Stat. 111.)

§ 213. Admission of aliens on giving bond or undertaking; return upon permanent departure [8 U.S.C.A. § 1183]

An alien inadmissible under paragraph (4) of section 212(a) [8 U.S.C.A. § 1182(a)] may, if otherwise admissible, be admitted in the discretion of the Attorney General (subject to the affidavit of support requirement and attribution of sponsor's income and resources under section 213A [8 U.S.C.A. § 1183a]) upon the giving of a suitable and proper bond or undertaking approved by the Attorney General, in such amount and containing such conditions as he may prescribe, to the United States, and to all States, territories, counties, towns, municipalities, and districts thereof holding the United States and all States, territories, counties, towns, municipalities, and districts thereof harmless against such alien becoming a public charge. Such bond or undertaking shall terminate upon the permanent departure from the United States, the naturalization, or the death of such alien, and any sums or other security held to secure performance thereof, except to the extent forfeited for violation of the terms thereof, shall be returned to the person by whom furnished, or to his legal representatives. Suit may be brought thereon in the name and by the proper law officers of the United States for the use of the United States, or of any State, territory, district, county, town or municipality in which such alien becomes a public charge, irrespective of whether a demand for payment of public expenses has been made.

(June 27, 1952, c. 477, Title II, ch. 2, § 213, 66 Stat. 188; July 10, 1970, Pub.L. 91–313, § 1, 84 Stat. 413; Nov. 29, 1990, Pub.L. 101–649, Title VI, § 603(a)(8), 104 Stat. 5083; Sept. 30, 1996, Pub.L. 104–208, Div. C, Title III, § 308(d)(3)(A), Title V, § 564(f), 110 Stat. 3009–617, 3009–684.)

§ 213A. Requirements for sponsor's affidavit of support [8 U.S.C.A. § 1183a]

(a) Enforceability

(1) Terms of affidavit

No affidavit of support may be accepted by the Attorney General or by any consular officer to establish that an alien is not excludable as a public charge under section 212(a)(4) [8 U.S.C.A. § 1182(a)(4)] unless such affidavit is executed by a sponsor of the alien as a contract—

(A) in which the sponsor agrees to provide support to maintain the sponsored alien at an annual income that is not less than 125 percent of the Federal poverty line during the period in which the affidavit is enforceable;

(B) that is legally enforceable against the sponsor by the sponsored alien, the Federal Government, any State (or any political subdivision of such State), or by any other entity that provides any means-tested public benefit (as defined in subsection (e)), consistent with the provisions of this section; and

(C) in which the sponsor agrees to submit to the jurisdiction of any Federal or State court for the purpose of actions brought under subsection (b)(2).

(2) Period of enforceability

An affidavit of support shall be enforceable with respect to benefits provided for an alien before the date the alien is naturalized as a citizen of the United States, or, if earlier, the termination date provided under paragraph (3).

(3) Termination of period of enforceability upon completion of required period of employment, etc.

(A) In general

An affidavit of support is not enforceable after such time as the alien (i) has worked 40 qualifying quarters of coverage as defined under title II of the Social Security Act [42 U.S.C.A § 401 et seq.] or can be credited with such qualifying quarters as provided under subparagraph (B), and (ii) in the case of any such qualifying quarter creditable for any period beginning after December 31, 1996, did not receive any Federal means-tested public benefit (as provided under section 403 of the Personal Responsibility and Work Opportunity Reconciliation Act of 1996 [8 U.S.C.A. § 1613]) during any such period.

(B) Qualifying quarters

For purposes of this section, in determining the number of qualifying quarters of coverage under title II of the Social Security Act [42 U.S.C.A. § 401 et seq.] an alien shall be credited with—

(i) all of the qualifying quarters of coverage as defined under title II of the Social Security Act worked by a parent of such alien while the alien was under age 18, and

(ii) all of the qualifying quarters worked by a spouse of such alien during their marriage and the alien remains married to such spouse or such spouse is deceased.

No such qualifying quarter of coverage that is creditable under title II of the Social Security Act [42 U.S.C.A. § 401 et seq.] for any period beginning after December 31, 1996, may be credited to an alien under clause (i) or (ii) if the parent or spouse (as the case may be) of such alien received any Federal means-tested public benefit (as provided under section 403 of the Personal Responsibility and Work Opportunity Reconciliation Act of 1996 [8 U.S.C.A. § 1613]) during the period for which such qualifying quarter of coverage is so credited.

(C) Provision of information to SAVE system

The Attorney General shall ensure that appropriate information regarding the application of this paragraph is provided to the system for alien verification of eligibility (SAVE) described in section 1137(d)(3) of the Social Security Act [42 U.S.C.A. § 1320b–7(d)(3)].

(b) Reimbursement of government expenses

(1) Request for reimbursement

(A) Requirement

Upon notification that a sponsored alien has received any means-tested public benefit, the appropriate nongovernmental entity which provided such benefit or the appropriate entity of the Federal Government, a State, or any political subdivision of a State shall request reimbursement by the sponsor in an amount which is equal to the unreimbursed costs of such benefit.

(B) Regulations

The Attorney General, in consultation with the heads of other appropriate Federal agencies, shall prescribe such regulations as may be necessary to carry out subparagraph (A).

(2) Actions to compel reimbursement

(A) In case of nonresponse

If within 45 days after a request for reimbursement under paragraph (1)(A), the appropriate entity has not received a response from the sponsor indicating a willingness to commence payment an action may be brought against the sponsor pursuant to the affidavit of support.

(B) In case of failure to pay

If the sponsor fails to abide by the repayment terms established by the appropriate entity, the entity may bring an action against the sponsor pursuant to the affidavit of support.

(C) Limitation on actions

No cause of action may be brought under this paragraph later than 10 years after the date on which the sponsored alien last received any means-tested public benefit to which the affidavit of support applies.

(3) Use of collection agencies

If the appropriate entity under paragraph (1)(A) requests reimbursement from the sponsor or brings an action against the sponsor pursuant to the affidavit of support, the appropriate entity may appoint or hire an individual or other person to act on behalf of such entity acting under the authority of law for purposes of collecting any amounts owed.

(c) Remedies

Remedies available to enforce an affidavit of support under this section include any or all of the remedies described in section 3201, 3203, 3204, or 3205 of Title 28, as well as an order for specific performance and payment of legal fees and other costs of collection, and include corresponding remedies available under State law. A Federal agency may seek to collect amounts owed under this section in accordance with the provisions of subchapter II of chapter 37 of Title 31.

(d) Notification of change of address

(1) General requirement

The sponsor shall notify the Attorney General and the State in which the sponsored alien is currently a resident within 30 days of any change of address of the sponsor during the period in which an affidavit of support is enforceable.

(2) Penalty

Any person subject to the requirement of paragraph (1) who fails to satisfy such requirement shall, after notice and opportunity to be heard, be subject to a civil penalty of—

(A) not less than $250 or more than $2,000, or

(B) if such failure occurs with knowledge that the sponsored alien has received any means-tested public benefits (other than benefits described in section 401(b), 403(c)(2), or 411(b) of the Personal Responsibility and Work Opportunity Reconciliation Act of 1996 [8 U.S.C.A. § 1611(b), 1613(c)(2), or 1621(b)]) not less than $2,000 or more than $5,000.

The Attorney General shall enforce this paragraph under appropriate regulations.

(e) Jurisdiction

An action to enforce an affidavit of support executed under subsection (a) may be brought against the sponsor in any appropriate court—

(1) by a sponsored alien, with respect to financial support; or

(2) by the appropriate entity of the Federal Government, a State or any political subdivision of a State, or by any other nongovernmental entity under subsection (b)(2), with respect to reimbursement.

(f) "Sponsor" defined

(1) In general

For purposes of this section the term "sponsor" in relation to a sponsored alien means an individual who executes an affidavit of support with respect to the sponsored alien and who—

(A) is a citizen or national of the United States or an alien who is lawfully admitted to the United States for permanent residence;

(B) is at least 18 years of age;

(C) is domiciled in any of the several States of the United States, the District of Columbia, or any territory or possession of the United States;

(D) is petitioning for the admission of the alien under section 204 [8 U.S.C.A. § 1154]; and

(E) demonstrates (as provided in paragraph (6)) the means to maintain an annual income equal to at least 125 percent of the Federal poverty line.

(2) Income requirement case

Such term also includes an individual who does not meet the requirement of paragraph (1)(E) but accepts joint and several liability together with an individual under paragraph (5)(A).

(3) Active duty armed services case

Such term also includes an individual who does not meet the requirement of paragraph (1)(E) but is on active duty (other than active duty for training) in the Armed Forces of the United States, is petitioning for the admission of the alien under section 204 [8 U.S.C.A. § 1154] as the spouse or child of the individual, and demonstrates (as provided in paragraph (6)) the means to maintain an annual income equal to at least 100 percent of the Federal poverty line.

(4) Certain employment-based immigrants case

Such term also includes an individual—

(A) who does not meet the requirement of paragraph (1)(D), but is the relative of the sponsored alien who filed a classification petition for the sponsored alien as an employment-based immigrant under section 203(b) [8 U.S.C.A. § 1153(b)] or who has a significant ownership interest in the entity that filed such a petition; and

(B)(i) who demonstrates (as provided under paragraph (6)) the means to maintain an annual income equal to at least 125 percent of the Federal poverty line, or

(ii) does not meet the requirement of paragraph (1)(E) but accepts joint and several liability together with an individual under paragraph (5)(A).

(5) Non-petitioning cases

Such term also includes an individual who does not meet the requirement of paragraph (1)(D) but who—

(A) accepts joint and several liability with a petitioning sponsor under paragraph (2) or relative of an employment-based immigrant under paragraph (4) and who demonstrates (as provided under paragraph (6)) the means to maintain an annual income equal to at least 125 percent of the Federal poverty line; or

(B) is a spouse, parent, mother-in-law, father-in-law, sibling, child (if at least 18 years of age), son, daughter, son-in-law, daughter-in-law, sister-in-law, brother-in-law, grandparent, or grandchild of a sponsored alien or a legal guardian of a sponsored alien, meets the requirements of paragraph (1) (other than subparagraph (D)), and executes an affidavit of support with respect to such alien in a case in which—

(i) the individual petitioning under section 204 [8 U.S.C.A. § 1154] for the classification of such alien died after the approval of such petition, and the Secretary of Homeland Security has determined for humanitarian reasons that revocation of such petition under section 205 [8 U.S.C.A. § 1155] would be inappropriate; or

(ii) the alien's petition is being adjudicated pursuant to section 204(*l*) [8 U.S.C.A. § 1154(*l*)] (surviving relative consideration).

(6) Demonstration of means to maintain income

(A) In general

(i) Method of demonstration

For purposes of this section, a demonstration of the means to maintain income shall include provision of a certified copy of the individual's Federal income tax return for the individual's 3 most recent taxable years and a written statement, executed under oath or as permitted under penalty of perjury under section 1746 of Title 28, that the copies are certified copies of such returns.

(ii) Flexibility

For purposes of this section, aliens may demonstrate the means to maintain income through demonstration of significant assets of the sponsored alien or of the sponsor, if such assets are available for the support of the sponsored alien.

(iii) Percent of poverty

For purposes of this section, a reference to an annual income equal to at least a particular percentage of the Federal poverty line means an annual income equal to at least such percentage of the Federal poverty line for a family unit of a size equal to the number of members of the sponsor's household (including family and non-family dependents) plus the total number of other dependents and aliens sponsored by that sponsor.

(B) Limitation

The Secretary of State, or the Attorney General in the case of adjustment of status, may provide that the demonstration under subparagraph (A) applies only to the most recent taxable year.

(h) [sic] Federal poverty line defined

For purposes of this section, the term "Federal poverty line" means the level of income equal to the official poverty line (as defined by the Director of the Office of Management and Budget, as revised annually by the Secretary of Health and Human Services, in accordance with section 9902(2) of Title 42) that is applicable to a family of the size involved.

(i) Sponsor's social security account number required to be provided

(1) An affidavit of support shall include the social security account number of each sponsor.

(2) The Attorney General shall develop an automated system to maintain the social security account number data provided under paragraph (1).

(3) The Attorney General shall submit an annual report to the Committees on the Judiciary of the House of Representatives and the Senate setting forth—

(A) for the most recent fiscal year for which data are available the number of sponsors under this section and the number of sponsors in compliance with the financial obligations of this section; and

(B) a comparison of such numbers with the numbers of such sponsors for the preceding fiscal year.

(June 27, 1952, c. 477, Title II, ch. 2, § 213A, as added Aug. 22, 1996, Pub.L. 104–193, Title IV, § 423(a), 110 Stat. 2271, and amended Sept. 30, 1996, Pub.L. 104–208, Div. C, Title V, § 551(a), 110 Stat. 3009–675; Mar. 13, 2002, Pub.L. 107–150, § 2(a)(1), (3), 116 Stat. 74, 75; Oct. 28, 2009, Pub.L. 111–83, Title V, § 568(e), 123 Stat. 2187.)

§ 214.   Admission   of   nonimmigrants   [8   U.S.C.A. § 1184]

(a) Regulations

(1) The admission to the United States of any alien as a nonimmigrant shall be for such time and under such conditions as the Attorney General may by regulations prescribe, including when he deems necessary the giving of a bond with sufficient surety in such sum and containing such conditions as the Attorney General shall prescribe, to insure that at the expiration of such time or upon failure to maintain the status under which he was admitted, or to maintain any status subsequently acquired under section 248 [8 U.S.C.A. § 1258], such alien will depart from the United States. No alien admitted to Guam or the Commonwealth of the Northern Mariana Islands without a visa pursuant to section 212(*l*) [8 U.S.C.A. § 1182(*l*)] may be authorized to enter or stay in the United States other than in Guam or the Commonwealth of the Northern Mariana Islands or to remain in Guam or the Commonwealth of the Northern Mariana Islands for a period exceeding 45 days from date of admission to Guam or the Commonwealth of the Northern Mariana Islands. No alien admitted to the United States without a visa pursuant to section 217 [8 U.S.C.A. § 1187] may be authorized to remain in the United States as a nonimmigrant visitor for a period exceeding 90 days from the date of admission.

(2)(A) The period of authorized status as a nonimmigrant described in section 101(a)(15)(O) [8 U.S.C.A. § 1101(a)(15)(O)] shall be for such period as the Attorney General may specify in order to provide for the event (or events) for which the nonimmigrant is admitted.

(B) The period of authorized status as a nonimmigrant described in section 101(a)(15)(P) [8 U.S.C.A. § 1101(a)(15)(P)] shall be for such period as the Attorney General may specify in order to provide for the competition, event, or performance for which the nonimmigrant is admitted. In the case of nonimmigrants admitted as individual athletes under section 101(a)(15)(P) [8 U.S.C.A. § 1101(a)(15)(P)], the period of authorized status may be for an initial period (not to exceed 5 years) during which the nonimmigrant will perform as an athlete and such period may be extended by the Attorney General for an additional period of up to 5 years.

(b) Presumption of status; written waiver

Every alien (other than a nonimmigrant described in subparagraph (L) or (V) of section 101(a)(15) [8 U.S.C.A. § 1101(a)(15)], and other than a nonimmigrant described in any provision of section 101(a)(15)(H)(i) [8 U.S.C.A. § 1101(a)(15)(H)(i)] except subclause (b1) of such section) shall be presumed to be an immigrant until he establishes to the satisfaction of the consular officer, at the time of application for a visa, and the immigration officers, at the time of application for admission, that he is entitled to a nonimmigrant status under section 101(a)(15) [8 U.S.C.A. § 1101(a)(15)]. An alien who is an officer or employee of any foreign government or of any international organization entitled to enjoy privileges, exemptions, and immunities under the International Organizations Immunities Act [22 U.S.C.A. § 288 et seq.], or an alien who is the attendant, servant, employee, or member of the immediate family of any such alien shall not be entitled to apply for or receive an immigrant visa, or to enter the United States as an immigrant unless he executes a written waiver in the same form and substance as is prescribed by section 247(b) [8 U.S.C.A. § 1257(b)].

(c) Petition of importing employer; involvement of Departments of Labor and Agriculture

(1) The question of importing any alien as a nonimmigrant under section subparagraph (H), (L), (O), or (P)(i) of section 101(a)(15) [8 U.S.C.A. § 1101(a)(15) (excluding nonimmigrants under section 101(a)(15)(H)(i)(b1) [8 U.S.C.A. § 1101(a)(15)(H)(i)(b1)]]) in any specific case or specific cases shall be determined by the Attorney General, after consultation with appropriate agencies of the Government, upon petition of the importing employer. Such petition, shall be made and approved before the visa is granted. The petition shall be in such form and contain such information as the Attorney General shall prescribe. The approval of such a petition shall not, of itself, be construed as establishing that the alien is a nonimmigrant. For purposes of this subsection with respect to nonimmigrants described in section 101(a)(15)(H)(ii)(a) [8 U.S.C.A. § 1101(a)(15)(H)(ii)(a)], the term "appropriate agencies of Government" means the Department of Labor and includes the Department of Agriculture. The provisions of section 218 [8 U.S.C.A. § 1188] shall apply to the question of importing any alien as a nonimmigrant under section 101(a)(15)(H)(ii)(a) [8 U.S.C.A. § 1101(a)(15)(H)(ii)(a)].

(2)(A) The Attorney General shall provide for a procedure under which an importing employer which meets requirements established by the Attorney General may file a blanket petition to import aliens as nonimmigrants described in section 101(a)(15)(L) [8 U.S.C.A. § 1101(a)(15)(L)] instead of filing individual petitions under paragraph (1) to import such aliens. Such procedure shall permit the expedited processing of visas for admission of aliens covered under such a petition.

(B) For purposes of section 101(a)(15)(L) [8 U.S.C.A. § 1101(a)(15)(L)], an alien is considered to be serving in a capacity involving specialized knowledge with respect to a company if the alien has a special knowledge of the company product and its application in international markets or has an advanced level of knowledge of processes and procedures of the company.

(C) The Attorney General shall provide a process for reviewing and acting upon petitions under this subsection with respect to nonimmigrants described in section 101(a)(15)(L) [8 U.S.C.A. § 1101(a)(15)(L)] within 30 days after the date a completed petition has been filed.

(D) The period of authorized admission for—

(i) a nonimmigrant admitted to render services in a managerial or executive capacity under section 101(a)(15)(L) [8 U.S.C.A. § 1101(a)(15)(L)] shall not exceed 7 years, or

(ii) a nonimmigrant admitted to render services in a capacity that involves specialized knowledge under section 101(a)(15)(L) [8 U.S.C.A. § 1101(a)(15)(L)] shall not exceed 5 years.

(E) In the case of an alien spouse admitted under section 101(a)(15)(L) [8 U.S.C.A. § 1101(a)(15)(L)], who is accompanying or following to join a principal alien admitted under such section, the Attorney General shall authorize the alien spouse to engage in employment in the United States and provide the spouse with an "employment authorized" endorsement or other appropriate work permit.

(F) An alien who will serve in a capacity involving specialized knowledge with respect to an employer for purposes of section 101(a)(15)(L) [8 U.S.C.A. § 1101(a)(15)(L)] and will be stationed primarily at the worksite of an employer other than the petitioning employer or its affiliate, subsidiary, or parent shall not be eligible for classification under section 101(a)(15)(L) [8 U.S.C.A. § 1101(a)(15)(L)] if—

(i) the alien will be controlled and supervised principally by such unaffiliated employer; or

(ii) the placement of the alien at the worksite of the unaffiliated employer is essentially an arrangement to provide labor for hire for the unaffiliated employer, rather than a placement in connection with the provision of a product or service for which specialized knowledge specific to the petitioning employer is necessary.

(3) The Attorney General shall approve a petition—

(A) with respect to a nonimmigrant described in section 101(a)(15)(O)(i) [8 U.S.C.A. § 1101(a)(15)(O)(i)] only after consultation in accordance with paragraph (6) or, with respect to aliens seeking entry for a motion picture or television production, after consultation with the appropriate union representing the alien's occupational peers and a management organization in the area of the alien's ability, or

(B) with respect to a nonimmigrant described in section 101(a)(15)(O)(ii) [8 U.S.C.A. § 1101(a)(15)(O)(ii)] after consultation in accordance with paragraph (6) or, in the case of such an alien seeking entry for a motion picture or television production, after consultation with such a labor organization and a management organization in the area of the alien's ability.

In the case of an alien seeking entry for a motion picture or television production, **(i)** any opinion under the previous sentence shall only be advisory, **(ii)** any such opinion that recommends denial must be in writing, **(iii)** in making the decision the Attorney General shall consider the exigencies and scheduling of the production, and (iv) the Attorney General shall append to the decision any such opinion. The Attorney General shall provide by regulation for the waiver of the consultation requirement under subparagraph (A) in the case of aliens who have been admitted as nonimmigrants under section 101(a)(15)(O)(i) [8 U.S.C.A. § 1101(a)(15)(O)(i)] because of extraordinary ability in the arts and who seek readmission to perform similar services within 2 years after the date of a consultation under such subparagraph. Not later than 5 days after the date such a waiver is provided, the Attorney General shall forward a copy of the petition and all supporting documentation to the national office of an appropriate labor organization.

(4)(A) For purposes of section 101(a)(15)(P)(i)(a) [8 U.S.C.A. § 1101(a)(15)(P)(i)(a)], an alien is described in this subparagraph if the alien—

(i)(I) performs as an athlete, individually or as part of a group or team, at an internationally recognized level of performance;

(II) is a professional athlete, as defined in section 204(i)(2) [8 U.S.C.A. § 1154(i)(2)];

(III) performs as an athlete, or as a coach, as part of a team or franchise that is located in the United States and a member of a foreign league or association of 15 or more amateur sports teams, if—

(aa) the foreign league or association is the highest level of amateur performance of that sport in the relevant foreign country;

(bb) participation in such league or association renders players ineligible, whether on a temporary or permanent basis, to earn a scholarship in, or participate in, that sport at a college or

186

university in the United States under the rules of the National Collegiate Athletic Association; and

(cc) a significant number of the individuals who play in such league or association are drafted by a major sports league or a minor league affiliate of such a sports league; or

(IV) is a professional athlete or amateur athlete who performs individually or as part of a group in a theatrical ice skating production; and

(ii) seeks to enter the United States temporarily and solely for the purpose of performing—

(I) as such an athlete with respect to a specific athletic competition; or

(II) in the case of an individual described in clause (i)(IV), in a specific theatrical ice skating production or tour.

(B)(i) For purposes of section 101(a)(15)(P)(i)(b) [8 U.S.C.A. § 1101(a)(15)(P)(i)(b)], an alien is described in this subparagraph if the alien—

(I) performs with or is an integral and essential part of the performance of an entertainment group that has (except as provided in clause (ii)) been recognized internationally as being outstanding in the discipline for a sustained and substantial period of time,

(II) in the case of a performer or entertainer, except as provided in clause (iii), has had a sustained and substantial relationship with that group (ordinarily for at least one year) and provides functions integral to the performance of the group, and

(III) seeks to enter the United States temporarily and solely for the purpose of performing as such a performer or entertainer or as an integral and essential part of a performance.

(ii) In the case of an entertainment group that is recognized nationally as being outstanding in its discipline for a sustained and substantial period of time, the Attorney General may, in consideration of special circumstances, waive the international recognition requirement of clause (i)(I).

(iii)(I) The one-year relationship requirement of clause (i)(II) shall not apply to 25 percent of the performers and entertainers in a group.

(II) The Attorney General may waive such one-year relationship requirement for an alien who because of illness or unanticipated and exigent circumstances replaces an essential member of the group and for an alien who augments the group by performing a critical role.

(iv) The requirements of subclauses (I) and (II) of clause (i) shall not apply to alien circus personnel who perform as part of a circus or circus group or who constitute an integral and essential part of the performance of such circus or circus group, but only if such personnel are entering the United States to join a circus that has been recognized nationally as outstanding for a sustained and substantial period of time or as part of such a circus.

(C) A person may petition the Attorney General for classification of an alien as a nonimmigrant under section 101(a)(15)(P) [8 U.S.C.A. § 1101(a)(15)(P)].

(D) The Attorney General shall approve petitions under this subsection with respect to nonimmigrants described in clause (i) or (iii) of section 101(a)(15)(P) [8 U.S.C.A. § 1101(a)(15)(P)] only after consultation in accordance with paragraph (6).

(E) The Attorney General shall approve petitions under this subsection for nonimmigrants described in section 101(a)(15)(P)(ii) [8 U.S.C.A. § 1101(a)(15)(P)(ii)] only after consultation with labor organizations representing artists and entertainers in the United States.

(F)(i) No nonimmigrant visa under section 101(a)(15)(P)(i)(a) [8 U.S.C.A. § 1101(a)(15)(P)(i)(a)] shall be issued to any alien who is a national of a country that is a state sponsor of international terrorism unless the Secretary of State determines, in consultation with the Secretary of Homeland Security and the heads of other appropriate United States agencies, that such alien does not pose a threat to the safety, national security, or national interest of the United States. In making a determination under this subparagraph, the Secretary of State shall apply standards developed by the Secretary of State, in consultation with the Secretary of Homeland Security and the heads of other appropriate United States agencies, that are applicable to the nationals of such states.

(ii) In this subparagraph, the term "state sponsor of international terrorism" means any country the government of which has been determined by the Secretary of State under any of the laws specified in clause (iii) to have repeatedly provided support for acts of international terrorism.

(iii) The laws specified in this clause are the following:

(I) Section 2405(j)(1)(A) of the Title 50, Appendix (or successor statute).

(II) Section 2780(d) of Title 22.

(III) Section 2371(a) of Title 22.

(G) The Secretary of Homeland Security shall permit a petition under this subsection to seek classification of more than 1 alien as a nonimmigrant under section 101(a)(15)(P)(i)(a) [8 U.S.C.A. § 1101(a)(15)(P)(i)(a)].

(H) The Secretary of Homeland Security shall permit an athlete, or the employer of an athlete, to seek admission to the United States for such athlete under a provision of this Act other than section 101(a)

(15)(P)(i) [8 U.S.C.A. § 1101(a)(15)(P)(i)] if the athlete is eligible under such other provision.

(5)(A) In the case of an alien who is provided nonimmigrant status under section 101(a)(15)(H)(i)(b) [8 U.S.C.A. § 1101(a)(15)(H)(i)(b)] or 101(a)(15)(H)(ii)(b) [8 U.S.C.A. § 1101(a)(15)(H)(ii)(b)] and who is dismissed from employment by the employer before the end of the period of authorized admission, the employer shall be liable for the reasonable costs of return transportation of the alien abroad.

(B) In the case of an alien who is admitted to the United States in nonimmigrant status under section 101(a)(15)(O) [8 U.S.C.A. § 1101(a)(15)(O)] or 101(a)(15)(P) [8 U.S.C.A. § 1101(a)(15)(P)] and whose employment terminates for reasons other than voluntary resignation, the employer whose offer of employment formed the basis of such nonimmigrant status and the petitioner are jointly and severally liable for the reasonable cost of return transportation of the alien abroad. The petitioner shall provide assurance satisfactory to the Attorney General that the reasonable cost of that transportation will be provided.

(6)(A)(i) To meet the consultation requirement of paragraph (3)(A) in the case of a petition for a nonimmigrant described in section 101(a)(15)(O)(i) [8 U.S.C.A. § 1101(a)(15)(O)(i)] (other than with respect to aliens seeking entry for a motion picture or television production), the petitioner shall submit with the petition an advisory opinion from a peer group (or other person or persons of its choosing, which may include a labor organization) with expertise in the specific field involved.

(ii) To meet the consultation requirement of paragraph (3)(B) in the case of a petition for a nonimmigrant described in section 101(a)(15)(O)(ii) [8 U.S.C.A. § 1101(a)(15)(O)(ii)] (other than with respect to aliens seeking entry for a motion picture or television production), the petitioner shall submit with the petition an advisory opinion from a labor organization with expertise in the skill area involved.

(iii) To meet the consultation requirement of paragraph (4)(D) in the case of a petition for a nonimmigrant described in section 101(a)(15)(P)(i) [8 U.S.C.A. § 1101(a)(15)(P)(i)] or 101(a)(15)(P)(iii) [8 U.S.C.A. § 1101(a)(15)(P)(iii)], the petitioner shall submit with the petition an advisory opinion from a labor organization with expertise in the specific field of athletics or entertainment involved.

(B) To meet the consultation requirements of subparagraph (A), unless the petitioner submits with the petition an advisory opinion from an appropriate labor organization, the Attorney General shall forward a copy of the petition and all supporting documentation to the national office of an appropriate labor organization within 5 days of the date of receipt of the petition. If there is a collective bargaining representative of an employer's employees in the occupational classification for which the alien is being sought, that representative shall be the appropriate labor organization.

(C) In those cases in which a petitioner described in subparagraph (A) establishes that an appropriate peer group (including a labor organization) does not exist, the Attorney General shall adjudicate the petition without requiring an advisory opinion.

(D) Any person or organization receiving a copy of a petition described in subparagraph (A) and supporting documents shall have no more than 15 days following the date of receipt of such documents within which to submit a written advisory opinion or comment or to provide a letter of no objection. Once the 15-day period has expired and the petitioner has had an opportunity, where appropriate, to supply rebuttal evidence, the Attorney General shall adjudicate such petition in no more than 14 days. The Attorney General may shorten any specified time period for emergency reasons if no unreasonable burden would be thus imposed on any participant in the process.

(E)(i) The Attorney General shall establish by regulation expedited consultation procedures in the case of nonimmigrant artists or entertainers described in section 101(a)(15)(O) [8 U.S.C.A. § 1101(a)(15)(O)] or 101(a)(15)(P) [8 U.S.C.A. § 1101(a)(15)(P)] to accommodate the exigencies and scheduling of a given production or event.

(ii) The Attorney General shall establish by regulation expedited consultation procedures in the case of nonimmigrant athletes described in section 101(a)(15)(O)(i) [8 U.S.C.A. § 1101(a)(15)(O)(i)] or 101(a)(15)(P)(i) [8 U.S.C.A. § 1101(a)(15)(P)(i)] in the case of emergency circumstances (including trades during a season).

(F) No consultation required under this subsection by the Attorney General with a nongovernmental entity shall be construed as permitting the Attorney General to delegate any authority under this subsection to such an entity. The Attorney General shall give such weight to advisory opinions provided under this section as the Attorney General determines, in his sole discretion, to be appropriate.

(7) If a petition is filed and denied under this subsection, the Attorney General shall notify the petitioner of the determination and the reasons for the denial and of the process by which the petitioner may appeal the determination.

(8) The Attorney General shall submit annually to the Committees on the Judiciary of the House of Representatives and of the Senate a report describing, with respect to petitions under each subcategory of subparagraphs (H), (O), (P), and (Q) of section 101(a)(15) [8 U.S.C.A. § 1101(a)(15)] the following:

(A) The number of such petitions which have been filed.

(B) The number of such petitions which have been approved and the number of workers (by occupation) included in such approved petitions.

(C) The number of such petitions which have been denied and the number of workers (by occupation) requested in such denied petitions.

(D) The number of such petitions which have been withdrawn.

(E) The number of such petitions which are awaiting final action.

(9)(A) The attorney general shall impose a fee on an employer (excluding any employer that is a primary or secondary education institution, an institution of higher education, as defined in section 1001(a) of Title 20, a nonprofit entity related to or affiliated with any such institution, a nonprofit entity which engages in established curriculum-related clinical training of students registered at any such institution, a nonprofit research organization, or a governmental research organization) filing before a petition under paragraph (1)

(i) initially to grant an alien nonimmigrant status described in section 101(a)(15)(H)(i)(b) [8 U.S.C.A. § 1101(a)(15)(H)(i)(b)];

(ii) to extend the stay of an alien having such status (unless the employer previously has obtained an extension for such alien); or

(iii) to obtain authorization for an alien having such status to change employers.

(B) The amount of the fee shall be $1,500 for each such petition except that the fee shall be half the amount for each such petition by any employer with not more than 25 full-time equivalent employees who are employed in the United States (determined by including any affiliate or subsidiary of such employer).

(C) Fees collected under this paragraph shall be deposited in the Treasury in accordance with section 286(s) [8 U.S.C.A. § 1356(s)].

(10) An amended H–1B petition shall not be required where the petitioning employer is involved in a corporate restructuring, including but not limited to a merger, acquisition, or consolidation, where a new corporate entity succeeds to the interests and obligations of the original petitioning employer and where the terms and conditions of employment remain the same but for the identity of the petitioner.

(11)(A) Subject to subparagraph (b), the Secretary of Homeland Security or the Secretary of State, as appropriate, shall impose a fee on an employer who has filed an attestation described in section 212(t) [8 U.S.C.A. § 1182(t)]—

(i) in order that an alien may be initially granted nonimmigrant status described in section 101(a)(15)(H)(i)(b1) [8 U.S.C.A. § 1101(a)(15)(H)(i)(b1)]; or

(ii) in order to satisfy the requirement of the second sentence of subsection (g)(8)(C) of this section for an alien having such status to obtain certain extensions of stay.

(B) The amount of the fee shall be the same as the amount imposed by the Secretary of Homeland Security under paragraph (9), except that if such paragraph does not authorize such Secretary to impose any fee, no fee shall be imposed under this paragraph.

(C) Fees collected under this paragraph shall be deposited in the Treasury in accordance with section 286(s) [8 U.S.C.A. § 1356(s)].

(12)(A) In addition to any other fees authorized by law, the Secretary of Homeland Security shall impose a fraud prevention and detection fee on an employer filing a petition under paragraph (1)—

(i) initially to grant an alien nonimmigrant status described in subparagraph (H)(i)(b) or (L) of section 101(a)(15) [8 U.S.C.A. § 1101(a)(15)]; or

(ii) to obtain authorization for an alien having such status to change employers.

(B) In addition to any other fees authorized by law, the Secretary of State shall impose a fraud prevention and detection fee on an alien filing an application abroad for a visa authorizing admission to the United States as a nonimmigrant described in section 101(a)(15)(L) [8 U.S.C.A. § 1101(a)(15)(L)], if the alien is covered under a blanket petition described in paragraph (2)(A).

(C) The amount of the fee imposed under subparagraph (A) or (B) shall be $500.

(D) The fee imposed under subparagraph (A) or (B) shall only apply to principal aliens and not to the spouses or children who are accompanying or following to join such principal aliens.

(E) Fees collected under this paragraph shall be deposited in the Treasury in accordance with section 286(v) [8 U.S.C.A. § 1356(v)].

(13)(A) In addition to any other fees authorized by law, the Secretary of Homeland Security shall impose a fraud prevention and detection fee on an employer filing a petition under paragraph (1) for nonimmigrant workers described in section 101(a)(15)(H)(ii)(b) [8 U.S.C.A. § 1101(a)(15)(H)(ii)(b)].

(B) The amount of the fee imposed under subparagraph (A) shall be $150.

(14)(A) If the Secretary of Homeland Security finds, after notice and an opportunity for a hearing, a substantial failure to meet any of the conditions of the petition to admit or otherwise provide status to a nonimmigrant worker under section 101(a)(15)(H)(ii)(b) [8 U.S.C.A. § 1101(a)(15)(H)(ii)(b)] or a willful misrepresentation of a material fact in such petition—

(i) the Secretary of Homeland Security may, in addition to any other remedy authorized by law, impose such administrative remedies (including civil monetary penalties in an amount not to exceed

$10,000 per violation) as the Secretary of Homeland Security determines to be appropriate; and

(ii) the Secretary of Homeland Security may deny petitions filed with respect to that employer under section 204 [8 U.S.C.A. § 1154] or paragraph (1) of this subsection during a period of at least 1 year but not more than 5 years for aliens to be employed by the employer.

(B) The Secretary of Homeland Security may delegate to the Secretary of Labor, with the agreement of the Secretary of Labor, any of the authority given to the Secretary of Homeland Security under subparagraph (A)(i).

(C) In determining the level of penalties to be assessed under subparagraph (A), the highest penalties shall be reserved for willful failures to meet any of the conditions of the petition that involve harm to United States workers.

(D) In this paragraph, the term "substantial failure" means the willful failure to comply with the requirements of this section that constitutes a significant deviation from the terms and conditions of a petition.

(d) Issuance of visa to fiancée or fiancé of citizen

(1) A visa shall not be issued under the provisions of section 101(a)(15)(K)(i) [8 U.S.C.A. § 1101(a)(15)(K)(i)] until the consular officer has received a petition filed in the United States by the fiancé or fiancée of the applying alien and approved by the Secretary of Homeland Security. The petition shall be in such form and contain such information as the Secretary of Homeland Security shall, by regulation, prescribe. Such information shall include information on any criminal convictions of the petitioner for any specified crime described in paragraph (3)(B) and information on any permanent protection or restraining order issued against the petitioner related to any specified crime described in paragraph (3)(B)(i). It shall be approved only after satisfactory evidence is submitted by the petitioner to establish that the parties have previously met in person within 2 years before the date of filing the petition, have a bona fide intention to marry, and are legally able and actually willing to conclude a valid marriage in the United States within a period of ninety days after the alien's arrival, except that the Secretary of Homeland Security in his discretion may waive the requirement that the parties have previously met in person. In the event the marriage with the petitioner does not occur within three months after the admission of the said alien and minor children, they shall be required to depart from the United States and upon failure to do so shall be removed in accordance with sections 240 [8 U.S.C.A. § 1229a] and 241 [8 U.S.C.A. § 1231].

(2)(A) Subject to subparagraphs (B) and (C), the Secretary of Homeland Security may not approve a petition under paragraph (1) unless the Secretary has verified that—

    (i) the petitioner has not, previous to the pending petition, petitioned under paragraph (1) with respect to two or more applying aliens; and

    (ii) if the petitioner has had such a petition previously approved, 2 years have elapsed since the filing of such previously approved petition.

(B) The Secretary of Homeland Security may, in the Secretary's discretion, waive the limitations in subparagraph (A) if justification exists for such a waiver. Except i n extraordinary circumstances and subject to subparagraph (C), such a waiver shall not be granted if the petitioner has a record of violent criminal offenses against a person or persons.

(C)(i) The Secretary of Homeland Security is not limited by the criminal court record and shall grant a waiver of the condition described in the second sentence of subparagraph (B) in the case of a petitioner described in clause (ii).

    (ii) A petitioner described in this clause is a petitioner who has been battered or subjected to extreme cruelty and who is or was not the primary perpetrator of violence in the relationship upon a determination that—

    (I) the petitioner was acting in self-defense;

    (II) the petitioner was found to have violated a protection order intended to protect the petitioner; or

    (III) the petitioner committed, was arrested for, was convicted of, or pled guilty to committing a crime that did not result in serious bodily injury and where there was a connection between the crime and the petitioner's having been battered or subjected to extreme cruelty.

    (iii) In acting on applications under this subparagraph, the Secretary of Homeland Security shall consider any credible evidence relevant to the application. The determination of what evidence is credible and the weight to be given that evidence shall be within the sole discretion of the Secretary.

(3) In this subsection:

    (A) The terms "domestic violence", "sexual assault", "child abuse and neglect", "dating violence", "elder abuse", and "stalking" have the meaning given such terms in section 13925 of Title 42.

    (B) The term "specified crime" means the following:

(i) Domestic violence, sexual assault, child abuse and neglect, dating violence, elder abuse, stalking, or an attempt to commit any such crime.

(ii) Homicide, murder, manslaughter, rape, abusive sexual contact, sexual exploitation, incest, torture, trafficking, peonage, holding hostage, involuntary servitude, slave trade, kidnapping, abduction, unlawful criminal restraint, false imprisonment, or an attempt to commit any of the crimes described in this clause.

(iii) At least three convictions for crimes relating to a controlled substance or alcohol not arising from a single act.

(e) Nonimmigrant professionals and annual numerical limit

(1) Notwithstanding any other provision of this Act, an alien who is a citizen of Canada and seeks to enter the United States under and pursuant to the provisions of Annex 1502.1 (United States of America), Part C—Professionals, of the United States-Canada Free-Trade Agreement to engage in business activities at a professional level as provided for therein may be admitted for such purpose under regulations of the Attorney General promulgated after consultation with the Secretaries of State and Labor.

(2) An alien who is a citizen of Canada or Mexico, and the spouse and children of any such alien if accompanying or following to join such alien, who seeks to enter the United States under and pursuant to the provisions of Section D of Annex 1603 of the North American Free Trade Agreement (in this subsection referred to as "NAFTA") to engage in business activities at a professional level as provided for in such Annex, may be admitted for such purpose under regulations of the Attorney General promulgated after consultation with the Secretaries of State and Labor. For purposes of this Act, including the issuance of entry documents and the application of subsection (b), such alien shall be treated as if seeking classification, or classifiable, as a nonimmigrant under section 101(a)(15) [8 U.S.C.A. § 1101(a)(15)]. The admission of an alien who is a citizen of Mexico shall be subject to paragraphs (3), (4), and (5). For purposes of this paragraph and paragraphs (3), (4), and (5), the term "citizen of Mexico" means "citizen" as defined in Annex 1608 of NAFTA.

(3) The Attorney General shall establish an annual numerical limit on admissions under paragraph (2) of aliens who are citizens of Mexico, as set forth in Appendix 1603.D.4 of Annex 1603 of the NAFTA. Subject to paragraph (4), the annual numerical limit—

(A) beginning with the second year that NAFTA is in force, may be increased in accordance with the provisions of paragraph 5(a) of Section D of such Annex, and

(B) shall cease to apply as provided for in paragraph 3 of such Appendix.

(4) The annual numerical limit referred to in paragraph (3) may be increased or shall cease to apply (other than by operation of paragraph 3 of such Appendix) only if—

(A) the President has obtained advice regarding the proposed action from the appropriate advisory committees established under section 2155 of Title 19.

(B) the President has submitted a report to the Committee on the Judiciary of the Senate and the Committee on the Judiciary of the House of Representatives that sets forth—

(i) the action proposed to be taken and the reasons therefor, and

(ii) the advice obtained under subparagraph (A);

(C) a period of at least 60 calendar days that begins on the first day on which the President has met the requirements of subparagraphs (A) and (B) with respect to such action has expired; and

(D) the President has consulted with such committees regarding the proposed action during the period referred to in subparagraph (C).

(5) During the period that the provisions of Appendix 1603.D.4 of Annex 1603 of the NAFTA apply, the entry of an alien who is a citizen of Mexico under and pursuant to the provisions of Section D of Annex 1603 of NAFTA shall be subject to the attestation requirement of section 212(m) [8 U.S.C.A. § 1182(m)], in the case of a registered nurse, or the application requirement of section 212(n) [8 U.S.C.A. § 1182(n)], in the case of all other professions set out in Appendix 1603.D.1 of Annex 1603 of NAFTA, and the petition requirement of subsection (c), to the extent and in the manner prescribed in regulations promulgated by the Secretary of Labor, with respect to sections 212(m) [8 U.S.C.A. § 1182(m)] and 212(n) [8 U.S.C.A. § 1182(n)], and the Attorney General, with respect to subsection (c).

(6) In the case of an alien spouse admitted under section 101(a)(15)(E) [8 U.S.C.A. § 1101(a)(15)(E)], who is accompanying or following to join a principal alien admitted under such section, the Attorney General shall authorize the alien spouse to engage in employment in the United States and provide the spouse with an "employment authorized" endorsement or other appropriate work permit.

(f) Denial of crewmember status in case of certain labor disputes

(1) Except as provided in paragraph (3), no alien shall be entitled to nonimmigrant status described in section 101(a)(15)(D) [8 U.S.C.A. § 1101(a)(15)(D)] if the alien intends to land for the purpose of performing service on board a vessel of the United States (as defined in section 2101(46) of Title 46) or on an aircraft of an air carrier (as defined in section 40102(a)(2) of Title 49) during a labor dispute where there is a strike or lockout in the bargaining unit of the employer in which the alien intends to perform such service.

(2) An alien described in paragraph (1)—

(A) may not be paroled into the United States pursuant to section 212(d)(5) [8 U.S.C.A. § 1182(d)(5)] unless the Attorney General determines that the parole of such alien is necessary to protect the national security of the United States; and

(B) shall be considered not to be a bona fide crewman for purposes of section 252(b) [8 U.S.C.A. § 1282(b)].

(3) Paragraph (1) shall not apply to an alien if the air carrier or owner or operator of such vessel that employs the alien provides documentation that satisfies the Attorney General that the alien—

(A) has been an employee of such employer for a period of not less than 1 year preceding the date that a strike or lawful lockout commenced;

(B) has served as a qualified crewman for such employer at least once in each of 3 months during the 12-month period preceding such date; and

(C) shall continue to provide the same services that such alien provided as such a crewman.

(g) Temporary workers and trainees; limitation on numbers

(1) The total number of aliens who may be issued visas or otherwise provided nonimmigrant status during any fiscal year (beginning with fiscal year 1992)—

(A) under section 101(a)(15)(H)(i)(b) [8 U.S.C.A. § 1101(a)(15)(H)(i)(b)], may not exceed—

(i) 65,000 in each fiscal year before fiscal year 1999;

(ii) 115,000 in fiscal year 1999;

(iii) 115,000 in fiscal year 2000;

(iv) 195,000 in fiscal year 2001;

(v) 195,000 in fiscal year 2002;

(vi) 195,000 in fiscal year 2003; and

(vii) 65,000 in each succeeding fiscal year;

(B) under section 101(a)(15)(H)(ii)(b) [8 U.S.C.A. § 1101(a)(15)(H)(ii)(b)] may not exceed 66,000.

(2) The numerical limitations of paragraph (1) shall only apply to principal aliens and not to the spouses or children of such aliens.

(3) Aliens who are subject to the numerical limitations of paragraph (1) shall be issued visas (or otherwise provided nonimmigrant status) in the order in which petitions are filed for such visas or status. If an alien who was issued a visa or otherwise provided nonimmigrant status and counted against the numerical limitations of paragraph (1) is found to have been issued such visa or otherwise provided such status by fraud or willfully misrepresenting a material fact and such visa or nonimmigrant status is revoked, then one number shall be restored to the total number of aliens who may be issued visas or otherwise provided such status under the numerical limitations of paragraph (1) in the fiscal year in which the petition is revoked, regardless of the fiscal year in which the petition was approved.

(4) In the case of a nonimmigrant described in section 101(a)(15)(H)(i)(b) [8 U.S.C.A. § 1101(a)(15)(H)(i)(b)], the period of authorized admission as such a nonimmigrant may not exceed 6 years.

(5) The numerical limitations contained in paragraph (1)(a) shall not apply to any nonimmigrant alien issued a visa or otherwise provided status under section 101(a)(15)(h)(i)(b) [8 U.S.C.A. § 1101(a)(15)(h)(i)(b)] who—

(A) is employed (or has received an offer of employment) at an institution of higher education (as defined in section 1001(a) of Title 20), or a related or affiliated nonprofit entity;

(B) is employed (or has received an offer of employment) at a nonprofit research organization or a governmental research organization; or

(C) has earned a master's or higher degree from a United States institution of higher education (as defined in section 1101(a) of Title 20), until the number of aliens who are exempted from such numerical limitation during such year exceeds 20,000.

(6) Any alien who ceases to be employed by an employer described in paragraph (5)(A) shall, if employed as a nonimmigrant alien described in section 101(a)(15)(H)(i)(b) [8 U.S.C.A. § 1101(a)(15)(H)(i)(b)], who has not previously been counted toward the numerical limitations contained in paragraph (1)(A), be counted toward those limitations the first time the alien is employed by an employer other than one described in paragraph (5).

(7) Any alien who has already been counted, within the 6 years prior to the approval of a petition described in subsection (c), toward the numerical limitations of paragraph (1)(A) shall not again be counted toward those limitations unless the alien would be eligible for a full 6 years of authorized admission at the time the petition is filed. Where multiple petitions are approved for 1 alien, that alien shall be counted only once.

(8)(A) The agreements referred to in section 101(a)(15)(H)(i)(b1) [8 U.S.C.A. § 1101(a)(15)(H)(i)(b1)] are—

(i) the United States-Chile Free Trade Agreement; and

(ii) the United States-Singapore Free Trade Agreement.

(B)(i) The Secretary of Homeland Security shall establish annual numerical limitations on approvals of initial applications by aliens for admission under section 101(a)(15)(H)(i)(b1) [8 U.S.C.A. § 1101(a)(15) (H)(i)(b1)].

(ii) The annual numerical limitations described in clause (i) shall not exceed

(I) 1,400 for nationals of Chile (as defined in article 14.9 of the United States-Chile Free Trade Agreement) for any fiscal year; and

(II) 5,400 for nationals of Singapore (as defined in Annex 1A of the United States-Singapore Free Trade Agreement) for any fiscal year.

(iii) The annual numerical limitations described in clause (i) shall only apply to principal aliens and not to the spouses or children of such aliens.

(iv) The annual numerical limitation described in paragraph (1)(A) is reduced by the amount of the annual numerical limitations established under clause (i). However, if a numerical limitation established under clause (i) has not been exhausted at the end of a given fiscal year, the Secretary of Homeland Security shall adjust upwards the numerical limitation in paragraph (1)(A) for that fiscal year by the amount remaining in the numerical limitation under clause (i). Visas under section 101(a)(15)(H)(i)(b1) [8 U.S.C.A. § 1101(a)(15)(H)(i)(b)] may be issued pursuant to such adjustment within the first 45 days of the next fiscal year to aliens who had applied for such visas during the fiscal year for which the adjustment was made.

(C) The period of authorized admission as a nonimmigrant under section 101(a)(15)(H)(i)(b1) [8 U.S.C.A. § 1101(a)(15)(H)(i)(b1)] shall be 1 year, and may be extended, but only in 1-year increments. After every second extension, the next following extension shall not be granted unless the Secretary of Labor had determined and certified to the Secretary of Homeland Security and the Secretary of State that the intending employer has filed with the Secretary of Labor an attestation under section 212(t)(1) [8 U.S.C.A. § 1182(t)(1)] for the purpose of permitting the nonimmigrant to obtain such extension.

(D) The numerical limitation described in paragraph (1)(A) for a fiscal year shall be reduced by one for each alien granted an extension under subparagraph (C) during such year who has obtained 5 or more consecutive prior extensions.

(9)(A) Subject to subparagraphs (B) and (C), an alien who has already been counted toward the numerical limitation of paragraph (1) (B) during fiscal year 2013, 2014, or 2015 shall not again be counted toward such limitation during fiscal year 2016. Such an alien shall be considered a returning worker.

(B) A petition to admit or otherwise provide status under section 101(a)(15)(H)(ii)(b) [8 U.S.C.A. § 1101(a)(15)(H)(ii)(b)] shall include, with respect to a returning worker

(i) all information and evidence that the Secretary of Homeland Security determines is required to support a petition for status under section 101(a)(15)(H)(ii)(b) [8 U.S.C.A. § 1101(a)(15)(H)(ii)(b)];

(ii) the full name of the alien; and

(iii) a certification to the Department of Homeland Security that the alien is a returning worker.

(C) An H–2B visa or grant of nonimmigrant status for a returning worker shall be approved only if the alien is confirmed to be a returning worker by—

(i) the Department of State; or

(ii) if the alien is visa exempt or seeking to change to status under section 101(a)(15)(H)(ii)(b) [8 U.S.C.A. § 1101(a)(15)(H)(ii)(b)], the Department of Homeland Security.

(10) The numerical limitations of paragraph (1)(B) shall be allocated for a fiscal year so that the total number of aliens subject to such numerical limits who enter the United States pursuant to a visa or are accorded nonimmigrant status under section 101(a)(15)(H)(ii)(b) [8 U.S.C.A. § 1101(a)(15)(H)(ii)(b)] during the first 6 months of such fiscal year is not more than 33,000.

(11)(A) The Secretary of State may not approve a number of initial applications submitted for aliens described in section 101(a)(15)(E)(iii) [8 U.S.C.A. § 1101(a)(15)(E)(iii)] that is more than the applicable numerical limitation set out in this paragraph.

(B) The applicable numerical limitation referred to in subparagraph (A) is 10,500 for each fiscal year.

(C) The applicable numerical limitation referred to in subparagraph (A) shall only apply to principal aliens and not to the spouses or children of such aliens.

(h) Intention to abandon foreign residence

The fact that an alien is the beneficiary of an application for a preference status filed under section 204 [8 U.S.C.A. § 1154] or has otherwise sought permanent residence in the United States shall not constitute evidence of an intention to abandon a foreign residence for purposes of obtaining a visa as a nonimmigrant described in subparagraph (H)(i)(b) or (c), (L), or (V) of section 101(a)(15) [8 U.S.C.A. § 1101(a)(15)] or otherwise obtaining or maintaining the status of a nonimmigrant described in such subparagraph, if the alien had obtained a change of status under section 248 [8 U.S.C.A. § 1258] to a classification as such a nonimmigrant before the alien's most recent departure from the United States.

(i) "Specialty occupation" defined

(1) Except as provided in paragraph (3), for purposes of section 101(a)(15)(H)(i)(b) [8 U.S.C.A. § 1101(a)(15)(H)(i)(b)], section 101(a)(15)(E)(iii) [8 U.S.C.A. § 1101(a)(15)(E)(iii)], and paragraph (2), the term "specialty occupation" means an occupation that requires—

(A) theoretical and practical application of a body of highly specialized knowledge, and

(B) attainment of a bachelor's or higher degree in the specific specialty (or its equivalent) as a minimum for entry into the occupation in the United States.

(2) For purposes of section 101(a)(15)(H)(i)(b) [8 U.S.C.A. § 1101(a)(15)(H)(i)(b)], the requirements of this paragraph, with respect to a specialty occupation, are—

(A) full state licensure to practice in the occupation, if such licensure is required to practice in the occupation,

(B) completion of the degree described in paragraph (1)(B) for the occupation, or

(C) (i) experience in the specialty equivalent to the completion of such degree, and **(ii)** recognition of expertise in the specialty through progressively responsible positions relating to the specialty.

(3) For purposes of section 101(a)(15)(H)(i)(b1) [8 U.S.C.A. § 1101(a)(15)(H)(i)(b1)], the term "specialty occupation" means an occupation that requires—

(A) theoretical and practical application of a body of specialized knowledge; and

(B) attainment of a bachelor's or higher degree in the specific specialty (or its equivalent) as a minimum for entry into the occupation in the United States.

(j) Labor disputes

(1) Notwithstanding any other provision of this chapter, an alien who is a citizen of Canada or Mexico who seeks to enter the United States under and pursuant to the provisions of Section B, Section C, or Section D of Annex 1603 of the North American Free Trade Agreement, shall not be classified as a nonimmigrant under such provisions if there is in progress a strike or lockout in the course of a labor dispute in the occupational classification at the place or intended place of employment, unless such alien establishes, pursuant to regulations promulgated by the Attorney General, that the alien's entry will not affect adversely the settlement of the strike or lockout or the employment of any person who is involved in the strike or lockout. Notice of a determination under this paragraph shall be given as may be required by paragraph 3 of article 1603 of such Agreement. For purposes of this paragraph, the term "citizen of Mexico" means "citizen" as defined in Annex 1608 of such Agreement.

(2) Notwithstanding any other provision of this chapter except section 212(t)(1) [8 U.S.C.A. § 1182(t)(1)], and subject to regulations promulgated by the Secretary of Homeland Security, an alien who seeks to enter the United States under and pursuant to the provisions of an agreement listed in subsection (g)(8)(A) of this section, and the spouse and children of such an alien if accompanying or following to join the alien, may be denied admission as a nonimmigrant under subparagraph (E), (L), or (H)(i)(b1) of section 101(a)(15) [8 U.S.C.A. § 1101(a)(15)] if there is in progress a labor dispute in the occupational classification at the place or intended place of employment, unless such alien establishes, pursuant to regulations promulgated by the Secretary of Homeland Security after consultation with the Secretary of Labor, that the alien's entry will not affect adversely the settlement of the labor dispute or the employment of any person who is involved in the labor dispute. Notice of a determination under this paragraph shall be given as may be required by such agreement.

(k) Numerical limitations; period of admission; conditions for admission and stay; annual report

(1) The number of aliens who may be provided a visa as nonimmigrants under section 101(a)(15)(S)(i) [8 U.S.C.A. § 1101(a)(15)(S)(i)] in any fiscal year may not exceed 200. The number of aliens who may be provided a visa as nonimmigrants under section 101(a)(15)(S)(ii) [8 U.S.C.A. § 1101(a)(15)(S)(ii)] in any fiscal year may not exceed 50.

(2) The period of admission of an alien as such a nonimmigrant may not exceed 3 years. Such period may not be extended by the Attorney General.

(3) As a condition for the admission, and continued stay in lawful status, of such a nonimmigrant, the nonimmigrant—

(A) shall report not less often than quarterly to the Attorney General such information concerning the alien's whereabouts and activities as the Attorney General may require;

(B) may not be convicted of any criminal offense punishable by a term of imprisonment of 1 year or more after the date of such admission;

(C) must have executed a form that waives the nonimmigrant's right to contest, other than on the basis of an application for withholding of removal, any action for removal of the alien instituted before the alien obtains lawful permanent resident status; and

(D) shall abide by any other condition, limitation, or restriction imposed by the Attorney General.

(4) The Attorney General shall submit a report annually to the Committee on the Judiciary of the House of Representatives and the Committee on the Judiciary of the Senate concerning—

(A) the number of such nonimmigrants admitted;

(B) the number of successful criminal prosecutions or investigations resulting from cooperation of such aliens;

(C) the number of terrorist acts prevented or frustrated resulting from cooperation of such aliens;

(D) the number of such nonimmigrants whose admission or cooperation has not resulted in successful criminal prosecution or investigation or the prevention or frustration of a terrorist act; and

(E) the number of such nonimmigrants who have failed to report quarterly (as required under paragraph (3)) or who have been convicted of crimes in the United States after the date of their admission as such a nonimmigrant.

(5) Redesignated (4)

(*l*) Restrictions on waiver

(1) In the case of a request by an interested State agency, or by an interested Federal agency, for a waiver of the 2-year foreign residence requirement under section 212(e) [8 U.S.C.A. § 1182(e)] on behalf of an alien described in clause (iii) of such section, the Attorney General shall not grant such waiver unless—

(A) in the case of an alien who is otherwise contractually obligated to return to a foreign country, the government of such country furnishes the Director of the United States Information Agency with a statement in writing that it has no objection to such waiver;

(B) in the case of a request by an interested State agency, the grant of such waiver would not cause the number of waivers allotted for that State for that fiscal year to exceed 30;

(C) in the case of a request by an interested Federal agency or by an interested State agency—

(i) the alien demonstrates a bona fide offer of full-time employment at a health facility or health care organization, which employment has been determined by the Attorney General to be in the public interest; and

(ii) the alien agrees to begin employment with the health facility or health care organization within 90 days of receiving such waiver, and agrees to continue to work for a total of not less than 3 years (unless the Attorney General determines that extenuating circumstances exist, such as closure of the facility or hardship to the alien, which would justify a lesser period of employment at such health facility or health care organization, in which case the alien must demonstrate another bona fide offer of employment at a health facility or health care organization for the remainder of such 3-year period); and

(D) in the case of a request by an interested Federal agency (other than a request by an interested Federal agency to employ the alien full-time in medical research or training) or by an interested

State agency, the alien agrees to practice primary care or specialty medicine in accordance with paragraph (2) for a total of not less than 3 years only in the geographic area or areas which are designated by the Secretary of Health and Human Services as having a shortage of health care professionals, except that—

(i) in the case of a request by the Department of Veterans Affairs, the alien shall not be required to practice medicine in a geographic area designated by the Secretary;

(ii) in the case of a request by an interested State agency, the head of such State agency determines that the alien is to practice medicine under such agreement in a facility that serves patients who reside in one or more geographic areas so designated by the Secretary of Health and Human Services (without regard to whether such facility is located within such a designated geographic area), and the grant of such waiver would not cause the number of the waivers granted on behalf of aliens for such State for a fiscal year (within the limitation in subparagraph (B)) in accordance with the conditions of this clause to exceed 10; and

(iii) in the case of a request by an interested Federal agency or by an interested State agency for a waiver for an alien who agrees to practice specialty medicine in a facility located in a geographic area so designated by the Secretary of Health and Human Services, the request shall demonstrate, based on criteria established by such agency, that there is a shortage of health care professionals able to provide services in the appropriate medical specialty to the patients who will be served by the alien.

(2)(A) Notwithstanding section 248(a)(2) [8 U.S.C.A § 1258(a)(2)], the Attorney General may change the status of an alien who qualifies under this subsection and section 212(e) [8 U.S.C.A § 1182(e)] to that of an alien described in section 101(a)(15)(H)(i)(b) [8 U.S.C.A § 1101(a)(15)(H)(i)(b)]. The numerical limitations contained in subsection (g)(1)(A) of this section shall not apply to any alien whose status is changed under the preceding sentence, if the alien obtained a waiver of the 2-year foreign residence requirement upon a request by an interested Federal agency or an interested State agency.

(B) No person who has obtained a change of status under subparagraph (A) and who has failed to fulfill the terms of the contract with the health facility or health care organization named in the waiver application shall be eligible to apply for an immigrant visa, for permanent residence, or for any other change of nonimmigrant status, until it is established that such person has resided and been physically present in the country of his nationality or his last residence for an aggregate of at least 2 years following departure from the United States.

(3) Notwithstanding any other provision of this subsection, the 2-year foreign residence requirement under section 212(e) [8 U.S.C.A.

§ 1182(e)] shall apply with respect to an alien described in clause (iii) of such section, who has not otherwise been accorded status under section 101(a)(27)(H) [8 U.S.C.A. § 1101(a)(27)(H)], if—

(A) at any time the alien ceases to comply with any agreement entered into under subparagraph (C) or (D) of paragraph (1); or

(B) the alien's employment ceases to benefit the public interest at any time during the 3-year period described in paragraph (1)(C).

(m) Nonimmigrant elementary and secondary school students

(1) An alien may not be accorded status as a nonimmigrant under clause (i) or (iii) of section 101(a)(15)(F) [8 U.S.C.A. § 1101(a)(15)(F)] in order to pursue a course of study—

(A) at a public elementary school or in a publicly funded adult education program; or

(B) at a public secondary school unless—

(i) the aggregate period of such status at such a school does not exceed 12 months with respect to any alien, and

(ii) the alien demonstrates that the alien has reimbursed the local educational agency that administers the school for the full, unsubsidized per capita cost of providing education at such school for the period of the alien's attendance.

(2) An alien who obtains the status of a nonimmigrant under clause (i) or (iii) of section 101(a)(15)(F) [8 U.S.C.A. § 1101(a)(15)(F)] in order to pursue a course of study at a private elementary or secondary school or in a language training program that is not publicly funded shall be considered to have violated such status, and the alien's visa under section 101(a)(15)(F) [8 U.S.C.A. § 1101(a)(15)(F)] shall be void, if the alien terminates or abandons such course of study at such a school and undertakes a course of study at a public elementary school, in a publicly funded adult education program, in a publicly funded adult education language training program, or at a public secondary school (unless the requirements of paragraph (1)(B) are met).

(n) Increased portability of H–1B status

(1) A nonimmigrant alien described in paragraph (2) who was previously issued a visa or otherwise provided nonimmigrant status under section 101(a)(15)(H)(i)(b) [8 U.S.C.A. § 1101(a)(15)(H)(i)(b)] is authorized to accept new employment upon the filing by the prospective employer of a new petition on behalf of such nonimmigrant as provided under subsection (a). Employment authorization shall continue for such alien until the new petition is adjudicated. If the new petition is denied, such authorization shall cease.

(2) A nonimmigrant alien described in this paragraph is a nonimmigrant alien—

(A) who has been lawfully admitted into the United States;

(B) on whose behalf an employer has filed a nonfrivolous petition for new employment before the date of expiration of the period of stay authorized by the Attorney General; and

(C) who, subsequent to such lawful admission, has not been employed without authorization in the United States before the filing of such petition.

(o) Trafficking in persons; conditions of nonimmigrant status

(1) No alien shall be eligible for admission to the United States under section 101(a)(15)(T) [8 U.S.C.A. § 1101(a)(15)(T)] if there is substantial reason to believe that the alien has committed an act of a severe form of trafficking in persons (as defined in section 103 of the Trafficking Victims Protection Act of 2000 [22 U.S.C.A. § 7102]).

(2) The total number of aliens who may be issued visas or otherwise provided nonimmigrant status during any fiscal year under section 101(a)(15)(T) [8 U.S.C.A. § 1101(a)(15)(T)] may not exceed 5,000.

(3) The numerical limitation of paragraph (2) shall only apply to principal aliens and not to the spouses, sons, daughters, siblings, or parents of such aliens.

(4) An unmarried alien who seeks to accompany, or follow to join, a parent granted status under section 101(a)(15)(T)(i) [8 U.S.C.A. § 1101(a)(15)(T)(i)], and who was under 21 years of age on the date on which such parent applied for such status, shall continue to be classified as a child for purposes of section 101(a)(15)(T)(ii) [8 U.S.C.A. § 1101(a)(15)(T)(ii)], if the alien attains 21 years of age after such parent's application was filed but while it was pending.

(5) An alien described in clause (i) of section 101(a)(15)(T) [8 U.S.C.A. § 1101(a)(15)(T)] shall continue to be treated as an alien described in clause (ii)(I) of such section if the alien attains 21 years of age after the alien's application for status under such clause (i) is filed but while it is pending.

(6) In making a determination under section 101(a)(15)(T)(i)(III)(aa) [8 U.S.C.A. § 1101(a)(15)(T)(i)(III)(aa)] with respect to an alien, statements from State and local law enforcement officials that the alien has complied with any reasonable request for assistance in the investigation or prosecution of crimes such as kidnapping, rape, slavery, or other forced labor offenses, where severe forms of trafficking in persons (as defined in section 7102 of Title 22) appear to have been involved, shall be considered.

(7)(A) Except as provided in subparagraph (B), an alien who is issued a visa or otherwise provided nonimmigrant status under section 101(a)(15)(T) [8 U.S.C.A § 1101(a)(15)(T)] may be granted such status for a period of not more than 4 years.

(B) An alien who is issued a visa or otherwise provided nonimmigrant status under section 101(a)(15)(T) [8 U.S.C.A. § 1101(a)

(15)(T)] may extend the period of such status beyond the period described in subparagraph (A) if—

(i) a Federal, State, or local law enforcement official, prosecutor, judge, or other authority investigating or prosecuting activity relating to human trafficking or certifies that the presence of the alien in the United States is necessary to assist in the investigation or prosecution of such activity;

(ii) the alien is eligible for relief under section 245(*l*) [8 U.S.C.A. § 1255(*l*)] and is unable to obtain such relief because regulations have not been issued to implement such section; or

(iii) the Secretary of Homeland Security determines that an extension of the period of such nonimmigrant status is warranted due to exceptional circumstances.

(C) Nonimmigrant status under section 101(a)(15)(T) [8 U.S.C.A. § 1101(a)(15)(T)] shall be extended during the pendency of an application for adjustment of status under section 245(*l*) [8 U.S.C.A. § 1255(*l*)].

(p) Requirements applicable to section 101(a)(15)(U) [8 U.S.C.A. § 1101(a)(15)(U)] visas

(1) Petitioning procedures for section 101(a)(15)(U) [8 U.S.C.A. § 1101(a)(15)(U)] visas

The petition filed by an alien under section 101(a)(15)(U)(i) [8 U.S.C.A. § 1101(a)(15)(U)(i)] shall contain a certification from a Federal, State, or local law enforcement official, prosecutor, judge, or other Federal, State, or local authority investigating criminal activity described in section 101(a)(15)(U)(iii) [8 U.S.C.A. § 1101(a)(15)(U)(iii)]. This certification may also be provided by an official of the Service whose ability to provide such certification is not limited to information concerning immigration violations. This certification shall state that the alien "has been helpful, is being helpful, or is likely to be helpful" in the investigation or prosecution of criminal activity described in section 101(a)(15)(U)(iii) [8 U.S.C.A. § 1101(a)(15)(U)(iii)].

(2) Numerical limitations

(A) The number of aliens who may be issued visas or otherwise provided status as nonimmigrants under section 101(a)(15)(U) [8 U.S.C.A. § 1101(a)(15)(U)] in any fiscal year shall not exceed 10,000.

(B) The numerical limitations in subparagraph (A) shall only apply to principal aliens described in section 101(a)(15)(U)(i) [8 U.S.C.A. § 1101(a)(15)(U)(i)], and not to spouses, children, or, in the case of alien children, the alien parents of such children.

(3) Duties of the Attorney General with respect to "U" visa nonimmigrants

With respect to nonimmigrant aliens described in subsection (a)(15) (U)[sic]—

(A) the Attorney General and other government officials, where appropriate, shall provide those aliens with referrals to nongovernmental organizations to advise the aliens regarding their options while in the United States and the resources available to them; and

(B) the Attorney General shall, during the period those aliens are in lawful temporary resident status under that subsection, provide the aliens with employment authorization.

(4) Credible evidence considered

In acting on any petition filed under this subsection, the consular officer or the Attorney General, as appropriate, shall consider any credible evidence relevant to the petition.

(5) Nonexclusive relief

Nothing in this subsection limits the ability of aliens who qualify for status under section 101(a)(15)(U) [8 U.S.C.A. § 1101(a)(15)(U)] to seek any other immigration benefit or status for which the alien may be eligible.

(6) Duration of status

The authorized period of status of an alien as a nonimmigrant under section 101(a)(15)(U) [8 U.S.C.A. § 1101(a)(15)(U)] shall be for a period of not more than 4 years, but shall be extended upon certification from a Federal, State, or local law enforcement official, prosecutor, judge, or other Federal, State, or local authority investigating or prosecuting criminal activity described in section 101(a)(15)(U)(iii) [8 U.S.C.A. § 1101(a)(15)(U)(iii)] that the alien's presence in the United States is required to assist in the investigation or prosecution of such criminal activity. The Secretary of Homeland Security may extend, beyond the 4-year period authorized under this section, the authorized period of status of an alien as a nonimmigrant under section 101(a)(15)(U) [8 U.S.C.A. § 1101(a)(15)(U)] if the Secretary determines that an extension of such period is warranted due to exceptional circumstances. Such alien's nonimmigrant status shall be extended beyond the 4-year period authorized under this section if the alien is eligible for relief under section 245(m) [8 U.S.C.A. § 1255(m)] and is unable to obtain such relief because regulations have not been issued to implement such section and shall be extended during the pendency of an application for adjustment of status under section 245(m) [8 U.S.C.A. § 1255(m)]. The Secretary may grant work authorization to any alien who has a pending, bona fide application for nonimmigrant status under section 101(a)(15)(U) [8 U.S.C.A. § 1101(a)(15)(U)].

(7) Age determinations

(A) Children

An unmarried alien who seeks to accompany, or follow to join, a parent granted status under section 101(a)(15)(U)(i) [8 U.S.C.A. § 1101(a)(15)(U)(i)], and who was under 21 years of age on the date on which such parent petitioned for such status, shall continue to be classified as a child for purposes of section 101(a)(15)(U)(ii) [8 U.S.C.A. § 1101(a)(15)(U)(ii)], if the alien attains 21 years of age after such parent's petition was filed but while it was pending.

(B) Principal aliens

An alien described in clause (i) of section 101(a)(15)(U) [8 U.S.C.A. § 1101(a)(15)(U)] shall continue to be treated as an alien described in clause (ii)(I) of such section if the alien attains 21 years of age after the alien's application for status under such clause (i) is filed but while it is pending.

(q) Nonimmigrant described in section 101(a)(15)(V) [8 U.S.C.A. § 1101(a)(15)(V)]

(1) In the case of a nonimmigrant described in section 101(a)(15)(V) [8 U.S.C.A. § 1101(a)(15)(V)]

(A) the Attorney General shall authorize the alien to engage in employment in the United States during the period of authorized admission and shall provide the alien with an "employment authorized" endorsement or other appropriate document signifying authorization of employment; and

(B) the period of authorized admission as such a nonimmigrant shall terminate 30 days after the date on which any of the following is denied:

(i) The petition filed under section 204 [8 U.S.C.A. § 1154] to accord the alien a status under section 203(a)(2)(A) [8 U.S.C.A. § 1153(a)(2)(A)] (or, in the case of a child granted nonimmigrant status based on eligibility to receive a visa under section 203(d) [8 U.S.C.A. § 1153(d)], the petition filed to accord the child's parent a status under section 203(a)(2)(A) [8 U.S.C.A. § 1153(a)(2)(A)]).

(ii) The alien's application for an immigrant visa pursuant to the approval of such petition.

(iii) The alien's application for adjustment of status under section 245 [8 U.S.C.A. § 1255] pursuant to the approval of such petition.

(2) In determining whether an alien is eligible to be admitted to the United States as a nonimmigrant under section 101(a)(15)(V) [8 U.S.C.A. § 1101(a)(15)(V)], the grounds for inadmissibility specified in section 212(a)(9)(B) [8 U.S.C.A. § 1182(a)(9)(B)] shall not apply.

(3) The status of an alien physically present in the United States may be adjusted by the attorney general, in the discretion of the attorney general and under such regulations as the attorney general may prescribe, to that of a nonimmigrant under section 101(a)(15)(v) [8 U.S.C.A. § 1101(a)(15)(v)], if the alien

(A) applies for such adjustment;

(B) satisfies the requirements of such section; and

(C) is eligible to be admitted to the United States, except in determining such admissibility, the grounds for inadmissibility specified in paragraphs (6)(A), (7), and (9)(B) of section 212(a) [8 U.S.C.A. § 1182(a)] shall not apply.

(r) Visas of nonimmigrants described in section 101(a)(15)(K) (ii) [8 U.S.C.A. § 1101(a)(15)(K)(ii)]

(1) A visa shall not be issued under the provisions of section 101(a) (15)(K)(ii) [8 U.S.C.A. § 1101(a)(15)(K)(ii)] until the consular officer has received a petition filed in the United States by the spouse of the applying alien and approved by the Attorney General. The petition shall be in such form and contain such information as the Attorney General shall, by regulation, prescribe. Such information shall include information on any criminal convictions of the petitioner for any specified crime described in paragraph (5)(B) and information on any permanent protection or restraining order issued against the petitioner related to any specified crime described in subsection (5)(B)(i).

(2) In the case of an alien seeking admission under section 101(a) (15)(K)(ii) [8 U.S.C.A. § 1101(a)(15)(K)(ii)] who concluded a marriage with a citizen of the United States outside the United States, the alien shall be considered inadmissible under section 212(a)(7)(B) [8 U.S.C.A. § 1182(a)(7)(B)] if the alien is not at the time of application for admission in possession of a valid nonimmigrant visa issued by a consular officer in the foreign state in which the marriage was concluded.

(3) In the case of a nonimmigrant described in section 101(a)(15)(K) (ii) [8 U.S.C.A. § 1101(a)(15)(K)(ii)], and any child of such a nonimmigrant who was admitted as accompanying, or following to join, such a nonimmigrant, the period of authorized admission shall terminate 30 days after the date on which any of the following is denied:

(A) The petition filed under section 204 [8 U.S.C.A. § 1154] to accord the principal alien status under section 201(b)(2)(A)(i) [8 U.S.C.A. § 1151(b)(2)(A)(i)].

(B) The principal alien's application for an immigrant visa pursuant to the approval of such petition.

(C) The principal alien's application for adjustment of status under section 245 [8 U.S.C.A. § 1255] pursuant to the approval of such petition.

(4)(A) The Secretary of Homeland Security shall create a database for the purpose of tracking multiple visa petitions filed for fiancé(e)s and spouses under clauses (i) and (ii) of section 101(a)(15)(K) [8 U.S.C.A § 1101(a)(15)(K)]. Upon approval of a second visa petition under section 101(a)(15)(K) [8 U.S.C.A § 1101(a)(15)(K)] for a fiancé(e) or spouse filed by the same United States citizen petitioner, the petitioner shall be notified by the Secretary that information concerning the petitioner has been entered into the multiple visa petition tracking database. All subsequent fiance(e) or spouse nonimmigrant visa petitions filed by that petitioner under such section shall be entered in the database.

(B)(i) Once a petitioner has had two fiance(e) or spousal petitions approved under clause (i) or (ii) of section 101(a)(15)(K) [8 U.S.C.A § 1101(a)(15)(K)], if a subsequent petition is filed under such section less than 10 years after the date the first visa petition was filed under such section, the Secretary of Homeland Security shall notify both the petitioner and beneficiary of any such subsequent petition about the number of previously approved fiance(e) or spousal petitions listed in the database.

(ii) To notify the beneficiary as required by clause (i), the Secretary of Homeland Security shall provide such notice to the Secretary of State for inclusion in the mailing to the beneficiary described in section 833(a)(5)(A)(i) of the International Marriage Broker Regulation Act of 2005 [8 U.S.C.A. § 1375a(a)(5)(A)(i)].

(5) In this subsection:

(A) The terms "domestic violence", "sexual assault", "child abuse and neglect", "dating violence", "elder abuse", and "stalking" have the meaning given such terms in section 13925 of Title 42.

(B) The term "specified crime" means the following:

(i) Domestic violence, sexual assault, child abuse and neglect, dating violence, elder abuse, stalking, or an attempt to commit any such crime.

(ii) Homicide, murder, manslaughter, rape, abusive sexual contact, sexual exploitation, incest, torture, trafficking, peonage, holding hostage, involuntary servitude, slave trade, kidnapping, abduction, unlawful criminal restraint, false imprisonment, or an attempt to commit any of the crimes described in this clause.

(iii) At least three convictions for crimes relating to a controlled substance or alcohol not arising from a single act.

(June 27, 1952, c. 477, Title II, ch. 2, § 214, 66 Stat. 189; Apr. 7, 1970, Pub.L. 91–225, § 3, 84 Stat. 117; Oct. 5, 1984, Pub.L. 98–454, Title VI, § 602(b), 98 Stat. 1737; Nov. 6, 1986, Pub.L. 99–603, Title III, §§ 301(b), 313(b), 100 Stat. 3411, 3438; Nov. 10, 1986, Pub.L. 99–639, § 3(a), (c), 100 Stat. 3542; Sept. 28, 1988, Pub.L. 100–449, Title III, § 307(b), 102 Stat. 1877; Nov. 6, 1986, Pub.L. 99–603, § 301(b); Oct. 24, 1988, Pub.L. 100–525, § 2(*l*) (1), 102 Stat. 2612; Nov. 29, 1990, Pub.L. 101–649, Title II, §§ 202(a), 205(a), (b), (c)(2), 206(b), 207(b), 104 Stat. 5014, 5019, 5020, 5023, 5025; Dec. 12, 1991, Pub.L. 102–232, Title II, §§ 202(a), 203(b), 204, 205(d), (e), 206(a), (c)(2), 207(a), (c)(1), Title III, § 303(a)(10), (11), (12), 105 Stat. 1737, 1738, 1740, 1741, 1748; Dec. 8, 1993, Pub.L. 103–182, Title III, § 341(b), (c), 107 Stat. 2116, 2117; Sept. 13, 1994, Pub.L. 103–322, Title XIII, § 130003(b) (2), 108 Stat. 2025; Oct. 25, 1994, Pub.L. 103–416, Title II, § 220(b), 108 Stat. 4319; Sept. 30, 1996, Pub.L. 104–208, Div. C, Title III, § 308(e)(1)(D), (2)(B), (f)(1)(G), (H), (3)(B), (g)(5) (A)(i), (g)(7)(A), Title VI, §§ 621, 622(c), 625(a)(1), 671(a)(3)(A), (e)(4)(A), 110 Stat. 3009–619, 3009–620, 3009–621, 3009–623, 3009–695, 3009–699, 3009–721, 3009–723; Oct. 27, 1997, Pub.L. 105–65, Title I, § 108, 111 Stat. 1350; Oct. 21, 1998, Pub.L. 105–277, Div. C, Title IV, §§ 411(a), 414(a), 112 Stat. 2681–642, 2681–651; Nov. 13, 1999, Pub.L. 106–104, § 2,

113 Stat. 1483; Oct. 17, 2000, Pub.L. 106–311, § 1, 114 Stat. 1247; Oct. 17, 2000, Pub.L. 106–313, Title I, §§ 102(a), 103, 105(a), 108, 114 Stat. 1251, 1252, 1253, 1255; Oct. 28, 2000, Pub.L. 106–386, Div. A, § 107(e)(2), Div. B, Title V, § 1513(c), 114 Stat. 1478, 1535; Oct. 30, 2000, Pub.L. 106–396, Title IV, § 401, 114 Stat. 1647; Dec. 21, 2000, Pub.L. 106–553, § 1(a)(2) [Title XI, §§ 1102(b), (d)(1), 1103(b), (c)(1)], 114 Stat. 2762; Oct. 1, 2001, Pub.L. 107–45, § 1, 115 Stat. 258; Jan. 16, 2002, Pub.L. 107–124, 115 Stat. 2402; Jan. 16, 2002, Pub.L. 107–125, §§ 1, 2(a), 115 Stat. 2403; Nov. 2, 2002, Pub.L. 107–274, § 2(c), 116 Stat. 1923; Nov. 2, 2002, Pub.L. 107–273, Div. C, Title I, § 11018(a), 116 Stat. 1825; Sept. 3, 2003, Pub.L. 108–77, Title IV, §§ 402(a)(2), (d)(1), 403, 404, 117 Stat. 940, 946, 947; Sept. 3, 2003, Pub.L. 108–78, Title IV, § 402, 117 Stat. 970; Dec. 19, 2003, Pub.L. 108–193, §§ 4(b)(2), 8(a)(3), 117 Stat. 2878, 2886; Dec. 3, 2004, Pub.L. 108–441, § 1(b), (c), (d), 118 Stat. 2630; Dec. 8, 2004, Pub.L. 108–447, Div. J, Title IV, §§ 412(a), 413(a), 422(b), 425(a), 426(a), 118 Stat. 3353, 3356, 3357; May 11, 2005, Pub.L. 109–13, Div. B, § 402(a), 403(a), 404(a), 405, 501(b), (c), 119 Stat. 231, 318–22; Jan. 5, 2006, Pub.L. 109–162, Title VIII, §§ 821(a), (b), (c)(2), 832(a)(1), (2), 119 Stat. 3062, 3066, 3067; Oct. 17, 2006, Pub.L. 109–364, Div. A, Title X, § 1074(a), 120 Stat. 2403; Dec. 22, 2006, Pub.L. 109–463, § 2, 120 Stat. 3477; May 8, 2008, Pub.L. 110–229, Title VII, Subtitle A, § 702(b)(1), 122 Stat. 860; Oct. 8, 2008, Pub.L. 110–362, § 2, 122 Stat. 4013; Dec. 23, 2008, Pub.L. 110–457, Title II, § 201(b), (c), 122 Stat. 5053; Pub.L. 113–4, Title VIII, §§ 805(a), 807(a), Mar. 7, 2013, 127 Stat. 111, 112; Pub.L. 114–113, Div. F, Title V, § 565, Dec. 18, 2015, 129 Stat. 2523.)

§ 215.   Travel control of citizens and aliens [8 U.S.C.A. § 1185]

(a) Restrictions and prohibitions

Unless otherwise ordered by the President, it shall be unlawful—

(1) for any alien to depart from or enter or attempt to depart from or enter the United States except under such reasonable rules, regulations, and orders, and subject to such limitations and exceptions as the President may prescribe;

(2) for any person to transport or attempt to transport from or into the United States another person with knowledge or reasonable cause to believe that the departure or entry of such other person is forbidden by this section;

(3) for any person knowingly to make any false statement in an application for permission to depart from or enter the United States with intent to induce or secure the granting of such permission either for himself or for another;

(4) for any person knowingly to furnish or attempt to furnish or assist in furnishing to another a permit or evidence of permission to depart or enter not issued and designed for such other person's use;

(5) for any person knowingly to use or attempt to use any permit or evidence of permission to depart or enter not issued and designed for his use;

(6) for any person to forge, counterfeit, mutilate, or alter, or cause or procure to be forged, counterfeited, mutilated, or altered, any permit or evidence of permission to depart from or enter the United States;

(7) for any person knowingly to use or attempt to use or furnish to another for use any false, forged, counterfeited, mutilated, or altered

8 U.S.C.A. § 1186a

permit, or evidence of permission, or any permit or evidence of permission which, though originally valid, has become or been made void or invalid.

(b) Citizens

Except as otherwise provided by the President and subject to such limitations and exceptions as the President may authorize and prescribe, it shall be unlawful for any citizen of the United States to depart from or enter, or attempt to depart from or enter, the United States unless he bears a valid United States passport.

(c) Definitions

The term "United States" as used in this section includes the Canal Zone, and all territory and waters, continental or insular, subject to the jurisdiction of the United States. The term "person" as used in this section shall be deemed to mean any individual, partnership, association, company, or other incorporated body of individuals, or corporation, or body politic.

(d) Nonadmission of certain aliens

Nothing in this section shall be construed to entitle an alien to whom a permit to enter the United States has been issued to enter the United States, if, upon arrival in the United States, he is found to be inadmissible under any of the provisions of this Act, or any other law, relative to the entry of aliens into the United States.

(e) Revocation of proclamation as affecting penalties

The revocation of any rule, regulation, or order issued in pursuance of this section shall not prevent prosecution for any offense committed, or the imposition of any penalties or forfeitures, liability for which was incurred under this section prior to the revocation of such rule, regulation, or order.

(f) Permits to enter

Passports, visas, reentry permits, and other documents required for entry under this Act may be considered as permits to enter for the purposes of this section.

(June 27, 1952, c. 477, Title II, ch. 2, § 215, 66 Stat. 190; Oct. 7, 1978, Pub.L. 95–426, Title VII, § 707(a)–(d), 92 Stat. 992, 993; Oct. 25, 1994, Pub.L. 103–416, Title II, § 204(a), 108 Stat. 4311.)

§ 216. Conditional permanent resident status for certain alien spouses and sons and daughters [8 U.S.C.A. § 1186a]

(a) In general

(1) Conditional basis for status

Notwithstanding any other provision of this chapter, an alien spouse (as defined in subsection (h)(1) of this section) and an alien son or daughter (as defined in subsection (h)(2) of this section) shall be considered, at the time of obtaining the status of an alien lawfully admitted for permanent residence, to have obtained such status on a conditional basis subject to the provisions of this section.

(2) Notice of requirements

(A) At time of obtaining permanent residence

At the time an alien spouse or alien son or daughter obtains permanent resident status on a conditional basis under paragraph (1), the Secretary of Homeland Security shall provide for notice to such a spouse, son, or daughter respecting the provisions of this section and the requirements of subsection (c)(1) of this section to have the conditional basis of such status removed.

(B) At time of required petition

In addition, the Secretary of Homeland Security shall attempt to provide notice to such a spouse, son, or daughter, at or about the beginning of the 90-day period described in subsection (d)(2)(A) of this section, of the requirements of subsections [sic] (c)(1) of this section.

(C) Effect of failure to provide notice

The failure of the Secretary of Homeland Security to provide a notice under this paragraph shall not affect the enforcement of the provisions of this section with respect to such a spouse, son, or daughter.

(b) Termination of status if finding that qualifying marriage improper

(1) In general

In the case of an alien with permanent resident status on a conditional basis under subsection (a) of this section, if the Secretary of Homeland Security determines, before the second anniversary of the alien's obtaining the status of lawful admission for permanent residence, that—

(A) the qualifying marriage—

(i) was entered into for the purpose of procuring an alien's admission as an immigrant, or

(ii) has been judicially annulled or terminated, other than through the death of a spouse; or

(B) a fee or other consideration was given (other than a fee or other consideration to an attorney for assistance in preparation of a lawful petition) for the filing of a petition under section 204(a) [8 U.S.C.A. § 1154(a)] or subsection (d) or (p) of section 214 [8 U.S.C.A. § 1184] with respect to the alien;

the Secretary of Homeland Security shall so notify the parties involved and, subject to paragraph (2), shall terminate the permanent resident status of the alien (or aliens) involved as of the date of the determination.

(2) Hearing in removal proceeding

Any alien whose permanent resident status is terminated under paragraph (1) may request a review of such determination in a proceeding to remove the alien. In such proceeding, the burden of proof shall be on the Secretary of Homeland Security to establish, by a preponderance of the evidence, that a condition described in paragraph (1) is met.

(c) Requirements of timely petition and interview for removal of condition

(1) In general

In order for the conditional basis established under subsection (a) for an alien spouse or an alien son or daughter to be removed—

(A) the alien spouse and the petitioning spouse (if not deceased) jointly must submit to the Secretary of Homeland Security, during the period described in subsection (d)(2) of this section, a petition which requests the removal of such conditional basis and which states, under penalty of perjury, the facts and information described in subsection (d)(1) of this section, and

(B) in accordance with subsection (d)(3) of this section, the alien spouse and the petitioning spouse (if not deceased) must appear for a personal interview before an officer or employee of the Department of Homeland Security respecting the facts and information described in subsection (d)(1) of this section.

(2) Termination of permanent resident status for failure to file petition or have personal interview

(A) In general

In the case of an alien with permanent resident status on a conditional basis under subsection (a), if—

(i) no petition is filed with respect to the alien in accordance with the provisions of paragraph (1)(A), or

(ii) unless there is good cause shown, the alien spouse and petitioning spouse fail to appear at the interview described in paragraph (1)(B),

the Secretary of Homeland Security shall terminate the permanent resident status of the alien as of the second anniversary of the alien's lawful admission for permanent residence.

(B) Hearing in removal proceeding

In any removal proceeding with respect to an alien whose permanent resident status is terminated under subparagraph (A), the burden of proof shall be on the alien to establish compliance with the conditions of paragraphs (1)(A) and (1)(B).

(3) Determination after petition and interview

(A) In general

If—

(i) a petition is filed in accordance with the provisions of paragraph (1)(A), and

(ii) the alien spouse and petitioning spouse appear at the interview described in paragraph (1)(B),

the Secretary of Homeland Security shall make a determination, within 90 days of the date of the interview, as to whether the facts and information described in subsection (d)(1) of this section and alleged in the petition are true with respect to the qualifying marriage.

(B) Removal of conditional basis if favorable determination

If the Secretary of Homeland Security determines that such facts and information are true, the Secretary of Homeland Security shall so notify the parties involved and shall remove the conditional basis of the parties effective as of the second anniversary of the alien's obtaining the status of lawful admission for permanent residence.

(C) Termination if adverse determination

If the Secretary of Homeland Security determines that such facts and information are not true, the Secretary of Homeland Security shall so notify the parties involved and, subject to subparagraph (D), shall terminate the permanent resident status of an alien spouse or an alien son or daughter as of the date of the determination.

(D) Hearing in removal proceeding

Any alien whose permanent resident status is terminated under subparagraph (C) may request a review of such determination in a proceeding to remove the alien. In such proceeding, the burden of proof shall be on the Secretary of Homeland Security to establish, by a preponderance of the evidence, that the facts and information described in subsection (d)(1) of this section and alleged in the petition are not true with respect to the qualifying marriage.

(4) Hardship waiver

The Secretary of Homeland Security, in the Secretary's discretion, may remove the conditional basis of the permanent resident status for an alien who fails to meet the requirements of paragraph (1) if the alien demonstrates that—

(A) extreme hardship would result if such alien is removed;

(B) the qualifying marriage was entered into in good faith by the alien spouse, but the qualifying marriage has been terminated (other than through the death of the spouse) and the alien was not at fault in failing to meet the requirements of paragraph (1); or

(C) the qualifying marriage was entered into in good faith by the alien spouse and during the marriage the alien spouse or child was battered by or was the subject of extreme cruelty perpetrated by his or her spouse or citizen or permanent resident parent and the alien was not at fault in failing to meet the requirements of paragraph (1); or

(D) the alien meets the requirements under section 204(a)(1)(A)(iii)(II)(aa)(BB) [8 U.S.C.A. § 1154(a)(1)(A)(iii)(II)(aa) (BB)] and following the marriage ceremony was battered by or subject to extreme cruelty perpetrated by the alien's intended spouse and was not at fault in failing to meet the requirements of paragraph (1).

In determining extreme hardship, the Secretary of Homeland Security shall consider circumstances occurring only during the period that the alien was admitted for permanent residence on a conditional basis. In acting on applications under this paragraph, the Secretary of Homeland Security shall consider any credible evidence relevant to the application. The determination of what evidence is credible and the weight to be given that evidence shall be within the sole discretion of the Secretary of Homeland Security. The Secretary of Homeland Security shall, by regulation, establish measures to protect the confidentiality of information concerning any abused alien spouse or child, including information regarding the whereabouts of such spouse or child.

(d) Details of petition and interview

(1) Contents of petition

Each petition under subsection (c)(1)(A) shall contain the following facts and information:

(A) Statement of proper marriage and petitioning process

The facts are that—

(i) the qualifying marriage—

(I) was entered into in accordance with the laws of the place where the marriage took place,

(II) has not been judicially annulled or terminated, other than through the death of a spouse, and

(III) was not entered into for the purpose of procuring an alien's admission as an immigrant; and

(ii) no fee or other consideration was given (other than a fee or other consideration to an attorney for assistance in preparation of a lawful petition) for the filing of a petition under section 204(a) [8 U.S.C.A. § 1154(a)] or subsection (d) or (p) of section 214 [8 U.S.C.A. § 1184] with respect to the alien spouse or alien son or daughter.

(B) Statement of additional information

The information is a statement of—

(i) the actual residence of each party to the qualifying marriage since the date the alien spouse obtained permanent resident status on a conditional basis under subsection (a), and

(ii) the place of employment (if any) of each such party since such date, and the name of the employer of such party.

(2) Period for filing petition

(A) 90-day period before second anniversary

Except as provided in subparagraph (B), the petition under subsection (c)(1)(A) must be filed during the 90-day period before the second anniversary of the alien's obtaining the status of lawful admission for permanent residence.

(B) Date petitions for good cause*

Such a petition may be considered if filed after such date, but only if the alien establishes to the satisfaction of the Secretary of Homeland Security good cause and extenuating circumstances for failure to file the petition during the period described in subparagraph (A).

(C) Filing of petitions during removal

In the case of an alien who is the subject of removal hearings as a result of failure to file a petition on a timely basis in accordance with subparagraph (A), the Secretary of Homeland Security may stay such removal proceedings against an alien pending the filing of the petition under subparagraph (B).

(3) Personal interview

The interview under subsection (c)(1)(B) of this section shall be conducted within 90 days after the date of submitting a petition under subsection (c)(1)(A) of this section and at a local office of the Department of Homeland Security, designated by the Secretary of Homeland Security, which is convenient to the parties involved. The Secretary of Homeland Security, in the Secretary's discretion, may waive the deadline for such an interview or the requirement for such an interview in such cases as may be appropriate.

(e) Treatment of period for purposes of naturalization

For purposes of title III, in the case of an alien who is in the United States as a lawful permanent resident on a conditional basis under this section, the alien shall be considered to have been admitted as an alien lawfully admitted for permanent residence and to be in the United States as an alien lawfully admitted to the United States for permanent residence.

(f) Treatment of certain waivers

* So in original.

In the case of an alien who has permanent residence status on a conditional basis under this section, if, in order to obtain such status, the alien obtained a waiver under subsection (h) or (i) of section 212 [8 U.S.C.A. § 1182] of certain grounds of inadmissibility, such waiver terminates upon the termination of such permanent residence status under this section.

(g) Service in armed forces

(1) Filing petition

The 90-day period described in subsection (d)(2)(A) shall be tolled during any period of time in which the alien spouse or petitioning spouse is a member of the Armed Forces of the United States and serving abroad in an active-duty status in the Armed Forces, except that, at the option of the petitioners, the petition may be filed during such active-duty service at any time after the commencement of such 90-day period.

(2) Personal interview

The 90-day period described in the first sentence of subsection (d)(3) shall be tolled during any period of time in which the alien spouse or petitioning spouse is a member of the Armed Forces of the United States and serving abroad in an active-duty status in the Armed Forces, except that nothing in this paragraph shall be construed to prohibit the Secretary of Homeland Security from waiving the requirement for an interview under subsection (c)(1)(B) pursuant to the Secretary's authority under the second sentence of subsection (d)(3).

(h) Definitions

In this section:

(1) The term "alien spouse" means an alien who obtains the status of an alien lawfully admitted for permanent residence (whether on a conditional basis or otherwise)—

    (A) as an immediate relative (described in section 201(b) [8 U.S.C.A. § 1151(b)]) as the spouse of a citizen of the United States,

    (B) under section 214(d) [8 U.S.C.A. § 1184(d)] as the fiancée or fiancé of a citizen of the United States, or

    (C) under section 203(a)(2) [8 U.S.C.A. § 1153(a)(2)] as the spouse of an alien lawfully admitted for permanent residence,

by virtue of a marriage which was entered into less than 24 months before the date the alien obtains such status by virtue of such marriage, but does not include such an alien who only obtains such status as a result of section 203(d) [8 U.S.C.A. § 1153(d)].

(2) The term "alien son or daughter" means an alien who obtains the status of an alien lawfully admitted for permanent residence (whether on a conditional basis or otherwise) by virtue of being the son or daughter of an individual through a qualifying marriage.

(3) The term "qualifying marriage" means the marriage described to [sic] in paragraph (1).

(4) The term "petitioning spouse" means the spouse of a qualifying marriage, other than the alien.

(June 27, 1952, c. 477, Title II, ch. 2, § 216, as added Nov. 6, 1986, Pub.L. 99–639, § 2(a), 100 Stat. 3537, and amended Oct. 24, 1988, Pub.L. 100–525, § 7(a)(1), 102 Stat. 2616; Oct. 24, 1988, Pub.L. 100–525, § 7(a)(2), 102 Stat. 2616; Nov. 29, 1990, Pub.L. 101–649, Title VII, § 701(a), 104 Stat. 5085; Dec.12, 1991, Pub.L. 102–232, Title III, § 302(e)(8)(B), 105 Stat. 1746; Sept. 13, 1994, Pub.L. 103–322, Title IV, § 40702(a), 108 Stat. 1955; Sept. 30, 1996, Pub.L. 104–208, Div. C, Title III, § 308(d)(4)(E), (e)(7), (f)(1)(I), (J), 110 Stat. 3009–618, 3009–620, 3009–621; Dec. 21, 2000, Pub.L. 106–553, § 1(a)(2) [Title XI, § 1103(c)(2)], 114 Stat. 2762; Pub.L. 112–58, § 1, Nov. 23, 2011, 125 Stat. 747; Pub.L. 113–4, Title VIII, § 806, Mar. 7, 2013, 127 Stat. 112.)

§ 216A. Conditional permanent resident status for certain alien entrepreneurs, spouses, and children [8 U.S.C.A. § 1186b]

(a) In general

(1) Conditional basis for status

Notwithstanding any other provision of this Act, an alien entrepreneur (as defined in subsection (f)(1) of this section), alien spouse, and alien child (as defined in subsection (f)(2) of this section) shall be considered, at the time of obtaining the status of an alien lawfully admitted for permanent residence, to have obtained such status on a conditional basis subject to the provisions of this section.

(2) Notice of requirements

(A) At time of obtaining permanent residence

At the time an alien entrepreneur, alien spouse, or alien child obtains permanent resident status on a conditional basis under paragraph (1), the Attorney General shall provide for notice to such an entrepreneur, spouse, or child respecting the provisions of this section and the requirements of subsection (c)(1) to have the conditional basis of such status removed.

(B) At time of required petition

In addition, the Attorney General shall attempt to provide notice to such an entrepreneur, spouse, or child, at or about the beginning of the 90-day period described in subsection (d)(2)(A), of the requirements of subsection (c)(1).

(C) Effect of failure to provide notice

The failure of the Attorney General to provide a notice under this paragraph shall not affect the enforcement of the provisions of this section with respect to such an entrepreneur, spouse, or child.

(b) Termination of status if finding that qualifying entrepreneurship improper

(1) In general

In the case of an alien entrepreneur with permanent resident status on a conditional basis under subsection (a), if the Attorney General determines, before the second anniversary of the alien's obtaining the status of lawful admission for permanent residence, that—

(A) the investment in the commercial enterprise was intended solely as a means of evading the immigration laws of the United States,

(B)(i) the alien did not invest, or was not actively in the process of investing, the requisite capital; or

(ii) the alien was not sustaining the actions described in clause (i) throughout the period of the alien's residence in the United States; or

(C) the alien was otherwise not conforming to the requirements of section 203(b)(5) [8 U.S.C.A. § 1153(b)(5)],

then the Attorney General shall so notify the alien involved and, subject to paragraph (2), shall terminate the permanent resident status of the alien (and the alien spouse and alien child) involved as of the date of the determination.

(2) Hearing in removal proceeding

Any alien whose permanent resident status is terminated under paragraph (1) may request a review of such determination in a proceeding to remove the alien. In such proceeding, the burden of proof shall be on the Attorney General to establish, by a preponderance of the evidence, that a condition described in paragraph (1) is met.

(c) Requirements of timely petition and interview for removal of condition

(1) In general

In order for the conditional basis established under subsection (a) for an alien entrepreneur, alien spouse, or alien child to be removed—

(A) the alien entrepreneur must submit to the Attorney General, during the period described in subsection (d)(2), a petition which requests the removal of such conditional basis and which states, under penalty of perjury, the facts and information described in subsection (d)(1), and

(B) in accordance with subsection (d)(3) of this section, the alien entrepreneur must appear for a personal interview before an officer or employee of the Service respecting the facts and information described in subsection (d)(1) of this section.

(2) Termination of permanent resident status for failure to file petition or have personal interview

(A) In general

In the case of an alien with permanent resident status on a conditional basis under subsection (a), if—

(i) no petition is filed with respect to the alien in accordance with the provisions of paragraph (1)(A), or

(ii) unless there is good cause shown, the alien entrepreneur fails to appear at the interview described in paragraph (1)(B) (if required under subsection (d)(3)),

the Attorney General shall terminate the permanent resident status of the alien (and the alien's spouse and children if it was obtained on a conditional basis under this section or section 216 [8 U.S.C.A. § 1186a]) as of the second anniversary of the alien's lawful admission for permanent residence.

(B) Hearing in removal proceeding

In any removal proceeding with respect to an alien whose permanent resident status is terminated under subparagraph (A), the burden of proof shall be on the alien to establish compliance with the conditions of paragraphs (1)(A) and (1)(B).

(3) Determination after petition and interview

(A) In general

If—

(i) a petition is filed in accordance with the provisions of paragraph (1)(A), and

(ii) the alien entrepreneur appears at any interview described in paragraph (1)(B),

the Attorney General shall make a determination, within 90 days of the date of the such filing or interview (whichever is later), as to whether the facts and information described in subsection (d)(1) and alleged in the petition are true with respect to the qualifying commercial enterprise.

(B) Removal of conditional basis if favorable determination

If the Attorney General determines that such facts and information are true, the Attorney General shall so notify the alien involved and shall remove the conditional basis of the alien's status effective as of the second anniversary of the alien's lawful admission for permanent residence.

(C) Termination if adverse determination

If the Attorney General determines that such facts and information are not true, the Attorney General shall so notify the alien involved and, subject to subparagraph (D), shall terminate the permanent resident status of an alien entrepreneur, alien spouse, or alien child as of the date of the determination.

(D) Hearing in removal proceeding

Any alien whose permanent resident status is terminated under subparagraph (C) may request a review of such determination in a proceeding to remove the alien. In such proceeding, the burden of proof shall be on the Attorney General to establish, by a preponderance of the evidence, that the facts and information described in subsection (d)(1) and alleged in the petition are not true with respect to the qualifying commercial enterprise.

(d) Details of petition and interview

(1) Contents of petition

Each petition under subsection (c)(1)(A) of this section shall contain facts and information demonstrating that the alien—

(A)(i) invested, or is actively in the process of investing, the requisite capital; and

(ii) sustained the actions described in clause (i) throughout the period of the alien's residence in the United States; and

(B) is otherwise conforming to the requirements of section 203(b) (5) [8 U.S.C.A. § 1153(b)(5)].

(2) Period for filing petition

(A) 90-day period before second anniversary

Except as provided in subparagraph (B), the petition under subsection (c)(1)(A) must be filed during the 90-day period before the second anniversary of the alien's lawful admission for permanent residence.

(B) Date petitions for good cause*

Such a petition may be considered if filed after such date, but only if the alien establishes to the satisfaction of the Attorney General good cause and extenuating circumstances for failure to file the petition during the period described in subparagraph (A).

(C) Filing of petitions during removal

In the case of an alien who is the subject of removal hearings as a result of failure to file a petition on a timely basis in accordance with subparagraph (A), the Attorney General may stay such removal proceedings against an alien pending the filing of the petition under subparagraph (B).

(3) Personal interview

The interview under subsection (c)(1)(B) of this section shall be conducted within 90 days after the date of submitting a petition under subsection (c)(1)(A) of this section and at a local office of the Service, designated by the Attorney General, which is convenient to the parties involved. The Attorney General, in the Attorney General's discretion,

---

* So in original.

may waive the deadline for such an interview or the requirement for such an interview in such cases as may be appropriate.

(e) Treatment of period for purposes of naturalization

For purposes of title III, in the case of an alien who is in the United States as a lawful permanent resident on a conditional basis under this section, the alien shall be considered to have been admitted as an alien lawfully admitted for permanent residence and to be in the United States as an alien lawfully admitted to the United States for permanent residence.

(f) Definitions

In this section:

(1) The term "alien entrepreneur" means an alien who obtains the status of an alien lawfully admitted for permanent residence (whether on a conditional basis or otherwise) under section 203(b)(5) [8 U.S.C.A. § 1153(b)(5)].

(2) The term "alien spouse" and the term "alien child" mean an alien who obtains the status of an alien lawfully admitted for permanent residence (whether on a conditional basis or otherwise) by virtue of being the spouse or child, respectively, of an alien entrepreneur.

(3) The term "commercial enterprise" includes a limited partnership.

(June 27, 1952, c. 477, Title II, ch. 2, § 216A, as added Nov. 29, 1990, Pub.L. 101–649, Title I, § 121(b)(1), 104 Stat. 4990, and amended Dec. 12, 1991, Pub.L. 102–232, Title III, § 302(b)(3), 105 Stat. 1743; Sept. 30, 1996, Pub.L. 104–208, Div. C, Title III, § 308(e)(8), 110 Stat. 3009–620; Nov. 2, 2002, Pub.L. 107–273, Div. C, Title I, § 11036(b), 116 Stat. 1847.)

§ 217.   Visa waiver program for certain visitors [8 U.S.C.A. § 1187]

(a) Establishment of program

The Secretary of Homeland Security and the Secretary of State are authorized to establish a program (hereinafter in this section referred to as the "program") under which the requirement of paragraph (7)(B)(i)(II) of section 212(a) [8 U.S.C.A. § 1182(a)] may be waived by the Secretary of Homeland Security, in consultation with the Secretary of State and in accordance with this section, in the case of an alien who meets the following requirements:

(1) Seeking entry as tourist for 90 days or less

The alien is applying for admission during the program as a nonimmigrant visitor (described in section 101(a)(15)(B) [8 U.S.C.A. § 1101(a)(15)(B)]) for a period not exceeding 90 days.

(2) National of program country

The alien is a national of, and presents a passport issued by, a country which—

(A) extends (or agrees to extend), either on its own or in conjunction with one or more other countries that are described in subparagraph (B) and that have established with it a common area for immigration admissions, reciprocal privileges to citizens and nationals of the United States, and

(B) is designated as a pilot [sic] program country under subsection (c) of this section.

(3) Passport requirements

The alien, at the time of application for admission, is in possession of a valid unexpired passport that satisfies the following:

(A) Machine readable

The passport is a machine-readable passport that is tamper-resistant, incorporates document authentication identifiers, and otherwise satisfies the internationally accepted standard for machine readability.

(B) Electronic

Beginning on April 1, 2016, the passport is an electronic passport that is fraud-resistant, contains relevant biographic and biometric information (as determined by the Secretary of Homeland Security), and otherwise satisfies internationally accepted standards for electronic passports.

(4) Executes immigration forms

The alien before the time of such admission completes such immigration form as the Secretary of Homeland Security shall establish.

(5) Entry into the United States

If arriving by sea or air, the alien arrives at the port of entry into the United States on a carrier, including any carrier conducting operations under part 135 of Title 14, Code of Federal Regulations, or a noncommercial aircraft that is owned or operated by a domestic corporation conducting operations under part 91 of Title 14, Code of Federal Regulations* which has entered into an agreement with the Secretary of Homeland Security pursuant to subsection (e) of this section. The Secretary of Homeland Security is authorized to require a carrier conducting operations under part 135 of Title 14, Code of Federal Regulations, or a domestic corporation conducting operations under part 91 of that title, to give suitable and proper bond, in such reasonable amount and containing such conditions as the Secretary of Homeland Security may deem sufficient to ensure compliance with the indemnification requirements of this section, as a term of such an agreement.

(6) Not a safety threat

---

* So in original. Probably should be followed by a comma.

The alien has been determined not to represent a threat to the welfare, health, safety, or security of the United States.

(7) No previous violation

If the alien previously was admitted without a visa under this section, the alien must not have failed to comply with the conditions of any previous admission as such a nonimmigrant.

(8) Round-trip ticket

The alien is in possession of a round-trip transportation ticket (unless this requirement is waived by the Secretary of Homeland Security under regulations or the alien is arriving at the port of entry on an aircraft operated under part 135 of title 14, Code of Federal Regulations, or a noncommercial aircraft that is owned or operated by a domestic corporation conducting operations under part 91 of title 14, Code of Federal Regulations).

(9) Automated system check

The identity of the alien has been checked using an automated electronic database containing information about the inadmissibility of aliens to uncover any grounds on which the alien may be inadmissible to the United States, and no such ground has been found.

(10) Electronic transmission of identification information

Operators of aircraft under part 135 of title 14, Code of Federal Regulations, or operators of noncommercial aircraft that are owned or operated by a domestic corporation conducting operations under part 91 of title 14, Code of Federal Regulations, carrying any alien passenger who will apply for admission under this section shall furnish such information as the Secretary of Homeland Security by regulation shall prescribe as necessary for the identification of any alien passenger being transported and for the enforcement of the immigration laws. Such information shall be electronically transmitted not less than one hour prior to arrival at the port of entry for purposes of checking for inadmissibility using the automated electronic database.

(11) Eligibility determination under the electronic system for travel authorization

Beginning on the date on which the electronic system for travel authorization developed under subsection (h)(3) of this section is fully operational, each alien traveling under the program shall, before applying for admission to the United States, electronically provide to the system biographical information and such other information as the Secretary of Homeland Security shall determine necessary to determine the eligibility of, and whether there exists a law enforcement or security risk in permitting, the alien to travel to the United States. Upon review of such biographical information, the Secretary of Homeland Security shall determine whether the alien is eligible to travel to the United States under the program.

(12) Not present in Iraq, Syria, or any other country or area of concern

(A) In general

Except as provided in subparagraphs (B) and (C)—

(i) the alien has not been present, at any time on or after March 1, 2011—

(I) in Iraq or Syria;

(II) in a country that is designated by the Secretary of State under section 4605(j) of Title 50 (as continued in effect under the International Emergency Economic Powers Act (50 U.S.C. 1701 et seq.)), section 2780 of Title 22, section 2371 of Title 22, or any other provision of law, as a country, the government of which has repeatedly provided support of acts of international terrorism; or

(III) in any other country or area of concern designated by the Secretary of Homeland Security under subparagraph (D); and

(ii) regardless of whether the alien is a national of a program country, the alien is not a national of—

(I) Iraq or Syria;

(II) a country that is designated, at the time the alien applies for admission, by the Secretary of State under section 4605(j) of Title 50 (as continued in effect under the International Emergency Economic Powers Act (50 U.S.C. 1701 et seq.)), section 2780 of Title 22, section 2371 of Title 22, or any other provision of law, as a country, the government of which has repeatedly provided support of acts of international terrorism; or

(III) any other country that is designated, at the time the alien applies for admission, by the Secretary of Homeland Security under subparagraph (D).

(B) Certain military personnel and Government employees

Subparagraph (A)(i) shall not apply in the case of an alien if the Secretary of Homeland Security determines that the alien was present—

(i) in order to perform military service in the armed forces of a program country; or

(ii) in order to carry out official duties as a full time employee of the government of a program country.

(C) Waiver

The Secretary of Homeland Security may waive the application of subparagraph (A) to an alien if the Secretary determines that such a waiver is in the law enforcement or national security interests of the United States.

(D) Countries or areas of concern

(i) In general

Not later than 60 days after December 18, 2015, the Secretary of Homeland Security, in consultation with the Secretary of State and the Director of National Intelligence, shall determine whether the requirement under subparagraph (A) shall apply to any other country or area.

(ii) Criteria

In making a determination under clause (i), the Secretary shall consider—

(I) whether the presence of an alien in the country or area increases the likelihood that the alien is a credible threat to the national security of the United States;

(II) whether a foreign terrorist organization has a significant presence in the country or area; and

(III) whether the country or area is a safe haven for terrorists.

(iii) Annual review

The Secretary shall conduct a review, on an annual basis, of any determination made under clause (i).

(E) Report

Beginning not later than one year after December 18, 2015, and annually thereafter, the Secretary of Homeland Security shall submit to the Committee on Homeland Security, the Committee on Foreign Affairs, the Permanent Select Committee on Intelligence, and the Committee on the Judiciary of the House of Representatives, and the Committee on Homeland Security and Governmental Affairs, the Committee on Foreign Relations, the Select Committee on Intelligence, and the Committee on the Judiciary of the Senate a report on each instance in which the Secretary exercised the waiver authority under subparagraph (C) during the previous year.

(b) Waiver of rights

An alien may not be provided a waiver under the program unless the alien has waived any right—

(1) to review or appeal under this Act of an immigration officer's determination as to the admissibility of the alien at the port of entry into the United States, or

(2) to contest, other than on the basis of an application for asylum, any action for removal of the alien.

(c) Designation of program countries

(1) In general

The Secretary of Homeland Security, in consultation with the Secretary of State, may designate any country as a program country if it meets the requirements of paragraph (2).

(2) Qualifications

Except as provided in subsection (f), a country may not be designated as a program country unless the following requirements are met:

(A) Low nonimmigrant visa refusal rate—Either—

(i) the average number of refusals of nonimmigrant visitor visas for nationals of that country during—

(I) the two previous full fiscal years was less than 2.0 percent of the total number of nonimmigrant visitor visas for nationals of that country which were granted or refused during those years; and

(II) either of such two previous full fiscal years was less than 2.5 percent of the total number of nonimmigrant visitor visas for nationals of that country which were granted or refused during that year; or

(ii) such refusal rate for nationals of that country during the previous full fiscal year was less than 3.0 percent.

(B) Passport program

(i) Issuance of passports

The government of the country certifies that it issues to its citizens passports described in subparagraph (A) of subsection (a)(3), and on or after April 1, 2016, passports described in subparagraph (B) of subsection (a)(3).

(ii) Validation of passports

Not later than October 1, 2016, the government of the country certifies that it has in place mechanisms to validate passports described in subparagraphs (A) and (B) of subsection (a)(3) at each key port of entry into that country. This requirement shall not apply to travel between countries which fall within the Schengen Zone.

(C) Law enforcement and security interests

The Secretary of Homeland Security, in consultation with the Secretary of State—

(i) evaluates the effect that the country's designation would have on the law enforcement and security interests of the United States (including the interest in enforcement of the immigration laws of the United States and the existence and effectiveness of its agreements and procedures for extraditing to the United States individuals, including its own nationals, who commit crimes that violate United States law);

(ii) determines that such interests would not be compromised by the designation of the country; and

(iii) submits a written report to the Committee on the Judiciary, the Committee on Foreign Affairs, and the Committee on Homeland Security of the House of Representatives and the Committee on the Judiciary, the Committee on Foreign Relations, and the Committee on Homeland Security and Governmental Affairs of the Senate regarding the country's qualification for designation that includes an explanation of such determination.

(D) Reporting lost and stolen passports

The government of the country enters into an agreement with the United States to report, or make available through Interpol or other means as designated by the Secretary of Homeland Security, to the United States Government information about the theft or loss of passports not later than 24 hours after becoming aware of the theft or loss and in a manner specified in the agreement.

(E) Repatriation of aliens

The government of the country accepts for repatriation any citizen, former citizen, or national of the country against whom a final executable order of removal is issued not later than three weeks after the issuance of the final order of removal. Nothing in this subparagraph creates any duty for the United States or any right for any alien with respect to removal or release. Nothing in this subparagraph gives rise to any cause of action or claim under this paragraph or any other law against any official of the United States or of any State to compel the release, removal, or consideration for release or removal of any alien.

(F) Passenger information exchange

The government of the country enters into an agreement with the United States to share information regarding whether citizens and nationals of that country traveling to the United States represent a threat to the security or welfare of the United States or its citizens, and fully implements such agreement.

(G) Interpol screening

Not later than 270 days after December 18, 2015, except in the case of a country in which there is not an international airport, the government of the country certifies to the Secretary of Homeland Security that, to the maximum extent allowed under the laws of the country, it is screening, for unlawful activity, each person who is not a citizen or national of that country who is admitted to or departs that country, by using relevant databases and notices maintained by Interpol, or other means designated by the Secretary of Homeland Security. This requirement shall not apply to travel between countries which fall within the Schengen Zone.

(3) Continuing and subsequent qualifications

For each fiscal year after the initial period—

(A) Continuing qualification

In the case of a country which was a program country in the previous fiscal year, a country may not be designated as a program country unless the sum of—

(i) the total of the number of nationals of that country who were denied admission at the time of arrival or withdrew their application for admission during such previous fiscal year as a nonimmigrant visitor, and

(ii) the total number of nationals of that country who were admitted as nonimmigrant visitors during such previous fiscal year and who violated the terms of such admission,

was less than 2 percent of the total number of nationals of that country who applied for admission as nonimmigrant visitors during such previous fiscal year.

(B) New countries

In the case of another country, the country may not be designated as a program country unless the following requirements are met:

(i) Low nonimmigrant visa refusal rate in previous 2-year period

The average number of refusals of nonimmigrant visitor visas for nationals of that country during the two previous full fiscal years was less than 2 percent of the total number of nonimmigrant visitor visas for nationals of that country which were granted or refused during those years.

(ii) Low nonimmigrant visa refusal rate in each of the 2 previous years

The average number of refusals of nonimmigrant visitor visas for nationals of that country during either of such two previous full fiscal years was less than 2.5 percent of the total number of nonimmigrant visitor visas for nationals of that country which were granted or refused during that year.

(4) Initial period

For purposes of paragraphs (2) and (3), the term "initial period" means the period beginning at the end of the 30-day period described in subsection (b)(1) [sic] of this section and ending on the last day of the first fiscal year which begins after such 30-day period.

(5) Written reports on continuing qualification; designation terminations

(A) Periodic evaluations

(i) In general

The Secretary of Homeland Security, in consultation with the Secretary of State, periodically (but not less than once every 2 years)—

(I) shall evaluate the effect of each program country's continued designation on the law enforcement and security interests of the United States (including the interest in enforcement of the immigration laws of the United States and the existence and effectiveness of its agreements and procedures for extraditing to the United States individuals, including its own nationals, who commit crimes that violate United States law);

(II) shall determine, based upon the evaluation in subclause (I), whether any such designation ought to be continued or terminated under subsection (d);

(III) shall submit a written report to the Committee on the Judiciary, the Committee on Foreign Affairs, the Permanent Select Committee on Intelligence, and the Committee on Homeland Security, of the House of Representatives and the Committee on the Judiciary, the Committee on Foreign Relations, the Select Committee on Intelligence and the Committee on Homeland Security and Governmental Affairs of the Senate regarding the continuation or termination of the country's designation that includes an explanation of such determination and the effects described in subclause (I);

(IV) shall submit to Congress a report regarding the implementation of the electronic system for travel authorization under subsection (h)(3) of this section and the participation of new countries in the program through a waiver under paragraph (8); and

(V) shall submit to the committees described in subclause (III), a report that includes an assessment of the threat to the national security of the United States of the designation of each country designated as a program country, including the compliance of the government of each such country with the requirements under subparagraphs (D) and (F) of paragraph (2), as well as each such government's capacity to comply with such requirements.

(ii) Effective date

A termination of the designation of a country under this subparagraph shall take effect on the date determined by the Secretary of Homeland Security, in consultation with the Secretary of State.

(iii) Redesignation

In the case of a termination under this subparagraph, the Secretary of Homeland Security shall redesignate the country as a program country, without regard to subsection (f) or paragraph (2) or (3), when the Secretary of Homeland Security, in consultation with the Secretary of State, determines that all causes of the termination have been eliminated.

(B) Emergency termination

(i) In general

In the case of a program country in which an emergency occurs that the Secretary of Homeland Security, in consultation with the Secretary of State, determines threatens the law enforcement or security interests of the United States (including the interest in enforcement of the immigration laws of the United States), the Secretary of Homeland Security shall immediately terminate the designation of the country as a program country.

(ii) Definition

For purposes of clause (i), the term "emergency" means—

(I) the overthrow of a democratically elected government;

(II) war (including undeclared war, civil war, or other military activity) on the territory of the program country;

(III) a severe breakdown in law and order affecting a significant portion of the program country's territory;

(IV) a severe economic collapse in the program country; or

(V) any other extraordinary event in the program country that threatens the law enforcement or security interests of the United States (including the interest in enforcement of the immigration laws of the United States) and where the country's participation in the program could contribute to that threat.

(iii) Redesignation

The Secretary of Homeland Security may redesignate the country as a program country, without regard to subsection (f) or paragraph (2) or (3), when the Secretary of Homeland Security, in consultation with the Secretary of State, determines that—

(I) at least 6 months have elapsed since the effective date of the termination;

(II) the emergency that caused the termination has ended; and

(III) the average number of refusals of nonimmigrant visitor visas for nationals of that country during the period of termination under this subparagraph was less than 3.0 percent of the total number of nonimmigrant visitor visas for nationals of that country which were granted or refused during such period.

(iv) Program suspension authority

The Director of National Intelligence shall immediately inform the Secretary of Homeland Security of any current and credible threat which poses an imminent danger to the United States or its citizens and originates from a country participating in the visa waiver program. Upon receiving such notification, the Secretary, in consultation with the Secretary of State—

(I) may suspend a country from the visa waiver program without prior notice;

(II) shall notify any country suspended under subclause (I) and, to the extent practicable without disclosing sensitive intelligence sources and methods, provide justification for the suspension; and

(III) shall restore the suspended country's participation in the visa waiver program upon a determination that the threat no longer poses an imminent danger to the United States or its citizens.

(C) Treatment of nationals after termination

For purposes of this paragraph—

(i) nationals of a country whose designation is terminated under subparagraph (A) or (B) shall remain eligible for a waiver under subsection (a) until the effective date of such termination; and

(ii) a waiver under this section that is provided to such a national for a period described in subsection (a)(1) shall not, by such termination, be deemed to have been rescinded or otherwise rendered invalid, if the waiver is granted prior to such termination.

(6) Computation of visa refusal rates

For purposes of determining the eligibility of a country to be designated as a program country, the calculation of visa refusal rates shall not include any visa refusals which incorporate any procedures based on, or are otherwise based on, race, sex, or disability, unless otherwise specifically authorized by law or regulation. No court shall have jurisdiction under this paragraph to review any visa refusal, the denial of admission to the United States of any alien by the Secretary of Homeland Security, the Secretary's computation of the visa refusal rate, or the designation or nondesignation of any country.

(7) Visa waiver information

(A) In general

In refusing the application of nationals of a program country for United States visas, or the applications of nationals of a country seeking entry into the visa waiver program, a consular officer shall not knowingly or intentionally classify the refusal of the visa under a category that is not included in the calculation of the visa refusal rate only so that the percentage of that country's visa refusals is less than the percentage limitation applicable to qualification for participation in the visa waiver program.

(B) Reporting requirement

On May 1 of each year, for each country under consideration for inclusion in the visa waiver program, the Secretary of State shall provide to the appropriate congressional committees—

(i) the total number of nationals of that country that applied for United States visas in that country during the previous calendar year;

(ii) the total number of such nationals who received United States visas during the previous calendar year;

(iii) the total number of such nationals who were refused United States visas during the previous calendar year;

(iv) the total number of such nationals who were refused United States visas during the previous calendar year under each provision of this Act under which the visas were refused; and

(v) the number of such nationals that were refused under section 214(b) [8 U.S.C.A. § 1184(b)] as a percentage of the visas that were issued to such nationals.

(C) Certification

Not later than May 1 of each year, the United States chief of mission, acting or permanent, to each country under consideration for inclusion in the visa waiver program shall certify to the appropriate congressional committees that the information described in subparagraph (B) is accurate and provide a copy of that certification to those committees.

(D) Consideration of countries in the visa waiver program

Upon notification to the Secretary of Homeland Security that a country is under consideration for inclusion in the visa waiver program, the Secretary of State shall provide all of the information described in subparagraph (B) to the Secretary of Homeland Security.

(E) Definition

In this paragraph, the term "appropriate congressional committees" means the Committee on the Judiciary and the Committee on

Foreign Relations of the Senate and the Committee on the Judiciary and the Committee on International Relations of the House of Representatives.

(8) Nonimmigrant visa refusal rate flexibility

(A) Certification

(i) In general

On the date on which an air exit system is in place that can verify the departure of not less than 97 percent of foreign nationals who exit through airports of the United States and the electronic system for travel authorization required under subsection (h)(3) of this section is fully operational, the Secretary of Homeland Security shall certify to Congress that such air exit system and electronic system for travel authorization are in place.

(ii) Notification to Congress

The Secretary shall notify Congress in writing of the date on which the air exit system under clause (i) fully satisfies the biometric requirements specified in subsection (i) of this section.

(iii) Temporary suspension of waiver authority

Notwithstanding any certification made under clause (i), if the Secretary has not notified Congress in accordance with clause (ii) by June 30, 2009, the Secretary's waiver authority under subparagraph (B) shall be suspended beginning on July 1, 2009, until such time as the Secretary makes such notification.

(iv) Rule of construction

Nothing in this paragraph shall be construed as in any way abrogating the reporting requirements under subsection (i)(3) of this section.

(B) Waiver

After certification by the Secretary under subparagraph (A), the Secretary, in consultation with the Secretary of State, may waive the application of paragraph (2)(A) for a country if—

(i) the country meets all security requirements of this section;

(ii) the Secretary of Homeland Security determines that the totality of the country's security risk mitigation measures provide assurance that the country's participation in the program would not compromise the law enforcement, security interests, or enforcement of the immigration laws of the United States;

(iii) there has been a sustained reduction in the rate of refusals for nonimmigrant visas for nationals of the country and conditions exist to continue such reduction;

(iv) the country cooperated with the Government of the United States on counterterrorism initiatives, information sharing, and preventing terrorist travel before the date of its designation as a program country, and the Secretary of Homeland Security and the Secretary of State determine that such cooperation will continue; and

(v)(I) the rate of refusals for nonimmigrant visitor visas for nationals of the country during the previous full fiscal year was not more than ten percent; or

(II) the visa overstay rate for the country for the previous full fiscal year does not exceed the maximum visa overstay rate, once such rate is established under subparagraph (C).

(C) Maximum visa overstay rate

(i) Requirement to establish

After certification by the Secretary under subparagraph (A), the Secretary and the Secretary of State jointly shall use information from the air exit system referred to in such subparagraph to establish a maximum visa overstay rate for countries participating in the program pursuant to a waiver under subparagraph (B). The Secretary of Homeland Security shall certify to Congress that such rate would not compromise the law enforcement, security interests, or enforcement of the immigration laws of the United States.

(ii) Visa overstay rate defined

In this paragraph the term "visa overstay rate" means, with respect to a country, the ratio of—

(I) the total number of nationals of that country who were admitted to the United States on the basis of a nonimmigrant visa whose periods of authorized stays ended during a fiscal year but who remained unlawfully in the United States beyond such periods; to

(II) the total number of nationals of that country who were admitted to the United States on the basis of a nonimmigrant visa during that fiscal year.

(iii) Report and publication

The Secretary of Homeland Security shall on the same date submit to Congress and publish in the Federal Register information relating to the maximum visa overstay rate established under clause (i). Not later than 60 days after such date, the Secretary shall issue a final maximum visa overstay rate above which a country may not participate in the program.

(9) Discretionary security-related considerations

In determining whether to waive the application of paragraph (2)(A) for a country, pursuant to paragraph (8), the Secretary of Homeland Security, in consultation with the Secretary of State, shall take into consideration other factors affecting the security of the United States, including—

(A) airport security standards in the country;

(B) whether the country assists in the operation of an effective air marshal program;

(C) the standards of passports and travel documents issued by the country; and

(D) other security-related factors, including the country's cooperation with the United States' initiatives toward combating terrorism and the country's cooperation with the United States intelligence community in sharing information regarding terrorist threats.

(10) Technical assistance

The Secretary of Homeland Security, in consultation with the Secretary of State, shall provide technical assistance to program countries to assist those countries in meeting the requirements under this section. The Secretary of Homeland Security shall ensure that the program office within the Department of Homeland Security is adequately staffed and has resources to be able to provide such technical assistance, in addition to its duties to effectively monitor compliance of the countries participating in the program with all the requirements of the program.

(11) Independent review

(A) In general

Prior to the admission of a new country into the program under this section, and in conjunction with the periodic evaluations required under subsection (c)(5)(A) of this section, the Director of National Intelligence shall conduct an independent intelligence assessment of a nominated country and member of the program.

(B) Reporting requirement

The Director shall provide to the Secretary of Homeland Security, the Secretary of State, and the Attorney General the independent intelligence assessment required under subparagraph (A).

(C) Contents

The independent intelligence assessment conducted by the Director shall include—

(i) a review of all current, credible terrorist threats of the subject country;

(ii) an evaluation of the subject country's counterterrorism efforts;

(iii) an evaluation as to the extent of the country's sharing of information beneficial to suppressing terrorist movements, financing, or actions;

(iv) an assessment of the risks associated with including the subject country in the program; and

(v) recommendations to mitigate the risks identified in clause (iv).

(12) Designation of high risk program countries

(A) In general

The Secretary of Homeland Security, in consultation with the Director of National Intelligence and the Secretary of State, shall evaluate program countries on an annual basis based on the criteria described in subparagraph (B) and shall identify any program country, the admission of nationals from which under the visa waiver program under this section, the Secretary determines presents a high risk to the national security of the United States.

(B) Criteria

In evaluating program countries under subparagraph (A), the Secretary of Homeland Security, in consultation with the Director of National Intelligence and the Secretary of State, shall consider the following criteria:

(i) The number of nationals of the country determined to be ineligible to travel to the United States under the program during the previous year.

(ii) The number of nationals of the country who were identified in United States Government databases related to the identities of known or suspected terrorists during the previous year.

(iii) The estimated number of nationals of the country who have traveled to Iraq or Syria at any time on or after March 1, 2011 to engage in terrorism.

(iv) The capacity of the country to combat passport fraud.

(v) The level of cooperation of the country with the counter-terrorism efforts of the United States.

(vi) The adequacy of the border and immigration control of the country.

(vii) Any other criteria the Secretary of Homeland Security determines to be appropriate.

(C) Suspension of designation

The Secretary of Homeland Security, in consultation with the Secretary of State, may suspend the designation of a program

239

country based on a determination that the country presents a high risk to the national security of the United States under subparagraph (A) until such time as the Secretary determines that the country no longer presents such a risk.

(D) Report

Not later than 60 days after December 18, 2015, and annually thereafter, the Secretary of Homeland Security, in consultation with the Director of National Intelligence and the Secretary of State, shall submit to the Committee on Homeland Security, the Committee on Foreign Affairs, the Permanent Select Committee on Intelligence, and the Committee on the Judiciary of the House of Representatives, and the Committee on Homeland Security and Governmental Affairs, the Committee on Foreign Relations, the Select Committee on Intelligence, and the Committee on the Judiciary of the Senate a report, which includes an evaluation and threat assessment of each country determined to present a high risk to the national security of the United States under subparagraph (A).

(d) Authority

Notwithstanding any other provision of this section, the Secretary of Homeland Security, in consultation with the Secretary of State, may for any reason (including national security) refrain from waiving the visa requirement in respect to nationals of any country which may otherwise qualify for designation or may, at any time, rescind any waiver or designation previously granted under this section. The Secretary of Homeland Security may not waive any eligibility requirement under this section unless the Secretary notifies, with respect to the House of Representatives, the Committee on Homeland Security, the Committee on the Judiciary, the Committee on Foreign Affairs, and the Committee on Appropriations, and with respect to the Senate, the Committee on Homeland Security and Governmental Affairs, the Committee on the Judiciary, the Committee on Foreign Relations, and the Committee on Appropriations not later than 30 days before the effective date of such waiver.

(e) Carrier agreements

(1) In general

The agreement referred to in subsection (a)(4) of this section is an agreement between a carrier (including any carrier conducting operations under part 135 of Title 14, Code of Federal Regulations) or a domestic corporation conducting operations under part 91 of that title and the Secretary of Homeland Security under which the carrier (including any carrier conducting operations under part 135 of Title 14, Code of Federal Regulations) or a domestic corporation conducting operations under part 91 of that title agrees, in consideration of the waiver of the visa requirement with respect to a nonimmigrant visitor under the program—

(A) to indemnify the United States against any costs for the transportation of the alien from the United States if the visitor is refused admission to the United States or remains in the United States unlawfully after the 90-day period described in subsection (a)(1)(A) of this section,

(B) to submit daily to immigration officers any immigration forms received with respect to nonimmigrant visitors provided a waiver under the program,

(C) to be subject to the imposition of fines resulting from the transporting into the United States of a national of a designated country without a passport pursuant to regulations promulgated by the Secretary of Homeland Security, and

(D) to collect, provide, and share passenger data as required under subsection (h)(1)(B).

(2) Termination of agreements

The Secretary of Homeland Security may terminate an agreement under paragraph (1) with five days' notice to the carrier (including any carrier conducting operations under part 135 of title 14, Code of Federal Regulations) or a domestic corporation conducting operations under part 91 of that title for the failure by a carrier (including any carrier conducting operations under part 135 of title 14, Code of Federal Regulations) or a domestic corporation conducting operations under part 91 of that title to meet the terms of such agreement.

(3) Business aircraft requirements

(A) In general

For purposes of this section, a domestic corporation conducting operations under part 91 of title 14, Code of Federal Regulations that owns or operates a noncommercial aircraft is a corporation that is organized under the laws of any of the States of the United States or the District of Columbia and is accredited by or a member of a national organization that sets business aviation standards. The Secretary of Homeland Security shall prescribe by regulation the provision of such information as the Secretary of Homeland Security deems necessary to identify the domestic corporation, its officers, employees, shareholders, its place of business, and its business activities.

(B) Collections

In addition to any other fee authorized by law, the Secretary of Homeland Security is authorized to charge and collect, on a periodic basis, an amount from each domestic corporation conducting operations under part 91 of title 14, Code of Federal Regulations, for nonimmigrant visa waiver admissions on noncommercial aircraft owned or operated by such domestic corporation equal to the total amount of fees assessed for issuance of nonimmigrant visa waiver arrival/departure forms at land border ports of entry. All fees collected under this paragraph shall be deposited into the Immigration User Fee Account established under section 286(h) [8 U.S.C.A. § 1356(h)].

(f) Duration and termination of designation

(1) In general

(A) Determination and notification of disqualification rate

Upon determination by the Secretary of Homeland Security that a program country's disqualification rate is 2 percent or more, the Secretary of Homeland Security shall notify the Secretary of State.

(B) Probationary status

If the program country's disqualification rate is greater than 2 percent but less than 3.5 percent, the Secretary of Homeland Security shall place the program country in probationary status for a period not to exceed 2 full fiscal years following the year in which the determination under subparagraph (A) is made.

(C) Termination of designation

Subject to paragraph (3), if the program country's disqualification rate is 3.5 percent or more, the Secretary of Homeland Security shall terminate the country's designation as a program country effective at the beginning of the second fiscal year following the fiscal year in which the determination under subparagraph (A) is made.

(2) Termination of probationary status

(A) In general

If the Secretary of Homeland Security determines at the end of the probationary period described in paragraph (1)(B) that the program country placed in probationary status under such paragraph has failed to develop a machine-readable passport program as required by section* (c)(2)(C) of this section, or has a disqualification rate of 2 percent or more, the Secretary of Homeland Security shall terminate the designation of the country as a program country. If the Secretary of Homeland Security determines that the program country has developed a machine-readable passport program and has a disqualification rate of less than 2 percent, the Secretary of Homeland Security shall redesignate the country as a program country.

(B) Effective date

A termination of the designation of a country under subparagraph (A) shall take effect on the first day of the first fiscal year following the fiscal year in which the determination under such sub-

* So in original. Probably should be "subsection."

paragraph is made. Until such date, nationals of the country shall remain eligible for a waiver under subsection (a) of this section.

(3) Nonapplicability of certain provisions

Paragraph (1)(C) shall not apply unless the total number of nationals of a program country described in paragraph (4)(A) exceeds 100.

(4) Definition of disqualification rate

For purposes of this subsection, the term "disqualification rate" means the percentage which—

(A) the total number of nationals of the program country who were—

(i) denied admission at the time of arrival or withdrew their application for admission during the most recent fiscal year for which data are available; and

(ii) admitted as nonimmigrant visitors during such fiscal year and who violated the terms of such admission; bears to

(B) the total number of nationals of such country who applied for admission as nonimmigrant visitors during such fiscal year.

(5) Failure to report passport thefts

If the Secretary of Homeland Security and the Secretary of State jointly determine that the program country is not reporting the theft or loss of passports, as required by subsection (c)(2)(D) of this section, the Secretary of Homeland Security shall terminate the designation of the country as a program country.

(6) Failure to share information

(A) In general

If the Secretary of Homeland Security and the Secretary of State jointly determine that the program country is not sharing information, as required by subsection (c)(2)(F), the Secretary of Homeland Security shall terminate the designation of the country as a program country.

(B) Redesignation

In the case of a termination under this paragraph, the Secretary of Homeland Security shall redesignate the country as a program country, without regard to paragraph (2) or (3) of subsection (c) or paragraphs (1) through (4), when the Secretary of Homeland Security, in consultation with the Secretary of State, determines that the country is sharing information, as required by subsection (c)(2) (F).

(7) Failure to screen

(A) In general

Beginning on the date that is 270 days after December 18, 2015, if the Secretary of Homeland Security and the Secretary of State jointly determine that the program country is not conducting the screening required by subsection (c)(2)(G), the Secretary of Homeland Security shall terminate the designation of the country as a program country.

(B) Redesignation

In the case of a termination under this paragraph, the Secretary of Homeland Security shall redesignate the country as a program country, without regard to paragraph (2) or (3) of subsection (c) or paragraphs (1) through (4), when the Secretary of Homeland Security, in consultation with the Secretary of State, determines that the country is conducting the screening required by subsection (c)(2)(G).

(g) Visa application sole method to dispute denial of waiver based on a ground of inadmissibility

In the case of an alien denied a waiver under the program by reason of a ground of inadmissibility described in section 212(a) [8 U.S.C.A. § 1182(a)] that is discovered at the time of the alien's application for the waiver or through the use of an automated electronic database required under subsection (a)(9), the alien may apply for a visa at an appropriate consular office outside the United States. There shall be no other means of administrative or judicial review of such a denial, and no court or person otherwise shall have jurisdiction to consider any claim attacking the validity of such a denial.

(h) Use of information technology systems

(1) Automated entry-exit control system

(A) System

Not later than October 1, 2001, the Secretary of Homeland Security shall develop and implement a fully automated entry and exit control system that will collect a record of arrival and departure for every alien who arrives and departs by sea or air at a port of entry into the United States and is provided a waiver under the program.

(B) Requirements

The system under subparagraph (A) shall satisfy the following requirements:

(i) Data collection by carriers

Not later than October 1, 2001, the records of arrival and departure described in subparagraph (A) shall be based, to the maximum extent practicable, on passenger data collected and electronically transmitted to the automated entry and exit control system by each carrier that has an agreement under subsection (a)(4).

(ii) Data provision by carriers

Not later than October 1, 2002, no waiver may be provided under this section to an alien arriving by sea or air at a port of entry into the United States on a carrier unless the carrier is electronically transmitting to the automated entry and exit control system passenger data determined by the Secretary of Homeland Security to be sufficient to permit the Secretary of Homeland Security to carry out this paragraph.

(iii) Calculation

The system shall contain sufficient data to permit the Secretary of Homeland Security to calculate, for each program country and each fiscal year, the portion of nationals of that country who are described in subparagraph (A) and for whom no record of departure exists, expressed as a percentage of the total number of such nationals who are so described.

(C) Reporting

(i) Percentage of nationals lacking departure record

As part of the annual report required to be submitted under section 1365a(e)(1) of this title [8 U.S.C.A. § 1365a(e)(1)], the Secretary of Homeland Security shall include a section containing the calculation described in subparagraph (B)(iii) for each program country for the previous fiscal year, together with an analysis of that information.

(ii) System effectiveness

Not later than December 31, 2004, the Secretary of Homeland Security shall submit a written report to the Committee on the Judiciary of the United States House of Representatives and of the Senate containing the following:

(I) The conclusions of the Secretary of Homeland Security regarding the effectiveness of the automated entry and exit control system to be developed and implemented under this paragraph.1

(II) The recommendations of the Secretary of Homeland Security regarding the use of the calculation described in subparagraph (B)(iii) as a basis for evaluating whether to terminate or continue the designation of a country as a program country.

The report required by this clause may be combined with the annual report required to be submitted on that date under section 1365a(e)(1) of this title [8 U.S.C.A. § 1365a(e)(1)].

(2) Automated data sharing system

(A) System

The Secretary of Homeland Security and the Secretary of State shall develop and implement an automated data sharing system that will permit them to share data in electronic form from their respective records systems regarding the admissibility of aliens who are nationals of a program country.

(B) Requirements

The system under subparagraph (A) shall satisfy the following requirements:

(i) Supplying information to immigration officers conducting inspections at ports of entry

Not later than October 1, 2002, the system shall enable immigration officers conducting inspections at ports of entry under section 235 [8 U.S.C.A. § 1225] to obtain from the system, with respect to aliens seeking a waiver under the program—

(I) any photograph of the alien that may be contained in the records of the Department of State or the Service; and

(II) information on whether the alien has ever been determined to be ineligible to receive a visa or ineligible to be admitted to the United States.

(ii) Supplying photographs of inadmissible aliens

The system shall permit the Secretary of Homeland Security electronically to obtain any photograph contained in the records of the Secretary of State pertaining to an alien who is a national of a program country and has been determined to be ineligible to receive a visa.

(iii) Maintaining records on applications for admission

The system shall maintain, for a minimum of 10 years, information about each application for admission made by an alien seeking a waiver under the program, including the following:

(I) The name or Service identification number of each immigration officer conducting the inspection of the alien at the port of entry.

(II) Any information described in clause (i) that is obtained from the system by any such officer.

(III) The results of the application.

(3) Electronic system for travel authorization

(A) System

The Secretary of Homeland Security, in consultation with the Secretary of State, shall develop and implement a fully automated electronic system for travel authorization (referred to in this paragraph as the "System") to collect such biographical and other information as the Secretary of Homeland Security determines necessary to determine, in advance of travel, the eligibility of, and whether there exists a law enforcement or security risk in permitting, the[*] alien to travel to the United States.

(B) Fees

(i) In general

No later than 6 months after March 4, 2010, the Secretary of Homeland Security shall establish a fee for the use of the System and begin assessment and collection of that fee. The initial fee shall be the sum of—

(I) $17 per travel authorization; and

(II) an amount that will at least ensure recovery of the full costs of providing and administering the System, as determined by the Secretary.

(ii) Disposition of amounts collected

Amounts collected under clause (i)(I) shall be credited to the Travel Promotion Fund established by subsection (d) of section 2131 of Title 22. Amounts collected under clause (i)(II) shall be transferred to the general fund of the Treasury and made available to pay the costs incurred to administer the System.

(iii) Sunset of Travel Promotion Fund fee

The Secretary may not collect the fee authorized by clause (i)(I) for fiscal years beginning after September 30, 2027.

(C) Validity

(i) Period

The Secretary of Homeland Security, in consultation with the Secretary of State, shall prescribe regulations that provide for a period, not to exceed three years, during which a determination of eligibility to travel under the program will be valid. Notwithstanding any other provision under this section, the Secretary of Homeland Security may revoke any such determination or shorten the period of eligibility under any such determination at any time and for any reason.

(ii) Limitation

A determination by the Secretary of Homeland Security that an alien is eligible to travel to the United States under the program is not a determination that the alien is admissible to the United States.

(iii) Not a determination of visa eligibility

A determination by the Secretary of Homeland Security that an alien who applied for authorization to travel to the United States through the System is not eligible to travel under the program is not a determination of eligibility for a visa to travel to

[*] So in original. Probably should be "an".

the United States and shall not preclude the alien from applying for a visa.

(iv) Judicial review

Notwithstanding any other provision of law, no court shall have jurisdiction to review an eligibility determination under the System.

(D) Fraud detection

The Secretary of Homeland Security shall research opportunities to incorporate into the System technology that will detect and prevent fraud and deception in the System.

(E) Additional and previous countries of citizenship

The Secretary of Homeland Security shall collect from an applicant for admission pursuant to this section information on any additional or previous countries of citizenship of that applicant. The Secretary shall take any information so collected into account when making determinations as to the eligibility of the alien for admission pursuant to this section.

(F) Report on certain limitations on travel

Not later than 30 days after December 18, 2015, and annually thereafter, the Secretary of Homeland Security, in consultation with the Secretary of State, shall submit to the Committee on Homeland Security, the Committee on the Judiciary, and the Committee on Foreign Affairs of the House of Representatives, and the Committee on Homeland Security and Governmental Affairs, the Committee on the Judiciary, and the Committee on Foreign Relations of the Senate a report on the number of individuals who were denied eligibility to travel under the program, or whose eligibility for such travel was revoked during the previous year, and the number of such individuals determined, in accordance with subsection (a)(6), to represent a threat to the national security of the United States, and shall include the country or countries of citizenship of each such individual.

(i) Exit system

(1) In general

Not later than one year after August 3, 2007, the Secretary of Homeland Security shall establish an exit system that records the departure on a flight leaving the United States of every alien participating in the visa waiver program established under this section.

(2) System requirements

The system established under paragraph (1) shall—

(A) match biometric information of the alien against relevant watch lists and immigration information; and

(B) compare such biometric information against manifest information collected by air carriers on passengers departing the United States to confirm such aliens have departed the United States.

(3) Report

Not later than 180 days after August 3, 2007, the Secretary shall submit to Congress a report that describes—

(A) the progress made in developing and deploying the exit system established under this subsection; and

(B) the procedures by which the Secretary shall improve the method of calculating the rates of nonimmigrants who overstay their authorized period of stay in the United States.

(June 27, 1952, c. 477, Title II, ch. 2, § 217, as added Nov. 6, 1986, Pub.L. 99–603, Title III, § 313(a), 100 Stat. 3435, and amended Oct. 24, 1988, Pub.L. 100–525, § 2(p)(1), 102 Stat. 2613; Oct. 24, 1988, Pub.L. 100–525, § 2(p)(2), 102 Stat. 2613; Nov. 29, 1990, Pub.L. 101–649, Title II, § 201(a), 104 Stat. 5012; Dec. 12, 1991, Pub.L. 102–232, Title III, §§ 303(a) (1),(2), 307(*l*)(3), 105 Stat. 1746, 1756; Oct. 25, 1994, Pub.L. 103–415, § 1(m), 108 Stat. 4301; Oct. 25, 1994, Pub.L. 103–416, Title II, §§ 210, 211, 108 Stat. 4312, 4313; Sept. 30, 1996, Pub.L. 104–208, Div. C, Title III, § 308(d)(4)(F), (e)(9), Title VI, § 635(a) to (c)(1), (3), 110 Stat. 3009–618, 3009–620, 3009–702, 3009–703; Nov. 26, 1997, Pub.L. 105–119, Title I, § 125, 111 Stat. 2471; Apr. 27, 1998, Pub.L. 105–173, §§ 1, 3, 112 Stat. 56; Oct. 30, 2000, Pub.L. 106–396, Title I, §§ 101(a), Title II, §§ 201 to 207, Title IV, § 403(a) to (d), 114 Stat. 1637 to 1644, 1647, 1648; Oct. 26, 2001, Pub.L. 107–56, Title IV, §§ 417(c), (d), 115 Stat. 355; May 14, 2002, Pub.L. 107–173, Title III, § 307; Aug. 3, 2007, Pub.L. 110–53, Title VII, § 711(c), (d)(1), 121 Stat. 339, 341; Mar. 4, 2010, Pub.L. 111–145, § 9(e), 124 Stat. 62; July 2, 2010, Pub.L. 111–198, § 5(a), 124 Stat. 1357; Pub.L. 113–235, Div. B, Title VI, 605(b), Dec. 16, 2014, 128 Stat. 2219; Pub.L. 114–113, Div. O, Title II, §§ 202(a), (b), 203 to 205(a), 206, 207(a), 209, Dec. 18, 2015, 129 Stat. 2989, 2993, 2995; Pub.L. 115–123, Div. C, Title II, § 30203(a), Feb. 9, 2018, 132 Stat. 126; Pub.L. 116–94, Div. I, Title VIII, § 806, Dec. 20, 2019, 133 Stat. 3029.)

§ 218.   Admission of temporary H–2A workers [8 U.S.C.A. § 1188]

(a) Conditions for approval of H–2A petitions

(1) A petition to import an alien as an H–2A worker (as defined in subsection (i)(2)) may not be approved by the Attorney General unless the petitioner has applied to the Secretary of Labor for a certification that—

(A) there are not sufficient workers who are able, willing, and qualified, and who will be available at the time and place needed, to perform the labor or services involved in the petition, and

(B) the employment of the alien in such labor or services will not adversely affect the wages and working conditions of workers in the United States similarly employed.

(2) The Secretary of Labor may require by regulation, as a condition of issuing the certification, the payment of a fee to recover the reasonable costs of processing applications for certification.

(b) Conditions for denial of labor certification

The Secretary of Labor may not issue a certification under subsection (a) with respect to an employer if the conditions described in that subsection are not met or if any of the following conditions are met:

(1) There is a strike or lockout in the course of a labor dispute which, under the regulations, precludes such certification.

(2)(A) The employer during the previous two-year period employed H–2A workers and the Secretary of Labor has determined, after notice and opportunity for a hearing, that the employer at any time during that period substantially violated a material term or condition of the labor certification with respect to the employment of domestic or nonimmigrant workers.

(B) No employer may be denied certification under subparagraph (A) for more than three years for any violation described in such subparagraph.

(3) The employer has not provided the Secretary with satisfactory assurances that if the employment for which the certification is sought is not covered by State workers' compensation law, the employer will provide, at no cost to the worker, insurance covering injury and disease arising out of and in the course of the worker's employment which will provide benefits at least equal to those provided under the State workers' compensation law for comparable employment.

(4) The Secretary determines that the employer has not made positive recruitment efforts within a multi-state region of traditional or expected labor supply where the Secretary finds that there are a significant number of qualified United States workers who, if recruited, would be willing to make themselves available for work at the time and place needed. Positive recruitment under this paragraph is in addition to, and shall be conducted within the same time period as, the circulation through the interstate employment service system of the employer's job offer. The obligation to engage in positive recruitment under this paragraph shall terminate on the date the H–2A workers depart for the employer's place of employment.

(c) Special rules for consideration of applications

The following rules shall apply in the case of the filing and consideration of an application for a labor certification under this section:

(1) Deadline for filing applications

The Secretary of Labor may not require that the application be filed more than 45 days before the first date the employer requires the labor or services of the H–2A worker.

(2) Notice within seven days of deficiencies

(A) The employer shall be notified in writing within seven days of the date of filing if the application does not meet the standards (other than that described in subsection (a)(1)(A)) for approval.

(B) If the application does not meet such standards, the notice shall include the reasons therefor and the Secretary shall provide an opportunity for the prompt resubmission of a modified application.

(3) Issuance of certification

(A) The Secretary of Labor shall make, not later than 30 days before the date such labor or services are first required to be performed, the certification described in subsection (a)(1) of this section if—

> **(i)** the employer has complied with the criteria for certification (including criteria for the recruitment of eligible individuals as prescribed by the Secretary), and

> **(ii)** the employer does not actually have, or has not been provided with referrals of, qualified eligible individuals who have indicated their availability to perform such labor or services on the terms and conditions of a job offer which meets the requirements of the Secretary.

In considering the question of whether a specific qualification is appropriate in a job offer, the Secretary shall apply the normal and accepted qualifications required by non-H–2A-employers in the same or comparable occupations and crops.

(B)(i) For a period of 3 years subsequent to the effective date of this section, labor certifications shall remain effective only if, from the time the foreign worker departs for the employer's place of employment, the employer will provide employment to any qualified United States worker who applies to the employer until 50 percent of the period of the work contract, under which the foreign worker who is in the job was hired, has elapsed. In addition, the employer will offer to provide benefits, wages and working conditions required pursuant to this section and regulations.

(ii) The requirement of clause (i) shall not apply to any employer who—

> **(I)** did not, during any calendar quarter during the preceding calendar year, use more than 500 man-days of agricultural labor, as defined in section 203(u) of Title 29,

> **(II)** is not a member of an association which has petitioned for certification under this section for its members, and

> **(III)** has not otherwise associated with other employers who are petitioning for temporary foreign workers under this section.

(iii) Six months before the end of the 3-year period described in clause (i), the Secretary of Labor shall consider the findings of the report mandated by section 403(a)(4)(D) of the Immigration Reform and Control Act of 1986 [8 U.S.C.A. § 1188 note] as well as other relevant materials, including evidence of benefits to United

States workers and costs to employers, addressing the advisability of continuing a policy which requires an employer, as a condition for certification under this section, to continue to accept qualified, eligible United States workers for employment after the date the H–2A workers depart for work with the employer. The Secretary's review of such findings and materials shall lead to the issuance of findings in furtherance of the Congressional policy that aliens not be admitted under this section unless there are not sufficient workers in the United States who are able, willing, and qualified to perform the labor or service needed and that the employment of the aliens in such labor or services will not adversely affect the wages and working conditions of workers in the United States similarly employed. In the absence of the enactment of Federal legislation prior to three months before the end of the 3-year period described in clause (i) which addresses the subject matter of this subparagraph, the Secretary shall immediately publish the findings required by this clause, and shall promulgate, on an interim or final basis, regulations based on his findings which shall be effective no later than three years from the effective date of this section.

(iv) In complying with clause (i) of this subparagraph, an association shall be allowed to refer or transfer workers among its members: Provided, That for purposes of this section an association acting as an agent for its members shall not be considered a joint employer merely because of such referral or transfer.

(v) United States workers referred or transferred pursuant to clause (iv) of this subparagraph shall not be treated disparately.

(vi) An employer shall not be liable for payments under section 655.202(b)(6) of title 20, Code of Federal Regulations (or any successor regulation) with respect to an H–2A worker who is displaced due to compliance with the requirement of this subparagraph, if the Secretary of Labor certifies that the H–2A worker was displaced because of the employer's compliance with clause (i) of this subparagraph.

(vii)(I) No person or entity shall willfully and knowingly withhold domestic workers prior to the arrival of H–2A workers in order to force the hiring of domestic workers under clause (i).

(II) Upon the receipt of a complaint by an employer that a violation of subclause (I) has occurred the Secretary shall immediately investigate. He shall within 36 hours of the receipt of the complaint issue findings concerning the alleged violation. Where the Secretary finds that a violation has occurred, he shall immediately suspend the application of clause (i) of this subparagraph with respect to that certification for that date of need.

(4) Housing

Employers shall furnish housing in accordance with regulations. The employer shall be permitted at the employer's option to provide housing meeting applicable Federal standards for temporary labor camps or to secure housing which meets the local standards for rental and/or public accommodations or other substantially similar class of habitation: Provided, That in the absence of applicable local standards, State standards for rental and/or public accommodations or other substantially similar class of habitation shall be met: Provided further, That in the absence of applicable local or State standards, Federal temporary labor camp standards shall apply: Provided further, That the Secretary of Labor shall issue regulations which address the specific requirements of housing for employees principally engaged in the range production of livestock: Provided further, That when it is the prevailing practice in the area and occupation of intended employment to provide family housing, family housing shall be provided to workers with families who request it: And provided further, That nothing in this paragraph shall require an employer to provide or secure housing for workers who are not entitled to it under the temporary labor certification regulations in effect on June 1, 1986. The determination as to whether the housing furnished by an employer for an H–2A worker meets the requirements imposed by this paragraph must be made prior to the date specified in paragraph (3)(A) by which the Secretary of Labor is required to make a certification described in subsection (a)(1) with respect to a petition for the importation of such worker.

(d) Roles of agricultural associations

(1) Permitting filing by agricultural associations

A petition to import an alien as a temporary agricultural worker, and an application for a labor certification with respect to such a worker, may be filed by an association of agricultural producers which use agricultural services.

(2) Treatment of associations acting as employers

If an association is a joint or sole employer of temporary agricultural workers, the certifications granted under this section to the association may be used for the certified job opportunities of any of its producer members and such workers may be transferred among its producer members to perform agricultural services of a temporary or seasonal nature for which the certifications were granted.

(3) Treatment of violations

(A) Member's violation does not necessarily disqualify association or other members

If an individual producer member of a joint employer association is determined to have committed an act that under subsection (b)(2) results in the denial of certification with respect to the member, the denial shall apply only to that member of the association unless the Secretary determines that the association or other member participated in, had knowledge of, or reason to know of, the violation.

(B) Association's violation does not necessarily disqualify members

(i) If an association representing agricultural producers as a joint employer is determined to have committed an act that under subsection (b)(2) results in the denial of certification with respect to the association, the denial shall apply only to the association and does not apply to any individual producer member of the association unless the Secretary determines that the member participated in, had knowledge of, or reason to know of, the violation.

(ii) If an association of agricultural producers certified as a sole employer is determined to have committed an act that under subsection (b)(2) results in the denial of certification with respect to the association, no individual producer member of such association may be the beneficiary of the services of temporary alien agricultural workers admitted under this section in the commodity and occupation in which such aliens were employed by the association which was denied certification during the period such denial is in force, unless such producer member employs such aliens in the commodity and occupation in question directly or through an association which is a joint employer of such workers with the producer member.

(e) Expedited administrative appeals of certain determinations

(1) Regulations shall provide for an expedited procedure for the review of a denial of certification under subsection (a)(1) of this section or a revocation of such a certification or, at the applicant's request, for a de novo administrative hearing respecting the denial or revocation.

(2) The Secretary of Labor shall expeditiously, but in no case later than 72 hours after the time a new determination is requested, make a new determination on the request for certification in the case of an H–2A worker if able, willing, and qualified eligible individuals are not actually available at the time such labor or services are required and a certification was denied in whole or in part because of the availability of qualified workers. If the employer asserts that any eligible individual who has been referred is not able, willing, or qualified, the burden of proof is on the employer to establish that the individual referred is not able, willing, or qualified because of employment-related reasons.

(f) Violators disqualified for 5 years

An alien may not be admitted to the United States as a temporary agricultural worker if the alien was admitted to the United States as such a worker within the previous five-year period and the alien during that period violated a term or condition of such previous admission.

(g) Authorizations of appropriations

(1) There are authorized to be appropriated for each fiscal year, beginning with fiscal year 1987, $10,000,000 for the purposes—

    (A) of recruiting domestic workers for temporary labor and services which might otherwise be performed by nonimmigrants described in section 101(a)(15)(H)(ii)(a) [8 U.S.C.A. § 1101(a)(15)(H)(ii)(a)], and

    (B) of monitoring terms and conditions under which such nonimmigrants (and domestic workers employed by the same employers) are employed in the United States.

(2) The Secretary of Labor is authorized to take such actions, including imposing appropriate penalties and seeking appropriate injunctive relief and specific performance of contractual obligations, as may be necessary to assure employer compliance with terms and conditions of employment under this section.

(3) There are authorized to be appropriated for each fiscal year, beginning with fiscal year 1987, such sums as may be necessary for the purpose of enabling the Secretary of Labor to make determinations and certifications under this section and under section 212(a)(5)(A)(i) [8 U.S.C.A. § 1182(a)(5)(A)(i)].

(4) There are authorized to be appropriated for each fiscal year, beginning with fiscal year 1987, such sums as may be necessary for the purposes of enabling the Secretary of Agriculture to carry out the Secretary's duties and responsibilities under this section.

(h) Miscellaneous provisions

(1) The Attorney General shall provide for such endorsement of entry and exit documents of nonimmigrants described in section 101(a)(15)(H)(ii) [8 U.S.C.A. § 1101(a)(15)(H)(ii)] as may be necessary to carry out this section and to provide notice for purposes of section 274A [8 U.S.C.A. § 1324a].

(2) The provisions of subsections (a) and (c) of section 214 [8 U.S.C.A. § 1184] and the provisions of this section preempt any State or local law regulating admissibility of nonimmigrant workers.

(i) Definitions

For purposes of this section:

(1) The term "eligible individual" means, with respect to employment, an individual who is not an unauthorized alien (as defined in section 274A(h)(3) [8 U.S.C.A. § 1324a(h)(3)]) with respect to that employment.

(2) The term "H–2A worker" means a nonimmigrant described in section 101(a)(15)(H)(ii)(a) [8 U.S.C.A. § 1101(a)(15)(H)(ii)(a)].

(June 27, 1952, c. 477, Title II, ch. 2, § 218, formerly § 216, as added Nov. 6, 1986, Pub.L. 99–603, Title III, § 301(c), 100 Stat. 3411, renumbered and amended Oct. 24, 1988, Pub.L.

100–525, § 2(*l*)(2), (3), 102 Stat. 2612; Dec. 12, 1991, Pub.L. 102–232, Title III, §§ 307(*l*)(4), 309(b)(8), 105 Stat. 1756, 1759; Oct. 25, 1994, Pub.L. 103–416, Title II, § 219(z)(8), 108 Stat. 4318; Oct. 22, 1999, Pub.L. 106–78, Title VII, § 748, 113 Stat. 1167; Dec. 21, 2000, Pub.L. 106–554, § 1(a)(1) [Title I, § 105], 114 Stat. 2763.)

§ 219. Designation of foreign terrorist organizations [8 U.S.C.A. § 1189]

(a) Designation

(1) In general

The Secretary is authorized to designate an organization as a foreign terrorist organization in accordance with this subsection if the Secretary finds that—

(A) the organization is a foreign organization;

(B) the organization engages in terrorist activity (as defined in section 212(a)(3)(B) [8 U.S.C.A. § 1182(a)(3)(B)]) or terrorism (as defined in section 2656f(d)(2) of Title 22), or retains the capability and intent to engage in terrorist activity or terrorism; and

(C) the terrorist activity or terrorism of the organization threatens the security of United States nationals or the national security of the United States.

(2) Procedure

(A) Notice

(i) To Congressional leaders

Seven days before making a designation under this subsection, the Secretary shall, by classified communication, notify the Speaker and Minority Leader of the House of Representatives, the President pro tempore, Majority Leader, and Minority Leader of the Senate, and the members of the relevant committees of the House of Representatives and the Senate, in writing, of the intent to designate an organization under this subsection, together with the findings made under paragraph (1) with respect to that organization, and the factual basis therefor.

(ii) Publication in Federal Register

The Secretary shall publish the designation in the Federal Register seven days after providing the notification under clause (i).

(B) Effect of designation

(i) For purposes of section 2339B of Title 18, a designation under this subsection shall take effect upon publication under subparagraph (A)(ii).

(ii) Any designation under this subsection shall cease to have effect upon an Act of Congress disapproving such designation.

(C) Freezing of assets

Upon notification under paragraph (2)(A)(i), the Secretary of the Treasury may require United States financial institutions possessing or controlling any assets of any foreign organization included in the notification to block all financial transactions involving those assets until further directive from either the Secretary of the Treasury, Act of Congress, or order of court.

(3) Record

(A) In general

In making a designation under this subsection, the Secretary shall create an administrative record.

(B) Classified information

The Secretary may consider classified information in making a designation under this subsection. Classified information shall not be subject to disclosure for such time as it remains classified, except that such information may be disclosed to a court ex parte and in camera for purposes of judicial review under subsection (c) of this section.

(4) Period of designation

(A) In general

A designation under this subsection shall be effective for all purposes until revoked under paragraph (5) or (6) or set aside pursuant to subsection (c).

(B) Review of designation upon petition

(i) In general

The Secretary shall review the designation of a foreign terrorist organization under the procedures set forth in clauses (iii) and (iv) if the designated organization files a petition for revocation within the petition period described in clause (ii).

(ii) Petition period

For purposes of clause (i)—

(I) if the designated organization has not previously filed a petition for revocation under this subparagraph, the petition period begins 2 years after the date on which the designation was made; or

(II) if the designated organization has previously filed a petition for revocation under this subparagraph, the petition period begins 2 years after the date of the determination made under clause (iv) on that petition.

(iii) Procedures

Any foreign terrorist organization that submits a petition for revocation under this subparagraph must provide evidence in that petition that the relevant circumstances described in paragraph (1) are sufficiently different from the circumstances that were the basis for the designation such that a revocation with respect to the organization is warranted.

(iv) Determination

(I) In general

Not later than 180 days after receiving a petition for revocation submitted under this subparagraph, the Secretary shall make a determination as to such revocation.

(II) Classified information

The Secretary may consider classified information in making a determination in response to a petition for revocation. Classified information shall not be subject to disclosure for such time as it remains classified, except that such information may be disclosed to a court ex parte and in camera for purposes of judicial review under subsection (c) of this section.

(III) Publication of determination

A determination made by the Secretary under this clause shall be published in the Federal Register.

(IV) Procedures

Any revocation by the Secretary shall be made in accordance with paragraph (6).

(C) Other review of designation

(i) In general

If in a 5-year period no review has taken place under subparagraph (B), the Secretary shall review the designation of the foreign terrorist organization in order to determine whether such designation should be revoked pursuant to paragraph (6).

(ii) Procedures

If a review does not take place pursuant to subparagraph (B) in response to a petition for revocation that is filed in accordance with that subparagraph, then the review shall be conducted pursuant to procedures established by the Secretary. The results of such review and the applicable procedures shall not be reviewable in any court.

(iii) Publication of results of review

The Secretary shall publish any determination made pursuant to this subparagraph in the Federal Register.

(5) Revocation by Act of Congress

The Congress, by an Act of Congress, may block or revoke a designation made under paragraph (1).

(6) Revocation based on change in circumstances

(A) In general

The Secretary may revoke a designation made under paragraph (1) at any time, and shall revoke a designation upon completion of a review conducted pursuant to subparagraphs (B) and (C) of paragraph (4) if the Secretary finds that—

(i) the circumstances that were the basis for the designation have changed in such a manner as to warrant revocation; or

(ii) the national security of the United States warrants a revocation.

(B) Procedure

The procedural requirements of paragraphs (2) and (3) shall apply to a revocation under this paragraph. Any revocation shall take effect on the date specified in the revocation or upon publication in the Federal Register if no effective date is specified.

(7) Effect of revocation

The revocation of a designation under paragraph (5) or (6) shall not affect any action or proceeding based on conduct committed prior to the effective date of such revocation.

(8) Use of designation in trial or hearing

If a designation under this subsection has become effective under paragraph (2)(B) a defendant in a criminal action or an alien in a removal proceeding shall not be permitted to raise any question concerning the validity of the issuance of such designation as a defense or an objection at any trial or hearing.

(b) Amendments to a designation

(1) In general

The Secretary may amend a designation under this subsection if the Secretary finds that the organization has changed its name, adopted a new alias, dissolved and then reconstituted itself under a different name or names, or merged with another organization.

(2) Procedure

Amendments made to a designation in accordance with paragraph (1) shall be effective upon publication in the Federal Register. Subparagraphs (B) and (C) of subsection (a)(2) of this section shall apply to an amended designation upon such publication. Paragraphs (2)(A)(i), (4), (5), (6), (7), and (8) of subsection (a) of this section shall also apply to an amended designation.

(3) Administrative record

The administrative record shall be corrected to include the amendments as well as any additional relevant information that supports those amendments.

(4) Classified information

The Secretary may consider classified information in amending a designation in accordance with this subsection. Classified information shall not be subject to disclosure for such time as it remains classified, except that such information may be disclosed to a court ex parte and in camera for purposes of judicial review under subsection (c).

(c) Judicial review of designation

(1) In general

Not later than 30 days after publication in the Federal Register of a designation, an amended designation, or a determination in response to a petition for revocation, the designated organization may seek judicial review in the United States Court of Appeals for the District of Columbia Circuit.

(2) Basis of review

Review under this subsection shall be based solely upon the administrative record, except that the Government may submit, for ex parte and in camera review, classified information used in making the designation, amended designation, or determination in response to a petition for revocation.

(3) Scope of review

The Court shall hold unlawful and set aside a designation, amended designation, or determination in response to a petition for revocation the court finds to be—

(A) arbitrary, capricious, an abuse of discretion, or otherwise not in accordance with law;

(B) contrary to constitutional right, power, privilege, or immunity;

(C) in excess of statutory jurisdiction, authority, or limitation, or short of statutory right;

(D) lacking substantial support in the administrative record taken as a whole or in classified information submitted to the court under paragraph (2), [sic]* or

(E) not in accord with the procedures required by law.

(4) Judicial review invoked

The pendency of an action for judicial review of a designation, amended designation, or determination in response to a petition for revocation shall not affect the application of this section, unless the court issues a final order setting aside the designation, amended designation, or determination in response to a petition for revocation.

(d) Definitions

As used in this section—

---

* So in original. The comma probably should be a semicolon.

(1) the term "classified information" has the meaning given that term in section 1(a) of the Classified Information Procedures Act (18 U.S.C. App.);

(2) the term "national security" means the national defense, foreign relations, or economic interests of the United States;

(3) the term "relevant committees" means the Committees on the Judiciary, Intelligence, and Foreign Relations of the Senate and the Committees on the Judiciary, Intelligence, and International Relations of the House of Representatives; and

(4) the term "Secretary" means the Secretary of State, in consultation with the Secretary of the Treasury and the Attorney General.

(June 27, 1952, c. 477, Title II, ch. 2, § 219, as added Apr. 24, 1996, Pub.L. 104–132, Title III, § 302(a), 110 Stat. 1248, and amended Sept. 30, 1996, Pub.L. 104–208, Div. C, Title III, § 356, Title VI, § 671(c)(1), 110 Stat. 3009–644, 3009–722; Oct. 26, 2001, Pub.L. 107–56, Title IV, § 411(c), 115 Stat. 349; Dec. 17, 2004, Pub.L. 108–458, Title VII, § 7119, 118 Stat. 3801 to 3803.)

CHAPTER III—ISSUANCE OF ENTRY DOCUMENTS

§ 221. Issuance of visas [8 U.S.C.A. § 1201]

(a) Immigrants; nonimmigrants

(1) Under the conditions hereinafter prescribed and subject to the limitations prescribed in this Act or regulations issued thereunder, a consular officer may issue

(A) to an immigrant who has made proper application therefor, an immigrant visa which shall consist of the application provided for in section 222 [8 U.S.C.A. § 1202], visaed by such consular officer, and shall specify the foreign state, if any, to which the immigrant is charged, the immigrant's particular status under such foreign state, the preference, immediate relative, or special immigrant classification to which the alien is charged, the date on which the validity of the visa shall expire, and such additional information as may be required; and

(B) to a nonimmigrant who has made proper application therefor, a nonimmigrant visa, which shall specify the classification under section 101(a)(15) [8 U.S.C.A. § 1101(a)(15)] of the nonimmigrant, the period during which the nonimmigrant visa shall be valid, and such additional information as may be required.

(2) The Secretary of State shall provide to the Service an electronic version of the visa file of each alien who has been issued a visa to ensure that the data in that visa file is available to immigration inspectors at the United States ports of entry before the arrival of the alien at such a port of entry.

(b) Registration; photographs; waiver of requirement

Each alien who applies for a visa shall be registered in connection with his application, and shall furnish copies of his photograph signed by him for such use as may be by regulations required. The requirements of this subsection may be waived in the discretion of the Secretary of State in the case of any alien who is within that class of nonimmigrants enumerated in sections 101(a)(15)(A) [8 U.S.C.A. § 1101(a)(15)(A)], and 101(a)(15)(G) [8 U.S.C.A. § 1101(a)(15)(G)], or in the case of any alien who is granted a diplomatic visa on a diplomatic passport or on the equivalent thereof.

(c) Period of validity; renewal or replacement

(1) Immigrant visas

An immigrant visa shall be valid for such period, not exceeding six months, as shall be by regulations prescribed, except that any visa issued to a child lawfully adopted by a United States citizen and spouse while such citizen is serving abroad in the United States Armed Forces, or is employed abroad by the United States Government, or is temporarily abroad on business, shall be valid until such time, for a period not to exceed three years, as the adoptive citizen parent returns to the United States in due course of his service, employment, or business.

(2) Nonimmigrant visas

A nonimmigrant visa shall be valid for such periods as shall be by regulations prescribed. In prescribing the period of validity of a nonimmigrant visa in the case of nationals of any foreign country who are eligible for such visas, the Secretary of State shall, insofar as practicable, accord to such nationals the same treatment upon a reciprocal basis as such foreign country accords to nationals of the United States who are within a similar class; except that in the case of aliens who are nationals of a foreign country and who either are granted refugee status and firmly resettled in another foreign country or are granted permanent residence and residing in another foreign country, the Secretary of State may prescribe the period of validity of such a visa based upon the treatment granted by that other foreign country to alien refugees and permanent residents, respectively, in the United States.

(3) Visa replacement

An immigrant visa may be replaced under the original number during the fiscal year in which the original visa was issued for an immigrant who establishes to the satisfaction of the consular officer that the immigrant—

> **(A)** was unable to use the original immigrant visa during the period of its validity because of reasons beyond his control and for which he was not responsible;

> **(B)** is found by a consular officer to be eligible for an immigrant visa; and

> **(C)** pays again the statutory fees for an application and an immigrant visa.

(4) Fee waiver

If an immigrant visa was issued, on or after March 27, 2013, for a child who has been lawfully adopted, or who is coming to the United States to be adopted, by a United States citizen, any statutory immigrant visa fees relating to a renewal or replacement of such visa may be waived or, if already paid, may be refunded upon request, subject to such criteria as the Secretary of State may prescribe, if—

(A) the immigrant child was unable to use the original immigrant visa during the period of its validity as a direct result of extraordinary circumstances, including the denial of an exit permit; and

(B) if such inability was attributable to factors beyond the control of the adopting parent or parents and of the immigrant.

(d) Physical examination

Prior to the issuance of an immigrant visa to any alien, the consular officer shall require such alien to submit to a physical and mental examination in accordance with such regulations as may be prescribed. Prior to the issuance of a nonimmigrant visa to any alien, the consular officer may require such alien to submit to a physical or mental examination, or both, if in his opinion such examination is necessary to ascertain whether such alien is eligible to receive a visa.

(e) Surrender of visa

Each immigrant shall surrender his immigrant visa to the immigration officer at the port of entry, who shall endorse on the visa the date and the port of arrival, the identity of the vessel or other means of transportation by which the immigrant arrived, and such other endorsements as may be by regulations required.

(f) Surrender of documents

Each nonimmigrant shall present or surrender to the immigration officer at the port of entry such documents as may be by regulation required. In the case of an alien crewman not in possession of any individual documents other than a passport and until such time as it becomes practicable to issue individual documents, such alien crewman may be admitted, subject to the provisions of this title, if his name appears in the crew list of the vessel or aircraft on which he arrives and the crew list is visaed by a consular officer, but the consular officer shall have the right to deny admission to any alien crewman from the crew list visa.

(g) Non-issuance of visas or other documents

No visa or other documentation shall be issued to an alien if **(1)** it appears to the consular officer, from statements in the application, or in the papers submitted therewith, that such alien is ineligible to receive a visa or such other documentation under section 212 [8 U.S.C.A. § 1182], or any other provision of law, **(2)** the application fails to comply with the provisions of this Act, or the regulations issued thereunder, or **(3)** the consular officer knows or has reason to believe that such alien is ineligible to receive a visa or such other documentation under section 212 [8 U.S.C.A. § 1182], or any other provision of law: Provided, That a visa or other documentation may be issued to an alien who is within the purview of section 212(a)(4) [8 U.S.C.A. § 1182(a)(4)], if such alien is otherwise entitled to receive a visa or other documentation, upon receipt of notice by the consular officer from the Attorney General of the giving of a bond or undertaking providing indemnity as in the case of aliens admitted under section 213 [8 U.S.C.A. § 1183]: Provided further, That a visa may be issued to an alien defined in section 101(a)(15)(B) or (F) [8 U.S.C.A. § 1101(a)(15)(B) or (F)], if such alien is otherwise entitled to receive a visa, upon receipt of a notice by the consular officer from the Attorney General of the giving of a bond with sufficient surety in such sum and containing such conditions as the consular officer shall prescribe, to insure that at the expiration of the time for which such alien has been admitted by the Attorney General, as provided in section 214(a) [8 U.S.C.A. § 1184(a)], or upon failure to maintain the status under which he was admitted, or to maintain any status subsequently acquired under section 248 [8 U.S.C.A. § 1258], such alien will depart from the United States.

(h) Nonadmission upon arrival

Nothing in this Act shall be construed to entitle any alien, to whom a visa or other documentation has been issued, to be admitted [sic] the United States, if, upon arrival at a port of entry in the United States, he is found to be inadmissible under this Act, or any other provision of law. The substance of this subsection shall appear upon every visa application.

(i) Revocation of visas or documents

After the issuance of a visa or other documentation to any alien, the consular officer or the Secretary of State may at any time, in his discretion, revoke such visa or other documentation. Notice of such revocation shall be communicated to the Attorney General, and such revocation shall invalidate the visa or other documentation from the date of issuance: Provided, That carriers or transportation companies, and masters, commanding officers, agents, owners, charterers, or consignees, shall not be penalized under section 273(b) [8 U.S.C.A. § 1323(b)] for action taken in reliance on such visas or other documentation, unless they received due notice of such revocation prior to the alien's embarkation. There shall be no means of judicial review (including review pursuant to section 2241 of Title 28 or any other habeas corpus provision, and sections 1361 and 1651 of such title) of a revocation under this subsection, except in the context of a removal proceeding if such revocation provides the sole ground for removal under section 237(a)(1)(B) [8 U.S.C.A. § 1227(a)(1)(B)].

(June 27, 1952, c. 477, Title II, ch. 3, § 221, 66 Stat. 191; Sept. 26, 1961, Pub.L. 87–301, § 4, 75 Stat. 651; Oct. 3, 1965, Pub.L. 89–236, §§ 11(a), (b), 17, 79 Stat. 918, 919; Dec. 29, 1981, Pub.L. 97–116, § 18(f), 95 Stat. 1620; Nov. 14, 1986, Pub.L. 99–653, § 5(a)(1) to (3), formerly § 5(a) to (c), 100 Stat. 3656; renumbered Oct. 24, 1988, Pub.L. 100–525, § 8 (d) (1), 102 Stat. 2617, and amended Nov. 29, 1990, Pub.L. 101–649, Title VI, § 603(a)(9), 104 Stat. 5083; Dec. 12, 1991, Pub.L. 102–232, Title III, § 302(e)(8)(C), 105 Stat. 1746; Sept. 30,

1996, Pub.L. 104–208, Div. C, Title III, § 308(d)(4)(G), (f)(2)(B), Title VI, § 631, 110 Stat. 3009–618, 3009–621, 3009–700; May 14, 2002, Pub.L. 107–173, Title III, § 301, 116 Stat. 552; Dec. 17, 2004, Pub.L. 108–458, Title V, § 5304(a), 118 Stat. 3736; Pub.L. 114–70, § 2, Oct. 16, 2015, 129 Stat. 561.)

§ 222. Application for visas [8 U.S.C.A. § 1202]

(a) Immigrant visas

Every alien applying for an immigrant visa and for alien registration shall make application therefor in such form and manner and at such place as shall be by regulations prescribed. In the application the alien shall state his full and true name, and any other name which he has used or by which he has been known; age and sex; the date and place of his birth; and such additional information necessary to the identification of the applicant and the enforcement of the immigration and nationality laws as may be by regulations prescribed.

(b) Other documentary evidence for immigrant visa

Every alien applying for an immigrant visa shall present a valid unexpired passport or other suitable travel document, or document of identity and nationality, if such document is required under the regulations issued by the Secretary of State. The immigrant shall furnish to the consular officer with his application a copy of a certification by the appropriate police authorities stating what their records show concerning the immigrant; a certified copy of any existing prison record, military record, and record of his birth; and a certified copy of all other records or documents concerning him or his case which may be required by the consular officer. The copy of each document so furnished shall be permanently attached to the application and become a part thereof. In the event that the immigrant establishes to the satisfaction of the consular officer that any document or record required by this subsection is unobtainable, the consular officer may permit the immigrant to submit in lieu of such document or record other satisfactory evidence of the fact to which such document or record would, if obtainable, pertain. All immigrant visa applications shall be reviewed and adjudicated by a consular officer.

(c) Nonimmigrant visas; nonimmigrant registration; form, manner and contents of application

Every alien applying for a nonimmigrant visa and for alien registration shall make application therefor in such form and manner as shall be by regulations prescribed. In the application the alien shall state his full and true name, the date and place of birth, his nationality, the purpose and length of his intended stay in the United States; his marital status; and such additional information necessary to the identification of the applicant, the determination of his eligibility for a nonimmigrant visa, and the enforcement of the immigration and nationality laws as may be by regulations prescribed. The alien shall provide complete and accurate information in response to any request for information contained in the application. At the discretion of the Secretary of State, application forms for the various classes of nonimmigrant admissions described in section 101(a)(15) [8 U.S.C.A. § 1101(a)(15)] may vary according to the class of visa being requested.

(d) Other documentary evidence for nonimmigrant visa

Every alien applying for a nonimmigrant visa and alien registration shall furnish to the consular officer, with his application, a certified copy of such documents pertaining to him as may be by regulations required. All nonimmigrant visa applications shall be reviewed and adjudicated by a consular officer.

(e) Signing and verification of application

Except as may be otherwise prescribed by regulations, each application for an immigrant visa shall be signed by the applicant in the presence of the consular officer, and verified by the oath of the applicant administered by the consular officer. The application for an immigrant visa, when visaed by the consular officer, shall become the immigrant visa. The application for a nonimmigrant visa or other documentation as a nonimmigrant shall be disposed of as may be by regulations prescribed. The issuance of a nonimmigrant visa shall, except as may be otherwise by regulations prescribed, be evidenced by a stamp, or other [sic] placed in the alien's passport.

(f) Confidential nature of records

The records of the Department of State and of diplomatic and consular offices of the United States pertaining to the issuance or refusal of visas or permits to enter the United States shall be considered confidential and shall be used only for the formulation, amendment, administration, or enforcement of the immigration, nationality, and other laws of the United States, except that—

(1) in the discretion of the Secretary of State certified copies of such records may be made available to a court which certifies that the information contained in such records is needed by the court in the interest of the ends of justice in a case pending before the court.

(2) the Secretary of State, in the Secretary's discretion and on the basis of reciprocity, may provide to a foreign government information in the Department of State's computerized visa lookout database and, when necessary and appropriate, other records covered by this section related to information in the database—

(A) with regard to individual aliens, at any time on a case-by-case basis for the purpose of preventing, investigating, or punishing acts that would constitute a crime in the United States, including, but not limited to, terrorism or trafficking in controlled substances, persons, or illicit weapons; or

(B) with regard to any or all aliens in the database, pursuant to such conditions as the Secretary of State shall establish in an agreement with the foreign government in which that government agrees to use such information and records for the purposes described in subparagraph (A) or to deny visas to persons who would be inadmissible to the United States.

(g) Voidness of nonimmigrant visa for stay beyond authorized period

(1) In the case of an alien who has been admitted on the basis of a nonimmigrant visa and remained in the United States beyond the period of stay authorized by the Attorney General, such visa shall be void beginning after the conclusion of such period of stay.

(2) An alien described in paragraph (1) shall be ineligible to be readmitted to the United States as a nonimmigrant, except—

(A) on the basis of a visa (other than the visa described in paragraph (1)) issued in a consular office located in the country of the alien's nationality (or, if there is no office in such country, in such other consular office as the Secretary of State shall specify); or

(B) where extraordinary circumstances are found by the Secretary of State to exist.

(h) Notwithstanding any other provision of this Act, the Secretary of State shall require every alien applying for a nonimmigrant visa—

(1) who is at least 14 years of age and not more than 79 years of age to submit to an in person interview with a consular officer unless the requirement for such interview is waived—

(A) by a consular official and such alien is—

(i) within that class of nonimmigrants enumerated in subparagraph (A) or (G) of section 101(a)(15) [8 U.S.C.A. § 1101(a)(15)];

(ii) within the NATO visa category;

(iii) within that class of nonimmigrants enumerated in section 101(a)(15)(C)(iii) [sic]* [8 U.S.C.A. § 1101(a)(15)(C)(iii)] (referred to as the "C–3 visa" category); or

(iv) granted a diplomatic or official visa on a diplomatic or official passport or on the equivalent thereof;

(B) by a consular official and such alien is applying for a visa—

(i) not more than 12 months after the date on which such alien's prior visa expired;

(ii) for the visa classification for which such prior visa was issued;

(iii) from the consular post located in the country of such alien's usual residence, unless otherwise prescribed in regulations that require an applicant to apply for a visa in the country of which such applicant is a national; and

* Section 101(a)(15)(C) does not have subparts.—eds.

(iv) the consular officer has no indication that such alien has not complied with the immigration laws and regulations of the United States; or

(C) by the Secretary of State if the Secretary determines that such waiver is—

(i) in the national interest of the United States; or

(ii) necessary as a result of unusual or emergent circumstances; and

(2) notwithstanding paragraph (1), to submit to an in person interview with a consular officer if such alien—

(A) is not a national or resident of the country in which such alien is applying for a visa;

(B) was previously refused a visa, unless such refusal was overcome or a waiver of ineligibility has been obtained;

(C) is listed in the Consular Lookout and Support System (or successor system at the Department of State);

(D) is a national of a country officially designated by the Secretary of State as a state sponsor of terrorism, except such nationals who possess nationalities of countries that are not designated as state sponsors of terrorism;

(E) requires a security advisory opinion or other Department of State clearance, unless such alien is—

(i) within that class of nonimmigrants enumerated in subparagraph (A) or (G) of section 101(a)(15) [8 U.S.C.A. § 1101(a)(15)];

(ii) within the NATO visa category;

(iii) within that class of nonimmigrants enumerated in section 101(a)(15)(C)(iii) [sic]* [8 U.S.C.A. § 1101(a)(15)(C)(iii)] (referred to as the "C–3 visa" category); or

(iv) an alien who qualifies for a diplomatic or official visa, or its equivalent; or

(F) is identified as a member of a group or sector that the Secretary of State determines—

(i) poses a substantial risk of submitting inaccurate information in order to obtain a visa;

(ii) has historically had visa applications denied at a rate that is higher than the average rate of such denials; or

(iii) poses a security threat to the United States.

(June 27, 1952, c. 477, Title II, ch. 3, § 222, 66 Stat. 193; Sept. 26, 1961, Pub.L. 87–301, § 6, 75 Stat. 653; Oct. 3, 1965, Pub.L. 89–236 § 11(c), 79 Stat. 918; Nov. 14, 1986, Pub.L.

* **Section 101(a)(15)(C) does not have subparts.—eds.**

99–653, § 6, 100 Stat. 3656; Oct. 24, 1988, Pub.L. 100–525, §§ 8(e), 9(j), 102 Stat. 2617, 2620; Oct. 25, 1994, Pub.L. 103–416, Title II, § 205(a), 108 Stat. 4311; Sept. 30, 1996, Pub.L. 104–208, Div. C, Title VI, §§ 632(a), 634, 110 Stat. 3009–701; Oct. 26, 2001, Pub.L. 107–56, Title IV, § 413, 115 Stat. 353; Dec. 17, 2004, Pub.L. 108–458, Title V, §§ 5301, 5302, Title VII, § 7203(b), 118 Stat. 3735, 3814.)

§ 223.   Re-entry permit [8 U.S.C.A. § 1203]

(a) Application; contents

(1) Any alien lawfully admitted for permanent residence, or (2) any alien lawfully admitted to the United States pursuant to clause 6 of section 3 of the Immigration Act of 1924, between July 1, 1924, and July 5, 1932, both dates inclusive, who intends to depart temporarily from the United States may make application to the Attorney General for a permit to reenter the United States, stating the length of his intended absence or absences, and the reasons therefor. Such applications shall be made under oath, and shall be in such form, contain such information, and be accompanied by such photographs of the applicant as may be by regulations prescribed.

(b) Issuance of permit; nonrenewability

If the Attorney General finds (1) that the applicant under subsection (a)(1) has been lawfully admitted to the United States for permanent residence, or that the applicant under subsection (a)(2) has since admission maintained the status required of him at the time of his admission and such applicant desires to visit abroad and to return to the United States to resume the status existing at the time of his departure for such visit, (2) that the application is made in good faith, and (3) that the alien's proposed departure from the United States would not be contrary to the interests of the United States, the Attorney General may, in his discretion, issue the permit, which shall be valid for not more than two years from the date of issuance and shall not be renewable. The permit shall be in such form as shall be by regulations prescribed for the complete identification of the alien.

(c) Multiple reentries

During the period of validity, such permit may be used by the alien in making one or more applications for reentry into the United States.

(d) Presented and surrendered

Upon the return of the alien to the United States the permit shall be presented to the immigration officer at the port of entry, and upon the expiration of its validity, the permit shall be surrendered to the Service.

(e) Permit in lieu of visa

A permit issued under this section in the possession of the person to whom issued, shall be accepted in lieu of any visa which otherwise would be required from such person under this Act. Otherwise a permit issued under this section shall have no effect under the immigration laws except to show that the alien to whom it was issued is returning from a temporary visit abroad; but nothing in this section shall be construed as making such permit the exclusive means of establishing that the alien is so returning.

(June 27, 1952, c. 477, Title II, ch. 3, § 223, 66 Stat. 194; Pub. L. 97–116, § 6, Dec. 29, 1981, 95 Stat. 1615.)

§ 224. Immediate relative and special immigrant visas [8 U.S.C.A. § 1204]

A consular officer may, subject to the limitations provided in section 221 [8 U.S.C.A. § 1201], issue an immigrant visa to a special immigrant or immediate relative as such upon satisfactory proof, under regulations prescribed under this Act, that the applicant is entitled to special immigrant or immediate relative status.

(June 27, 1952, c. 477, Title II, ch. 3, § 224, 66 Stat. 195; Pub. L. 89–236, § 11(d), Oct. 3, 1965, 79 Stat. 918.)

CHAPTER IV—INSPECTION, APPREHENSION, EXAMINATION, EXCLUSION, AND REMOVAL

§ 231. Lists of alien and citizen passengers arriving and departing [8 U.S.C.A. § 1221]

(a) Arrival manifest

For each commercial vessel or aircraft transporting any person to any seaport or airport of the United States from any place outside the United States, it shall be the duty of an appropriate official specified in subsection (d) to provide to any United States border officer (as defined in subsection (i)) at that port manifest information about each passenger, crew member, and other occupant transported on such vessel or aircraft prior to arrival at that port.

(b) Departure manifests

For each commercial vessel or aircraft taking passengers on board at any seaport or airport of the United States, who are destined to any place outside the United States, it shall be the duty of an appropriate official specified in subsection (d) to provide any United States border officer (as defined in subsection (i)) before departure from such port manifest information about each passenger, crew member, and other occupant to be transported.

(c) Contents of manifest

The information to be provided with respect to each person listed on a manifest required to be provided under subsection (a) or (b) shall include—

    (1) complete name;

    (2) date of birth;

(3) citizenship;

(4) sex;

(5) passport number and country of issuance;

(6) country of residence;

(7) United States visa number, date, and place of issuance, where applicable;

(8) alien registration number, where applicable;

(9) United States address while in the United States; and

(10) such other information the Attorney General, in consultation with the Secretary of State, and the Secretary of Treasury determines as being necessary for the identification of the persons transported and for the enforcement of the immigration laws and to protect safety and national security.

(d) Appropriate officials specified

An appropriate official specified in this subsection is the master or commanding officer, or authorized agent, owner, or consignee, of the commercial vessel or aircraft concerned.

(e) Deadline for requirement of electronic transmission of manifest information

Not later than January 1, 2003, manifest information required to be provided under subsection (a) or (b) shall be transmitted electronically by the appropriate official specified in subsection (d) to an immigration officer.

(f) Prohibition

No operator of any private or public carrier that is under a duty to provide manifest information under this section shall be granted clearance papers until the appropriate official specified in subsection (d) has complied with the requirements of this subsection, except that, in the case of commercial vessels or aircraft that the Attorney General determines are making regular trips to the United States, the Attorney General may, when expedient, arrange for the provision of manifest information of persons departing the United States at a later date.

(g) Penalties against noncomplying shipments, aircraft, or carriers

If it shall appear to the satisfaction of the Attorney General that an appropriate official specified in subsection (d), any public or private carrier, or the agent of any transportation line, as the case may be, has refused or failed to provide manifest information required by subsection (a) or (b), or that the manifest information provided is not accurate and full based on information provided to the carrier, such official, carrier, or agent, as the case may be, shall pay to the Commissioner the sum of $1,000 for each person with respect to whom such accurate and full manifest information is not provided, or with respect to whom the manifest information is not prepared as prescribed by this section or by regulations issued pursuant thereto. No commercial vessel or aircraft shall be granted clearance pending determination of the question of the liability to the payment of such penalty, or while it remains unpaid, and no such penalty shall be remitted or refunded, except that clearance may be granted prior to the determination of such question upon the deposit with the Commissioner of a bond or undertaking approved by the Attorney General or a sum sufficient to cover such penalty.

(h) Waiver

The Attorney General may waive the requirements of subsection (a) or (b) upon such circumstances and conditions as the Attorney General may by regulation prescribe.

(i) United States border officer defined

In this section, the term "United States border officer" means, with respect to a particular port of entry into the United States, any United States official who is performing duties at that port of entry.

(j) Record of citizens and resident aliens leaving permanently for foreign countries

The Attorney General may authorize immigration officers to record the following information regarding every resident person leaving the United States by way of the Canadian or Mexican borders for permanent residence in a foreign country: Names, age, and sex; whether married or single; calling or occupation; whether able to read or write; nationality; country of birth; country of which citizen or subject; race; last permanent residence in the United States; intended future permanent residence; and time and port of last arrival in the United States; and if a United States citizen or national, the facts on which claim to that status is based.

(June 27, 1952, c. 477, Title II, ch. 4, § 231, 66 Stat. 195; Dec. 29, 1981, Pub.L. 97–116, § 18(g), 95 Stat. 1620; Nov. 29, 1990, Pub.L. 101–649, Title V, § 543(a)(1), 104 Stat. 5057; Dec. 12, 1991, Pub.L. 102–232, Title III, § 306(c)(4)(A), 105 Stat. 1752; Pub.L. 104–208, Div. C, Title III, § 308(g)(1), Sept. 30, 1996, 110 Stat. 3009–622; Nov. 28, 2001, Pub.L. 107–77, Title I, § 115, 115 Stat. 768; May 14, 2002, Pub.L. 107–173, Title IV, § 402.)

§ 232. Detention of aliens for physical and mental examination [8 U.S.C.A. § 1222]

(a) Detention of aliens

For the purpose of determining whether aliens (including alien crewmen) arriving at ports of the United States belong to any of the classes inadmissible under this Act, by reason of being afflicted with any of the diseases or mental or physical defects or disabilities set forth in section 212(a) [8 U.S.C.A. § 1182(a)], or whenever the Attorney General has received information showing that any aliens are coming from a country or have embarked at a place where any of such diseases are prevalent or epidemic, such aliens shall be detained by the Attorney General, for a sufficient time to enable the immigration officers and medical officers to subject such aliens to observation and an examination sufficient to determine whether or not they belong to the inadmissible classes.

(b) Physical and mental examination

The physical and mental examination of arriving aliens (including alien crewmen) shall be made by medical officers of the United States Public Health Service, who shall conduct all medical examinations and shall certify, for the information of the immigration officers and the immigration judges, any physical and mental defect or disease observed by such medical officers in any such alien. If medical officers of the United States Public Health Service are not available, civil surgeons of not less than four years' professional experience may be employed for such service upon such terms as may be prescribed by the Attorney General. Aliens (including alien crewmen) arriving at ports of the United States shall be examined by at least one such medical officer or civil surgeon under such administrative regulations as the Attorney General may prescribe, and under medical regulations prepared by the Secretary of Health and Human Services. Medical officers of the United States Public Health Service who have had special training in the diagnosis of insanity and mental defects shall be detailed for duty or employed at such ports of entry as the Attorney General may designate, and such medical officers shall be provided with suitable facilities for the detention and examination of all arriving aliens who it is suspected may be inadmissible under paragraph (1) of section 212(a) [8 U.S.C.A. § 1182(a)], and the services of interpreters shall be provided for such examination. Any alien certified under paragraph (1) of section 212(a) [8 U.S.C.A. § 1182(a)], may appeal to a board of medical officers of the United States Public Health Service, which shall be convened by the Secretary of Health and Human Services, and any such alien may introduce before such board one expert medical witness at his own cost and expense.

(c) Certification of certain helpless aliens

If an examining medical officer determines that an alien arriving in the United States is inadmissible, is helpless from sickness, mental or physical disability, or infancy, and is accompanied by another alien whose protection or guardianship may be required, the officer may certify such fact for purposes of applying section 212(a)(10)(B) [8 U.S.C.A. § 1182(a)(10)(B)] with respect to the other alien.

(June 27, 1952, c. 477, Title II, ch. 4, § 232, 66 Stat. 196; Oct. 18, 1986, Pub.L. 99–500, Title I, § 101(b) [Title II, § 206(a), formerly § 206], 100 Stat. 1783–56 as renumbered and amended Oct. 24, 1988, Pub.L. 100–525, § 4(b)(1), (2), (d), 102 Stat. 2615; Sept. 30, 1996, Pub.L. 104–208, Div. C, Title III, §§ 308(b)(2), (3), (c)(2)(A), (d)(3)(A), (4)(H), 371(b)(3), 110 Stat. 3009–615, 3009–616, 3009–617, 3009–618, 3009–645.)

§ 233. Entry through or from foreign territory and adjacent islands [8 U.S.C.A. § 1223]

(a) Necessity of transportation contract

The Attorney General shall have power to enter into contracts with transportation lines for the inspection and admission of aliens coming to the United States from foreign territory or from adjacent islands. No such transportation line shall be allowed to land any such alien in the United States until and unless it has entered into any such contracts which may be required by the Attorney General.

(b) Landing stations

Every transportation line engaged in carrying alien passengers for hire to the United States from foreign territory of from adjacent islands shall provide and maintain at its expense suitable landing stations, approved by the Attorney General, conveniently located at the point or points of entry. No such transportation line shall be allowed to land any alien passengers in the United States until such landing stations are provided, and unless such stations are thereafter maintained to the satisfaction of the Attorney General.

(c) Landing agreements

The Attorney General shall have power to enter into contracts including bonding agreements with transportation lines to guarantee the passage through the United States in immediate and continuous transit of aliens destined to foreign countries. Notwithstanding any other provision of this Act, such aliens may not have their classification changed under section 248 [8 U.S.C.A. § 1258].

(d) Definitions

As used in this section the terms "transportation line" and "transportation company" include, but are not limited to, the owner, charterer, consignee, or authorized agent operating any vessel or aircraft or railroad train bringing aliens to the United States, to foreign territory, or to adjacent islands.

(e) Redesignated (d).

(June 27, 1952, c. 477, Title II, ch. 4, § 233, formerly § 238, 66 Stat. 202, as amended Nov. 14, 1986, Pub.L. 99–653, § 7(b), 100 Stat. 3657; redesignated § 233 and amended, Sept. 30, 1996, Pub.L. 104–208, Div. C, Title III, §§ 308(b)(4), (f)(4), 362, 110 Stat. 3009–615, 3009–622, 3009–645.)

§ 234. Designation of ports of entry for aliens arriving by aircraft [8 U.S.C.A. § 1224]

The Attorney General is authorized (1) by regulation to designate as ports of entry for aliens arriving by aircraft any of the ports of entry for civil aircraft designated as such in accordance with law; (2) by regulation to provide such reasonable requirements for aircraft in civil air navigation with respect to giving notice of intention to land in advance of landing, or notice of landing, as shall be deemed necessary for purposes of administration and enforcement of this Act; and **(3)** by regulation to provide for the application to civil air navigation of the provisions of this Act where not expressly so provided in this Act to such extent and upon such conditions as he deems necessary. Any person who violates any regulation made under this section shall be subject to a civil penalty of $2,000 which may be remitted or mitigated by the Attorney General in accordance with such proceedings as the Attorney General shall by regulation prescribe. In case the violation is by the owner or person in command of the aircraft, the penalty shall be a lien upon the aircraft, and such aircraft may be libeled therefor in the appropriate United States court. The determination by the Attorney General and remission or mitigation of the civil penalty shall be final. In case the violation is by the owner or person in command of the aircraft, the penalty shall be a lien upon the aircraft and may be collected by proceedings in rem which shall conform as nearly as may be to civil suits in admiralty. The Supreme Court of the United States, and under its direction other courts of the United States, are authorized to prescribe rules regulating such proceedings against aircraft in any particular not otherwise provided by law. Any aircraft made subject to a lien by this section may be summarily seized by, and placed in the custody of such persons as the Attorney General may by regulation prescribe. The aircraft may be released from such custody upon deposit of such amount not exceeding $2000 as the Attorney General may prescribe, or of a bond in such sum and with such sureties as the Attorney General may prescribe, conditioned upon the payment of the penalty which may be finally determined by the Attorney General.

(June 27, 1952, c. 477, Title II, ch. 4, § 234, formerly § 239, 66 Stat. 203, as amended Nov. 29, 1990, Pub.L. 101–649, Title V, § 543(a)(3), 104 Stat. 5058; Dec. 12, 1991, Pub.L. 102–232, Title III, § 306(c)(2), 105 Stat. 1752; renumbered § 234, Pub.L. 104–208, Div. C, Title III, § 304(a)(1), Sept. 30, 1996, 110 Stat. 3009–587.)

§ 235. Inspection by immigration officers; expedited removal of inadmissible arriving aliens; referral for hearing [8 U.S.C.A. § 1225]

(a) Inspection

(1) Aliens treated as applicants for admission

An alien present in the United States who has not been admitted or who arrives in the United States (whether or not at a designated port of arrival and including an alien who is brought to the United States after having been interdicted in international or United States waters) shall be deemed for purposes of this Act an applicant for admission.

(2) Stowaways

An arriving alien who is a stowaway is not eligible to apply for admission or to be admitted and shall be ordered removed upon inspection by an immigration officer. Upon such inspection if the alien indicates an intention to apply for asylum under section 208 [8 U.S.C.A.

§ 1158] or a fear of persecution, the officer shall refer the alien for an interview under subsection (b)(1)(B). A stowaway may apply for asylum only if the stowaway is found to have a credible fear of persecution under subsection (b)(1)(B). In no case may a stowaway be considered an applicant for admission or eligible for a hearing under section 240 [8 U.S.C.A. § 1229a].

(3) Inspection

All aliens (including alien crewmen) who are applicants for admission or otherwise seeking admission or readmission to or transit through the United States shall be inspected by immigration officers.

(4) Withdrawal of application for admission

An alien applying for admission may, in the discretion of the Attorney General and at any time, be permitted to withdraw the application for admission and depart immediately from the United States.

(5) Statements

An applicant for admission may be required to state under oath any information sought by an immigration officer regarding the purposes and intentions of the applicant in seeking admission to the United States, including the applicant's intended length of stay and whether the applicant intends to remain permanently or become a United States citizen, and whether the applicant is inadmissible.

(b) Inspection of applicants for admission

(1) Inspection of aliens arriving in the United States and certain other aliens who have not been admitted or paroled

(A) Screening

(i) In general

If an immigration officer determines that an alien (other than an alien described in subparagraph (F)) who is arriving in the United States or is described in clause (iii) is inadmissible under section 212(a)(6)(C) [8 U.S.C.A. § 1182(a)(6)(C)] or 212(a)(7) [8 U.S.C.A. § 1182(a)(7)], the officer shall order the alien removed from the United States without further hearing or review unless the alien indicates either an intention to apply for asylum under section 208 [8 U.S.C.A. § 1158] or a fear of persecution.

(ii) Claims for asylum

If an immigration officer determines that an alien (other than an alien described in subparagraph (F)) who is arriving in the United States or is described in clause (iii) is inadmissible under section 212(a)(6)(C) [8 U.S.C.A. § 1182(a)(6)(C)] or 212(a)(7) [8 U.S.C.A. § 1182(a)(7)] and the alien indicates either an intention to apply for asylum under section 208 [8 U.S.C.A. § 1158] or a fear of persecution, the officer shall refer the alien for an interview by an asylum officer under subparagraph (B).

(iii) Application to certain other aliens

(I) In general

The Attorney General may apply clauses (i) and (ii) of this subparagraph to any or all aliens described in subclause (II) as designated by the Attorney General. Such designation shall be in the sole and unreviewable discretion of the Attorney General and may be modified at any time.

(II) Aliens described

An alien described in this clause is an alien who is not described in subparagraph (F), who has not been admitted or paroled into the United States, and who has not affirmatively shown, to the satisfaction of an immigration officer, that the alien has been physically present in the United States continuously for the 2-year period immediately prior to the date of the determination of inadmissibility under this subparagraph.

(B) Asylum interviews

(i) Conduct by asylum officers

An asylum officer shall conduct interviews of aliens referred under subparagraph (A)(ii), either at a port of entry or at such other place designated by the Attorney General.

(ii) Referral of certain aliens

If the officer determines at the time of the interview that an alien has a credible fear of persecution (within the meaning of clause (v)), the alien shall be detained for further consideration of the application for asylum.

(iii) Removal without further review if no credible fear of persecution

(I) In general

Subject to subclause (III), if the officer determines that an alien does not have a credible fear of persecution, the officer shall order the alien removed from the United States without further hearing or review.

(II) Record of determination

The officer shall prepare a written record of a determination under subclause (I). Such record shall include a summary of the material facts as stated by the applicant, such additional facts (if any) relied upon by the officer, and the officer's analysis of why, in the light of such facts, the alien has not established a credible fear of persecution. A copy of the officer's interview notes shall be attached to the written summary.

(III) Review of determination

The Attorney General shall provide by regulation and upon the alien's request for prompt review by an immigration judge of a determination under subclause (I) that the alien does not have a credible fear of persecution. Such review shall include an opportunity for the alien to be heard and questioned by the immigration judge, either in person or by telephonic or video connection. Review shall be concluded as expeditiously as possible, to the maximum extent practicable within 24 hours, but in no case later than 7 days after the date of the determination under subclause (I).

(IV) Mandatory detention

Any alien subject to the procedures under this clause shall be detained pending a final determination of credible fear of persecution and, if found not to have such a fear, until removed.

(iv) Information about interviews

The Attorney General shall provide information concerning the asylum interview described in this subparagraph to aliens who may be eligible. An alien who is eligible for such interview may consult with a person or persons of the alien's choosing prior to the interview or any review thereof, according to regulations prescribed by the Attorney General. Such consultation shall be at no expense to the Government and shall not unreasonably delay the process.

(v) Credible fear of persecution defined

For purposes of this subparagraph, the term "credible fear of persecution" means that there is a significant possibility, taking into account the credibility of the statements made by the alien in support of the alien's claim and such other facts as are known to the officer, that the alien could establish eligibility for asylum under section 208 [8 U.S.C.A. § 1158].

(C) Limitation on administrative review

Except as provided in subparagraph (B)(iii)(III), a removal order entered in accordance with subparagraph (A)(i) or (B)(iii)(I) is not subject to administrative appeal, except that the Attorney General shall provide by regulation for prompt review of such an order under subparagraph (A)(i) against an alien who claims under oath, or as permitted under penalty of perjury under section 1746 of Title 28, after having been warned of the penalties for falsely making such claim under such conditions, to have been lawfully admitted for permanent residence, to have been admitted as a refugee under section 207 [8 U.S.C.A. § 1157], or to have been granted asylum under section 208 [8 U.S.C.A. § 1158].

(D) Limit on collateral attacks

In any action brought against an alien under section 275(a) [8 U.S.C.A. § 1325(a)] or section 276 [8 U.S.C.A. § 1326], the court shall not have jurisdiction to hear any claim attacking the validity of an order of removal entered under subparagraph (A)(i) or (B)(iii).

(E) Asylum officer defined

As used in this paragraph, the term "asylum officer" means an immigration officer who—

(i) has had professional training in country conditions, asylum law, and interview techniques comparable to that provided to full-time adjudicators of applications under section 208 [8 U.S.C.A. § 1158], and

(ii) is supervised by an officer who meets the condition described in clause (i) and has had substantial experience adjudicating asylum applications.

(F) Exception

Subparagraph (A) shall not apply to an alien who is a native or citizen of a country in the Western Hemisphere with whose government the United States does not have full diplomatic relations and who arrives by aircraft at a port of entry.

(G) Commonwealth of the Northern Mariana Islands

Nothing in this subsection shall be construed to authorize or require any person described in section 208(e) [8 U.S.C.A. § 1158(e)] to be permitted to apply for asylum under section 208 [8 U.S.C.A. § 1158] at any time before January 1, 2014.

(2) Inspection of other aliens

(A) In general

Subject to subparagraphs (B) and (C), in the case of an alien who is an applicant for admission, if the examining immigration officer determines that an alien seeking admission is not clearly and beyond a doubt entitled to be admitted, the alien shall be detained for a proceeding under section 240 [8 U.S.C.A. § 1229a].

(B) Exception

Subparagraph (A) shall not apply to an alien—

(i) who is a crewman,

(ii) to whom paragraph (1) applies, or

(iii) who is a stowaway.

(C) Treatment of aliens arriving from contiguous territory

In the case of an alien described in subparagraph (A) who is arriving on land (whether or not at a designated port of arrival) from a foreign territory contiguous to the United States, the Attorney

General may return the alien to that territory pending a proceeding under section 240 [8 U.S.C.A. § 1229a].

(3) Challenge of decision

The decision of the examining immigration officer, if favorable to the admission of any alien, shall be subject to challenge by any other immigration officer and such challenge shall operate to take the alien whose privilege to be admitted is so challenged, before an immigration judge for a proceeding under section 240 [8 U.S.C.A. § 1229a].

(c) Removal of aliens inadmissible on security and related grounds

(1) Removal without further hearing

If an immigration officer or an immigration judge suspects that an arriving alien may be inadmissible under subparagraph (A) (other than clause (ii)), (B), or (C) of section 212(a)(3) [8 U.S.C.A. § 1182(a)(3)], the officer or judge shall—

(A) order the alien removed, subject to review under paragraph (2);

(B) report the order of removal to the Attorney General; and

(C) not conduct any further inquiry or hearing until ordered by the Attorney General.

(2) Review of order

(A) The Attorney General shall review orders issued under paragraph (1).

(B) If the Attorney General—

(i) is satisfied on the basis of confidential information that the alien is inadmissible under subparagraph (A) (other than clause (ii)), (B), or (C) of section 212(a)(3) [8 U.S.C.A. § 1182(a)(3)], and

(ii) after consulting with appropriate security agencies of the United States Government, concludes that disclosure of the information would be prejudicial to the public interest, safety, or security,

the Attorney General may order the alien removed without further inquiry or hearing by an immigration judge.

(C) If the Attorney General does not order the removal of the alien under subparagraph (B), the Attorney General shall specify the further inquiry or hearing that shall be conducted in the case.

(3) Submission of statement and information

The alien or the alien's representative may submit a written statement and additional information for consideration by the Attorney General.

(d) Authority relating to inspections

(1) Authority to search conveyances

Immigration officers are authorized to board and search any vessel, aircraft, railway car, or other conveyance or vehicle in which they believe aliens are being brought into the United States.

(2) Authority to order detention and delivery of arriving aliens

Immigration officers are authorized to order an owner, agent, master, commanding officer, person in charge, purser, or consignee of a vessel or aircraft bringing an alien (except an alien crewmember) to the United States—

(A) to detain the alien on the vessel or at the airport of arrival, and

(B) to deliver the alien to an immigration officer for inspection or to a medical officer for examination.

(3) Administration of oath and consideration of evidence

The Attorney General and any immigration officer shall have power to administer oaths and to take and consider evidence of or from any person touching the privilege of any alien or person he believes or suspects to be an alien to enter, reenter, transit through, or reside in the United States or concerning any matter which is material and relevant to the enforcement of this Act and the administration of the Service.

(4) Subpoena authority

(A) The Attorney General and any immigration officer shall have power to require by subpoena the attendance and testimony of witnesses before immigration officers and the production of books, papers, and documents relating to the privilege of any person to enter, reenter, reside in, or pass through the United States or concerning any matter which is material and relevant to the enforcement of this Act and the administration of the Service, and to that end may invoke the aid of any court of the United States.

(B) Any United States district court within the jurisdiction of which investigations or inquiries are being conducted by an immigration officer may, in the event of neglect or refusal to respond to a subpoena issued under this paragraph or refusal to testify before an immigration officer, issue an order requiring such persons to appear before an immigration officer, produce books, papers, and documents if demanded, and testify, and any failure to obey such order of the court may be punished by the court as a contempt thereof.

(June 27, 1952, c. 477, Title II, ch. 4, § 235, 66 Stat. 198; Nov. 29, 1990, Pub.L. 101–649, Title VI, § 603(a)(11), 104 Stat. 5083; Apr. 24, 1996, Pub.L. 104–132, Title IV, §§ 422(a), 423(b), 110 Stat. 1270, 1272; Sept. 30, 1996, Pub.L. 104–208, Div. C, Title III, §§ 302(a), 308(d)(5), 371(b)(4), 110 Stat. 3009–579, 3009–619, 3009–645; May 8, 2008, Pub.L. 110–229, Title VII, Subtitle A, § 702(j)(5), 122 Stat. 867.)

§ 235A. Preinspection at foreign airports [8 U.S.C.A. § 1225a]

(a) Establishment of preinspection stations

(1) New stations

Subject to paragraph (5), not later than October 31, 1998, the Attorney General, in consultation with the Secretary of State, shall establish and maintain preinspection stations in at least 5 of the foreign airports that are among the 10 foreign airports which the Attorney General identifies as serving as last points of departure for the greatest numbers of inadmissible alien passengers who arrive from abroad by air at ports of entry within the United States. Such preinspection stations shall be in addition to any preinspection stations established prior to the date of the enactment of such Act.

(2) Report

Not later than October 31, 1998, the Attorney General shall report to the Committees on the Judiciary of the House of Representatives and of the Senate on the implementation of paragraph (1).

(3) Data collection

Not later than November 1, 1997, and each subsequent November 1, the Attorney General shall compile data identifying—

(A) the foreign airports which served as last points of departure for aliens who arrived by air at United States ports of entry without valid documentation during the preceding fiscal years;

(B) the number and nationality of such aliens arriving from each such foreign airport; and

(C) the primary routes such aliens followed from their country of origin to the United States.

(4) Additional stations

Subject to paragraph (5), not later than January 1, 2008, the Secretary of Homeland Security, in consultation with the Secretary of State, shall establish preinspection stations in at least 25 additional foreign airports, which the Secretary of Homeland Security, in consultation with the Secretary of State, determines, based on the data compiled under paragraph (3) and such other information as may be available, would most effectively facilitate the travel of admissible aliens and reduce the number of inadmissible aliens, especially aliens who are potential terrorists, who arrive from abroad by air at points of entry within the United States. Such preinspection stations shall be in addition to those established before September 30, 1996, or pursuant to paragraph (1).

(5) Conditions

Prior to the establishment of a preinspection station, the Attorney General, in consultation with the Secretary of State, shall ensure that—

(A) employees of the United States stationed at the preinspection station and their accompanying family members will receive appropriate protection;

(B) such employees and their families will not be subject to unreasonable risks to their welfare and safety; and

(C) the country in which the preinspection station is to be established maintains practices and procedures with respect to asylum seekers and refugees in accordance with the Convention Relating to the Status of Refugees (done at Geneva, July 28, 1951), or the Protocol Relating to the Status of Refugees (done at New York, January 31, 1967), or that an alien in the country otherwise has recourse to avenues of protection from return to persecution.

(b) Establishment of carrier consultant program and immigration security initiative

The Secretary of Homeland Security shall assign additional immigration officers to assist air carriers in the detection of fraudulent documents at foreign airports which, based on the records maintained pursuant to subsection (a)(3) of this section, served as a point of departure for a significant number of arrivals at United States ports of entry without valid documentation, but where no preinspection station exists. Beginning not later than December 31, 2006, the number of airports selected for an assignment under this subsection shall be at least 50.

(June 27, 1952, c. 477, Title II, ch. 4, § 235A, as added Sept. 30, 1996, Pub.L. 104–208, Div.C, Title I, § 123(a), 110 Stat. 3009–560; Pub.L. 108–458, Title VII, §§ 7206(a), 7210(d), Dec. 17, 2004, 118 Stat. 3817, 3824.)

§ 236.   Apprehension and detention of aliens [8 U.S.C.A. § 1226]

(a) Arrest, detention, and release

On a warrant issued by the Attorney General, an alien may be arrested and detained pending a decision on whether the alien is to be removed from the United States. Except as provided in subsection (c) and pending such decision, the Attorney General—

(1) may continue to detain the arrested alien; and

(2) may release the alien on—

(A) bond of at least $1,500 with security approved by, and containing conditions prescribed by, the Attorney General; or

(B) conditional parole; but

(3) may not provide the alien with work authorization (including an "employment authorized" endorsement or other appropriate work permit), unless the alien is lawfully admitted for permanent residence or otherwise would (without regard to removal proceedings) be provided such authorization.

(b) Revocation of bond or parole

The Attorney General at any time may revoke a bond or parole authorized under subsection (a), rearrest the alien under the original warrant, and detain the alien.

(c) Detention of criminal aliens

(1) Custody

The Attorney General shall take into custody any alien who—

(A) is inadmissible by reason of having committed any offense covered in section 212(a)(2) [8 U.S.C.A. § 1182(a)(2)],

(B) is deportable by reason of having committed any offense covered in section 237(a)(2)(A)(ii), (A)(iii), (B), (C), or (D) [8 U.S.C.A. § 1227(a)(2)(A)(ii), (A)(iii), (B), (C), or (D)],

(C) is deportable under section 237(a)(2)(A)(i) [8 U.S.C.A. § 1227(a)(2)(A)(i)] on the basis of an offense for which the alien has been sentence [sic] to a term of imprisonment of at least 1 year, or

(D) is inadmissible under section 212(a)(3)(B) [8 U.S.C.A. § 1182(a)(3)(B)] or deportable under section 237(a)(4)(B) [8 U.S.C.A. § 1227(a)(4)(B)],

when the alien is released, without regard to whether the alien is released on parole, supervised release, or probation, and without regard to whether the alien may be arrested or imprisoned again for the same offense.

(2) Release

The Attorney General may release an alien described in paragraph (1) only if the Attorney General decides pursuant to section 3521 of Title 18, that release of the alien from custody is necessary to provide protection to a witness, a potential witness, a person cooperating with an investigation into major criminal activity, or an immediate family member or close associate of a witness, potential witness, or person cooperating with such an investigation, and the alien satisfies the Attorney General that the alien will not pose a danger to the safety of other persons or of property and is likely to appear for any scheduled proceeding. A decision relating to such release shall take place in accordance with a procedure that considers the severity of the offense committed by the alien.

(d) Identification of criminal aliens

(1) The Attorney General shall devise and implement a system—

(A) to make available, daily (on a 24-hour basis), to Federal, State, and local authorities the investigative resources of the Service to determine whether individuals arrested by such authorities for aggravated felonies are aliens;

(B) to designate and train officers and employees of the Service to serve as a liaison to Federal, State, and local law enforcement and correctional agencies and courts with respect to the arrest, conviction, and release of any alien charged with an aggravated felony; and

(C) which uses computer resources to maintain a current record of aliens who have been convicted of an aggravated felony, and indicates those who have been removed.

(2) The record under paragraph (1)(C) shall be made available—

(A) to inspectors at ports of entry and to border patrol agents at sector headquarters for purposes of immediate identification of any alien who was previously ordered removed and is seeking to reenter the United States, and

(B) to officials of the Department of State for use in its automated visa lookout system.

(3) Upon the request of the governor or chief executive officer of any State, the Service shall provide assistance to State courts in the identification of aliens unlawfully present in the United States pending criminal prosecution.

(e) Judicial review

The Attorney General's discretionary judgment regarding the application of this section shall not be subject to review. No court may set aside any action or decision by the Attorney General under this section regarding the detention or release of any alien or the grant, revocation, or denial of bond or parole.

(June 27, 1952, c. 477, Title II, ch. 4, § 236, 66 Stat. 200; Nov. 29, 1990, Pub.L. 101–649, Title V, § 504(b), Title VI, § 603(a)(12), 104 Stat. 5050, 5083; Dec. 12, 1991, Pub.L. 102–232, Title III, § 306(a)(5), 105 Stat. 1751; Sept. 30, 1996, Pub.L. 104–208, Div. C, Title III, §§ 303(a), 371(b)(5), 110 Stat. 3009–585, 3009–645.)

§ 236A. Mandatory detention of suspected terrorists; habeas corpus; judicial review [8 U.S.C.A. § 1226a]

(a) Detention of terrorist aliens

(1) Custody

The Attorney General shall take into custody any alien who is certified under paragraph (3).

(2) Release

Except as provided in paragraphs (5) and (6), the Attorney General shall maintain custody of such an alien until the alien is removed from the United States. Except as provided in paragraph (6), such custody shall be maintained irrespective of any relief from removal for which the alien may be eligible, or any relief from removal granted the alien, until the Attorney General determines that the alien is no longer an alien who may be certified under paragraph (3). If the alien is finally determined not to be removable, detention pursuant to this subsection shall terminate.

(3) Certification

The Attorney General may certify an alien under this paragraph if the Attorney General has reasonable grounds to believe that the alien—

(A) is described in section 212(a)(3)(A)(i), 212(a)(3)(A)(iii), 212(a)(3)(B), 237(a)(4)(A)(i), 237(a)(4)(A)(iii), or 237(a)(4)(B) [8 U.S.C.A. § 1182(a)(3)(A)(i), 1182(a)(3)(A)(iii), 1182(a)(3)(B), 1227(a)(4)(A)(i), 1227(a)(4)(A)(iii), or 1227(a)(4)(B)]; or

(B) is engaged in any other activity that endangers the national security of the United States.

(4) Nondelegation

The Attorney General may delegate the authority provided under paragraph (3) only to the Deputy Attorney General. The Deputy Attorney General may not delegate such authority.

(5) Commencement of proceedings

The Attorney General shall place an alien detained under paragraph (1) in removal proceedings, or shall charge the alien with a criminal offense, not later than 7 days after the commencement of such detention. If the requirement of the preceding sentence is not satisfied, the Attorney General shall release the alien.

(6) Limitation on indefinite detention

An alien detained solely under paragraph (1) who has not been removed under section 241(a)(1)(A) [8 U.S.C.A. § 1231(a)(1)(A)], and whose removal is unlikely in the reasonably foreseeable future, may be detained for additional periods of up to six months only if the release of the alien will threaten the national security of the United States or the safety of the community or any person.

(7) Review of certification

The Attorney General shall review the certification made under paragraph (3) every 6 months. If the Attorney General determines, in the Attorney General's discretion, that the certification should be revoked, the alien may be released on such conditions as the Attorney General deems appropriate, unless such release is otherwise prohibited by law. The alien may request each 6 months in writing that the Attorney General reconsider the certification and may submit documents or other evidence in support of that request.

(b) Habeas corpus and judicial review

(1) In general

Judicial review of any action or decision relating to this section (including judicial review of the merits of a determination made under subsection (a)(3) or (a)(6)) is available exclusively in habeas corpus proceedings consistent with this subsection. Except as provided in the preceding sentence, no court shall have jurisdiction to review, by habeas corpus petition or otherwise, any such action or decision.

(2) Application

(A) In general

Notwithstanding any other provision of law, including section 2241(a) of Title 28, habeas corpus proceedings described in paragraph (1) may be initiated only by an application filed with—

(i) the Supreme Court;

(ii) any justice of the Supreme Court;

(iii) any circuit judge of the United States Court of Appeals for the District of Columbia Circuit; or

(iv) any district court otherwise having jurisdiction to entertain it.

(B) Application transfer

Section 2241(b) of Title 28 shall apply to an application for a writ of habeas corpus described in subparagraph (A).

(3) Appeals

Notwithstanding any other provision of law, including section 2253 of Title 28, in habeas corpus proceedings described in paragraph (1) before a circuit or district judge, the final order shall be subject to review, on appeal, by the United States Court of Appeals for the District of Columbia Circuit. There shall be no right of appeal in such proceedings to any other circuit court of appeals.

(4) Rule of decision

The law applied by the Supreme Court and the United States Court of Appeals for the District of Columbia Circuit shall be regarded as the rule of decision in habeas corpus proceedings described in paragraph (1).

(c) Statutory construction

The provisions of this section shall not be applicable to any other provision of this Act.

(June 27, 1952, c. 477, Title II, ch. 4, § 236A, as added Oct. 26, 2001, Pub.L. 107–56, Title IV, § 412(a), 115 Stat. 350.)

§ 237.   Deportable aliens [8 U.S.C.A. § 1227]

(a) Classes of deportable aliens

Any alien (including an alien crewman) in and admitted to the United States shall, upon the order of the Attorney General, be removed if the alien is within one or more of the following classes of deportable aliens:

(1) Inadmissible at time of entry or of adjustment of status or violates status

(A) Inadmissible aliens

Any alien who at the time of entry or adjustment of status was within one or more of the classes of aliens inadmissible by the law existing at such time is deportable.

(B) Present in violation of law

Any alien who is present in the United States in violation of this Act or any other law of the United States, or whose nonimmigrant visa (or other documentation authorizing admission into the United States as a nonimmigrant) has been revoked under section 221(i) [8 U.S.C.A. § 1201(i)], is deportable.

(C) Violated nonimmigrant status or condition of admission

(i) Nonimmigrant status violators

Any alien who was admitted as a nonimmigrant and who has failed to maintain the nonimmigrant status in which the alien was admitted or to which it was changed under section 248 [8 U.S.C.A. § 1258], or to comply with the conditions of any such status, is deportable.

(ii) Violators of conditions of admission

Any alien whom the Secretary of Health and Human Services certifies has failed to comply with terms, conditions, and controls that were imposed under section 212(g) [8 U.S.C.A. § 1182(g)] is deportable.

(D) Termination of conditional permanent residence

(i) In general

Any alien with permanent resident status on a conditional basis under section 216 [8 U.S.C.A. § 1186a] (relating to conditional permanent resident status for certain alien spouses and sons and daughters) or under section 216A [8 U.S.C.A. § 1186b] (relating to conditional permanent resident status for certain alien entrepreneurs, spouses, and children) who has had such status terminated under such respective section is deportable.

(ii) Exception

Clause (i) shall not apply in the cases described in section 216(c)(4) [8 U.S.C.A. § 1186a(c)(4)] (relating to certain hardship waivers).

(E) Smuggling

(i) In general

Any alien who (prior to the date of entry, at the time of any entry, or within 5 years of the date of any entry) knowingly has encouraged, induced, assisted, abetted, or aided any other alien to enter or to try to enter the United States in violation of law is deportable.

(ii) Special rule in the case of family reunification

Clause (i) shall not apply in the case of alien who is an eligible immigrant (as defined in section 301(b)(1) of the Immigration Act of 1990), was physically present in the United States on May 5, 1988, and is seeking admission as an immediate relative or under section 203(a)(2) [8 U.S.C.A. § 1153(a)(2)] (including under section 112 of the Immigration Act of 1990) or benefits under section 301(a) of the Immigration Act of 1990 if the alien, before May 5, 1988, has encouraged, induced, assisted, abetted, or aided only the alien's spouse, parent, son, or daughter (and no other individual) to enter the United States in violation of law.

(iii) Waiver authorized

The Attorney General may, in his discretion for humanitarian purposes, to assure family unity, or when it is otherwise in the public interest, waive application of clause (i) in the case of any alien lawfully admitted for permanent residence if the alien has encouraged, induced, assisted, abetted, or aided only an individual who at the time of the offense was the alien's spouse, parent, son, or daughter (and no other individual) to enter the United States in violation of law.

(F) Repealed. Pub.L. 104–208, Div. C, Title VI, § 671(d)(1)(C), Sept. 30, 1996, 110 Stat. 3009–723.

(G) Marriage fraud

An alien shall be considered to be deportable as having procured a visa or other documentation by fraud (within the meaning of section 212(a)(6)(C)(i) [8 U.S.C.A. § 1182(a)(6)(C)(i)]) and to be in the United States in violation of this Act (within the meaning of subparagraph (B)) if—

   (i) the alien obtains any admission into the United States with an immigrant visa or other documentation procured on the basis of a marriage entered into less than 2 years prior to such admission of the alien and which, within 2 years subsequent to any admission of the alien in the United States, shall be judicially annulled or terminated, unless the alien establishes to the satisfaction of the Attorney General that such marriage was not contracted for the purpose of evading any provisions of the immigration laws, or

   (ii) it appears to the satisfaction of the Attorney General that the alien has failed or refused to fulfill the alien's marital agreement which in the opinion of the Attorney General was made for the purpose of procuring the alien's admission as an immigrant.

(H) Waiver authorized for certain misrepresentations

The provisions of this paragraph relating to the removal of aliens within the United States on the ground that they were inadmissible at the time of admission as aliens, described in section 212(a)(6)(C)(i) [8 U.S.C.A. § 1182(a)(6)(C)(i)], whether willful or innocent, may, in the discretion of the Attorney General, be waived for any alien (other than an alien described in paragraph (4)(D)) who—

(i)(I) is the spouse, parent, son, or daughter of a citizen of the United States or of an alien lawfully admitted to the United States for permanent residence; and

(II) was in possession of an immigrant visa or equivalent document and was otherwise admissible to the United States at the time of such admission except for those grounds of inadmissibility specified under paragraphs (5)(A) and (7)(A) of section 212(a) [8 U.S.C.A. § 1182(a)] which were a direct result of that fraud or misrepresentation.

(ii) is a VAWA self-petitioner.

A waiver of removal for fraud or misrepresentation granted under this subparagraph shall also operate to waive removal based on the grounds of inadmissibility directly resulting from such fraud or misrepresentation.

(2) Criminal offenses

(A) General crimes

(i) Crimes of moral turpitude

Any alien who—

(I) is convicted of a crime involving moral turpitude committed within five years (or 10 years in the case of an alien provided lawful permanent resident status under section 245(j) [8 U.S.C.A. § 1255(j)]) after the date of admission, and

(II) is convicted of a crime for which a sentence of one year or longer may be imposed,

is deportable.

(ii) Multiple criminal convictions

Any alien who at any time after admission is convicted of two or more crimes involving moral turpitude, not arising out of a single scheme of criminal misconduct, regardless of whether confined therefor and regardless of whether the convictions were in a single trial, is deportable.

(iii) Aggravated felony

Any alien who is convicted of an aggravated felony at any time after admission is deportable.

(iv) High speed flight

Any alien who is convicted of a violation of section 758 of Title 18, (relating to high speed flight from an immigration checkpoint) is deportable.

(v) Failure to register as a sex offender

Any alien who is convicted under section 2250 of title 18, United States Code, is deportable.

(vi) Waiver authorized

Clauses (i), (ii), (iii), and (iv) shall not apply in the case of an alien with respect to a criminal conviction if the alien subsequent to the criminal conviction has been granted a full and unconditional pardon by the President of the United States or by the Governor of any of the several States.

(B) Controlled substances

(i) Conviction

Any alien who at any time after admission has been convicted of a violation of (or a conspiracy or attempt to violate) any law or regulation of a State, the United States, or a foreign country relating to a controlled substance (as defined in section 802 of Title 21), other than a single offense involving possession for one's own use of 30 grams or less of marijuana, is deportable.

(ii) Drug abusers and addicts

Any alien who is, or at any time after admission has been, a drug abuser or addict is deportable.

(C) Certain firearm offenses

Any alien who at any time after admission is convicted under any law of purchasing, selling, offering for sale, exchanging, using, owning, possessing, or carrying, or of attempting or conspiring to purchase, sell, offer for sale, exchange, use, own, possess, or carry, any weapon, part, or accessory which is a firearm or destructive device (as defined in section 921(a) of Title 18) in violation of any law is deportable.

(D) Miscellaneous crimes

Any alien who at any time has been convicted (the judgment on such conviction becoming final) of, or has been so convicted of a conspiracy or attempt to violate—

(i) any offense under chapter 37 (relating to espionage), chapter 105 (relating to sabotage), or chapter 115 (relating to treason and sedition) of Title 18, for which a term of imprisonment of five or more years may be imposed;

(ii) any offense under section 871 or 960 of Title 18;

(iii) a violation of any provision of the Military Selective Service Act (50 U.S.C. App. 451 et seq.) or the Trading With the Enemy Act (50 U.S.C. App. 1 et seq.); or

(iv) a violation of section 215 [8 U.S.C.A. § 1185] or 278 [8 U.S.C.A. § 1328],

is deportable.

(E) Crimes of domestic violence, stalking, or violation of protection order, crimes against children and*

(i) Domestic violence, stalking, and child abuse

Any alien who at any time after admission is convicted of a crime of domestic violence, a crime of stalking, or a crime of child abuse, child neglect, or child abandonment is deportable. For purposes of this clause, the term "crime of domestic violence" means any crime of violence (as defined in section 16 of Title 18) against a person committed by a current or former spouse of the person, by an individual with whom the person shares a child in common, by an individual who is cohabiting with or has cohabited with the person as a spouse, by an individual similarly situated to a spouse of the person under the domestic or family violence laws of the jurisdiction where the offense occurs, or by any other individual against a person who is protected from that individual's acts under the domestic or family violence laws of the United States or any State, Indian tribal government, or unit of local government.

(ii) Violators of protection orders

Any alien who at any time after admission is enjoined under a protection order issued by a court and whom the court determines has engaged in conduct that violates the portion of a protection order that involves protection against credible threats of violence, repeated harassment, or bodily injury to the person or persons for whom the protection order was issued is deportable. For purposes of this clause, the term "protection order" means any injunction issued for the purpose of preventing violent or threatening acts of domestic violence, including temporary or final orders issued by civil or criminal courts (other than support or child custody orders or provisions) whether obtained by filing an independent action or as a pendente lite order in another proceeding.

(F) Trafficking

Any alien described in section 212(a)(2)(H) [8 U.S.C.A. § 1182(a)(2)(H)] is deportable.

(3) Failure to register and falsification of documents

(A) Change of address

* So in original.

An alien who has failed to comply with the provisions of section 265 [8 U.S.C.A. § 1305] is deportable, unless the alien establishes to the satisfaction of the Attorney General that such failure was reasonably excusable or was not willful.

(B) Failure to register or falsification of documents

Any alien who at any time has been convicted—

(i) under section 266(c) [8 U.S.C.A. § 1306(c)] or under section 36(c) of the Alien Registration Act, 1940,

(ii) of a violation of, or an attempt or a conspiracy to violate, any provision of the Foreign Agents Registration Act of 1938 (22 U.S.C. 611 et seq.), or

(iii) of a violation of, or an attempt or a conspiracy to violate, section 1546 of Title 18 (relating to fraud and misuse of visas, permits, and other entry documents),

is deportable.

(C) Document fraud

(i) In general

An alien who is the subject of a final order for violation of section 274C [8 U.S.C.A. § 1324C] is deportable.

(ii) Waiver authorized

The Attorney General may waive clause (i) in the case of an alien lawfully admitted for permanent residence if no previous civil money penalty was imposed against the alien under section 274C [8 U.S.C.A. § 1324C] and the offense was incurred solely to assist, aid, or support the alien's spouse or child (and no other individual). No court shall have jurisdiction to review a decision of the Attorney General to grant or deny a waiver under this clause.

(D) Falsely claiming citizenship

(i) In general

Any alien who falsely represents, or has falsely represented, himself to be a citizen of the United States for any purpose or benefit under this Act (including section 274A [8 U.S.C.A. § 1324a]) or any Federal or State law is deportable.

(ii) Exception

In the case of an alien making a representation described in clause (i), if each natural parent of the alien (or, in the case of an adopted alien, each adoptive parent of the alien) is or was a citizen (whether by birth or naturalization), the alien permanently resided in the United States prior to attaining the age of 16, and the alien reasonably believed at the time of making such representation that he or she was a citizen, the alien shall not be considered to be deportable under any provision of this subsection based on such representation.

(4) Security and related grounds

(A) In general

Any alien who has engaged, is engaged, or at any time after admission engages in—

(i) any activity to violate any law of the United States relating to espionage or sabotage or to violate or evade any law prohibiting the export from the United States of goods, technology, or sensitive information,

(ii) any other criminal activity which endangers public safety or national security, or

(iii) any activity a purpose of which is the opposition to, or the control or overthrow of, the Government of the United States by force, violence, or other unlawful means,

is deportable.

(B) Terrorist activities

Any alien who is described in subparagraph (B) or (F) of section 212(a)(3) [8 U.S.C.A. § 1182(a)(3)] is deportable.

(C) Foreign policy

(i) In general

An alien whose presence or activities in the United States the Secretary of State has reasonable ground to believe would have potentially serious adverse foreign policy consequences for the United States is deportable.

(ii) Exceptions

The exceptions described in clauses (ii) and (iii) of section 212(a)(3)(C) [8 U.S.C.A. § 1182(a)(3)(C)] shall apply to deportability under clause (i) in the same manner as they apply to inadmissibility under section 212(a)(3)(C)(i) [8 U.S.C.A. § 1182(a)(3)(C)(i)].

(D) Participated in Nazi persecution, genocide, or the commission of any act of torture or extrajudicial killing

Any alien described in clause (i), (ii), or (iii) of section 212(a)(3)(E) [8 U.S.C.A. § 1182(a)(3)(E)] is deportable.

(E) Participated in the Commission of severe violations of religious freedom

Any alien described in section 212(a)(2)(G) [8 U.S.C.A. § 1182(a)(2)(G)] is deportable.

(F) Recruitment or use of child soldiers

Any alien who has engaged in the recruitment or use of child soldiers in violation of section 2442 of Title 18, United States Code, is deportable.

(5) Public charge

Any alien who, within five years after the date of entry, has become a public charge from causes not affirmatively shown to have arisen since entry is deportable.

(6) Unlawful voters

(A) In general

Any alien who has voted in violation of any Federal, State, or local constitutional provision, statute, ordinance, or regulation is deportable.

(B) Exception

In the case of an alien who voted in a Federal, State, or local election (including an initiative, recall, or referendum) in violation of a lawful restriction of voting to citizens, if each natural parent of the alien (or, in the case of an adopted alien, each adoptive parent of the alien) is or was a citizen (whether by birth or naturalization), the alien permanently resided in the United States prior to attaining the age of 16, and the alien reasonably believed at the time of such violation that he or she was a citizen, the alien shall not be considered to be deportable under any provision of this subsection based on such violation.

(7) Waiver for victims of domestic violence

(A) In general

The Attorney General is not limited by the criminal court record and may waive the application of paragraph (2)(E)(i) (with respect to crimes of domestic violence and crimes of stalking) and (ii) in the case of an alien who has been battered or subjected to extreme cruelty and who is not and was not the primary perpetrator of violence in the relationship—

(i) upon a determination that—

(I) the alien was acting is* self-defense;

(II) the alien was found to have violated a protection order intended to protect the alien; or

(III) the alien committed, was arrested for, was convicted of, or pled guilty to committing a crime—

(aa) that did not result in serious bodily injury; and

(bb) where there was a connection between the crime and the alien's having been battered or subjected to extreme cruelty.

---

* So in original. Probably should be "in".

(B) Credible evidence considered

In acting on applications under this paragraph, the Attorney General shall consider any credible evidence relevant to the application. The determination of what evidence is credible and the weight to be given that evidence shall be within the sole discretion of the Attorney General.

(b) Deportation of certain nonimmigrants

An alien, admitted as a nonimmigrant under the provisions of either section 101(a)(15)(A)(i) [8 U.S.C.A. § 1101(a)(15)(A)(i)] or 101(a)(15)(G)(i) [8 U.S.C.A. § 1101(a)(15)(G)(i)], and who fails to maintain a status under either of those provisions, shall not be required to depart from the United States without the approval of the Secretary of State, unless such alien is subject to deportation under paragraph (4) of subsection (a).

(c) Waiver of grounds for deportation

Paragraphs (1)(A), (1)(B), (1)(C), (1)(D), and (3)(A) of subsection (a) (other than so much of paragraph (1) as relates to a ground of inadmissibility described in paragraph (2) or (3) of section 212(a) [8 U.S.C.A. § 1182(a)]) shall not apply to a special immigrant described in section 101(a)(27)(J) [8 U.S.C.A. § 1101(a)(27)(J)] based upon circumstances that existed before the date the alien was provided such special immigrant status.

(d)(1) If the Secretary of Homeland Security determines that an application for nonimmigrant status under subparagraph (T) or (U) of section 101(a)(15) [8 U.S.C.A. § 1101(a)(15)] filed for an alien in the United States sets forth a prima facie case for approval, the Secretary may grant the alien an administrative stay of a final order of removal under section 241(c)(2) [8 U.S.C.A. § 1231(c)(2)] until

(A) the application for nonimmigrant status under such subparagraph (T) or (U) is approved; or

(B) there is a final administrative denial of the application for such nonimmigrant status after the exhaustion of administrative appeals.

(2) The denial of a request for an administrative stay of removal under this subsection shall not preclude the alien from applying for a stay of removal, deferred action, or a continuance or abeyance of removal proceedings under any other provision of the immigration laws of the United States.

(3) During any period in which the administrative stay of removal is in effect, the alien shall not be removed.

(4) Nothing in this subsection may be construed to limit the authority of the Secretary of Homeland Security or the Attorney General to grant a stay of removal or deportation in any case not described in this subsection.

(e) Redesignated (b).

(f) and (g) Repealed. Pub.L. 101–649, § 602(b)(1), Nov. 29, 1990, 104 Stat. 5081.

(h) Redesignated (c).

(June 27, 1952, c. 477, Title II, ch. 5, § 237, formerly § 241, 66 Stat. 204; July 18, 1956, c. 629, Title III, § 301(b), (c), 70 Stat. 575; July 14, 1960, Pub.L. 86–648, § 9, 74 Stat. 505; Sept. 26, 1961, Pub.L. 87–301, § 16, 75 Stat. 655; Oct. 3, 1965, Pub.L. 89–236, § 11(e), 79 Stat. 918; Oct. 20, 1976, Pub.L. 94–571, § 7(e), 90 Stat. 2706; Oct. 30, 1978; Pub.L. 95–549, Title I, § 103, 92 Stat. 2065; Dec. 29, 1981, Pub.L. 97–116, § 8, 95 Stat. 1616; Oct. 27, 1986, Pub.L. 99–570, Title I, § 1751(b), 100 Stat. 3207–47; Nov. 6, 1986, Pub.L. 99–603, Title III, § 303(b), 100 Stat. 3431; Nov. 10, 1986, Pub.L. 99–639, § 2(b), 100 Stat. 3541; Nov. 14, 1986, Pub.L. 99–653, § 7(c), 100 Stat. 3657; Oct. 24, 1988, Pub.L. 100–525, §§ 2(n)(2), 9(m), 102 Stat. 2613, 2620; Nov. 18, 1988, Pub.L. 100–690, Title VII, §§ 7344(a), 7348(a), 102 Stat. 4471, 4473; Nov. 29, 1990, Pub.L. 101–649, Title I, § 153(b), Title V, §§ 505(a), 508(a), 544(b), Title VI, § 602(a), (b), 104 Stat. 5006, 5050, 5051, 5061, 5077, 5081; Dec. 12, 1991, Pub.L. 102–232, Title III, §§ 302(d)(3), 307(h), (k), 105 Stat. 1745, 1755, 1756; Sept. 13, 1994, Pub.L. 103–322, Title XIII, § 130003(d), 108 Stat. 2026; Oct. 25, 1994, Pub.L. 103–416, Title II, §§ 203(b), 219(g), 108 Stat. 4311, 4317; Apr. 24, 1996, Pub.L. 104–132, Title IV, §§ 414(a), 435(a), 110 Stat. 1270, 1274; renumbered § 237 and amended Sept. 30, 1996, Pub.L. 104–208, Div. C, Title I, § 108(c), Title III, §§ 301(d), 305(a)(2), 308(d)(2), (3)(A), (e)(1)(E), (2)(C), (f)(1)(L) to (N), (5), 344(b), 345(b), 347(b), 350(a), 351(b), Title VI, § 671(a)(4)(B), (d)(1)(C), 110 Stat. 3009–558, 3009–579, 3009–598, 3009–617, 3009–619 to 3009–622, 3009–637 to 3009–640, 3009–721, 3009–723; Oct. 28, 2000, Pub.L. 106–386, Div. B, Title V, § 1505(b)(1), (c)(2), 114 Stat. 1525, 1526; Oct. 30, 2000, Pub.L. 106–395, Title II, § 201(c)(1), (2), 114 Stat. 1634, 1635; Oct. 26, 2001, Pub.L. 107–56, Title IV, § 411(b)(1), 115 Stat. 348; Dec. 17, 2004, Pub.L. 108–458, Title V, §§ 5304(b), 5402, 5501(b), 5502(b), 118 Stat. 3736, 3737, 3740, 3741; May 11, 2005, Pub.L. 109–13, Div. B, § 105(a), 119 Stat. 231, 309; July 27, 2006, Pub.L. 109–248, Title IV, § 401, 120 Stat. 622; Aug. 12, 2006, Pub.L. 109–271, § 6(c), 120 Stat. 763; Oct. 3, 2008, Pub.L. 110–340, § 2(c), 122 Stat. 3736; Dec. 23, 2008, Pub.L. 110–457, Title II, § 204, 122 Stat. 5060; Dec. 23, 2008, Pub.L. 110–457, Title II, § 222(f)(2), 122 Stat. 5071.)

§ 238. Expedited removal of aliens convicted of committing aggravated felonies [8 U.S.C.A. § 1228]

(a) Removal of criminal aliens

(1) In general

The Attorney General shall provide for the availability of special removal proceedings at certain Federal, State, and local correctional facilities for aliens convicted of any criminal offense covered in section 237(a)(2)(A)(iii), (B), (C), or (D) [8 U.S.C.A. § 1227(a)(2)(A)(iii), (B), (C), or (D)], or any offense covered by section 237(a)(2)(A)(ii) [8 U.S.C.A. § 1227(a)(2)(A)(ii)] for which both predicate offenses are, without regard to the date of their commission, otherwise covered by section 237(a)(2)(A)(i) [8 U.S.C.A. § 1227(a)(2)(A)(i)]. Such proceedings shall be conducted in conformity with section 240 [8 U.S.C.A. § 1229a] (except as otherwise provided in this section), and in a manner which eliminates the need for additional detention at any processing center of the Service and in a manner which assures expeditious removal following the end of the alien's incarceration for the underlying sentence. Nothing in this section shall be construed to create any substantive or procedural right or benefit that is legally enforceable by any party against the United States or its agencies or officers or any other person.

(2) Implementation

With respect to an alien convicted of an aggravated felony who is taken into custody by the Attorney General pursuant to section 236(c) [8 U.S.C.A. § 1226(c)], the Attorney General shall, to the maximum extent practicable, detain any such felon at a facility at which other such aliens are detained. In the selection of such facility, the Attorney General shall make reasonable efforts to ensure that the alien's access to counsel and right to counsel under section 292 [8 U.S.C.A. § 1362] are not impaired.

(3) Expedited proceedings

(A) Notwithstanding any other provision of law, the Attorney General shall provide for the initiation and, to the extent possible, the completion of removal proceedings, and any administrative appeals thereof, in the case of any alien convicted of an aggravated felony before the alien's release from incarceration for the underlying aggravated felony.

(B) Nothing in this section shall be construed as requiring the Attorney General to effect the removal of any alien sentenced to actual incarceration, before release from the penitentiary or correctional institution where such alien is confined.

(4) Review

(A) The Attorney General shall review and evaluate removal proceedings conducted under this section.

(B) The Comptroller General shall monitor, review, and evaluate removal proceedings conducted under this section. Within 18 months after the effective date of this section, the Comptroller General shall submit a report to such Committees concerning the extent to which removal proceedings conducted under this section may adversely affect the ability of such aliens to contest removal effectively.

(b) Removal of aliens who are not permanent residents

(1) The Attorney General may, in the case of an alien described in paragraph (2), determine the deportability of such alien under section 237(a)(2)(A)(iii) [8 U.S.C.A. § 1227(a)(2)(A)(iii)] (relating to conviction of an aggravated felony) and issue an order of removal pursuant to the procedures set forth in this subsection or section 240 [8 U.S.C.A. § 1229a].

(2) An alien is described in this paragraph if the alien—

(A) was not lawfully admitted for permanent residence at the time at which proceedings under this section commenced; or

(B) had permanent resident status on a conditional basis (as described in section 216 [8 U.S.C.A. § 1186a]) at the time that proceedings under this section commenced.

(3) The Attorney General may not execute any order described in paragraph (1) until 14 calendar days have passed from the date that such order was issued, unless waived by the alien, in order that the alien has an opportunity to apply for judicial review under section 242 [8 U.S.C.A. § 1252].

(4) Proceedings before the Attorney General under this subsection shall be in accordance with such regulations as the Attorney General shall prescribe. The Attorney General shall provide that—

    (A) the alien is given reasonable notice of the charges and of the opportunity described in subparagraph (C);

    (B) the alien shall have the privilege of being represented (at no expense to the government) by such counsel, authorized to practice in such proceedings, as the alien shall choose;

    (C) the alien has a reasonable opportunity to inspect the evidence and rebut the charges;

    (D) a determination is made for the record that the individual upon whom the notice for the proceeding under this section is served (either in person or by mail) is, in fact, the alien named in such notice;

    (E) a record is maintained for judicial review; and

    (F) the final order of removal is not adjudicated by the same person who issues the charges.

    (G) Redesignated (F).

(5) No alien described in this section shall be eligible for any relief from removal that the Attorney General may grant in the Attorney General's discretion.

(c)* [sic] Presumption of deportability

An alien convicted of an aggravated felony shall be conclusively presumed to be deportable from the United States.

(c)** [sic] Judicial removal

(1) Authority

Notwithstanding any other provision of this Act, a United States district court shall have jurisdiction to enter a judicial order of removal at the time of sentencing against an alien who is deportable, if such an order has been requested by the United States Attorney with the concurrence of the Commissioner and if the court chooses to exercise such jurisdiction.

---

* So in original. Two subsecs. (c) have been enacted.
** So in original. Two subsecs. (c) have been enacted.

(2) Procedure

(A) The United States Attorney shall file with the United States district court, and serve upon the defendant and the Service, prior to commencement of the trial or entry of a guilty plea a notice of intent to request judicial removal.

(B) Notwithstanding section 242B [8 U.S.C.A. § 1252b] [sic], the United States Attorney, with the concurrence of the Commissioner, shall file at least 30 days prior to the date set for sentencing a charge containing factual allegations regarding the alienage of the defendant and identifying the crime or crimes which make the defendant deportable under section 237(a)(2)(A) [8 U.S.C.A. § 1227(a)(2)(A)].

(C) If the court determines that the defendant has presented substantial evidence to establish prima facie eligibility for relief from removal under this Act, the Commissioner shall provide the court with a recommendation and report regarding the alien's eligibility for relief. The court shall either grant or deny the relief sought.

(D)(i) The alien shall have a reasonable opportunity to examine the evidence against him or her, to present evidence on his or her own behalf, and to cross-examine witnesses presented by the Government.

(ii) The court, for the purposes of determining whether to enter an order described in paragraph (1), shall only consider evidence that would be admissible in proceedings conducted pursuant to section 240 [8 U.S.C.A. § 1229a].

(iii) Nothing in this subsection shall limit the information a court of the United States may receive or consider for the purposes of imposing an appropriate sentence.

(iv) The court may order the alien removed if the Attorney General demonstrates that the alien is deportable under this Act.

(3) Notice, appeal, and execution of judicial order of removal

(A)(i) A judicial order of removal or denial of such order may be appealed by either party to the court of appeals for the circuit in which the district court is located.

(ii) Except as provided in clause (iii), such appeal shall be considered consistent with the requirements described in section 242 [8 U.S.C.A. § 1252].

(iii) Upon execution by the defendant of a valid waiver of the right to appeal the conviction on which the order of removal is based, the expiration of the period described in section 242(b)(1) [8 U.S.C.A. § 1252(b)(1)], or the final dismissal of an appeal from such conviction, the order of removal shall become final and shall be executed at the end of the prison term in accordance with the terms of the order. If the conviction is reversed on direct appeal, the order entered pursuant to this section shall be void.

(B) As soon as is practicable after entry of a judicial order of removal, the Commissioner shall provide the defendant with written notice of the order of removal, which shall designate the defendant's country of choice for removal and any alternate country pursuant to section 243(a) [8 U.S.C.A. § 1253(a)].

(4) Denial of judicial order

Denial of a request for a judicial order of removal shall not preclude the Attorney General from initiating removal proceedings pursuant to section 240 [8 U.S.C.A. § 1229a] upon the same ground of deportability or upon any other ground of deportability provided under section 237(a) [8 U.S.C.A. § 1227(a)].

(5) Stipulated judicial order of removal

The United States Attorney, with the concurrence of the Commissioner, may, pursuant to Federal Rule of Criminal Procedure 11, enter into a plea agreement which calls for the alien, who is deportable under this Act, to waive the right to notice and a hearing under this section, and stipulate to the entry of a judicial order of removal from the United States as a condition of the plea agreement or as a condition of probation or supervised release, or both. The United States district court, in both felony and misdemeanor cases, and a United States magistrate judge in misdemeanor cases, may accept such a stipulation and shall have jurisdiction to enter a judicial order of removal pursuant to the terms of such stipulation.

(d) Redesignated (c).

(June 27, 1952, c. 477, Title II, ch. 5, § 238, formerly § 242A, as added Nov. 18, 1988, Pub.L. 100–690, Title VII, § 7347(a), 102 Stat. 4471, and amended Nov. 29, 1990, Pub.L. 101–649, Title V, § 506(a), 104 Stat. 5050; Dec. 12, 1991, Pub.L. 102–232, Title III, § 309(b) (10), 105 Stat. 1759; Sept. 13, 1994, Pub.L. 103–322, Title XIII, § 130004(a), (c), 108 Stat. 2026, 2028; Oct. 25, 1994, Pub.L. 103–416, Title II, §§ 223(a), 224(a), 108 Stat. 4322; Apr. 24, 1996, Pub.L. 104–132, Title IV, §§ 440(g), 442(a), (c), 110 Stat. 1278, 1279, 1280; redesignated § 238 and amended Sept. 30, 1996, Pub.L. 104–208, Div. C, Title III, §§ 304(c)(1), 306(d), 308(b)(5), (c)(1), (4)(A), (e)(1)(F), (2)(D), (10), (g)(1), (2)(A), (C), (5)(A)(ii), (C), (D), (10) (H), 374(a), Title VI, § 671(b)(13), (c)(5), (6), 110 Stat. 3009–597, 3009–612, 3009–615, 3009–616, 3009–619, 3009–620, 3009–622, 3009–623, 3009–625, 3009–647, 3009–722, 3009–723.)

§ 239. Initiation of removal proceedings [8 U.S.C.A. § 1229]

(a) Notice to appear

(1) In general

In removal proceedings under section 240 [8 U.S.C.A. § 1229a], written notice (in this section referred to as a "notice to appear") shall be given in person to the alien (or, if personal service is not practicable, through service by mail to the alien or to the alien's counsel of record, if any) specifying the following:

(A) The nature of the proceedings against the alien.

(B) The legal authority under which the proceedings are conducted.

(C) The acts or conduct alleged to be in violation of law.

(D) The charges against the alien and the statutory provisions alleged to have been violated.

(E) The alien may be represented by counsel and the alien will be provided (i) a period of time to secure counsel under subsection (b)(1) and (ii) a current list of counsel prepared under subsection (b)(2).

(F)(i) The requirement that the alien must immediately provide (or have provided) the Attorney General with a written record of an address and telephone number (if any) at which the alien may be contacted respecting proceedings under section 240 [8 U.S.C.A. § 1229a].

(ii) The requirement that the alien must provide the Attorney General immediately with a written record of any change of the alien's address or telephone number.

(iii) The consequences under section 240(b)(5) [8 U.S.C.A. § 1229a(b)(5)] of failure to provide address and telephone information pursuant to this subparagraph.

(G)(i) The time and place at which the proceedings will be held.

(ii) The consequences under section 240(b)(5) [8 U.S.C.A. § 1229a(b)(5)] of the failure, except under exceptional circumstances, to appear at such proceedings.

(2) Notice of change in time or place of proceedings

(A) In general

In removal proceedings under section 240(b)(5) [8 U.S.C.A. § 1229a(b)(5)], in the case of any change or postponement in the time and place of such proceedings, subject to subparagraph (B) a written notice shall be given in person to the alien (or, if personal service is not practicable, through service by mail to the alien or to the alien's counsel of record, if any) specifying—

(i) the new time or place of the proceedings, and

(ii) the consequences under section 240(b)(5) [8 U.S.C.A. § 1229a(b)(5)] of failing, except under exceptional circumstances, to attend such proceedings.

(B) Exception

In the case of an alien not in detention, a written notice shall not be required under this paragraph if the alien has failed to provide the address required under paragraph (1)(F).

(3) Central address files

The Attorney General shall create a system to record and preserve on a timely basis notices of addresses and telephone numbers (and changes) provided under paragraph (1)(F).

(b) Securing of counsel

(1) In general

In order that an alien be permitted the opportunity to secure counsel before the first hearing date in proceedings under section 240 [8 U.S.C.A. § 1229a], the hearing date shall not be scheduled earlier than 10 days after the service of the notice to appear, unless the alien requests in writing an earlier hearing date.

(2) Current lists of counsel

The Attorney General shall provide for lists (updated not less often than quarterly) of persons who have indicated their availability to represent pro bono aliens in proceedings under section 240 [8 U.S.C.A. § 1229a]. Such lists shall be provided under subsection (a)(1)(E) and otherwise made generally available.

(3) Rule of construction

Nothing in this subsection may be construed to prevent the Attorney General from proceeding against an alien pursuant to section 240 [8 U.S.C.A. § 1229a] if the time period described in paragraph (1) has elapsed and the alien has failed to secure counsel.

(c) Service by mail

Service by mail under this section shall be sufficient if there is proof of attempted delivery to the last address provided by the alien in accordance with subsection (a)(1)(F).

(d) Prompt initiation of removal

(1) In the case of an alien who is convicted of an offense which makes the alien deportable, the Attorney General shall begin any removal proceeding as expeditiously as possible after the date of the conviction.

(2) Nothing in this subsection shall be construed to create any substantive or procedural right or benefit that is legally enforceable by any party against the United States or its agencies or officers or any other person.

(e) Certification of compliance with restrictions on disclosure

(1) In general

In cases where an enforcement action leading to a removal proceeding was taken against an alien at any of the locations specified in paragraph (2), the Notice to Appear shall include a statement that the provisions of section 384 of the Illegal Immigration Reform and Immigrant Responsibility Act of 1996 [8 U.S.C.A § 1367] have been complied with.

(2) Locations

The locations specified in this paragraph are as follows:

(A) At a domestic violence shelter, a rape crisis center, supervised visitation center, family justice center, a victim services, or victim services provider, or a community-based organization.

(B) At a courthouse (or in connection with that appearance of the alien at a courthouse) if the alien is appearing in connection with a protection order case, child custody case, or other civil or criminal case relating to domestic violence, sexual assault, trafficking, or stalking in which the alien has been battered or subject to extreme cruelty or if the alien is described in subparagraph (T) or (U) of section 101(a)(15) [8 U.S.C.A. § 1101(a)(15)].

(June 27, 1952, c. 477, Title II, § 239, as added Sept. 30, 1996, Pub.L. 104–208, Div. C, Title III, § 304(a)(3), 110 Stat. 3009–587, and amended Jan. 5, 2006, Pub.L. 109–162, Title VIII, § 825(c)(1), 119 Stat. 3065; Aug. 12, 2006, Pub.L. 109–271, § 6(d), 120 Stat. 763.)

§ 240. Removal proceedings [8 U.S.C.A. § 1229a]

(a) Proceeding

(1) In general

An immigration judge shall conduct proceedings for deciding the inadmissibility or deportability of an alien.

(2) Charges

An alien placed in proceedings under this section may be charged with any applicable ground of inadmissibility under section 212(a) [8 U.S.C.A. § 1182(a)] or any applicable ground of deportability under section 237(a) [8 U.S.C.A. § 1227(a)].

(3) Exclusive procedures

Unless otherwise specified in this Act, a proceeding under this section shall be the sole and exclusive procedure for determining whether an alien may be admitted to the United States or, if the alien has been so admitted, removed from the United States. Nothing in this section shall affect proceedings conducted pursuant to section 238 [8 U.S.C.A. § 1228].

(b) Conduct of proceeding

(1) Authority of immigration judge

The immigration judge shall administer oaths, receive evidence, and interrogate, examine, and cross-examine the alien and any witnesses. The immigration judge may issue subpoenas for the attendance of witnesses and presentation of evidence. The immigration judge shall have authority (under regulations prescribed by the Attorney General) to sanction by civil money penalty any action (or inaction) in contempt of the judge's proper exercise of authority under this Act.

(2) Form of proceeding

(A) In general

The proceeding may take place—

(i) in person,

(ii) where agreed to by the parties, in the absence of the alien,

(iii) through video conference, or

(iv) subject to subparagraph (B), through telephone conference.

(B) Consent required in certain cases

An evidentiary hearing on the merits may only be conducted through a telephone conference with the consent of the alien involved after the alien has been advised of the right to proceed in person or through video conference.

(3) Presence of alien

If it is impracticable by reason of an alien's mental incompetency for the alien to be present at the proceeding, the Attorney General shall prescribe safeguards to protect the rights and privileges of the alien.

(4) Aliens [sic] rights in proceeding

In proceedings under this section, under regulations of the Attorney General—

(A) the alien shall have the privilege of being represented, at no expense to the Government, by counsel of the alien's choosing who is authorized to practice in such proceedings,

(B) the alien shall have a reasonable opportunity to examine the evidence against the alien, to present evidence on the alien's own behalf, and to cross-examine witnesses presented by the Government but these rights shall not entitle the alien to examine such national security information as the Government may proffer in opposition to the alien's admission to the United States or to an application by the alien for discretionary relief under this Act, and

(C) a complete record shall be kept of all testimony and evidence produced at the proceeding.

(5) Consequences of failure to appear

(A) In general

Any alien who, after written notice required under paragraph (1) or (2) of section 239(a) [8 U.S.C.A. § 1229(a)] has been provided to the alien or the alien's counsel of record, does not attend a proceeding under this section, shall be ordered removed in absentia if the Service establishes by clear, unequivocal, and convincing evidence that the written notice was so provided and that the alien is removable (as defined in subsection (e)(2)). The written notice by the Attorney General shall be considered sufficient for purposes of this subparagraph if provided at the most recent address provided under section 239(a)(1)(F) [8 U.S.C.A. § 1229(a)(1)(F)].

(B) No notice if failure to provide address information

No written notice shall be required under subparagraph (A) if the alien has failed to provide the address required under section 239(a)(1)(F) [8 U.S.C.A. § 1229(a)(1)(F)].

(C) Rescission of order

Such an order may be rescinded only—

(i) upon a motion to reopen filed within 180 days after the date of the order of removal if the alien demonstrates that the failure to appear was because of exceptional circumstances (as defined in subsection (e)(1)), or

(ii) upon a motion to reopen filed at any time if the alien demonstrates that the alien did not receive notice in accordance with paragraph (1) or (2) of section 239(a) [8 U.S.C.A. § 1229(a)] or the alien demonstrates that the alien was in Federal or State custody and the failure to appear was through no fault of the alien.

The filing of the motion to reopen described in clause (i) or (ii) shall stay the removal of the alien pending disposition of the motion by the immigration judge.

(D) Effect on judicial review

Any petition for review under section 242 [8 U.S.C.A. § 1252] of an order entered in absentia under this paragraph shall (except in cases described in section 242(b)(5) [8 U.S.C.A. § 1252(b)(5)]) be confined to (i) the validity of the notice provided to the alien, (ii) the reasons for the alien's not attending the proceeding, and (iii) whether or not the alien is removable.

(E) Additional application to certain aliens in contiguous territory

The preceding provisions of this paragraph shall apply to all aliens placed in proceedings under this section, including any alien who remains in a contiguous foreign territory pursuant to section 235(b)(2)(C) [8 U.S.C.A. § 1225(b)(2)(C)].

(6) Treatment of frivolous behavior

The Attorney General shall, by regulation—

(A) define in a proceeding before an immigration judge or before an appellate administrative body under this title, frivolous behavior for which attorneys may be sanctioned,

(B) specify the circumstances under which an administrative appeal of a decision or ruling will be considered frivolous and will be summarily dismissed, and

(C) impose appropriate sanctions (which may include suspension and disbarment) in the case of frivolous behavior.

Nothing in this paragraph shall be construed as limiting the authority of the Attorney General to take actions with respect to inappropriate behavior.

(7) Limitation on discretionary relief for failure to appear

Any alien against whom a final order of removal is entered in absentia under this subsection and who, at the time of the notice described in paragraph (1) or (2) of section 239(a) [8 U.S.C.A. § 1229(a)], was provided oral notice, either in the alien's native language or in another language the alien understands, of the time and place of the proceedings and of the consequences under this paragraph of failing, other than because of exceptional circumstances (as defined in subsection (e)(1)) to attend a proceeding under this section, shall not be eligible for relief under section 240A [8 U.S.C.A. § 1229b], 240B [8 U.S.C.A. § 1229c], 245 [8 U.S.C.A. § 1255], 248 [8 U.S.C.A. § 1258], or 249 [8 U.S.C.A. § 1259] for a period of 10 years after the date of the entry of the final order of removal.

(c) Decision and burden of proof

(1) Decision

(A) In general

At the conclusion of the proceeding the immigration judge shall decide whether an alien is removable from the United States. The determination of the immigration judge shall be based only on the evidence produced at the hearing.

(B) Certain medical decisions

If a medical officer or civil surgeon or board of medical officers has certified under section 232(b) [8 U.S.C.A. § 1222(b)] that an alien has a disease, illness, or addiction which would make the alien inadmissible under paragraph (1) of section 212(a) [8 U.S.C.A. § 1182(a)], the decision of the immigration judge shall be based solely upon such certification.

(2) Burden on alien

In the proceeding the alien has the burden of establishing—

(A) if the alien is an applicant for admission, that the alien is clearly and beyond doubt entitled to be admitted and is not inadmissible under section 212 [8 U.S.C.A. § 1182]; or

(B) by clear and convincing evidence, that the alien is lawfully present in the United States pursuant to a prior admission.

In meeting the burden of proof under subparagraph (B), the alien shall have access to the alien's visa or other entry document, if any, and any other records and documents, not considered by the Attorney General to be confidential, pertaining to the alien's admission or presence in the United States.

(3) Burden on service in cases of deportable aliens

(A) In general

In the proceeding the Service has the burden of establishing by clear and convincing evidence that, in the case of an alien who has been admitted to the United States, the alien is deportable. No decision on deportability shall be valid unless it is based upon reasonable, substantial, and probative evidence.

(B) Proof of convictions

In any proceeding under this Act, any of the following documents or records (or a certified copy of such an official document or record) shall constitute proof of a criminal conviction:

(i) An official record of judgment and conviction.

(ii) An official record of plea, verdict, and sentence.

(iii) A docket entry from court records that indicates the existence of the conviction.

(iv) Official minutes of a court proceeding or a transcript of a court hearing in which the court takes notice of the existence of the conviction.

(v) An abstract of a record of conviction prepared by the court in which the conviction was entered, or by a State official associated with the State's repository of criminal justice records, that indicates the charge or section of law violated, the disposition of the case, the existence and date of conviction, and the sentence.

(vi) Any document or record prepared by, or under the direction of, the court in which the conviction was entered that indicates the existence of a conviction.

(vii) Any document or record attesting to the conviction that is maintained by an official of a State or Federal penal institution, which is the basis for that institution's authority to assume custody of the individual named in the record.

(C) Electronic records

In any proceeding under this Act, any record of conviction or abstract that has been submitted by electronic means to the Service from a State or court shall be admissible as evidence to prove a criminal conviction if it is—

(i) certified by a State official associated with the State's repository of criminal justice records as an official record from its repository or by a court official from the court in which the conviction was entered as an official record from its repository, and

(ii) certified in writing by a Service official as having been received electronically from the State's record repository or the court's record repository.

A certification under clause (i) may be by means of a computer-generated signature and statement of authenticity.

(4) Applications for relief from removal

(A) In general

An alien applying for relief or protection from removal has the burden of proof to establish that the alien—

(i) satisfies the applicable eligibility requirements; and

(ii) with respect to any form of relief that is granted in the exercise of discretion, that the alien merits a favorable exercise of discretion.

(B) Sustaining burden

The applicant must comply with the applicable requirements to submit information or documentation in support of the applicant's application for relief or protection as provided by law or by regulation or in the instructions for the application form. In evaluating the testimony of the applicant or other witness in support of the application, the immigration judge will determine whether or not the testimony is credible, is persuasive, and refers to specific facts sufficient to demonstrate that the applicant has satisfied the applicant's burden of proof. In determining whether the applicant has met such burden, the immigration judge shall weigh the credible testimony along with other evidence of record. Where the immigration judge determines that the applicant should provide evidence which corroborates otherwise credible testimony, such evidence must be provided unless the applicant demonstrates that the applicant does not have the evidence and cannot reasonably obtain the evidence.

(C) Credibility determination

Considering the totality of the circumstances, and all relevant factors, the immigration judge may base a credibility determination on the demeanor, candor, or responsiveness of the applicant or witness, the inherent plausibility of the applicant's or witness's account, the consistency between the applicant's or witness's written and oral statements (whenever made and whether or not under oath, and considering the circumstances under which the statements were made), the internal consistency of each such statement, the consistency of such statements with other evidence of record (including the reports of the Department of State on country conditions), and any inaccuracies or falsehoods in such statements, without regard to whether an inconsistency, inaccuracy, or falsehood goes to the heart of the applicant's claim, or any other relevant factor. There is no presumption of credibility, however, if no adverse credibility determination is explicitly made, the applicant or witness shall have a rebuttable presumption of credibility on appeal.

(5) Notice

If the immigration judge decides that the alien is removable and orders the alien to be removed, the judge shall inform the alien of the right to appeal that decision and of the consequences for failure to depart under the order of removal, including civil and criminal penalties.

(6) Motions to reconsider

(A) In general

The alien may file one motion to reconsider a decision that the alien is removable from the United States.

(B) Deadline

The motion must be filed within 30 days of the date of entry of a final administrative order of removal.

(C) Contents

The motion shall specify the errors of law or fact in the previous order and shall be supported by pertinent authority.

(7) Motions to reopen

(A) In general

An alien may file one motion to reopen proceedings under this section, except that this limitation shall not apply so as to prevent the filing of one motion to reopen described in subparagraph (C)(iv).

(B) Contents

The motion to reopen shall state the new facts that will be proven at a hearing to be held if the motion is granted, and shall be supported by affidavits or other evidentiary material.

(C) Deadline

(i) In general

Except as provided in this subparagraph, the motion to reopen shall be filed within 90 days of the date of entry of a final administrative order of removal.

(ii) Asylum

There is no time limit on the filing of a motion to reopen if the basis of the motion is to apply for relief under sections 208 [8 U.S.C.A. § 1158] or 241(b)(3) [8 U.S.C.A. § 1231(b)(3)] and is based on changed country conditions arising in the country of nationality or the country to which removal has been ordered, if such evidence is material and was not available and would not have been discovered or presented at the previous proceeding.

(iii) Failure to appear

The filing of a motion to reopen an order entered pursuant to subsection (b)(5) is subject to the deadline specified in subparagraph (C) of such subsection.

(iv) Special rule for battered spouses, children, and parents

Any limitation under this section on the deadlines for filing such motions shall not apply—

(I) if the basis for the motion is to apply for relief under clause (iii) or (iv) of section 204(a)(1)(A) [8 U.S.C.A § 1154(a)(1)(A)], clause (ii) or (iii) of section 204(a)(1)(B) [8 U.S.C.A § 1154(a)(1)(B)], section 240A(b) [8 U.S.C.A § 1229b(b)], or section 244(a)(3) [8 U.S.C.A § 1254(a)(3)] (as in effect on March 31, 1997);

(II) if the motion is accompanied by a cancellation of removal application to be filed with the Attorney General or by a copy of the self-petition that has been or will be filed with the Immigration and Naturalization Service upon the granting of the motion to reopen;

(III) if the motion to reopen is filed within 1 year of the entry of the final order of removal, except that the Attorney General may, in the Attorney General's discretion, waive this time limitation in the case of an alien who demonstrates extraordinary circumstances or extreme hardship to the alien's child; and

(IV) if the alien is physically present in the United States at the time of filing the motion.

The filing of a motion to reopen under this clause shall only stay the removal of a qualified alien (as defined in section 431(c)(1)(B) of the Personal Responsibility and Work Opportunity Reconciliation Act of 1996 [8 U.S.C. 1641(c)(1)(B)]) pending the final disposition of the motion, including exhaustion of all appeals if the motion establishes that the alien is a qualified alien.

(d) Stipulated removal

The Attorney General shall provide by regulation for the entry by an immigration judge of an order of removal stipulated to by the alien (or the alien's representative) and the Service. A stipulated order shall constitute a conclusive determination of the alien's removability from the United States.

(e) Definitions

In this section and section 240A [8 U.S.C.A. § 1229b]:

(1) Exceptional circumstances

The term "exceptional circumstances" refers to exceptional circumstances (such as battery or extreme cruelty to the alien or any child or parent of the alien, serious illness of the alien, or serious illness or death of the spouse, child, or parent of the alien, but not including less compelling circumstances) beyond the control of the alien.

(2) Removable

The term "removable" means—

(A) in the case of an alien not admitted to the United States, that the alien is inadmissible under section 212 [8 U.S.C.A. § 1182], or

(B) in the case of an alien admitted to the United States, that the alien is deportable under section 237 [8 U.S.C.A. § 1227].

(June 27, 1952, c. 477, Title II, Ch. 4, § 240 as added Sept. 30, 1996, Pub.L. 104–208, Div. C, Title III, § 304(a)(3), 110 Stat. 3009–589, and amended Oct. 28, 2000, Pub.L. 106–386, Title V, § 1506(c)(1)(A), 114 Stat. 1528; May 11, 2005, Pub.L. 109–13, Div. B, § 101(d), 119 Stat. 231, 304–05; Jan. 5, 2006, Pub.L. 109–162, Title VIII, §§ 813(a)(1), 825(a), 119 Stat. 3057, 3063.)

§ 240A. Cancellation of removal; adjustment of status [8 U.S.C.A. § 1229b]

(a) Cancellation of removal for certain permanent residents

The Attorney General may cancel removal in the case of an alien who is inadmissible or deportable from the United States if the alien—

(1) has been an alien lawfully admitted for permanent residence for not less than 5 years,

(2) has resided in the United States continuously for 7 years after having been admitted in any status, and

(3) has not been convicted of any aggravated felony.

(b) Cancellation of removal and adjustment of status for certain nonpermanent residents

(1) In general

The Attorney General may cancel removal of, and adjust to the status of an alien lawfully admitted for permanent residence, an alien who is inadmissible or deportable from the United States if the alien—

(A) has been physically present in the United States for a continuous period of not less than 10 years immediately preceding the date of such application;

(B) has been a person of good moral character during such period;

(C) has not been convicted of an offense under section 212(a) (2) [8 U.S.C.A § 1182(a)(2)], 237(a)(2) [8 U.S.C.A § 1227(a)(2)], or 237(a)(3) [8 U.S.C.A § 1227(a)(3)], subject to paragraph (5); and

(D) establishes that removal would result in exceptional and extremely unusual hardship to the alien's spouse, parent, or child, who is a citizen of the United States or an alien lawfully admitted for permanent residence.

(2) Special rule for battered spouse or child

(A) Authority

The Attorney General may cancel removal of, and adjust to the status of an alien lawfully admitted for permanent residence, an alien who is inadmissible or deportable from the United States if the alien demonstrates that—

(i)(I) the alien has been battered or subjected to extreme cruelty by a spouse or parent who is or was a United States citizen (or is the parent of a child of a United States citizen and the child has been battered or subjected to extreme cruelty by such citizen parent);

(II) the alien has been battered or subjected to extreme cruelty by a spouse or parent who is or was a lawful permanent resident (or is the parent of a child of an alien who is or was a lawful permanent resident and the child has been battered or subjected to extreme cruelty by such permanent resident parent); or

(III) the alien has been battered or subjected to extreme cruelty by a United States citizen or lawful permanent resident whom the alien intended to marry, but whose marriage is not legitimate because of that United States citizen's or lawful permanent resident's bigamy;

(ii) the alien has been physically present in the United States for a continuous period of not less than 3 years immediately preceding the date of such application, and the issuance of a charging document for removal proceedings shall not toll the 3-year period of continuous physical presence in the United States;

(iii) the alien has been a person of good moral character during such period, subject to the provisions of subparagraph (C);

(iv) the alien is not inadmissible under paragraph (2) or (3) of section 212(a) [8 U.S.C.A § 1182(a)], is not deportable under paragraphs (1)(G) or (2) through (4) of section 237(a) [8 U.S.C.A § 1227(a)], subject to paragraph (5), and has not been convicted of an aggravated felony; and

(v) the removal would result in extreme hardship to the alien, the alien's child, or the alien's parent.

(B) Physical presence

Notwithstanding subsection (d)(2) of this section, for purposes of subparagraph (A)(ii) or for purposes of section 244(a)(3) [8 U.S.C.A § 1254(a)(3)] (as in effect before the title III–A effective date in section 309 of the Illegal Immigration Reform and Immigrant Responsibility Act of 1996), an alien shall not be considered to have failed to maintain continuous physical presence by reason of an absence if the alien demonstrates a connection between the absence and the battering or extreme cruelty perpetrated against the alien. No absence or portion of an absence connected to the battering or extreme cruelty shall count toward the 90-day or 180-day limits established in subsection (d)(2) of this section. If any absence or aggregate absences exceed 180 days, the absences or portions of the absences will not be considered to break the period of continuous presence. Any such period of time excluded from the 180-day limit shall be excluded in computing the time during which the alien has been physically present for purposes of the 3-year requirement set forth in this subparagraph, subparagraph (A)(ii), and section 244(a)(3) [8 U.S.C.A § 1254(a)(3)] (as in effect before the title III–A effective date in section 309 of the Illegal Immigration Reform and Immigrant Responsibility Act of 1996).

(C) Good moral character

Notwithstanding section 101(f) [8 U.S.C.A § 1101(f)], an act or conviction that does not bar the Attorney General from granting relief under this paragraph by reason of subparagraph (A)(iv) shall not bar the Attorney General from finding the alien to be of good moral character under subparagraph (A)(iii) or section 244(a)(3) [8 U.S.C.A § 1254(a)(3)] (as in effect before the title III–A effective date in section 309 of the Illegal Immigration Reform and Immigrant Responsibility Act of 1996), if the Attorney General finds that the act or conviction was connected to the alien's having been battered or subjected to extreme cruelty and determines that a waiver is otherwise warranted.

(D) Credible evidence considered

In acting on applications under this paragraph, the Attorney General shall consider any credible evidence relevant to the application. The determination of what evidence is credible and the weight to be given that evidence shall be within the sole discretion of the Attorney General.

(3) Recordation of date

With respect to aliens who the Attorney General adjusts to the status of an alien lawfully admitted for permanent residence under paragraph (1) or (2), the Attorney General shall record the alien's lawful admission for permanent residence as of the date of the Attorney General's cancellation of removal under paragraph (1) or (2).

(4) Children of battered aliens and parents of battered alien children

(A) In general

The Attorney General shall grant parole under section 212(d)(5) [8 U.S.C.A. § 1182(d)(5)] to any alien who is a—

(i) child of an alien granted relief under section 240A(b)(2) [8 U.S.C.A. § 1229b(b)(2)] or section 244(a)(3) (as in effect before the title III–A effective date in section 309 of the Illegal Immigration Reform and Immigrant Responsibility Act of 1996); or

(ii) parent of a child alien granted relief under section 240A(b)(2) [8 U.S.C.A. § 1229b(b)(2)] or section 244(a)(3) (as in effect before the title III–A effective date in section 309 of the Illegal Immigration Reform and Immigrant Responsibility Act of 1996).

(B) Duration of parole

The grant of parole shall extend from the time of the grant of relief under subsection (b)(2) of this section or section 244(a)(3) [8 U.S.C.A. § 1254(a)(3)] (as in effect before the title III–A effective date in section 309 of the Illegal Immigration Reform and Immigrant Responsibility Act of 1996) to the time the application for adjustment of status filed by aliens covered under this paragraph has been finally adjudicated. Applications for adjustment of status filed by aliens covered under this paragraph shall be treated as if the applicants were VAWA self-petitioners. Failure by the alien granted relief under subsection (b)(2) of this section or section 244(a)(3) [8 U.S.C.A. § 1254(a)(3)] (as in effect before the title III–A effective date in section 309 of the Illegal Immigration Reform and Immigrant Responsibility Act of 1996) to exercise due diligence in filing a visa petition on behalf of an alien described in clause (i) or (ii) may result in revocation of parole.

(5) Application of domestic violence waiver authority

The authority provided under section 237(a)(7) [8 U.S.C.A § 1227(a)(7)] may apply under paragraphs (1)(B), (1)(C), and (2)(A)(iv) in a cancellation of removal and adjustment of status proceeding.

(6) Relatives of trafficking victims

(A) In general

Upon written request by a law enforcement official, the Secretary of Homeland Security may parole under section 212(d)(5) [8 U.S.C.A. § 1182(d)(5)] any alien who is a relative of an alien granted continued presence under section 107(c)(3)(A) of the Trafficking Victims Protection Act [22 U.S.C.A. § 7105(c)(3)(A)], if the relative—

(i) was, on the date on which law enforcement applied for such continued presence—

(I) in the case of an alien granted continued presence who is under 21 years of age, the spouse, child, parent, or unmarried sibling under 18 years of age, of the alien; or

(II) in the case of an alien granted continued presence who is 21 years of age or older, the spouse or child of the alien; or

(ii) is a parent or sibling of the alien who the requesting law enforcement official, in consultation with the Secretary of Homeland Security, as appropriate, determines to be in present danger of retaliation as a result of the alien's escape from the severe form of trafficking or cooperation with law enforcement, irrespective of age.

(B) Duration of parole

(i) In general

The Secretary may extend the parole granted under subparagraph (A) until the final adjudication of the application filed by the principal alien under section 101(a)(15)(T)(ii) [8 U.S.C.A. § 1101(a)(15)(T)(ii)].

(ii) Other limits on duration

If an application described in clause (i) is not filed, the parole granted under subparagraph (A) may extend until the later of—

(I) the date on which the principal alien's authority to remain in the United States under section 107(c)(3)(A) of the Trafficking Victims Protection Act [22 U.S.C.A. § 7105(c)(3)(A)] is is terminated; or

(II) the date on which a civil action filed by the principal alien under section 1595 of Title 18, United States Code, is concluded.

(iii) Due diligence

Failure by the principal alien to exercise due diligence in filing a visa petition on behalf of an alien described in clause (i) or (ii) of subparagraph (A), or in pursuing the civil action described in clause (ii)(II) (as determined by the Secretary of Homeland Security in consultation with the Attorney General), may result in revocation of parole.

(C) Other limitations

A relative may not be granted parole under this paragraph if—

(i) the Secretary of Homeland Security or the Attorney General has reason to believe that the relative was knowingly complicit in the trafficking of an alien permitted to remain in the United States under section 107(c)(3)(A) of the Trafficking Victims Protection Act [22 U.S.C.A. § 7105(c)(3)(A)]; or

(ii) the relative is an alien described in paragraph (2) or (3) of section 212(a) [8 U.S.C.A. § 1182(a)] or paragraph (2) or (4) of section 237(a) [8 U.S.C.A. § 1227(a)].

(c) Aliens ineligible for relief

The provisions of subsections (a) and (b)(1) shall not apply to any of the following aliens:

(1) An alien who entered the United States as a crewman subsequent to June 30, 1964.

(2) An alien who was admitted to the United States as a nonimmigrant exchange alien as defined in section 101(a)(15)(J) [8 U.S.C.A. § 1101(a)(15)(J)], or has acquired the status of such a nonimmigrant exchange alien after admission, in order to receive graduate medical education or training, regardless of whether or not the alien is subject to or has fulfilled the two-year foreign residence requirement of section 212(c) [8 U.S.C.A. § 1182(c)].

(3) An alien who—

(A) was admitted to the United States as a nonimmigrant exchange alien as defined in section 101(a)(15)(J) [8 U.S.C.A. § 1101(a)(15)(J)] or has acquired the status of such a nonimmigrant exchange alien after admission other than to receive graduate medical education or training,

(B) is subject to the two-year foreign residence requirement of section 212(e) [8 U.S.C.A. § 1182(e)], and

(C) has not fulfilled that requirement or received a waiver thereof.

(4) An alien who is inadmissible under section 212(a)(3) [8 U.S.C.A. § 1182(a)(3)] or deportable under section 237(a)(4) [8 U.S.C.A. § 1227(a)(4)].

(5) An alien who is described in section 241(b)(3)(B)(i) [8 U.S.C.A. § 1231(b)(3)(B)(i)].

(6) An alien whose removal has previously been cancelled under this section or whose deportation was suspended under section 244(a) [8 U.S.C.A. § 1254(a)] or who has been granted relief under section 212(c) [8 U.S.C.A. § 1182(c)], as such sections were in effect before the date of the enactment of the Illegal Immigration Reform and Immigrant Responsibility Act of 1996 [September 30, 1996].

(d) Special rules relating to continuous residence or physical presence

(1) Termination of continuous period

For purposes of this section, any period of continuous residence or continuous physical presence in the United States shall be deemed to end (A) except in the case of an alien who applies for cancellation of removal under subsection (b)(2), when the alien is served a notice to appear under section 239(a) [8 U.S.C.A. § 1229(a)], or (B) when the alien has committed an offense referred to in section 212(a)(2) [8 U.S.C.A. § 1182(a)(2)] that renders the alien inadmissible to the United States under section 212(a)(2) [8 U.S.C.A. § 1182(a)(2)] or removable from the United States under section 237(a)(2) [8 U.S.C.A. § 1227(a)(2)] or 237(a)(4) [8 U.S.C.A. § 1227(a)(4)], whichever is earliest.

(2) Treatment of certain breaks in presence

An alien shall be considered to have failed to maintain continuous physical presence in the United States under subsections (b)(1) and (b)(2) if the alien has departed from the United States for any period in excess of 90 days or for any periods in the aggregate exceeding 180 days.

(3) Continuity not required because of honorable service in armed forces and presence upon entry into service

The requirements of continuous residence or continuous physical presence in the United States under subsections (a) and (b) shall not apply to an alien who—

(A) has served for a minimum period of 24 months in an active-duty status in the Armed Forces of the United States and, if separated from such service, was separated under honorable conditions, and

(B) at the time of the alien's enlistment or induction was in the United States.

(e) Annual limitation

(1) Aggregate limitation

Subject to paragraphs (2) and (3), the Attorney General may not cancel the removal and adjust the status under this section, nor suspend the deportation and adjust the status under section 244(a) [8 U.S.C.A. § 1254(a)] (as in effect before the enactment of the Illegal Immigration Reform and Immigrant Responsibility Act of 1996), of a total of more than 4,000 aliens in any fiscal year. The previous sentence shall apply regardless of when an alien applied for such cancellation and adjustment, or such suspension and adjustment, and whether such an alien had previously applied for suspension of deportation under such section 244(a) [8 U.S.C.A. § 1254(a)]. The numerical limitation under this paragraph shall apply to the aggregate number of decisions in any fiscal year to cancel the removal (and adjust the status) of an alien, or suspend the deportation (and adjust the status) of an alien, under this section or such section 244(a) [8 U.S.C.A. § 1254(a)].

(2) Fiscal year 1997

For fiscal year 1997, paragraph (1) shall only apply to decisions to cancel the removal of an alien, or suspend the deportation of an alien, made after April 1, 1997. Notwithstanding any other provision of law, the Attorney General may cancel the removal or suspend the deportation, in addition to the normal allotment for fiscal year 1998, of a number of aliens equal to 4,000 less the number of such cancellations of removal and suspensions of deportation granted in fiscal year 1997 after April 1, 1997.

(3) Exception for certain aliens

Paragraph (1) shall not apply to the following:

(A) Aliens described in section 309(c)(5)(C)(i) of the Illegal Immigration Reform and Immigrant Responsibility Act of 1996 (as amended by the Nicaraguan Adjustment and Central American Relief Act).

(B) Aliens in deportation proceedings prior to April 1, 1997, who applied for suspension of deportation under section 244(a)(3) [8 U.S.C.A. § 1254(a)(3)] (as in effect before Sept. 30, 1996).

(June 27, 1952, c. 477, Title II, ch. 4, § 240A, as added Sept. 30, 1996, Pub.L. 104–208, Div. C, Title III, § 304(a)(3), 110 Stat. 3009–594; Nov. 19, 1997, Pub.L. 105–100, Title I, § 204(a) to (c), 111 Stat. 2200; Oct. 28, 2000, Pub.L. 106–386, Div. B, Title V, §§ 1504(a), (b), 1505(b)(2), 1506(b)(1), 114 Stat. 1522, 1525, 1527; Jan. 5, 2006, Pub.L. 109–162, Title VIII, §§ 813(c), 822(a), (b), 119 Stat. 3058, 3062, 3063; Aug. 12, 2006, Pub.L. 109–271, § 6(e), 120 Stat. 763; Dec. 23, 2008, Pub.L. 110–457, Title II, § 205(b), 122 Stat. 5062.)

§ 240B. Voluntary departure [8 U.S.C.A. § 1229c]

(a) Certain conditions

(1) In general

The Attorney General may permit an alien voluntarily to depart the United States at the alien's own expense under this subsection, in lieu of being subject to proceedings under section 240 [8 U.S.C.A. § 1229a] or prior to the completion of such proceedings, if the alien is not deportable under section 237(a)(2)(A)(iii) [8 U.S.C.A. § 1227(a)(2)(A)(iii)] or section 237(a)(4)(B) [8 U.S.C.A. § 1227(a)(4)(B)].

(2) Period

(A) In general

Subject to subparagraph (B), permission to depart voluntarily under this subsection shall not be valid for a period exceeding 120 days.

(B) Three-year pilot program waiver

During the period October 1, 2000, through September 30, 2003, and subject to subparagraphs (C) and (D)(ii), the Attorney General may, in the discretion of the Attorney General for humanitarian purposes, waive application of subparagraph (A) in the case of an alien—

(i) who was admitted to the United States as a nonimmigrant visitor (described in section 101(a)(15)(B) [8 U.S.C.A. § 1101(a)(15)(B)]) under the provisions of the visa waiver pilot program established pursuant to section 217 [8 U.S.C.A. § 1187], seeks the waiver for the purpose of continuing to receive medical treatment in the United States from a physician associated with a health care facility, and submits to the Attorney General

(I) a detailed diagnosis statement from the physician, which includes the treatment being sought and the expected time period the alien will be required to remain in the United States;

(II) a statement from the health care facility containing an assurance that the alien's treatment is not being paid through any Federal or State public health assistance, that the alien's account has no outstanding balance, and that such facility will notify the Service when the alien is released or treatment is terminated; and

(III) evidence of financial ability to support the alien's day-to-day expenses while in the United States (including the expenses of any family member described in clause (ii)) and evidence that any such alien or family member is not receiving any form of public assistance; or

(ii) who—

(I) is a spouse, parent, brother, sister, son, daughter, or other family member of a principal alien described in clause (i); and

(II) entered the United States accompanying, and with the same status as, such principal alien.

(C) Waiver limitations

(i) Waivers under subparagraph (B) may be granted only upon a request submitted by a Service district office to Service headquarters.

(ii) Not more than 300 waivers may be granted for any fiscal year for a principal alien under subparagraph (B)(i).

(iii)(I) Except as provided in subclause (II), in the case of each principal alien described in subparagraph (B)(i) not more than one adult may be granted a waiver under subparagraph (B)(ii).

(II) Not more than two adults may be granted a waiver under subparagraph (b)(ii) in a case in which—

(aa) the principal alien described in subparagraph (B)(i) is a dependent under the age of 18; or

(bb) one such adult is age 55 or older or is physically handicapped.

(D) Report to Congress; suspension of waiver authority

(i) Not later than March 30 of each year, the Commissioner shall submit to the Congress an annual report regarding all waivers granted under subparagraph (B) during the preceding fiscal year.

(ii) Notwithstanding any other provision of law, the authority of the Attorney General under subparagraph (B) shall be suspended during any period in which an annual report under clause (i) is past due and has not been submitted.

(3) Bond

The Attorney General may require an alien permitted to depart voluntarily under this subsection to post a voluntary departure bond, to be surrendered upon proof that the alien has departed the United States within the time specified.

(4) Treatment of aliens arriving in the United States

In the case of an alien who is arriving in the United States and with respect to whom proceedings under section 240 [8 U.S.C.A. § 1229a] are (or would otherwise be) initiated at the time of such alien's arrival, paragraph (1) shall not apply. Nothing in this paragraph shall be construed as preventing such an alien from withdrawing the application for admission in accordance with section 235(a)(4) [8 U.S.C.A. § 1225(a)(4)].

(b) At conclusion of proceedings

(1) In general

The Attorney General may permit an alien voluntarily to depart the United States at the alien's own expense if, at the conclusion of a proceeding under section 240 [8 U.S.C.A. § 1229a], the immigration judge enters an order granting voluntary departure in lieu of removal and finds that—

(A) the alien has been physically present in the United States for a period of at least one year immediately preceding the date the notice to appear was served under section 239(a) [8 U.S.C.A. § 1229(a)];

(B) the alien is, and has been, a person of good moral character for at least 5 years immediately preceding the alien's application for voluntary departure;

(C) the alien is not deportable under section 237(a)(2)(A)(iii) [8 U.S.C.A. § 1227(a)(2)(A)(iii)] or section 237(a)(4) [8 U.S.C.A. § 1227(a)(4)]; and

(D) the alien has established by clear and convincing evidence that the alien has the means to depart the United States and intends to do so.

(2) Period

Permission to depart voluntarily under this subsection shall not be valid for a period exceeding 60 days.

(3) Bond

An alien permitted to depart voluntarily under this subsection shall be required to post a voluntary departure bond, in an amount necessary to ensure that the alien will depart, to be surrendered upon proof that the alien has departed the United States within the time specified.

(c) Aliens not eligible

The Attorney General shall not permit an alien to depart voluntarily under this section if the alien was previously permitted to so depart after having been found inadmissible under section 212(a)(6)(A) [8 U.S.C.A. § 1182(a)(6)(A)].

(d) Civil penalty for failure to depart

(1) In general

Subject to paragraph (2), if an alien is permitted to depart voluntarily under this section and voluntarily fails to depart the United States within the time period specified, the alien—

(A) shall be subject to a civil penalty of not less than $1,000 and not more than $5,000; and

(B) shall be ineligible, for a period of 10 years, to receive any further relief under this section and sections 240A [8 U.S.C.A § 1229b], 245 [8 U.S.C.A § 1255], 248 [8 U.S.C.A § 1258], and 249 [8 U.S.C.A § 1259].

(2) Application of VAWA protections

The restrictions on relief under paragraph (1) shall not apply to relief under section 240A [8 U.S.C.A § 1229b] or 245 [8 U.S.C.A § 1255] on the basis of a petition filed by a VAWA self-petitioner, or a petition filed under section 240A(b)(2) [8 U.S.C.A § 1229b(b)(2)], or under section 244(a)(3) [8 U.S.C.A § 1254(a)(3)] (as in effect prior to March 31, 1997), if the extreme cruelty or battery was at least one central reason for the alien's overstaying the grant of voluntary departure.

(3) Notice of penalties

The order permitting an alien to depart voluntarily shall inform the alien of the penalties under this subsection.

(e) Additional conditions

The Attorney General may by regulation limit eligibility for voluntary departure under this section for any class or classes of aliens. No court may review any regulation issued under this subsection.

(f) Judicial review

No court shall have jurisdiction over an appeal from denial of a request for an order of voluntary departure under subsection (b), nor shall any court order a stay of an alien's removal pending consideration of any claim with respect to voluntary departure.

(June 27, 1952, c. 477, Title II, ch. 4, § 240B, as added Sept. 30, 1996, Pub.L. 104–208, Div. C, Title III, § 304(a)(3), 110 Stat. 3009–596, and amended Nov. 1, 2000, Pub.L. 106–406, § 2, 114 Stat. 1755; Jan. 5, 2006, Pub.L. 109–162, Title VIII, § 812, 119 Stat. 3057).

§ 240C. Records of admission [8 U.S.C.A. § 1230]

(a) The Attorney General shall cause to be filed, as a record of admission of each immigrant, the immigrant visa required by section 211(e) [8

U.S.C.A. § 1201(e)] to be surrendered at the port of entry by the arriving alien to an immigration officer.

(b) The Attorney General shall cause to be filed such record of the admission into the United States of each immigrant admitted under section 211(b) [8 U.S.C.A. § 1181(b)] and of each nonimmigrant as the Attorney General deems necessary for the enforcement of the immigration laws.

(June 27, 1952, c. 477, Title II, ch. 4, § 240C, formerly § 240, 66 Stat. 204, redesignated and amended Sept. 30, 1996, Pub.L. 104–208, Div. C, Title III, §§ 304(a)(2), 308(f)(1)(K), 110 Stat. 3009–587, 3009–621.)

§ 241. Detention and removal of aliens ordered removed [8 U.S.C.A. § 1231]

(a) Detention, release, and removal of aliens ordered removed

(1) Removal period

(A) In general

Except as otherwise provided in this section, when an alien is ordered removed, the Attorney General shall remove the alien from the United States within a period of 90 days (in this section referred to as the "removal period").

(B) Beginning of period

The removal period begins on the latest of the following:

(i) The date the order of removal becomes administratively final.

(ii) If the removal order is judicially reviewed and if a court orders a stay of the removal of the alien, the date of the court's final order.

(iii) If the alien is detained or confined (except under an immigration process), the date the alien is released from detention or confinement.

(C) Suspension of period

The removal period shall be extended beyond a period of 90 days and the alien may remain in detention during such extended period if the alien fails or refuses to make timely application in good faith for travel or other documents necessary to the alien's departure or conspires or acts to prevent the alien's removal subject to an order of removal.

(2) Detention

During the removal period, the Attorney General shall detain the alien. Under no circumstance during the removal period shall the Attorney General release an alien who has been found inadmissible under section 212(a)(2) [8 U.S.C.A. § 1182(a)(2)] or 212(a)(3)(B) [8 U.S.C.A. § 1182(a)(3)(B)] or deportable under section 237(a)(2) [8 U.S.C.A. § 1227(a)(2)] or 237(a)(4)(B) [8 U.S.C.A. § 1227(a)(4)(B)].

(3) Supervision after 90-day period

If the alien does not leave or is not removed within the removal period, the alien, pending removal, shall be subject to supervision under regulations prescribed by the Attorney General. The regulations shall include provisions requiring the alien—

(A) to appear before an immigration officer periodically for identification;

(B) to submit, if necessary, to a medical and psychiatric examination at the expense of the United States Government;

(C) to give information under oath about the alien's nationality, circumstances, habits, associations, and activities, and other information the Attorney General considers appropriate; and

(D) to obey reasonable written restrictions on the alien's conduct or activities that the Attorney General prescribes for the alien.

(4) Aliens imprisoned, arrested, or on parole, supervised release, or probation

(A) In general

Except as provided in section 259(a) of Title 42 and paragraph (2), the Attorney General may not remove an alien who is sentenced to imprisonment until the alien is released from imprisonment. Parole, supervised release, probation, or possibility of arrest or further imprisonment is not a reason to defer removal.

(B) Exception for removal of nonviolent offenders prior to completion of sentence of imprisonment

The Attorney General is authorized to remove an alien in accordance with applicable procedures under this Act before the alien has completed a sentence of imprisonment—

(i) in the case of an alien in the custody of the Attorney General, if the Attorney General determines that (I) the alien is confined pursuant to a final conviction for a nonviolent offense (other than an offense related to smuggling or harboring of aliens or an offense described in section 101(a)(43)(B), (C), (E), (I), or (L) [8 U.S.C.A. § 1101(a)(43)(B), (C), (E), (I), or (L)] [sic] and (II) the removal of the alien is appropriate and in the best interest of the United States); or

(ii) in the case of an alien in the custody of a State (or a political subdivision of a State), if the chief State official exercising authority with respect to the incarceration of the alien determines that (I) the alien is confined pursuant to a final conviction for a nonviolent offense (other than an offense described in section 101(a)(43)(C) or (E) [8 U.S.C.A. § 1101(a)(43)(C) or (E)]), (II) the removal is appropriate and in the best interest of the State, and (III) submits a written request to the Attorney General that such alien be so removed.

(C) Notice

Any alien removed pursuant to this paragraph shall be notified of the penalties under the laws of the United States relating to the reentry of deported aliens, particularly the expanded penalties for aliens removed under subparagraph (B).

(D) No private right

No cause or claim may be asserted under this paragraph against any official of the United States or of any State to compel the release, removal, or consideration for release or removal of any alien.

(5) Reinstatement of removal orders against aliens illegally reentering

If the Attorney General finds that an alien has reentered the United States illegally after having been removed or having departed voluntarily, under an order of removal, the prior order of removal is reinstated from its original date and is not subject to being reopened or reviewed, the alien is not eligible and may not apply for any relief under this Act, and the alien shall be removed under the prior order at any time after the reentry.

(6) Inadmissible or criminal aliens

An alien ordered removed who is inadmissible under section 212 [8 U.S.C.A. § 1182], removable under section 237(a)(1)(C) [8 U.S.C.A. § 1227(a)(1)(C)], 237(a)(2) [8 U.S.C.A. § 1227(a)(2)], or 237(a)(4) [8 U.S.C.A. § 1227(a)(4)] or who has been determined by the Attorney General to be a risk to the community or unlikely to comply with the order of removal, may be detained beyond the removal period and, if released, shall be subject to the terms of supervision in paragraph (3).

(7) Employment authorization

No alien ordered removed shall be eligible to receive authorization to be employed in the United States unless the Attorney General makes a specific finding that—

(A) the alien cannot be removed due to the refusal of all countries designated by the alien or under this section to receive the alien, or

(B) the removal of the alien is otherwise impracticable or contrary to the public interest.

(b) Countries to which aliens may be removed

(1) Aliens arriving at the United States

Subject to paragraph (3)—

(A) In general

Except as provided by subparagraphs (B) and (C), an alien who arrives at the United States and with respect to whom proceedings under section 240 [8 U.S.C.A. § 1229a] were initiated at the time of such alien's arrival shall be removed to the country in which the alien boarded the vessel or aircraft on which the alien arrived in the United States.

(B) Travel from contiguous territory

If the alien boarded the vessel or aircraft on which the alien arrived in the United States in a foreign territory contiguous to the United States, an island adjacent to the United States, or an island adjacent to a foreign territory contiguous to the United States, and the alien is not a native, citizen, subject, or national of, or does not reside in, the territory or island, removal shall be to the country in which the alien boarded the vessel that transported the alien to the territory or island.

(C) Alternative countries

If the government of the country designated in subparagraph (A) or (B) is unwilling to accept the alien into that country's territory, removal shall be to any of the following countries, as directed by the Attorney General:

    (i) The country of which the alien is a citizen, subject, or national.

    (ii) The country in which the alien was born.

    (iii) The country in which the alien has a residence.

    (iv) A country with a government that will accept the alien into the country's territory if removal to each country described in a previous clause of this subparagraph is impracticable, inadvisable, or impossible.

(2) Other aliens

Subject to paragraph (3)—

(A) Selection of country by alien

Except as otherwise provided in this paragraph—

    (i) any alien not described in paragraph (1) who has been ordered removed may designate one country to which the alien wants to be removed, and

    (ii) the Attorney General shall remove the alien to the country the alien so designates.

(B) Limitation on designation

An alien may designate under subparagraph (A)(i) a foreign territory contiguous to the United States, an adjacent island, or an island adjacent to a foreign territory contiguous to the United States as the place to which the alien is to be removed only if the alien is a native, citizen, subject, or national of, or has resided in, that designated territory or island.

(C) Disregarding designation

The Attorney General may disregard a designation under subparagraph (A)(i) if—

(i) the alien fails to designate a country promptly;

(ii) the government of the country does not inform the Attorney General finally, within 30 days after the date the Attorney General first inquires, whether the government will accept the alien into the country;

(iii) the government of the country is not willing to accept the alien into the country; or

(iv) the Attorney General decides that removing the alien to the country is prejudicial to the United States.

(D) Alternative country

If an alien is not removed to a country designated under subparagraph (A)(i), the Attorney General shall remove the alien to a country of which the alien is a subject, national, or citizen unless the government of the country—

(i) does not inform the Attorney General or the alien finally, within 30 days after the date the Attorney General first inquires or within another period of time the Attorney General decides is reasonable, whether the government will accept the alien into the country; or

(ii) is not willing to accept the alien into the country.

(E) Additional removal countries

If an alien is not removed to a country under the previous subparagraphs of this paragraph, the Attorney General shall remove the alien to any of the following countries:

(i) The country from which the alien was admitted to the United States.

(ii) The country in which is located the foreign port from which the alien left for the United States or for a foreign territory contiguous to the United States.

(iii) A country in which the alien resided before the alien entered the country from which the alien entered the United States.

(iv) The country in which the alien was born.

(v) The country that had sovereignty over the alien's birthplace when the alien was born.

(vi) The country in which the alien's birthplace is located when the alien is ordered removed.

(vii) If impracticable, inadvisable, or impossible to remove the alien to each country described in a previous clause of this subparagraph, another country whose government will accept the alien into that country.

(F) Removal country when United States is at war

When the United States is at war and the Attorney General decides that it is impracticable, inadvisable, inconvenient, or impossible to remove an alien under this subsection because of the war, the Attorney General may remove the alien—

(i) to the country that is host to a government in exile of the country of which the alien is a citizen or subject if the government of the host country will permit the alien's entry; or

(ii) if the recognized government of the country of which the alien is a citizen or subject is not in exile, to a country, or a political or territorial subdivision of a country, that is very near the country of which the alien is a citizen or subject, or, with the consent of the government of the country of which the alien is a citizen or subject, to another country.

(3) Restriction on removal to a country where alien's life or freedom would be threatened

(A) In general

Notwithstanding paragraphs (1) and (2), the Attorney General may not remove an alien to a country if the Attorney General decides that the alien's life or freedom would be threatened in that country because of the alien's race, religion, nationality, membership in a particular social group, or political opinion.

(B) Exception

Subparagraph (A) does not apply to an alien deportable under section 237(a)(4)(D) [8 U.S.C.A. § 1227(a)(4)(D)] or if the Attorney General decides that—

(i) the alien ordered, incited, assisted, or otherwise participated in the persecution of an individual because of the individual's race, religion, nationality, membership in a particular social group, or political opinion;

(ii) the alien, having been convicted by a final judgment of a particularly serious crime is a danger to the community of the United States;

(iii) there are serious reasons to believe that the alien committed a serious nonpolitical crime outside the United States before the alien arrived in the United States; or

(iv) there are reasonable grounds to believe that the alien is a danger to the security of the United States.

For purposes of clause (ii), an alien who has been convicted of an aggravated felony (or felonies) for which the alien has been sentenced to an aggregate term of imprisonment of at least 5 years shall be considered to have committed a particularly serious crime. The previous sentence shall not preclude the Attorney General from determining that, notwithstanding the length of sentence imposed, an alien has been convicted of a particularly serious crime. For purposes of clause (iv), an alien who is described in section 237(a)(4)(B) [8 U.S.C.A. § 1227(a)(4)(B)] shall be considered to be an alien with respect to whom there are reasonable grounds for regarding as a danger to the security of the United States.

(C) Sustaining burden of proof; credibility determinations

In determining whether an alien has demonstrated that the alien's life or freedom would be threatened for a reason described in subparagraph (A), the trier of fact shall determine whether the alien has sustained the alien's burden of proof, and shall make credibility determinations, in the manner described in clauses (ii) and (iii) of section 208(b)(1)(B) [8 U.S.C.A. § 1158(b)(1)(B)].

(c) Removal of aliens arriving at port of entry

(1) Vessels and aircraft

An alien arriving at a port of entry of the United States who is ordered removed either without a hearing under section 235(b)(1) [8 U.S.C.A. § 1225(b)(1)] or 235(c) [8 U.S.C.A. § 1225(c)] or pursuant to proceedings under section 240 [8 U.S.C.A. § 1229a] initiated at the time of such alien's arrival shall be removed immediately on a vessel or aircraft owned by the owner of the vessel or aircraft on which the alien arrived in the United States, unless—

(A) it is impracticable to remove the alien on one of those vessels or aircraft within a reasonable time, or

(B) the alien is a stowaway—

(i) who has been ordered removed in accordance with section 235(a)(1) [8 U.S.C.A. § 1225(a)(1)],

(ii) who has requested asylum, and

(iii) whose application has not been adjudicated or whose asylum application has been denied but who has not exhausted all appeal rights.

(2) Stay of removal

(A) In general

The Attorney General may stay the removal of an alien under this subsection if the Attorney General decides that—

(i) immediate removal is not practicable or proper; or

(ii) the alien is needed to testify in the prosecution of a person for a violation of a law of the United States or of any State.

(B) Payment of detention costs

During the period an alien is detained because of a stay of removal under subparagraph (A)(ii), the Attorney General may pay from the appropriation "Immigration and Naturalization Service— Salaries and Expenses"—

(i) the cost of maintenance of the alien; and

(ii) a witness fee of $1 a day.

(C) Release during stay

The Attorney General may release an alien whose removal is stayed under subparagraph (A)(ii) on—

(i) the alien's filing a bond of at least $500 with security approved by the Attorney General;

(ii) condition that the alien appear when required as a witness and for removal; and

(iii) other conditions the Attorney General may prescribe.

(3) Costs of detention and maintenance pending removal

(A) In general

Except as provided in subparagraph (B) and subsection (d), an owner of a vessel or aircraft bringing an alien to the United States shall pay the costs of detaining and maintaining the alien—

(i) while the alien is detained under subsection (d)(1), and

(ii) in the case of an alien who is a stowaway, while the alien is being detained pursuant to—

(I) subsection (d)(2)(A) or (d)(2)(B)(i),

(II) subsection (d)(2)(B)(ii) or (iii) for the period of time reasonably necessary for the owner to arrange for repatriation or removal of the stowaway, including obtaining necessary travel documents, but not to extend beyond the date on which it is ascertained that such travel documents cannot be obtained from the country to which the stowaway is to be returned, or

(III) section 235(b)(1)(B)(ii), for a period not to exceed 15 days (excluding Saturdays, Sundays, and holidays) commencing on the first such day which begins on the earlier of 72 hours after the time of the initial presentation of the stowaway for inspection or at the time the stowaway is determined to have a credible fear of persecution.

(B) Nonapplication

Subparagraph (A) shall not apply if—

(i) the alien is a crewmember;

(ii) the alien has an immigrant visa;

(iii) the alien has a nonimmigrant visa or other documentation authorizing the alien to apply for temporary admission to the United States and applies for admission not later than 120 days after the date the visa or documentation was issued;

(iv) the alien has a reentry permit and applies for admission not later than 120 days after the date of the alien's last inspection and admission;

(v)(I) the alien has a nonimmigrant visa or other documentation authorizing the alien to apply for temporary admission to the United States or a reentry permit;

(II) the alien applies for admission more than 120 days after the date the visa or documentation was issued or after the date of the last inspection and admission under the reentry permit; and

(III) the owner of the vessel or aircraft satisfies the Attorney General that the existence of the condition relating to inadmissibility could not have been discovered by exercising reasonable care before the alien boarded the vessel or aircraft; or

(vi) the individual claims to be a national of the United States and has a United States passport.

(d) Requirements of persons providing transportation

(1) Removal at time of arrival

An owner, agent, master, commanding officer, person in charge, purser, or consignee of a vessel or aircraft bringing an alien (except an alien crewmember) to the United States shall—

(A) receive an alien back on the vessel or aircraft or another vessel or aircraft owned or operated by the same interests if the alien is ordered removed under this part; and

(B) take the alien to the foreign country to which the alien is ordered removed.

(2) Alien stowaways

An owner, agent, master, commanding officer, charterer, or consignee of a vessel or aircraft arriving in the United States with an alien stowaway—

(A) shall detain the alien on board the vessel or aircraft, or at such place as the Attorney General shall designate, until completion of the inspection of the alien by an immigration officer;

(B) may not permit the stowaway to land in the United States, except pursuant to regulations of the Attorney General temporarily—

(i) for medical treatment,

(ii) for detention of the stowaway by the Attorney General, or

(iii) for departure or removal of the stowaway; and

(C) if ordered by an immigration officer, shall remove the stowaway on the vessel or aircraft or on another vessel or aircraft.

The Attorney General shall grant a timely request to remove the stowaway under subparagraph (C) on a vessel or aircraft other than that on which the stowaway arrived if the requester has obtained any travel documents necessary for departure or repatriation of the stowaway and removal of the stowaway will not be unreasonably delayed.

(3) Removal upon order

An owner, agent, master, commanding officer, person in charge, purser, or consignee of a vessel, aircraft, or other transportation line shall comply with an order of the Attorney General to take on board, guard safely, and transport to the destination specified any alien ordered to be removed under this Act.

(e) Payment of expenses of removal

(1) Costs of removal at time of arrival

In the case of an alien who is a stowaway or who is ordered removed either without a hearing under section 235(a)(1) [8 U.S.C.A. § 1225(a)(1)] or 235(c) [8 U.S.C.A. § 1225(c)] or pursuant to proceedings under section 240 [8 U.S.C.A. § 1229a] initiated at the time of such alien's arrival, the owner of the vessel or aircraft (if any) on which the alien arrived in the United States shall pay the transportation cost of removing the alien. If removal is on a vessel or aircraft not owned by the owner of the vessel or aircraft on which the alien arrived in the United States, the Attorney General may—

(A) pay the cost from the appropriation "Immigration and Naturalization Service—Salaries and Expenses"; and

(B) recover the amount of the cost in a civil action from the owner, agent, or consignee of the vessel or aircraft (if any) on which the alien arrived in the United States.

(2) Costs of removal to port of removal for aliens admitted or permitted to land

In the case of an alien who has been admitted or permitted to land and is ordered removed, the cost (if any) of removal of the alien to the port of removal shall be at the expense of the appropriation for the enforcement of this Act.

(3) Costs of removal from port of removal for aliens admitted or permitted to land

(A) Through appropriation

Except as provided in subparagraph (B), in the case of an alien who has been admitted or permitted to land and is ordered removed, the cost (if any) of removal of the alien from the port of removal shall be at the expense of the appropriation for the enforcement of this Act.

(B) Through owner

(i) In general

In the case of an alien described in clause (ii), the cost of removal of the alien from the port of removal may be charged to any owner of the vessel, aircraft, or other transportation line by which the alien came to the United States.

(ii) Aliens described

An alien described in this clause is an alien who—

(I) is admitted to the United States (other than lawfully admitted for permanent residence) and is ordered removed within 5 years of the date of admission based on a ground that existed before or at the time of admission, or

(II) is an alien crewman permitted to land temporarily under section 252 [8 U.S.C.A. § 1282] and is ordered removed within 5 years of the date of landing.

(C) Costs of removal of certain aliens granted voluntary departure

In the case of an alien who has been granted voluntary departure under section 240B [8 U.S.C.A. § 1229c] and who is financially unable to depart at the alien's own expense and whose removal the Attorney General deems to be in the best interest of the United States, the expense of such removal may be paid from the appropriation for the enforcement of this Act.

(f) Aliens requiring personal care during removal

(1) In general

If the Attorney General believes that an alien being removed requires personal care because of the alien's mental or physical condition, the Attorney General may employ a suitable person for that purpose who shall accompany and care for the alien until the alien arrives at the final destination.

(2) Costs

The costs of providing the service described in paragraph (1) shall be defrayed in the same manner as the expense of removing the accompanied alien is defrayed under this section.

(g) Places of detention

(1) In general

The Attorney General shall arrange for appropriate places of detention for aliens detained pending removal or a decision on removal. When United States Government facilities are unavailable or facilities adapted or suitably located for detention are unavailable for rental, the Attorney General may expend from the appropriation "Immigration and Naturalization Service—Salaries and Expenses", without regard to section 5 of Title 41, amounts necessary to acquire land and to acquire, build, remodel, repair, and operate facilities (including living quarters for immigration officers if not otherwise available) necessary for detention.

(2) Detention facilities of the immigration and naturalization service

Prior to initiating any project for the construction of any new detention facility for the Service, the Commissioner shall consider the availability for purchase or lease of any existing prison, jail, detention center, or other comparable facility suitable for such use.

(h) Statutory construction

Nothing in this section shall be construed to create any substantive or procedural right or benefit that is legally enforceable by any party against the United States or its agencies or officers or any other person.

(i) Incarceration

(1) If the chief executive officer of a State (or, if appropriate, a political subdivision of the State) exercising authority with respect to the incarceration of an undocumented criminal alien submits a written request to the Attorney General, the Attorney General shall, as determined by the Attorney General—

(A) enter into a contractual arrangement which provides for compensation to the State or a political subdivision of the State, as may be appropriate, with respect to the incarceration of the undocumented criminal alien; or

(B) take the undocumented criminal alien into the custody of the Federal Government and incarcerate the alien.

(2) Compensation under paragraph (1)(A) shall be the average cost of incarceration of a prisoner in the relevant State as determined by the Attorney General.

(3) For purposes of this subsection, the term "undocumented criminal alien" means an alien who—

(A) has been convicted of a felony or two or more misdemeanors; and

(B)(i) entered the United States without inspection or at any time or place other than as designated by the Attorney General;

(ii) was the subject of exclusion or deportation proceedings at the time he or she was taken into custody by the State or a political subdivision of the State; or

(iii) was admitted as a nonimmigrant and at the time he or she was taken into custody by the State or a political subdivision of the State has failed to maintain the nonimmigrant status in which the alien was admitted or to which it was changed under section 248

[8 U.S.C.A. § 1258], or to comply with the conditions of any such status.

(4)(A) In carrying out paragraph (1), the Attorney General shall give priority to the Federal incarceration of undocumented criminal aliens who have committed aggravated felonies.

(B) The Attorney General shall ensure that undocumented criminal aliens incarcerated in Federal facilities pursuant to this subsection are held in facilities which provide a level of security appropriate to the crimes for which they were convicted.

(5) There are authorized to be appropriated to carry out this subsection—

(A) $750,000,000 for fiscal year 2006;

(B) $850,000,000 for fiscal year 2007; and

(C) $950,000,000 for each of the fiscal years 2008 through 2011.

(6) Amounts appropriated pursuant to the authorization of appropriations in paragraph (5) that are distributed to a State or political subdivision of a State, including a municipality, may be used only for correctional purposes.

(June 27, 1952, c. 477, Title II, ch. 4, § 241, as added and amended Sept. 30, 1996, Pub.L. 104–208, Div. C, Title III, §§ 305(a)(3), 306(a)(1), 328(a)(1), 110 Stat. 3009–598, 3009–607, 3009–630; Nov. 2, 2002, Pub.L. 107–273, Div. C, Title I, § 11014, 116 Stat. 1824; May 11, 2005, Pub.L. 109–13, Div. B, § 101(c), 119 Stat. 231, 303–04; Jan. 5, 2006, Pub.L. 109–162, Title XI, § 1196(a), (b), 119 Stat. 3130.)

§ 242. Judicial review of orders of removal [8 U.S.C.A. § 1252]

(a) Applicable provisions

(1) General orders of removal

Judicial review of a final order of removal (other than an order of removal without a hearing pursuant to section 235(b)(1) [8 U.S.C.A. § 1225(b)(1)]) is governed only by chapter 158 of Title 28, except as provided in subsection (b) and except that the court may not order the taking of additional evidence under section 2347(c) of Title 28.

(2) Matters not subject to judicial review

(A) Review relating to section 235(b)(1) [8 U.S.C.A. § 1225(b)(1)]

Notwithstanding any other provision of law (statutory or nonstatutory), including section 2241 of title 28, United States Code, or any other habeas corpus provision, and sections 1361 and 1651 of such title, no court shall have jurisdiction to review—

(i) except as provided in subsection (e), any individual determination or to entertain any other cause or claim arising from or relating to the implementation or operation of an order of removal pursuant to section 235(b)(1) [8 U.S.C.A. § 1225(b)(1)],

(ii) except as provided in subsection (e), a decision by the Attorney General to invoke the provisions of such section,

(iii) the application of such section to individual aliens, including the determination made under section 235(b)(1)(B) [8 U.S.C.A. § 1225(b)(1)(B)], or

(iv) except as provided in subsection (e), procedures and policies adopted by the Attorney General to implement the provisions of section 235(b)(1) [8 U.S.C.A. § 1225(b)(1)].

(B) Denials of discretionary relief

Notwithstanding any other provision of law (statutory or nonstatutory), including section 2241 of title 28, United States Code, or any other habeas corpus provision, and sections 1361 and 1651 of such title, and except as provided in subparagraph (D), and regardless of whether the judgment, decision, or action is made in removal proceedings, no court shall have jurisdiction to review—

(i) any judgment regarding the granting of relief under section 212(h) [8 U.S.C.A. § 1182(h)], 212(i) [8 U.S.C.A. § 1182(i)], 240A [8 U.S.C.A. § 1229b], 240B [8 U.S.C.A. § 1229c], or 245 [8 U.S.C.A. § 1255], or

(ii) any other decision or action of the Attorney General or the Secretary of Homeland Security the authority for which is specified under this title to be in the discretion of the Attorney General or the Secretary of Homeland Security, other than the granting of relief under section 208(a) [8 U.S.C.A. § 1158(a)].

(C) Orders against criminal aliens

Notwithstanding any other provision of law (statutory or nonstatutory), including section 2241 of title 28, United States Code, or any other habeas corpus provision, and sections 1361 and 1651 of such title, and except as provided in subparagraph (D), no court shall have jurisdiction to review any final order of removal against an alien who is removable by reason of having committed a criminal offense covered in section 212(a)(2) [8 U.S.C.A. § 1182(a)(2)] or 237(a)(2)(A)(iii), (B), (C), or (D) [8 U.S.C.A. § 1227(a)(2)(A)(iii), (B), (C), or (D)], or any offense covered by section 237(a)(2)(A)(ii) [8 U.S.C.A. § 1227(a)(2)(A)(ii)] for which both predicate offenses are, without regard to their date of commission, otherwise covered by section 237(a)(2)(A)(i) [8 U.S.C.A. § 1227(a)(2)(A)(i)].

(D) Judicial review of certain legal claims

Nothing in subparagraph (B) or (C), or in any other provision of this Act (other than this section) which limits or eliminates judicial review, shall be construed as precluding review of constitutional claims or questions of law raised upon a petition for review filed with an appropriate court of appeals in accordance with this section.

(3) Treatment of certain decisions

No alien shall have a right to appeal from a decision of an immigration judge which is based solely on a certification described in section 240(c)(1)(B) [8 U.S.C.A. § 1229a(c)(1)(B)].

(4) Claims under the United Nations Convention

Notwithstanding any other provision of law (statutory or nonstatutory), including section 2241 of title 28, United States Code, or any other habeas corpus provision, and sections 1361 and 1651 of such title, a petition for review filed with an appropriate court of appeals in accordance with this section shall be the sole and exclusive means for judicial review of any cause or claim under the United Nations Convention Against Torture and Other Forms of Cruel, Inhuman, or Degrading Treatment or Punishment, except as provided in subsection (e).

(5) Exclusive means of review

Notwithstanding any other provision of law (statutory or nonstatutory), including section 2241 of title 28, United States Code, or any other habeas corpus provision, and sections 1361 and 1651 of such title, a petition for review filed with an appropriate court of appeals in accordance with this section shall be the sole and exclusive means for judicial review of an order of removal entered or issued under any provision of this Act, except as provided in subsection (e). For purposes of this Act, in every provision that limits or eliminates judicial review or jurisdiction to review, the terms "judicial review" and "jurisdiction to review" include habeas corpus review pursuant to section 2241 of title 28, United States Code, or any other habeas corpus provision, sections 1361 and 1651 of such title, and review pursuant to any other provision of law (statutory or nonstatutory).

(b) Requirements for review of orders of removal

With respect to review of an order of removal under subsection (a)(1), the following requirements apply:

(1) Deadline

The petition for review must be filed not later than 30 days after the date of the final order of removal.

(2) Venue and forms

The petition for review shall be filed with the court of appeals for the judicial circuit in which the immigration judge completed the proceedings. The record and briefs do not have to be printed. The court of appeals shall review the proceeding on a typewritten record and on typewritten briefs.

(3) Service

(A) In general

The respondent is the Attorney General. The petition shall be served on the Attorney General and on the officer or employee of the Service in charge of the Service district in which the final order of removal under section 240 [8 U.S.C.A. § 1229a] was entered.

(B) Stay of order

Service of the petition on the officer or employee does not stay the removal of an alien pending the court's decision on the petition, unless the court orders otherwise.

(C) Alien's brief

The alien shall serve and file a brief in connection with a petition for judicial review not later than 40 days after the date on which the administrative record is available, and may serve and file a reply brief not later than 14 days after service of the brief of the Attorney General, and the court may not extend these deadlines except upon motion for good cause shown. If an alien fails to file a brief within the time provided in this paragraph, the court shall dismiss the appeal unless a manifest injustice would result.

(4) Scope and standard for review

Except as provided in paragraph (5)(B)—

(A) the court of appeals shall decide the petition only on the administrative record on which the order of removal is based,

(B) the administrative findings of fact are conclusive unless any reasonable adjudicator would be compelled to conclude to the contrary,

(C) a decision that an alien is not eligible for admission to the United States is conclusive unless manifestly contrary to law, and

(D) the Attorney General's discretionary judgment whether to grant relief under section 208(a) [8 U.S.C.A. § 1158(a)] shall be conclusive unless manifestly contrary to the law and an abuse of discretion.

No court shall reverse a determination made by a trier of fact with respect to the availability of corroborating evidence, as described in section 208(b)(1)(B) [8 U.S.C.A. § 1158(b)(1)(B)], 240(c)(4)(B) [8 U.S.C.A. § 1229a(c)(4)(B)], or 241(b)(3)(C) [8 U.S.C.A. § 1231(b)(3)(C)], unless the court finds, pursuant to section 242(b)(4)(B) [8 U.S.C.A. § 1252(b)(4)(B)], that a reasonable trier of fact is compelled to conclude that such corroborating evidence is unavailable.

(5) Treatment of nationality claims

(A) Court determination if no issue of fact

If the petitioner claims to be a national of the United States and the court of appeals finds from the pleadings and affidavits that no genuine issue of material fact about the petitioner's nationality is presented, the court shall decide the nationality claim.

(B) Transfer if issue of fact

If the petitioner claims to be a national of the United States and the court of appeals finds that a genuine issue of material fact about the petitioner's nationality is presented, the court shall transfer the proceeding to the district court of the United States for the judicial district in which the petitioner resides for a new hearing on the nationality claim and a decision on that claim as if an action had been brought in the district court under section 2201 of Title 28.

(C) Limitation on determination

The petitioner may have such nationality claim decided only as provided in this paragraph.

(6) Consolidation with review of motions to reopen or reconsider

When a petitioner seeks review of an order under this section, any review sought of a motion to reopen or reconsider the order shall be consolidated with the review of the order.

(7) Challenge to validity of orders in certain criminal proceedings

(A) In general

If the validity of an order of removal has not been judicially decided, a defendant in a criminal proceeding charged with violating section 243(a) [8 U.S.C.A. § 1253(a)] may challenge the validity of the order in the criminal proceeding only by filing a separate motion before trial. The district court, without a jury, shall decide the motion before trial.

(B) Claims of United States nationality

If the defendant claims in the motion to be a national of the United States and the district court finds that—

(i) no genuine issue of material fact about the defendant's nationality is presented, the court shall decide the motion only on the administrative record on which the removal order is based and the administrative findings of fact are conclusive if supported by reasonable, substantial, and probative evidence on the record considered as a whole; or

(ii) a genuine issue of material fact about the defendant's nationality is presented, the court shall hold a new hearing on the nationality claim and decide that claim as if an action had been brought under section 2201 of Title 28, United States Code.

The defendant may have such nationality claim decided only as provided in this subparagraph.

(C) Consequence of invalidation

If the district court rules that the removal order is invalid, the court shall dismiss the indictment for violation of section 243(a) [8 U.S.C.A. § 1253(a)]. The United States Government may appeal the dismissal to the court of appeals for the appropriate circuit within 30 days after the date of the dismissal.

(D) Limitation on filing petitions for review

The defendant in a criminal proceeding under section 243(a) [8 U.S.C.A. § 1253(a)] may not file a petition for review under subsection (a) during the criminal proceeding.

(8) Construction

This subsection—

(A) does not prevent the Attorney General, after a final order of removal has been issued, from detaining the alien under section 241(a) [8 U.S.C.A. § 1231(a)];

(B) does not relieve the alien from complying with section 241(a)(4) [8 U.S.C.A. § 1231(a)(4)] and section 243(g) [8 U.S.C.A. § 1253(g)]; and

(C) does not require the Attorney General to defer removal of the alien.

(9) Consolidation of questions for judicial review

Judicial review of all questions of law and fact, including interpretation and application of constitutional and statutory provisions, arising from any action taken or proceeding brought to remove an alien from the United States under this title shall be available only in judicial review of a final order under this section. Except as otherwise provided in this section, no court shall have jurisdiction, by habeas corpus under section 2241 of title 28, United States Code, or any other habeas corpus provision, by section 1361 or 1651 of such title, or by any other provision of law (statutory or nonstatutory), to review such an order or such questions of law or fact.

(c) Requirements for petition

A petition for review or for habeas corpus of an order of removal—

(1) shall attach a copy of such order, and

(2) shall state whether a court has upheld the validity of the order, and, if so, shall state the name of the court, the date of the court's ruling, and the kind of proceeding.

(d) Review of final orders

A court may review a final order of removal only if—

(1) the alien has exhausted all administrative remedies available to the alien as of right, and

(2) another court has not decided the validity of the order, unless the reviewing court finds that the petition presents grounds that could not have been presented in the prior judicial proceeding or that the remedy provided by the prior proceeding was inadequate or ineffective to test the validity of the order.

(e) Judicial review of orders under section 235(b)(1) [8 U.S.C.A. § 1225(b)(1)]

(1) Limitations on relief

Without regard to the nature of the action or claim and without regard to the identity of the party or parties bringing the action, no court may—

(A) enter declaratory, injunctive, or other equitable relief in any action pertaining to an order to exclude an alien in accordance with section 235(b)(1) [8 U.S.C.A. § 1225(b)(1)] except as specifically authorized in a subsequent paragraph of this subsection, or

(B) certify a class under Rule 23 of the Federal Rules of Civil Procedure in any action for which judicial review is authorized under a subsequent paragraph of this subsection.

(2) Habeas corpus proceedings

Judicial review of any determination made under section 235(b)(1) [8 U.S.C.A. § 1225(b)(1)] is available in habeas corpus proceedings, but shall be limited to determinations of—

(A) whether the petitioner is an alien,

(B) whether the petitioner was ordered removed under such section, and

(C) whether the petitioner can prove by a preponderance of the evidence that the petitioner is an alien lawfully admitted for permanent residence, has been admitted as a refugee under section 207 [8 U.S.C.A. § 1157], or has been granted asylum under section 208 [8 U.S.C.A. § 1158], such status not having been terminated, and is entitled to such further inquiry as prescribed by the Attorney General pursuant to section 235(b)(1)(C) [8 U.S.C.A. § 1225(b)(1)(C)].

(3) Challenges on validity of the system

(A) In general

Judicial review of determinations under section 235(b) [8 U.S.C.A. § 1225(b)] and its implementation is available in an action instituted in the United States District Court for the District of Columbia, but shall be limited to determinations of—

(i) whether such section, or any regulation issued to implement such section, is constitutional; or

(ii) whether such a regulation, or a written policy directive, written policy guideline, or written procedure issued by or under the authority of the Attorney General to implement such section, is not consistent with applicable provisions of this title or is otherwise in violation of law.

(B) Deadlines for bringing actions

Any action instituted under this paragraph must be filed no later than 60 days after the date the challenged section, regulation, directive, guideline, or procedure described in clause (i) or (ii) of subparagraph (A) is first implemented.

(C) Notice of appeal

A notice of appeal of an order issued by the District Court under this paragraph may be filed not later than 30 days after the date of issuance of such order.

(D) Expeditious consideration of cases

It shall be the duty of the District Court, the Court of Appeals, and the Supreme Court of the United States to advance on the docket and to expedite to the greatest possible extent the disposition of any case considered under this paragraph.

(4) Decision

In any case where the court determines that the petitioner—

(A) is an alien who was not ordered removed under section 235(b)(1) [8 U.S.C.A. § 1225(b)(1)], or

(B) has demonstrated by a preponderance of the evidence that the alien is an alien lawfully admitted for permanent residence, has been admitted as a refugee under section 207 [8 U.S.C.A. § 1157], or has been granted asylum under section 208 [8 U.S.C.A. § 1158],

the court may order no remedy or relief other than to require that the petitioner be provided a hearing in accordance with section 240 [8 U.S.C.A. § 1229a]. Any alien who is provided a hearing under section 240 [8 U.S.C.A. § 1229a] pursuant to this paragraph may thereafter obtain judicial review of any resulting final order of removal pursuant to subsection (a)(1) of this section.

(5) Scope of inquiry

In determining whether an alien has been ordered removed under section 235(b)(1) [8 U.S.C.A. § 1225(b)(1)], the court's inquiry shall be limited to whether such an order in fact was issued and whether it relates to the petitioner. There shall be no review of whether the alien is actually inadmissible or entitled to any relief from removal.

(f) Limit on injunctive relief

(1) In general

Regardless of the nature of the action or claim or of the identity of the party or parties bringing the action, no court (other than the Supreme Court) shall have jurisdiction or authority to enjoin or restrain the operation of the provisions of chapter 4 of title II, as amended by the Illegal Immigration Reform and Immigrant Responsibility Act of 1996, other than with respect to the application of such provisions to an individual alien against whom proceedings under such part have been initiated.

(2) Particular cases

Notwithstanding any other provision of law, no court shall enjoin the removal of any alien pursuant to a final order under this section unless the alien shows by clear and convincing evidence that the entry or execution of such order is prohibited as a matter of law.

(g) Exclusive jurisdiction

Except as provided in this section and notwithstanding any other provision of law (statutory or nonstatutory), including section 2241 of title 28, United States Code, or any other habeas corpus provision, and sections 1361 and 1651 of such title, no court shall have jurisdiction to hear any cause or claim by or on behalf of any alien arising from the decision or action by the Attorney General to commence proceedings, adjudicate cases, or execute removal orders against any alien under this Act.

(June 27, 1952, c. 477, Title II, ch. 5, § 242, 66 Stat. 208; Sept. 3, 1954, c. 1263, § 17, 68 Stat. 1232; Dec. 29, 1981, Pub.L. 97–116, § 18(h)(1), 95 Stat. 1620; Oct. 12, 1984, Pub.L. 98–473, Title II, § 220(b), 98 Stat. 2028; Nov. 6, 1986, Pub.L. 99–603, Title VII, § 701, 100 Stat. 3445; Oct. 24, 1988, Pub.L. 100–525, § 9(n) 102 Stat. 2620; Nov. 18, 1988, Pub.L. 100–690, Title VII, § 7343(a), 102 Stat. 4470; Nov. 29, 1990, Pub.L. 101–649, Title V, §§ 504(a), 545(e), Title VI, § 603(b)(2), 104 Stat. 5049, 5066, 5085; Dec. 12, 1991, Pub.L. 102–232, Title III, §§ 306(a)(4), (c)(7), 307(m)(2), 309(b)(9), 105 Stat. 1751, 1753, 1757, 1759; Sept. 13, 1994, Pub.L. 103–322, Title II, § 20301(a), Title XIII, § 130001(a), 108 Stat. 1823, 2023; Oct. 25, 1994, Pub.L. 103–416, Title II, §§ 219(h), 224(b), 108 Stat. 4317, 4324; Apr. 24, 1996, Pub.L. 104–132, Title IV, §§ 436(a), (b)(1), 438(a), 440(c), (h), 110 Stat. 1275, 1277, 1279; Sept. 30, 1996, Pub.L. 104–208, Div. C, Title III, §§ 306(a), (d), 308(g)(10)(H), 371(b)(6), 110 Stat. 3009–607, 3009–612, 3009–625, 3009–645; May 11, 2005, Pub.L. 109–13, Div. B, § 101(e), (f), 106, 119 Stat. 231, 305, 310–11.)

§ 243.   Penalties related to removal [8 U.S.C.A. § 1253]

(a) Penalty for failure to depart

(1) In general

Any alien against whom a final order of removal is outstanding by reason of being a member of any of the classes described in section 237(a) [8 U.S.C.A. § 1227(a)], who—

(A) willfully fails or refuses to depart from the United States within a period of 90 days from the date of the final order of removal under administrative processes, or if judicial review is had, then from the date of the final order of the court,

(B) willfully fails or refuses to make timely application in good faith for travel or other documents necessary to the alien's departure,

(C) connives or conspires, or takes any other action, designed to prevent or hamper or with the purpose of preventing or hampering the alien's departure pursuant to such, or

(D) willfully fails or refuses to present himself or herself for removal at the time and place required by the Attorney General pursuant to such order,

shall be fined under Title 18, or imprisoned not more than four years (or 10 years if the alien is a member of any of the classes described in paragraph (1)(E), (2), (3), or (4) of section 237(a) [8 U.S.C.A. § 1227(a)]), or both.

(2) Exception

It is not a violation of paragraph (1) to take any proper steps for the purpose of securing cancellation of or exemption from such order of removal or for the purpose of securing the alien's release from incarceration or custody.

(3) Suspension

The court may for good cause suspend the sentence of an alien under this subsection and order the alien's release under such conditions as the court may prescribe. In determining whether good cause has been shown to justify releasing the alien, the court shall take into account such factors as—

(A) the age, health, and period of detention of the alien;

(B) the effect of the alien's release upon the national security and public peace or safety;

(C) the likelihood of the alien's resuming or following a course of conduct which made or would make the alien deportable;

(D) the character of the efforts made by such alien himself and by representatives of the country or countries to which the alien's removal is directed to expedite the alien's departure from the United States;

(E) the reason for the inability of the Government of the United States to secure passports, other travel documents, or removal facilities from the country or countries to which the alien has been ordered removed; and

(F) the eligibility of the alien for discretionary relief under the immigration laws.

(b) Willful failure to comply with terms of release under supervision

An alien who shall willfully fail to comply with regulations or requirements issued pursuant to section 241(a)(3) [8 U.S.C.A. § 1231(a)(3)] or knowingly give false information in response to an inquiry under such section shall be fined not more than $1,000 or imprisoned for not more than one year, or both.

(c) Penalties relating to vessels and aircraft

(1) Civil penalties

(A) Failure to carry out certain orders

If the Attorney General is satisfied that a person has violated subsection (d) or (e) of section 241 [8 U.S.C.A. § 1231], the person shall pay to the Commissioner the sum of $2,000 for each violation.

(B) Failure to remove alien stowaways

If the Attorney General is satisfied that a person has failed to remove an alien stowaway as required under section 241(d)(2) [8 U.S.C.A. § 1231(d)(2)], the person shall pay to the Commissioner the sum of $5,000 for each alien stowaway not removed.

(C) No compromise

The Attorney General may not compromise the amount of such penalty under this paragraph.

(2) Clearing vessels and aircraft

(A) Clearance before decision on liability

A vessel or aircraft may be granted clearance before a decision on liability is made under paragraph (1) only if a bond approved by the Attorney General or an amount sufficient to pay the civil penalty is deposited with the Commissioner.

(B) Prohibition on clearance while penalty unpaid

A vessel or aircraft may not be granted clearance if a civil penalty imposed under paragraph (1) is not paid.

(d) Discontinuing granting visas to nationals of country denying or delaying accepting alien

On being notified by the Attorney General that the government of a foreign country denies or unreasonably delays accepting an alien who is a citizen, subject, national, or resident of that country after the Attorney General asks whether the government will accept the alien under this section, the Secretary of State shall order consular officers in that foreign country to discontinue granting immigrant visas or nonimmigrant visas, or both, to citizens, subjects, nationals, and residents of that country until the Attorney General notifies the Secretary that the country has accepted the alien.

(June 27, 1952, c. 477, Title II, ch. 5, § 243, 66 Stat. 212; Oct. 3, 1965, Pub.L. 89–236, § 11(f), 79 Stat. 918; Oct. 30, 1978, Pub.L. 95–549, Title I, § 104, 92 Stat. 2066; Mar. 17, 1980, Pub.L. 96–212, Title II, § 203(e), 94 Stat. 107; Dec. 29, 1981, Pub.L. 97–116, § 18(i), 95 Stat. 1620; Nov. 29, 1990, Pub.L. 101–649, Title V, § 515(a)(2), Title VI, § 603(b)(3), 104 Stat. 5053, 5085; Apr. 24, 1996, Pub.L. 104–132, Title IV, § 413(a), (f), 110 Stat. 1269; Sept. 30, 1996, Pub.L. 104–208, Div. C, Title III, § 307(a), 110 Stat. 3009–612.)

§ 244. Temporary protected status [8 U.S.C.A. § 1254a]

(a) Granting of status

(1) In general

In the case of an alien who is a national of a foreign state designated under subsection (b) (or in the case of an alien having no nationality, is a person who last habitually resided in such designated state) and who meets the requirements of subsection (c), the Attorney General, in accordance with this section—

(A) may grant the alien temporary protected status in the United States and shall not remove the alien from the United States during the period in which such status is in effect, and

(B) shall authorize the alien to engage in employment in the United States and provide the alien with an "employment authorized" endorsement or other appropriate work permit.

(2) Duration of work authorization

Work authorization provided under this section shall be effective throughout the period the alien is in temporary protected status under this section.

(3) Notice

(A) Upon the granting of temporary protected status under this section, the Attorney General shall provide the alien with information concerning such status under this section.

(B) If, at the time of initiation of a removal proceeding against an alien, the foreign state (of which the alien is a national) is designated under subsection (b), the Attorney General shall promptly notify the alien of the temporary protected status that may be available under this section.

(C) If, at the time of designation of a foreign state under subsection (b), an alien (who is a national of such state) is in a removal proceeding under this title, the Attorney General shall promptly notify the alien of the temporary protected status that may be available under this section.

(D) Notices under this paragraph shall be provided in a form and language that the alien can understand.

(4) Temporary treatment for eligible aliens

(A) In the case of an alien who can establish a prima facie case of eligibility for benefits under paragraph (1), but for the fact that the period of registration under subsection (c)(1)(A)(iv) has not begun, until the alien has had a reasonable opportunity to register during the first 30 days of such period, the Attorney General shall provide for the benefits of paragraph (1).

(B) In the case of an alien who establishes a prima facie case of eligibility for benefits under paragraph (1), until a final determination with respect to the alien's eligibility for such benefits under paragraph (1) has been made, the alien shall be provided such benefits.

(5) Clarification

Nothing in this section shall be construed as authorizing the Attorney General to deny temporary protected status to an alien based on the alien's immigration status or to require any alien, as a condition of being granted such status, either to relinquish nonimmigrant or other status the alien may have or to execute any waiver of other rights under this Act. The granting of temporary protected status under this section shall not be considered to be inconsistent with the granting of nonimmigrant status under this Act.

(b) Designations

(1) In general

The Attorney General, after consultation with appropriate agencies of the Government, may designate any foreign state (or any part of such foreign state) under this subsection only if—

(A) the Attorney General finds that there is an ongoing armed conflict within the state and, due to such conflict, requiring the return of aliens who are nationals of that state to that state (or to the part of the state) would pose a serious threat to their personal safety;

(B) the Attorney General finds that—

(i) there has been an earthquake, flood, drought, epidemic, or other environmental disaster in the state resulting in a substantial, but temporary, disruption of living conditions in the area affected,

(ii) the foreign state is unable, temporarily, to handle adequately the return to the state of aliens who are nationals of the state, and

(iii) the foreign state officially has requested designation under this subparagraph; or

(C) the Attorney General finds that there exist extraordinary and temporary conditions in the foreign state that prevent aliens who are nationals of the state from returning to the state in safety, unless the Attorney General finds that permitting the aliens to remain temporarily in the United States is contrary to the national interest of the United States.

A designation of a foreign state (or part of such foreign state) under this paragraph shall not become effective unless notice of the designation (including a statement of the findings under this paragraph and the effective date of the designation) is published in the Federal Register. In such notice, the Attorney General shall also state an estimate of the number of nationals of the foreign state designated who are (or within the effective period of the designation are likely to become) eligible for temporary protected status under this section and their immigration status in the United States.

(2) Effective period of designation for foreign states

The designation of a foreign state (or part of such foreign state) under paragraph (1) shall—

(A) take effect upon the date of publication of the designation under such paragraph, or such later date as the Attorney General may specify in the notice published under such paragraph, and

(B) shall remain in effect until the effective date of the termination of the designation under paragraph (3)(B).

For purposes of this section, the initial period of designation of a foreign state (or part thereof) under paragraph (1) is the period, specified by the Attorney General, of not less than 6 months and not more than 18 months.

(3) Periodic review, terminations, and extensions of designations

(A) Periodic review

At least 60 days before end of the initial period of designation, and any extended period of designation, of a foreign state (or part thereof) under this section the Attorney General, after consultation with appropriate agencies of the Government, shall review the conditions in the foreign state (or part of such foreign state) for which a designation is in effect under this subsection and shall determine whether the conditions for such designation under this subsection continue to be met. The Attorney General shall provide on a timely basis for the publication of notice of each such determination (including the basis for the determination, and, in the case of an affirmative determination, the period of extension of designation under subparagraph (C)) in the Federal Register.

(B) Termination of designation

If the Attorney General determines under subparagraph (A) that a foreign state (or part of such foreign state) no longer continues to meet the conditions for designation under paragraph (1), the Attorney General shall terminate the designation by publishing notice in the Federal Register of the determination under this subparagraph (including the basis for the determination). Such termination is effective in accordance with subsection (d)(3), but shall not be effective earlier than 60 days after the date the notice is published or, if later, the expiration of the most recent previous extension under subparagraph (C).

(C) Extension of designation

If the Attorney General does not determine under subparagraph (A) that a foreign state (or part of such foreign state) no longer meets the conditions for designation under paragraph (1), the period of designation of the foreign state is extended for an additional period of 6 months (or, in the discretion of the Attorney General, a period of 12 or 18 months).

(4) Information concerning protected status at time of designations

At the time of a designation of a foreign state under this subsection, the Attorney General shall make available information respecting the temporary protected status made available to aliens who are nationals of such designated foreign state.

(5) Review

(A) Designations

There is no judicial review of any determination of the Attorney General with respect to the designation, or termination or extension of a designation, of a foreign state under this subsection.

(B) Application to individuals

The Attorney General shall establish an administrative procedure for the review of the denial of benefits to aliens under this subsection. Such procedure shall not prevent an alien from asserting protection under this section in removal proceedings if the alien demonstrates that the alien is a national of a state designated under paragraph (1).

(c) Aliens eligible for temporary protected status

(1) In general

(A) Nationals of designated foreign states

Subject to paragraph (3), an alien, who is a national of a state designated under subsection (b)(1) (or in the case of an alien having no nationality, is a person who last habitually resided in such designated state) meets the requirements of this paragraph only if—

(i) the alien has been continuously physically present in the United States since the effective date of the most recent designation of that state;

(ii) the alien has continuously resided in the United States since such date as the Attorney General may designate;

(iii) the alien is admissible as an immigrant, except as otherwise provided under paragraph (2)(A), and is not ineligible for temporary protected status under paragraph (2)(B); and

(iv) to the extent and in a manner which the Attorney General establishes, the alien registers for the temporary protected status under this section during a registration period of not less than 180 days.

(B) Registration fee

The Attorney General may require payment of a reasonable fee as a condition of registering an alien under subparagraph (A)(iv) (including providing an alien with an "employment authorized" endorsement or other appropriate work permit under this section). The amount of any such fee shall not exceed $50. In the case of aliens registered pursuant to a designation under this section made after July 17, 1991, the Attorney General may impose a separate, additional fee for providing an alien with documentation of work authorization. Notwithstanding section 3302 of Title 31, all fees collected under this subparagraph shall be credited to the appropriation to be used in carrying out this section.

(2) Eligibility standards

(A) Waiver of certain grounds for inadmissibility

In the determination of an alien's admissibility for purposes of subparagraph (A)(iii) of paragraph (1)—

(i) the provisions of paragraphs (5) and (7)(A) of section 212(a) [8 U.S.C.A. § 1182(a)] shall not apply;

(ii) except as provided in clause (iii), the Attorney General may waive any other provision of section 212(a) [8 U.S.C.A. § 1182(a)] in the case of individual aliens for humanitarian purposes, to assure family unity, or when it is otherwise in the public interest; but

(iii) the Attorney General may not waive—

(I) paragraphs (2)(A) and (2)(B) (relating to criminals) of such section,

(II) paragraph (2)(C) of such section (relating to drug offenses), except for so much of such paragraph as relates to a single offense of simple possession of 30 grams or less of marijuana, or

(III) paragraphs (3)(A), (3)(B), (3)(C), and (3)(E) of such section (relating to national security and participation in the Nazi persecutions or those who have engaged in genocide).

(B) Aliens ineligible

An alien shall not be eligible for temporary protected status under this section if the Attorney General finds that—

(i) the alien has been convicted of any felony or 2 or more misdemeanors committed in the United States, or

(ii) the alien is described in section 208(b)(2)(A) [8 U.S.C.A. § 1158(b)(2)(A)].

(3) Withdrawal of temporary protected status

The Attorney General shall withdraw temporary protected status granted to an alien under this section if—

(A) the Attorney General finds that the alien was not in fact eligible for such status under this section,

(B) except as provided in paragraph (4) and permitted in subsection (f)(3), the alien has not remained continuously physically present in the United States from the date the alien first was granted temporary protected status under this section, or

(C) the alien fails, without good cause, to register with the Attorney General annually, at the end of each 12-month period after the granting of such status, in a form and manner specified by the Attorney General.

(4) Treatment of brief, casual, and innocent departures and certain other absences

(A) For purposes of paragraphs (1)(A)(i) and (3)(B), an alien shall not be considered to have failed to maintain continuous physical presence in the United States by virtue of brief, casual, and innocent absences from the United States, without regard to whether such absences were authorized by the Attorney General.

(B) For purposes of paragraph (1)(A)(ii), an alien shall not be considered to have failed to maintain continuous residence in the United States by reason of a brief, casual, and innocent absence described in subparagraph (A) or due merely to a brief temporary trip abroad required by emergency or extenuating circumstances outside the control of the alien.

(5) Construction

Nothing in this section shall be construed as authorizing an alien to apply for admission to, or to be admitted to, the United States in order to apply for temporary protected status under this section.

(6) Confidentiality of information

The Attorney General shall establish procedures to protect the confidentiality of information provided by aliens under this section.

(d) Documentation

(1) Initial issuance

Upon the granting of temporary protected status to an alien under this section, the Attorney General shall provide for the issuance of such temporary documentation and authorization as may be necessary to carry out the purposes of this section.

(2) Period of validity

Subject to paragraph (3), such documentation shall be valid during the initial period of designation of the foreign state (or part thereof) involved and any extension of such period. The Attorney General may stagger the periods of validity of the documentation and authorization in order to provide for an orderly renewal of such documentation and authorization and for an orderly transition (under paragraph (3)) upon the termination of a designation of a foreign state (or any part of such foreign state).

(3) Effective date of terminations

If the Attorney General terminates the designation of a foreign state (or part of such foreign state) under subsection (b)(3)(B), such termination shall only apply to documentation and authorization issued or renewed after the effective date of the publication of notice of the determination under that subsection (or, at the Attorney General's option, after such period after the effective date of the determination as the Attorney General determines to be appropriate in order to provide for an orderly transition).

(4) Detention of the alien

An alien provided temporary protected status under this section shall not be detained by the Attorney General on the basis of the alien's immigration status in the United States.

(e) Relation of period of temporary protected status to cancellation of removal

With respect to an alien granted temporary protected status under this section, the period of such status shall not be counted as a period of physical presence in the United States for purposes of section 240A(a) [8 U.S.C.A. § 1229b(a)], unless the Attorney General determines that extreme hardship exists. Such period shall not cause a break in the continuity of residence of the period before and after such period for purposes of such section.

(f) Benefits and status during period of temporary protected status

During a period in which an alien is granted temporary protected status under this section—

(1) the alien shall not be considered to be permanently residing in the United States under color of law;

(2) the alien may be deemed ineligible for public assistance by a State (as defined in section 101(a)(36) [8 U.S.C.A. § 1101(a)(36)]) or any political subdivision thereof which furnishes such assistance;

(3) the alien may travel abroad with the prior consent of the Attorney General; and

(4) for purposes of adjustment of status under section 245 [8 U.S.C.A. § 1255] and change of status under section 248 [8 U.S.C.A. § 1258], the alien shall be considered as being in, and maintaining, lawful status as a nonimmigrant.

(g) Exclusive remedy

Except as otherwise specifically provided, this section shall constitute the exclusive authority of the Attorney General under law to permit aliens who are or may become otherwise deportable or have been paroled into the United States to remain in the United States temporarily because of their particular nationality or region of foreign state of nationality.

(h) Limitation on consideration in Senate of legislation adjusting status

(1) In general

Except as provided in paragraph (2), it shall not be in order in the Senate to consider any bill, resolution, or amendment that—

(A) provides for adjustment to lawful temporary or permanent resident alien status for any alien receiving temporary protected status under this section, or

(B) has the effect of amending this subsection or limiting the application of this subsection.

(2) Supermajority required

Paragraph (1) may be waived or suspended in the Senate only by the affirmative vote of three-fifths of the Members duly chosen and sworn. An affirmative vote of three-fifths of the Members of the Senate duly chosen and sworn shall be required in the Senate to sustain an appeal of the ruling of the Chair on a point of order raised under paragraph (1).

(3) Rules

Paragraphs (1) and (2) are enacted—

(A) as an exercise of the rulemaking power of the Senate and as such they are deemed a part of the rules of the Senate, but applicable only with respect to the matters described in paragraph (1) and supersede other rules of the Senate only to the extent that such paragraphs are inconsistent therewith; and

(B) with full recognition of the constitutional right of the Senate to change such rules at any time, in the same manner as in the case of any other rule of the Senate.

(i) Annual report and review

(1) Annual report

Not later than March 1 of each year (beginning with 1992), the Attorney General, after consultation with the appropriate agencies of the Government, shall submit a report to the Committees on the Judiciary of the House of Representatives and of the Senate on the operation of this section during the previous year. Each report shall include—

(A) a listing of the foreign states or parts thereof designated under this section,

(B) the number of nationals of each such state who have been granted temporary protected status under this section and their immigration status before being granted such status, and

(C) an explanation of the reasons why foreign states or parts thereof were designated under subsection (b)(1) and, with respect to foreign states or parts thereof previously designated, why the designation was terminated or extended under subsection (b)(3).

(2) Committee report

No later than 180 days after the date of receipt of such a report, the Committee on the Judiciary of each House of Congress shall report to its respective House such oversight findings and legislation as it deems appropriate.

(June 27, 1952, c. 477, Title II, ch. 5, § 244, formerly § 244A, as added and amended Nov. 29, 1990, Pub.L. 101–649, Title III, § 302(a), Title VI, § 603(a)(24), 104 Stat. 5030, 5084; Dec. 12, 1991, Pub.L. 102–232, Title III, §§ 304(b), 307(*l*)(5), 105 Stat. 1749, 1756; Oct. 25, 1994, Pub.L. 103–416, Title II, § 219(j), (z)(2), 108 Stat. 4317, 4318; renumbered § 244 and amended Sept. 30, 1996, Pub.L. 104–208, Div. C, Title III, § 308(b)(7), (e)(1)(G), (11), (g)(7) (E)(i), (g)(8)(A)(i), 110 Stat. 3009–615, 3009–619, 3009–620, 3009–624.)

Chapter V—Adjustment and Change of Status[*]

§ 245. Adjustment of status of nonimmigrant to that of person admitted for permanent residence [8 U.S.C.A. § 1255]

(a) Status as person admitted for permanent residence on application and eligibility for immigrant visa

The status of an alien who was inspected and admitted or paroled into the United States or the status of any other alien having an approved petition for classification as a VAWA self-petitioner may be adjusted by the Attorney General, in his discretion and under such regulations as he may prescribe, to that of an alien lawfully admitted for permanent residence if **(1)** the alien makes an application for such adjustment, **(2)** the alien is eligible to receive an immigrant visa and is admissible to the United States for permanent residence, and **(3)** an immigrant visa is immediately available to him at the time his application is filed.

(b) Record of lawful admission for permanent residence; reduction of preference visas

Upon the approval of an application for adjustment made under subsection (a), the Attorney General shall record the alien's lawful admission for permanent residence as of the date the order of the Attorney General

[*] Pub.L. 104–208, section 308(a)(2), amended the table of contents of the Immigration and Nationality Act to show that renumbered §§ 242 to 244 are part of chapter IV, with chapter V starting with § 245. This suggests Congressional intent to move §§ 242 to 244 to chapter IV, but there is no specific directory language that actually moves these sections.

approving the application for the adjustment of status is made, and the Secretary of State shall reduce by one the number of the preference visas authorized to be issued under sections 202 [8 U.S.C.A. § 1152] and 203 [8 U.S.C.A. § 1153] within the class to which the alien is chargeable for the fiscal year then current.

(c) Alien crewmen, aliens continuing or accepting unauthorized employment, and aliens admitted in transit without visa

Other than an alien having an approved petition for classification as a VAWA self-petitioner, subsection (a) of this section shall not be applicable to **(1)** an alien crewman; **(2)** subject to subsection (k) of this section, an alien (other than an immediate relative as defined in section 201(b) [8 U.S.C.A. § 1151(b)] or a special immigrant described in section 101(a)(27) (H), (I), (J), or (K) [8 U.S.C.A. § 1101(a)(27)(H), (I), (J), or (K)]) who hereafter continues in or accepts unauthorized employment prior to filing an application for adjustment of status or who is in unlawful immigration status on the date of filing the application for adjustment of status or who has failed (other than through no fault of his own or for technical reasons) to maintain continuously a lawful status since entry into the United States; **(3)** any alien admitted in transit without visa under section 212(d) (4)(C) [8 U.S.C.A. § 1182(d)(4)(C)]; **(4)** an alien (other than an immediate relative as defined in section 201(b) [8 U.S.C.A. § 1151(b)]) who was admitted as a nonimmigrant visitor without a visa under section 212(*l*) [8 U.S.C.A. § 1182(*l*)] or section 217 [8 U.S.C.A. § 1187]; **(5)** an alien who was admitted as a nonimmigrant described in section 101(a)(15)(S) [8 U.S.C.A. § 1101(a)(15)(S)], [sic]* **(6)** an alien who is deportable under section 237(a)(4)(B) [8 U.S.C.A. § 1227(a)(4)(B)]; **(7)** any alien who seeks adjustment of status to that of an immigrant under section 203(b) [8 U.S.C.A. § 1153(b)] and is not in a lawful nonimmigrant status; or **(8)** any alien who was employed while the alien was an unauthorized alien, as defined in section 274A(h)(3) [8 U.S.C.A. § 1324a(h)(3)], or who has otherwise violated the terms of a nonimmigrant visa.

(d) Alien admitted for permanent residence on conditional basis; fiancée or fiancé of citizen

The Attorney General may not adjust, under subsection (a), the status of an alien lawfully admitted to the United States for permanent residence on a conditional basis under section 216 [8 U.S.C.A. § 1186a]. The Attorney General may not adjust, under subsection (a), the status of a nonimmigrant alien described in section 101(a)(15)(K) [8 U.S.C.A. § 1101(a)(15)(K)] except to that of an alien lawfully admitted to the United States on a conditional basis under section 216 [8 U.S.C.A. § 1186a] as a result of the marriage of the nonimmigrant (or, in the case of a minor child, the parent) to the citizen who filed the petition to accord that alien's nonimmigrant status under section 101(a)(15)(K) [8 U.S.C.A. § 1101(a) (15)(K)].

---

* **Comma probably should be a semi-colon.**

(e) Restrictions on adjustment of status based on marriages entered while in exclusion or deportation proceedings; bona fide marriage exception

(1) Except as provided in paragraph (3), an alien who is seeking to receive an immigrant visa on the basis of a marriage which was entered into during the period described in paragraph (2) may not have the alien's status adjusted under subsection (a).

(2) The period described in this paragraph is the period during which administrative or judicial proceedings are pending regarding the alien's right to be admitted or remain in the United States.

(3) Paragraph (1) and section 204(g) [8 U.S.C.A. § 1154(g)] shall not apply with respect to a marriage if the alien establishes by clear and convincing evidence to the satisfaction of the Attorney General that the marriage was entered into in good faith and in accordance with the laws of the place where the marriage took place and the marriage was not entered into for the purpose of procuring the alien's admission as an immigrant and no fee or other consideration was given (other than a fee or other consideration to an attorney for assistance in preparation of a lawful petition) for the filing of a petition under section 204(a) [8 U.S.C.A. § 1154(a)] or subsection (d) or (p) of section 214 [8 U.S.C.A. § 1184] with respect to the alien spouse or alien son or daughter. In accordance with regulations, there shall be only one level of administrative appellate review for each alien under the previous sentence.

(f) Limitation on adjustment of status

The Attorney General may not adjust, under subsection (a), the status of an alien lawfully admitted to the United States for permanent residence on a conditional basis under section 216A [8 U.S.C.A. § 1186b].

(g) Special immigrants

In applying this section to a special immigrant described in section 101(a)(27)(K) [8 U.S.C.A. § 1101(a)(27)(K)], such an immigrant shall be deemed, for purposes of subsection (a), to have been paroled into the United States.

(h) Application with respect to special immigrants

In applying this section to a special immigrant described in section 101(a)(27)(J) [8 U.S.C.A. § 1101(a)(27)(J)]—

(1) such an immigrant shall be deemed, for purposes of subsection (a), to have been paroled into the United States; and

(2) in determining the alien's admissibility as an immigrant—

(A) paragraphs (4), (5)(A), (6)(A), (6)(C), (6)(D), (7)(A), and (9)(B) of section 212(a) [8 U.S.C.A. § 1182(a)] shall not apply; and

(B) the Attorney General may waive other paragraphs of section 212(a) [8 U.S.C.A. § 1182(a)] (other than paragraphs (2)(A), (2)(B), (2)(C) (except for so much of such paragraph as related to a single

offense of simple possession of 30 grams or less of marijuana), (3)
(A), (3)(B), (3)(C), and (3)(E)) in the case of individual aliens for
humanitarian purposes, family unity, or when it is otherwise in the
public interest.

The relationship between an alien and the alien's natural parents or
prior adoptive parents shall not be considered a factor in making a
waiver under paragraph (2)(B). Nothing in this subsection or section
101(a)(27)(J) [8 U.S.C.A. § 1101(a)(27)(J)] shall be construed as authorizing an alien to apply for admission or be admitted to the United
States in order to obtain special immigrant status described in such
section.

**(i) Adjustment of status of certain aliens physically present in
United States**

   (1) Notwithstanding the provisions of subsections (a) and (c) of this
section, an alien physically present in the United States—

      (A) who—

         (i) entered the United States without inspection; or

         (ii) is within one of the classes enumerated in subsection (c)
      of this section;

      (B) who is the beneficiary (including a spouse or child of the
   principal alien, if eligible to receive a visa under section 203(d) [8
   U.S.C.A. § 1153(d)]) of—

         (i) a petition for classification under section 204 [8 U.S.C.A.
      § 1154] that was filed with the Attorney General on or before
      April 30, 2001; or

         (ii) an application for a labor certification under section 212(a)
      (5)(A) [8 U.S.C.A. § 1182(a)(5)(A)] that was filed pursuant to the
      regulations of the Secretary of Labor on or before such date; and

      (C) who, in the case of a beneficiary of a petition for classifica-
   tion, or an application for labor certification, described in subparagraph (B) that was filed after January 14, 1998, is physically present in the United States on the date of the enactment of the LIFE
   Act Amendments of 2000 [December 21, 2000];

may apply to the Attorney General for the adjustment of his or her status to that of an alien lawfully admitted for permanent residence. The
Attorney General may accept such application only if the alien remits
with such application a sum equalling $1,000 as of the date of receipt
of the application, but such sum shall not be required from a child
under the age of seventeen, or an alien who is the spouse or unmarried child of an individual who obtained temporary or permanent resident status under section 210 [8 U.S.C.A. § 1160] or 245A [8 U.S.C.A.
§ 1255a] or section 202 of the Immigration Reform and Control Act of
1986 at any date, who—

(i) as of May 5, 1988, was the unmarried child or spouse of the individual who obtained temporary or permanent resident status under section 210 [8 U.S.C.A. § 1160] or 245A [8 U.S.C.A. § 1255a] or section 202 of the Immigration Reform and Control Act of 1986;

(ii) entered the United States before May 5, 1988, resided in the United States on May 5, 1988, and is not a lawful permanent resident; and

(iii) applied for benefits under section 301(a) of the Immigration Act of 1990. The sum specified herein shall be in addition to the fee normally required for the processing of an application under this section.

(2) Upon receipt of such an application and the sum hereby required, the Attorney General may adjust the status of the alien to that of an alien lawfully admitted for permanent residence if—

(A) the alien is eligible to receive an immigrant visa and is admissible to the United States for permanent residence; and

(B) an immigrant visa is immediately available to the alien at the time the application is filed.

(3)(A) The portion of each application fee (not to exceed $200) that the Attorney General determines is required to process an application under this section and is remitted to the Attorney General pursuant to paragraphs (1) and (2) of this subsection shall be disposed of by the Attorney General as provided in subsections (m), (n), and (o) of section 286 [8 U.S.C.A. § 1356].

(B) Any remaining portion of such fees remitted under such paragraphs shall be deposited by the Attorney General into the Breached Bond/Detention Fund established under section 286(r) [8 U.S.C.A. § 1356(r)], except that in the case of fees attributable to applications for a beneficiary with respect to whom a petition for classification, or an application for labor certification, described in paragraph (1)(B) was filed after January 14, 1998, one-half of such remaining portion shall be deposited by the Attorney General into the Immigration Examinations Fee Account established under section 286(m) [8 U.S.C.A. § 1356(m)].

(j) Adjustment to permanent resident status of "S" visa nonimmigrants

(1) If, in the opinion of the Attorney General—

(A) a nonimmigrant admitted into the United States under section 101(a)(15)(S)(i) [8 U.S.C.A. § 1101(a)(15)(S)(i)] has supplied information described in subclause (I) of such section; and

(B) the provision of such information has substantially contributed to the success of an authorized criminal investigation or the prosecution of an individual described in subclause (III) of that section,

the Attorney General may adjust the status of the alien (and the spouse, married and unmarried sons and daughters, and parents of the alien if admitted under that section) to that of an alien lawfully admitted for permanent residence if the alien is not described in section 212(a)(3)(E) [8 U.S.C.A. § 1182(a)(3)(E)].

(2) If, in the sole discretion of the Attorney General—

(A) a nonimmigrant admitted into the United States under section 101(a)(15)(S)(ii) [8 U.S.C.A. § 1101(a)(15)(S)(ii)] has supplied information described in subclause (I) of such section, and

(B) the provision of such information has substantially contributed to—

(i) the prevention or frustration of an act of terrorism against a United States person or United States property, or

(ii) the success of an authorized criminal investigation of, or the prosecution of, an individual involved in such an act of terrorism, and

(C) the nonimmigrant has received a reward under section 2708(a) of Title 22,

the Attorney General may adjust the status of the alien (and the spouse, married and unmarried sons and daughters, and parents of the alien if admitted under such section) to that of an alien lawfully admitted for permanent residence if the alien is not described in section 212(a)(3)(E) [8 U.S.C.A. § 1182(a)(3)(E)].

(3) Upon the approval of adjustment of status under paragraph (1) or (2), the Attorney General shall record the alien's lawful admission for permanent residence as of the date of such approval and the Secretary of State shall reduce by one the number of visas authorized to be issued under sections 201(d) [8 U.S.C.A. § 1151(d)] and 203(b)(4) [8 U.S.C.A. § 1153(b)(4)] for the fiscal year then current.

(k) Inapplicability of certain provisions for certain employment-based immigrants

An alien who is eligible to receive an immigrant visa under paragraph (1), (2), or (3) of section 203(b) [8 U.S.C.A. § 1153(b)] (or, in the case of an alien who is an immigrant described in section 101(a)(27)(C) [8 U.S.C.A. § 1101(a)(27)(C)], under section 203(b)(4) [8 U.S.C.A. § 1153(b)(4)]) may adjust status pursuant to subsection (a) and notwithstanding subsection (c)(2), (c)(7), and (c)(8), if—

(1) the alien, on the date of filing an application for adjustment of status, is present in the United States pursuant to a lawful admission;

(2) the alien, subsequent to such lawful admission has not, for an aggregate period exceeding 180 days—

(A) failed to maintain, continuously, a lawful status;

(B) engaged in unauthorized employment; or

(C) otherwise violated the terms and conditions of the alien's admission.

(*l*) Adjustment of status for victims of trafficking

(1) If, in the opinion of the Secretary of Homeland Security, or in the case of subparagraph (C)(i), in the opinion of the Secretary of Homeland Security, in consultation with the Attorney General, as appropriate a nonimmigrant admitted into the United States under section 101(a)(15)(T)(i) [8 U.S.C.A. § 1101(a)(15)(T)(i)]—

(A) has been physically present in the United States for a continuous period of at least 3 years since the date of admission as a nonimmigrant under section 101(a)(15)(T)(i) [8 U.S.C.A. § 1101(a)(15)(T)(i)], or has been physically present in the United States for a continuous period during the investigation or prosecution of acts of trafficking and that, in the opinion of the Attorney General, the investigation or prosecution is complete, whichever period of time is less;

(B) subject to paragraph (6), has, throughout such period, been a person of good moral character; and

(C)(i) has, during such period, complied with any reasonable request for assistance in the investigation or prosecution of acts of trafficking;

(ii) the alien would suffer extreme hardship involving unusual and severe harm upon removal from the United States,

the Secretary of Homeland Security may adjust the status of the alien (and any person admitted under section 101(a)(15)(T)(ii) [8 U.S.C.A. § 1101(a)(15)(T)(ii)] as the spouse, parent, sibling, or child of the alien) to that of an alien lawfully admitted for permanent residence; or

(iii) was younger than 18 years of age at the time of the victimization qualifying the alien for relief under section 101(a)(15)(T) [8 U.S.C.A. § 1101(a)(15)(T)].*

(2) Paragraph (1) shall not apply to an alien admitted under section 101(a)(15)(T) [8 U.S.C.A § 1101(a)(15)(T)] who is inadmissible to the United States by reason of a ground that has not been waived under section 212 [8 U.S.C.A § 1182], except that, if the Secretary of Homeland Security considers it to be in the National interest to do so, the Secretary of Homeland Security, in the Attorney General's discretion,** may waive the application of

(A) paragraphs (1) and (4) of section 212(a) [8 U.S.C.A. § 1182(a)]; and

---

** So in original. The term "Attorney General's" probably should be "Secretary's".

(B) any other provision of such section (excluding paragraphs (3), (10)(C), and (10)(E)) [sic], if the activities rendering the alien inadmissible under the provision were caused by, or were incident to, the victimization described in section 101(a)(15)(T)(i)(I) [8 U.S.C.A. § 1101(a)(15)(T)(i)(I)].

(3) An alien shall be considered to have failed to maintain continuous physical presence in the United States under paragraph (1)(A) if the alien has departed from the United States for any period in excess of 90 days or for any periods in the aggregate exceeding 180 days, unless—

(A) the absence was necessary to assist in the investigation or prosecution described in paragraph (1)(A); or

(B) an official involved in the investigation or prosecution certifies that the absence was otherwise justified.

(4)(A) The total number of aliens whose status may be adjusted under paragraph (1) during any fiscal year may not exceed 5,000.

(B) The numerical limitation of subparagraph (A) shall only apply to principal aliens and not to the spouses, sons, daughters, siblings, or parents of such aliens.

(5) Upon the approval of adjustment of status under paragraph (1), the Secretary of Homeland Security shall record the alien's lawful admission for permanent residence as of the date of such approval.

(6) For purposes of paragraph (1)(B), the Secretary of Homeland Security may waive consideration of a disqualification from good moral character with respect to an alien if the disqualification was caused by, or incident to, the trafficking described in section 101(a)(15)(T)(i)(I) [8 U.S.C.A. § 1101(a)(15)(T)(i)(I)].

(7) The Secretary of Homeland Security shall permit aliens to apply for a waiver of any fees associated with filing an application for relief through final adjudication of the adjustment of status for a VAWA self-petitioner and for relief under sections 101(a)(15)(T) [8 U.S.C.A. § 1101(a)(15)(T)], 101(a)(15)(U) [8 U.S.C.A. § 1101(a)(15)(U)], 106 [8 U.S.C.A. § 1105a], 240A(b)(2) [8 U.S.C.A. § 1229b(b)(2)], and 244(a)(3) [8 U.S.C.A. § 1254a] (as in effect on March 31, 1997).

(m) Adjustment of status for victims of crimes against women

(1) The Secretary of Homeland Security may adjust the status of an alien admitted into the United States (or otherwise provided nonimmigrant status) under section 101(a)(15)(U) [8 U.S.C.A. § 1101(a)(15)(U)] to that of an alien lawfully admitted for permanent residence if the alien is not described in section 212(a)(3)(E) [8 U.S.C.A. § 1182(a)(3)(E)], unless the Secretary determines based on affirmative evidence that the alien unreasonably refused to provide assistance in a criminal investigation or prosecution, if—

(A) the alien has been physically present in the United States for a continuous period of at least 3 years since the date of admission as a nonimmigrant under clause (i) or (ii) of section 101(a)(15)(U) [8 U.S.C.A. § 1101(a)(15)(U)]; and

(B) in the opinion of the Secretary of Homeland Security, the alien's continued presence in the United States is justified on humanitarian grounds, to ensure family unity, or is otherwise in the public interest.

(2) An alien shall be considered to have failed to maintain continuous physical presence in the United States under paragraph (1)(A) if the alien has departed from the United States for any period in excess of 90 days or for any periods in the aggregate exceeding 180 days unless the absence is in order to assist in the investigation or prosecution or unless an official involved in the investigation or prosecution certifies that the absence was otherwise justified.

(3) Upon approval of adjustment of status under paragraph (1) of an alien described in section 101(a)(15)(U)(i) [8 U.S.C.A § 1101(a)(15)(U)(i)] the Secretary of Homeland Security may adjust the status of or issue an immigrant visa to a spouse, a child, or, in the case of an alien child, a parent who did not receive a nonimmigrant visa under section 101(a)(15)(U)(ii) [8 U.S.C.A § 1101(a)(15)(U)(ii)] if the Secretary considers the grant of such status or visa necessary to avoid extreme hardship.

(4) Upon the approval of adjustment of status under paragraph (1) or (3), the Secretary of Homeland Security shall record the alien's lawful admission for permanent residence as of the date of such approval.

(5)(A) The Secretary of Homeland Security shall consult with the Attorney General, as appropriate, in making a determination under paragraph (1) whether affirmative evidence demonstrates that the alien unreasonably refused to provide assistance to a Federal law enforcement official, Federal prosecutor, Federal judge, or other Federal authority investigating or prosecuting criminal activity described in section 101(a)(15)(U)(iii) [8 U.S.C.A. § 1101(a)(15)(U)(iii)].

(B) Nothing in paragraph (1)(B) may be construed to prevent the Secretary from consulting with the Attorney General in making a determination whether affirmative evidence demonstrates that the alien unreasonably refused to provide assistance to a State or local law enforcement official, State or local prosecutor, State or local judge, or other State or local authority investigating or prosecuting criminal activity described in section 101(a)(15)(U)(iii) [8 U.S.C.A. § 1101(a)(15)(U)(iii)].

(June 27, 1952, c. 477, Title II, ch. 5, § 245, 66 Stat. 217; Aug. 21, 1958, Pub.L. 85–700, § 1, 72 Stat. 699; July 14, 1960, Pub.L. 86–648, § 10, 74 Stat. 505; Oct. 3, 1965, Pub.L. 89–236, § 13, 79 Stat. 918; Oct. 20, 1976, Pub.L. 94–571, § 6, 90 Stat. 2705; Dec. 29, 1981, Pub.L. 97–116, § 5(d)(2), 95 Stat. 1614; Nov. 6, 1986, Pub.L. 99–603, Title III, §§ 117, 313(c), 100 Stat. 3384, 3438; Nov. 6, 1986, Pub.L. 99–603, Title III, § 313(c), as amended Oct. 24, 1988, Pub.L. 100–525, § 2(p)(3), 102 Stat. 2613; Nov. 10, 1986, Pub.L. 99–639, §§ 2(e), 3(b),

5(a), 100 Stat. 3542, 3543; Nov. 10, 1986, Pub.L. 99–639, § 3(b), as amended Oct. 24, 1988, Pub.L. 100–525, § 7(b), 102 Stat. 2616; Oct. 24, 1988, Pub.L. 100–525, § 2(f)(1), 102 Stat. 2611; Nov. 29, 1990, Pub.L. 101–649, Title I, §§ 121(b)(4), 162(e)(3), Title VII, § 702(a), 104 Stat. 4994, 5011, 5086; Oct. 1, 1991, Pub.L. 102–110, § 2(c), 105 Stat. 556; Dec. 12, 1991, Pub.L. 102–232, Title III, §§ 302(d)(2), (e)(7), 308(a), 105 Stat. 1744, 1746, 1757; Aug. 26, 1994, Pub.L. 103–317, Title V, § 506(b), 108 Stat. 1765; Sept. 13, 1994, Pub.L. 103–322, Title XIII, § 130003(c), 108 Stat. 2025; Oct. 25, 1994, Pub.L. 103–416, Title II, § 219(k), 108 Stat. 4317; Apr. 24, 1996, Pub.L. 104–132, Title IV, § 413(d), 110 Stat. 1269; Sept. 30, 1996, Pub.L. 104–208, Div. C, Title III, §§ 308(f)(1)(O), (2)(C), (g)(10)(B), 375, 376(a), Title VI, § 671(a)(4)(A), (5), 110 Stat. 3009–621, 3009–625, 3009–648, 3009–721; Nov. 26, 1997, Pub.L. 105–119, Title I, §§ 110(3), 111(a), (c), 111 Stat. 2458; Oct. 28, 2000, Pub.L. 106–386, Div. A, § 107(f), Div. B, Title V, §§ 1506(a), 1513(f), 114 Stat. 1479, 1527, 1536; Dec. 21, 2000, Pub.L. 106–553, § 1(a)(2) [Title XI, §§ 1102(c), (d)(2), 1103(c)(3)], 114 Stat. 2762; Dec. 21, 2000, Pub.L. 106–554, § 1(a)(4) [Div. B, Title XV, § 1502], 114 Stat. 2763, 2763A–324; Pub.L. 108–193, § 4(b)(3), 8(a)(4), Dec. 19, 2003, 117 Stat. 2879; Jan. 5, 2006, Pub.L. 109–162, Title VIII, § 803, 119 Stat. 3054; Aug. 12, 2006, Pub.L. 109–271, § 6(f), 120 Stat. 763; Dec. 23, 2008, Pub.L. 110–457, Title II, §§ 201(d), (e), 235(d)(3), 122 Stat. 5053, 5080.)

§ 245A. Adjustment of status of certain entrants before January 1, 1982, to that of person admitted for lawful residence [8 U.S.C.A. § 1255a]

(a) Temporary resident status

The Attorney General shall adjust the status of an alien to that of an alien lawfully admitted for temporary residence if the alien meets the following requirements:

(1) Timely application

(A) During application period

Except as provided in subparagraph (B), the alien must apply for such adjustment during the 12-month period beginning on a date (not later than 180 days after November 6, 1986) designated by the Attorney General.

(B) Application within 30 days of show-cause order

An alien who, at any time during the first 11 months of the 12-month period described in subparagraph (A) is the subject of an order to show cause issued under section 242 [8 U.S.C.A. § 1252] (as in effect before October 1, 1996), must make application under this section not later than the end of the 30-day period beginning either on the first day of such 12-month period or on the date of the issuance of such order, whichever day is later.

(C) Information included in application

Each application under this subsection shall contain such information as the Attorney General may require, including information on living relatives of the applicant with respect to whom a petition for preference or other status may be filed by the applicant at any later date under section 204(a) [8 U.S.C.A. § 1154(a)].

(2) Continuous unlawful residence since 1982

(A) In general

The alien must establish that he entered the United States before January 1, 1982, and that he has resided continuously in the United States in an unlawful status since such date and through the date the application is filed under this subsection.

(B) Nonimmigrants

In the case of an alien who entered the United States as a nonimmigrant before January 1, 1982, the alien must establish that the alien's period of authorized stay as a nonimmigrant expired before such date through the passage of time or the alien's unlawful status was known to the Government as of such date.

(C) Exchange visitors

If the alien was at any time a nonimmigrant exchange alien (as defined in section 101(a)(15)(J) [8 U.S.C.A. § 1101(a)(15)(J)]), the alien must establish that the alien was not subject to the two-year foreign residence requirement of section 212(e) [8 U.S.C.A. § 1182(e)] or has fulfilled that requirement or received a waiver thereof.

(3) Continuous physical presence since November 6, 1986

(A) In general

The alien must establish that the alien has been continuously physically present in the United States since November 6, 1986.

(B) Treatment of brief, casual, and innocent absences

An alien shall not be considered to have failed to maintain continuous physical presence in the United States for purposes of subparagraph (A) by virtue of brief, casual, and innocent absences from the United States.

(C) Admissions

Nothing in this section shall be construed as authorizing an alien to apply for admission to, or to be admitted to, the United States in order to apply for adjustment of status under this subsection.

(4) Admissible as immigrant

The alien must establish that he—

(A) is admissible to the United States as an immigrant, except as otherwise provided under subsection (d)(2),

(B) has not been convicted of any felony or of three or more misdemeanors committed in the United States,

(C) has not assisted in the persecution of any person or persons on account of race, religion, nationality, membership in a particular social group, or political opinion, and

(D) is registered or registering under the Military Selective Service Act [50 U.S.C.A.App. § 451 et seq.], if the alien is required to be so registered under that Act.

For purposes of this subsection, an alien in the status of a Cuban and Haitian entrant described in paragraph (1) or (2)(A) of section 501(e) of Public Law 96–422 [8 U.S.C.A. § 1522 note] shall be considered to have entered the United States and to be in an unlawful status in the United States.

(b) Subsequent adjustment to permanent residence and nature of temporary resident status

(1) Adjustment to permanent residence

The Attorney General shall adjust the status of any alien provided lawful temporary resident status under subsection (a) to that of an alien lawfully admitted for permanent residence if the alien meets the following requirements:

(A) Timely application after one year's residence

The alien must apply for such adjustment during the 2-year period beginning with the nineteenth month that begins after the date the alien was granted such temporary resident status.

(B) Continuous residence

(i) In general

The alien must establish that he has continuously resided in the United States since the date the alien was granted such temporary resident status.

(ii) Treatment of certain absences

An alien shall not be considered to have lost the continuous residence referred to in clause (i) by reason of an absence from the United States permitted under paragraph (3)(A).

(C) Admissible as immigrant

The alien must establish that he—

(i) is admissible to the United States as an immigrant, except as otherwise provided under subsection (d)(2), and

(ii) has not been convicted of any felony or three or more misdemeanors committed in the United States.

(D) Basic citizenship skills

(i) In general

The alien must demonstrate that he either—

(I) meets the requirements of section 312(a) [8 U.S.C.A. § 1423(a)] (relating to minimal understanding of ordinary English and a knowledge and understanding of the history and government of the United States), or

(II) is satisfactorily pursuing a course of study (recognized by the Attorney General) to achieve such an understanding of English and such a knowledge and understanding of the history and government of the United States.

(ii) Exception for elderly or developmentally disabled individuals

The Attorney General may, in his discretion, waive all or part of the requirements of clause (i) in the case of an alien who is 65 years of age or older or who is developmentally disabled.

(iii) Relation to naturalization examination

In accordance with regulations of the Attorney General, an alien who has demonstrated under clause (i)(I) that the alien meets the requirements of section 312(a) [8 U.S.C.A. § 1423(a)] may be considered to have satisfied the requirements of that section for purposes of becoming naturalized as a citizen of the United States under title III.

(2) Termination of temporary residence

The Attorney General shall provide for termination of temporary resident status granted an alien under subsection (a)—

(A) if it appears to the Attorney General that the alien was in fact not eligible for such status;

(B) if the alien commits an act that **(i)** makes the alien inadmissible to the United States as an immigrant, except as otherwise provided under subsection (d)(2), or **(ii)** is convicted of any felony or three or more misdemeanors committed in the United States; or

(C) at the end of the 43rd month beginning after the date the alien is granted such status, unless the alien has filed an application for adjustment of such status pursuant to paragraph (1) and such application has not been denied.

(3) Authorized travel and employment during temporary residence

During the period an alien is in lawful temporary resident status granted under subsection (a)—

(A) Authorization of travel abroad

The Attorney General shall, in accordance with regulations, permit the alien to return to the United States after such brief and casual trips abroad as reflect an intention on the part of the alien to adjust to lawful permanent resident status under paragraph (1) and after brief temporary trips abroad occasioned by a family obligation involving an occurrence such as the illness or death of a close relative or other family need.

(B) Authorization of employment

The Attorney General shall grant the alien authorization to engage in employment in the United States and provide to that alien an "employment authorized" endorsement or other appropriate work permit.

(c) Applications for adjustment of status

(1) To whom may be made

The Attorney General shall provide that applications for adjustment of status under subsection (a) may be filed—

(A) with the Attorney General, or

(B) with a qualified designated entity, but only if the applicant consents to the forwarding of the application to the Attorney General.

As used in this section, the term "qualified designated entity" means an organization or person designated under paragraph (2).

(2) Designation of qualified entities to receive applications

For purposes of assisting in the program of legalization provided under this section, the Attorney General—

(A) shall designate qualified voluntary organizations and other qualified State, local, and community organizations, and

(B) may designate such other persons as the Attorney General determines are qualified and have substantial experience, demonstrated competence, and traditional long-term involvement in the preparation and submittal of applications for adjustment of status under section 209 [8 U.S.C.A. § 1159] or 245 [8 U.S.C.A. § 1255], Public Law 89–732 [8 U.S.C.A. § 1255 note], or Public Law 95–145.

(3) Treatment of applications by designated entities

Each qualified designated entity must agree to forward to the Attorney General applications filed with it in accordance with paragraph (1)(B) but not to forward to the Attorney General applications filed with it unless the applicant has consented to such forwarding. No such entity may make a determination required by this section to be made by the Attorney General.

(4) Limitation on access to information

Files and records of qualified designated entities relating to an alien's seeking assistance or information with respect to filing an application under this section are confidential and the Attorney General and the Service shall not have access to such files or records relating to an alien without the consent of the alien.

(5) Confidentiality of information

(A) In general

Except as provided in this paragraph, neither the Attorney General, nor any other official or employee of the Department of Justice, or bureau or agency thereof, may—

(i) use the information furnished by the applicant pursuant to an application filed under this section for any purpose other than to make a determination on the application, for enforcement of paragraph (6), or for the preparation of reports to Congress under section 404 of the Immigration Reform and Control Act of 1986;

(ii) make any publication whereby the information furnished by any particular applicant can be identified; or

(iii) permit anyone other than the sworn officers and employees of the Department or bureau or agency or, with respect to applications filed with a designated entity, that designated entity, to examine individual applications.

(B) Required disclosures

The Attorney General shall provide the information furnished under this section, and any other information derived from such furnished information, to a duly recognized law enforcement entity in connection with a criminal investigation or prosecution, when such information is requested in writing by such entity, or to an official coroner for purposes of affirmatively identifying a deceased individual (whether or not such individual is deceased as a result of a crime).

(C) Authorized disclosures

The Attorney General may provide, in the Attorney General's discretion, for the furnishing of information furnished under this section in the same manner and circumstances as census information may be disclosed by the Secretary of Commerce under section 8 of Title 13.

(D) Construction

(i) In general

Nothing in this paragraph shall be construed to limit the use, or release, for immigration enforcement purposes or law enforcement purposes of information contained in files or records of the Service pertaining to an application filed under this section, other than information furnished by an applicant pursuant to the application, or any other information derived from the application, that is not available from any other source.

(ii) Criminal convictions

Information concerning whether the applicant has at any time been convicted of a crime may be used or released for immigration enforcement or law enforcement purposes.

(E) Crime

Whoever knowingly uses, publishes, or permits information to be examined in violation of this paragraph shall be fined not more than $10,000.

(6) Penalties for false statements in applications

Whoever files an application for adjustment of status under this section and knowingly and willfully falsifies, misrepresents, conceals, or covers up a material fact or makes any false, fictitious, or fraudulent statements or representations, or makes or uses any false writing or document knowing the same to contain any false, fictitious, or fraudulent statement or entry, shall be fined in accordance with Title 18, or imprisoned not more than five years, or both.

(7) Application fees

(A) Fee schedule

The Attorney General shall provide for a schedule of fees to be charged for the filing of applications for adjustment under subsection (a) or (b)(1). The Attorney General shall provide for an additional fee for filing an application for adjustment under subsection (b)(1) after the end of the first year of the 2-year period described in subsection (b)(1)(A).

(B) Use of fees

The Attorney General shall deposit payments received under this paragraph in a separate account and amounts in such account shall be available, without fiscal year limitation, to cover administrative and other expenses incurred in connection with the review of applications filed under this section.

(C) Immigration-related unfair employment practices

Not to exceed $3,000,000 of the unobligated balances remaining in the account established in subparagraph (B) shall be available in fiscal year 1992 and each fiscal year thereafter for grants, contracts, and cooperative agreements to community-based organizations for outreach programs, to be administered by the Office of Special Counsel for Immigration-Related Unfair Employment Practices: Provided, That such amounts shall be in addition to any funds appropriated to the Office of Special Counsel for such purposes: Provided further, That none of the funds made available by this section shall be used by the Office of Special Counsel to establish regional offices.

(d) Waiver of numerical limitations and certain grounds for exclusion

(1) Numerical limitations do not apply

The numerical limitations of sections 201 [8 U.S.C.A. § 1151] and 202 [8 U.S.C.A. § 1152] shall not apply to the adjustment of aliens to lawful permanent resident status under this section.

(2) Waiver of grounds for exclusion

In the determination of an alien's admissibility under subsections (a)(4)(A), (b)(1)(C)(i), and (b)(2)(B)—

(A) Grounds of exclusion not applicable

The provisions of paragraphs (5) and (7)(A) of section 212(a) [8 U.S.C.A. § 1182(a)] shall not apply.

(B) Waiver of other grounds

(i) In general

Except as provided in clause (ii), the Attorney General may waive any other provision of section 212(a) [8 U.S.C.A. § 1182(a)] in the case of individual aliens for humanitarian purposes, to assure family unity, or when it is otherwise in the public interest.

(ii) Grounds that may not be waived

The following provisions of section 212(a) [8 U.S.C.A. § 1182(a)] may not be waived by the Attorney General under clause (i):

(I) Paragraphs (2)(A) and (2)(B) (relating to criminals).

(II) Paragraph (2)(C) (relating to drug offenses), except for so much of such paragraph as relates to a single offense of simple possession of 30 grams or less of marihuana.

(III) Paragraph (3) (relating to security and related grounds).

(IV) Paragraph (4) (relating to aliens likely to become public charges) insofar as it relates to an application for adjustment to permanent residence.

Subclause (IV) (prohibiting the waiver of section 212(a)(4) [8 U.S.C.A. § 1182(a)(4)]) shall not apply to an alien who is or was an aged, blind, or disabled individual (as defined in section 1382c(a)(1) of Title 42).

(iii) Special rule for determination of public charge

An alien is not ineligible for adjustment of status under this section due to being inadmissible under section 212(a)(4) [8 U.S.C.A. § 1182(a)(4)] if the alien demonstrates a history of employment in the United States evidencing self-support without receipt of public cash assistance.

(C) Medical examination

The alien shall be required, at the alien's expense, to undergo such a medical examination (including a determination of immunization status) as is appropriate and conforms to generally accepted professional standards of medical practice.

(e) Temporary stay of deportation and work authorization for certain applicants

(1) Before application period

The Attorney General shall provide that in the case of an alien who is apprehended before the beginning of the application period described in subsection (a)(1)(A) and who can establish a prima facie case of eligibility to have his status adjusted under subsection (a) (but for the fact that he may not apply for such adjustment until the beginning of such period), until the alien has had the opportunity during the first 30 days of the application period to complete the filing of an application for adjustment, the alien—

(A) may not be deported, and

(B) shall be granted authorization to engage in employment in the United States and be provided an "employment authorized" endorsement or other appropriate work permit.

(2) During application period

The Attorney General shall provide that in the case of an alien who presents a prima facie application for adjustment of status under subsection (a) during the application period, and until a final determination on the application has been made in accordance with this section, the alien—

(A) may not be deported, and

(B) shall be granted authorization to engage in employment in the United States and be provided an "employment authorized" endorsement or other appropriate work permit.

(f) Administrative and judicial review

(1) Administrative and judicial review

There shall be no administrative or judicial review of a determination respecting an application for adjustment of status under this section except in accordance with this subsection.

(2) No review for late filings

No denial of adjustment of status under this section based on a late filing of an application for such adjustment may be reviewed by a court of the United States or of any State or reviewed in any administrative proceeding of the United States Government.

(3) Administrative review

(A) Single level of administrative appellate review

The Attorney General shall establish an appellate authority to provide for a single level of administrative appellate review of a determination described in paragraph (1).

(B) Standard for review

Such administrative appellate review shall be based solely upon the administrative record established at the time of the determination on the application and upon such additional or newly discovered evidence as may not have been available at the time of the determination.

(4) Judicial review

(A) Limitation to review of deportation

There shall be judicial review of such a denial only in the judicial review of an order of deportation under section 106 [8 U.S.C.A. § 1105a] (as in effect before October 1, 1996).

(B) Standard for judicial review

Such judicial review shall be based solely upon the administrative record established at the time of the review by the appellate authority and the findings of fact and determinations contained in such record shall be conclusive unless the applicant can establish abuse of discretion or that the findings are directly contrary to clear and convincing facts contained in the record considered as a whole.

(C) Jurisdiction of courts

Notwithstanding any other provision of law, no court shall have jurisdiction of any cause of action or claim by or on behalf of any person asserting an interest under this section unless such person in fact filed an application under this section within the period specified by subsection (a)(1), or attempted to file a complete application and application fee with an authorized legalization officer of the Service but had the application and fee refused by that officer.

(g) Implementation of section

(1) Regulations

The Attorney General, after consultation with the Committees on the Judiciary of the House of Representatives and of the Senate, shall prescribe—

(A) regulations establishing a definition of the term "resided continuously", as used in this section, and the evidence needed to establish that an alien has resided continuously in the United States for purposes of this section, and

(B) such other regulations as may be necessary to carry out this section.

(2) Considerations

In prescribing regulations described in paragraph (1)(A)—

(A) Periods of continuous residence

The Attorney General shall specify individual periods, and aggregate periods, of absence from the United States which will be considered to break a period of continuous residence in the United

States and shall take into account absences due merely to brief and casual trips abroad.

(B) Absences caused by deportation or advanced parole

The Attorney General shall provide that—

(i) an alien shall not be considered to have resided continuously in the United States, if, during any period for which continuous residence is required, the alien was outside the United States as a result of a departure under an order of deportation, and

(ii) any period of time during which an alien is outside the United States pursuant to the advance parole procedures of the Service shall not be considered as part of the period of time during which an alien is outside the United States for purposes of this section.

(C) Waivers of certain absences

The Attorney General may provide for a waiver, in the discretion of the Attorney General, of the periods specified under subparagraph (A) in the case of an absence from the United States due merely to a brief temporary trip abroad required by emergency or extenuating circumstances outside the control of the alien.

(D) Use of certain documentation

The Attorney General shall require that—

(i) continuous residence and physical presence in the United States must be established through documents, together with independent corroboration of the information contained in such documents, and

(ii) the documents provided under clause (i) be employment-related if employment-related documents with respect to the alien are available to the applicant.

(3) Interim final regulations

Regulations prescribed under this section may be prescribed to take effect on an interim final basis if the Attorney General determines that this is necessary in order to implement this section in a timely manner.

(h) Temporary disqualification of newly legalized aliens from receiving certain public welfare assistance

(1) In general

During the five-year period beginning on the date an alien was granted lawful temporary resident status under subsection (a), and notwithstanding any other provision of law—

(A) except as provided in paragraphs (2) and (3), the alien is not eligible for—

(i) any program of financial assistance furnished under Federal law (whether through grant, loan, guarantee, or otherwise) on the basis of financial need, as such programs are identified by the Attorney General in consultation with other appropriate heads of the various departments and agencies of Government (but in any event including the program of aid to families with dependent children under part A of title IV of the Social Security Act [42 U.S.C.A. § 601 et seq.]),

(ii) medical assistance under a State plan approved under title XIX of the Social Security Act [42 U.S.C.A. § 1396 et seq.], and

(iii) assistance under the Food and Nutrition Act of 2008 [7 U.S.C.A. § 2011 et seq.]; and

(B) a State or political subdivision therein may, to the extent consistent with subparagraph (A) and paragraphs (2) and (3), provide that the alien is not eligible for the programs of financial assistance or for medical assistance described in subparagraph (A)(ii) furnished under the law of that State or political subdivision.

Unless otherwise specifically provided by this section or other law, an alien in temporary lawful residence status granted under subsection (a) shall not be considered (for purposes of any law of a State or political subdivision providing for a program of financial assistance) to be permanently residing in the United States under color of law.

(2) Exceptions

Paragraph (1) shall not apply—

(A) to a Cuban and Haitian entrant (as defined in paragraph (1) or (2)(A) of section 501(e) of Public Law 96–422 [8 U.S.C.A. § 1522 note], as in effect on April 1, 1983), or

(B) in the case of assistance (other than aid to families with dependent children) which is furnished to an alien who is an aged, blind, or disabled individual (as defined in section 1614(a)(1) of the Social Security Act [42 U.S.C.A. § 1382c(a)(1)]).

(3) Restricted medicaid benefits

(A) Clarification of entitlement

Subject to the restrictions under subparagraph (B), for the purpose of providing aliens with eligibility to receive medical assistance—

(i) paragraph (1) shall not apply,

(ii) aliens who would be eligible for medical assistance but for the provisions of paragraph (1) shall be deemed, for purposes of title XIX of the Social Security Act [42 U.S.C.A. § 1396 et seq.], to be so eligible, and

(iii) aliens lawfully admitted for temporary residence under this section, such status not having changed, shall be considered to be permanently residing in the United States under color of law.

(B) Restriction of benefits

(i) Limitation to emergency services and services for pregnant women

Notwithstanding any provision of title XIX of the Social Security Act (including subparagraphs (B) and (C) of section 1902(a)(10) of such Act [42 U.S.C.A. § 1396a(a)(10)]) aliens who, but for subparagraph (A), would be ineligible for medical assistance under paragraph (1), are only eligible for such assistance with respect to—

(I) emergency services (as defined for purposes of section 1916(a)(2)(D) of the Social Security Act [42 U.S.C.A. § 1396o(a)(2)(D)]), and

(II) services described in section 1916(a)(2)(B) of such Act [42 U.S.C.A. § 1396o(a)(2)(B)] (relating to service for pregnant women).

(ii) No restriction for exempt aliens and children

The restrictions of clause (i) shall not apply to aliens who are described in paragraph (2) or who are under 18 years of age.

(C) Definition of medical assistance

In this paragraph, the term "medical assistance" refers to medical assistance under a State plan approved under title XIX of the Social Security Act.

(4) Treatment of certain programs

Assistance furnished under any of the following provisions of law shall not be construed to be financial assistance described in paragraph (1)(A)(i):

(A) The Richard B. Russell National School Lunch Act [42 U.S.C.A. § 1751 et seq.].

(B) The Child Nutrition Act of 1966 [42 U.S.C.A. § 1771 et seq.].

(C) The Carl D. Perkins Career and Technical Education Act of 2006 [20 U.S.C.A. § 2301 et seq.].

(D) Title I of the Elementary and Secondary Education Act of 1965 [20U.S.C.A. § 6301 et seq.].

(E) The Headstart–Follow Through Act.

(F) Title I of the Workforce Innovation and Opportunity Act.

(G) Title IV of the Higher Education Act of 1965 [20 U.S.C.A. § 1070 et seq.].

(H) The Public Health Service Act [42 U.S.C.A. § 1201 et seq.].

(I) Titles V, XVI, and XX, and parts B, D, and E of title IV, of the Social Security Act [42 U.S.C.A. §§ 701 et seq., 1381 et seq., 1391 et seq., 620 et seq., 651 et seq., and 670 et seq., respectively] (and titles I, X, XIV, and XVI of such Act [42 U.S.C.A. §§ 301 et seq., 1201 et seq., 1351 et seq., and 1381 et seq., respectively] as in effect without regard to the amendment made by section 301 of the Social Security Amendments of 1972).

(5) Adjustment not affecting Fascell-Stone benefits

For the purpose of section 501 of the Refugee Education Assistance Act of 1980 (Public Law 96–122) [sic] [8 U.S.C.A. § 1522 note]; assistance shall be continued under such section with respect to an alien without regard to the alien's adjustment of status under this section.

(i) Dissemination of information on legalization program

Beginning not later than the date designated by the Attorney General under subsection (a)(1)(A), the Attorney General, in cooperation with qualified designated entities, shall broadly disseminate information respecting the benefits which aliens may receive under this section and the requirements to obtain such benefits.

(June 27, 1952, c. 477, Title II, ch. 5, § 245A, as added Nov. 6, 1986, Pub.L. 99–603, Title II, § 201(a), 100 Stat. 3394, and amended Oct. 24, 1988, Pub.L. 100–525, § 2(h)(1), 102 Stat. 2611; Nov. 5, 1990, Pub.L. 101–649, Title VI, § 603(a)(13), Title VII, § 703, 104 Stat. 5083, 5086; Oct. 28, 1991, Pub.L. 102–140, Title I, 105 Stat. 785; Dec. 12, 1991, Pub.L. 102–232, Title III, § 307(*l*)(6), 105 Stat. 1756; Oct. 20, 1994, Pub.L. 103–382, Title III, § 394(g), 108 Stat. 4028; Oct. 25, 1994, Pub.L. 103–416, Title I, § 108(b), Title II, § 219(*l*)(1), 108 Stat. 4310, 4317; Apr. 24, 1996, Pub.L. 104–132, Title IV, § 431(a), 110 Stat. 1273; Aug. 22, 1996, Pub.L. 104–193, Title I, § 110(s)(2), 110 Stat. 2175; Sept. 30, 1996, Pub.L. 104–208, Div. C, Title III, §§ 308(g)(2)(B), (5)(A)(iii), 377(a), 384(d)(1), Title VI, § 623(a), 110 Stat. 3009–622, 3009–623, 3009–649, 3009–653, 3009–696; Oct. 21, 1998, 112 Stat. 2681–419, 2681–430; Oct. 31, 1998, Pub.L. 105–332, § 3(a), 112 Stat. 3125, Pub.L. 105–277, Div. A, § 101(f) [Title VIII, § 405(d)(4)]; Oct. 22, 1999, Pub.L. 106–78, Title VII, § 752(b)(5), 113 Stat. 1169; Aug. 12, 2006, Pub.L. 109–270, § 2(a), 120 Stat. 746; May 22, 2008, Pub.L. 110–234, Title IV, § 4002(b)(1)(B), (2)(J), 122 Stat. 1096, 1097; June 18, 2008, Pub.L. 110–246, Title IV, § 4002(b)(1)(B), (2)(J), 122 Stat. 1857, 1858; Pub.L. 113–128, Title V, § 512(q), July 22, 2014, 128 Stat. 1712.)

§ 246. Rescission of adjustment of status; effect upon naturalized citizen [8 U.S.C.A. § 1256]

(a) If, at any time within five years after the status of a person has been otherwise adjusted under the provisions of section 245 [8 U.S.C.A. § 1255] or 249 [8 U.S.C.A. § 1259] or any other provision of law to that of an alien lawfully admitted for permanent residence, it shall appear to the satisfaction of the Attorney General that the person was not in fact eligible for such adjustment of status, the Attorney General shall rescind the action taken granting an adjustment of status to such person and cancelling removal in the case of such person if that occurred and the person shall thereupon be subject to all provisions of this Act to the same extent as if the adjustment of status had not been made. Nothing in this subsection shall require the Attorney General to rescind the alien's status prior to commencement of procedures to remove the alien under section 240 [8 U.S.C.A. § 1229a], and an order of removal issued by an immigration judge shall be sufficient to rescind the alien's status.

(b) Any person who has become a naturalized citizen of the United States upon the basis of a record of a lawful admission for permanent residence, created as a result of an adjustment of status for which such person was not in fact eligible, and which is subsequently rescinded under subsection (a) of this section, shall be subject to the provisions of section 340 of this Act [8 U.S.C.A. § 1451] as a person whose naturalization was procured by concealment of a material fact or by willful misrepresentation.

(June 27, 1952, c. 477, Title II, ch. 5, § 246, 66 Stat. 217; Oct. 25, 1994, Pub.L. 103–416, Title II, § 219(m), 108 Stat. 4317; Sept. 30, 1996, Pub.L. 104–208, Div. C, Title III, §§ 308(e)(1)(H), 378(a), 110 Stat. 3009–619, 3009–649.)

§ 247.   Adjustment of status of certain resident aliens to nonimmigrant status; exceptions [8 U.S.C.A. § 1257]

(a) The status of an alien lawfully admitted for permanent residence shall be adjusted by the Attorney General, under such regulations as he may prescribe, to that of a nonimmigrant under paragraph (15)(A), (E), or (G) of section 101(a) [8 U.S.C.A. § 1101(a)], if such alien had at the time of admission or subsequently acquires an occupational status which would, if he were seeking admission to the United States, entitle him to a non-immigrant status under such paragraphs. As of the date of the Attorney General's order making such adjustment of status, the Attorney General shall cancel the record of the alien's admission for permanent residence, and the immigrant status of such alien shall thereby be terminated.

(b) The adjustment of status required by subsection (a) shall not be applicable in the case of any alien who requests that he be permitted to retain his status as an immigrant and who, in such form as the Attorney General may require, executes and files with the Attorney General a written waiver of all rights, privileges, exemptions, and immunities under any law or any executive order which would otherwise accrue to him because of the acquisition of an occupational status entitling him to a nonimmigrant status under paragraph (15)(A), (E), or (G) of section 101(a) [8 U.S.C.A. § 1101(a)].

(June 27, 1952, c. 477, Title II, ch. 5, § 247, 66 Stat. 218; Sept. 30, 1996, Pub.L. 104–208, Div. C, Title III, § 308(f)(1)(P), 110 Stat. 3009–621.)

§ 248.   Change of nonimmigrant classification [8 U.S.C.A. § 1258]

(a) The Secretary of Homeland Security may, under such conditions as he may prescribe, authorize a change from any nonimmigrant classification to any other nonimmigrant classification in the case of any alien lawfully admitted to the United States as a nonimmigrant who is continuing to maintain that status and who is not inadmissible under section 212(a)(9)(B)(i) [8 U.S.C.A § 1182(a)(9)(B)(i)] (or whose inadmissibility under such section is waived under section 212(a)(9)(B)(v) [8 U.S.C.A § 1182(a)(9)(B)(v)]), except (subject to subsection (b)) in the case of—

(1) an alien classified as a nonimmigrant under subparagraph (C), (D), (K), or (S) of section 101(a)(15) [8 U.S.C.A. § 1101(a)(15)],

(2) an alien classified as a nonimmigrant under subparagraph (J) of section 101(a)(15) [8 U.S.C.A. § 1101(a)(15)] who came to the United States or acquired such classification in order to receive graduate medical education or training,

(3) an alien (other than an alien described in paragraph (2)) classified as a nonimmigrant under subparagraph (J) of section 101(a)(15) [8 U.S.C.A. § 1101(a)(15)] who is subject to the two-year foreign residence requirement of section 212(e) [8 U.S.C.A. § 1182(e)] and has not received a waiver thereof, unless such alien applies to have the alien's classification changed from classification under subparagraph (J) of section 101(a)(15) [8 U.S.C.A. § 1101(a)(15)] to a classification under subparagraph (A) or (G) of such section and

(4) an alien admitted as a nonimmigrant visitor without a visa under section 212(*l*) [8 U.S.C.A. § 1182(*l*)] or section 217 [8 U.S.C.A. § 1187].

(b) The exceptions specified in paragraphs (1) through (4) of subsection (a) of this section shall not apply to a change of nonimmigrant classification to that of a nonimmigrant under subparagraph (T) or (U) of section 101(a)(15) [8 U.S.C.A § 1101(a)(15)].

(June 27, 1952, c. 477, Title II, ch. 5, § 248, 66 Stat. 218; Sept. 21, 1961, Pub.L. 87–256, § 109(d), 75 Stat. 535; Dec. 29, 1981, Pub.L. 97–116, § 10, 95 Stat. 1617; Nov. 6, 1986, Pub.L. 99–603, Title III, § 313(d), 100 Stat. 3439; Sept. 13, 1994, Pub.L. 103–322, Title XIII, § 130003(b)(3), 108 Stat. 2025; Sept. 30, 1996, Pub.L. 104–208, Div. C, Title III, § 301(b)(2), Title VI, § 671(a)(2), 110 Stat. 3009–578, 3009–721; Jan. 5, 2006, Pub.L. 109–162, Title VIII, § 821(c)(1), 119 Stat. 3062.)

§ 249. Record of admission for permanent residence in the case of certain aliens who entered the United States prior to January 1, 1972 [8 U.S.C.A. § 1259]

A record of lawful admission for permanent residence may, in the discretion of the Attorney General and under such regulations as he may prescribe, be made in the case of any alien, as of the date of the approval of his application or, if entry occurred prior to July 1, 1924, as of the date of such entry, if no such record is otherwise available and such alien shall satisfy the Attorney General that he is not inadmissible under section 212(a)(3)(E) [8 U.S.C.A. § 1182(a)(3)(E)] or under section 212(a) [8 U.S.C.A. § 1182(a)] insofar as it relates to criminals, procurers and other immoral persons, subversives, violators of the narcotic laws or smugglers of aliens, and he establishes that he—

(a) entered the United States prior to January 1, 1972;

(b) has had his residence in the United States continuously since such entry;

(c) is a person of good moral character; and

(d) is not ineligible to citizenship and is not deportable under section 237(a)(4)(B) [8 U.S.C.A. § 1227(a)(4)(B)].

(June 27, 1952, c. 477, Title II, ch. 5, § 249, 66 Stat. 219; Aug. 8, 1958, Pub.L. 85–616, 72 Stat. 546; Oct. 3, 1965, Pub.L. 89–236, § 19, 79 Stat. 920; Nov. 6, 1986, Pub.L. 99–603, Title II, § 203(a), 100 Stat. 3405; Oct. 24, 1988, Pub.L. 100–525, § 2(j), 102 Stat. 2612; Nov. 29, 1990, Pub.L. 101–649, Title VI, § 603(a)(14), 104 Stat. 5083; Apr. 24, 1996, Pub.L. 104–132, Title IV, § 413(e), 110 Stat. 1269; Sept. 30, 1996, Pub.L. 104–208, Div. C, Title III, § 308(g) (10)(C), 110 Stat. 3009–625.)

§ 250. Removal of aliens falling into distress [8 U.S.C.A. § 1260]

The Attorney General may remove from the United States any alien who falls into distress or who needs public aid from causes arising subsequent to his entry, and is desirous of being so removed, to the native country of such alien, or to the country from which he came, or to the country of which he is a citizen or subject, or to any other country to which he wishes to go and which will receive him, at the expense of the appropriation for the enforcement of this Act. Any alien so removed shall be ineligible to apply for or receive a visa or other documentation for readmission, or to apply for admission to the United States except with the prior approval of the Attorney General.

(June 27, 1952, c. 477, Title II, ch. 5, § 250, 66 Stat. 219.)

CHAPTER VI—SPECIAL PROVISIONS
RELATING TO ALIEN CREWMEN

§ 251.   Alien crewmen [8 U.S.C.A. § 1281]

(a) Arrival; submission of list; exceptions

Upon arrival of any vessel or aircraft in the United States from any place outside the United States it shall be the duty of the owner, agent, consignee, master, or commanding officer thereof to deliver to an immigration officer at the port of arrival **(1)** a complete, true, and correct list containing the names of all aliens employed on such vessel or aircraft, the positions they respectively hold in the crew of the vessel or aircraft, when and where they were respectively shipped or engaged, and those to be paid off or discharged in the port of arrival; or **(2)** in the discretion of the Attorney General, such a list containing so much of such information, or such additional or supplemental information, as the Attorney General shall by regulations prescribe. In the case of a vessel engaged solely in traffic on the Great Lakes, Saint Lawrence River, and connecting waterways, such lists shall be furnished at such times as the Attorney General may require.

(b) Reports of illegal landings

It shall be the duty of any owner, agent, consignee, master, or commanding officer of any vessel or aircraft to report to an immigration officer, in writing, as soon as discovered, all cases in which any alien crewman has illegally landed in the United States from the vessel or aircraft, together with a description of such alien and any information likely to lead to his apprehension.

(c) Departure; submission of list; exceptions

Before the departure of any vessel or aircraft from any port in the United States, it shall be the duty of the owner, agent, consignee, master, or commanding officer thereof, to deliver to an immigration officer at that port **(1)** a list containing the names of all alien employees who were not employed thereon at the time of the arrival at that port but who will leave such port thereon at the time of the departure of such vessel or aircraft and the names of those, if any, who have been paid off or discharged, and of those, if any, who have deserted or landed at that port, or **(2)** in the discretion of the Attorney General, such a list containing so much of such information, or such additional or supplemental information, as the Attorney General shall by regulations prescribe. In the case of a vessel engaged solely in traffic on the Great Lakes, Saint Lawrence River, and connecting waterways, such lists shall be furnished at such times as the Attorney General may require.

(d) Violations

In case any owner, agent, consignee, master, or commanding officer shall fail to deliver complete, true, and correct lists or reports of aliens, or to report cases of desertion or landing, as required by subsections (a), (b), and (c), such owner, agent, consignee, master, or commanding officer, shall, if required by the Attorney General, pay to the Commissioner the sum of $200 for each alien concerning whom such lists are not delivered or such reports are not made as required in the preceding subsections. In the case that any owner, agent, consignee, master, or commanding officer of a vessel shall secure services of an alien crewman described in section 101(a)(15)(D)(i) [8 U.S.C.A. § 1101(a)(15)(D)(i)] to perform long-shore work not included in the normal operation and service on board the vessel under section 258 [8 U.S.C.A. § 1288], the owner, agent, consignee, master, or commanding officer shall pay to the Commissioner the sum of $5,000, and such fine shall be a lien against the vessel. No such vessel or aircraft shall be granted clearance from any port at which it arrives pending the determination of the question of the liability to the payment of such fine, and if such fine is imposed, while it remains unpaid. No such fine shall be remitted or refunded. Clearance may be granted prior to the determination of such question upon deposit of a bond or a sum sufficient to cover such fine.

(e) Regulations

The Attorney General is authorized to prescribe by regulations the circumstances under which a vessel or aircraft shall be deemed to be arriving in, or departing from the United States or any port thereof within the meaning of any provision of this chapter.

(June 27, 1952, c. 477, Title II, ch. 6, § 251, 66 Stat. 219; Nov. 29, 1990, Pub.L. 101–649, Title II, § 203(b), 104 Stat. 5018; Dec. 12, 1991, Pub.L. 102–232, Title III, § 303(a)(3), 105 Stat. 1746.)

§ 252.   Conditional permits to land temporarily [8 U.S.C.A. § 1282]

(a) Period of time

No alien crewman shall be permitted to land temporarily in the United States except as provided in this section and sections 212(d)(3), (5) [8 U.S.C.A. § 1182(d)(3), (5)] and 253 [8 U.S.C.A. § 1283]. If an immigration officer finds upon examination that an alien crewman is a nonimmigrant under paragraph (15)(D) of section 101(a) [8 U.S.C.A. § 1101(a)] and is otherwise admissible and has agreed to accept such permit, he may, in his discretion, grant the crewman a conditional permit to land temporarily pursuant to regulations prescribed by the Attorney General, subject to revocation in subsequent proceedings as provided in subsection (b), and for a period of time, in any event, not to exceed—

  (1) the period of time (not exceeding twenty-nine days) during which the vessel or aircraft on which he arrived remains in port, if the immigration officer is satisfied that the crewman intends to depart on the vessel or aircraft on which he arrived; or

(2) twenty-nine days, if the immigration officer is satisfied that the crewman intends to depart, within the period for which he is permitted to land, on a vessel or aircraft other than the one on which he arrived.

(b) Revocation; expenses of detention

Pursuant to regulations prescribed by the Attorney General, any immigration officer may, in his discretion, if he determines that an alien is not a bona fide crewman, or does not intend to depart on the vessel or aircraft which brought him, revoke the conditional permit to land which was granted such crewman under the provisions of subsection (a)(1), take such crewman into custody, and require the master or commanding officer of the vessel or aircraft on which the crewman arrived to receive and detain him on board such vessel or aircraft, if practicable, and such crewman shall be removed from the United States at the expense of the transportation line which brought him to the United States. Until such alien is so removed, any expenses of his detention shall be borne by such transportation company. Nothing in this section shall be construed to require the procedure prescribed in section 240 [8 U.S.C.A. § 1229a] to cases falling within the provisions of this subsection.

(c) Penalties

Any alien crewman who willfully remains in the United States in excess of the number of days allowed in any conditional permit issued under subsection (a) shall be fined under Title 18 or imprisoned not more than 6 months, or both.

(June 27, 1952, c. 477, Title II, ch. 6, § 252, 66 Stat. 220; Nov. 29, 1990, Pub.L. 101–649, Title V, § 543(b)(1), 104 Stat. 5059; Dec. 12, 1991, Pub.L. 102–232, Title III, § 306(c)(3), 105 Stat. 1752; Sept. 30, 1996, Pub.L. 104–208, Div. C, Title III, § 308(e)(2)(E), (g)(5)(A)(i), 110 Stat. 3009–620, 3009–623.)

§ 253. Hospital treatment of alien crewmen afflicted with certain diseases [8 U.S.C.A. § 1283]

An alien crewman, including an alien crewman ineligible for a conditional permit to land under section 252(a) [8 U.S.C.A. § 1282(a)], who is found on arrival in a port of the United States to be afflicted with any of the disabilities or diseases mentioned in section 255 [8 U.S.C.A. § 1285], shall be placed in a hospital designated by the immigration officer in charge at the port of arrival and treated, all expenses connected therewith, including burial in the event of death, to be borne by the owner, agent, consignee, commanding officer, or master of the vessel or aircraft, and not to be deducted from the crewman's wages. No such vessel or aircraft shall be granted clearance until such expenses are paid, or their payment appropriately guaranteed, and the collector of customs is so notified by the immigration officer in charge. An alien crewman suspected of being afflicted with any such disability or disease may be removed from the vessel or aircraft on which he arrived to an immigration station, or other appropriate place, for such observation as will enable the examining surgeons to determine definitely whether or not he is so afflicted, all expenses connected therewith to be borne in the manner hereinbefore prescribed. In cases in which it appears to the satisfaction of the immigration officer in charge that it will not be possible within a reasonable time to effect a cure, the return of the alien crewman shall be enforced on, or at the expense of, the transportation line on which he came, upon such conditions as the Attorney General shall prescribe, to insure that the alien shall be properly cared for and protected, and that the spread of contagion shall be guarded against.

(June 27, 1952, c. 477, Title II, ch. 6, § 253, 66 Stat. 221.)

§ 254. Control of alien crewmen [8 U.S.C.A. § 1284]

(a) Penalties for failure

The owner, agent, consignee, charterer, master, or commanding officer of any vessel or aircraft arriving in the United States from any place outside thereof who fails **(1)** to detain on board the vessel, or in the case of an aircraft to detain at a place specified by an immigration officer at the expense of the airline, any alien crewman employed thereon until an immigration officer has completely inspected such alien crewman, including a physical examination by the medical examiner, or **(2)** to detain any alien crewman on board the vessel, or in the case of an aircraft at a place specified by an immigration officer at the expense of the airline, after such inspection unless a conditional permit to land temporarily has been granted such alien crewman under section 252 [8 U.S.C.A. § 1282] or unless an alien crewman has been permitted to land temporarily under section 212(d)(5) [8 U.S.C.A. § 1182(d)(5)] or 253 [8 U.S.C.A. § 1283] for medical or hospital treatment, or **(3)** to remove such alien crewman if required to do so by an immigration officer, whether such removal requirement is imposed before or after the crewman is permitted to land temporarily under section 212(d)(5) [8 U.S.C.A. § 1182(d)(5)], 252 [8 U.S.C.A. § 1282], or 253 [8 U.S.C.A. § 1283], shall pay to the Commissioner the sum of $3,000 for each alien crewman in respect to whom any such failure occurs. No such vessel or aircraft shall be granted clearance pending the determination of the liability to the payment of such fine, or while the fine remains unpaid, except that clearance may be granted prior to the determination of such question upon the deposit of a sum sufficient to cover such fine, or of a bond with sufficient surety to secure the payment thereof approved by the Commissioner. The Attorney General may, upon application in writing therefor, mitigate such penalty to not less than $500 for each alien crewman in respect of whom such failure occurs, upon such terms as he shall think proper.

(b) Prima facie evidence against transportation line

Except as may be otherwise prescribed by regulations issued by the Attorney General, proof that an alien crewman did not appear upon the outgoing manifest of the vessel or aircraft on which he arrived in the United States from any place outside thereof, or that he was reported by the master or commanding officer of such vessel or aircraft as a deserter, shall be prima facie evidence of a failure to detain or remove such alien crewman.

(c) Removal on other than arriving vessel or aircraft; expenses

If the Attorney General finds that removal of an alien crewman under this section on the vessel or aircraft on which he arrived is impracticable or impossible, or would cause undue hardship to such alien crewman, he may cause the alien crewman to be removed from the port of arrival or any other port on another vessel or aircraft of the same transportation line, unless the Attorney General finds this to be impracticable. All expenses incurred in connection with such removal, including expenses incurred in transferring an alien crewman from one place in the United States to another under such conditions and safeguards as the Attorney General shall impose, shall be paid by the owner or owners of the vessel or aircraft on which the alien arrived in the United States. The vessel or aircraft on which the alien arrived shall not be granted clearance until such expenses have been paid or their payment guaranteed to the satisfaction of the Attorney General. An alien crewman who is transferred within the United States in accordance with this subsection shall not be regarded as having been landed in the United States.

(June 27, 1952, c. 477, Title II, ch. 6, § 254, 66 Stat. 221; Nov. 29, 1990, Pub.L. 101–649, Title V, § 543(a)(4), 104 Stat. 5058; Dec. 12, 1991, Pub.L. 102–232, Title III, § 306(c)(4)(C), 105 Stat. 1752; Sept. 30, 1996, Pub.L. 104–208, Div. C, Title III, § 308(e)(1)(I), (2)(F), (12), 110 Stat. 3009–619, 3009–620.)

§ 255. Employment on passenger vessels of aliens afflicted with certain disabilities [8 U.S.C.A. § 1285]

It shall be unlawful for any vessel or aircraft carrying passengers between a port of the United States and a port outside thereof to have employed on board upon arrival in the United States any alien afflicted with feeble-mindedness, insanity, epilepsy, tuberculosis in any form, leprosy, or any dangerous contagious disease. If it appears to the satisfaction of the Attorney General, from an examination made by a medical officer of the United States Public Health Service, and is so certified by such officer, that any such alien was so afflicted at the time he was shipped or engaged and taken on board such vessel or aircraft and that the existence of such affliction might have been detected by means of a competent medical examination at such time, the owner, commanding officer, agent, consignee, or master thereof shall pay for each alien so afflicted to the Commissioner the sum of $1,000. No vessel or aircraft shall be granted clearance pending the determination of the question of the liability to the payment of such sums, or while such sums remain unpaid, except that clearance may be granted prior to the determination of such question upon the deposit of an amount sufficient to cover such sums or of a bond approved by the Commissioner with sufficient surety to secure the payment thereof. Any such fine may, in the discretion of the Attorney General, be mitigated or remitted.

(June 27, 1952, c. 477, Title II, ch. 6, § 255, 66 Stat. 222; Nov. 29, 1990, Pub.L. 101–649, Title V, § 543(a)(5), 104 Stat. 5058.)

§ 256. Discharge of alien crewmen; penalties [8 U.S.C.A. § 1286]

It shall be unlawful for any person, including the owner, agent, consignee, charterer, master, or commanding officer of any vessel or aircraft, to pay off or discharge any alien crewman, except an alien lawfully admitted for permanent residence, employed on board a vessel or aircraft arriving in the United States without first having obtained the consent of the Attorney General. If it shall appear to the satisfaction of the Attorney General that any alien crewman has been paid off or discharged in the United States in violation of the provisions of this section, such owner, agent, consignee, charterer, master, commanding officer, or other person, shall pay to the Commissioner the sum of $3,000 for each such violation. No vessel or aircraft shall be granted clearance pending the determination of the question of the liability to the payment of such sums, or while such sums remain unpaid, except that clearance may be granted prior to the determination of such question upon the deposit of an amount sufficient to cover such sums, or of a bond approved by the Commissioner with sufficient surety to secure the payment thereof. Such fine may, in the discretion of the Attorney General, be mitigated to not less than $1,500 for each violation, upon such terms as he shall think proper.

(June 27, 1952, c. 477, Title II, ch. 6, § 256, 66 Stat. 223; Nov. 29, 1990, Pub.L. 101–649, Title V, § 543(a)(6), 104 Stat. 5058.)

§ 257. Alien crewmen brought into the United States with intent to evade immigration laws; penalties [8 U.S.C.A. § 1287]

Any person, including the owner, agent, master, or commanding officer of any vessel or aircraft arriving in the United States from any place outside thereof, who shall knowingly sign on the vessel's articles, or bring to the United States as one of the crew of such vessel or aircraft, any alien, with intent to permit or assist such alien to enter or land in the United States in violation of law, or who shall falsely and knowingly represent to a consular officer at the time of application for visa, or to the immigration officer at the port of arrival in the United States, that such alien is a bona fide member of the crew employed in any capacity regularly required for normal operation and services aboard such vessel or aircraft, shall be liable to a penalty not exceeding $10,000 for each such violation, for which sum such vessel or aircraft shall be liable and may be seized and proceeded against by way of libel in any district court of the United States having jurisdiction of the offense.

(June 27, 1952, c. 477, Title II, ch. 6, § 257, 66 Stat. 223; Nov. 29, 1990, Pub.L. 101–649, Title V, § 543(a)(7), 104 Stat. 5058.)

§ 258.   Limitations on performance of longshore work by alien crewmen [8 U.S.C.A. § 1288]

(a) In general

For purposes of section 101(a)(15)(D)(i) [8 U.S.C.A. § 1101(a)(15)(D)(i)], the term "normal operation and service on board a vessel" does not include any activity that is longshore work (as defined in subsection (b)), except as provided under subsection (c), (d), or (e).

(b) Longshore work defined

(1) In general

In this section, except as provided in paragraph (2), the term "longshore work" means any activity relating to the loading or unloading of cargo, the operation of cargo-related equipment (whether or not integral to the vessel), and the handling of mooring lines on the dock when the vessel is made fast or let go, in the United States or the coastal waters thereof.

(2) Exception for safety and environmental protection

The term "longshore work" does not include the loading or unloading of any cargo for which the Secretary of Transportation has, under the authority contained in chapter 37 of Title 46 (relating to Carriage of Liquid Bulk Dangerous Cargoes), section 311 of the Federal Water Pollution Control Act (33 U.S.C. 1321), section 4106 of the Oil Pollution Act of 1990, or section 5103(b), 5104, 5106, 5107, or 5110 of Title 49 prescribed regulations which govern—

(A) the handling or stowage of such cargo,

(B) the manning of vessels and the duties, qualifications, and training of the officers and crew of vessels carrying such cargo, and

(C) the reduction or elimination of discharge during ballasting, tank cleaning, handling of such cargo.

(3) Construction

Nothing in this section shall be construed as broadening, limiting, or otherwise modifying the meaning or scope of longshore work for purposes of any other law, collective bargaining agreement, or international agreement.

(c) Prevailing practice exception

(1) Subsection (a) shall not apply to a particular activity of longshore work in and about a local port if—

(A) (i) there is in effect in the local port one or more collective bargaining agreements each covering at least 30 percent of the number of individuals employed in performing longshore work and (ii) each such agreement (covering such percentage of longshore workers) permits the activity to be performed by alien crewmen under the terms of such agreement; or

(B) there is no collective bargaining agreement in effect in the local port covering at least 30 percent of the number of individuals employed in performing longshore work, and an employer of alien crewmen (or the employer's designated agent or representative) has filed with the Secretary of Labor at least 14 days before the date of performance of the activity (or later, if necessary due to an unanticipated emergency, but not later than the date of performance of the activity) an attestation setting forth facts and evidence to show that—

    (i) the performance of the activity by alien crewmen is permitted under the prevailing practice of the particular port as of the date of filing of the attestation and that the use of alien crewmen for such activity—

        (I) is not during a strike or lockout in the course of a labor dispute, and

        (II) is not intended or designed to influence an election of a bargaining representative for workers in the local port; and

    (ii) notice of the attestation has been provided by the owner, agent, consignee, master, or commanding officer to the bargaining representative of longshore workers in the local port, or, where there is no such bargaining representative, notice of the attestation has been provided to longshore workers employed at the local port.

In applying subparagraph (B) in the case of a particular activity of longshore work consisting of the use of an automated self-unloading conveyor belt or vacuum-actuated system on a vessel, the attestation shall be required to be filed only if the Secretary of Labor finds, based on a preponderance of the evidence which may be submitted by any interested party, that the performance of such particular activity is not described in clause (i) of such subparagraph.

(2) Subject to paragraph (4), an attestation under paragraph (1) shall—

    (A) expire at the end of the 1-year period beginning on the date of its filing with the Secretary of Labor, and

    (B) apply to aliens arriving in the United States during such 1-year period if the owner, agent, consignee, master, or commanding officer states in each list under section 251 [8 U.S.C.A. § 1281] that it continues to comply with the conditions in the attestation.

(3) An owner, agent, consignee, master, or commanding officer may meet the requirements under this subsection with respect to more than one alien crewman in a single list.

(4)(A) The Secretary of Labor shall compile and make available for public examination in a timely manner in Washington, D.C., a list identifying owners, agents, consignees, masters, or commanding of-

387

ficers which have filed lists for nonimmigrants described in section 101(a)(15)(D)(i) [8 U.S.C.A. § 1101(a)(15)(D)(i)] with respect to whom an attestation under paragraph (1) or subsection (d)(1) is made and, for each such entity, a copy of the entity's attestation under paragraph (1) or subsection (d)(1) (and accompanying documentation) and each such list filed by the entity.

(B)(i) The Secretary of Labor shall establish a process for the receipt, investigation, and disposition of complaints respecting an entity's failure to meet conditions attested to, an entity's misrepresentation of a material fact in an attestation, or, in the case described in the last sentence of paragraph (1), whether the performance of the particular activity is or is not described in paragraph (1)(B)(i).

(ii) Complaints may be filed by any aggrieved person or organization (including bargaining representatives, associations deemed appropriate by the Secretary, and other aggrieved parties as determined under regulations of the Secretary).

(iii) The Secretary shall promptly conduct an investigation under this subparagraph if there is reasonable cause to believe that an entity fails to meet conditions attested to, an entity has misrepresented a material fact in the attestation, or, in the case described in the last sentence of paragraph (1), the performance of the particular activity is not described in paragraph (1)(B)(i).

(C)(i) If the Secretary determines that reasonable cause exists to conduct an investigation with respect to an attestation, a complaining party may request that the activities attested to by the employer cease during the hearing process described in subparagraph (D). If such a request is made, the attesting employer shall be issued notice of such request and shall respond within 14 days to the notice. If the Secretary makes an initial determination that the complaining party's position is supported by a preponderance of the evidence submitted, the Secretary shall require immediately that the employer cease and desist from such activities until completion of the process described in subparagraph (D).

(ii) If the Secretary determines that reasonable cause exists to conduct an investigation with respect to a matter under the last sentence of paragraph (1), a complaining party may request that the activities of the employer cease during the hearing process described in subparagraph (D) unless the employer files with the Secretary of Labor an attestation under paragraph (1). If such a request is made, the employer shall be issued notice of such request and shall respond within 14 days to the notice. If the Secretary makes an initial determination that the complaining party's position is supported by a preponderance of the evidence submitted, the Secretary shall require immediately that the employer cease and desist from such activities until completion of the process described in subparagraph (D) unless the employer files with the Secretary of Labor an attestation under paragraph (1).

(D) Under the process established under subparagraph (B), the Secretary shall provide, within 180 days after the date a complaint is filed (or later for good cause shown), for a determination as to whether or not a basis exists to make a finding described in subparagraph (E). The Secretary shall provide notice of such determination to the interested parties and an opportunity for a hearing on the complaint within 60 days of the date of the determination.

(E)(i) If the Secretary of Labor finds, after notice and opportunity for a hearing, that an entity has failed to meet a condition attested to or has made a misrepresentation of material fact in the attestation, the Secretary shall notify the Attorney General of such finding and may, in addition, impose such other administrative remedies (including civil monetary penalties in an amount not to exceed $5,000 for each alien crewman performing unauthorized longshore work) as the Secretary determines to be appropriate. Upon receipt of such notice, the Attorney General shall not permit the vessels owned or chartered by such entity to enter any port of the United States during a period of up to 1 year.

(ii) If the Secretary of Labor finds, after notice and opportunity for a hearing, that, in the case described in the last sentence of paragraph (1), the performance of the particular activity is not described in subparagraph (B)(i), the Secretary shall notify the Attorney General of such finding and, thereafter, the attestation described in paragraph (1) shall be required of the employer for the performance of the particular activity.

(F) A finding by the Secretary of Labor under this paragraph that the performance of an activity by alien crewmen is not permitted under the prevailing practice of a local port shall preclude for one year the filing of a subsequent attestation concerning such activity in the port under paragraph (1).

(5) Except as provided in paragraph (5) of subsection (d), this subsection shall not apply to longshore work performed in the State of Alaska.

(d) State of Alaska exception

(1) Subsection (a) shall not apply to a particular activity of longshore work at a particular location in the State of Alaska if an employer of alien crewmen has filed an attestation with the Secretary of Labor at least 30 days before the date of the first performance of the activity (or anytime up to 24 hours before the first performance of the activity, upon a showing that the employer could not have reasonably anticipated the need to file an attestation for that location at that time) setting forth facts and evidence to show that—

(A) the employer will make a bona fide request for United States longshore workers who are qualified and available in sufficient numbers to perform the activity at the particular time and location from the parties to whom notice has been provided under clauses (ii) and (iii) of subparagraph (D), except that—

    (i) wherever two or more contract stevedoring companies have signed a joint collective bargaining agreement with a single labor organization described in subparagraph (D)(i), the employer may request longshore workers from only one of such contract stevedoring companies, and

    (ii) a request for longshore workers to an operator of a private dock may be made only for longshore work to be performed at that dock and only if the operator meets the requirements of section 932 of Title 33;

(B) the employer will employ all those United States longshore workers made available in response to the request made pursuant to subparagraph (A) who are qualified and available in sufficient numbers and who are needed to perform the longshore activity at the particular time and location;

(C) the use of alien crewmembers for such activity is not intended or designed to influence an election of a bargaining representative for workers in the State of Alaska; and

(D) notice of the attestation has been provided by the employer to—

    (i) labor organizations which have been recognized as exclusive bargaining representatives of United States longshore workers within the meaning of the National Labor Relations Act [29 U.S.C.A. § 151 et seq.] and which make available or intend to make available workers to the particular location where the longshore work is to be performed,

    (ii) contract stevedoring companies which employ or intend to employ United States longshore workers at that location, and

    (iii) operators of private docks at which the employer will use longshore workers.

(2)(A) An employer filing an attestation under paragraph (1) who seeks to use alien crewmen to perform longshore work shall be responsible while the attestation is valid to make bona fide requests for United States longshore workers under paragraph (1)(A) and to employ United States longshore workers, as provided in paragraph (1)(B), before using alien crewmen to perform the activity or activities specified in the attestation, except that an employer shall not be required to request longshore workers from a party if that party has notified the employer in writing that it does not intend to make available United States longshore workers to the location at which the longshore work is to be performed.

(B) If a party that has provided such notice subsequently notifies the employer in writing that it is prepared to make available

United States longshore workers who are qualified and available in sufficient numbers to perform the longshore activity to the location at which the longshore work is to be performed, then the employer's obligations to that party under subparagraphs (A) and (B) of paragraph (1) shall begin 60 days following the issuance of such notice.

(3)(A) In no case shall an employer filing an attestation be required—

(i) to hire less than a full work unit of United States longshore workers needed to perform the longshore activity;

(ii) to provide overnight accommodations for the longshore workers while employed; or

(iii) to provide transportation to the place of work, except where—

(I) surface transportation is available;

(II) such transportation may be safely accomplished;

(III) travel time to the vessel does not exceed one-half hour each way; and

(IV) travel distance to the vessel from the point of embarkation does not exceed 5 miles.

(B) In the cases of Wide Bay, Alaska, and Klawock/Craig, Alaska, the travel times and travel distances specified in subclauses (III) and (IV) of subparagraph (A)(iii) shall be extended to 45 minutes and 7.5 miles, respectively, unless the party responding to the request for longshore workers agrees to the lesser time and distance limitations specified in those subclauses.

(4) Subject to subparagraphs (A) through (D) of subsection (c)(4), attestations filed under paragraph (1) of this subsection shall—

(A) expire at the end of the 1-year period beginning on the date the employer anticipates the longshore work to begin, as specified in the attestation filed with the Secretary of Labor, and

(B) apply to aliens arriving in the United States during such 1-year period if the owner, agent, consignee, master, or commanding officer states in each list under section 251 [8 U.S.C.A. § 1281] that it continues to comply with the conditions in the attestation.

(5)(A) Except as otherwise provided by subparagraph (B), subsection (c)(3) and subparagraphs (A) through (E) of subsection (c)(4) shall apply to attestations filed under this subsection.

(B) The use of alien crewmen to perform longshore work in Alaska consisting of the use of an automated self-unloading conveyor belt or vacuum-actuated system on a vessel shall be governed by the provisions of subsection (c).

(6) For purposes of this subsection—

(A) the term "contract stevedoring companies" means those stevedoring companies licensed to do business in the State of Alaska that meet the requirements of section 932 of Title 33;

(B) the term "employer" includes any agent or representative designated by the employer; and

(C) the terms "qualified" and "available in sufficient numbers" shall be defined by reference to industry standards in the State of Alaska, including safety considerations.

(e) Reciprocity exception

(1) In general

Subject to the determination of the Secretary of State pursuant to paragraph (2), the Attorney General shall permit an alien crewman to perform an activity constituting longshore work if—

(A) the vessel is registered in a country that by law, regulation, or in practice does not prohibit such activity by crewmembers aboard United States vessels; and

(B) nationals of a country (or countries) which by law, regulation, or in practice does not prohibit such activity by crewmembers aboard United States vessels hold a majority of the ownership interest in the vessel.

(2) Establishment of list

The Secretary of State shall, in accordance with section 553 of Title 5, compile and annually maintain a list, of longshore work by particular activity, or countries where performance of such a particular activity by crewmembers aboard United States vessels is prohibited by law, regulation, or in practice in the country. By not later than 90 days after November 29, 1990, the Secretary shall publish a notice of proposed rulemaking to establish such list. The Secretary shall first establish such list by not later than 180 days after November 29, 1990.

(3) In practice defined

For purposes of this subsection, the term "in practice" refers to an activity normally performed in such country during the one-year period preceding the arrival of such vessel into the United States or coastal waters thereof.

(June 27, 1952, c. 477, Title II, ch. 6, § 258, as added Nov. 29, 1990, Pub.L. 101–649, Title II, § 203(a)(1), 104 Stat. 5015, and amended Dec. 12, 1991, Pub.L. 102–232, Title III, § 303(a)(4), 105 Stat. 1747; Dec. 17, 1993, Pub.L. 103–198, § 8(a), (b), 107 Stat. 2313, 2315; Dec. 20, 1993, Pub.L. 103–206, Title III, § 323(a), (b), 107 Stat. 2428, 2430; Oct. 25, 1994, Pub.L. 103–416, Title II, § 219(f), (gg), 108 Stat. 4317, 4319; Sept. 30, 1996, Pub.L. 104–208, Div. C, Title VI, § 671(e)(4)(B), 110 Stat. 3009–723.)

Chapter VII—Registration of Aliens

§ 261.   Alien seeking entry; contents [8 U.S.C.A. § 1301]

No visa shall be issued to any alien seeking to enter the United States until such alien has been registered in accordance with section 221(b) [8 U.S.C.A. § 1201(b)].

(June 27, 1952, c. 477, Title II, ch. 7, § 261, 66 Stat. 223; Pub.L. 99–653, § 8, Nov. 14, 1986, 100 Stat. 3657, as amended Pub.L. 100–525, § 8(g), Oct. 24, 1988, 102 Stat. 2617.)

§ 262.   Registration of aliens [8 U.S.C.A. § 1302]

(a) It shall be the duty of every alien now or hereafter in the United States, who **(1)** is fourteen years of age or older, **(2)** has not been registered and fingerprinted under section 221(b) [8 U.S.C.A. § 1201(b)] or section 30 or 31 of the Alien Registration Act, 1940, and **(3)** remains in the United States for thirty days or longer, to apply for registration and to be fingerprinted before the expiration of such thirty days.

(b) It shall be the duty of every parent or legal guardian of any alien now or hereafter in the United States, who **(1)** is less than fourteen years of age, **(2)** has not been registered under section 221(b) [8 U.S.C.A. § 1201(b)] or section 30 or 31 of the Alien Registration Act, 1940, and **(3)** remains in the United States for thirty days or longer, to apply for the registration of such alien before the expiration of such thirty days. Whenever any alien attains his fourteenth birthday in the United States he shall, within thirty days thereafter, apply in person for registration and to be fingerprinted.

(c) The Attorney General may, in his discretion and on the basis of reciprocity pursuant to such regulations as he may prescribe, waive the requirement of fingerprinting specified in subsections (a) and (b) in the case of any nonimmigrant.

(June 27, 1952, c. 477, Title II, ch. 7, § 262, 66 Stat. 224; Nov. 14, 1986, Pub.L. 99–653, § 9, 100 Stat. 3657; Oct. 24, 1988, Pub.L. 100–525, § 8(h), 102 Stat. 2617; Oct. 25, 1994, Pub.L. 103–416, Title II, § 219(n), 108 Stat. 4317.)

§ 263.   Registration of special groups [8 U.S.C.A. § 1303]

(a) Notwithstanding the provisions of sections 261 [8 U.S.C.A. § 1301] and 262 [8 U.S.C.A. § 1302], the Attorney General is authorized to prescribe special regulations and forms for the registration and fingerprinting of **(1)** alien crewmen, **(2)** holders of border-crossing identification cards, **(3)** aliens confined in institutions within the United States, **(4)** aliens under order of removal, **(5)** aliens who are or have been on criminal probation or criminal parole within the United States, and **(6)** aliens of any other class not lawfully admitted to the United States for permanent residence.

(b) The provisions of section 262 [8 U.S.C.A. § 1302] and of this section shall not be applicable to any alien who is in the United States as a non-immigrant under section 101(a)(15)(A) or (a)(15)(G) [8 U.S.C.A. § 1101(a)(15)(A) or (a)(15)(G)] until the alien ceases to be entitled to such a nonimmigrant status.

(June 27, 1952, c. 477, Title II, ch. 7, § 263, 66 Stat. 224; Sept. 30, 1996, Pub.L. 104–208, Div. C, Title III, §§ 308(e)(1)(J), 323, 110 Stat. 3009–619, 3009–629.)

§ 264. Forms for registration and fingerprinting [8 U.S.C.A. § 1304]

(a) Preparation; contents

The Attorney General and the Secretary of State jointly are authorized and directed to prepare forms for the registration of aliens under section 261 [8 U.S.C.A. § 1301], and the Attorney General is authorized and directed to prepare forms for the registration and fingerprinting of aliens under section 262 [8 U.S.C.A. § 1302]. Such forms shall contain inquiries with respect to **(1)** the date and place of entry of the alien into the United States; **(2)** activities in which he has been and intends to be engaged; **(3)** the length of time he expects to remain in the United States; **(4)** the police and criminal record, if any, of such alien; and **(5)** such additional matters as may be prescribed.

(b) Confidential nature

All registration and fingerprint records made under the provisions of this title shall be confidential, and shall be made available only **(1)** pursuant to section 287(f)(2) [8 U.S.C.A. § 1357(f)(2)], and **(2)** to such persons or agencies as may be designated by the Attorney General.

(c) Information under oath

Every person required to apply for the registration of himself or another under this title shall submit under oath the information required for such registration. Any person authorized under regulations issued by the Attorney General to register aliens under this title shall be authorized to administer oaths for such purpose.

(d) Certificate of alien registration or alien receipt card

Every alien in the United States who has been registered and fingerprinted under the provisions of the Alien Registration Act, 1940, or under the provisions of this Act shall be issued a certificate of alien registration or an alien registration receipt card in such form and manner and at such time as shall be prescribed under regulations issued by the Attorney General.

(e) Personal possession of registration or receipt card; penalties

Every alien, eighteen years of age and over, shall at all times carry with him and have in his personal possession any certificate of alien registration or alien registration receipt card issued to him pursuant to subsection (d). Any alien who fails to comply with the provisions of this subsection shall be guilty of a misdemeanor and shall upon conviction for each offense be fined not to exceed $100 or be imprisoned not more than thirty days, or both.

(f) Social security account number

Notwithstanding any other provision of law, the Attorney General is authorized to require any alien to provide the alien's social security account number for purposes of inclusion in any record of the alien maintained by the Attorney General or the Service.

(June 27, 1952, c. 477, Title II, ch. 7, § 264, 66 Stat. 224; Nov. 14, 1986, Pub.L. 99–653, § 10, 100 Stat. 3657; Oct. 24, 1988, Pub.L. 100–525, § 8(i), 102 Stat. 2617; Nov. 29, 1990, Pub.L. 101–649, Title V, § 503(b)(2), 104 Stat. 5049; Sept. 30, 1996, Pub.L. 104–208, Div. C, Title IV, § 415, 110 Stat. 3009–669.)

§ 265.   Notices of change of address [8 U.S.C.A. § 1305]

(a) Notification of change

Each alien required to be registered under this title who is within the United States shall notify the Attorney General in writing of each change of address and new address within ten days from the date of such change and furnish with such notice such additional information as the Attorney General may require by regulation.

(b) Current address of natives of any one or more foreign states

The Attorney General may in his discretion, upon ten days notice, require the natives of any one or more foreign states, or any class or group thereof, who are within the United States and who are required to be registered under this title, to notify the Attorney General of their current addresses and furnish such additional information as the Attorney General may require.

(c) Notice to parent or legal guardian

In the case of an alien for whom a parent or legal guardian is required to apply for registration, the notice required by this section shall be given to such parent or legal guardian.

(June 27, 1952, c. 477, Title II, c. 7, § 265, 66 Stat. 225; Pub.L. 97–116, § 11, Dec. 29, 1981, 95 Stat. 1617; Pub.L. 100–525, § 9(*o*), Oct. 24, 1988, 102 Stat. 2620.)

§ 266.   Penalties [8 U.S.C.A. § 1306]

(a) Willful failure to register

Any alien required to apply for registration and to be fingerprinted in the United States who willfully fails or refuses to make such application or to be fingerprinted, and any parent or legal guardian required to apply for the registration of any alien who willfully fails or refuses to file application for the registration of such alien shall be guilty of a misdemeanor and shall, upon conviction thereof, be fined not to exceed $1,000 or be imprisoned not more than six months, or both.

(b) Failure to notify change of address

Any alien or any parent or legal guardian in the United States of any alien who fails to give written notice to the Attorney General, as required by section 265 [8 U.S.C.A. § 1305], shall be guilty of a misdemeanor and shall, upon conviction thereof, be fined not to exceed $200 or be imprisoned not more than thirty days, or both. Irrespective of whether an alien is convicted and punished as herein provided, any alien who fails to give written notice to the Attorney General, as required by section 265 [8 U.S.C.A. § 1305], shall be taken into custody and removed in the manner provided by chapter 4 of the title, unless such alien establishes to the satisfaction of the Attorney General that such failure was reasonably excusable or was not willful.

(c) Fraudulent statements

Any alien or any parent or legal guardian of any alien, who files an application for registration containing statements known by him to be false, or who procures or attempts to procure registration of himself or another person through fraud, shall be guilty of a misdemeanor and shall, upon conviction thereof, be fined not to exceed $1,000, or be imprisoned not more than six months, or both; and any alien so convicted shall, upon the warrant of the Attorney General, be taken into custody and be removed in the manner provided in part IV of this title.

(d) Counterfeiting

Any person who with unlawful intent photographs, prints, or in any other manner makes, or executes, any engraving, photograph, print, or impression in the likeness of any certificate of alien registration or an alien registration receipt card or any colorable imitation thereof, except when and as authorized under such rules and regulations as may be prescribed by the Attorney General, shall upon conviction be fined not to exceed $5,000 or be imprisoned not more than five years, or both.

(June 27, 1952, c. 477, Title II, ch. 7, § 266, 66 Stat. 225; Sept. 30, 1996, Pub.L. 104–208, Div. C, Title III, § 308(e)(2)(G), (g)(9)(A), 110 Stat. 3009–620, 3009–624.)

CHAPTER VIII—GENERAL PENALTY PROVISIONS

§ 271.   Prevention of unauthorized landing of aliens [8 U.S.C.A. § 1321]

(a) Failure to report; penalties

It shall be the duty of every person, including the owners, masters, officers, and agents of vessels, aircraft, transportation lines, or international bridges or toll roads, other than transportation lines which may enter into a contract as provided in section 233 [8 U.S.C.A. § 1223], bringing an alien to, or providing a means for an alien to come to, the United States (including an alien crewman whose case is not covered by section 254(a) [8 U.S.C.A. § 1284(a)]) to prevent the landing of such alien in the United States at a port of entry other than as designated by the Attorney General

or at any time or place other than as designated by the immigration officers. Any such person, owner, master, officer, or agent who fails to comply
with the foregoing requirements shall be liable to a penalty to be imposed
by the Attorney General of $3,000 for each such violation, which may, in
the discretion of the Attorney General, be remitted or mitigated by him
in accordance with such proceedings as he shall by regulation prescribe.
Such penalty shall be a lien upon the vessel or aircraft whose owner, master, officer, or agent violates the provisions of this section, and such vessel
or aircraft may be libeled therefor in the appropriate United States court.

(b) Prima facie evidence

Proof that the alien failed to present himself at the time and place
designated by the immigration officers shall be prima facie evidence that
such alien has landed in the United States at a time or place other than
as designated by the immigration officers.

(c) Liability of owners and operators of international bridges and toll roads

(1) Any owner or operator of a railroad line, international bridge,
or toll road who establishes to the satisfaction of the Attorney General
that the person has acted diligently and reasonably to fulfill the duty
imposed by subsection (a) shall not be liable for the penalty described
in such subsection, notwithstanding the failure of the person to prevent the unauthorized landing of any alien.

(2)(A) At the request of any person described in paragraph (1), the
Attorney General shall inspect any facility established, or any method
utilized, at a point of entry into the United States by such person for
the purpose of complying with subsection (a). The Attorney General
shall approve any such facility or method (for such period of time as
the Attorney General may prescribe) which the Attorney General determines is satisfactory for such purpose.

(B) Proof that any person described in paragraph (1) has diligently
maintained any facility, or utilized any method, which has been approved by the Attorney General under subparagraph (A) (within the
period for which the approval is effective) shall be prima facie evidence
that such person acted diligently and reasonably to fulfill the duty
imposed by subsection (a) (within the meaning of paragraph (1) of this
subsection).

(June 27, 1952, c. 477, Title II, ch. 8, § 271, 66 Stat. 226; Nov. 6, 1986, Pub.L. 99–603,
Title I, § 114, 100 Stat. 3383; Nov. 29, 1990, Pub.L. 101–649, Title V, § 543(a)(8), 104 Stat.
5058; Sept. 30, 1996, Pub.L. 104–208, Div. C, Title III, § 308(g)(1), 110 Stat. 3009–622.)

§ 272. Bringing in aliens subject to denial of admission on a health-related ground; persons liable; clearance papers; exceptions; "person" defined [8 U.S.C.A. § 1322]

(a) Any person who shall bring to the United States an alien (other than an alien crewman) who is inadmissible under section 212(a)(1) [8 U.S.C.A. § 1182(a)(1)] shall pay to the Commissioner for each and every alien so afflicted the sum of $3,000 unless (1) the alien was in possession of a valid, unexpired immigrant visa, or **(2)** the alien was allowed to land in the United States, or **(3)** the alien was in possession of a valid unexpired non-immigrant visa or other document authorizing such alien to apply for temporary admission to the United States or an unexpired reentry permit issued to him, and **(A)** such application was made within one hundred and twenty days of the date of issuance of the visa or other document, or in the case of an alien in possession of a reentry permit, within one hundred and twenty days of the date on which the alien was last examined and admitted by the Service, or **(B)** in the event the application was made later than one hundred and twenty days of the date of issuance of the visa or other document or such examination and admission, if such person establishes to the satisfaction of the Attorney General that the existence of the condition causing inadmissibility could not have been detected by the exercise of due diligence prior to the alien's embarkation.

(b) No vessel or aircraft shall be granted clearance papers pending determination of the question of liability to the payment of any fine under this section, or while the fines remain unpaid, nor shall such fines be remitted or refunded; but clearance may be granted prior to the determination of such question upon the deposit of a sum sufficient to cover such fines or of a bond with sufficient surety to secure the payment thereof, approved by the Commissioner.

(c) Nothing contained in this section shall be construed to subject transportation companies to a fine for bringing to ports of entry in the United States aliens who are entitled by law to exemption from the provisions of section 212(a) [8 U.S.C.A. § 1182(a)].

(d) As used in this section, the term "person" means the owner, master, agent, commanding officer, charterer, or consignee of any vessel or aircraft.

(June 27, 1952, c. 477, Title II, ch. 8, § 272, 66 Stat. 226; Oct. 3, 1965, Pub.L. 89–236, § 18, 79 Stat. 920; Nov. 29, 1990, Pub.L. 101–649, Title V, § 543(a)(9), Title VI, § 603(a)(15), 104 Stat. 5058, 5084; Dec. 12, 1991, Pub.L. 102–232, Title III, § 307(*l*)(7), 105 Stat. 1757; Oct. 25, 1994, Pub.L. 103–416, Title II, § 219(*o*), 108 Stat. 4317; Sept. 30, 1996, Pub.L. 104–208, Div. C, Title III, § 308(d)(3)(A), (4)(I)(i), 110 Stat. 3009–617, 3009–618.)

§ 273. Unlawful bringing of aliens into United States [8 U.S.C.A. § 1323]

(a) Persons liable

(1) It shall be unlawful for any person, including any transportation company, or the owner, master, commanding officer, agent, charterer, or consignee of any vessel or aircraft, to bring to the United States from any place outside thereof (other than from foreign contiguous territory) any alien who does not have a valid passport and an unexpired visa, if a visa was required under this Act or regulations issued thereunder.

(2) It is unlawful for an owner, agent, master, commanding officer, person in charge, purser, or consignee of a vessel or aircraft who is bringing an alien (except an alien crewmember) to the United States to take any consideration to be kept or returned contingent on whether an alien is admitted to, or ordered removed from, the United States.

(b) Evidence

If it appears to the satisfaction of the Attorney General that any alien has been so brought, such person, or transportation company, or the master, commanding officer, agent, owner, charterer, or consignee of any such vessel or aircraft, shall pay to the Commissioner a fine of $3,000 for each alien so brought and, except in the case of any such alien who is admitted, or permitted to land temporarily, in addition, an amount equal to that paid by such alien for his transportation from the initial point of departure, indicated in his ticket, to the port of the arrival, such latter fine to be delivered by the Commissioner to the alien on whose account the assessment is made. No vessel or aircraft shall be granted clearance pending the determination of the liability to the payment of such fine or while such fine remains unpaid, except that clearance may be granted prior to the determination of such question upon the deposit of an amount sufficient to cover such fine, or of a bond with sufficient surety to secure the payment thereof approved by the Commissioner.

(c) Remission or refund

Except as provided in subsection (e), such fine shall not be remitted or refunded, unless it appears to the satisfaction of the Attorney General that such person, and the owner, master, commanding officer, agent, charterer, and consignee of the vessel or aircraft, prior to the departure of the vessel or aircraft from the last port outside the United States, did not know, and could not have ascertained by the exercise of reasonable diligence, that the individual transported was an alien and that a valid passport or visa was required.

(d) Repealed. Pub.L. 104–208, Div. C, Title III, § 308(e)(13), Sept. 30, 1996, 110 Stat. 3009–620.

(e) Reduction, refund, or waiver 8 U.S.C.A.

A fine under this section may be reduced, refunded, or waived under such regulations as the Attorney General shall prescribe in cases in which—

> **(1)** the carrier demonstrates that it had screened all passengers on the vessel or aircraft in accordance with procedures prescribed by the Attorney General, or

> **(2)** circumstances exist that the Attorney General determines would justify such reduction, refund, or waiver.

(June 27, 1952, c. 477, Title II, ch. 8, § 273, 66 Stat. 227; Nov. 29, 1990, Pub.L. 101–649, Title II, § 201(b), Title V, § 543(a)(10), 104 Stat. 5014, 5058; Dec. 12, 1991, Pub.L. 102–232, Title III, § 306(c)(4)(D), 105 Stat. 1752; Oct. 25, 1994, Pub.L. 103–416, Title II, §§ 209(a), 216, 219(p), 108 Stat. 4312, 4315, 4317; Sept. 30, 1996, Pub.L. 104–208, Div. C, Title III, §§ 308(c)(3), (e)(13), 371(b)(8), Title VI, § 671(b)(6), (7), 110 Stat. 3009–616, 3009–620, 3009–645, 3009–722.)

§ 274. Bringing in and harboring certain aliens [8 U.S.C.A. § 1324]

(a) Criminal penalties

(1)(A) Any person who—

> **(i)** knowing that a person is an alien, brings to or attempts to bring to the United States in any manner whatsoever such person at a place other than a designated port of entry or place other than as designated by the Commissioner, regardless of whether such alien has received prior official authorization to come to, enter, or reside in the United States and regardless of any future official action which may be taken with respect to such alien;

> **(ii)** knowing or in reckless disregard of the fact that an alien has come to, entered, or remains in the United States in violation of law, transports, or moves or attempts to transport or move such alien within the United States by means of transportation or otherwise, in furtherance of such violation of law;

> **(iii)** knowing or in reckless disregard of the fact that an alien has come to, entered, or remains in the United States in violation of law, conceals, harbors, or shields from detection, or attempts to conceal, harbor, or shield from detection, such alien in any place, including any building or any means of transportation;

> **(iv)** encourages or induces an alien to come to, enter, or reside in the United States, knowing or in reckless disregard of the fact that such coming to, entry, or residence is or will be in violation of law; or

> **(v)(I)** engages in any conspiracy to commit any of the preceding acts, or

> **(II)** aids or abets the commission of any of the preceding acts,

shall be punished as provided in subparagraph (B).

(B) A person who violates subparagraph (A) shall, for each alien in respect to whom such a violation occurs—

(i) in the case of a violation of subparagraph (A)(i) or (v)(I) or in the case of a violation of subparagraph (A)(ii), (iii), or (iv) in which the offense was done for the purpose of commercial advantage or private financial gain, be fined under Title 18, imprisoned not more than 10 years, or both;

(ii) in the case of a violation of subparagraph (A)(ii), (iii), (iv), or (v)(II), be fined under Title 18, imprisoned not more than 5 years, or both;

(iii) in the case of a violation of subparagraph (A)(i), (ii), (iii), (iv), or (v) during and in relation to which the person causes serious bodily injury (as defined in section 1365 of Title 18) to, or places in jeopardy the life of, any person, be fined under Title 18, imprisoned not more than 20 years, or both; and

(iv) in the case of a violation of subparagraph (A)(i), (ii), (iii), (iv), or (v) resulting in the death of any person, be punished by death or imprisoned for any term of years or for life, fined under Title 18, or both.

(C) It is not a violation of clauses (ii) or (iii) of subparagraph (A), or of clause (iv) of subparagraph (A) except where a person encourages or induces an alien to come to or enter the United States, for a religious denomination having a bona fide nonprofit, religious organization in the United States, or the agents or officers of such denomination or organization, to encourage, invite, call, allow, or enable an alien who is present in the United States to perform the vocation of a minister or missionary for the denomination or organization in the United States as a volunteer who is not compensated as an employee, notwithstanding the provision of room, board, travel, medical assistance, and other basic living expenses, provided the minister or missionary has been a member of the denomination for at least one year.

(2) Any person who, knowing or in reckless disregard of the fact that an alien has not received prior official authorization to come to, enter, or reside in the United States, brings to or attempts to bring to the United States in any manner whatsoever, such alien, regardless of any official action which may later be taken with respect to such alien shall, for each alien in respect to whom a violation of this paragraph occurs—

(A) be fined in accordance with Title 18, or imprisoned not more than one year, or both; or

(B) in the case of—

(i) an offense committed with the intent or with reason to believe that the alien unlawfully brought into the United States will commit an offense against the United States or any State punishable by imprisonment for more than 1 year,

(ii) an offense done for the purpose of commercial advantage or private financial gain, or

(iii) an offense in which the alien is not upon arrival immediately brought and presented to an appropriate immigration officer at a designated port of entry,

be fined under Title 18, and shall be imprisoned, in the case of a first or second violation of subparagraph (B)(iii), not more than 10 years, in the case of a first or second violation of subparagraph (B)(i) or (B)(ii), not less than 3 nor more than 10 years, and for any other violation, not less than 5 nor more than 15 years.

(3)(A) Any person who, during any 12-month period, knowingly hires for employment at least 10 individuals with actual knowledge that the individuals are aliens described in subparagraph (B) shall be fined under Title 18, or imprisoned for not more than 5 years, or both.

(B) An alien described in this subparagraph is an alien who—

(i) is an unauthorized alien (as defined in section 274A(h)(3) [8 U.S.C.A. § 1324a(h)(3)]), and

(ii) has been brought into the United States in violation of this subsection.

(4) In the case of a person who has brought aliens into the United States in violation of this subsection, the sentence otherwise provided for may be increased by up to 10 years if—

(A) the offense was part of an ongoing commercial organization or enterprise;

(B) aliens were transported in groups of 10 or more; and

(C)(i) aliens were transported in a manner that endangered their lives; or

(ii) the aliens presented a life-threatening health risk to people in the United States.

(b) Seizure and forfeiture

(1) Any conveyance, including any vessel, vehicle, or aircraft, that has been or is being used in the commission of a violation of subsection (a), the gross proceeds of such violation, and any property traceable to such conveyance or proceeds, shall be seized and subject to forfeiture.

(2) Seizures and forfeitures under this subsection shall be governed by the provisions of chapter 46 of title 18, United States Code, relating to civil forfeitures, including section 981(d) of such title, except that such duties as are imposed upon the Secretary of the Treasury under the customs laws described in that section shall be performed by such officers, agents, and other persons as may be designated for that purpose by the Attorney General.

(3) In determining whether a violation of subsection (a) has occurred, any of the following shall be prima facie evidence that an alien involved in the alleged violation had not received prior official authorization to come to, enter, or reside in the United States or that such alien had come to, entered, or remained in the United States in violation of law:

(A) Records of any judicial or administrative proceeding in which that alien's status was an issue and in which it was determined that the alien had not received prior official authorization to come to, enter, or reside in the United States or that such alien had come to, entered, or remained in the United States in violation of law.

(B) Official records of the Service or of the Department of State showing that the alien had not received prior official authorization to come to, enter, or reside in the United States or that such alien had come to, entered, or remained in the United States in violation of law.

(C) Testimony, by an immigration officer having personal knowledge of the facts concerning that alien's status, that the alien had not received prior official authorization to come to, enter, or reside in the United States or that such alien had come to, entered, or remained in the United States in violation of law.

(c) Authority to arrest

No officer or person shall have authority to make any arrest for a violation of any provision of this section except officers and employees of the Service designated by the Attorney General, either individually or as a member of a class, and all other officers whose duty it is to enforce criminal laws.

(d) Admissibility of videotaped witness testimony

Notwithstanding any provision of the Federal Rules of Evidence, the videotaped (or otherwise audiovisually preserved) deposition of a witness to a violation of subsection (a) who has been deported or otherwise expelled from the United States, or is otherwise unable to testify, may be admitted into evidence in an action brought for that violation if the witness was available for cross examination and the deposition otherwise complies with the Federal Rules of Evidence.

(e) Outreach program

The Secretary of Homeland Security, in consultation with the Attorney General and the Secretary of State, as appropriate, shall develop and implement an outreach program to educate the public in the United States and abroad about the penalties for bringing in and harboring aliens in violation of this section.

(June 27, 1952, c. 477, Title II, ch. 8, § 274, 66 Stat. 228; Nov. 2, 1978, Pub.L. 95–582, § 2, 92 Stat. 2479; Dec. 29, 1981, Pub.L. 97–116, § 12, 95 Stat. 1617; Nov. 6, 1986, Pub.L. 99–603, § 112, 100 Stat. 3381; Oct. 24, 1988, Pub.L. 100–525, § 2(d), 102 Stat. 2610; Sept. 13, 1994, Pub.L. 103–322, Title VI, § 60024, 108 Stat. 1981; Sept. 30, 1996, Pub.L. 104–208,

Div. C, Title II, §§ 203(a) to (d), 219, Title VI, § 671(a)(1), 110 Stat. 3009–565, 3009–566, 3009–574, 3009–721; April 25, 2000, Pub.L. 106–185, § 18, 114 Stat. 222; Dec. 17, 2004, Pub.L. 108–458, Title V, § 5401, 118 Stat. 3737; Nov. 10, 2005, Pub.L. 109–97, Title VII, § 796, 119 Stat. 2165.)

§ 274A. Unlawful employment of aliens [8 U.S.C.A. § 1324a]

(a) Making employment of unauthorized aliens unlawful

(1) In general

It is unlawful for a person or other entity—

(A) to hire, or to recruit or refer for a fee, for employment in the United States an alien knowing the alien is an unauthorized alien (as defined in subsection (h)(3)) with respect to such employment, or

(B) (i) to hire for employment in the United States an individual without complying with the requirements of subsection (b) or **(ii)** if the person or entity is an agricultural association, agricultural employer, or farm labor contractor (as defined in section 1802 of Title 29) to hire, or to recruit or refer for a fee, for employment in the United States an individual without complying with the requirements of subsection (b).

(2) Continuing employment

It is unlawful for a person or other entity, after hiring an alien for employment in accordance with paragraph (1), to continue to employ the alien in the United States knowing the alien is (or has become) an unauthorized alien with respect to such employment.

(3) Defense

A person or entity that establishes that it has complied in good faith with the requirements of subsection (b) with respect to the hiring, recruiting, or referral for employment of an alien in the United States has established an affirmative defense that the person or entity has not violated paragraph (1)(A) with respect to such hiring, recruiting, or referral.

(4) Use of labor through contract

For purposes of this section, a person or other entity who uses a contract, subcontract, or exchange, entered into, renegotiated, or extended after the date of the enactment of this section, to obtain the labor of an alien in the United States knowing that the alien is an unauthorized alien (as defined in subsection (h)(3)) with respect to performing such labor, shall be considered to have hired the alien for employment in the United States in violation of paragraph (1)(A).

(5) Use of State employment agency documentation

For purposes of paragraphs (1)(B) and (3), a person or entity shall be deemed to have complied with the requirements of subsection (b)

with respect to the hiring of an individual who was referred for such employment by a State employment agency (as defined by the Attorney General), if the person or entity has and retains (for the period and in the manner described in subsection (b)(3)) appropriate documentation of such referral by that agency, which documentation certifies that the agency has complied with the procedures specified in subsection (b) with respect to the individual's referral.

(6) Treatment of documentation for certain employees

(A) In general

For purposes of this section, if—

(i) an individual is a member of a collective-bargaining unit and is employed, under a collective bargaining agreement entered into between one or more employee organizations and an association of two or more employers, by an employer that is a member of such association, and

(ii) within the period specified in subparagraph (B), another employer that is a member of the association (or an agent of such association on behalf of the employer) has complied with the requirements of subsection (b) with respect to the employment of the individual,

the subsequent employer shall be deemed to have complied with the requirements of subsection (b) with respect to the hiring of the employee and shall not be liable for civil penalties described in subsection (e)(5).

(B) Period

The period described in this subparagraph is 3 years, or, if less, the period of time that the individual is authorized to be employed in the United States.

(C) Liability

(i) In general

If any employer that is a member of an association hires for employment in the United States an individual and relies upon the provisions of subparagraph (A) to comply with the requirements of subsection (b) and the individual is an alien not authorized to work in the United States, then for the purposes of paragraph (1)(A), subject to clause (ii), the employer shall be presumed to have known at the time of hiring or afterward that the individual was an alien not authorized to work in the United States.

(ii) Rebuttal of presumption

The presumption established by clause (i) may be rebutted by the employer only through the presentation of clear and convincing evidence that the employer did not know (and could not reasonably have known) that the individual at the time of hiring or afterward was an alien not authorized to work in the United States.

(iii) Exception

Clause (i) shall not apply in any prosecution under subsection (f)(1).

(7) Application to Federal Government

For purposes of this section, the term "entity" includes an entity in any branch of the Federal Government.

(b) Employment verification system

The requirements referred to in paragraphs (1)(B) and (3) of subsection (a) are, in the case of a person or other entity hiring, recruiting, or referring an individual for employment in the United States, the requirements specified in the following three paragraphs:

(1) Attestation after examination of documentation

(A) In general

The person or entity must attest, under penalty of perjury and on a form designated or established by the Attorney General by regulation, that it has verified that the individual is not an unauthorized alien by examining—

(i) a document described in subparagraph (B), or

(ii) a document described in subparagraph (C) and a document described in subparagraph (D).

A person or entity has complied with the requirement of this paragraph with respect to examination of a document if the document reasonably appears on its face to be genuine. If an individual provides a document or combination of documents that reasonably appears on its face to be genuine and that is sufficient to meet the requirements of the first sentence of this paragraph, nothing in this paragraph shall be construed as requiring the person or entity to solicit the production of any other document or as requiring the individual to produce such another document.

(B) Documents establishing both employment authorization and identity

A document described in this subparagraph is an individual's—

(i) United States passport;

(ii) resident alien card, alien registration card, or other document designated by the Attorney General, if the document—

(I) contains a photograph of the individual and such other personal identifying information relating to the individual as the Attorney General finds, by regulation, sufficient for purposes of this subsection,

(II) is evidence of authorization of employment in the United States, and

(III) contains security features to make it resistant to tampering, counterfeiting, and fraudulent use.

(iii), (iv) Repealed. Pub.L. 104–208, Div. C, Title IV, § 412(a)(1)(A), Sept. 30, 1996, 110 Stat. 3009–666.

(v) Redesignated (ii).

(C) Documents evidencing employment authorization

A document described in this subparagraph is an individual's—

(i) social security account number card (other than such a card which specifies on the face that the issuance of the card does not authorize employment in the United States); or

(ii) other documentation evidencing authorization of employment in the United States which the Attorney General finds, by regulation, to be acceptable for purposes of this section.

(iii) Redesignated (ii).

(D) Documents establishing identity of individual

A document described in this subparagraph is an individual's—

(i) driver's license or similar document issued for the purpose of identification by a State, if it contains a photograph of the individual or such other personal identifying information relating to the individual as the Attorney General finds, by regulation, sufficient for purposes of this section; or

(ii) in the case of individuals under 16 years of age or in a State which does not provide for issuance of an identification document (other than a driver's license) referred to in clause (i), documentation of personal identity of such other type as the Attorney General finds, by regulation, provides a reliable means of identification.

(E) Authority to prohibit use of certain documents

If the Attorney General finds, by regulation, that any document described in subparagraph (B), (C), or (D) as establishing employment authorization or identity does not reliably establish such authorization or identity or is being used fraudulently to an unacceptable degree, the Attorney General may prohibit or place conditions on its use for purposes of this subsection.

(2) Individual attestation of employment authorization

The individual must attest, under penalty of perjury on the form designated or established for purposes of paragraph (1), that the individual is a citizen or national of the United States, an alien lawfully admitted for permanent residence, or an alien who is authorized under this Act or by the Attorney General to be hired, recruited, or referred for such employment.

(3) Retention of verification form

After completion of such form in accordance with paragraphs (1) and (2), the person or entity must retain the form and make it available for inspection by officers of the Service, the Special Counsel for Immigration-Related Unfair Employment Practices, or the Department of Labor during a period beginning on the date of the hiring, recruiting, or referral of the individual and ending—

(A) in the case of the recruiting or referral for a fee (without hiring) of an individual, three years after the date of the recruiting or referral, and

(B) in the case of the hiring of an individual—

(i) three years after the date of such hiring, or

(ii) one year after the date the individual's employment is terminated,

whichever is later.

(4) Copying of documentation permitted

Notwithstanding any other provision of law, the person or entity may copy a document presented by an individual pursuant to this subsection and may retain the copy, but only (except as otherwise permitted under law) for the purpose of complying with the requirements of this subsection.

(5) Limitation on use of attestation form

A form designated or established by the Attorney General under this subsection and any information contained in or appended to such form, may not be used for purposes other than for enforcement of this Act and sections 1001, 1028, 1546, and 1621 of Title 18.

(6) Good faith compliance

(A) In general

Except as provided in subparagraphs (B) and (C), a person or entity is considered to have complied with a requirement of this subsection notwithstanding a technical or procedural failure to meet such requirement if there was a good faith attempt to comply with the requirement.

(B) Exception if failure to correct after notice

Subparagraph (A) shall not apply if—

(i) the Service (or another enforcement agency) has explained to the person or entity the basis for the failure,

(ii) the person or entity has been provided a period of not less than 10 business days (beginning after the date of the explanation) within which to correct the failure, and

(iii) the person or entity has not corrected the failure voluntarily within such period.

(C) Exception for pattern or practice violators

Subparagraph (A) shall not apply to a person or entity that has or is engaging in a pattern or practice of violations of subsection (a)(1)(A) or (a)(2).

(c) No authorization of national identification cards

Nothing in this section shall be construed to authorize, directly or indirectly, the issuance or use of national identification cards or the establishment of a national identification card.

(d) Evaluation and changes in employment verification system

(1) Presidential monitoring and improvements in system

(A) Monitoring

The President shall provide for the monitoring and evaluation of the degree to which the employment verification system established under subsection (b) provides a secure system to determine employment eligibility in the United States and shall examine the suitability of existing Federal and State identification systems for use for this purpose.

(B) Improvements to establish secure system

To the extent that the system established under subsection (b) is found not to be a secure system to determine employment eligibility in the United States, the President shall, subject to paragraph (3) and taking into account the results of any demonstration projects conducted under paragraph (4), implement such changes in (including additions to) the requirements of subsection (b) as may be necessary to establish a secure system to determine employment eligibility in the United States. Such changes in the system may be implemented only if the changes conform to the requirements of paragraph (2).

(2) Restrictions on changes in system

Any change the President proposes to implement under paragraph (1) in the verification system must be designed in a manner so the verification system, as so changed, meets the following requirements:

(A) Reliable determination of identity

The system must be capable of reliably determining whether—

(i) a person with the identity claimed by an employee or prospective employee is eligible to work, and

(ii) the employee or prospective employee is claiming the identity of another individual.

(B) Using of counterfeit-resistant documents

If the system requires that a document be presented to or examined by an employer, the document must be in a form which is resistant to counterfeiting and tampering.

(C) Limited use of system

Any personal information utilized by the system may not be made available to Government agencies, employers, and other persons except to the extent necessary to verify that an individual is not an unauthorized alien.

(D) Privacy of information

The system must protect the privacy and security of personal information and identifiers utilized in the system.

(E) Limited denial of verification

A verification that an employee or prospective employee is eligible to be employed in the United States may not be withheld or revoked under the system for any reason other than that the employee or prospective employee is an unauthorized alien.

(F) Limited use for law enforcement purposes

The system may not be used for law enforcement purposes, other than for enforcement of this Act or sections 1001, 1028, 1546, and 1621 of Title 18.

(G) Restriction on use of new documents

If the system requires individuals to present a new card or other document (designed specifically for use for this purpose) at the time of hiring, recruitment, or referral, then such document may not be required to be presented for any purpose other than under this Act (or enforcement of sections 1001, 1028, 1546, and 1621 of Title 18) nor to be carried on one's person.

(3) Notice to Congress before implementing changes

(A) In general

The President may not implement any change under paragraph (1) unless at least—

> **(i)** 60 days,

> **(ii)** one year, in the case of a major change described in subparagraph (D)(iii), or

> **(iii)** two years, in the case of a major change described in clause (i) or (ii) of subparagraph (D),

before the date of implementation of the change, the President has prepared and transmitted to the Committee on the Judiciary of the House of Representatives and to the Committee on the Judiciary of the Senate a written report setting forth the proposed change. If the President proposes to make any change regarding social security account number cards, the President shall transmit to the Committee on Ways and Means of the House of Representatives and to the Committee on Finance of the Senate a written report setting forth the proposed change. The President promptly shall cause to have printed in the Federal Register the substance of any major change (described in subparagraph (D)) proposed and reported to Congress.

(B) Contents of report

In any report under subparagraph (A) the President shall include recommendations for the establishment of civil and criminal sanctions for unauthorized use or disclosure of the information or identifiers contained in such system.

(C) Congressional review of major changes

(i) Hearings and review

The Committees on the Judiciary of the House of Representatives and of the Senate shall cause to have printed in the Congressional Record the substance of any major change described in subparagraph (D), shall hold hearings respecting the feasibility and desirability of implementing such a change, and, within the two year period before implementation, shall report to their respective Houses findings on whether or not such a change should be implemented.

(ii) Congressional action

No major change may be implemented unless the Congress specifically provides, in an appropriations or other Act, for funds for implementation of the change.

(D) Major changes defined

As used in this paragraph, the term "major change" means a change which would—

(i) require an individual to present a new card or other document (designed specifically for use for this purpose) at the time of hiring, recruitment, or referral,

(ii) provide for a telephone verification system under which an employer, recruiter, or referrer must transmit to a Federal official information concerning the immigration status of prospective employees and the official transmits to the person, and the person must record, a verification code, or

(iii) require any change in any card used for accounting purposes under the Social Security Act [42 U.S.C.A. § 301 et seq.]; including any change requiring that the only social security account number cards which may be presented in order to comply with subsection (b)(1)(C)(i) are such cards as are in a counterfeit-resistant form consistent with the second sentence of section 205(c)(2) (D) of the Social Security Act [42 U.S.C.A. § 405(c)(2)(D)].

(E) General revenue funding of social security card changes

Any costs incurred in developing and implementing any change described in subparagraph (D)(iii) for purposes of this subsection shall not be paid for out of any trust fund established under the Social Security Act.

(4) Demonstration projects

(A) Authority

The President may undertake demonstration projects (consistent with paragraph (2)) of different changes in the requirements of subsection (b). No such project may extend over a period of longer than five years.

(B) Reports on projects

The President shall report to the Congress on the results of demonstration projects conducted under this paragraph.

(e) Compliance

(1) Complaints and investigations

The Attorney General shall establish procedures—

(A) for individuals and entities to file written, signed complaints respecting potential violations of subsection (a) or (g)(1),

(B) for the investigation of those complaints which, on their face, have a substantial probability of validity,

(C) for the investigation of such other violations of subsection (a) or (g)(1) as the Attorney General determines to be appropriate, and

(D) for the designation in the Service of a unit which has, as its primary duty, the prosecution of cases of violations of subsection (a) or (g)(1) under this subsection.

(2) Authority in investigations

In conducting investigations and hearings under this subsection—

(A) immigration officers and administrative law judges shall have reasonable access to examine evidence of any person or entity being investigated,

(B) administrative law judges may, if necessary, compel by subpoena the attendance of witnesses and the production of evidence at any designated place or hearing, and

(C) immigration officers designated by the Commissioner may compel by subpoena the attendance of witnesses and the production of evidence at any designated place prior to the filing of a complaint in a case under paragraph (2).

In case of contumacy or refusal to obey a subpoena lawfully issued under this paragraph and upon application of the Attorney General, an appropriate district court of the United States may issue an order requiring compliance with such subpoena and any failure to obey such order may be punished by such court as a contempt thereof.

(3) Hearing

(A) In general

Before imposing an order described in paragraph (4), (5), or (6) against a person or entity under this subsection for a violation of subsection (a) or (g)(1), the Attorney General shall provide the person or entity with notice and, upon request made within a reasonable time (of not less than 30 days, as established by the Attorney General) of the date of the notice, a hearing respecting the violation.

(B) Conduct of hearing

Any hearing so requested shall be conducted before an administrative law judge. The hearing shall be conducted in accordance with the requirements of section 554 of Title 5. The hearing shall be held at the nearest practicable place to the place where the person or entity resides or of the place where the alleged violation occurred. If no hearing is so requested, the Attorney General's imposition of the order shall constitute a final and unappealable order.

(C) Issuance of orders

If the administrative law judge determines, upon the preponderance of the evidence received, that a person or entity named in the complaint has violated subsection (a) or (g)(1), the administrative law judge shall state his findings of fact and issue and cause to be served on such person or entity an order described in paragraph (4), (5), or (6).

(4) Cease and desist order with civil money penalty for hiring, recruiting, and referral violations

With respect to a violation of subsection (a)(1)(A) or (a)(2), the order under this subsection—

(A) shall require the person or entity to cease and desist from such violations and to pay a civil penalty in an amount of—

(i) not less than $250 and not more than $2,000 for each unauthorized alien with respect to whom a violation of either such subsection occurred.

(ii) not less than $2,000 and not more than $5,000 for each such alien in the case of a person or entity previously subject to one order under this paragraph, or

(iii) not less than $3,000 and not more than $10,000 for each such alien in the case of a person or entity previously subject to more than one order under this paragraph; and

(B) may require the person or entity—

(i) to comply with the requirements of subsection (b) (or subsection (d) if applicable) with respect to individuals hired (or recruited or referred for employment for a fee) during a period of up to three years, and

(ii) to take such other remedial action as is appropriate.

In applying this subsection in the case of a person or entity composed of distinct, physically separate subdivisions each of which provides separately for the hiring, recruiting, or referring for employment, without reference to the practices of, and not under the control of or common control with, another subdivision, each such subdivision shall be considered a separate person or entity.

(5) Order for civil money penalty for paperwork violations

With respect to a violation of subsection (a)(1)(B), the order under this subsection shall require the person or entity to pay a civil penalty in an amount of not less than $100 and not more than $1,000 for each individual with respect to whom such violation occurred. In determining the amount of the penalty, due consideration shall be given to the size of the business of the employer being charged, the good faith of the employer, the seriousness of the violation, whether or not the individual was an unauthorized alien, and the history of previous violations.

(6) Order for prohibited indemnity bonds

With respect to a violation of subsection (g)(1), the order under this subsection may provide for the remedy described in subsection (g)(2).

(7) Administrative appellate review

The decision and order of an administrative law judge shall become the final agency decision and order of the Attorney General unless either **(A)** within 30 days, an official delegated by regulation to exercise review authority over the decision and order modifies or vacates the decision and order, or **(B)** within 30 days of the date of such a modification or vacation (or within 60 days of the date of decision and order of an administrative law judge if not so modified or vacated) the decision and order is referred to the Attorney General pursuant to regulations, in which case the decision and order of the Attorney General shall become the final agency decision and order under this subsection. The Attorney General may not delegate the Attorney General's authority under this paragraph to any entity which has review authority over immigration-related matters.

(8) Judicial review

A person or entity adversely affected by a final order respecting an assessment may, within 45 days after the date the final order is issued, file a petition in the Court of Appeals for the appropriate circuit for review of the order.

(9) Enforcement of orders

If a person or entity fails to comply with a final order issued under this subsection against the person or entity, the Attorney General shall file a suit to seek compliance with the order in any appropriate district court of the United States. In any such suit, the validity and appropriateness of the final order shall not be subject to review.

(f) Criminal penalties and injunctions for pattern or practice violations

(1) Criminal penalty

Any person or entity which engages in a pattern or practice of violations of subsection (a)(1)(A) or (a)(2) shall be fined not more than $3,000 for each unauthorized alien with respect to whom such a violation occurs, imprisoned for not more than six months for the entire pattern or practice, or both, notwithstanding the provisions of any other Federal law relating to fine levels.

(2) Enjoining of pattern or practice violations

Whenever the Attorney General has reasonable cause to believe that a person or entity is engaged in a pattern or practice of employment, recruitment, or referral in violation of paragraph (1)(A) or (2) of subsection (a), the Attorney General may bring a civil action in the appropriate district court of the United States requesting such relief, including a permanent or temporary injunction, restraining order, or other order against the person or entity, as the Attorney General deems necessary.

(g) Prohibition of indemnity bonds

(1) Prohibition

It is unlawful for a person or other entity, in the hiring, recruiting, or referring for employment of any individual, to require the individual to post a bond or security, to pay or agree to pay an amount, or otherwise to provide a financial guarantee or indemnity, against any potential liability arising under this section relating to such hiring, recruiting, or referring of the individual.

(2) Civil penalty

Any person or entity which is determined, after notice and opportunity for an administrative hearing under subsection (e), to have violated paragraph (1) shall be subject to a civil penalty of $1,000 for each violation and to an administrative order requiring the return of any amounts received in violation of such paragraph to the employee or, if the employee cannot be located, to the general fund of the Treasury.

(h) Miscellaneous provisions

(1) Documentation

In providing documentation or endorsement of authorization of aliens (other than aliens lawfully admitted for permanent residence) authorized to be employed in the United States, the Attorney General shall provide that any limitations with respect to the period or type of employment or employer shall be conspicuously stated on the documentation or endorsement.

(2) Preemption

The provisions of this section preempt any State or local law imposing civil or criminal sanctions (other than through licensing and similar laws) upon those who employ, or recruit or refer for a fee for employment, unauthorized aliens.

(3) Definition of unauthorized alien

As used in this section, the term "unauthorized alien" means, with respect to the employment of an alien at a particular time, that the alien is not at that time either (A) an alien lawfully admitted for permanent residence, or (B) authorized to be so employed by this Act or by the Attorney General.

(i) to (n) Repealed. Pub.L. 104–208, Div. C, Title IV, § 412(c), Sept. 30, 1996, 110 Stat. 3009–668.

(June 27, 1952, c. 477, Title II, ch. 8, § 274A, as added Nov. 6, 1986, Pub.L. 99–603, Title I, § 101(a)(1), 100 Stat. 3360, and amended Oct. 24, 1988, Pub.L. 100–525, § 2(a)(1), 102 Stat. 2609; Nov. 29, 1990, Pub.L. 101–649, Title V, §§ 521(a), 538(a), 104 Stat. 5053, 5056; Dec. 12, 1991, Pub.L. 102–232, Title III, §§ 306(b)(2), 309(b)(11), 105 Stat. 1752, 1759; Oct. 25, 1994, Pub.L. 103–416, Title II, §§ 213, 219(z)(4), 108 Stat. 4314, 4318; Sept. 30, 1996, Pub.L. 104–208, Div. C, Title III, § 379(a), Title IV, §§ 411(a), 412(a) to (d), 416, 110 Stat. 3009–649, 3009–666 to 3009–669.)

§ 274B. Unfair immigration-related employment practices [8 U.S.C.A. § 1324b]

(a) Prohibition of discrimination based on national origin or citizenship status

(1) General rule

It is an unfair immigration-related employment practice for a person or other entity to discriminate against any individual (other than an unauthorized alien, as defined in section 274A(h)(3) [8 U.S.C.A. § 1324a(h)(3)]) with respect to the hiring, or recruitment or referral for a fee, of the individual for employment or the discharging of the individual from employment—

(A) because of such individual's national origin, or

(B) in the case of a protected individual (as defined in paragraph (3)), because of such individual's citizenship status.

(2) Exceptions

Paragraph (1) shall not apply to—

(A) a person or other entity that employs three or fewer employees,

(B) a person's or entity's discrimination because of an individual's national origin if the discrimination with respect to that person or entity and that individual is covered under section 2000e–2 of Title 42, or

(C) discrimination because of citizenship status which is otherwise required in order to comply with law, regulation, or executive order, or required by Federal, State, or local government contract, or which the Attorney General determines to be essential for an employer to do business with an agency or department of the Federal, State, or local government.

(3) Definition of protected individual

As used in paragraph (1), the term "protected individual" means an individual who—

(A) is a citizen or national of the United States, or

(B) is an alien who is lawfully admitted for permanent residence, is granted the status of an alien lawfully admitted for temporary residence under section 210(a) [8 U.S.C.A. § 1160(a)] or 245A(a)(1) [8 U.S.C.A. § 1255a(a)(1)], is admitted as a refugee under section 207 [8 U.S.C.A. § 1157], or is granted asylum under section 208 [8 U.S.C.A. § 1158]; but does not include **(i)** an alien who fails to apply for naturalization within six months of the date the alien first becomes eligible (by virtue of period of lawful permanent residence) to apply for naturalization or, if later, within six months after November 6, 1986 and **(ii)** an alien who has applied on a timely basis, but has not been naturalized as a citizen within 2 years after the date of the application, unless the alien can establish that the alien is actively pursuing naturalization, except that time consumed in the Service's processing the application shall not be counted toward the 2-year period.

(4) Additional exception providing right to prefer equally qualified citizens

Notwithstanding any other provision of this section, it is not an unfair immigration-related employment practice for a person or other entity to prefer to hire, recruit, or refer an individual who is a citizen or national of the United States over another individual who is an alien if the two individuals are equally qualified.

(5) Prohibition of intimidation or retaliation

It is also an unfair immigration-related employment practice for a person or other entity to intimidate, threaten, coerce, or retaliate against any individual for the purpose of interfering with any right or privilege secured under this section or because the individual intends to file or has filed a charge or a complaint, testified, assisted, or participated in any manner in an investigation, proceeding, or hearing under this section. An individual so intimidated, threatened, coerced, or retaliated against shall be considered, for purposes of subsections (d) and (g), to have been discriminated against.

417

(6) Treatment of certain documentary practices as employment practices

A person's or other entity's request, for purposes of satisfying the requirements of section 274A(b) [8 U.S.C.A. § 1324a(b)], for more or different documents than are required under such section or refusing to honor documents tendered that on their face reasonably appear to be genuine shall be treated as an unfair immigration-related employment practice if made for the purpose or with the intent of discriminating against an individual in violation of paragraph (1).

(b) Charges of violations

(1) In general

Except as provided in paragraph (2), any person alleging that the person is adversely affected directly by an unfair immigration-related employment practice (or a person on that person's behalf) or an officer of the Service alleging that an unfair immigration-related employment practice has occurred or is occurring may file a charge respecting such practice or violation with the Special Counsel (appointed under subsection (c)). Charges shall be in writing under oath or affirmation and shall contain such information as the Attorney General requires. The Special Counsel by certified mail shall serve a notice of the charge (including the date, place, and circumstances of the alleged unfair immigration-related employment practice) on the person or entity involved within 10 days.

(2) No overlap with EEOC complaints

No charge may be filed respecting an unfair immigration-related employment practice described in subsection (a)(1)(A) if a charge with respect to that practice based on the same set of facts has been filed with the Equal Employment Opportunity Commission under title VII of the Civil Rights Act of 1964 [42 U.S.C.A. § 2000e et seq.], unless the charge is dismissed as being outside the scope of such title. No charge respecting an employment practice may be filed with the Equal Employment Opportunity Commission under such title if a charge with respect to such practice based on the same set of facts has been filed under this subsection, unless the charge is dismissed under this section as being outside the scope of this section.

(c) Special Counsel

(1) Appointment

The President shall appoint, by and with the advice and consent of the Senate, a Special Counsel for Immigration-Related Unfair Employment Practices (hereinafter in this section referred to as the "Special Counsel") within the Department of Justice to serve for a term of four years. In the case of a vacancy in the office of the Special Counsel the President may designate the officer or employee who shall act as Special Counsel during such vacancy.

(2) Duties

The Special Counsel shall be responsible for investigation of charges and issuance of complaints under this section and in respect of the prosecution of all such complaints before administrative law judges and the exercise of certain functions under subsection (j)(1).

(3) Compensation

The Special Counsel is entitled to receive compensation at a rate not to exceed the rate now or hereafter provided for grade GS–17 of the General Schedule, under section 5332 of Title 5.

(4) Regional offices

The Special Counsel, in accordance with regulations of the Attorney General, shall establish such regional offices as may be necessary to carry out his duties.

(d) Investigation of charges

(1) By Special Counsel

The Special Counsel shall investigate each charge received and, within 120 days of the date of the receipt of the charge, determine whether or not there is reasonable cause to believe that the charge is true and whether nor not to bring a complaint with respect to the charge before an administrative law judge. The Special Counsel may, on his own initiative, conduct investigations respecting unfair immigration-related employment practices and, based on such an investigation and subject to paragraph (3), file a complaint before such a judge.

(2) Private actions

If the Special Counsel, after receiving such a charge respecting an unfair immigration-related employment practice which alleges knowing and intentional discriminatory activity or a pattern or practice of discriminatory activity, has not filed a complaint before an administrative law judge with respect to such charge within such 120-day period, the Special Counsel shall notify the person making the charge of the determination not to file such a complaint during such period and the person making the charge may (subject to paragraph (3)) file a complaint directly before such a judge within 90 days after the date of receipt of the notice. The Special Counsel's failure to file such a complaint within such 120-day period shall not affect the right of the Special Counsel to investigate the charge or to bring a complaint before an administrative law judge during such 90-day period.

(3) Time limitations on complaints

No complaint may be filed respecting any unfair immigration-related employment practice occurring more than 180 days prior to the date of the filing of the charge with the Special Counsel. This subparagraph shall not prevent the subsequent amending of a charge or complaint under subsection (e)(1).

(e) Hearings

(1) Notice

Whenever a complaint is made that a person or entity has engaged in or is engaging in any such unfair immigration-related employment practice, an administrative law judge shall have power to issue and cause to be served upon such person or entity a copy of the complaint and a notice of hearing before the judge at a place therein fixed, not less than five days after the serving of the complaint. Any such complaint may be amended by the judge conducting the hearing, upon the motion of the party filing the complaint, in the judge's discretion at any time prior to the issuance of an order based thereon. The person or entity so complained of shall have the right to file an answer to the original or amended complaint and to appear in person or otherwise and give testimony at the place and time fixed in the complaint.

(2) Judges hearing cases

Hearings on complaints under this subsection shall be considered before administrative law judges who are specially designated by the Attorney General as having special training respecting employment discrimination and, to the extent practicable, before such judges who only consider cases under this section.

(3) Complainant as party

Any person filing a charge with the Special Counsel respecting an unfair immigration-related employment practice shall be considered a party to any complaint before an administrative law judge respecting such practice and any subsequent appeal respecting that complaint. In the discretion of the judge conducting the hearing, any other person may be allowed to intervene in the proceeding and to present testimony.

(f) Testimony and authority of hearing officers

(1) Testimony

The testimony taken by the administrative law judge shall be reduced to writing. Thereafter, the judge, in his discretion, upon notice may provide for the taking of further testimony or hear argument.

(2) Authority of administrative law judges

In conducting investigations and hearings under this subsection and in accordance with regulations of the Attorney General, the Special Counsel and administrative law judges shall have reasonable access to examine evidence of any person or entity being investigated. The administrative law judges by subpoena may compel the attendance of witnesses and the production of evidence at any designated place or hearing. In case of contumacy or refusal to obey a subpoena lawfully issued under this paragraph and upon application of the administrative law judge, an appropriate district court of the United States may issue an order requiring compliance with such subpoena and any failure to obey such order may be punished by such court as a contempt thereof.

(g) Determinations

(1) Order

The administrative law judge shall issue and cause to be served on the parties to the proceeding an order, which shall be final unless appealed as provided under subsection (i).

(2) Orders finding violations

(A) In general

If, upon the preponderance of the evidence, an administrative law judge determines that any person or entity named in the complaint has engaged in or is engaging in any such unfair immigration-related employment practice, then the judge shall state his findings of fact and shall issue and cause to be served on such person or entity an order which requires such person or entity to cease and desist from such unfair immigration-related employment practice.

(B) Contents of order

Such an order also may require the person or entity—

(i) to comply with the requirements of section 274A(b) [8 U.S.C.A. § 1324a(b)] with respect to individuals hired (or recruited or referred for employment for a fee) during a period of up to three years;

(ii) to retain for the period referred to in clause (i) and only for purposes consistent with section 274A(b)(5) [8 U.S.C.A. § 1324a(b)(5)], the name and address of each individual who applies, in person or in writing, for hiring for an existing position, or for recruiting or referring for a fee, for employment in the United States;

(iii) to hire individuals directly and adversely affected, with or without back pay;

(iv)(I) except as provided in subclauses (III) through (IV), to pay a civil penalty of not less than $250 and not more than $2,000 for each individual discriminated against,

(II) except as provided in subclauses (III) and (IV), in the case of a person or entity previously subject to a single order under this paragraph, to pay a civil penalty of not less than $2,000 and not more than $5,000 for each individual discriminated against,

(III) except as provided in subclause (IV), in the case of a person or entity previously subject to more than one order under this paragraph, to pay a civil penalty of not less than $3,000 and not more than $10,000 for each individual discriminated against, and

(IV) in the case of an unfair immigration-related employment practice described in subsection (a)(6) of this section, to pay a civil penalty of not less than $100 and not more than $1,000 for each individual discriminated against;

(v) to post notices to employees about their rights under this section and employers' obligations under section 274A [8 U.S.C.A. § 1324a];

(vi) to educate all personnel involved in hiring and complying with this section or section 274A [8 U.S.C.A. § 1324a] about the requirements of this section or such section;

(vii) to remove (in an appropriate case) a false performance review or false warning from an employee's personnel file; and

(viii) to lift (in an appropriate case) any restrictions on an employee's assignments, work shifts, or movements.

(C) Limitation on back pay remedy

In providing a remedy under subparagraph (B)(iii), back pay liability shall not accrue from a date more than two years prior to the date of the filing of a charge with the Special Counsel. Interim earnings or amounts earnable with reasonable diligence by the individual or individuals discriminated against shall operate to reduce the back pay otherwise allowable under such subparagraph. No order shall require the hiring of an individual as an employee or the payment to an individual of any back pay, if the individual was refused employment for any reason other than discrimination on account of national origin or citizenship status.

(D) Treatment of distinct entities

In applying this subsection in the case of a person or entity composed of distinct, physically separate subdivisions each of which provides separately for the hiring, recruiting, or referring for employment, without reference to the practices of, and not under the control of or common control with, another subdivision, each such subdivision shall be considered a separate person or entity.

(3) Orders not finding violations

If upon the preponderance of the evidence an administrative law judge determines that the person or entity named in the complaint has not engaged and is not engaging in any such unfair immigration-related employment practice, then the judge shall state his findings of fact and shall issue an order dismissing the complaint.

(h) Awarding of attorney's fees

In any complaint respecting an unfair immigration-related employment practice, an administrative law judge, in the judge's discretion, may allow a prevailing party, other than the United States, a reasonable attorney's fee, if the losing party's argument is without reasonable foundation in law and fact.

(i) Review of final orders

(1) In general

Not later than 60 days after the entry of such final order, any person aggrieved by such final order may seek a review of such order in the United States court of appeals for the circuit in which the violation is alleged to have occurred or in which the employer resides or transacts business.

(2) Further review

Upon the filing of the record with the court, the jurisdiction of the court shall be exclusive and its judgment shall be final, except that the same shall be subject to review by the Supreme Court of the United States upon writ of certiorari or certification as provided in section 1254 of Title 28.

(j) Court enforcement of administrative orders

(1) In general

If an order of the agency is not appealed under subsection (i)(1), the Special Counsel (or, if the Special Counsel fails to act, the person filing the charge) may petition the United States district court for the district in which a violation of the order is alleged to have occurred, or in which the respondent resides or transacts business, for the enforcement of the order of the administrative law judge, by filing in such court a written petition praying that such order be enforced.

(2) Court enforcement order

Upon the filing of such petition, the court shall have jurisdiction to make and enter a decree enforcing the order of the administrative law judge. In such a proceeding, the order of the administrative law judge shall not be subject to review.

(3) Enforcement decree in original review

If, upon appeal of an order under subsection (i)(1), the United States court of appeals does not reverse such order, such court shall have the jurisdiction to make and enter a decree enforcing the order of the administrative law judge.

(4) Awarding of attorney's fees

In any judicial proceeding under subsection (i) or this subsection, the court, in its discretion, may allow a prevailing party, other than the United States, a reasonable attorney's fee as part of costs but only if the losing party's argument is without reasonable foundation in law and fact.

(k) Termination dates

(1) This section shall not apply to discrimination in hiring, recruiting, referring, or discharging of individuals occurring after the date of any termination of the provisions of section 274A [8 U.S.C.A. § 1324a], under subsection (*l*) of that section.

(2) The provisions of this section shall terminate 30 calendar days after receipt of the last report required to be transmitted under section 274A(i) [8 U.S.C.A. § 1324a(i)] if—

(A) the Comptroller General determines, and so reports in such report that—

(i) no significant discrimination has resulted, against citizens or nationals of the United States or against any eligible workers seeking employment, from the implementation of section 274A [8 U.S.C.A. § 1324a], or

(ii) such section has created an unreasonable burden on employers hiring such workers; and

(B) there has been enacted, within such period of 30 calendar days, a joint resolution stating in substance that the Congress approves the findings of the Comptroller General contained in such report.

The provisions of subsections (m) and (n) of section 274A [8 U.S.C.A. § 1324a] shall apply to any joint resolution under subparagraph (B) in the same manner as they apply to a joint resolution under subsection (*l*) of such section.

(*l*) Dissemination of information concerning anti-discrimination provisions

(1) Not later than 3 months after November 29, 1990, the Special Counsel, in cooperation with the chairman of the Equal Employment Opportunity Commission, the Secretary of Labor, and the Administrator of the Small Business Administration, shall conduct a campaign to disseminate information respecting the rights and remedies prescribed under this section and under title VII of the Civil Rights Act of 1964 [42 U.S.C.A. § 2000e et seq.] in connection with unfair immigration-related employment practices. Such campaign shall be aimed at increasing the knowledge of employers, employees, and the general public concerning employer and employee rights, responsibilities, and remedies under this section and such title.

(2) In order to carry out the campaign under this subsection, the Special Counsel—

(A) may, to the extent deemed appropriate and subject to the availability of appropriations, contract with public and private organizations for outreach activities under the campaign, and

(B) shall consult with the Secretary of Labor, the chairman of the Equal Employment Opportunity Commission, and the heads of such other agencies as may be appropriate.

(3) There are authorized to be appropriated to carry out this subsection $10,000,000 for each fiscal year (beginning with fiscal year 1991).

(June 27, 1952, c. 477, Title II, ch. 8, § 274B, as added Nov. 6, 1986, Pub.L. 99–603, Title I, 102(a), 100 Stat. 3374, and amended Oct. 24, 1988, Pub.L. 100–525, § 2(b), 102 Stat.

2610; Nov. 29, 1990, Pub.L. 101–649, Title V, §§ 531, 532(a), 533(a), 534(a), 535(a), 536(a), 537(a), 539(a), 104 Stat. 5054, 5055, 5056; Dec. 12, 1991, Pub.L. 102–232, Title III, § 306(b) (1),(3),(c)(1), 105 Stat. 1752; Oct. 25, 1994, Pub.L. 103–416, Title II, § 219(q), 108 Stat. 4317; Sept. 30, 1996, Pub.L. 104–208, Div. C, Title IV, § 421(a), Title VI, § 671(d)(1)(B), 110 Stat. 3009–670, 3009–723.)

§ 274C. Penalties for document fraud [8 U.S.C.A. § 1324c]

(a) Activities prohibited

It is unlawful for any person or entity knowingly—

(1) to forge, counterfeit, alter, or falsely make any document for the purpose of satisfying a requirement of this Act or to obtain a benefit under this Act,

(2) to use, attempt to use, possess, obtain, accept, or receive or to provide any forged, counterfeit, altered, or falsely made document in order to satisfy any requirement of this Act or to obtain a benefit under this Act,

(3) to use or attempt to use or to provide or attempt to provide any document lawfully issued to or with respect to a person other than the possessor (including a deceased individual) for the purpose of satisfying a requirement of this Act or obtaining a benefit under this Act,

(4) to accept or receive or to provide any document lawfully issued to or with respect to a person other than the possessor (including a deceased individual) for the purpose of complying with section 274A(b) [8 U.S.C.A. § 1324a(b)] or obtaining a benefit under this Act, or

(5) to prepare, file, or assist another in preparing or filing, any application for benefits under this Act, or any document required under this Act, or any document submitted in connection with such application or document, with knowledge or in reckless disregard of the fact that such application or document was falsely made or, in whole or in part, does not relate to the person on whose behalf it was or is being submitted, or

(6) (A) to present before boarding a common carrier for the purpose of coming to the United States a document which relates to the alien's eligibility to enter the United States, and (B) to fail to present such document to an immigration officer upon arrival at a United States port of entry.

(b) Exception

This section does not prohibit any lawfully authorized investigative, protective, or intelligence activity of a law enforcement agency of the United States, a State, or a subdivision of a State, or of an intelligence agency of the United States, or any activity authorized under chapter 224 of Title 18.

(c) Construction

Nothing in this section shall be construed to diminish or qualify any of the penalties available for activities prohibited by this section but proscribed as well in Title 18.

(d) Enforcement

(1) Authority in investigations

In conducting investigations and hearings under this subsection—

(A) immigration officers and administrative law judges shall have reasonable access to examine evidence of any person or entity being investigated,

(B) administrative law judges, may, if necessary, compel by subpoena the attendance of witnesses and the production of evidence at any designated place or hearing, and

(C) immigration officers designated by the Commissioner may compel by subpoena the attendance of witnesses and the production of evidence at any designated place prior to the filing of a complaint in a case under paragraph (2).

In case of contumacy or refusal to obey a subpoena lawfully issued under this paragraph and upon application of the Attorney General, an appropriate district court of the United States may issue an order requiring compliance with such subpoena and any failure to obey such order may be punished by such court as a contempt thereof.

(2) Hearing

(A) In general

Before imposing an order described in paragraph (3) against a person or entity under this subsection for a violation of subsection (a), the Attorney General shall provide the person or entity with notice and, upon request made within a reasonable time (of not less than 30 days, as established by the Attorney General) of the date of the notice, a hearing respecting the violation.

(B) Conduct of hearing

Any hearing so requested shall be conducted before an administrative law judge. The hearing shall be conducted in accordance with the requirements of section 554 of Title 5. The hearing shall be held at the nearest practicable place to the place where the person or entity resides or of the place where the alleged violation occurred. If no hearing is so requested, the Attorney General's imposition of the order shall constitute a final and unappealable order.

(C) Issuance of orders

If the administrative law judge determines, upon the preponderance of the evidence received, that a person or entity has violated subsection (a), the administrative law judge shall state his findings

426

of fact and issue and cause to be served on such person or entity an order described in paragraph (3).

(3) Cease and desist order with civil money penalty

With respect to a violation of subsection (a), the order under this subsection shall require the person or entity to cease and desist from such violations and to pay a civil penalty in an amount of—

(A) not less than $250 and not more than $2,000 for each document that is the subject of a violation under subsection (a), or

(B) in the case of a person or entity previously subject to an order under this paragraph, not less than $2,000 and not more than $5,000 for each document that is the subject of a violation under subsection (a).

In applying this subsection in the case of a person or entity composed of distinct, physically separate subdivisions each of which provides separately for the hiring, recruiting, or referring for employment, without reference to the practices of, and not under the control of or common control with, another subdivision, each such subdivision shall be considered a separate person or entity.

(4) Administrative appellate review

The decision and order of an administrative law judge shall become the final agency decision and order of the Attorney General unless either **(A)** within 30 days, an official delegated by regulation to exercise review authority over the decision and order modifies or vacates the decision and order, or **(B)** within 30 days of the date of such a modification or vacation (or within 60 days of the date of decision and order of an administrative law judge if not so modified or vacated) the decision and order is referred to the Attorney General pursuant to regulations, in which case the decision and order of the Attorney General shall become the final agency decision and order under this subsection.

(5) Judicial review

A person or entity adversely affected by a final order under this section may, within 45 days after the date the final order is issued, file a petition in the Court of Appeals for the appropriate circuit for review of the order.

(6) Enforcement of orders

If a person or entity fails to comply with a final order issued under this section against the person or entity, the Attorney General shall file a suit to seek compliance with the order in any appropriate district court of the United States. In any such suit, the validity and appropriateness of the final order shall not be subject to review.

(7) Waiver by Attorney General

The Attorney General may waive the penalties imposed by this section with respect to an alien who knowingly violates subsection (a)(6)

if the alien is granted asylum under section 208 [8 U.S.C.A. § 1158] or withholding of removal under section 241(b)(3) [8 U.S.C.A. § 1231(b)(3)].

(e) Criminal penalties for failure to disclose role as document preparer

(1) Whoever, in any matter within the jurisdiction of the Service, knowingly and willfully fails to disclose, conceals, or covers up the fact that they have, on behalf of any person and for a fee or other remuneration, prepared or assisted in preparing an application which was falsely made (as defined in subsection (f)) for immigration benefits, shall be fined in accordance with Title 18, imprisoned for not more than 5 years, or both, and prohibited from preparing or assisting in preparing, whether or not for a fee or other remuneration, any other such application.

(2) Whoever, having been convicted of a violation of paragraph (1), knowingly and willfully prepares or assists in preparing an application for immigration benefits pursuant to this Act, or the regulations promulgated thereunder, whether or not for a fee or other remuneration and regardless of whether in any matter within the jurisdiction of the Service, shall be fined in accordance with Title 18, imprisoned for not more than 15 years, or both, and prohibited from preparing or assisting in preparing any other such application.

(f) Falsely make

For purposes of this section, the term "falsely make" means to prepare or provide an application or document, with knowledge or in reckless disregard of the fact that the application or document contains a false, fictitious, or fraudulent statement or material representation, or has no basis in law or fact, or otherwise fails to state a fact which is material to the purpose for which it was submitted.

(June 27, 1952, c. 477, Title II, ch. 8, § 274C, as added Nov. 29, 1990, Pub.L. 101–649, Title V, § 544(a), 104 Stat. 5059, and amended Dec. 12, 1991, Pub.L. 102–232, Title III, § 306(c)(5)(A), 105 Stat. 1752; Oct. 25, 1994, Pub.L. 103–416, Title II, § 219(r), 108 Stat. 4317; Sept. 30, 1996, Pub.L. 104–208, Div. C, Title II, §§ 212(a) to (d), 213, 220, Title III, §§ 308(g)(10)(D), 379(a), 110 Stat. 3009–570, 3009–571, 3009–575, 3009–625, 3009–649.)

§ 274D. Civil penalties for failure to depart [8 U.S.C.A. § 1324d]

(a) In general

Any alien subject to a final order of removal who—

(1) willfully fails or refuses to—

(A) depart from the United States pursuant to the order,

(B) make timely application in good faith for travel or other documents necessary for departure, or

(C) present for removal at the time and place required by the Attorney General; or

(2) conspires to or takes any action designed to prevent or hamper the alien's departure pursuant to the order,

shall pay a civil penalty of not more than $500 to the Commissioner for each day the alien is in violation of this section.

(b) Construction

Nothing in this section shall be construed to diminish or qualify any penalties to which an alien may be subject for activities proscribed by section 243(a) [8 U.S.C.A. § 1253(a)] or any other section of this Act.

(June 27, 1952, c. 477, Title II, ch. 8, § 274D, as added Sept. 30, 1996, Pub.L. 104–208, Div. C, Title III, § 380(a), 110 Stat. 3009–650.)

§ 275.   Improper entry by alien [8 U.S.C.A. § 1325]

(a) Improper time or place; avoidance of examination or inspection; misrepresentation and concealment of facts

Any alien who **(1)** enters or attempts to enter the United States at any time or place other than as designated by immigration officers, or **(2)** eludes examination or inspection by immigration officers, or **(3)** attempts to enter or obtains entry to the United States by a willfully false or misleading representation or the willful concealment of a material fact, shall, for the first commission of any such offense, be fined under Title 18 or imprisoned not more than 6 months, or both, and, for a subsequent commission of any such offense, be fined under Title 18, or imprisoned not more than 2 years, or both.

(b) Civil penalty for illegal entry

Any alien who is apprehended while entering (or attempting to enter) the United States at a time or place other than as designated by immigration officers shall be subject to a civil penalty of—

(1) at least $50 and not more than $250 for each such entry (or attempted entry); or

(2) twice the amount specified in paragraph (1) in the case of an alien who has been previously subject to a civil penalty under this subsection.

Civil penalties under this subsection are in addition to, and not in lieu of, any criminal or other civil penalties that may be imposed.

(c) Marriage fraud

Any individual who knowingly enters into a marriage for the purpose of evading any provision of the immigration laws shall be imprisoned for not more than 5 years, or fined not more than $250,000, or both.

(d) Immigration-related entrepreneurship fraud

Any individual who knowingly establishes a commercial enterprise for the purpose of evading any provision of the immigration laws shall be imprisoned for not more than 5 years, fined in accordance with Title 18, or both.

(June 27, 1952, c. 477, Title II, ch. 8, § 275, 66 Stat. 229; Nov. 10, 1986, Pub.L. 99–639, § 2(d), 100 Stat. 3542; Nov. 29, 1990, Pub.L. 101–649, Title I, § 121(b)(3), Title V, § 543(b)(2), 104 Stat. 4994, 5059; Dec. 12, 1991, Pub.L. 102–232, Title III, § 306(c)(3), 105 Stat. 1752; Sept. 30, 1996, Pub.L. 104–208, Div C, Title I, § 105(a), 110 Stat. 3009–556.)

§ 276. Reentry of deported alien; criminal penalties for reentry of certain deported aliens [8 U.S.C.A. § 1326]

(a) Subject to subsection (b), any alien who—

(1) has been denied admission, excluded, deported, or removed or has departed the United States while an order of exclusion, deportation, or removal is outstanding, and thereafter

(2) enters, attempts to enter, or is at any time found in, the United States, unless **(A)** prior to his reembarkation at a place outside the United States or his application for admission from foreign contiguous territory, the Attorney General has expressly consented to such alien's reapplying for admission; or **(B)** with respect to an alien previously denied admission and removed, unless such alien shall establish that he was not required to obtain such advance consent under this or any prior Act,

shall be fined under Title 18, or imprisoned not more than 2 years, or both.

(b) Notwithstanding subsection (a), in the case of any alien described in such subsection—

(1) whose removal was subsequent to a conviction for commission of three or more misdemeanors involving drugs, crimes against the person, or both, or a felony (other than an aggravated felony), such alien shall be fined under Title 18, imprisoned not more than 10 years, or both;

(2) whose removal was subsequent to a conviction for commission of an aggravated felony, such alien shall be fined under such Title, imprisoned not more than 20 years, or both;

(3) who has been excluded from the United States pursuant to section 235(c) [8 U.S.C.A. § 1225(c)] because the alien was excludable under section 212(a)(3)(B) [8 U.S.C.A. § 1182(a)(3)(B)] or who has been removed from the United States pursuant to the provisions of title V, and who thereafter, without the permission of the Attorney General, enters the United States, or attempts to do so, shall be fined under Title 18, and imprisoned for a period of 10 years, which sentence shall not run concurrently with any other sentence; or

(4) who was removed from the United States pursuant to section 241(a)(4)(B) [8 U.S.C.A. § 1231(a)(4)(B)] who thereafter, without the permission of the Attorney General, enters, attempts to enter, or is at any time found in, the United States (unless the Attorney General has expressly consented to such alien's reentry) shall be fined under Title 18, imprisoned for not more than 10 years, or both.

For the purposes of this subsection, the term "removal" includes any agreement in which an alien stipulates to removal during (or not during) a criminal trial under either Federal or State law.

(c) Any alien deported pursuant to section 242(h)(2) [8 U.S.C.A. § 1252(h)(2)]* who enters, attempts to enter, or is at any time found in, the United States (unless the Attorney General has expressly consented to such alien's reentry) shall be incarcerated for the remainder of the sentence of imprisonment which was pending at the time of deportation without any reduction for parole or supervised release. Such alien shall be subject to such other penalties relating to the reentry of deported aliens as may be available under this section or any other provision of law.

(d) In a criminal proceeding under this section, an alien may not challenge the validity of the deportation order described in subsection (a)(1) or subsection (b) unless the alien demonstrates that—

(1) the alien exhausted any administrative remedies that may have been available to seek relief against the order;

(2) the deportation proceedings at which the order was issued improperly deprived the alien of the opportunity for judicial review; and

(3) the entry of the order was fundamentally unfair.

(June 27, 1952, c. 477, Title II, ch. 8, § 276, 66 Stat. 229; Nov. 18, 1988, Pub.L. 100–690, Title VII, § 7345(a), 102 Stat. 4471; Nov. 29, 1990, Pub.L. 101–649, Title V, § 543(b)(3), 104 Stat. 5059; Sept. 13, 1994, Pub.L. 103–322, Title XIII, § 130001(b), 108 Stat. 2023; Apr. 24, 1996, Pub.L. 104–132, Title IV, §§ 401(c), 438(b), 441(a), 110 Stat. 1267, 1276, 1279; Sept. 30, 1996, Pub.L. 104–208, Div. C, Title III, §§ 305(b), 308(d)(4)(J), (e)(1)(K), (14)(A), 324(a), (b), 110 Stat. 3009–606, 3009–618, 3009–619, 3009–620, 3009–629.)

§ 277. Aiding or assisting certain aliens to enter [8 U.S.C.A. § 1327]

Any person who knowingly aids or assists any alien inadmissible under section 212(a)(2) [8 U.S.C.A. § 1182(a)(2)] (insofar as an alien inadmissible under such section has been convicted of an aggravated felony) or 212(a)(3) [8 U.S.C.A. § 1182(a)(3)] (other than subparagraph (E) thereof) to enter the United States, or who connives or conspires with any person or persons to allow, procure, or permit any such alien to enter the United States, shall be fined under Title 18, or imprisoned not more than 10 years, or both.

(June 27, 1952, c. 477, Title II, ch. 8, § 277, 66 Stat. 229; Nov. 18, 1988, Pub.L. 100–690, Title VII, § 7346(a), (c)(1), 102 Stat. 4471; Nov. 29, 1990, Pub.L. 101–649, Title V, § 543(b)

* Section 242 does not contain a subsec. (h). For provisions similar to those contained in former section 242(h), see section 241(a)(4).

(4), Title VI, § 603(a)(16), 104 Stat. 5059, 5084; Sept. 30, 1996, Pub.L. 104–208, Div. C, Title III, § 308(d)(3)(A), 110 Stat. 3009–617.)

§ 278.   Importation of alien for immoral purpose [8 U.S.C.A. § 1328]

The importation into the United States of any alien for the purpose of prostitution, or for any other immoral purpose, is forbidden. Whoever shall, directly or indirectly, import, or attempt to import into the United States any alien for the purpose of prostitution or for any other immoral purpose, or shall hold or attempt to hold any alien for any such purpose in pursuance of such illegal importation, or shall keep, maintain, control, support, employ, or harbor in any house or other place, for the purpose of prostitution or for any other immoral purpose, any alien, in pursuance of such illegal importation, shall be fined under Title 18, or imprisoned not more than 10 years, or both. The trial and punishment of offenses under this section may be in any district to or into which such alien is brought in pursuance of importation by the person or persons accused, or in any district in which a violation of any of the provisions of this section occurs. In all prosecutions under this section, the testimony of a husband or wife shall be admissible and competent evidence against each other.

(June 27, 1952, c. 477, Title II, ch. 8, § 278, 66 Stat. 230; Nov. 29, 1990, Pub.L. 101–649, Title V, § 543(b)(5), 104 Stat. 5059.)

§ 279.   Jurisdiction of district courts [8 U.S.C.A. § 1329]

The district courts of the United States shall have jurisdiction of all causes, civil and criminal, brought by the United States that arise under the provisions of this title. It shall be the duty of the United States attorney of the proper district to prosecute every such suit when brought by the United States. Notwithstanding any other law, such prosecutions or suits may be instituted at any place in the United States at which the violation may occur or at which the person charged with a violation under section 275 [8 U.S.C.A. § 1325] or 276 [8 U.S.C.A. § 1326] may be apprehended. No suit or proceeding for a violation of any of the provisions of this title shall be settled, compromised, or discontinued without the consent of the court in which it is pending and any such settlement, compromise, or discontinuance shall be entered of record with the reasons therefor. Nothing in this section shall be construed as providing jurisdiction for suits against the United States or its agencies or officers.

(June 27, 1952, c. 477, Title II, ch. 8, § 279, 66 Stat. 230; Sept. 30, 1996, Pub.L. 104–208, Div. C, Title III, § 381(a), 110 Stat. 3009–650.)

§ 280.   Collection of penalties and expenses [8 U.S.C.A. § 1330]

(a) Notwithstanding any other provisions of this title, the withholding or denial of clearance of or a lien upon any vessel or aircraft provided for in section 231 [8 U.S.C.A. § 1221], 234 [8 U.S.C.A. § 1224], 243(c)(2) [8 U.S.C.A. § 1253(c)(2)], 251 [8 U.S.C.A. § 1281], 253 [8 U.S.C.A. § 1283], 254 [8 U.S.C.A. § 1284], 255 [8 U.S.C.A. § 1285], 256 [8 U.S.C.A. § 1286], 271 [8 U.S.C.A. § 1321], 272 [8 U.S.C.A. § 1322], or 273 [8 U.S.C.A. § 1323] shall not be regarded as the sole and exclusive means or remedy for the enforcement of payments of any fine, penalty or expenses imposed or incurred under such sections, but, in the discretion of the Attorney General, the amount thereof may be recovered by civil suit, in the name of the United States, from any person made liable under any of such sections.

(b)(1) There is established in the general fund of the Treasury a separate account which shall be known as the "Immigration Enforcement Account". Notwithstanding any other section of this title, there shall be deposited as offsetting receipts into the Immigration Enforcement Account amounts described in paragraph (2) to remain available until expended.

(2) The amounts described in this paragraph are the following:

(A) The increase in penalties collected resulting from the amendments made by sections 203(b) and 543(a) of the Immigration Act of 1990.

(B) Civil penalties collected under sections 240B(d) [8 U.S.C.A. § 1229c(d)], 274C [8 U.S.C.A. § 1324c], 274D [8 U.S.C.A. § 1324d], and 275(b) [8 U.S.C.A. § 1325(b)].

(3)(A) The Secretary of the Treasury shall refund out of the Immigration Enforcement Account to any appropriation the amount paid out of such appropriation for expenses incurred by the Attorney General for activities that enhance enforcement of provisions of this title. Such activities include—

(i) the identification, investigation, apprehension, detention, and removal of criminal aliens;

(ii) the maintenance and updating of a system to identify and track criminal aliens, deportable aliens, inadmissible aliens, and aliens illegally entering the United States; and

(iii) for the repair, maintenance, or construction on the United States border, in areas experiencing high levels of apprehensions of illegal aliens, of structures to deter illegal entry into the United States.

(B) The amounts which are required to be refunded under subparagraph (A) shall be refunded at least quarterly on the basis of estimates made by the Attorney General of the expenses referred to in subparagraph (A). Proper adjustments shall be made in the amounts subsequently refunded under subparagraph (A) to the extent prior estimates were in excess of, or less than, the amount required to be refunded under subparagraph (A).

(C) The amounts required to be refunded from the Immigration Enforcement Account for fiscal year 1996 and thereafter shall be refunded in accordance with estimates made in the budget request of the Attorney

General for those fiscal years. Any proposed changes in the amounts designated in such budget requests shall only be made after notification to the Committees on Appropriations of the House of Representatives and the Senate in accordance with section 605 of Public Law 104–134.

(D) The Attorney General shall prepare and submit annually to the Congress statements of financial condition of the Immigration Enforcement Account, including beginning account balance, revenues, withdrawals, and ending account balance and projection for the ensuing fiscal year.

(June 27, 1952, c. 477, Title II, ch. 8, § 280, 66 Stat. 230; Nov. 29, 1990, Pub.L. 101–649, Title V, § 542(a), 104 Stat. 5057; Oct. 25, 1994, Pub.L. 103–416, Title II, § 219(s), 108 Stat. 4317; Sept. 30, 1996, Pub.L. 104–208, Div. C, Title III, §§ 308(g)(4)(C), 382(a), 110 Stat. 3009–623, 3009–651; Pub.L. 113–235, Div. H, Title I, § 1301(d), Dec. 16, 2014, 128 Stat. 2537.)

CHAPTER IX. MISCELLANEOUS

§ 281.   Nonimmigrant visa fees [8 U.S.C.A. § 1351]

The fees for the furnishing and verification of applications for visas by nonimmigrants of each foreign country and for the issuance of visas to nonimmigrants of each foreign country shall be prescribed by the Secretary of State, if practicable, in amounts corresponding to the total of all visa, entry, residence, or other similar fees, taxes, or charges assessed or levied against nationals of the United States by the foreign countries of which such nonimmigrants are nationals or stateless residents: *Provided,* That nonimmigrant visas issued to aliens coming to the United States in transit to and from the headquarters district of the United Nations in accordance with the provisions of the Headquarters Agreement shall be gratis. Subject to such criteria as the Secretary of State may prescribe, including the duration of stay of the alien and the financial burden upon the charitable organization, the Secretary of State shall waive or reduce the fee for application and issuance of a nonimmigrant visa for any alien coming to the United States primarily for, or in activities related to, a charitable purpose involving health or nursing care, the provision of food or housing, job training, or any other similar direct service or assistance to poor or otherwise needy individuals in the United States.

(June 27, 1952, c. 477, Title II, ch. 9, § 281, 66 Stat. 230; Oct. 3, 1965, Pub. L. 89–236, § 14, 79 Stat. 919; Oct. 21, 1968, Pub. L. 90–609, § 1, 82 Stat. 1199; Oct. 6, 1997, Pub.L. 105–54, § 2(a), 111 Stat. 1175.)

§ 282.   Printing of reentry permits and blank forms of manifest and crew lists; sale to public [8 U.S.C.A. § 1352]

(a) Reentry permits issued under section 223 [8 U.S.C.A. § 1203] shall be printed on distinctive safety paper and shall be prepared and issued under regulations prescribed by the Attorney General.

(b) The Director of the Government Publishing Office is authorized to print for sale to the public by the Superintendent of Documents, upon prepayment, copies of blank forms of manifests and crew lists and such other forms as may be prescribed and authorized by the Attorney General to be sold pursuant to the provisions of this title.

(June 27, 1952, c. 477, Title II, ch. 9, § 282, 66 Stat. 231; Pub.L. 113–235, Div. H, Title I, § 1301(d), Dec. 16, 2014, 128 Stat. 2537.)

§ 283. Travel expenses and expense of transporting remains of officers and employees dying outside of United States [8 U.S.C.A. § 1353]

When officers, inspectors, or other employees of the Service are ordered to perform duties in a foreign country, or are transferred from one station to another, in the United States or in a foreign country, or while performing duties in any foreign country become eligible for voluntary retirement and return to the United States, they shall be allowed their traveling expenses in accordance with such regulations as the Attorney General may deem advisable, and they may also be allowed, within the discretion and under written orders of the Attorney General, the expenses incurred for the transfer of their wives and dependent children, their household effects and other personal property, including the expenses for packing, crating, freight, unpacking, temporary storage, and drayage thereof in accordance with subchapter II of chapter 57 of Title 5. The expense of transporting the remains of such officers, inspectors, or other employees who die while in, or in transit to, a foreign country in the discharge of their official duties, to their former homes in this country for interment, and the ordinary and necessary expenses of such interment and of preparation for shipment, are authorized to be paid on the written order of the Attorney General.

(June 27, 1952, c. 477, Title II, ch. 9, § 283, 66 Stat. 231; Pub.L. 100–525, § 9(p), Oct. 24, 1988, 102 Stat. 2621.)

§ 284. Applicability to members of the armed forces [8 U.S.C.A. § 1354]

(a) Nothing contained in this title shall be construed so as to limit, restrict, deny, or affect the coming into or departure from the United States of an alien member of the Armed Forces of the United States who is in the uniform of, or who bears documents identifying him as a member of, such Armed Forces, and who is coming to or departing from the United States under official orders or permit of such Armed Forces: *Provided,* That nothing contained in this section shall be construed to give to or confer upon any such alien any other privileges, rights, benefits, exemptions, or immunities under this Act, which are not otherwise specifically granted by this Act.

(b) If a person lawfully admitted for permanent residence is the spouse or child of a member of the armed forces of the United States, is authorized to accompany the member and reside abroad with the member pursuant to the member's official orders, and is so accompanying and residing with the member (in marital union if a spouse), then the residence and physical presence of the person abroad shall not be treated as

(1) an abandonment or relinquishment of lawful permanent resident status for purposes of clause (i) of section 101(a)(13)(C) [8 U.S.C.A. § 1101(a)(13)(C)]; or

(2) an absence from the United States for purposes of clause (ii) of such section.

(June 27, 1952, c. 477, Title II, ch. 9, § 284, 66 Stat. 232; Jan. 28, 2008, Pub.L. 110–181, Div. A, Title VI, § 673, 122 Stat. 185.)

§ 285.   Disposal of privileges at immigrant stations; rentals; retail sale; disposition of receipts [8 U.S.C.A. § 1355]

(a) Subject to such conditions and limitations as the Attorney General shall prescribe, all exclusive privileges of exchanging money, transporting passengers or baggage, keeping eating houses, or other like privileges in connection with any United States immigrant station, shall be disposed of to the lowest responsible and capable bidder (other than an alien) in accordance with the provisions of section 5 of Title 41 and for the use of Government property in connection with the exercise of such exclusive privileges a reasonable rental may be charged. The feeding of aliens, or the furnishing of any other necessary service in connection with any United States immigrant station, may be performed by the Service without regard to the foregoing provisions of this subsection if the Attorney General shall find that it would be advantageous to the Government in terms of economy and efficiency. No intoxicating liquors shall be sold at any immigrant station.

(b) Such articles determined by the Attorney General to be necessary to the health and welfare of aliens detained at any immigrant station, when not otherwise readily procurable by such aliens, may be sold at reasonable prices to such aliens through Government canteens operated by the Service, under such conditions and limitations as the Attorney General shall prescribe.

(c) All rentals or other receipts accruing from the disposal of privileges, and all moneys arising from the sale of articles through Service-operated canteens, authorized by this section, shall be covered into the Treasury to the credit of the appropriation for the enforcement of this title.

(June 27, 1952, c. 477, Title II, ch. 9, § 285, 66 Stat. 232.)

§ 286.   Disposition of monies collected under the provisions of this title [8 U.S.C.A. § 1356]

(a) Detention, transportation, hospitalization, and all other expenses of detained aliens; expenses of landing stations

All moneys paid into the Treasury to reimburse the Service for detention, transportation, hospitalization, and all other expenses of detained aliens paid from the appropriation for the enforcement of this Act, and all moneys paid into the Treasury to reimburse the Service for expenses of landing stations referred to in section 233(b) [8 U.S.C.A. § 1223(b)] paid by the Service from the appropriation for the enforcement of this Act, shall be credited to the appropriation for the enforcement of this Act for the fiscal year in which the expenses were incurred.

(b) Purchase of evidence

Moneys expended from appropriations for the Service for the purchase of evidence and subsequently recovered shall be reimbursed to the current appropriation for the Service.

(c) Fees and administrative fines and penalties; exception

Except as otherwise provided in subsection (a) and subsection (b), or in any other provision of this title, all moneys received in payment of fees and administrative fines and penalties under this title shall be covered into the Treasury as miscellaneous receipts: Provided, however, That all fees received from applicants residing in the Virgin Islands of the United States, and in Guam, required to be paid under section 281 [8 U.S.C.A. § 1351], shall be paid over to the Treasury of the Virgin Islands and to the Treasury of Guam, respectively.

(d) Schedule of fees

In addition to any other fee authorized by law, the Attorney General shall charge and collect $7 per individual for the immigration inspection of each passenger arriving at a port of entry in the United States, or for the preinspection of a passenger in a place outside of the United States prior to such arrival, aboard a commercial aircraft or commercial vessel.

(e) Limitations on fees

(1) Except as provided in paragraph (3), no fee shall be charged under subsection (d) for immigration inspection or preinspection provided in connection with the arrival of any passenger, other than aircraft passengers, whose journey originated in the following:

(A) Canada,

(B) Mexico,

(C) a State, territory or possession of the United States, or

(D) any adjacent island (within the meaning of section 101(b)(5) [8 U.S.C.A. § 1101(b)(5)]).

(2) No fee may be charged under subsection (d) with respect to the arrival of any passenger—

(A) who is in transit to a destination outside the United States, and

(B) for whom immigration inspection services are not provided.

437

(3) The Attorney General shall charge and collect $3 per individual for the immigration inspection or pre-inspection of each commercial vessel passenger whose journey originated in the United States or in any place set forth in paragraph (1): Provided, That this requirement shall not apply to immigration inspection at designated ports of entry of passengers arriving by ferry, or by Great Lakes vessels on the Great Lakes and connecting waterways when operating on a regular schedule. For the purposes of this paragraph, the term "ferry" means a vessel, in other than ocean or coastwise service, having provisions only for deck passengers and/or vehicles, operating on a short run on a frequent schedule between two points over the most direct water route, and offering a public service of a type normally attributed to a bridge or tunnel.

(f) Collection

(1) Each person that issues a document or ticket to an individual for transportation by a commercial vessel or commercial aircraft into the United States shall—

(A) collect from that individual the fee charged under subsection (d) at the time the document or ticket is issued; and

(B) identify on that document or ticket the fee charged under subsection (d) as a Federal inspection fee.

(2) If—

(A) a document or ticket for transportation of a passenger into the United States is issued in a foreign country; and

(B) the fee charged under subsection (d) is not collected at the time such document or ticket is issued;

the person providing transportation to such passenger shall collect such fee at the time such passenger departs from the United States and shall provide such passenger a receipt for the payment of such fee.

(3) The person who collects fees under paragraph (1) or (2) shall remit those fees to the Attorney General at any time before the date that is thirty-one days after the close of the calendar quarter in which the fees are collected, except the fourth quarter payment for fees collected from airline passengers shall be made on the date that is ten days before the end of the fiscal year, and the first quarter payment shall include any collections made in the preceding quarter that were not remitted with the previous payment. Regulations issued by the Attorney General under this subsection with respect to the collection of the fees charged under subsection (d) and the remittance of such fees to the Treasury of the United States shall be consistent with the regulations issued by the Secretary of the Treasury for the collection and remittance of the taxes imposed by subchapter C of chapter 33 of Title 26, but only to the extent the regulations issued with respect to such taxes do not conflict with the provisions of this section.

(g) Provision of immigration inspection and preinspection services

Notwithstanding the Act of March 2, 1931, 46 Stat. 1467 [8 U.S.C.A. § 1353b] or any other provision of law, the immigration services required to be provided to passengers upon arrival in the United States on scheduled airline flights shall be adequately provided when needed and at no cost (other than the fees imposed under subsection (d)) to airlines and airline passengers at:

(1) immigration serviced airports, and

(2) places located outside of the United States at which an immigration officer is stationed for the purpose of providing such immigration services.

(h) Disposition of receipts

(1)(A) There is established in the general fund of the Treasury a separate account which shall be known as the "Immigration User Fee Account". Notwithstanding any other section of this title, there shall be deposited as offsetting receipts into the Immigration User Fee Account all fees collected under subsection (d) of this section, to remain available until expended. At the end of each 2-year period, beginning with the creation of this account, the Attorney General, following a public rulemaking with opportunity for notice and comment, shall submit a report to the Congress concerning the status of the account, including any balances therein, and recommend any adjustment in the prescribed fee that may be required to ensure that the receipts collected from the fee charged for the succeeding two years equal, as closely as possible, the cost of providing these services.

(B) Notwithstanding any other provisions of law, all civil fines or penalties collected pursuant to sections 243(c) [8 U.S.C.A. § 1253(c)], 271 [8 U.S.C.A. § 1321], and 273 [8 U.S.C.A. § 1323] and all liquidated damages and expenses collected pursuant to this Act shall be deposited in the Immigration User Fee Account.

(2)(A) The Secretary of the Treasury shall refund out of the Immigration User Fee Account to any appropriation the amount paid out of such appropriation for expenses incurred by the Attorney General in providing immigration inspection and preinspection services for commercial aircraft or vessels and in—

(i) providing overtime immigration inspection services for commercial aircraft or vessels;

(ii) administration of debt recovery, including the establishment and operation of a national collections office;

(iii) expansion, operation and maintenance of information systems for nonimmigrant control and debt collection;

439

(iv) detection of fraudulent documents used by passengers traveling to the United States, including training of, and technical assistance to, commercial airline personnel regarding such detection;

(v) providing detention and removal services for inadmissible aliens arriving on commercial aircraft and vessels and for any alien who is inadmissible under section 212(a) [8 U.S.C.A. § 1182(a)] who has attempted illegal entry into the United States through avoidance of immigration inspection at air or sea ports-of-entry; and

(vi) providing removal and asylum proceedings at air or sea ports-of-entry for inadmissible aliens arriving on commercial aircraft and vessels including immigration removal proceedings resulting from presentation of fraudulent documents and failure to present documentation and for any alien who is inadmissible under section 212(a) [8 U.S.C.A. § 1182(a)] who has attempted illegal entry into the United States through avoidance of immigration inspection at air or sea ports-of-entry.

(B) The amounts which are required to be refunded under subparagraph (A) shall be refunded at least quarterly on the basis of estimates made by the Attorney General of the expenses referred to in subparagraph (A). Proper adjustments shall be made in the amounts subsequently refunded under subparagraph (A) to the extent prior estimates were in excess of, or less than, the amount required to be refunded under subparagraph (A).

The Attorney General shall provide for expenditures for training and assistance described in clause (iv) in an amount, for any fiscal year, not less than 5 percent of the total of the expenses incurred that are described in the previous sentence.

(i) Reimbursement

Notwithstanding any other provision of law, the Attorney General is authorized to receive reimbursement from the owner, operator, or agent of a private or commercial aircraft, train, or vessel, or from any airport, rail line, or seaport authority for expenses incurred by the Attorney General in providing immigration inspection services which are rendered at the request of such person or authority (including the salary and expenses of individuals employed by the Attorney General to provide such immigration inspection services). Reimbursements under this subsection may be collected in advance of the provision of such immigration inspection services. Notwithstanding subsection (h)(1)(B), and only to the extent provided in appropriations Acts, any amounts collected under this subsection shall be credited as offsetting collections to the currently applicable appropriation, account, or fund of U.S. Customs and Border Protection, remain available until expended, and be available for the purposes for which such appropriation, account, or fund is authorized to be used.

(j) Regulations

The Attorney General may prescribe such rules and regulations as may be necessary to carry out the provisions of this section.

(k) Advisory committee

In accordance with the provisions of the Federal Advisory Committee Act [5 U.S.C.A.App. § 1 et seq.], the Attorney General shall establish an advisory committee, whose membership shall consist of representatives from the airline and other transportation industries who may be subject to any fee or charge authorized by law or proposed by the Immigration and Naturalization Service for the purpose of covering expenses incurred by the Immigration and Naturalization Service. The advisory committee shall meet on a periodic basis and shall advise the Attorney General on issues related to the performance of the inspectional services of the Immigration and Naturalization Service. This advice shall include, but not be limited to, such issues as the time periods during which such services should be performed, the proper number and deployment of inspection officers, the level of fees, and the appropriateness of any proposed fee. The Attorney General shall give substantial consideration to the views of the advisory committee in the exercise of his duties.

(*l*) Report to Congress

In addition to the reporting requirements established pursuant to subsection (h), the Attorney General shall prepare and submit annually to the Congress, not later than March 31st of each year, a statement of the financial condition of the "Immigration User Fee Account" including beginning account balance, revenues, withdrawals and their purpose, ending balance, projections for the ensuing fiscal year and a full and complete workload analysis showing on a port by port basis the current and projected need for inspectors. The statement shall indicate the success rate of the Immigration and Naturalization Service in meeting the forty-five minute inspection standard and shall provide detailed statistics regarding the number of passengers inspected within the standard, progress that is being made to expand the utilization of United States citizen by-pass, the number of passengers for whom the standard is not met and the length of their delay, locational breakdown of these statistics and the steps being taken to correct any nonconformity.

(m) Immigration Examinations Fee Account

Notwithstanding any other provisions of law, all adjudication fees as are designated by the Attorney General in regulations shall be deposited as offsetting receipts into a separate account entitled "Immigration Examinations Fee Account" in the Treasury of the United States, whether collected directly by the Attorney General or through clerks of courts: *Provided, however,* That all fees received by the Attorney General from applicants residing in the Virgin Islands of the United States, and in Guam, under this subsection shall be paid over to the treasury of the Virgin Islands and to the treasury of Guam: *Provided further,* That fees for providing adjudication and naturalization services may be set at a level that will ensure recovery of the full costs of providing all such services, including the costs of similar services provided without charge to asylum applicants or other immigrants. Such fees may also be set at a level that will recover any additional costs associated with the administration of the fees collected.

(n) Reimbursement of administrative expenses; transfer of deposits to General Fund of United States Treasury

All deposits into the "Immigration Examinations Fee Account" shall remain available until expended to the Attorney General to reimburse any appropriation the amount paid out of such appropriation for expenses in providing immigration adjudication and naturalization services and the collection, safeguarding and accounting for fees deposited in and funds reimbursed from the "Immigration Examinations Fee Account". [sic]

(o) Annual financial reports to Congress

The Attorney General shall prepare and submit annually to Congress statements of financial condition of the "Immigration Examinations Fee Account", including beginning account balance, revenues, withdrawals, and ending account balance and projections for the ensuing fiscal year.

(p) Additional effective dates

The provisions set forth in subsections (m), (n), and (o) apply to adjudication and naturalization services performed and to related fees collected on or after October 1, 1988.

(q) Land Border Inspection Fee Account

(1)(A)(i) Notwithstanding any other provision of law, the Attorney General is authorized to establish, by regulation, not more than 96 projects under which a fee may be charged and collected for inspection services provided at one or more land border points of entry. Such projects may include the establishment of commuter lanes to be made available to qualified United States citizens and aliens, as determined by the Attorney General.

(ii) This subparagraph shall take effect, with respect to any project described in clause (1)* that was not authorized to be commenced before the date of the enactment of the Illegal Immigration Reform and Immigrant Responsibility Act of 1996 [September 30, 1996], 30 days after submission of a written plan by the Attorney General detailing the proposed implementation of such project.

(iii) The Attorney General shall prepare and submit on a quarterly basis a status report on each land border inspection project implemented under this subparagraph.

(iv) Redesignated (iii).

(B) The Attorney General, in consultation with the Secretary of the Treasury, may conduct pilot projects to demonstrate the use of

* So in original; probably should be clause "(i)".

designated ports of entry after working hours through the use of card reading machines or other appropriate technology.

(2) All of the fees collected under this subsection, including receipts for services performed in processing forms I–94, I–94W, and I–68, and other similar applications processed at land border ports of entry, shall be deposited as offsetting receipts in a separate account within the general fund of the Treasury of the United States, to remain available until expended. Such account shall be known as the Land Border Inspection Fee Account.

(3)(A) The Secretary of the Treasury shall refund, at least on a quarterly basis amounts to any appropriations for expenses incurred in providing inspection services at land border points of entry. Such expenses shall include—

(i) the providing of overtime inspection services;

(ii) the expansion, operation and maintenance of information systems for nonimmigrant control;

(iii) the hire of additional permanent and temporary inspectors;

(iv) the minor construction costs associated with the addition of new traffic lanes (with the concurrence of the General Services Administration);

(v) the detection of fraudulent documents used by passengers travelling to the United States;

(vi) providing for the administration of said account.

(B) The amounts required to be refunded from the Land Border Inspection Fee Account for fiscal years 1992 and thereafter shall be refunded in accordance with estimates made in the budget request of the Attorney General for those fiscal years: Provided, That any proposed changes in the amounts designated in said budget requests shall only be made after notification to the Committees on Appropriations of the House of Representatives and the Senate in accordance with section 606 of Public Law 101–162.

(4) The Attorney General will prepare and submit annually to the Congress statements of financial condition of the Land Border Immigration Fee Account, including beginning account balance, revenues, withdrawals, and ending account balance and projection for the ensuing fiscal year.

(5) Repealed. Pub.L. 104–208, Div. C, Title I, § 122(a)(2), Sept. 30, 1996, 110 Stat. 3009–560.

(r) Breached Bond/Detention Fund

(1) Notwithstanding any other provision of law, there is established in the general fund of the Treasury a separate account which shall be known as the Breached Bond/Detention Fund (in this subsection referred to as the "Fund").

(2) There shall be deposited as offsetting receipts into the Fund all breached cash and surety bonds, in excess of $8,000,000, posted under this Act, which are recovered by the Department of Justice, and amount [sic] described in section 245(i)(3)(B) [8 U.S.C.A. § 1255(i)(3)(B)].

(3) Such amounts as are deposited into the Fund shall remain available until expended and shall be refunded out of the Fund by the Secretary of the Treasury, at least on a quarterly basis, to the Attorney General for the following purposes—

> **(i)** for expenses incurred in the collection of breached bonds, and

> **(ii)** for expenses associated with the detention of illegal aliens.

(4) The amounts required to be refunded from the Fund for fiscal year 1998 and thereafter shall be refunded in accordance with estimates made in the budget request of the President for those fiscal years. Any proposed changes in the amounts designated in such budget requests shall only be made after Congressional reprogramming notification in accordance with the reprogramming guidelines for the applicable fiscal year.

(5) The Attorney General shall prepare and submit annually to the Congress, statements of financial condition of the Fund, including the beginning balance, receipts, refunds to appropriations, transfers to the general fund, and the ending balance.

(6) For fiscal year 1993 only, the Attorney General may transfer up to $1,000,000 from the Immigration User Fee Account to the Fund for initial expenses necessary to enhance collection efforts: Provided, That any such transfers shall be refunded from the Fund back to the Immigration User Fee Account by December 31, 1993.

(s) H–1B nonimmigrant petitioner account

(1) In general

There is established in the general fund of the Treasury a separate account, which shall be known as the "H–1B Nonimmigrant Petitioner Account". Notwithstanding any other section of this subchapter, there shall be deposited as offsetting receipts into the account all fees collected under paragraphs (9) and (11) of section 214(c) [8 U.S.C.A. § 1184(c)].

(2) Use of fees for job training

50 percent of amounts deposited into the H–1B Nonimmigrant Petitioner Account shall remain available to the Secretary of Labor until expended for demonstration programs and projects described in section 414(c) of the American Competitiveness and Workforce Improvement Act of 1998 [29 U.S.C.A. § 2916a].

(3) Use of fees for low-income scholarship program

30 percent of the amounts deposited into the H–1B Nonimmigrant Petitioner Account shall remain available to the Director of the National Science Foundation until expended for scholarships described in section 1869c of Title 42 for low-income students enrolled in a program of study leading to a degree in mathematics, engineering, or computer science.

(4) National Science Foundation competitive grant program for K–12 math, science and technology education

(A) In general

10 percent of the amounts deposited into the H–1B Nonimmigrant Petitioner Account shall remain available to the Director of the National Science Foundation until expended to carry out a direct or matching grant program to support private-public partnerships in K–12 education.

(B) Types of programs covered

The Director shall award grants to such programs, including those which support the development and implementation of standards-based instructional materials models and related student assessments that enable K–12 students to acquire an understanding of science, mathematics, and technology, as well as to develop critical thinking skills; provide systemic improvement in training K–12 teachers and education for students in science, mathematics, and technology; support the professional development of K–12 math and science teachers in the use of technology in the classroom; stimulate system-wide K–12 reform of science, mathematics, and technology in rural, economically disadvantaged regions of the United States; provide externships and other opportunities for students to increase their appreciation and understanding of science, mathematics, engineering, and technology (including summer institutes sponsored by an institution of higher education for students in grades 7–12 that provide instruction in such fields); involve partnerships of industry, educational institutions, and community organizations to address the educational needs of disadvantaged communities; provide college preparatory support to expose and prepare students for careers in science, mathematics, engineering, and technology; and provide for carrying out systemic reform activities under section 1862(a)(1) of Title 42.

(5) Use of fees for duties relating to petitions

5 percent of the amounts deposited into the H–1B Nonimmigrant Petitioner Account shall remain available to the Secretary of Homeland Security until expended to carry out duties under paragraphs (1) and (9) of section 214(c) [8 U.S.C.A. § 1184(c)] related to petitions made for nonimmigrants described in section 101(a)(15)(H)(i)(b) [8 U.S.C.A. § 1101(a)(15)(H)(i)(b)], under paragraph (1)(C) or (D) of section 204 [8

U.S.C.A. § 1154] [sic]* related to petitions for immigrants described in section 203(b) [8 U.S.C.A. § 1153(b)].

(6) Use of fees for application processing and enforcement

For fiscal year 1999, 4 percent of the amounts deposited into the H–1B Nonimmigrant Petitioner Account shall remain available to the Secretary of Labor until expended for decreasing the processing time for applications under section 212(n)(1) [8 U.S.C.A. § 1182(n)(1)] and for carrying out section 212(n)(2) [8 U.S.C.A. § 1182(n)(2)]. Beginning with fiscal year 2000, 5 percent of the amounts deposited into the H–1B Nonimmigrant Petitioner Account shall remain available to the Secretary of Labor until expended for decreasing the processing time for applications under section 212(n)(1) [8 U.S.C.A. § 1182(n)(1)] and section 212(a)(5)(A) [8 U.S.C.A. § 1182(a)(5)(A)].

(t) Genealogy fee

(1) There is hereby established the Genealogy Fee for providing genealogy research and information services. This fee shall be deposited as offsetting collections into the Examinations Fee Account. Fees for such research and information services may be set at a level that will ensure the recovery of the full costs of providing all such services.

(2) The Attorney General will prepare and submit annually to Congress statements of the financial condition of the Genealogy Fee.

(3) Any officer or employee of the Immigration and Naturalization Service shall collect fees prescribed under regulation before disseminating any requested genealogical information.

(u) Premium fee for employment-based petitions and applications

The Attorney General is authorized to establish and collect a premium fee for employment-based petitions and applications. This fee shall be used to provide certain premium-processing services to business customers, and to make infrastructure improvements in the adjudications and customer-service processes. For approval of the benefit applied for, the petitioner/applicant must meet the legal criteria for such benefit. This fee shall be set at $1,000, shall be paid in addition to any normal petition/application fee that may be applicable, and shall be deposited as offsetting collections in the Immigration Examinations Fee Account. The Attorney General may adjust this fee according to the Consumer Price Index.

(v) Fraud Prevention and Detection Account

(1) In general

There is established in the general fund of the Treasury a separate account, which shall be known as the "Fraud Prevention and Detection Account". Notwithstanding any other provision of law, there shall be

---

* So in original. Probably should be "204(a) [1154(a)]".

deposited as offsetting receipts into the account all fees collected under paragraph (12) or (13) of section 214(c) [8 U.S.C.A. § 1184(c)].

(2) Use of fees to combat fraud

(A) Secretary of State

One-third of the amounts deposited into Fraud Prevention and Detection Account shall remain available to the Secretary of State until expended for programs and activities at United States embassies and consulates abroad—

(i) to increase the number* diplomatic security personnel assigned exclusively or primarily to the function of preventing and detecting fraud by applicants for visas described in subparagraph (H)(i), (H)(ii), or (L) of section 101(a)(15) [8 U.S.C.A. § 1101(a)(15)];

(ii) otherwise to prevent and detect visa fraud, including primarily fraud by applicants for visas described in subparagraph (H)(i), (H)(ii), or (L) of section 101(a)(15) [8 U.S.C.A. § 1101(a)(15)], in cooperation with the Secretary of Homeland Security or pursuant to the terms of a memorandum of understanding or other agreement between the Secretary of State and the Secretary of Homeland Security; and

(iii) upon request by the Secretary of Homeland Security, to assist such Secretary in carrying out the fraud prevention and detection programs and activities described in subparagraph (B).

(B) Secretary of Homeland Security

One-third of the amounts deposited into the Fraud Prevention and Detection Account shall remain available to the Secretary of Homeland Security until expended for programs and activities to prevent and detect immigration benefit fraud, including fraud with respect to petitions filed under paragraph (1) or (2)(A) of section 214(c) [8 U.S.C.A. § 1184(c)] to grant an alien nonimmigrant status described in subparagraph (H) or(L) of section 101(a)(15) [8 U.S.C.A. § 1101(a)(15)].

(C) Secretary of Labor

One-third of the amounts deposited into the Fraud Prevention and Detection Account shall remain available to the Secretary of Labor until expended for wage and hour enforcement programs and activities otherwise authorized to be conducted by the Secretary of Labor that focus on industries likely to employ nonimmigrants, including enforcement programs and activities described in section 212(n) [8 U.S.C.A. § 1182(n)] and enforcement programs and activities related to section 214(c)(14)(A)(i) [8 U.S.C.A. § 1184(c)(14)(A)(i)].

---

* So in original. Probably should be followed by "of".

(D) Consultation

The Secretary of State, the Secretary of Homeland Security, and the Secretary of Labor shall consult one another with respect to the use of the funds in the Fraud Prevention and Detection Account or for programs and activities to prevent and detect fraud with respect to petitions under paragraph (1) or (2)(A) of section 214(c) [8 U.S.C.A. § 1184(c)] to grant an alien nonimmigrant status described in section 101(a)(15)(H)(ii) [8 U.S.C.A. § 1101(a)(15)(H)(ii)].

(June 27, 1952, c. 477, Title II, ch. 9, § 286, 66 Stat. 232; Dec. 29, 1981, Pub.L. 97–116, § 13, 95 Stat. 1618; Oct. 18, 1986, Pub.L. 99–500, Title I, § 101(b) [Title II, § 205(a), formerly § 205], 100 Stat. 1783–39, 1783–53, as amended Oct. 24, 1988, Pub.L. 100–525, § 4(a)(2)(A), 102 Stat. 2615; Nov. 14, 1986, Pub.L. 99–653, § 7(d)(1), as added Oct. 24, 1988, Pub.L. 100–525, § 8(f), 102 Stat. 2617; July 11, 1987, Pub.L. 100–71, Title I, § 1, 101 Stat. 394; Oct. 1, 1988, Pub.L. 100–459, § 209(a), 102 Stat. 2203, as amended Dec. 12, 1991, Pub.L. 102–232, Title III, § 309(a)(1)(A)(i)(I), 105 Stat. 1757; Oct. 24, 1988, Pub.L. 100–525, § 4(a)(1), 102 Stat. 2614; Nov. 21, 1989, Pub. L. 101–162, Title II, 103 Stat. 1000, as amended Dec. 12, 1991, Pub.L. 102–232, Title III, § 309(a)(1)(B), 105 Stat. 1758; Nov. 5, 1990, Pub.L. 101–515, Title II, § 210(a), (d), 104 Stat. 2120, 2121; Dec. 12, 1991, Pub.L. 102–232, Title III, § 309(a)(1)(A)(i), (B), (2), (b)(12), 105 Stat. 1758, 1759; Oct. 6, 1992, Pub.L. 102–395, Title I, § 112, 106 Stat. 1843; Oct. 27, 1993, Pub.L. 103–121, Title I, 107 Stat. 1161; Oct. 25, 1994, Pub.L. 103–416, Title II, § 219(t), 108 Stat. 4317; Sept. 30, 1996, Pub.L. 104–208, Div. C, Title I, §§ 122(a), 124(a)(1), Title III, §§ 308(d)(3)(A), (4)(K), (e)(1)(L), (g)(1), 376(b), 382(b), Title VI, § 671(b)(11), (e)(5), (6), 110 Stat. 3009–560, 3009–562, 3009–617 to 3009–619, 3009–622, 3009–648, 3009–651, 3009–722, 3009–723; Nov. 26, 1997, Pub.L. 105–119, Title I, § 110(1), (2), 111 Stat. 2457; Oct. 21, 1998, Pub.L. 105–277, Div. A, § 101(b) [Title I, § 114], Div. C, Title IV, § 414(b), 112 Stat. 2681–68, 2681–652; Nov. 29, 1999, Pub.L. 106–113, Div. B, § 1000(a)(1) [H.R. 3421, Title I, § 118], 113 Stat. 1535, 1537; Oct. 17, 2000, Pub.L. 106–313, Title I, §§ 110(a), 113, 114 Stat. 1255, 1261; Dec. 21, 2000, Pub.L. 106–553, § 1(a)(2) [Title I, § 112], 114 Stat. 2762; Dec. 21, 2000, Pub.L. 106–554, § 1(a)(1) [Title I, § 106], 114 Stat. 2763; Nov. 28, 2001, Pub.L. 107–77, Title I, §§ 109, 110, 115 Stat. 765; May 14, 2002, Pub.L. 107–173, Title IV, § 403; Aug. 2, 2002, Pub.L. 107–206, Title I, § 202, 116 Stat. 832; Nov. 2, 2002, Pub.L. 107–273, Div. C, Title I, § 11016(2), 116 Stat. 1824; Nov. 25, 2002, Pub.L. 107–296, Title IV, § 457, 116 Stat. 2201; Feb. 20, 2003, Pub.L. 108–7, Div. B, Title I, § 108, Div. L, § 107, 117 Stat. 67, 532; Sept. 3, 2003, Pub.L. 108–77, Title IV, § 402(d)(2), 117 Stat. 946; Dec. 8, 2004, Pub.L. 108–447, Div. J, Title IV, §§ 426(b), 427, 118 Stat. 3357,3358, as amended by Dec. 16, 2009, Pub.L. 111–117, Div. D, Title V, § 524(a), 123 Stat. 3283; May 11, 2005, Pub.L. 109–13, Div. A, Title VI, § 6046, Div. B, Title IV, § 403(b), 119 Stat. 295, 319; Jan. 11, 2007, Pub.L. 109–472, § 2, 120 Stat. 3554; Pub.L. 114–125, Title VIII, § 818(a), Feb. 24, 2016, 130 Stat. 222; Pub.L. 115–254, Div. B, Title V, § 573, Oct. 5, 2018, 132 Stat. 3389.)

§ 287. Powers of immigration officers and employees [8 U.S.C.A. § 1357]

(a) Powers without warrant

Any officer or employee of the Service authorized under regulations prescribed by the Attorney General shall have power without warrant—

(1) to interrogate any alien or person believed to be an alien as to his right to be or to remain in the United States;

(2) to arrest any alien who in his presence or view is entering or attempting to enter the United States in violation of any law or regulation made in pursuance of law regulating the admission, exclusion, expulsion, or removal of aliens, or to arrest any alien in the United States, if he has reason to believe that the alien so arrested is in the United States in violation of any such law or regulation and is likely to escape before a warrant can be obtained for his arrest, but the alien arrested shall be taken without unnecessary delay for examination before an officer of the Service having authority to examine aliens as to their right to enter or remain in the United States;

(3) within a reasonable distance from any external boundary of the United States, to board and search for aliens any vessel within the territorial waters of the United States and any railway car, aircraft, conveyance, or vehicle, and within a distance of twenty-five miles from any such external boundary to have access to private lands, but not dwellings, for the purpose of patrolling the border to prevent the illegal entry of aliens into the United States;

(4) to make arrests for felonies which have been committed and which are cognizable under any law of the United States regulating the admission, exclusion, expulsion, or removal of aliens, if he has reason to believe that the person so arrested is guilty of such felony and if there is likelihood of the person escaping before a warrant can be obtained for his arrest, but the person arrested shall be taken without unnecessary delay before the nearest available officer empowered to commit persons charged with offenses against the laws of the United States; and

(5) to make arrests—

(A) for any offense against the United States, if the offense is committed in the officer's or employee's presence, or

(B) for any felony cognizable under the laws of the United States, if the officer or employee has reasonable grounds to believe that the person to be arrested has committed or is committing such a felony,

if the officer or employee is performing duties relating to the enforcement of the immigration laws at the time of the arrest and if there is a likelihood of the person escaping before a warrant can be obtained for his arrest.

Under regulations prescribed by the Attorney General, an officer or employee of the Service may carry a firearm and may execute and serve any order, warrant, subpoena, summons, or other process issued under the authority of the United States. The authority to make arrests under paragraph (5)(B) shall only be effective on and after the date on which the Attorney General publishes final regulations which **(i)** prescribe the categories of officers and employees of the Service who may use force (including deadly force) and the circumstances under which such force may be used, **(ii)** establish standards with respect to enforcement activities of the Service, **(iii)** require that any officer or employee of the Service is not authorized to make arrests under paragraph (5)(B) unless the officer or employee has received certification as having completed a training program which covers such arrests and standards described in clause (ii), and **(iv)** establish an expedited, internal review process for violations of such standards, which process is consistent with standard agency procedure regarding confidentiality of matters related to internal investigations.

(b) Administration of oath; taking of evidence

Any officer or employee of the Service designated by the Attorney General, whether individually or as one of a class, shall have power and authority to administer oaths and to take and consider evidence concerning the privilege of any person to enter, reenter, pass through, or reside in the United States, or concerning any matter which is material or relevant to the enforcement of this Act and the administration of the Service; and any person to whom such oath has been administered (or who has executed an unsworn declaration, certificate, verification, or statement under penalty of perjury as permitted under section 1746 of Title 28), under the provisions of this Act, who shall knowingly or willfully give false evidence or swear (or subscribe under penalty of perjury as permitted under section 1746 of Title 28) to any false statement concerning any matter referred to in this subsection shall be guilty of perjury and shall be punished as provided by section 1621 of Title 18.

(c) Search without warrant

Any officer or employee of the Service authorized and designated under regulations prescribed by the Attorney General, whether individually or as one of a class, shall have power to conduct a search, without warrant, of the person, and of the personal effects in the possession of any person seeking admission to the United States, concerning whom such officer or employee may have reasonable cause to suspect that grounds exist for denial of admission to the United States under this Act which would be disclosed by such search.

(d) Detainer of aliens for violation of controlled substances laws

In the case of an alien who is arrested by a Federal, State, or local law enforcement official for a violation of any law relating to controlled substances, if the official (or another official)—

(1) has reason to believe that the alien may not have been lawfully admitted to the United States or otherwise is not lawfully present in the United States,

(2) expeditiously informs an appropriate officer or employee of the Service authorized and designated by the Attorney General of the arrest and of facts concerning the status of the alien, and

(3) requests the Service to determine promptly whether or not to issue a detainer to detain the alien,

the officer or employee of the Service shall promptly determine whether or not to issue such a detainer. If such a detainer is issued and the alien is not otherwise detained by Federal, State, or local officials, the Attorney General shall effectively and expeditiously take custody of the alien.

(e) Restriction on warrantless entry in case of outdoor agricultural operations

Notwithstanding any other provision of this section other than paragraph (3) of subsection (a) an officer or employee of the Service may not enter without the consent of the owner (or agent thereof) or a properly executed warrant onto the premises of a farm or other outdoor agricultural operation for the purpose of interrogating a person believed to be an alien as to the person's right to be or to remain in the United States.

(f) Fingerprinting and photographing of certain aliens

(1) Under regulations of the Attorney General, the Commissioner shall provide for the fingerprinting and photographing of each alien 14 years of age or older against whom a proceeding is commenced under section 240 [8 U.S.C.A. § 1229a].

(2) Such fingerprints and photographs shall be made available to Federal, State, and local law enforcement agencies, upon request.

(g) Acceptance of State services to carry out immigration enforcement

(1) Notwithstanding section 1342 of Title 31, the Attorney General may enter into a written agreement with a State, or any political subdivision of a State, pursuant to which an officer or employee of the State or subdivision, who is determined by the Attorney General to be qualified to perform a function of an immigration officer in relation to the investigation, apprehension, or detention of aliens in the United States (including the transportation of such aliens across State lines to detention centers), may carry out such function at the expense of the State or political subdivision and to the extent consistent with State and local law.

(2) An agreement under this subsection shall require that an officer or employee of a State or political subdivision of a State performing a function under the agreement shall have knowledge of, and adhere to, Federal law relating to the function, and shall contain a written certification that the officers or employees performing the function under the agreement have received adequate training regarding the enforcement of relevant Federal immigration laws.

(3) In performing a function under this subsection, an officer or employee of a State or political subdivision of a State shall be subject to the direction and supervision of the Attorney General.

(4) In performing a function under this subsection, an officer or employee of a State or political subdivision of a State may use Federal property or facilities, as provided in a written agreement between the Attorney General and the State or subdivision.

(5) With respect to each officer or employee of a State or political subdivision who is authorized to perform a function under this subsection, the specific powers and duties that may be, or are required to be, exercised or performed by the individual, the duration of the authority of the individual, and the position of the agency of the Attorney General who is required to supervise and direct the individual, shall be set forth in a written agreement between the Attorney General and the State or political subdivision.

(6) The Attorney General may not accept a service under this subsection if the service will be used to displace any Federal employee.

(7) Except as provided in paragraph (8), an officer or employee of a State or political subdivision of a State performing functions under this subsection shall not be treated as a Federal employee for any purpose other than for purposes of chapter 81 of Title 5 (relating to compensation for injury) and sections 2671 through 2680 of Title 28 (relating to tort claims).

(8) An officer or employee of a State or political subdivision of a State acting under color of authority under this subsection, or any agreement entered into under this subsection, shall be considered to be acting under color of Federal authority for purposes of determining the liability, and immunity from suit, of the officer or employee in a civil action brought under Federal or State law.

(9) Nothing in this subsection shall be construed to require any State or political subdivision of a State to enter into an agreement with the Attorney General under this subsection.

(10) Nothing in this subsection shall be construed to require an agreement under this subsection in order for any officer or employee of a State or political subdivision of a State—

(A) to communicate with the Attorney General regarding the immigration status of any individual, including reporting knowledge that a particular alien is not lawfully present in the United States; or

(B) otherwise to cooperate with the Attorney General in the identification, apprehension, detention, or removal of aliens not lawfully present in the United States.

(h) An alien described in section 101(a)(27)(J) [8 U.S.C.A § 1101(a)(27)(J)] who has been battered, abused, neglected, or abandoned, shall not be compelled to contact the alleged abuser (or family member of the alleged abuser) at any stage of applying for special immigrant juvenile status, including after a request for the consent of the Secretary of Homeland Security under section 101(a)(27)(J)(iii)(I) [8 U.S.C.A § 1101(a)(27)(J)(iii)(I)] of such Act.

(June 27, 1952, c. 477, Title II, ch. 9, § 287, 66 Stat. 233; Oct. 18, 1976, Pub.L. 94–550, § 7, 90 Stat. 2535; Oct. 27, 1986, Pub.L. 99–570, Title I, § 1751(d), 100 Stat. 3207–47; Nov. 6, 1986, Pub.L. 99–603, Title I, § 116, 100 Stat. 3384; Oct. 24, 1988, Pub.L. 100–525, §§ 2(e),

5, 102 Stat. 2610, 2615; Nov. 29, 1990, Pub.L. 101–649, Title V, § 503(a), (b)(1), 104 Stat. 5048; Dec. 12, 1991, Pub.L. 102–232, Title III, § 306(a)(3), 105 Stat. 1751; Sept. 30, 1996, Pub.L. 104–208, Div. C, Title I, § 133, Title III, § 308(d)(4)(L), (e)(1)(M), (g)(5)(A)(i), 110 Stat. 3009–563, 3009–618, 3009–619, 3009–623; Jan. 5, 2006, Pub.L. 109–162, Title VIII, § 826, 119 Stat. 3065; Aug. 12, 2006, Pub.L. 109–271, § 6(g), 120 Stat. 763.)

§ 288. Local jurisdiction over immigrant stations [8 U.S.C.A. § 1358]

The officers in charge of the various immigrant stations shall admit therein the proper State and local officers charged with the enforcement of the laws of the State or Territory of the United States in which any such immigrant station is located in order that such State and local officers may preserve the peace and make arrests for crimes under the laws of the States and Territories. For the purpose of this section the jurisdiction of such State and local officers and of the State and local courts shall extend over such immigrant stations.

(June 27, 1952, c. 477, Title II, ch. 9, § 288, 66 Stat. 234.)

§ 289. Application to American Indians born in Canada [8 U.S.C.A. § 1359]

Nothing in this title shall be construed to affect the right of American Indians born in Canada to pass the borders of the United States, but such right shall extend only to persons who possess at least 50 per centum of blood of the American Indian race.

(June 27, 1952, c. 477, Title II, ch. 9, § 289, 66 Stat. 234.)

§ 290. Establishment of central file; information from other departments and agencies [8 U.S.C.A. § 1360]

(a) There shall be established in the office of the Commissioner, for the use of security and enforcement agencies of the Government of the United States, a central index, which shall contain the names of all aliens heretofore admitted or denied admission to the United States, insofar as such information is available from the existing records of the Service, and the names of all aliens hereafter admitted or denied admission to the United States, the names of their sponsors of record, if any, and such other relevant information as the Attorney General shall require as an aid to the proper enforcement of this Act.

(b) Any information in any records kept by any department or agency of the Government as to the identity and location of aliens in the United States shall be made available to the Service upon request made by the Attorney General to the head of any such department or agency.

(c)(1) Not later than 3 months after the end of each fiscal year (beginning with fiscal year 1996), the Commissioner of Social Security shall report to the Committees on the Judiciary of the House of Representatives and the Senate on the aggregate quantity of social security account numbers issued to aliens not authorized to be employed, with respect to which, in such fiscal year, earnings were reported to the Social Security Administration.

(2) If earnings are reported on or after January 1, 1997, to the Social Security Administration on a social security account number issued to an alien not authorized to work in the United States, the Commissioner of Social Security shall provide the Attorney General with information regarding the name and address of the alien, the name and address of the person reporting the earnings, and the amount of the earnings. The information shall be provided in an electronic form agreed upon by the Commissioner and the Attorney General.

(d) A written certification signed by the Attorney General or by any officer of the Service designated by the Attorney General to make such certification, that after diligent search no record or entry of a specified nature is found to exist in the records of the Service, shall be admissible as evidence in any proceeding as evidence that the records of the Service contain no such record or entry, and shall have the same effect as the testimony of a witness given in open court.

(June 27, 1952, c. 477, Title II, ch. 9, § 290, 66 Stat. 234; 1953 Reorg. Plan No. 1, §§ 5, 8, eff. Apr. 11, 1953, 18 F.R. 2053, 67 Stat. 631; Oct. 24, 1988, Pub.L. 100–525, § 9(q), 102 Stat. 2621; Sept. 30, 1996, Pub.L. 104–208, Div. C, Title III, § 308(d)(4)(M), Title IV, § 414(a), 110 Stat. 3009–618, 3009–669.)

§ 291.   Burden of proof upon alien [8 U.S.C.A. § 1361]

Whenever any person makes application for a visa or any other document required for entry, or makes application for admission, or otherwise attempts to enter the United States, the burden of proof shall be upon such person to establish that he is eligible to receive such visa or such document, or is not inadmissible under any provision of this Act, and, if an alien, that he is entitled to the nonimmigrant, immigrant, special immigrant, immediate relative, or refugee status claimed, as the case may be. If such person fails to establish to the satisfaction of the consular officer that he is eligible to receive a visa or other document required for entry, no visa or other document required for entry shall be issued to such person, nor shall such person be admitted to the United States unless he establishes to the satisfaction of the Attorney General that he is not inadmissible under any provision of this Act. In any removal proceeding under chapter 4 against any person, the burden of proof shall be upon such person to show the time, place, and manner of his entry into the United States, but in presenting such proof he shall be entitled to the production of his visa or other entry document, if any, and of any other documents and records, not considered by the Attorney General to be confidential, pertaining to such entry in the custody of the Service. If such burden of proof is not sustained, such person shall be presumed to be in the United States in violation of law.

(June 27, 1952, c. 477, Title II, ch. 9, § 291, 66 Stat. 234; Dec. 29, 1981, Pub.L. 97–116, § 18(k)(1), 95 Stat. 1620; Sept. 30, 1996, Pub.L. 104–208, Div. C, Title III, § 308(d)(4)(N), (e) (1)(N), (g)(9)(A), 110 Stat. 3009–618, 3009–619, 3009–624.)

§ 292.　Right to counsel [8 U.S.C.A. § 1362]

In any removal proceedings before an immigration judge and in any appeal proceedings before the Attorney General from any such removal proceedings, the person concerned shall have the privilege of being represented (at no expense to the Government) by such counsel, authorized to practice in such proceedings, as he shall choose.

(June 27, 1952, c. 477, Title II, ch. 9, § 292, 66 Stat. 235; Sept. 30, 1996, Pub.L. 104–208, Div. C, Title III, §§ 308(d)(4)(O), 371(b)(9), 110 Stat. 3009–619, 3009–645.)

§ 293.　Deposit of and interest on cash received to secure immigration bonds [8 U.S.C.A. § 1363]

(a) Cash received by the Attorney General as security on an immigration bond shall be deposited in the Treasury of the United States in trust for the obligor on the bond, and shall bear interest payable at a rate determined by the Secretary of the Treasury, except that in no case shall the interest rate exceed 3 per centum per annum. Such interest shall accrue from date of deposit occurring after April 27, 1966, to and including date of withdrawal or date of breach of the immigration bond, whichever occurs first: *Provided,* That cash received by the Attorney General as security on an immigration bond, and deposited by him in the postal savings system prior to discontinuance of the system, shall accrue interest as provided in this section from the date such cash ceased to accrue interest under the system. Appropriations to the Treasury Department for interest on uninvested funds shall be available for payment of said interest.

(b) The interest accruing on cash received by the Attorney General as security on an immigration bond shall be subject to the same disposition as prescribed for the principal cash, except that interest accruing to the date of breach of the immigration bond shall be paid to the obligor on the bond.

(June 27, 1952, c. 477, Title II, ch. 9, § 293; as added Pub.L. 91–313, § 2, July 10, 1970, 84 Stat. 413.)

§ 294.　Undercover investigation authority [8 U.S.C.A. § 1363a]

(a) In general

With respect to any undercover investigative operation of the Service which is necessary for the detection and prosecution of crimes against the United States—

(1) sums appropriated for the Service may be used for leasing space within the United States and the territories and possessions of the United States without regard to the following provisions of law:

(A) section 3679(a) of the Revised Statutes (31 U.S.C. 1341),

(B) section 3732(a) of the Revised Statutes (41 U.S.C. 11(a)),

(C) section 305 of the Act of June 30, 1949 (63 Stat. 396; 41 U.S.C. 255),

(D) the third undesignated paragraph under the heading "Miscellaneous" of the Act of March 3, 1877 (19 Stat. 370; 40 U.S.C. 34),

(E) section 3648 of the Revised Statutes (31 U.S.C. 3324),

(F) section 3741 of the Revised Statutes (41 U.S.C. 22), and

(G) subsections (a) and (c) of section 304 of the Federal Property and Administrative Services Act of 1949 (63 Stat. 395; 41 U.S.C. 254(a) and (c));

(2) sums appropriated for the Service may be used to establish or to acquire proprietary corporations or business entities as part of an undercover operation, and to operate such corporations or business entities on a commercial basis, without regard to the provisions of section 304 of the Government Corporation Control Act (31 U.S.C. 9102);

(3) sums appropriated for the Service, and the proceeds from the undercover operation, may be deposited in banks or other financial institutions without regard to the provisions of section 648 of Title 18, and of section 3639 of the Revised Statutes (31 U.S.C. 3302); and

(4) the proceeds from the undercover operation may be used to offset necessary and reasonable expenses incurred in such operation without regard to the provisions of section 3617 of the Revised Statutes (31 U.S.C. 3302).

The authority set forth in this subsection may be exercised only upon written certification of the Commissioner, in consultation with the Deputy Attorney General, that any action authorized by paragraph (1), (2), (3), or (4) is necessary for the conduct of the undercover operation.

(b) Disposition of proceeds no longer required

As soon as practicable after the proceeds from an undercover investigative operation, carried out under paragraphs (3) and (4) of subsection (a), are no longer necessary for the conduct of the operation, the proceeds or the balance of the proceeds remaining at the time shall be deposited into the Treasury of the United States as miscellaneous receipts.

(c) Disposition of certain corporations and business entities

If a corporation or business entity established or acquired as part of an undercover operation under paragraph (2) of subsection (a) with a net value of over $50,000 is to be liquidated, sold, or otherwise disposed of, the Service, as much in advance as the Commissioner or Commissioner's designee determines practicable, shall report the circumstances to the Attorney General, the Director of the Office of Management and Budget, and the Comptroller General. The proceeds of the liquidation, sale, or other disposition, after obligations are met, shall be deposited in the Treasury of the United States as miscellaneous receipts.

(d) Financial audits

The Service shall conduct detailed financial audits of closed undercover operations on a quarterly basis and shall report the results of the audits in writing to the Deputy Attorney General.

(June 27, 1952, c. 477, Title II, ch. 9, § 294, as added Sept. 30, 1996, Pub.L. 104–208, Div. C, Title II, § 205(a), 110 Stat. 3009–567.)

TITLE III

NATIONALITY AND NATURALIZATION

Chapter I—Nationality at Birth and Collective Naturalization

§ 301. Nationals and citizens of United States at birth [8 U.S.C.A. § 1401]

The following shall be nationals and citizens of the United States at birth:

(a) a person born in the United States, and subject to the jurisdiction thereof;

(b) a person born in the United States to a member of an Indian, Eskimo, Aleutian, or other aboriginal tribe: Provided, That the granting of citizenship under this subsection shall not in any manner impair or otherwise affect the right of such person to tribal or other property;

(c) a person born outside of the United States and its outlying possessions of parents both of whom are citizens of the United States and one of whom has had a residence in the United States or one of its outlying possessions, prior to the birth of such person;

(d) a person born outside of the United States and its outlying possessions of parents one of whom is a citizen of the United States who has been physically present in the United States or one of its outlying possessions for a continuous period of one year prior to the birth of such person, and the other of whom is a national, but not a citizen of the United States;

(e) a person born in an outlying possession of the United States of parents one of whom is a citizen of the United States who has been physically present in the United States or one of its outlying possessions for a continuous period of one year at any time prior to the birth of such person;

(f) a person of unknown parentage found in the United States while under the age of five years, until shown, prior to his attaining the age of twenty-one years, not to have been born in the United States;

(g) a person born outside the geographical limits of the United States and its outlying possessions of parents one of whom is an alien, and the other a citizen of the United States who, prior to the birth of such person, was physically present in the United States or its outlying possessions for a period or periods totaling not less than five years, at least two of which were after attaining the age of fourteen years: Provided, That any periods of honorable service in the Armed Forces of the United States, or periods of employment with the United States Government or with an international organization as that term is defined in section 288 of Title 22 by such citizen parent, or any periods during which such citizen parent is physically present abroad as the dependent unmarried son or daughter and a member of the household of a person **(A)** honorably serving with the Armed Forces of the United States, or **(B)** employed by the United States Government or an international organization as defined in section 288 of Title 22, may be included in order to satisfy the physical-presence requirement of this paragraph. This proviso shall be applicable to persons born on or after December 24, 1952, to the same extent as if it had become effective in its present form on that date; and

(h) a person born before noon (Eastern Standard Time) May 24, 1934, outside the limits and jurisdiction of the United States of an alien father and a mother who is a citizen of the United States who, prior to the birth of such person, had resided in the United States.

(June 27, 1952, c. 477, Title III, ch. 1, § 301, 66 Stat. 235; Nov. 6, 1966, Pub.L. 89–770, 80 Stat. 1322; Oct. 27, 1972, Pub.L. 92–584, §§ 1, 3, 86 Stat. 1289; Oct. 10, 1978, Pub.L. 95–432, §§ 1, 3, 92 Stat. 1046; Nov. 14, 1986, Pub.L. 99–653, § 12, 100 Stat. 3657; Oct. 25, 1994, Pub.L. 103–416, Title I, § 101(a), 108 Stat. 4306.)

§ 302. Persons born in Puerto Rico on or after April 11, 1899 [8 U.S.C.A. § 1402]

All persons born in Puerto Rico on or after April 11, 1899, and prior to January 13, 1941, subject to the jurisdiction of the United States, residing on January 13, 1941, in Puerto Rico or other territory over which the United States exercises rights of sovereignty and not citizens of the United States under any other Act, are declared to be citizens of the United States as of January 13, 1941. All persons born in Puerto Rico on or after January 13, 1941, and subject to the jurisdiction of the United States, are citizens of the United States at birth.

(June 27, 1952, c. 477, Title III, ch. 1, § 302, 66 Stat. 236.)

§ 303.   Persons born in the Canal Zone or Republic of Panama on or after February 26, 1904 [8 U.S.C.A. § 1403]

(a) Any person born in the Canal Zone on or after February 26, 1904, and whether before or after the effective date of this Act, whose father or mother or both at the time of the birth of such person was or is a citizen of the United States, is declared to be a citizen of the United States.

(b) Any person born in the Republic of Panama on or after February 26, 1904, and whether before or after the effective date of this Act, whose father or mother or both at the time of the birth of such person was or is a citizen of the United States employed by the Government of the United States or by the Panama Railroad Company, or its successor in title, is declared to be a citizen of the United States.

(June 27, 1952, c. 477, Title III, ch. 1, § 303, 66 Stat. 236.)

§ 304.   Persons born in Alaska on or after March 30, 1867 [8 U.S.C.A. § 1404]

A person born in Alaska on or after March 30, 1867, except a noncitizen Indian, is a citizen of the United States at birth. A noncitizen Indian born in Alaska on or after March 30, 1867, and prior to June 2, 1924, is declared to be a citizen of the United States as of June 2, 1924. An Indian born in Alaska on or after June 2, 1924, is a citizen of the United States at birth.

(June 27, 1952, c. 477, Title III, ch. 1, § 304, 66 Stat. 237.)

§ 305.   Persons born in Hawaii [8 U.S.C.A. § 1405]

A person born in Hawaii on or after August 12, 1898, and before April 30, 1900, is declared to be a citizen of the United States as of April 30, 1900. A person born in Hawaii on or after April 30, 1900, is a citizen of the United States at birth. A person who was a citizen of the Republic of Hawaii on August 12, 1898, is declared to be a citizen of the United States as of April 30, 1900.

(June 27, 1952, c. 477, Title III, ch. 1, § 305, 66 Stat. 237.)

§ 306.   Persons living in and born in the Virgin Islands [8 U.S.C.A. § 1406]

(a) The following persons and their children born subsequent to January 17, 1917, and prior to February 25, 1927, are declared to be citizens of the United States as of February 25, 1927:

(1) All former Danish citizens who, on January 17, 1917, resided in the Virgin Islands of the United States, and were residing in those islands or in the United States or Puerto Rico on February 25, 1927, and who did not make the declaration required to preserve their Danish citizenship by article 6 of the treaty entered into on August 4, 1916, between the United States and Denmark, or who, having made such a declaration have heretofore renounced or may hereafter renounce it by a declaration before a court of record;

(2) All natives of the Virgin Islands of the United States who, on January 17, 1917, resided in those islands, and were residing in those islands or in the United States or Puerto Rico on February 25, 1927, and who were not on February 25, 1927, citizens or subjects of any foreign country;

(3) All natives of the Virgin Islands of the United States who, on January 17, 1917, resided in the United States, and were residing in those islands on February 25, 1927, and who were not on February 25, 1927, citizens or subjects of any foreign country; and

(4) All natives of the Virgin Islands of the United States who, on June 28, 1932, were residing in continental United States, the Virgin Islands of the United States, Puerto Rico, the Canal Zone, or any other insular possession or territory of the United States, and who, on June 28, 1932, were not citizens or subjects of any foreign country, regardless of their place of residence on January 17, 1917.

(b) All persons born in the Virgin Islands of the United States on or after January 17, 1917, and prior to February 25, 1927, and subject to the jurisdiction of the United States are declared to be citizens of the United States as of February 25, 1927; and all persons born in those islands on or after February 25, 1927, and subject to the jurisdiction of the United States, are declared to be citizens of the United States at birth.

(June 27, 1952, c. 477, Title III, ch. 1, § 306, 66 Stat. 237.)

§ 307. Persons living in and born in Guam [8 U.S.C.A. § 1407]

(a) The following persons, and their children born after April 11, 1899, are declared to be citizens of the United States as of August 1, 1950, if they were residing on August 1, 1950, on the island of Guam or other territory over which the United States exercises rights of sovereignty:

(1) All inhabitants of the island of Guam on April 11, 1899, including those temporarily absent from the island on that date, who were Spanish subjects, who after that date continued to reside in Guam or other territory over which the United States exercises sovereignty, and who have taken no affirmative steps to preserve or acquire foreign nationality; and

(2) All persons born in the island of Guam who resided in Guam on April 11, 1899, including those temporarily absent from the island on that date, who after that date continued to reside in Guam or other territory over which the United States exercises sovereignty, and who have taken no affirmative steps to preserve or acquire foreign nationality.

(b) All persons born in the island of Guam on or after April 11, 1899 (whether before or after August 1, 1950) subject to the jurisdiction of the United States, are declared to be citizens of the United States: *Provided,* That in the case of any person born before August 1, 1950, he has taken no affirmative steps to preserve or acquire foreign nationality.

(c) Any person hereinbefore described who is a citizen or national of a country other than the United States and desires to retain his present political status shall have made, prior to August 1, 1952, a declaration under oath of such desire, said declaration to be in form and executed in the manner prescribed by regulations. From and after the making of such a declaration any such person shall be held not to be a national of the United States by virtue of this Act.

(June 27, 1952, c. 477, Title III, ch. 1, § 307, 66 Stat. 237.)

§ 308. Nationals but not citizens of the United States at birth [8 U.S.C.A. § 1408]

Unless otherwise provided in section 301 [8 U.S.C.A. § 1401], the following shall be nationals, but not citizens, of the United States at birth:

(1) A person born in an outlying possession of the United States on or after the date of formal acquisition of such possession;

(2) A person born outside the United States and its outlying possessions of parents both of whom are nationals, but not citizens, of the United States, and have had a residence in the United States, or one of its outlying possessions prior to the birth of such person;

(3) A person of unknown parentage found in an outlying possession of the United States while under the age of five years, until shown, prior to his attaining the age of twenty-one years, not to have been born in such outlying possession; and

(4) A person born outside the United States and its outlying possessions of parents one of whom is an alien, and the other a national, but not a citizen, of the United States who, prior to the birth of such person, was physically present in the United States or its outlying possessions for a period or periods totaling not less than seven years in any continuous period of ten years—

(A) during which the national parent was not outside the United States or its outlying possessions for a continuous period of more than one year, and

(B) at least five years of which were after attaining the age of fourteen years.

The proviso of section 301(g) [8 U.S.C.A. § 1401(g)] shall apply to the national parent under this paragraph in the same manner as it applies to the citizen parent under that section.

(June 27, 1952, c. 477, Title III, ch. 1, § 308, 66 Stat. 238; Pub. L. 99–396, § 15(a), Aug. 27, 1986, 100 Stat. 842, as amended Pub.L. 100–525, § 3(2), Oct. 24, 1988, 102 Stat. 2614.)

§ 309. Children born out of wedlock [8 U.S.C.A. § 1409]

(a) The provisions of paragraphs (c), (d), (e), and (g) of section 301 [8 U.S.C.A. § 1401(c), (d), (e), and (g)], and of paragraph (2) of section 308 [8 U.S.C.A. § 1408], shall apply as of the date of birth to a person born out of wedlock if—

(1) a blood relationship between the person and the father is established by clear and convincing evidence,

(2) the father had the nationality of the United States at the time of the person's birth,

(3) the father (unless deceased) has agreed in writing to provide financial support for the person until the person reaches the age of 18 years, and

(4) while the person is under the age of 18 years—

(A) the person is legitimated under the law of the person's residence or domicile,

(B) the father acknowledges paternity of the person in writing under oath, or

(C) the paternity of the person is established by adjudication of a competent court.

(b) Except as otherwise provided in section 405 of this Act, the provisions of section 301(g) [8 U.S.C.A. § 1401(g)] shall apply to a child born out of wedlock on or after January 13, 1941, and before December 24, 1952, as of the date of birth, if the paternity of such child is established at any time and while such child is under the age of twenty-one years by legitimation.

(c) Notwithstanding the provision of subsection (a) of this section, a person born after December 23, 1952, outside the United States and out of wedlock shall be held to have acquired at birth the nationality status of his mother, if the mother had the nationality of the United States at the time of such person's birth, and if the mother had previously been physically present in the United States or one of its outlying possessions for a continuous period of one year.

(June 27, 1952, c. 477, Title III, ch. 1, § 309, 66 Stat. 238; Pub. L. 97–116, § 18(*l*), Dec. 29, 1981, 95 Stat. 1620; Pub.L. 99–653, § 13, Nov. 14, 1986, 100 Stat. 3657, as amended Pub.L. 100–525, § 8(k), Oct. 24, 1988, 102 Stat. 2617; Pub.L. 100–525, § 9(r), Oct. 24, 1988, 102 Stat. 2621.)

CHAPTER II—NATIONALITY THROUGH NATURALIZATION

§ 310.   Naturalization authority [8 U.S.C.A. § 1421]

(a) Authority in Attorney General

The sole authority to naturalize persons as citizens of the United States is conferred upon the Attorney General.

(b) Court authority to administer oaths

(1) Jurisdiction

Subject to section 337(c) [8 U.S.C.A. § 1448(c)]—

(A) General jurisdiction

Except as provided in subparagraph (B), each applicant for naturalization may choose to have the oath of allegiance under section 337(a) [8 U.S.C.A. § 1448(a)] administered by the Attorney General or by an eligible court described in paragraph (5). Each such eligible court shall have authority to administer such oath of allegiance to persons residing within the jurisdiction of the court.

(B) Exclusive authority

An eligible court described in paragraph (5) that wishes to have exclusive authority to administer the oath of allegiance under section 337(a) [8 U.S.C.A. § 1448(a)] to persons residing within the jurisdiction of the court during the period described in paragraph (3)(A)(i) shall notify the Attorney General of such wish and, subject to this subsection, shall have such exclusive authority with respect to such persons during such period.

(2) Information

(A) General information

In the case of a court exercising authority under paragraph (1), in accordance with procedures established by the Attorney General—

(i) the applicant for naturalization shall notify the Attorney General of the intent to be naturalized before the court, and

(ii) the Attorney General—

(I) shall forward to the court (not later than 10 days after the date of approval of an application for naturalization in the case of a court which has provided notice under paragraph (1)(B)) such information as may be necessary to administer the oath of allegiance under section 337(a) [8 U.S.C.A. § 1448(a)], and

(II) shall promptly forward to the court a certificate of naturalization (prepared by the Attorney General).

(B) Assignment of individuals in the case of exclusive authority

If an eligible court has provided notice under paragraph (1)(B), the Attorney General shall inform each person (residing within the jurisdiction of the court), at the time of the approval of the person's application for naturalization, of—

(i) the court's exclusive authority to administer the oath of allegiance under section 337(a) [8 U.S.C.A. § 1448(a)] to such a person during the period specified in paragraph (3)(A)(i), and

(ii) the date or dates (if any) under paragraph (3)(B) on which the court has scheduled oath administration ceremonies.

If more than one eligible court in an area has provided notice under paragraph (1)(B), the Attorney General shall permit the person, at the time of the approval, to choose the court to which the information will be forwarded for administration of the oath of allegiance under this section.

(3) Scope of exclusive authority

(A) Limited period and advance notice required

The exclusive authority of a court to administer the oath of allegiance under paragraph (1)(B) shall apply with respect to a person—

(i) only during the 45-day period beginning on the date on which the Attorney General certifies to the court that an applicant is eligible for naturalization, and

(ii) only if the court has notified the Attorney General, prior to the date of certification of eligibility, of the day or days (during such 45-day period) on which the court has scheduled oath administration ceremonies.

(B) Authority of attorney general

Subject to subparagraph (C), the Attorney General shall not administer the oath of allegiance to a person under subsection (a) during the period in which exclusive authority to administer the oath of allegiance may be exercised by an eligible court under this subsection with respect to that person.

(C) Waiver of exclusive authority

Notwithstanding the previous provisions of this paragraph, a court may waive exclusive authority to administer the oath of allegiance under section 337(a) [8 U.S.C.A. § 1448(a)] to a person under this subsection if the Attorney General has not provided the court with the certification described in subparagraph (A)(i) within a reasonable time before the date scheduled by the court for oath administration ceremonies. Upon notification of a court's waiver of jurisdiction, the Attorney General shall promptly notify the applicant.

(4) Issuance of certificates

The Attorney General shall provide for the issuance of certificates of naturalization at the time of administration of the oath of allegiance.

(5) Eligible courts

For purposes of this section, the term "eligible court" means—

(A) a district court of the United States in any State, or

(B) any court of record in any State having a seal, a clerk, and jurisdiction in actions in law or equity, or law and equity, in which the amount in controversy is unlimited.

(c) Judicial review

A person whose application for naturalization under this title is denied, after a hearing before an immigration officer under section 336(a) [8 U.S.C.A. § 1447(a)], may seek review of such denial before the United States district court for the district in which such person resides in accordance with chapter 7 of Title 5. Such review shall be de novo, and the court shall make its own findings of fact and conclusions of law and shall, at the request of the petitioner, conduct a hearing de novo on the application.

(d) Sole procedure

A person may only be naturalized as a citizen of the United States in the manner and under the conditions prescribed in this title and not otherwise.

(June 27, 1952, c. 477, Title III, ch. 2, § 310, 66 Stat. 239; July 7, 1958, Pub.L. 85–508, § 25, 72 Stat. 351; Mar. 18, 1959, Pub.L. 86–3, § 20(c), 73 Stat. 13; Sept. 26, 1961, Pub.L. 87–301, § 17, 75 Stat. 656; Oct. 24, 1988, Pub.L. 100–525, § 9(s), 102 Stat. 2621; Nov. 29, 1990, Pub.L. 101–649, Title IV, § 401(a), 104 Stat. 5038; Dec. 12, 1991, Pub.L. 102–232, Title I, § 102(a), Title III, § 305(a), 105 Stat. 1734, 1749; Oct. 25, 1994, Pub.L. 103–416, Title II, § 219(u), 108 Stat. 4318.)

§ 311. Eligibility for naturalization [8 U.S.C.A. § 1422]

The right of a person to become a naturalized citizen of the United States shall not be denied or abridged because of race or sex or because such person is married.

(June 27, 1952, c. 477, Title III, ch. 2, § 311, 66 Stat. 239; Pub.L. 100–525, § 9(t), Oct. 24, 1988, 102 Stat. 2621.)

§ 312. Requirements as to understanding the English language, history, principles and form of government of the United States [8 U.S.C.A. § 1423]

(a) No person except as otherwise provided in this title shall hereafter be naturalized as a citizen of the United States upon his own application who cannot demonstrate—

(1) an understanding of the English language, including an ability to read, write, and speak words in ordinary usage in the English language: Provided, That the requirements of this paragraph relating to ability to read and write shall be met if the applicant can read or write simple words and phrases to the end that a reasonable test of his literacy shall be made and that no extraordinary or unreasonable condition shall be imposed upon the applicant; and

(2) a knowledge and understanding of the fundamentals of the history, and of the principles and form of government, of the United States.

(b)(1) The requirements of subsection (a) shall not apply to any person who is unable because of physical or developmental disability or mental impairment to comply therewith.

(2) The requirement of subsection (a)(1) shall not apply to any person who, on the date of the filing of the person's application for naturalization as provided in section 334 [8 U.S.C.A. § 1445], either—

(A) is over fifty years of age and has been living in the United States for periods totaling at least twenty years subsequent to a lawful admission for permanent residence, or

(B) is over fifty-five years of age and has been living in the United States for periods totaling at least fifteen years subsequent to a lawful admission for permanent residence.

(3) The Attorney General, pursuant to regulations, shall provide for special consideration, as determined by the Attorney General, concerning the requirement of subsection (a)(2) with respect to any person who, on the date of the filing of the person's application for naturalization as provided in section 334 [8 U.S.C.A. § 1445], is over sixty-five years of age and has been living in the United States for periods totaling at least twenty years subsequent to a lawful admission for permanent residence.

(June 27, 1952, c. 477, Title III, ch. 2, § 312, 66 Stat. 239; Nov. 2, 1978, Pub.L. 95–579, § 3, 92 Stat. 2474; Nov. 29, 1990, Pub.L. 101–649, Title IV, § 403, 104 Stat. 5039; Dec. 12, 1991, Pub.L. 102–232, Title III, § 305(m)(2), 105 Stat. 1750; Oct. 25, 1994, Pub.L. 103–416, Title I, § 108(a), 108 Stat. 4309.)

§ 313. Prohibition upon the naturalization of persons opposed to government or law, or who favor totalitarian forms of government [8 U.S.C.A. § 1424]

(a) Notwithstanding the provisions of section 405(b) of this Act [8 U.S.C.A. § 1101 note], no person shall hereafter be naturalized as a citizen of the United States—

(1) who advocates or teaches, or who is a member of or affiliated with any organization that advocates or teaches, opposition to all organized government; or

(2) who is a member of or affiliated with **(A)** the Communist Party of the United States; **(B)** any other totalitarian party of the United States; **(C)** the Communist Political Association; **(D)** the Communist or other totalitarian party of any State of the United States, of any foreign state, or of any political or geographical subdivision of any foreign state; **(E)** any section, subsidiary, branch, affiliate, or subdivision of any such association or party; or **(F)** the direct predecessors or successors of any such association or party, regardless of what name such group or organization may have used, may now bear, or may hereafter adopt, unless such alien establishes that he did not have knowledge or reason to believe at the time he became a member of or affiliated with such an organization (and did not thereafter and prior to the date upon which such organization was so registered or so required to be registered have such knowledge or reason to believe) that such organization was a Communist-front organization; or

(3) who, although not within any of the other provisions of this section, advocates the economic, international, and governmental doctrines of world communism or the establishment in the United States of a totalitarian dictatorship, or who is a member of or affiliated with any organization that advocates the economic, international, and governmental doctrines of world communism or the establishment in the United States of a totalitarian dictatorship, either through its own utterances or through any written or printed publications issued or published by or with the permission or consent of or under authority of such organization or paid for by the funds of such organization; or

(4) who advocates or teaches or who is a member of or affiliated with any organization that advocates or teaches **(A)** the overthrow by force or violence or other unconstitutional means of the Government of the United States or of all forms of law; or **(B)** the duty, necessity, or propriety of the unlawful assaulting or killing of any officer or officers (either of specific individuals or of officers generally) of the Government of the United States or of any other organized government because of his or their official character; or **(C)** the unlawful damage, injury, or destruction of property; or **(D)** sabotage; or

(5) who writes or publishes or causes to be written or published, or who knowingly circulates, distributes, prints, or displays, or knowingly causes to be circulated, distributed, printed, published, or displayed, or who knowingly has in his possession for the purpose of circulation, publication, distribution, or display, any written or printed matter, advocating or teaching opposition to all organized government, or advocating **(A)** the overthrow by force, violence, or other unconstitutional means of the Government of the United States or of all forms of law; or **(B)** the duty, necessity, or propriety of the unlawful assaulting or killing of any officer or officers (either of specific individuals or of officers generally) of the Government of the United States or of any other organized government, because of his or their official character; or **(C)**

the unlawful damage, injury, or destruction of property; or **(D)** sabotage; or **(E)** the economic, international, and governmental doctrines of world communism or the establishment in the United States of a totalitarian dictatorship; or

(6) who is a member of or affiliated with any organization that writes, circulates, distributes, prints, publishes, or displays, or causes to be written, circulated, distributed, printed, published, or displayed, or that has in its possession for the purpose of circulation, distribution, publication, issue, or display, any written or printed matter of the character described in subparagraph (5) of this subsection.

(b) The provisions of this section or of any other section of this title shall not be construed as declaring that any of the organizations referred to in this section or in any other section of this title do not advocate the overthrow of the Government of the United States by force, violence, or other unconstitutional means.

(c) The provisions of this section shall be applicable to any applicant for naturalization who at any time within a period of ten years immediately preceding the filing of the application for naturalization or after such filing and before taking the final oath of citizenship is, or has been found to be within any of the classes enumerated within this section, notwithstanding that at the time the application is filed he may not be included within such classes.

(d) Any person who is within any of the classes described in subsection (a) solely because of past membership in, or past affiliation with, a party or organization may be naturalized without regard to the provisions of subsection (c) if such person establishes that such membership or affiliation is or was involuntary, or occurred and terminated prior to the attainment by such alien of the age of sixteen years, or that such membership or affiliation is or was by operation of law, or was for purposes of obtaining employment, food rations, or other essentials of living and where necessary for such purposes.

(e) A person may be naturalized under this title without regard to the prohibitions in subsections (a)(2) and (c) of this section if the person—

(1) is otherwise eligible for naturalization;

(2) is within the class described in subsection (a)(2) solely because of past membership in, or past affiliation with, a party or organization described in that subsection;

(3) does not fall within any other of the classes described in that subsection; and

(4) is determined by the Director of Central Intelligence, in consultation with the Secretary of Defense when Department of Defense activities are relevant to the determination, and with the concurrence of the Attorney General and the Secretary of Homeland Security, to have made a contribution to the national security or to the national intelligence mission of the United States.

(June 27, 1952, c. 477, Title III, ch. 2, § 313, 66 Stat. 240; Oct. 24, 1988, Pub.L. 100–525, § 9(u), 102 Stat. 2621; Nov. 29, 1990, Pub.L. 101–649, Title IV, § 407(c), 104 Stat. 5041; Dec. 12, 1991, Pub.L. 102–232, Title III, § 309(b)(13), 105 Stat. 1759; Oct. 25, 1994, Pub.L. 103–416, Title II, § 219(v), 108 Stat. 4318; Dec. 3, 1999, Pub.L. 106–120, Title III, § 306, 113 Stat. 1612; Dec. 13, 2003, Pub.L. 108–177, Title III, § 373, 117 Stat. 2628.)

§ 314. Ineligibility to naturalization of deserters from the armed forces [8 U.S.C.A. § 1425]

A person who, at any time during which the United States has been or shall be at war, deserted or shall desert the military, air, or naval forces of the United States, or who, having been duly enrolled, departed, or shall depart from the jurisdiction of the district in which enrolled, or who, whether or not having been duly enrolled, went or shall go beyond the limits of the United States, with intent to avoid any draft into the military, air, or naval service, lawfully ordered, shall, upon conviction thereof by a court martial or a court of competent jurisdiction, be permanently ineligible to become a citizen of the United States; and such deserters and evaders shall be forever incapable of holding any office of trust or of profit under the United States, or of exercising any rights of citizens thereof.

(June 27, 1952, c. 477, Title III, ch. 2, § 314, 66 Stat. 241.)

§ 315. Citizenship denied alien relieved of service in armed forces because of alienage [8 U.S.C.A. § 1426]

(a) Permanent ineligibility

Notwithstanding the provisions of section 405(b) of this Act but subject to subsection (c), any alien who applies or has applied for exemption or discharge from training or service in the Armed Forces or in the National Security Training Corps of the United States on the ground that he is an alien, and is or was relieved or discharged from such training or service on such ground, shall be permanently ineligible to become a citizen of the United States.

(b) Conclusiveness of records

The records of the Selective Service System or of the Department of Defense shall be conclusive as to whether an alien was relieved or discharged from such liability for training or service because he was an alien.

(c) Service in armed forces of a foreign country

An alien shall not be ineligible for citizenship under this section or otherwise because of an exemption from training or service in the Armed Forces of the United States pursuant to the exercise of rights under a treaty, if before the time of the exercise of such rights the alien served in the Armed Forces of a foreign country of which the alien was a national.

(June 27, 1952, c. 477, Title III, ch. 2, § 315, 66 Stat. 242; Pub.L. 100–525, § 9(v), Oct. 24, 1988, 102 Stat. 2621; Pub.L. 101–649, Title IV, § 404, Nov. 29, 1990, 104 Stat. 5039.)

§ 316. Requirements of naturalization [8 U.S.C.A. § 1427]

(a) Residence

No person, except as otherwise provided in this title, shall be naturalized unless such applicant, **(1)** immediately preceding the date of filing his application for naturalization has resided continuously, after being lawfully admitted for permanent residence, within the United States for at least five years and during the five years immediately preceding the date of filing his application has been physically present therein for periods totaling at least half of that time, and who has resided within the State or within the district of the Service in the United States in which the applicant filed the application for at least three months, **(2)** has resided continuously within the United States from the date of the application up to the time of admission to citizenship, and **(3)** during all the period referred to in this subsection has been and still is a person of good moral character, attached to the principles of the Constitution of the United States, and well disposed to the good order and happiness of the United States.

(b) Absences

Absence from the United States of more than six months but less than one year during the period for which continuous residence is required for admission to citizenship, immediately preceding the date of filing the application for naturalization, or during the period between the date of filing the application and the date of any hearing under section 336(a) [8 U.S.C.A. § 1447(a)], shall break the continuity of such residence, unless the applicant shall establish to the satisfaction of the Attorney General that he did not in fact abandon his residence in the United States during such period.

Absence from the United States for a continuous period of one year or more during the period for which continuous residence is required for admission to citizenship (whether preceding or subsequent to the filing of the application for naturalization) shall break the continuity of such residence, except that in the case of a person who has been physically present and residing in the United States, after being lawfully admitted for permanent residence, for an uninterrupted period of at least one year, and who thereafter is employed by or under contract with the Government of the United States or an American institution of research recognized as such by the Attorney General, or is employed by an American firm or corporation engaged in whole or in part in the development of foreign trade and commerce of the United States, or a subsidiary thereof more than 50 per centum of whose stock is owned by an American firm or corporation, or is employed by a public international organization of which the United States is a member by treaty or statute and by which the alien was not employed until after being lawfully admitted for permanent residence, no period of absence from the United States shall break the continuity of residence if—

(1) prior to the beginning of such period of employment (whether such period begins before or after his departure from the United States), but prior to the expiration of one year of continuous absence from the United States, the person has established to the satisfaction of the Attorney General that his absence from the United States for such period is to be on behalf of such Government, or for the purpose of carrying on scientific research on behalf of such institution, or to be engaged in the development of such foreign trade and commerce or whose residence abroad is necessary to the protection of the property rights in such countries in such firm or corporation, or to be employed by a public international organization of which the United States is a member by treaty or statute and by which the alien was not employed until after being lawfully admitted for permanent residence; and

(2) such person proves to the satisfaction of the Attorney General that his absence from the United States for such period has been for such purpose.

The spouse and dependent unmarried sons and daughters who are members of the household of a person who qualifies for the benefits of this subsection shall also be entitled to such benefits during the period for which they were residing abroad as dependent members of the household of the person.

(c) Physical presence

The granting of the benefits of subsection (b) of this section shall not relieve the applicant from the requirement of physical presence within the United States for the period specified in subsection (a) of this section, except in the case of those persons who are employed by, or under contract with, the Government of the United States. In the case of a person employed by or under contract with Central Intelligence Agency, the requirement in subsection (b) of an uninterrupted period of at least one year of physical presence in the United States may be complied with by such person at any time prior to filing an application for naturalization.

(d) Moral character

No finding by the Attorney General that the applicant is not deportable shall be accepted as conclusive evidence of good moral character.

(e) Determination

In determining whether the applicant has sustained the burden of establishing good moral character and the other qualifications for citizenship specified in subsection (a) of this section, the Attorney General shall not be limited to the applicant's conduct during the five years preceding the filing of the application, but may take into consideration as a basis for such determination the applicant's conduct and acts at any time prior to that period.

(f) Persons making extraordinary contributions to national security

(1) Whenever the Director of Central Intelligence, the Attorney General and the Commissioner of Immigration determine that an applicant otherwise eligible for naturalization has made an extraordinary contribution to the national security of the United States or to the conduct of United States intelligence activities, the applicant may be naturalized without regard to the residence and physical presence requirements of this section, or to the prohibitions of section 313 [8 U.S.C.A. § 1424], and no residence within a particular State or district of the Service in the United States shall be required: Provided, That the applicant has continuously resided in the United States for at least one year prior to naturalization: Provided, further, That the provisions of this subsection shall not apply to any alien described in clauses (i) through (iv) of section 208(b)(2)(A) [8 U.S.C.A. § 1158(b)(2)(A)].

(2) An applicant for naturalization under this subsection may be administered the oath of allegiance under section 337(a) [8 U.S.C.A. § 1448(a)] by any district court of the United States, without regard to the residence of the applicant. Proceedings under this subsection shall be conducted in a manner consistent with the protection of intelligence sources, methods and activities.

(3) The number of aliens naturalized pursuant to this subsection in any fiscal year shall not exceed five. The Director of Central Intelligence shall inform the Select Committee on Intelligence and the Committee on the Judiciary of the Senate and the Permanent Select Committee on Intelligence and the Committee on the Judiciary of the House of Representatives within a reasonable time prior to the filing of each application under the provisions of this subsection.

(g) Repealed.

(June 27, 1952, c. 477, Title III, ch. 2, § 316, 66 Stat. 242; Dec. 29, 1981, Pub.L. 97–116, § 14, 95 Stat. 1619; Dec. 4, 1985, Pub.L. 99–169, Title VI, § 601, 99 Stat. 1007; Nov. 29, 1990, Pub.L. 101–649, Title IV, §§ 402, 407(c)(2), (d)(1), (e)(1), 104 Stat. 5038, 5041, 5046; Sept. 30, 1996, Pub.L. 104–208, Div. C, Title III, § 308(g)(7)(F), 110 Stat. 3009–624; Dec. 30, 2005, Pub.L. 109–149, Title IV, § 518, 119 Stat. 2882.)

§ 317.   Temporary absence of persons performing religious duties [8 U.S.C.A. § 1428]

Any person who is authorized to perform the ministerial or priestly functions of a religious denomination having a bona fide organization within the United States, or any person who is engaged solely by a religious denomination or by an interdenominational mission organization having a bona fide organization within the United States as a missionary, brother, nun, or sister, who **(1)** has been lawfully admitted to the United States for permanent residence, **(2)** has at any time thereafter and before filing an application for naturalization been physically present and residing within the United States for an uninterrupted period of at least one year, and **(3)** has heretofore been or may hereafter be absent temporarily from the United States in connection with or for the purpose of performing the ministerial or priestly functions of such religious denomination, or serving as a missionary, brother, nun, or sister, shall be considered as being physically present and residing in the United States for the purpose of naturalization within the meaning of section 316(a) [8 U.S.C.A. § 1427(a)], notwithstanding any such absence from the United States, if he shall in all other respects comply with the requirements of the naturalization law. Such person shall prove to the satisfaction of the Attorney General that his absence from the United States has been solely for the purpose of performing the ministerial or priestly functions of such religious denomination, or of serving as a missionary, brother, nun, or sister.

(June 27, 1952, c. 477, Title III, ch. 2, § 317, 66 Stat. 243; Nov. 29, 1990, Pub.L. 101–649, Title IV, § 407(c), (d)(2), 104 Stat. 5041.)

§ 318.   Prerequisite to naturalization; burden of proof [8 U.S.C.A. § 1429]

Except as otherwise provided in this title, no person shall be naturalized unless he has been lawfully admitted to the United States for permanent residence in accordance with all applicable provisions of this Act. The burden of proof shall be upon such person to show that he entered the United States lawfully, and the time, place, and manner of such entry into the United States, but in presenting such proof he shall be entitled to the production of his immigrant visa, if any, or of other entry document, if any, and of any other documents and records, not considered by the Attorney General to be confidential, pertaining to such entry, in the custody of the Service. Notwithstanding the provisions of section 405(b) of this Act, and except as provided in sections 328 [8 U.S.C.A. § 1439] and 329 [8 U.S.C.A. § 1440] no person shall be naturalized against whom there is outstanding a final finding of deportability pursuant to a warrant of arrest issued under the provisions of this or any other Act; and no application for naturalization shall be considered by the Attorney General if there is pending against the applicant a removal proceeding pursuant to a warrant of arrest issued under the provisions of this or any other Act: Provided, That the findings of the Attorney General in terminating removal proceedings or in canceling the removal of an alien pursuant to the provisions of this Act, shall not be deemed binding in any way upon the Attorney General with respect to the question of whether such person has established his eligibility for naturalization as required by this title.

(June 27, 1952, c. 477, Title III, ch. 2, § 318, 66 Stat. 244; Oct. 24, 1968, Pub.L. 90–633, § 4, 82 Stat. 1344; Nov. 29, 1990, Pub.L. 101–649, Title IV, § 407(c)(4), (d)(3), 104 Stat. 5041; Sept. 30, 1996, Pub.L. 104–208, Div. C, Title III, § 308(e)(1)(O), (15), 110 Stat. 3009–620, 3009–621.)

§ 319.   Married persons and employees of certain nonprofit organizations [8 U.S.C.A. § 1430]

(a) Any person whose spouse is a citizen of the United States, or any person who obtained status as a lawful permanent resident by reason of his or her status as a spouse or child of a United States citizen who battered him or her or subjected him or her to extreme cruelty, may be naturalized upon compliance with all the requirements of this title except the provisions of paragraph (1) of section 316(a) [8 U.S.C.A. § 1427(a)] if such person immediately preceding the date of filing his application for naturalization has resided continuously, after being lawfully admitted for permanent residence, within the United States for at least three years, and during the three years immediately preceding the date of filing his application has been living in marital union with the citizen spouse (except in the case of a person who has been battered or subjected to extreme cruelty by a United States citizen spouse or parent), who has been a United States citizen during all of such period, and has been physically present in the United States for periods totaling at least half of that time and has resided within the State or the district of the Service in the United States in which the applicant filed his application for at least three months.

(b) Any person, **(1)** whose spouse is **(A)** a citizen of the United States, **(B)** in the employment of the Government of the United States, or of an American institution of research recognized as such by the Attorney General, or of an American firm or corporation engaged in whole or in part in the development of foreign trade and commerce of the United States, or a subsidiary thereof, or of a public international organization in which the United States participates by treaty or statute, or is authorized to perform the ministerial or priestly functions of a religious denomination having a bona fide organization within the United States, or is engaged solely as a missionary by a religious denomination or by an interdenominational mission organization having a bona fide organization within the United States, and **(C)** regularly stationed abroad in such employment, and **(2)** who is in the United States at the time of naturalization, and **(3)** who declares before the Attorney General in good faith an intention to take up residence within the United States immediately upon the termination of such employment abroad of the citizen spouse, may be naturalized upon compliance with all the requirements of the naturalization laws, except that no prior residence or specified period of physical presence within the United States or within a State or a district of the Service in the United States or proof thereof shall be required.

(c) Any person who **(1)** is employed by a bona fide United States incorporated nonprofit organization which is principally engaged in conducting abroad through communications media the dissemination of information which significantly promotes United States interests abroad and which is recognized as such by the Attorney General, and **(2)** has been so employed continuously for a period of not less than five years after a lawful admission for permanent residence, and **(3)** who files his application for naturalization while so employed or within six months following the termination thereof, and **(4)** who is in the United States at the time of naturalization, and **(5)** who declares before the Attorney General in good faith an intention to take up residence within the United States immediately upon termination of such employment, may be naturalized upon compliance with all the requirements of this title except that no prior residence or specified period of physical presence within the United States or any State or district of the Service in the United States, or proof thereof, shall be required.

(d) Any person who is the surviving spouse, child, or parent of a United States citizen, whose citizen spouse, parent, or child dies during a period of honorable service in an active duty status in the Armed Forces of the United States and who, in the case of a surviving spouse, was living in marital union with the citizen spouse at the time of his death, may be naturalized upon compliance with all the requirements of this subchapter except that no prior residence or specified physical presence within the United States, or within a State or a district of the Service in the United States shall be required. For purposes of this subsection, the terms "United States citizen" and "citizen spouse" include a person granted posthumous citizenship under section 329A [8 U.S.C.A. § 1440–1].

(e)(1) In the case of a person lawfully admitted for permanent residence in the United States who is the spouse of a member of the armed forces of the United States, is authorized to accompany such member and reside abroad with the member pursuant to the member's official orders, and is so accompanying and residing with the member in marital union, such residence and physical presence abroad shall be treated, for purposes of subsection (a) of this section and section 316 [8 U.S.C.A. § 1427(a)], as residence and physical presence in

(A) the United States; and

(B) any State or district of the Department of Homeland Security in the United States.

(2) Notwithstanding any other provision of law, a spouse described in paragraph (1) shall be eligible for naturalization proceedings overseas pursuant to section 1701(d) of the National Defense Authorization Act for Fiscal Year 2004 [Public Law 108–136; 8 U.S.C.A. § 1443a].

(June 27, 1952, c. 477, Title III, ch. 2, § 319, 66 Stat. 244; Pub. L. 85–697, § 2, Aug. 20, 1958, 72 Stat. 687; Pub. L. 90–215, § 1(a), Dec. 18, 1967, 81 Stat. 661; Pub. L. 90–369, June 29, 1968, 82 Stat. 279; Pub.L. 101–649, Title IV, § 407(b)(1), (c), (d)(4), 104 Stat. 5040, 5041; Oct. 28, 2000, Pub.L. 106–386, Div. B, Title V, § 1503(e), 114 Stat. 1522; Nov. 24, 2003, Pub.L. 108–136, Div. A, Title XVII, § 1703(f)(1), (h), 117 Stat. 1695, 1696; Jan. 28, 2008, Pub.L. 110–181, Div. A, Title VI, § 674(a), 122 Stat. 185.)

§ 320. Children born outside the United States and lawfully admitted for permanent residence; conditions under which citizenship automatically acquired [8 U.S.C.A. § 1431]

(a) In general

A child born outside of the United States automatically becomes a citizen of the United States when all of the following conditions have been fulfilled:

(1) At least one parent of the child is a citizen of the United States, whether by birth or naturalization.

(2) The child is under the age of eighteen years.

(3) The child is residing in the United States in the legal and physical custody of the citizen parent pursuant to a lawful admission for permanent residence.

(b) Adoption

Subsection (a) shall apply to a child adopted by a United States citizen parent if the child satisfies the requirements applicable to adopted children under section 101(b)(1) [8 U.S.C.A. § 1101(b)(1)].

(c) Subsection (a)(3) is deemed satisfied in the case of a child who is lawfully admitted for permanent residence in the United States if—

(1) the child is residing in the legal and physical custody of a citizen parent who is—

(A) stationed and residing abroad as an employee of the Government of the United States; or

(B) residing abroad in marital union with an employee of the Government of the United States who is stationed abroad; or

(2) the child is—

(A) residing in the legal and physical custody of a citizen parent who is—

(i) stationed and residing abroad as a member of the Armed Forces of the United States; or

(ii) authorized to accompany and reside abroad with a member of the Armed Forces of the United States pursuant to the member's official orders, and is so accompanying and residing abroad with the member in marital union; and

(B) authorized to accompany such member and reside abroad with the member pursuant to the member's official orders, and is so accompanying and residing with the member.

(d) Name and birth date

A Certificate of Citizenship or other Federal document issued or requested to be amended under this section shall reflect the child's name and date of birth as indicated on a State court order, birth certificate, certificate of foreign birth, certificate of birth abroad, or similar State vital records document issued by the child's State of residence in the United States after the child has been adopted or readopted in that State.

(June 27, 1952, c. 477, Title III, ch. 2, § 320, 66 Stat. 245; Pub. L. 95–417, § 4, Oct. 5, 1978, 92 Stat. 917; Pub. L. 97–116, § 18(m), Dec. 29, 1981, 95 Stat. 1620; Pub.L. 99–653, § 14, Nov. 14, 1986, 100 Stat. 3658; Pub.L. 100–525, §§ 8(*l*), 9(w), Oct. 24, 1988, 102 Stat. 2618, 2621; Oct. 30, 2000, Pub.L. 106–395, Title I, § 101(a), 114 Stat. 1631; Pub.L. 113–74, § 2, Jan. 16, 2014, 127 Stat. 1212; Pub.L. 116–133, § 2(a), Mar. 26, 2020, 134 Stat. 274.)

§ 321.   Repealed. Pub.L. 106–395, Title I, § 103(a), Oct. 30, 2000, 114 Stat. 1632 [8 U.S.C.A. § 1432]

§ 322.   Child born and residing outside United States; conditions for acquiring certificate of citizenship [8 U.S.C.A. § 1433]

(a) Application by citizen parents; requirements

A parent who is a citizen of the United States (or, if the citizen parent has died during the preceding 5 years, a citizen grandparent or citizen legal guardian) may apply for naturalization on behalf of a child born outside of the United States who has not acquired citizenship automatically under section 320 [8 U.S.C.A. § 1431]. The Attorney General shall issue a certificate of citizenship to such applicant upon proof, to the satisfaction of the Attorney General, that the following conditions have been fulfilled:

(1) At least one parent (or, at the time of his or her death, was) is a citizen of the United States, whether by birth or naturalization.

(2) The United States citizen parent—

(A) has (or, at the time of his or her death, had) been physically present in the United States or its outlying possessions for a period or periods totaling not less than five years, at least two of which were after attaining the age of fourteen years; or

(B) has (or, at the time of his or her death, had) a citizen parent who has been physically present in the United States or its outlying possessions for a period or periods totaling not less than five years, at least two of which were after attaining the age of fourteen years.

(3) The child is under the age of eighteen years.

(4) The child is residing outside of the United States in the legal and physical custody of the applicant (or, if the citizen parent is deceased, an individual who does not object to the application).

(5) The child is temporarily present in the United States pursuant to a lawful admission, and is maintaining such lawful status.

(b) Attainment of citizenship status; receipt of certificate

Upon approval of the application (which may be filed from abroad) and, except as provided in the last sentence of section 337(a) [8 U.S.C.A.

§ 1448(a)], upon taking and subscribing before an officer of the Service within the United States to the oath of allegiance required by this Act of an applicant for naturalization, the child shall become a citizen of the United States and shall be furnished by the Attorney General with a certificate of citizenship.

(c) Adopted children

Subsections (a) and (b) shall apply to a child adopted by a United States citizen parent if the child satisfies the requirements applicable to adopted children under section 101(b)(1) [8 U.S.C.A. § 1101(b)(1)].

(d) In the case of a child of a member of the armed forces of the United States who is authorized to accompany such member and reside abroad with the member pursuant to the member's official orders, and is so accompanying and residing with the member

> **(1)** any period of time during which the member of the Armed Forces is residing abroad pursuant to official orders shall be treated, for purposes of subsection (a)(2)(A) of this section, as physical presence in the United States;

> **(2)** subsection (a)(5) of this section shall not apply; and

> **(3)** the oath of allegiance described in subsection (b) of this section may be subscribed to abroad pursuant to section 1701(d) of the National Defense Authorization Act for Fiscal Year 2004 [Public Law 108–136; 8 U.S.C.A. § 1443a].

(June 27, 1952, c. 477, Title III, ch. 2, § 322, 66 Stat. 246; Oct. 5, 1978, Pub.L. 95–417, § 6, 92 Stat. 918; Dec. 29, 1981, Pub.L. 97–116, § 18(m), (n), 95 Stat. 1620, 1621; Nov. 14, 1986, Pub.L. 99–653, § 16, 100 Stat. 3658; Oct. 24, 1988, Pub.L. 100–525, § 8(*l*), 102 Stat. 2618; Nov. 29, 1990, Pub.L. 101–649, Title IV, § 407(b)(2), (c)(6), (d)(5), 104 Stat. 5040 to 5042; Dec. 12, 1991, Pub.L. 102–232, Title III, § 305(m)(3), 105 Stat. 1750; Oct. 25, 1994, Pub.L. 103–416, Title I, § 102(a), 108 Stat. 4306; Dec. 7, 1999, Pub.L. 106–139, § 1(b)(2), 113 Stat. 1697; Oct. 30, 2000, Pub.L. 106–395, Title I, § 102(a), 114 Stat. 1632; Nov. 2, 2002, Pub.L. 107–273, Div. C, Title I, § 11030B, 116 Stat. 1837; Jan. 28, 2008, Pub.L. 110–181, Div. A, Title VI, § 674(b), 122 Stat. 186.)

§ 323.   Repealed. Pub. L. 95–417, § 7, Oct. 5, 1978, 92 Stat. 918 [8 U.S.C.A. § 1434]

§ 324.   Former citizens regaining citizenship [8 U.S.C.A. § 1435]

(a) Requirements

Any person formerly a citizen of the United States who **(1)** prior to September 22, 1922, lost United States citizenship by marriage to an alien, or by the loss of United States citizenship of such person's spouse, or **(2)** on or after September 22, 1922, lost United States citizenship by marriage to an alien ineligible to citizenship, may if no other nationality was acquired by an affirmative act of such person other than by marriage be naturalized upon compliance with all requirements of this title, except—

(1) no period of residence or specified period of physical presence within the United States or within the State or district of the Service in the United States where the application is filed shall be required; and

(2) the application need not set forth that it is the intention of the applicant to reside permanently within the United States.

Such person, or any person who was naturalized in accordance with the provisions of section 317(a) of the Nationality Act of 1940, shall have, from and after her naturalization, the status of a native-born or naturalized citizen of the United States, whichever status existed in the case of such person prior to the loss of citizenship: Provided, That nothing contained herein or in any other provision of law shall be construed as conferring United States citizenship retroactively upon such person, or upon any person who was naturalized in accordance with the provisions of section 317(a) of the Nationality Act of 1940, during any period in which such person was not a citizen.

(b) Additional requirements

No person who is otherwise eligible for naturalization in accordance with the provisions of subsection (a) of this section shall be naturalized unless such person shall establish to the satisfaction of the Attorney General that she has been a person of good moral character, attached to the principles of the Constitution of the United States, and well disposed to the good order and happiness of the United States for a period of not less than five years immediately preceding the date of filing an application for naturalization and up to the time of admission to citizenship, and, unless she has resided continuously in the United States since the date of her marriage, has been lawfully admitted for permanent residence prior to filing her application for naturalization.

(c) Oath of allegiance

(1) A woman who was a citizen of the United States at birth and **(A)** who has or is believed to have lost her United States citizenship solely by reason of her marriage prior to September 22, 1922, to an alien, or by her marriage on or after such date to an alien ineligible to citizenship, **(B)** whose marriage to such alien shall have terminated subsequent to January 12, 1941, and **(C)** who has not acquired by an affirmative act other than by marriage any other nationality, shall, from and after taking the oath of allegiance required by section 337 [8 U.S.C.A. § 1448], be a citizen of the United States and have the status of a citizen of the United States by birth, without filing an application for naturalization, and notwithstanding any of the other provisions of this title except the provisions of section 313 [8 U.S.C.A. § 1424]: Provided, That nothing contained herein or in any other provision of law shall be construed as conferring United States citizenship retroactively upon such person, or upon any person who was naturalized in accordance with the provisions of section 317(b) of the Nationality Act of 1940, during any period in which such person was not a citizen.

(2) Such oath of allegiance may be taken abroad before a diplomatic or consular officer of the United States, or in the United States before the Attorney General or the judge or clerk of a court described in section 310(b) [8 U.S.C.A. § 1421(b)].

(3) Such oath of allegiance shall be entered in the records of the appropriate embassy, legation, consulate, court, or the Attorney General, and, upon demand, a certified copy of the proceedings, including a copy of the oath administered, under the seal of the embassy, legation, consulate, court, or the Attorney General, shall be delivered to such woman at a cost not exceeding $5, which certified copy shall be evidence of the facts stated therein before any court of record or judicial tribunal and in any department or agency of the Government of the United States.

(d) Persons losing citizenship for failure to meet physical presence retention requirement

(1) A person who was a citizen of the United States at birth and lost such citizenship for failure to meet the physical presence retention requirements under section 301(b) [8 U.S.C.A. § 1401(b)] (as in effect before October 10, 1978), shall, from and after taking the oath of allegiance required by section 337 [8 U.S.C.A. § 1448] be a citizen of the United States and have the status of a citizen of the United States by birth, without filing an application for naturalization, and notwithstanding any of the other provisions of this title except the provisions of section 313 [8 U.S.C.A. § 1424]. Nothing in this subsection or any other provision of law shall be construed as conferring United States citizenship retroactively upon such person during any period in which such person was not a citizen.

(2) The provisions of paragraphs (2) and (3) of subsection (c) shall apply to a person regaining citizenship under paragraph (1) in the same manner as they apply under subsection (c)(1).

(June 27, 1952, c. 477, Title III, ch. 2, § 324, 66 Stat. 246; Oct. 24, 1988, Pub.L. 100–525, § 9(x), 102 Stat. 2621; Nov. 29, 1990, Pub.L. 101–649, Title IV, § 407(b)(3), (c)(7), (d)(6), 104 Stat. 5040–5042; Oct. 25, 1994, Pub.L. 103–416, Title I, § 103(a), 108 Stat. 4307.)

§ 325. Nationals but not citizens; residence within outlying possessions [8 U.S.C.A. § 1436]

A person not a citizen who owes permanent allegiance to the United States, and who is otherwise qualified, may, if he becomes a resident of any State, be naturalized upon compliance with the applicable requirements of this title, except that in applications for naturalization filed under the provisions of this section residence and physical presence within the United States within the meaning of this title shall include residence and physical presence within any of the outlying possessions of the United States.

(June 27, 1952, c. 477, Title III, ch. 2, § 325, 66 Stat. 248; Nov. 29, 1990, Pub.L. 101–649, Title IV, § 407(c)(8), 104 Stat. 5041.)

§ 326. Resident Philippine citizens excepted from certain requirements [8 U.S.C.A. § 1437]

Any person who **(1)** was a citizen of the Commonwealth of the Philippines on July 2, 1946, **(2)** entered the United States prior to May 1, 1934, and **(3)** has, since such entry, resided continuously in the United States shall be regarded as having been lawfully admitted to the United States for permanent residence for the purpose of applying for naturalization under this title.

(June 27, 1952, c. 477, Title III, ch. 2, § 326, 66 Stat. 248; Nov. 29, 1990, Pub.L. 101–649, Title IV, § 407(c)(9), 104 Stat. 5041.)

§ 327. Former citizens losing citizenship by entering armed forces of foreign countries during World War II [8 U.S.C.A. § 1438]

(a) Requirements; oath; certified copies of oath

Any person who, **(1)** during World War II and while a citizen of the United States, served in the military, air, or naval forces of any country at war with a country with which the United States was at war after December 7, 1941, and before September 2, 1945, and **(2)** has lost United States citizenship by reason of entering or serving in such forces, or taking an oath or obligation for the purpose of entering such forces, may, upon compliance with all the provisions of title III of this Act, except section 316(a) [8 U.S.C.A. § 1427(a)], and except as otherwise provided in subsection (b), be naturalized by taking before the Attorney General or before a court described in section 310(b) [8 U.S.C.A. § 1421(b)] the oath required by section 337 [8 U.S.C.A. § 1448]. Certified copies of such oath shall be sent by such court to the Department of State and to the Department of Justice and by the Attorney General to the Secretary of State.

(b) Exceptions

No person shall be naturalized under subsection (a) of this section unless he—

(1) is, and has been for a period of at least five years immediately preceding taking the oath required in subsection (a), a person of good moral character, attached to the principles of the Constitution of the United States and well disposed to the good order and happiness of the United States; and

(2) has been lawfully admitted to the United States for permanent residence and intends to reside permanently in the United States.

(c) Status

Any person naturalized in accordance with the provisions of this section, or any person who was naturalized in accordance with the provisions of section 323 of the Nationality Act of 1940, shall have, from and after such naturalization, the status of a native-born, or naturalized, citizen of the United States, whichever status existed in the case of such person prior to the loss of citizenship: *Provided,* That nothing contained herein, or in any other provision of law, shall be construed as conferring United States citizenship retroactively upon any such person during any period in which such person was not a citizen.

(d) Span of World War II

For the purposes of this section, World War II shall be deemed to have begun on September 1, 1939, and to have terminated on September 2, 1945.

(e) Inapplicability to certain persons

This section shall not apply to any person who during World War II served in the armed forces of a country while such country was at war with the United States.

(June 27, 1952, c. 477, Title III, ch. 2, § 327, 66 Stat. 248; Nov. 29, 1990, Pub.L. 101–649, Title IV, § 407(d)(7), 104 Stat. 5042.)

§ 328. Naturalization through service in the armed forces [8 U.S.C.A. § 1439]

(a) Requirements

A person who has served honorably at any time in the armed forces of the United States for a period or periods aggregating one year, and, who, if separated from such service, was never separated except under honorable conditions, may be naturalized without having resided, continuously immediately preceding the date of filing such person's application, in the United States for at least five years, and in the State or district of the Service in the United States in which the application for naturalization is filed for at least three months, and without having been physically present in the United States for any specified period, if such application is filed while the applicant is still in the service or within six months after the termination of such service.

(b) Exceptions

A person filing an application under subsection (a) of this section shall comply in all other respects with the requirements of this subchapter, except that—

(1) no residence within a State or district of the Service in the United States shall be required;

(2) notwithstanding section 318 [8 U.S.C.A. § 1429] insofar as it relates to deportability, such applicant may be naturalized immediately if the applicant be then actually in the Armed Forces of the United States, and if prior to the filing of the application, the applicant shall have appeared before and been examined by a representative of the Service;

(3) the applicant shall furnish to the Secretary of Homeland Security, prior to any hearing upon his application, a certified statement from the proper executive department for each period of his service upon which he relies for the benefits of this section, clearly showing that such service was honorable and that no discharges from service, including periods of service not relied upon by him for the benefits of this section, were other than honorable (the certificate or certificates herein provided for shall be conclusive evidence of such service and discharge); and

(4) notwithstanding any other provision of law, no fee shall be charged or collected from the applicant for filing a petition for naturalization or for the issuance of a certificate of naturalization upon citizenship being granted to the applicant, and no clerk of any State court shall charge or collect any fee for such services unless the laws of the State require such charge to be made, in which case nothing more than the portion of the fee required to be paid to the State shall be charged or collected.

(c) Periods when not in service

In the case such applicant's service was not continuous, the applicant's residence in the United States and State or district of the Service in the United States, good moral character, attachment to the principles of the Constitution of the United States, and favorable disposition toward the good order and happiness of the United States, during any period within five years immediately preceding the date of filing such application between the periods of applicant's service in the Armed Forces, shall be alleged in the application filed under the provisions of subsection (a) of this section, and proved at any hearing thereon. Such allegation and proof shall also be made as to any period between the termination of applicant's service and the filing of the application for naturalization.

(d) Residence requirements

The applicant shall comply with the requirements of section 316(a) [8 U.S.C.A. § 1427(a)], if the termination of such service has been more than six months preceding the date of filing the application for naturalization, except that such service within five years immediately preceding the date of filing such application shall be considered as residence and physical presence within the United States.

(e) Moral character

Any such period or periods of service under honorable conditions, and good moral character, attachment to the principles of the Constitution of the United States, and favorable disposition toward the good order and happiness of the United States, during such service, shall be proved by duly authenticated copies of the records of the executive departments having custody of the records of such service, and such authenticated copies of records shall be accepted in lieu of compliance with the provisions of section 316(a) [8 U.S.C.A. § 1427(a)].

(f) Revocation

Citizenship granted pursuant to this section may be revoked in accordance with section 340 [8 U.S.C.A. § 1451] if the person is separated from the Armed Forces under other than honorable conditions before the person has served honorably for a period or periods aggregating five years. Such ground for revocation shall be in addition to any other provided by law, including the grounds described in section 340 [8 U.S.C.A. § 1451]. The fact that the naturalized person was separated from the service under other than honorable conditions shall be proved by a duly authenticated certification from the executive department under which the person was serving at the time of separation. Any period or periods of service shall be proved by duly authenticated copies of the records of the executive departments having custody of the records of such service.

(g), (h) Repealed. Oct. 9, 2008, Pub.L. 110–382, §§ 3(a), 4, 122 Stat. 4088, 4089.

(June 27, 1952, c. 477, Title III, ch. 2, § 328, 66 Stat. 249; Oct. 24, 1968, Pub.L. 90–633, § 5, 82 Stat. 1344; Dec. 29, 1981, Pub.L. 97–116, § 15(e), 95 Stat. 1619; Nov. 29, 1990, Pub.L. 101–649, Title IV, § 407(b)(4), (c)(10), (d)(8), 104 Stat. 5040 to 5042; Nov. 29, 1990, Pub.L. 101–649, Title IV, § 407(d)(8); Dec. 12, 1991, Pub.L. 102–232, Title III, § 305(c), 105 Stat. 1750; Nov. 24, 2003, Pub.L. 108–136, Div. A, Title XVII, § 1701(a), 1701(b)(1), (c)(1)(A), (f), 1705(b), 117 Stat. 1691, 1692, 1696; Oct. 9, 2008, Pub.L. 110–382, § 3(a), 122 Stat. 4088.)

§ 329.   Naturalization through active-duty service in the armed forces during World War I, World War II, Korean hostilities, Vietnam hostilities, or other periods of military hostilities [8 U.S.C.A. § 1440]

(a) Requirements

Any person who, while an alien or a noncitizen national of the United States, has served honorably as a member of the Selected Reserve of the Ready Reserve or in an active-duty status in the military, air, or naval forces of the United States during either World War I or during a period beginning September 1, 1939, and ending December 31, 1946, or during a period beginning June 25, 1950, and ending July 1, 1955, or during a period beginning February 28, 1961, and ending on a date designated by the President by Executive order as of the date of termination of the Vietnam hostilities, or thereafter during any other period which the President by Executive order shall designate as a period in which Armed Forces of the United States are or were engaged in military operations involving armed conflict with a hostile foreign force, and who, if separated from such service, was separated under honorable conditions, may be naturalized as provided in this section if **(1)** at the time of enlistment, reenlistment, extension of enlistment, or induction such person shall have been in the United States, the Canal Zone, American Samoa, or Swains Island, or on board a public vessel owned or operated by the United States for noncommercial service, whether or not he has been lawfully admitted to the United States for permanent residence, or **(2)** at any time subsequent to enlistment or induction such person shall have been lawfully admitted to the United States for permanent residence. The executive department under which such person served shall determine whether persons have served honorably in an active-duty status, and whether separation from such service was under honorable conditions: *Provided, however,* That no person who is or has been separated from such service on account of alienage, or who was a conscientious objector who performed no military, air, or naval duty whatever or refused to wear the uniform, shall be regarded as having served honorably or having been separated under honorable conditions for the purposes of this section. No period of service in the Armed Forces shall be made the basis of an application for naturalization under this section if the applicant has previously been naturalized on the basis of the same period of service.

(b) Exceptions

A person filing an application under subsection (a) of this section shall comply in all other respects with the requirements of this title, except that—

(1) he may be naturalized regardless of age, and notwithstanding the provisions of section 318 [8 U.S.C.A. § 1429] as they relate to deportability and the provisions of section 331 [8 U.S.C.A. § 1442];

(2) no period of residence or specified period of physical presence within the United States or any State or district of the Service in the United States shall be required;

(3) service in the military, air or naval forces of the United States shall be proved by a duly authenticated certification from the executive department under which the applicant served or is serving, which shall state whether the applicant served honorably in an active-duty status during either World War I or during a period beginning September 1, 1939, and ending December 31, 1946, or during a period beginning June 25, 1950, and ending July 1, 1955, or during a period beginning February 28, 1961, and ending on a date designated by the President by Executive order as the date of termination of the Vietnam hostilities, or thereafter during any other period which the President by Executive order shall designate as a period in which Armed Forces of the United States are or were engaged in military operations involving armed conflict with a hostile foreign force, and was separated from such service under honorable conditions; and

(4) notwithstanding any other provision of law, no fee shall be charged or collected from the applicant for filing a petition for naturalization or for the issuance of a certificate of naturalization upon citizenship being granted to the applicant, and no clerk of any State court shall charge or collect any fee for such services unless the laws of the State require such charge to be made, in which case nothing more than the portion of the fee required to be paid to the State shall be charged or collected.

(5) Repealed.

(c) Revocation

Citizenship granted pursuant to this section may be revoked in accordance with section 340 [8 U.S.C.A. § 1451] if the person is separated from the Armed Forces under other than honorable conditions before the person has served honorably for a period or periods aggregating five years. Such ground for revocation shall be in addition to any other provided by law, including the grounds described in section 340 [8 U.S.C.A. § 1451]. The fact that the naturalized person was separated from the service under other than honorable conditions shall be proved by a duly authenticated certification from the executive department under which the person was serving at the time of separation. Any period or periods of service shall be proved by duly authenticated copies of the records of the executive departments having custody of the records of such service.

(d) Repealed.

(June 27, 1952, c. 477, Title III, ch. 2, § 329, 66 Stat. 250; Pub. L. 87–301, § 8, Sept. 26, 1961, 75 Stat. 654; Pub. L. 90–633, §§ 1, 2, 6, Oct. 24, 1968, 82 Stat. 1343, 1344; Pub. L. 97–116, § 15(a), Dec. 29, 1981, 95 Stat. 1619; Pub.L. 100–525, § 9(y), Oct. 24, 1988, 102 Stat. 2621; Pub.L. 101–649, Title IV, § 407(b)(5), (c)(11), Nov. 29, 1990, 104 Stat. 5040, 5041; Dec. 12, 1991, Pub.L. 102–232, Title III, § 305(b), 105 Stat. 1749; Nov. 18, 1997, Pub.L. 105–85, Div. A, Title X, § 1080(a), 111 Stat. 1916; Nov. 24, 2003, Pub.L. 108–136, Div. A, Title XVII, §§ 1701(b)(2), 1701(c)(1)(B), 1702, 1705(b), 117 Stat. 1691, 1692, 1693, 1696.)

§ 329A. Posthumous citizenship through death while on active-duty service in the armed forces during World War I, World War II, the Korean hostilities, the Vietnam hostilities, or in other periods of military hostilities [8 U.S.C.A. § 1440–1]

(a) Permitting granting of posthumous citizenship

Notwithstanding any other provision of this subchapter, the Secretary of Homeland Security shall provide, in accordance with this section, for the granting of posthumous citizenship at the time of death to a person described in subsection (b) of this section if the Secretary of Homeland Security approves an application for that posthumous citizenship under subsection (c) of this section.

(b) Noncitizens eligible for posthumous citizenship

A person referred to in subsection (a) of this section is a person who, while an alien or a noncitizen national of the United States—

(1) served honorably in an active-duty status in the military, air, or naval forces of the United States during any period described in the first sentence of section 329(a) [8 U.S.C.A. § 1440(a)],

(2) died as a result of injury or disease incurred in or aggravated by that service, and

(3) satisfied the requirements of clause (1) or (2) of the first sentence of section 329(a) [8 U.S.C.A. § 1440(a)].

The executive department under which the person so served shall determine whether the person satisfied the requirements of paragraphs (1) and (2).

(c) Requests for posthumous citizenship

(1) In general

A request for the granting of posthumous citizenship to a person described in subsection (b) of this section may be filed on behalf of that person—

(A) upon locating the next-of-kin, and if so requested by the next-of-kin, by the Secretary of Defense or the Secretary's designee with the Bureau of Citizenship and Immigration Services in the Department of Homeland Security immediately upon the death of that person; or

(B) by the next-of-kin.

(2) Approval

The Director of the Bureau of Citizenship and Immigration Services shall approve a request for posthumous citizenship filed by the next-of-kin in accordance with paragraph (1)(B) if—

(A) the request is filed not later than 2 years after—

(i) November 24, 2003; or

(ii) the date of the person's death;

whichever date is later;

(B) the request is accompanied by a duly authenticated certificate from the executive department under which the person served which states that the person satisfied the requirements of paragraphs (1) and (2) of subsection (b) of this section; and

(C) the Director finds that the person satisfied the requirement of subsection (b)(3) of this section.

(d) Documentation of posthumous citizenship

If the Director of the Bureau of Citizenship and Immigration Services approves the request referred to in subsection (c) of this section, the Director shall send to the next-of-kin of the person who is granted citizenship, a suitable document which states that the United States considers the person to have been a citizen of the United States at the time of the person's death.

(e) Repealed. Pub.L. 108–136, Div. A, Title XVII, § 1703(g)(1), Nov. 24, 2003, 117 Stat. 1695.

(June 27, 1952, c. 477, Title III, ch. 2, § 329A, as added Mar. 6, 1990, Pub.L. 101–249, § 2(a), 104 Stat. 94; Nov. 2, 2002, Pub.L. 107–273, Div. C, Title I, § 11030(b), 116 Stat. 1836; Nov. 24, 2003, Pub.L. 108–136, Div. A, Title XVII, §§ 1703(g), 1704, 117 Stat. 1695, 1696.)

§ 330. Constructive residence through service on certain United States vessels [8 U.S.C.A. § 1441]

Any periods of time during all of which a person who was previously lawfully admitted for permanent residence has served honorably or with good conduct, in any capacity other than as a member of the Armed Forces of the United States, **(A)** on board a vessel operated by the United States, or an agency thereof, the full legal and equitable title to which is in the United States; or **(B)** on board a vessel whose home port is in the United States, and **(i)** which is registered under the laws of the United States, or **(ii)** the full legal and equitable title to which is in a citizen of the United States, or a corporation organized under the laws of any of the several States of the United States, shall be deemed residence and physical presence within the United States within the meaning of section 316(a) [8 U.S.C.A. § 1427(a)], if such service occurred within five years immediately preceding the date such person shall file an application for naturalization. Service on vessels described in clause (A) of this section shall be proved by duly authenticated copies of the records of the executive departments or agency having custody of the records of such service. Service on vessels described in clause (B) of this section may be proved by certificates from the masters of such vessels.

(June 27, 1952, c. 477, Title III, ch. 2, § 330, 66 Stat. 251; Pub.L. 100–525, § 9(z), Oct. 24, 1988, 102 Stat. 2621; Pub.L. 101–649, Title IV, § 407(c)(12), Nov. 29, 1990, 104 Stat. 5041; Pub.L. 102–232, Title III, § 305(m)(5), Dec. 12, 1991, 105 Stat. 1750.)

§ 331. Alien enemies [8 U.S.C.A. § 1442]

(a) Naturalization under specified conditions

An alien who is a native, citizen, subject, or denizen of any country, state, or sovereignty with which the United States is at war may, after his loyalty has been fully established upon investigation by the Attorney General, be naturalized as a citizen of the United States if such alien's application for naturalization shall be pending at the beginning of the state of war and the applicant is otherwise entitled to admission to citizenship.

(b) Procedure

An alien embraced within this section shall not have his application for naturalization considered or heard except after 90 days' notice to the Attorney General to be considered at the examination or hearing, and the Attorney General's objection to such consideration shall cause the application to be continued from time to time for so long as the Attorney General may require.

(c) Exceptions from classification

The Attorney General may, in his discretion, upon investigation fully establishing the loyalty of any alien enemy who did not have an application for naturalization pending at the beginning of the state of war, except such alien enemy from the classification of alien enemy for the purposes of this title, and thereupon such alien shall have the privilege of filing an application for naturalization.

(d) Effect of cessation of hostilities

An alien who is a native, citizen, subject, or denizen of any country, state, or sovereignty with which the United States is at war shall cease to be an alien enemy within the meaning of this section upon the determination by proclamation of the President, or by concurrent resolution of the Congress, that hostilities between the United States and such country, state, or sovereignty have ended.

(e) Apprehension and removal

Nothing contained herein shall be taken or construed to interfere with or prevent the apprehension and removal, consistent with law, of any alien enemy at any time prior to the actual naturalization of such alien.

(June 27, 1952, c. 477, Title III, ch. 2, § 331, 66 Stat. 252; Nov. 29, 1990, Pub.L. 101–649, Title IV, § 407(c)(13), (d)(9), (e)(2), 104 Stat. 5041, 5042, 5046.)

§ 332. Administration [8 U.S.C.A. § 1443]

(a) Rules and regulations governing examination of petitioners

The Attorney General shall make such rules and regulations as may be necessary to carry into effect the provisions of this part and is authorized to prescribe the scope and nature of the examination of applicants for naturalization as to their admissibility to citizenship. Such examination shall be limited to inquiry concerning the applicant's residence, physical presence in the United States, good moral character, understanding of and attachment to the fundamental principles of the Constitution of the United States, ability to read, write, and speak English, and other qualifications to become a naturalized citizen as required by law, and shall be uniform throughout the United States.

(b) Instruction in citizenship

The Attorney General is authorized to promote instruction and training in citizenship responsibilities of applicants for naturalization including the sending of names of candidates for naturalization to the public schools, preparing and distributing citizenship textbooks to such candidates as are receiving instruction in preparation for citizenship within or under the supervision of the public schools, preparing and distributing monthly an immigration and naturalization bulletin and securing the aid of and cooperating with official State and national organizations, including those concerned with vocational education.

(c) Prescription of forms

The Attorney General shall prescribe and furnish such forms as may be required to give effect to the provisions of this part, and only such forms as may be so provided shall be legal. All certificates of naturalization and of citizenship shall be printed on safety paper and shall be consecutively numbered in separate series.

(d) Administration of oaths and depositions

Employees of the Service may be designated by the Attorney General to administer oaths and to take depositions without charge in matters relating to the administration of the naturalization and citizenship laws. In cases where there is a likelihood of unusual delay or of hardship, the Attorney General may, in his discretion, authorize such depositions to be taken before a postmaster without charge, or before a notary public or other person authorized to administer oaths for general purposes.

(e) Issuance of certificate of naturalization or citizenship

A certificate of naturalization or of citizenship issued by the Attorney General under the authority of this title shall have the same effect in all courts, tribunals, and public offices of the United States, at home and abroad, of the District of Columbia, and of each State, Territory, and outlying possession of the United States, as a certificate of naturalization or of citizenship issued by a court having naturalization jurisdiction.

(f) Copies of records

Certifications and certified copies of all papers, documents, certificates, and records required or authorized to be issued, used, filed, recorded, or kept under any and all provisions of this Act shall be admitted in evidence equally with the originals in any and all cases and proceedings under this Act and in all cases and proceedings in which the originals thereof might be admissible as evidence.

(g) Furnished quarters for photographic studios

The officers in charge of property owned or leased by the Government are authorized, upon the recommendation of the Attorney General, to provide quarters, without payment of rent, in any building occupied by the Service, for a photographic studio, operated by welfare organizations without profit and solely for the benefit of persons seeking to comply with requirements under the immigration and nationality laws. Such studio shall be under the supervision of the Attorney General.

(h) Public education regarding naturalization benefits

In order to promote the opportunities and responsibilities of United States citizenship, the Attorney General shall broadly distribute information concerning the benefits which persons may receive under this title and the requirements to obtain such benefits. In carrying out this subsection, the Attorney General shall seek the assistance of appropriate community groups, private voluntary agencies, and other relevant organizations. There are authorized to be appropriated (for each fiscal year beginning with fiscal year 1991) such sums as may be necessary to carry out this subsection.

(June 27, 1952, c. 477, Title III, ch. 2, § 332, 66 Stat. 252; Nov. 29, 1990, Pub.L. 101–649, Title IV, §§ 406, 407(d)(10), 104 Stat. 5040, 5042; Dec. 12, 1991, Pub.L. 102–232, Title III, § 305(m)(6), 105 Stat. 1750.)

§ 333. Photographs; number [8 U.S.C.A. § 1444]

(a) Three identical photographs of the applicant shall be signed by and furnished by each applicant for naturalization or citizenship. One of such photographs shall be affixed by the Attorney General to the original certificate of naturalization issued to the naturalized citizen and one to the duplicate certificate of naturalization required to be forwarded to the Service.

(b) Three identical photographs of the applicant shall be furnished by each applicant for—

(1) a record of lawful admission for permanent residence to be made under section 249 [8 U.S.C.A. § 1259];

(2) a certificate of derivative citizenship;

(3) a certificate of naturalization or of citizenship;

(4) a special certificate of naturalization;

(5) a certificate of naturalization or of citizenship, in lieu of one lost, mutilated, or destroyed;

(6) a new certificate of citizenship in the new name of any naturalized citizen who, subsequent to naturalization, has had his name changed by order of a court of competent jurisdiction or by marriage; and

(7) a declaration of intention.

One such photograph shall be affixed to each such certificate issued by the Attorney General and one shall be affixed to the copy of such certificate retained by the Service.

(June 27, 1952, c. 477, Title III, ch. 2, § 333, 66 Stat. 253; Nov. 29, 1990, Pub.L. 101–649, Title IV, § 407(c)(14), (d)(11), 104 Stat. 5041, 5042; Oct. 25, 1994, Pub.L. 103–416, Title II, § 219(w), 108 Stat. 4318.)

§ 334. Application for naturalization; declaration of intention [8 U.S.C.A. § 1445]

(a) Evidence and form

An applicant for naturalization shall make and file with the Attorney General a sworn application in writing, signed by the applicant in the applicant's own handwriting if physically able to write, which application shall be on a form prescribed by the Attorney General and shall include averments of all facts which in the opinion of the Attorney General may be material to the applicant's naturalization, and required to be proved under this title. In the case of an applicant subject to a requirement of continuous residence under section 316(a) or 319(a) [8 U.S.C.A. §§ 1427(a) or 1430(a)], the application for naturalization may be filed up to 3 months before the date the applicant would first otherwise meet such continuous residence requirement.

(b) Who may file

No person shall file a valid application for naturalization unless he shall have attained the age of eighteen years. An application for naturalization by an alien shall contain an averment of lawful admission for permanent residence.

(c) Hearings

Hearings under section 336(a) [8 U.S.C.A. § 1447(a)] on applications for naturalization shall be held at regular intervals specified by the Attorney General.

(d) Filing of application

Except as provided in subsection (e), an application for naturalization shall be filed in the office of the Attorney General.

(e) Substitute filing place and administering oath other than before Attorney General

A person may file an application for naturalization other than in the office of the Attorney General, and an oath of allegiance administered other than in a public ceremony before the Attorney General or a court, if the Attorney General determines that the person has an illness or other disability which—

(1) is of a permanent nature and is sufficiently serious to prevent the person's personal appearance, or

(2) is of a nature which so incapacitates the person as to prevent him from personally appearing.

(f) Declaration of intention

An alien over 18 years of age who is residing in the United States pursuant to a lawful admission for permanent residence may file with the Attorney General a declaration of intention to become a citizen of the United States. Such a declaration shall be filed in duplicate and in a form prescribed by the Attorney General and shall be accompanied by an application prescribed and approved by the Attorney General. Nothing in this subsection shall be construed as requiring any such alien to make and file a declaration of intention as a condition precedent to filing an application for naturalization nor shall any such declaration of intention be regarded as conferring or having conferred upon any such alien United States citizenship or nationality or the right to United States citizenship or nationality, nor shall such declaration be regarded as evidence of such alien's lawful admission for permanent residence in any proceeding, action, or matter arising under this or any other Act.

(June 27, 1952, c. 477, Title III, ch. 2, § 334, 66 Stat. 254; Pub. L. 97–116, § 15(b), Dec. 29, 1981, 95 Stat. 1619; Pub.L. 101–649, Title IV, §§ 401(b), 407(c)(15), (d)(12), Nov. 29, 1990, 104 Stat. 5038, 5041, 5042; Pub.L. 102–232, Title III, § 305(d), (e), (m)(7), Dec. 12, 1991, 105 Stat. 1750.)

§ 335. Investigation of applicants; examination of applications [8 U.S.C.A. § 1446]

(a) Waiver

Before a person may be naturalized, an employee of the Service, or of the United States designated by the Attorney General, shall conduct a personal investigation of the person applying for naturalization in the vicinity or vicinities in which such person has maintained his actual place of abode and in the vicinity or vicinities in which such person has been employed or has engaged in business or work for at least five years immediately preceding the filing of his application for naturalization. The Attorney General may, in his discretion, waive a personal investigation in an individual case or in such cases or classes of cases as may be designated by him.

(b) Conduct of examinations; authority of designees; record

The Attorney General shall designate employees of the Service to conduct examinations upon petitions for naturalization. For such purposes any such employee so designated is authorized to take testimony concerning any matter touching or in any way affecting the admissibility of any applicant for naturalization, to administer oaths, including the oath of the applicant for naturalization, and to require by subpoena the attendance and testimony of witnesses, including applicant, before such employee so designated and the production of relevant books, papers, and documents, and to that end may invoke the aid of any district court of the United States; and any such court may, in the event of neglect or refusal to respond to a subpoena issued by any such employee so designated or refusal to testify before such employee so designated issue an order requiring such person to appear before such employee so designated, produce relevant books, papers, and documents if demanded, and testify; and any failure to obey such order of the court may be punished by the court as a contempt thereof. The record of the examination authorized by this subsection shall be admissible as evidence in any hearing conducted by an immigration officer under section 336(a) [8 U.S.C.A. § 1447(a)]. Any such employee shall, at the examination, inform the petitioner of the remedies available to the petitioner under section 336 [8 U.S.C.A. § 1447].

(c) Transmittal of record of examination

The record of the examination upon any application for naturalization may, in the discretion of the Attorney General be transmitted to the Attorney General and the determination with respect thereto of the employee designated to conduct such examination shall when made also be transmitted to the Attorney General.

(d) Determination to grant or deny application

The employee designated to conduct any such examination shall make a determination as to whether the application should be granted or denied, with reasons therefor.

(e) Withdrawal of application

After an application for naturalization has been filed with the Attorney General, the applicant shall not be permitted to withdraw his application, except with the consent of the Attorney General. In cases where the Attorney General does not consent to the withdrawal of the application, the application shall be determined on its merits and a final order determination made accordingly. In cases where the applicant fails to prosecute his application, the application shall be decided on the merits unless the Attorney General dismisses it for lack of prosecution.

(f) Transfer of application

An applicant for naturalization who moves from the district of the Service in the United States in which the application is pending may, at any time thereafter, request the Service to transfer the application to any district of the Service in the United States which may act on the application. The transfer shall not be made without the consent of the Attorney General. In the case of such a transfer, the proceedings on the application shall continue as though the application had originally been filed in the district of the Service to which the application is transferred.

(g), (h) Repealed. Pub. L. 97–116, § 15(c)(2), Dec. 29, 1981, 95 Stat. 1619.

(i) Redesignated (f).

(June 27, 1952, c. 477, Title III, ch. 2, § 335, 66 Stat. 255; Pub. L. 97–116, § 15(c), Dec. 29, 1981, 95 Stat. 1619; Pub.L. 100–525, § 9(aa), (bb), Oct. 24, 1988, 102 Stat. 2621; Pub.L. 101–649, Title IV, §§ 401(c), 407(c)(16), (d)(13), Nov. 29, 1990, 104 Stat. 5038, 5041, 5043; Dec. 12, 1991, Pub.L. 102–232, Title III, § 305(f), 105 Stat. 1750.)

§ 336. Hearings on denials of applications for naturalization [8 U.S.C.A. § 1447]

(a) Request for hearing before immigration officer

If, after an examination under section 335 [8 U.S.C.A. § 1446], an application for naturalization is denied, the applicant may request a hearing before an immigration officer.

(b) Request for hearing before district court

If there is a failure to make a determination under section 335 [8 U.S.C.A. § 1446] before the end of the 120-day period after the date on which the examination is conducted under such section, the applicant may apply to the United States district court for the district in which the applicant resides for a hearing on the matter. Such court has jurisdiction over the matter and may either determine the matter or remand the matter, with appropriate instructions, to the Service to determine the matter.

(c) Appearance of Attorney General

494

The Attorney General shall have the right to appear before any immigration officer in any naturalization proceedings for the purpose of cross-examining the applicant and the witnesses produced in support of the application concerning any matter touching or in any way affecting the applicant's right to admission to citizenship, and shall have the right to call witnesses, including the applicant, produce evidence, and be heard in opposition to, or in favor of, the granting of any application in naturalization proceedings.

(d) Subpoena of witness

The immigration officer shall, if the applicant requests it at the time of filing the request for the hearing, issue a subpoena for the witnesses named by such applicant to appear upon the day set for the hearing, but in case such witnesses cannot be produced upon the hearing other witnesses may be summoned upon notice to the Attorney General, in such manner and at such time as the Attorney General may by regulation prescribe. Such subpoenas may be enforced in the same manner as subpoenas under section 335(b) [8 U.S.C.A. § 1446(b)] may be enforced.

(e) Change of name of applicant

It shall be lawful at the time and as a part of the administration by a court of the oath of allegiance under section 337(a) [8 U.S.C.A. § 1448(a)] for the court, in its discretion, upon the bona fide prayer of the applicant included in an appropriate petition to the court, to make a decree changing the name of said person, and the certificate of naturalization shall be issued in accordance therewith.

(f) Redesignated (e).

(June 27, 1952, c. 477, Title III, ch. 2, § 336, 66 Stat. 257; Pub. L. 91–136, Dec. 5, 1969, 83 Stat. 283; Pub. L. 97–116, § 15(d), Dec. 29, 1981, 95 Stat. 1619; Pub.L. 100–525, § 9(cc), Oct. 24, 1988, 102 Stat. 2621; Pub.L. 101–649, Title IV, § 407(c)(17), (d)(14), Nov. 29, 1990, 104 Stat. 5041, 5044; Dec. 12, 1991, Pub.L. 102–232, Title III, § 305(g), (h), 105 Stat. 1750.)

§ 337.   Oath of renunciation and allegiance [8 U.S.C.A. § 1448]

(a) Public ceremony

A person who has applied for naturalization shall, in order to be and before being admitted to citizenship, take in a public ceremony before the Attorney General or a court with jurisdiction under section 310(b) [8 U.S.C.A. § 1421(b)] an oath (1) to support the Constitution of the United States; (2) to renounce and abjure absolutely and entirely all allegiance and fidelity to any foreign prince, potentate, state, or sovereignty of whom or which the applicant was before a subject or citizen; (3) to support and defend the Constitution and the laws of the United States against all enemies, foreign and domestic; (4) to bear true faith and allegiance to the same; and (5)(A) to bear arms on behalf of the United States when required by the law, or (B) to perform noncombatant service in the Armed Forces of the United States when required by the law, or (C) to perform work of national importance under civilian direction when required by the law. Any such person shall be required to take an oath containing the substance of clauses (1) to (5) of the preceding sentence, except that a person who shows by clear and convincing evidence to the satisfaction of the Attorney General that he is opposed to the bearing of arms in the Armed Forces of the United States by reason of religious training and belief shall be required to take an oath containing the substance of clauses (1) to (4) and clauses (5)(B) and (5)(C) of this subsection, and a person who shows by clear and convincing evidence to the satisfaction of the Attorney General that he is opposed to any type of service in the Armed Forces of the United States by reason of religious training and belief shall be required to take an oath containing the substance of said clauses (1) to (4) and clause (5)(C). The term "religious training and belief" as used in this section shall mean an individual's belief in a relation to a Supreme Being involving duties superior to those arising from any human relation, but does not include essentially political, sociological, or philosophical views or a merely personal moral code. In the case of the naturalization of a child under the provisions of section 322 [8 U.S.C.A. § 1433] the Attorney General may waive the taking of the oath if in the opinion of the Attorney General the child is unable to understand its meaning. The Attorney General may waive the taking of the oath by a person if in the opinion of the Attorney General the person is unable to understand, or to communicate an understanding of, its meaning because of a physical or developmental disability or mental impairment. If the Attorney General waives the taking of the oath by a person under the preceding sentence, the person shall be considered to have met the requirements of section 316(a)(3) [8 U.S.C.A. § 1427(a)(3)] with respect to attachment to the principles of the Constitution and well disposition to the good order and happiness of the United States.

(b) Hereditary titles or orders of nobility

In case the person applying for naturalization has borne any hereditary title, or has been of any of the orders of nobility in any foreign state, the applicant shall in addition to complying with the requirements of subsection (a) of this section, make under oath in the same public ceremony in which the oath of allegiance is administered, an express renunciation of such title or order of nobility, and such renunciation shall be recorded as a part of such proceedings.

(c) Expedited administration of oath

Notwithstanding section 310(b) [8 U.S.C.A. § 1421(b)], an individual may be granted an expedited judicial oath administration ceremony or administrative naturalization by the Attorney General upon demonstrating sufficient cause. In determining whether to grant an expedited judicial oath administration ceremony, a court shall consider special circumstances (such as serious illness of the applicant or a member of the applicant's immediate family, permanent disability sufficiently incapacitating as to prevent the applicant's personal appearance at the scheduled ceremony, developmental disability or advanced age, or exigent circumstances relating to travel or employment). If an expedited judicial oath administration ceremony is impracticable, the court shall refer such individual to the Attorney General who may provide for immediate administrative naturalization.

(d) Rules and regulations

The Attorney General shall prescribe rules and procedures to ensure that the ceremonies conducted by the Attorney General for the administration of oaths of allegiance under this section are public, conducted frequently and at regular intervals, and are in keeping with the dignity of the occasion.

(June 27, 1952, c. 477, Title III, ch. 2, § 337, 66 Stat. 258; Pub. L. 97–116, § 18(o), Dec. 29, 1981, 95 Stat. 1621; Pub.L. 101–649, Title IV, § 407(c)(18), (d)(15), Nov. 29, 1990, 104 Stat. 5041, 5044; Pub.L. 102–232, Title I, § 102(b)(2), Title III, § 305(i), Dec. 12, 1991, 105 Stat. 1736, 1750; Nov. 6, 2000, Pub.L. 106–448, § 1, 114 Stat. 1939.)

§ 338.   Certificate   of   naturalization;   contents [8 U.S.C.A. § 1449]

A person admitted to citizenship in conformity with the provisions of this title shall be entitled upon such admission to receive from the Attorney General a certificate of naturalization, which shall contain substantially the following information: Number of application for naturalization; number of certificate of naturalization; date of naturalization; name, signature, place of residence, autographed photograph, and personal description of the naturalized person, including age, sex, marital status, and country of former nationality; location of the district office of the Service in which the application was filed and the title, authority, and location of the official or court administering the oath of allegiance; statement that the Attorney General having found that the applicant had complied in all respects with all of the applicable provisions of the naturalization laws of the United States, and was entitled to be admitted a citizen of the United States of America, thereupon ordered that the applicant be admitted as a citizen of the United States of America; attestation of an immigration officer; and the seal of the Department of Justice.

(June 27, 1952, c. 447, Title III, ch. 2, § 338, 66 Stat. 259; Nov. 29, 1990, Pub.L. 101–649, Title IV, § 407(c)(19), (d)(16), 104 Stat. 5041, 5045; Dec. 12, 1991, Pub.L. 102–232, Title III, § 305(j), 105 Stat. 1750; Oct. 25, 1994, Pub.L. 103–416, Title I, § 104(a), Title II, § 219(z)(3), 108 Stat. 4308, 4318.)

§ 339. Functions and duties of clerks and records of declarations of intention and applications for naturalization [8 U.S.C.A. § 1450]

(a) The clerk of each court that administers oaths of allegiance under section 337 [8 U.S.C.A. § 1448] shall—

(1) deliver to each person administered the oath of allegiance by the court pursuant to section 337(a) [8 U.S.C.A. § 1448(a)] the certificate of naturalization prepared by the Attorney General pursuant to section 310(b)(2)(A)(ii) [8 U.S.C.A. § 1421(b)(2)(A)(ii)],

(2) forward to the Attorney General a list of applicants actually taking the oath as each scheduled ceremony and information concerning each person to whom such an oath is administered by the court, within 30 days after the close of the month in which the oath was administered,

(3) forward to the Attorney General certified copies of such other proceedings and orders instituted in or issued out of the court affecting or relating to the naturalization of persons as may be required from time to time by the Attorney General, and

(4) be responsible for all blank certificates of naturalization received by them from time to time from the Attorney General and shall account to the Attorney General for them whenever required to do so.

No certificate of naturalization received by any clerk of court which may be defaced or injured in such manner as to prevent its use as herein provided shall in any case be destroyed, but such certificates shall be returned to the Attorney General.

(b) Each district office of the Service in the United States shall maintain, in chronological order, indexed, and consecutively numbered, as part of its permanent records, all declarations of intention and applications for naturalization filed with the office.

(June 27, 1952, c. 477, Title III, ch. 2, § 339, 66 Stat. 259; Nov. 29, 1990, Pub.L. 101–649, Title IV, § 407(d)(17), 104 Stat. 5045; Dec. 12, 1991, Pub.L. 102–232, Title I, § 102(b)(1), 105 Stat. 1735.)

§ 340. Revocation of naturalization [8 U.S.C.A. § 1451]

(a) Concealment of material evidence; refusal to testify

It shall be the duty of the United States attorneys for the respective districts, upon affidavit showing good cause therefor, to institute proceedings in any district court of the United States in the judicial district in which the naturalized citizen may reside at the time of bringing suit, for the purpose of revoking and setting aside the order admitting such person to citizenship and canceling the certificate of naturalization on the ground that such order and certificate of naturalization were illegally procured or were procured by concealment of a material fact or by willful misrepresentation, and such revocation and setting aside of the order admitting such person to citizenship and such canceling of certificate of naturalization shall be effective as of the original date of the order and certificate, respectively: Provided, That refusal on the part of a naturalized citizen within a period of ten years following his naturalization to testify as a witness in any proceeding before a congressional committee concerning his subversive activities, in a case where such person has been convicted of contempt for such refusal, shall be held to constitute a ground for revocation of such person's naturalization under this subsection as having been procured by concealment of a material fact or by willful misrepresentation. If the naturalized citizen does not reside in any judicial district in the United States at the time of bringing such suit, the proceedings may be instituted in the United States District Court for the District of Columbia or in the United States district court in the judicial district in which such person last had his residence.

(b) Notice to party

The party to whom was granted the naturalization alleged to have been illegally procured or procured by concealment of a material fact or by willful misrepresentation shall, in any such proceedings under subsection (a) of this section, have sixty days' personal notice, unless waived by such party, in which to make answers to the petition of the United States; and if such naturalized person be absent from the United States or from the judicial district in which such person last had his residence, such notice shall be given either by personal service upon him or by publication in the manner provided for the service of summons by publication or upon absentees by the laws of the State or the place where such suit is brought.

(c) Membership in certain organizations; prima facie evidence

If a person who shall have been naturalized after December 24, 1952 shall within five years next following such naturalization become a member of or affiliated with any organization, membership in or affiliation with which at the time of naturalization would have precluded such person from naturalization under the provisions of section 313 [8 U.S.C.A. § 1424], it shall be considered prima facie evidence that such person was not attached to the principles of the Constitution of the United States and was not well disposed to the good order and happiness of the United States at the time of naturalization, and, in the absence of countervailing evidence, it shall be sufficient in the proper proceeding to authorize the revocation and setting aside of the order admitting such person to citizenship and the cancellation of the certificate of naturalization as having been obtained by concealment of a material fact or by willful misrepresentation, and such revocation and setting aside of the order admitting such person to citizenship and such canceling of certificate of naturalization shall be effective as of the original date of the order and certificate, respectively.

(d) Applicability to citizenship through naturalization of parent or spouse

Any person who claims United States citizenship through the naturalization of a parent or spouse in whose case there is a revocation and setting aside of the order admitting such parent or spouse to citizenship under the provisions of subsection (a) of this section on the ground that the order and certificate of naturalization were procured by concealment of a material fact or by willful misrepresentation shall be deemed to have lost and to lose his citizenship and any right or privilege of citizenship which he may have, now has, or may hereafter acquire under and by virtue of such naturalization of such parent or spouse, regardless of whether such person is residing within or without the United States at the time of the revocation and setting aside of the order admitting such parent or spouse to citizenship. Any person who claims United States citizenship through the naturalization of a parent or spouse in whose case there is a revocation and setting aside of the order admitting such parent or spouse to citizenship and the cancellation of the certificate of naturalization under the provisions of subsection (c) of this section, or under the provisions of section 329(c) [8 U.S.C.A. § 1440 (c)] on any ground other than that the order and certificate of naturalization were procured by concealment of a material fact or by willful misrepresentation, shall be deemed to have lost and to lose his citizenship and any right or privilege of citizenship which would have been enjoyed by such person had there not been a revocation and setting aside of the order admitting such parent or spouse to citizenship and the cancellation of the certificate of naturalization, unless such person is residing in the United States at the time of the revocation and setting aside of the order admitting such parent or spouse to citizenship and the cancellation of the certificate of naturalization.

(e) Citizenship unlawfully procured

When a person shall be convicted under section 1425 of Title 18 of knowingly procuring naturalization in violation of law, the court in which such conviction is had shall thereupon revoke, set aside, and declare void the final order admitting such person to citizenship, and shall declare the certificate of naturalization of such person to be canceled. Jurisdiction is conferred on the courts having jurisdiction of the trial of such offense to make such adjudication.

(f) Cancellation of certificate of naturalization

Whenever an order admitting an alien to citizenship shall be revoked and set aside or a certificate of naturalization shall be canceled, or both, as provided in this section, the court in which such judgment or decree is rendered shall make an order canceling such certificate and shall send a certified copy of such order to the Attorney General. The clerk of court shall transmit a copy of such order and judgment to the Attorney General. A person holding a certificate of naturalization or citizenship which has been canceled as provided by this section shall upon notice by the court by which the decree of cancellation was made, or by the Attorney General, surrender the same to the Attorney General.

(g) Applicability of certificates of naturalization and citizenship

The provisions of this section shall apply not only to any naturalization granted and to certificates of naturalization and citizenship issued under the provisions of this title, but to any naturalization heretofore granted by any court, and to all certificates of naturalization and citizenship which may have been issued heretofore by any court or by the Commissioner based upon naturalization granted by any court, or by a designated representative of the Commissioner under the provisions of section 702 of the Nationality Act of 1940, as amended, or by such designated representative under any other act.

(h) Power to correct, reopen, alter, modify, or vacate order

Nothing contained in this section shall be regarded as limiting, denying, or restricting the power of the Attorney General to correct, reopen, alter, modify, or vacate an order naturalizing the person.

(June 27, 1952, c. 477, Title III, ch. 2, § 340, 66 Stat. 260; Sept. 3, 1954, c. 1263, § 18, 68 Stat. 1232; Sept. 26, 1961, Pub.L. 87–301, § 18, 75 Stat. 656; Nov. 14, 1986, Pub.L. 99–653, § 17, 100 Stat. 3658; Oct. 24, 1988, Pub.L. 100–525, § 9(dd), 102 Stat. 2621; Nov. 29, 1990, Pub.L. 101–649, Title IV, § 407(d)(18), 104 Stat. 5046; Dec. 12, 1991, Pub.L. 102–232, Title III, § 305(k), 105 Stat. 1750; Oct. 25, 1994, Pub.L. 103–416, Title I, § 104(b), (c), 108 Stat. 4308.)

§ 341. Certificates of citizenship or U.S. non-citizen national status; procedure [8 U.S.C.A. § 1452]

(a) Application to Attorney General for certificate of citizenship; proof; oath of allegiance

A person who claims to have derived United States citizenship through the naturalization of a parent or through the naturalization or citizenship of a husband, or who is a citizen of the United States by virtue of the provisions of section 1993 of the United States Revised Statutes, or of section 1993 of the United States Revised Statutes, as amended by section 1 of the Act of May 24, 1934 (48 Stat. 797), or who is a citizen of the United States by virtue of the provisions of subsection (c), (d), (e), (g), or (i) of section 201 of the Nationality Act of 1940, as amended (54 Stat. 1138), or of the Act of May 7, 1934 (48 Stat. 667), or of paragraph (c), (d), (e), or (g) of section 301 [8 U.S.C.A. § 1401], or under the provisions of the Act of August 4, 1937 (50 Stat. 558), or under the provisions of section 203 or 205 of the Nationality Act of 1940 (54 Stat. 1139), or under the provisions of section 303 [8 U.S.C.A. § 1403], may apply to the Attorney General for a certificate of citizenship. Upon proof to the satisfaction of the Attorney General that the applicant is a citizen, and that the applicant's alleged citizenship was derived as claimed, or acquired, as the case may be, and upon taking and subscribing before a member of the Service within the United States to the oath of allegiance required by this chapter of an applicant for naturalization, such individual shall be furnished by the Attorney General with a certificate of citizenship, but only if such individual is at the time within the United States.

(b) Application to Secretary of State for certificate of non-citizen national status; proof; oath of allegiance

A person who claims to be a national, but not a citizen, of the United States may apply to the Secretary of State for a certificate of non-citizen national status. Upon—

(1) proof to the satisfaction of the Secretary of State that the applicant is a national, but not a citizen, of the United States, and

(2) in the case of such a person born outside of the United States or its outlying possessions, taking and subscribing, before an immigration officer within the United States or its outlying possessions, to the oath of allegiance required by this chapter of a petitioner for naturalization, the individual shall be furnished by the Secretary of State with a certificate of non-citizen national status, but only if the individual is at the time within the United States or its outlying possessions.

(June 27, 1952, c. 477, Title III, ch. 2, § 341, 66 Stat. 263; Dec. 29, 1981, Pub.L. 97–116, § 18(p), 95 Stat. 1621; Aug. 27, 1986, Pub.L. 99–396, § 16(a), 100 Stat. 843; Nov. 14, 1986, Pub.L. 99–653, § 22, 100 Stat. 3658; Oct. 24, 1988, Pub.L. 100–525, § 8(q), 102 Stat. 2618; Dec. 12, 1991, Pub.L. 102–232, Title III, § 305(m)(8), 105 Stat. 1750; Oct. 25, 1994, Pub.L. 103–416, Title I, § 102(b), 108 Stat. 4307.)

§ 342. Cancellation of certificates issued by Attorney General, the Commissioner or a Deputy Commissioner; action not to affect citizenship status [8 U.S.C.A. § 1453]

The Attorney General is authorized to cancel any certificate of citizenship, certificate of naturalization, copy of a declaration of intention, or other certificate, document or record heretofore issued or made by the Commissioner or a Deputy Commissioner or hereafter made by the Attorney General if it shall appear to the Attorney General's satisfaction that such document or record was illegally or fraudulently obtained from, or was created through illegality or by fraud practiced upon, him or the Commissioner or a Deputy Commissioner; but the person for or to whom such document or record has been issued or made shall be given at such person's last-known place of address written notice of the intention to cancel such document or record with the reasons therefor and shall be given at least sixty days in which to show cause why such document or record should not be canceled. The cancellation under this section of any document purporting to show the citizenship status of the person to whom it was issued shall affect only the document and not the citizenship status of the person in whose name the document was issued.

(June 27, 1952, c. 477, Title III, ch. 2, § 342, 66 Stat. 263.)

§ 343. Documents and copies issued by Attorney General [8 U.S.C.A. § 1454]

(a) If any certificate of naturalization or citizenship issued to any citizen or any declaration of intention furnished to any declarant is lost, mutilated, or destroyed, the citizen or declarant may make application to the Attorney General for a new certificate or declaration. If the Attorney General finds that the certificate or declaration is lost, mutilated, or destroyed, he shall issue to the applicant a new certificate or declaration. If the certificate or declaration has been mutilated, it shall be surrendered to the Attorney General before the applicant may receive such new certificate or declaration. If the certificate or declaration has been lost, the applicant or any other person who shall have, or may come into possession of it is required to surrender it to the Attorney General.

(b) The Attorney General shall issue for any naturalized citizen, on such citizen's application therefor, a special certificate of naturalization for use by such citizen only for the purpose of obtaining recognition as a citizen of the United States by a foreign state. Such certificate when issued shall be furnished to the Secretary of State for transmission to the proper authority in such foreign state.

(c) If the name of any naturalized citizen has, subsequent to naturalization, been changed by order of any court of competent jurisdiction, or by marriage, the citizen may make application for a new certificate of naturalization in the new name of such citizen. If the Attorney General finds the name of the applicant to have been changed as claimed, the Attorney General shall issue to the applicant a new certificate and shall notify the naturalization court of such action.

(d) The Attorney General is authorized to make and issue certifications of any part of the naturalization records of any court, or of any certificate of naturalization or citizenship, for use in complying with any statute, State or Federal, or in any judicial proceeding. No such certification shall be made by any clerk of court except upon order of the court.

(June 27, 1952, c. 477, Title III, ch. 2, § 343, 66 Stat. 263; Pub.L. 100–525, § 9(ee), Oct. 24, 1988, 102 Stat. 2621.)

§ 344. Fiscal provisions [8 U.S.C.A. § 1455]

(a) The Attorney General shall charge, collect, and account for fees prescribed by the Attorney General pursuant to section 9701 of Title 31 for the following:

(1) Making, filing, and docketing an application for naturalization, including the hearing on such application, if such hearing be held, and a certificate of naturalization, if the issuance of such certificate is authorized by the Attorney General.

(2) Receiving and filing a declaration of intention, and issuing a duplicate thereof.

(b) Notwithstanding the provisions of this Act or any other law, no fee shall be charged or collected for an application for declaration of intention or a certificate of naturalization in lieu of a declaration or a certificate alleged to have been lost, mutilated, or destroyed, submitted by a person who was a member of the military or naval forces of the United States at any time after April 20, 1898, and before July 5, 1902; or at any time after April 5, 1917, and before November 12, 1918; or who served on the Mexican border as a member of the Regular Army or National Guard between June 1916 and April 1917; or who has served or hereafter serves in the military, air, or naval forces of the United States after September 16, 1940, and who was not at any time during such period or thereafter separated from such forces under other than honorable conditions, who was not a conscientious objector who performed no military duty whatever or refused to wear the uniform, or who was not at any time during such period or thereafter discharged from such military, air, or naval forces on account of alienage.

(c) Except as provided by section 286(q)(2) [8 U.S.C.A. § 1356(q)(2)] or any other law, all fees collected by the Attorney General shall be deposited by the Attorney General in the Treasury of the United States except that all such fees collected or paid over on or after October 1, 1988, shall be deposited in the Immigration Examinations Fee Account established under section 286(m) [8 U.S.C.A. § 1356(m)]: *Provided, however*, That all fees received by the Attorney General from applicants residing in the Virgin Islands of the United States, and in Guam, under this title, shall be paid over to the treasury of the Virgin Islands and to the treasury of Guam, respectively.

(d) During the time when the United States is at war the Attorney General may not charge or collect a naturalization fee from an alien in the military, air, or naval service of the United States for filing an application for naturalization or issuing a certificate of naturalization upon admission to citizenship.

(e) In addition to the other fees required by this title, the applicant for naturalization shall, upon the filing of an application for naturalization, deposit with and pay to the Attorney General a sum of money sufficient to cover the expenses of subpoenaing and paying the legal fees of any witnesses for whom such applicant may request a subpoena, and upon the final discharge of such witnesses, they shall receive, if they demand the same from the Attorney General, the customary and usual witness fees from the moneys which the applicant shall have paid to the Attorney General for such purpose, and the residue, if any, shall be returned by the Attorney General to the applicant.

(f)(1) The Attorney General shall pay over to courts administering oaths of allegiance to persons under this title a specified percentage of all fees described in subsection (a)(1) collected by the Attorney General with respect to persons administered the oath of allegiance by the respective courts. The Attorney General, annually and in consultation with the courts, shall determine the specified percentage based on the proportion, of the total costs incurred by the Service and courts for essential services directly related to the naturalization process, which are incurred by courts.

(2) The Attorney General shall provide on an annual basis to the Committees on the Judiciary of the House of Representatives and of the Senate a detailed report on the use of the fees described in paragraph (1) and shall consult with such Committees before increasing such fees.

(g) to (i) Redesignated (c) to (e).

(June 27, 1952, c. 477, Title III, ch. 2, § 344, 66 Stat. 264; Pub. L. 85–508, § 26, July 7, 1958, 72 Stat. 351; Pub. L. 90–609, § 3, Oct. 21, 1968, 82 Stat. 1200; Pub. L. 97–116, § 16, Dec. 29, 1981, 95 Stat. 1619; Pub.L. 100–459, Title II, § 209(b), Oct. 1, 1988, 102 Stat. 2203; Pub.L. 100–525, § 9(ff), Oct. 24, 1988, 102 Stat. 2621; Pub.L. 101–649, Title IV, § 407(c)(20), (d)(19), Nov. 29, 1990, 104 Stat. 5041, 5046; Pub.L. 100–459, Title II, § 209(b), amended Pub.L. 102–232, Title I, § 102(b)(3), Title III, §§ 305(*l*),309(a)(1)(A)(ii), Dec. 12, 1991, 105 Stat. 1758; Pub.L. 102–232 309(b)(14), Dec. 12, 1991, 105 Stat. 1736, 1750, 1758, 1759; Nov. 2, 2002, Pub.L. 107–273, Div. C, Title I, § 11016(1), 116 Stat. 1824.)

§ 345. Repealed. Pub. L. 86–682, § 12(c), Sept. 2, 1960, 74 Stat. 708, eff. Sept. 1, 1960 [8 U.S.C.A. § 1456]

§ 346. Publication and distribution of citizenship textbooks; use of naturalization fees [8 U.S.C.A. § 1457]

Authorization is granted for the publication and distribution of the citizenship textbook described in subsection (b) of section 332 [8 U.S.C.A. § 1443(b)] and for the reimbursement of the appropriation of the Department of Justice upon the records of the Treasury Department from the naturalization fees deposited in the Treasury through the Service for the cost of such publication and distribution, such reimbursement to be made upon statements by the Attorney General of books so published and distributed.

(June 27, 1952, c. 477, Title III, ch. 2, § 346, 66 Stat. 266.)

§ 347. Compilation of naturalization statistics and payment for equipment [8 U.S.C.A. § 1458]

The Attorney General is authorized and directed to prepare from the records in the custody of the Service a report upon those heretofore seeking citizenship to show by nationalities their relation to the numbers of aliens annually arriving and to the prevailing census populations of the foreign-born, their economic, vocational, and other classification, in statistical form, with analytical comment thereon, and to prepare such report annually hereafter. Payment for the equipment used in preparing such compilation shall be made from the appropriation for the enforcement of this Act by the Service.

(June 27, 1952, c. 477, Title III, ch. 2, § 347, 66 Stat. 266.)

§ 348.   Repealed [8 U.S.C.A. § 1459].

Chapter III—Loss of Nationality

§ 349.   Loss of nationality by native-born or natural-ized citizen; voluntary action; burden of proof; presumptions [8 U.S.C.A. § 1481]

(a) A person who is a national of the United States whether by birth or naturalization, shall lose his nationality by voluntarily performing any of the following acts with the intention of relinquishing United States nationality—

(1) obtaining naturalization in a foreign state upon his own appli-cation, or upon an application filed by a duly authorized agent, after having attained the age of eighteen years; or

(2) taking an oath or making an affirmation or other formal decla-ration of allegiance to a foreign state or a political subdivision thereof, after having attained the age of eighteen years; or

(3) entering, or serving in, the armed forces of a foreign state if **(A)** such armed forces are engaged in hostilities against the United States, or **(B)** such persons serve as a commissioned or noncommissioned of-ficer; or

(4)(A) accepting, serving in, or performing the duties of any office, post, or employment under the government of a foreign state or a po-litical subdivision thereof, after attaining the age of eighteen years, if he has or acquires the nationality of such foreign state; or

(B) accepting, serving in, or performing the duties of any office, post, or employment under the government of a foreign state or a po-litical subdivision thereof, after attaining the age of eighteen years for which office, post, or employment an oath, affirmation, or declaration of allegiance is required; or

(5) making a formal renunciation of nationality before a diplomatic or consular officer of the United States in a foreign state, in such form as may be prescribed by the Secretary of State; or

(6) making in the United States a formal written renunciation of nationality in such form as may be prescribed by, and before such of-ficer as may be designated by, the Attorney General, whenever the United States shall be in a state of war and the Attorney General shall approve such renunciation as not contrary to the interests of national defense; or

(7) committing any act of treason against, or attempting by force to overthrow, or bearing arms against, the United States, violating or conspiring to violate any of the provisions of section 2383 of Title 18, or willfully performing any act in violation of section 2385 of Title 18, or violating section 2384 of Title 18 by engaging in a conspiracy to over-throw, put down, or to destroy by force the Government of the United States, or to levy war against them, if and when he is convicted thereof by a court martial or by a court of competent jurisdiction.

(b) Whenever the loss of United States nationality is put in issue in any action or proceeding commenced on or after September 26, 1961 un-der, or by virtue of, the provisions of this Act or any other Act, the burden shall be upon the person or party claiming that such loss occurred, to establish such claim by a preponderance of the evidence. Any person who commits or performs, or who has committed or performed, any act of ex-patriation under the provisions of this or any other Act shall be presumed to have done so voluntarily, but such presumption may be rebutted upon a showing, by a preponderance of the evidence, that the act or acts com-mitted or performed were not done voluntarily.

(June 27, 1952, c. 477, Title III, ch. 3, § 349, 66 Stat. 267; Sept. 3, 1954, c. 1256, § 2, 68 Stat. 1146; Pub.L. 87–301, § 19, Sept. 26, 1961, 75 Stat. 656; Pub.L. 94–412, Title V, § 501(a), Sept. 14, 1976, 90 Stat. 1258; Pub.L. 95–432, §§ 2, 4, Oct. 10, 1978, 92 Stat. 1046; Pub.L. 97–116, § 18(k)(2), (q), Dec. 29, 1981, 95 Stat. 1620, 1621; Pub.L. 99–653, §§ 18, 19, Nov. 14, 1986, 100 Stat. 3658, as amended Pub.L. 100–525, §§ 8(m), (n), 9(hh), Oct. 24, 1988, 102 Stat. 2618, 2622.)

§ 350.   Repealed. Pub. L. 95–432, § 1, Oct. 10, 1978, 92 Stat. 1046 [8 U.S.C.A. § 1482]

§ 351.   Restrictions on loss of nationality [8 U.S.C.A. § 1483]

(a) Except as provided in paragraphs (6) and (7) of section 349(a) of this title [8 U.S.C.A. § 1481(a)], no national of the United States can lose United States nationality under this Act while within the United States or any of its outlying possessions, but loss of nationality shall result from the performance within the United States or any of its outlying posses-sions of any of the acts or the fulfillment of any of the conditions specified in this part if and when the national thereafter takes up a residence out-side the United States and its outlying possessions.

(b) A national who within six months after attaining the age of eigh-teen years asserts his claim to United States nationality, in such man-ner as the Secretary of State shall by regulation prescribe, shall not be deemed to have lost United States nationality by the commission, prior to his eighteenth birthday, of any of the acts specified in paragraphs (3) and (5) of section 349(a) [8 U.S.C.A. § 1481(a)].

(June 27, 1952, c. 477, Title III, ch. 3, § 351, 66 Stat. 269; Dec. 29, 1981, Pub.L. 97–116, § 18(r), 95 Stat. 1621; Nov. 14, 1986, Pub.L. 99–653, § 20, 100 Stat. 3658; Oct. 24, 1988, Pub.L. 100–525, § 8(o), 102 Stat. 2618; Oct. 25, 1994, Pub.L. 103–416, Title I, § 105(a), 108 Stat. 4308; Sept. 30, 1996, Pub.L. 104–208, Div. C, Title VI, § 671(b)(3), 110 Stat. 3009–721.)

§§ 352 to 355.   Repealed. Pub. L. 95–432, § 2, Oct. 10, 1978, 92 Stat. 1046 [8 U.S.C.A. §§ 1484 to 1487]

§ 356.   Nationality lost solely from performance of acts or fulfillment of conditions [8 U.S.C.A. § 1488]

The loss of nationality under this part shall result solely from the performance by a national of the acts or fulfillment of the conditions specified in this Part.

(June 27, 1952, c. 477, Title III, ch. 3, § 356, 66 Stat. 272.)

§ 357.   Application of treaties; exceptions [8 U.S.C.A. § 1489]

Nothing in this title shall be applied in contravention of the provisions of any treaty or convention to which the United States is a party and which has been ratified by the Senate before December 25, 1952: *Provided, however,* That no woman who was a national of the United States shall be deemed to have lost her nationality solely by reason of her marriage to an alien on or after September 22, 1922, or to an alien racially ineligible to citizenship on or after March 3, 1931, or, in the case of a woman who was a United States citizen at birth, through residence abroad following such marriage, notwithstanding the provisions of any existing treaty or convention.

(June 27, 1952, c. 477, Title III, ch. 3, § 357, 66 Stat. 272; Pub.L. 100–525, § 9(ii), Oct. 24, 1988, 102 Stat. 2622.)

CHAPTER IV—MISCELLANEOUS

§ 358.   Certificate of diplomatic or consular officer of United States as to loss of American nationality [8 U.S.C.A. § 1501]

Whenever a diplomatic or consular officer of the United States has reason to believe that a person while in a foreign state has lost his United States nationality under any provision of chapter 3 of this title, or under any provision of chapter IV of the Nationality Act of 1940, as amended, he shall certify the facts upon which such belief is based to the Department of State, in writing, under regulations prescribed by the Secretary of State. If the report of the diplomatic or consular officer is approved by the Secretary of State, a copy of the certificate shall be forwarded to the Attorney General, for his information, and the diplomatic or consular office in which the report was made shall be directed to forward a copy of the certificate to the person to whom it relates. Approval by the Secretary of State of a certificate under this section shall constitute a final administrative determination of loss of United States nationality under this Act, subject to such procedures for administrative appeal as the Secretary may prescribe by regulation, and also shall constitute a denial of a right or privilege of United States nationality for purposes of section 360 [8 U.S.C.A. § 1503].

(June 27, 1952, c. 477, Title III, ch. 3, § 358, 66 Stat. 272; Oct. 25, 1994, Pub.L. 103–416, Title I, § 106, 108 Stat. 4309.)

§ 359.   Certificate of nationality issued by Secretary of State for person not a naturalized citizen of United States for use in proceedings of a foreign state [8 U.S.C.A. § 1502]

The Secretary of State is authorized to issue, in his discretion and in accordance with rules and regulations prescribed by him, a certificate of nationality for any person not a naturalized citizen of the United States who presents satisfactory evidence that he is an American national and that such certificate is needed for use in judicial or administrative proceedings in a foreign state. Such certificate shall be solely for use in the case for which it was issued and shall be transmitted by the Secretary of State through appropriate official channels to the judicial or administrative officers of the foreign state in which it is to be used.

(June 27, 1952, c. 477, Title III, ch. 4, § 359, 66 Stat. 273.)

§ 360.   Denial of rights and privileges as national [8 U.S.C.A. § 1503]

(a) Proceedings for declaration of United States nationality

If any person who is within the United States claims a right or privilege as a national of the United States and is denied such right or privilege by any department or independent agency, or official thereof, upon the ground that he is not a national of the United States, such person may institute an action under the provisions of section 2201 of Title 28 against the head of such department or independent agency for a judgment declaring him to be a national of the United States, except that no such action may be instituted in any case if the issue of such person's status as a national of the United States **(1)** arose by reason of, or in connection with any removal proceeding under the provisions of this or any other act, or **(2)** is in issue in any such removal proceeding. An action under this subsection may be instituted only within five years after the final administrative denial of such right or privilege and shall be filed in the district court of the United States for the district in which such person resides or claims a residence, and jurisdiction over such officials in such cases is conferred upon those courts.

(b) Application for certificate of identity; appeal

If any person who is not within the United States claims a right or privilege as a national of the United States and is denied such right or privilege by any department or independent agency, or official thereof, upon the ground that he is not a national of the United States, such person may make application to a diplomatic or consular officer of the United States in the foreign country in which he is residing for a certificate of identity for the purpose of traveling to a port of entry in the United States and applying for admission. Upon proof to the satisfaction of such diplomatic or consular officer that such application is made in good faith and has a substantial basis, he shall issue to such person a certificate of identity. From any denial of an application for such certificate the applicant shall be entitled to an appeal to the Secretary of State, who, if he approves the denial, shall state in writing his reasons for his decision. The Secretary of State shall prescribe rules and regulations for the issuance of certificates of identity as above provided. The provisions of this subsection shall be applicable only to a person who at some time prior to his application for the certificate of identity has been physically present in the United States, or to a person under sixteen years of age who was born abroad of a United States citizen parent.

(c) Application for admission to United States under certificate of identity; revision of determination

A person who has been issued a certificate of identity under the provisions of subsection (b), and while in possession thereof, may apply for admission to the United States at any port of entry, and shall be subject to all the provisions of this Act relating to the conduct of proceedings involving aliens seeking admission to the United States. A final determination by the Attorney General that any such person is not entitled to admission to the United States shall be subject to review by any court of competent jurisdiction in habeas corpus proceedings and not otherwise. Any person described in this section who is finally denied admission to the United States shall be subject to all the provisions of this Act relating to aliens seeking admission to the United States.

(June 27, 1952, c. 477, Title III, ch. 3, § 360, 66 Stat. 273; Sept. 30, 1996, Pub.L. 104–208, Div. C, Title III, § 308(d)(4)(P), 110 Stat. 3009–619.)

§ 361. Cancellation of United States passports and Consular Reports of Birth [8 U.S.C.A. § 1504]

(a) The Secretary of State is authorized to cancel any United States passport or Consular Report of Birth, or certified copy thereof, if it appears that such document was illegally, fraudulently, or erroneously obtained from, or was created through illegality or fraud practiced upon, the Secretary. The person for or to whom such document has been issued or made shall be given, at such person's last known address, written notice of the cancellation of such document, together with the procedures for seeking a prompt post-cancellation hearing. The cancellation under this section of any document purporting to show the citizenship status of the person to whom it was issued shall affect only the document and not the citizenship status of the person in whose name the document was issued.

(b) For purposes of this section, the term "Consular Report of Birth" refers to the report, designated as a "Report of Birth Abroad of a Citizen of the United States", issued by a consular officer to document a citizen born abroad.

(June 27, 1952, c. 477, Title III, ch. 3, § 361, as added Oct. 25, 1994, Pub.L. 103–416, Title I, § 107(a), 108 Stat. 4309.)

TITLE IV

MISCELLANEOUS AND REFUGEE ASSISTANCE

§ 404.   Authorization of appropriations [8 U.S.C.A. § 1101, note]

(a) There are authorized to be appropriated such sums as may be necessary to carry out the provisions of this Act (other than chapter 2 of title IV).

(b)(1) There are authorized to be appropriated (for fiscal year 1991 and any subsequent fiscal year) to an immigration emergency fund, to be established in the Treasury, an amount sufficient to provide for a balance of $35,000,000 in such fund, to be used to carry out paragraph (2) and to provide for an increase in border patrol or other enforcement activities of the Service and for reimbursement of State and localities in providing assistance as requested by the Attorney General in meeting an immigration emergency, except that no amounts may be withdrawn from such fund with respect to an emergency unless the President has determined that the immigration emergency exists and has certified such fact to the Judiciary Committees of the House of Representatives and of the Senate.

(2)(A) Funds which are authorized to be appropriated by paragraph (1), subject to the dollar limitation contained in subparagraph (B), shall be available, by application for the reimbursement of States and localities providing assistance as required by the Attorney General, to States and localities whenever—

(i) a district director of the Service certifies to the Commissioner that the number of asylum applications filed in the respective district during a calendar quarter exceeds by at least 1,000 the number of such applications filed in that district during the preceding calendar quarter,

(ii) the lives, property, safety, or welfare of the residents of a State or locality are endangered, or

(iii) in any other circumstances as determined by the Attorney General.

In applying clause (i), the providing of parole at a point of entry in a district shall be deemed to constitute an application for asylum in the district.

(B) Not more than $20,000,000 shall be made available for all localities under this paragraph.

(C) For purposes of subparagraph (A), the requirement of paragraph (1) that an immigration emergency be determined shall not apply.

(D) A decision with respect to an application for reimbursement under subparagraph (A) shall be made by the Attorney General within 15 days after the date of receipt of the application.

(June 27, 1952, c. 477, Title IV, ch. 2, § 404, as amended Pub.L. 97–116, § 18(s), Dec. 29, 1981, 95 Stat. 1621; Pub.L. 99–603, Title I, § 113, Nov. 6, 1986, 100 Stat. 3383; Pub.L. 101–649, Title VII, § 705(a), Nov. 29, 1990, 104 Stat. 5087; Pub.L. 102–232, Title III, § 308(d), Dec. 12, 1991, 105 Stat. 1757.)

§ 405.   Savings clause [8 U.S.C.A. § 1101, note]

(a) Nothing contained in this Act, unless otherwise specifically provided therein, shall be construed to affect the validity of any declaration of intention, petition for naturalization, certificate of naturalization, certificate of citizenship, warrant of arrest, order or warrant of deportation, order of exclusion, or other document or proceeding which shall be valid at the time this Act shall take effect; or to affect any prosecution, suit, action, or proceedings, civil or criminal, brought, or any status, condition, right in process of acquisition, act, thing, liability, obligation, or matter, civil or criminal, done or existing, at the time this Act shall take effect; but as to all such prosecutions, suits, actions, proceedings, statutes [sic] conditions, rights, acts, things, liabilities, obligations, or matters the statutes or parts of statutes repealed by this Act are, unless otherwise specifically provided therein, hereby continued in force and effect. When an immigrant, in possession of an unexpired immigrant visa issued prior to the effective date of this Act, makes application for admission, his admissibility shall be determined under the provisions of law in effect on the date of the issuance of such visa. An application for suspension of deportation under § 19 of the Immigration Act of 1917, as amended, or for adjustment of status under § 4 of the Displaced Persons Act of 1948, as amended, which is pending on the date of enactment of this Act [June 27, 1952], shall be regarded as a proceeding within the meaning of this subsection.

(b) Except as otherwise specifically provided in title III, any petition for naturalization heretofore filed which may be pending at the time this Act shall take effect shall be heard and determined in accordance with the requirements of law in effect when such petition was filed.

(c) Except as otherwise specifically provided in this Act, the repeal of any statute by this Act shall not terminate nationality heretofore lawfully acquired nor restore nationality heretofore lost under any law of the United States or any treaty to which the United States may have been a party.

(d) Except as otherwise specifically provided in this Act, or any amendment thereto, fees, charges and prices for purposes specified in title V of the Independent Offices Appropriation Act, 1952 (Public Law

137, Eighty-second Congress, approved August 31, 1951), may be fixed and established in the manner and by the head of any Federal Agency as specified in that Act.

(e) This Act shall not be construed to repeal, alter, or amend section 231(a) of the Act of April 30, 1946 (60 Stat. 148; 22 U.S.C. 1281(a)), the Act of June 20, 1949 (Public Law 110, section 8, Eighty-first Congress, first session; 63 Stat. 208 [section 403h of Title 50]), the Act of June 5, 1950 (Public Law 535, Eighty-first Congress, second session [former section 1501 et seq. of Title 22]), nor Title V of the Agricultural Act of 1949, as amended (Public Law 78, Eighty-second Congress, first session [sections 1461 to 1468 of Title 7]).

(June 27, 1952, c. 477, Title IV, ch. 2, § 405, 66 Stat. 274.)

§ 406.   Separability clause [8 U.S.C.A. § 1101, note]

If any particular provision of this Act, or the application thereof to any person or circumstance, is held invalid, the remainder of the Act and the application of such provision to other persons or circumstances shall not be affected thereby.

(June 27, 1952, c. 477, Title IV, ch. 2, § 406, 66 Stat. 275.)

§ 411.   Office of Refugee Resettlement; establishment; appointment of Director; functions [8 U.S.C.A. § 1521]

(a) There is established, within the Department of Health and Human Services, an office to be known as the Office of Refugee Resettlement (hereinafter in this chapter referred to as the "Office"). The head of the Office shall be a Director (hereinafter in this chapter referred to as the "Director"), to be appointed by the Secretary of Health and Human Services (hereinafter in this chapter referred to as the "Secretary").

(b) The function of the Office and its Director is to fund and administer (directly or through arrangements with other Federal agencies), in consultation with the Secretary of State, programs of the Federal Government under this chapter.

(June 27, 1952, c. 477, Title IV, ch. 2, § 411, as added Mar. 17, 1980, Pub.L. 96–212, Title III, § 311(a)(2), 94 Stat. 110, and amended Apr. 30, 1994, Pub.L. 103–236, Title I, § 162(n)(1), 108 Stat. 409.)

§ 412.   Authorization for programs for domestic resettlement of and assistance to refugees [8 U.S.C.A. § 1522]

(a) Conditions and considerations

(1)(A) In providing assistance under this section, the Director shall, to the extent of available appropriations, **(i)** make available sufficient resources for employment training and placement in order to achieve economic self-sufficiency among refugees as quickly as possible, **(ii)**

provide refugees with the opportunity to acquire sufficient English language training to enable them to become effectively resettled as quickly as possible, **(iii)** insure that cash assistance is made available to refugees in such a manner as not to discourage their economic self-sufficiency, in accordance with subsection (e)(2), and **(iv)** insure that women have the same opportunities as men to participate in training and instruction.

(B) it is the intent of Congress that in providing refugee assistance under this section—

(i) employable refugees should be placed on jobs as soon as possible after their arrival in the United States;

(ii) social service funds should be focused on employment-related services, English-as-a-second-language training (in nonwork hours where possible), and case-management services; and

(iii) local voluntary agency activities should be conducted in close cooperation and advance consultation with State and local governments.

(2)(A) The Director and the Federal agency administering subsection (b)(1) shall consult regularly (not less often than quarterly) with State and local governments and private nonprofit voluntary agencies concerning the sponsorship process and the intended distribution of refugees among the States and localities before their placement in those States and localities.

(B) The Director shall develop and implement, in consultation with representatives of voluntary agencies and State and local governments, policies and strategies for the placement and resettlement of refugees within the United States.

(C) Such policies and strategies, to the extent practicable and except under such unusual circumstances as the Director may recognize, shall—

(i) insure that a refugee is not initially placed or resettled in an area highly impacted (as determined under regulations prescribed by the Director after consultation with such agencies and governments) by the presence of refugees or comparable populations unless the refugee has a spouse, parent, sibling, son, or daughter residing in that area,

(ii) provide for a mechanism whereby representatives of local affiliates of voluntary agencies regularly (not less often than quarterly) meet with representatives of State and local governments to plan and coordinate in advance of their arrival the appropriate placement of refugees among the various States and localities, and

(iii) take into account—

(I) the proportion of refugees and comparable entrants in the population in the area,

(II) the availability of employment opportunities, affordable housing, and public and private resources (including educational, health care, and mental health services) for refugees in the area,

(III) the likelihood of refugees placed in the area becoming self-sufficient and free from long-term dependence on public assistance, and

(IV) the secondary migration of refugees to and from the area that is likely to occur.

(D) With respect to the location of placement of refugees within a State, the Federal agency administering subsection (b)(1) shall, consistent with such policies and strategies and to the maximum extent possible, take into account recommendations of the State.

(3) In the provision of domestic assistance under this section, the Director shall make a periodic assessment, based on refugee population and other relevant factors, of the relative needs of refugees for assistance and services under this chapter and the resources available to meet such needs. The Director shall compile and maintain data on secondary migration of refugees within the United States and, by State of residence and nationality, on the proportion of refugees receiving cash or medical assistance described in subsection (e). In allocating resources, the Director shall avoid duplication of services and provide for maximum coordination between agencies providing related services.

(4)(A) No grant or contract may be awarded under this section unless an appropriate proposal and application (including a description of the agency's ability to perform the services specified in the proposal) are submitted to, and approved by, the appropriate administering official. Grants and contracts under this section shall be made to those agencies which the appropriate administering official determines can best perform the services. Payments may be made for activities authorized under this chapter in advance or by way of reimbursement. In carrying out this section, the Director, the Secretary of State, and any such other appropriate administering official are authorized—

(i) to make loans, and

(ii) to accept and use money, funds, property, and services of any kind made available by gift, devise, bequest, grant, or otherwise for the purpose of carrying out this section.

(B) No funds may be made available under this chapter (other than under subsection (b)(1)) to States or political subdivisions in the form of block grants, per capita grants, or similar consolidated grants or contracts. Such funds shall be made available under separate grants or contracts—

(i) for medical screening and initial medical treatment under subsection (b)(5),

(ii) for services for refugees under subsection (c)(1),

(iii) for targeted assistance project grants under subsection (c)(2), and

(iv) for assistance for refugee children under subsection (d)(2).

(C) The Director may not delegate to a State or political subdivision his authority to review or approve grants or contracts under this chapter or the terms under which such grants or contracts are made.

(5) Assistance and services funded under this section shall be provided to refugees without regard to race, religion, nationality, sex, or political opinion.

(6) As a condition for receiving assistance under this section, a State must—

(A) submit to the Director a plan which provides—

(i) a description of how the State intends to encourage effective refugee resettlement and to promote economic self-sufficiency as quickly as possible,

(ii) a description of how the State will insure that language training and employment services are made available to refugees receiving cash assistance,

(iii) for the designation of an individual, employed by the State, who will be responsible for insuring coordination of public and private resources in refugee resettlement,

(iv) for the care and supervision of and legal responsibility for unaccompanied refugee children in the State, and

(v) for the identification of refugees who at the time of resettlement in the State are determined to have medical conditions requiring, or medical histories indicating a need for, treatment or observation and such monitoring of such treatment or observation as may be necessary;

(B) meet standards, goals, and priorities, developed by the Director, which assure the effective resettlement of refugees and which promote their economic self-sufficiency as quickly as possible and the efficient provision of services; and

(C) submit to the Director, within a reasonable period of time after the end of each fiscal year, a report on the uses of funds provided under this chapter which the State is responsible for administering.

(7) The Secretary, together with the Secretary of State with respect to assistance provided by the Secretary of State under subsection (b), shall develop a system of monitoring the assistance provided under this section. This system shall include—

(A) evaluations of the effectiveness of the programs funded under this section and the performance of States, grantees, and contractors;

(B) financial auditing and other appropriate monitoring to detect any fraud, abuse, or mismanagement in the operation of such programs; and

(C) data collection on the services provided and the results achieved.

(8) The Attorney General shall provide the Director with information supplied by refugees in conjunction with their applications to the Attorney General for adjustment of status, and the Director shall compile, summarize, and evaluate such information.

(9) The Secretary, the Secretary of Education, the Attorney General, and the Secretary of State may issue such regulations as each deems appropriate to carry out this chapter.

(10) For purposes of this chapter, the term "refugee" includes any alien described in section 207(c)(2) [8 U.S.C.A. § 1157(c)(2)].

(b) Program of initial resettlement

(1)(A) For—

(i) fiscal years 1980 and 1981, the Secretary of State is authorized, and

(ii) fiscal year 1982 and succeeding fiscal years, the Director (except as provided in subparagraph (B)) is authorized,

to make grants to, and contracts with, public or private nonprofit agencies for initial resettlement (including initial reception and placement with sponsors) of refugees in the United States. Grants to, or contracts with, private nonprofit voluntary agencies under this paragraph shall be made consistent with the objectives of this chapter, taking into account the different resettlement approaches and practices of such agencies. Resettlement assistance under this paragraph shall be provided in coordination with the Director's provision of other assistance under this chapter. Funds provided to agencies under such grants and contracts may only be obligated or expended during the fiscal year in which they are provided (or the subsequent fiscal year or such subsequent fiscal period as the Federal contracting agency may approve) to carry out the purposes of this subsection.

(B) If the President determines that the Director should not administer the program under this paragraph, the authority of the Director under the first sentence of subparagraph (A) shall be exercised by such officer as the President shall from time to time specify.

(2) The Director is authorized to develop programs for such orientation, instruction in English, and job training for refugees, and such other education and training of refugees, as facilitates their resettlement in the United States. The Director is authorized to implement such programs, in accordance with the provisions of this section, with respect to refugees in the United States. The Secretary of State is authorized to implement such programs with respect to refugees awaiting entry into the United States.

(3) The Secretary is authorized to make arrangements (including cooperative arrangements with other Federal agencies) for the temporary care of refugees in the United States in emergency circumstances, including the establishment of processing centers, if necessary, without regard to such provisions of law (other than the Renegotiation Act of 1951 [50 App. U.S.C.A. § 1211 et seq.] and section 414(b) [8 U.S.C.A. § 1524(b)]) regulating the making, performance amendment, or modification of contracts and the expenditure of funds of the United States Government as the Secretary may specify.

(4) The Secretary shall—

(A) assure that an adequate number of trained staff are available at the location at which the refugees enter the United States to assure that all necessary medical records are available and in proper order;

(B) provide for the identification of refugees who have been determined to have medical conditions affecting the public health and requiring treatment;

(C) assure that State or local health officials at the resettlement destination within the United States of each refugee are promptly notified of the refugee's arrival and provided with all applicable medical records; and

(D) provide for such monitoring of refugees identified under subparagraph (B) as will insure that they receive appropriate and timely treatment.

The Secretary shall develop and implement methods for monitoring and assessing the quality of medical screening and related health services provided to refugees awaiting resettlement in the United States.

(5) The Director is authorized to make grants to, and enter into contracts with, State and local health agencies for payments to meet their costs of providing medical screening and initial medical treatment to refugees.

(6) The Comptroller General shall directly conduct an annual financial audit of funds expended under each grant or contract made under paragraph (1) for fiscal year 1986 and for fiscal year 1987.

(7) Each grant or contract with an agency under paragraph (1) shall require the agency to do the following:

(A) To provide quarterly performance and financial status reports to the Federal agency administering paragraph (1).

(B)(i) To provide, directly or through its local affiliate, notice to the appropriate county or other local welfare office at the time that the agency becomes aware that a refugee is offered employment and to provide notice to the refugee that such notice has been provided, and

(ii) upon request of such a welfare office to which a refugee has applied for cash assistance, to furnish that office with documentation respecting any cash or other resources provided directly by the agency to the refugee under this subsection.

(C) To assure that refugees, known to the agency as having been identified pursuant to paragraph (4)(B) as having medical conditions affecting the public health and requiring treatment, report to the appropriate county or other health agency upon their resettlement in an area.

(D) To fulfill its responsibility to provide for the basic needs (including food, clothing, shelter, and transportation for job interviews and training) of each refugee resettled and to develop and implement a resettlement plan including the early employment of each refugee resettled and to monitor the implementation of such plan.

(E) To transmit to the Federal agency administering paragraph (1) an annual report describing the following:

(i) The number of refugees placed (by county of placement) and the expenditures made in the year under the grant or contract, including the proportion of such expenditures used for administrative purposes and for provision of services.

(ii) The proportion of refugees placed by the agency in the previous year who are receiving cash or medical assistance described in subsection (e).

(iii) The efforts made by the agency to monitor placement of the refugees and the activities of local affiliates of the agency.

(iv) The extent to which the agency has coordinated its activities with local social service providers in a manner which avoids duplication of activities and has provided notices to local welfare offices and the reporting of medical conditions of certain aliens to local health departments in accordance with subparagraphs (B)(i) and (C).

(v) Such other information as the agency administering paragraph (1) deems to be appropriate in monitoring the effectiveness of agencies in carrying out their functions under such grants and contracts.

The agency administering paragraph (1) shall promptly forward a copy of each annual report transmitted under subparagraph (E) to the Committees on the Judiciary of the House of Representatives and of the Senate.

(8) The Federal agency administering paragraph (1) shall establish criteria for the performance of agencies under grants and contracts under that paragraph, and shall include criteria relating to an agency's—

(A) efforts to reduce welfare dependency among refugees resettled by that agency,

(B) collection of travel loans made to refugees resettled by that agency for travel to the United States,

(C) arranging for effective local sponsorship and other nonpublic assistance for refugees resettled by that agency,

(D) cooperation with refugee mutual assistance associations, local social service providers, health agencies, and welfare offices,

(E) compliance with the guidelines established by the Director for the placement and resettlement of refugees within the United States, and

(F) compliance with other requirements contained in the grant or contract, including the reporting and other requirements under subsection (b)(7).

The Federal administering agency shall use the criteria in the process of awarding or renewing grants and contracts under paragraph (1).

(c) Project grants and contracts for services for refugees

(1)(A) The Director is authorized to make grants to, and enter into contracts with, public or private nonprofit agencies for projects specifically designed—

(i) to assist refugees in obtaining the skills which are necessary for economic self-sufficiency, including projects for job training, employment services, day care, professional refresher training, and other recertification services;

(ii) to provide training in English where necessary (regardless of whether the refugees are employed or receiving cash or other assistance); and

(iii) to provide where specific needs have been shown and recognized by the Director, health (including mental health) services, social services, educational and other services.

(B) The funds available for a fiscal year for grants and contracts under subparagraph (A) shall be allocated among the States based on the total number or refugees (including children and adults) who arrived in the United States not more than 36 months before the beginning of such fiscal year and who are actually residing in each State (taking into account secondary migration) as of the beginning of the fiscal year.

(C) Any limitation which the Director establishes on the proportion of funds allocated to a State under this paragraph that the State may use for services other than those described in subsection (a)(1)(B)(ii) shall not apply if the Director receives a plan (established by or in consultation with local governments) and determines that the plan provides for the maximum appropriate provision of employment-related services for, and the maximum placement of, employable refugees consistent with performance standards established under section 1516 of Title 29.

(2)(A) The Director is authorized to make grants to States for assistance to counties and similar areas in the States where, because of factors such as unusually large refugee populations (including secondary migration), high refugee concentrations, and high use of public assistance by refugees, there exists and can be demonstrated a specific need for supplementation of available resources for services to refugees.

(B) Grants shall be made available under this paragraph—

(i) primarily for the purpose of facilitating refugee employment and achievement of self-sufficiency,

(ii) in a manner that does not supplant other refugee program funds and that assures that not less than 95 percent of the amount of the grant award is made available to the county or other local entity.

(d) Assistance for refugee children

(1) The Secretary of Education is authorized to make grants, and enter into contracts, for payments for projects to provide special educational services (including English language training) to refugee children in elementary and secondary schools where a demonstrated need has been shown.

(2)(A) The Director is authorized to provide assistance, reimbursement to States, and grants to and contracts with public and private nonprofit agencies, for the provision of child welfare services, including foster care maintenance payments and services and health care, furnished to any refugee child (except as provided in subparagraph (B)) during the thirty-six month period beginning with the first month in which such refugee child is in the United States.

(B)(i) In the case of a refugee child who is unaccompanied by a parent or other close adult relative (as defined by the Director), the services described in subparagraph (A) may be furnished until the month after the child attains eighteen years of age (or such higher age as the State's child welfare services plan under part B of title IV of the Social Security Act [42 U.S.C.A. § 620 et seq.] prescribes for the availability of such services to any other child in that State).

(ii) The Director shall attempt to arrange for the placement under the laws of the States of such unaccompanied refugee children, who have been accepted for admission to the United States, before (or as soon as possible after) their arrival in the United States. During any interim period while such a child is in the United States or in transit to the United States but before the child is so placed, the Director shall assume legal responsibility (including financial responsibility) for the child, if necessary, and is authorized to make necessary decisions to provide for the child's immediate care.

(iii) In carrying out the Director's responsibilities under clause (ii), the Director is authorized to enter into contracts with appropriate public or private nonprofit agencies under such conditions as the Director determines to be appropriate.

(iv) The Director shall prepare and maintain a list of (I) all such unaccompanied children who have entered the United States after April 1, 1975, (II) the names and last known residences of their parents (if living) at the time of arrival, and (III) the children's location, status, and progress.

(e) Cash assistance and medical assistance to refugees

(1) The Director is authorized to provide assistance, reimbursement to States, and grants to, and contracts with, public or private nonprofit agencies for 100 per centum of the cash assistance and medical assistance provided to any refugee during the thirty-six month period beginning with the first month in which such refugee has entered the United States and for the identifiable and reasonable administrative costs of providing this assistance.

(2)(A) Cash assistance provided under this subsection to an employable refugee is conditioned, except for good cause shown—

(i) on the refugee's registration with an appropriate agency providing employment services described in subsection (c)(1)(A)(i), or, if there is no such agency available, with an appropriate State or local employment service;

(ii) on the refugee's participation in any available and appropriate social service or targeted assistance program (funded under subsection (c)) providing job or language training in the area in which the refugee resides; and

(iii) on the refugee's acceptance of appropriate offers of employment.

(B) Cash assistance shall not be made available to refugees who are full-time students in institutions of higher education (as defined by the Director after consultation with the Secretary of Education).

(C) In the case of a refugee who—

(i) refuses an offer of employment which has been determined to be appropriate either by the agency responsible for the initial resettlement of the refugee under subsection (b) or by the appropriate State or local employment service,

(ii) refuses to go to a job interview which has been arranged through such agency or service, or

(iii) refuses to participate in a social service or targeted assistance program referred to in subparagraph (A)(ii) which such agency or service determines to be available and appropriate, cash assistance to the refugee shall be terminated (after opportunity for an administrative hearing) for a period of three months (for the first such refusal) or for a period of six months for any subsequent refusal.

(3) The Director shall develop plans to provide English training and other appropriate services and training to refugees receiving cash assistance.

(4) If a refugee is eligible for aid or assistance under a State plan approved under part A of title IV or under title XIX of the Social Security Act [42 U.S.C.A §§ 601 et seq., 1396 et seq.], or for supplemental security income benefits (including State supplementary payments) under the program established under title XVI of that Act [42 U.S.C.A. § 1381 et seq.], funds authorized under this subsection shall only be used for the non-Federal share of such aid or assistance, or for such supplementary payments, with respect to cash and medical assistance provided with respect to such refugee under this paragraph.

(5) The Director is authorized to allow for the provision of medical assistance under paragraph (1) to any refugee, during the one-year period after entry, who does not qualify for assistance under a State plan approved under title XIX of the Social Security Act [42 U.S.C.A. § 1396 et seq.] on account of any resources or income requirement of such plan, but only if the Director determines that—

(A) this will **(i)** encourage economic self-sufficiency, or **(ii)** avoid a significant burden on State and local governments; and

(B) the refugee meets such alternative financial resources and income requirements as the Director shall establish.

(6) As a condition for receiving assistance, reimbursement, or a contract under this subsection and notwithstanding any other provision of law, a State or agency must provide assurances that whenever a refugee applies for cash or medical assistance for which assistance or reimbursement is provided under this subsection, the State or agency must notify promptly the agency (or local affiliate) which provided for the initial resettlement of the refugee under subsection (b) of the fact that the refugee has so applied.

(7)(A) The Secretary shall develop and implement alternative projects for refugees who have been in the United States less than thirty-six months, under which refugees are provided interim support, medical services, support services, and case management, as needed, in a manner that encourages self-sufficiency, reduces welfare dependency, and fosters greater coordination among the resettlement agencies and service providers. The Secretary may permit alternative projects to cover specific groups of refugees who have been in the United States 36 months or longer if the Secretary determines that refugees in the group have been significantly and disproportionately dependent on welfare and need the services provided under the project in order to become self-sufficient and that their coverage under the projects would be cost-effective.

(B) Refugees covered under such alternative projects shall be precluded from receiving cash or medical assistance under any other paragraph of this subsection or under title XIX or part A of title IV of the Social Security Act [42 U.S.C.A. §§ 601 et seq., 1396 et seq.].

(C) The Secretary shall report to Congress not later than October 31, 1985, on the results of these projects and on any recommendations respecting changes in the refugee assistance program under this section to take into account such results.

(D) To the extent that the use of such funds is consistent with the purposes of such provisions, funds appropriated under section 414(a) [8 U.S.C.A. § 1524(a)], part A of title IV of the Social Security Act [42 U.S.C.A. § 601 et seq.], or title XIX of such Act [42 U.S.C.A. § 1396 et seq.], may be used for the purpose of implementing and evaluating alternative projects under this paragraph.

(8) In its provision of assistance to refugees, a State or political subdivision shall consider the recommendations of, and assistance provided by, agencies with grants or contracts under subsection (b)(1).

(f) Assistance to States and counties for incarceration of certain Cuban nationals; priority for removal and return to Cuba

(1) The Attorney General shall pay compensation to States and to counties for costs incurred by the States and counties to confine in prisons, during the fiscal year for which such payment is made, nationals of Cuba who—

(A) were paroled into the United States in 1980 by the Attorney General,

(B) after such parole committed any violation of State or county law for which a term of imprisonment was imposed, and

(C) at the time of such parole and such violation were not aliens lawfully admitted to the United States—

(i) for permanent residence, or

(ii) under the terms of an immigrant or a nonimmigrant visa issued,

under this Act.

(2) For a State or county to be eligible to receive compensation under this subsection, the chief executive officer of the State or county shall submit to the Attorney General, in accordance with rules to be issued by the Attorney General, an application containing—

(A) the number and names of the Cuban nationals with respect to whom the State or county is entitled to such compensation, and

(B) such other information as the Attorney General may require.

(3) For a fiscal year the Attorney General shall pay the costs described in paragraph (1) to each State and county determined by the Attorney General to be eligible under paragraph (2); except that if the amounts appropriated for the fiscal year to carry out this subsection are insufficient to cover all such payments, each of such payments shall be ratably reduced so that the total of such payments equals the amount so appropriated.

(4) The authority of the Attorney General to pay compensation under this subsection shall be effective for any fiscal year only to the extent and in such amounts as may be provided in advance in appropriation Acts.

(5) Priority for removal and return to Cuba of certain Cuban nationals.

It shall be the policy of the United States Government that the President, in consultation with the Attorney General and all other appropriate Federal officials and all appropriate State and county officials referred to in paragraph (2), shall place top priority on seeking the expeditious removal from this country and the return to Cuba of Cuban nationals described in paragraph (1) by any reasonable and responsible means, and to this end the Attorney General may use the funds authorized to carry out this subsection to conduct such policy.

(June 27, 1952, c. 477, Title IV, ch. 2, § 412, as added Mar. 17, 1980, Pub.L. 96–212, Title III, § 311(a)(2), 94 Stat. 111, and amended Oct. 25, 1982, Pub.L. 97–363, §§ 3(a), 4 to 6, 96 Stat. 1734 to 1736; Nov. 22, 1983, Pub.L. 98–164, Title X, § 1011 (b), 97 Stat. 1061; Oct. 12, 1984, Pub.L. 98–473 Title I, § 101(d), 98 Stat. 1877; Pub.L. 99–605, §§ 3, 4, 5(a), (b), (c), 6(a), (b), (d), 8, 9(a), (b), 10, 12, 13, Nov. 6, 1986, 100 Stat. 3449 to 3451, 3453 to 3455; Oct. 24, 1988, Pub.L. 100–525, § 6(b), 102 Stat. 2616; Apr. 30, 1994, Pub.L. 103–236, Title I, § 162(n) (2), 108 Stat. 409; Oct. 25, 1994, Pub.L. 103–416, Title II, § 219(x), 108 Stat. 4318; Aug. 22, 1996, Pub.L. 104–193, Title I, § 110(s)(3), 110 Stat. 2175; Sept. 30, 1996, Pub.L. 104–208, Div. C, Title VI, § 671(e)(7), 110 Stat. 3009–723.)

§ 413. Congressional reports [8 U.S.C.A. § 1523]

(a) The Secretary shall submit a report on activities under this chapter to the Committees on the Judiciary of the House of Representatives and of the Senate not later than the January 31 following the end of each fiscal year, beginning with fiscal year 1980.

(b) Each such report shall contain—

(1) an updated profile of the employment and labor force statistics for refugees who have entered the United States within the five-fiscal-year period immediately preceding the fiscal year within which the report is to be made and for refugees who entered earlier and who have shown themselves to be significantly and disproportionately dependent on welfare, as well as a description of the extent to which refugees received the forms of assistance or services under this chapter during that period;

(2) a description of the geographic location of refugees;

(3) a summary of the results of the monitoring and evaluation conducted under section 412(a)(7) [8 U.S.C.A. § 1522(a)(7)] during the period for which the report is submitted;

(4) a description of **(A)** the activities, expenditures, and policies of the Office under this chapter and of the activities of States, voluntary agencies, and sponsors, and **(B)** the Director's plans for improvement of refugee resettlement;

(5) evaluations of the extent to which **(A)** the services provided under this chapter are assisting refugees in achieving economic self-sufficiency, achieving ability in English, and achieving employment commensurate with their skills and abilities, and **(B)** any fraud, abuse, or mismanagement has been reported in the provisions of services or assistance;

(6) a description of any assistance provided by the Director pursuant to section 412(e)(5) [8 U.S.C.A. § 1522(e)(5)];

(7) a summary of the location and status of unaccompanied refugee children admitted to the United States; and

(8) a summary of the information compiled and evaluation made under section 412(a)(8) [8 U.S.C.A. § 1522(a)(8)].

(June 27, 1952, c. 477, Title IV, ch. 2, § 413, as added Mar. 17, 1980, Pub.L. 96–212, Title III, § 311(a)(2), 94 Stat. 115, and amended Oct. 25, 1982, Pub.L. 97–363, §§ 3(b), 7, 96 Stat. 1734, 1737; Pub.L. 99–605, § 11, Nov. 6, 1986, 100 Stat. 3455; Oct. 24, 1988, Pub.L. 100–525, § 9(jj), 102 Stat. 2622; Apr. 30, 1994, Pub.L. 103–236, Title I, § 162(n)(3), 108 Stat. 409.)

TITLE V

ALIEN TERRORIST REMOVAL PROCEDURES

§ 501. Definitions [8 U.S.C.A. § 1531]

As used in this title—

(1) the term "alien terrorist" means any alien described in section 237(a)(4)(B) [8 U.S.C.A. § 1227(a)(4)(B)];

(2) the term "classified information" has the same meaning as in section 1(a) of the Classified Information Procedures Act (18 U.S.C. App.);

(3) the term "national security" has the same meaning as in section 1(b) of the Classified Information Procedures Act (18 U.S.C. App.);

(4) the term "removal court" means the court described in section 502 [8 U.S.C.A. § 1532];

(5) the term "removal hearing" means the hearing described in section 504 [8 U.S.C.A. § 1534];

(6) the term "removal proceeding" means a proceeding under this title; and

(7) the term "special attorney" means an attorney who is on the panel established under section 502(e) [8 U.S.C.A. § 1532(e)].

(June 27, 1952, c. 477, Title V, § 501, as added Apr. 24, 1996, Pub.L. 104–132, Title IV, § 401(a), 110 Stat. 1259, and amended Sept. 30, 1996, Pub.L. 104–208, Title III, §§ 308(g) (1), 354(a)(5), 110 Stat. 3009–622, 3009–643.)

§ 502. Establishment of removal court [8 U.S.C.A. § 1532]

(a) Designation of judges

The Chief Justice of the United States shall publicly designate 5 district court judges from 5 of the United States judicial circuits who shall constitute a court that shall have jurisdiction to conduct all removal proceedings. The Chief Justice may, in the Chief Justice's discretion, designate the same judges under this section as are designated pursuant to section 103(a) of the Foreign Intelligence Surveillance Act of 1978 (50 U.S.C. 1803(a)).

(b) Terms

Each judge designated under subsection (a) shall serve for a term of 5 years and shall be eligible for redesignation, except that of the members first designated—

(1) 1 member shall serve for a term of 1 year;

(2) 1 member shall serve for a term of 2 years;

(3) 1 member shall serve for a term of 3 years; and

(4) 1 member shall serve for a term of 4 years.

(c) Chief judge

(1) Designation

The Chief Justice shall publicly designate one of the judges of the removal court to be the chief judge of the removal court.

(2) Responsibilities

The chief judge shall—

(A) promulgate rules to facilitate the functioning of the removal court; and

(B) assign the consideration of cases to the various judges on the removal court.

(d) Expeditious and confidential nature of proceedings

The provisions of section 103(c) of the Foreign Intelligence Surveillance Act of 1978 (50 U.S.C. 1803(c)) shall apply to removal proceedings in the same manner as they apply to proceedings under that Act.

(e) Establishment of panel of special attorneys

The removal court shall provide for the designation of a panel of attorneys each of whom—

(1) has a security clearance which affords the attorney access to classified information, and

(2) has agreed to represent permanent resident aliens with respect to classified information under section 504(e)(3) [8 U.S.C.A. § 1534(e)(3)] in accordance with (and subject to the penalties under) this title.

(June 27, 1952, c. 477, Title V, § 502, as added Apr. 24, 1996, Pub.L. 104–132, Title IV, § 401(a), 110 Stat. 1259, and amended Sept. 30, 1996, Pub.L. 104–208, Div. C, Title III, § 354(a)(4), 110 Stat. 3009–643.)

§ 503.   Removal court procedure [8 U.S.C.A. § 1533]

(a) Application

(1) In general

In any case in which the Attorney General has classified information that an alien is an alien terrorist, the Attorney General may seek removal of the alien under this title by filing an application with the removal court that contains—

(A) the identity of the attorney in the Department of Justice making the application;

(B) a certification by the Attorney General or the Deputy Attorney General that the application satisfies the criteria and requirements of this section;

(C) the identity of the alien for whom authorization for the removal proceeding is sought; and

(D) a statement of the facts and circumstances relied on by the Department of Justice to establish probable cause that—

(i) the alien is an alien terrorist;

(ii) the alien is physically present in the United States; and

(iii) with respect to such alien, removal under title II would pose a risk to the national security of the United States.

(2) Filing

An application under this section shall be submitted ex parte and in camera, and shall be filed under seal with the removal court.

(b) Right to dismiss

The Attorney General may dismiss a removal action under this title at any stage of the proceeding.

(c) Consideration of application

(1) Basis for decision

In determining whether to grant an application under this section, a single judge of the removal court may consider, ex parte and in camera, in addition to the information contained in the application—

(A) other information, including classified information, presented under oath or affirmation; and

(B) testimony received in any hearing on the application, of which a verbatim record shall be kept.

(2) Approval of order

The judge shall issue an order granting the application, if the judge finds that there is probable cause to believe that—

(A) the alien who is the subject of the application has been correctly identified and is an alien terrorist present in the United States; and

(B) removal under title II would pose a risk to the national security of the United States.

(3) Denial of order

If the judge denies the order requested in the application, the judge shall prepare a written statement of the reasons for the denial, taking all necessary precautions not to disclose any classified information contained in the Government's application.

(d) Exclusive provisions

If an order is issued under this section granting an application, the rights of the alien regarding removal and expulsion shall be governed solely by this title, and except as they are specifically referenced in this title, no other provisions of this Act shall be applicable.

(June 27, 1952, c. 477, Title V, § 503, as added Apr. 24, 1996, Pub.L. 104–132, Title IV, § 401(a), 110 Stat. 1259.)

§ 504.   Removal hearing [8 U.S.C.A. § 1534]

(a) In general

(1) Expeditious hearing

In any case in which an application for an order is approved under section 503(c)(2) [8 U.S.C.A. § 1533(c)(2)], a removal hearing shall be conducted under this section as expeditiously as practicable for the purpose of determining whether the alien to whom the order pertains should be removed from the United States on the grounds that the alien is an alien terrorist.

(2) Public hearing

The removal hearing shall be open to the public.

(b) Notice

An alien who is the subject of a removal hearing under this title shall be given reasonable notice of—

(1) the nature of the charges against the alien, including a general account of the basis for the charges; and

(2) the time and place at which the hearing will be held.

(c) Rights in hearing

(1) Right of counsel

The alien shall have a right to be present at such hearing and to be represented by counsel. Any alien financially unable to obtain counsel shall be entitled to have counsel assigned to represent the alien. Such counsel shall be appointed by the judge pursuant to the plan for furnishing representation for any person financially unable to obtain adequate representation for the district in which the hearing is conducted, as provided for in section 3006A of Title 18. All provisions of that section shall apply and, for purposes of determining the maximum amount of compensation, the matter shall be treated as if a felony was charged.

(2) Introduction of evidence

Subject to the limitations in subsection (e), the alien shall have a reasonable opportunity to introduce evidence on the alien's own behalf.

(3) Examination of witnesses

Subject to the limitations in subsection (e), the alien shall have a reasonable opportunity to examine the evidence against the alien and to cross-examine any witness.

(4) Record

A verbatim record of the proceedings and of all testimony and evidence offered or produced at such a hearing shall be kept.

(5) Removal decision based on evidence at hearing

The decision of the judge regarding removal shall be based only on that evidence introduced at the removal hearing.

(d) Subpoenas

(1) Request

At any time prior to the conclusion of the removal hearing, either the alien or the Department of Justice may request the judge to issue a subpoena for the presence of a named witness (which subpoena may also command the person to whom it is directed to produce books, papers, documents, or other objects designated therein) upon a satisfactory showing that the presence of the witness is necessary for the determination of any material matter. Such a request may be made ex parte except that the judge shall inform the Department of Justice of any request for a subpoena by the alien for a witness or material if compliance with such a subpoena would reveal classified evidence or the source of that evidence. The Department of Justice shall be given a reasonable opportunity to oppose the issuance of such a subpoena.

(2) Payment for attendance

If an application for a subpoena by the alien also makes a showing that the alien is financially unable to pay for the attendance of a witness so requested, the court may order the costs incurred by the process and the fees of the witness so subpoenaed to be paid from funds appropriated for the enforcement of title II.

(3) Nationwide service

A subpoena under this subsection may be served anywhere in the United States.

(4) Witness fees

A witness subpoenaed under this subsection shall receive the same fees and expenses as a witness subpoenaed in connection with a civil proceeding in a court of the United States.

(5) No access to classified information

Nothing in this subsection is intended to allow an alien to have access to classified information.

(e) Discovery

(1) In general

For purposes of this title—

(A) the Government is authorized to use in a removal proceedings [sic] the fruits of electronic surveillance and unconsented physical searches authorized under the Foreign Intelligence Surveillance Act of 1978 (50 U.S.C. 1801 et seq.) without regard to subsections (c), (e), (f), (g), and (h) of section 106 of that Act [50 U.S.C.A. § 1806(c), (e), (f), (g), (h)] and discovery of information derived pursuant to such Act, or otherwise collected for national security purposes, shall not be authorized if disclosure would present a risk to the national security of the United States;

(B) an alien subject to removal under this title shall not be entitled to suppress evidence that the alien alleges was unlawfully obtained; and

(C) section 3504 of Title 18, and section 1806(c) of Title 50, shall not apply if the Attorney General determines that public disclosure would pose a risk to the national security of the United States because it would disclose classified information or otherwise threaten the integrity of a pending investigation.

(2) Protective orders

Nothing in this title shall prevent the United States from seeking protective orders and from asserting privileges ordinarily available to the United States to protect against the disclosure of classified information, including the invocation of the military and State secrets privileges.

(3) Treatment of classified information

(A) Use

The judge shall examine, ex parte and in camera, any evidence for which the Attorney General determines that public disclosure would pose a risk to the national security of the United States or to the security of any individual because it would disclose classified information and neither the alien nor the public shall be informed of such evidence or its sources other than through reference to the summary provided pursuant to this paragraph. Notwithstanding the previous sentence, the Department of Justice may, in its discretion and, in the case of classified information, after coordination with the originating agency, elect to introduce such evidence in open session.

(B) Submission

With respect to such information, the Government shall submit to the removal court an unclassified summary of the specific evidence that does not pose that risk.

(C) Approval

Not later than 15 days after submission, the judge shall approve the summary if the judge finds that it is sufficient to enable the alien to prepare a defense. The Government shall deliver to the alien a copy of the unclassified summary approved under this subparagraph.

(D) Disapproval

(i) In general

If an unclassified summary is not approved by the removal court under subparagraph (C), the Government shall be afforded 15 days to correct the deficiencies identified by the court and submit a revised unclassified summary.

(ii) Revised summary

If the revised unclassified summary is not approved by the court within 15 days of its submission pursuant to subparagraph (C), the removal hearing shall be terminated unless the judge makes the findings under clause (iii).

(iii) Findings

The findings described in this clause are, with respect to an alien, that—

(I) the continued presence of the alien in the United States would likely cause serious and irreparable harm to the national security or death or serious bodily injury to any person, and

(II) the provision of the summary would likely cause serious and irreparable harm to the national security or death or serious bodily injury to any person.

(E) Continuation of hearing without summary

If a judge makes the findings described in subparagraph (D) (iii)—

(i) if the alien involved is an alien lawfully admitted for permanent residence, the procedures described in subparagraph (F) shall apply; and

(ii) in all cases the special removal hearing shall continue, the Department of Justice shall cause to be delivered to the alien a statement that no summary is possible, and the classified information submitted in camera and ex parte may be used pursuant to this paragraph.

(F) Special procedures for access and challenges to classified information by special attorneys in case of lawful permanent aliens

(i) In general

The procedures described in this subparagraph are that the judge (under rules of the removal court) shall designate a special attorney to assist the alien—

(I) by reviewing in camera the classified information on behalf of the alien, and

(II) by challenging through an in camera proceeding the veracity of the evidence contained in the classified information.

(ii) Restrictions on disclosure

A special attorney receiving classified information under clause (i)—

(I) shall not disclose the information to the alien or to any other attorney representing the alien, and

(II) who discloses such information in violation of subclause (I) shall be subject to a fine under Title 18, imprisoned for not less than 10 years nor more than 25 years, or both.

(f) Arguments

Following the receipt of evidence, the Government and the alien shall be given fair opportunity to present argument as to whether the evidence is sufficient to justify the removal of the alien. The Government shall open the argument. The alien shall be permitted to reply. The Government shall then be permitted to reply in rebuttal. The judge may allow any part of the argument that refers to evidence received in camera and ex parte to be heard in camera and ex parte.

(g) Burden of proof

In the hearing, it is the Government's burden to prove, by the preponderance of the evidence, that the alien is subject to removal because the alien is an alien terrorist.

(h) Rules of evidence

The Federal Rules of Evidence shall not apply in a removal hearing.

(i) Determination of deportation

If the judge, after considering the evidence on the record as a whole, finds that the Government has met its burden, the judge shall order the alien removed and detained pending removal from the United States. If the alien was released pending the removal hearing, the judge shall order the Attorney General to take the alien into custody.

(j) Written order

At the time of issuing a decision as to whether the alien shall be removed, the judge shall prepare a written order containing a statement of facts found and conclusions of law. Any portion of the order that would reveal the substance or source of information received in camera and ex parte pursuant to subsection (e) shall not be made available to the alien or the public.

(k) No right to ancillary relief

At no time shall the judge consider or provide for relief from removal based on—

> **(1)** asylum under section 208 [8 U.S.C.A. § 1158];
>
> **(2)** by [sic] withholding of removal under section 237(b)(3)* [8 U.S.C.A. § 1227(b)(3)];
>
> **(3)** cancellation of removal under section 240A [8 U.S.C.A. § 1229b];
>
> **(4)** voluntary departure under section 244(e)** [8 U.S.C.A. § 1254(e)];
>
> **(5)** adjustment of status under section 245 [8 U.S.C.A. § 1255]; or
>
> **(6)** registry under section 249 [8 U.S.C.A. § 1259].

(*l*) Report on alien terrorist removal proceedings

Not later than 3 months from the date of the enactment of this subsection, the Attorney General shall submit to Congress a report concerning the effect and efficacy of alien terrorist removal proceedings, including the reasons why proceedings pursuant to this section have not been used by the Attorney General in the past and the effect on the use of these proceedings after the enactment of the USA PATRIOT Act of 2001 (Public Law 107–56).

(June 27, 1952, c. 477, Title V, § 504, as added Apr. 24, 1996, Pub.L. 104–132, Title IV, § 401(a), 110 Stat. 1260, and amended Sept. 30, 1996, Pub.L. 104–208, Div. C, Title III, §§ 308(g)(7)(B), (8)(B), 354(a)(1), (2), (b), 357, 110 Stat. 3009–623, 3009–624, 3009–641 to 3009–644; Dec. 28, 2001, Pub.L. 107–108, Title III, § 313, 115 Stat. 1401.)

§ 505. Appeals [8 U.S.C.A. § 1535]

(a) Appeal of denial of application for removal proceedings

(1) In general

---

* So in original; probably should refer to section 241(b)(3).
** So in original; probably should refer to section 240B.

The Attorney General may seek a review of the denial of an order sought in an application filed pursuant to section 503 [8 U.S.C.A. § 1533]. The appeal shall be filed in the United States Court of Appeals for the District of Columbia Circuit by notice of appeal filed not later than 20 days after the date of such denial.

(2) Record on appeal

The entire record of the proceeding shall be transmitted to the Court of Appeals under seal, and the Court of Appeals shall hear the matter ex parte.

(3) Standard of review

The Court of Appeals shall—

(A) review questions of law de novo; and

(B) set aside a finding of fact only if such finding was clearly erroneous.

(b) Appeal of determination regarding summary of classified information

(1) In general

The United States may take an interlocutory appeal to the United States Court of Appeals for the District of Columbia Circuit of—

(A) any determination by the judge pursuant to section 504(e)(3) [8 U.S.C.A. § 1534(e)(3)]; or

(B) the refusal of the court to make the findings permitted by section 504(e)(3) [8 U.S.C.A. § 1534(e)(3)].

(2) Record

In any interlocutory appeal taken pursuant to this subsection, the entire record, including any proposed order of the judge, any classified information and the summary of evidence, shall be transmitted to the Court of Appeals. The classified information shall be transmitted under seal. A verbatim record of such appeal shall be kept under seal in the event of any other judicial review.

(c) Appeal of decision in hearing

(1) In general

Subject to paragraph (2), the decision of the judge after a removal hearing may be appealed by either the alien or the Attorney General to the United States Court of Appeals for the District of Columbia Circuit by notice of appeal filed not later than 20 days after the date on which the order is issued. The order shall not be enforced during the pendency of an appeal under this subsection.

(2) Automatic appeals in cases of permanent resident aliens in which no summary provided

(A) In general

Unless the alien waives the right to a review under this paragraph, in any case involving an alien lawfully admitted for permanent residence who is denied a written summary of classified information under section 504(e)(3) [8 U.S.C.A. § 1534(e)(3)] and with respect to which the procedures described in section 504(e)(3)(F) [8 U.S.C.A. § 1534(e)(3)(F)] apply, any order issued by the judge shall be reviewed by the Court of Appeals for the District of Columbia Circuit.

(B) Use of special attorney

With respect to any issue relating to classified information that arises in such review, the alien shall be represented only by the special attorney designated under section 504(e)(3)(F)(i) [8 U.S.C.A. § 1534(e)(3)(F)(i)] on behalf of the alien.

(3) Transmittal of record

In an appeal or review to the Court of Appeals pursuant to this subsection—

(A) the entire record shall be transmitted to the Court of Appeals; and

(B) information received in camera and ex parte, and any portion of the order that would reveal the substance or source of such information, shall be transmitted under seal.

(4) Expedited appellate proceeding

In an appeal or review to the Court of Appeals under this subsection—

(A) the appeal or review shall be heard as expeditiously as practicable and the court may dispense with full briefing and hear the matter solely on the record of the judge of the removal court and on such briefs or motions as the court may require to be filed by the parties;

(B) the Court of Appeals shall issue an opinion not later than 60 days after the date of the issuance of the final order of the district court;

(C) the court shall review all questions of law de novo; and

(D) a finding of fact shall be accorded deference by the reviewing court and shall not be set aside unless such finding was clearly erroneous, except that in the case of a review under paragraph (2) in which an alien lawfully admitted for permanent residence was denied a written summary of classified information under section 504(c)(3) [8 U.S.C.A. § 1534(c)(3)], the Court of Appeals shall review questions of fact de novo.

(d) Certiorari

Following a decision by the Court of Appeals pursuant to subsection (c), the alien or the Attorney General may petition the Supreme Court for a writ of certiorari. In any such case, any information transmitted to the Court of Appeals under seal shall, if such information is also submitted to the Supreme Court, be transmitted under seal. Any order of removal shall not be stayed pending disposition of a writ of certiorari, except as provided by the Court of Appeals or a Justice of the Supreme Court.

(e) Appeal of detention order

(1) In general

Sections 3145 through 3148 of Title 18, pertaining to review and appeal of a release or detention order, penalties for failure to appear, penalties for an offense committed while on release, and sanctions for violation of a release condition shall apply to an alien to whom section 507(b)(1) [8 U.S.C.A. § 1537(b)(1)] applies. In applying the previous sentence—

(A) for purposes of section 3145 of Title 18 an appeal shall be taken to the United States Court of Appeals for the District of Columbia Circuit; and

(B) for purposes of section 3146 of Title 18 the alien shall be considered released in connection with a charge of an offense punishable by life imprisonment.

(2) No review of continued detention

The determinations and actions of the Attorney General pursuant to section 507(b)(2)(C) [8 U.S.C.A. § 1537(b)(2)(C)] shall not be subject to judicial review, including application for a writ of habeas corpus, except for a claim by the alien that continued detention violates the alien's rights under the Constitution. Jurisdiction over any such challenge shall lie exclusively in the United States Court of Appeals for the District of Columbia Circuit.

(June 27, 1952, c. 477, Title V, § 505, as added Apr. 24, 1996, Pub.L. 104–132, Title IV, § 401(a), 110 Stat. 1263, and amended Sept. 30, 1996, Pub.L. 104–208, Div. C, Title III, § 354(a)(3), 110 Stat. 3009–642.)

§ 506. Custody and release pending removal hearing [8 U.S.C.A. § 1536]

(a) Upon filing application

(1) In general

Subject to paragraphs (2) and (3), the Attorney General may—

(A) take into custody any alien with respect to whom an application under section 503 [8 U.S.C.A. § 1533] has been filed; and

(B) retain such an alien in custody in accordance with the procedures authorized by this title.

(2) Special rules for permanent resident aliens

(A) Release hearing

An alien lawfully admitted for permanent residence shall be entitled to a release hearing before the judge assigned to hear the removal hearing. Such an alien shall be detained pending the removal hearing, unless the alien demonstrates to the court that the alien—

(i) is a person lawfully admitted for permanent residence in the United States;

(ii) if released upon such terms and conditions as the court may prescribe (including the posting of any monetary amount), is not likely to flee; and

(iii) will not endanger national security, or the safety of any person or the community, if released.

(B) Information considered

The judge may consider classified information submitted in camera and ex parte in making a determination whether to release an alien pending the removal hearing.

(3) Release if order denied and no review sought

(A) In general

Subject to subparagraph (B), if a judge of the removal court denies the order sought in an application filed pursuant to section 503 [8 U.S.C.A. § 1533], and the Attorney General does not seek review of such denial, the alien shall be released from custody.

(B) Application of regular procedures

Subparagraph (A) shall not prevent the arrest and detention of the alien pursuant to title II.

(b) Conditional release if order denied and review sought

(1) In general

If a judge of the removal court denies the order sought in an application filed pursuant to section 503 [8 U.S.C.A. § 1533] and the Attorney General seeks review of such denial, the judge shall release the alien from custody subject to the least restrictive condition, or combination of conditions, of release described in section 3142(b) and clauses (i) through (xiv) of section 3142(c)(1)(B) of Title 18, that—

(A) will reasonably assure the appearance of the alien at any future proceeding pursuant to this title; and

(B) will not endanger the safety of any other person or the community.

(2) No release for certain aliens

If the judge finds no such condition or combination of conditions, as described in paragraph (1), the alien shall remain in custody until the completion of any appeal authorized by this title.

(June 27, 1952, c. 477, Title V, § 506, as added Apr. 24, 1996, Pub.L. 104–132, Title IV, § 401(a), 110 Stat. 1265.)

§ 507. Custody and release after removal hearing [8 U.S.C.A. § 1537]

(a) Release

(1) In general

Subject to paragraph (2), if the judge decides that an alien should not be removed, the alien shall be released from custody.

(2) Custody pending appeal

If the Attorney General takes an appeal from such decision, the alien shall remain in custody, subject to the provisions of section 3142 of Title 18.

(b) Custody and removal

(1) Custody

If the judge decides that an alien shall be removed, the alien shall be detained pending the outcome of any appeal. After the conclusion of any judicial review thereof which affirms the removal order, the Attorney General shall retain the alien in custody and remove the alien to a country specified under paragraph (2).

(2) Removal

(A) In general

The removal of an alien shall be to any country which the alien shall designate if such designation does not, in the judgment of the Attorney General, in consultation with the Secretary of State, impair the obligation of the United States under any treaty (including a treaty pertaining to extradition) or otherwise adversely affect the foreign policy of the United States.

(B) Alternate countries

If the alien refuses to designate a country to which the alien wishes to be removed or if the Attorney General, in consultation with the Secretary of State, determines that removal of the alien to the country so designated would impair a treaty obligation or adversely affect United States foreign policy, the Attorney General shall cause the alien to be removed to any country willing to receive such alien.

(C) Continued detention

If no country is willing to receive such an alien, the Attorney General may, notwithstanding any other provision of law, retain the alien in custody. The Attorney General, in coordination with the Secretary of State, shall make periodic efforts to reach agreement with other countries to accept such an alien and at least every 6 months shall provide to the attorney representing the alien at the removal hearing a written report on the Attorney General's efforts. Any alien in custody pursuant to this subparagraph shall be released from custody solely at the discretion of the Attorney General and subject to such conditions as the Attorney General shall deem appropriate.

(D) Fingerprinting

Before an alien is removed from the United States pursuant to this subsection, or pursuant to an order of removal because such alien is inadmissible under section 212(a)(3)(B) [8 U.S.C.A. § 1182(a)(3)(B)], the alien shall be photographed and fingerprinted, and shall be advised of the provisions of section 276(b) [8 U.S.C.A. § 1326(b)].

(c) Continued detention pending trial

(1) Delay in removal

The Attorney General may hold in abeyance the removal of an alien who has been ordered removed, pursuant to this title, to allow the trial of such alien on any Federal or State criminal charge and the service of any sentence of confinement resulting from such a trial.

(2) Maintenance of custody

Pending the commencement of any service of a sentence of confinement by an alien described in paragraph (1), such an alien shall remain in the custody of the Attorney General, unless the Attorney General determines that temporary release of the alien to the custody of State authorities for confinement in a State facility is appropriate and would not endanger national security or public safety.

(3) Subsequent removal

Following the completion of a sentence of confinement by an alien described in paragraph (1), or following the completion of State criminal proceedings which do not result in a sentence of confinement of an alien released to the custody of State authorities pursuant to paragraph (2), such an alien shall be returned to the custody of the Attorney General who shall proceed to the removal of the alien under this title.

(d) Application of certain provisions relating to escape of prisoners

For purposes of sections 751 and 752 of Title 18, an alien in the custody of the Attorney General pursuant to this title shall be subject to the penalties provided by those sections in relation to a person committed to the custody of the Attorney General by virtue of an arrest on a charge of a felony.

(e) Rights of aliens in custody

(1) Family and attorney visits

An alien in the custody of the Attorney General pursuant to this title shall be given reasonable opportunity, as determined by the Attorney General, to communicate with and receive visits from members of the alien's family, and to contact, retain, and communicate with an attorney.

(2) Diplomatic contact

An alien in the custody of the Attorney General pursuant to this title shall have the right to contact an appropriate diplomatic or consular official of the alien's country of citizenship or nationality or of any country providing representation services therefore. The Attorney General shall notify the appropriate embassy, mission, or consular office of the alien's detention.

(June 27, 1952, c. 477, Title V, § 507, as added Apr. 24, 1996, Pub.L. 104–132, Title IV, § 401(a), 110 Stat. 1266, and amended Pub.L. 104–208, Div. C, Title III, § 308(d)(4)(Q), Sept. 30, 1996, 110 Stat. 3009–619.)

II. ADDITIONAL STATUTES

Title 8, U.S. Code, Aliens and Nationality
Selected Sections Not Codified
in the Immigration and Nationality Act

Designation and Adjustment of Status of Soviet and Indochinese Refugees (Lautenberg Amendment)

Foreign Affairs Reform and Restructuring Act

Consolidated Appropriations Act of 2008

Administrative Procedure Act
Selected Sections

TITLE 8, U.S. CODE

TITLE 8, U.S. CODE, ALIENS AND NATIONALITY SELECTED SECTIONS NOT CODIFIED IN THE IMMIGRATION AND NATIONALITY ACT

§ 1373.   Communication between Government agencies and the Immigration and Naturalization Service. [Illegal Immigration Reform and Immigrant Responsibility Act of 1996 § 642]

(a) In general

Notwithstanding any other provision of Federal, State, or local law, a Federal, State, or local government entity or official may not prohibit, or in any way restrict, any government entity or official from sending to, or receiving from, the Immigration and Naturalization Service information regarding the citizenship or immigration status, lawful or unlawful, of any individual.

(b) Additional authority of Government entities

Notwithstanding any other provision of Federal, State, or local law, no person or agency may prohibit, or in any way restrict, a Federal, State, or local government entity from doing any of the following with respect to information regarding the immigration status, lawful or unlawful, of any individual:

(1) Sending such information to, or requesting or receiving such information from, the Immigration and Naturalization Service.

(2) Maintaining such information.

(3) Exchanging such information with any other Federal, State, or local government entity.

(c) Obligation to respond to inquiries

The Immigration and Naturalization Service shall respond to an inquiry by a Federal, State, or local government agency, seeking to verify or ascertain the citizenship or immigration status of any individual within the jurisdiction of the agency for any purpose authorized by law, by providing the requested verification or status information.

(Pub.L. 104–208, Div. C, Title VI, § 642, Sept. 30, 1996, 110 Stat. 3009–707.)

§ 1621.   Aliens who are not qualified aliens or nonimmigrants ineligible for State and local public benefits. [Personal Responsibility and Work Opportunity Reconciliation Act of 1996, § 411]

(a) In general

Notwithstanding any other provisions of law and except as provided in subsections (b) and (d) of this section, an alien who is not—

(1) a qualified alien (as defined in section 1641 of this title [8 U.S.C.A. § 1641]),

(2) a nonimmigrant under the Immigration and Nationality Act [8 U.S.C.A. § 1101 et seq.], or

(3) an alien who is paroled into the United States under section 212(d)(5) of such Act [8 U.S.C.A. § 1182(d)(5)] for less than one year,

is not eligible for any State or local public benefit (as defined in subsection (c) of this section).

(b) Exceptions

Subsection (a) of this section shall not apply with respect to the following State or local public benefits:

(1) Assistance for health care items and services that are necessary for the treatment of an emergency medical condition (as defined in section 1396b(v)(3) of Title 42) of the alien involved and are not related to an organ transplant procedure.

(2) Short-term, non-cash, in-kind emergency disaster relief.

(3) Public health assistance for immunizations with respect to immunizable diseases and for testing and treatment of symptoms of communicable diseases whether or not such symptoms are caused by a communicable disease.

(4) Programs, services, or assistance (such as soup kitchens, crisis counseling and intervention, and short-term shelter) specified by the Attorney General, in the Attorney General's sole and unreviewable discretion after consultation with appropriate Federal agencies and departments, which **(A)** deliver in-kind services at the community level, including through public or private nonprofit agencies; **(B)** do not condition the provision of assistance, the amount of assistance provided, or the cost of assistance provided on the individual recipient's income or resources; and **(C)** are necessary for the protection of life or safety.

(c) "State or local public benefit" defined

(1) Except as provided in paragraphs (2) and (3), for purposes of this subchapter the term "State or local public benefit" means—

(A) any grant, contract, loan, professional license, or commercial license provided by an agency of a State or local government or by appropriated funds of a State or local government; and

(B) any retirement, welfare, health, disability, public or assisted housing, postsecondary education, food assistance, unemployment benefit, or any other similar benefit for which payments or assistance are provided to an individual, household, or family eligibility unit by an agency of a State or local government or by appropriated funds of a State or local government.

(2) Such term shall not apply—

(A) to any contract, professional license, or commercial license for a nonimmigrant whose visa for entry is related to such employment in the United States, or to a citizen of a freely associated state, if section 141 of the applicable compact of free association approved in Public Law 99–239 [48 U.S.C.A. § 1901 note] or 99–658 [48 U.S.C.A. § 1931 note] (or a successor provision) is in effect;

(B) with respect to benefits for an alien who as a work authorized nonimmigrant or as an alien lawfully admitted for permanent residence under the Immigration and Nationality Act [8 U.S.C.A. § 1101 et seq.] qualified for such benefits and for whom the United States under reciprocal treaty agreements is required to pay benefits, as determined by the Secretary of State, after consultation with the Attorney General; or

(C) to the issuance of a professional license to, or the renewal of a professional license by, a foreign national not physically present in the United States.

(3) Such term does not include any Federal public benefit under section 1611(c) of this title [8 U.S.C.A. § 1611(c)].

(d) State authority to provide for eligibility of illegal aliens for State and local public benefits

A State may provide that an alien who is not lawfully present in the United States is eligible for any State or local public benefit for which such alien would otherwise be ineligible under subsection (a) of this section only through the enactment of a State law after August 22, 1996, which affirmatively provides for such eligibility.

(Pub.L. 104–193, Title IV, § 411, Aug. 22, 1996, 110 Stat. 2268; Pub.L. 105–33, Title V, §§ 5565, 5581(b)(1), Aug. 5, 1997, 111 Stat. 639, 642; Pub.L. 105–306, § 5(b), Oct. 28, 1998, 112 Stat. 2927.)

§ 1623. Limitation on eligibility for preferential treatment of aliens not lawfully present on basis of residence for higher education benefits. [Illegal Immigration Reform and Immigrant Responsibility Act of 1996, § 505]

(a) In general

Notwithstanding any other provision of law, an alien who is not lawfully present in the United States shall not be eligible on the basis of residence within a State (or a political subdivision) for any postsecondary education benefit unless a citizen or national of the United States is eligible for such a benefit (in no less an amount, duration, and scope) without regard to whether the citizen or national is such a resident.

(b) Effective date

This section shall apply to benefits provided on or after July 1, 1998.

(Pub.L. 104–208, Div. C, Title V, § 505, Sept. 30, 1996, 110 Stat. 3009–672.)

§ 1624. Authority of States and political subdivisions of States to limit assistance to aliens and to distinguish among classes of aliens in providing general cash public assistance. [Illegal Immigration Reform and Immigrant Responsibility Act of 1996, § 553]

(a) In general

Subject to subsection (b) of this section and notwithstanding any other provision of law, a State or political subdivision of a State is authorized to prohibit or otherwise limit or restrict the eligibility of aliens or classes of aliens for programs of general cash public assistance furnished under the law of the State or a political subdivision of a State.

(b) Limitation

The authority provided for under subsection (a) of this section may be exercised only to the extent that any prohibitions, limitations, or restrictions imposed by a State or political subdivision of a State are not more restrictive than the prohibitions, limitations, or restrictions imposed under comparable Federal programs. For purposes of this section, attribution to an alien of a sponsor's income and resources (as described in section 1631 of this title) for purposes of determining eligibility for, and the amount of, benefits shall be considered less restrictive than a prohibition of eligibility for such benefits.

(Pub.L. 104–208, Div. C, Title V, § 553, Sept. 30, 1996, 110 Stat. 3009–681.)

§ 1644. Communication between State and local government agencies and the Immigration and Naturalization Service. [Personal Responsibility and Work Opportunity Reconciliation Act of 1996, § 434]

Notwithstanding any other provision of Federal, State, or local law, no State or local government entity may be prohibited, or in any way restricted, from sending to or receiving from the Immigration and Naturalization Service information regarding the immigration status, lawful or unlawful, of an alien in the United States.

(Pub.L. 104–193, Title IV, § 434, Aug. 22, 1996, 110 Stat. 2275.)

DESIGNATION AND ADJUSTMENT OF STATUS OF SOVIET AND INDOCHINESE REFUGEES (LAUTENBERG AMENDMENT)

§ 599D. Establishing Categories of Aliens for Purposes of Refugee Determinations [8 U.S.C.A. § 1157, Note]

(a) In General.—In the case of an alien who is within a category of aliens established under subsection (b), the alien may establish, for purposes of admission as a refugee under section 207 of the Immigration and Nationality Act, that the alien has a well-founded fear of persecution on account of race, religion, nationality, membership in a particular social group, or political opinion by asserting such a fear and asserting a credible basis for concern about the possibility of such persecution.

(b) Establishment of Categories.—

(1) For purposes of subsection (a), the Attorney General, in consultation with the Secretary of State and the Coordinator for Refugee Affairs, shall establish—

(A) one or more categories of aliens who are or were nationals and residents of an independent state of the former Soviet Union or of Estonia, Latvia, or Lithuania and who share common characteristics that identify them as targets of persecution in that state on account of race, religion, nationality, membership in a particular social group, or political opinion,

(B) one or more categories of aliens who are or were nationals and residents of Vietnam, Laos, or Cambodia and who share common characteristics that identify them as targets of persecution in such respective foreign state on such an account; and

(C) one or more categories of aliens who are or were nationals and residents of the Islamic Republic or Iran who, as members of a religious minority in Iran, share common characteristics that identify them as targets of persecution in that state on account of race, religion, nationality, membership in a particular social group, or political opinion.

(2)(A) Aliens who are (or were) nationals and residents of an independent state of the former Soviet Union or of Estonia, Latvia, or Lithuania and who are Jews or Evangelical Christians shall be deemed a category of alien established under paragraph (1)(A).

(B) Aliens who are (or were) nationals of an independent state of the former Soviet Union or of Estonia, Latvia, or Lithuania and who are current members of, and demonstrate public, active, and continuous participation (or attempted participation) in the religious activities of, the Ukrainian Catholic Church or the Ukrainian Orthodox

Church, shall be deemed a category of alien established under paragraph (1)(A).

(C) Aliens who are (or were) nationals and residents of Vietnam, Laos, or Cambodia and who are members of categories of individuals determined, by the Attorney General in accordance with "Immigration and Naturalization Service Worldwide Guidelines for Overseas Refugee Processing" (issued by the Immigration and Naturalization Service in August 1983) shall be deemed a category of alien established under paragraph (1)(B).

(3) Within the number of admissions of refugees allocated for for [sic] each of fiscal years 1990, 1991, and 1992 for refugees who are nationals of the Soviet Union under section 207(a)(3) of the Immigration and Nationality Act [subsec. (a)(3) of this section] and within the number of such admissions allocated for each of fiscal years 1993, 1994, 1995, 1996, 1997, 1998, 1999, 2000, 2001, 2002, 2003, 2004, 2005, 2006, 2007, 2008, 2009, 2010, 2011, 2012, 2013, 2014, 2015, 2016, 2017, 2018, 2019, and 2020 for refugees who are nationals of the independent states of the former Soviet Union, Estonia, Latvia, and Lithuania under such section, notwithstanding any other provision of law, the President shall allocate one thousand of such admissions for such fiscal year to refugees who are within the category of aliens described in paragraph (2)(B).

(c) Written Reasons for Denials of Refugee Status.—Each decision to deny an application for refugee status of an alien who is within a category established under this section shall be in writing and shall state, to the maximum extent feasible, the reason for the denial.

(d) Permitting Certain Aliens Within Categories to Reapply for Refugee Status.—Each alien who is within a category established under this section and who (after August 14, 1988, and before the date of the enactment of this Act [Nov. 21, 1989]) was denied refugee status shall be permitted to reapply for such status. Such an application shall be determined taking into account the application of this section.

(e) Period of Application.—

(1) Subsections (a) and (b) shall take effect on the date of the enactment of this Act [Nov. 21, 1989] and shall only apply to applications for refugee status submitted before October 1, 2020.

(2) Subsection (c) shall apply to decisions made after the date of the enactment of this Act [Nov. 21, 1989] and before October 1, 2020.

(3) Subsection (d) shall take effect on the date of the enactment of this Act [Nov. 21, 1989] and shall only apply to reapplications for refugee status submitted before October 1, 2020.

(f) Repealed. Pub.L. 102–391, Title V, § 582(c), Oct. 6, 1992, 106 Stat. 1686; Pub.L. 102–511, Title IX, § 905(c), Oct. 24, 1992, 106 Stat. 3356.

(Pub.L. 101–167, Title V, § 599D, Nov. 21, 1989, 103 Stat. 1261, as amended Pub.L. 101–513, Title V, § 598(a), Nov. 5, 1990, 104 Stat. 2063; Pub.L. 102–391, Title V, § 582(a)(1), (b)(1), and (c), Oct. 6, 1992, 106 Stat. 1686; Pub.L. 102–511, Title IX, § 905(a), (b)(1), and (c), Oct. 24, 1992,

106 Stat. 3356; Pub.L. 103–236, Title V, § 512(1), Apr. 30, 1994, 108 Stat. 466; Pub.L. 104–208, Div. A, Title I, § 101(c) [Title V, § 575(1)], Sept. 30, 1996, 110 Stat. 3009–168; Pub.L. 104–319, Title I, § 101(1), Oct. 19, 1996, 110 Stat. 3865; Pub.L. 105–118, Title V, § 574(1), Nov. 26, 1997, 111 Stat. 2432; Pub.L. 105–277, Div. A, § 101(f) [Title VII, § 705(1)], Oct. 21, 1998, 112 Stat. 2681–389; Nov. 29, 1999, Pub.L. 106–113, Div. B, § 1000(a)(4) [H.R. 3424, Title II, § 214(1)], 113 Stat. 1535, 1537; Pub.L. 106–554, § 1(a)(1) [Title II, § 212(1)], Dec. 21, 2000, 114 Stat. 2763; Pub.L. 107–116, Title II, § 213(1), Jan. 10, 2002, 115 Stat. 2177, 2200; Pub.L. 108–7, Div. G, Title II, § 213(1), Feb. 20, 2003, 117 Stat. 324; Pub. L. 108–199, Div. E, Title II, § 213(1), Jan. 23, 2004, 118 Stat. 253; Pub.L. 108–447, Div. F, Title II, § 213(1), Dec. 8, 2004, 118 Stat. 3139; Pub.L. 109–102, Title V, § 534(m)(1), Nov. 14, 2005, 119 Stat. 2211; Pub.L. 109–289, Div. B, Title II, § 20412(b)(1), as added Pub.L. 110–5, § 2, Feb. 15, 2007, 121 Stat. 25; Pub.L. 110–161, Div. J, Title VI, § 634(k)(1), Dec. 26, 2007, 121 Stat. 2329; Pub.L. 111–8, Div. H, Title VII, § 7034(g)(1), Mar. 11, 2009, 123 Stat. 878; Pub.L. 111–117 Div. F, Title VII, § 7034(f)(1), Dec. 16, 2009, 123 Stat. 3361; Pub.L. 112–10, Div. B, Title XI, § 2121(m), Apr. 15, 2011, 125 Stat. 186; Pub.L. 112–74, Div. I, Title VII, § 7034(r)(1), Dec. 23, 2011, 125 Stat. 1218; Pub.L. 113–6, Div. F, Title VII, § 1706(h)(1), Mar. 26, 2013, 127 Stat. 430; Pub.L. 113–76, Div. K, Title VII, § 7034(m)(8)(A), Jan. 17, 2014, 128 Stat. 516; Pub.L. 113–235, Div. J, Title VII, § 7034(*l*)(8)(A), Dec. 16, 2014, 128 Stat. 2625; Pub.L. 114–113, Div. K, Title VII, § 7034(k)(8)(A), Dec. 18, 2015, 129 Stat. 2765; Pub.L. 115–31, Div. J, Title VII, § 7034(k)(5)(A), May 5, 2017; 131 Stat. 651; Pub.L. 115–141, Div. K, Title VII, § 7034(*l*)(5)(A), Mar. 23, 2018, 132 Stat. 895; Pub.L. 116–6, Div. F, Title VII, § 7034(m)(5)(A), Feb. 15, 2019, 133 Stat. 327; Pub.L. 116–94, Div. G, Title VII, § 7034(*l*)(5)(A), Dec. 20, 2019, 133 Stat. 2873.)

§ 599E. Adjustment of Status for Certain Soviet and Indochinese Parolees [8 U.S.C.A. § 1255, Note]

(a) In general.—The Attorney General shall adjust the status of an alien described in subsection (b) to that of an alien lawfully admitted for permanent residence if the alien—

(1) applies for such adjustment,

(2) has been physically present in the United States for at least 1 year and is physically present in the United States on the date the application for such adjustment is filed,

(3) is admissible to the United States as an immigrant, except as provided in subsection (c), and

(4) pays a fee (determined by the Attorney General) for the processing of such application.

(b) Aliens eligible for adjustment of status.—The benefits provided in subsection (a) shall only apply to an alien who—

(1) was a national of an independent state of the former Soviet Union, Estonia, Latvia, Lithuania, Vietnam, Laos, or Cambodia, and

(2) was inspected and granted parole into the United States during the period beginning on August 15, 1988, and ending on September 30, 2020, after being denied refugee status.

(c) Waiver of certain grounds for inadmissibility.—The provisions of paragraphs (4), (5), and (7)(A) of section 212(a) of the Immigration and Nationality Act [8 U.S.C.A. § 1182(a)] shall not apply to adjustment of status under this section and the Attorney General may waive any other provision of such section (other than paragraph (2)(C) or sub-paragraph (A), (B), (C), or (E) of paragraph (3)) with respect to such an adjustment for humanitarian purposes, to assure family unity, or when it is otherwise in the public interest.

(d) Date of approval.—Upon the approval of such an application for adjustment of status, the Attorney General shall create a record of the alien's admission as a lawful permanent resident as of the date of the alien's inspection and parole described in subsection (b)(2).

(e) No offset in number of visas available.—When an alien is granted the status of having been lawfully admitted for permanent residence under this section, the Secretary of State shall not be required to reduce the number of immigrant visas authorized to be issued under the Immigration and Nationality Act.

(Pub.L. 101–167, Title V, § 599E, Nov. 21, 1989, 103 Stat. 1263, as amended Pub.L. 101–513, Title V, § 598(b), Nov. 5, 1990, 104 Stat. 2063, Pub.L. 101–649, Title VI, § 603(a)(22), Nov. 29, 1990, 104 Stat. 5084; Pub.L. 102–232, Title III, 307(*l*)(9), Dec. 12, 1991, 105 Stat. 1757; Pub.L. 102–391, Title V, § 582(a)(2), (b)(2), Oct. 6, 1992, 106 Stat. 1686; Pub.L. 102–511, Title IX, § 905(b)(2), Oct. 24, 1992, 106 Stat. 3356; Pub.L. 103–236, Title V, § 512(2), Apr. 30, 1994, 108 Stat. 466; Pub.L. 103–416, Title II, § 219(bb), Oct. 25, 1994, 108 Stat. 4319; Pub.L. 104–208, Div. A, Title I, § 101(c) [Title V, § 575(2)], Sept. 30, 1996, 110 Stat. 3009–168; Pub.L. 104–319, Title I, § 101(2), Oct. 19, 1996, 110 Stat. 3865; Pub.L. 105–118, Title V, § 574(2), Nov. 26, 1997, 111 Stat. 2432; Pub.L. 105–277, Div. A, § 101(f) [Title VII, § 705(2)], Oct. 21, 1998, 112 Stat. 2681; Nov. 29, 1999, Pub.L. 106–113, Div. B, § 1000(a) (4) [H.R. 3424, Title I, § 214(2)], 113 Stat. 1535, 1537; Pub.L. 106–554, § 1(a)(1) [Title II, § 212(2)], Dec. 21, 2000, 114 Stat. 2763; Pub.L. 107–116, Title II, § 213(2), Jan. 10, 2002, 115 Stat. 2177, 2200; Pub.L. 108–7, Div. G, Title II, § 213(2), Feb. 20, 2003, 117 Stat. 324; Pub.L. 108–199, Div. E, Title II, § 213(2), Jan. 23, 2004, 118 Stat. 253; Pub.L. 108–447, Div. F, Title II, § 213(2), Dec. 8, 2004, 118 Stat. 3140; Pub.L. 109–102, Title V, § 534(m)(2), Nov. 14, 2005, 119 Stat. 2211; Pub.L. 109–289, Div. B, Title II, § 20412(b)(2), as added Pub.L. 110–5, § 2, Feb. 15, 2007, 121 Stat. 25; Pub.L. 110–161, Div. J, Title VI, § 634(k)(2), Dec. 26, 2007, 121 Stat. 2329; Pub.L. 111–8, Div. H, Title VII, § 7034(g)(2), Mar. 11, 2009, 123 Stat. 878; Pub.L. 111–117, Div. F, Title VII, § 7034(f)(2), Dec. 16, 2009, 123 Stat. 3361; Pub.L. 112–10, Div. B, Title XI, § 2121(m), Apr. 15, 2011, 125 Stat. 186; Pub.L. 112–74. Div. I, Title VII, § 7034(r)(2), Dec. 23, 2011, 125 Stat. 1218; Pub.L. 113–6, Div. F, Title VII, § 1706(h) (2), Mar. 26, 2013, 127 Stat. 430; Pub.L. 113–76, Div. K, Title VII, § 7034(m)(8)(B), Jan. 17, 2014, 128 Stat. 516; Pub.L. 113–235, Div. J, Title VII, § 7034(*l*)(8)(B), Dec. 16, 2014, 128 Stat. 2625; Pub.L. 114–113, Div. K, Title VII, § 7034(k)(8)(B), Dec. 18, 2015, 129 Stat. 2765; Pub.L. 115–31, Div. J, Title VII, § 7034(k)(5)(A), May 5, 2017, 131 Stat. 651; Pub.L. 115–141, Div. K, Title VII, § 7034(*l*)(5)(B), Mar. 23, 2018, 132 Stat. 895; Pub.L. 116–6, Div. F, Title VII, § 7034(m)(5)(B), Feb. 15, 2019, 133 Stat. 327; Pub.L. 116–94, Div. G, Title VII, § 7034(*l*)(5)(B), Dec. 20, 2019, 133 Stat. 2873.)

FOREIGN AFFAIRS REFORM AND RESTRUCTURING ACT

§ 2242.   United States Policy with Respect to the Involuntary Return of Persons in Danger of Subjection to Torture [8 U.S.C.A § 1231, Note]

(a) Policy.—It shall be the policy of the United States not to expel, extradite, or otherwise effect the involuntary return of any person to a country in which there are substantial grounds for believing the person would be in danger of being subjected to torture, regardless of whether the person is physically present in the United States.

(b) Regulations.—Not later than 120 days after the date of enactment of this Act [Oct. 21, 1998], the heads of the appropriate agencies shall prescribe regulations to implement the obligations of the United States under Article 3 of the United Nations Convention Against Torture and Other Forms of Cruel, Inhuman or Degrading Treatment or Punishment, subject to any reservations, understandings, declarations, and provisos contained in the United States Senate resolution of ratification of the Convention.

(c) Exclusion of certain aliens.—To the maximum extent consistent with the obligations of the United States under the Convention, subject to any reservations, understandings, declarations, and provisos contained in the United States Senate resolution of ratification of the Convention, the regulations described in subsection (b) shall exclude from the protection of such regulations aliens described in section 241(b)(3)(B) of the Immigration and Nationality Act (8 U.S.C. 1231(b)(3)(B)).

(d) Review and construction.—Notwithstanding any other provision of law, and except as provided in the regulations described in subsection (b), no court shall have jurisdiction to review the regulations adopted to implement this section, and nothing in this section shall be construed as providing any court jurisdiction to consider or review claims raised under the Convention or this section, or any other determination made with respect to the application of the policy set forth in subsection (a), except as part of the review of a final order of removal pursuant to section 242 of the Immigration and Nationality Act (8 U.S.C. 1252).

(e) Authority to detain.—Nothing in this section shall be construed as limiting the authority of the Attorney General to detain any person under any provision of law, including, but not limited to, any provision of the Immigration and Nationality Act.

(f) Definitions.—

(1) Convention defined.—In this section, the term "Convention" means the United Nations Convention Against Torture and Other

Forms of Cruel, Inhuman or Degrading Treatment or Punishment, done at New York on December 10, 1984.

(2) Same terms as in the Convention.—Except as otherwise provided, the terms used in this section have the meanings given those terms in the Convention, subject to any reservations, understandings, declarations, and provisos contained in the United States Senate resolution of ratification of the Convention.

(Pub.L. 105–277, Div. G, Title XXII, § 2242, Oct. 21, 1998, 112 Stat. 2681–822.)

CONSOLIDATED APPROPRIATIONS ACT OF 2008

§ 691.   Relief for Iraqi, Montagnards, Hmong and Other Refugees Who Do Not Pose a Threat to the United States

* * *

(b) Automatic relief for the Hmong and other groups that do not pose a threat to the United States.—For purposes of section 212(a)(3)(B) of the Immigration and Nationality Act (8 U.S.C.A. § 1182(a)(3)(B)), the Karen National Union/Karen Liberation Army (KNU/KNLA), the Chin National Front/Chin National Army (CNF/CNA), the Chin National League for Democracy (CNLD), the Kayan New Land Party (KNLP), the Arakan Liberation Party (ALP), the Mustangs, the Alzados, the Karenni National Progressive Party, and appropriate groups affiliated with the Hmong and the Montagnards shall not be considered to be a terrorist organization on the basis of any act or event occurring before the date of enactment of this section. Nothing in this subsection may be construed to alter or limit the authority of the Secretary of State or the Secretary of Homeland Security to exercise his discretionary authority pursuant to section 212(d)(3)(B)(i) of the Immigration and Nationality Act (8 U.S.C.A. § 1182(d)(3)(B)(i)).

* * *

(d) Designation of the Taliban as a terrorist organization.—For purposes of section 212(a)(3)(B) of the Immigration and Nationality Act (8 U.S.C.A. § 1182(a)(3)(B)), the Taliban shall be considered to be a terrorist organization described in subclause (I) of clause (vi) of that section.

(e) Report on duress waivers.—The Secretary of Homeland Security shall provide to the Committees on the Judiciary of the United States Senate and House of Representatives a report, not less than 180 days after the enactment of this Act and every year thereafter, which may include a classified annex, if appropriate, describing—

(1) the number of individuals subject to removal from the United States for having provided material support to a terrorist group who allege that such support was provided under duress;

(2) a breakdown of the types of terrorist organizations to which the individuals described in paragraph (1) have provided material support;

(3) a description of the factors that the Department of Homeland Security considers when evaluating duress waivers; and

(4) any other information that the Secretary believes that the Congress should consider while overseeing the Department's application of duress waivers.

(f) Effective date.—The amendments made by this section shall take effect on the date of enactment of this section, and these amendments and sections 212(a)(3)(B) and 212(d)(3)(B) of the Immigration and Nationality Act (8 U.S.C.A. § 1182(a)(3)(B) and § 1182(d)(3)(B)), as amended by these sections, shall apply to—

(1) removal proceedings instituted before, on, or after the date of enactment of this section; and

(2) acts and conditions constituting a ground for inadmissibility, excludability, deportation, or removal occurring or existing before, on, or after such date.

(Pub. L. 110–161, Dec. 26, 2007, 121 Stat. 1844.)

ADMINISTRATIVE PROCEDURE ACT

Selected Sections

[Title 5, U.S. Code. Government Organization and Employees]

§ 551.   Definitions

For the purpose of this subchapter—

(1) "agency" means each authority of the Government of the United States, whether or not it is within or subject to review by another agency, but does not include—

    (A) the Congress;

    (B) the courts of the United States;

    (C) the governments of the territories or possessions of the United States;

    (D) the government of the District of Columbia;

or except as to the requirements of section 552 of this title—

    (E) agencies composed of representatives of the parties or of representatives of organizations of the parties to the disputes determined by them;

    (F) courts martial and military commissions;

    (G) military authority exercised in the field in time of war or in occupied territory; or

    (H) functions conferred by sections 1738, 1739, 1743, and 1744 of title 12; subchapter II of chapter 471 of title 49; or sections 1884, 1891–1902, and former section 1641(b)(2), of title 50, appendix;

(2) "person" includes an individual, partnership, corporation, association, or public or private organization other than an agency;

(3) "party" includes a person or agency named or admitted as a party, or properly seeking and entitled as of right to be admitted as a party, in an agency proceeding, and a person or agency admitted by an agency as a party for limited purposes;

(4) "rule" means the whole or a part of an agency statement of general or particular applicability and future effect designed to implement, interpret, or prescribe law or policy or describing the organization, procedure, or practice requirements of an agency and includes the approval or prescription for the future of rates, wages, corporate or financial structures or reorganizations thereof, prices, facilities, appliances, services or allowances therefor or of valuations, costs, or accounting, or practices bearing on any of the foregoing;

(5) "rule making" means agency process for formulating, amending, or repealing a rule;

(6) "order" means the whole or a part of a final disposition, whether affirmative, negative, injunctive, or declaratory in form, of an agency in a matter other than rule making but including licensing;

(7) "adjudication" means agency process for the formulation of an order;

(8) "license" includes the whole or a part of an agency permit, certificate, approval, registration, charter, membership, statutory exemption or other form of permission;

(9) "licensing" includes agency process respecting the grant, renewal, denial, revocation, suspension, annulment, withdrawal, limitation, amendment, modification, or conditioning of a license;

(10) "sanction" includes the whole or a part of an agency—

(A) prohibition, requirement, limitation, or other condition affecting the freedom of a person;

(B) withholding of relief;

(C) imposition of penalty or fine;

(D) destruction, taking, seizure, or withholding of property;

(E) assessment of damages, reimbursement, restitution, compensation, costs, charges, or fees;

(F) requirement, revocation, or suspension of a license; or

(G) taking other compulsory or restrictive action;

(11) "relief" includes the whole or a part of an agency—

(A) grant of money, assistance, license, authority, exemption, exception, privilege, or remedy;

(B) recognition of a claim, right, immunity, privilege, exemption, or exception; or

(C) taking of other action on the application or petition of, and beneficial to, a person;

(12) "agency proceeding" means an agency process as defined by paragraphs (5), (7), and (9) of this section;

(13) "agency action" includes the whole or a part of an agency rule, order, license, sanction, relief, or the equivalent or denial thereof, or failure to act; and

(14) "ex parte communication" means an oral or written communication not on the public record with respect to which reasonable prior notice to all parties is not given, but it shall not include requests for status reports on any matter or proceeding covered by this subchapter.

(Pub.L. 89–554, Sept. 6, 1966, 80 Stat. 381; Pub.L. 94–409, § 4(b), Sept. 13, 1976, 90 Stat. 1247; Pub.L. 103–272, § 5(a), July 5, 1994, 108 Stat. 1373; Pub.L. 111–350, § 5(a)(2), Jan. 4, 2011, 124 Stat. 3841.)

§ 553.   Rule making

(a) This section applies, according to the provisions thereof, except to the extent that there is involved—

    (1) a military or foreign affairs function of the United States; or

    (2) a matter relating to agency management or personnel or to public property, loans, grants, benefits, or contracts.

(b) General notice of proposed rule making shall be published in the Federal Register, unless persons subject thereto are named and either personally served or otherwise have actual notice thereof in accordance with law. The notice shall include—

    (1) a statement of the time, place, and nature of public rule making proceedings;

    (2) reference to the legal authority under which the rule is proposed; and

    (3) either the terms or substance of the proposed rule or a description of the subjects and issues involved.

Except when notice or hearing is required by statute, this subsection does not apply—

    (A) to interpretative rules, general statements of policy, or rules of agency organization, procedure, or practice; or

    (B) when the agency for good cause finds (and incorporates the finding and a brief statement of reasons therefor in the rules issued) that notice and public procedure thereon are impracticable, unnecessary, or contrary to the public interest.

(c) After notice required by this section, the agency shall give interested persons an opportunity to participate in the rule making through submission of written data, views, or arguments with or without opportunity for oral presentation. After consideration of the relevant matter presented, the agency shall incorporate in the rules adopted a concise general statement of their basis and purpose. When rules are required by statute to be made on the record after opportunity for an agency hearing, sections 556 and 557 of this title apply instead of this subsection.

(d) The required publication or service of a substantive rule shall be made not less than 30 days before its effective date, except—

    (1) a substantive rule which grants or recognizes an exemption or relieves a restriction;

    (2) interpretative rules and statements of policy; or

    (3) as otherwise provided by the agency for good cause found and published with the rule.

(e) Each agency shall give an interested person the right to petition for the issuance, amendment, or repeal of a rule.

(Pub.L. 89–554, Sept. 6, 1966, 80 Stat. 383.)

§ 701.   Application; definitions

(a) This chapter applies, according to the provisions thereof, except to the extent that—

(1) statutes preclude judicial review; or

(2) agency action is committed to agency discretion by law.

(b) For the purpose of this chapter—

(1) "agency" means each authority of the Government of the United States, whether or not it is within or subject to review by another agency, but does not include—

(A) the Congress;

(B) the courts of the United States;

(C) the governments of the territories or possessions of the United States;

(D) the government of the District of Columbia;

(E) agencies composed of representatives of the parties or of representatives of organizations of the parties to the disputes determined by them;

(F) courts martial and military commissions;

(G) military authority exercised in the field in time of war or in occupied territory; or

(H) functions conferred by sections 1738, 1739, 1743, and 1744 of title 12; subchapter II of chapter 471 of title 49; or sections 1884, 1891–1902, and former section 1641(b)(2), of title 50, appendix; and

(2) "person", "rule", "order", "license", "sanction", "relief", and "agency action" have the meanings given them by section 551 of this title.

(Pub.L. 89–554, Sept. 6, 1966, 80 Stat. 392; Pub.L. 103–272, § 5(a), July 5, 1994, 108 Stat. 1373; Pub.L. 111–350, § 5(a)(3), Jan. 4, 2011, 124 Stat. 3841.)

§ 702.   Right of review

A person suffering legal wrong because of agency action, or adversely affected or aggrieved by agency action within the meaning of a relevant statute, is entitled to judicial review thereof. An action in a court of the United States seeking relief other than money damages and stating a claim that an agency or an officer or employee thereof acted or failed to act in an official capacity or under color of legal authority shall not be dismissed nor relief therein be denied on the ground that it is against the United States or that the United States is an indispensable party. The United States may be named as a defendant in any such action, and a judgment or decree may be entered against the United States: *Provided,* That any mandatory or injunctive decree shall specify the Federal officer or officers (by name or by title), and their successors in office, personally responsible for compliance. Nothing herein **(1)** affects other limitations on judicial review or the power or duty of the court to dismiss any action or deny relief on any other appropriate legal or equitable ground; or **(2)** confers authority to grant relief if any other statute that grants consent to suit expressly or impliedly forbids the relief which is sought.

(Pub.L. 89–554, Sept. 6, 1966, 80 Stat. 392; Pub.L. 94–574, § 1, Oct. 21, 1976, 90 Stat. 2721.)

§ 703.   Form and venue of proceeding

The form of proceeding for judicial review is the special statutory review proceeding relevant to the subject matter in a court specified by statute or, in the absence or inadequacy thereof, any applicable form of legal action, including actions for declaratory judgments or writs of prohibitory or mandatory injunction or habeas corpus, in a court of competent jurisdiction. If no special statutory review proceeding is applicable, the action for judicial review may be brought against the United States, the agency by its official title, or the appropriate officer. Except to the extent that prior, adequate, and exclusive opportunity for judicial review is provided by law, agency action is subject to judicial review in civil or criminal proceedings for judicial enforcement.

(Pub.L. 89–554, Sept. 6, 1966, 80 Stat. 392; Pub.L. 94–574, § 1, Oct. 21, 1976, 90 Stat. 2721.)

§ 704.   Actions reviewable

Agency action made reviewable by statute and final agency action for which there is no other adequate remedy in a court are subject to judicial review. A preliminary, procedural, or intermediate agency action or ruling not directly reviewable is subject to review on the review of the final agency action. Except as otherwise expressly required by statute, agency action otherwise final is final for the purposes of this section whether or not there has been presented or determined an application for a declaratory order, for any form of reconsideration, or, unless the agency otherwise requires by rule and provides that the action meanwhile is inoperative, for an appeal to superior agency authority.

(Pub.L. 89–554, Sept. 6, 1966, 80 Stat. 392.)

§ 705.   Relief pending review

When an agency finds that justice so requires, it may postpone the effective date of action taken by it, pending judicial review. On such conditions as may be required and to the extent necessary to prevent irreparable injury, the reviewing court, including the court to which a case may be taken on appeal from or on application for certiorari or other writ to a reviewing court, may issue all necessary and appropriate process to postpone the effective date of an agency action or to preserve status or rights pending conclusion of the review proceedings.

(Pub.L. 89–554, Sept. 6, 1966, 80 Stat. 393.)

§ 706.   Scope of review

To the extent necessary to decision and when presented, the reviewing court shall decide all relevant questions of law, interpret constitutional and statutory provisions, and determine the meaning or applicability of the terms of an agency action. The reviewing court shall—

(1) compel agency action unlawfully withheld or unreasonably delayed; and

(2) hold unlawful and set aside agency action, findings, and conclusions found to be—

(A) arbitrary, capricious, an abuse of discretion, or otherwise not in accordance with law;

(B) contrary to constitutional right, power, privilege, or immunity;

(C) in excess of statutory jurisdiction, authority, or limitations, or short of statutory right;

(D) without observance of procedure required by law;

(E) unsupported by substantial evidence in a case subject to sections 556 and 557 of this title or otherwise reviewed on the record of an agency hearing provided by statute; or

(F) unwarranted by the facts to the extent that the facts are subject to trial de novo by the reviewing court.

In making the foregoing determinations, the court shall review the whole record or those parts of it cited by a party, and due account shall be taken of the rule of prejudicial error.

(Pub.L. 89–554, Sept. 6, 1966, 80 Stat. 393.)

TITLE 18, U.S. CODE, CRIMES AND CRIMINAL PROCEDURE

§ 16.   Crime of violence defined

The term "crime of violence" means—

(a) an offense that has as an element the use, attempted use, or threatened use of physical force against the person or property of another, or

(b) any other offense that is a felony and that, by its nature, involves a substantial risk that physical force against the person or property of another may be used in the course of committing the offense.

(Pub.L. 98–473, Title II, § 1001(a), Oct. 12, 1984, 98 Stat. 2136.)

§ 1546.   Fraud and misuse of visas, permits, and other documents

(a) Whoever knowingly forges, counterfeits, alters, or falsely makes any immigrant or nonimmigrant visa, permit, border crossing card, alien registration receipt card, or other document prescribed by statute or regulation for entry into or as evidence of authorized stay or employment in the United States, or utters, uses, attempts to use, possesses, obtains, accepts, or receives any such visa, permit, border crossing card, alien registration receipt card, or other document prescribed by statute or regulation for entry into or as evidence of authorized stay or employment in the United States, knowing it to be forged, counterfeited, altered, or falsely made, or to have been procured by means of any false claim or statement, or to have been otherwise procured by fraud or unlawfully obtained; or

Whoever, except under direction of the Attorney General or the Commissioner of the Immigration and Naturalization Service, or other proper officer, knowingly possesses any blank permit, or engraves, sells, brings into the United States, or has in his control or possession any plate in the likeness of a plate designed for the printing of permits, or makes any print, photograph, or impression in the likeness of any immigrant or nonimmigrant visa, permit or other document required for entry into the United States, or has in his possession a distinctive paper which has been adopted by the Attorney General or the Commissioner of the Immigration and Naturalization Service for the printing of such visas, permits, or documents; or

Whoever, when applying for an immigrant or nonimmigrant visa, permit, or other document required for entry into the United States, or for admission to the United States personates another, or falsely appears in the name of a deceased individual, or evades or attempts to evade the immigration laws by appearing under an assumed or fictitious name without disclosing his true identity, or sells or otherwise disposes of, or offers to sell or otherwise dispose of, or utters, such visa, permit, or other document, to any person not authorized by law to receive such document; or

Whoever knowingly makes under oath, or as permitted under penalty of perjury under section 1746 of title 28, United States Code, knowingly subscribes as true, any false statement with respect to a material fact in any application, affidavit, or other document required by the immigration laws or regulations prescribed thereunder, or knowingly presents any such application, affidavit, or other document which contains any such false statement or which fails to contain any reasonable basis in law or fact—

Shall be fined under this title or imprisoned not more than 25 years (if the offense was committed to facilitate an act of international terrorism (as defined in section 2331 of this title)), 20 years (if the offense was committed to facilitate a drug trafficking crime (as defined in section 929(a) of this title)), 10 years (in the case of the first or second such offense, if the offense was not committed to facilitate such an act of international terrorism or a drug trafficking crime), or 15 years (in the case of any other offense), or both.

(b) Whoever uses—

(1) an identification document, knowing (or having reason to know) that the document was not issued lawfully for the use of the possessor,

(2) an identification document knowing (or having reason to know) that the document is false, or

(3) a false attestation,

for the purpose of satisfying a requirement of section 274A(b) of the Immigration and Nationality Act [8 U.S.C.A. § 1324a(b)], shall be fined under this title, imprisoned not more than 5 years, or both.

(c) This section does not prohibit any lawfully authorized investigative, protective, or intelligence activity of a law enforcement agency of the United States, a State, or a subdivision of a State, or of an intelligence agency of the United States, or any activity authorized under title V of the Organized Crime Control Act of 1970 (18 U.S.C.A. note prec. 3481). For purposes of this section, the term "State" means a State of the United States, the District of Columbia, and any commonwealth, territory, or possession of the United States.

(June 25, 1948, c. 645, 62 Stat. 771; June 27, 1952, c. 477, Title IV, § 402(a), 66 Stat. 275; Oct. 18, 1976, Pub.L. 94–550, § 5, 90 Stat. 2535; Nov. 6, 1986, Pub.L. 99–603, Title I, § 103(a), 100 Stat. 3380; Oct. 24, 1988, Pub.L. 100–525, Title I, § 2(c), 102 Stat. 2610; Nov. 29, 1990, Pub.L. 101–647, Title XXXV, § 3550, 104 Stat. 4926; Sept. 13, 1994, Pub.L. 103–322, Title XIII, § 130009(a)(4), (5), Title XXXIII, § 330011(p), 108 Stat. 2030, 2145; Sept. 30, 1996, Pub.L. 104–208, Div. C, Title II, §§ 211(a)(2), 214, 110 Stat. 3009–569, 3009–572; Oct. 11, 1996, Pub.L. 104–294, Title VI, § 607(m), 110 Stat. 3512; Nov. 2, 2002, Pub.L. 107–273, Div. B, Title IV, § 4002(a)(3), 116 Stat. 1806.)

§ 2331. Definitions

As used in this chapter—

(1) the term "international terrorism" means activities that—

(A) involve violent acts or acts dangerous to human life that are a violation of the criminal laws of the United States or of any State, or that would be a criminal violation if committed within the jurisdiction of the United States or of any State;

(B) appear to be intended—

    (i) to intimidate or coerce a civilian population;

    (ii) to influence the policy of a government by intimidation or coercion; or

    (iii) to affect the conduct of a government by mass destruction, assassination, or kidnapping; and

(C) occur primarily outside the territorial jurisdiction of the United States, or transcend national boundaries in terms of the means by which they are accomplished, the persons they appear intended to intimidate or coerce, or the locale in which their perpetrators operate or seek asylum;

(2) the term "national of the United States" has the meaning given such term in section 101(a)(22) of the Immigration and Nationality Act;

(3) the term "person" means any individual or entity capable of holding a legal or beneficial interest in property;

(4) the term "act of war" means any act occurring in the course of—

(A) declared war;

(B) armed conflict, whether or not war has been declared, between two or more nations; or

(C) armed conflict between military forces of any origin;

(5) the term "domestic terrorism" means activities that—

(A) involve acts dangerous to human life that are a violation of the criminal laws of the United States or of any State;

(B) appear to be intended—

    (i) to intimidate or coerce a civilian population;

    (ii) to influence the policy of a government by intimidation or coercion; or

    (iii) to affect the conduct of a government by mass destruction, assassination, or kidnapping; and

(C) occur primarily within the territorial jurisdiction of the United States; and

(6) the term "military force" does not include any person that—

(A) has been designated as a—

    (i) foreign terrorist organization by the Secretary of State under section 219 of the Immigration and Nationality Act (8 U.S.C. 1189); or

(ii) specially designated global terrorist (as such term is defined in section 594.310 of title 31, Code of Federal Regulations) by the Secretary of State or the Secretary of the Treasury; or

(B) has been determined by the court to not be a "military force".

(Pub.L. 102–572, Title X, § 1003(a)(3), Oct. 29, 1992, 106 Stat. 4521; as amended Pub.L. 107–56, Title VIII, § 802(a), Oct. 26, 2001, 115 Stat. 376; Pub.L. 115–253, § 2(a), Oct. 3, 2018, 132 Stat. 3183.)

§ 2339A. Providing material support to terrorists

(a) Offense.—Whoever provides material support or resources or conceals or disguises the nature, location, source, or ownership of material support or resources, knowing or intending that they are to be used in preparation for, or in carrying out, a violation of section 32, 37, 81, 175, 229, 351, 831, 842(m)or (n), 844(f) or (i), 930(c), 956, 1091, 1114, 1116, 1203, 1361, 1362, 1363, 1366, 1751, 1992, 2155,2156, 2280, 2281, 2332, 2332a, 2332b, 2332f, 2340A, or 2442 of this title, section 236 of the Atomic Energy Act of 1954 (42 U.S.C. 2284), section 46502 or 60123(b) of title 49, or any offense listed in section 2332b(g)(5)(B) (except for sections 2339A and 2339B) or in preparation for, or in carrying out, the concealment of an escape from the commission of any such violation, or attempts or conspires to do such an act, shall be fined under this title, imprisoned not more than 15 years, or both, and, if the death of any person results, shall be imprisoned for any term of years or for life. A violation of this section may be prosecuted in any Federal judicial district in which the underlying offense was committed, or in any other Federal judicial district as provided by law.

(b) Definitions.—As used in this section—

(1) the term "material support or resources" means any property, tangible or intangible, or service, including currency or monetary instruments or financial securities, financial services, lodging, training, expert advice or assistance, safehouses, false documentation or identification, communications equipment, facilities, weapons, lethal substances, explosives, personnel (1 or more individuals who may be or include oneself), and transportation, except medicine or religious materials;

(2) the term "training" means instruction or teaching designed to impart a specific skill, as opposed to general knowledge; and

(3) the term "expert advice or assistance" means advice or assistance derived from scientific, technical or other specialized knowledge.

(Pub.L. 103–322, Title XII, § 120005(a), Sept. 13, 1994, 108 Stat. 2022, and amended Pub.L. 104–132, Title III, § 323, Apr. 24, 1996, 110 Stat. 1255; Pub.L. 104–294, Title VI, §§ 601(b)(2), (s)(2), (3), 604(b)(5), Oct. 11, 1996, 110 Stat. 3498, 3502, 3506; as amended Pub.L. 107–56, Title VIII, §§ 805(a), 810(c), 811(f), Oct. 26, 2001, 115 Stat. 377, 380, 381; Pub.L. 107–197, Title III, § 301(c), June 25, 2002, 116 Stat. 728; Pub.L. 107–273, Div. B, Title IV, § 4002(a)(7), (c)(1), (e)(11), Nov. 2, 2002, 116 Stat. 1807, 1808, 1811; Pub.L. 108–458, Title VI, § 6603(a)(2), (b), Dec. 17, 2004, 118 Stat. 3762; Pub.L. 109–177, Title I, § 110(b)(3) (B), Mar. 9, 2006, 120 Stat. 208; Pub.L. 111–122, § 3(d), Dec. 22, 2009, 123 Stat. 3481.)

§ 2339B. Providing material support or resources to designated foreign terrorist organizations

(a) Prohibited activities.—

(1) Unlawful conduct.—Whoever knowingly provides material support or resources to a foreign terrorist organization, or attempts or conspires to do so, shall be fined under this title or imprisoned not more than 20 years, or both, and, if the death of any person results, shall be imprisoned for any term of years or for life. To violate this paragraph, a person must have knowledge that the organization is a designated terrorist organization (as defined in subsection (g)(6)), that the organization has engaged or engages in terrorist activity (as defined in section 212(a)(3)(B) of the Immigration and Nationality Act [8 U.S.C.A. § 1182(a)(3)(B)]), or that the organization has engaged or engages in terrorism (as defined in section 140(d)(2) of the Foreign Relations Authorization Act, Fiscal Years 1988 and 1989).

(2) Financial institutions.—Except as authorized by the Secretary, any financial institution that becomes aware that it has possession of, or control over, any funds in which a foreign terrorist organization, or its agent, has an interest, shall—

(A) retain possession of, or maintain control over, such funds; and

(B) report to the Secretary the existence of such funds in accordance with regulations issued by the Secretary.

(b) Civil penalty.—Any financial institution that knowingly fails to comply with subsection (a)(2) shall be subject to a civil penalty in an amount that is the greater of—

(A) $50,000 per violation; or

(B) twice the amount of which the financial institution was required under subsection (a)(2) to retain possession or control.

(c) Injunction.—Whenever it appears to the Secretary or the Attorney General that any person is engaged in, or is about to engage in, any act that constitutes, or would constitute, a violation of this section, the Attorney General may initiate civil action in a district court of the United States to enjoin such violation.

(d) Extraterritorial jurisdiction.—

(1) In general.—There is jurisdiction over an offense under subsection (a) if—

(A) an offender is a national of the United States (as defined in section 101(a)(22) of the Immigration and Nationality Act (8 U.S.C. 1101(a)(22))) or an alien lawfully admitted for permanent residence in the United States (as defined in section 101(a)(20) of the Immigration and Nationality Act (8 U.S.C. 1101(a)(20)));

(B) an offender is a stateless person whose habitual residence is in the United States;

(C) after the conduct required for the offense occurs an offender is brought into or found in the United States, even if the conduct required for the offense occurs outside the United States;

(D) the offense occurs in whole or in part within the United States;

(E) the offense occurs in or affects interstate or foreign commerce; or

(F) an offender aids or abets any person over whom jurisdiction exists under this paragraph in committing an offense under subsection (a) or conspires with any person over whom jurisdiction exists under this paragraph to commit an offense under subsection (a).

(2) Extraterritorial jurisdiction.—There is extraterritorial Federal jurisdiction over an offense under this section.

(e) Investigations.—

(1) In general.—The Attorney General shall conduct any investigation of a possible violation of this section, or of any license, order, or regulation issued pursuant to this section.

(2) Coordination with the Department of the Treasury.—The Attorney General shall work in coordination with the Secretary in investigations relating to—

(A) the compliance or noncompliance by a financial institution with the requirements of subsection (a)(2); and

(B) civil penalty proceedings authorized under subsection (b).

(3) Referral.—Any evidence of a criminal violation of this section arising in the course of an investigation by the Secretary or any other Federal agency shall be referred immediately to the Attorney General for further investigation. The Attorney General shall timely notify the Secretary of any action taken on referrals from the Secretary, and may refer investigations to the Secretary for remedial licensing or civil penalty action.

(f) Classified information in civil proceedings brought by the United States.—

(1) Discovery of classified information by defendants.—

(A) Request by United States.—In any civil proceeding under this section, upon request made ex parte and in writing by the United States, a court, upon a sufficient showing, may authorize the United States to—

(i) redact specified items of classified information from documents to be introduced into evidence or made available to the defendant through discovery under the Federal Rules of Civil Procedure;

(ii) substitute a summary of the information for such classified documents; or

(iii) substitute a statement admitting relevant facts that the classified information would tend to prove.

(B) Order granting request.—If the court enters an order granting a request under this paragraph, the entire text of the documents to which the request relates shall be sealed and preserved in the records of the court to be made available to the appellate court in the event of an appeal.

(C) Denial of request.—If the court enters an order denying a request of the United States under this paragraph, the United States may take an immediate, interlocutory appeal in accordance with paragraph (5). For purposes of such an appeal, the entire text of the documents to which the request relates, together with any transcripts of arguments made ex parte to the court in connection therewith, shall be maintained under seal and delivered to the appellate court.

(2) Introduction of classified information; precautions by court.—

(A) Exhibits.—To prevent unnecessary or inadvertent disclosure of classified information in a civil proceeding brought by the United States under this section, the United States may petition the court ex parte to admit, in lieu of classified writings, recordings, or photographs, one or more of the following:

(i) Copies of items from which classified information has been redacted.

(ii) Stipulations admitting relevant facts that specific classified information would tend to prove.

(iii) A declassified summary of the specific classified information.

(B) Determination by court.—The court shall grant a request under this paragraph if the court finds that the redacted item, stipulation, or summary is sufficient to allow the defendant to prepare a defense.

(3) Taking of trial testimony.—

(A) Objection.—During the examination of a witness in any civil proceeding brought by the United States under this subsection, the United States may object to any question or line of inquiry that may require the witness to disclose classified information not previously found to be admissible.

(B) Action by court.—In determining whether a response is admissible, the court shall take precautions to guard against the compromise of any classified information, including—

(i) permitting the United States to provide the court, ex parte, with a proffer of the witness's response to the question or line of inquiry; and

(ii) requiring the defendant to provide the court with a proffer of the nature of the information that the defendant seeks to elicit.

(C) Obligation of defendant.—In any civil proceeding under this section, it shall be the defendant's obligation to establish the relevance and materiality of any classified information sought to be introduced.

(4) Appeal.—If the court enters an order denying a request of the United States under this subsection, the United States may take an immediate interlocutory appeal in accordance with paragraph (5).

(5) Interlocutory appeal.—

(A) Subject of appeal.—An interlocutory appeal by the United States shall lie to a court of appeals from a decision or order of a district court—

(i) authorizing the disclosure of classified information;

(ii) imposing sanctions for nondisclosure of classified information; or

(iii) refusing a protective order sought by the United States to prevent the disclosure of classified information.

(B) Expedited consideration.—

(i) In general.—An appeal taken pursuant to this paragraph, either before or during trial, shall be expedited by the court of appeals.

(ii) Appeals prior to trial.—If an appeal is of an order made prior to trial, an appeal shall be taken not later than 14 days after the decision or order appealed from, and the trial shall not commence until the appeal is resolved.

(iii) Appeals during trial.—If an appeal is taken during trial, the trial court shall adjourn the trial until the appeal is resolved, and the court of appeals—

(I) shall hear argument on such appeal not later than 4 days after the adjournment of the trial, excluding intermediate weekends and holidays;

(II) may dispense with written briefs other than the supporting materials previously submitted to the trial court;

(III) shall render its decision not later than 4 days after argument on appeal, excluding intermediate weekends and holidays; and

(IV) may dispense with the issuance of a written opinion in rendering its decision.

(C) Effect of ruling.—An interlocutory appeal and decision shall not affect the right of the defendant, in a subsequent appeal from a final judgment, to claim as error reversal by the trial court on remand of a ruling appealed from during trial.

(6) Construction.—Nothing in this subsection shall prevent the United States from seeking protective orders or asserting privileges ordinarily available to the United States to protect against the disclosure of classified information, including the invocation of the military and State secrets privilege.

(g) Definitions.—As used in this section—

(1) the term "classified information" has the meaning given that term in section 1(a) of the Classified Information Procedures Act (18 U.S.C. App.);

(2) the term "financial institution" has the same meaning as in section 5312(a)(2) of title 31, United States Code;

(3) the term "funds" includes coin or currency of the United States or any other country, traveler's checks, personal checks, bank checks, money orders, stocks, bonds, debentures, drafts, letters of credit, any other negotiable instrument, and any electronic representation of any of the foregoing;

(4) the term "material support or resources" has the same meaning given that term in section 2339A (including the definitions of "training" and "expert advice or assistance" in that section);

(5) the term "Secretary" means the Secretary of the Treasury; and

(6) the term "terrorist organization" means an organization designated as a terrorist organization under section 219 of the Immigration and Nationality Act.

(h) Provision of personnel.—No person may be prosecuted under this section in connection with the term "personnel" unless that person has knowingly provided, attempted to provide, or conspired to provide a foreign terrorist organization with 1 or more individuals (who may be or include himself) to work under that terrorist organization's direction or control or to organize, manage, supervise, or otherwise direct the operation of that organization. Individuals who act entirely independently of the foreign terrorist organization to advance its goals or objectives shall not be considered to be working under the foreign terrorist organization's direction and control.

(i) Rule of construction.—Nothing in this section shall be construed or applied so as to abridge the exercise of rights guaranteed under the First Amendment to the Constitution of the United States.

(j) Exception.—No person may be prosecuted under this section in connection with the term "personnel", "training", or "expert advice or assistance" if the provision of that material support or resources to a foreign terrorist organization was approved by the Secretary of State with the concurrence of the Attorney General. The Secretary of State may not approve the provision of any material support that may be used to carry out terrorist activity (as defined in section 212(a)(3)(B)(iii) of the Immigration and Nationality Act [8 U.S.C.A. § 1182(a)(3)(B)(iii)]).

(Pub.L. 104–132, Title III, § 303(a), Apr. 24, 1996, 110 Stat. 1250; as amended Pub.L. 107–56, Title VIII, § 810(d), Oct. 26, 2001, 115 Stat. 380; Pub.L. 108–458, Title VI, § 6603(c) to (f), Dec. 17, 2004, 118 Stat. 3762, 3763; Pub.L. 111–16, § 3(6) to (8), May 7, 2009, 123 Stat. 1608; Pub.L. 114–23, Title VII, § 704, June 2, 2015, 129 Stat. 300.)

III. EXCERPTS FROM CODE OF FEDERAL REGULATIONS

TITLE 8—(ALIENS AND NATIONALITY) AND TITLE 20 (EMPLOYEES' BENEFITS)

Part 204—Immigrant Petitions

EXCERPTS FROM C.F.R.

PART 204—IMMIGRANT PETITIONS

§ 204.5 Petitions for employment-based immigrants.

(a) General. A petition to classify an alien under section 203(b)(1), 203(b)(2), or 203(b)(3) of the Act must be filed on Form I–140, Petition for Immigrant Worker. A petition to classify an alien under section 203(b)(4) (as it relates to special immigrants under section 101(a)(27)(C)) must be filed on Form I–360, Petition for Amerasian, Widow, or Special Immigrant. A separate Form I–140 or I–360 must be filed for each beneficiary, accompanied by the applicable fee. A petition is considered properly filed if it is:

(1) Accepted for processing under the provisions of part 103;

(2) Accompanied by any required individual labor certification, application for Schedule A designation, or evidence that the alien's occupation qualifies as a shortage occupation within the Department of Labor's Labor Market Information Pilot Program; and

(3) Accompanied by any other required supporting documentation.

(b) Jurisdiction. Form I–140 or I–360 must be filed in accordance with the instructions on the form.

(c) Filing petition. Any United States employer desiring and intending to employ an alien may file a petition for classification of the alien under section 203(b)(1)(B), 203(b)(1)(C), 203(b)(2), or 203(b)(3) of the Act. An alien, or any person in the alien's behalf, may file a petition for classification under section 203(b)(1)(A) or 203(b)(4) of the Act (as it relates to special immigrants under section 101(a)(27)(C) of the Act).

(d) Priority date. The priority date of any petition filed for classification under section 203(b) of the Act which is accompanied by an individual labor certification from the Department of Labor shall be the date the labor certification application was accepted for processing by any office of the Department of Labor. The priority date of any petition filed for a classification under section 203(b) of the Act which does not require a labor certification from the Department of Labor shall be the date the completed, signed petition (including all initial evidence and the correct fee) is properly filed with USCIS. The priority date of any petition filed for classification under section 203(b) of the Act which is accompanied by an application for Schedule A designation shall be the date the completed, signed petition (including all initial evidence and the correct fee) is properly filed with USCIS. The priority date of an alien who filed for classification as a special immigrant under section 203(b)(4) of the Act prior to October 1, 1991, and who is the beneficiary of an approved petition for special immigrant status after October 1, 1991, shall be the date the alien applied for an immigrant visa or adjustment of status.

(e) Retention of section 203(b)(1), (2), or (3) priority date.

(1) A petition approved on behalf of an alien under sections 203(b) (1), (2), or (3) of the Act accords the alien the priority date of the ap-

proved petition for any subsequently filed petition for any classification under sections 203(b)(1), (2), or (3) of the Act for which the alien may qualify. In the event that the alien is the beneficiary of multiple approved petitions under sections 203(b)(1), (2), or (3) of the Act, the alien shall be entitled to the earliest priority date.

(2) The priority date of a petition may not be retained under paragraph (e)(1) of this section if at any time USCIS revokes the approval of the petition because of:

(i) Fraud, or a willful misrepresentation of a material fact;

(ii) Revocation by the Department of Labor of the approved permanent labor certification that accompanied the petition;

(iii) Invalidation by USCIS or the Department of State of the permanent labor certification that accompanied the petition; or

(iv) A determination by USCIS that petition approval was based on a material error.

(3) A denied petition will not establish a priority date.

(4) A priority date is not transferable to another alien.

(5) A petition filed under section 204(a)(1)(F) of the Act for an alien shall remain valid with respect to a new employment offer as determined by USCIS under section 204(j) of the Act and 8 CFR 245.25. An alien will continue to be afforded the priority date of such petition, if the requirements of paragraph (e) of this section are met.

(f) Maintaining the priority date of a third or sixth preference petition filed prior to October 1, 1991—Any petition filed before October 1, 1991, and approved on any date, to accord status under section 203(a)(3) or 203(a)(6) of the Act, as in effect before October 1, 1991, shall be deemed a petition approved to accord status under section 203(b)(2) or within the appropriate classification under section 203(b)(3), respectively, of the Act as in effect on or after October 1, 1991, provided that the alien applies for an immigrant visa or adjustment of status within the two years following notification that an immigrant visa is immediately available for his or her use.

(g) Initial evidence—

(1) General. Specific requirements for initial supporting documents for the various employment-based immigrant classifications are set forth in this section. In general, ordinary legible photocopies of such documents (except for labor certifications from the Department of Labor) will be acceptable for initial filing and approval. However, at the discretion of the director, original documents may be required in individual cases. Evidence relating to qualifying experience or training shall be in the form of letter(s) from current or former employer(s) or trainer(s) and shall include the name, address, and title of the writer, and a specific description of the duties performed by the alien or of the training received. If such evidence is unavailable, other documentation relating to the alien's experience or training will be considered.

(2) Ability of prospective employer to pay wage. Any petition filed by or for an employment-based immigrant which requires an offer of employment must be accompanied by evidence that the prospective United States employer has the ability to pay the proffered wage. The petitioner must demonstrate this ability at the time the priority date is established and continuing until the beneficiary obtains lawful permanent residence. Evidence of this ability shall be either in the form of copies of annual reports, federal tax returns, or audited financial statements. In a case where the prospective United States employer employs 100 or more workers, the director may accept a statement from a financial officer of the organization which establishes the prospective employer's ability to pay the proffered wage. In appropriate cases, additional evidence, such as profit/loss statements, bank account records, or personnel records, may be submitted by the petitioner or requested by the Service.

(h) Aliens with extraordinary ability—

(1) An alien, or any person on behalf of the alien, may file an I–140 visa petition for classification under section 203(b)(1)(A) of the Act as an alien of extraordinary ability in the sciences, arts, education, business, or athletics.

(2) Definition. As used in this section:

Extraordinary ability means a level of expertise indicating that the individual is one of that small percentage who have risen to the very top of the field of endeavor.

(3) Initial evidence. A petition for an alien of extraordinary ability must be accompanied by evidence that the alien has sustained national or international acclaim and that his or her achievements have been recognized in the field of expertise. Such evidence shall include evidence of a one-time achievement (that is, a major, international recognized award), or at least three of the following:

(i) Documentation of the alien's receipt of lesser nationally or internationally recognized prizes or awards for excellence in the field of endeavor;

(ii) Documentation of the alien's membership in associations in the field for which classification is sought, which require outstanding achievements of their members, as judged by recognized national or international experts in their disciplines or fields;

(iii) Published material about the alien in professional or major trade publications or other major media, relating to the alien's work in the field for which classification is sought. Such evidence shall include the title, date, and author of the material, and any necessary translation;

(iv) Evidence of the alien's participation, either individually or on a panel, as a judge of the work of others in the same or an allied field of specification for which classification is sought;

(v) Evidence of the alien's original scientific, scholarly, artistic, athletic, or business-related contributions of major significance in the field;

(vi) Evidence of the alien's authorship of scholarly articles in the field, in professional or major trade publications or other major media;

(vii) Evidence of the display of the alien's work in the field at artistic exhibitions or showcases;

(viii) Evidence that the alien has performed in a leading or critical role for organizations or establishments that have a distinguished reputation;

(ix) Evidence that the alien has commanded a high salary or other significantly high remuneration for services, in relation to others in the field; or

(x) Evidence of commercial successes in the performing arts, as shown by box office receipts or record, cassette, compact disk, or video sales.

(4) If the above standards do not readily apply to the beneficiary's occupation, the petitioner may submit comparable evidence to establish the beneficiary's eligibility.

(5) No offer of employment required. Neither an offer for employment in the United States nor a labor certification is required for this classification; however, the petition must be accompanied by clear evidence that the alien is coming to the United States to continue work in the area of expertise. Such evidence may include letter(s) from prospective employer(s), evidence of prearranged commitments such as contracts, or a statement from the beneficiary detailing plans on how he or she intends to continue his or her work in the United States.

(i) Outstanding professors and researchers.

(1) Any United States employer desiring and intending to employ a professor or researcher who is outstanding in an academic field under section 203(b)(1)(B) of the Act may file an I–140 visa petition for such classification.

(2) Definitions. As used in this section:

Academic field means a body of specialized knowledge offered for study at an accredited United States university or institution of higher education.

Permanent, in reference to a research position, means either tenured, tenure-track, or for a term of indefinite or unlimited duration, and in which the employee will ordinarily have an expectation of continued employment unless there is good cause for termination.

(3) Initial evidence. A petition for an outstanding professor or researcher must be accompanied by:

(i) Evidence that the professor or researcher is recognized internationally as outstanding in the academic field specified in the petition. Such evidence shall consist of at least two of the following:

(A) Documentation of the alien's receipt of major prizes or awards for outstanding achievement in the academic field;

(B) Documentation of the alien's membership in associations in the academic field which require outstanding achievements of their members;

(C) Published material in professional publications written by others about the alien's work in the academic field. Such material shall include the title, date, and author of the material, and any necessary translation;

(D) Evidence of the alien's participation, either individually or on a panel, as the judge of the work of others in the same or an allied academic field;

(E) Evidence of the alien's original scientific or scholarly research contributions to the academic field; or

(F) Evidence of the alien's authorship of scholarly books or articles (in scholarly journals with international circulation) in the academic field;

(ii) If the standards in paragraph (i)(3)(i) of this section do not readily apply, the petitioner may submit comparable evidence to establish the beneficiary's eligibility.

(iii) Evidence that the alien has at least three years of experience in teaching and/or research in the academic field. Experience in teaching or research while working on an advanced degree will only be acceptable if the alien has acquired the degree, and if the teaching duties were such that he or she had full responsibility for the class taught or if the research conducted toward the degree has been recognized within the academic field as outstanding. Evidence of teaching and/or research experience shall be in the form of letter(s) from current or former employer(s) and shall include the name, address, and title of the writer, and a specific description of the duties performed by the alien; and

(iv) An offer of employment from a prospective United States employer. A labor certification is not required for this classification. The offer of employment shall be in the form of a letter from:

(A) A United States university or institution of higher learning offering the alien a tenured or tenure-track teaching position in the alien's academic field;

(B) A United States university or institution of higher learning offering the alien a permanent research position in the alien's academic field; or

(C) A department, division, or institute of a private employer offering the alien a permanent research position in the alien's academic field. The department, division, or institute must demonstrate that it employs at least three persons full-time in research positions, and that it has achieved documented accomplishments in an academic field.

(j) Certain multinational executives and managers.

(1) A United States employer may file a petition on Form I–140 for classification of an alien under section 203(b)(1)(C) of the Act as a multinational executive or manager.

(2) Definitions. As used in this section:

Affiliate means:

(A) One of two subsidiaries both of which are owned and controlled by the same parent or individual;

(B) One of two legal entities owned and controlled by the same group of individuals, each individual owning and controlling approximately the same share or proportion of each entity; or

(C) In the case of a partnership that is organized in the United States to provide accounting services, along with managerial and/or consulting services, and markets its accounting services under an internationally recognized name under an agreement with a worldwide coordinating organization that is owned and controlled by the member accounting firms, a partnership (or similar organization) that is organized outside the United States to provide accounting' services shall be considered to be an affiliate of the United States partnership if it markets its accounting services under the same internationally recognized name under the agreement with the worldwide coordinating organization of which the United States partnership is also a member.

Doing business means the regular, systematic, and continuous provision of goods and/or services by a firm, corporation, or other entity and does not include the mere presence of an agent or office.

Executive capacity means an assignment within an organization in which the employee primarily:

(A) Directs the management of the organization or a major component or function of the organization;

(B) Establishes the goals and policies of the organization, component, or function;

(C) Exercises wide latitude in discretionary decisionmaking; and

(D) Receives only general supervision or direction from higher level executives, the board of directors, or stockholders of the organization.

Managerial capacity means an assignment within an organization in which the employee primarily:

(A) Manages the organization, or a department, subdivision, function, or component of the organization;

(B) Supervises and controls the work of other supervisory, professional, or managerial employees, or manages an essential function within the organization, or a department or subdivision of the organization;

(C) If another employee or other employees are directly supervised, has the authority to hire and fire or recommend those as well as other personnel actions (such as promotion and leave authorization), or, if no other employee is directly supervised, functions at a senior level within the organizational hierarchy or with respect to the function managed; and

(D) Exercises direction over the day-to-day operations of the activity or function for which the employee has authority.

Multinational means that the qualifying entity, or its affiliate, or subsidiary, conducts business in two or more countries, one of which is the United States.

Subsidiary means a firm, corporation, or other legal entity of which a parent owns, directly or indirectly, more than half of the entity and controls the entity; or owns, directly or indirectly, half of the entity and controls the entity; or owns, directly or indirectly, 50 percent of a 50–50 joint venture and has equal control and veto power over the entity; or owns, directly or indirectly, less than half of the entity, but in fact controls the entity.

(3) Initial evidence—

(i) Required evidence. A petition for a multinational executive or manager must be accompanied by a statement from an authorized official of the petitioning United States employer which demonstrates that:

(A) If the alien is outside the United States, in the three years immediately preceding the filing of the petition the alien has been employed outside the United States for at least one year in a managerial or executive capacity by a firm or corporation, or other legal entity, or by an affiliate or subsidiary of such a firm or corporation or other legal entity; or

(B) If the alien is already in the United States working for the same employer or a subsidiary or affiliate of the firm or corporation, or other legal entity by which the alien was employed overseas, in the three years preceding entry as a nonimmigrant, the alien was employed by the entity abroad for at least one year in a managerial or executive capacity;

(C) The prospective employer in the United States is the same employer or a subsidiary or affiliate of the firm or corporation or other legal entity by which the alien was employed overseas; and

(D) The prospective United States employer has been doing business for at least one year.

(ii) Appropriate additional evidence. In appropriate cases, the director may request additional evidence.

(4) Determining managerial or executive capacities.—

(i) Supervisors as managers. A first-line supervisor is not considered to be acting in a managerial capacity merely by virtue of his or her supervisory duties unless the employees supervised are professional.

(ii) Staffing levels. If staffing levels are used as a factor in determining whether an individual is acting in a managerial or executive capacity, the reasonable needs of the organization, component, or function, in light of the overall purpose and stage of development of the organization, component, or function, shall be taken into account. An individual shall not be considered to be acting in a managerial or executive capacity merely on the basis of the number of employees that the individual supervises or has supervised or directs or has directed.

(5) Offer of employment. No labor certification is required for this classification; however, the prospective employer in the United States must furnish a job offer in the form of a statement which indicates that the alien is to be employed in the United States in a managerial or executive capacity. Such letter must clearly describe the duties to be performed by the alien.

(k) Aliens who are members of the professions holding advanced degrees or aliens of exceptional ability.

(1) Any United States employer may file a petition on Form I–140 for classification of an alien under section 203(b)(2) of the Act as an alien who is a member of the professions holding an advanced degree or an alien of exceptional ability in the sciences, arts, or business. If an alien is claiming exceptional ability in the sciences, arts, or business and is seeking an exemption from the requirement of a job offer in the United States pursuant to section 203(b)(2)(B) of the Act, then the alien, or anyone in the alien's behalf, may be the petitioner.

(2) Definitions. As used in this section: Advanced degree means any United States academic or professional degree or a foreign equivalent degree above that of baccalaureate. A United States baccalaureate degree or a foreign equivalent degree followed by at least five years of progressive experience in the specialty shall be considered the equivalent of a master's degree. If a doctoral degree is customarily required by the specialty, the alien must have a United States doctorate or a foreign equivalent degree.

Exceptional ability in the sciences, arts, or business means a degree of expertise significantly above that ordinarily encountered in the sciences, arts, or business.

Profession means one of the occupations listed in section 101(a)(32) of the Act, as well as any occupation for which a United States baccalaureate degree or its foreign equivalent is the minimum requirement for entry into the occupation.

(3) Initial evidence. The petition must be accompanied by documentation showing that the alien is a professional holding an advanced degree or an alien of exceptional ability in the sciences, the arts, or business.

(i) To show that the alien is a professional holding an advanced degree, the petition must be accompanied by:

(A) An official academic record showing that the alien has a United States advanced degree or a foreign equivalent degree; or

(B) An official academic record showing that the alien has a United States baccalaureate degree or a foreign equivalent degree, and evidence in the form of letters from current or former employer(s) showing that the alien has at least five years of progressive post-baccalaureate experience in the specialty.

(ii) To show that the alien is an alien of exceptional ability in the sciences, arts, or business, the petition must be accompanied by at least three of the following:

(A) An official academic record showing that the alien has a degree, diploma, certificate, or similar award from a college, university, school, or other institution of learning relating to the area of exceptional ability;

(B) Evidence in the form of letter(s) from current or former employer(s) showing that the alien has at least ten years of full-time experience in the occupation for which he or she is being sought;

(C) A license to practice the profession or certification for a particular profession or occupation;

(D) Evidence that the alien has commanded a salary, or other remuneration for services, which demonstrates exceptional ability;

(E) Evidence of membership in professional associations; or

(F) Evidence of recognition for achievements and significant contributions to the industry or field by peers, governmental entities, or professional or business organizations.

(iii) If the above standards do not readily apply to the beneficiary's occupation, the petitioner may submit comparable evidence to establish the beneficiary's eligibility.

(4) Labor certification or evidence that alien qualifies for Labor Market Information Pilot Program—

(i) General. Every petition under this classification must be accompanied by an individual labor certification from the Department of Labor, by an application for Schedule A designation (if applicable), or by documentation to establish that the alien qualifies for one of the shortage occupations in the Department of Labor's Labor Market Information Pilot Program. To apply for Schedule A designation or to establish that the alien's occupation is within the Labor Market Information Program, a fully executed uncertified Form ETA–750 in duplicate must accompany the petition. The job offer portion of the individual labor certification, Schedule A application, or Pilot Program application must demonstrate that the job requires a professional holding an advanced degree or the equivalent or an alien of exceptional ability.

(ii) Exemption from job offer. The director may exempt the requirement of a job offer, and thus of a labor certification, for aliens of exceptional ability in the sciences, arts, or business if exemption would be in the national interest. To apply for the exemption, the petitioner must submit Form ETA–750B, Statement of Qualifications of Alien, in duplicate, as well as evidence to support the claim that such exemption would be in the national interest.

(*l*) Skilled workers, professionals, and other workers.

(1) Any United States employer may file a petition on Form I–140 for classification of an alien under section 203(b)(3) as a skilled worker, professional, or other (unskilled) worker.

(2) Definitions. As used in this part:

Other worker means a qualified alien who is capable, at the time of petitioning for this classification, of performing unskilled labor (requiring less than two years training or experience), not of a temporary or seasonal nature, for which qualified workers are not available in the United States.

Professional means a qualified alien who holds at least a United States baccalaureate degree or a foreign equivalent degree and who is a member of the professions.

Skilled worker means an alien who is capable, at the time of petitioning for this classification, of performing skilled labor (requiring at least two years training or experience), not of a temporary or seasonal nature, for which qualified workers are not available in the United States. Relevant post-secondary education may be considered as training for the purposes of this provision.

(3) Initial evidence—

(i) Labor certification or evidence that alien qualifies for Labor Market Information Pilot Program. Every petition under this classification must be accompanied by an individual labor certification from the Department of Labor, by an application for Schedule A designation, or by documentation to establish that the alien qualifies for one of the shortage occupations in the Department of Labor's Labor Market Information Pilot Program. To apply for Schedule A designation or to establish that the alien's occupation is a shortage occupation with the Labor Market Pilot Program, a fully executed uncertified Form ETA–750 in duplicate must accompany the petition. The job offer portion of an individual labor certification, Schedule A application, or Pilot Program application for a professional must demonstrate that the job requires the minimum of a baccalaureate degree.

(ii) Other documentation—

(A) General. Any requirements of training or experience for skilled workers, professionals, or other workers must be supported by letters from trainers or employers giving the name, address, and title of the trainer or employer, and a description of the training received or the experience of the alien.

(B) Skilled workers. If the petition is for a skilled worker, the petition must be accompanied by evidence that the alien meets the educational, training or experience, and any other requirements of the individual labor certification, meets the requirements for Schedule A designation, or meets the requirements for the Labor Market Information Pilot Program occupation designation. The minimum requirements for this classification are at least two years of training or experience.

(C) Professionals. If the petition is for a professional, the petition must be accompanied by evidence that the alien holds a United States baccalaureate degree or a foreign equivalent degree and by evidence that the alien is a member of the professions. Evidence of a baccalaureate degree shall be in the form of an official college or university record showing the date the baccalaureate degree was awarded and the area of concentration of study. To show that the alien is a member of the professions, the petitioner must submit evidence showing that the minimum of a baccalaureate degree is required for entry into the occupation.

(D) Other workers. If the petition is for an unskilled (other) worker, it must be accompanied by evidence that the alien meets any educational, training and experience, and other requirements of the labor certification.

(4) Differentiating between skilled and other workers. The determination of whether a worker is a skilled or other worker will be based on the requirements of training and/or experience placed on the job by the prospective employer, as certified by the Department of Labor. In the case of a Schedule A occupation or a shortage occupation within the Labor Market Pilot Program, the petitioner will be required to establish to the director that the job is a skilled job, i.e., one which requires at least two years of training and/or experience.

(m) Religious workers. This paragraph governs classification of an alien as a special immigrant religious worker as defined in section 101(a)(27)(C) of the Act and under section 203(b)(4) of the Act. To be eligible for classification as a special immigrant religious worker, the alien (either abroad or in the United States) must:

(1) For at least the two years immediately preceding the filing of the petition have been a member of a religious denomination that has a bona fide non-profit religious organization in the United States.

(2) Be coming to the United States to work in a full time (average of at least 35 hours per week) compensated position in one of the following occupations as they are defined in paragraph (m)(5) of this section:

(i) Solely in the vocation of a minister of that religious denomination;

(ii) A religious vocation either in a professional or nonprofessional capacity; or

(iii) A religious occupation either in a professional or nonprofessional capacity.

(3) Be coming to work for a bona fide non-profit religious organization in the United States, or a bona fide organization which is affiliated with the religious denomination in the United States.

(4) Have been working in one of the positions described in paragraph (m)(2) of this section, either abroad or in lawful immigration status in the United States, and after the age of 14 years continuously for at least the two-year period immediately preceding the filing of the petition. The prior religious work need not correspond precisely to the type of work to be performed. A break in the continuity of the work during the preceding two years will not affect eligibility so long as:

(i) The alien was still employed as a religious worker;

(ii) The break did not exceed two years; and

(iii) The nature of the break was for further religious training or for sabbatical that did not involve unauthorized work in the United States. However, the alien must have been a member of the petitioner's denomination throughout the two years of qualifying employment.

(5) Definitions. As used in paragraph (m) of this section, the term:

Bona fide non-profit religious organization in the United States means a religious organization exempt from taxation as described in section 501(c)(3) of the Internal Revenue Code of 1986, subsequent amendment or equivalent sections of prior enactments of the Internal Revenue Code, and possessing a currently valid determination letter from the IRS confirming such exemption.

Bona fide organization which is affiliated with the religious denomination means an organization which is closely associated with the religious denomination and which is exempt from taxation as described in section 501(c)(3) of the Internal Revenue Code of 1986, subsequent amendment or equivalent sections of prior enactments of the Internal Revenue Code and possessing a currently valid *72292 determination letter from the IRS confirming such exemption.

Denominational membership means membership during at least the two-year period immediately preceding the filing date of the petition, in the same type of religious denomination as the United States religious organization where the alien will work.

Minister means an individual who:

(A) Is fully authorized by a religious denomination, and fully trained according to the denomination's standards, to conduct such religious worship and perform other duties usually performed by authorized members of the clergy of that denomination;

(B) Is not a lay preacher or a person not authorized to perform duties usually performed by clergy;

(C) Performs activities with a rational relationship to the religious calling of the minister; and

(D) Works solely as a minister in the United States, which may include administrative duties incidental to the duties of a minister.

Petition means USCIS Form I–360, Petition for Amerasian, Widow(er), or Special Immigrant, a successor form, or other form as may be prescribed by USCIS, along with a supplement containing attestations required by this section, the fee specified in 8 CFR 103.7(b)(1), and supporting evidence filed as provided by this part.

Religious denomination means a religious group or community of believers that is governed or administered under a common type of ecclesiastical government and includes one or more of the following:

(A) A recognized common creed or statement of faith shared among the denomination's members;

(B) A common form of worship;

(C) A common formal code of doctrine and discipline;

(D) Common religious services and ceremonies;

(E) Common established places of religious worship or religious congregations; or

(F) Comparable indicia of a bona fide religious denomination.

Religious occupation means an occupation that meets all of the following requirements:

(A) The duties must primarily relate to a traditional religious function and be recognized as a religious occupation within the denomination.

(B) The duties must be primarily related to, and must clearly involve, inculcating or carrying out the religious creed and beliefs of the denomination.

(C) The duties do not include positions that are primarily administrative or support such as janitors, maintenance workers, clerical employees, fund raisers, persons solely involved in the solicitation of donations, or similar positions, although limited administrative duties that are only incidental to religious functions are permissible.

(D) Religious study or training for religious work does not constitute a religious occupation, but a religious worker may pursue study or training incident to status.

Religious vocation means a formal lifetime commitment, through vows, investitures, ceremonies, or similar indicia, to a religious way of life. The religious denomination must have a class of individuals whose lives are dedicated to religious practices and functions, as distinguished from the secular members of the religion. Examples of individuals practicing religious vocations include nuns, monks, and religious brothers and sisters.

Religious worker means an individual engaged in and, according to the denomination's standards, qualified for a religious occupation or vocation, whether or not in a professional capacity, or as a minister.

Tax-exempt organization means an organization that has received a determination letter from the IRS establishing that it, or a group that it belongs to, is exempt from taxation in accordance with sections 501(c)(3) of the Internal Revenue Code of 1986 or subsequent amendments or equivalent sections of prior enactments of the Internal Revenue Code.

(6) Filing requirements. A petition must be filed as provided in the petition form instructions either by the alien or by his or her prospective United States employer. After the date stated in section 101(a)(27)(C) of the Act, immigration or adjustment of status on the basis of this section is limited solely to ministers.

(7) Attestation. An authorized official of the prospective employer of an alien seeking religious worker status must complete, sign and date an attestation prescribed by USCIS and submit it along with the petition. If the alien is a self-petitioner and is also an authorized official of the prospective employer, the self-petitioner may sign the attestation. The prospective employer must specifically attest to all of the following:

(i) That the prospective employer is a bona fide non-profit religious organization or a bona fide organization which is affiliated with the religious denomination and is exempt from taxation;

(ii) The number of members of the prospective employer's organization;

(iii) The number of employees who work at the same location where the beneficiary will be employed and a summary of the type of responsibilities of those employees. USCIS may request a list of all employees, their titles, and a brief description of their duties at its discretion;

(iv) The number of aliens holding special immigrant or nonimmigrant religious worker status currently employed or employed within the past five years by the prospective employer's organization;

(v) The number of special immigrant religious worker and nonimmigrant religious worker petitions and applications filed by or on behalf of any aliens for employment by the prospective employer in the past five years;

(vi) The title of the position offered to the alien, the complete package of salaried or non-salaried compensation being offered, and a detailed description of the alien's proposed daily duties;

(vii) That the alien will be employed at least 35 hours per week;

(viii) The specific location(s) of the proposed employment;

(ix) That the alien has worked as a religious worker for the two years immediately preceding the filing of the application and is otherwise qualified for the position offered;

(x) That the alien has been a member of the denomination for at least two years immediately preceding the filing of the application;

(xi) That the alien will not be engaged in secular employment, and any salaried or non-salaried compensation for the work will be paid to the alien by the attesting employer; and

(xii) That the prospective employer has the ability and intention to compensate the alien at a level at which the alien and accompanying family members will not become public charges, and that funds to pay the alien's compensation do not include any monies obtained from the alien, excluding reasonable donations or tithing to the religious organization.

(8) **Evidence relating to the petitioning organization.** A petition shall include the following initial evidence relating to the petitioning organization:

(i) A currently valid determination letter from the Internal Revenue Service (IRS) establishing that the organization is a tax-exempt organization; or

(ii) For a religious organization that is recognized as tax-exempt under a group tax-exemption, a currently valid determination letter from the IRS *72293 establishing that the group is tax-exempt; or

(iii) For a bona fide organization that is affiliated with the religious denomination, if the organization was granted tax-exempt status under section 501(c)(3) of the Internal Revenue Code of 1986, or subsequent amendment or equivalent sections of prior enactments of the Internal Revenue Code, as something other than a religious organization:

(A) A currently valid determination letter from the IRS establishing that the organization is a tax-exempt organization;

(B) Documentation that establishes the religious nature and purpose of the organization, such as a copy of the organizing instrument of the organization that specifies the purposes of the organization;

(C) Organizational literature, such as books, articles, brochures, calendars, flyers and other literature describing the religious purpose and nature of the activities of the organization; and

(D) A religious denomination certification. The religious organization must complete, sign and date a religious denomination certification certifying that the petitioning organization is affiliated with the religious denomination. The certification is to be submitted by the petitioner along with the petition.

(9) Evidence relating to the qualifications of a minister. If the alien is a minister, the petitioner must submit the following:

(i) A copy of the alien's certificate of ordination or similar documents reflecting acceptance of the alien's qualifications as a minister in the religious denomination; and

(ii) Documents reflecting acceptance of the alien's qualifications as a minister in the religious denomination, as well as evidence that the alien has completed any course of prescribed theological education at an accredited theological institution normally required or recognized by that religious denomination, including transcripts, curriculum, and documentation that establishes that the theological institution is accredited by the denomination, or

(iii) For denominations that do not require a prescribed theological education, evidence of:

(A) The denomination's requirements for ordination to minister;

(B) The duties allowed to be performed by virtue of ordination;

(C) The denomination's levels of ordination, if any; and

(D) The alien's completion of the denomination's requirements for ordination.

(10) Evidence relating to compensation. Initial evidence must include verifiable evidence of how the petitioner intends to compensate the alien. Such compensation may include salaried or non-salaried compensation. This evidence may include past evidence of compensation for similar positions; budgets showing monies set aside for salaries, leases, etc.; verifiable documentation that room and board will be provided; or other evidence acceptable to USCIS. If IRS documentation, such as IRS Form W–2 or certified tax returns, is available, it must be provided. If IRS documentation is not available, an explanation for its absence must be provided, along with comparable, verifiable documentation.

(11) Evidence relating to the alien's prior employment. Qualifying prior experience during the two years immediately preceding the petition or preceding any acceptable break in the continuity of the religious work, must have occurred after the age of 14, and if acquired in the United States, must have been authorized under United States immigration law. If the alien was employed in the United States during the two years immediately preceding the filing of the application and:

(i) Received salaried compensation, the petitioner must submit IRS documentation that the alien received a salary, such as an IRS Form W–2 or certified copies of income tax returns.

(ii) Received non-salaried compensation, the petitioner must submit IRS documentation of the non-salaried compensation if available.

(iii) Received no salary but provided for his or her own support, and provided support for any dependents, the petitioner must show how support was maintained by submitting with the petition additional documents such as audited financial statements, financial institution records, brokerage account statements, trust documents signed by an attorney, or other verifiable evidence acceptable to USCIS.

If the alien was employed outside the United States during such two years, the petitioner must submit comparable evidence of the religious work.

(12) Inspections, evaluations, verifications, and compliance reviews. The supporting evidence submitted may be verified by USCIS through any means determined appropriate by USCIS, up to and including an on-site inspection of the petitioning organization. The inspection may include a tour of the organization's facilities, an interview with the organization's officials, a review of selected organization records relating to compliance with immigration laws and regulations, and an interview with any other individuals or review of any other records that the USCIS considers pertinent to the integrity of the organization. An inspection may include the organization headquarters, satellite locations, or the work locations planned for the applicable employee. If USCIS decides to conduct a pre-approval inspection, satisfactory completion of such inspection will be a condition for approval of any petition.

(n) Closing action—

(1) Approval. An approved employment-based petition will be forwarded to the National Visa Center of the Department of State if the beneficiary resides outside of the United States. If the Form I–140 petition indicates that the alien has filed or will file an application for adjustment to permanent residence in the United States (Form I–485) the approved visa petition (Form I–140), will be retained by the Service for consideration with the application for permanent residence (Form I–485). If a visa is available, and Form I–485 has not been filed, the alien will be instructed on the Form I–797, Notice of Action, (mailed out upon approval of the Form I–140 petition) to file the Form I–485.

(2) Denial. The denial of a petition for classification under section 203(b)(1), 203(b)(2), 203(b)(3), or 203(b)(4) of the Act (as it relates to special immigrants under section 101(a)(27)(C) of the Act) shall be appealable to the Associate Commissioner for Examinations. The petitioner shall be informed in plain language of the reasons for denial and of his or her right to appeal.

(3) Validity of approved petitions. Unless approval is revoked under section 203(g) or 205 of the Act, an employment-based petition is valid indefinitely.

(*o*) Denial of petitions under section 204 of the Act based on a finding by the Department of Labor. Upon debarment by the Department of Labor pursuant to 20 CFR 655.31, USCIS may deny any employment-based immigrant petition filed by that petitioner for a period of at least 1 year but not more than 5 years. The time period of such bar to petition approval shall be based on the severity of the violation or violations. The decision to deny petitions, the time period for the bar to petitions, and the reasons for the time period will be explained in a written notice to the petitioner.

(p) Eligibility for employment authorization in compelling circumstances—

(1) Eligibility of principal alien. An individual who is the principal beneficiary of an approved immigrant petition for classification under sections 203(b)(1), 203(b)(2) or 203(b)(3) of the Act may be eligible to receive employment authorization, upon application, if:

(i) In the case of an initial request for employment authorization, the individual is in E–3, H–1B, H–1B1, O–1, or L–1 nonimmigrant status, including the periods authorized by § 214.1(l)(1) and (2), as well as any other periods of admission authorized by this chapter before a validity period begins or after the expiration of a validity period, on the date the application for employment authorization (Form I–765) is filed;

(ii) An immigrant visa is not authorized for issuance to the principal beneficiary based on his or her priority date on the date the application for employment authorization is filed; and

(iii) USCIS determines, as a matter of discretion, that the principal beneficiary demonstrates compelling circumstances that justify the issuance of employment authorization.

(2) Eligibility of spouses and children. The family members, as described in section 203(d) of the Act, of a principal beneficiary, who are in nonimmigrant status at the time the principal beneficiary applies for employment authorization under paragraph (p)(1) of this section, are eligible to apply for employment authorization provided that the principal beneficiary has been granted employment authorization under paragraph (p) of this section and such employment authorization has not been terminated or revoked. Such family members may apply for employment authorization concurrently with the principal beneficiary, but cannot be granted employment authorization until the principal beneficiary is so authorized. The validity period of employment authorization granted to family members may not extend beyond the validity period of employment authorization granted to the principal beneficiary.

(3) Eligibility for renewal of employment authorization. An alien may be eligible to renew employment authorization granted under paragraph (p) of this section, upon submission of a new application before the expiration of such employment authorization, if:

(i) He or she is the principal beneficiary of an approved immigrant petition for classification under section 203(b)(1), 203(b)(2) or 203(b)(3) of the Act and either:

(A) An immigrant visa is not authorized for issuance to the principal beneficiary based on his or her priority date on the date the application for employment authorization, (Form I–765) is filed; and USCIS determines, as a matter of discretion that the principal beneficiary demonstrates compelling circumstances that justify the issuance of employment authorization; or

(B) The difference between the principal beneficiary's priority date and the date upon which immigrant visas are authorized for issuance for the principal beneficiary's preference category and country of chargeability is 1 year or less according to the Department of State Visa Bulletin in effect on the date the application for employment authorization (Form I–765), is filed. For example, if the Department of State Visa Bulletin in effect on the date the renewal application is filed indicates immigrant visas are authorized for issuance for the applicable preference category and country of chargeability to individuals with priority dates earlier than November 1, 2000, USCIS may grant a renewal to a principal beneficiary whose priority date is on or between October 31, 1999 and October 31, 2001; or

(ii) He or she is a family member, as described under paragraph (p)(2) of this section, of a principal beneficiary granted a renewal of employment authorization under paragraph (p)(3)(i) that remains valid, except that the family member need not be maintaining nonimmigrant status at the time the principal beneficiary applies for renewal of employment authorization under paragraph (p) of this section. A family member may file an application to renew employment authorization concurrently with an application to renew employment authorization filed by the principal beneficiary or while such application by the principal beneficiary is pending, but the family member's renewal application cannot be approved unless the principal beneficiary's application is granted. The validity period of a renewal of employment authorization granted to family members may not extend beyond the validity period of the renewal of employment authorization granted to the principal beneficiary.

(4) Application for employment authorization. To request employment authorization, an eligible applicant described in paragraph (p)(1), (2), or (3) of this section must file an application for employment authorization (Form I–765), with USCIS, in accordance with 8 CFR 274a.13(a) and the form instructions. Such applicant is subject to the collection of his or her biometric information and the payment of any biometric services fee as provided in the form instructions. Employment authorization under this paragraph may be granted solely in 1-year increments.

(5) Ineligibility for employment authorization. An alien is not eligible for employment authorization, including renewal of employment authorization, under this paragraph if the alien has been convicted of any felony or two or more misdemeanors.

[30 FR 14775, Nov. 30, 1965, as amended at 41 FR 55849, Dec. 23, 1976; 52 FR 33797, Sept. 8, 1987; 53 FR 2824, Feb. 2, 1988; 56 FR 60905, Nov. 29, 1991; 59 FR 502, Jan. 5, 1994; 59 FR 27229, May 26, 1994; 59 FR 51360, Oct. 11, 1994; 60 FR 29753, June 6, 1995; 61 FR 33305, June 27, 1996; 62 FR 4631, Jan. 31, 1997; 62 Fed. Reg. 67 FR 49563, July 31, 2002; 73 FR 72291, Nov. 26, 2008; 73 FR 78127, Dec. 19, 2008; 74 FR 26936, June 5, 2009; 81 FR 2083, Jan. 15, 2016; 81 FR 82484, Nov. 18, 2016]

PART 208—PROCEDURES FOR ASYLUM AND WITHHOLDING OF REMOVAL

SUBPART A—ASYLUM AND WITHHOLDING OF REMOVAL

§ 208.1 General. [also 8 C.F.R. § 1208.1, which has minor wording changes and cross-references to part 1208]

(a) Applicability.

(1) General. Unless otherwise provided in this chapter I, this subpart A shall apply to all applications for asylum under section 208 of the Act or for withholding of deportation or withholding of removal under section 241(b)(3) of the Act, or under the Convention Against Torture, whether before an asylum officer or an immigration judge, regardless of the date of filing. For purposes of this chapter I, withholding of removal shall also mean withholding of deportation under section 243(h) of the Act, as it appeared prior to April 1, 1997, except as provided in § 208.16(d). Such applications are referred to as "asylum applications." The provisions of this part 208 shall not affect the finality or validity of any decision made by a district director, an immigration judge, or the Board of Immigration Appeals in any such case prior to April 1, 1997. No asylum application that was filed with a district director, asylum officer, or immigration judge prior to April 1, 1997, may be reopened or otherwise reconsidered under the provisions of this part 208 except by motion granted in the exercise of discretion by the Board of Immigration Appeals, an immigration judge, or an asylum officer for proper cause shown. Motions to reopen or reconsider must meet the requirements of sections 240(c)(6) and (c)(7) of the Act, and 8 CFR parts 103 and 1003, as applicable.

(2) Commonwealth of the Northern Mariana Islands. The provisions of this subpart A shall not apply prior to January 1, 2015, to an alien physically present in or arriving in the Commonwealth of the Northern Mariana Islands seeking to apply for asylum. No application for asylum may be filed prior to January 1, 2015, pursuant to section 208 of the Act by an alien physically present in or arriving in the Commonwealth of the Northern Mariana Islands. Effective on the transition program effective date, the provisions of this subpart A shall apply to aliens physically present in or arriving in the CNMI with respect to withholding of removal under section 241(b)(3) of the Act and withholding and deferral of removal under the Convention Against Torture.

(b) Training of asylum officers. The Associate Director of USCIS Refugee, Asylum, and International Operations (RAIO) shall ensure that asylum officers receive special training in international human rights law, nonadversarial interview techniques, and other relevant national and international refugee laws and principles. The Associate Director of USCIS Refugee, Asylum, and International Operations (RAIO) shall also, in cooperation with the Department of State and other appropriate sources, compile and disseminate to asylum officers information concerning the persecution of persons in other countries on account of race, religion, nationality, membership in a particular social group, or political opinion, torture of persons in other countries, and other information relevant to asylum determinations, and shall maintain a documentation center with information on human rights conditions.

[64 FR 8487, Feb. 19, 1999; 74 FR 55736, Oct. 28, 2009; 76 FR 53784, Aug. 29, 2011]

§ 208.2 Jurisdiction. [also 8 C.F.R. § 1208.2, which has minor wording changes and cross-references to part 1208]

(a) Refugee, Asylum, and International Operations (RAIO). Except as provided in paragraph (b) or (c) of this section, RAIO shall have initial jurisdiction over an asylum application filed by an alien physically present in the United States or seeking admission at a port-of-entry. RAIO shall also have initial jurisdiction over credible fear determinations under § 208.30 and reasonable fear determinations under § 208.31.

(b) Jurisdiction of Immigration Court in general. Immigration judges shall have exclusive jurisdiction over asylum applications filed by an alien who has been served a Form I–221, Order to Show Cause; Form I–122, Notice to Applicant for Admission Detained for a Hearing before an Immigration Judge; or Form I–862, Notice to Appear, after the charging document has been filed with the Immigration Court. Immigration judges shall also have jurisdiction over any asylum applications filed prior to April 1, 1997, by alien crewmembers who have remained in the United States longer than authorized, by applicants for admission under the Visa Waiver Pilot Program, and by aliens who have been admitted to the United States under the Visa Waiver Pilot Program. Immigration judges shall also have the authority to review reasonable fear determinations referred to the Immigration Court under § 208.31, and credible fear determinations referred to the Immigration Court under § 208.30.

(c) Certain aliens not entitled to proceedings under section 240 of the Act.

(1) Asylum applications and withholding of removal applications only. After Form I–863, Notice of Referral to Immigration Judge, has been filed with the Immigration Court, an immigration judge shall have exclusive jurisdiction over any asylum application filed on or after April 1, 1997, by:

(i) An alien crewmember who:

(A) Is an applicant for a landing permit;

(B) Has been refused permission to land under section 252 of the Act; or

(C) On or after April 1, 1997, was granted permission to land under section 252 of the Act, regardless of whether the alien has remained in the United States longer than authorized;

(ii) An alien stowaway who has been found to have a credible fear of persecution or torture pursuant to the procedures set forth in subpart B of this part;

(iii) An alien who is an applicant for admission pursuant to the Visa Waiver Program under section 217 of the Act, except that if such an alien is an applicant for admission to the Commonwealth of the Northern Mariana Islands, then he or she shall not be eligible for asylum prior to January 1, 2015;

(iv) An alien who was admitted to the United States pursuant to the Visa Waiver Program under section 217 of the Act and has remained longer than authorized or has otherwise violated his or her immigration status, except that if such an alien was admitted to the Commonwealth of the Northern Mariana Islands, then he or she shall not be eligible for asylum in the Commonwealth of the Northern Mariana Islands prior to January 1, 2015;

(v) An alien who has been ordered removed under § 235(c) of the Act, as described in § 235.8(a) of this chapter (applicable only in the event that the alien is referred for proceedings under this paragraph by the Regional Director pursuant to section 235.8(b)(2)(ii) of this chapter);

(vi) An alien who is an applicant for admission, or has been admitted, as an alien classified under section 101(a)(15)(S) of the Act (applicable only in the event that the alien is referred for proceedings under this paragraph by the district director);

(vii) An alien who is an applicant for admission to Guam or the Commonwealth of the Northern Mariana Islands pursuant to the Guam-CNMI Visa Waiver Program under section 212(*l*) of the Act, except that if such an alien is an applicant for admission to the Commonwealth of the Northern Mariana Islands, then he or she shall not be eligible for asylum prior to January 1, 2015; or

(viii) An alien who was admitted to Guam or the Commonwealth of the Northern Mariana Islands pursuant to the Guam-CNMI Visa Waiver Program under section 212(*l*) of the Act and has remained longer than authorized or has otherwise violated his or her immigration status, except that if such an alien was admitted to the Commonwealth of the Northern Mariana Islands, then he or she shall not be eligible for asylum in the Commonwealth of the Northern Mariana Islands prior to January 1, 2015.

(2) Withholding of removal applications only. After Form I–863, Notice of Referral to Immigration Judge, has been filed with the Immigration Court, an immigration judge shall have exclusive jurisdiction over any application for withholding of removal filed by:

(i) An alien who is the subject of a reinstated removal order pursuant to section 241(a)(5) of the Act; or

(ii) An alien who has been issued an administrative removal order pursuant to section 238 of the Act as an alien convicted of committing an aggravated felony.

(3) Rules of procedure.

(i) General. Except as provided in this section, proceedings falling under the jurisdiction of the immigration judge pursuant to paragraph (c)(1) or (c)(2) of this section shall be conducted in accordance with the same rules of procedure as proceedings conducted under 8 CFR part 240, subpart A. The scope of review in proceedings conducted pursuant to paragraph (c)(1) of this section shall be limited to a determination of whether the alien is eligible for asylum or withholding or deferral of removal, and whether asylum shall be granted in the exercise of discretion. The scope of review in proceedings conducted pursuant to paragraph (c)(2) of this section shall be limited to a determination of whether the alien is eligible for withholding or deferral of removal. During such proceedings, all parties are prohibited from raising or considering any other issues, including but not limited to issues of admissibility, deportability, eligibility for waivers, and eligibility for any other form of relief.

(ii) Notice of hearing procedures and in-absentia decisions. The alien will be provided with notice of the time and place of the proceeding. The request for asylum and withholding of removal submitted by an alien who fails to appear for the hearing shall be denied. The denial of asylum and withholding of removal for failure to appear may be reopened only upon a motion filed with the immigration judge with jurisdiction over the case. Only one motion to reopen may be filed, and it must be filed within 90 days, unless the alien establishes that he or she did not receive notice of the hearing date or was in Federal or State custody on the date directed to appear. The motion must include documentary evidence, which demonstrates that:

(A) The alien did not receive the notice;

(B) The alien was in Federal or State custody and the failure to appear was through no fault of the alien; or

(C) "Exceptional circumstances," as defined in section 240(e)(1) of the Act, caused the failure to appear.

(iii) Relief. The filing of a motion to reopen shall not stay removal of the alien unless the immigration judge issues an order granting a stay pending disposition of the motion. An alien who fails to appear for a proceeding under this section shall not be eligible for relief under section 240A, 240B, 245, 248, or 249 of the Act for a period of 10 years after the date of the denial, unless the applicant can show exceptional circumstances resulted in his or her failure to appear.

[62 FR 15362, April 1, 1997; 64 FR 8487, Feb. 19, 1999; 65 FR 76130, Dec. 6, 2000; 74 FR 55736, Oct. 28, 2009; 76 FR 53784, Aug. 29, 2011.]

§ 208.3 Form of application. [also 8 C.F.R. § 1208.3, which is identical except for cross-references to part 1208]

(a) An asylum applicant must file Form I–589, Application for Asylum and for Withholding of Removal, together with any additional supporting evidence in accordance with the instructions on the form. The applicant's spouse and children shall be listed on the application and may be included in the request for asylum if they are in the United States. One additional copy of the principal applicant's Form I–589 must be submitted for each dependent included in the principal's application.

(b) An asylum application shall be deemed to constitute at the same time an application for withholding of removal, unless adjudicated in deportation or exclusion proceedings commenced prior to April 1, 1997. In such instances, the asylum application shall be deemed to constitute an application for withholding of deportation under section 243(h) of the Act, as that section existed prior to April 1, 1997. Where a determination is made that an applicant is ineligible to apply for asylum under section 208(a)(2) of the Act, an asylum application shall be construed as an application for withholding of removal.

(c) Form I–589 shall be filed under the following conditions and shall have the following consequences:

(1) If the application was filed on or after January 4, 1995, information provided in the application may be used as a basis for the initiation of removal proceedings, or to satisfy any burden of proof in exclusion, deportation, or removal proceedings;

(2) The applicant and anyone other than a spouse, parent, son, or daughter of the applicant who assists the applicant in preparing the application must sign the application under penalty of perjury. The applicant's signature establishes a presumption that the applicant is aware of the contents of the application. A person other than a relative specified in this paragraph who assists the applicant in preparing the application also must provide his or her full mailing address;

(3) An asylum application that does not include a response to each of the questions contained in the Form I–589, is unsigned, or is unaccompanied by the required materials specified in paragraph (a) of this section is incomplete. The filing of an incomplete application shall not commence the 150-day period after which the applicant may file an application for employment authorization in accordance with § 208.7. An application that is incomplete shall be returned by mail to the applicant within 30 days of the receipt of the application by the Service.

If the Service has not mailed the incomplete application back to the applicant within 30 days, it shall be deemed complete. An application returned to the applicant as incomplete shall be resubmitted by the applicant with the additional information if he or she wishes to have the application considered;

(4) Knowing placement of false information on the application may subject the person placing that information on the application to criminal penalties under title 18 of the United States Code and to civil or criminal penalties under section 274C of the Act; and

(5) Knowingly filing a frivolous application on or after April 1, 1997, so long as the applicant has received the notice required by section 208(d)(4) of the Act, shall render the applicant permanently ineligible for any benefits under the Act pursuant to § 208.20.

[62 FR 10338, March 6, 1997; 65 FR 76131, Dec. 6, 2000]

§ 208.4   Filing the application. [also 8 C.F.R. § 1208.4, which has minor wording changes and cross-references to part 1208]

Except as prohibited in paragraph (a) of this section, asylum applications shall be filed in accordance with paragraph (b) of this section.

(a) Prohibitions on filing. Section 208(a)(2) of the Act prohibits certain aliens from filing for asylum on or after April 1, 1997, unless the alien can demonstrate to the satisfaction of the Attorney General that one of the exceptions in section 208(a)(2)(D) of the Act applies. Such prohibition applies only to asylum applications under section 208 of the Act and not to applications for withholding of removal under § 208.16. If an applicant files an asylum application and it appears that one or more of the prohibitions contained in section 208(a)(2) of the Act apply, an asylum officer, in an interview, or an immigration judge, in a hearing, shall review the application and give the applicant the opportunity to present any relevant and useful information bearing on any prohibitions on filing to determine if the application should be rejected. For the purpose of making determinations under section 208(a)(2) of the Act, the following rules shall apply:

(1) Authority. Only an asylum officer, an immigration judge, or the Board of Immigration Appeals is authorized to make determinations regarding the prohibitions contained in section 208(a)(2)(B) or (C) of the Act.

(2) One-year filing deadline.

(i) For purposes of section 208(a)(2)(B) of the Act, an applicant has the burden of proving:

(A) By clear and convincing evidence that the application has been filed within 1 year of the date of the alien's arrival in the United States, or

(B) To the satisfaction of the asylum officer, the immigration judge, or the Board that he or she qualifies for an exception to the 1-year deadline.

(ii) The 1-year period shall be calculated from the date of the alien's last arrival in the United States or April 1, 1997, whichever is later. When the last day of the period so computed falls on a Saturday, Sunday, or legal holiday, the period shall run until the end of the next day that is not a Saturday, Sunday, or legal holiday. For the purpose of making determinations under section 208(a)(2)(B) of the Act only, an application is considered to have been filed on the date it is received by the Service, pursuant to § 103.2(a)(7) of this chapter. In a case in which the application has not been received by the Service within 1 year from the applicant's date of entry into the United States, but the applicant provides clear and convincing documentary evidence of mailing the application within the 1-year period, the mailing date shall be considered the filing date. For cases before the Immigration Court in accordance with § 3.13 of this chapter, the application is considered to have been filed on the date it is received by the Immigration Court. For cases before the Board of Immigration Appeals, the application is considered to have been filed on the date it is received by the Board. In the case of an application that appears to have been filed more than a year after the applicant arrived in the United States, the asylum officer, the immigration judge, or the Board will determine whether the applicant qualifies for an exception to the deadline. For aliens present in or arriving in the Commonwealth of the Northern Mariana Islands, the 1-year period shall be calculated from either January 1, 2015, or from the date of the alien's last arrival in the United States (including the Commonwealth of the Northern Mariana Islands), whichever is later. No period of physical presence in the Commonwealth of the Northern Mariana Islands prior to January 1, 2015, shall count toward the 1-year period. After November 28, 2009, any travel to the Commonwealth of the Northern Mariana Islands from any other State shall not re-start the calculation of the 1-year period.

(3) Prior denial of application. For purposes of section 208(a)(2)(C) of the Act, an asylum application has not been denied unless denied by an immigration judge or the Board of Immigration Appeals.

(4) Changed circumstances.

(i) The term "changed circumstances" in section 208(a)(2)(D) of the Act shall refer to circumstances materially affecting the applicant's eligibility for asylum. They may include, but are not limited to:

(A) Changes in conditions in the applicant's country of nationality or, if the applicant is stateless, country of last habitual residence;

(B) Changes in the applicant's circumstances that materially affect the applicant's eligibility for asylum, including changes in applicable U.S. law and activities the applicant becomes involved in outside the country of feared persecution that place the applicant at risk; or

(C) In the case of an alien who had previously been included as a dependent in another alien's pending asylum application, the loss of the spousal or parent-child relationship to the principal applicant through marriage, divorce, death, or attainment of age 21.

(ii) The applicant shall file an asylum application within a reasonable period given those "changed circumstances." If the applicant can establish that he or she did not become aware of the changed circumstances until after they occurred, such delayed awareness shall be taken into account in determining what constitutes a "reasonable period."

(5) The term "extraordinary circumstances" in section 208(a)(2)(D) of the Act shall refer to events or factors directly related to the failure to meet the 1-year deadline. Such circumstances may excuse the failure to file within the 1-year period as long as the alien filed the application within a reasonable period given those circumstances. The burden of proof is on the applicant to establish to the satisfaction of the asylum officer, the immigration judge, or the Board of Immigration Appeals that the circumstances were not intentionally created by the alien through his or her own action or inaction, that those circumstances were directly related to the alien's failure to file the application within the 1-year period, and that the delay was reasonable under the circumstances. Those circumstances may include but are not limited to:

(i) Serious illness or mental or physical disability, including any effects of persecution or violent harm suffered in the past, during the 1-year period after arrival;

(ii) Legal disability (e.g., the applicant was an unaccompanied minor or suffered from a mental impairment) during the 1-year period after arrival;

(iii) Ineffective assistance of counsel, provided that:

(A) The alien files an affidavit setting forth in detail the agreement that was entered into with counsel with respect to the actions to be taken and what representations counsel did or did not make to the respondent in this regard;

(B) The counsel whose integrity or competence is being impugned has been informed of the allegations leveled against him or her and given an opportunity to respond; and

(C) The alien indicates whether a complaint has been filed with appropriate disciplinary authorities with respect to any violation of counsel's ethical or legal responsibilities, and if not, why not;

(iv) The applicant maintained Temporary Protected Status, lawful immigrant or nonimmigrant status, or was given parole, until a reasonable period before the filing of the asylum application;

(v) The applicant filed an asylum application prior to the expiration of the 1-year deadline, but that application was rejected by the Service as not properly filed, was returned to the applicant for corrections, and was refiled within a reasonable period thereafter; and

(vi) The death or serious illness or incapacity of the applicant's legal representative or a member of the applicant's immediate family.

(6) Asylum Cooperative Agreements. Immigration officers have authority to apply section 208(a)(2)(A) of the Act, relating to the determination that the alien may be removed to a third country pursuant to a bilateral or multilateral agreement, as provided in § 208.30(e). For provisions relating to the authority of immigration judges with respect to section 208(a)(2)(A), see 8 CFR 1240.11(g) and (h).

(b) Filing location—Form I–589, Application for Asylum and Withholding of Removal, must be filed in accordance with the instructions on the form.

(c) Amending an application after filing. Upon request of the alien and as a matter of discretion, the asylum officer or immigration judge having jurisdiction may permit an asylum applicant to amend or supplement the application, but any delay caused by such request shall extend the period within which the applicant may not apply for employment authorization in accordance with § 208.7(a).

[64 FR 8488, Feb. 19, 1999; 64 FR 13881, March 23, 1999; 65 FR 76131, Dec. 6, 2000; 69 FR 69488, Nov. 29, 2004; 74 FR 26937, June 5, 2009; 74 FR 55737, Oct. 28, 2009; 84 FR 64008, Nov. 19, 2019]

§ 208.5   Special duties toward aliens in custody of DHS. [also 8 C.F.R. § 1208.5, which has minor wording changes and cross-references to part 1208]

(a) General. When an alien in the custody of DHS requests asylum or withholding of removal, or expresses a fear of persecution or harm upon return to his or her country of origin or to agents thereof, DHS shall make available the appropriate application forms and shall provide the applicant with the information required by section 208(d)(4) of the Act, except in the case of an alien who is in custody pending a credible fear determination under 8 CFR 208.30 or a reasonable fear determination pursuant to 8 CFR 208.31. Although DHS does not have a duty in the case of an alien who is in custody pending a credible fear or reasonable fear determination under either 8 CFR 208.30 or 8 CFR 208.31, DHS may provide the appropriate forms, upon request. Where possible, expedited consideration shall be given to applications of detained aliens. Except as provided in paragraph (c) of this section, such alien shall not be excluded, deported, or removed before a decision is rendered on his or her asylum application. Furthermore, except as provided in paragraph (c) of this section, an alien physically present in or arriving in the Commonwealth of the Northern Mariana Islands shall not be excluded, deported, or removed before a decision is rendered on his or her application for withholding of removal pursuant to section 241(b)(3) of the Act and withholding of removal under the Convention Against Torture. No application for asylum may be filed prior to January 1, 2015, under section 208 of the Act by an alien physically present in or arriving in the Commonwealth of the Northern Mariana Islands.

(b) Certain aliens aboard vessels.

(1) If an alien crewmember or alien stowaway on board a vessel or other conveyance alleges, claims, or otherwise makes known to an immigration inspector or other official making an examination on the conveyance that he or she is unable or unwilling to return to his or her country of nationality or last habitual residence (if not a national of any country) because of persecution or a fear of persecution in that country on account of race, religion, nationality, membership in a particular social group, or political opinion, or if the alien expresses a fear of torture upon return to that country, the alien shall be promptly removed from the conveyance. If the alien makes such fear known to an official while off such conveyance, the alien shall not be returned to the conveyance but shall be retained in or transferred to the custody of the Service.

(i) An alien stowaway will be referred to an asylum officer for a credible fear determination under § 208.30.

(ii) An alien crewmember shall be provided the appropriate application forms and information required by section 208(d)(4) of the Act and may then have 10 days within which to submit an asylum application in accordance with the instructions on the form. DHS may extend the 10-day filing period for good cause. Once the application has been filed, DHS shall serve Form I–863 on the alien and immediately forward any such application to the appropriate Immigration Court with a copy of the Form I–863 being filed with that court.

(iii) An alien crewmember physically present in or arriving in the Commonwealth of the Northern Mariana Islands can request withholding of removal pursuant to section 241(b)(3) of the Act and withholding of removal under the Convention Against Torture. However, such an alien crewmember is not eligible to request asylum pursuant to section 208 of the Act prior to January 1, 2015.

(2) Pending adjudication of the application, and, in the case of a stowaway the credible fear determination and any review thereof, the alien may be detained by the Service or otherwise paroled in accordance with § 212.5 of this chapter. However, pending the credible fear determination, parole of an alien stowaway may be permitted only when the Secretary determines, in the exercise of discretion, that parole is required to meet a medical emergency or is necessary for a legitimate law enforcement objective.

(c) Exception to prohibition on removal. A motion to reopen or an order to remand accompanied by an asylum application pursuant to § 208.4(b)(3)(iii) shall not stay execution of a final exclusion, deportation, or removal order unless such stay is specifically granted by the Board of Immigration Appeals or the immigration judge having jurisdiction over the motion.

[64 FR 8488, Feb. 19, 1999; 65 FR 76132, Dec. 6, 2000; 74 FR 26937, June 5, 2009; 74 FR 55737, Oct. 28, 2009; 76 FR 53784, Aug. 29, 2011.]

§ 208.6   Disclosure to third parties. [also 8 C.F.R. § 1208.6, which is identical except for cross-references to part 1208]

(a) Information contained in or pertaining to any asylum application, records pertaining to any credible fear determination conducted pursuant to § 208.30, and records pertaining to any reasonable fear determination conducted pursuant to § 208.31, shall not be disclosed without the written consent of the applicant, except as permitted by this section or at the discretion of the Attorney General.

(b) The confidentiality of other records kept by the Service and the Executive Office for Immigration Review that indicate that a specific alien has applied for asylum, received a credible fear or reasonable fear interview, or received a credible fear or reasonable fear review shall also be protected from disclosure. The Service will coordinate with the Department of State to ensure that the confidentiality of those records is maintained if they are transmitted to Department of State offices in other countries.

(c) This section shall not apply to any disclosure to:

(1) Any United States Government official or contractor having a need to examine information in connection with:

(i) The adjudication of asylum applications;

(ii) The consideration of a request for a credible fear or reasonable fear interview, or a credible fear or reasonable fear review;

(iii) The defense of any legal action arising from the adjudication of, or failure to adjudicate, the asylum application, or from a credible fear determination or reasonable fear determination under § 208.30 or § 208.31;

(iv) The defense of any legal action of which the asylum application, credible fear determination, or reasonable fear determination is a part; or

(v) Any United States Government investigation concerning any criminal or civil matter; or

(2) Any Federal, State, or local court in the United States considering any legal action:

(i) Arising from the adjudication of, or failure to adjudicate, the asylum application, or from a credible fear or reasonable fear determination under § 208.30 or § 208.31; or

(ii) Arising from the proceedings of which the asylum application, credible fear determination, or reasonable fear determination is a part.

[62 Fed.Reg. 10340, March 6, 1997; 65 FR 76133, Dec. 6, 2000]

§ 208.7 Employment authorization. [also 8 C.F.R. § 1208.7, which has minor wording changes and cross-references to part 1208]

(a) Application and approval.

(1) Subject to the restrictions contained in sections 208(d) and 236(a) of the Act, an applicant for asylum who is not an aggravated felon shall be eligible pursuant to §§ 274a.12(c)(8) and 274a.13(a) of this chapter to request employment authorization. Except in the case of an alien whose asylum application has been recommended for approval, or in the case of an alien who filed an asylum application prior to January 4, 1995, the application shall be submitted no earlier than 150 days after the date on which a complete asylum application submitted in accordance with §§ 208.3 and 208.4 has been received. In the case of an applicant whose asylum application has been recommended for approval, the applicant may apply for employment authorization when he or she receives notice of the recommended approval. If an asylum application has been returned as incomplete in accordance with § 208.3(c)(3), the 150-day period will commence upon receipt by the Service of a complete asylum application. An applicant whose asylum application has been denied by an asylum officer or by an immigration judge within the 150-day period shall not be eligible to apply for employment authorization. If an asylum application is denied prior to a decision on the application for employment authorization, the application for employment authorization shall be denied. If the asylum application is not so denied, the Service shall have 30 days from the date of filing of the employment authorization request to grant or deny that application, except that no employment authorization shall be issued to an asylum applicant prior to the expiration of the 180-day period following the filing of the asylum application filed on or after April 1, 1997.

(2) The time periods within which the alien may not apply for employment authorization and within which USCIS must respond to any such application and within which the asylum application must be adjudicated pursuant to section 208(d)(5)(A)(iii) of the Act shall begin when the alien has filed a complete asylum application in accordance with SS208.3 and 208.4. Any delay requested or caused by the applicant shall not be counted as part of these time periods, including delays caused by failure without good cause to follow the requirements for fingerprint processing. Such time periods shall also be extended by the equivalent of the time between issuance of a request for evidence pursuant to § 103.2(b)(8) of this chapter and the receipt of the applicant's response to such request.

(3) The provisions of paragraphs (a)(1) and (a)(2) of this section apply to applications for asylum filed on or after January 4, 1995.

(4) Employment authorization pursuant to § 274a.12(c)(8) of this chapter may not be granted to an alien who fails to appear for a scheduled interview before an asylum officer or a hearing before an immigration judge, unless the applicant demonstrates that the failure to appear was the result of exceptional circumstances.

(b) Renewal and termination. Employment authorization shall be renewable, in increments to be determined by USCIS, for the continuous period of time necessary for the asylum officer or immigration judge to decide the asylum application and, if necessary, for completion of any administrative or judicial review.

(1) If the asylum application is denied by the asylum officer, the employment authorization shall terminate at the expiration of the employment authorization document or 60 days after the denial of asylum, whichever is longer.

(2) If the application is denied by the immigration judge, the Board of Immigration Appeals, or a Federal court, the employment authorization terminates upon the expiration of the employment authorization document, unless the applicant has filed an appropriate request for administrative or judicial review.

(c) Supporting evidence for renewal of employment authorization. In order for employment authorization to be renewed under this section, the alien must request employment authorization in accordance with the form instructions. USCIS may require that an alien establish that he or she has continued to pursue an asylum application before an immigration judge or sought administrative or judicial review. For purposes of employment authorization, pursuit of an asylum application is established by presenting one of the following, depending on the stage of the alien's immigration proceedings:

(1) If the alien's case is pending in proceedings before the immigration judge, and the alien wishes to continue to pursue his or her asylum application, a copy of any asylum denial, referral notice, or charging document placing the alien in such proceedings;

(2) If the immigration judge has denied asylum, a copy of the document issued by the Board of Immigration Appeals to show that a timely appeal has been filed from a denial of the asylum application by the immigration judge; or

(3) If the Board of Immigration Appeals has dismissed the alien's appeal of a denial of asylum, or sustained an appeal by the Service of a grant of asylum, a copy of the petition for judicial review or for habeas corpus pursuant to section 242 of the Act, date stamped by the appropriate court.

(d) In order for employment authorization to be renewed before its expiration, the application for renewal must be received by the Service 90 days prior to expiration of the employment authorization.

[62 FR 10340, March 6, 1997; as amended at 63 FR 12986, March 17, 1998; 76 FR 53784, Aug. 29, 2011.]

§ 208.8   Limitations on travel outside the United States. [also 8 C.F.R. § 1208.8, which is identical except for cross-references to part 1208]

(a) An applicant who leaves the United States without first obtaining advance parole under § 212.5(f) of this chapter shall be presumed to have abandoned his or her application under this section.

(b) An applicant who leaves the United States pursuant to advance parole under § 212.5(f) of this chapter and returns to the country of claimed persecution shall be presumed to have abandoned his or her application, unless the applicant is able to establish compelling reasons for such return.

[62 Fed. Reg. 10341, March 6, 1997; 65 FR 82255, Dec. 28, 2000; 66 FR 7863, Jan. 26, 2001]

§ 208.9   Procedure for interview before an asylum officer. [also 8 C.F.R. § 1208.9, which has minor wording changes and cross-references to part 1208]

(a) The Service shall adjudicate the claim of each asylum applicant whose application is complete within the meaning of § 208.3(c)(3) and is within the jurisdiction of the Service.

(b) The asylum officer shall conduct the interview in a nonadversarial manner and, except at the request of the applicant, separate and apart from the general public. The purpose of the interview shall be to elicit all relevant and useful information bearing on the applicant's eligibility for asylum. At the time of the interview, the applicant must provide complete information regarding his or her identity, including name, date and place of birth, and nationality, and may be required to register this identity. The applicant may have counsel or a representative present, may present witnesses, and may submit affidavits of witnesses and other evidence.

(c) The asylum officer shall have authority to administer oaths, verify the identity of the applicant (including through the use of electronic means), verify the identity of any interpreter, present and receive evidence, and question the applicant and any witnesses.

(d) Upon completion of the interview, the applicant or the applicant's representative shall have an opportunity to make a statement or comment on the evidence presented. The asylum officer may, in his or her discretion, limit the length of such statement or comment and may require its submission in writing. Upon completion of the interview, the applicant shall be informed that he or she must appear in person to receive and to acknowledge receipt of the decision of the asylum officer and any other accompanying material at a time and place designated by the asylum officer, except as otherwise provided by the asylum officer. An applicant's failure to appear to receive and acknowledge receipt of the decision shall be treated as delay caused by the applicant for purposes of § 208.7(a)(3) and shall extend the period within which the applicant may not apply for employment authorization by the number of days until the applicant does appear to receive and acknowledge receipt of the decision or until the applicant appears before an immigration judge in response to the issuance of a charging document under § 208.14(c).

(e) The asylum officer shall consider evidence submitted by the applicant together with his or her asylum application, as well as any evidence submitted by the applicant before or at the interview. As a matter of discretion, the asylum officer may grant the applicant a brief extension of time following an interview during which the applicant may submit additional evidence. Any such extension shall extend by an equivalent time the periods specified by § 208.7 for the filing and adjudication of any employment authorization application.

(f) The asylum application, all supporting information provided by the applicant, any comments submitted by the Department of State or by the Service, and any other information specific to the applicant's case and considered by the asylum officer shall comprise the record.

(g) An applicant unable to proceed with the interview in English must provide, at no expense to the Service, a competent interpreter fluent in both English and the applicant's native language or any other language in which the applicant is fluent. The interpreter must be at least 18 years of age. Neither the applicant's attorney or representative of record, a witness testifying on the applicant's behalf, nor a representative or employee of the applicant's country of nationality, or if stateless, country of last habitual residence, may serve as the applicant's interpreter. Failure without good cause to comply with this paragraph may be considered a failure to appear for the interview for purposes of § 208.10.

[62 FR 10341, March 6, 1997; 65 FR 76133, Dec. 6, 2000; 76 FR 53784, Aug. 29, 2011.]

§ 208.10 Failure to appear at an interview before an asylum officer or failure to follow requirements for fingerprint processing. [also 8 C.F.R. § 1208.10, which has similar details]

Failure to appear for a scheduled interview without prior authorization may result in dismissal of the application or waiver of the right to an interview. Failure to comply with fingerprint processing requirements without good cause may result in dismissal of the application or waiver of the right to an adjudication by an asylum officer. Failure to appear shall be excused if the notice of the interview or fingerprint appointment was not mailed to the applicant's current address and such address had been provided to the USCIS by the applicant prior to the date of mailing in accordance with section 265 of the Act and regulations promulgated thereunder, unless the asylum officer determines that the applicant received reasonable notice of the interview or fingerprinting appointment. Failure to appear at the interview or fingerprint appointment will be excused if the applicant demonstrates that such failure was the result of exceptional circumstances.

[62 FR 10341, March 6, 1997; as amended at 63 FR 12986, March 17, 1998; 76 FR 53784, Aug. 29, 2011.]

§ 208.11 Comments from the Department of State. [also 8 C.F.R. § 1208.11, which has minor wording changes and cross-references to part 1208]

(a) U.S. Citizenship and Immigration Services (USCIS) may request, at its discretion, specific comments from the Department of State regarding individual cases or types of claims under consideration, or such other information as USCIS deems appropriate.

(b) With respect to any asylum application, the Department of State may provide, at its discretion, to USCIS:

(1) Detailed country conditions information relevant to eligibility for asylum or withholding of removal;

(2) An assessment of the accuracy of the applicant's assertions about conditions in his or her country of nationality or habitual residence and his or her particular situation;

(3) Information about whether persons who are similarly situated to the applicant are persecuted or tortured in the applicant's country of nationality or habitual residence and the frequency of such persecution or torture; or

(4) Such other information as it deems relevant.

(c) Any comments received pursuant to paragraph (b) of this section shall be made part of the record. Unless the comments are classified under the applicable Executive Order, the applicant shall be provided an opportunity to review and respond to such comments prior to the issuance of any decision to deny the application.

[64 FR 8488, Feb. 19, 1999; 74 FR 15369, April 6, 2009]

§ 208.12 Reliance on information compiled by other sources. [also 8 C.F.R. § 1208.12, which has minor wording changes and cross-references to part 1208]

(a) In deciding an asylum application, or in deciding whether the alien has a credible fear of persecution or torture pursuant to § 208.30 of this part, or a reasonable fear of persecution or torture pursuant to § 208.31, the asylum officer may rely on material provided by the Department of State, other USCIS offices, or other credible sources, such as international organizations, private voluntary agencies, news organizations, or academic institutions.

(b) Nothing in this part shall be construed to entitle the applicant to conduct discovery directed toward the records, officers, agents, or employees of the Service, the Department of Justice, or the Department of State. Persons may continue to seek documents available through a Freedom of Information Act (FOIA) request pursuant to 8 CFR part 103.

[64 FR 8488, Feb. 19, 1999; 65 FR 76133, Dec. 6, 2000; 76 FR 53784, Aug. 29, 2011.]

§ 208.13 Establishing asylum eligibility. [also 8 C.F.R. § 1208.13, which is identical except for cross-references to part 1208]

(a) Burden of proof. The burden of proof is on the applicant for asylum to establish that he or she is a refugee as defined in section 101(a)(42) of the Act. The testimony of the applicant, if credible, may be sufficient to sustain the burden of proof without corroboration. The fact that the applicant previously established a credible fear of persecution for purposes of section 235(b)(1)(B) of the Act does not relieve the alien of the additional burden of establishing eligibility for asylum.

(b) Eligibility. The applicant may qualify as a refugee either because he or she has suffered past persecution or because he or she has a well-founded fear of future persecution.

(1) Past persecution. An applicant shall be found to be a refugee on the basis of past persecution if the applicant can establish that he or she has suffered persecution in the past in the applicant's country of nationality or, if stateless, in his or her country of last habitual residence, on account of race, religion, nationality, membership in a particular social group, or political opinion, and is unable or unwilling to return to, or avail himself or herself of the protection of, that country owing to such persecution. An applicant who has been found to have established such past persecution shall also be presumed to have a well-founded fear of persecution on the basis of the original claim. That presumption may be rebutted if an asylum officer or immigration judge makes one of the findings described in paragraph (b)(1)(i) of this section. If the applicant's fear of future persecution is unrelated to the past persecution, the applicant bears the burden of establishing that the fear is well-founded.

(i) **Discretionary referral or denial.** Except as provided in paragraph (b)(1)(iii) of this section, an asylum officer shall, in the exercise of his or her discretion, refer or deny, or an immigration judge, in the exercise of his or her discretion, shall deny the asylum application of an alien found to be a refugee on the basis of past persecution if any of the following is found by a preponderance of the evidence:

(A) There has been a fundamental change in circumstances such that the applicant no longer has a well-founded fear of persecution in the applicant's country of nationality or, if stateless, in the applicant's country of last habitual residence, on account of race, religion, nationality, membership in a particular social group, or political opinion; or

(B) The applicant could avoid future persecution by relocating to another part of the applicant's country of nationality or, if stateless, another part of the applicant's country of last habitual residence, and under all the circumstances, it would be reasonable to expect the applicant to do so.

(ii) **Burden of proof.** In cases in which an applicant has demonstrated past persecution under paragraph (b)(1) of this section, the Service shall bear the burden of establishing by a preponderance of the evidence the requirements of paragraphs (b)(1)(i)(A) or (B) of this section.

(iii) **Grant in the absence of well-founded fear of persecution.** An applicant described in paragraph (b)(1)(i) of this section who is not barred from a grant of asylum under paragraph (c) of this section, may be granted asylum, in the exercise of the decision-maker's discretion, if:

(A) The applicant has demonstrated compelling reasons for being unwilling or unable to return to the country arising out of the severity of the past persecution; or

(B) The applicant has established that there is a reasonable possibility that he or she may suffer other serious harm upon removal to that country.

(2) **Well-founded fear of persecution.**

(i) An applicant has a well-founded fear of persecution if:

(A) The applicant has a fear of persecution in his or her country of nationality or, if stateless, in his or her country of last habitual residence, on account of race, religion, nationality, membership in a particular social group, or political opinion;

(B) There is a reasonable possibility of suffering such persecution if he or she were to return to that country; and

(C) He or she is unable or unwilling to return to, or avail himself or herself of the protection of, that country because of such fear.

(ii) An applicant does not have a well-founded fear of persecution if the applicant could avoid persecution by relocating to another part of the applicant's country of nationality or, if stateless, another part of the applicant's country of last habitual residence, if under all the circumstances it would be reasonable to expect the applicant to do so.

(iii) In evaluating whether the applicant has sustained the burden of proving that he or she has a well-founded fear of persecution, the asylum officer or immigration judge shall not require the applicant to provide evidence that there is a reasonable possibility he or she would be singled out individually for persecution if:

(A) The applicant establishes that there is a pattern or practice in his or her country of nationality or, if stateless, in his or her country of last habitual residence, of persecution of a group of persons similarly situated to the applicant on account of race, religion, nationality, membership in a particular social group, or political opinion; and

(B) The applicant establishes his or her own inclusion in, and identification with, such group of persons such that his or her fear of persecution upon return is reasonable.

(3) Reasonableness of internal relocation. For purposes of determinations under paragraphs (b)(1)(i), (b)(1)(ii), and (b)(2) of this section, adjudicators should consider, but are not limited to considering, whether the applicant would face other serious harm in the place of suggested relocation; any ongoing civil strife within the country; administrative, economic, or judicial infrastructure; geographical limitations; and social and cultural constraints, such as age, gender, health, and social and familial ties. Those factors may, or may not, be relevant, depending on all the circumstances of the case, and are not necessarily determinative of whether it would be reasonable for the applicant to relocate.

(i) In cases in which the applicant has not established past persecution, the applicant shall bear the burden of establishing that it would not be reasonable for him or her to relocate, unless the persecution is by a government or is government-sponsored.

(ii) In cases in which the persecutor is a government or is government-sponsored, or the applicant has established persecution in the past, it shall be presumed that internal relocation would not be reasonable, unless the Service establishes by a preponderance of the evidence that, under all the circumstances, it would be reasonable for the applicant to relocate.

(c) Mandatory denials.

(1) Applications filed on or after April 1, 1997. For applications filed on or after April 1, 1997, an applicant shall not qualify for asylum if section 208(a)(2) or 208(b)(2) of the Act applies to the applicant. If the applicant is found to be ineligible for asylum under either section 208(a)(2) or 208(b)(2) of the Act, the applicant shall be considered for eligibility for withholding of removal under section 241(b)(3) of the Act. The applicant shall also be considered for eligibility for withholding of removal under the Convention Against Torture if the applicant requests such consideration or if the evidence presented by the alien indicates that the alien may be tortured in the country of removal.

(2) Applications filed before April 1, 1997.

(i) An immigration judge or asylum officer shall not grant asylum to any applicant who filed his or her application before April 1, 1997, if the alien:

(A) Having been convicted by a final judgment of a particularly serious crime in the United States, constitutes a danger to the community;

(B) Has been firmly resettled within the meaning of § 208.15;

(C) Can reasonably be regarded as a danger to the security of the United States;

(D) Has been convicted of an aggravated felony, as defined in section 101(a)(43) of the Act; or

(E) Ordered, incited, assisted, or otherwise participated in the persecution of any person on account of race, religion, nationality, membership in a particular social group, or political opinion.

(F) Is described within section 212(a)(3)(B)(i)(I), (II), and (III) of the Act as it existed prior to April 1, 1997, and as amended by the Anti-terrorist and Effective Death Penalty Act of 1996 (AEDPA), unless it is determined that there are no reasonable grounds to believe that the individual is a danger to the security of the United States.

(ii) If the evidence indicates that one of the above grounds apply to the applicant, he or she shall have the burden of proving by a preponderance of the evidence that he or she did not so act.

(3) Additional limitation on eligibility for asylum. For applications filed after November 9, 2018, an alien shall be ineligible for asylum if the alien is subject to a presidential proclamation or other presidential order suspending or limiting the entry of aliens along the southern border with Mexico that is issued pursuant to subsection 212(f) or 215(a)(1) of the Act on or after November 9, 2018 and the alien enters the United States after the effective date of the proclamation or order contrary to the terms of the proclamation or order. This limitation on eligibility does not apply if the proclamation or order expressly provides that it does not affect eligibility for asylum, or expressly provides for a waiver or exception that makes the suspension or limitation inapplicable to the alien.

(4) Additional limitation on eligibility for asylum. Notwithstanding the provisions of § 208.15, any alien who enters, attempts to enter, or arrives in the United States across the southern land border on or after July 16, 2019, after transiting through at least one country outside the alien's country of citizenship, nationality, or last lawful habitual residence en route to the United States, shall be found ineligible for asylum unless:

(i) The alien demonstrates that he or she applied for protection from persecution or torture in at least one country outside the alien's country of citizenship, nationality, or last lawful habitual residence through which the alien transited en route to the United States, and the alien received a final judgment denying the alien protection in such country;

(ii) The alien demonstrates that he or she satisfies the definition of "victim of a severe form of trafficking in persons" provided in 8 CFR 214.11; or

(iii) The only countries through which the alien transited en route to the United States were, at the time of the transit, not parties to the 1951 United Nations Convention relating to the Status of Refugees, the 1967 Protocol Relating to the Status of Refugees, or the United Nations Convention against Torture and Other Cruel, Inhuman or Degrading Treatment or Punishment.

(5) Non-binding determinations. Determinations made with respect to paragraph (c)(4)(ii) of this section are not binding on Federal departments or agencies in subsequent determinations of eligibility for T or U nonimmigrant status under section 101(a)(15)(T) or (U) of the INA or for benefits or services under 22 U.S.C. 7105 or 8 U.S.C. 1641(c)(4).

[64 FR 8488, Feb. 19, 1999; 65 FR 76133, Dec. 6, 2000; 78 FR 42863, July 18, 2013; 83 FR 55952, Nov. 9, 2018; 84 FR 33843, July 16, 2019]

§ 208.14 Approval, denial, referral, or dismissal of application. [also 8 C.F.R. § 1208.14, which has minor wording changes and cross-references to part 1208]

(a) **By an immigration judge.** Unless otherwise prohibited in § 208.13(c), an immigration judge may grant or deny asylum in the exercise of discretion to an applicant who qualifies as a refugee under section 101(a)(42) of the Act.

(b) **Approval by an asylum officer.** In any case within the jurisdiction of the RAIO, unless otherwise prohibited in § 208.13(c), an asylum officer may grant, in the exercise of his or her discretion, asylum to an applicant who qualifies as a refugee under section 101(a)(42) of the Act, and whose identity has been checked pursuant to section 208(d)(5)(A)(i) of the Act.

(c) **Denial, referral, or dismissal by an asylum officer.** If the asylum officer does not grant asylum to an applicant after an interview conducted in accordance with § 208.9, or if, as provided in § 208.10, the applicant is deemed to have waived his or her right to an interview or an adjudication by an asylum officer, the asylum officer shall deny, refer, or dismiss the application, as follows:

(1) **Inadmissible or deportable aliens.** Except as provided in paragraph (c)(4) of this section, in the case of an applicant who appears to be inadmissible or deportable under section 212(a) or 237(a) of the Act, the asylum officer shall refer the application to an immigration judge, together with the appropriate charging document, for adjudication in removal proceedings (or, where charging documents may not be issued, shall dismiss the application).

(2) **Alien in valid status.** In the case of an applicant who is maintaining valid immigrant, nonimmigrant, or Temporary Protected Status at the time the application is decided, the asylum officer shall deny the application for asylum.

(3) **Alien with valid parole.** If an applicant has been paroled into the United States and the parole has not expired or been terminated by the Service, the asylum officer shall deny the application for asylum.

(4) **Alien paroled into the United States whose parole has expired or is terminated.**

(i) **Alien paroled prior to April 1, 1997, or with advance authorization for parole.** In the case of an applicant who was paroled into the United States prior to April 1, 1997, or who, prior to departure from the United States, had received an advance authorization for parole, the asylum officer shall refer the application, together with the appropriate charging documents, to an immigration judge for adjudication in removal proceedings if the parole has expired, the Service has terminated parole, or the Service is terminating parole through issuance of the charging documents, pursuant to § 212.5(d)(2)(i) of this chapter.

(ii) Alien paroled on or after April 1, 1997, without advance authorization for parole. In the case of an applicant who is an arriving alien or is otherwise subject to removal under § 235.3(b) of this chapter, and was paroled into the United States on or after April 1, 1997, without advance authorization for parole prior to departure from the United States, the asylum officer will take the following actions, if the parole has expired or been terminated:

(A) Inadmissible under section 212(a)(6)(C) or 212(a)(7) of the Act. If the applicant appears inadmissible to the United States under section 212(a)(6)(C) or 212(a)(7) of the Act and the asylum officer does not intend to lodge any additional charges of inadmissibility, the asylum officer shall proceed in accordance with § 235.3(b) of this chapter. If such applicant is found to have a credible fear of persecution or torture based on information elicited from the asylum interview, an asylum officer may refer the applicant directly to an immigration judge in removal proceedings under section 240 of the Act, without conducting a separate credible fear interview pursuant to § 208.30. If such applicant is not found to have a credible fear based on information elicited at the asylum interview, an asylum officer will conduct a credible fear interview and the applicant will be subject to the credible fear process specified at § 208.30(b).

(B) Inadmissible on other grounds. In the case of an applicant who was paroled into the United States on or after April 1, 1997, and will be charged as inadmissible to the United States under provisions of the Act other than, or in addition to, sections 212(a)(6)(C) or 212(a)(7), the asylum officer shall refer the application to an immigration judge for adjudication in removal proceedings.

(d) Applicability of § 103.2(b) of this chapter. No application for asylum or withholding of deportation shall be subject to denial pursuant to § 103.2(b) of this chapter.

(e) Duration. If the applicant is granted asylum, the grant will be effective for an indefinite period, subject to termination as provided in § 208.24.

(f) Effect of denial of principal's application on separate applications by dependents. The denial of an asylum application filed by a principal applicant for asylum shall also result in the denial of asylum status to any dependents of that principal applicant who are included in that same application. Such denial shall not preclude a grant of asylum for an otherwise eligible dependent who has filed a separate asylum application, nor shall such denial result in an otherwise eligible dependent becoming ineligible to apply for asylum due to the provisions of section 208(a)(2)(C) of the Act.

(g) Applicants granted lawful permanent residence status. If an asylum applicant is granted adjustment of status to lawful permanent resident, the Service may provide written notice to the applicant that his or her asylum application will be presumed abandoned and dismissed without prejudice, unless the applicant submits a written request within 30 days of the notice, that the asylum application be adjudicated. If an applicant does not respond within 30 days of the date the written notice was sent or served, the Service may presume the asylum application abandoned and dismiss it without prejudice.

[62 FR 10342, March 6, 1997; as amended at 63 FR 12986, March 17, 1998; 64 FR 27875, May 21, 1999; 65 FR 76134, Dec. 6, 2000; 76 FR 53784, Aug. 29, 2011.]

§ 208.15 Definition of "firm resettlement." [also 8 C.F.R. § 1208.15]

An alien is considered to be firmly resettled if, prior to arrival in the United States, he or she entered into another country with, or while in that country received, an offer of permanent resident status, citizenship, or some other type of permanent resettlement unless he or she establishes:

(a) That his or her entry into that country was a necessary consequence of his or her flight from persecution, that he or she remained in that country only as long as was necessary to arrange onward travel, and that he or she did not establish significant ties in that country; or

(b) That the conditions of his or her residence in that country were so substantially and consciously restricted by the authority of the country of refuge that he or she was not in fact resettled. In making his or her determination, the asylum officer or immigration judge shall consider the conditions under which other residents of the country live; the type of housing, whether permanent or temporary, made available to the refugee; the types and extent of employment available to the refugee; and the extent to which the refugee received permission to hold property and to enjoy other rights and privileges, such as travel documentation that includes a right of entry or reentry, education, public relief, or naturalization, ordinarily available to others resident in the country.

[62 Fed. Reg. 10343, March 6, 1997; 65 FR 76135, Dec. 6, 2000]

§ 208.16 Withholding of removal under section 241(b) (3)(B) of the Act and withholding of removal under the Convention Against Torture. [also 8 C.F.R. § 1208.16, which is identical except for cross-references to part 1208]

(a) **Consideration of application for withholding of removal.** An asylum officer shall not decide whether the exclusion, deportation, or removal of an alien to a country where the alien's life or freedom would be threatened must be withheld, except in the case of an alien who is otherwise eligible for asylum but is precluded from being granted such status due solely to section 207(a)(5) of the Act*. In exclusion, deportation, or removal proceedings, an immigration judge may adjudicate both an asylum claim and a request for withholding of removal whether or not asylum is granted.

(b) **Eligibility for withholding of removal under section 241(b) (3) of the Act; burden of proof.** The burden of proof is on the applicant for withholding of removal under section 241(b)(3) of the Act to establish that his or her life or freedom would be threatened in the proposed country of removal on account of race, religion, nationality, membership in a particular social group, or political opinion. The testimony of the applicant, if credible, may be sufficient to sustain the burden of proof without corroboration. The evidence shall be evaluated as follows:

(1) **Past threat to life or freedom.**

(i) If the applicant is determined to have suffered past persecution in the proposed country of removal on account of race, religion, nationality, membership in a particular social group, or political opinion, it shall be presumed that the applicant's life or freedom would be threatened in the future in the country of removal on the basis of the original claim. This presumption may be rebutted if an asylum officer or immigration judge finds by a preponderance of the evidence:

(A) There has been a fundamental change in circumstances such that the applicant's life or freedom would not be threatened on account of any of the five grounds mentioned in this paragraph upon the applicant's removal to that country; or

(B) The applicant could avoid a future threat to his or her life or freedom by relocating to another part of the proposed country of removal and, under all the circumstances, it would be reasonable to expect the applicant to do so.

(ii) In cases in which the applicant has established past persecution, the Service shall bear the burden of establishing by a prepon-

* Because INA § 207(a)(5) has been repealed, asylum officers no longer decide applications for withholding of removal.

derance of the evidence the requirements of paragraphs (b)(1)(i)(A) or (b)(1)(i)(B) of this section.

(iii) If the applicant's fear of future threat to life or freedom is unrelated to the past persecution, the applicant bears the burden of establishing that it is more likely than not that he or she would suffer such harm.

(2) Future threat to life or freedom. An applicant who has not suffered past persecution may demonstrate that his or her life or freedom would be threatened in the future in a country if he or she can establish that it is more likely than not that he or she would be persecuted on account of race, religion, nationality, membership in a particular social group, or political opinion upon removal to that country. Such an applicant cannot demonstrate that his or her life or freedom would be threatened if the asylum officer or immigration judge finds that the applicant could avoid a future threat to his or her life or freedom by relocating to another part of the proposed country of removal and, under all the circumstances, it would be reasonable to expect the applicant to do so. In evaluating whether it is more likely than not that the applicant's life or freedom would be threatened in a particular country on account of race, religion, nationality, membership in a particular social group, or political opinion, the asylum officer or immigration judge shall not require the applicant to provide evidence that he or she would be singled out individually for such persecution if:

(i) The applicant establishes that in that country there is a pattern or practice of persecution of a group of persons similarly situated to the applicant on account of race, religion, nationality, membership in a particular social group, or political opinion; and

(ii) The applicant establishes his or her own inclusion in and identification with such group of persons such that it is more likely than not that his or her life or freedom would be threatened upon return to that country.

(3) Reasonableness of internal relocation. For purposes of determinations under paragraphs (b)(1) and (b)(2) of this section, adjudicators should consider, among other things, whether the applicant would face other serious harm in the place of suggested relocation; any ongoing civil strife within the country; administrative, economic, or judicial infrastructure; geographical limitations; and social and cultural constraints, such as age, gender, health, and social and familial ties. These factors may or may not be relevant, depending on all the circumstances of the case, and are not necessarily determinative of whether it would be reasonable for the applicant to relocate.

(i) In cases in which the applicant has not established past persecution, the applicant shall bear the burden of establishing that it would not be reasonable for him or her to relocate, unless the persecutor is a government or is government-sponsored.

(ii) In cases in which the persecutor is a government or is government-sponsored, or the applicant has established persecution in the past, it shall be presumed that internal relocation would not be reasonable, unless the Service establishes by a preponderance of the evidence that under all the circumstances it would be reasonable for the applicant to relocate.

(c) Eligibility for withholding of removal under the Convention Against Torture.

(1) For purposes of regulations under Title II of the Act, "Convention Against Torture" shall refer to the United Nations Convention Against Torture and Other Cruel, Inhuman or Degrading Treatment or Punishment, subject to any reservations, understandings, declarations, and provisos contained in the United States Senate resolution of ratification of the Convention, as implemented by section 2242 of the Foreign Affairs Reform and Restructuring Act of 1998 (Pub.L. 105–277, 112 Stat. 2681, 2681–821). The definition of torture contained in § 208.18(a) of this part shall govern all decisions made under regulations under Title II of the Act about the applicability of Article 3 of the Convention Against Torture.

(2) The burden of proof is on the applicant for withholding of removal under this paragraph to establish that it is more likely than not that he or she would be tortured if removed to the proposed country of removal. The testimony of the applicant, if credible, may be sufficient to sustain the burden of proof without corroboration.

(3) In assessing whether it is more likely than not that an applicant would be tortured in the proposed country of removal, all evidence relevant to the possibility of future torture shall be considered, including, but not limited to:

(i) Evidence of past torture inflicted upon the applicant;

(ii) Evidence that the applicant could relocate to a part of the country of removal where he or she is not likely to be tortured;

(iii) Evidence of gross, flagrant or mass violations of human rights within the country of removal, where applicable; and

(iv) Other relevant information regarding conditions in the country of removal.

(4) In considering an application for withholding of removal under the Convention Against Torture, the immigration judge shall first determine whether the alien is more likely than not to be tortured in the country of removal. If the immigration judge determines that the alien is more likely than not to be tortured in the country of removal, the alien is entitled to protection under the Convention Against Torture. Protection under the Convention Against Torture will be granted either in the form of withholding of removal or in the form of deferral of removal. An alien entitled to such protection shall be granted with-

holding of removal unless the alien is subject to mandatory denial of withholding of removal under paragraphs (d)(2) or (d)(3) of this section. If an alien entitled to such protection is subject to mandatory denial of withholding of removal under paragraphs (d)(2) or (d)(3) of this section, the alien's removal shall be deferred under § 208.17(a).

(d) Approval or denial of application.

(1) General. Subject to paragraphs (d)(2) and (d)(3) of this section, an application for withholding of deportation or removal to a country of proposed removal shall be granted if the applicant's eligibility for withholding is established pursuant to paragraphs (b) or (c) of this section.

(2) Mandatory denials. Except as provided in paragraph (d)(3) of this section, an application for withholding of removal under section 241(b)(3) of the Act or under the Convention Against Torture shall be denied if the applicant falls within section 241(b)(3)(B) of the Act or, for applications for withholding of deportation adjudicated in proceedings commenced prior to April 1, 1997, within section 243(h)(2) of the Act as it appeared prior to that date. For purposes of section 241(b)(3)(B)(ii) of the Act, or section 243(h)(2)(B) of the Act as it appeared prior to April 1, 1997, an alien who has been convicted of a particularly serious crime shall be considered to constitute a danger to the community. If the evidence indicates the applicability of one or more of the grounds for denial of withholding enumerated in the Act, the applicant shall have the burden of proving by a preponderance of the evidence that such grounds do not apply.

(3) Exception to the prohibition on withholding of deportation in certain cases. Section 243(h)(3) of the Act, as added by section 413 of Pub.L. 104–132 (110 Stat. 1214), shall apply only to applications adjudicated in proceedings commenced before April 1, 1997, and in which final action had not been taken before April 24, 1996. The discretion permitted by that section to override section 243(h)(2) of the Act shall be exercised only in the case of an applicant convicted of an aggravated felony (or felonies) where he or she was sentenced to an aggregate term of imprisonment of less than 5 years and the immigration judge determines on an individual basis that the crime (or crimes) of which the applicant was convicted does not constitute a particularly serious crime. Nevertheless, it shall be presumed that an alien convicted of an aggravated felony has been convicted of a particularly serious crime. Except in the cases specified in this paragraph, the grounds for denial of withholding of deportation in section 243(h)(2) of the Act as it appeared prior to April 1, 1997, shall be deemed to comply with the Protocol Relating to the Status of Refugees, Jan. 31, 1967, T.I.A.S. No. 6577.

(e) Reconsideration of discretionary denial of asylum. In the event that an applicant is denied asylum solely in the exercise of discretion, and the applicant is subsequently granted withholding of deportation or removal under this section, thereby effectively precluding admission of the applicant's spouse or minor children following to join him or her, the denial of asylum shall be reconsidered. Factors to be considered will include the reasons for the denial and reasonable alternatives available to the applicant such as reunification with his or her spouse or minor children in a third country.

(f) Removal to third country. Nothing in this section or § 208.17 shall prevent the Service from removing an alien to a third country other than the country to which removal has been withheld or deferred.

[64 FR 8488, Feb. 19, 1999; 65 FR 76135, Dec. 6, 2000]

§ 208.17 Deferral of removal under the Convention Against Torture. [also 8 C.F.R. § 1208.17, which is identical except for cross-references to part 1208]

(a) Grant of deferral of removal. An alien who: has been ordered removed; has been found under § 208.16(c)(3) to be entitled to protection under the Convention Against Torture; and is subject to the provisions for mandatory denial of withholding of removal under § 208.16(d)(2) or (d)(3), shall be granted deferral of removal to the country where he or she is more likely than not to be tortured.

(b) Notice to Alien.

(1) After an immigration judge orders an alien described in paragraph (a) of this section removed, the immigration judge shall inform the alien that his or her removal to the country where he or she is more likely than not to be tortured shall be deferred until such time as the deferral is terminated under this section. The immigration judge shall inform the alien that deferral of removal:

(i) Does not confer upon the alien any lawful or permanent immigration status in the United States;

(ii) Will not necessarily result in the alien being released from the custody of the Service if the alien is subject to such custody;

(iii) Is effective only until terminated; and

(iv) Is subject to review and termination if the immigration judge determines that it is not likely that the alien would be tortured in the country to which removal has been deferred, or if the alien requests that deferral be terminated.

(2) The immigration judge shall also inform the alien that removal has been deferred only to the country in which it has been determined that the alien is likely to be tortured, and that the alien may be removed at any time to another country where he or she is not likely to be tortured.

(c) Detention of an alien granted deferral of removal under this section. Nothing in this section shall alter the authority of the Service to detain an alien whose removal has been deferred under this section and who is otherwise subject to detention. In the case of such an alien, decisions about the alien's release shall be made according to part 241 of this chapter.

(d) Termination of deferral of removal.

(1) At any time while deferral of removal is in effect, the INS District Counsel for the District with jurisdiction over an alien whose removal has been deferred under paragraph (a) of this section may file a motion with the Immigration Court having administrative control pursuant to § 3.11 of this chapter to schedule a hearing to consider whether deferral of removal should be terminated. The Service motion shall be granted if it is accompanied by evidence that is relevant to the possibility that the alien would be tortured in the country to which removal has been deferred and that was not presented at the previous hearing. The Service motion shall not be subject to the requirements for reopening in §§ 3.2 and 3.23 of this chapter.

(2) The Immigration Court shall provide notice to the alien and the Service of the time, place, and date of the termination hearing. Such notice shall inform the alien that the alien may supplement the information in his or her initial application for withholding of removal under the Convention Against Torture and shall provide that the alien must submit any such supplemental information within 10 calendar days of service of such notice (or 13 calendar days if service of such notice was by mail). At the expiration of this 10 or 13 day period, the Immigration Court shall forward a copy of the original application, and any supplemental information the alien or the Service has submitted, to the Department of State, together with notice to the Department of State of the time, place and date of the termination hearing. At its option, the Department of State may provide comments on the case, according to the provisions of § 208.11 of this part.

(3) The immigration judge shall conduct a hearing and make a de novo determination, based on the record of proceeding and initial application in addition to any new evidence submitted by the Service or the alien, as to whether the alien is more likely than not to be tortured in the country to which removal has been deferred. This determination shall be made under the standards for eligibility set out in § 208.16(c). The burden is on the alien to establish that it is more likely than not that he or she would be tortured in the country to which removal has been deferred.

(4) If the immigration judge determines that the alien is more likely than not to be tortured in the country to which removal has been deferred, the order of deferral shall remain in place. If the immigration judge determines that the alien has not established that he or she is more likely than not to be tortured in the country to which removal has been deferred, the deferral of removal shall be terminated and the alien may be removed to that country. Appeal of the immigration judge's decision shall lie to the Board.

(e) Termination at the request of the alien.

(1) At any time while deferral of removal is in effect, the alien may make a written request to the Immigration Court having administrative control pursuant to § 3.11 of this chapter to terminate the deferral order. If satisfied on the basis of the written submission that the alien's request is knowing and voluntary, the immigration judge shall terminate the order of deferral and the alien may be removed.

(2) If necessary the immigration judge may calendar a hearing for the sole purpose of determining whether the alien's request is knowing and voluntary. If the immigration judge determines that the alien's request is knowing and voluntary, the order of deferral shall be terminated. If the immigration judge determines that the alien's request is not knowing and voluntary, the alien's request shall not serve as the basis for terminating the order of deferral.

(f) Termination pursuant to § 208.18(c). At any time while deferral of removal is in effect, the Attorney General may determine whether deferral should be terminated based on diplomatic assurances forwarded by the Secretary of State pursuant to the procedures in § 208.18(c).

[64 FR 8489, Feb. 19, 1999]

§ 208.18 Implementation of the Convention Against Torture. [also 8 C.F.R. § 1208.18, which is identical except for cross-references to part 1208]

(a) Definitions. The definitions in this subsection incorporate the definition of torture contained in Article 1 of the Convention Against Torture, subject to the reservations, understandings, declarations, and provisos contained in the United States Senate resolution of ratification of the Convention.

(1) Torture is defined as any act by which severe pain or suffering, whether physical or mental, is intentionally inflicted on a person for such purposes as obtaining from him or her or a third person information or a confession, punishing him or her for an act he or she or a third person has committed or is suspected of having committed, or intimidating or coercing him or her or a third person, or for any reason based on discrimination of any kind, when such pain or suffering is inflicted by or at the instigation of or with the consent or acquiescence of a public official or other person acting in an official capacity.

(2) Torture is an extreme form of cruel and inhuman treatment and does not include lesser forms of cruel, inhuman or degrading treatment or punishment that do not amount to torture.

(3) Torture does not include pain or suffering arising only from, inherent in or incidental to lawful sanctions. Lawful sanctions include judicially imposed sanctions and other enforcement actions authorized by law, including the death penalty, but do not include sanctions that defeat the object and purpose of the Convention Against Torture to prohibit torture.

(4) In order to constitute torture, mental pain or suffering must be prolonged mental harm caused by or resulting from:

(i) The intentional infliction or threatened infliction of severe physical pain or suffering;

(ii) The administration or application, or threatened administration or application, of mind altering substances or other procedures calculated to disrupt profoundly the senses or the personality;

(iii) The threat of imminent death; or

(iv) The threat that another person will imminently be subjected to death, severe physical pain or suffering, or the administration or application of mind altering substances or other procedures calculated to disrupt profoundly the sense or personality.

(5) In order to constitute torture, an act must be specifically intended to inflict severe physical or mental pain or suffering. An act that results in unanticipated or unintended severity of pain and suffering is not torture.

(6) In order to constitute torture an act must be directed against a person in the offender's custody or physical control.

(7) Acquiescence of a public official requires that the public official, prior to the activity constituting torture, have awareness of such activity and thereafter breach his or her legal responsibility to intervene to prevent such activity.

(8) Noncompliance with applicable legal procedural standards does not per se constitute torture.

(b) Applicability of §§ 208.16(c) and 208.17(a).

(1) Aliens in proceedings on or after March 22, 1999. An alien who is in exclusion, deportation, or removal proceedings on or after March 22, 1999 may apply for withholding of removal under § 208.16(c), and, if applicable, may be considered for deferral of removal under § 208.17(a).

(2) Aliens who were ordered removed, or whose removal orders became final, before March 22, 1999. An alien under a final order of deportation, exclusion, or removal that became final prior to March 22, 1999 may move to reopen proceedings for the sole purpose of seeking protection under § 208.16(c). Such motions shall be governed by §§ 3.23 and 3.2 of this chapter, except that the time and numerical limitations on motions to reopen shall not apply and the alien shall not be required to demonstrate that the evidence sought to be offered was unavailable and could not have been discovered or presented at the former hearing. The motion to reopen shall not be granted unless:

(i) The motion is filed within June 21, 1999; and

(ii) The evidence sought to be offered establishes a prima facie case that the applicant's removal must be withheld or deferred under §§ 208.16(c) or 208.17(a).

(3) Aliens who, on March 22, 1999, have requests pending with the Service for protection under Article 3 of the Convention Against Torture.

(i) Except as otherwise provided, after March 22, 1999, the Service will not:

(A) Consider, under its pre-regulatory administrative policy to ensure compliance with the Convention Against Torture, whether Article 3 of that Convention prohibits the removal of an alien to a particular country, or

(B) Stay the removal of an alien based on a request filed with the Service for protection under Article 3 of that Convention.

(ii) For each alien who, on or before March 22, 1999, filed a request with the Service for protection under Article 3 of the Convention Against Torture, and whose request has not been finally decided by the Service, the Service shall provide written notice that, after March 22, 1999, consideration for protection under Article 3 can be obtained only through the provisions of this rule.

(A) The notice shall inform an alien who is under an order of removal issued by EOIR that, in order to seek consideration of a claim under §§ 208.16(c) or 208.17(a), such an alien must file a motion to reopen with the immigration court or the Board of Immigration Appeals. This notice shall be accompanied by a stay of removal, effective until 30 days after service of the notice on the alien. A motion to reopen filed under this paragraph for the limited purpose of asserting a claim under §§ 208.16(c) or 208.17(a) shall not be subject to the requirements for reopening in §§ 3.2 and 3.23 of this chapter. Such a motion shall be granted if it is accompanied by a copy of the notice described in paragraph (b)(3)(ii) or by other convincing evidence that the alien had a request pending with the Service for protection under Article 3 of the Convention Against Torture on March 22, 1999. The filing of such a motion shall extend the stay of removal during the pendency of the adjudication of this motion.

(B) The notice shall inform an alien who is under an administrative order of removal issued by the Service under section 238(b) of the Act or an exclusion, deportation, or removal order reinstated by the Service under section 241(a)(5) of the Act that the alien's claim to withholding of removal under § 208.16(c) or deferral of removal under § 208.17(a) will be considered under § 208.31.

(C) The notice shall inform an alien who is under an administrative order of removal issued by the Service under section 235(c) of the Act that the alien's claim to protection under the Convention Against Torture will be decided by the Service as provided in § 208.18(d) and 235.8(b)(4) and will not be considered under the provisions of this part relating to consideration or review by an immigration judge, the Board of Immigration Appeals, or an asylum officer.

(4) Aliens whose claims to protection under the Convention Against Torture were finally decided by the Service prior to March 22, 1999. Sections 208.16(c) and 208.17 (a) and paragraphs (b)(1) through (b)(3) of this section do not apply to cases in which, prior to March 22, 1999, the Service has made a final administrative determination about the applicability of Article 3 of the Convention Against Torture to the case of an alien who filed a request with the Service for protection under Article 3. If, prior to March 22, 1999, the Service determined that an applicant cannot be removed consistent with the Convention Against Torture, the alien shall be considered to have been granted withholding of removal under § 208.16(c), unless the alien is subject to mandatory denial of withholding of removal under § 208.16(d)(2) or (d)(3), in which case the alien will be considered to have been granted deferral of removal under 208.17(a). If, prior to March 22, 1999, the Service determined that an alien can be removed consistent with the Convention Against Torture, the alien will be considered to have been finally denied withholding of removal under § 208.16(c) and deferral of removal under § 208.17(a).

(c) Diplomatic assurances against torture obtained by the Secretary of State.

(1) The Secretary of State may forward to the Attorney General assurances that the Secretary has obtained from the government of a specific country that an alien would not be tortured there if the alien were removed to that country.

(2) If the Secretary of State forwards assurances described in paragraph (c)(1) of this section to the Attorney General for consideration by the Attorney General or her delegates under this paragraph, the Attorney General shall determine, in consultation with the Secretary of State, whether the assurances are sufficiently reliable to allow the alien's removal to that country consistent with Article 3 of the Convention Against Torture. The Attorney General's authority under this paragraph may be exercised by the Deputy Attorney General or by the Commissioner, Immigration and Naturalization Service, but may not be further delegated.

(3) Once assurances are provided under paragraph (c)(2) of this section, the alien's claim for protection under the Convention Against Torture shall not be considered further by an immigration judge, the Board of Immigration Appeals, or an asylum officer.

(d) Cases involving aliens ordered removed under section 235(c) of the Act. With respect to an alien terrorist or other alien subject to administrative removal under section 235(c) of the Act who requests protection under Article 3 of the Convention Against Torture, the Service will assess the applicability of Article 3 through the removal process to ensure that a removal order will not be executed under circumstances that would violate the obligations of the United States under Article 3. In such cases, the provisions of Part 208 relating to consideration or review by an immigration judge, the Board of Immigration Appeals, or an asylum officer shall not apply.

(e) Judicial review of claims for protection from removal under Article 3 of the Convention Against Torture.

(1) Pursuant to the provisions of section 2242(d) of the Foreign Affairs Reform and Restructuring Act of 1998, there shall be no judicial appeal or review of any action, decision, or claim raised under the Convention or that section, except as part of the review of a final order of removal pursuant to section 242 of the Act; provided however, that any appeal or petition regarding an action, decision, or claim under the Convention or under section 2242 of the Foreign Affairs Reform and Restructuring Act of 1998 shall not be deemed to include or authorize the consideration of any administrative order or decision, or portion thereof, the appeal or review of which is restricted or prohibited by the Act.

(2) Except as otherwise expressly provided, nothing in this paragraph shall be construed to create a private right of action or to authorize the consideration or issuance of administrative or judicial relief.

[64 FR 8490, Feb. 19, 1999; 64 FR 13881, March 23, 1999]

§ 208.19 Decisions. [also 8 C.F.R. § 1208.19, which is identical except for cross-references to part 1208]

The decision of an asylum officer to grant or to deny asylum or to refer an asylum application, in accordance with § 208.14(b) or (c), shall be communicated in writing to the applicant. Pursuant to § 208.9(d), an applicant must appear in person to receive and to acknowledge receipt of the decision to grant or deny asylum, or to refer an asylum application unless, in the discretion of the asylum office director, service by mail is appropriate. A letter communicating denial of asylum or referral of the application shall state the basis for denial or referral and include an assessment of the applicant's credibility.

[65 FR 76136, Dec. 6, 2000]

§ 208.20 Determining if an asylum application is frivolous. [also 8 C.F.R. § 1208.20]

For applications filed on or after April 1, 1997, an applicant is subject to the provisions of section 208(d)(6) of the Act only if a final order by an immigration judge or the Board of Immigration Appeals specifically finds that the alien knowingly filed a frivolous asylum application. For purposes of this section, an asylum application is frivolous if any of its material elements is deliberately fabricated. Such finding shall only be made if the immigration judge or the Board is satisfied that the applicant, during the course of the proceedings, has had sufficient opportunity to account for any discrepancies or implausible aspects of the claim. For purposes of this section, a finding that an alien filed a frivolous asylum application shall not preclude the alien from seeking withholding of removal.

[64 FR 8490, 8492, Feb. 19, 1999; 65 FR 76136, Dec. 6, 2000]

§ 208.21 Admission of the asylee's spouse and children. [also 8 C.F.R. § 1208.21, which has minor wording changes and cross-references to part 1208]

(a) Eligibility. In accordance with section 208(b)(3) of the Act, a spouse, as defined in section 101(a)(35) of the Act, 8 U.S.C. 1101(a)(35), or child, as defined in section 101(b)(1) of the Act, also may be granted asylum if accompanying, or following to join, the principal alien who was granted asylum, unless it is determined that the spouse or child is ineligible for asylum under section 208(b)(2)(A)(i), (ii), (iii), (iv) or (v) of the Act for applications filed on or after April 1, 1997, or under § 208.13(c)(2)(i)(A), (C), (D), (E), or (F) for applications filed before April 1, 1997.

(b) Relationship. The relationship of spouse and child as defined in sections 101(a)(35) and 101(b)(1) of the Act must have existed at the time the principal alien's asylum application was approved and must continue to exist at the time of filing for accompanying or following-to-join benefits and at the time of the spouse or child's subsequent admission to the United States. If the asylee proves that the asylee is the parent of a child who was born after asylum was granted, but who was in utero on the date of the asylum grant, the child shall be eligible to accompany or follow-to-join the asylee. The child's mother, if not the principal asylee, shall not be eligible to accompany or follow-to-join the principal asylee unless the child's mother was the principal asylee's spouse on the date the principal asylee was granted asylum.

(c) Spouse or child in the United States. When a spouse or child of an alien granted asylum is in the United States, but was not included in the asylee's benefit request, the asylee may request accompanying or following-to-join benefits for his or her spouse or child, by filing for each qualifying family member a Request for Refugee/Asylee Relative, with supporting evidence, and in accordance with the form instructions, regardless of the status of that spouse or child in the United States. A separate Request for Refugee/Asylee Relative must be filed by the asylee for each qualifying family member within two years of the date in which he or she was granted asylum status, unless it is determined by USCIS that this period should be extended for humanitarian reasons. Upon approval of the Request for Refugee/Asylee Relative, USCIS will notify the asylee of such approval. Employment will be authorized incident to status. To demonstrate employment authorization, USCIS will issue a document reflecting the derivative's current status as an asylee, or the derivative may apply, under 8 CFR 274a.12(a), for employment authorization. The approval of the Request for Refugee/Asylee Relative will remain valid for the duration of the relationship to the asylee and, in the case of a child, while the child is under 21 years of age and unmarried, provided also that the principal's status has not been revoked. However, the approved Request for Refugee/Asylee Relative will cease to confer immigration benefits after it has been used by the beneficiary for admission to the United States as a derivative of an asylee.

(d) Spouse or child outside the United States. When a spouse or child of an alien granted asylum is outside the United States, the asylee may request accompanying or following-to-join benefits for his or her spouse or child(ren) by filing a separate Request for Refugee/Asylee Relative for each qualifying family member in accordance with the form instructions. A separate Request for Refugee/Asylee Relative for each qualifying family member must be filed within two years of the date in which the asylee was granted asylum, unless USCIS determines that the filing period should be extended for humanitarian reasons. When the Request for Refugee/Asylee Relative is approved, USCIS will notify the asylee of such approval. USCIS also will send the approved request to the Department of State for transmission to the U.S. Embassy or Consulate having jurisdiction over the area in which the asylee's spouse or child is located. The approval of the Request for Refugee/Asylee Relative will remain valid for the duration of the relationship to the asylee and, in the case of a child, while the child is under 21 years of age and unmarried, provided also that the principal's status has not been revoked. However, the approved Request for Refugee/Asylee Relative will cease to confer immigration benefits after it has been used by the beneficiary for admission to the United States as a derivative of an asylee.

(e) Denial. If the spouse or child is found to be ineligible for the status accorded under section 208(c) of the Act, a written notice stating the basis for denial shall be forwarded to the principal alien. No appeal shall lie from this decision.

(f) Burden of proof. To establish the claimed relationship of spouse or child as defined in sections 101(a)(35) and 101(b)(1) of the Act, evidence must be submitted with the request as set forth in part 204 of this chapter. Where possible this will consist of the documents specified in § 204.2 (a)(1)(i)(B), (a)(1)(iii)(B), (a)(2), (d)(2), and (d)(5) of this chapter. The burden of proof is on the principal alien to establish by a preponderance of the evidence that any person on whose behalf he or she is making a request under this section is an eligible spouse or child.

(g) Duration. The spouse or child qualifying under section 208(c) of the Act shall be granted asylum for an indefinite period unless the principal's status is revoked.

[63 FR 3796, Jan. 27, 1998; 64 FR 8490, Feb. 19, 1999; 65 FR 76136, Dec. 6, 2000; 76 FR 53784, Aug. 29, 2011; 76 FR 73476, Nov. 29, 2011.]

§ 208.22 Effect on exclusion, deportation, and removal proceedings. [also 8 C.F.R. § 1208.22, which is identical except for cross-references to part 1208]

An alien who has been granted asylum may not be deported or removed unless his or her asylum status is terminated pursuant to § 208.24. An alien in exclusion, deportation, or removal proceedings who is granted withholding of removal or deportation, or deferral of removal, may not be deported or removed to the country to which his or her deportation or removal is ordered withheld or deferred unless the withholding order is terminated pursuant to § 208.24 or deferral is terminated pursuant to § 208.17(d) or (e).

[64 FR 8490, 8492, Feb. 19, 1999; 65 FR 76136, Dec. 6, 2000]

§ 208.23 Restoration of status. [also 8 C.F.R. § 1208.23]

An alien who was maintaining his or her nonimmigrant status at the time of filing an asylum application and has such application denied may continue in or be restored to that status, if it has not expired.

[64 FR 8490, Feb. 19, 1999; 65 FR 76136, Dec. 6, 2000]

§ 208.24 Termination of asylum or withholding of removal or deportation. [also 8 C.F.R. § 1208.24, which has minor wording changes and cross-references to part 1208]

(a) Termination of asylum by USCIS. Except as provided in paragraph (e) of this section, an asylum officer may terminate a grant of asylum made under the jurisdiction of USCIS if, following an interview, the asylum officer determines that:

(1) There is a showing of fraud in the alien's application such that he or she was not eligible for asylum at the time it was granted;

(2) As to applications filed on or after April 1, 1997, one or more of the conditions described in section 208(c)(2) of the Act exist; or

(3) As to applications filed before April 1, 1997, the alien no longer has a well-founded fear of persecution upon return due to a change of country conditions in the alien's country of nationality or habitual residence or the alien has committed any act that would have been grounds for denial of asylum under § 208.13(c)(2).

(b) Termination of withholding of deportation or removal by USCIS. Except as provided in paragraph (e) of this section, an asylum officer may terminate a grant of withholding of deportation or removal made under the jurisdiction of USCIS if the asylum officer determines, following an interview, that:

(1) The alien is no longer entitled to withholding of deportation or removal because, owing to a fundamental change in circumstances relating to the original claim, the alien's life or freedom no longer would be threatened on account of race, religion, nationality, membership in a particular social group, or political opinion in the country from which deportation or removal was withheld.

(2) There is a showing of fraud in the alien's application such that the alien was not eligible for withholding of removal at the time it was granted;

(3) The alien has committed any other act that would have been grounds for denial of withholding of removal under section 241(b)(3)(B) of the Act had it occurred prior to the grant of withholding of removal; or

(4) For applications filed in proceedings commenced before April 1, 1997, the alien has committed any act that would have been grounds for denial of withholding of deportation under section 243(h)(2) of the Act.

(c) Procedure. Prior to the termination of a grant of asylum or withholding of deportation or removal, the alien shall be given notice of intent to terminate, with the reasons therefor, at least 30 days prior to the interview specified in paragraph (a) of this section before an asylum officer. The alien shall be provided the opportunity to present evidence showing that he or she is still eligible for asylum or withholding of deportation or removal. If the asylum officer determines that the alien is no longer eligible for asylum or withholding of deportation or removal, the alien shall be given written notice that asylum status or withholding of deportation or removal and any employment authorization issued pursuant thereto, are terminated.

(d) Termination of derivative status. The termination of asylum status for a person who was the principal applicant shall result in termination of the asylum status of a spouse or child whose status was based on the asylum application of the principal. Such termination shall not preclude the spouse or child of such alien from separately asserting an asylum or withholding of deportation or removal claim.

(e) Removal proceedings. When an alien's asylum status or withholding of removal or deportation is terminated under this section, the Service shall initiate removal proceedings, as appropriate, if the alien is not already in exclusion, deportation, or removal proceedings. Removal proceedings may take place in conjunction with a termination hearing scheduled under § 208.24(f).

(f) Termination of asylum, or withholding of deportation or removal, by an immigration judge or the Board of Immigration Appeals. An immigration judge or the Board of Immigration Appeals may reopen a case pursuant to 8 CFR 1003.2 and 8 CFR 1003.23 for the purpose of terminating a grant of asylum, or a withholding of deportation or removal. In such a reopened proceeding, the Service must establish, by a preponderance of evidence, one or more of the grounds set forth in paragraphs (a) or (b) of this section. In addition, an immigration judge may terminate a grant of asylum, or a withholding of deportation or removal, made under the jurisdiction of the Service at any time after the alien has been provided a notice of intent to terminate by the Service. Any termination under this paragraph may occur in conjunction with an exclusion, deportation, or removal proceeding.

(g) Termination of asylum for arriving aliens. If the Service determines that an applicant for admission who had previously been granted asylum in the United States falls within conditions set forth in § 208.24 and is inadmissible, the Service shall issue a notice of intent to terminate asylum and initiate removal proceedings under section 240 of the Act. The alien shall present his or her response to the intent to terminate during proceedings before the immigration judge.

[64 FR 8490, Feb. 19, 1999; 65 FR 76136, Dec. 6, 2000; 76 FR 53784, Aug. 29, 2011; 78 FR 22771, April 17, 2013.]

§§ 208.25–29 [Reserved.] [also 8 C.F.R. § 1208.25–29]

SUBPART B—CREDIBLE FEAR OF PERSECUTION

§ 208.30 Credible fear determinations involving stowaways and applicants for admission who are found inadmissible pursuant to section 212(a)(6)(C) or 212(a)(7) of the Act, whose entry is limited or suspended under section 212(f) or 215(a)(1) of the Act, or who failed to apply for protection from persecution in a third country where potential relief is available while en route to the United States. [also 8 C.F.R. § 1208.30, which has similar details and cross-references to part 1208]

(a) Jurisdiction. The provisions of this subpart B apply to aliens subject to sections 235(a)(2) and 235(b)(1) of the Act. Pursuant to section 235(b)(1)(B) of the Act, DHS has exclusive jurisdiction to make credible fear determinations, and the Executive Office for Immigration Review has exclusive jurisdiction to review such determinations. Except as otherwise provided in this subpart B, paragraphs (b) through (g) of this section are the exclusive procedures applicable to credible fear interviews, determinations, and reviews under section 235(b)(1)(B) of the Act. Prior to January 1, 2015, an alien present in or arriving in the Commonwealth of the Northern Mariana Islands is ineligible to apply for asylum and may only establish eligibility for withholding of removal pursuant to section 241(b)(3) of the Act or withholding or deferral of removal under the Convention Against Torture.

(b) Treatment of dependents. A spouse or child of an alien may be included in that alien's credible fear evaluation and determination, if such spouse or child:

(1) Arrived in the United States concurrently with the principal alien; and

(2) Desires to be included in the principal alien's determination. However, any alien may have his or her credible fear evaluation and determination made separately, if he or she expresses such a desire.

(c) Authority. Asylum officers conducting credible fear interviews shall have the authorities described in § 208.9(c).

(d) Interview. The asylum officer, as defined in section 235(b)(1)(E) of the Act, will conduct the interview in a nonadversarial manner, separate and apart from the general public. The purpose of the interview shall be to elicit all relevant and useful information bearing on whether the applicant has a credible fear of persecution or torture, and shall conduct the interview as follows:

(1) If the officer conducting the credible fear interview determines that the alien is unable to participate effectively in the interview because of illness, fatigue, or other impediments, the officer may reschedule the interview.

(2) At the time of the interview, the asylum officer shall verify that the alien has received Form M–444, Information about Credible Fear Interview in Expedited Removal Cases. The officer shall also determine that the alien has an understanding of the credible fear determination process.

(3) The alien may be required to register his or her identity.

(4) The alien may consult with a person or persons of the alien's choosing prior to the interview or any review thereof, and may present other evidence, if available. Such consultation shall be at no expense to the Government and shall not unreasonably delay the process. Any person or persons with whom the alien chooses to consult may be present at the interview and may be permitted, in the discretion of the asylum officer, to present a statement at the end of the interview. The asylum officer, in his or her discretion, may place reasonable limits on the number of persons who may be present at the interview and on the length of the statement.

(5) If the alien is unable to proceed effectively in English, and if the asylum officer is unable to proceed competently in a language chosen by the alien, the asylum officer shall arrange for the assistance of an interpreter in conducting the interview. The interpreter must be at least 18 years of age and may not be the applicant's attorney or representative of record, a witness testifying on the applicant's behalf, a representative or employee of the applicant's country of nationality, or, if the applicant is stateless, the applicant's country of last habitual residence.

(6) The asylum officer shall create a summary of the material facts as stated by the applicant. At the conclusion of the interview, the officer shall review the summary with the alien and provide the alien with an opportunity to correct any errors therein.

(e) Determination.

(1) The asylum officer shall create a written record of his or her determination, including a summary of the material facts as stated by the applicant, any additional facts relied on by the officer, and the officer's determination of whether, in light of such facts, the alien has established a credible fear of persecution or torture.

(2) Subject to paragraph (e)(5) of this section, an alien will be found to have a credible fear of persecution if there is a significant possibility, taking into account the credibility of the statements made by the alien in support of the alien's claim and such other facts as are known to the officer, the alien can establish eligibility for asylum under section 208 of the Act or for withholding of removal under section 241(b)(3) of the Act. However, prior to January 1, 2015, in the case of an alien physically present in or arriving in the Commonwealth of the Northern Mariana Islands, the officer may only find a credible fear of persecution if there is a significant possibility that the alien can establish eligibility for withholding of removal pursuant to section 241(b)(3) of the Act.

(3) Subject to paragraph (e)(5) of this section, an alien will be found to have a credible fear of torture if the alien shows that there is a significant possibility that he or she is eligible for withholding of removal or deferral of removal under the Convention Against Torture, pursuant to § 208.16 or § 208.17.

(4) In determining whether the alien has a credible fear of persecution, as defined in section 235(b)(1)(B)(v) of the Act, or a credible fear of torture, the asylum officer shall consider whether the alien's case presents novel or unique issues that merit consideration in a full hearing before an immigration judge.

(5)(i) Except as provided in this paragraph (e)(5)(i) or paragraph (e)(6) of this section, if an alien is able to establish a credible fear of persecution but appears to be subject to one or more of the mandatory bars to applying for, or being granted, asylum contained in section 208(a)(2) and 208(b)(2) of the Act, or to withholding of removal contained in section 241(b)(3)(B) of the Act, the Department of Homeland Security shall nonetheless place the alien in proceedings under section 240 of the Act for full consideration of the alien's claim, if the alien is not a stowaway. If the alien is a stowaway, the Department shall place the alien in proceedings for consideration of the alien's claim pursuant to § 208.2(c)(3).

(ii) If the alien is found to be an alien described in § 208.13(c)(3), then the asylum officer shall enter a negative credible fear determination with respect to the alien's intention to apply for asylum. The Department shall nonetheless place the alien in proceedings under section 240 of the Act for full consideration of the alien's claim for withholding of removal under section 241(b)(3) of the Act, or for withholding or deferral of removal under the Convention Against Torture, if the alien establishes, respectively, a reasonable fear of persecution or torture. However, if an alien fails to establish, during the interview with the asylum officer, a reasonable fear of either persecution or torture, the asylum officer will provide the alien with a written notice of decision, which will be subject to immigration judge review consistent with paragraph (g) of this section, except that the immigration judge will review the reasonable fear findings under the reasonable fear standard instead of the credible fear standard described in paragraph (g) and in 8 CFR 1208.30(g).

(iii) If the alien is found to be an alien described as ineligible for asylum in § 208.13(c)(4), then the asylum officer shall enter a negative credible fear determination with respect to the alien's application for asylum. The Department shall nonetheless place the alien in proceedings under section 240 of the Act for consideration of the alien's claim for withholding of removal under section 241(b)(3) of the Act, or for withholding or deferral of removal under the Convention Against Torture, if the alien establishes, respectively, a reasonable fear of persecution or torture. The scope of review shall be limited to a determination of whether the alien is eligible for withholding or deferral of removal, accordingly. However, if an alien fails to establish, during the interview with the asylum officer, a reasonable fear of either persecution or torture, the asylum officer will provide the alien with a written notice of decision, which will be subject to immigration judge review consistent with paragraph (g) of this section, except that the immigration judge will review the reasonable fear findings under the reasonable fear standard instead of the credible fear standard described in paragraph (g) and in 8 CFR 1208.30(g).

(6) Prior to any determination concerning whether an alien arriving in the United States at a U.S.-Canada land border port-of-entry

or in transit through the U.S. during removal by Canada has a credible fear of persecution or torture, the asylum officer shall conduct a threshold screening interview to determine whether such an alien is ineligible to apply for asylum pursuant to section 208(a)(2)(A) of the Act and subject to removal to Canada by operation of the Agreement Between the Government of the United States and the Government of Canada For Cooperation in the Examination of Refugee Status Claims from Nationals of Third Countries ("Agreement"). In conducting this threshold screening interview, the asylum officer shall apply all relevant interview procedures outlined in paragraph (d) of this section, provided, however, that paragraph (d)(2) of this section shall not apply to aliens described in this paragraph. The asylum officer shall advise the alien of the Agreement's exceptions and question the alien as to applicability of any of these exceptions to the alien's case.

(i) If the asylum officer, with concurrence from a supervisory asylum officer, determines that an alien does not qualify for an exception under the Agreement during this threshold screening interview, the alien is ineligible to apply for asylum in the United States. After the asylum officer's documented finding is reviewed by a supervisory asylum officer, the alien shall be advised that he or she will be removed to Canada in order to pursue his or her claims relating to a fear of persecution or torture under Canadian law. Aliens found ineligible to apply for asylum under this paragraph shall be removed to Canada.

(ii) If the alien establishes by a preponderance of the evidence that he or she qualifies for an exception under the terms of the Agreement, the asylum officer shall make a written notation of the basis of the exception, and then proceed immediately to a determination concerning whether the alien has a credible fear of persecution or torture under paragraph (d) of this section.

(iii) An alien qualifies for an exception to the Agreement if the alien is not being removed from Canada in transit through the United States and

(A) Is a citizen of Canada or, not having a country of nationality, is a habitual resident of Canada;

(B) Has in the United States a spouse, son, daughter, parent, legal guardian, sibling, grandparent, grandchild, aunt, uncle, niece, or nephew who has been granted asylum, refugee, or other lawful status in the United States, provided, however, that this exception shall not apply to an alien whose relative maintains only nonimmigrant visitor status, as defined in section 101(a)(15)(B) of the Act, or whose relative maintains only visitor status based on admission to the United States pursuant to the Visa Waiver Program;

(C) Has in the United States a spouse, son, daughter, parent, legal guardian, sibling, grandparent, grandchild, aunt, uncle, niece, or nephew who is at least 18 years of age and has an asylum application pending before U.S. Citizenship and Immigration Services, the Executive Office for Immigration Review, or on appeal in federal court in the United States;

(D) Is unmarried, under 18 years of age, and does not have a parent or legal guardian in either Canada or the United States;

(E) Arrived in the United States with a validly issued visa or other valid admission document, other than for transit, issued by the United States to the alien, or, being required to hold a visa to enter Canada, was not required to obtain a visa to enter the United States; or

(F) The Director of USCIS, or the Director's designee, determines, in the exercise of unreviewable discretion, that it is in the public interest to allow the alien to pursue a claim for asylum, withholding of removal, or protection under the Convention Against Torture, in the United States.

(iv) As used in 8 CFR 208.30(e)(6)(iii)(B), (C) and (D) only, "legal guardian" means a person currently vested with legal custody of such an alien or vested with legal authority to act on the alien's behalf, provided that such an alien is both unmarried and less than 18 years of age, and provided further that any dispute with respect to whether an individual is a legal guardian will be resolved on the basis of U.S. law.

(7) When an immigration officer has made an initial determination that an alien, other than an alien described in paragraph (e)(6) of this section and regardless of whether the alien is arriving at a port of entry, appears to be subject to the terms of an agreement authorized by section 208(a)(2)(A) of the Act, and seeks the alien's removal consistent with this provision, prior to any determination concerning whether the alien has a credible fear of persecution or torture, the asylum officer shall conduct a threshold screening interview to determine whether the alien is ineligible to apply for asylum in the United States and is subject to removal to a country ("receiving country") that is a signatory to the applicable agreement authorized by section 208(a)(2)(A) of the Act, other than the U.S.-Canada Agreement effectuated in 2004. In conducting this threshold screening interview, the asylum officer shall apply all relevant interview procedures outlined in paragraph (d) of this section, except that paragraphs (d)(2) and (4) of this section shall not apply to aliens described in this paragraph (e)(7). The asylum officer shall advise the alien of the applicable agreement's exceptions and question the alien as to applicability of any of these exceptions to the alien's case. The alien shall be provided written notice that if he or she fears removal to the prospective receiving country because of the likelihood of persecution on account of a protected ground or torture in that country and wants the officer to determine whether it is more likely than not that the alien would be persecuted on account of a protected ground or tortured in that country, the alien should affirmatively state to the officer such a fear of removal. If the alien affirmatively states such a fear, the asylum officer will determine whether the individual has demonstrated that it is more likely than not that he or she would be persecuted on account of a protected ground or tortured in that country.

(i)(A) If the asylum officer, with concurrence from a supervisory asylum officer, determines during the threshold screening interview that an alien does not qualify for an exception under the applicable agreement, and, if applicable, that the alien has not demonstrated that it is more likely than not that he or she would be persecuted on account of a protected ground or tortured in the receiving country, the alien is ineligible to apply for asylum in the United States. Subject to paragraph (e)(7)(i)(B) of this section, after the asylum officer's documented finding is reviewed by a supervisory asylum officer, the alien shall be advised that he or she will be removed to the receiving country, as appropriate under the applicable agreement, in order to pursue his or her claims relating to a fear of persecution or torture under the law of the receiving country. Prior to removal to a receiving country under an agreement authorized by section 208(a)(2)(A), the alien shall be informed that, in the receiving country, the alien will have an opportunity to pursue the alien's claim for asylum or equivalent temporary protection.

(B) Aliens found ineligible to apply for asylum under this paragraph (e)(7) shall be removed to the receiving country, depending on the applicable agreement, unless the alien voluntarily withdraws his or her request for asylum.

(ii) If the alien establishes by a preponderance of the evidence that he or she qualifies for an exception under the terms of the applicable agreement, or would more likely than not be persecuted on account of a protected ground delineated in section 208(a)(2)(A) of the Act or tortured in the receiving country, the asylum officer shall make a written notation to that effect, and may then proceed to determine whether any other agreement is applicable to the alien under the procedures set forth in this paragraph (e)(7). If the alien establishes by a preponderance of the evidence that he or she qualifies for an exception under the terms of each of the applicable agreements, or would more likely than not be persecuted on account of a protected ground or tortured in each of the prospective receiving countries, the asylum officer shall make a written notation to that effect, and then proceed immediately to a determination concerning whether the alien has a credible fear of persecution or torture under paragraph (d) of this section.

(iii) An exception to an applicable agreement is defined under the terms of the agreement itself. Each agreement, including any exceptions, will be announced in a Federal Register document. If the asylum officer determines that an alien is within one of the classes covered by a section 208(a)(2)(A) agreement, the officer shall next determine whether the alien meets any of the applicable agreement's exceptions. Regardless of whether the text of the applicable agreement provides for the following exceptions, all such agreements, by operation of section 208(a)(2)(A) of the Act, and as applicable to the United States, are deemed to contain the following provisions:

(A) No alien may be removed, pursuant to an agreement authorized by section 208(a)(2)(A), to the alien's country of nationality, or, if the alien has no nationality, to the alien's country of last habitual residence; and

(B) No alien may be removed, pursuant to an agreement authorized by section 208(a)(2)(A), where the Director of USCIS, or the Director's designee, determines, in the exercise of unreviewable discretion, that it is in the public interest for the alien to receive asylum in the United States, and that the alien therefore may apply for asylum, withholding of removal, or protection under the Convention Against Torture, in the United States.

(iv) If the asylum officer determines the alien meets an exception under the applicable agreement, or would more likely than not be persecuted on account of a protected ground or tortured in the prospective receiving country, the officer may consider whether the alien is subject to another agreement and its exceptions or would more likely than not be persecuted on account of a protected ground or tortured in another receiving country. If another section 208(a)(2)(A) agreement may not be applied to the alien, the officer should immediately proceed to a credible fear interview.

(8) An asylum officer's determination shall not become final until reviewed by a supervisory asylum officer.

(f) Procedures for a positive credible fear finding. If an alien, other than an alien stowaway, is found to have a credible fear of persecution or torture, the asylum officer will so inform the alien and issue a Form I–862, Notice to Appear, for full consideration of the asylum and withholding of removal claim in proceedings under section 240 of the Act. If an alien stowaway is found to have a credible fear of persecution or torture, the asylum officer will so inform the alien and issue a Form I–863, Notice of Referral to Immigration Judge, for full consideration of the asylum claim, or the withholding of removal claim, in proceedings under § 208.2(c). Parole of the alien may be considered only in accordance with section 212(d)(5) of the Act and § 212.5 of this chapter.

(g) Procedures for a negative credible fear finding.

(1) If an alien is found not to have a credible fear of persecution or torture, the asylum officer shall provide the alien with a written notice of decision and inquire whether the alien wishes to have an immigration judge review the negative decision, using Form I–869, Record of Negative Credible Fear Finding and Request for Review by Immigration Judge. The alien shall indicate whether he or she desires such review on Form I–869. A refusal by the alien to make such indication shall be considered a request for review.

(i) If the alien requests such review, or refuses to either request or decline such review, the asylum officer shall arrange for detention of the alien and serve him or her with a Form I–863, Notice of Referral to Immigration Judge, for review of the credible fear determination in accordance with paragraph (f)(2) of this section.

(ii) If the alien is not a stowaway and does not request a review by an immigration judge, the officer shall order the alien removed and issue a Form I–860, Notice and Order of Expedited Removal, after review by a supervisory asylum officer.

(iii) If the alien is a stowaway and the alien does not request a review by an immigration judge, the asylum officer shall refer the alien to the district director for completion of removal proceedings in accordance with section 235(a)(2) of the Act.

(2) Review by immigration judge of a negative credible fear finding.

(i) Immigration judges will review negative credible fear findings as provided in 8 CFR 1208.30(g)(2).

(ii) The record of the negative credible fear determination, including copies of the Form I–863, the asylum officer's notes, the summary of the material facts, and other materials upon which the determination was based shall be provided to the immigration judge with the negative determination.

[64 FR 8492, Feb. 19, 1999; 65 FR 76136, Dec. 6, 2000; 69 FR 69488, Nov. 29, 2004; 74 FR 55737, Oct. 28, 2009; 76 FR 53784, Aug. 29, 2011; 83 FR 55952, Nov. 9, 2018; 84 FR 33843, July 16, 2019; 84 FR 64008, Nov. 19, 2019.]

§ 208.31 Reasonable fear of persecution or torture determinations involving aliens ordered removed under section 238(b) of the Act and aliens whose removal is reinstated under section 241(a)(5) of the Act. [also 8 C.F.R. § 1208.31, which has minor wording changes and cross-references to part 1208]

(a) Jurisdiction. This section shall apply to any alien ordered removed under section 238(b) of the Act or whose deportation, exclusion, or removal order is reinstated under section 241(a)(5) of the Act who, in the course of the administrative removal or reinstatement process, expresses a fear of returning to the country of removal. USCIS has exclusive jurisdiction to make reasonable fear determinations, and EOIR has exclusive jurisdiction to review such determinations.

(b) Initiation of reasonable fear determination process. Upon issuance of a Final Administrative Removal Order under § 238.1 of this chapter, or notice under § 241.8(b) of this chapter that an alien is subject to removal, an alien described in paragraph (a) of this section shall be referred to an asylum officer for a reasonable fear determination. In the absence of exceptional circumstances, this determination will be conducted within 10 days of the referral.

(c) Interview and Procedure. The asylum officer shall conduct the interview in a non-adversarial manner, separate and apart from the general public. At the time of the interview, the asylum officer shall determine that the alien has an understanding of the reasonable fear determination process. The alien may be represented by counsel or an accredited representative at the interview, at no expense to the Government, and may present evidence, if available, relevant to the possibility of persecution or torture. The alien's representative may present a statement at the end of the interview. The asylum officer, in his or her discretion, may place reasonable limits on the number of persons who may be present at the interview and the length of the statement. If the alien is unable to proceed effectively in English, and if the asylum officer is unable to proceed competently in a language chosen by the alien, the asylum officer shall arrange for the assistance of an interpreter in conducting the interview. The interpreter may not be a representative or employee of the applicant's country or [sic] nationality, or if the applicant is stateless, the applicant's country of last habitual residence. The asylum officer shall create a summary of the material facts as stated by the applicant. At the conclusion of the interview, the officer shall review the summary with the alien and provide the alien with an opportunity to correct errors therein. The asylum officer shall create a written record of his or her determination, including a summary of the material facts as stated by the applicant, any additional facts relied on by the officers, and the officer's determination of whether, in light of such facts, the alien has established a reasonable fear of persecution or torture. The alien shall be determined to have a reasonable fear of persecution or torture if the alien establishes a reasonable possibility that he or she would be persecuted on account of his or her race, religion, nationality, membership in a particular social group or political opinion, or a reasonable possibility that he or she would be tortured in the country of removal. For purposes of the screening determination, the bars to eligibility for withholding of removal under section 241(b)(3)(B) of the Act shall not be considered.

(d) Authority. Asylum officers conducting screening determinations under this section shall have the authority described in § 208.9(c).

(e) Referral to Immigration Judge. If an asylum officer determines that an alien described in this section has a reasonable fear of persecution or torture, the officer shall so inform the alien and issue a Form I–863,

Notice of Referral to the Immigration Judge, for full consideration of the request for withholding of removal only. Such cases shall be adjudicated by the immigration judge in accordance with the provisions of § 208.16. Appeal of the immigration judge's decision shall lie to the Board of Immigration Appeals.

(f) Removal of aliens with no reasonable fear of persecution or torture. If the asylum officer determines that the alien has not established a reasonable fear of persecution or torture, the asylum officer shall inform the alien in writing of the decision and shall inquire whether the alien wishes to have an immigration judge review the negative decision, using Form I–898, Record of Negative Reasonable Fear Finding and Request for Review by Immigration Judge, on which the alien shall indicate whether he or she desires such review.

(g) Review by immigration judge. The asylum officer's negative decision regarding reasonable fear shall be subject to review by an immigration judge upon the alien's request. If the alien requests such review, the asylum officer shall serve him or her with a Form I–863. The record of determination, including copies of the Form I–863, the asylum officer's notes, the summary of the material facts, and other materials upon which the determination was based shall be provided to the immigration judge with the negative determination. In the absence of exceptional circumstances, such review shall be conducted by the immigration judge within 10 days of the filing of the Form I–863 with the immigration court. Upon review of the asylum officer's negative reasonable fear determination:

(1) If the immigration judge concurs with the asylum officer's determination that the alien does not have a reasonable fear of persecution or torture, the case shall be returned to the Service for removal of the alien. No appeal shall lie from the immigration judge's decision.

(2) If the immigration judge finds that the alien has a reasonable fear of persecution or torture, the alien may submit Form I–589, Application for Asylum and Withholding of Removal.

(i) The immigration judge shall consider only the alien's application for withholding of removal under § 208.16 and shall determine whether the alien's removal to the country of removal must be withheld or deferred.

(ii) Appeal of the immigration judge's decision whether removal must be withheld or deferred lies to the Board of Immigration Appeals. If the alien or the Service appeals the immigration judge's decision, the Board shall review only the immigration judge's decision regarding the alien's eligibility for withholding or deferral of removal under § 208.16.

[64 FR 8493, Feb. 19, 1999; 64 FR 13881, March 23, 1999; 76 FR 53784, Aug. 29, 2011.]

PART 1003—EXECUTIVE OFFICE FOR IMMIGRATION REVIEW

SUBPART C—IMMIGRATION COURT—RULES OF PROCEDURE

§ 1003.42   Review of credible fear determination. [subsection (h)]

(h) Asylum cooperative agreement—

(1) Arriving alien. An asylum judge has no jurisdiction to review a determination by an immigration officer that an arriving alien is not eligible to apply for asylum pursuant to the 2002 U.S.-Canada Agreement formed under section 208(a)(2)(A) of the Act and should be returned to Canada to pursue his or her claims for asylum or other protection under the laws of Canada. See 8 CFR 208.30(e)(6). However, in any case where an asylum officer has found that an arriving alien qualifies for an exception to that Agreement, an immigration judge does have jurisdiction to review a negative credible fear finding made thereafter by the asylum officer as provided in this section.

(2) Aliens in transit. An immigration judge has no jurisdiction to review any determination by DHS that an alien being removed from Canada in transit through the United States should be returned to Canada to pursue asylum claims under Canadian law, under the terms of the 2002 U.S.-Canada Agreement.

(3) Applicants for admission. An immigration judge has no jurisdiction to review a determination by an asylum officer that an alien is not eligible to apply for asylum pursuant to a bilateral or multilateral agreement with a third country under section 208(a)(2)(A) of the Act and should be removed to the third country to pursue his or her claims for asylum or other protection under the laws of that country. See 8 CFR 208.30(e)(7). However, if the asylum officer has determined that the alien may not or should not be removed to a third country under section 208(a)(2)(A) of the Act and subsequently makes a negative credible fear determination, an immigration judge has jurisdiction to review the negative credible fear finding as provided in this section.

(4) Aliens in transit through the United States from countries other than Canada. An immigration judge has no jurisdiction to review any determination by DHS that an alien being removed from a receiving country in transit through the United States should be returned to pursue asylum claims under the receiving country's law, under the terms of the applicable cooperative agreement. See 8 CFR 208.30(e)(7).

[62 FR 10335, Mar. 6, 1997, as amended at 64 FR 8487, Feb. 19, 1999; 69 FR 69496, Nov. 29, 2004; 83 FR 55952, Nov. 9, 2018; 84 FR 33844, July 16, 2019; 84 FR 64009, Nov. 19, 2019]

PART 1208—PROCEDURES FOR ASYLUM AND WITHHOLDING OF REMOVAL

SUBPART A—ASYLUM AND WITHHOLDING OF REMOVAL

§ 1208.4 Filing the application. [subsection (a)(6)]

(a) (6) Asylum cooperative agreements. Immigration judges have authority to consider issues under section 208(a)(2)(A) of the Act, relating to the determination of whether an alien is ineligible to apply for asylum and should be removed to a third country pursuant to a bilateral or multilateral agreement, only with respect to aliens whom DHS has chosen to place in removal proceedings under section 240 of the Act, as provided in 8 CFR 1240.11(g) and (h). For DHS regulations relating to determinations by immigration officers on this subject, see 8 CFR 208.30(e)(6) and (7).

[62 FR 10337, Mar. 6, 1997, as amended at 64 FR 8488, Feb. 19, 1999; 64 FR 13881, Mar. 23, 1999; 65 FR 76131, Dec. 6, 2000; 69 FR 69497, Nov. 29, 2004; 70 FR 4754, Jan. 31, 2005; 74 FR 55741, Oct. 28, 2009; 84 FR 64010, Nov. 19, 2019]

PART 1240—PROCEEDINGS TO DETERMINE REMOVABILITY OF ALIENS IN THE UNITED STATES

SUBPART A REMOVAL PROCEEDINGS

§ 1240.11   Ancillary matters, applications. [subsections (g) and (h)]

(g) U.S.-Canada safe third country agreement.

(1) The immigration judge has authority to apply section 208(a)(2)(A) of the Act, relating to a determination that an alien may be removed to Canada pursuant to the 2002 Agreement Between the Government of the United States of America and the Government of Canada For Cooperation in the Examination of Refugee Status Claims from Nationals of Third Countries ("Agreement"), in the case of an alien who is subject to the terms of the Agreement and is placed in proceedings pursuant to section 240 of the Act. In an appropriate case, the immigration judge shall determine whether under that Agreement the alien should be returned to Canada, or whether the alien should be permitted to pursue asylum or other protection claims in the United States.

* * *

(4) An alien who is found to be ineligible to apply for asylum under section 208(a)(2)(A) of the Act is ineligible to apply for withholding of removal pursuant to section 241(b)(3) of the Act and the Convention against Torture. However, the alien may apply for any other relief from removal for which the alien may be eligible. If an alien who is subject to the Agreement and section 208(a)(2)(A) of the Act is ordered removed, the alien shall be ordered removed to Canada, in which the alien will be able to pursue his or her claims for asylum or protection against persecution or torture under the laws of Canada.

(h) Other asylum cooperative agreements.

(1) The immigration judge has authority to apply section 208(a)(2)(A) of the Act, relating to a determination that an alien may be removed to a third country pursuant to a bilateral or multilateral agreement—other than the 2002 U.S.-Canada Agreement—in the case of an alien who is subject to the terms of the relevant agreement and is placed in proceedings pursuant to section 240 of the Act. In an appropriate case, the immigration judge shall determine whether under the relevant agreement the alien should be removed to the third country, or whether the alien should be permitted to pursue asylum or other protection claims in the United States. If more than one agreement applies to the alien and the alien is ordered removed, the immigration judge shall enter alternate orders of removal to each relevant country.

(2) An alien described in paragraph (h)(1) of this section is ineligible to apply for asylum pursuant to section 208(a)(2)(A) of the Act, or for withholding of removal or CAT protection in the United States, unless the immigration judge determines, by a preponderance of the evidence, that:

(i) The relevant agreement does not apply to the alien or does not preclude the alien from applying for asylum in the United States;

(ii) The alien qualifies for an exception to the relevant agreement as set forth in paragraph (h)(3) of this section and the Federal Register document specifying the exceptions particular to the relevant agreement; or

(iii) The alien has demonstrated that it is more likely than not that he or she would be persecuted on account of a protected ground or tortured in the third country.

(3) The immigration judge shall apply the applicable regulations in deciding whether an alien described in paragraph (h)(1) of this section qualifies for an exception under the relevant agreement that would permit the United States to exercise authority over the alien's asylum claim. The exceptions for agreements with countries other than Canada are further explained by the applicable published Federal Register document setting out each Agreement and its exceptions. The immigration judge shall not review, consider, or decide any issues pertaining to any discretionary determination on whether an alien described in paragraph (h)(1) of this section should be allowed to pursue an application for asylum in the United States notwithstanding the general terms of an agreement, as section 208(a)(2)(A) of the Act reserves to the Secretary or his delegates the determination whether it is in the public interest for the alien to receive asylum in the United States. However, an alien in removal proceedings who is otherwise ineligible to apply for asylum under an agreement may apply for asylum if DHS files a written notice in the proceedings before the immigration judge that DHS has decided in the public interest that the alien may pursue an application for asylum or withholding of removal in the United States.

(4) If the immigration judge determines that an alien described in paragraph (h)(1) of this section is subject to the terms of agreements formed pursuant to section 208(a)(2)(A) of the Act, and that the alien has failed to demonstrate that it is more likely than not that the alien would be persecuted on account of a protected ground or tortured in those third countries, then the alien is ineligible to apply for withholding of removal pursuant to section 241(b)(3) of the Act and the Convention Against Torture notwithstanding any other provision in this chapter. However, the alien may apply for any other relief from removal for which the alien may be eligible. If an alien who is subject to section 208(a)(2)(A) of the Act is ordered removed, the alien shall be ordered removed to the relevant third country in which the alien will be able to pursue his or her claims for asylum or protection against persecution or torture under the laws of that country.

[62 FR 10367, Mar. 6, 1997, as amended at 62 FR 45150, Aug. 26, 1997; 63 FR 27829, May 21, 1998; 64 FR 25766, May 12, 1999; 69 FR 69497, Nov. 29, 2004; 71 FR 35757, June 21, 2006; 73 FR 76937, Dec. 18, 2008; 78 FR 19080, Mar. 29, 2013; 84 FR 64010, Nov. 19, 2019]

PART 212—DOCUMENTARY REQUIREMENTS: NONIMMIGRANTS; WAIVERS; ADMISSION OF CERTAIN INADMISSIBLE ALIENS; PAROLE

§ 212.21 Definitions.

For the purposes of 8 CFR 212.20 through 212.23, the following definitions apply:

(a) Public Charge. Public charge means an alien who receives one or more public benefits, as defined in paragraph (b) of this section, for more than 12 months in the aggregate within any 36-month period (such that, for instance, receipt of two benefits in one month counts as two months).

(b) Public benefit. Public benefit means:

(1) Any Federal, State, local, or tribal cash assistance for income maintenance (other than tax credits), including:

(i) Supplemental Security Income (SSI), 42 U.S.C. 1381 et seq.;

(ii) Temporary Assistance for Needy Families (TANF), 42 U.S.C. 601 et seq.; or

(iii) Federal, State or local cash benefit programs for income maintenance (often called "General Assistance" in the State context, but which also exist under other names); and

(2) Supplemental Nutrition Assistance Program (SNAP), 7 U.S.C. 2011 to 2036c;

(3) Section 8 Housing Assistance under the Housing Choice Voucher Program, as administered by HUD under 42 U.S.C. 1437f;

(4) Section 8 Project-Based Rental Assistance (including Moderate Rehabilitation) under Section 8 of the U.S. Housing Act of 1937 (42 U.S.C. 1437f);

(5) Medicaid under 42 U.S.C. 1396 et seq., except for:

(i) Benefits received for an emergency medical condition as described in 42 U.S.C. 1396b(v)(2)–(3), 42 CFR 440.255(c);

(ii) Services or benefits funded by Medicaid but provided under the Individuals with Disabilities Education Act (IDEA) 20 U.S.C. 1400 et seq.;

(iii) School-based services or benefits provided to individuals who are at or below the oldest age eligible for secondary education as determined under State or local law; and

(iv) Benefits received by an alien under 21 years of age, or a woman during pregnancy (and during the 60-day period beginning on the last day of the pregnancy);

(6) Public Housing under section 9 of the U.S. Housing Act of 1937.

(7) Public benefits, as defined in paragraphs (b)(1) through (b)(6) of this section, do not include any public benefits received by—

(i) An alien who at the time of receipt of the public benefit, or at the time of filing or adjudication of the application for admission or adjustment of status, or application or request for extension of stay or change of status is—

(A) Enlisted in the U.S. Armed Forces under the authority of 10 U.S.C. 504(b)(1)(B) or 10 U.S.C. 504(b)(2), or

(B) Serving in active duty or in the Ready Reserve component of the U.S. Armed Forces, or

(ii) The spouse or child, as defined in section 101(b) of the Act, of an individual who at the time of receipt of the public benefit by such spouse or child, or at the time of filing or adjudication of the spouse's or child's application for admission or adjustment of status, or application or request for extension of stay or change of status, had been:

(A) Enlisted in the U.S. Armed Forces under the authority of 10 U.S.C. 504(b)(1)(B) or 10 U.S.C. 504(b)(2), or

(B) Serving in active duty or in the Ready Reserve component of the U.S. Armed Forces.

(8) In a subsequent adjudication for a benefit for which the public charge ground of inadmissibility applies, public benefits, as defined in paragraph (b) of this section, do not include any public benefits received by an alien during periods in which the alien was present in the United States in an immigration category that is exempt from the public charge ground of inadmissibility, as set forth in 8 CFR 212.23(a), or for which the alien received a waiver of public charge inadmissibility, as set forth in 8 CFR 212.23(b).

(9) Public benefits, as defined in paragraph (b) of this section, do not include any public benefits that were or will be received by—

(i) Children of U.S. citizens whose lawful admission for permanent residence and subsequent residence in the legal and physical custody of their U.S. citizen parent will result automatically in the child's acquisition of citizenship, upon meeting the eligibility criteria of section 320(a)–(b) of the Act, in accordance with 8 CFR part 320; or

(ii) Children of U.S. citizens whose lawful admission for permanent residence will result automatically in the child's acquisition of citizenship upon finalization of adoption (if the child satisfies the requirements applicable to adopted children under INA 101(b)(1)), in the United States by the U.S. citizen parent(s), upon meeting the eligibility criteria of section 320(a)–(b) of the Act, in accordance with 8 CFR part 320; or

(iii) Children of U.S. citizens who are entering the United States for the purpose of attending an interview under section 322 of the Act in accordance with 8 CFR part 322.

(c) Likely at any time to become a public charge. Likely at any time to become a public charge means more likely than not at any time in the future to become a public charge, as defined in 212.21(a), based on the totality of the alien's circumstances.

(d) Alien's household. For purposes of public charge inadmissibility determinations under section 212(a)(4) of the Act:

(1) If the alien is 21 years of age or older, or under the age of 21 and married, the alien's household includes:

(i) The alien;

(ii) The alien's spouse, if physically residing with the alien;

(iii) The alien's children, as defined in section 101(b)(1) of the Act, physically residing with the alien;

(iv) The alien's other children, as defined in section 101(b)(1) of the Act, not physically residing with the alien, for whom the alien provides or is required to provide at least 50 percent of financial support, as evidenced by a child support order or agreement, a custody order or agreement, or any other order or agreement specifying the amount of financial support to be provided by the alien;

(v) Any other individuals (including a spouse not physically residing with the alien) to whom the alien provides, or is required to provide, at least 50 percent of the individual's financial support or who are listed as dependents on the alien's federal income tax return; and

(vi) Any individual who provides to the alien at least 50 percent of the alien's financial support, or who lists the alien as a dependent on his or her federal income tax return.

(2) If the alien is a child as defined in section 101(b)(1) of the Act, the alien's household includes the following individuals:

(i) The alien;

(ii) The alien's children as defined in section 101(b)(1) of the Act physically residing with the alien;

(iii) The alien's other children as defined in section 101(b)(1) of the Act not physically residing with the alien for whom the alien provides or is required to provide at least 50 percent of the children's financial support, as evidenced by a child support order or agreement, a custody order or agreement, or any other order or agreement specifying the amount of financial support to be provided by the alien;

(iv) The alien's parents, legal guardians, or any other individual providing or required to provide at least 50 percent of the alien's

650

financial support to the alien as evidenced by a child support order or agreement, a custody order or agreement, or any other order or agreement specifying the amount of financial support to be provided to the alien;

(v) The parents' or legal guardians' other children as defined in section 101(b)(1) of the Act physically residing with the alien;

(vi) The alien's parents' or legal guardians' other children as defined in section 101(b)(1) of the Act, not physically residing with the alien for whom the parent or legal guardian provides or is required to provide at least 50 percent of the other children's financial support, as evidenced by a child support order or agreement, a custody order or agreement, or any other order or agreement specifying the amount of financial support to be provided by the parents or legal guardians; and

(vii) Any other individuals to whom the alien's parents or legal guardians provide, or are required to provide at least 50 percent of each individual's financial support, or who is listed as a dependent on the parent's or legal guardian's federal income tax return.

(e) **Receipt of public benefits.** Receipt of public benefits occurs when a public benefit-granting agency provides a public benefit, as defined in paragraph (b) of this section, to an alien as a beneficiary, whether in the form of cash, voucher, services, or insurance coverage. Applying for a public benefit does not constitute receipt of public benefits although it may suggest a likelihood of future receipt. Certification for future receipt of a public benefit does not constitute receipt of public benefits, although it may suggest a likelihood of future receipt. An alien's receipt of, application for, or certification for public benefits solely on behalf of another individual does not constitute receipt of, application for, or certification for such alien.

(f) Primary caregiver means an alien who is 18 years of age or older and has significant responsibility for actively caring for and managing the well-being of a child or an elderly, ill, or disabled person in the alien's household.

§ 212.22 Public charge inadmissibility determination.

(a) **Prospective determination based on the totality of circumstances**. The determination of an alien's likelihood of becoming a public charge at any time in the future must be based on the totality of the alien's circumstances by weighing all factors that are relevant to whether the alien is more likely than not at any time in the future to receive one or more public benefits, as defined in 8 CFR 212.21(b), for more than 12 months in the aggregate within any 36-month period (such that, for instance, receipt of two benefits in one month counts as two months). Except as necessary to fully evaluate evidence provided in paragraph (b) (4)(ii)(E)(3) of this section, DHS will not specifically assess whether an alien qualifies or would qualify for any public benefit, as defined in 8 CFR 212.21(b).

(b) Minimum factors to consider. A public charge inadmissibility determination must at least entail consideration of the alien's age; health; family status; education and skills; and assets, resources, and financial status, as follows:

(1) The alien's age—

(i) Standard. When considering an alien's age, DHS will consider whether the alien's age makes the alien more likely than not to become a public charge at any time in the future, such as by impacting the alien's ability to work, including whether the alien is between the age of 18 and the minimum "early retirement age" for Social Security set forth in 42 U.S.C. 416(l)(2).

(ii) [Reserved]

(2) The alien's health—

(i) Standard. DHS will consider whether the alien's health makes the alien more likely than not to become a public charge at any time in the future, including whether the alien has been diagnosed with a medical condition that is likely to require extensive medical treatment or institutionalization or that will interfere with the alien's ability to provide and care for himself or herself, to attend school, or to work upon admission or adjustment of status.

(ii) Evidence. USCIS' consideration includes but is not limited to the following:

(A) A report of an immigration medical examination performed by a civil surgeon or panel physician where such examination is required (to which USCIS will generally defer absent evidence that such report is incomplete); or

(B) Evidence of a medical condition that is likely to require extensive medical treatment or institutionalization or that will interfere with the alien's ability to provide and care for himself or herself, to attend school, or to work upon admission or adjustment of status.

(3) The alien's family status—

(i) Standard. When considering an alien's family status, DHS will consider the alien's household size, as defined in 8 CFR 212.21(d), and whether the alien's household size makes the alien more likely than not to become a public charge at any time in the future.

(ii) [Reserved]

(4) The alien's assets, resources, and financial status—

(i) Standard. When considering an alien's assets, resources, and financial status, DHS will consider whether such assets, resources, and financial status excluding any income from illegal activities or sources (e.g., proceeds from illegal gambling or drug sales, and income from public benefits listed in 8 CFR 212.21(b)), make the alien more likely than not to become a public charge at any time in the future, including whether:

(A) The alien's household's annual gross income is at least 125 percent of the most recent Federal Poverty Guideline (100 percent for an alien on active duty, other than training, in the U.S. Armed Forces) based on the alien's household size as defined by section 212.21(d);

(B) If the alien's household's annual gross income is less than 125 percent of the most recent Federal Poverty Guideline (100 percent for an alien on active duty, other than training, in the U.S. Armed Forces), the alien may submit evidence of ownership of significant assets. For purposes of this paragraph, an alien may establish ownership of significant assets, such as savings accounts, stocks, bonds, certificates of deposit, real estate or other assets, in which the combined cash value of all the assets (the total value of the assets less any offsetting liabilities) exceeds:

(1) If the intending immigrant is the spouse or child of a United States citizen (and the child has reached his or her 18th birthday), three times the difference between the alien's household income and 125 percent of the FPG (100 percent for those on active duty, other than training, in the U.S. Armed Forces) for the alien's household size;

(2) If the intending immigrant is an orphan who will be adopted in the United States after the alien orphan acquires permanent residence (or in whose case the parents will need to seek a formal recognition of a foreign adoption under the law of the State of the intending immigrant's proposed residence because at least one of the parents did not see the child before or during the adoption), and who will, as a result of the adoption or formal recognition of the foreign adoption, acquire citizenship under section 320 of the Act, the difference between the alien's household income and 125 percent of the FPG (100 percent for those on active duty, other than training, in the U.S. Armed Forces) for the alien's household size; or

(3) In all other cases, five times the difference between the alien's household income and 125 percent of the FPG (100 percent for those on active duty, other than training, in the U.S. Armed Forces) for the alien's household size.

(C) The alien has sufficient household assets and resources to cover any reasonably foreseeable medical costs, including as related to a medical condition that is likely to require extensive medical treatment or institutionalization or that will interfere with the alien's ability to provide care for himself or herself, to attend school, or to work;

(D) The alien has any financial liabilities; and

(E) The alien has applied for, been certified to receive, or received public benefits, as defined in 8 CFR 212.21(b), on or after October 15, 2019.

(ii) Evidence. USCIS' consideration includes, but is not limited to the following:

(A) The alien's annual gross household income including, but not limited to:

(1) For each member of the household whose income will be considered, the most recent tax-year transcript from the U.S. Internal Revenue Service (IRS) of such household member's IRS Form 1040, U.S. Individual Income Tax Return; or

(2) If the evidence in paragraph (b)(4)(ii)(A)(1) of this section is unavailable for a household member, other credible and probative evidence of such household member's income, including an explanation of why such transcript is not available, such as if the household member is not subject to taxation in the United States.

(B) Any additional income from individuals not included in the alien's household provided to the alien's household on a continuing monthly or yearly basis for the most recent calendar year and on which the alien relies or will rely to meet the standard at 8 CFR 212.22(b)(4)(i);

(C) The household's cash assets and resources. Evidence of such cash assets and resources may include checking and savings account statements covering 12 months prior to filing the application;

(D) The household's non-cash assets and resources, that can be converted into cash within 12 months, such as net cash value of real estate holdings minus the sum of all loans secured by a mortgage, trust deed, or other lien on the home; annuities; securities; retirement and educational accounts; and any other assets that can easily be converted into cash;

(E) Evidence that the alien has:

(1) Applied for or received any public benefit, as defined in 8 CFR 212.21(b), on or after October 15, 2019 or disenrolled or requested to be disenrolled from such benefit(s); or

(2) Been certified or approved to receive any public benefit, as defined in 8 CFR 212.21(b), on or after October 15, 2019 or withdrew his or her application or disenrolled or requested to be to [sic] disenrolled from such benefit(s);

(3) Submitted evidence from a Federal, State, local, or tribal agency administering a public benefit, as defined in 212.21(b), that the alien has specifically identified as showing that the alien does not qualify or would not qualify for such public benefit by virtue of, for instance, the alien's annual gross household income or prospective immigration status or length of stay;

(F) Whether the alien has applied for or has received a USCIS fee waiver for an immigration benefit request on or after October 15, 2019, unless the fee waiver was applied for or granted as part of an application for which a public charge inadmissibility determination under section 212(a)(4) of the Act was not required.

(G) The alien's credit history and credit score in the United States, and other evidence of the alien's liabilities not reflected in the credit history and credit score (e.g., any mortgages, car loans, unpaid child or spousal support, unpaid taxes, and credit card debt); and

(H) Whether the alien has sufficient household assets and resources (including, for instance, health insurance not designated as a public benefit under 8 CFR 212.21(b)) to pay for reasonably foreseeable medical costs, such as costs related to a medical condition that is likely to require extensive medical treatment or institutionalization or that will interfere with the alien's ability to provide care for himself or herself, to attend school, or to work;

(5) The alien's education and skills—

(i) Standard. When considering an alien's education and skills, DHS will consider whether the alien has adequate education and skills to either obtain or maintain lawful employment with an income sufficient to avoid being more likely than not to become a public charge.

(ii) Evidence. USCIS' consideration includes but is not limited to the following:

(A) The alien's history of employment, excluding employment involving illegal activities, e.g., illegal gambling or drug sales. The alien must provide the following:

(1) The last 3 years of the alien's tax transcripts from the U.S. Internal Revenue Service (IRS) of the alien's IRS Form 1040, U.S. Individual Income Tax Return; or

(2) If the evidence in paragraph (b)(5)(ii)(A)(1) of this section is unavailable, other credible and probative evidence of the alien's history of employment for the last 3 years, including an explanation of why such transcripts are not available, such as if the alien is not subject to taxation in the United States;

(B) Whether the alien has a high school diploma (or its equivalent) or has a higher education degree;

(C) Whether the alien has any occupational skills, certifications, or licenses;

(D) Whether the alien is proficient in English or proficient in other languages in addition to English; and

(E) Whether the alien is a primary caregiver as defined in 8 CFR 212.21(f), such that the alien lacks an employment history, is not currently employed, or is not employed full time. Only one alien within a household can be considered a primary caregiver of the same individual within the household. USCIS' consideration with respect this paragraph includes but is not limited to evidence that an individual the alien is caring for resides in the alien's household, evidence of the individual's age, and evidence of the individual's medical condition, including disability, if any.

(6) The alien's prospective immigration status and expected period of admission—

(i) Standard. DHS will consider the immigration status that the alien seeks and the expected period of admission as it relates to the alien's ability to financially support himself or herself during the duration of the alien's stay, including:

(A) Whether the alien is applying for adjustment of status or admission in a nonimmigrant or immigrant classification; and

(B) If the alien is seeking admission as a nonimmigrant, the nonimmigrant classification and the anticipated period of temporary stay.

(ii) [Reserved]

(7) An affidavit of support under section 213A of the Act, when required under section 212(a)(4) of the Act, that meets the requirements of section 213A of the Act and 8 CFR 213a—

(i) Standard. If the alien is required under sections 212(a)(4)(C) or (D) to submit an affidavit of support under section 213A of the Act and 8 CFR part 213a, and submits such a sufficient affidavit of support, DHS will consider the likelihood that the sponsor would actually provide the statutorily-required amount of financial support to the alien, and any other related considerations.

(ii) Evidence. USCIS consideration includes but is not limited to the following:

(A) The sponsor's annual income, assets, and resources;

(B) The sponsor's relationship to the applicant, including but not limited to whether the sponsor lives with the alien; and

(C) Whether the sponsor has submitted an affidavit of support with respect to other individuals.

(c) Heavily weighted factors. The factors below will weigh heavily in a public charge inadmissibility determination. The mere presence of any one heavily weighted factor does not, alone, make the alien more or less likely than not to become a public charge.

(1) Heavily weighted negative factors. The following factors will weigh heavily in favor of a finding that an alien is likely at any time in the future to become a public charge:

(i) The alien is not a full-time student and is authorized to work, but is unable to demonstrate current employment, recent employment history, or a reasonable prospect of future employment;

(ii) The alien has received or has been certified or approved to receive one or more public benefits, as defined in § 212.21(b), for more than 12 months in the aggregate within any 36-month period (such that, for instance, receipt of two benefits in one month counts as two months), beginning no earlier than 36 months prior to the alien's application for admission or adjustment of status on or after October 15, 2019;

(iii)

(A) The alien has been diagnosed with a medical condition that is likely to require extensive medical treatment or institutionalization or that will interfere with the alien's ability to provide for himself or herself, attend school, or work; and

(B) The alien is uninsured and has neither the prospect of obtaining private health insurance, nor the financial resources to pay for reasonably foreseeable medical costs related to such medical condition; or

(iv) The alien was previously found inadmissible or deportable on public charge grounds by an Immigration Judge or the Board of Immigration Appeals.

(2) Heavily weighted positive factors. The following factors will weigh heavily in favor of a finding that an alien is not likely to become a public charge:

(i) The alien's household has income, assets, or resources, and support (excluding any income from illegal activities, e.g., proceeds from illegal gambling or drug sales, and any income from public benefits as defined in § 212.21(b)) of at least 250 percent of the Federal Poverty Guidelines for the alien's household size;

(ii) The alien is authorized to work and is currently employed in a legal industry with an annual income, excluding any income from illegal activities such as proceeds from illegal gambling or drug sales, of at least 250 percent of the Federal Poverty Guidelines for the alien's household size; or

(iii) The alien has private health insurance, except that for purposes of this paragraph (c)(2)(iii), private health insurance must be appropriate for the expected period of admission, and does not include health insurance for which the alien receives subsidies in the form of premium tax credits under the Patient Protection and Affordable Care Act, as amended.

(d) Treatment of benefits received before October 15, 2019. For purposes of this regulation, DHS will consider, as a negative factor, but not as a heavily weighted negative factor as described in paragraph (c)(1) of this section, any amount of cash assistance for income maintenance, including Supplemental Security Income (SSI), Temporary Assistance for Needy Families (TANF), State and local cash assistance programs that provide benefits for income maintenance (often called "General Assistance" programs), and programs (including Medicaid) supporting aliens who are institutionalized for long-term care, received, or certified for receipt, before October 15, 2019, as provided under the 1999 Interim Field Guidance, also known as the 1999 Field Guidance on Deportability and Inadmissibility on Public Charge Grounds. DHS will not consider as a negative factor any other public benefits received, or certified for receipt, before October 15, 2019.

§ 212.23 Exemptions and waivers for public charge ground of inadmissibility

(a) Exemptions. The public charge ground of inadmissibility under section 212(a)(4) of the Act does not apply, based on statutory or regulatory authority, to the following categories of aliens:

(1) Refugees at the time of admission under section 207 of the Act and at the time of adjustment of status to lawful permanent resident under section 209 of the Act;

(2) Asylees at the time of grant under section 208 of the Act and at the time of adjustment of status to lawful permanent resident under section 209 of the Act;

(3) Amerasian immigrants at the time of application for admission as described in sections 584 of the Foreign Operations, Export Financing, and Related Programs Appropriations Act of 1988, Public Law 100–202, 101 Stat. 1329–183, section 101(e) (Dec. 22, 1987), as amended, 8 U.S.C. 1101 note;

(4) Afghan and Iraqi Interpreter, or Afghan or Iraqi national employed by or on behalf of the U.S. Government as described in section 1059(a)(2) of the National Defense Authorization Act for Fiscal Year 2006 Public Law 109–163 (Jan. 6, 2006), as amended, and section 602(b) of the Afghan Allies Protection Act of 2009, Public Law 111–8, title VI (Mar. 11, 2009), as amended, 8 U.S.C. 1101 note, and section 1244(g) of the National Defense Authorization Act for Fiscal Year 2008, as amended Public Law 110–181 (Jan. 28, 2008);

(5) Cuban and Haitian entrants applying for adjustment of status under section 202 of the Immigration Reform and Control Act of 1986 (IRCA), Public Law 99–603, 100 Stat. 3359 (Nov. 6, 1986), as amended, 8 U.S.C. 1255a note;

(6) Aliens applying for adjustment of status under the Cuban Adjustment Act, Public Law 89–732 (Nov. 2, 1966), as amended, 8 U.S.C. 1255 note;

(7) Nicaraguans and other Central Americans applying for adjustment of status under sections 202(a) and section 203 of the Nicaraguan Adjustment and Central American Relief Act (NACARA), Public Law 105–100, 111 Stat. 2193 (Nov. 19, 1997), as amended, 8 U.S.C. 1255 note;

(8) Haitians applying for adjustment of status under section 902 of the Haitian Refugee Immigration Fairness Act of 1998, Public Law 105–277, 112 Stat. 2681 (Oct. 21, 1998), as amended, 8 U.S.C. 1255 note;

(9) Lautenberg parolees as described in section 599E of the Foreign Operations, Export Financing, and Related Programs Appropriations Act of 1990, Public Law 101–167, 103 Stat. 1195, title V (Nov. 21, 1989), as amended, 8 U.S.C. 1255 note;

(10) Special immigrant juveniles as described in section 245(h) of the Act;

(11) Aliens who entered the United States prior to January 1, 1972, and who meet the other conditions for being granted lawful permanent residence under section 249 of the Act and 8 CFR part 249 (Registry);

(12) Aliens applying for or re-registering for Temporary Protected Status as described in section 244 of the Act in accordance with section 244(c)(2)(A)(ii) of the Act and 8 CFR 244.3(a);

(13) A nonimmigrant described in section 101(a)(15)(A)(i) and (A)(ii) of the Act (Ambassador, Public Minister, Career Diplomat or Consular Officer, or Immediate Family or Other Foreign Government Official or Employee, or Immediate Family), in accordance with section 102 of the Act and 22 CFR 41.21(d);

(14) A nonimmigrant classifiable as C–2 (alien in transit to U.N. Headquarters) or C–3 (foreign government official), 22 CFR 41.21(d);

(15) A nonimmigrant described in section 101(a)(15)(G)(i), (G)(ii), (G)(iii), and (G)(iv), of the Act (Principal Resident Representative of Recognized Foreign Government to International Organization, and related categories), in accordance with section 102 of the Act and 22 CFR 41.21(d);

(16) A nonimmigrant classifiable as NATO–1, NATO–2, NATO–3, NATO–4 (NATO representatives), and NATO–6 in accordance with 22 CFR 41.21(d);

(17) An applicant for nonimmigrant status under section 101(a)(15) (T) of the Act, in accordance with 8 CFR 212.16(b);

(18) Except as provided in section 212.23(b), an individual who is seeking an immigration benefit for which admissibility is required, including but not limited to adjustment of status under section 245(a) of the Act and section 245(*l*) of the Act and who:

(i) Has a pending application that sets forth a prima facie case for eligibility for nonimmigrant status under section 101(a)(15)(T) of the Act, or

(ii) Has been granted nonimmigrant status under section 101(a)(15)(T) of the Act, provided that the individual is in valid T nonimmigrant status at the time the benefit request is properly filed with USCIS and at the time the benefit request is adjudicated;

(19) Except as provided in § 212.23(b),

(i) A petitioner for nonimmigrant status under section 101(a)(15)(U) of the Act, in accordance with section 212(a)(4)(E)(ii) of the Act; or

(ii) An individual who is granted nonimmigrant status under section 101(a)(15)(U) of the Act in accordance with section 212(a)(4)(E)(ii) of the Act, who is seeking an immigration benefit for which admissibility is required, including, but not limited to, adjustment of status under section 245(a) of the Act, provided that the individual is in valid U nonimmigrant status at the time the benefit request is properly filed with USCIS and at the time the benefit request is adjudicated;

(20) Except as provided in section 212.23(b), any alien who is a VAWA self-petitioner under section 212(a)(4)(E)(i) of the Act;

(21) Except as provided in section 212.23(b), a qualified alien described in section 431(c) of the Personal Responsibility and Work Opportunity Reconciliation Act of 1996, 8 U.S.C. 1641(c), under section 212(a)(4)(E)(iii) of the Act;

(22) Applicants adjusting status who qualify for a benefit under section 1703 of the National Defense Authorization Act, Public Law 108–136, 117 Stat. 1392 (Nov. 24, 2003), 8 U.S.C. 1151 note (posthumous benefits to surviving spouses, children, and parents);

(23) American Indians born in Canada determined to fall under section 289 of the Act;

(24) Texas Band of Kickapoo Indians of the Kickapoo Tribe of Oklahoma, Public Law 97–429 (Jan. 8, 1983);

(25) Nationals of Vietnam, Cambodia, and Laos applying for adjustment of status under section 586 of Public Law 106–429 under 8 CFR 245.21;

(26) Polish and Hungarian Parolees who were paroled into the United States from November 1, 1989 to December 31, 1991 under section 646(b) of the IIRIRA, Public Law 104–208, Div. C, Title VI, Subtitle D (Sept. 30, 1996), 8 U.S.C. 1255 note; and

(27) Any other categories of aliens exempt under any other law from the public charge ground of inadmissibility provisions under section 212(a)(4) of the Act.

(b) Limited Exemption. Aliens described in §§ 212.23(a)(18) through (21) must submit an affidavit of support as described in section 213A of the Act if they are applying for adjustment of status based on an employment-based petition that requires such an affidavit of support as described in section 212(a)(4)(D) of the Act.

(c) Waivers. A waiver for the public charge ground of inadmissibility may be authorized based on statutory or regulatory authority, for the following categories of aliens:

(1) Applicants for admission as nonimmigrants under 101(a)(15)(S) of the Act;

(2) Nonimmigrants admitted under section 101(a)(15)(S) of the Act applying for adjustment of status under section 245(j) of the Act (witnesses or informants); and

(3) Any other waiver of the public charge ground of inadmissibility that is authorized by law or regulation.

[84 FR 41501, 41504, Aug. 14, 2019; 84 FR 52363, Oct. 2, 2019]

PART 214—NONIMMIGRANT CLASSES

§ 214.1   Requirements for admission, extension, and maintenance of status.

(a) General.

(1) Nonimmigrant classes. For the purpose of administering the nonimmigrant provisions of the Act, the following administrative sub-classifications of nonimmigrant classifications as defined in section 101(a)(15) of the Act are established:

(i) Section 101(a)(15)(B) is divided into (B)(i) for visitors for business and (B)(ii) for visitors for pleasure;

(ii) Section 101(a)(15)(C) is divided into (C)(i) for aliens who are not diplomats and are in transit through the United States; (C)(ii) for aliens in transit to and from the United Nations Headquarters District; and (C)(iii) for alien diplomats in transit through the United States;

(iii) Section 101(a)(15)(H) is divided to create an (H)(iv) subclassification for the spouse and children of a nonimmigrant classified under section 101(a)(15)(H)(i), (ii), or (iii);

(iv) Section 101(a)(15)(J) is divided into (J)(i) for principal aliens and (J)(ii) for such alien's spouse and children;

(v) Section 101(a)(15)(K) is divided into (K)(i) for the fiance(e), (K)(ii) for the spouse, and (K)(iii) for the children of either;

(vi) Section 101(a)(15)(L) is divided into (L)(i) for principal aliens and (L)(ii) for such alien's spouse and children;

(vii) Section 101(a)(15)(Q)(ii) is divided to create a (Q)(iii) for subclassification for the spouse and children of a nonimmigrant classified under section 101(a)(15)(Q)(ii) of the Act;

(viii) Section 101(a)(15)(T)(ii) is divided into (T)(ii), (T)(iii), (T)(iv), and (T)(v) for the spouse, child, parent, and unmarried sibling under 18 years of age, respectively, of a principal nonimmigrant classified under section 101(a)(15)(T)(i); and T(vi) for the adult or minor child of a derivative nonimmigrant classified under section 101(a)(15)(T)(ii); and

(ix) Section 101(a)(15)(U)(ii) is divided into (U)(ii), (U)(iii), (U)(iv), and (U)(v) for the spouse, child, parent, and siblings, respectively, of a nonimmigrant classified under section 101(a)(15)(U)(i); and

(2) Classification designations. For the purpose of this chapter the following nonimmigrant designations are established. The designation in the second column may be used to refer to the appropriate nonimmigrant classification.

Section	Designation
101(a)(15)(A)(i)	A–1.
101(a)(15)(A)(ii)	A–2.
101(a)(15)(A)(iii)	A–3.
101(a)(15)(B)(i)	B–1.
101(a)(15)(B)(ii)	B–2.
101(a)(15)(C)(i)	C–1.
101(a)(15)(C)(ii)	C–2.
101(a)(15)(C)(iii)	C–3.
101(a)(15)(D)(i)	D–1.
101(a)(15)(D)(ii)	D–2.
101(a)(15)(E)(i)	E–1.
101(a)(15)(E)(ii)	E–2.
101(a)(15)(F)(i)	F–1.
101(a)(15)(F)(ii)	F–2.
101(a)(15)(G)(i)	G–1.
101(a)(15)(G)(ii)	G–2.
101(a)(15)(G)(iii)	G–3.
101(a)(15)(G)(iv)	G–4.
101(a)(15)(G)(v)	G–5.
101(a)(15)(H)(i)(B)	H–1B.
101(a)(15)(H)(i)(C)	H–1C.
101(a)(15)(H)(ii)(A)	H–2A.
101(a)(15)(H)(ii)(B)	H–2B.
101(a)(15)(H)(iii)	H–3.
101(a)(15)(H)(iv)	H–4.
101(a)(15)(I)	I.
101(a)(15)(J)(i)	J–1.
101(a)(15)(J)(ii)	J–2.
101(a)(15)(K)(i)	K–1.
101(a)(15)(K)(ii)	K–3.
101(a)(15)(K)(iii)	K–2; K–4.
101(a)(15)(L)(i)	L–1.
101(a)(15)(L)(ii)	L–2.
101(a)(15)(M)(i)	M–1.
101(a)(15)(M)(ii)	M–2.

101(a)(15)(N)(i)	N–8.
101(a)(15)(N)(ii)	N–9.
101(a)(15)(O)(i)	O–1.
101(a)(15)(O)(ii)	O–2.
101(a)(15)(O)(iii)	O–3.
101(a)(15)(P)(i)	P–1.
101(a)(15)(P)(ii)	P–2.
101(a)(15)(P)(iii)	P–3.
101(a)(15)(P)(iv)	P–4.
101(a)(15)(Q)(i)	Q–1.
101(a)(15)(Q)(ii)	Q–2.
101(a)(15)(Q)(iii)	Q–3.
101(a)(15)(R)(i)	R–1.
101(a)(15)(R)(ii)	R–2.
101(a)(15)(S)(i)	S–5.
101(a)(15)(S)(ii)	S–6.
101(a)(15)(S) qualified family members	S–7.
101(a)(15)(T)(i)	T–1.
101(a)(15)(T)(ii)	T–2.
101(a)(15)(T)(iii)	T–3.
101(a)(15)(T)(iv)	T–4.
101(a)(15)(T)(v)	T–5.
101(a)(15)(T)(vi)	T–6.
101(a)(15)(U)(i)	U–1.
101(a)(15)(U)(ii)	U–2, U–3, U–4, U–5.
101(a)(15)(V)	V–1, V–2, or V–3.
NAFTA, Principal	TN.
NAFTA, Dependent	TD.
Visa Waiver, Business	WB.
Visa Waiver, Tourist	WT.

Note 1: The classification designation K–2 is for the child of a K–1. The classification designation K–4 is for the child of a K–3.

Note 2: The classification designation V–1 is for the spouse of a lawful permanent resident; the classification designation V–2 is for the principal beneficiary of an I–130 who is the child of an LPR; the classification V–3 is for the derivative child of a V–1 or V–2 alien.

(3) General requirements.

(i) Every nonimmigrant alien who applies for admission to, or an extension of stay in, the United States, must establish that he or she is admissible to the United States, or that any ground of inadmissibility has been waived under section 212(d)(3) of the Act. Upon application for admission, the alien must present a valid passport and valid visa unless either or both documents have been waived. A nonimmigrant alien's admission to the United States is conditioned on compliance with any inspection requirement in § 235.1(d) or of this chapter, as well as compliance with part 215, subpart B, of this chapter, if applicable. The passport of an alien applying for admission must be valid for a minimum of six months from the expiration date of the contemplated period of stay, unless otherwise provided in this chapter, and the alien must agree to abide by the terms and conditions of his or her admission. An alien applying for extension of stay must present a passport only if requested to do so by the Department of Homeland Security. The passport of an alien applying for extension of stay must be valid at the time of application for extension, unless otherwise provided in this chapter, and the alien must agree to maintain the validity of his or her passport and to abide by all the terms and conditions of his extension.

(ii) At the time of admission or extension of stay, every nonimmigrant alien must also agree to depart the United States at the expiration of his or her authorized period of admission or extension of stay, or upon abandonment of his or her authorized nonimmigrant status, and to comply with the departure procedures at section 215.8 of this chapter if such procedures apply to the particular alien. The nonimmigrant alien's failure to comply with those departure requirements, including any requirement that the alien provide biometric identifiers, may constitute a failure of the alien to maintain the terms of his or her nonimmigrant status.

(iii) At the time a nonimmigrant alien applies for admission or extension of stay, he or she must post a bond on Form I–352 in the sum of not less than $500, to ensure the maintenance of his or her nonimmigrant status and departure from the United States, if required to do so by the Commissioner of CBP, the Director of U.S. Citizenship and Immigration Services, an immigration judge, or the Board of Immigration Appeals.

(iv) Except where the nonimmigrant classification for which the alien seeks to extend is exempt from section 212(a)(4) of the Act or that section has been waived, as a condition for approval of extension of status, the alien must demonstrate that he or she has not received since obtaining the nonimmigrant status he or she seeks to extend one or more public benefits as defined in 8 CFR 212.21(b), for more than 12 months in the aggregate within any 36-month period (such that, for instance, receipt of two benefits in one month counts as two months). For the purposes of this determination, DHS will only consider public benefits received on or after October

15, 2019 for petitions or applications postmarked (or, if applicable, submitted electronically) on or after that date.

(b) Readmission of nonimmigrants under section 101(a)(15)(F), (J), (M), or (Q)(ii) to complete unexpired periods of previous admission or extension of stay—

(1) Section 101(a)(15)(F). The inspecting immigration officer shall readmit for duration of status as defined in § 214.2(f)(5)(iii), any nonimmigrant alien whose nonimmigrant visa is considered automatically revalidated pursuant to 22 CFR 41.125(f) and who is applying for readmission under section 101(a)(15)(F) of the Act, if the alien:

(i) Is admissible;

(ii) Is applying for readmission after an absence from the United States not exceeding thirty days solely in contiguous territory or adjacent islands;

(iii) Is in possession of a valid passport unless exempt from the requirement for presentation of a passport; and

(iv) Presents, or is the accompanying spouse or child of an alien who presents, an Arrival-Departure Record, Form I–94 (see § 1.4), issued to the alien in connection with the previous admission or stay, the alien's Form I–20 ID copy, and either:

(A) A properly endorsed page 4 of Form I–20A–B if there has been no substantive change in the information on the student's most recent Form I–20A since the form was initially issued; or

(B) A new Form I–20A–B if there has been any substantive change in the information on the student's most recent Form I–20A since the form was initially issued.

(2) Section 101(a)(15)(J). The inspecting immigration officer shall readmit for the unexpired period of stay authorized prior to the alien's departure, any nonimmigrant alien whose nonimmigrant visa is considered automatically revalidated pursuant to 22 CFR 41.125(f) and who is applying for readmission under section 101(a)(15)(J) of the Act, if the alien:

(i) Is admissible;

(ii) Is applying for readmission after an absence from the United States not exceeding thirty days solely in contiguous territory or adjacent islands;

(iii) Is in possession of a valid passport unless exempt from the requirement for the presentation of a passport; and

(iv) Presents, or is the accompanying spouse or child of an alien who presents, Form I–94 issued to the alien in connection with the previous admission or stay or copy three of the last Form IAP–66 issued to the alien. Form I–94 or Form IAP–66 must show the unexpired period of the alien's stay endorsed by the Service.

(3) Section 101(a)(15)(M). The inspecting immigration officer shall readmit for the unexpired period of stay authorized prior to the alien's departure, any nonimmigrant alien whose nonimmigrant visa is considered automatically revalidated pursuant to 22 CFR 41.125(f) and who is applying for readmission under section 101(a)(15)(M) of the Act, if the alien:

(i) Is admissible;

(ii) Is applying for readmission after an absence not exceeding thirty days solely in contiguous territory;

(iii) Is in possession of a valid passport unless exempt from the requirement for the presentation of a passport; and

(iv) Presents, or is the accompanying spouse or child of an alien who presents, Form I–94 issued to the alien in connection with the previous admission or stay, the alien's Form I–20 ID copy, and a properly endorsed page 4 of Form I–20M–N.

(4) Section 101(a)(15)(Q)(ii). The inspecting immigration officer shall readmit for the unexpired period of stay authorized prior to the alien's departure, if the alien:

(i) Is admissible;

(ii) Is applying for readmission after an absence from the United States not exceeding 30 days solely in contiguous territory or adjacent islands;

(iii) Is in possession of a valid passport;

(iv) Presents, or is the accompanying spouse or child of an alien who presents, an Arrival-Departure Record, Form I–94, issued to the alien in connection with the previous admission or stay. The principal alien must also present a Certification Letter issued by the Department of State's Program Administrator.

(c) Extensions of stay—

(1) Extension of stay for certain employment-based nonimmigrant workers. A petitioner seeking the services of an E–1, E–2, E–3, H–1B, H–1B1, H–2A, H–2B, H–3, L–1, O–1, O–2, P–1, P–2, P–3, Q–1, R–1, or TN nonimmigrant beyond the period previously granted, must apply for an extension of stay on the form designated by USCIS, with the fee prescribed in 8 CFR 103.7(b)(1), with the initial evidence specified in § 214.2, and in accordance with the form instructions. Dependents holding derivative status may be included in the petition if it is for only one worker and the form version specifically provides for their inclusion. In all other cases dependents of the worker should file on Form I–539.

(2) Filing on Form I–539. Any other nonimmigrant alien, except an alien in F or J status who has been granted duration of status, who seeks to extend his or her stay beyond the currently authorized period of admission, must apply for an extension of stay on Form I–539 with the fee required in § 103.7 of this chapter together with any initial evidence specified in the applicable provisions of § 214.2, and on the application form. More than one person may be included in an application where the co-applicants are all members of a single family group and either all hold the same nonimmigrant status or one holds a nonimmigrant status and the other co-applicants are his or her spouse and/or children who hold derivative nonimmigrant status based on his or her status. Extensions granted to members of a family group must be for the same period of time. The shortest period granted to any member of the family shall be granted to all members of the family. In order to be eligible for an extension of stay, nonimmigrant aliens in K–3/K–4 status must do so in accordance with § 214.2(k)(10).

(3) Ineligible for extension of stay. A nonimmigrant in any of the following classes is ineligible for an extension of stay:

(i) B–1 or B–2 where admission was pursuant to the Visa Waiver Pilot Program;

(ii) C–1, C–2, C–3;

(iii) D–1, D–2;

(iv) K–1, K–2;

(v) Any nonimmigrant admitted for duration of status, other than as provided in § 214.2(f)(7);

(vi) Any nonimmigrant who is classified pursuant to section 101(a)(15)(S) of the Act beyond a total of 3 years; or

(vii) Any nonimmigrant who is classified according to section 101(a)(15)(Q)(ii) of the Act beyond a total of 3 years.

(viii) Any nonimmigrant admitted pursuant to the Guam-CNMI Visa Waiver Program, as provided in section 212(*l*) of the Act.

(4) Timely filing and maintenance of status. An extension of stay may not be approved for an applicant who failed to maintain the previously accorded status or where such status expired before the application or petition was filed, except that failure to file before the period of previously authorized status expired may be excused in the discretion of the Service and without separate application, with any extension granted from the date the previously authorized stay expired, where it is demonstrated at the time of filing that:

(i) The delay was due to extraordinary circumstances beyond the control of the applicant or petitioner, and the Service finds the delay commensurate with the circumstances;

(ii) The alien has not otherwise violated his or her nonimmigrant status;

(iii) The alien remains a bona fide nonimmigrant;

(iv) The alien is not the subject of deportation proceedings under section 242 of the Act (prior to April 1, 1997) or removal proceedings under section 240 of the Act.

(5) Decision in Form I–129 or I–539 extension proceedings. Where an applicant or petitioner demonstrates eligibility for a requested extension, it may be granted at the discretion of the Service. There is no appeal from the denial of an application for extension of stay filed on Form I–129 or I–539.

(d) Termination of status. Within the period of initial admission or extension of stay, the nonimmigrant status of an alien shall be terminated by the revocation of a waiver authorized on his or her behalf under section 212(d)(3) or (4) of the Act; by the introduction of a private bill to confer permanent resident status on such alien; or, pursuant to notification in the Federal Register, on the basis of national security, diplomatic, or public safety reasons.

(e) Employment. A nonimmigrant in the United States in a class defined in section 101(a)(15)(B) of the Act as a temporary visitor for pleasure, or section 101(a)(15)(C) of the Act as an alien in transit through this country, may not engage in any employment. Any other nonimmigrant in the United States may not engage in any employment unless he has been accorded a nonimmigrant classification which authorizes employment or he has been granted permission to engage in employment in accordance with the provisions of this chapter. A nonimmigrant who is permitted to engage in employment may engage only in such employment as has been authorized. Any unauthorized employment by a nonimmigrant constitutes a failure to maintain status within the meaning of section 241(a)(1)(C)(i) of the Act.

(f) False information. A condition of a nonimmigrant's admission and continued stay in the United States is the full and truthful disclosure of all information requested by DHS. A nonimmigrant's willful failure to provide full and truthful information requested by DHS (regardless of whether or not the information requested was material) constitutes a failure to maintain nonimmigrant status under section 237(a)(1)(C)(i) of the Act.

(g) Criminal activity. A condition of a nonimmigrant's admission and continued stay in the United States is obedience to all laws of United States jurisdictions which prohibit the commission of crimes of violence and for which a sentence of more than one year imprisonment may be imposed. A nonimmigrant's conviction in a jurisdiction in the United States for a crime of violence for which a sentence of more than one year imprisonment may be imposed (regardless of whether such sentence is in fact imposed) constitutes a failure to maintain status under Section 241(a)(1)(C)(i) of the Act.

(h) Education privacy and F, J, and M nonimmigrants. As authorized by section 641(c)(2) of Division C of Pub. L. 104–208, 8 U.S.C. § 1372, and § 2.1(a) of this chapter, the Service has determined that, with respect to F and M nonimmigrant students and J nonimmigrant exchange visitors, waiving the provisions of the Family Educational Rights and Privacy Act (FERPA), 20 U.S.C. § 1232g, is necessary for the proper implementation of 8 U.S.C. § 1372. An educational agency or institution may not refuse to report information concerning an F or M nonimmigrant student or a J nonimmigrant exchange visitor that the educational agency or institution is required to report under 8 U.S.C. § 1372 and § 214.3(g) (or any corresponding Department of State regulation concerning J nonimmigrants) on the basis of FERPA and any regulation implementing FERPA. The waiver of FERPA under this paragraph authorizes and requires an educational agency or institution to report information concerning an F, J or M nonimmigrant that would ordinarily be protected by FERPA, but only to the extent that 8 U.S.C. § 1372 and § 214.3(g) (or any corresponding Department of State regulation concerning J nonimmigrants) requires the educational agency or institution to report information.

(i) Employment in a health care occupation.

(1) Except as provided in 8 CFR 212.15(n), any alien described in 8 CFR 212.15(a) who is coming to the United States to perform labor in a health care occupation described in 8 CFR 212.15(c) must obtain a certificate from a credentialing organization described in 8 CFR 212.15(e). The certificate or certified statement must be presented to the Department of Homeland Security in accordance with 8 CFR 212.15(d). In the alternative, an eligible alien seeking admission as a nurse may obtain a certified statement as provided in 8 CFR 212.15(h).

(2) A TN nonimmigrant may establish that he or she is eligible for a waiver described at 8 CFR 212.15(n) by providing evidence that his or her initial admission as a TN (or TC) nonimmigrant health care worker occurred before September 23, 2003, and he or she was licensed and employed in the United States as a health care worker before September 23, 2003. Evidence may include, but is not limited to, copies of TN or TC approval notices, copies of Form I–94 Arrival/Departure Records, employment verification letters and/or pay-stubs or other employment records, and state health care worker licenses.

(j) Extension of stay or change of status for health care worker.

In the case of any alien admitted temporarily as a nonimmigrant under section 212(d)(3) of the Act and 8 CFR 212.15(n) for the primary purpose of the providing labor in a health care occupation described in 8 CFR 212.15(c), the petitioning employer may file a Form I–129 to extend the approval period for the alien's classification for the nonimmigrant status. If the alien is in the United States and is eligible for an extension of stay or change of status, the Form I–129 also serves as an application to extend the period of the alien's authorized stay or to change the alien's status. Although the Form I–129 petition may be approved, as it relates to the employer's request to classify the alien, the application for an extension of stay or change of status shall be denied if:

(1) The petitioner or applicant fails to submit the certification required by 8 CFR 212.15(a) with the petition or application to extend the alien's stay or change the alien's status; or

(2) The petition or application to extend the alien's stay or change the alien's status does include the certification required by 8 CFR 212.15(a), but the alien obtained the certification more than 1 year after the date of the alien's admission under section 212(d)(3) of the Act and 8 CFR 212.15(n). While DHS may admit, extend the period of authorized stay, or change the status of a nonimmigrant health care worker for a period of 1 year if the alien does not have certification on or before July 26, 2004 (or on or before July 26, 2005, in the case of a citizen of Canada or Mexico, who, before September 23, 2003, was employed as a TN or TC nonimmigrant health care worker and held a valid license from a U.S. jurisdiction), the alien will not be eligible for a subsequent admission, change of status, or extension of stay as a health care worker if the alien has not obtained the requisite certification 1 year after the initial date of admission, change of status, or extension of stay as a health care worker.

(k) Denial of petitions under section 214(c) of the Act based on a finding by the Department of Labor. Upon debarment by the Department of Labor pursuant to 20 CFR part 655, USCIS may deny any petition filed by that petitioner for nonimmigrant status under section 101(a)(15)(H) (except for status under sections 101(a)(15)(H)(i)(b1)), (L), (O), and (P)(i) of the Act) for a period of at least 1 year but not more than 5 years. The length of the period shall be based on the severity of the violation or violations. The decision to deny petitions, the time period for the bar to petitions, and the reasons for the time period will be explained in a written notice to the petitioner.

(*l*) Period of stay.

(1) An alien admissible in E–1, E–2, E–3, H–1B, L–1, or TN classification and his or her dependents may be admitted to the United States or otherwise provided such status for the validity period of the petition, or for a validity period otherwise authorized for the E–1, E–2, E–3, and TN classifications, plus an additional period of up to 10 days before the validity period begins and 10 days after the validity period ends. Unless authorized under 8 CFR 274a.12, the alien may not work except during the validity period.

(2) An alien admitted or otherwise provided status in E–1, E–2, E–3, H–1B, H–1B1, L–1, O–1 or TN classification and his or her dependents shall not be considered to have failed to maintain nonimmigrant status solely on the basis of a cessation of the employment on which the alien's classification was based, for up to 60 consecutive days or until the end of the authorized validity period, whichever is shorter, once during each authorized validity period. DHS may eliminate or shorten this 60-day period as a matter of discretion. Unless otherwise authorized under 8 CFR 274a.12, the alien may not work during such a period.

(3) An alien in any authorized period described in paragraph (*l*) of this section may apply for and be granted an extension of stay under paragraph (c)(4) of this section or change of status under 8 CFR 248.1, if otherwise eligible.

[26 FR 12067, Dec. 16, 1961, as amended at 36 FR 8048, April 29, 1971; 37 FR 14288, June 19, 1972; 43 FR 12674, March 27, 1978; 44 FR 65727, Nov. 14, 1979; 45 FR 48867, July 22, 1980; 46 FR 25597, May 8, 1981; 48 FR 14582, April 5, 1983; 48 FR 20685, May 9, 1983; 48 FR 30350, July 1, 1983; 52 FR 45446, Nov. 30, 1987; 56 FR 38333, Aug. 13, 1991; 59 FR 1463, Jan. 11, 1994; 59 FR 26594, May 23, 1994; 60 FR 44266, Aug. 25, 1995; 62 FR 10349, March 6, 1997; 65 FR 14777, March 17, 2000; 65 FR 43531, July 13, 2000; 65 FR 67617, Nov. 13, 2000; 66 FR 31112, June 11, 2001; 66 FR 42593, Aug. 14, 2001; 66 FR 46702, Sept. 7, 2001; 66 FR 49514, Sept. 28, 2001; 67 FR 4795, Jan. 31, 2002; 67 FR 52591, Aug. 12, 2002; 67 FR 61476, Oct. 1, 2002; 67 FR 76270, Dec. 11, 2002; 68 FR 43920, July 25, 2003; 69 FR 480, Jan. 5, 2004; 69 FR 43732, July 22, 2004; 72 FR 53036, Sept. 17, 2007; 73 FR 61334, Oct. 16, 2008; 73 FR 78127, Dec. 19, 2008; 74 FR 2835, Jan. 16, 2009; 78 FR 18472, March 27, 2013; 80 FR 24108, April 29, 2015; 81 FR 2083, Jan. 15, 2016; 81 FR 72491, Oct. 20, 2016; 81 FR 82486, Nov. 18, 2016; 81 FR 91670, Dec. 19, 2016; 81 FR 92304, Dec. 19, 2016; 81 FR 94234, Dec. 23, 2016; 84 FR 41507, Aug. 14, 2019]

PART 235—INSPECTION OF PERSONS APPLYING FOR ADMISSION

§ 235.1 Scope of examination.

(a) General. Application to lawfully enter the United States shall be made in person to an immigration officer at a U.S. port-of-entry when the port is open for inspection, or as otherwise designated in this section.

(b) U.S. Citizens. A person claiming U.S. citizenship must establish that fact to the examining officer's satisfaction and must present a U.S. passport or alternative documentation as required by 22 CFR part 53. If such applicant for admission fails to satisfy the examining immigration officer that he or she is a U.S. citizen, he or she shall thereafter be inspected as an alien. A U.S. citizen must present a valid unexpired U.S. passport book upon entering the United States, unless he or she presents one of the following documents:

(1) Passport Card. A U.S. citizen who possesses a valid unexpired United States passport card, as defined in 22 CFR 53.1, may present the passport card when entering the United States from contiguous territory or adjacent islands at land or sea ports-of-entry.

(2) Merchant Mariner Document. A U.S. citizen who holds a valid Merchant Mariner Document (MMD) issued by the U.S. Coast Guard may present an unexpired MMD used in conjunction with official maritime business when entering the United States.

(3) Military Identification. Any U.S. citizen member of the U.S. Armed Forces who is in the uniform of, or bears documents identifying him or her as a member of, such Armed Forces, and who is coming to or departing from the United States under official orders or permit of such Armed Forces, may present a military identification card and the official orders when entering the United States.

(4) Trusted Traveler Programs. A U.S. citizen who travels as a participant in the NEXUS, FAST, or SENTRI programs may present a valid NEXUS program card when using a NEXUS Air kiosk or a valid NEXUS, FAST, or SENTRI card at a land or sea port-of-entry prior to entering the United States from contiguous territory or adjacent islands. A U.S. citizen who enters the United States by pleasure vessel from Canada using the remote inspection system may present a NEXUS program card.

(5) Certain Cruise Ship Passengers. A U.S. citizen traveling entirely within the Western Hemisphere is permitted to present a government-issued photo identification document in combination with either an original or a copy of his or her birth certificate, a Consular Report of Birth Abroad issued by the Department of State, or a Certificate of Naturalization issued by U.S. Citizenship and Immigration Services for entering the United States when the United States citizen:

(i) Boards a cruise ship at a port or place within the United States; and,

(ii) Returns on the return voyage of the same cruise ship to the same United States port or place from where he or she originally departed.

On such cruises, U.S. Citizens under the age of 16 may present an original or a copy of a birth certificate, a Consular Report of Birth Abroad, or a Certificate of Naturalization issued by U.S. Citizenship and Immigration Services.

(6) Native American Holders of an American Indian Card. A Native American holder of a Form I–872 American Indian Card arriving from contiguous territory or adjacent islands may present the Form I–872 card prior to entering the United States at a land or sea port-of-entry.

(7) Native American Holders of Tribal Documents. A U.S. citizen holder of a tribal document issued by a United States qualifying tribal entity or group of United States qualifying tribal entities, as provided in paragraph (e) of this section, who is arriving from contiguous territory or adjacent islands may present the tribal document prior to entering the United States at a land or sea port-of-entry.

(8) Children. A child who is a United States citizen entering the United States from contiguous territory at a sea or land ports-of-entry may present certain other documents, if the arrival falls under subsection (i) or (ii).

(i) Children Under Age 16. A U.S. citizen who is under the age of 16 is permitted to present either an original or a copy of his or her birth certificate, a Consular Report of Birth Abroad issued by the Department of State, or a Certificate of Naturalization issued by U.S. Citizenship and Immigration Services when entering the United States from contiguous territory at land or sea ports-of-entry.

(ii) Groups of Children Under Age 19. A U.S. citizen, who is under age 19 and is traveling with a public or private school group, religious group, social or cultural organization, or team associated with a youth sport organization is permitted to present either an original or a copy of his or her birth certificate, a Consular Report of Birth Abroad issued by the Department of State, or a Certificate of Naturalization issued by U.S. Citizenship and Immigration Services when arriving from contiguous territory at land or sea ports-of-entry, when the group, organization, or team is under the supervision of an adult affiliated with the group, organization, or team and when the child has parental or legal guardian consent to travel. For purposes of this paragraph, an adult is considered to be a person age 19 or older. The following requirements will apply:

(A) The group or organization must provide to CBP upon crossing the border, on organizational letterhead:

(1) The name of the group, organization or team, and the name of the supervising adult;

(2) A list of the children on the trip;

(3) For each child, the primary address, primary phone number, date of birth, place of birth, and name of a parent or legal guardian.

(B) The adult leading the group, organization, or team must demonstrate parental or legal guardian consent by certifying in the writing submitted in paragraph (b)(8)(ii)(A) of this section that he or she has obtained for each child the consent of at least one parent or legal guardian.

(C) The inspection procedure described in this paragraph is limited to members of the group, organization, or team who are under age 19. Other members of the group, organization, or team must comply with other applicable document and/or inspection requirements found in this part.

(c) Alien members of United States Armed Forces and members of a force of a NATO country. Any alien member of the United States Armed Forces who is in the uniform of, or bears documents identifying him or her as a member of, such Armed Forces, and who is coming to or departing from the United States under official orders or permit of such Armed Forces is not subject to the removal provisions of the Act. A member of the force of a NATO country signatory to Article III of the Status of Forces Agreement seeking to enter the United States under official orders is exempt from the control provision of the Act. Any alien who is a member of either of the foregoing classes may, upon request, be inspected and his or her entry as an alien may be recorded. If the alien does not appear to the examining immigration officer to be clearly and beyond a doubt entitled to enter the United States under the provisions of the Act, the alien shall be so informed and his or her entry shall not be recorded.

(d) Enhanced Driver's License Projects; alternative requirements. Upon the designation by the Secretary of Homeland Security of an enhanced driver's license as an acceptable document to denote identity and citizenship for purposes of entering the United States, U.S. and Canadian citizens may be permitted to present these documents in lieu of a passport upon entering or seeking admission to the United States according to the terms of the agreements entered between the Secretary of Homeland Security and the entity. The Secretary of Homeland Security will announce, by publication of a notice in the Federal Register, documents designated under this paragraph. A list of the documents designated under this paragraph will also be made available to the public.

(e) Native American Tribal Cards; alternative requirements. Upon the designation by the Secretary of Homeland Security of a United States qualifying tribal entity document as an acceptable document to denote identity and citizenship for purposes of entering the United States,

Native Americans may be permitted to present tribal cards upon entering or seeking admission to the United States according to the terms of the voluntary agreement entered between the Secretary of Homeland Security and the tribe. The Secretary of Homeland Security will announce, by publication of a notice in the Federal Register, documents designated under this paragraph. A list of the documents designated under this paragraph will also be made available to the public.

(f) Alien applicants for admission.

(1) Each alien seeking admission at a United States port-of-entry must present whatever documents are required and must establish to the satisfaction of the inspecting officer that the alien is not subject to removal under the immigration laws, Executive Orders, or Presidential Proclamations, and is entitled, under all of the applicable provisions of the immigration laws and this chapter, to enter the United States.

(i) A person claiming to have been lawfully admitted for permanent residence must establish that fact to the satisfaction of the inspecting officer and must present proper documents in accordance with § 211.1 of this chapter.

(ii) The Secretary of Homeland Security or his designee may require any alien, other than aliens exempted under paragraph (iv) of this section or Canadian citizens under section 101(a)(15)(B) of the Act who are not otherwise required to present a visa or be issued Form I–94 (see § 1.4) or Form I–95 for admission or parole into the United States, to provide fingerprints, photograph(s) or other specified biometric identifiers, documentation of his or her immigration status in the United States, and such other evidence as may be requested to determine the alien's identity and whether he or she has properly maintained his or her status while in the United States and/or whether he or she is admissible. The failure of an alien at the time of inspection to comply with any requirement to provide biometric identifiers may result in a determination that the alien is inadmissible under section 212(a) of the Immigration and Nationality Act or any other law.

(iii) Aliens who are required under paragraph (d)(1)(ii) to provide biometric identifier(s) at inspection may also be subject to the departure requirements for biometrics contained in § 215.8 of this chapter, unless otherwise exempted.

(iv) The requirements of paragraph (d)(1)(ii) shall not apply to:

(A) Aliens younger than 14 or older than 79 on date of admission;

(B) Aliens admitted on A–1, A–2, C–3 (except for attendants, servants, or personal employees of accredited officials), G–1, G–2, G–3, G–4, NATO–1, NATO–2, NATO–3, NATO–4, NATO–5, or NATO–6 visas, and certain Taiwan officials who hold E–1 visas and members of their immediate families who hold E–1 visas unless the Secretary of State and the Secretary of Homeland Security jointly determine that a class of such aliens should be subject to the requirements of paragraph (d)(1)(ii);

(C) Classes of aliens to whom the Secretary of Homeland Security and the Secretary of State jointly determine it shall not apply; or

(D) An individual alien to whom the Secretary of Homeland Security, the Secretary of State, or the Director of Central Intelligence determines it shall not apply.

(2) An alien present in the United States who has not been admitted or paroled or an alien who seeks entry at other than an open, designated port-of-entry, except as otherwise permitted in this section, is subject to the provisions of section 212(a) of the Act and to removal under section 235(b) or 240 of the Act.

(3) An alien who is brought to the United States, whether or not to a designated port-of-entry and regardless of the means of transportation, after having been interdicted in international or United States waters, is considered an applicant for admission and shall be examined under section 235(b) of the Act.

(4) An alien stowaway is not an applicant for admission and may not be admitted to the United States. A stowaway shall be removed from the United States under section 235(a)(2) of the Act. The provisions of section 240 of the Act are not applicable to stowaways, nor is the stowaway entitled to further hearing or review of the removal, except that an alien stowaway who indicates an intention to apply for asylum, or expresses a fear of persecution, a fear of torture, or a fear of return to the country of proposed removal shall be referred to an asylum officer for a determination of credible fear of persecution or torture in accordance with section 235(b)(1)(B) of the Act and § 208.30 of this chapter. An alien stowaway who is determined to have a credible fear of persecution or torture shall have his or her asylum application adjudicated in accordance with § 208.2(b)(2) of this chapter.

(g) U.S. citizens, lawful permanent residents of the United States, and other aliens, entering the United States along the northern border, other than at a port-of-entry. A citizen of Canada or a permanent resident of Canada who is a national of a country listed in § 217.2(a) of this chapter may, if in possession of a valid, unexpired, Canadian Border Boat Landing Permit (Form I–68) or evidence of enrollment in any other Service Alternative Inspections program (e.g., the Immigration and Naturalization Service Passenger Accelerated Service System (INSPASS) or the Port Passenger Accelerated Service System (PORTPASS)), enter the United States by means of a pleasure craft along the northern border of the United States from time-to-time without further inspection. No persons other than those described in this paragraph may participate in this program. Permanent residents of Canada who are nationals of a designated Visa Waiver Program country listed in § 217.2(a) of this chapter must be in possession of a valid, unexpired passport issued by his or her country of nationality, and an unexpired multiple entry Form I–94W, Nonimmigrant Visa Waiver Arrival/Departure Form, or an unexpired passport, valid unexpired United States visa and I–94 Arrival/Departure Form. When an entry to the United States is made by a person who is a Canadian citizen or a permanent resident of *5194 Canada who is a national of a designated Visa Waiver Program country listed in § 217.2(a) of this chapter, entry may be made under this program only for a purpose as described in section 101(a)(15)(B)(ii) of the Act as a visitor for pleasure. Persons seeking to enter the United States for any other purpose must do so at a port-of-entry staffed by immigration inspectors. Persons aboard a vessel which has crossed the international boundary between the United States and Canada and who do not intend to land in the United States, other than at a staffed port-of-entry, are not required to be in possession of Form I–68, Canadian Border Boat Landing Permit, or evidence of enrollment in an Alternative Inspections program merely because they have crossed the international boundary. However, the Service retains the right to conduct inspections or examinations of all persons applying for admission or readmission to or seeking transit through the United States in accordance with the Act.

(1) Application. An eligible applicant may apply for a Canadian Border Boat Landing Permit by completing the Form I–68 in triplicate. Application forms will be made readily available through the Internet, from a Service office, or by mail. A family may apply on a single application. For the purposes of this paragraph, a family is defined as a husband, wife, unmarried children under the age of 21, and the parents of either husband or wife, who reside at the same address. In order for the I–68 application to be considered complete, it must be accompanied by the following:

(i) For each person included on the application, evidence of citizenship, and, if not a citizen of the United States or Canada, evidence of legal permanent resident status in either the United States or Canada. Evidence of residency must be submitted by all applicants. It is not required that all persons on the application be of the same nationality; however, they must all be individually eligible to participate in this program.

(ii) If multiple members of a family, as defined in paragraph (e)(1) of this section, are included on a single application, evidence of the familial relationship.

(iii) A fee as prescribed in § 103.7(b)(1) of this chapter.

(iv) A copy of any previously approved Form I–68.

(v) A permanent resident of Canada who is a national of a Visa Waiver Program may apply for admission simultaneously with the Form I–68 application and thereby obtain a Form I–94 or I–94W.

(2) Submission of Form I–68. Except as indicated in this paragraph, Form I–68 shall be properly completed and submitted in person, along with the documentary evidence and the required fee as specified in § 103.7(b)(1) of this chapter, to a United States immigration officer at a Canadian border Port-of-Entry located within the district having jurisdiction over the applicant's residence or intended place of landing. Persons previously granted Form I–68 approval may apply by mail to the issuing Service office for renewal if a copy of the previous Form I–68 is included in the application. At the discretion of the district director concerned, any applicant for renewal of Form I–68 may be required to appear for an interview in person if the applicant does not appear to be clearly eligible for renewal.

(3) Denial of Form I–68. If the applicant has committed a violation of any immigration or customs regulation or, in the case of an alien, is inadmissible to the United States, approval of the Form I–68 shall be denied. However, if, in the exercise of discretion, the district director waives under section 212(d)(3) of the Act all applicable grounds of inadmissibility, the I–68 application may be approved for such non-citizens. If the Form I–68 application is denied, the applicant shall be given written notice of and the reasons for the denial by letter from the district director. There is no appeal from the denial of the Form I–68 application, but the denial is without prejudice to a subsequent application for this program or any other Service benefit, except that the applicant may not submit a subsequent Form I–68 application for 90 days after the date of the last denial.

(4) Validity. Form I–68 shall be valid for 1 year from the date of issuance, or until revoked or violated [sic] by the Service.

(5) Conditions for participation in the I–68 program. Upon being inspected and positively identified by an immigration officer and found admissible and eligible for participation in the I–68 program, a participant must agree to abide by the following conditions:

(i) Form I–68 may be used only when entering the United States by means of a vessel exclusively used for pleasure, including chartered vessels when such vessel has been chartered by an approved Form I–68 holder. When used by a person who is a not a citizen or a lawful permanent resident of the United States, admission shall be for a period not to exceed 72 hours to visit within 25 miles of the shore line along the northern border of the United States, including the shore line of Lake Michigan and Puget Sound.

(ii) Participants must be in possession of any authorization documents issued for participation in this program or another Service Alternative Inspections program (INSPASS or PORTPASS). Participants over the age of 15 years and who are not in possession of an INSPASS or PORTPASS enrollment card must also be in possession of a photographic identification document issued by a governmental agency. Participants who are permanent residents of Canada who are nationals of a Visa Waiver Program country listed in § 217.2(a) of this chapter must also be in possession of proper documentation as described in paragraph (e) of this section.

(iii) Participants may not import merchandise or transport controlled or restricted items while entering the United States under this program. The entry of any merchandise or goods must be in accordance with the laws and regulations of all Federal Inspection Services.

(iv) Participants must agree to random checks or inspections that may be conducted by the Service, at any time and at any location, to ensure compliance.

(v) Participants must abide by all Federal, state, and local laws regarding the importation of alcohol or agricultural products or the importation or possession of controlled substances as defined in section 101 of the Controlled Substance Act (21 U.S.C. 802).

(vi) Participants acknowledge that all devices, decals, cards, or other Federal Government supplied identification or technology used to identify or inspect persons or vessels seeking entry via this program remain the property of the United States Government at all times, and must be surrendered upon request by a Border Patrol Agent or any other officer of a Federal Inspection Service.

(vii) The captain, charterer, master, or owner (if aboard) of each vessel bringing persons into the United States is responsible for determining that all persons aboard the vessel are in possession of a valid, unexpired Form I–68 or other evidence of participation in a Service Alternative Inspections program (INSPASS or PORTPASS) prior to entry into the territorial waters of the United States. If any person on board is not in possession of such evidence, the captain, charterer, master, or owner must transport such person to a staffed United States Port-of-Entry for an in-person immigration inspection.

(6) Revocation. The district director, the chief patrol agent, or their designated representatives may revoke the designation of any participant who violates any condition of this program, as contained in paragraph (e)(5) of this section, or who has violated any immigration law or regulation, or a law or regulation of the United States Customs Service or other Federal Inspection Service, has abandoned his or her residence in the United States or Canada, is inadmissible to the United States, or who is otherwise determined by an immigration officer to be ineligible for continued participation in this program. Such persons may be subject to other applicable sanctions, such as criminal and/

or administrative prosecution or deportation, as well as possible seizure of goods and/or vessels. If permission to participate is revoked, a written request to the district director for restoration of permission to participate may be made. The district director will notify the person of his or her decision and the reasons therefore in writing.

(7) Compliance checking. Participation in this program does not relieve the holder from responsibility to comply with all other aspects of United States Immigration, Customs, or other Federal inspection service laws or regulations. To prevent abuse, the United States Immigration and Naturalization Service retains the right to conduct inspections or examinations of all persons applying for admission or readmission to or seeking transit through the United States in accordance with the Immigration and Nationality Act.

(h) Form 1–94, Arrival-Departure Record.

(1) Unless otherwise exempted, each arriving nonimmigrant who is admitted to the United States will be issued a Form I–94 as evidence of the terms of admission. For land border admission, a Form I–94 will be issued only upon payment of a fee, and will be considered issued for multiple entries unless specifically annotated for a limited number of entries. A Form I–94 issued at other than a land border port-of-entry, unless issued for multiple entries, must be surrendered upon departure from the United States in accordance with the instructions on the form. Form I–94 is not required by:

(i) Any nonimmigrant alien described in § 212.1(a) of this chapter and 22 CFR 41.33 who is admitted as a visitor for business or pleasure or admitted to proceed in direct transit through the United States;

(ii) Any nonimmigrant alien residing in the British Virgin Islands who was admitted only to the U.S. Virgin Islands as a visitor for business or pleasure under § 212.1(b) of this chapter;

(iii) Except as provided in paragraph (h)(1)(v) of this section, any Mexican national admitted as a nonimmigrant visitor who is:

(A) Exempt from a visa and passport pursuant to § 212.1(c)(1) of this chapter and is admitted for a period not to exceed 30 days to visit within 25 miles of the border; or

(B) In possession of a valid visa and passport and is admitted for a period not to exceed 72 hours to visit within 25 miles of the border;

(iv) Bearers of Mexican diplomatic or official passports described in § 212.1(c) of this chapter; or

(v) Any Mexican national admitted as a nonimmigrant visitor who is:

(A) Exempt from a visa and passport pursuant to § 212.1(c)(1) of this chapter and is admitted at the Mexican border POEs in the State of Arizona at Sasabe, Nogales, Mariposa, Naco or Douglas to visit within the State of Arizona within 75 miles of the border for a period not to exceed 30 days; or

(B) In possession of a valid visa and passport and is admitted at the Mexican border POEs in the State of Arizona at Sasabe, Nogales, Mariposa, Naco or Douglas to visit within the State of Arizona within 75 miles of the border for a period not to exceed 72 hours; or

(C) Exempt from visa and passport pursuant to § 212.1(c)(1) of this chapter and is admitted for a period not to exceed 30 days to visit within the State of New Mexico within 55 miles of the border or the area south of and including Interstate Highway I–10, whichever is further north; or

(D) In possession of a valid visa and passport and is admitted for a period not to exceed 72 hours to visit within the State of New Mexico within 55 miles of the border or the area south of and including Interstate Highway I–10, whichever is further north.

(2) Paroled aliens. Any alien paroled into the United States under section 212(d)(5) of the Act, including any alien crewmember, shall be issued a completely executed Form I–94, endorsed with the parole stamp.

[32 FR 9627, July 4, 1967; 32 FR 11628, Aug. 11, 1967; 42 FR 41848, Aug. 19, 1977; 45 FR 19545, March 26, 1980; 45 FR 63483, Sept. 25, 1980; 45 FR 70428, Oct. 24, 1980; 46 FR 43826, Sept. 1, 1981; 47 FR 49953, Nov. 4, 1982; 49 FR 33434, Aug. 23, 1984; 58 FR 69217, Dec. 30, 1993; 60 FR 40068, Aug. 7, 1995; 60 FR 50389, Sept. 29, 1995; 61 FR 53831, Oct. 16, 1996; 62 FR 10353, March 6, 1997; 62 FR 47751, Sept. 11, 1997; 63 FR 1334, Jan. 9, 1998; 64 FR 8494, Feb. 19, 1999; 64 FR 36561, July 7, 1999; 64 FR 68617, Dec. 8, 1999; 67 FR 71449, Dec. 2, 2002; 68 FR 5193, Jan. 31, 2003; 69 FR 480, Jan. 5, 2004; 69 FR 50053, Aug. 13, 2004; 69 FR 53333, Aug. 31, 2004; 69 FR 58037, Sept. 29, 2004; 71 FR 68429, Nov. 24, 2006; 73 FR 18416, Apr. 3, 2008; 73 FR 77491, Dec. 19, 2008; 74 FR 2837, Jan. 16, 2009; 78 FR 18472, March 27, 2013; 78 FR 35107, June 12, 2013; 81 FR 91670, Dec. 19, 2016]

§ 235.2   Parole for deferred inspection. [also 8 C.F.R. § 1235.2]

(a) A district director may, in his or her discretion, defer the inspection of any vessel or aircraft, or of any alien, to another Service office or port-of-entry. Any alien coming to a United States port from a foreign port, from an outlying possession of the United States, from Guam, Puerto Rico, or the Virgin Islands of the United States, or from another port of the United States at which examination under this part was deferred, shall be regarded as an applicant for admission at that onward port.

(b) An examining immigration officer may defer further examination and refer the alien's case to the district director having jurisdiction over the place where the alien is seeking admission, or over the place of the alien's residence or destination in the United States, if the examining immigration officer has reason to believe that the alien can overcome a finding of inadmissibility by:

(1) Posting a bond under section 213 of the Act;

(2) Seeking and obtaining a waiver under section211 or 212(d)(3) or (4) of the Act; or

(3) Presenting additional evidence of admissibility not available at the time and place of the initial examination.

(c) Such deferral shall be accomplished pursuant to the provisions of section 212(d)(5) of the Act for the period of time necessary to complete the deferred inspection.

(d) Refusal of a district director to authorize admission under section 213 of the Act, or to grant an application for the benefits of section 211 or section 212(d)(3) or (4) of the Act, shall be without prejudice to the renewal of such application or the authorizing of such admission by the immigration judge without additional fee.

(e) Whenever an alien on arrival is found or believed to be suffering from a disability that renders it impractical to proceed with the examination under the Act, the examination of such alien, members of his or her family concerning whose admissibility it is necessary to have such alien testify, and any accompanying aliens whose protection or guardianship will be required should such alien be found inadmissible shall be deferred for such time and under such conditions as the district director in whose district the port is located imposes.

[22 FR 9791, Dec. 6, 1957; 62 FR 10355, March 6, 1997]

§ 235.3 Inadmissible aliens and expedited removal. [also 8 C.F.R. § 1235.3]

(a) Detention prior to inspection. All persons arriving at a port-of-entry in the United States by vessel or aircraft shall be detained aboard the vessel or at the airport of arrival by the owner, agent, master, commanding officer, person in charge, purser, or consignee of such vessel or aircraft until admitted or otherwise permitted to land by an officer of the Service. Notice or order to detain shall not be required. The owner, agent, master, commanding officer, person in charge, purser, or consignee of such vessel or aircraft shall deliver every alien requiring examination to an immigration officer for inspection or to a medical officer for examination. The Service will not be liable for any expenses related to such detention or presentation or for any expenses of a passenger who has not been presented for inspection and for whom a determination has not been made concerning admissibility by a Service officer.

(b) Expedited removal.

(1) Applicability. The expedited removal provisions shall apply to the following classes of aliens who are determined to be inadmissible under section 212(a)(6)(C) or (7) of the Act:

(i) Arriving aliens, as defined in 8 CFR 1.2;

(ii) As specifically designated by the Commissioner, aliens who arrive in, attempt to enter, or have entered the United States without having been admitted or paroled following inspection by an immigration officer at a designated port-of-entry, and who have not established to the satisfaction of the immigration officer that they have been physically present in the United States continuously for the 2-year period immediately prior to the date of determination of inadmissibility. The Commissioner shall have the sole discretion to apply the provisions of section 235(b)(1) of the Act, at any time, to any class of aliens described in this section. The Commissioner's designation shall become effective upon publication of a notice in the Federal Register. However, if the Commissioner determines, in the exercise of discretion, that the delay caused by publication would adversely affect the interests of the United States or the effective enforcement of the immigration laws, the Commissioner's designation shall become effective immediately upon issuance, and shall be published in the Federal Register as soon as practicable thereafter. When these provisions are in effect for aliens who enter without inspection, the burden of proof rests with the alien to affirmatively show that he or she has the required continuous physical presence in the United States. Any absence from the United States shall serve to break the period of continuous physical presence. An alien who was not inspected and admitted or paroled into the United States but who establishes that he or she has been continuously physically present in the United States for the 2-year period immediately prior to the date of determination of inadmissibility shall be detained in accordance with section 235(b)(2) of the Act for a proceeding under section 240 of the Act.

(2) Determination of inadmissibility.

(i) Record of proceeding. An alien who is arriving in the United States, or other alien as designated pursuant to paragraph (b)(1)(ii) of this section, who is determined to be inadmissible under section 212(a)(6)(C) or 212(a)(7) of the Act (except an alien for whom documentary requirements are waived under § 211.1(b)(3) or § 212.1 of this chapter), shall be ordered removed from the United States in accordance with section 235(b)(1) of the Act. In every case in which the expedited removal provisions will be applied and before removing an alien from the United States pursuant to this section, the examining immigration officer shall create a record of the facts of the case and statements made by the alien. This shall be accomplished by means of a sworn statement using Form I–867AB, Record of Sworn Statement in Proceedings under Section 235(b)(1) of the Act. The examining immigration officer shall read (or have read) to the alien all information contained on Form I–867A. Following questioning and recording of the alien's statement regarding identity, alienage, and inadmissibility, the examining immigration officer shall record the alien's response to the questions contained on Form I–867B, and have the alien read (or have read to him or her) the statement, and the alien shall sign and initial each page of the statement and each correction. The examining immigration officer shall advise the alien of the charges against him or her on Form I–860, Notice and Order of Expedited Removal, and the alien shall be given an opportunity to respond to those charges in the sworn statement. After obtaining supervisory concurrence in accordance with paragraph (b)(7) of this section, the examining immigration official shall serve the alien with Form I–860 and the alien shall sign the reverse of the form acknowledging receipt. Interpretative assistance shall be used if necessary to communicate with the alien.

(ii) No entitlement to hearings and appeals. Except as otherwise provided in this section, such alien is not entitled to a hearing before an immigration judge in proceedings conducted pursuant to section 240 of the Act, or to an appeal of the expedited removal order to the Board of Immigration Appeals.

(iii) Detention and parole of alien in expedited removal. An alien whose inadmissibility is being considered under this section or who has been ordered removed pursuant to this section shall be detained pending determination and removal, except that parole of such alien, in accordance with section 212(d)(5) of the Act, may be permitted only when the Attorney General determines, in the exercise of discretion, that parole is required to meet a medical emergency or is necessary for a legitimate law enforcement objective.

(3) Additional charges of inadmissibility. In the expedited removal process, the Service may not charge an alien with any additional grounds of inadmissibility other than section 212(a)(6)(C) or 212(a)(7) of the Act. If an alien appears to be inadmissible under other grounds contained in section 212(a) of the Act, and if the Service wishes to pursue such additional grounds of inadmissibility, the alien shall be detained and referred for a removal hearing before an immigration judge pursuant to sections 235(b)(2) and 240 of the Act for inquiry into all charges. Once the alien is in removal proceedings under section 240 of the Act, the Service is not precluded from lodging additional charges against the alien. Nothing in this paragraph shall preclude the Service from pursuing such additional grounds of inadmissibility against the alien in any subsequent attempt to reenter the United States, provided the additional grounds of inadmissibility still exist.

(4) Claim of asylum or fear of persecution or torture. If an alien subject to the expedited removal provisions indicates an intention to apply for asylum, or expresses a fear of persecution or torture, or a fear of return to his or her country, the inspecting officer shall not proceed further with removal of the alien until the alien has been referred for an interview by an asylum officer in accordance with 8

CFR 208.30. The examining immigration officer shall record sufficient information in the sworn statement to establish and record that the alien has indicated such intention, fear, or concern, and to establish the alien's inadmissibility.

(i) **Referral.** The referring officer shall provide the alien with a written disclosure on Form M–444, Information About Credible Fear Interview, describing:

(A) The purpose of the referral and description of the credible fear interview process;

(B) The right to consult with other persons prior to the interview and any review thereof at no expense to the United States Government;

(C) The right to request a review by an immigration judge of the asylum officer's credible fear determination; and

(D) The consequences of failure to establish a credible fear of persecution or torture.

(ii) **Detention pending credible fear interview.** Pending the credible fear determination by an asylum officer and any review of that determination by an immigration judge, the alien shall be detained. Parole of such alien in accordance with section 212(d)(5) of the Act may be permitted only when the Attorney General determines, in the exercise of discretion, that parole is required to meet a medical emergency or is necessary for a legitimate law enforcement objective. Prior to the interview, the alien shall be given time to contact and consult with any person or persons of his or her choosing. Such consultation shall be made available in accordance with the policies and procedures of the detention facility where the alien is detained, shall be at no expense to the government, and shall not unreasonably delay the process.

(5) **Claim to lawful permanent resident, refugee, or asylee status or U.S. citizenship.—**

(i) **Verification of status.** If an applicant for admission who is subject to expedited removal pursuant to section 235(b)(1) of the Act claims to have been lawfully admitted for permanent residence, admitted as a refugee under section 207 of the Act, granted asylum under section 208 of the Act, or claims to be a U.S. citizen, the immigration officer shall attempt to verify the alien's claim. Such verification shall include a check of all available Service data systems and any other means available to the officer. An alien whose claim to lawful permanent resident, refugee, asylee status, or U.S. citizen status cannot be verified will be advised of the penalties for perjury, and will be placed under oath or allowed to make a declaration as permitted under 28 U.S.C. 1746, concerning his or her lawful admission for permanent residence, admission as a refugee under section 207 of the Act, grant of asylum status under section 208 of the Act, or claim to U.S. citizenship. A written statement shall be taken from the alien in the alien's own language and handwriting, stating that he or she declares, certifies, verifies, or states that the claim is true and correct. The immigration officer shall issue an expedited order of removal under section 235(b)(1)(A)(i) of the Act and refer the alien to the immigration judge for review of the order in accordance with paragraph (b)(5)(iv) of this section and § 235.6(a)(2)(ii). The person shall be detained pending review of the expedited removal order under this section. Parole of such person, in accordance with section 212(d)(5) of the Act, may be permitted only when the Attorney General determines, in the exercise of discretion, that parole is required to meet a medical emergency or is necessary for a legitimate law enforcement objective.

(ii) Verified lawful permanent residents. If the claim to lawful permanent resident status is verified, and such status has not been terminated in exclusion, deportation, or removal proceedings, the examining immigration officer shall not order the alien removed pursuant to section 235(b)(1) of the Act. The examining immigration officer will determine in accordance with section 101(a)(13)(C) of the Act whether the alien is considered to be making an application for admission. If the alien is determined to be seeking admission and the alien is otherwise admissible, except that he or she is not in possession of the required documentation, a discretionary waiver of documentary requirements may be considered in accordance with section 211(b) of the Act and § 211.1(b)(3) of this chapter or the alien's inspection may be deferred to an onward office for presentation of the required documents. If the alien appears to be inadmissible, the immigration officer may initiate removal proceedings against the alien under section 240 of the Act.

(iii) Verified refugees and asylees. If a check of Service records or other means indicates that the alien has been granted refugee status or asylee status, and such status has not been terminated in deportation, exclusion, or removal proceedings, the immigration officer shall not order the alien removed pursuant to section 235(b)(1) of the Act. If the alien is not in possession of a valid, unexpired refugee travel document, the examining immigration officer may accept an application for a refugee travel document in accordance with § 223.2(b)(2)(ii) of this chapter. If accepted, the immigration officer shall readmit the refugee or asylee in accordance with § 223.3(d)(2)(i) of this chapter. If the alien is determined not to be eligible to file an application for a refugee travel document the immigration officer may initiate removal proceedings against the alien under section 240 of the Act.

(iv) Review of order for claimed lawful permanent residents, refugees, asylees, or U.S. citizens. A person whose claim to U.S. citizenship has been verified may not be ordered removed.

When an alien whose status has not been verified but who is claiming under oath or under penalty of perjury to be a lawful permanent resident, refugee, asylee, or U.S. citizen is ordered removed pursuant to section 235(b)(1) of the Act, the case will be referred to an immigration judge for review of the expedited removal order under section 235(b)(1)(C) of the Act and § 235.6(a)(2)(ii). If the immigration judge determines that the alien has never been admitted as a lawful permanent resident or as a refugee, granted asylum status, or is not a U.S. citizen, the order issued by the immigration officer will be affirmed and the Service will remove the alien. There is no appeal from the decision of the immigration judge. If the immigration judge determines that the alien was once so admitted as a lawful permanent resident or as a refugee, or was granted asylum status, or is a U.S. citizen, and such status has not been terminated by final administrative action, the immigration judge will terminate proceedings and vacate the expedited removal order. The Service may initiate removal proceedings against such an alien, but not against a person determined to be a U.S. citizen, in proceedings under section 240 of the Act. During removal proceedings, the immigration judge may consider any waivers, exceptions, or requests for relief for which the alien is eligible.

(6) Opportunity for alien to establish that he or she was admitted or paroled into the United States. If the Commissioner determines that the expedited removal provisions of section 235(b)(1) of the Act shall apply to any or all aliens described in paragraph (b)(2)(ii) of this section, such alien will be given a reasonable opportunity to establish to the satisfaction of the examining immigration officer that he or she was admitted or paroled into the United States following inspection at a port-of-entry. The alien will be allowed to present evidence or provide sufficient information to support the claim. Such evidence may consist of documentation in the possession of the alien, the Service, or a third party. The examining immigration officer will consider all such evidence and information, make further inquiry if necessary, and will attempt to verify the alien's status through a check of all available Service data systems. The burden rests with the alien to satisfy the examining immigration officer of the claim of lawful admission or parole. If the alien establishes that he or she was lawfully admitted or paroled, the case will be examined to determine if grounds of deportability under section 237(a) of the Act are applicable, or if paroled, whether such parole has been, or should be, terminated, and whether the alien is inadmissible under section 212(a) of the Act. An alien who cannot satisfy the examining officer that he or she was lawfully admitted or paroled will be ordered removed pursuant to section 235(b)(1) of the Act.

(7) Review of expedited removal orders. Any removal order entered by an examining immigration officer pursuant to section 235(b)(1) of the Act must be reviewed and approved by the appropriate supervisor before the order is considered final. Such supervisory review shall not be delegated below the level of the second line supervisor, or a person acting in that capacity. The supervisory review shall include a review of the sworn statement and any answers and statements made by the alien regarding a fear of removal or return. The supervisory review and approval of an expedited removal order for an alien described in section 235(b)(1)(A)(iii) of the Act must include a review of any claim of lawful admission or parole and any evidence or information presented to support such a claim, prior to approval of the order. In such cases, the supervisor may request additional information from any source and may require further interview of the alien.

(8) Removal procedures relating to expedited removal. An alien ordered removed pursuant to section 235(b)(1) of the Act shall be removed from the United States in accordance with section 241(c) of the Act and 8 CFR part 241.

(9) Waivers of documentary requirements. Nothing in this section limits the discretionary authority of the Attorney General, including authority under sections 211(b) or 212(d) of the Act, to waive the documentary requirements for arriving aliens.

(10) Applicant for admission under section 217 of the Act. The provisions of § 235.3(b) do not apply to an applicant for admission under section 217 of the Act.

(c) Arriving aliens placed in proceedings under section 240 of the Act. Except as otherwise provided in this chapter, any arriving alien who appears to the inspecting officer to be inadmissible, and who is placed in removal proceedings pursuant to section 240 of the Act shall be detained in accordance with section 235(b) of the Act. Parole of such alien shall only be considered in accordance with § 212.5(b) of this chapter. This paragraph shall also apply to any alien who arrived before April 1, 1997, and who was placed in exclusion proceedings.

(d) Service custody. The Service will assume custody of any alien subject to detention under paragraph (b) or (c) of this section. In its discretion, the Service may require any alien who appears inadmissible and who arrives at a land border port-of-entry from Canada or Mexico, to remain in that country while awaiting a removal hearing. Such alien shall be considered detained for a proceeding within the meaning of section 235(b) of the Act and may be ordered removed in absentia by an immigration judge if the alien fails to appear for the hearing.

(e) Detention in non-Service facility. Whenever an alien is taken into Service custody and detained at a facility other than at a Service Processing Center, the public or private entities contracted to perform such service shall have been approved for such use by the Service's Jail Inspection Program or shall be performing such service under contract in compliance with the Standard Statement of Work for Contract Detention Facilities. Both programs are administered by the Detention and Deportation section having jurisdiction over the alien's place of detention. Under no circumstances shall an alien be detained in facilities not meeting the four mandatory criteria for usage. These are:

    (1) 24-Hour supervision,

    (2) Conformance with safety and emergency codes,

    (3) Food service, and

    (4) Availability of emergency medical care.

    (f) Privilege of communication. The mandatory notification requirements of consular and diplomatic officers pursuant to § 236.1(e) of this chapter apply when an inadmissible alien is detained for removal proceedings, including for purpose of conducting the credible fear determination.

    [32 FR 9628, July 4, 1967, as amended at 34 FR 14727, Sept. 24, 1969; 47 FR 30046, July 9, 1982; 47 FR 46494, Oct. 19, 1982; 54 FR 101, Jan. 4, 1989; 54 FR 6365, Feb. 9, 1989; 60 FR 16043, March 29, 1995; 62 FR 10355, March 6, 1997; 64 FR 8494, Feb. 19, 1999; 65 FR 82256, Dec. 28, 2000; 66 FR 7863, Jan. 26, 2001; 69 FR 69490, Nov. 29, 2004; 76 FR 53784, Aug. 29, 2011; 82 FR 4771, Jan. 17, 2017]

§ 235.4 Withdrawal of application for admission. [also 8 C.F.R. § 1235.4]

    The Attorney General may, in his or her discretion, permit any alien applicant for admission to withdraw his or her application for admission in lieu of removal proceedings under section 240 of the Act or expedited removal under section 235(b)(1) of the Act. The alien's decision to withdraw his or her application for admission must be made voluntarily, but nothing in this section shall be construed as to give an alien the right to withdraw his or her application for admission. Permission to withdraw an application for admission should not normally be granted unless the alien intends and is able to depart the United States immediately. An alien permitted to withdraw his or her application for admission shall normally remain in carrier or Service custody pending departure, unless the district director determines that parole of the alien is warranted in accordance with § 212.5(b) of this chapter.

    [22 FR 9791, Dec. 6, 1957, as amended at 33 FR 4562, March 15, 1968; 48 FR 35349, Aug. 4, 1983; 62 FR 10358, March 6, 1997; 62 FR 15363, April 1, 1997; 65 FR 82256, Dec. 28, 2000; 66 FR 7863, Jan. 26, 2001]

§ 235.5 Preinspection. [also 8 C.F.R. § 1235.5]

    (a) In United States territories and possessions. In the case of any aircraft proceeding from Guam, the Commonwealth of the Northern Mariana Islands (beginning November 28, 2009), Puerto Rico, or the United States Virgin Islands destined directly and without touching at a foreign port or place, to any other of such places, or to one of the States of the United States or the District of Columbia, the examination of the passengers and crew required by the Act may be made prior to the departure of the aircraft, and in such event, final determination of admissibility will be made immediately prior to such departure. The examination will be conducted in accordance with sections 232, 235, and 240 of the Act and 8 CFR parts 235 and 240. If it appears to the immigration officer that any person in the United States being examined under this section is prima facie removable from the United States, further action with respect to his or her examination will be deferred and further proceedings regarding removability conducted as provided in section 240 of the Act and 8 CFR part 240. When the foregoing inspection procedure is applied to any aircraft, persons examined and found admissible will be placed aboard the aircraft, or kept at the airport separate and apart from the general public until they are permitted to board the aircraft. No other person will be permitted to depart on such aircraft until and unless he or she is found to be admissible as provided in this section.

(b) In foreign territory. In the case of any aircraft, vessel, or train proceeding directly, without stopping, from a port or place in foreign territory to a port-of-entry in the United States, the examination and inspection of passengers and crew required by the Act and final determination of admissibility may be made immediately prior to such departure at the port or place in the foreign territory and shall have the same effect under the Act as though made at the destined port-of-entry in the United States.

[23 FR 3997, June 7, 1958, as amended at 24 FR 2583, Apr. 3, 1959; 50 FR 11842, March 26, 1985; 54 FR 101, Jan. 4, 1989; 62 FR 10358, March 6, 1997; 74 FR 2836, Jan. 16, 2009; 74 FR 25388, May 28, 2009]

§ 235.6 Referral to immigration judge. [also 8 C.F.R. § 1235.6]

(a) Notice.

(1) Referral by Form I–862, Notice to Appear. An immigration officer or asylum officer will sign and deliver a Form I–862 to an alien in the following cases:

(i) If, in accordance with the provisions of section 235(b)(2)(A) of the Act, the examining immigration officer detains an alien for a proceeding before an immigration judge under section 240 of the Act; or

(ii) If an asylum officer determines that an alien in expedited removal proceedings has a credible fear of persecution or torture and refers the case to the immigration judge for consideration of the application for asylum, except that, prior to January 1, 2015, an alien arriving in the Commonwealth of the Northern Mariana Islands is not eligible to apply for asylum but the immigration judge may consider eligibility for withholding of removal pursuant to section 241(b)(3) of the Act or withholding or deferral of removal under the Convention Against Torture.

(iii) If the immigration judge determines that an alien in expedited removal proceedings has a credible fear of persecution or torture and vacates the expedited removal order issued by the asylum officer, except that, prior to January 1, 2015, an alien physically present in or arriving in the Commonwealth of the Northern Mariana Islands is not eligible to apply for asylum but an immigration judge may consider eligibility for withholding of removal pursuant to section 241(b)(3) of the Act or withholding or deferral of removal under the Convention Against Torture.

(iv) If an immigration officer verifies that an alien subject to expedited removal under section 235(b)(1) of the Act has been admitted as a lawful permanent resident refugee, or asylee, or upon review pursuant to § 235.3(b)(5)(iv) an immigration judge determines that the alien was once so admitted, provided that such status has not been terminated by final administrative action, and the Service initiates removal proceedings against the alien under section 240 of the Act.

(2) Referral by Form I–863, Notice of Referral to Immigration Judge. An immigration officer will sign and deliver a Form I–863 to an alien in the following cases:

(i) If an asylum officer determines that an alien does not have a credible fear of persecution or torture, and the alien requests a review of that determination by an immigration judge; or

(ii) If, in accordance with section 235(b)(1)(C) of the Act, an immigration officer refers an expedited removal order entered on an alien claiming to be a lawful permanent resident, refugee, asylee, or U.S. citizen for whom the officer could not verify such status to an immigration judge for review of the order.

(iii) If an immigration officer refers an applicant described in § 208.2(b)(1) of this chapter to an immigration judge for an asylum hearing under § 208.2(b)(2) of this chapter.

(b) Certification for mental condition; medical appeal. An alien certified under sections 212(a)(1) and 232(b) of the Act shall be advised by the examining immigration officer that he or she may appeal to a board of medical examiners of the United States Public Health Service pursuant to section 232 of the Act. If such appeal is taken, the district director shall arrange for the convening of the medical board.

[24 FR 6477, Aug. 12, 1959, as amended at 44 FR 4653, Jan. 23, 1979; 56 FR 50812, Oct. 9, 1991; 62 FR 9074, Feb. 28, 1997; 62 FR 10358, March 6, 1997; 64 FR 8494, Feb. 19, 1999; 74 FR 55739, Oct. 28, 2009]

PART 248—CHANGE OF NONIMMIGRANT CLASSIFICATION

§ 248.1   Eligibility.

(a) General. Except for those classes enumerated in § 248.2 of this part, any alien lawfully admitted to the United States as a nonimmigrant, including an alien who acquired such status in accordance with section 247 of the Act who is continuing to maintain his or her nonimmigrant status, may apply to have his or her nonimmigrant classification changed to any nonimmigrant classification other than that of a spouse or fiance(e), or the child of such alien, under section 101(a)(15)(K) of the Act or as an alien in transit under section 101(a)(15)(C) of the Act. Except where the nonimmigrant classification to which the alien seeks to change is exempted by law or regulation from section 212(a)(4) of the Act or that section has been waived, as a condition for approval of a change of nonimmigrant status, the alien must demonstrate that he or she has not received since obtaining the nonimmigrant status from which he or she seeks to change, public benefits, as described in 8 CFR 212.21(b), for more than 12 months in the aggregate within any 36-month period (such that, for instance, receipt of two benefits in one month counts as two months). DHS will only consider public benefits received on or after October 15, 2019 for petitions or applications postmarked (or, if applicable, submitted electronically) on or after that date. An alien defined by section 101(a)(15)(V) or 101(a)(15)(U) of the Act may be accorded nonimmigrant status in the United States by following the procedures set forth in 8 CFR 214.15(f) and 214.14, respectively.

(b) Decision in change of status proceedings. Where an applicant or petitioner demonstrates eligibility for a requested change of status, it may be granted at the discretion of DHS. There is no appeal from the denial of an application for change of status.

(c) Except in the case of an alien applying to obtain V nonimmigrant status in the United States under § 214.15(f) of this chapter, a change of status may not be approved for an alien who failed to maintain the previously accorded status or whose status expired before the application or petition was filed, except that failure to file before the period of previously authorized status expired may be excused in the discretion of USCIS, and without separate application, where it is demonstrated at the time of filing that:

(1) The failure to file a timely application was due to extraordinary circumstances beyond the control of the applicant or petitioner, and USCIS finds the delay commensurate with the circumstances;

(2) The alien has not otherwise violated his or her nonimmigrant status;

(3) The alien remains a bona fide nonimmigrant; and

693

(4) As a condition for approval, an alien seeking to change nonimmigrant classification must demonstrate that he or she has not received, since obtaining the nonimmigrant status from which he or she seeks to change, one or more public benefits, as defined in 8 CFR 212.21(b), for more than 12 months in the aggregate within any 36-month period (such that, for instance, receipt of two benefits in one month counts as two months). For purposes of this determination, DHS will only consider public benefits received on or after October 15, 2019 for petitions or applications postmarked (or, if applicable, submitted electronically) on or after that date. This provision does not apply where the nonimmigrant classification from which the alien seeks to change or to which the alien seeks to change is exempt from section 212(a)(4) of the Act, or where that section has been waived.

(d) Change of nonimmigrant classification to that of a nonimmigrant student.

(1) Except as provided in paragraph (c)(3) of this section, a nonimmigrant applying for a change of classification as an F–1 or M–1 student is not considered ineligible for such a change solely because the applicant may have started attendance at school before the application was submitted. USCIS will deny an application for a change to classification as an M–1 student if the applicant intends to pursue the course of study solely in order to qualify for a subsequent change of nonimmigrant classification to that of an alien temporary worker under section 101(a)(15)(H) of the Act. Furthermore, an alien may not change from classification as an M–1 student to that of an F–1 student.

(2) [Reserved]

(3) A nonimmigrant who is admitted as, or changes status to, a B–1 or B–2 nonimmigrant on or after April 12, 2002, or who files a request to extend the period of authorized stay as a B–1 or B–2 nonimmigrant on or after such date, may not pursue a course of study at an approved school unless the Service has approved his or her application for change of status to a classification as an F–1 or M–1 student. USCIS will deny the change of status if the B–1 or B–2 nonimmigrant enrolled in a course of study before filing the application for change of status or while the application is pending.

(e) Application for change of nonimmigrant classification from that of a student under section 101(a)(15)(M)(i) to that described in section 101(a)(15)(H). A district director shall deny an application for change of nonimmigrant classification from that of an M–1 student to that of an alien temporary worker under section 101(a)(15)(H) of the Act if the education or training which the student received while an M–1 student enables the student to meet the qualifications for temporary worker classification under section 101(a)(15)(H) of the Act.

(f) Change of nonimmigrant classification to that as described in section 101(a)(15)(N). An application for change to N status shall not be denied on the grounds the applicant is an intending immigrant. Change of status shall be granted for three years not to exceed termination of eligibility under section 101(a)(15)(N) of the Act. Employment authorization pursuant to section 274(A) of the Act may be granted to an alien accorded nonimmigrant status under section 101(a)(15)(N) of the Act. Employment authorization is automatically terminated when the alien changes status or is no longer eligible for classification under section 101(a)(15)(N) of the Act.

[36 FR 9001, May 18, 1971; 48 FR 14592, April 5, 1983; 52 FR 11621, April 10, 1987; 59 FR 1465, Jan. 11, 1994; 62 FR 10386, March 6, 1997; 66 FR 42595, Aug. 14, 2001; 66 FR 46704, Sept. 7, 2001; 67 FR 18064, April 12, 2002; 72 FR 53041, Sept. 17, 2007; 76 FR 53794, Aug. 29, 2011; 80 FR 79459, Dec. 22, 2015; 84 FR 41508, Aug. 14, 2019; 84 FR 52363, Oct. 2, 2019]

PART 274a—CONTROL OF EMPLOYMENT OF ALIENS

SUBPART B—EMPLOYMENT AUTHORIZATION

§ 274a.12   Classes of aliens authorized to accept employment. [also 8 C.F.R. § 1274a.12]

(a) Aliens authorized employment incident to status. Pursuant to the statutory or regulatory reference cited, the following classes of aliens are authorized to be employed in the United States without restrictions as to location or type of employment as a condition of their admission or subsequent change to one of the indicated classes. Any alien who is within a class of aliens described in paragraphs (a)(3), (a)(4), (a)(6)–(a)(8), (a)(10)–(a)(15), or (a)(20) of this section, and who seeks to be employed in the United States, must apply to U.S. Citizenship and Immigration Services (USCIS) for a document evidencing such employment authorization. USCIS may, in its discretion, determine the validity period assigned to any document issued evidencing an alien's authorization to work in the United States.

(1) An alien who is a lawful permanent resident (with or without conditions pursuant to section 216 of the Act), as evidenced by Form I–551 issued by the Service. An expiration date on the Form I–551 reflects only that the card must be renewed, not that the bearer's work authorization has expired;

(2) An alien admitted to the United States as a lawful temporary resident pursuant to section 245A or 210 of the Act, as evidenced by an employment authorization document issued by the Service;

(3) An alien admitted to the United States as a refugee pursuant to section 207 of the Act for the period of time in that status, as evidenced by an employment authorization document issued by the Service;

(4) An alien paroled into the United States as a refugee for the period of time in that status, as evidenced by an employment authorization document issued by the Service;

(5) An alien granted asylum under section 208 of the Act for the period of time in that status, as evidenced by an employment authorization document, issued by USCIS to the alien. An expiration date on the employment authorization document issued by USCIS reflects only that the document must be renewed, and not that the bearer's work authorization has expired. Evidence of employment authorization shall be granted in increments not exceeding 5 years for the period of time the alien remains in that status;

(6) An alien admitted to the United States as a nonimmigrant fiancé or fiancée pursuant to section 101(a)(15)(K)(i) of the Act, or an alien admitted as a child of such alien, for the period of admission in that status, as evidenced by an employment authorization document issued by the Service;

(7) An alien admitted as a parent (N–8) or dependent child (N–9) of an alien granted permanent residence under section 101(a)(27)(I) of the Act, as evidenced by an employment authorization document issued by the Service;

(8) An alien admitted to the United States as a nonimmigrant pursuant to the Compact of Free Association between the United States and of the Federated States of Micronesia, the Republic of the Marshall Islands, or the Republic of Palau;

(9) Any alien admitted as a nonimmigrant spouse pursuant to section 101(a)(15)(K)(ii) of the Act, or an alien admitted as a child of such alien, for the period of admission in that status, as evidenced by an employment authorization document, with an expiration date issued by the Service;

(10) An alien granted withholding of deportation or removal for the period of time in that status, as evidenced by an employment authorization document issued by the Service;

(11) An alien whose enforced departure from the United States has been deferred in accordance with a directive from the President of the United States to the Secretary. Employment is authorized for the period of time and under the conditions established by the Secretary pursuant to the Presidential directive;

(12) An alien granted Temporary Protected Status under section 244 of the Act for the period of time in that status, as evidenced by an employment authorization document issued by the Service;

(13) An alien granted voluntary departure by the Attorney General under the Family Unity Program established by section 301 of the Immigration Act of 1990, as evidenced by an employment authorization document issued by the Service;

(14) An alien granted Family Unity benefits under section 1504 of the Legal Immigrant Family Equity (LIFE) Act Amendments, Public Law 106–554, and the provisions of 8 CFR part 245a, Subpart C of this chapter, as evidenced by an employment authorization document issued by the Service; or

(15) Any alien in V nonimmigrant status as defined in section 101(a)(15)(V) of the Act and 8 CFR 214.15;

(16) Any alien in T–1 nonimmigrant status, pursuant to 8 CFR 214.11, for the period in that status, as evidenced by an employment authorization document issued by USCIS to the alien.

(17) [Reserved]

(18) [Reserved]

(19) Any alien in U–1 nonimmigrant status, pursuant to 8 CFR 214.14, for the period of time in that status, as evidenced by an employment authorization document issued by USCIS to the alien.

(20) Any alien in U–2, U–3, U–4, or U–5 nonimmigrant status, pursuant to 8 CFR 214.14, for the period of time in that status, as evidenced by an employment authorization document issued by USCIS to the alien.

(b) Aliens authorized for employment with a specific employer incident to status or parole. The following classes of aliens are authorized to be employed in the United States by the specific employer and subject to any restrictions described in the section(s) of this chapter indicated as a condition of their parole or of their admission in, or subsequent change to, the designated nonimmigrant classification. An alien in one of these classes is not issued an employment authorization document by DHS:

(1) A foreign government official (A–1 or A–2), pursuant to § 214.2(a) of this chapter. An alien in this status may be employed only by the foreign government entity;

(2) An employee of a foreign government official (A–3), pursuant to § 214.2(a) of this chapter. An alien in this status may be employed only by the foreign government official;

(3) A foreign government official in transit (C–2 or C–3), pursuant to § 214.2(c) of this chapter. An alien in this status may be employed only by the foreign government entity;

(4) [Reserved]

(5) A nonimmigrant treaty trader (E–1) or treaty investor (E–2), pursuant to § 214.2(e) of this chapter. An alien in this status may be employed only by the treaty-qualifying company through which the alien attained the status. Employment authorization does not extend to the dependents of the principal treaty trader or treaty investor (also designated "E–1" or "E–2"), other than those specified in paragraph (c)(2) of this section;

(6) A nonimmigrant (F–1) student who is in valid nonimmigrant student status and pursuant to 8 CFR 214.2(f) is seeking:

(i) On-campus employment for not more than twenty hours per week when school is in session or full-time employment when school is not in session if the student intends and is eligible to register for the next term or session. Part-time on-campus employment is authorized by the school and no specific endorsement by a school official or Service officer is necessary;

(ii) [Reserved].

(iii) Curricular practical training (internships, cooperative training programs, or work-study programs which are part of an established curriculum) after having been enrolled full-time in a Service approved institution for one full academic year. Curricular practical training (part-time or full-time) is authorized by the Designated School Official on the student's Form I–20. No Service endorsement is necessary.

(iv) An Employment Authorization Document, Form I–766 or successor form, under paragraph (c)(3)(i)(C) of this section based on a STEM Optional Practical Training extension, and whose timely filed Form I–765 or successor form is pending and employment authorization and accompanying Form I–766 or successor form issued under paragraph (c)(3)(i)(B) of this section have expired. Employment is authorized beginning on the expiration date of the Form I–766 or successor form issued under paragraph (c)(3)(i)(B) of this section and ending on the date of USCIS' written decision on the current Form I–765 or successor form, but not to exceed 180 days. For this same period, such Form I–766 or successor form is automatically extended and is considered unexpired when combined with a Certificate of Eligibility for Nonimmigrant (F–1/M–1) Students, Form I–20 or successor form, endorsed by the Designated School Official recommending such an extension; or

(v) Pursuant to 8 CFR 214.2(h) is seeking H–1B nonimmigrant status and whose duration of status and employment authorization have been extended pursuant to 8 CFR 214.2(f)(5)(vi).

(7) A representative of an international organization (G–1, G–2, G–3, or G–4), pursuant to § 214.2(g) of this chapter. An alien in this status may be employed only by the foreign government entity or the international organization;

(8) A personal employee of an official or representative of an international organization (G–5), pursuant to § 214.2(g) of this chapter. An alien in this status may be employed only by the official or representative of the international organization;

(9) A temporary worker or trainee (H–1, H–2A, H–2B, or H–3), pursuant to § 214.2(h) of this chapter, or a nonimmigrant specialty occupation worker pursuant to section 101(a)(15)(H)(i)(b1) of the Act. An alien in this status may be employed only by the petitioner through whom the status was obtained. In the case of a professional H–2B athlete who is traded from one organization to another organization, employment authorization for the player will automatically continue for a period of 30 days after acquisition by the new organization, within which time the new organization is expected to file a new Form I–129 to petition for H–2B classification. If a new Form I–129 is not filed within 30 days, employment authorization will cease. If a new Form I–129 is filed within 30 days, the professional athlete's employment authorization will continue until the petition is adjudicated. If the new petition is denied, employment authorization will cease;[sic] In the case of a nonimmigrant with H–1B status, employment authorization will automatically continue upon the filing of a qualifying petition under 8 CFR 214.2(h)(2)(i)(H) until such petition is adjudicated, in accordance with section 214(n) of the Act and 8 CFR 214.2(h)(2)(i)(H);

(10) An information media representative (I), pursuant to § 214.2(i) of this chapter. An alien in this status may be employed only for the sponsoring foreign news agency or bureau. Employment authorization does not extend to the dependents of an information media representative (also designated "I");

(11) An exchange visitor (J–1), pursuant to § 214.2(j) of this chapter and 22 CFR part 62. An alien in this status may be employed only by the exchange visitor program sponsor or appropriate designee and within the guidelines of the program approved by the Department of State as set forth in the Form DS–2019, Certificate of Eligibility, issued by the program sponsor;

(12) An intra-company transferee (L–1), pursuant to § 214.2(1) of this chapter. An alien in this status may be employed only by the petitioner through whom the status was obtained;

(13) An alien having extraordinary ability in the sciences, arts, education, business, or athletics (O–1), and an accompanying alien (O–2), pursuant to § 214.2(o) of this chapter. An alien in this status may be employed only by the petitioner through whom the status was obtained. In the case of a professional O–1 athlete who is traded from one organization to another organization, employment authorization for the player will automatically continue for a period of 30 days after the acquisition by the new organization, within which time the new organization is expected to file a new Form I–129 petition for O nonimmigrant classification. If a new Form I–129 is not filed within 30 days, employment authorization will cease. If a new Form I–129 is filed within 30 days, the professional athlete's employment authorization will continue until the petition is adjudicated. If the new petition is denied, employment authorization will cease.

(14) An athlete, artist, or entertainer (P–1, P–2, or P–3), pursuant to § 214.2(p) of this chapter. An alien in this status may be employed only by the petitioner through whom the status was obtained. In the case of a professional P–1 athlete who is traded from one organization to another organization, employment authorization for the player will automatically continue for a period of 30 days after the acquisition by the new organization, within which time the new organization is expected to file a new Form I–129 for P–1 nonimmigrant classification. If a new Form I–129 is not filed within 30 days, employment authorization will cease. If a new Form I–129 is filed within 30 days, the professional athlete's employment authorization will continue until the petition is adjudicated. If the new petition is denied, employment authorization will cease;

(15) An international cultural exchange visitor (Q–1), according to § 214.2(q)(1) of this chapter. An alien may only be employed by the petitioner through whom the status was obtained;

(16) An alien having a religious occupation, pursuant to § 214.2(r) of this chapter. An alien in this status may be employed only by the religious organization through whom the status was obtained;

(17) Officers and personnel of the armed services of nations of the North Atlantic Treaty Organization, and representatives, officials, and staff employees of NATO (NATO–1, NATO–2, NATO–3, NATO–4, NATO–5 and NATO–6), pursuant to § 214.2(*o*) of this chapter. An alien in this status may be employed only by NATO;

(18) An attendant, servant or personal employee (NATO–7) of an alien admitted as a NATO–1, NATO–2, NATO–3, NATO–4, NATO–5, or NATO–6, pursuant to § 214.2(*o*) of this chapter. An alien admitted under this classification may be employed only by the NATO alien through whom the status was obtained;

(19) A nonimmigrant pursuant to section 214(e) of the Act. An alien in this status must be engaged in business activities at a professional level in accordance with the provisions of Chapter 16 of the North American Free Trade Agreement (NAFTA);

(20) A nonimmigrant alien within the class of aliens described in paragraphs (b)(2), (b)(5), (b)(8), (b)(9), (b)(10), (b)(11), (b)(12), (b)(13), (b)(14), (b)(16), (b)(19), (b)(23) and (b)(25) of this section whose status has expired but on whose behalf an application for an extension of stay was timely filed pursuant to § 214.2 or § 214.6 of this chapter. These aliens are authorized to continue employment with the same employer for a period not to exceed 240 days beginning on the date of the expiration of the authorized period of stay. Such authorization shall be subject to any conditions and limitations noted on the initial authorization. However, if the district director or service center director adjudicates the application prior to the expiration of this 240 day period and denies the application for extension of stay, the employment authorization under this paragraph shall automatically terminate upon notification of the denial decision;

(21) A nonimmigrant alien within the class of aliens described in 8 CFR 14.2(h)(1)(ii)(C) who filed an application for an extension of stay pursuant to 8 CFR 214.2 during his or her period of admission. Such alien is authorized to be employed by a new employer that has filed an H–2A petition naming the alien as a beneficiary and requesting an extension of stay for the alien for a period not to exceed 120 days beginning from the "Received Date" on Form I–797 (Notice of Action) acknowledging receipt of the petition requesting an extension of stay, provided that the employer has enrolled in and is a participant in good standing in the E-Verify program, as determined by USCIS in its discretion. Such authorization will be subject to any conditions and limitations noted on the initial authorization, except as to the employer and place of employment. However, if the District Director or Service Center director adjudicates the application prior to the expiration of this 120-day period and denies the application for extension of stay, the employment authorization under this paragraph (b)(21) shall automatically terminate upon 15 days after the date of the denial decision. The employment authorization shall also terminate automatically if the employer fails to remain a participant in good standing in the E-Verify program, as determined by USCIS in its discretion;

(22) An alien in E–2 CNMI Investor nonimmigrant status pursuant to 8 CFR 214.2(e)(23). An alien in this status may be employed only by the qualifying company through which the alien attained the status. An alien in E–2 CNMI Investor nonimmigrant status may be employed only in the Commonwealth of the Northern Mariana Islands for a qualifying entity. An alien who attained E–2 CNMI Investor nonimmigrant status based upon a Foreign Retiree Investment Certificate or Certification is not employment-authorized. Employment authorization does not extend to the dependents of the principal investor (also designated E–2 CNMI Investor nonimmigrants) other than those specified in paragraph (c)(12) of this section;

(23) A Commonwealth of the Northern Mariana Islands transitional worker (CW–1) pursuant to 8 CFR 214.2(w). An alien in this status may be employed only in the CNMI during the transition period, and only by the petitioner through whom the status was obtained, or as otherwise authorized by 8 CFR 214.2(w). An alien who is lawfully present in the CNMI (as defined by 8 CFR 214.2(w)(1)(v)) on or before November 27, 2011, is authorized to be employed in the CNMI, and is so employed in the CNMI by an employer properly filing an application under 8 CFR 214.2(w)(14)(ii) on or before such date for a grant of CW–1 status to its employee in the CNMI for the purpose of the alien continuing the employment, is authorized to continue such employment on or after November 27, 2011, until a decision is made on the application;

(24) An alien who is authorized to be employed in the Commonwealth of the Northern Mariana Islands for a period of up to 2 years following the transition program effective date, under section 6(e)(2) of Public Law 94–241, as added by section 702(a) of Public Law 110–229. Such alien is only authorized to continue in the same employment that he or she had on the transition program effective date as defined in 8 CFR 1.1 until the earlier of the date that is 2 years after the transition program effective date or the date of expiration of the alien's employment authorization, unless the alien had unrestricted employment authorization or was otherwise authorized as of the transition program effective date to change employers, in which case the alien may have such employment privileges as were authorized as of the transition program effective date for up to 2 years;

(25) A nonimmigrant treaty alien in a specialty occupation (E–3) pursuant to section 101(a)(15)(E)(iii) of the Act; or

(26)(i) Pursuant to 8 CFR 214.2(h)(21) and notwithstanding 8 CFR 214.2(h)(2)(i)(D) and paragraph (b)(21) of this section, an alien is authorized to be employed, but no earlier than the start date of employment indicated in the H–2A petition, by a new employer that has filed an H–2A petition naming the alien as a beneficiary and requesting an extension of stay for the alien, for a period not to exceed 45 days beginning from the "Received Date" on Form I–797 (Notice of Action) acknowledging receipt of the petition requesting an extension of stay, or 45 days beginning on the start date of employment if the start date of employment indicated in the H–2A petition occurs after the filing. The length of the period (up to 45 days) is to be determined by USCIS in its discretion. However, if USCIS adjudicates the petition prior to the expiration of this 45-day period and denies the petition for extension of stay, or if the petitioner withdraws the petition before the expiration of the 45-day period, the employment authorization under this paragraph (b)(26) will automatically terminate upon 15 days after the date of the denial decision or the date on which the petition is withdrawn.

(ii) This paragraph (b)(26) is in effect for the period set forth in 8 CFR 214.2(h)(21)(iii).

(27) to (36) [Reserved]

(37) An alien paroled into the United States as an entrepreneur pursuant to 8 CFR 212.19 for the period of authorized parole. An entrepreneur who has timely filed a non-frivolous application requesting re-parole with respect to the same start-up entity in accordance with 8 CFR 212.19 prior to the expiration of his or her parole, but whose authorized parole period expires during the pendency of such application, is authorized to continue employment with the same start-up entity for a period not to exceed 240 days beginning on the date of expiration of parole. Such authorization shall be subject to any conditions and limitations on such expired parole. If DHS adjudicates the application prior to the expiration of this 240-day period and denies the application for re-parole, the employment authorization under this paragraph shall automatically terminate upon notification to the alien of the denial decision.

(c) Aliens who must apply for employment authorization. An alien within a class of aliens described in this section must apply for work authorization. If authorized, such an alien may accept employment subject to any restrictions stated in the regulations or cited on the employment authorization document. USCIS, in its discretion, may establish a specific validity period for an employment authorization document, which may include any period when an administrative appeal or judicial review of an application or petition is pending.

(1) An alien spouse or unmarried dependent child; son or daughter of a foreign government official (A–1 or A–2) pursuant to 8 CFR 214.2(a)(2) and who presents an endorsement from an authorized representative of the Department of State;

(2) An alien spouse or unmarried dependent son or daughter of an alien employee of the Coordination Council for North American Affairs (E–1) pursuant to § 214.2(e) of this chapter;

(3) A nonimmigrant (F–1) student who:

(i)(A) Is seeking pre-completion practical training pursuant to 8 CFR 214.2(f)(10)(ii)(A)(1) and (2);

(B) Is seeking authorization to engage in up to 12 months of post-completion Optional Practical Training (OPT) pursuant to 8 CFR 214.2(f)(10)(ii)(A)(3); or

(C) Is seeking a 24-month OPT extension pursuant to 8 CFR 214.2(f)(10)(ii)(C);

(ii) Has been offered employment under the sponsorship of an international organization within the meaning of the International Organization Immunities Act (59 Stat. 669) and who presents a written certification from the international organization that the proposed employment is within the scope of the organization's sponsorship. The F–1 student must also present a Form I–20 ID or SEVIS Form I–20 with employment page completed by DSO certifying eligibility for employment; or

(iii) Is seeking employment because of severe economic hardship pursuant to 8 CFR 214.2(f)(9)(ii)(C) and has filed the Form I–20 ID and Form I–538 (for non-SEVIS schools), or SEVIS Form I–20 with employment page completed by the DSO certifying eligibility, and any other supporting materials such as affidavits which further detail the unforeseen economic circumstances that require the student to seek employment authorization.

(4) An alien spouse or unmarried dependent child; son or daughter of a foreign government official (G–1, G–3 or G–4) pursuant to 8 CFR 214.2(g) and who presents an endorsement from an authorized representative of the Department of State;

(5) An alien spouse or minor child of an exchange visitor (J–2) pursuant to § 214.2(j) of this chapter;

(6) A nonimmigrant (M–1) student seeking employment for practical training pursuant to 8 CFR 214.2(m) following completion of studies. The alien may be employed only in an occupation or vocation directly related to his or her course of study as recommended by the endorsement of the designated school official on the I–20 ID;

(7) A dependent of an alien classified as NATO–1 through NATO–7 pursuant to § 214.2(n) of this chapter;

(8) An alien who has filed a complete application for asylum or withholding of deportation or removal pursuant to 8 CFR part 208, whose application:

(i) Has not been decided, and who is eligible to apply for employment authorization under § 208.7 of this chapter because the 150-day period set forth in that section has expired. Employment authorization may be granted according to the provisions of § 208.7 of this chapter in increments to be determined by the Commissioner and shall expire on a specified date; or

(ii) Has been recommended for approval, but who has not yet received a grant of asylum or withholding or deportation or removal;

(9) An alien who has filed an application for adjustment of status to lawful permanent resident pursuant to part 245 of this chapter. For purposes of section 245(c)(8) of the Act, an alien will not be deemed to be an "unauthorized alien" as defined in section 274A(h)(3) of the Act while his or her properly filed Form I–485 application is pending final adjudication, if the alien has otherwise obtained permission from the Service pursuant to 8 CFR 274a.12 to engage in employment, or if the alien had been granted employment authorization prior to the filing of the adjustment application and such authorization does not expire during the pendency of the adjustment application. Upon meeting these conditions, the adjustment applicant need not file an application for employment authorization to continue employment during the period described in the preceding sentence;

(10) An alien who has filed an application for suspension of deportation under section 244 of the Act (as it existed prior to April 1, 1997), cancellation of removal pursuant to section 240A of the Act, or special rule cancellation of removal under section 309(f)(1) of the Illegal Immigration Reform and Immigrant Responsibility Act of 1996, enacted as Pub.L. 104–208 (110 Stat. 3009–625) (as amended by the Nicaraguan Adjustment and Central American Relief Act (NACARA)), title II of Pub.L. 105–100 (111 Stat. 2160, 2193) and whose properly filed application has been accepted by the Service or EOIR;

(11) Except as provided in paragraphs (b)(37) and (c)(34) of this section and § 212.19(h)(4) of this chapter, an alien paroled into the United States temporarily for urgent humanitarian reasons or significant public benefit pursuant to section 212(d)(5) of the Act.

(12) An alien spouse of a long-term investor in the Commonwealth of the Northern Mariana Islands (E–2 CNMI Investor) other than an E–2 CNMI investor who obtained such status based upon a Foreign Retiree Investment Certificate, pursuant to 8 CFR 214.2(e)(23). An alien spouse of an E–2 CNMI Investor is eligible for employment in the CNMI only;

(13) [Reserved]

(14) An alien who has been granted deferred action, an act of administrative convenience to the government which gives some cases lower priority, if the alien establishes an economic necessity for employment;

(15) [Reserved]

(16) Any alien who has filed an application for creation of record of lawful admission for permanent residence pursuant to part 249 of this chapter;

(17) A nonimmigrant visitor for business (B–1) who:

(i) Is a personal or domestic servant who is accompanying or following to join an employer who seeks admission into, or is already in, the United States as a nonimmigrant defined under sections 101(a)(15)(B), (E), (F), (H), (I), (J), (L) or section 214(e) of the Act. The personal or domestic servant shall have a residence abroad which he or she has no intention of abandoning and shall demonstrate at least one year's experience as a personal or domestic servant. The nonimmigrant's employer shall demonstrate that the employer/employee relationship has existed for at least one year prior to the employer's admission to the United States; or, if the employer/employee relationship existed for less than one year, that the employer has regularly employed (either year-round or seasonally) personal or domestic servants over a period of several years preceding the employer's admission to the United States;

(ii) Is a domestic servant of a United States citizen accompanying or following to join his or her United States citizen employer who has a permanent home or is stationed in a foreign country, and who is visiting temporarily in the United States. The employer/employee relationship shall have existed prior to the commencement of the employer's visit to the United States; or

(iii) Is an employee of a foreign airline engaged in international transportation of passengers freight, whose position with the foreign airline would otherwise entitle the employee to classification under section 101(a)(15)(E)(i) of the Immigration and Nationality Act, and who is precluded from such classification solely because the employee is not a national of the country of the airline's nationality or because there is no treaty of commerce and navigation in effect between the United States and the country of the airline's nationality.

(18) An alien against whom a final order of deportation or removal exists and who is released on an order of supervision under the authority contained in section 241(a)(3) of the Act may be granted employment authorization in the discretion of the district director only if the alien cannot be removed due to the refusal of all countries designated by the alien or under section 241 of the Act to receive the alien, or because the removal of the alien is otherwise impracticable or contrary to the public interest. Additional factors which may be considered by the district director in adjudicating the application for employment authorization include, but are not limited to, the following:

(i) The existence of economic necessity to be employed;

(ii) The existence of a dependent spouse and/or children in the United States who rely on the alien for support; and

(iii) The anticipated length of time before the alien can be removed from the United States.

(19) An alien applying for Temporary Protected Status pursuant to section 244 of the Act shall apply for employment authorization only in accordance with the procedures set forth in part 244 of this chapter.

(20) Any alien who has filed a completed legalization application pursuant to section 210 of the Act (and part 210 of this chapter).

(21) A principal nonimmigrant witness or informant in S classification, and qualified dependent family members.

(22) Any alien who has filed a completed legalization application pursuant to section 245A of the Act (and part 245a of this chapter). Employment authorization shall be granted in increments not exceeding 1 year during the period the application is pending (including any period when an administrative appeal is pending) and shall expire on a specified date.

(23) Reserved.

(24) An alien who has filed an application for adjustment pursuant to section 1104 of the LIFE Act, Public Law 106–553, and the provisions of 8 CFR part 245a, Subpart B of this chapter.

(25) Any alien in T–2, T–3, T–4, T–5, or T–6 nonimmigrant status, pursuant to 8 CFR 214.11, for the period in that status, as evidenced by an employment authorization document issued by USCIS to the alien.

(26) An H–4 nonimmigrant spouse of an H–1B nonimmigrant described as eligible for employment authorization in 8 CFR 214.2(h)(9)(iv).

(27) to (33) [Reserved]

(34) A spouse of an entrepreneur parolee described as eligible for employment authorization in § 212.19(h)(3) of this chapter.

(35) An alien who is the principal beneficiary of a valid immigrant petition under section 203(b)(1), 203(b)(2) or 203(b)(3) of the Act described as eligible for employment authorization in 8 CFR 204.5(p).

(36) A spouse or child of a principal beneficiary of a valid immigrant petition under section 203(b)(1), 203(b)(2) or 203(b)(3) of the Act described as eligible for employment authorization in 8 CFR 204.5(p).

(d) An alien lawfully enlisted in one of the Armed Forces, or whose enlistment the Secretary with jurisdiction over such Armed Force has determined would be vital to the national interest under 10 U.S.C. 504(b)(2), is authorized to be employed by that Armed Force in military service, if such employment is not otherwise authorized under this section and the immigration laws. An alien described in this section is not issued an employment authorization document.

(e) Basic criteria to establish economic necessity. Title 45—Public Welfare, Poverty Guidelines, 45 CFR 1060.2 should be used as the basic criteria to establish eligibility for employment authorization when the alien's economic necessity is identified as a factor. The alien shall submit an application for employee authorization listing his or her assets, income, and expenses as evidence of his or her economic need to work. Permission to work granted on the basis of the alien's application for employment authorization may be revoked under § 274a.14 of this chapter upon a showing that the information contained in the statement was not true and correct.

[53 FR 8614, March 16, 1988; 53 FR 46855, Nov. 21, 1988; 54 FR 16, Jan. 3, 1989; 54 FR 48577, Nov. 24, 1989; 55 FR 5576, Feb. 16, 1990; 55 FR 25935, 25936, June 25, 1990; 56 FR 624, Jan. 7, 1991; 56 FR 23496, 23499, May 22, 1991; 56 FR 41782, 41786, 41787, Aug. 23, 1991; 56 FR 55616, Oct. 29, 1991; 57 FR 6462, Feb. 25, 1992; 57 FR 31956, July 20, 1992; 57 FR 42884, Sept. 17, 1992; 58 FR 48780, Sept. 20, 1993; 58 FR 69217, Dec. 30, 1993; 59 FR 42487, Aug. 15, 1994; 59 FR 47063, Sept. 14, 1994; 59 FR 52894, Oct. 20, 1994; 59 FR 62302, Dec. 5, 1994; 60 FR 14353, March 17, 1995; 60 FR 21976, May 4, 1995; 60 FR 44271, Aug. 25, 1995; 60 FR 66067, 66069, Dec. 21, 1995; 61 FR 46537, Sept. 4, 1996; 62 FR 10389, March 6, 1997; 62 FR 18514, April 16, 1997; 62 FR 39425, July 23, 1997; 62 FR 46553, Sept. 3, 1997; 63 FR 1334, Jan. 9, 1998; 63 FR 27833, May 21, 1998; 63 FR 63597, Nov. 16, 1998; 64 FR 25773, May 12, 1999; 64 FR 27881, May 21, 1999; 65 FR 14780, March 17, 2000; 65 FR 14774, March 24, 2000; 65 FR 43680, July 14, 2000; 66 FR 29681, June 1, 2001; 66 FR 42595, Aug. 14, 2001; 66 FR 46704, Sept. 7, 2001; 67 FR 4803, Jan. 31, 2002; 67 FR 38350, June 4, 2002; 67 FR 76280, Dec. 11, 2002; 69 FR 45557, July 30, 2004; 69 FR 47763, Aug. 6, 2004; 72 FR 53041, Sept. 17, 2007; 73 FR 18956, Apr. 8, 2008; 73 FR 76914, Dec. 18, 2008; 74 FR 7995, Feb. 23, 2009; 74 FR 26515, June 3, 2009; 74 FR 55111, Oct. 27, 2009; 74 FR 55740, Oct. 28, 2009; 75 FR 47701, Aug. 9, 2010; 75 FR 58990, Sept. 24, 2010; 75 FR 79277, Dec. 20, 2010; 76 FR 53784, Aug. 29, 2011; 76 FR 55538, Sept. 7, 2011; 80 FR 10311, Feb. 25, 2015; 81 FR 2068–01, Jan. 15, 2016; 81 FR 13121, March 11, 2016; 81 FR 82491, Nov. 18, 2016; 81 FR 92312, Dec. 19, 2016; 82 FR 5289, Jan. 17, 2017; 82 FR 31887, July 11, 2017; 85 FR 21744, April 20, 2020]

TITLE 20—EMPLOYEES' BENEFITS

Part 656—Labor Certification Process for Permanent
Employment of Aliens in the United States

PART 656—LABOR CERTIFICATION PROCESS FOR PERMANENT EMPLOYMENT OF ALIENS IN THE UNITED STATES

§ 656.3   Definitions, for purposes of this part, of terms used in this part.

Act means the Immigration and Nationality Act, as amended, 8 U.S.C. 1101 et seq.

Agent means a person who is not an employee of an employer, and who has been designated in writing to act on behalf of an alien or employer in connection with an application for labor certification.

Applicant means a U.S. worker (see definition of U.S. worker below) who is applying for a job opportunity for which an employer has filed an Application for Permanent Employment Certification (ETA Form 9089).

Application means an Application for Permanent Employment Certification submitted by an employer (or its agent or attorney) in applying for a labor certification under this part.

Area of intended employment means the area within normal commuting distance of the place (address) of intended employment. There is no rigid measure of distance which constitutes a normal commuting distance or normal commuting area, because there may be widely varying factual circumstances among different areas (e.g., normal commuting distances might be 20, 30, or 50 miles). If the place of intended employment is within a Metropolitan Statistical Area (MSA) or a Primary Metropolitan Statistical Area (PMSA), any place within the MSA or PMSA is deemed to be within normal commuting distance of the place of intended employment; however, not all locations within a Consolidated Metropolitan Statistical Area (CMSA) will be deemed automatically to be within normal commuting distance. The borders of MSA's and PMSA's are not controlling in the identification of the normal commuting area; a location outside of an MSA or PMSA (or a CMSA) may be within normal commuting distance of a location that is inside (e.g., near the border of) the MSA or PMSA (or CMSA). The terminology CMSAs and PMSAs are being replaced by the

Office of Management and Budget (OMB). However, ETA will continue to recognize the use of these area concepts as well as their replacements.

Attorney means any person who is a member in good standing of the bar of the highest court of any state, possession, territory, or commonwealth of the United States, or the District of Columbia, and who is not under suspension or disbarment from practice before any court or before DHS or the United States Department of Justice's Executive Office for Immigration Review. Such a person is permitted to act as an agent, representative, or attorney for an employer and/or alien under this part.

Barter, for purposes of an Application for Permanent Employment Certification (Form ETA 9089) or an Application for Alien Labor Certification (Form ETA 750), means the transfer of ownership of a labor certification application or certification from one person to another by voluntary act or agreement in exchange for a commodity, service, property or other valuable consideration.

Board of Alien Labor Certification Appeals (BALCA or Board) means the permanent Board established by this part, chaired by the Chief Administrative Law Judge, and consisting of Administrative Law Judges assigned to the Department of Labor and designated by the Chief Administrative Law Judge to be members of the Board of Alien Labor Certification Appeals. The Board of Alien Labor Certification Appeals is located in Washington, DC, and reviews and decides appeals in Washington, DC.

Certifying Officer (CO) means a Department of Labor official who makes determinations about whether or not to grant applications for labor certifications.

Closely-held Corporation means a corporation that typically has relatively few shareholders and whose shares are not generally traded in the securities market.

Employer means:

(1) A person, association, firm, or a corporation that currently has a location within the United States to which U.S. workers may be referred for employment and that proposes to employ a full-time employee at a place within the United States, or the authorized representative of such a person, association, firm, or corporation. An employer must possess a valid Federal Employer Identification Number (FEIN). For purposes of this definition, an "authorized representative" means an employee of the employer whose position or legal status authorizes the employee to act for the employer in labor certification matters. A labor certification can not be granted for an Application for Permanent Employment Certification filed on behalf of an independent contractor.

(2) Persons who are temporarily in the United States, including but not limited to, foreign diplomats, intra-company transferees, students, and exchange visitors, visitors for business or pleasure, and representatives of foreign information media can not be employers for the purpose of obtaining a labor certification for permanent employment.

Employment means:

(1) Permanent, full-time work by an employee for an employer other than oneself. For purposes of this definition, an investor is not an employee. In the event of an audit, the employer must be prepared to document the permanent and full-time nature of the position by furnishing position descriptions and payroll records for the job opportunity involved in the Application for Permanent Employment Certification.

(2) Job opportunities consisting solely of job duties that will be performed totally outside the United States, its territories, possessions, or commonwealths can not be the subject of an Application for Permanent Employment Certification.

Employment and Training Administration (ETA) means the agency within the Department of Labor (DOL) that includes the Office of Foreign Labor Certification (OFLC).

Immigration Officer means an official of the Department of Homeland Security, United States Citizenship and Immigration Services (USCIS) who handles applications for labor certifications under this part.

Job opportunity means a job opening for employment at a place in the United States to which U.S. workers can be referred.

Nonprofessional occupation means any occupation for which the attainment of a bachelor's or higher degree is not a usual requirement for the occupation.

Non-profit or tax-exempt organization for the purposes of § 656.40 means an organization that:

(1) Is defined as a tax exempt organization under the Internal Revenue Code of 1986, section 501(c)(3), (c)(4), or (c)(6) (26 U.S.C. 501(c) (3), (c)(4) or (c)(6)); and

(2) Has been approved as a tax-exempt organization for research or educational purposes by the Internal Revenue Service.

O*NET means the system developed by the Department of Labor, Employment and Training Administration, to provide to the general public information on skills, abilities, knowledge, work activities, interests and specific vocational preparation levels associated with occupations. O*NET is based on the Standard Occupational Classification system. Further information about O*NET can be found at http://www.onetcenter.org.

Office of Foreign Labor Certification means the organizational component within the Employment and Training Administration that provides national leadership and policy guidance and develops regulations and procedures to carry out the responsibilities of the Secretary of Labor under the Immigration and Nationality Act, as amended, concerning alien workers seeking admission to the United States in order to work under section 212(a)(5)(A) of the Immigration and Nationality Act, as amended.

Prevailing wage determination (PWD) means the prevailing wage provided or approved by an OFLC National Processing Center (NPC), in accordance with OFLC guidance governing foreign labor certification programs. This includes PWD requests processed for purposes of employer petitions filed with DHS under Schedule A or for sheepherders.

Professional occupation means an occupation for which the attainment of a bachelor's or higher degree is a usual education requirement. A beneficiary of an application for permanent alien employment certification involving a professional occupation need not have a bachelor's or higher degree to qualify for the professional occupation. However, if the employer is willing to accept work experience in lieu of a baccalaureate or higher degree, such work experience must be attainable in the U.S. labor market and must be stated on the application form. If the employer is willing to accept an equivalent foreign degree, it must be clearly stated on the Application for Permanent Employment Certification form.

"Purchase" for purposes of an Application for Permanent Employment Certification (Form ETA 9089) or an Application for Alien Labor Certification (Form ETA 750), means the transfer of ownership of a labor certification application or certification from one person to another by voluntary act and agreement, based on a valuable consideration.

"Sale" for purposes of an Application for Permanent Employment Certification (Form ETA 9089) or an Application for Alien Labor Certification (Form ETA 750), means an agreement between two parties, called, respectively, the seller (or vendor) and the buyer (or purchaser) by which the seller, in consideration of the payment or promise of payment of a certain price in money terms, transfers ownership of a labor certification application or certification to the buyer.

Secretary means the Secretary of Labor, the chief official of the U.S. Department of Labor, or the Secretary's designee.

Secretary of Homeland Security means the chief official of the U.S. Department of Homeland Security or the Secretary of Homeland Security's designee.

Secretary of State means the chief official of the U.S. Department of State or the Secretary of State's designee.

Specific vocational preparation (SVP) means the amount of lapsed time required by a typical worker to learn the techniques, acquire the information, and develop the facility needed for average performance in a specific job-worker situation. Lapsed time is not the same as work time. For example, 30 days is approximately 1 month of lapsed time and not six 5-day work weeks, and 3 months refers to 3 calendar months and not 90 work days. The various levels of specific vocational preparation are provided below.

Level Time

---

1 . . . Short demonstration.

2 . . . Anything beyond short demonstration up to and including 30 days.

3 . . . Over 30 days up to and including 3 months.

4 . . . Over 3 months up to and including 6 months.

5 . . . Over 6 months up to and including 1 year.

6 . . . Over 1 year up to and including 2 years.

7 . . . Over 2 years up to and including 4 years.

8 . . . Over 4 years up to and including 10 years.

9 . . . Over 10 years.

"State Workforce Agency (SWA)", formerly known as State Employment Security Agency (SESA), means the state agency that receives funds under the Wagner-Peyser Act to provide employment-related services to U.S. workers and employers and/or administers the public labor exchange delivered through the state's one-stop delivery system in accordance with the Wagner-Peyser Act.

United States, when used in a geographic sense, means the 50 states, the District of Columbia, Puerto Rico, the U.S. Virgin Islands, and Guam.

United States worker means any worker who is:

(1) A U.S. citizen;

(2) A U.S. national;

(3) Lawfully admitted for permanent residence;

(4) Granted the status of an alien lawfully admitted for temporary residence under 8 U.S.C. 1160(a), 1161(a), or 1255a(a)(1);

(5) Admitted as a refugee under 8 U.S.C. 1157; or

(6) Granted asylum under 8 U.S.C. 1158.

[71 FR 35522, June 21, 2006; 72 FR 27944, May 17, 2007; 73 FR 78068, Dec. 19, 2008]

§ 656.5   Schedule A.

We have determined there are not sufficient United States workers who are able, willing, qualified, and available for the occupations listed below on Schedule A and the wages and working conditions of United States workers similarly employed will not be adversely affected by the employment of aliens in Schedule A occupations. An employer seeking a labor certification for an occupation listed on Schedule A may apply for that labor certification under § 656.15.

Schedule A

(a) Group I:

(1) Persons who will be employed as physical therapists, and who possess all the qualifications necessary to take the physical therapist licensing examination in the state in which they propose to practice physical therapy.

(2) Aliens who will be employed as professional nurses; and

(i) Who have received a Certificate from the Commission on Graduates of Foreign Nursing Schools (CGFNS);

(ii) Who hold a permanent, full and unrestricted license to practice professional nursing in the state of intended employment; or

(iii) Who have passed the National Council Licensure Examination for Registered Nurses (NCLEX–RN), administered by the National Council of State Boards of Nursing.

(3) Definitions of Group I occupations:

(i) Physical therapist means a person who applies the art and science of physical therapy to the treatment of patients with disabilities, disorders and injuries to relieve pain, develop or restore function, and maintain performance, using physical means, such as exercise, massage, heat, water, light, and electricity, as prescribed by a physician (or a surgeon).

(ii) Professional nurse means a person who applies the art and science of nursing which reflects comprehension of principles derived from the physical, biological and behavioral sciences. Professional nursing generally includes making clinical judgments involving the observation, care and counsel of persons requiring nursing care; administering of medicines and treatments prescribed by the physician or dentist; and participation in the activities for the promotion of health and prevention of illness in others. A program of study for professional nurses generally includes theory and practice in clinical areas such as obstetrics, surgery, pediatrics, psychiatry, and medicine.

(b) Group II:

(1) Sciences or arts (except performing arts). Aliens (except for aliens in the performing arts) of exceptional ability in the sciences or arts including college and university teachers of exceptional ability who have been practicing their science or art during the year prior to application and who intend to practice the same science or art in the United States. For purposes of this group, the term "science or art" means any field of knowledge and/or skill with respect to which colleges and universities commonly offer specialized courses leading to a degree in the knowledge and/or skill. An alien, however, need not have studied at a college or university in order to qualify for the Group II occupation.

714

(2) Performing arts. Aliens of exceptional ability in the performing arts whose work during the past 12 months did require, and whose intended work in the United States will require, exceptional ability.

[69 FR 77326, 77389, Dec. 27, 2004]

§ 656.10 General instructions.

(a) Filing of applications. A request for a labor certification on behalf of any alien who is required by the Act to be a beneficiary of a labor certification in order to obtain permanent resident status in the United States may be filed as follows:

(1) Except as provided in paragraphs (a)(2), (3), and (4) of this section, an employer seeking a labor certification must file under this section and § 656.17.

(2) An employer seeking a labor certification for a college or university teacher must apply for a labor certification under this section and must also file under either § 656.17 or § 656.18.

(3) An employer seeking labor certification for an occupation listed on Schedule A must apply for a labor certification under this section and § 656.15.

(4) An employer seeking labor certification for a sheepherder must apply for a labor certification under this section and must also choose to file under either § 656.16 or § 656.17.

(b) Representation.

(1) Employers may have agents or attorneys represent them throughout the labor certification process. If an employer intends to be represented by an agent or attorney, the employer must sign the statement set forth on the Application for Permanent Employment Certification form: That the attorney or agent is representing the employer and the employer takes full responsibility for the accuracy of any representations made by the attorney or agent. Whenever, under this part, any notice or other document is required to be sent to the employer, the document will be sent to the attorney or agent who has been authorized to represent the employer on the Application for Permanent Employment Certification form.

(2)(i) It is contrary to the best interests of U.S. workers to have the alien and/or agents or attorneys for either the employer or the alien participate in interviewing or considering U.S. workers for the job offered the alien. As the beneficiary of a labor certification application, the alien can not represent the best interests of U.S. workers in the job opportunity. The alien's agent and/or attorney can not represent the alien effectively and at the same time truly be seeking U.S. workers for the job opportunity. Therefore, the alien and/or the alien's agent and/or attorney may not interview or consider U.S. workers for the job offered to the alien, unless the agent and/or attorney is the employer's representative, as described in paragraph (b)(2)(ii) of this section.

(ii) The employer's representative who interviews or considers U.S. workers for the job offered to the alien must be the person who normally interviews or considers, on behalf of the employer, applicants for job opportunities such as that offered the alien, but which do not involve labor certifications.

(3) No person under suspension or disbarment from practice before any court or before the DHS or the United States Department of Justice's Executive Office for Immigration Review is permitted to act as an agent, representative, or attorney for an employer and/or alien under this part.

(c) Attestations. The employer must certify to the conditions of employment listed below on the Application for Permanent Employment Certification under penalty of perjury under 18 U.S.C. 1621(2). Failure to attest to any of the conditions listed below results in a denial of the application.

(1) The offered wage equals or exceeds the prevailing wage determined pursuant to § 656.40 and § 656.41, and the wage the employer will pay to the alien to begin work will equal or exceed the prevailing wage that is applicable at the time the alien begins work or from the time the alien is admitted to take up the certified employment;

(2) The wage offered is not based on commissions, bonuses or other incentives, unless the employer guarantees a prevailing wage paid on a weekly, bi-weekly, or monthly basis that equals or exceeds the prevailing wage;

(3) The employer has enough funds available to pay the wage or salary offered the alien;

(4) The employer will be able to place the alien on the payroll on or before the date of the alien's proposed entrance into the United States;

(5) The job opportunity does not involve unlawful discrimination by race, creed, color, national origin, age, sex, religion, handicap, or citizenship;

(6) The employer's job opportunity is not:

    (i) Vacant because the former occupant is on strike or locked out in the course of a labor dispute involving a work stoppage;

    (ii) At issue in a labor dispute involving a work stoppage.

(7) The job opportunity's terms, conditions and occupational environment are not contrary to Federal, state or local law;

(8) The job opportunity has been and is clearly open to any U.S. worker;

(9) The U.S. workers who applied for the job opportunity were rejected for lawful job-related reasons;

(10) The job opportunity is for full-time, permanent employment for an employer other than the alien.

(d) Notice.

(1) In applications filed under §§ 656.15 (Schedule A), 656.16 (Sheepherders), 656.17 (Basic Process), 656.18 (College and University Teachers), and 656.21 (Supervised Recruitment), the employer must give notice of the filing of the Application for Permanent Employment Certification and be able to document that notice was provided, if requested by the Certifying Officer, as follows:

(i) To the bargaining representative(s) (if any) of the employer's employees in the occupational classification for which certification of the job opportunity is sought in the employer's location(s) in the area of intended employment. Documentation may consist of a copy of the letter and a copy of the Application for Permanent Employment Certification form that was sent to the bargaining representative.

(ii) If there is no such bargaining representative, by posted notice to the employer's employees at the facility or location of the employment. The notice must be posted for at least 10 consecutive business days. The notice must be clearly visible and unobstructed while posted and must be posted in conspicuous places where the employer's U.S. workers can readily read the posted notice on their way to or from their place of employment. Appropriate locations for posting notices of the job opportunity include locations in the immediate vicinity of the wage and hour notices required by 29 CFR 516.4 or occupational safety and health notices required by 29 CFR 1903.2(a). In addition, the employer must publish the notice in any and all in-house media, whether electronic or printed, in accordance with the normal procedures used for the recruitment of similar positions in the employer's organization. The documentation requirement may be satisfied by providing a copy of the posted notice and stating where it was posted, and by providing copies of all the in-house media, whether electronic or print, that were used to distribute notice of the application in accordance with the procedures used for similar positions within the employer's organization.

(2) In the case of a private household, notice is required under this paragraph (d) only if the household employs one or more U.S. workers at the time the application for labor certification is filed. The documentation requirement may be satisfied by providing a copy of the posted notice to the Certifying Officer.

(3) The notice of the filing of an Application for Permanent Employment Certification must:

(i) State the notice is being provided as a result of the filing of an application for permanent alien labor certification for the relevant job opportunity;

(ii) State any person may provide documentary evidence bearing on the application to the Certifying Officer of the Department of Labor;

(iii) Provide the address of the appropriate Certifying Officer; and

(iv) Be provided between 30 and 180 days before filing the application.

(4) If an application is filed under § 656.17, the notice must contain the information required for advertisements by § 656.17(f), must state the rate of pay (which must equal or exceed the prevailing wage entered by the SWA on the prevailing wage request form), and must contain the information required by paragraph (d)(3) of this section.

(5) If an application is filed on behalf of a college and university teacher selected in a competitive selection and recruitment process, as provided by § 656.18, the notice must include the information required for advertisements by § 656.18(b)(3), and must include the information required by paragraph (d)(3) of this section.

(6) If an application is filed under the Schedule A procedures at § 656.15, or the procedures for sheepherders at § 656.16, the notice must contain a description of the job and rate of pay, and must meet the requirements of this section.

(e)(1)(i) Submission of evidence. Any person may submit to the Certifying Officer documentary evidence bearing on an application for permanent alien labor certification filed under the basic labor certification process at § 656.17 or an application involving a college and university teacher selected in a competitive recruitment and selection process under § 656.18.

(ii) Documentary evidence submitted under paragraph (e)(1)(i) of this section may include information on available workers, information on wages and working conditions, and information on the employer's failure to meet the terms and conditions for the employment of alien workers and co-workers. The Certifying Officer must consider this information in making his or her determination.

(2)(i) Any person may submit to the appropriate DHS office documentary evidence of fraud or willful misrepresentation in a Schedule A application filed under § 656.15 or a sheepherder application filed under § 656.16.

(ii) Documentary evidence submitted under paragraph (e)(2) of this section is limited to information relating to possible fraud or willful misrepresentation. The DHS may consider this information under § 656.31.

(f) Retention of Documents. Copies of applications for permanent employment certification filed with the Department of Labor and all supporting documentation must be retained by the employer for 5 years from the date of filing the Application for Permanent Employment Certification.

[71 FR 35523, June 21, 2006]

§ 656.15 Applications for labor certification for Schedule A occupations.

(a) **Filing application.** An employer must apply for a labor certification for a Schedule A occupation by filing an application with the appropriate DHS office, and not with an ETA application processing center.

(b) **General documentation requirements.** A Schedule A application must include:

(1) An Application for Permanent Employment Certification form, which includes a prevailing wage determination in accordance with § 656.40 and § 656.41.

(2) Evidence that notice of filing the Application for Permanent Employment Certification was provided to the bargaining representative or the employer's employees as prescribed in § 656.10(d).

(c) **Group I documentation.** An employer seeking labor certification under Group I of Schedule A must file with DHS, as part of its labor certification application, documentary evidence of the following:

(1) An employer seeking Schedule A labor certification for an alien to be employed as a physical therapist (§ 656.5(a)(1)) must file as part of its labor certification application a letter or statement, signed by an authorized state physical therapy licensing official in the state of intended employment, stating the alien is qualified to take that state's written licensing examination for physical therapists. Application for certification of permanent employment as a physical therapist may be made only under this § 656.15 and not under § 656.17.

(2) An employer seeking a Schedule A labor certification for an alien to be employed as a professional nurse (§ 656.5(a)(2)) must file as part of its labor certification application documentation that the alien has received a Certificate from the Commission on Graduates of Foreign Nursing Schools (CGFNS); that the alien holds a full and unrestricted (permanent) license to practice nursing in the state of intended employment; or that the alien has passed the National Council Licensure Examination for Registered Nurses (NCLEX–RN). Application for certification of employment as a professional nurse may be made only under this § 656.15(c) and not under § 656.17.

(d) **Group II documentation.** An employer seeking a Schedule A labor certification under Group II of Schedule A must file with DHS, as part of its labor certification application, documentary evidence of the following:

(1) An employer seeking labor certification on behalf of an alien to be employed as an alien of exceptional ability in the sciences or arts (excluding those in the performing arts) must file documentary evidence showing the widespread acclaim and international recognition accorded the alien by recognized experts in the alien's field; and documentation showing the alien's work in that field during the past year

did, and the alien's intended work in the United States will, require exceptional ability. In addition, the employer must file documentation about the alien from at least two of the following seven groups:

(i) Documentation of the alien's receipt of internationally recognized prizes or awards for excellence in the field for which certification is sought;

(ii) Documentation of the alien's membership in international associations, in the field for which certification is sought, which require outstanding achievement of their members, as judged by recognized international experts in their disciplines or fields;

(iii) Published material in professional publications about the alien, about the alien's work in the field for which certification is sought, which shall include the title, date, and author of such published material;

(iv) Evidence of the alien's participation on a panel, or individually, as a judge of the work of others in the same or in an allied field of specialization to that for which certification is sought;

(v) Evidence of the alien's original scientific or scholarly research contributions of major significance in the field for which certification is sought;

(vi) Evidence of the alien's authorship of published scientific or scholarly articles in the field for which certification is sought, in international professional journals or professional journals with an international circulation;

(vii) Evidence of the display of the alien's work, in the field for which certification is sought, at artistic exhibitions in more than one country.

(2) An employer seeking labor certification on behalf of an alien of exceptional ability in the performing arts must file documentary evidence that the alien's work experience during the past twelve months did require, and the alien's intended work in the United States will require, exceptional ability; and must submit documentation to show this exceptional ability, such as:

(i) Documentation attesting to the current widespread acclaim and international recognition accorded to the alien, and receipt of internationally recognized prizes or awards for excellence;

(ii) Published material by or about the alien, such as critical reviews or articles in major newspapers, periodicals, and/or trade journals (the title, date, and author of such material shall be indicated);

(iii) Documentary evidence of earnings commensurate with the claimed level of ability;

(iv) Playbills and star billings;

(v) Documents attesting to the outstanding reputation of theaters, concert halls, night clubs, and other establishments in which the alien has appeared or is scheduled to appear; and/or

(vi) Documents attesting to the outstanding reputation of theaters or repertory companies, ballet troupes, orchestras, or other organizations in which or with which the alien has performed during the past year in a leading or starring capacity.

(e) **Determination.** An Immigration Officer determines whether the employer and alien have met the applicable requirements of § 656.10 and of Schedule A (§ 656.5); reviews the application; and determines whether or not the alien is qualified for and intends to pursue the Schedule A occupation. The Schedule A determination of DHS is conclusive and final. The employer, therefore, may not appeal from any such determination under the review procedures at § 656.26.

(f) **Refiling after denial.** If an application for a Schedule A occupation is denied, the employer, except where the occupation is as a physical therapist or a professional nurse, may at any time file for a labor certification on the alien beneficiary's behalf under § 656.17. Labor certifications for professional nurses and for physical therapists shall not be considered under § 656.17.

[69 FR 77326, 77390, Dec. 27, 2004; 72 FR 27944, May 17, 2007; 73 FR 78068, Dec. 19, 2008]

§ 656.17 Basic labor certification process.

(a) Filing applications.

(1) Except as otherwise provided by §§ 656.15, 656.16, and 656.18, an employer who desires to apply for a labor certification on behalf of an alien must file a completed Department of Labor Application for Permanent Employment Certification form (ETA Form 9089). The application must be filed with an ETA application processing center. Incomplete applications will be denied. Applications filed and certified electronically must, upon receipt of the labor certification, be signed immediately by the employer in order to be valid. Applications submitted by mail must contain the original signature of the employer, alien, attorney, and/or agent when they are received by the application processing center. DHS will not process petitions unless they are supported by an original certified ETA Form 9089 that has been signed by the employer, alien, attorney and/or agent.

(2) The Department of Labor may issue or require the use of certain identifying information, including user identifiers, passwords, or personal identification numbers (PINS). The purpose of these personal identifiers is to allow the Department of Labor to associate a given electronic submission with a single, specific individual. Personal identifiers can not be issued to a company or business. Rather, a personal identifier can only be issued to specific individual. Any personal iden-

tifiers must be used solely by the individual to whom they are assigned and can not be used or transferred to any other individual. An individual assigned a personal identifier must take all reasonable steps to ensure that his or her personal identifier can not be compromised. If an individual assigned a personal identifier suspects, or becomes aware, that his or her personal identifier has been compromised or is being used by someone else, then the individual must notify the Department of Labor immediately of the incident and cease the electronic transmission of any further submissions under that personal identifier until such time as a new personal identifier is provided. Any electronic transmissions submitted with a personal identifier will be presumed to be a submission by the individual assigned that personal identifier. The Department of Labor's system will notify those making submissions of these requirements at the time of each submission.

(3) Documentation supporting the application for labor certification should not be filed with the application, however in the event the Certifying Officer notifies the employer that its application is to be audited, the employer must furnish required supporting documentation prior to a final determination.

(b) Processing.

(1) Applications are screened and are certified, are denied, or are selected for audit.

(2) Employers will be notified if their applications have been selected for audit by the issuance of an audit letter under § 656.20.

(3) Applications may be selected for audit in accordance with selection criteria or may be randomly selected.

(c) Filing date. Non-electronically filed applications accepted for processing shall be date stamped. Electronically filed applications will be considered filed when submitted.

(d) Refiling Procedures.

(1) Employers that filed applications under the regulations in effect prior to March 28, 2005, may, if a job order has not been placed pursuant to those regulations, refile such applications under this part without loss of the original filing date by:

(i) Submitting an application for an identical job opportunity after complying with all of the filing and recruiting requirements of this part 656; and

(ii) Withdrawing the original application in accordance with ETA procedures. Filing an application under this part stating the employer's desire to use the original filing date will be deemed to be a withdrawal of the original application. The original application will be deemed withdrawn regardless of whether the employer's request to use the original filing date is approved.

(2) Refilings under this paragraph must be made within 210 days of the withdrawal of the prior application.

(3) A copy of the original application, including amendments, must be sent to the appropriate ETA application processing center when requested by the CO under § 656.20.

(4) For purposes of paragraph (d)(1)(i) of this section, a job opportunity shall be considered identical if the employer, alien, job title, job location, job requirements, and job description are the same as those stated in the original application filed under the regulations in effect prior to March 28, 2005. For purposes of determining identical job opportunity, the original application includes all accepted amendments up to the time the application was withdrawn, including amendments in response to an assessment notice from a SWA pursuant to § 656.21(h) of the regulations in effect prior to March 28, 2005.

(e) Required pre-filing recruitment. Except for labor certification applications involving college or university teachers selected pursuant to a competitive recruitment and selection process (§ 656.18), Schedule A occupations (§§ 656.5 and 656.15), and sheepherders (§ 656.16), an employer must attest to having conducted the following recruitment prior to filing the application:

(1) Professional occupations. If the application is for a professional occupation, the employer must conduct the recruitment steps within 6 months of filing the application for alien employment certification. The employer must maintain documentation of the recruitment and be prepared to submit this documentation in the event of an audit or in response to a request from the Certifying Officer prior to rendering a final determination.

(i) Mandatory steps. Two of the steps, a job order and two print advertisements, are mandatory for all applications involving professional occupations, except applications for college or university teachers selected in a competitive selection and recruitment process as provided in § 656.18. The mandatory recruitment steps must be conducted at least 30 days, but no more than 180 days, before the filing of the application.

(A) Job order. Placement of a job order with the SWA serving the area of intended employment for a period of 30 days. The start and end dates of the job order entered on the application shall serve as documentation of this step.

(B) Advertisements in newspaper or professional journals.

(1) Placing an advertisement on two different Sundays in the newspaper of general circulation in the area of intended employment most appropriate to the occupation and the workers likely to apply for the job opportunity and most likely to bring responses from able, willing, qualified, and available U.S. workers.

(2) If the job opportunity is located in a rural area of intended employment that does not have a newspaper with a Sunday edition, the employer may use the edition with the widest circulation in the area of intended employment.

(3) The advertisements must satisfy the requirements of paragraph (f) of this section. Documentation of this step can be satisfied by furnishing copies of the newspaper pages in which the advertisements appeared or proof of publication furnished by the newspaper.

(4) If the job involved in the application requires experience and an advanced degree, and a professional journal normally would be used to advertise the job opportunity, the employer may, in lieu of one of the Sunday advertisements, place an advertisement in the professional journal most likely to bring responses from able, willing, qualified, and available U.S. workers. Documentation of this step can be satisfied by providing a copy of the page in which the advertisement appeared.

(ii) Additional recruitment steps. The employer must select three additional recruitment steps from the alternatives listed in paragraphs (e)(1)(ii)(A)–(J) of this section. Only one of the additional steps may consist solely of activity that took place within 30 days of the filing of the application. None of the steps may have taken place more than 180 days prior to filing the application.

(A) Job fairs. Recruitment at job fairs for the occupation involved in the application, which can be documented by brochures advertising the fair and newspaper advertisements in which the employer is named as a participant in the job fair.

(B) Employer's Web site. The use of the employer's Web site as a recruitment medium can be documented by providing dated copies of pages from the site that advertise the occupation involved in the application.

(C) Job search Web site other than the employer's. The use of a job search Web site other than the employer's can be documented by providing dated copies of pages from one or more website(s) that advertise the occupation involved in the application. Copies of web pages generated in conjunction with the newspaper advertisements required by paragraph (e)(1)(i)(B) of this section can serve as documentation of the use of a Web site other than the employer's.

(D) On-campus recruiting. The employer's on-campus recruiting can be documented by providing copies of the notification issued or posted by the college's or university's placement office naming the employer and the date it conducted interviews for employment in the occupation.

(E) Trade or professional organizations. The use of professional or trade organizations as a recruitment source can be documented by providing copies of pages of newsletters or trade journals containing advertisements for the occupation involved in the application for alien employment certification.

(F) Private employment firms. The use of private employment firms or placement agencies can be documented by providing documentation sufficient to demonstrate that recruitment has been conducted by a private firm for the occupation for which certification is sought. For example, documentation might consist of copies of contracts between the employer and the private employment firm and copies of advertisements placed by the private employment firm for the occupation involved in the application.

(G) Employee referral program with incentives. The use of an employee referral program with incentives can be documented by providing dated copies of employer notices or memoranda advertising the program and specifying the incentives offered.

(H) Campus placement offices. The use of a campus placement office can be documented by providing a copy of the employer's notice of the job opportunity provided to the campus placement office.

(I) Local and ethnic newspapers. The use of local and ethnic newspapers can be documented by providing a copy of the page in the newspaper that contains the employer's advertisement.

(J) Radio and television advertisements. The use of radio and television advertisements can be documented by providing a copy of the employer's text of the employer's advertisement along with a written confirmation from the radio or television station stating when the advertisement was aired.

(2) Nonprofessional occupations. If the application is for a nonprofessional occupation, the employer must at a minimum, place a job order and two newspaper advertisements within 6 months of filing the application. The steps must be conducted at least 30 days but no more that 180 days before the filing of the application.

(i) Job order. Placing a job order with the SWA serving the area of intended employment for a period of 30 days. The start and end dates of the job order entered on the application serve as documentation of this step.

(ii) Newspaper advertisements.

(A) Placing an advertisement on two different Sundays in the newspaper of general circulation in the area of intended employment most appropriate to the occupation and the workers likely to apply for the job opportunity.

(B) If the job opportunity is located in a rural area of intended employment that does not have a newspaper that publishes a Sunday edition, the employer may use the newspaper edition with the widest circulation in the area of intended employment.

(C) Placement of the newspaper advertisements can be documented in the same way as provided in paragraph (e)(1)(i)(B)(3) of this section for professional occupations.

(D) The advertisements must satisfy the requirements of paragraph (f) of this section.

(f) Advertising requirements. Advertisements placed in newspapers of general circulation or in professional journals before filing the Application for Permanent Employment Certification must:

(1) Name the employer;

(2) Direct applicants to report or send resumes, as appropriate for the occupation, to the employer;

(3) Provide a description of the vacancy specific enough to apprise the U.S. workers of the job opportunity for which certification is sought;

(4) Indicate the geographic area of employment with enough specificity to apprise applicants of any travel requirements and where applicants will likely have to reside to perform the job opportunity;

(5) Not contain a wage rate lower than the prevailing wage rate;

(6) Not contain any job requirements or duties which exceed the job requirements or duties listed on the ETA Form 9089; and

(7) Not contain wages or terms and conditions of employment that are less favorable than those offered to the alien.

(g) Recruitment report.

(1) The employer must prepare a recruitment report signed by the employer or the employer's representative noted in § 656.10(b)(2)(ii) describing the recruitment steps undertaken and the results achieved, the number of hires, and, if applicable, the number of U.S. workers rejected, categorized by the lawful job related reasons for such rejections. The Certifying Officer, after reviewing the employer's recruitment report, may request the U.S. workers' resumes or applications, sorted by the reasons the workers were rejected.

(2) A U.S. worker is able and qualified for the job opportunity if the worker can acquire the skills necessary to perform the duties involved in the occupation during a reasonable period of on-the-job training. Rejecting U.S. workers for lacking skills necessary to perform the duties involved in the occupation, where the U.S. workers are capable of acquiring the skills during a reasonable period of on-the-job training is not a lawful job-related reason for rejection of the U.S. workers.

(h) Job duties and requirements.

(1) The job opportunity's requirements, unless adequately documented as arising from business necessity, must be those normally required for the occupation and must not exceed the Specific Vocational Preparation level assigned to the occupation as shown in the O*NET Job Zones. To establish a business necessity, an employer must demonstrate the job duties and requirements bear a reasonable relationship to the occupation in the context of the employer's business and are essential to perform the job in a reasonable manner.

(2) A foreign language requirement can not be included, unless it is justified by business necessity. Demonstrating business necessity for a foreign language requirement may be based upon the following:

(i) The nature of the occupation, e.g., translator; or

(ii) The need to communicate with a large majority of the employer's customers, contractors, or employees who can not communicate effectively in English, as documented by:

(A) The employer furnishing the number and proportion of its clients, contractors, or employees who can not communicate in English, and/or a detailed plan to market products or services in a foreign country; and

(B) A detailed explanation of why the duties of the position for which certification is sought requires frequent contact and communication with customers, employees or contractors who can not communicate in English and why it is reasonable to believe the allegedly foreign-language-speaking customers, employees, and contractors can not communicate in English.

(3) If the job opportunity involves a combination of occupations, the employer must document that it has normally employed persons for that combination of occupations, and/or workers customarily perform the combination of occupations in the area of intended employment, and/or the combination job opportunity is based on a business necessity. Combination occupations can be documented by position descriptions and relevant payroll records, and/or letters from other employers stating their workers normally perform the combination of occupations in the area of intended employment, and/or documentation that the combination occupation arises from a business necessity.

(4)(i) Alternative experience requirements must be substantially equivalent to the primary requirements of the job opportunity for which certification is sought; and

(ii) If the alien beneficiary already is employed by the employer, and the alien does not meet the primary job requirements and only potentially qualifies for the job by virtue of the employer's alternative requirements, certification will be denied unless the application states that any suitable combination of education, training, or experience is acceptable.

(i) Actual minimum requirements. DOL will evaluate the employer's actual minimum requirements in accordance with this paragraph (i).

(1) The job requirements, as described, must represent the employer's actual minimum requirements for the job opportunity.

(2) The employer must not have hired workers with less training or experience for jobs substantially comparable to that involved in the job opportunity.

(3) If the alien beneficiary already is employed by the employer, in considering whether the job requirements represent the employer's actual minimums, DOL will review the training and experience possessed by the alien beneficiary at the time of hiring by the employer, including as a contract employee. The employer can not require domestic worker applicants to possess training and/or experience beyond what the alien possessed at the time of hire unless:

(i) The alien gained the experience while working for the employer, including as a contract employee, in a position not substantially comparable to the position for which certification is being sought, or

(ii) The employer can demonstrate that it is no longer feasible to train a worker to qualify for the position.

(4) In evaluating whether the alien beneficiary satisfies the employer's actual minimum requirements, DOL will not consider any education or training obtained by the alien beneficiary at the employer's expense unless the employer offers similar training to domestic worker applicants.

(5) For purposes of this paragraph (i):

(i) The term "employer" means an entity with the same Federal Employer Identification Number (FEIN), provided it meets the definition of an employer at § 656.3.

(ii) A "substantially comparable" job or position means a job or position requiring performance of the same job duties more than 50 percent of the time. This requirement can be documented by furnishing position descriptions, the percentage of time spent on the various duties, organization charts, and payroll records.

(j) Conditions of employment.

(1) Working conditions must be normal to the occupation in the area and industry.

(2) Live-in requirements are acceptable for household domestic service workers only if the employer can demonstrate the requirement is essential to perform, in a reasonable manner, the job duties as described by the employer and there are not cost-effective alternatives to a live-in household requirement. Mere employer assertions do not constitute acceptable documentation. For example, a live-in requirement could be supported by documenting two working parents and young children in the household, and/or the existence of erratic work schedules requiring frequent travel and a need to entertain business associates and clients on short notice. Depending upon the situation, acceptable documentation could consist of travel vouchers, written estimates of costs of alternatives such as babysitters, or a detailed listing of the frequency and length of absences of the employer from the home.

(k) Layoffs.

(1) If there has been a layoff by the employer applicant in the area of intended employment within 6 months of filing an application involving the occupation for which certification is sought or in a related occupation, the employer must document it has notified and considered all potentially qualified laid off (employer applicant) U.S. workers of the job opportunity involved in the application and the results of the notification and consideration. A layoff shall be considered any involuntary separation of one or more employees without cause or prejudice.

(2) For the purposes of paragraph (k)(1) of this section, a related occupation is any occupation that requires workers to perform a majority of the essential duties involved in the occupation for which certification is sought.

(*l*) Alien influence and control over job opportunity. If the employer is a closely held corporation or partnership in which the alien has an ownership interest, or if there is a familial relationship between the stockholders, corporate officers, incorporators, or partners, and the alien, or if the alien is one of a small number of employees, the employer in the event of an audit must be able to demonstrate the existence of a bona fide job opportunity, i.e. the job is available to all U.S. workers, and must provide to the Certifying Officer, the following supporting documentation:

(1) A copy of the articles of incorporation, partnership agreement, business license or similar documents that establish the business entity;

(2) A list of all corporate/company officers and shareholders/partners of the corporation/firm/business, their titles and positions in the business' structure, and a description of the relationships to each other and to the alien beneficiary;

(3) The financial history of the corporation/company/partnership, including the total investment in the business entity and the amount of investment of each officer, incorporator/partner and the alien beneficiary; and

(4) The name of the business' official with primary responsibility for interviewing and hiring applicants for positions within the organization and the name(s) of the business' official(s) having control or influence over hiring decisions involving the position for which labor certification is sought.

(5) If the alien is one of 10 or fewer employees, the employer must document any family relationship between the employees and the alien.

[69 FR 77326, 77392, Dec. 27, 2004]

IV. OTHER FEDERAL MATERIALS

List of Significant Federal Materials
Arranged by Subject Matter

OTHER FEDERAL MATERIALS

SUSPENSION OF ENTRY

DEFERRED ACTION

U.S. Dep't of Homeland Sec., Rescission of the June 15, 2012 Memorandum Entitled "Exercising Prosecutorial Discretion with Respect to Individuals Who Came to the United States as Children" (Sept. 5, 2017)

Release Date:

September 5, 2017

MEMORANDUM FOR:

> James W. McCament
> Acting Director
> U.S. Citizenship and Immigration Services
>
> Thomas D. Homan
> Acting Director
> U.S. Immigration and Customs Enforcement
>
> Kevin K. McAleenan
> Acting Commissioner
> U.S. Customs and Border Protection
>
> Joseph B. Maher
> Acting General Counsel
>
> Ambassador James D. Nealon
> Assistant Secretary, International Engagement
>
> Julie M. Kirchner
> Citizenship and Immigration Services Ombudsman

FROM: Elaine C. Duke
            Acting Secretary

SUBJECT: **Rescission of the June 15, 2012 Memorandum Entitled "Exercising Prosecutorial Discretion with Respect to Individuals Who Came to the United States as Children"**

This memorandum rescinds the June 15, 2012 memorandum entitled "Exercising Prosecutorial Discretion with Respect to Individuals Who Came to the United States as Children," which established the program known

733

as Deferred Action for Childhood Arrivals ("DACA"). For the reasons and in the manner outlined below, Department of Homeland Security personnel shall take all appropriate actions to execute a wind-down of the program, consistent with the parameters established in this memorandum.

Background

The Department of Homeland Security established DACA through the issuance of a memorandum on June 15, 2012. The program purported to use deferred action—an act of prosecutorial discretion meant to be applied only on an individualized case-by-case basis—to confer certain benefits to illegal aliens that Congress had not otherwise acted to provide by law.[1] Specifically, DACA provided certain illegal aliens who entered the United States before the age of sixteen a period of deferred action and eligibility to request employment authorization.

On November 20, 2014, the Department issued a new memorandum, expanding the parameters of DACA and creating a new policy called Deferred Action for Parents of Americans and Lawful Permanent Residents ("DAPA"). Among other things—such as the expansion of the coverage criteria under the 2012 DACA policy to encompass aliens with a wider range of ages and arrival dates, and lengthening the period of deferred action and work authorization from two years to three—the November 20, 2014 memorandum directed USCIS "to establish a process, similar to DACA, for exercising prosecutorial discretion through the use of deferred action, on a case-by-case basis," to certain aliens who have "a son or daughter who is a U.S. citizen or lawful permanent resident."

Prior to the implementation of DAPA, twenty-six states—led by Texas—challenged the policies announced in the November 20, 2014 memorandum in the U.S. District Court for the Southern District of Texas. In an order issued on February 16, 2015, the district court preliminarily enjoined the policies nationwide.[2] The district court held that the plaintiff states were likely to succeed on their claim that the DAPA program did not comply with relevant authorities.

The United States Court of Appeals for the Fifth Circuit affirmed, holding that Texas and the other states had demonstrated a substantial likelihood of success on the merits and satisfied the other requirements for a preliminary injunction.[3] The Fifth Circuit concluded that the Department's DAPA policy conflicted with the discretion authorized by Congress. In considering the DAPA program, the court noted that the Immigration and Nationality Act "flatly does not permit the reclassification of millions of illegal aliens as lawfully present and thereby make them newly eligible for a host of federal and state benefits, including work authorization." According to the court, "DAPA is foreclosed by Congress's careful plan; the program is 'manifestly contrary to the statute' and therefore was properly enjoined."

Although the original DACA policy was not challenged in the lawsuit, both the district and appellate court decisions relied on factual findings about the implementation of the 2012 DACA memorandum. The Fifth Circuit agreed with the lower court that DACA decisions were not truly discretionary,[4] and that DAPA and expanded DACA would be substantially similar in execution. Both the district court and the Fifth Circuit concluded that implementation of the program did not comply with the Administrative Procedure Act because the Department did not implement it through notice-and-comment rulemaking.

The Supreme Court affirmed the Fifth Circuit's ruling by equally divided vote (4–4).[5] The evenly divided ruling resulted in the Fifth Circuit order being affirmed. The preliminary injunction therefore remains in place today. In October 2016, the Supreme Court denied a request from DHS to rehear the case upon the appointment of a new Justice. After the 2016 election, both parties agreed to a stay in litigation to allow the new administration to review these issues.

On January 25, 2017, President Trump issued Executive Order No. 13,768, "Enhancing Public Safety in the Interior of the United States." In that Order, the President directed federal agencies to "[e]nsure the faithful execution of the immigration laws . . . against all removable aliens," and established new immigration enforcement priorities. On February 20, 2017, then Secretary of Homeland Security John F. Kelly issued an implementing memorandum, stating "the Department no longer will exempt classes or categories of removable aliens from potential enforcement," except as provided in the Department's June 15, 2012 memorandum establishing DACA,[6] and the November 20, 2014 memorandum establishing DAPA and expanding DACA.[7]

On June 15, 2017, after consulting with the Attorney General, and considering the likelihood of success on the merits of the ongoing litigation, then Secretary John F. Kelly issued a memorandum rescinding DAPA and the expansion of DACA—but temporarily left in place the June 15, 2012 memorandum that initially created the DACA program.

Then, on June 29, 2017, Texas, along with several other states, sent a letter to Attorney General Sessions asserting that the original 2012 DACA memorandum is unlawful for the same reasons stated in the Fifth Circuit and district court opinions regarding DAPA and expanded DACA. The letter notes that if DHS does not rescind the DACA memo by September 5, 2017, the States will seek to amend the DAPA lawsuit to include a challenge to DACA.

The Attorney General sent a letter to the Department on September 4, 2017, articulating his legal determination that DACA "was effectuated by the previous administration through executive action, without proper statutory authority and with no established end-date, after Congress' repeated rejection of proposed legislation that would have accomplished a similar result. Such an open-ended circumvention of immigration laws was an unconstitutional exercise of authority by the Executive Branch." The letter further stated that because DACA "has the same legal and constitutional defects that the courts recognized as to DAPA, it is likely that potentially imminent litigation would yield similar results with respect to DACA." Nevertheless, in light of the administrative complexities associated with ending the program, he recommended that the Department wind it down in an efficient and orderly fashion, and his office has reviewed the terms on which our Department will do so.

Rescission of the June 15, 2012 DACA Memorandum

Taking into consideration the Supreme Court's and the Fifth Circuit's rulings in the ongoing litigation, and the September 4, 2017 letter from the Attorney General, it is clear that the June 15, 2012 DACA program should be terminated. In the exercise of my authority in establishing national immigration policies and priorities, except for the purposes explicitly identified below, I hereby rescind the June 15, 2012 memorandum.

Recognizing the complexities associated with winding down the program, the Department will provide a limited window in which it will adjudicate certain requests for DACA and associated applications meeting certain parameters specified below. Accordingly, effective immediately, the Department:

- Will adjudicate—on an individual, case-by-case basis—properly filed pending DACA initial requests and associated applications for Employment Authorization Documents that have been accepted by the Department as of the date of this memorandum.

- Will reject all DACA initial requests and associated applications for Employment Authorization Documents filed after the date of this memorandum.

- Will adjudicate—on an individual, case by case basis—properly filed pending DACA renewal requests and associated applications for Employment Authorization Documents from current beneficiaries that have been accepted by the Department as of the date of this memorandum, and from current beneficiaries whose benefits will expire between the date of this memorandum and March 5, 2018 that have been accepted by the Department as of October 5, 2017.

- Will reject all DACA renewal requests and associated applications for Employment Authorization Documents filed outside of the parameters specified above.

- Will not terminate the grants of previously issued deferred action or revoke Employment Authorization Documents solely based on the directives in this memorandum for the remaining duration of their validity periods.

- Will not approve any new Form I–131 applications for advance parole under standards associated with the DACA program, although it will generally honor the stated validity period for previously approved applications for advance parole. Notwithstanding the continued validity of advance parole approvals previously granted, CBP will—of course—retain the authority it has always had and exercised in determining the admissibility of any person presenting at the border and the eligibility of such persons for parole. Further, USCIS will—of course—retain the authority to revoke or terminate an advance parole document at any time.

- Will administratively close all pending Form I–131 applications for advance parole filed under standards associated with the DACA program, and will refund all associated fees.

- Will continue to exercise its discretionary authority to terminate or deny deferred action at any time when immigration officials determine termination or denial of deferred action is appropriate.

This document is not intended to, does not, and may not be relied upon to create any right or benefit, substantive or procedural, enforceable at law by any party in any administrative, civil, or criminal matter. Likewise, no limitations are placed by this guidance on the otherwise lawful enforcement or litigation prerogatives of DHS.

---

[1] Significantly, while the DACA denial notice indicates the decision to deny is made in the unreviewable discretion of USCIS, USCIS has not been able to identify specific denial cases where an applicant appeared to satisfy the programmatic categorical criteria as outlined in the June 15, 2012 memorandum, but still had his or her application denied based solely upon discretion.

[2] Texas v. United States, 86 F. Supp. 3d 591 (S.D. Tex. 2015).

[3] Texas v. United States, 809 F.3d 134 (5th Cir. 2015).

[4] Id.

[5] United States v. Texas, 136 S. Ct. 2271 (2016) (per curiam).

[6] Memorandum from Janet Napolitano, Secretary, DHS to David Aguilar, Acting Comm'r, CBP, et al., "Exercising Prosecutorial Discretion with Respect to Individuals Who Came to the United States as Children" (June 15, 2012).

[7] Memorandum from Jeh Johnson, Secretary, DHS, to Leon Rodriguez, Dir., USCIS, et al., "Exercising Prosecutorial Discretion with Respect to Individuals Who Came to the United States as Children and with Respect to Certain Individuals Whose Parents are U.S. Citizens or Permanent Residents" (Nov. 20, 2014).

U.S. Dep't of Homeland Sec., Memorandum from Secretary of Dep't of Homeland Security, Kirstjen M. Nielsen (June 22, 2018)

Memorandum from Secretary Kirstjen M. Nielsen on the Rescission of Deferred Action for Childhood Arrivals (DACA)

On September 5, 2017, Acting Secretary of Homeland Security Elaine C. Duke issued a memorandum (the "Duke memorandum") rescinding the enforcement policy known as Deferred Action for Childhood Arrivals (DACA). Acting Secretary Duke concluded that, "[t]aking into consideration the Supreme Court's and the Fifth Circuit's rulings in the ongoing litigation [over the enforcement policy known as Deferred Action for Parents of Americans and Lawful Permanent Residents (DAPA)], and the September 4, 2017 letter from the Attorney General [concerning DACA], it is clear that the June 15, 2012 DACA program should be terminated." Accordingly, "in the exercise of [her] authority in establishing national immigration policies and priorities," she "rescind[ed] the June 15, 2012 memorandum," subject to certain exceptions.

On April 24, 2018, the U.S. District Court for the District of Columbia held that the Duke memorandum was subject to judicial review under the Administrative Procedure Act and that it provided insufficient justification for rescinding the DACA policy. The court vacated the Duke memorandum and remanded to the Department of Homeland Security (DHS). The court issued a 90-day stay of vacatur, however, to afford DHS an opportunity to provide further explanation for rescinding the DACA policy.

Because the D.C. district court has requested further explanation, I am providing such explanation here. Having considered the Duke memorandum and Acting Secretary Duke's accompanying statement, the administrative record for the Duke memorandum that was produced in litigation, and the judicial opinions reviewing the Duke memorandum, I decline to disturb the Duke memorandum's rescission of the DACA policy, and it is my understanding that the Department of Justice will continue to seek appellate review of preliminary injunctions that restrict DHS from implementing the Duke memorandum and rescinding the DACA policy. This explanation reflects my understanding of the Duke memorandum and why the decision to rescind the DACA policy was, and remains, sound.

The Secretary of Homeland Security is vested with authority over "the administration and enforcement" of the immigration laws, 8 U.S.C. § 1103(a)(1), including the discretion to "[e]stablish[ ] national immigration enforcement policies and priorities," 6 U.S.C. § 202(5). The DACA policy of deferred action was cast as an exercise of enforcement discretion to forbear from removing a certain class of aliens who are subject to removal under law. DHS also had concluded that under pre-existing statutory and regulatory provisions a grant of deferred action would trigger certain collateral benefits for such aliens, such as eligibility for employment authorization. In considering how DHS's discretion to establish enforcement policies and priorities should be exercised, the DACA policy properly was—and should be—rescinded, for several separate and independently sufficient reasons.

First, as the Attorney General concluded, the DACA policy was contrary to law. The Fifth Circuit ruled that DAPA should be enjoined on a nationwide basis on the ground, among other things, that it likely was contrary to the statutory scheme of the Immigration and Nationality Act (INA). As the Fifth Circuit held, "the INA does not grant the Secretary discretion to grant deferred action and lawful presence on a class-wide basis to 4.3 million otherwise removable aliens." *Texas v. United States,* 809 F.3d 134, 186 n.202 (5th Cir. 2015). An equally divided Supreme Court affirmed that decision. In light of those decisions and other factors, Secretary Kelly rescinded the DAPA policy in June 2017. Any arguable distinctions between the DAPA and DACA policies are not sufficiently material to convince me that the DACA policy is lawful.

The memorandum announcing the DAPA policy both expanded the DACA policy by loosening the age and residency criteria and adopted a similar deferred action policy for parents of U.S. citizens and lawful permanent residents. The Fifth Circuit's rejection of DAPA and expanded DACA did not turn on whether the covered aliens had a pathway to lawful status (which not all of them had). Rather, it turned on the incompatibility of such a major non enforcement policy with the INA's comprehensive scheme. The Attorney General concluded that the DACA policy has the same statutory defects that the Fifth Circuit identified with DAPA—a determination and ruling by the Attorney General that, in any event, I am bound by pursuant to 8 U.S.C. § II 03(a)(l).

Second, regardless of whether the DACA policy is ultimately illegal, it was appropriately rescinded by DHS because there are, at a minimum, serious doubts about its legality. A central aspect of the exercise of a discretionary enforcement policy is a judgment concerning whether DHS has sufficient confidence in the legality of such policy. Like Acting Secretary Duke, I lack sufficient confidence in the DACA policy's legality to continue this non-enforcement policy, whether the courts would ultimately uphold it or not.

There are sound reasons for a law enforcement agency to avoid discretionary policies that are legally questionable. Those reasons include the risk that such policies may undermine public confidence in and reliance on the agency and the rule of law, and the threat of burdensome litigation that distracts from the agency's work. The fact that some courts have recently held or suggested that the DACA policy is legal does not change my view that the DACA policy's legality is too questionable to warrant continuing the policy, especially in light of the Attorney General's contrary determination and ruling about the DACA policy and the contrary implication of the decisions of the Fifth Circuit Court of Appeals and the Supreme Court invalidating the DAPA policy.

Third, regardless of whether these concerns about the DACA policy render it illegal or legally questionable, there are sound reasons of enforcement policy to rescind the DACA policy. To start, DHS should enforce the policies reflected in the laws adopted by Congress and should not adopt public policies of non-enforcement of those laws for broad classes and categories of aliens under the guise of prosecutorial discretion-particularly a class that Congress has repeatedly considered but declined to protect. Even if a policy such as DACA could be implemented lawfully through the exercise of prosecutorial discretion, it would necessarily lack the permanence and detail of statutory law. DACA recipients continue to be illegally present, unless and until Congress gives them permanent status.

Accordingly, I agree with Acting Secretary Duke and the Attorney General that if a policy concerning the ability of this class of aliens to remain in the United States is to be adopted, it should be enacted legislatively.

In addition, DHS should only exercise its prosecutorial discretion not to enforce the immigration laws on a truly individualized, case-by-case basis. While the DACA policy on its face did allow for individual considerations, a categorical deferred-action policy, at the very least, tilts the scales significantly and has the practical effect of inhibiting assessments of whether deferred action is appropriate in a particular case. Without the DACA policy, DHS may consider deferred action on a case-by-case basis, consistent with the INA. Moreover, considering the fact that tens of thousands of minor aliens have illegally crossed or been smuggled across our border in recent years and then have been released into the country owing to loopholes in our laws-and that pattern continues to occur at unacceptably high levels to the detriment of the immigration system-it is critically important for DHS to project a message that leaves no doubt regarding the clear, consistent, and transparent enforcement of the immigration laws against all classes and categories of aliens. All of those considerations lead me to conclude that Acting Secretary Duke's decision to rescind the DACA policy was, and remains, sound as a matter of both legal judgment and enforcement policy discretion.

I do not come to these conclusions lightly. I am keenly aware that DACA recipients have availed themselves of the policy in continuing their presence in this country and pursuing their lives. Nevertheless, in considering DHS enforcement policy, I do not believe that the asserted reliance interests outweigh the questionable legality of the DACA policy and the other reasons for ending the policy discussed above. That is especially so because issues of reliance would best be considered by Congress, which can assess and weigh a range of options. In contrast, the DACA policy was announced as a temporary stopgap measure, not a permanent fix; it was expressly limited to two-year renewal periods, it expressly conferred no substantive rights, and it was revocable at any time. In my judgment, neither any individual's reliance on the expected continuation of the DACA policy nor the sympathetic circumstances of DACA recipients as a class overcomes the legal and institutional concerns with sanctioning the continued presence of hundreds of thousands of aliens who are illegally present in violation of the laws passed by Congress, a status that the DACA non-enforcement policy did not change. And in all events, the rescission of the DACA policy does not preclude the exercise of deferred action in individual cases if circumstances warrant.

For these reasons, in setting DHS enforcement policies and priorities, I concur with and decline to disturb Acting Secretary Duke's decision to rescind the DACA policy.

Kirstjen M. Nielsen
Secretary

ENFORCEMENT AND REMOVAL

Border Security and Immigration Enforcement Improvements, Exec. Order No. 13767, 82 Fed. Reg. 8,793 (Jan. 25, 2017)

By the authority vested in me as President by the Constitution and the laws of the United States of America, including the Immigration and Nationality Act (8 U.S.C. 1101 *et seq.*) (INA), the Secure Fence Act of 2006 (Public Law 109–367) (Secure Fence Act), and the Illegal Immigration Reform and Immigrant Responsibility Act of 1996 (Public Law 104–208 Div. C) (IIRIRA), and in order to ensure the safety and territorial integrity of the United States as well as to ensure that the Nation's immigration laws are faithfully executed, I hereby order as follows:

Section 1. *Purpose.* Border security is critically important to the national security of the United States. Aliens who illegally enter the United States without inspection or admission present a significant threat to national security and public safety. Such aliens have not been identified or inspected by Federal immigration officers to determine their admissibility to the United States. The recent surge of illegal immigration at the southern border with Mexico has placed a significant strain on Federal resources and overwhelmed agencies charged with border security and immigration enforcement, as well as the local communities into which many of the aliens are placed.

Transnational criminal organizations operate sophisticated drug- and human-trafficking networks and smuggling operations on both sides of the southern border, contributing to a significant increase in violent crime and United States deaths from dangerous drugs. Among those who illegally enter are those who seek to harm Americans through acts of terror or criminal conduct. Continued illegal immigration presents a clear and present danger to the interests of the United States.

Federal immigration law both imposes the responsibility and provides the means for the Federal Government, in cooperation with border States, to secure the Nation's southern border. Although Federal immigration law provides a robust framework for Federal-State partnership in enforcing our immigration laws—and the Congress has authorized and provided appropriations to secure our borders—the Federal Government has failed to discharge this basic sovereign responsibility. The purpose of this order is to direct executive departments and agencies (agencies) to deploy all lawful means to secure the Nation's southern border, to prevent further illegal immigration into the United States, and to repatriate illegal aliens swiftly, consistently, and humanely.

Sec. 2. *Policy.* It is the policy of the executive branch to:

(a) secure the southern border of the United States through the immediate construction of a physical wall on the southern border, monitored and supported by adequate personnel so as to prevent illegal immigration, drug and human trafficking, and acts of terrorism;

(b) detain individuals apprehended on suspicion of violating Federal or State law, including Federal immigration law, pending further proceedings regarding those violations;

(c) expedite determinations of apprehended individuals' claims of eligibility to remain in the United States;

(d) remove promptly those individuals whose legal claims to remain in the United States have been lawfully rejected, after any appropriate civil or criminal sanctions have been imposed; and

(e) cooperate fully with States and local law enforcement in enacting Federal-State partnerships to enforce Federal immigration priorities, as well as State monitoring and detention programs that are consistent with Federal law and do not undermine Federal immigration priorities.

Sec. 3. *Definitions.* (a) "Asylum officer" has the meaning given the term in section 235(b)(1)(E) of the INA (8 U.S.C. 1225(b)(1)).

(b) "Southern border" shall mean the contiguous land border between the United States and Mexico, including all points of entry.

(c) "Border States" shall mean the States of the United States immediately adjacent to the contiguous land border between the United States and Mexico.

(d) Except as otherwise noted, "the Secretary" shall refer to the Secretary of Homeland Security.

(e) "Wall" shall mean a contiguous, physical wall or other similarly secure, contiguous, and impassable physical barrier.

(f) "Executive department" shall have the meaning given in section 101 of title 5, United States Code.

(g) "Regulations" shall mean any and all Federal rules, regulations, and directives lawfully promulgated by agencies.

(h) "Operational control" shall mean the prevention of all unlawful entries into the United States, including entries by terrorists, other unlawful aliens, instruments of terrorism, narcotics, and other contraband.

Sec. 4. *Physical Security of the Southern Border of the United States.* The Secretary shall immediately take the following steps to obtain complete operational control, as determined by the Secretary, of the southern border:

(a) In accordance with existing law, including the Secure Fence Act and IIRIRA, take all appropriate steps to immediately plan, design, and construct a physical wall along the southern border, using appropriate materials and technology to most effectively achieve complete operational control of the southern border;

(b) Identify and, to the extent permitted by law, allocate all sources of Federal funds for the planning, designing, and constructing of a physical wall along the southern border;

(c) Project and develop long-term funding requirements for the wall, including preparing Congressional budget requests for the current and upcoming fiscal years; and

(d) Produce a comprehensive study of the security of the southern border, to be completed within 180 days of this order, that shall include the current state of southern border security, all geophysical and topographical aspects of the southern border, the availability of Federal and State resources necessary to achieve complete operational control of the southern border, and a strategy to obtain and maintain complete operational control of the southern border.

Sec. 5. *Detention Facilities*. (a) The Secretary shall take all appropriate action and allocate all legally available resources to immediately construct, operate, control, or establish contracts to construct, operate, or control facilities to detain aliens at or near the land border with Mexico.

(b) The Secretary shall take all appropriate action and allocate all legally available resources to immediately assign asylum officers to immigration detention facilities for the purpose of accepting asylum referrals and conducting credible fear determinations pursuant to section 235(b)(1) of the INA (8 U.S.C. 1225(b)(1)) and applicable regulations and reasonable fear determinations pursuant to applicable regulations.

(c) The Attorney General shall take all appropriate action and allocate all legally available resources to immediately assign immigration judges to immigration detention facilities operated or controlled by the Secretary, or operated or controlled pursuant to contract by the Secretary, for the purpose of conducting proceedings authorized under title 8, chapter 12, subchapter II, United States Code.

Sec. 6. *Detention for Illegal Entry*. The Secretary shall immediately take all appropriate actions to ensure the detention of aliens apprehended for violations of immigration law pending the outcome of their removal proceedings or their removal from the country to the extent permitted by law. The Secretary shall issue new policy guidance to all Department of Homeland Security personnel regarding the appropriate and consistent use of lawful detention authority under the INA, including the termination of the practice commonly known as "catch and release," whereby aliens are routinely released in the United States shortly after their apprehension for violations of immigration law.

Sec. 7. *Return to Territory*. The Secretary shall take appropriate action, consistent with the requirements of section 1232 of title 8, United States Code, to ensure that aliens described in section 235(b)(2)(C) of the INA (8 U.S.C. 1225(b)(2)(C)) are returned to the territory from which they came pending a formal removal proceeding.

Sec. 8. *Additional Border Patrol Agents.* Subject to available appropriations, the Secretary, through the Commissioner of U.S. Customs and Border Protection, shall take all appropriate action to hire 5,000 additional Border Patrol agents, and all appropriate action to ensure that such agents enter on duty and are assigned to duty stations as soon as is practicable.

Sec. 9. *Foreign Aid Reporting Requirements.* The head of each executive department and agency shall identify and quantify all sources of direct and indirect Federal aid or assistance to the Government of Mexico on an annual basis over the past five years, including all bilateral and multilateral development aid, economic assistance, humanitarian aid, and military aid. Within 30 days of the date of this order, the head of each executive department and agency shall submit this information to the Secretary of State. Within 60 days of the date of this order, the Secretary shall submit to the President a consolidated report reflecting the levels of such aid and assistance that has been provided annually, over each of the past five years.

Sec. 10. *Federal-State Agreements.* It is the policy of the executive branch to empower State and local law enforcement agencies across the country to perform the functions of an immigration officer in the interior of the United States to the maximum extent permitted by law.

(a) In furtherance of this policy, the Secretary shall immediately take appropriate action to engage with the Governors of the States, as well as local officials, for the purpose of preparing to enter into agreements under section 287(g) of the INA (8 U.S.C. 1357(g)).

(b) To the extent permitted by law, and with the consent of State or local officials, as appropriate, the Secretary shall take appropriate action, through agreements under section 287(g) of the INA, or otherwise, to authorize State and local law enforcement officials, as the Secretary determines are qualified and appropriate, to perform the functions of immigration officers in relation to the investigation, apprehension, or detention of aliens in the United States under the direction and the supervision of the Secretary. Such authorization shall be in addition to, rather than in place of, Federal performance of these duties.

(c) To the extent permitted by law, the Secretary may structure each agreement under section 287(g) of the INA in the manner that provides the most effective model for enforcing Federal immigration laws and obtaining operational control over the border for that jurisdiction.

Sec. 11. *Parole, Asylum, and Removal.* It is the policy of the executive branch to end the abuse of parole and asylum provisions currently used to prevent the lawful removal of removable aliens.

(a) The Secretary shall immediately take all appropriate action to ensure that the parole and asylum provisions of Federal immigration law are not illegally exploited to prevent the removal of otherwise removable aliens.

(b) The Secretary shall take all appropriate action, including by promulgating any appropriate regulations, to ensure that asylum referrals and credible fear determinations pursuant to section 235(b)(1) of the INA (8 U.S.C. 1125(b)(1)) and 8 CFR 208.30, and reasonable fear determinations pursuant to 8 CFR 208.31, are conducted in a manner consistent with the plain language of those provisions.

(c) Pursuant to section 235(b)(1)(A)(iii)(I) of the INA, the Secretary shall take appropriate action to apply, in his sole and unreviewable discretion, the provisions of section 235(b)(1)(A)(i) and (ii) of the INA to the aliens designated under section 235(b)(1)(A)(iii)(II).

(d) The Secretary shall take appropriate action to ensure that parole authority under section 212(d)(5) of the INA (8 U.S.C. 1182(d)(5)) is exercised only on a case-by-case basis in accordance with the plain language of the statute, and in all circumstances only when an individual demonstrates urgent humanitarian reasons or a significant public benefit derived from such parole.

(e) The Secretary shall take appropriate action to require that all Department of Homeland Security personnel are properly trained on the proper application of section 235 of the William Wilberforce Trafficking Victims Protection Reauthorization Act of 2008 (8 U.S.C. 1232) and section 462(g)(2) of the Homeland Security Act of 2002 (6 U.S.C. 279(g)(2)), to ensure that unaccompanied alien children are properly processed, receive appropriate care and placement while in the custody of the Department of Homeland Security, and, when appropriate, are safely repatriated in accordance with law.

Sec. 12. *Authorization to Enter Federal Lands.* The Secretary, in conjunction with the Secretary of the Interior and any other heads of agencies as necessary, shall take all appropriate action to:

(a) permit all officers and employees of the United States, as well as all State and local officers as authorized by the Secretary, to have access to all Federal lands as necessary and appropriate to implement this order; and

(b) enable those officers and employees of the United States, as well as all State and local officers as authorized by the Secretary, to perform such actions on Federal lands as the Secretary deems necessary and appropriate to implement this order.

Sec. 13. *Priority Enforcement.* The Attorney General shall take all appropriate steps to establish prosecution guidelines and allocate appropriate resources to ensure that Federal prosecutors accord a high priority to prosecutions of offenses having a nexus to the southern border.

Sec. 14. *Government Transparency.* The Secretary shall, on a monthly basis and in a publicly available way, report statistical data on aliens apprehended at or near the southern border using a uniform method of reporting by all Department of Homeland Security components, in a format that is easily understandable by the public.

Sec. 15. *Reporting.* Except as otherwise provided in this order, the Secretary, within 90 days of the date of this order, and the Attorney General, within 180 days, shall each submit to the President a report on the progress of the directives contained in this order.

Sec. 16. *Hiring.* The Office of Personnel Management shall take appropriate action as may be necessary to facilitate hiring personnel to implement this order.

Sec. 17. *General Provisions.* (a) Nothing in this order shall be construed to impair or otherwise affect:

(i) the authority granted by law to an executive department or agency, or the head thereof; or

(ii) the functions of the Director of the Office of Management and Budget relating to budgetary, administrative, or legislative proposals.

(b) This order shall be implemented consistent with applicable law and subject to the availability of appropriations.

(c) This order is not intended to, and does not, create any right or benefit, substantive or procedural, enforceable at law or in equity by any party against the United States, its departments, agencies, or entities, its officers, employees, or agents, or any other person.

THE WHITE HOUSE,
January 25, 2017.

Enhancing Public Safety in the Interior of the United States, Exec. Order No. 13768, 82 Fed. Reg. 8,799 (Jan. 25, 2017)

By the authority vested in me as President by the Constitution and the laws of the United States of America, including the Immigration and Nationality Act (INA) (8 U.S.C. 1101 et seq.), and in order to ensure the public safety of the American people in communities across the United States as well as to ensure that our Nation's immigration laws are faithfully executed, I hereby declare the policy of the executive branch to be, and order, as follows:

Section 1. *Purpose.* Interior enforcement of our Nation's immigration laws is critically important to the national security and public safety of the United States. Many aliens who illegally enter the United States and those who overstay or otherwise violate the terms of their visas present a significant threat to national security and public safety. This is particularly so for aliens who engage in criminal conduct in the United States.

Sanctuary jurisdictions across the United States willfully violate Federal law in an attempt to shield aliens from removal from the United States. These jurisdictions have caused immeasurable harm to the American people and to the very fabric of our Republic.

Tens of thousands of removable aliens have been released into communities across the country, solely because their home countries refuse to accept their repatriation. Many of these aliens are criminals who have served time in our Federal, State, and local jails. The presence of such individuals in the United States, and the practices of foreign nations that refuse the repatriation of their nationals, are contrary to the national interest.

Although Federal immigration law provides a framework for Federal-State partnerships in enforcing our immigration laws to ensure the removal of aliens who have no right to be in the United States, the Federal Government has failed to discharge this basic sovereign responsibility. We cannot faithfully execute the immigration laws of the United States if we exempt classes or categories of removable aliens from potential enforcement. The purpose of this order is to direct executive departments and agencies (agencies) to employ all lawful means to enforce the immigration laws of the United States.

Sec. 2. *Policy.* It is the policy of the executive branch to:

(a) Ensure the faithful execution of the immigration laws of the United States, including the INA, against all removable aliens, consistent with Article II, Section 3 of the United States Constitution and section 3331 of title 5, United States Code;

(b) Make use of all available systems and resources to ensure the efficient and faithful execution of the immigration laws of the United States;

(c) Ensure that jurisdictions that fail to comply with applicable Federal law do not receive Federal funds, except as mandated by law;

(d) Ensure that aliens ordered removed from the United States are promptly removed; and

(e) Support victims, and the families of victims, of crimes committed by removable aliens.

Sec. 3. *Definitions.* The terms of this order, where applicable, shall have the meaning provided by section 1101 of title 8, United States Code.

Sec. 4. *Enforcement of the Immigration Laws in the Interior of the United States.* In furtherance of the policy described in section 2 of this order, I hereby direct agencies to employ all lawful means to ensure the faithful execution of the immigration laws of the United States against all removable aliens.

Sec. 5. *Enforcement Priorities.* In executing faithfully the immigration laws of the United States, the Secretary of Homeland Security (Secretary) shall prioritize for removal those aliens described by the Congress in sections 212(a)(2), (a)(3), and (a)(6)(C), 235, and 237(a)(2) and (4) of the INA (8 U.S.C. 1182(a)(2), (a)(3), and (a)(6)(C), 1225, and 1227(a)(2) and (4)), as well as removable aliens who:

(a) Have been convicted of any criminal offense;

(b) Have been charged with any criminal offense, where such charge has not been resolved;

(c) Have committed acts that constitute a chargeable criminal offense;

(d) Have engaged in fraud or willful misrepresentation in connection with any official matter or application before a governmental agency;

(e) Have abused any program related to receipt of public benefits;

(f) Are subject to a final order of removal, but who have not complied with their legal obligation to depart the United States; or

(g) In the judgment of an immigration officer, otherwise pose a risk to public safety or national security.

Sec. 6. *Civil Fines and Penalties.* As soon as practicable, and by no later than one year after the date of this order, the Secretary shall issue guidance and promulgate regulations, where required by law, to ensure the assessment and collection of all fines and penalties that the Secretary is authorized under the law to assess and collect from aliens unlawfully present in the United States and from those who facilitate their presence in the United States.

Sec. 7. *Additional Enforcement and Removal Officers.* The Secretary, through the Director of U.S. Immigration and Customs Enforcement, shall, to the extent permitted by law and subject to the availability of appropriations, take all appropriate action to hire 10,000 additional immigration officers, who shall complete relevant training and be authorized to perform the law enforcement functions described in section 287 of the INA (8 U.S.C. 1357).

Sec. 8. *Federal-State Agreements*. It is the policy of the executive branch to empower State and local law enforcement agencies across the country to perform the functions of an immigration officer in the interior of the United States to the maximum extent permitted by law.

(a) In furtherance of this policy, the Secretary shall immediately take appropriate action to engage with the Governors of the States, as well as local officials, for the purpose of preparing to enter into agreements under section 287(g) of the INA (8 U.S.C. 1357(g)).

(b) To the extent permitted by law and with the consent of State or local officials, as appropriate, the Secretary shall take appropriate action, through agreements under section 287(g) of the INA, or otherwise, to authorize State and local law enforcement officials, as the Secretary determines are qualified and appropriate, to perform the functions of immigration officers in relation to the investigation, apprehension, or detention of aliens in the United States under the direction and the supervision of the Secretary. Such authorization shall be in addition to, rather than in place of, Federal performance of these duties.

(c) To the extent permitted by law, the Secretary may structure each agreement under section 287(g) of the INA in a manner that provides the most effective model for enforcing Federal immigration laws for that jurisdiction.

Sec. 9. *Sanctuary Jurisdictions*. It is the policy of the executive branch to ensure, to the fullest extent of the law that a State, or a political subdivision of a State, shall comply with 8 U.S.C. 1373.

(a) In furtherance of this policy, the Attorney General and the Secretary, in their discretion and to the extent consistent with law, shall ensure that jurisdictions that willfully refuse to comply with 8 U.S.C. 1373 (sanctuary jurisdictions) are not eligible to receive Federal grants, except as deemed necessary for law enforcement purposes by the Attorney General or the Secretary. The Secretary has the authority to designate, in his discretion and to the extent consistent with law, a jurisdiction as a sanctuary jurisdiction. The Attorney General shall take appropriate enforcement action against any entity that violates 8 U.S.C. 1373, or which has in effect a statute, policy, or practice that prevents or hinders the enforcement of Federal law.

(b) To better inform the public regarding the public safety threats associated with sanctuary jurisdictions, the Secretary shall utilize the Declined Detainer Outcome Report or its equivalent and, on a weekly basis, make public a comprehensive list of criminal actions committed by aliens and any jurisdiction that ignored or otherwise failed to honor any detainers with respect to such aliens.

(c) The Director of the Office of Management and Budget is directed to obtain and provide relevant and responsive information on all Federal grant money that currently is received by any sanctuary jurisdiction.

Sec. 10. *Review of Previous Immigration Actions and Policies.* (a) The Secretary shall immediately take all appropriate action to terminate the Priority Enforcement Program (PEP) described in the memorandum issued by the Secretary on November 20, 2014, and to reinstitute the immigration program known as "Secure Communities" referenced in that memorandum.

(b) The Secretary shall review agency regulations, policies, and procedures for consistency with this order and, if required, publish for notice and comment proposed regulations rescinding or revising any regulations inconsistent with this order and shall consider whether to withdraw or modify any inconsistent policies and procedures, as appropriate and consistent with the law.

(c) To protect our communities and better facilitate the identification, detention, and removal of criminal aliens within constitutional and statutory parameters, the Secretary shall consolidate and revise any applicable forms to more effectively communicate with recipient law enforcement agencies.

Sec. 11. *Department of Justice Prosecutions of Immigration Violators.* The Attorney General and the Secretary shall work together to develop and implement a program that ensures that adequate resources are devoted to the prosecution of criminal immigration offenses in the United States, and to develop cooperative strategies to reduce violent crime and the reach of transnational criminal organizations into the United States.

Sec. 12. *Recalcitrant Countries.* The Secretary of Homeland Security and the Secretary of State shall cooperate to effectively implement the sanctions provided by section 243(d) of the INA (8 U.S.C. 1253(d)), as appropriate. The Secretary of State shall, to the maximum extent permitted by law, ensure that diplomatic efforts and negotiations with foreign states include as a condition precedent the acceptance by those foreign states of their nationals who are subject to removal from the United States.

Sec. 13. *Office for Victims of Crimes Committed by Removable Aliens.* The Secretary shall direct the Director of U.S. Immigration and Customs Enforcement to take all appropriate and lawful action to establish within U.S. Immigration and Customs Enforcement an office to provide proactive, timely, adequate, and professional services to victims of crimes committed by removable aliens and the family members of such victims. This office shall provide quarterly reports studying the effects of the victimization by criminal aliens present in the United States.

Sec. 14. *Privacy Act.* Agencies shall, to the extent consistent with applicable law, ensure that their privacy policies exclude persons who are not United States citizens or lawful permanent residents from the protections of the Privacy Act regarding personally identifiable information.

Sec. 15. *Reporting.* Except as otherwise provided in this order, the Secretary and the Attorney General shall each submit to the President a report on the progress of the directives contained in this order within 90 days of the date of this order and again within 180 days of the date of this order.

Sec. 16. *Transparency*. To promote the transparency and situational awareness of criminal aliens in the United States, the Secretary and the Attorney General are hereby directed to collect relevant data and provide quarterly reports on the following:

(a) the immigration status of all aliens incarcerated under the supervision of the Federal Bureau of Prisons;

(b) the immigration status of all aliens incarcerated as Federal pretrial detainees under the supervision of the United States Marshals Service; and

(c) the immigration status of all convicted aliens incarcerated in State prisons and local detention centers throughout the United States.

Sec. 17. *Personnel Actions*. The Office of Personnel Management shall take appropriate and lawful action to facilitate hiring personnel to implement this order.

Sec. 18. *General Provisions*. (a) Nothing in this order shall be construed to impair or otherwise affect:

(i) the authority granted by law to an executive department or agency, or the head thereof; or

(ii) the functions of the Director of the Office of Management and Budget relating to budgetary, administrative, or legislative proposals.

(b) This order shall be implemented consistent with applicable law and subject to the availability of appropriations.

(c) This order is not intended to, and does not, create any right or benefit, substantive or procedural, enforceable at law or in equity by any party against the United States, its departments, agencies, or entities, its officers, employees, or agents, or any other person.

THE WHITE HOUSE,
January 25, 2017.

U.S. Dep't of Homeland Sec., Implementing the President's Border Security and Immigration Enforcement Improvements Policies (Feb. 20, 2017)

Release Date:

February 20, 2017

MEMORANDUM FOR:

> Kevin McAleenan
> Acting Commissioner
> U.S. Customs and Border Protection
>
> Thomas D. Homan Acting Director
> U.S. Immigration and Customs Enforcement
>
> Lori Scialabba Acting Director
> U.S. Citizenship and Immigration Services
>
> Joseph B. Maher
> Acting General Counsel
>
> Dimple Shah
> Acting Assistant Secretary for International Affairs
>
> Chip Fulghum
> Acting Undersecretary for Management

FROM: John Kelly
          Secretary

SUBJECT: Implementing the President's Border Security and Immigration Enforcement Improvements Policies

This memorandum implements the Executive Order entitled "Border Security and Immigration Enforcement Improvements," issued by the President on January 25, 2017, which establishes the President's policy regarding effective border security and immigration enforcement through faithful execution of the laws of the United States. It implements new policies designed to stem illegal immigration and facilitate the detection, apprehension, detention, and removal of aliens who have no lawful basis to enter or remain in the United States. It constitutes guidance to all Department personnel, and supersedes all existing conflicting policy, directives, memoranda, and other guidance regarding this subject matter—to the extent of the conflict—except as otherwise expressly stated in this memorandum.

A. Policies Regarding the Apprehension and Detention of Aliens Described in Section 235 of the Immigration and Nationality Act.

The President has determined that the lawful detention of aliens arriving in the United States and deemed inadmissible or otherwise described in section 235(b) of the Immigration and Nationality Act (INA) pending a final determination of whether to order them removed, including determining eligibility for immigration relief, is the most efficient means by which to enforce the immigration laws at our borders. Detention also prevents such aliens from committing crimes while at large in the United States, ensures that aliens will appear for their removal proceedings, and substantially increases the likelihood that aliens lawfully ordered removed will be removed.

These policies are consistent with INA provisions that mandate detention of such aliens and allow me or my designee to exercise discretionary parole authority pursuant to section 212(d)(5) of the INA only on a case-by-case basis, and only for urgent humanitarian reasons or significant public benefit. Policies that facilitate the release of removable aliens apprehended at and between the ports of entry, which allow them to abscond and fail to appear at their removal hearings, undermine the border security mission. Such policies, collectively referred to as "catch-and-release," shall end.

Accordingly, effective upon my determination of (1) the establishment and deployment of a joint plan with the Department of Justice to surge the deployment of immigration judges and asylum officers to interview and adjudicate claims asserted by recent border entrants; and, (2) the establishment of appropriate processing and detention facilities, U.S. Customs and Border Protection (CBP) and U.S. Immigration and Customs Enforcement (ICE) personnel should only release from detention an alien detained pursuant to section 235(b) of the INA, who was apprehended or encountered after illegally entering or attempting to illegally enter the United States, in the following situations on a case-by-case basis, to the extent consistent with applicable statutes and regulations:

1.　When removing the alien from the United States pursuant to statute or regulation;

2.   When the alien obtains an order granting relief or protection from removal or the Department of Homeland Security (DHS) determines that the individual is a U.S. citizen, national of the United States, or an alien who is a lawful permanent resident, refugee, asylee, holds temporary protected status, or holds a valid immigration status in the United States;

3.   When an ICE Field Office Director, ICE Special Agent-in-Charge, U.S. Border Patrol Sector Chief, CBP Director of Field Operations, or CBP Air & Marine Operations Director consents to the alien's withdrawal of an application for admission, and the alien contemporaneously departs from the United States;

4.   When required to do so by statute, or to comply with a binding settlement agreement or order issued by a competent judicial or administrative authority;

5.   When an ICE Field Office Director, ICE Special Agent-in-Charge, U.S. Border Patrol Sector Chief, CBP Director of Field Operations, or CBP Air & Marine Operations Director authorizes the alien's parole pursuant to section 212(d)(5) of the INA with the written concurrence of the Deputy Director of ICE or the Deputy Commissioner of CBP, except in exigent circumstances such as medical emergencies where seeking prior approval is not practicable. In those exceptional instances, any such parole will be reported to the Deputy Director or Deputy Commissioner as expeditiously as possible; or

6.   When an arriving alien processed under the expedited removal provisions of section 235(b) has been found to have established a "credible fear" of persecution or torture by an asylum officer or an immigration judge, provided that such an alien affirmatively establishes to the satisfaction of an ICE immigration officer his or her identity, that he or she presents neither a security risk nor a risk of absconding, and provided that he or she agrees to comply with any additional conditions of release imposed by ICE to ensure public safety and appearance at any removal hearings.

To the extent current regulations are inconsistent with this guidance, components will develop or revise regulations as appropriate. Until such regulations are revised or removed, Department officials shall continue to operate according to regulations currently in place.

As the Department works to expand detention capabilities, detention of all such individuals may not be immediately possible, and detention resources should be prioritized based upon potential danger and risk of flight if an individual alien is not detained, and parole determinations will be made in accordance with current regulations and guidance. See

8 C.F.R. §§ 212.5, 235.3. This guidance does not prohibit the return of an alien who is arriving on land to the foreign territory contiguous to the United States from which the alien is arriving pending a removal proceeding under section 240 of the INA consistent with the direction of an ICE Field Office Director, ICE Special Agent-in-Charge, CBP Chief Patrol Agent, or CBP Director of Field Operations.

B. Hiring More CBP Agents/Officers

CBP has insufficient agents/officers to effectively detect, track, and apprehend all aliens illegally entering the United States. The United States needs additional agents and officers to ensure complete operational control of the border. Accordingly, the Commissioner of CBP shall—while ensuring consistency in training and standards—immediately begin the process of hiring 5,000 additional Border Patrol agents, as well as 500 Air & Marine Agents/Officers, subject to the availability of resources, and take all actions necessary to ensure that such agents/officers enter on duty and are assigned to appropriate duty stations, including providing for the attendant resources and additional personnel necessary to support such agents, as soon as practicable.

Human Capital leadership in CBP and ICE, in coordination with the Under Secretary for Management, Chief Financial Officer, and Chief Human Capital Officer, shall develop hiring plans that balance growth and interagency attrition by integrating workforce shaping and career paths for incumbents and new hires.

C. Identifying and Quantifying Sources of Aid to Mexico

The President has directed the heads of all executive departments to identify and quantify all sources of direct and indirect Federal aid or assistance to the Government of Mexico. Accordingly, the Under Secretary for Management shall identify all sources of direct or indirect aid and assistance, excluding intelligence activities, from every departmental component to the Government of Mexico on an annual basis, for the last five fiscal years, and quantify such aid or assistance. The Under Secretary for Management shall submit a report to me reflecting historic levels of such aid or assistance provided annually within 30 days of the date of this memorandum.

D. Expansion of the 287(g) Program in the Border Region

Section 287(g) of the INA authorizes me to enter into a written agreement with a state or political subdivision thereof, for the purpose of authorizing qualified officers or employees of the state or subdivision to perform the functions of an immigration officer in relation to the investigation, apprehension, or detention of aliens in the United States. This grant of authority, known as the 287(g) Program, has been a highly successful force multiplier that authorizes state or local law enforcement personnel to perform all law enforcement functions specified in section 287(a) of the INA, including the authority to investigate, identify, apprehend, arrest, detain, transport and conduct searches of an alien for the purposes of enforcing the immigration laws. From January 2006 through September 2015, the 287(g) Program led to the identification of more than 402,000 removable aliens, primarily through encounters at local jails.

Empowering state and local law enforcement agencies to assist in the enforcement of federal immigration law is critical to an effective enforcement strategy. Aliens who engage in criminal conduct are priorities for arrest and removal and will often be encountered by state and local law enforcement officers during the course of their routine duties. It is in the interest of the Department to partner with those state and local jurisdictions through 287(g) agreements to assist in the arrest and removal of criminal aliens.

To maximize participation by state and local jurisdictions in the enforcement of federal immigration law near the southern border, I am directing the Director of ICE and the Commissioner of CBP to engage immediately with all willing and qualified law enforcement jurisdictions that meet all program requirements for the purpose of entering into agreements under 287(g) of the INA.

The Commissioner of CBP and the Director of ICE should consider the operational functions and capabilities of the jurisdictions willing to enter into 287(g) agreements and structure such agreements in a manner that employs the most effective enforcement model for that jurisdiction, including the jail enforcement model, task force officer model, or joint jail enforcement-task force officer model. In furtherance of my direction herein, the Commissioner of CBP is authorized, in addition to the Director of ICE, to accept state services and take other actions as appropriate to carry out immigration enforcement pursuant to 287(g).

E. Commissioning a Comprehensive Study of Border Security

The Under Secretary for Management, in consultation with the Commissioner of CBP, Joint Task Force (Border), and Commandant of the Coast Guard, is directed to commission an immediate, comprehensive study of the security of the southern border (air, land and maritime) to identify vulnerabilities and provide recommendations to enhance border security. The study should include all aspects of the current border security environment, including the availability of federal and state resources to develop and implement an effective border security strategy that will achieve complete operational control of the border.

F. Border Wall Construction and Funding

A wall along the southern border is necessary to deter and prevent the illegal entry of aliens and is a critical component of the President's overall border security strategy. Congress has authorized the construction of physical barriers and roads at the border to prevent illegal immigration in several statutory provisions, including section 102 of the Illegal Immigration Reform and Immigrant Responsibility Act of 1996, as amended, 8 U.S.C. § 1103 note.

Consistent with the President's Executive Order, the will of Congress and the need to secure the border in the national interest, CBP, in consultation with the appropriate executive departments and agencies, and nongovernmental entities having relevant expertise—and using materials originating in the United States to the maximum extent permitted by law—shall immediately begin planning, design, construction and maintenance of a wall, including the attendant lighting, technology (including sensors), as well as patrol and access roads, along the land border with Mexico in accordance with existing law, in the most appropriate locations and utilizing appropriate materials and technology to most effectively achieve operational control of the border.

The Under Secretary for Management, in consultation with the Commissioner of CBP shall immediately identify and allocate all sources of available funding for the planning, design, construction and maintenance of a wall, including the attendant lighting, technology (including sensors), as well as patrol and access roads, and develop requirements for total ownership cost of this project, including preparing Congressional budget requests for the current fiscal year (e.g., supplemental budget requests) and subsequent fiscal years.

G. Expanding Expedited Removal Pursuant to Section 235(b)(1)(A)(iii)(I) of the INA

It is in the national interest to detain and expeditiously remove from the United States aliens apprehended at the border, who have been ordered removed after consideration and denial of their claims for relief or protection. Pursuant to section 235(b)(1)(A)(i) of the INA, if an immigration officer determines that an arriving alien is inadmissible to the United States under section 212(a)(6)(C) or section 212(a)(7) of the INA, the officer shall, consistent with all applicable laws, order the alien removed from the United States without further hearing or review, unless the alien is an unaccompanied alien child as defined in 6 U.S.C. § 279(g)(2), indicates an intention to apply for asylum or a fear of persecution or torture or a fear of return to his or her country, or claims to have a valid immigration status within the United States or to be a citizen or national of the United States.

Pursuant to section 235(b)(1)(A)(iii)(I) of the INA and other provisions of law, I have been granted the authority to apply, by designation in my sole and unreviewable discretion, the expedited removal provisions in section 235(b)(1)(A)(i) and (ii) of the INA to aliens who have not been admitted or paroled into the United States, who are inadmissible to the United States under section 212(a)(6)(C) or section 212(a)(7) of the INA, and who have not affirmatively shown, to the satisfaction of an immigration officer, that they have been continuously physically present in the United States for the two-year period immediately prior to the determination of their inadmissibility. To date, this authority has only been exercised to designate for application of expedited removal, aliens encountered within 100 air miles of the border and 14 days of entry, and aliens who arrived in the United States by sea other than at a port of entry.[1]

The surge of illegal immigration at the southern border has overwhelmed federal agencies and resources and has created a significant national security vulnerability to the United States. Thousands of aliens apprehended at the border, placed in removal proceedings, and released from custody have absconded and failed to appear at their removal hearings. Immigration courts are experiencing a historic backlog of removal cases, primarily proceedings under section 240 of the INA for individuals who are not currently detained.

During October 2016 and November 2016, there were 46,184 and 47,215 apprehensions, respectively, between ports of entry on our southern border. In comparison, during October 2015 and November 2015 there were 32,724 and 32,838 apprehensions, respectively, between ports of entry on our southern border. This increase of 10,000–15,000 apprehensions per month has significantly strained DHS resources.

Furthermore, according to EOIR information provided to DHS, there are more than 534,000 cases currently pending on immigration court

---

[1] Notice Designating Aliens Subject to Expedited Removal Under Section 235(b)(I)(a)(iii) of the Immigration and Nationality Act, 67 Fed. Reg. 68924 (Nov. 13, 2002); Designating Aliens For Expedited Removal, 69 Fed. Reg. 48877 (Aug. 11, 2004); Eliminating Exception to Expedited Removal Authority for Cuban Nationals Encountered in the United States or Arriving by Sea, 82 Fed. Reg. 4902 (Jan. 17, 2017).

dockets nationwide—a record high. By contrast, according to some reports, there were nearly 168,000 cases pending at the end of fiscal year
(FY) 2004 when section 235(b)(1)(A)(i) was last expanded.[2] This represents an increase of more than 200% in the number of cases pending
completion. The average removal case for an alien who is not detained
has been pending for more than two years before an immigration judge.[3]
In some immigration courts, aliens who are not detained will not have
their cases heard by an immigration judge for as long as five years. This
unacceptable delay affords removable aliens with no plausible claim for
relief to remain unlawfully in the United States for many years.

To ensure the prompt removal of aliens apprehended soon after crossing the border illegally, the Department will publish in the Federal Register a new Notice Designating Aliens Subject to Expedited Removal Under
Section 235(b)(1)(a)(iii) of the Immigration and Nationality Act, which
may, to the extent I determine is appropriate, depart from the limitations
set forth in the designation currently in force. I direct the Commissioner
of CBP and the Director of ICE to conform the use of expedited removal
procedures to the designations made in this notice upon its publication.

H. Implementing the Provisions of Section 235(b)(2)(C) of the INA to Return Aliens to Contiguous Countries

Section 235(b)(2)(C) of the INA authorizes the Department to return
aliens arriving on land from a foreign territory contiguous to the United
States, to the territory from which they arrived, pending a formal removal proceeding under section 240 of the INA. When aliens so apprehended
do not pose a risk of a subsequent illegal entry or attempted illegal entry, returning them to the foreign contiguous territory from which they
arrived, pending the outcome of removal proceedings saves the Department's detention and adjudication resources for other priority aliens.

Accordingly, subject to the requirements of section 1232, Title 8, United States Code, related to unaccompanied alien children and to the extent otherwise consistent with the law and U.S. international treaty obligations, CBP and ICE personnel shall, to the extent appropriate and
reasonably practicable, return aliens described in section 235(b)(2)(A) of
the INA, who are placed in removal proceedings under section 240 of the
INA—and who, consistent with the guidance of an ICE Field Office Director, CBP Chief Patrol Agent, or CBP Director of Field Operations, pose no
risk of recidivism—to the territory of the foreign contiguous country from
which they arrived pending such removal proceedings.

---

[2] Syracuse University, *Transactional Records Access Clearinghouse (TRAC) Data Research*; available at
http://trac.syr.edu/phptools/immigration/court_backlog/.
[3] *Id.*

To facilitate the completion of removal proceedings for aliens so returned to the contiguous country, ICE Field Office Directors, ICE Special
Agents-in-Charge, CBP Chief Patrol Agent, and CBP Directors of Field
Operations shall make available facilities for such aliens to appear via
video teleconference. The Director of ICE and the Commissioner of CBP
shall consult with the Director of EOIR to establish a functional, interop-
erable video teleconference system to ensure maximum capability to conduct video teleconference removal hearings for those aliens so returned to
the contiguous country.

I. Enhancing Asylum Referrals and Credible Fear Determina-
tions Pursuant to Section 235(b)(1) of the INA

With certain exceptions, any alien who is physically present in the
United States or who arrives in the United States (whether or not at a
designated port of arrival and including an alien who is brought to the
United States after having been interdicted in international or United
States waters), irrespective of such alien's status, may apply for asylum. For those aliens who are subject to expedited removal under section
235(b) of the INA, aliens who claim a fear of return must be referred to
an asylum officer to determine whether they have established a credible
fear of persecution or torture.[4] To establish a credible fear of persecution,
an alien must demonstrate that there is a "significant possibility" that
the alien could establish eligibility for asylum, taking into account the
credibility of the statements made by the alien in support of the claim and
such other facts as are known to the officer.[5]

The Director of USCIS shall ensure that asylum officers conduct credible fear interviews in a manner that allows the interviewing officer to
elicit all relevant information from the alien as is necessary to make a
legally sufficient determination. In determining whether the alien has
demonstrated a significant possibility that the alien could establish eligibility for asylum, or for withholding or deferral of removal under the Convention Against Torture, the asylum officer shall consider the statements
of the alien and determine the credibility of the alien's statements made
in support of his or her claim and shall consider other facts known to the
officer, as required by statute.[6]

The asylum officer shall make a positive credible fear finding only after the officer has considered all relevant evidence and determined, based
on credible evidence, that the alien has a significant possibility of estab-

---

[4] *See* INA § 235(b)(1)(A)–(B); 8 C.F.R. §§ 235.3, 208.30.
[5] *See* INA § 235(b)(1)(B)(v).
[6] *See id.*

lishing eligibility for asylum, or for withholding or deferral of removal under the Convention Against Torture, based on established legal authority.[7]

The Director of USCIS shall also increase the operational capacity of the Fraud Detection and National Security (FDNS) Directorate and continue to strengthen the integration of its operations to support the Field Operations, Refugee, Asylum, and International Operations, and Service Center Operations Directorate, to detect and prevent fraud in the asylum and benefits adjudication processes, and in consultation with the USCIS Office of Policy and Strategy as operationally appropriate.

The Director of USCIS, the Commissioner of CBP, and the Director of ICE shall review fraud detection, deterrence, and prevention measures throughout their respective agencies and provide me with a consolidated report within 90 days of the date of this memorandum regarding fraud vulnerabilities in the asylum and benefits adjudication processes, and propose measures to enhance fraud detection, deterrence, and prevention in these processes.

J. Allocation of Resources and Personnel to the Southern Border for Detention of Aliens and Adjudication of Claims

The detention of aliens apprehended at the border is critical to the effective enforcement of the immigration laws. Aliens who are released from custody pending a determination of their removability are highly likely to abscond and fail to attend their removal hearings. Moreover, the screening of credible fear claims by USCIS and adjudication of asylum claims by EOIR at detention facilities located at or near the point of apprehension will facilitate an expedited resolution of those claims and result in lower detention and transportation costs.

Accordingly, the Director of ICE and the Commissioner of CBP should take all necessary action and allocate all available resources to expand their detention capabilities and capacities at or near the border with Mexico to the greatest extent practicable. CBP shall focus these actions on expansion of "short-term detention" (defined as 72 hours or less under 6 U.S.C. § 21 l(m)) capability, and ICE will focus these actions on expansion of all other detention capabilities. CBP and ICE should also explore options for joint temporary structures that meet appropriate standards for detention given the length of stay in those facilities.

In addition, to the greatest extent practicable, the Director of USCIS is directed to increase the number of asylum officers and FDNS officers

---

[7] *Id.*

assigned to detention facilities located at or near the border with Mexico to properly and efficiently adjudicate credible fear and reasonable fear claims and to counter asylum-related fraud.

K. Proper Use of Parole Authority Pursuant to Section 212(d)(S) of the INA

The authority to parole aliens into the United States is set forth in section 212(d)(5) of the INA, which provides that the Secretary may, in his discretion and on a case-by-case basis, temporarily parole into the United States any alien who is an applicant for admission for urgent humanitarian reasons or significant public benefit. The statutory language authorizes parole in individual cases only where, after careful consideration of the circumstances, it is necessary because of demonstrated urgent humanitarian reasons or significant public benefit. In my judgment, such authority should be exercised sparingly.

The practice of granting parole to certain aliens in pre-designated categories in order to create immigration programs not established by Congress, has contributed to a border security crisis, undermined the integrity of the immigration laws and the parole process, and created an incentive for additional illegal immigration.

Therefore, the Director of USCIS, the Commissioner of CBP, and the Director of ICE shall ensure that, pending the issuance of final regulations clarifying the appropriate use of the parole power, appropriate written policy guidance and training is provided to employees within those agencies exercising parole authority, including advance parole, so that such employees are familiar with the proper exercise of parole under section 212(d)(5) of the INA and exercise such parole authority only on a case-by-case basis, consistent with the law and written policy guidance.

Notwithstanding any other provision of this memorandum, pending my further review and evaluation of the impact of operational changes to implement the Executive Order, and additional guidance on the issue by the Director of ICE, the ICE policy directive establishing standards and procedures for the parole of certain arriving aliens found to have a credible fear of persecution or torture shall remain in full force and effect.[8] The ICE policy directive shall be implemented in a manner consistent with its plain language. In every case, the burden to establish that his or her release would neither pose a danger to the community, nor a risk of flight remains on the individual alien, and ICE retains ultimate discretion whether it grants parole in a particular case.

---

[8] ICE Policy No. 11002.1: Parole of Arriving Aliens Found to Have a Credible Fear of Persecution or Torture (Dec. 8, 2009).

L. Proper Processing and Treatment of Unaccompanied Alien Minors Encountered at the Border

In accordance with section 235 of the William Wilberforce Trafficking Victims Protection Reauthorization Act of 2008 (codified in part at 8 U.S.C. § 1232) and section 462 of the Homeland Security Act of 2002 (6 U.S.C. § 279), unaccompanied alien children are provided special protections to ensure that they are properly processed and receive the appropriate care and placement when they are encountered by an immigration officer. An unaccompanied alien child, as defined in section 279(g)(2), Title 6, United States Code, is an alien who has no lawful immigration status in the United States, has not attained 18 years of age; and with respect to whom, (1) there is no parent or legal guardian in the United States, or (2) no parent of [sic] legal guardian in the United States is available to provide care and physical custody.

Approximately 155,000 unaccompanied alien children have been apprehended at the southern border in the last three years. Most of these minors are from El Salvador, Honduras, and Guatemala, many of whom travel overland to the southern border with the assistance of a smuggler who is paid several thousand dollars by one or both parents, who reside illegally in the United States.

With limited exceptions, upon apprehension, CBP or ICE must promptly determine if a child meets the definition of an "unaccompanied alien child" and, if so, the child must be transferred to the custody of the Office of Refugee Resettlement within the Department of Health and Human Services (HHS) within 72 hours, absent exceptional circumstances.[9] The determination that the child is an "unaccompanied alien child" entitles the child to special protections, including placement in a suitable care facility, access to social services, removal proceedings before an immigration judge under section 240 of the INA, rather than expedited removal proceedings under section 235(b) of the INA, and initial adjudication of any asylum claim by USCIS.[10]

Approximately 60% of minors initially determined to be "unaccompanied alien children" are placed in the care of one or more parents illegally residing in the United States. However, by Department policy and practice, such minors maintained their status as "unaccompanied alien children," notwithstanding that they may no longer meet the statutory definition once they have been placed by HHS in the custody of a parent in

---

[9] *See* 8 U.S.C. § 1232(b)(3).
[10] *See generally* 8 U.S.C. § 1232; INA § 208(b)(3)(C).

the United States who can care for the minor. Exploitation of that policy led to abuses by many of the parents and legal guardians of those minors and has contributed to significant administrative delays in adjudications by immigration courts and USCIS.

To ensure identification of abuses and the processing of unaccompanied alien children consistent with the statutory framework and any applicable court order, the Director of USCIS, the Commissioner of CBP, and the Director of ICE are directed to develop uniform written guidance and training for all employees and contractors of those agencies regarding the proper processing of unaccompanied alien children, the timely and fair adjudication of their claims for relief from removal, and, if appropriate, their safe repatriation at the conclusion of removal proceedings. In developing such guidance and training, they shall establish standardized review procedures to confirm that alien children who are initially determined to be "unaccompanied alien child[ren]," as defined in section 279(g)(2), Title 6, United States Code, continue to fall within the statutory definition when being considered for the legal protections afforded to such children as they go through the removal process.

M. Accountability Measures to Protect Alien Children from Exploitation and Prevent Abuses of Our Immigration Laws

Although the Department's personnel must process unaccompanied alien children pursuant to the requirements described above, we have an obligation to ensure that those who conspire to violate our immigration laws do not do so with impunity—particularly in light of the unique vulnerabilities of alien children who are smuggled or trafficked into the United States.

The parents and family members of these children, who are often illegally present in the United States, often pay smugglers several thousand dollars to bring their children into this country. Tragically, many of these children fall victim to robbery, extortion, kidnapping, sexual assault, and other crimes of violence by the smugglers and other criminal elements along the dangerous journey through Mexico to the United States. Regardless of the desires for family reunification, or conditions in other countries, the smuggling or trafficking of alien children is intolerable.

Accordingly, the Director of ICE and the Commissioner of CBP shall ensure the proper enforcement of our immigration laws against any individual who—directly or indirectly—facilitates the illegal smuggling or trafficking of an alien child into the United States. In appropriate cases, taking into account the risk of harm to the child from the specific smuggling or trafficking activity that the individual facilitated and other factors relevant to the individual's culpability and the child's welfare, proper enforcement includes (but is not limited to) placing any such individual who is a removable alien into removal proceedings, or referring the individual for criminal prosecution.

N. Prioritizing Criminal Prosecutions for Immigration Offenses Committed at the Border

The surge of illegal immigration at the southern border has produced a significant increase in organized criminal activity in the border region. Mexican drug cartels, Central American gangs, and other violent transnational criminal organizations have established sophisticated criminal enterprises on both sides of the border. The large-scale movement of Central Americans, Mexicans, and other foreign nationals into the border area has significantly strained federal agencies and resources dedicated to border security. These criminal organizations have monopolized the human trafficking, human smuggling, and drug trafficking trades in the border region.

It is in the national interest of the United States to prevent criminals and criminal organizations from destabilizing border security through the proliferation of illicit transactions and violence perpetrated by criminal organizations.

To counter this substantial and ongoing threat to the security of the southern border—including threats to our maritime border and the approaches—the Directors of the Joint Task Forces-West, -East, and -Investigations, as well as the ICE-led Border Enforcement Security Task Forces (BESTs), are directed to plan and implement enhanced counter-network operations directed at disrupting transnational criminal organizations, focused on those involved in human smuggling. The Department will support this work through the Office of Intelligence and Analysis, CBP's National Targeting Center, and the OHS Human Smuggling Cell.

In addition, the task forces should include participants from other federal, state, and local agencies, and should target individuals and organizations whose criminal conduct undermines border security or the integrity of the immigration system, including offenses related to alien smuggling or trafficking, drug trafficking, illegal entry and reentry, visa fraud, identity theft, unlawful possession or use of official documents, and acts of violence committed against persons or property at or near the border.

In order to support the efforts of the BESTs and counter network operations of the Joint Task Forces, the Director of ICE shall increase of [sic] the number of special agents and analysts in the Northern Triangle ICE Attaché Offices and increase the number of vetted Transnational Criminal Investigative Unit international partners. This expansion of ICE' s international footprint will focus both domestic and international efforts to dismantle transnational criminal organizations that are facilitating and profiting from the smuggling routes to the United States.

O. Public Reporting of Border Apprehensions Data

The Department has an obligation to perform its mission in a transparent and forthright manner. The public is entitled to know, with a reasonable degree of detail, information pertaining to the aliens unlawfully entering at our borders.

Therefore, consistent with law, in an effort to promote transparency and renew confidence in the Department's border security mission, the Commissioner of CBP and the Director of ICE shall develop a standardized method for public reporting of statistical data regarding aliens apprehended at or near the border for violating the immigration law. The reporting method shall include uniform terminology and shall utilize a format that is easily understandable by the public in a medium that can be readily accessed.

At a minimum, in addition to statistical information currently being publicly reported regarding apprehended aliens, the following information must be included: the number of convicted criminals and the nature of their offenses; the prevalence of gang members and prior immigration violators; the custody status of aliens and, if released, the reason for release and location of that release; and the number of aliens ordered removed and those aliens physically removed.

P. No Private Right of Action

This document provides only internal DHS policy guidance, which may be modified, rescinded, or superseded at any time without notice. This guidance is not intended to, does not, and may not be relied upon to create any right or benefit, substantive or procedural, enforceable at law by any party in any administrative, civil, or criminal matter. Likewise, no limitations are placed by this guidance on the otherwise lawful enforcement or litigation prerogatives of DHS.

In implementing this guidance, I direct DHS Components to consult with legal counsel to ensure compliance with all applicable laws, including the Administrative Procedure Act.

U.S. Dep't of Homeland Sec., Enforcement of the Immigration Laws to Serve the National Interest (Feb. 20, 2017)

Release Date:

February 20, 2017

MEMORANDUM FOR:

> Kevin McAleenan
> Acting Commissioner
> U.S. Customs and Border Protection
>
> Thomas D. Homan Acting Director
> U.S. Immigration and Customs Enforcement
>
> Lori Scialabba Acting Director
> U.S. Citizenship and Immigration Services
>
> Joseph B. Maher
> Acting General Counsel
>
> Dimple Shah
> Acting Assistant Secretary for International Affairs
>
> Chip Fulghum
> Acting Undersecretary for Management

FROM: John Kelly
              Secretary

SUBJECT: Enforcement of the Immigration Laws to Serve the National Interest

This memorandum implements the Executive Order entitled "Enhancing Public Safety in the Interior of the United States," issued by the President on January 25, 2017. It constitutes guidance for all Department personnel regarding the enforcement of the immigration laws of the United States, and is applicable to the activities of U.S. Immigration and Customs Enforcement (ICE), U.S. Customs and Border Protection (CBP), and U.S. Citizenship and Immigration Services (USCIS). As such, it should inform enforcement and removal activities, detention decisions, administrative litigation, budget requests and execution, and strategic planning.

With the exception of the June 15, 2012, memorandum entitled "Exercising Prosecutorial Discretion with Respect to Individuals Who Came to the United States as Children," and the November 20, 2014 memorandum entitled "Exercising Prosecutorial Discretion with Respect to Individuals Who Came to the United States as Children and with Respect to Certain Individuals Who Are the Parents of U.S. Citizens or Permanent Residents,"[1] all existing conflicting directives, memoranda, or field guidance regarding the enforcement of our immigration laws and priorities for removal are hereby immediately rescinded—to the extent of the conflict—including, but not limited to, the November 20, 2014, memoranda entitled "Policies for the Apprehension, Detention and Removal of Undocumented Immigrants," and "Secure Communities."

A. The Department's Enforcement Priorities

Congress has defined the Department's role and responsibilities regarding the enforcement of the immigration laws of the United States. Effective immediately, and consistent with Article II, Section 3 of the United States Constitution and Section 3331 of Title 5, United States Code, Department personnel shall faithfully execute the immigration laws of the United States against all removable aliens.

Except as specifically noted above, the Department no longer will exempt classes or categories of removable aliens from potential enforcement. In faithfully executing the immigration laws, Department personnel should take enforcement actions in accordance with applicable law. In order to achieve this goal, as noted below, I have directed ICE to hire 10,000 officers and agents expeditiously, subject to available resources, and to take enforcement actions consistent with available resources. However, in order to maximize the benefit to public safety, to stem unlawful migration and to prevent fraud and misrepresentation, Department personnel should prioritize for removal those aliens described by Congress in Sections 212(a)(2), (a)(3), and (a)(6)(C), 235(b) and (c), and 237(a)(2) and (4) of the Immigration and Nationality Act (INA).

Additionally, regardless of the basis of removability, Department personnel should prioritize removable aliens who: (1) have been convicted of any criminal offense; (2) have been charged with any criminal offense that has not been resolved; (3) have committed acts which constitute a chargeable criminal offense; (4) have engaged in fraud or willful misrep-

---

[1] The November 20, 2014, memorandum will be addressed in future guidance.

resentation in connection with any official matter before a governmental agency; (5) have abused any program related to receipt of public benefits; (6) are subject to a final order of removal but have not complied with their legal obligation to depart the United States; or (7) in the judgment of an immigration officer, otherwise pose a risk to public safety or national security. The Director of ICE, the Commissioner of CBP, and the Director of USCIS may, as they determine is appropriate, issue further guidance to allocate appropriate resources to prioritize enforcement activities within these categories—for example, by prioritizing enforcement activities against removable aliens who are convicted felons or who are involved in gang activity or drug trafficking.

B. Strengthening Programs to Facilitate the Efficient and Faithful Execution of the Immigration Laws of the United States

Facilitating the efficient and faithful execution of the immigration laws of the United States—and prioritizing the Department's resources—requires the use of all available systems and enforcement tools by Department personnel.

Through passage of the immigration laws, Congress established a comprehensive statutory regime to remove aliens expeditiously from the United States in accordance with all applicable due process of law. I determine that the faithful execution of our immigration laws is best achieved by using all these statutory authorities to the greatest extent practicable. Accordingly, Department personnel shall make full use of these authorities.

Criminal aliens have demonstrated their disregard for the rule of law and pose a threat to persons residing in the United States. As such, criminal aliens are a priority for removal. The Priority Enforcement Program failed to achieve its stated objectives, added an unnecessary layer of uncertainty for the Department's personnel, and hampered the Department's enforcement of the immigration laws in the interior of the United States. Effective immediately, the Priority Enforcement Program is terminated and the Secure Communities Program shall be restored. To protect our communities and better facilitate the identification, detention, and removal of criminal aliens within constitutional and statutory parameters, the Department shall eliminate the existing Forms I–247D, I–247N, and I–247X, and replace them with a new form to more effectively communicate with recipient law enforcement agencies. However, until such forms are updated they may be used as an interim measure to ensure that detainers may still be issued, as appropriate.

ICE's Criminal Alien Program is an effective tool to facilitate the removal of criminal aliens from the United States, while also protecting our communities and conserving the Department's detention resources. Accordingly, ICE should devote available resources to expanding the use of the Criminal Alien Program in any willing jurisdiction in the United States. To the maximum extent possible, in coordination with the Executive Office for Immigration Review (EOIR), removal proceedings shall be initiated against aliens incarcerated in federal, state, and local correctional facilities under the Institutional Hearing and Removal Program pursuant to section 238(a) of the INA, and administrative removal processes, such as those under section 238(b) of the INA, shall be used in all eligible cases.

The INA § 287(g) Program has been a highly successful force multiplier that allows a qualified state or local law enforcement officer to be designated as an "immigration officer" for purposes of enforcing federal immigration law. Such officers have the authority to perform all law enforcement functions specified in section 287(a) of the INA, including the authority to investigate, identify, apprehend, arrest, detain, and conduct searches authorized under the INA, under the direction and supervision of the Department.

There are currently 32 law enforcement agencies in 16 states participating in the 287(g) Program. In previous years, there were significantly more law enforcement agencies participating in the 287(g) Program. To the greatest extent practicable, the Director of ICE and Commissioner of CBP shall expand the 287(g) Program to include all qualified law enforcement agencies that request to participate and meet all program requirements. In furtherance of this direction and the guidance memorandum, "Implementing the President's Border Security and Immigration Enforcement Improvements Policies" (Feb. 20, 2017), the Commissioner of CBP is authorized, in addition to the Director of ICE, to accept State services and take other actions as appropriate to carry out immigration enforcement pursuant to section 287(g) of the INA.

C. Exercise of Prosecutorial Discretion

Unless otherwise directed, Department personnel may initiate enforcement actions against removable aliens encountered during the performance of their official duties and should act consistently with the President's enforcement priorities identified in his Executive Order and any further guidance issued pursuant to this memorandum. Department personnel have full authority to arrest or apprehend an alien whom an immigration officer has probable cause to believe is in violation of the immigration laws. They also have full authority to initiate removal proceedings against any alien who is subject to removal under any provision of the INA, and to refer appropriate cases for criminal prosecution. The Department shall prioritize aliens described in the Department's Enforcement Priorities (Section A) for arrest and removal. This is not intended to remove the individual, case-by-case decisions of immigration officers.

The exercise of prosecutorial discretion with regard to any alien who is subject to arrest, criminal prosecution, or removal in accordance with law shall be made on a case-by-case basis in consultation with the head of the field office component, where appropriate, of CBP, ICE, or USCIS that initiated or will initiate the enforcement action, regardless of which entity actually files any applicable charging documents: CBP Chief Patrol Agent, CBP Director of Field Operations, ICE Field Office Director, ICE Special Agent-in-Charge, or the USCIS Field Office Director, Asylum Office Director or Service Center Director.

Except as specifically provided in this memorandum, prosecutorial discretion shall not be exercised in a manner that exempts or excludes a specified class or category of aliens from enforcement of the immigration laws. The General Counsel shall issue guidance consistent with these principles to all attorneys involved in immigration proceedings.

D. Establishing the Victims of Immigration Crime Engagement (VOICE) Office

Criminal aliens routinely victimize Americans and other legal residents. Often, these victims are not provided adequate information about the offender, the offender's immigration status, or any enforcement action taken by ICE against the offender. Efforts by ICE to engage these victims have been hampered by prior Department of Homeland Security (DHS) policy extending certain Privacy Act protections to persons other than U.S. citizens and lawful permanent residents, leaving victims feeling marginalized and without a voice. Accordingly, I am establishing the Victims of Immigration Crime Engagement (VOICE) Office within the Office of the Director of ICE, which will create a programmatic liaison between ICE and the known victims of crimes committed by removable aliens. The liaison will facilitate engagement with the victims and their families to ensure, to the extent permitted by law, that they are provided information about the offender, including the offender's immigration status and custody status, and that their questions and concerns regarding immigration enforcement efforts are addressed.

To that end, I direct the Director of ICE to immediately reallocate any and all resources that are currently used to advocate on behalf of illegal aliens (except as necessary to comply with a judicial order) to the new

VOICE Office, and to immediately terminate the provision of such out-reach or advocacy services to illegal aliens.

Nothing herein may be construed to authorize disclosures that are pro-hibited by law or may relate to information that is Classified, Sensitive but Unclassified (SBU), Law Enforcement Sensitive (LES), For Official Use Only (FOUO), or similarly designated information that may relate to national security, law enforcement, or intelligence programs or oper-ations, or disclosures that are reasonably likely to cause harm to any person.

E. Hiring Additional ICE Officers and Agents

To enforce the immigration laws effectively in the interior of the Unit-ed States in accordance with the President's directives, additional ICE agents and officers are necessary. The Director of ICE shall—while en-suring consistency in training and standards—take all appropriate ac-tion to expeditiously hire 10,000 agents and officers, as well as additional operational and mission support and legal staff necessary to hire and support their activities. Human Capital leadership in CBP and ICE, in coordination with the Under Secretary for Management and the Chief Human Capital Officer, shall develop hiring plans that balance growth and interagency attrition by integrating workforce shaping and career paths for incumbents and new hires.

F. Establishment of Programs to Collect Authorized Civil Fines and Penalties

As soon as practicable, the Director of ICE, the Commissioner of CBP, and the Director of USCIS shall issue guidance and promulgate regula-tions, where required by law, to ensure the assessment and collection of all fines and penalties which the Department is authorized under the law to assess and collect from aliens and from those who facilitate their unlawful presence in the United States.

G. Aligning the Department's Privacy Policies With the Law

The Department will no longer afford Privacy Act rights and protec-tions to persons who are neither U.S. citizens nor lawful permanent resi-dents. The DHS Privacy Office will rescind the DHS Privacy Policy Guid-ance memorandum, dated January 7, 2009, which implemented the DHS "mixed systems" policy of administratively treating all personal informa-tion contained in DHS record systems as being subject to the Privacy Act regardless of the subject's immigration status. The DHS Privacy Office, with the assistance of the Office of the General Counsel, will develop new guidance specifying the appropriate treatment of personal information DHS maintains in its record systems.

H. Collecting and Reporting Data on Alien Apprehensions and Releases

The collection of data regarding aliens apprehended by ICE and the disposition of their cases will assist in the development of agency performance metrics and provide transparency in the immigration enforcement mission. Accordingly, to the extent permitted by law, the Director of ICE shall develop a standardized method of reporting statistical data regarding aliens apprehended by ICE and, at the earliest practicable time, provide monthly reports of such data to the public without charge.

The reporting method shall include uniform terminology and shall utilize a format that is easily understandable by the public and a medium that can be readily accessed. At a minimum, in addition to statistical information currently being publicly reported regarding apprehended aliens, the following categories of information must be included: country of citizenship, convicted criminals and the nature of their offenses, gang members, prior immigration violators, custody status of aliens and, if released, the reason for release and location of their release, aliens ordered removed, and aliens physically removed or returned.

The ICE Director shall also develop and provide a weekly report to the public, utilizing a medium that can be readily accessed without charge, of non-Federal jurisdictions that release aliens from their custody, notwithstanding that such aliens are subject to a detainer or similar request for custody issued by ICE to that jurisdiction. In addition to other relevant information, to the extent that such information is readily available, the report shall reflect the name of the jurisdiction, the citizenship and immigration status of the alien, the arrest, charge, or conviction for which each alien was in the custody of that jurisdiction, the date on which the ICE detainer or similar request for custody was served on the jurisdiction by ICE, the date of the alien's release from the custody of that jurisdiction and the reason for the release, an explanation concerning why the detainer or similar request for custody was not honored, and all arrests, charges, or convictions occurring after the alien's release from the custody of that jurisdiction.

I. No Private Right of Action

This document provides only internal OHS policy guidance, which may be modified, rescinded, or superseded at any time without notice.

This guidance is not intended to, does not, and may not be relied upon to create any right or benefit, substantive or procedural, enforceable at law by any party in any administrative, civil, or criminal matter. Likewise, no limitations are placed by this guidance on the otherwise lawful enforcement or litigation prerogatives of DHS.

In implementing these policies, I direct DHS Components to consult with legal counsel to ensure compliance with all applicable laws, including the Administrative Procedure Act.

U.S. Dep't. of Just., Memorandum for All Federal Prosecutors: Renewed Commitment to Criminal Immigration Enforcement (Apr. 11, 2017)

FROM: THE ATTORNEY GENERAL

SUBJECT: Renewed Commitment to Criminal Immigration Enforcement

Charging Practices

It is a high priority of the Department of Justice to establish lawfulness in our immigration system. While dramatic progress has been made at the border in recent months, much remains to be done. It is critical that our work focus on criminal cases that will further reduce illegality. Consistent and vigorous enforcement of key laws will disrupt organizations and deter unlawful conduct. I ask that you increase your efforts in this area making the following immigration offenses higher priorities. Further guidance and support of executing this priority—including an updated memorandum on charging for all criminal cases—will be forthcoming.

8 U.S.C. § 1324 ("[b]ringing in and harboring certain aliens") and related offenses: Each District shall consider for prosecution any case involving the unlawful transportation or harboring of aliens, or any other conduct proscribed pursuant to 8 U.S.C. § 1324. If a determination must be made regarding use of finite resources, a priority should be given to those who are bringing in three or more aliens into the United States and those who are transporting or harboring three or more aliens, as well as offenses where there are aggravating circumstances, such as those involving serious bodily injury, physical or sexual assault, or the death of any person. Priority should also be given to prosecuting any offenses under section 1327 ("aiding or assisting criminal aliens to enter") and section 1328 ("importation of aliens for immoral purposes").

8 U.S.C. § 1325 ("[i]mproper entry by alien"): Each District shall consider for felony prosecution under 8 U.S.C. § 1325 any case where a defendant has two or more prior misdemeanor improper entry convictions or one or more prior misdemeanor improper entry convictions with aggravating circumstances, such as felony criminal history, gang membership or affiliation, multiple prior voluntary returns, prior removal, deportation or exclusion, or other aggravating circumstances. Each District shall also consider for felony prosecution under 8 U.S.C. § 1325 any case where a defendant knowingly enters into a marriage for the purpose of evading any provision of the immigration laws.

Regarding misdemeanor violations of 8 U.S.C. § 1325, I ask that each U.S. Attorney's Office on the Southwest Border (i.e., District of Arizona, District of New Mexico, Southern District of California, Southern District of Texas, and Western District of Texas) work with the U.S. Department of Homeland Security and any other appropriate agency to develop a set of guidelines for prosecuting such violations. These guidelines should aim to accomplish the goal of deterring first-time improper entrants. Each District should submit its guidelines to the Office of the Deputy Attorney General by April 24, 2017.

8 U.S.C. § 1326 ("[r]eentry of removed aliens"): Each District shall consider prosecution of 8 U.S.C. § 1326 for each illegal reentrant. Priority, however, must be given to defendants who have been convicted of an aggravated felony, have any prior criminal history indicating the defendant poses a danger to public safety, have one or more administrative or criminal immigration violations, gang membership or affiliation, or where other aggravating circumstances are present.

18 U.S.C. § 1028A ("[a]ggravated identity theft") & 18 U.S.C. § 1546 ("[f]raud and misuse of visas, permits, and other documents"): Each District shall consider, to the extent practicable, prosecution of both aggravated identity theft under Section 1028A and document fraud under Section 1546 in relation to the immigration offenses listed above.

18 U.S.C. § 111 ("[a]ssaulting, resisting, or impeding" officers): Each District shall consider, to the extent practicable, prosecution of assault, resisting or impeding officers under Section 111, while they are engaging in the performance of their official duties in the administrative and criminal immigration context. More information on this to follow.

Sentencing Practices

At the sentencing phase of each federal case, prosecutors should seek, to the extent practicable, judicial orders of removal and a term of supervised release that is consistent with the factors set forth in 18 U.S.C. § 3553(a). I know many of you are already seeking these measures from District Courts, and I ask that you continue this effort to achieve the results consistent with this guidance.

Border Security Coordinators

In furtherance of these objectives, I also direct every District to designate a Border Security Coordinator ("Coordinator") by close of business on April 18, 2017. These Coordinators will be responsible for:

- overseeing the investigation and prosecution of the offenses listed above;

- attending training programs with other Coordinators regarding these offenses;
- providing legal advice and training to AUSAs regarding these offenses; and
- maintaining and routinely reporting prosecution statistics related to these offenses.

Each Coordinator will be responsible for convening meetings with representatives from the Department of Homeland Security—including Immigration and Customs Enforcement, Homeland Security Investigations, U.S. Customs and Border Protection, and United States Citizenship and Immigration Services as well as other law enforcement partners deemed necessary to accomplish this criminal immigration enforcement effort. The Coordinators will work with this group to (1) coordinate specific immigration enforcement initiatives, emphasizing those initiatives that will have the greatest impact on public safety; (2) initiate training programs; and (3) facilitate information sharing.

Bureau of Justice Assistance, Office of Justice Programs, Dep't of Justice (FY 2017)

Edward Byrne Memorial
Justice Assistance Grant Program
FY 2017 Local Solicitation

* * *

A. Program Description

Overview

The Edward Byrne Memorial Justice Assistance Grant (JAG) Program is the primary provider of federal criminal justice funding to States and units of local government. BJA will award JAG Program funds to eligible units of local government under this FY 2017 JAG Program Local Solicitation. * * *

* * *

Program-Specific Information

Permissible uses of JAG Funds—In general

In general, JAG funds awarded to a unit of local government under this FY 2017 solicitation may be used to provide additional personnel, equipment, supplies, contractual support, training, technical assistance, and information systems for criminal justice, including for any one or more of the following:

- Law enforcement programs
- Prosecution and court programs
- Prevention and education programs
- Corrections and community corrections programs
- Drug treatment and enforcement programs
- Planning, evaluation, and technology improvement programs
- Crime victim and witness programs (other than compensation)
- Mental health programs and related law enforcement and corrections programs, including behavioral programs and crisis intervention teams

Under the JAG Program, units of local government may use award funds for broadband deployment and adoption activities as they relate to criminal justice activities.

* * *

Required compliance with applicable federal laws

By law, the chief executive (e.g., the mayor) of each unit of local government that applies for an FY 2017 JAG award must certify that the unit of local government will "comply with all provisions of [the JAG program statute] and all other applicable Federal laws." To satisfy this requirement, each unit of local government applicant must submit two properly executed certifications using the forms shown in Appendix I and Appendix II.

All applicants should understand that OJP awards, including certifications provided in connection with such awards, are subject to review by DOJ, including by OJP and by the DOJ Office of the Inspector General. Applicants also should understand that a materially false, fictitious, or fraudulent statement (or concealment or omission of a material fact) in a certification submitted to OJP in support of an application may be the subject of criminal prosecution, and also may result in civil penalties and administrative remedies for false claims or otherwise. Administrative remedies that may be available to OJP with respect to an FY 2017 award include suspension or termination of the award, placement on the DOJ high risk grantee list, disallowance of costs, and suspension or debarment of the recipient.

* * *

C. Eligibility Information

For information on eligibility, see the title page of this solicitation.

Note that, as discussed in more detail below, the certification regarding compliance with 8 U.S.C. § 1373 must be executed and submitted before a unit of local government (other than an Indian tribal government) can make a valid award acceptance. Also, a unit of local government may not receive award funds (and its award will include a condition that withholds funds) until it submits a properly executed "Certifications and Assurances by Chief Executive of Applicant Government."

* * *

F. Federal Award Administration Information

* * *

NOTE: In order validly to accept an award under the FY 2017 JAG Program, a unit of local government (other than an Indian tribal government) must submit to GMS the certification by its chief legal officer regarding compliance with 8 U.S.C. § 1373[.] * * * Unless the executed certification either (1) is submitted to OJP together with the signed award document or (2) is uploaded in GMS no later than the day the signed award document is submitted, **OJP will reject as invalid** any submission by a unit of local government (other than an Indian tribal government) that purports to accept an award under this solicitation.

Rejection of an initial submission as an invalid award acceptance is not a denial of the award. Consistent with award requirements, once the unit of local government **does** submit the necessary certification regarding 8 U.S.C. § 1373, the unit of local government **will** be permitted to submit an award document executed by the unit of local government on or after the date of that certification.

Also, in order for a unit of local government applicant validly to accept an award under the FY 2017 JAG Program, an individual with the necessary authority to bind the applicant will be required to log in; execute a set of legal certifications and a set of legal assurances; designate a financial point of contact; thoroughly review the award, including **all** award conditions; and sign and accept the award. The award acceptance process requires physical signature of the award document by the authorized representative and the scanning of the fully executed award document (along with the required certification regarding 8 U.S.C. § 1373, if not already uploaded in GMS) to OJP.

Statutory and Regulatory Requirements; Award Conditions

* * *

Individual FY 2017 JAG awards will include two new express conditions that, with respect to the "program or activity" that would be funded by the FY 2017 award, are designed to ensure that States and units of local government that receive funds from the FY 2017 JAG award: (1) permit personnel of the U.S. Department of Homeland Security (DHS) to access any correctional or detention facility in order to meet with an alien (or an individual believed to be an alien) and inquire as to his or her right to be or remain in the United States and (2) provide at least 48 hours' advance notice to DHS regarding the scheduled release date and time of an alien in the jurisdiction's custody when DHS requests such notice in order to take custody of the alien pursuant to the Immigration and Nationality Act.

Compliance with the requirements of the two foregoing new award conditions will be an authorized and priority purpose of the award. The reasonable costs (to the extent not reimbursed under any other federal program) of developing and putting into place statutes, rules, regulations, policies, or practices as required by these conditions, and to honor any duly authorized requests from DHS that is encompassed by these conditions, will be allowable costs under the award.

* * *

APPENDIX I

Certifications and Assurances by the Chief Executive of the Applicant Government

Template for use by *chief executive* of the "Unit of local government" (e.g., the mayor)

. . .

U.S. DEPARTMENT OF JUSTICE
OFFICE OF JUSTICE PROGRAMS

Edward Byrne Justice Assistance Grant Program
FY 2017 Local Solicitation

Certifications and Assurances
by the Chief Executive of the Applicant Government

On behalf of the applicant unit of local government named below, in support of that locality's application for an award under the FY 2017 Edward Byrne Justice Assistance Grant ("JAG") Program, and further to 42 U.S.C. § 3752(a), I certify under penalty of perjury to the Office of Justice Programs ("OJP"), U.S. Department of Justice ("USDOJ"), that all of the following are true and correct:

1. I am the chief executive of the applicant unit of local government named below, and I have the authority to make the following representations on my own behalf and on behalf of the applicant unit of local government. I understand that these representations will be relied upon as material in any OJP decision to make an award, under the application described above, to the applicant unit of local government.

2. I certify that no federal funds made available by the award (if any) that OJP makes based on the application described above will be used to supplant local funds, but will be used to increase the amounts of such funds that would, in the absence of federal funds, be made available for law enforcement activities.

3. I assure that the application described above (and any amendment to that application) was submitted for review to the governing body of the unit of local government (e.g., city council or county commission), or to an organization designated by that governing body, not less than 30 days before the date of this certification.

4. I assure that, before the date of this certification— (a) the application described above (and any amendment to that application) was made public; and (b) an opportunity to comment on that application (or amendment) was provided to citizens and to neighborhood or community-based organizations, to the extent applicable law or established procedure made such an opportunity available.

5. I assure that, for each fiscal year of the award (if any) that OJP makes based on the application described above, the applicant unit of local government will maintain and report such data, records, and information (programmatic and financial), as OJP may reasonably require.

6. I certify that— (a) the programs to be funded by the award (if any) that OJP makes based on the application described above meet all the requirements of the JAG Program statute (42 U.S.C. §§ 3750-3758); (b) all the information contained in that application is correct; (c) in connection with that application, there has been appropriate coordination with affected agencies; and (d) in connection with that award (if any), the applicant unit of local government will comply with all provisions of the JAG Program statute and all other applicable federal laws.

7. I have examined certification entitled "State or Local Government: FY 2017 Certification of Compliance with 8 U.S.C. § 1373" executed by the chief legal officer of the applicant government with respect to the FY 2017 JAG program and submitted in support of the application described above, and I hereby adopt that certification as my own on behalf of that government.

I acknowledge that a materially false, fictitious, or fraudulent statement (or concealment or omission of a material fact) in this certification, or in the application that it "supports, may be the subject of criminal prosecution (including under 18 U.S.C. §§ 1001 and/or 1621, and/or 42 U.S.C. § 3795a), and also may subject me and the applicant unit of local government to civil penalties and administrative remedies for false claims or otherwise (including under 31 U.S.C. §§ 3729-3730 and §§ 3801-3812). I also acknowledge that OJP awards, including certifications provided in connection with such awards, are subject to review by USDOJ, including by OJP and by the USDOJ Office of the Inspector General.

_____
Signature of Chief Executive of the Applicant Unit of
Local Government

_____
Printed Name of Chief Executive

_____
Date of Certification

_____
Title of Chief Executive

_____
Name of Applicant Unit of Local Government

January 17, 1997

UNITED STATES DISTRICT COURT
CENTRAL DISTRICT OF CALIFORNIA

JENNY LISETTE FLORES, et al, Plaintiffs

v.

JANET RENO, Attorney General of the United States, et al., Defendants

Case No. CV 85-4544-RJK(Px)

STIPULATED SETTLEMENT AGREEMENT

WHEREAS, Plaintiffs have filed this action against Defendants, challenging, *inter alia*, the constitutionality of Defendants' policies, practices and regulations regarding the detention and release of unaccompanied minors taken into the custody of the Immigration and Naturalization Service (INS) in the Western Region; and

WHEREAS, the district court has certified this case as a class action on behalf of all minors apprehended by the INS in the Western Region of the United States; and

WHEREAS, this litigation has been pending for nine (9) years, all parties have conducted extensive discovery, and the United States Supreme Court has upheld the constitutionality of the challenged INS regulations on their face and has remanded for further proceedings consistent with its opinion; and

* * *

NOW, THEREFORE, Plaintiffs and Defendants enter into this Stipulated Settlement Agreement (the Agreement), stipulate that it constitutes a full and complete resolution of the issues raised in this action, and agree to the following:

* * *

II. SCOPE OF SETTLEMENT, EFFECTIVE DATE, AND PUBLICATION

9. This Agreement sets out nationwide policy for the detention, release, and treatment of minors in the custody of the INS and shall supersede

all previous INS policies that are inconsistent with the terms of this Agreement.* * *

III. CLASS DEFINITION

10. The certified class in this action shall be defined as follows: "All minors who are detained in the legal custody of the INS."

IV. STATEMENTS OF GENERAL APPLICABILITY

11. The INS treats, and shall continue to treat, all minors in its custody with dignity, respect and special concern for their particular vulnerability as minors. The INS shall place each detained minor in the least restrictive setting appropriate to the minor's age and special needs, provided that such setting is consistent with its interests to ensure the minor's timely appearance before the INS and the immigration courts and to protect the minor's well-being and that of others. Nothing herein shall require the INS to release a minor to any person or agency whom the INS has reason to believe may harm or neglect the minor or fail to present him or her before the INS or the immigration courts when requested to do so.

V. PROCEDURES AND TEMPORARY PLACEMENT FOLLOWING ARREST

12.

A. Whenever the INS takes a minor into custody, it shall expeditiously process the minor and shall provide the minor with a notice of rights, including the right to a bond redetermination hearing if applicable. Following arrest, the INS shall hold minors in facilities that are safe and sanitary and that are consistent with the INS's concern for the particular vulnerability of minors. Facilities will provide access to toilets and sinks, drinking water and food as appropriate, medical assistance if the minor is in need of emergency services, adequate temperature control and ventilation, adequate supervision to protect minors from others, and contact with family members who were arrested with the minor. The INS will segregate unaccompanied minors from unrelated adults. Where such segregation is not immediately possible, an unaccompanied minor will not be detained with an unrelated adult for more than 24 hours. If there is no one to whom the INS may release the minor pursuant to Paragraph 14, and no appropriate licensed program is immediately available for placement pursuant to Paragraph 19, the minor may be placed in an INS detention facility, or other INS-contracted facility, having separate accommodations for minors, or a State or county juvenile detention facility. However, minors shall be separated from delinquent offenders. Every effort must be taken to ensure that the safety and well-being of the minors detained in these facilities are satisfactorily provided for by the staff. The INS will transfer a minor from a placement under this paragraph to a placement under Paragraph 19 (i) within three (3) days, if the minor was apprehended in an INS district in which a licensed program is located and has space available; or (ii) within five (5) days in all other cases; except:

1. as otherwise provided under Paragraph 13 or Paragraph 21;

2. as otherwise required by any court decree or court-approved settlement;

3. in the event of an emergency or influx of minors into the United States, in which case the INS shall place all minors pursuant to Paragraph 19 as expeditiously as possible; or

4. where individuals must be transported from remote areas for processing or speak unusual languages such that the INS must locate interpreters in order to complete processing, in which case the INS shall place all such minors pursuant to Paragraph 19 within five (5) business days.

B. For purposes of this Paragraph, the term "emergency" shall be defined as any act or event that prevents the placement of minors pursuant to Paragraph 19 within the time frame provided. Such emergencies include natural disasters (e.g., earthquakes, hurricanes, etc.), facility fires, civil disturbances, and medical emergencies (e.g., a chicken pox epidemic among a group of minors). The term "influx of minors into the United States" shall be defined as those circumstances where the INS has, at any given time, more than 130 minors eligible for placement in a licensed program under Paragraph 19, including those who have been so placed or are awaiting such placement.

C. In preparation for an "emergency" or "influx," as described in Subparagraph B, the INS shall have a written plan that describes the reasonable efforts that it will take to place all minors as expeditiously as possible. This plan shall include the identification of 80 beds that are potentially available for INS placements and that are licensed by an appropriate State agency to provide residential, group, or foster care services for dependent children. The plan, without identification of the additional beds available, is attached as Exhibit 3. The INS shall not be obligated to fund these additional beds on an ongoing basis. The INS shall update this listing of additional beds on a quarterly basis and provide Plaintiffs' counsel with a copy of this listing.

13. If a reasonable person would conclude that an alien detained by the INS is an adult despite his claims to be a minor, the INS shall treat

the person as an adult for all purposes, including confinement and release on bond or recognizance. The INS may require the alien to submit to a medical or dental examination conducted by a medical professional or to submit to other appropriate procedures to verify his or her age. If the INS subsequently determines that such an individual is a minor, he or she will be treated as a minor in accordance with this Agreement for all purposes.

VI. GENERAL POLICY FAVORING RELEASE

14. Where the INS determines that the detention of the minor is not required either to secure his or her timely appearance before the INS or the immigration court, or to ensure the minor's safety or that of others, the INS shall release a minor from its custody without unnecessary delay, in the following order of preference, to:

   A. a parent;

   B. a legal guardian;

   C. an adult relative (brother, sister, aunt, uncle, or grandparent);

   D. an adult individual or entity designated by the parent or legal guardian as capable and willing to care for the minor's well-being in (i) a declaration signed under penalty of perjury before an immigration or consular officer or (ii) such other document(s) that establish(es) to the satisfaction of the INS, in its discretion, the affiant's paternity or guardianship;

   E. a licensed program willing to accept legal custody; or

   F. an adult individual or entity seeking custody, in the discretion of the INS, when it appears that there is no other likely alternative to long term detention and family reunification does not appear to be a reasonable possibility.

15. Before a minor is released from INS custody pursuant to Paragraph 14 above, the custodian must execute an Affidavit of Support (Form I–134) and an agreement to:

   A. provide for the minor's physical, mental, and financial well-being;

   B. ensure the minor's presence at all future proceedings before the INS and the immigration court;

   C. notify the INS of any change of address within five (5) days following a move;

   D. in the case of custodians other than parents or legal guardians, not transfer custody of the minor to another party without the prior written permission of the District Director;

E. notify the INS at least five days prior to the custodian's departing the United States of such departure, whether the departure is voluntary or pursuant to a grant of voluntary departure or order of deportation; and

F. if dependency proceedings involving the minor are initiated, notify the INS of the initiation of a such proceedings and the dependency court of any immigration proceedings pending against the minor.

In the event of an emergency, a custodian may transfer temporary physical custody of a minor prior to securing permission from the INS but shall notify the INS of the transfer as soon as is practicable thereafter, but in all cases within 72 hours. For purposes of this Paragraph, examples of an "emergency" shall include the serious illness of the custodian, destruction of the home, etc. In all cases where the custodian in writing seeks written permission for a transfer, the District Director shall promptly respond to the request.

16. The INS may terminate the custody arrangements and assume legal custody of any minor whose custodian fails to comply with the agreement required under Paragraph 15. The INS, however, shall not terminate the custody arrangements for minor violations of that part of the custodial agreement outlined at Subparagraph 15.C above.

17. A positive suitability assessment may be required prior to release to any individual or program pursuant to Paragraph 14. A suitability assessment may include such components as an investigation of the living conditions in which the minor would be placed and the standard of care he would receive, verification of identity and employment of the individuals offering support, interviews of members of the household, and a home visit. Any such assessment should also take into consideration the wishes and concerns of the minor.

18. Upon taking a minor into custody, the INS, or the licensed program in which the minor is placed, shall make and record the prompt and continuous efforts on its part toward family reunification and the release of the minor pursuant to Paragraph 14 above. Such efforts at family reunification shall continue so long as the minor is in INS custody.

VII. INS CUSTODY

19. In any case in which the INS does not release a minor pursuant to Paragraph 14, the minor shall remain in INS legal custody. Except as provided in Paragraphs 12 or 21, such minor shall be placed temporarily in a licensed program until such time as release can be effected in accordance with Paragraph 14 above or until the minor's immigration proceedings are concluded, whichever occurs earlier. All minors placed in such a licensed program remain in the legal custody of the INS and may only be transferred or released under the authority

of the INS; provided, however, that in the event of an emergency a licensed program may transfer temporary physical custody of a minor prior to securing permission from the INS but shall notify the INS of the transfer as soon as is practicable thereafter, but in all cases within 8 hours.

20. Within 60 days of final court approval of this Agreement, the INS shall authorize the United States Department of Justice Community Relations Service to publish in the Commerce Business Daily and/or the Federal Register a Program Announcement to solicit proposals for the care of 100 minors in licensed programs.

21. A minor may be held in or transferred to a suitable State or county juvenile detention facility or a secure INS detention facility, or INS-contracted facility, having separate accommodations for minors whenever the District Director or Chief Patrol Agent determines that the minor:

A. has been charged with, is chargeable, or has been convicted of a crime, or is the subject of delinquency proceedings, has been adjudicated delinquent, or is chargeable with a delinquent act; provided, however, that this provision shall not apply to any minor whose offense(s) fall(s) within either of the following categories:

    i. Isolated offenses that (1) were not within a pattern or practice of criminal activity and (2) did not involve violence against a person or the use or carrying of a weapon (Examples: breaking and entering, vandalism, DUI, etc. This list is not exhaustive.);

    ii. Petty offenses, which are not considered grounds for stricter means of detention in any case (Examples: shoplifting, joy riding, disturbing the peace, etc. This list is not exhaustive.);

As used in this paragraph, "chargeable" means that the INS has probable cause to believe that the individual has committed a specified offense;

B. has committed, or has made credible threats to commit, a violent or malicious act (whether directed at himself or others) while in INS legal custody or while in the presence of an INS officer;

C. has engaged, while in a licensed program, in conduct that has proven to be unacceptably disruptive of the normal functioning of the licensed program in which he or she has been placed and removal is necessary to ensure the welfare of the minor or others, as determined by the staff of the licensed program (Examples: drug or alcohol abuse, stealing, fighting, intimidation of others, etc. This list is not exhaustive.);

D. is an escape-risk; or

E. must be held in a secure facility for his or her own safety, such as when the INS has reason to believe that a smuggler would abduct or coerce a particular minor to secure payment of smuggling fees.

22. The term "escape-risk" means that there is a serious risk that the minor will attempt to escape from custody. Factors to consider when determining whether a minor is an escape-risk or not include, but are not limited to, whether:

A. the minor is currently under a final order of deportation or exclusion;

B. the minor's immigration history includes: a prior breach of a bond; a failure to appear before the INS or the immigration court; evidence that the minor is indebted to organized smugglers for his transport; or a voluntary departure or a previous removal from the United States pursuant to a final order of deportation or exclusion;

C. the minor has previously absconded or attempted to abscond from INS custody.

23. The INS will not place a minor in a secure facility pursuant to Paragraph 21 if there are less restrictive alternatives that are available and appropriate in the circumstances, such as transfer to (a) a medium security facility which would provide intensive staff supervision and counseling services or (b) another licensed program. All determinations to place a minor in a secure facility will be reviewed and approved by the regional juvenile coordinator.

24.

A. A minor in deportation proceedings shall be afforded a bond redetermination hearing before an immigration judge in every case, unless the minor indicates on the Notice of Custody Determination form that he or she refuses such a hearing.

B. Any minor who disagrees with the INS's determination to place that minor in particular type of facility, or who asserts that the licensed program in which he or she has been placed does not comply with the standards set forth in Exhibit 1 attached hereto, may seek judicial review in any United States District Court with jurisdiction and venue over the matter to challenge that placement determination or to allege noncompliance with the standards set forth in Exhibit 1. In such an action, the United States District Court shall be limited to entering an order solely affecting the individual claims of the minor bringing the action.

C. In order to permit judicial review of Defendants' placement decisions as provided in this Agreement, Defendants shall provide minors not placed in licensed programs with a notice of the reasons for housing the minor in a detention or medium security facility. With respect to placement decisions reviewed under this paragraph, the standard of review for the INS's exercise of its discretion shall be the abuse of discretion standard of review. With respect to all other matters for which this paragraph provides judicial review, the standard of review shall be *de novo* review.

D. The INS shall promptly provide each minor not released with (a) INS Form I–770; (b) an explanation of the right of judicial review as set out in Exhibit 6, and (c) the list of free legal services providers compiled pursuant to INS regulation (unless previously given to the minor).

E. Exhausting the procedures established in Paragraph 37 of this Agreement shall not be a precondition to the bringing of an action under this paragraph in any United District Court. Prior to initiating any such action, however, the minor and/or the minors' attorney shall confer telephonically or in person with the United States Attorney's office in the judicial district where the action is to be filed, in an effort to informally resolve the minor's complaints without the need of federal court intervention.

* * *

XI. ATTORNEY-CLIENT VISITS

32.

A. Plaintiffs' counsel are entitled to attorney-client visits with class members even though they may not have the names of class members who are housed at a particular location. All visits shall occur in accordance with generally applicable policies and procedures relating to attorney-client visits at the facility in question. Upon Plaintiffs' counsel's arrival at a facility for attorney-client visits, the facility staff shall provide Plaintiffs' counsel with a list of names and alien registration numbers for the minors housed at that facility. In all instances, in order to memorialize any visit to a minor by Plaintiffs' counsel, Plaintiffs' counsel must file a notice of appearance with the INS prior to any attorney-client meeting. Plaintiffs' counsel may limit any such notice of appearance to representation of the minor in connection with this Agreement. Plaintiffs' counsel must submit a copy of the notice of appearance by hand or by mail to the local INS juvenile coordinator and a copy by hand to the staff of the facility.

B. Every six months, Plaintiffs' counsel shall provide the INS with a list of those attorneys who may make such attorney-client visits, as Plaintiffs' counsel, to minors during the following six month period. Attorney-client visits may also be conducted by any staff attorney employed by the Center for Human Rights & Constitutional Law in Los Angeles, California or the National Center for Youth Law in San Francisco, California, provided that such attorney presents credentials establishing his or her employment prior to any visit.

C. Agreements for the placement of minor in non-INS facilities shall permit attorney-client visits, including by class counsel in this case.

D. Nothing in Paragraph 32 shall affect a minor's right to refuse to meet with Plaintiffs' counsel. Further, the minor's parent or legal guardian may deny Plaintiffs' counsel permission to meet with the minor.

XII. FACILITY VISITS

33. In addition to the attorney-client visits permitted pursuant to Paragraph 32, Plaintiffs' counsel may request access to any licensed program's facility in which a minor has been placed pursuant to Paragraph 19 or to any medium security facility or detention facility in which a minor has been placed pursuant to Paragraphs 21 or 23. Plaintiffs' counsel shall submit a request to visit a facility under this paragraph to the INS district juvenile coordinator who will provide reasonable assistance to Plaintiffs' counsel by conveying the request to the facility's staff and coordinating the visit. The rules and procedures to be followed in connection with any visit approved by a facility under this paragraph are set forth in Exhibit 4 attached, except as may be otherwise agreed by Plaintiffs' counsel and the facility's staff. In all visits to any facility pursuant to this Agreement, Plaintiffs' counsel and their associated experts shall treat minors and staff with courtesy and dignity and shall not disrupt the normal functioning of the facility.

* * *

EXHIBIT 1

Minimum Standards for Licensed Programs

A. Licensed programs shall comply with all applicable state child welfare laws and regulations and all state and local building, fire, health and safety codes and shall provide or arrange for the following services for each minor in its care:

1. Proper physical care and maintenance, including suitable living accommodations, food, appropriate clothing, and personal grooming items.

2. Appropriate routine medical and dental care, family planning services, and emergency health care services, including a complete medical examination (including screening for infectious disease) within 48 hours of admission, excluding weekends and holidays, unless the minor was recently examined at another facility;

appropriate immunizations in accordance with the U.S. Public Health Service (PHS), Center for Disease Control; administration of prescribed medication and special diets; appropriate mental health interventions when necessary.

3. An individualized needs assessment which shall include: (a) various initial intake forms; (b) essential data relating to the identification and history of the minor and family; (c) identification of the minors' special needs including any specific problem(s) which appear to require immediate intervention; (d) an educational assessment and plan; (e) an assessment of family relationships and interaction with adults, peers and authority figures; (f) a statement of religious preference and practice; (g) an assessment of the minor's personal goals, strengths and weaknesses; and (h) identifying information regarding immediate family members, other relatives, godparents or friends who may be residing in the United States and may be able to assist in family reunification.

4. Educational services appropriate to the minor's level of development, and communication skills in a structured classroom setting, Monday through Friday, which concentrates primarily on the development of basic academic competencies and secondarily on English Language Training (ELT). The educational program shall include instruction and educational and other reading materials in such languages as needed. Basic academic areas should include Science, Social Studies, Math, Reading, Writing and Physical Education. The program shall provide minors with appropriate reading materials in languages other than English for use during the minor's leisure time.

5. Activities according to a recreation and leisure time plan which shall include daily outdoor activity, weather permitting, at least one hour per day of large muscle activity and one hour per day of structured leisure time activities (this should not include time spent watching television). Activities should be increased to a total of three hours on days when school is not in session.

6. At least one (1) individual counseling session per week conducted by trained social work staff with the specific objectives of reviewing the minor's progress, establishing new short term objectives, and addressing both the developmental and crisis-related needs of each minor.

7. Group counseling sessions at least twice a week. This is usually an informal process and takes place with all the minors present. It is a time when new minors are given the opportunity to get acquainted with the staff, other children, and the rules of the program. It is an open forum where everyone gets a chance to speak. Daily program management is discussed and decisions are made about recreational activities, etc. It is a time for staff

and minors to discuss whatever is on their minds and to resolve problems.

8. Acculturation and adaptation services which include information regarding the development of social and inter-personal skills which contribute to those abilities necessary to live independently and responsibly.

9. Upon admission, a comprehensive orientation regarding program intent, services, rules (written and verbal), expectations and the availability of legal assistance.

10. Whenever possible, access to religious services of the minor's choice.

11. Visitation and contact with family members (regardless of their immigration status) which is structured to encourage such visitation. The staff shall respect the minor's privacy while reasonably preventing the unauthorized release of the minor.

12. A reasonable right to privacy, which shall include the right to: (a) wear his or her own clothes, when available; (b) retain a private space in the residential facility, group or foster home for the storage of personal belongings; (c) talk privately on the phone, as permitted by the house rules and regulations; (d) visit privately with guests, as permitted by the house rules and regulations; and (e) receive and send uncensored mail unless there is a reasonable belief that the mail contains contraband.

13. Family reunification services designed to identify relatives in the United States as well as in foreign countries and assistance in obtaining legal guardianship when necessary for the release of the minor.

14. Legal services information regarding the availability of free legal assistance, the right to be represented by counsel at no expense to the government, the right to a deportation or exclusion hearing before an immigration judge, the right to apply for political asylum or to request voluntary departure in lieu of deportation.

B. Service delivery is to be accomplished in a manner which is sensitive to the age, culture, native language and the complex needs of each minor.

C. Program rules and discipline standards shall be formulated with consideration for the range of ages and maturity in the program and shall be culturally sensitive to the needs of alien minors. Minors shall not be subjected to corporal punishment, humiliation, mental abuse, or punitive interference with the daily functions of living, such as eating or sleeping. Any sanctions employed shall not: (1) adversely affect either a minor's health, or physical or psychological well-being; or (2) deny minors regular meals, sufficient sleep, exercise, medical care, correspondence privileges, or legal assistance.

D. A comprehensive and realistic individual plan for the care of each minor must be developed in accordance with the minor's needs as determined by the individualized need assessment. Individual plans shall be implemented and closely coordinated through an operative case management system.

E. Programs shall develop, maintain and safeguard individual client case records. Agencies and organizations are required to develop a system of accountability which preserves the confidentiality of client information and protects the records from unauthorized use or disclosure.

F. Programs shall maintain adequate records and make regular reports as required by the INS that permit the INS to monitor and enforce this order and other requirements and standards as the INS may determine are in the best interests of the minors.

EXHIBIT 2

Instructions to Service Officers re:
Processing, Treatment, and Placement of Minors

These instructions are to advise Service officers of INS policy regarding the way in which minors in INS custody are processed, housed and released. These instructions are applicable nationwide and supersede all prior inconsistent instructions regarding minors.

(a) Minors. A minor is a person under the age of eighteen years. However, individuals who have been "emancipated" by a state court or convicted and incarcerated for a criminal offense as an adult are not considered minors. Such individuals must be treated as adults for all purposes, including confinement and release on bond.

Similarly, if a reasonable person would conclude that an individual is an adult despite his claims to be a minor, the INS shall treat such person as an adult for all purposes, including confinement and release on bond or recognizance. The INS may require such an individual to submit to a medical or dental examination conducted by a medical professional or to submit to other appropriate procedures to verify his or her age. If the INS subsequently determines that such an individual is a minor, he or she will be treated as a minor for all purposes.

(b) General policy. The INS treats and shall continue to treat minors with dignity, respect and special concern for their particular vulnerability. INS policy is to place each detained minor in the least restrictive setting appropriate to the minor's age and special needs, provided that such setting is consistent with the need to ensure the minor's timely appearance and to protect the minor's well-being and that of others. INS officers are not required to release a minor to any person or agency whom they have reason to believe may harm or neglect the minor or fail to present him or her before the INS or the immigration courts when requested to do so.

(c) Processing. The INS will expeditiously process minors and will provide them a Form I–770 notice of rights, including the right to a bond redetermination hearing, if applicable.

Following arrest, the INS will hold minors in a facility that is safe and sanitary and that is consistent with the INS's concern for the particular vulnerability of minors. Such facilities will have access to toilets and sinks, drinking water and food as appropriate, medical assistance if the minor is in need of emergency services, adequate temperature control and ventilation, adequate supervision to protect minors from others, and contact with family members who were arrested with the minor. The INS will separate unaccompanied minors from unrelated adults whenever possible. Where such segregation is not immediately possible, an unaccompanied minor will not be detained with an unrelated adult for more than 24 hours.

If the minor cannot be immediately released, and no licensed program (described below) is available to care for him, he should be placed in an INS or INS-contract facility that has separate accommodations for minors, or in a State or county juvenile detention facility that separates minors in INS custody from delinquent offenders. The INS will make every effort to ensure the safety and well-being of juveniles placed in these facilities.

(d) Release. The INS will release minors from its custody without unnecessary delay, unless detention of a juvenile is required to secure her timely appearance or to ensure the minor's safety or that of others.

Minors shall be released in the following order of preference, to:

(i) a parent;

(ii) a legal guardian;

(iii) an adult relative (brother, sister, aunt, uncle, or grandparent);

(iv) an adult individual or entity designated by the parent or legal guardian as capable and willing to care for the minor's well-being in (i) a declaration signed under penalty of perjury before an immigration or consular officer, or (ii) such other documentation that establishes to the satisfaction of the INS, in its discretion, that the individual designating the individual or entity as the minor's custodian is in fact the minor's parent or guardian;

(v) a state-licensed juvenile shelter, group home, or foster home willing to accept legal custody; or

(vi) an adult individual or entity seeking custody, in the discretion of the INS, when it appears that there is no other likely alternative to long term detention and family reunification does not appear to be a reasonable possibility.

795

(e) Certification of custodian. Before a minor is released, the custodian must execute an Affidavit of Support (Form I–134) and an agreement to:

(i) provide for the minor's physical, mental, and financial well-being;

(ii) ensure the minor's presence at all future proceedings before the INS and the immigration court;

(iii) notify the INS of any change of address within five (5) days following a move;

(iv) if the custodian is not a parent or legal guardian, not transfer custody of the minor to another party without the prior written permission of the District Director, except in the event of an emergency;

(v) notify the INS at least five days prior to the custodian's departing the United States of such departure, whether the departure is voluntary or pursuant to a grant of voluntary departure or order of deportation; and

(vi) if dependency proceedings involving the minor are initiated, notify the INS of the initiation of a such proceedings and the dependency court of any deportation proceedings pending against the minor.

In an emergency, a custodian may transfer temporary physical custody of a minor prior to securing permission from the INS, but must notify the INS of the transfer as soon as is practicable, and in all cases within 72 hours. Examples of an "emergency" include the serious illness of the custodian, destruction of the home, etc. In all cases where the custodian seeks written permission for a transfer, the District Director shall promptly respond to the request.

The INS may terminate the custody arrangements and assume legal custody of any minor whose custodian fails to comply with the agreement. However, custody arrangements will not be terminated for minor violations of the custodian's obligation to notify the INS of any change of address within five days following a move.

(f) Suitability assessment. An INS officer may require a positive suitability assessment prior to releasing a minor to any individual or program. A suitability assessment may include an investigation of the living conditions in which the minor is to be placed and the standard of care he would receive, verification of identity and employment of the individuals offering support, interviews of members of the household, and a home visit. The assessment will also take into consideration the wishes and concerns of the minor.

(g) Family reunification. Upon taking a minor into custody, the INS, or the licensed program in which the minor is placed, will promptly attempt to reunite the minor with his or her family to permit the release of the minor under Paragraph (d) above. Such efforts at family reunification will continue so long as the minor is in INS or licensed program custody and will be recorded by the INS or the licensed program in which the minor is placed.

(h) Placement in licensed programs. A "licensed program" is any program, agency or organization licensed by an appropriate state agency to provide residential group, or foster care services for dependent children, including a program operating group homes, foster homes or facilities for special needs minors. Exhibit 1 of the Flores v. Reno Settlement Agreement describes the standards required of licensed programs. Juveniles who remain in INS custody must be placed in a licensed program within three days if the minor was apprehended in an INS district in which a licensed program is located and has space available, or within five days in all other cases, except when:

(i) the minor is an escape risk or delinquent, as defined in Paragraph (*l*) below;

(ii) a court decree or court-approved settlement requires otherwise;

(iii) an emergency or influx of minors into the United States prevents compliance, in which case all minors should be placed in licensed programs as expeditiously as possible; or

(iv) where the minor must be transported from remote areas for processing or speaks an unusual language such that a special interpreter is required to process the minor, in which case the minor must be placed in a licensed program within five business days.

(i) Secure and supervised detention. A minor may be held in or transferred to a State or county juvenile detention facility or in a secure INS facility or INS-contracted facility having separate accommodations for minors, whenever the District Director or Chief Patrol Agent determines that the minor

(i) has been charged with, is chargeable, or has been convicted of a crime, or is the subject of delinquency proceedings, has been adjudicated delinquent, or is chargeable with a delinquent act, unless the minor's offense is

(a) an isolated offense not within a pattern of criminal activity which did not involve violence against a person or the use or carrying of a weapon (Examples: breaking and entering, vandalism, DUI, etc.); or

(b) a petty offense, which is not considered grounds for stricter means of detention in any case (Examples: shoplifting, joy riding, disturbing the peace, etc.);

(ii) has committed, or has made credible threats to commit, a violent or malicious act (whether directed at himself or others) while in INS legal custody or while in the presence of an INS officer;

(iii) has engaged, while in a licensed program, in conduct that has proven to be unacceptably disruptive of the normal functioning of the licensed program in which he or she has been placed and removal is necessary to ensure the welfare of the minor or others, as determined by the staff of the licensed program (Examples: drug or alcohol abuse, stealing, fighting, intimidation of others, etc.);

(iv) is an escape-risk; or

(v) must be held in a secure facility for his or her own safety, such as when the INS has reason to believe that a smuggler would abduct or coerce a particular minor to secure payment of smuggling fees.

"Chargeable" means that the INS has probable cause to believe that the individual has committed a specified offense.

The term "escape-risk" means that there is a serious risk that the minor will attempt to escape from custody. Factors to consider when determining whether a minor is an escape-risk or not include, but are not limited to, whether:

(a) the minor is currently under a final order of deportation or exclusion;

(b) the minor's immigration history includes: a prior breach of a bond; a failure to appear before the INS or the immigration court; evidence that the minor is indebted to organized smugglers for his transport; or a voluntary departure or a previous removal from the United States pursuant to a final order of deportation or exclusion;

(c) the minor has previously absconded or attempted to abscond from INS custody.

The INS will not place a minor in a State or county juvenile detention facility, secure INS detention facility or secure INS-contracted facility if less restrictive alternatives are available and appropriate in the circumstances, such as transfer to a medium security facility that provides intensive staff supervision and counseling services or transfer to another licensed program. All determinations to place a minor in a secure facility must be reviewed and approved by the regional Juvenile Coordinator.

(j) **Notice of right to bond redetermination and judicial review of placement.** A minor in deportation proceedings shall be afforded a bond redetermination hearing before an immigration judge in every case in which he either affirmatively requests, or fails to request or refuse, such a hearing on the Notice of Custody Determination. A juvenile who is not released or placed in a licensed placement shall be provided (1) a written explanation of the right of judicial review in the form attached, and (2) the list of free legal services providers compiled pursuant to 8 C.F.R. § 292a.

* * *

EXHIBIT 3

Contingency Plan

In the event of an emergency or influx that prevents the prompt placement of minors in licensed programs with which the Community Relations Service has contracted, INS policy is to make all reasonable efforts to place minors in licensed programs licensed by an appropriate state agency as expeditiously as possible. An emergency is an act or event, such as a natural disaster (e.g. earthquake, fire, hurricane), facility fire, civil disturbance, or medical emergency (e.g. a chicken pox epidemic among a group of minors) that prevents the prompt placement of minors in licensed facilities. An influx is defined as any situation in which there are more than 130 minors in the custody of the INS who are eligible for placement in licensed programs.

1. The Juvenile Coordinator will establish and maintain an Emergency Placement List of at least 80 beds at programs licensed by an appropriate state agency that are potentially available to accept emergency placements. These 80 placements would supplement the 130 placements that INS normally has available, and whenever possible, would meet all standards applicable to juvenile placements the INS normally uses. The Juvenile Coordinator may consult with child welfare specialists, group home operators, and others in developing the list. The Emergency Placement List will include the facility name; the number of beds at the facility; the name and telephone number of contact persons; the name and telephone number of contact persons for nights, holidays, and weekends if different; any restrictions on minors accepted (e.g. age); and any special services that are available.

2. The Juvenile Coordinator will maintain a list of minors affected by the emergency or influx, including (1) the minor's name, (2) date and country of birth, (3) date placed in INS custody, and (4) place and date of current placement.

3. Within one business day of the emergency or influx the Juvenile Coordinator, or his or her designee will contact the programs on the Emergency Placement List to determine available placements. As soon as available placements are identified, the Juvenile Coordinator will advise appropriate INS staff of their availability. To the extent practicable, the INS will attempt to locate emergency placements in geographic areas where culturally and linguistically appropriate community services are available.

4. In the event that the number of minors needing emergency placement exceeds the available appropriate placements on the Emergency Placement List, the Juvenile Coordinator will work with the Community Relations Service to locate additional placements through licensed programs, county social services departments, and foster family agencies.

5. Each year, the INS will reevaluate the number of regular placements needed for detained minors to determine whether the number of regular placements should be adjusted to accommodate an increased or decreased number of minors eligible for placement in licensed programs. However, any decision to increase the number of placements available shall be subject to the availability of INS resources. The Juvenile Coordinator shall promptly provide Plaintiffs' counsel with any reevaluation made by INS pursuant to this paragraph.

6. The Juvenile Coordinator shall provide to Plaintiffs' counsel copies of the Emergency Placement List within six months after the court's final approval of the Settlement Agreement.

EXHIBIT 4

Agreement Concerning Facility Visits Under Paragraph 33

The purpose of facility visits under paragraph 33 is to interview class members and staff and to observe conditions at the facility. Visits under paragraph 33 shall be conducted in accordance with the generally applicable policies and procedures of the facility to the extent that those policies and procedures are consistent with this Exhibit.

Visits authorized under paragraph 33 shall be scheduled no less than seven (7) business days in advance. The names, positions, credentials, and professional association (e.g., Center for Human Rights and Constitutional Law) of the visitors will be provided at that time.

All visits with class members shall take place during normal business hours.

No video recording equipment or cameras of any type shall be permitted. Audio recording equipment shall be limited to hand-held tape recorders.

The number of visitors will not exceed six (6) or, in the case of a family foster home, four (4), including interpreters, in any instance. Up to two (2) of the visitors may be non-attorney experts in juvenile justice and/or child welfare.

No visit will extend beyond three (3) hours per day in length. Visits shall minimize disruption to the routine that minors and staff follow.

* * *

EXHIBIT 6

Notice of Right to Judicial Review

"The INS usually houses persons under the age of 18 in an open setting, such as a foster or group home and not in detention facilities. If you believe you have not been properly placed or that you have been treated improperly, you may ask a federal judge to review your case. You may call a lawyer to help you do this. If you cannot afford a lawyer, you may call one from the list of free legal services given to you with this form."

REFUGEES AND ASYLUM

Addressing Mass Migration Through the Southern Border of the United States, Proclamation No. 9822, 83 Fed. Reg. 57,661 (Nov. 9, 2018)

A Proclamation

The United States expects the arrival at the border between the United States and Mexico (southern border) of a substantial number of aliens primarily from Central America who appear to have no lawful basis for admission into our country. They are traveling in large, organized groups through Mexico and reportedly intend to enter the United States unlawfully or without proper documentation and to seek asylum, despite the fact that, based on past experience, a significant majority will not be eligible for or be granted that benefit. Many entered Mexico unlawfully some with violence and have rejected opportunities to apply for asylum and benefits in Mexico. The arrival of large numbers of aliens will contribute to the overloading of our immigration and asylum system and to the release of thousands of aliens into the interior of the United States. The continuing and threatened mass migration of aliens with no basis for admission into the United States through our southern border has precipitated a crisis and undermines the integrity of our borders. I therefore must take immediate action to protect the national interest, and to maintain the effectiveness of the asylum system for legitimate asylum seekers who demonstrate that they have fled persecution and warrant the many special benefits associated with asylum.

In recent weeks, an average of approximately 2,000 inadmissible aliens have entered each day at our southern border. In Fiscal Year 2018 overall, 124,511 aliens were found inadmissible at ports of entry on the southern border, while 396,579 aliens were apprehended entering the United States unlawfully between such ports of entry. The great number of aliens who cross unlawfully into the United States through the southern border consumes tremendous resources as the Government seeks to surveil, apprehend, screen, process, and detain them.

Aliens who enter the United States unlawfully or without proper documentation and are subject to expedited removal may avoid being promptly removed by demonstrating, during an initial screening process, a credible fear of persecution or torture. Approximately 2 decades ago, most aliens deemed inadmissible at a port of entry or apprehended after unlawfully entering the United States through the southern border were single adults who were promptly returned to Mexico, and very few asserted a fear of return. Since then, however, there has been a massive increase in fear-of-persecution or torture claims by aliens who enter the United States through the southern border. The vast majority of such aliens are found to satisfy the credible-fear threshold, although only a fraction of the claimants whose claims are adjudicated ultimately qualify for asylum or other protection. Aliens found to have a credible fear are often released into the interior of the United States, as a result of a lack of detention space and a variety of other legal and practical difficulties, pending adjudication of their claims in a full removal proceeding in immigration court. The immigration adjudication process often takes years to complete because of the growing volume of claims and because of the need to expedite proceedings for detained aliens. During that time, many released aliens fail to appear for hearings, do not comply with subsequent orders of removal, or are difficult to locate and remove.

Members of family units pose particular challenges. The Federal Government lacks sufficient facilities to house families together. Virtually all members of family units who enter the United States through the southern border, unlawfully or without proper documentation, and that are found to have a credible fear of persecution, are thus released into the United States. Against this backdrop of near-assurance of release, the number of such aliens traveling as family units who enter through the southern border and claim a credible fear of persecution has greatly increased. And large numbers of family units decide to make the dangerous and unlawful border crossing with their children.

The United States has a long and proud history of offering protection to aliens who are fleeing persecution and torture and who qualify under the standards articulated in our immigration laws, including through our asylum system and the Refugee Admissions Program. But our system is being overwhelmed by migration through our southern border. Crossing the border to avoid detection and then, if apprehended, claiming a fear of persecution is in too many instances an avenue to near-automatic release into the interior of the United States. Once released, such aliens are very difficult to remove. An additional influx of large groups of aliens arriving at once through the southern border would add tremendous strain to an already taxed system, especially if they avoid orderly processing by unlawfully crossing the southern border.

The entry of large numbers of aliens into the United States unlawfully between ports of entry on the southern border is contrary to the national interest, and our law has long recognized that aliens who seek to lawfully enter the United States must do so at ports of entry. Unlawful entry puts lives of both law enforcement and aliens at risk. By contrast, entry at ports of entry at the southern border allows for orderly processing, which enables the efficient deployment of law enforcement resources across our vast southern border.

Failing to take immediate action to stem the mass migration the United States is currently experiencing and anticipating would only encourage additional mass unlawful migration and further overwhelming of the system.

Other presidents have taken strong action to prevent mass migration. In Proclamation 4865 of September 29, 1981 (High Seas Interdiction of

Illegal Aliens), in response to an influx of Haitian nationals traveling to the United States by sea, President Reagan suspended the entry of undocumented aliens from the high seas and ordered the Coast Guard to intercept such aliens before they reached United States shores and to return them to their point of origin. In Executive Order 12807 of May 24, 1992 (Interdiction of Illegal Aliens), in response to a dramatic increase in the unlawful mass migration of Haitian nationals to the United States, President Bush ordered additional measures to interdict such Haitian nationals and return them to their home country. The Supreme Court upheld the legality of those measures in Sale v. Haitian Centers Council, Inc., 509 U.S. 155 (1993).

I am similarly acting to suspend, for a limited period, the entry of certain aliens in order to address the problem of large numbers of aliens traveling through Mexico to enter our country unlawfully or without proper documentation. I am tailoring the suspension to channel these aliens to ports of entry, so that, if they enter the United States, they do so in an orderly and controlled manner instead of unlawfully. Under this suspension, aliens entering through the southern border, even those without proper documentation, may, consistent with this proclamation, avail themselves of our asylum system, provided that they properly present themselves for inspection at a port of entry. In anticipation of a large group of aliens arriving in the coming weeks, I am directing the Secretary of Homeland Security to commit additional resources to support our ports of entry at the southern border to assist in processing those aliens and all others arriving at our ports of entry as efficiently as possible.

But aliens who enter the United States unlawfully through the southern border in contravention of this proclamation will be ineligible to be granted asylum under the regulation promulgated by the Attorney General and the Secretary of Homeland Security that became effective earlier today. Those aliens may, however, still seek other forms of protection from persecution or torture. In addition, this limited suspension will facilitate ongoing negotiations with Mexico and other countries regarding appropriate cooperative arrangements to prevent unlawful mass migration to the United States through the southern border. Thus, this proclamation is also necessary to manage and conduct the foreign affairs of the United States effectively.

NOW, THEREFORE, I, DONALD J. TRUMP, by the authority vested in me by the Constitution and the laws of the United States of America, including sections 212(f) and 215(a) of the Immigration and Nationality Act (INA) (8 U.S.C. 1182(f) and 1185(a), respectively) hereby find that, absent the measures set forth in this proclamation, the entry into the United States of persons described in section 1 of this proclamation would be detrimental to the interests of the United States, and that their entry should be subject to certain restrictions, limitations, and exceptions. I therefore hereby proclaim the following:

Section 1. *Suspension and Limitation on Entry.* The entry of any alien into the United States across the international boundary between the United States and Mexico is hereby suspended and limited, subject to section 2 of this proclamation. That suspension and limitation shall expire 90 days after the date of this proclamation or the date on which an agreement permits the United States to remove aliens to Mexico in compliance with the terms of section 208(a)(2)(A) of the INA (8 U.S.C. 1158(a)(2)(A)), whichever is earlier.

Sec. 2. *Scope and Implementation of Suspension and Limitation on Entry.* (a) The suspension and limitation on entry pursuant to section 1 of this proclamation shall apply only to aliens who enter the United States after the date of this proclamation.

(b) The suspension and limitation on entry pursuant to section 1 of this proclamation shall not apply to any alien who enters the United States at a port of entry and properly presents for inspection, or to any lawful permanent resident of the United States.

(c) Nothing in this proclamation shall limit an alien entering the United States from being considered for withholding of removal under section 241(b)(3) of the INA (8 U.S.C. 1231(b)(3)) or protection pursuant to the regulations promulgated under the authority of the implementing legislation regarding the Convention Against Torture and Other Cruel, Inhuman or Degrading Treatment or Punishment, or limit the statutory processes afforded to unaccompanied alien children upon entering the United States under section 279 of title 6, United States Code, and section 1232 of title 8, United States Code.

(d) No later than 90 days after the date of this proclamation, the Secretary of State, the Attorney General, and the Secretary of Homeland Security shall jointly submit to the President, through the Assistant to the President for National Security Affairs, a recommendation on whether an extension or renewal of the suspension or limitation on entry in section 1 of this proclamation is in the interests of the United States.

Sec. 3. *Interdiction.* The Secretary of State and the Secretary of Homeland Security shall consult with the Government of Mexico regarding appropriate steps consistent with applicable law and the foreign policy, national security, and public-safety interests of the United States to address the approach of large groups of aliens traveling through Mexico with the intent of entering the United States unlawfully, including efforts to deter, dissuade, and return such aliens before they physically enter United States territory through the southern border.

Sec. 4. *Severability.* It is the policy of the United States to enforce this proclamation to the maximum extent possible to advance the interests of the United States. Accordingly:

(a) if any provision of this proclamation, or the application of any provision to any person or circumstance, is held to be invalid, the remainder of this proclamation and the application of its other provisions to any other persons or circumstances shall not be affected thereby; and

(b) if any provision of this proclamation, or the application of any provision to any person or circumstance, is held to be invalid because of the failure to follow certain procedures, the relevant executive branch officials shall implement those procedural requirements to conform with existing law and with any applicable court orders.

Sec. 5. *General Provisions*. (a) Nothing in this proclamation shall be construed to impair or otherwise affect:

(i) the authority granted by law to an executive department or agency, or the head thereof; or

(ii) the functions of the Director of the Office of Management and Budget relating to budgetary, administrative, or legislative proposals.

(b) This proclamation shall be implemented consistent with applicable law and subject to the availability of appropriations.

(c) This proclamation is not intended to, and does not, create any right or benefit, substantive or procedural, enforceable at law or in equity by any party against the United States, its departments, agencies, or entities, its officers, employees, or agents, or any other person.

IN WITNESS WHEREOF, I have hereunto set my hand this ninth day of November, in the year of our Lord two thousand eighteen, and of the Independence of the United States of America the two hundred and forty-third.

Dep't of Homeland Sec., Policy Guidance for Implementation of the Migrant Protection Protocols (Jan. 25, 2019)

MEMORANDUM FOR:

L. Francis Cissna

Director

U.S. Citizenship and Immigration Services

Kevin K. McAleenan

Commissioner

U.S. Customs and Border Protection

Ronald D. Vitiello

Deputy Director and Senior Official Performing the Duties of Director

U.S. Immigration and Customs Enforcement

FROM: Kirstjen M. Nielsen

Secretary

SUBJECT: **Policy Guidance for Implementation of the Migrant Protection Protocols**

On December 20, 2018, I announced that the Department of Homeland Security (DHS), consistent with the Migrant Protection Protocols (MPP), will begin implementation of Section 235(b)(2)(C) of the Immigration and Nationality Act (INA) on a large-scale basis to address the migration crisis along our southern border. In 1996, Congress added Section 235(b)(2)(C) to the INA. This statutory authority allows the Secretary of Homeland Security to return certain applicants for admission to the contiguous country from which they are arriving on land (whether or not at a designated port of entry) pending removal proceedings under Section 240 of the INA. Consistent with the MPP, citizens and nationals of countries other than Mexico ("third-country nationals") arriving in the United States by land from Mexico-illegally or without proper documentation-may be returned to Mexico pursuant to Section 235(b)(2)(C) for the duration of their Section 240 removal proceedings.

Section 235(b)(2)(C) and the MPP

The United States issued the following statement on December 20, 2018, regarding implementation of the Migrant Protection Protocols:

[T]he United States will begin the process of implementing Section 235(b)(2)(C) . . . with respect to non-Mexican nationals who may be arriving on land (whether or not at a designated port of entry) seeking to enter the United States from Mexico illegally or without proper documentation. Such implementation will be done consistent with applicable domestic and international legal obligations. Individuals subject to this action may return to the United States as necessary and appropriate to attend their immigration court proceedings.

The United States understands that, according to the Mexican law of migration, the Government of Mexico will afford such individuals all legal and procedural protection[s] provided for under applicable domestic and international law. That includes applicable international human rights law and obligations as a party to the 1951 Convention relating to the Status of Refugees (and its 1967 Protocol) and the Convention Against Torture.

The United States further recognizes that Mexico is implementing its own, sovereign, migrant protection protocols providing humanitarian support for and humanitarian visas to migrants.

The United States proposes a joint effort with the Government of Mexico to develop a comprehensive regional plan in consultation with foreign partners to address irregular migration, smuggling, and trafficking with the goal of promoting human rights, economic development, and security.[1]

The Government of Mexico, in response, issued a statement on December 20, 2018. That statement provides, in part, as follows:

1. For humanitarian reasons, [the Government of Mexico] will authorize the temporary entrance of certain foreign individuals coming from the United States who entered that country at a port of entry or who were detained between ports of entry, have been interviewed by U.S. immigration authorities, and have received a notice to appear before an immigration judge. This is based on current Mexican legislation and the international commitments Mexico has signed, such as the Convention Relating to the Status of Refugees, its Protocol, and the Convention against Torture and Other Cruel, Inhuman or Degrading Treatment or Punishment, among others.

2. It will allow foreigners who have received a notice to appear to request admission into Mexican territory for humanitarian reasons at locations designated for the international transit of individuals and to remain in national territory. This would be a "stay for humanitarian reasons" and they would be able to enter and leave national territory multiple times.

3. It will ensure that foreigners who have received their notice to appear have all the rights and freedoms recognized in the Constitution, the international treaties to which Mexico is a party, and its Migration

---

[1] Letter from Chargé d'Affaires John S. Creamer to Sr. Jesus Seade, Subsecretaria para America del Norte, Secretaria de Relaciones Exteriores (Dec. 20, 2018).

Law. They will be entitled to equal treatment with no discrimination whatsoever and due respect will be paid to their human rights. They will also have the opportunity to apply for a work permit for paid employment, which will allow them to meet their basic needs.

4. It will ensure that the measures taken by each government are coordinated at a technical and operational level in order to put mechanisms in place that allow migrants who have receive[d] a notice to appear before a U.S. immigration judge have access without interference to information and legal services, and to prevent fraud and abuse.[2]

Prosecutorial Discretion and *Non-Refoulement* in the Context of the MPP

In exercising their prosecutorial discretion regarding whether to place an alien arriving by land from Mexico in Section 240 removal proceedings (rather than another applicable proceeding pursuant to the INA), and, if doing so, whether to return the alien to the contiguous country from which he or she is arriving pursuant to Section 235(b)(2)(C), DHS officials should act consistent with the *non-refoulement* principles contained in Article 33 of the 1951 Convention Relating to the Status of Refugees[3] (1951 Convention) and Article 3 of the Convention Against Torture and Other Cruel, Inhuman or Degrading Treatment or Punishment (CAT).[4] Specifically, a third-country national should not be involuntarily returned to Mexico pursuant to Section 235(b)(2)(C) of the INA if the alien would more likely than not be persecuted on account of race, religion, nationality, membership in a particular social group, or political opinion (unless such alien has engaged in criminal, persecutory, or terrorist activity described in Section 241(b)(3)(B) of the INA), or would more likely than not be tortured, if so returned pending removal proceedings. The United States expects that the Government of Mexico will comply with the commitments articulated in its statement of December 20, 2018.

---

[2] Secretaría de Relaciones Exteriores, *Position of Mexico on the Decision of the U.S. Government to Invoke Section 235(b)(2)(C) of its Immigration and Nationality Act* (Dec. 20, 2018).

[3] The United States is not a party to the 1951 Convention but is a party to the 1967 Protocol Relating to the Status of Refugees, which incorporates Articles 2 to 34 of the 1951 Convention. Article 33 of the 1951 Convention provides that: "[n]o Contracting State shall expel or return *('refouler')* a refugee in any manner whatsoever to the frontiers of territories where his life or freedom would be threatened on account of his race, religion, nationality, membership of a particular social group or political opinion."

[4] Article 3 of the CAT states, "No State Party shall expel, return *('refouler')* or extradite a person to another State where there are substantial grounds for believing that he would be in danger of being subjected to torture." *See also* Foreign Affairs Reform and Restructuring Act of 1998 (FARRA), Pub. L. No. 105–277, Div. G, Title XXII, § 2242(a) (8 U.S.C. § 1231 note) ("It shall be the policy of the United States not to expel, extradite, or otherwise effect the involuntary return of any person to a country in which there are substantial grounds for believing the person would be in danger of being subjected to torture, regardless of whether the person is physically present in the United States.").

U.S. Citizenship and Immigration Services, U.S. Customs and Border Protection, and U.S. Immigration and Customs Enforcement will issue appropriate internal procedural guidance to carry out the policy set forth in this memorandum.[5]

This memorandum is not intended to, and does not, create any right or benefit, substantive or procedural, enforceable at law or in equity by any party against the United States, its departments, agencies, or entities, its officers, employees, or agents, or any other person.

---

[5] A DHS immigration officer, when processing an alien for Section 235(b)(2)(C), should refer to USCIS any alien who has expressed a fear of return to Mexico for a *non-refoulement* assessment by an asylum officer.

Executive Office for Immigration Review, Dep't of Justice; U.S. Citizenship and Immigration Services, Dep't of Homeland Sec. (Nov. 19, 2019)

Interim Final Rule re:

Implementing Bilateral and Multilateral Asylum Cooperative Agreements Under the Immigration and Nationality Act

* * *

II. Executive Summary

The Departments are adopting an interim final rule to modify existing regulations to provide for the implementation of agreements that the United States enters into pursuant to section 208(a)(2)(A) of the INA. 8 U.S.C. 1158(a)(2)(A). Such agreements—referred to by the Departments as Asylum Cooperative Agreements and alternatively described as safe third country agreements in existing regulations—are formed between the United States and foreign countries where aliens removed to those countries would have access to a full and fair procedure for determining a claim to asylum or equivalent temporary protection. In certain circumstances, an ACA, in conjunction with section 208(a)(2)(A), bars an alien subject to the agreement from applying for asylum in the United States and provides for the removal of the alien, pursuant to the agreement, to a country that will provide access to a full and fair procedure for determining the alien's protection claim. Removal pursuant to these agreements will be ordered within ER proceedings or, in certain instances, within INA section 240 removal proceedings. But because the underlying purpose of section 208(a)(2)(A) is to provide asylum seekers with access to only one of the ACA signatory countries' protection systems, this rule adopts a modified approach to the ER and section 240 processes in the form of a threshold screening as to which country will consider the alien's claim. This rule will apply to all ACAs between the United States and countries other than Canada. * * *

Although various recent regulatory reforms have reduced the burdens associated with adjudicating asylum claims (and others hold out promise to do so should injunctions on their implementation be lifted), the U.S. asylum system remains overtaxed. Hundreds of thousands of migrants have reached the United States in recent years and have claimed a fear of persecution or torture. They often do not ultimately establish legal qualification for such relief or even actually applying for protection after being released into the United States, which has contributed to a backlog of 987,198 cases before the Executive Office for Immigration Review (including 474,327 asylum cases), each taking an average of 816 days to complete. Asylum claims by aliens from El Salvador, Guatemala, and Honduras account for over half of the pending asylum cases.

To help alleviate those burdens and promote regional migration cooperation, the United States recently signed bilateral ACAs with El Salvador, Guatemala, and Honduras in an effort to share the distribution of asylum claims. Pending the Department of State's publication of the ACAs in the United States Treaties and Other International Agreements series in accordance with 1 U.S.C. 112a, the agreements will be published in a document in the Federal Register. This rule will establish the authority of DHS asylum officers to make threshold determinations as to whether aliens are ineligible to apply for asylum under those three ACAs, and any future ones, in the course of ER proceedings under section 235(b)(1) of the Act, 8 U.S.C. 1225(b)(1), once the agreements enter into force. As a practical matter, this rule will also establish the authority of immigration judges ("IJs") to make such determinations in the context of removal proceedings under INA section 240, 8 U.S.C. 1229a. To the extent that an alien in ER proceedings is rendered ineligible to apply for asylum by more than one ACA, the immigration officer will assess which agreement is most appropriately applicable to the alien.* * * The rule will apply only prospectively to aliens who arrive at a U.S. port of entry, or enter or attempt to enter the United States between ports of entry, on or after the effective date of the rule.

III. Purpose of This Interim Final Rule

Asylum is a discretionary immigration benefit that generally can be sought by eligible aliens who are physically present or arriving in the United States. See INA 208(a)(1), 8 U.S.C. 1158(a)(1). Throughout the past decade, the United States has experienced a significant increase in the number of aliens encountered at or near its borders, particularly the southern land border with Mexico, as described by the Departments' recent joint rule requiring certain aliens seeking to apply for asylum to have first applied for equivalent protection in at least one country through which they transited en route to the United States, see Asylum Eligibility and Procedural Modifications, 84 FR 33829, 33830 (July 16, 2019). This increase has been accompanied by a sharp increase in the number and percentage of aliens requesting asylum or claiming a fear of persecution or torture when apprehended or encountered by DHS. As noted by the third-country-transit rule, for example, over the past decade the percentage of aliens referred for credible fear interviews within ER proceedings jumped from approximately 5 percent to above 40 percent. Id. at 33830–31. The number of asylum cases filed with DOJ also rose sharply, more than tripling between 2013 and 2018. Id. at 33831. During that same period, the filing of affirmative asylum applications rose from 44,453 in 2013 to 106,147 in 2018.

This increase reflects high rises in both defensive asylum claims (i.e., asylum claims raised after removal proceedings have begun) and affirmative asylum claims (i.e., asylum claims raised apart from or before removal proceedings have begun). In Fiscal Year ("FY") 2018, 110,136 individuals in ER proceedings raised claims of persecution or torture and were referred for credible fear interviews (99,035 individuals) or reasonable fear interviews (11,101 individuals). These individuals, combined with individuals who filed for asylum while in INA section 240 removal proceedings, resulted in 114,532 defensive asylum applications filed with DOJ in FY2018. Additionally, in FY2018, 48,922 affirmative asylum applications were also referred to DOJ.* * *

This has led to a backlog that, as of October 11, 2019, included more than 476,000 asylum cases before DOJ's Executive Office for Immigration Review ("EOIR"). The backlog of affirmative asylum applications pending with USCIS sits at 340,810, as of the end of FY2019. Historically, only a small minority of the individuals claiming a fear of return on the basis of persecution or torture were ultimately granted asylum or had even applied for it. Indeed, over the years, many aliens who initially claimed a fear of return upon entry or arrival abandoned those claims altogether.

Immigration detention centers have often been pushed to capacity, making even temporary detention for arriving aliens difficult to sustain. Or aliens have been released into the interior of the country, after which they often fail to appear for their removal proceedings, or unlawfully abscond after receiving removal orders, becoming fugitives. To help ease some of the burden on the immigration detention system and to reduce the numbers of aliens illegally entering the country, the Administration has worked with Mexico to permit people attempting to enter the United States from Mexico on land to remain in Mexico while awaiting their removal proceedings, pursuant to section 235(b)(2)(C) of the INA, 8 U.S.C. 1225(b)(2)(C).

Arresting the significant number of aliens who illegally enter the United States or arrive at ports of entry without the necessary documents to enter the United States legally, and processing and adjudicating their fear of return claims for ER, and processing and adjudicating their asylum claims in removal proceedings under INA section 240, consumes a tremendous amount of resources within the Departments of Justice and Homeland Security.* * *

The large number of aliens seeking relief in the United States also consumes substantial DOJ resources. Within DOJ, IJs adjudicate aliens' asylum claims in INA section 240 proceedings, prosecutors and law enforcement officials must prosecute and maintain custody of aliens who violate Federal criminal law, and DOJ attorneys represent the United States in civil cases involving immigration and detention issues. Despite DOJ deploying 80% more immigration judges than in 2010, and completing nearly double the number of asylum cases in FY2018 as in FY2010, more than 476,000 asylum cases remain pending before the immigration courts.* * *

The large majority of fear of persecution or torture claims raised by those arrested at the southern border either have not led to actual claims for asylum or have been ultimately determined to be without legal merit. For example, in FY2018, 34,031 individuals who had received credible fear interviews before asylum officers were referred to DOJ for asylum hearings. Approximately 39%, or 13,369, of these individuals failed to file an asylum application, and thus abandoned their claims. Only 5,577 individuals were granted asylum, a number equal to 16.4% of all individuals referred to DOJ after credible fear interviews, or 27% of individuals who were referred to DOJ following a credible fear interview and filed an asylum application. The success rate declines when one looks at all asylum applications adjudicated by DOJ. In FY2018, 64,223 asylum applications were adjudicated by DOJ's immigration judges. Only 13,173, or 20.5%, were granted. The strain on the U.S. immigration system, and the wait times for aliens seeking to process legitimate claims through the U.S. asylum system, is extreme.* * *

In section 208(a)(2)(A) of the INA, 8 U.S.C. 1158(a)(2)(A), Congress provided a mechanism to help ease this strain on the immigration system by authorizing the Executive Branch to enter into agreements with other countries to distribute the burdens associated with adjudicating claims for asylum or equivalent temporary protection. Specifically, section 208(a)(2)(A) authorizes the Executive Branch to bar an alien from applying for asylum in the United States where, pursuant to a bilateral or multilateral agreement, the alien may be removed to a third country (i.e., a country other than the alien's country of nationality or last habitual residence, see INA 208(a)(2)(A), 8 U.S.C. 1158(a)(2)(A)), that affords the alien access to a full and fair procedure for determining claims for asylum or equivalent temporary protection. Consistent with the President's extensive foreign affairs authority, see, e.g., Zivotofsky v. Kerry, 135 S. Ct. 2076, 2084–94 (2015); United States v. Curtiss-Wright Exp. Corp., 299 U.S. 304, 319 (1936) (emphasizing the President's extensive role representing U.S. interests in relations with foreign nations), section 208(a)(2)(A), by its terms, provides substantial flexibility to the Executive Branch in negotiating and implementing ACAs. Accord INA 208(d)(5)(B), 8 U.S.C. 1158(d)(5)(B) (authorizing the Attorney General and Secretary to "provide by regulation for any other conditions or limitations on the consideration of an application for asylum not inconsistent with this chapter"); see also Youngstown Sheet & Tube Co. v. Sawyer, 343 U.S. 579, 635 (Jackson, J., concurring) ("When the President acts pursuant to an express or implied authorization of Congress, his authority is at its maximum, for it includes all that he possesses in his own right plus all that Congress can delegate."); id. at 637 (observing that an exercise of federal affairs power "pursuant to an Act of congress would be supported by the strongest of presumptions and the widest latitude of judicial interpretation").

In contrast to statutory and regulatory bars providing that certain aliens are ineligible to receive asylum, see, e.g., INA 208(b)(2)(A), (C), 8 U.S.C. 1158(b)(2)(A), (C), the ACA bar relates to whether an alien may even apply for asylum. Unlike the restrictions on asylum eligibility, application of the ACA bar does not involve an evaluation of whether an alien would ultimately receive asylum relief if able to apply, or even whether the alien has made a preliminary showing of a significant possibility that the alien would be eligible for asylum. Rather, section 208(a)(2)(A) bars an alien from applying for asylum in the United States when the following four requirements are satisfied: (i) The United States has entered into a requisite "bilateral or multilateral agreement"; (ii) at least one of the signatory countries to the agreement is a "third country" with respect to the alien; (iii) "the alien's life or freedom would not be threatened" in that third country "on account of race, religion, nationality, membership in a particular social group, or political opinion"; and (iv) that third country provides aliens removed there pursuant to the agreement "access to a full and fair procedure for determining a claim to asylum or equivalent temporary protection." Even if all of these elements are satisfied, the Secretary nonetheless may determine in his discretion "that it is in the public interest for the alien to receive asylum in the United States." INA 208(a)(2)(A), 8 U.S.C. 1158(a)(2)(A).

This interim rule will amend DHS and DOJ regulations implementing section 208(a)(2)(A) to effectuate ACAs other than the agreement already formed with Canada in 2002 and implemented by regulation in 2004.* * *

In particular, this rule will broaden the procedures (implemented in ER and INA section 240 proceedings) for determining whether an alien is subject to an ACA or within one of its exceptions to account for ACAs other than the U.S.-Canada Agreement. Additionally, this rule will establish a screening mechanism to evaluate whether an alien who would otherwise be removable to a third country under an ACA other than the U.S.-Canada Agreement can establish that it is more likely than not that he or she would be persecuted on account of race, religion, nationality, membership in a particular social group, or political opinion, or would be tortured in that third country. This rule consequently will provide a general mechanism for implementation of all existing and future ACAs not previously implemented.* * *

ACAs entered pursuant to section 208(a)(2)(A) will be published in the Federal Register. Prior to implementation of an ACA, the Attorney General and the Secretary of Homeland Security ("Secretary") will evaluate and make a categorical determination whether a country to which aliens would be removed under such an agreement provides "access to a full and fair procedure for determining a claim to asylum or equivalent temporary protection." INA 208(a)(2)(A), 8 U.S.C. 1158(a)(2)(A). Section 208(a)(2)(A) of the INA also requires a determination that an alien's life and freedom would not be threatened on account of a protected ground in a third country with which the United States has entered into an ACA. This rule effectuates such a determination via individualized threshold screening that provides an opportunity for an alien to establish fear of persecution in the third country to which he would be removed pursuant to an ACA.

The INA's ACA provision provides authority to pursue significant policy interests by entering into bilateral or multilateral agreements allowing for burden-sharing between the United States and other countries with respect to refugee-protection claims.

Consistent with this compelling policy aim, this interim rule is intended to aid the United States in its negotiations with foreign nations on migration issues. Specifically, the rule will aid the United States as it seeks to develop a regional framework with other countries to more equitably distribute the burden of processing the protection claims of the hundreds of thousands of irregular migrants who now seek to enter the United States every year and claim a fear of return. Addressing the eligibility for asylum of aliens who enter or attempt to enter the United States will better position the United States as it engages in ongoing diplomatic negotiations with Mexico and the Northern Triangle countries (El Salvador, Guatemala, and Honduras) regarding migration issues in general, and related measures employed to curtail the irregular flow of aliens into the United States.

IV. Background and Legal Basis for Regulatory Changes

* * *

B. Adjudication of Asylum Applications and the Section 208(a)(2) (A) Bar

* * *

3. Protection Screening With Respect to Removal to the Third Country

Where section 208(a)(2)(A) applies, it bars an alien from applying for asylum in the United States and authorizes the removal of the alien to a third country that will provide procedures for asylum or equivalent temporary protection in the place of the United States. . . . The terms of section 208(a)(2)(A) do not specify the precise procedural mechanism by which the Attorney General and Secretary must determine that an alien's life or freedom will not be threatened on account of a protected ground in the third country. As the relevant text of section 208(a)(2)(A) ("the alien's life or freedom would not be threatened [in the third country] on account of race, religion, nationality, membership in a particular social group, or political opinion") mirrors the standard for protection contained in the INA's withholding-of-removal provision, INA 241(b)(3)(A), 8 U.S.C. 1231(b)(3)(A), this regulation adopts the burden of proof that applies in the withholding-of-removal context.* * * Accordingly, under the threshold screening implemented by this rule, an alien will not be removed to a third country under INA section 208(a)(2)(A) if the alien establishes that it is more likely than not that the alien would be persecuted on account of a protected ground in that country.

* * * Article 33 of the 1951 Refugee Convention, as understood in U.S. law, generally precludes state parties from removing individuals to any country where their lives or freedom would be threatened on account of their race, religion, nationality, political opinion, or membership in a particular social group. Consistent with these obligations, Congress has precluded removal of an alien to a third country under section 208(a)(2)(A) if "the alien's life or freedom would . . . be threatened on account of race, religion, nationality, membership in a particular social group, or political opinion." 8 U.S.C. 1158(a)(2)(A).

* * * Removing an alien to a third country pursuant to an ACA for consideration of the alien's protection claim in that country is consistent with U.S. obligations under CAT, in the absence of grounds for believing that the alien would be persecuted on account of a protected ground or tortured in the third country. * * *

Congress enacted section 208(a)(2)(A) as a mechanism for countries to burden-share the responsibility for providing protection to refugees. Such agreements allocate responsibility between the United States and the third country with which it has formed an ACA whereby one country or the other (but not both) will bear responsibility for processing the asylum and other protection claims of refugees subject to the terms of the ACA. . . . [citations omitted] The salient factor for the formulation and application of a section 208(a)(2)(A) agreement is whether the country sharing responsibility with the United States for refugee protection has laws and mechanisms in place that adhere to international treaty obligations to protect refugees. * * *

Accordingly, this interim rule provides that an alien who will potentially be subject to an ACA will be advised that he or she may be removed to a third country pursuant to a bilateral or multilateral agreement. If the alien affirmatively states a fear of removal to or persecution or torture in that third country, a DHS asylum officer will interview the alien to determine whether it is more likely than not that the alien would be persecuted on account of a protected ground or tortured in the third country. See 8 CFR 208.30. DOJ immigration judges will apply a similar procedure to determine whether a removal pursuant to an ACA cannot proceed because the individual has established that it is more likely than not that he or she would be persecuted on account of a protected ground or tortured in the third country. See id. 1240.11.

4. Additional Consequences of the Applicability of Section 208(a)(2)(A) to an Alien's Asylum Application

If an asylum officer or IJ determines that an alien is barred from applying for asylum under section 208(a)(2)(A), then the alien is also barred from applying for withholding of removal under section 241(b)(3)(A) of the INA, 8 U.S.C. 1231(b)(3)(A), and protection under the regulations implementing CAT. The purpose of section 208(a)(2)(A)—and an agreement between the United States and another country formed thereunder—is to vest "one country or the other (but not both) [with the] responsibility for processing" an alien's claims related to fear of persecution or torture in the alien's home country. . . .

* * *

V. Detailed Discussion of Regulatory Changes

A. *Summary of the New and Amended Regulatory Provisions and Their Import*

* * *

The scope of the U.S.-Canada Agreement, and, consequently, the U.S.-Canada Agreement regulations, is limited to aliens arriving at ports of entry along the U.S. border with Canada. In contrast, this generalized rule for the implementation of all ACAs (with countries other than Canada) will cover ACAs to the full extent permitted by section 208(a)(2)(A), which contains no limitation to only those aliens who have transited through the relevant third country or who arrive at ports of entry. To accommodate for the expanded applicability of the ACAs implemented under this current rule beyond the narrower class of aliens subject to the U.S.-Canada Agreement after traveling through Canada, this rule expands the threshold screening of aliens potentially subject to ACAs other than the U.S.-Canada Agreement. The rule gives aliens subject to an ACA an opportunity, during threshold screening, to establish that it would be "more likely than not" that the alien's life or freedom would be threatened in the third country on account of a protected ground or that the alien would be tortured in the third country. If DHS officers or IJs determine that an alien establishes such a fear by a preponderance of the evidence, the alien will not be removed to the third country pursuant to the ACA formed with that particular country. * * *

In contrast to many of the countries listed as potential countries of removal in section 241(b) of the INA, the third country to which an alien would be removed under an ACA is a country to which an alien does not necessarily have preexisting ties or any preexisting reason to fear persecution or torture. Compare INA 208(a)(2)(A), 8 U.S.C. 1158(a)(2)(A), with

INA 241(b)(1)–(2), 8 U.S.C. 1231(b)(1)–(2). Moreover, unlike the countries to which aliens typically would be removed under section 241(b) of the INA, these third countries of removal would have pre-committed, per binding agreements with the United States, to provide access to a "full and fair procedure" for the alien to acquire "asylum or equivalent temporary protection," INA 208(a)(2)(A), 8 U.S.C. 1158(a)(2)(A). Aliens subject to an ACA thus would have an avenue for protection in the third country of removal not necessarily available in an INA section 241(b) country of removal—a country that may not have entered a binding agreement to provide the alien procedures for requesting safe haven and that may have originally prompted the alien's flight and application for asylum.

* * * [T]his rule also replicates several key aspects of implementation of the U.S.-Canada Agreement. First, as with the regulatory scheme for the U.S.-Canada Agreement, prior to implementation of an ACA subject to this rule, the Departments will make a generalized determination as to whether the third country grants asylum seekers "access to a full and fair procedure" within the meaning of INA 208(a)(2)(A). This finding is required by the text of section 208(a)(2)(A), and the Departments will make the "full and fair" third country determination separate and apart from the regulatory provisions provided for here, to address this threshold statutory element that must be satisfied before any section 208(a)(2)(A) bilateral or multilateral agreement is effectuated. Second, under this rule, there will be an individualized screening process within the preexisting ER and INA section 240 frameworks to evaluate whether an alien falls within the terms of an agreement and, if so, whether the alien nonetheless meets one of its exceptions. * * *

* * *

* * * [T]he terms of section 208(a)(2)(A) do not limit the applicability of ACAs to aliens who have traveled through the third country in transit to the United States. Consequently, in contrast to the U.S.-Canada provisions, this rule provides that the screening procedures for ACAs with countries other than Canada (which, with one possible exception, would not be contiguous to the United States) will afford aliens an opportunity to establish that it is more likely than not that they would be persecuted or tortured if removed to the applicable third country.* * *

B. New 8 CFR 208.30(e)(7)

The regulations at 8 CFR 208.30 govern interviews, conducted by DHS asylum officers, of stowaways and aliens subject to ER. See 8 CFR 208.30(a). New paragraph (e)(7) requires an asylum officer, in an appropriate case, to make several threshold screening determinations before assessing the merits of an alien's claims for asylum, withholding of removal, or CAT protection. * * *

After identifying the third country or countries to which the alien may be removed, if the alien does not affirmatively state a fear of persecution or torture in, or removal to, the country or countries, the asylum officer will refer the determination—i.e., that the alien is barred from applying for asylum, withholding of removal, and CAT protection in the United States, and subject to removal to the third country or countries—to a supervisory officer for review. If the supervisory asylum officer disagrees, that officer will remand the case to the asylum officer for a credible fear interview.

If, on the other hand, the alien affirmatively states a fear of persecution or torture in, or removal to, the third country or countries, the asylum officer will then determine whether the alien can establish, by a preponderance of the evidence, that, if the alien were removed to the third country or countries, it is more likely than not that he or she would be persecuted on account of a protected ground or tortured. * * *

* * *

In contrast to the final rule implementing the U.S.-Canada Agreement that provided an alien with a minimal consultation period prior to the threshold screening interview to determine the applicability of the Agreement, this rule does not mandate such a period.* * *

The bilateral ACAs that the United States has signed as of the effective date of this rule include agreements with El Salvador, Guatemala, and Honduras and incorporate fewer and less complex exceptions than the U.S.-Canada Agreement, eliminating the need for a consultation period analogous to the consultation period permitted by the U.S.-Canada Agreement. Further, this rule's expansion of the underlying threshold screening procedures to provide an opportunity for aliens to establish "more likely than not" persecution or torture in the receiving country provides additional process beyond that which is available under the regulations implementing the U.S.-Canada Agreement.

* * *

C. Amended 8 CFR 1003.42(h)(1)–(2) and New 8 CFR 1003.42(h) (3)–(4)

This rule will amend 8 CFR 1003.42(h) to reflect the implementation of ACAs other than the U.S.-Canada Agreement. . . .[omitted]. Under the new paragraph (h)(3), an IJ is prohibited from reviewing an officer's determination that section 208(a)(2)(A) bars an alien from applying for asylum. But an IJ acquires jurisdiction to review a negative credible fear finding in any case where an alien either establishes that he or she qualifies for an ACA exception, or establishes more-likely-than-not harm in the relevant third country, thus prohibiting the application of the ACA to that alien. * * *

* * *

* * * [E]valuating whether an asylum seeker would face persecution or torture in a country to which he has no substantial connections is more

straightforward. The third country with which the United States has formed an ACA is, by definition, not an alien's country of nationality or last habitual residence. * * *

Finally, Congress chose not to mandate IJ review of decisions as to whether an alien is subject to an ACA. * * *

Therefore, it is unnecessary—and indeed would be inconsistent with the INA removal statutory scheme—to mandate IJ review of a determination that section 208(a)(2)(A) bars an alien from applying for asylum. In section 208(a)(2)(A), Congress authorized the Executive Branch to operate within the President's foreign affairs authority to enter international agreements more evenly distributing the load of providing access to potential asylum for international refugees and asylees. By its terms, section 208(a)(2)(A) preserves flexibility for the Executive Branch in entering such agreements. The provision imposes two clear requirements, limiting such international agreements only to countries that provide access to full and fair protection procedures and are places in which an alien's life or freedom would not be harmed on account of a protected ground. Beyond those specifications, the Executive Branch's utilization of its statutory authority under section 208(a)(2)(A) is subject to no express procedural stipulations.

* * *

D. Amended 8 CFR 1240.11(g) and New 8 CFR 1240.11(h)

This rule will amend 8 CFR 1240.11(g) to reflect that the section will now apply only to the U.S.-Canada Agreement. The rule will also create a new 8 CFR 1240.11(h) to provide for the implementation of all other existing and future ACAs within the context of section 240 proceedings. Similar to the threshold determinations that asylum officers must make in ER proceedings, as described above, this new regulatory section will require IJs to determine whether an alien falls within an exception to an otherwise applicable ACA, and will authorize IJs to provide an alien subject to the terms of an ACA an opportunity to establish that it is more likely than not that the alien would be persecuted on account of a protected ground or tortured in the applicable third country.1

* * *

[NOTE: For regulatory amendments implementing this interim final rule re: asylum procedures for applicants from countries with bilateral and multilateral cooperative agreements, *see* Part III (Excerpts from Code of Federal Regulations), 8 C.F.R. §§ 208.4, 208.30, 1003.42, 1208.4, and 1240.11]

Agreement Between the Government of the United States of America and the Government of the Republic of Guatemala on Cooperation Regarding the Examination of Protection Claims (July 26, 2019)

THE GOVERNMENT OF THE UNITED STATES OF AMERICA AND THE GOVERNMENT OF THE REPUBLIC OF GUATEMALA, hereinafter referred to individually as "Party" or collectively "the Parties".

CONSIDERING that Guatemala regulates its relations with other countries in accordance with international principles, rules and practices, with the purpose of contributing to the maintenance of peace and freedom, the respect and defense of human rights, and the strengthening of democratic processes and international institutions that guarantee the mutual and equitable benefit among the states. On the other hand, Guatemala will maintain relations of friendship, solidarity and cooperation with those states whose economic, social and cultural development is analogous to that of Guatemala, such as the right of people to migrate and their need for protection.

WHEREAS Guatemala currently incorporates a dynamic immigration law into its domestic legislation, which requires Guatemala to recognize the right of every person to emigrate or immigrate, thereby allowing any migrant to enter, remain, transit, leave and return to its territory in accordance with its domestic laws. Likewise, in situations not provided for by domestic legislation, the norm that most favors the migrant must be applied. As such, temporary shelter and care should be given to those who wish to enter Guatemala legally. For the above reasons it is necessary to promote cooperation agreements with other states that uphold the same values outlined in Guatemala's migration policy, which is regulated by the National Migration Authority.

CONSIDERING that Guatemala is a party to the 1951 Convention relating to the Status of Refugees, done at Geneva on July 28, 1951 (the "1951 Convention") and the Protocol Relating to the Status of Refugees, done at New York on January 31, 1967 (the "1967 Protocol"), to which the United States of America is a party and reaffirming the obligation of the Parties to provide protection to refugees who meet the requirements and who are physically in their respective territories, in accordance with their obligations under those instruments and subject to the respective laws, treaties, and declarations of the Parties.

RECOGNIZING, in particular, the obligation of the Parties to comply with the principle of non-refoulement, as outlined in the 1951 Convention and the 1967 Protocol, as well as the Convention against Torture and Other Treatment or Cruel, Inhuman or Degrading Penalties, signed in New York on December 10, 1984 (the "Convention against Torture"), subject to the Parties respective reservations, understandings, and declarations and reaffirming their respective obligations to promote and protect human rights and fundamental freedoms consistent with their international obligations;

RECOGNIZING and respecting the obligations of each Party in accordance with its domestic laws and policies, and international agreements and arrangements;

UNDERSCORING that the United States and Guatemala offer refugee protection systems that are consistent with their obligations under the 1951 Convention and/or the 1967 Protocols;

DETERMINED to maintain the status of refuge or equivalent temporary protection, as an essential measure of the protection of refugees or asylees, and at the same time wishing to prevent fraud in the refugee or asylum application process—an action that undermines its legitimate purpose—and determined to strengthen the integrity of the official process for requesting asylum or refugee status as well as public support for said processes;

AWARE that the distribution of responsibility for requests for protection must guarantee in practice, that people in need of protection be identified and that violations of the basic principle of non-refoulement be avoided; and, therefore, committed to safeguarding for each applicant the status of refuge or asylum that meets the required conditions, access to a full and fair procedure for the determination of their claim;

AGREE to the following:

ARTICLE 1

For the purposes of this Agreement:

1. "Request for Protection" refers to the request of a person of any nationality, to the government of one of the Parties to receive protection in accordance with their respective institutional obligations derived from the 1951 Convention, the 1967 Protocol or the Convention against Torture, and in accordance with the respective laws and policies of the Parties, enforcing compliance with said international obligations; as well as to receive any other type of equivalent temporary protection available under the migration law of the receiving party.

2. "Protection Applicant" refers to any person who submits a request for protection in the territory of one of the Parties.

3. "System to Determine Protection" refers to the set of policies, laws, administrative and judicial practices that the Government of each Party uses to make a decision on requests for protection.

4. "Unaccompanied Minor" refers to an applicant for protection who has not reached the age of eighteen (18) and whose parent or legal guardian is not present or available to provide care and physical custody in the United States, or in Guatemala, where the unaccompanied minor is located.

5. In the case of Guatemala immigration, law and migration policy refers to the rights of persons to enter, remain, transit and leave its territory in accordance with its domestic laws and international agreements and arrangements, and immigration stay means the authorized period of time according to the immigration status granted to individuals.

ARTICLE 2

This Agreement does not apply to applicants for protection who are citizens or nationals of Guatemala; or stateless individuals habitually residing in Guatemala.

ARTICLE 3

1. To ensure that protection applicants transferred to Guatemala by the United States have access to a system to determine protection, Guatemala will not return or expel applicants for protection in Guatemala, unless the application is abandoned by the applicant or is formally rejected through an administrative decision.

2. During the transfer process, the persons subject to this Agreement will be the responsibility of the United States until the transfer process is completed.

ARTICLE 4

1. The responsibility for determining and concluding requests for protection within its territory shall rest with the United States, when the United States establishes that that person:

   a. is an unaccompanied minor; or

   b. has arrived in the territory of the United States:

      i. with a validly-issued visa or other valid admission document, other than a transit visa, issued by the United States; or

      ii. without the United States requiring him to obtain a visa.

2. Notwithstanding paragraph 1 of this article, Guatemala will evaluate the request for protection on an individual basis, in accordance with what is established and authorized by the competent authority on immigration matters in its migration policies and laws and in its territory, of persons who meet the appropriate requirements under this Agreement and who arrive in the United States at a port of entry or between ports of entry, on or after the effective date of this Agreement. Guatemala will evaluate the request for protection, in keeping with the Initial Implementation Plan and the standard operating procedures referenced in Article 7.1 and 7.5.

3. The Parties shall apply this Agreement with respect to unaccompanied minors, in accordance with their respective domestic laws.

4. The Parties shall have procedures in place to ensure that the transfers from the United States to Guatemala of the persons covered by this

Agreement are compatible with their respective obligations, domestic and international laws, and migration policies.

5. The United States shall make the final decision that an individual qualifies for an exception under Articles 4 and 5 of this Agreement.

ARTICLE 5

Notwithstanding any provision of this Agreement, any Party may, at its discretion, examine any request for protection that has been submitted to that Party when it decides that it is in the public interest to do so.

ARTICLE 6

The Parties may:

1. Exchange information when necessary for the effective implementation of this Agreement, subject to national laws and regulations. Such information will not be disclosed by the recipient country except in accordance with its national laws and regulations.

2. The Parties may regularly exchange information regarding laws, regulations, and practices related to their respective systems to determine migration protection.

ARTICLE 7

1. The Parties shall develop standard operating procedures to assist in the implementation of this Agreement. These procedures shall incorporate provisions to notify Guatemala in advance of the transfer of any person pursuant to this Agreement. The United States will collaborate with Guatemala to identify the appropriate individuals to be transferred to Guatemala's territory.

2. The operating procedures shall incorporate mechanisms to resolve disputes that respect the interpretation and implementation of the terms of this Agreement. Unforeseen cases that cannot be resolved through these mechanisms will be resolved through diplomatic channels.

3. The United States plans to cooperate to strengthen the institutional capacities of Guatemala.

4. The Parties agree to regularly evaluate this Agreement and its implementation to correct any deficiencies found. The evaluations will be carried out jointly by the Parties, the first within a maximum period of three (3) months from the date of entry into operation of the Agreement with following evaluations occurring by the same terms. The Parties may invite, by mutual agreement, other relevant organizations with specialized knowledge on the subject, to participate in the initial evaluation and/or cooperate for the implementation of this Agreement.

5. The Parties intend to complete an initial implementation plan, which will contain gradual steps, and address, among other things: (a) procedures necessary to effectuate the transfer of individuals under this agree-

ment; (b) the volume or number of individuals to be transferred; and (c) institutional capacity requirements. The Parties plan to operationalize this Agreement upon the completion of a phased implementation plan.

ARTICLE 8

1. This Agreement shall enter into force by means of an exchange of notes between the Parties indicating that each party has complied with the necessary domestic legal procedures for the Agreement to enter into force. For the term of two (2) years, renewable before its expiration with the exchange of diplomatic notes.

2. Any Party may terminate this Agreement by giving written notice to the other Party three (3) months in advance.

3. Any Party may, immediately after notifying the other Party in writing, suspend for an initial period of up to three (3) months the implementation of this Agreement. This suspension may be extended for additional periods of up to three (3) months, by means of written notification to the other Party. Any Party may, with the written consent of the other, suspend any part of this Agreement.

4. The Parties may in writing, by mutual agreement, make any modification or addition to this Agreement. These shall enter into force in accordance with the relevant legal procedures of each Party and the amendment or addition shall constitute an integral part of this Agreement.

5. Nothing in this Agreement shall be construed in such a way as to oblige the Parties to disburse or obligate funds.

IN FAITH WHEREOF, the undersigned, duly authorized by their respective governments, sign this Agreement.

SIGNED on the _____ day of _____ of the year 2019 in the English and Spanish languages, with both texts being authentic.

FOR THE GOVERNMENT OF THE UNITED STATES OF AMERICA:
Kevin K. McAleenan,
Acting Secretary of Homeland Security

FOR THE GOVERNMENT OF THE REPUBLIC OF GUATEMALA:
Enrique A. Degenhart Asturias
Minister of Government

INADMISSIBILITY

U.S. Citizenship and Immigration Services, Dep't of Homeland Sec. (Aug. 14, 2019)

Final Rule re:

Inadmissibility on Public Charge Grounds

I. Executive Summary

A. *Purpose of the Regulatory Action*

This rule changes how the Department of Homeland Security (DHS) interprets and implements the public charge ground of inadmissibility. The Immigration and Nationality Act (INA or the Act) renders inadmissible and therefore (1) ineligible for a visa, (2) ineligible for admission and (3) ineligible for adjustment of status, any alien who, in the opinion of the DHS (or the Departments of State (DOS) or Justice (DOJ), as applicable), is likely at any time to become a public charge. The statute does not define the term "public charge," but in a related statute, Congress has articulated a national policy that (1) "aliens within the Nation's borders not depend on public resources to meet their needs, but rather rely on their own capabilities and the resources of their families, their sponsors, and private organizations," and (2) "the availability of public benefits not constitute an incentive for immigration to the United States." In addition, the public charge statute provides that in making the inadmissibility determination, administering agencies must "at a minimum consider the alien's age; health; family status; assets, resources, and financial status; and education and skills." The agencies may also consider any affidavit of support under section 213A of the Act, 8 U.S.C. 1183a, i.e., Form I–864, Affidavit of Support Under Section 213A of the INA, submitted on the alien's behalf.

Since 1999, the prevailing approach to public charge inadmissibility has been dictated primarily by the May 26, 1999, Field Guidance on Deportability and Inadmissibility on Public Charge Grounds (1999 Interim Field Guidance), issued by the former Immigration and Naturalization Service (INS). Under that approach, "public charge" has been interpreted to mean a person who is "primarily dependent on the Government for subsistence, as demonstrated by either the receipt of public cash assistance for income maintenance or institutionalization for long-term care at Government expense." As a consequence, an alien's reliance on or receipt of non-cash benefits such as the Supplemental Nutrition Assistance Program (SNAP), or food stamps; Medicaid; and housing vouchers and other housing subsidies are not currently considered by DHS in determining whether an alien is deemed likely at any time to become a public charge.

INADMISSIBILITY

DHS is revising its interpretation of "public charge" to incorporate consideration of such benefits, and to better ensure that aliens subject to the public charge inadmissibility ground are self-sufficient, i.e., do not depend on public resources to meet their needs, but rather rely on their own capabilities, as well as the resources of family members, sponsors, and private organizations. This rule redefines the term "public charge" to mean an alien who receives one or more designated public benefits for more than 12 months in the aggregate within any 36-month period (such that, for instance, receipt of two benefits in one month counts as two months). This rule defines the term "public benefit" to include cash benefits for income maintenance, SNAP, most forms of Medicaid, Section 8 Housing Assistance under the Housing Choice Voucher (HCV) Program, Section 8 Project-Based Rental Assistance, and certain other forms of subsidized housing. DHS has tailored the rule to limit its effects in certain ways, such as for active duty military members and their families, and children in certain contexts.

This rule also explains how DHS will interpret the minimum statutory factors for determining whether "in the opinion of" the officer, the alien is likely at any time to become a public charge. Specifically, the rule contains a list of negative and positive factors that DHS will consider as part of this determination, and directs officers to consider these factors in the totality of the alien's circumstances. For instance, with respect to the statutory factor for the alien's age, DHS would generally consider it to be a negative factor if the alien is younger than 18 or older than 61, and a positive factor if the alien is between the ages of 18 and 61. These positive or negative factors operate as guidelines to help the officer determine whether the alien is likely at any time to become a public charge, i.e., is more likely than not at any time in the future to receive one or more designated public benefits for more than 12 months in the aggregate within any 36-month period. The rule also contains lists of heavily weighted negative factors and heavily weighted positive factors.* * * The presence of a single positive or negative factor, or heavily weighted negative or positive factor, will never, on its own, create a presumption that an applicant is inadmissible as likely to become a public charge or determine the outcome of the public charge inadmissibility determination. Rather, a public charge inadmissibility determination must be based on the totality of the circumstances presented in an applicant's case.

With respect to applications for adjustment of status in particular, this rule also provides a more comprehensive evidentiary framework under which U.S. Citizenship and Immigration Services (USCIS) will consider public charge inadmissibility. Under this rule, applicants for adjustment of status who are subject to the public charge ground of inadmissibility must file a Declaration of Self-Sufficiency (Form I–944) with their Application to Register Permanent Residence or Adjust Status (Form I–485) to demonstrate they are not likely to become a public charge. The Form I–944 only applies to adjustment applicants and not applicants for admission at a port of entry.

* * *

E. Summary of Costs and Benefits

This rule will impose new costs on the population applying to adjust status using Form I–485 that are subject to the public charge ground of inadmissibility. DHS will now require any adjustment applicants subject to the public charge ground of inadmissibility and who are applying for adjustment of status on or after the effective date of this final rule to submit a Form I–944 with their Form I–485 to demonstrate they are not likely to become a public charge. Failure to submit the form, where required, may result in a rejection or a denial of the Form I–485 without a prior issuance of a Request for Evidence or Notice of Intent to Deny.* * *

* * *

DHS estimates that the additional total cost of the rule will be approximately $35,202,698 annually. This cost includes the population applying to adjust status who are also required to file Form I–944, the opportunity costs of time associated with such filings, as well the increased time burden estimates for completing Forms I–485, I–129, I–129CW, and I–539, and for requesting or cancelling a public charge bond using Form I–945 and Form I–356, respectively.

* * *

The final rule will also potentially impose new costs on obligors (individuals or companies) if an alien has been determined to be likely at any time in the future to become a public charge and will be permitted to submit a public charge bond, for which USCIS will use the new Form I–945.* * *

* * *

The final rule will also result in a reduction in transfer payments from the Federal Government to individuals who may choose to disenroll from or forego enrollment in a public benefits program. Individuals who might choose to disenroll from or forego future enrollment in a public benefits program include foreign-born non-citizens, as well as U.S. citizens who are members of mixed-status households,* * * who may otherwise be eligible for public benefits. DHS estimates that the total reduction in transfer payments from the Federal and State governments will be approximately $2.47 billion annually due to disenrollment or foregone enrollment in public benefits programs by foreign-born non-citizens who may be receiving public benefits. DHS estimates that the 10-year discounted federal and state transfer payments reduction of this final rule will be approximately $21.0 billion at a 3 percent discount rate and about $17.3 billion at a 7 percent discount rate. However, DHS notes there may be additional reductions in transfer payments that we are unable to quantify.

There also may be additional reductions in transfer payments from states to individuals who may choose to disenroll from or forego enrollment in public benefits program. For example, the Federal Government funds all SNAP food expenses, but only 50 percent of allowable administrative costs for regular operating expenses.* * * Similarly, Federal Medical Assistance Percentages (FMAP) in some U.S. Department of Health and Human Services (HHS) programs, like Medicaid, can vary from between 50 percent to an enhanced rate of 100 percent in some cases.* * * Since the state share of federal financial participation (FFP) varies from state to state, DHS uses the average FMAP across all states and U.S. territories of 59 percent to estimate the amount of state transfer payments. Therefore, the 10-year undiscounted amount of state transfer payments of the provisions of this final rule is about $1.01 billion annually. The 10-year discounted amount of state transfer payments of the provisions of this final rule would be approximately $8.63 billion at a 3 percent discount rate, and about $7.12 billion at a 7 percent discount rate. Finally, DHS recognizes that reductions in federal and state transfers under federal benefit programs may have impacts on state and local economies, large and small businesses, and individuals. For example, the rule might result in reduced revenues for healthcare providers participating in Medicaid, companies that manufacture medical supplies or pharmaceuticals, grocery retailers participating in SNAP, agricultural producers who grow foods that are eligible for purchase using SNAP benefits, or landlords participating in federally funded housing programs.

Additionally, the final rule will have new direct and indirect impacts on various entities and individuals associated with regulatory familiarization with the provisions of the rule.* * *

* * *

The final rule will produce some quantified benefits due to the regulatory changes DHS is making. The final rule will produce some benefits for T nonimmigrants applying for adjustment of status based on their T nonimmigrant status, as this population will no longer need to submit Application for Waiver of Grounds of Inadmissibility (Form I–601) seeking a waiver of the public charge ground of inadmissibility. DHS estimates the total benefit for this population is $15,176 annually.* * *

The primary benefit of the final rule would be to better ensure that aliens who are admitted to the United States, seek extension of stay or change of status, or apply for adjustment of status will be self-sufficient, i.e., will rely on their own financial resources, as well as the financial resources of the family, sponsors, and private organizations.* * * DHS also anticipates that the final rule will produce some benefits from the elimination of Form I–864W. The elimination of this form will potentially reduce the number of forms USCIS would have to process.* * * Additionally, a public charge bond process will also provide benefits to applicants as they potentially will be given the opportunity for adjustment if otherwise admissible, at the discretion of DHS, after a determination that he or she is likely to become a public charge.

[Note: For regulatory amendments implementing portions of this final rule re: inadmissibility on public charge grounds, see Part III (Excerpts from Code of Federal Regulations), 8 C.F.R. §§ 212.21, 212.22, 212.23, 214.1, and 248.1]

SUSPENSION OF ENTRY

Enhancing Vetting Capabilities and Processes for Detecting Attempted Entry into the United States by Terrorists or Other Public Safety Threats, Proclamation No. 9645, 82 Fed. Reg. 45,161 (Sept. 24, 2017)

A Proclamation

In Executive Order 13780 of March 6, 2017 (Protecting the Nation from Foreign Terrorist Entry into the United States), on the recommendations of the Secretary of Homeland Security and the Attorney General, I ordered a worldwide review of whether, and if so what, additional information would be needed from each foreign country to assess adequately whether their nationals seeking to enter the United States pose a security or safety threat. This was the first such review of its kind in United States history. As part of the review, the Secretary of Homeland Security established global requirements for information sharing in support of immigration screening and vetting. The Secretary of Homeland Security developed a comprehensive set of criteria and applied it to the information-sharing practices, policies, and capabilities of foreign governments. The Secretary of State thereafter engaged with the countries reviewed in an effort to address deficiencies and achieve improvements. In many instances, those efforts produced positive results. By obtaining additional information and formal commitments from foreign governments, the United States Government has improved its capacity and ability to assess whether foreign nationals attempting to enter the United States pose a security or safety threat. Our Nation is safer as a result of this work.

Despite those efforts, the Secretary of Homeland Security, in consultation with the Secretary of State and the Attorney General, has determined that a small number of countries—out of nearly 200 evaluated—remain deficient at this time with respect to their identity-management and information-sharing capabilities, protocols, and practices. In some cases, these countries also have a significant terrorist presence within their territory.

As President, I must act to protect the security and interests of the United States and its people. I am committed to our ongoing efforts to engage those countries willing to cooperate, improve information-sharing and identity-management protocols and procedures, and address both terrorism-related and public-safety risks. Some of the countries with remaining inadequacies face significant challenges. Others have made strides to improve their protocols and procedures, and I commend them for these efforts. But until they satisfactorily address the identified inadequacies, I have determined, on the basis of recommendations from the Secretary of Homeland Security and other members of my Cabinet, to impose certain conditional restrictions and limitations, as set forth more fully below, on entry into the United States of nationals of the countries identified in section 2 of this proclamation.

NOW, THEREFORE, I, DONALD J. TRUMP, by the authority vested in me by the Constitution and the laws of the United States of America, including sections 212(f) and 215(a) of the Immigration and Nationality Act (INA), 8 U.S.C. 1182(f) and 1185(a), and section 301 of title 3, United States Code, hereby find that, absent the measures set forth in this proclamation, the immigrant and nonimmigrant entry into the United States of persons described in section 2 of this proclamation would be detrimental to the interests of the United States, and that their entry should be subject to certain restrictions, limitations, and exceptions. I therefore hereby proclaim the following:

Section 1. *Policy and Purpose*. (a) It is the policy of the United States to protect its citizens from terrorist attacks and other public-safety threats. Screening and vetting protocols and procedures associated with visa adjudications and other immigration processes play a critical role in implementing that policy. They enhance our ability to detect foreign nationals who may commit, aid, or support acts of terrorism, or otherwise pose a safety threat, and they aid our efforts to prevent such individuals from entering the United States.

(b) Information-sharing and identity-management protocols and practices of foreign governments are important for the effectiveness of the screening and vetting protocols and procedures of the United States. Governments manage the identity and travel documents of their nationals and residents. They also control the circumstances under which they provide information about their nationals to other governments, including information about known or suspected terrorists and criminal-history information. It is, therefore, the policy of the United States to take all necessary and appropriate steps to encourage foreign governments to improve their information-sharing and identity-management protocols and practices and to regularly share identity and threat information with our immigration screening and vetting systems.

(c) Section 2(a) of Executive Order 13780 directed a "worldwide review to identify whether, and if so what, additional information will be needed from each foreign country to adjudicate an application by a national of that country for a visa, admission, or other benefit under the INA (adjudications) in order to determine that the individual is not a security or public-safety threat." That review culminated in a report submitted to the President by the Secretary of Homeland Security on July 9, 2017. In that review, the Secretary of Homeland Security, in consultation with the Secretary of State and the Director of National Intelligence, developed a baseline for the kinds of information required from foreign governments to support the United States Government's ability to confirm the identity of individuals seeking entry into the United States as immigrants and nonimmigrants, as well as individuals applying for any other benefit under the immigration laws, and to assess whether they are a security or public-safety threat. That baseline incorporates three categories of criteria:

(i) *Identity-management information.* The United States expects foreign governments to provide the information needed to determine whether individuals seeking benefits under the immigration laws are who they claim to be. The identity-management information category focuses on the integrity of documents required for travel to the United States. The criteria assessed in this category include whether the country issues electronic passports embedded with data to enable confirmation of identity, reports lost and stolen passports to appropriate entities, and makes available upon request identity-related information not included in its passports.

(ii) *National security and public-safety information.* The United States expects foreign governments to provide information about whether persons who seek entry to this country pose national security or public-safety risks. The criteria assessed in this category include whether the country makes available, directly or indirectly, known or suspected terrorist and criminal-history information upon request, whether the country provides passport and national-identity document exemplars, and whether the country impedes the United States Government's receipt of information about passengers and crew traveling to the United States.

(iii) *National security and public-safety risk assessment.* The national security and public-safety risk assessment category focuses on national security risk indicators. The criteria assessed in this category include whether the country is a known or potential terrorist safe haven, whether it is a participant in the Visa Waiver Program established under section 217 of the INA, 8 U.S.C. 1187, that meets all of its requirements, and whether it regularly fails to receive its nationals subject to final orders of removal from the United States.

(d) The Department of Homeland Security, in coordination with the Department of State, collected data on the performance of all foreign governments and assessed each country against the baseline described in subsection (c) of this section. The assessment focused, in particular, on identity management, security and public-safety threats, and national security risks. Through this assessment, the agencies measured each country's performance with respect to issuing reliable travel documents and implementing adequate identity-management and information-sharing protocols and procedures, and evaluated terrorism-related and public-safety risks associated with foreign nationals seeking entry into the United States from each country.

(e) The Department of Homeland Security evaluated each country against the baseline described in subsection (c) of this section. The Secretary of Homeland Security identified 16 countries as being "inadequate" based on an analysis of their identity-management protocols, information-sharing practices, and risk factors. Thirty-one additional countries were classified "at risk" of becoming "inadequate" based on those criteria.

(f) As required by section 2(d) of Executive Order 13780, the Department of State conducted a 50-day engagement period to encourage all foreign governments, not just the 47 identified as either "inadequate" or "at risk," to improve their performance with respect to the baseline described in subsection (c) of this section. Those engagements yielded significant improvements in many countries. Twenty-nine countries, for example, provided travel document exemplars for use by Department of Homeland Security officials to combat fraud. Eleven countries agreed to share information on known or suspected terrorists.

(g) The Secretary of Homeland Security assesses that the following countries continue to have "inadequate" identity-management protocols, information-sharing practices, and risk factors, with respect to the baseline described in subsection (c) of this section, such that entry restrictions and limitations are recommended: Chad, Iran, Libya, North Korea, Syria, Venezuela, and Yemen. The Secretary of Homeland Security also assesses that Iraq did not meet the baseline, but that entry restrictions and limitations under a Presidential proclamation are not warranted. The Secretary of Homeland Security recommends, however, that nationals of Iraq who seek to enter the United States be subject to additional scrutiny to determine if they pose risks to the national security or public safety of the United States. In reaching these conclusions, the Secretary of Homeland Security considered the close cooperative relationship between the United States and the democratically elected government of Iraq, the strong United States diplomatic presence in Iraq, the significant presence of United States forces in Iraq, and Iraq's commitment to combating the Islamic State of Iraq and Syria (ISIS).

(h) Section 2(e) of Executive Order 13780 directed the Secretary of Homeland Security to "submit to the President a list of countries recommended for inclusion in a Presidential proclamation that would prohibit the entry of appropriate categories of foreign nationals of countries that have not provided the information requested until they do so or until the Secretary of Homeland Security certifies that the country has an adequate plan to do so, or has adequately shared information through other means." On September 15, 2017, the Secretary of Homeland Security submitted a report to me recommending entry restrictions and limitations on certain nationals of 7 countries determined to be "inadequate" in providing such information and in light of other factors discussed in the report. According to the report, the recommended restrictions would help address the threats that the countries' identity-management protocols, information-sharing inadequacies, and other risk factors pose to the security and welfare of the United States. The restrictions also encourage the countries to work with the United States to address those inadequacies and risks so that the restrictions and limitations imposed by this proclamation may be relaxed or removed as soon as possible.

(i) In evaluating the recommendations of the Secretary of Homeland Security and in determining what restrictions to impose for each country,

I consulted with appropriate Assistants to the President and members of the Cabinet, including the Secretaries of State, Defense, and Homeland Security, and the Attorney General. I considered several factors, including each country's capacity, ability, and willingness to cooperate with our identity-management and information-sharing policies and each country's risk factors, such as whether it has a significant terrorist presence within its territory. I also considered foreign policy, national security, and counterterrorism goals. I reviewed these factors and assessed these goals, with a particular focus on crafting those country-specific restrictions that would be most likely to encourage cooperation given each country's distinct circumstances, and that would, at the same time, protect the United States until such time as improvements occur. The restrictions and limitations imposed by this proclamation are, in my judgment, necessary to prevent the entry of those foreign nationals about whom the United States Government lacks sufficient information to assess the risks they pose to the United States. These restrictions and limitations are also needed to elicit improved identity-management and information-sharing protocols and practices from foreign governments; and to advance foreign policy, national security, and counterterrorism objectives.

(ii) After reviewing the Secretary of Homeland Security's report of September 15, 2017, and accounting for the foreign policy, national security, and counterterrorism objectives of the United States, I have determined to restrict and limit the entry of nationals of 7 countries found to be "inadequate" with respect to the baseline described in subsection (c) of this section: Chad, Iran, Libya, North Korea, Syria, Venezuela, and Yemen. These restrictions distinguish between the entry of immigrants and nonimmigrants. Persons admitted on immigrant visas become lawful permanent residents of the United States. Such persons may present national security or public-safety concerns that may be distinct from those admitted as nonimmigrants. The United States affords lawful permanent residents more enduring rights than it does to nonimmigrants. Lawful permanent residents are more difficult to remove than nonimmigrants even after national security concerns arise, which heightens the costs and dangers of errors associated with admitting such individuals. And although immigrants generally receive more extensive vetting than non-immigrants, such vetting is less reliable when the country from which someone seeks to emigrate exhibits significant gaps in its identity-management or information-sharing policies, or presents risks to the national security of the United States. For all but one of those 7 countries, therefore, I am restricting the entry of all immigrants.

(iii) I am adopting a more tailored approach with respect to nonimmigrants, in accordance with the recommendations of the Secretary of Homeland Security. For some countries found to be "inadequate" with respect to the baseline described in subsection (c) of this section, I am restricting the entry of all nonimmigrants. For countries with certain mitigating factors, such as a willingness to cooperate or play a substantial role in combatting terrorism, I am restricting the entry only of certain categories of nonimmigrants, which will mitigate the security threats presented by their entry into the United States. In those cases in which future cooperation seems reasonably likely, and accounting for foreign policy, national security, and counterterrorism objectives, I have tailored the restrictions to encourage such improvements.

(i) Section 2(e) of Executive Order 13780 also provided that the "Secretary of State, the Attorney General, or the Secretary of Homeland Security may also submit to the President the names of additional countries for which any of them recommends other lawful restrictions or limitations deemed necessary for the security or welfare of the United States." The Secretary of Homeland Security determined that Somalia generally satisfies the information-sharing requirements of the baseline described in subsection (c) of this section, but its government's inability to effectively and consistently cooperate, combined with the terrorist threat that emanates from its territory, present special circumstances that warrant restrictions and limitations on the entry of its nationals into the United States. Somalia's identity-management deficiencies and the significant terrorist presence within its territory make it a source of particular risks to the national security and public safety of the United States. Based on the considerations mentioned above, and as described further in section 2(h) of this proclamation, I have determined that entry restrictions, limitations, and other measures designed to ensure proper screening and vetting for nationals of Somalia are necessary for the security and welfare of the United States.

(j) Section 2 of this proclamation describes some of the inadequacies that led me to impose restrictions on the specified countries. Describing all of those reasons publicly, however, would cause serious damage to the national security of the United States, and many such descriptions are classified.

Sec. 2. *Suspension of Entry for Nationals of Countries of Identified Concern.* The entry into the United States of nationals of the following countries is hereby suspended and limited, as follows, subject to categorical exceptions and case-by-case waivers, as described in sections 3 and 6 of this proclamation:

(a) *Chad.*

(i) The government of Chad is an important and valuable counterterrorism partner of the United States, and the United States Government looks forward to expanding that cooperation, including in the areas of immigration and border management. Chad has shown a clear willingness to improve in these areas. Nonetheless, Chad does not adequately share public-safety and terrorism-related information and fails to satisfy at least one key risk criterion. Additionally, several terrorist groups are active within Chad or in the surrounding region, including elements of Boko Haram, ISIS-West Africa, and al-Qa'ida in the Islamic Maghreb. At this time, additional information sharing to identify those foreign nationals applying for visas or seeking entry into the United States who represent national security and public-safety threats is necessary given the significant terrorism-related risk from this country.

(ii) The entry into the United States of nationals of Chad, as immigrants, and as nonimmigrants on business (B–1), tourist (B–2), and business/ tourist (B–1/B–2) visas, is hereby suspended.

(b) *Iran.*

(i) Iran regularly fails to cooperate with the United States Government in identifying security risks, fails to satisfy at least one key risk criterion, is the source of significant terrorist threats, and fails to receive its nationals subject to final orders of removal from the United States. The Department of State has also designated Iran as a state sponsor of terrorism.

(ii) The entry into the United States of nationals of Iran as immigrants and as nonimmigrants is hereby suspended, except that entry by such nationals under valid student (F and M) and exchange visitor (J) visas is not suspended, although such individuals should be subject to enhanced screening and vetting requirements.

(c) *Libya.*

(i) The government of Libya is an important and valuable counterterrorism partner of the United States, and the United States Government looks forward to expanding on that cooperation, including in the areas of immigration and border management. Libya, nonetheless, faces significant challenges in sharing several types of information, including public-safety and terrorism-related information necessary for the protection of the national security and public safety of the United States. Libya also has significant inadequacies in its identity-management protocols. Further, Libya fails to satisfy at least one key risk criterion and has been assessed to be not fully cooperative with respect to receiving its nationals subject to final orders of removal from the United States. The substantial terrorist presence within Libya's territory amplifies the risks posed by the entry into the United States of its nationals.

(ii) The entry into the United States of nationals of Libya, as immigrants, and as nonimmigrants on business (B–1), tourist (B–2), and business/ tourist (B–1/B–2) visas, is hereby suspended.

(d) *North Korea.*

(i) North Korea does not cooperate with the United States Government in any respect and fails to satisfy all information-sharing requirements.

(ii) The entry into the United States of nationals of North Korea as immigrants and nonimmigrants is hereby suspended.

(e) *Syria.*

(i) Syria regularly fails to cooperate with the United States Government in identifying security risks, is the source of significant terrorist threats, and has been designated by the Department of State as a state sponsor of terrorism. Syria has significant inadequacies in identity-management protocols, fails to share public-safety and terrorism information, and fails to satisfy at least one key risk criterion.

(ii) The entry into the United States of nationals of Syria as immigrants and nonimmigrants is hereby suspended.

(f) *Venezuela.*

(i) Venezuela has adopted many of the baseline standards identified by the Secretary of Homeland Security and in section 1 of this proclamation, but its government is uncooperative in verifying whether its citizens pose national security or public-safety threats. Venezuela's government fails to share public-safety and terrorism-related information adequately, fails to satisfy at least one key risk criterion, and has been assessed to be not fully cooperative with respect to receiving its nationals subject to final orders of removal from the United States. There are, however, alternative sources for obtaining information to verify the citizenship and identity of nationals from Venezuela. As a result, the restrictions imposed by this proclamation focus on government officials of Venezuela who are responsible for the identified inadequacies.

(ii) Notwithstanding section 3(b)(v) of this proclamation, the entry into the United States of officials of government agencies of Venezuela involved in screening and vetting procedures—including the Ministry of the Popular Power for Interior, Justice and Peace; the Administrative Service of Identification, Migration and Immigration; the Scientific, Penal and Criminal Investigation Service Corps; the Bolivarian National Intelligence Service; and the Ministry of the Popular Power for Foreign Relations—and their immediate family members, as nonimmigrants on business (B–1), tourist (B–2), and business/tourist (B–1/B–2) visas, is hereby suspended. Further, nationals of Venezuela who are visa holders should be subject to appropriate additional measures to ensure traveler information remains current.

(g) *Yemen.*

(i) The government of Yemen is an important and valuable counterterrorism partner, and the United States Government looks forward to expanding that cooperation, including in the areas of immigration and border management. Yemen, nonetheless, faces significant identity-management challenges, which are amplified by the notable terrorist presence within its territory. The government of Yemen fails to satisfy critical identity-management requirements, does not share public-safety and terrorism-related information adequately, and fails to satisfy at least one key risk criterion.

(ii) The entry into the United States of nationals of Yemen as immigrants, and as nonimmigrants on business (B–1), tourist (B–2), and business/ tourist (B–1/B–2) visas, is hereby suspended.

(h) *Somalia.*

(i) The Secretary of Homeland Security's report of September 15, 2017, determined that Somalia satisfies the information-sharing requirements of the baseline described in section 1(c) of this proclamation. But several other considerations support imposing entry restrictions and limitations on Somalia. Somalia has significant identity-management deficiencies. For example, while Somalia issues an electronic passport, the United States and many other countries do not recognize it. A persistent terrorist threat also emanates from Somalia's territory. The United States Government has identified Somalia as a terrorist safe haven. Somalia stands apart from other countries in the degree to which its government lacks command and control of its territory, which greatly limits the effectiveness of its national capabilities in a variety of respects. Terrorists use undergoverned areas in northern, central, and southern Somalia as safe havens from which to plan, facilitate, and conduct their operations. Somalia also remains a destination for individuals attempting to join terrorist groups that threaten the national security of the United States. The State Department's 2016 Country Reports on Terrorism observed that Somalia has not sufficiently degraded the ability of terrorist groups to plan and mount attacks from its territory. Further, despite having made significant progress toward formally federating its member states, and its willingness to fight terrorism, Somalia continues to struggle to provide the governance needed to limit terrorists' freedom of movement, access to resources, and capacity to operate. The government of Somalia's lack of territorial control also compromises Somalia's ability, already limited because of poor record-keeping, to share information about its nationals who pose criminal or terrorist risks. As a result of these and other factors, Somalia presents special concerns that distinguish it from other countries.

(ii) The entry into the United States of nationals of Somalia as immigrants is hereby suspended. Additionally, visa adjudications for nationals of Somalia and decisions regarding their entry as nonimmigrants should be subject to additional scrutiny to determine if applicants are connected to terrorist organizations or otherwise pose a threat to the national security or public safety of the United States.

Sec. 3. *Scope and Implementation of Suspensions and Limitations. (a) Scope.* Subject to the exceptions set forth in subsection (b) of this section and any waiver under subsection (c) of this section, the suspensions of and limitations on entry pursuant to section 2 of this proclamation shall apply only to foreign nationals of the designated countries who:

(i) are outside the United States on the applicable effective date under section 7 of this proclamation;

(ii) do not have a valid visa on the applicable effective date under section 7 of this proclamation; and

(iii) do not qualify for a visa or other valid travel document under section 6(d) of this proclamation.

(b) *Exceptions.* The suspension of entry pursuant to section 2 of this proclamation shall not apply to:

(i) any lawful permanent resident of the United States;

(ii) any foreign national who is admitted to or paroled into the United States on or after the applicable effective date under section 7 of this proclamation;

(iii) any foreign national who has a document other than a visa—such as a transportation letter, an appropriate boarding foil, or an advance parole document—valid on the applicable effective date under section 7 of this proclamation or issued on any date thereafter, that permits him or her to travel to the United States and seek entry or admission;

(iv) any dual national of a country designated under section 2 of this proclamation when the individual is traveling on a passport issued by a non-designated country;

(v) any foreign national traveling on a diplomatic or diplomatic-type visa, North Atlantic Treaty Organization visa, C–2 visa for travel to the United Nations, or G–1, G–2, G–3, or G–4 visa; or

(vi) any foreign national who has been granted asylum by the United States; any refugee who has already been admitted to the United States; or any individual who has been granted withholding of removal, advance parole, or protection under the Convention Against Torture.

(c) *Waivers.* Notwithstanding the suspensions of and limitations on entry set forth in section 2 of this proclamation, a consular officer, or the Commissioner, United States Customs and Border Protection (CBP), or the Commissioner's designee, as appropriate, may, in their discretion, grant waivers on a case-by-case basis to permit the entry of foreign nationals for whom entry is otherwise suspended or limited if such foreign nationals demonstrate that waivers would be appropriate and consistent with subsections (i) through (iv) of this subsection. The Secretary of State and the Secretary of Homeland Security shall coordinate to adopt guidance addressing the circumstances in which waivers may be appropriate for foreign nationals seeking entry as immigrants or nonimmigrants.

(i) A waiver may be granted only if a foreign national demonstrates to the consular officer's or CBP official's satisfaction that:

(A) denying entry would cause the foreign national undue hardship;

(B) entry would not pose a threat to the national security or public safety of the United States; and

(C) entry would be in the national interest.

(ii) The guidance issued by the Secretary of State and the Secretary of Homeland Security under this subsection shall address the standards, policies, and procedures for:

(A) determining whether the entry of a foreign national would not pose a threat to the national security or public safety of the United States;

(B) determining whether the entry of a foreign national would be in the national interest;

(C) addressing and managing the risks of making such a determination in light of the inadequacies in information sharing, identity management, and other potential dangers posed by the nationals of individual countries subject to the restrictions and limitations imposed by this proclamation;

(D) assessing whether the United States has access, at the time of the waiver determination, to sufficient information about the foreign national to determine whether entry would satisfy the requirements of subsection (i) of this subsection; and

(E) determining the special circumstances that would justify granting a waiver under subsection (iv)(E) of this subsection.

(iii) Unless otherwise specified by the Secretary of Homeland Security, any waiver issued by a consular officer as part of the visa adjudication process will be effective both for the issuance of a visa and for any subsequent entry on that visa, but will leave unchanged all other requirements for admission or entry.

(iv) Case-by-case waivers may not be granted categorically, but may be appropriate, subject to the limitations, conditions, and requirements set forth under subsection (i) of this subsection and the guidance issued under subsection (ii) of this subsection, in individual circumstances such as the following:

(A) the foreign national has previously been admitted to the United States for a continuous period of work, study, or other long-term activity, is outside the United States on the applicable effective date under section 7 of this proclamation, seeks to reenter the United States to resume that activity, and the denial of reentry would impair that activity;

(B) the foreign national has previously established significant contacts with the United States but is outside the United States on the applicable effective date under section 7 of this proclamation for work, study, or other lawful activity;

(C) the foreign national seeks to enter the United States for significant business or professional obligations and the denial of entry would impair those obligations;

(D) the foreign national seeks to enter the United States to visit or reside with a close family member (e.g., a spouse, child, or parent) who is a United States citizen, lawful permanent resident, or alien lawfully admitted on a valid nonimmigrant visa, and the denial of entry would cause the foreign national undue hardship;

(E) the foreign national is an infant, a young child or adoptee, an individual needing urgent medical care, or someone whose entry is otherwise justified by the special circumstances of the case;

(F) the foreign national has been employed by, or on behalf of, the United States Government (or is an eligible dependent of such an employee), and the foreign national can document that he or she has provided faithful and valuable service to the United States Government;

(G) the foreign national is traveling for purposes related to an international organization designated under the International Organizations Immunities Act (IOIA), 22 U.S.C. 288 et seq., traveling for purposes of conducting meetings or business with the United States Government, or traveling to conduct business on behalf of an international organization not designated under the IOIA;

(H) the foreign national is a Canadian permanent resident who applies for a visa at a location within Canada;

(I) the foreign national is traveling as a United States Government–sponsored exchange visitor; or

(J) the foreign national is traveling to the United States, at the request of a United States Government department or agency, for legitimate law enforcement, foreign policy, or national security purposes.

Sec. 4. *Adjustments to and Removal of Suspensions and Limitations.* (a) The Secretary of Homeland Security shall, in consultation with the Secretary of State, devise a process to assess whether any suspensions and limitations imposed by section 2 of this proclamation should be continued, terminated, modified, or supplemented. The process shall account for whether countries have improved their identity-management and information-sharing protocols and procedures based on the criteria set forth in section 1 of this proclamation and the Secretary of Homeland Security's report of September 15, 2017. Within 180 days of the date of this proclamation, and every 180 days thereafter, the Secretary of Homeland Security, in consultation with the Secretary of State, the Attorney General, the Director of National Intelligence, and other appropriate heads of agencies, shall submit a report with recommendations to the President, through appropriate Assistants to the President, regarding the following:

(i) the interests of the United States, if any, that continue to require the suspension of, or limitations on, the entry on certain classes of nationals of countries identified in section 2 of this proclamation and whether the restrictions and limitations imposed by section 2 of this proclamation should be continued, modified, terminated, or supplemented; and

(ii) the interests of the United States, if any, that require the suspension of, or limitations on, the entry of certain classes of nationals of countries not identified in this proclamation.

(b) The Secretary of State, in consultation with the Secretary of Homeland Security, the Secretary of Defense, the Attorney General, the Director of National Intelligence, and the head of any other executive department or agency (agency) that the Secretary of State deems appropriate, shall engage the countries listed in section 2 of this proclamation, and any other countries that have information-sharing, identity-management, or risk-factor deficiencies as practicable, appropriate, and consistent with the foreign policy, national security, and public-safety objectives of the United States.

(c) Notwithstanding the process described above, and consistent with the process described in section 2(f) of Executive Order 13780, if the Secretary of Homeland Security, in consultation with the Secretary of State, the Attorney General, and the Director of National Intelligence, determines, at any time, that a country meets the standards of the baseline described in section 1(c) of this proclamation, that a country has an adequate plan to provide such information, or that one or more of the restrictions or limitations imposed on the entry of a country's nationals are no longer necessary for the security or welfare of the United States, the Secretary of Homeland Security may recommend to the President the removal or modification of any or all such restrictions and limitations. The Secretary of Homeland Security, the Secretary of State, or the Attorney General may also, as provided for in Executive Order 13780, submit to the President the names of additional countries for which any of them recommends any lawful restrictions or limitations deemed necessary for the security or welfare of the United States.

Sec. 5. *Reports on Screening and Vetting Procedures.* (a) The Secretary of Homeland Security, in coordination with the Secretary of State, the Attorney General, the Director of National Intelligence, and other appropriate heads of agencies shall submit periodic reports to the President, through appropriate Assistants to the President, that:

(i) describe the steps the United States Government has taken to improve vetting for nationals of all foreign countries, including through improved collection of biometric and biographic data;

(ii) describe the scope and magnitude of fraud, errors, false information, and unverifiable claims, as determined by the Secretary of Homeland Security on the basis of a validation study, made in applications for immigration benefits under the immigration laws; and

(iii) evaluate the procedures related to screening and vetting established by the Department of State's Bureau of Consular Affairs in order to enhance the safety and security of the United States and to ensure sufficient review of applications for immigration benefits.

(b) The initial report required under subsection (a) of this section shall be submitted within 180 days of the date of this proclamation; the second report shall be submitted within 270 days of the first report; and reports shall be submitted annually thereafter.

(c) The agency heads identified in subsection (a) of this section shall coordinate any policy developments associated with the reports described in subsection (a) of this section through the appropriate Assistants to the President.

Sec. 6. *Enforcement.* (a) The Secretary of State and the Secretary of Homeland Security shall consult with appropriate domestic and international partners, including countries and organizations, to ensure efficient, effective, and appropriate implementation of this proclamation.

(b) In implementing this proclamation, the Secretary of State and the Secretary of Homeland Security shall comply with all applicable laws and regulations, including those that provide an opportunity for individuals to enter the United States on the basis of a credible claim of fear of persecution or torture.

(c) No immigrant or nonimmigrant visa issued before the applicable effective date under section 7 of this proclamation shall be revoked pursuant to this proclamation.

(d) Any individual whose visa was marked revoked or marked canceled as a result of Executive Order 13769 of January 27, 2017 (Protecting the Nation from Foreign Terrorist Entry into the United States), shall be entitled to a travel document confirming that the individual is permitted to travel to the United States and seek entry under the terms and conditions of the visa marked revoked or marked canceled. Any prior cancellation or revocation of a visa that was solely pursuant to Executive Order 13769 shall not be the basis of inadmissibility for any future determination about entry or admissibility.

(e) This proclamation shall not apply to an individual who has been granted asylum by the United States, to a refugee who has already been admitted to the United States, or to an individual granted withholding of removal or protection under the Convention Against Torture. Nothing in this proclamation shall be construed to limit the ability of an individual to seek asylum, refugee status, withholding of removal, or protection under the Convention Against Torture, consistent with the laws of the United States.

Sec. 7. *Effective Dates*. Executive Order 13780 ordered a temporary pause on the entry of foreign nationals from certain foreign countries. In two cases, however, Federal courts have enjoined those restrictions. The Supreme Court has stayed those injunctions as to foreign nationals who lack a credible claim of a bona fide relationship with a person or entity in the United States, pending its review of the decisions of the lower courts.

(a) The restrictions and limitations established in section 2 of this proclamation are effective at 3:30 p.m. eastern daylight time on September 24, 2017, for foreign nationals who:

(i) were subject to entry restrictions under section 2 of Executive Order 13780, or would have been subject to the restrictions but for section 3 of that Executive Order, and

(ii) lack a credible claim of a bona fide relationship with a person or entity in the United States.

(b) The restrictions and limitations established in section 2 of this proclamation are effective at 12:01 a.m. eastern daylight time on October 18, 2017, for all other persons subject to this proclamation, including nationals of:

(i) Iran, Libya, Syria, Yemen, and Somalia who have a credible claim of a bona fide relationship with a person or entity in the United States; and

(ii) Chad, North Korea, and Venezuela.

Sec. 8. *Severability.* It is the policy of the United States to enforce this proclamation to the maximum extent possible to advance the national security, foreign policy, and counterterrorism interests of the United States. Accordingly:

(a) if any provision of this proclamation, or the application of any provision to any person or circumstance, is held to be invalid, the remainder of this proclamation and the application of its other provisions to any other persons or circumstances shall not be affected thereby; and

(b) if any provision of this proclamation, or the application of any provision to any person or circumstance, is held to be invalid because of the lack of certain procedural requirements, the relevant executive branch officials shall implement those procedural requirements to conform with existing law and with any applicable court orders.

Sec. 9. *General Provisions.* (a) Nothing in this proclamation shall be construed to impair or otherwise affect:

(i) the authority granted by law to an executive department or agency, or the head thereof; or

(ii) the functions of the Director of the Office of Management and Budget relating to budgetary, administrative, or legislative proposals.

(b) This proclamation shall be implemented consistent with applicable law and subject to the availability of appropriations.

(c) This proclamation is not intended to, and does not, create any right or benefit, substantive or procedural, enforceable at law or in equity by any party against the United States, its departments, agencies, or entities, its officers, employees, or agents, or any other person.

IN WITNESS WHEREOF, I have hereunto set my hand this twenty-fourth day of September, in the year of our Lord two thousand seventeen, and of the Independence of the United States of America the two hundred and forty-second.

Addressing Suspension of Entry of Immigrants Who Will Financially Burden the United States Healthcare System, in order to Protect the Availability of Healthcare Benefits for Americans, Proclamation No. 9945, 84 Fed. Reg. 53991 (Oct. 4, 2019)

A Proclamation

Healthcare providers and taxpayers bear substantial costs in paying for medical expenses incurred by people who lack health insurance or the ability to pay for their healthcare. Hospitals and other providers often administer care to the uninsured without any hope of receiving reimbursement from them. The costs associated with this care are passed on to the American people in the form of higher taxes, higher premiums, and higher fees for medical services. In total, uncompensated care costs the overall measure of unreimbursed services that hospitals give their patients have exceeded $35 billion in each of the last 10 years. These costs amount to approximately $7 million on average for each hospital in the United States, and can drive hospitals into insolvency. Beyond uncompensated care costs, the uninsured strain Federal and State government budgets through their reliance on publicly funded programs, which ultimately are financed by taxpayers.

Beyond imposing higher costs on hospitals and other healthcare infrastructure, uninsured individuals often use emergency rooms to seek remedies for a variety of non-emergency conditions, causing overcrowding and delays for those who truly need emergency services. This non-emergency usage places a large burden on taxpayers, who reimburse hospitals for a portion of their uncompensated emergency care costs.

While our healthcare system grapples with the challenges caused by uncompensated care, the United States Government is making the problem worse by admitting thousands of aliens who have not demonstrated any ability to pay for their healthcare costs. Notably, data show that lawful immigrants are about three times more likely than United States citizens to lack health insurance. Immigrants who enter this country should not further saddle our healthcare system, and subsequently American taxpayers, with higher costs.

The United States has a long history of welcoming immigrants who come lawfully in search of brighter futures. We must continue that tradition while also addressing the challenges facing our healthcare system, including protecting both it and the American taxpayer from the burdens of uncompensated care. Continuing to allow entry into the United States of certain immigrants who lack health insurance or the demonstrated ability to pay for their healthcare would be detrimental to these interests.

NOW, THEREFORE, I, DONALD J. TRUMP, by the authority vested in me by the Constitution and the laws of the United States of America, including sections 212(f) and 215(a) of the Immigration and Nationality Act (8 U.S.C. 1182(f) and 1185(a)) and section 301 of title 3, United States Code, hereby find that the unrestricted immigrant entry into the United States of persons described in section 1 of this proclamation would, except as provided for in section 2 of this proclamation, be detrimental to the interests of the United States, and that their entry should be subject to certain restrictions, limitations, and exceptions. I therefore hereby proclaim the following:

Section 1. *Suspension and Limitation on Entry.* (a) The entry into the United States as immigrants of aliens who will financially burden the United States healthcare system is hereby suspended and limited subject to section 2 of this proclamation. An alien will financially burden the United States healthcare system unless the alien will be covered by approved health insurance, as defined in subsection (b) of this section, within 30 days of the alien's entry into the United States, or unless the alien possesses the financial resources to pay for reasonably foreseeable medical costs.

(b) Approved health insurance means coverage under any of the following plans or programs:

(i) an employer-sponsored plan, including a retiree plan, association health plan, and coverage provided by the Consolidated Omnibus Budget Reconciliation Act of 1985;

(ii) an unsubsidized health plan offered in the individual market within a State;

(iii) a short-term limited duration health policy effective for a minimum of 364 days or until the beginning of planned, extended travel outside the United States;

(iv) a catastrophic plan;

(v) a family member's plan;

(vi) a medical plan under chapter 55 of title 10, United States Code, including coverage under the TRICARE program;

(vii) a visitor health insurance plan that provides adequate coverage for medical care for a minimum of 364 days or until the beginning of planned, extended travel outside the United States;

(viii) a medical plan under the Medicare program; or

(ix) any other health plan that provides adequate coverage for medical care as determined by the Secretary of Health and Human Services or his designee.

(c) For persons over the age of 18, approved health insurance does not include coverage under the Medicaid program.

Sec. 2. *Scope of Suspension and Limitation on Entry.* (a) Section 1 of this proclamation shall apply only to aliens seeking to enter the United States pursuant to an immigrant visa.

(b) Section 1 of this proclamation shall not apply to:

(i) any alien holding a valid immigrant visa issued before the effective date of this proclamation;

(ii) any alien seeking to enter the United States pursuant to a Special Immigrant Visa, in either the SI or SQ classification, who is also a national of Afghanistan or Iraq, or his or her spouse and children, if any;

(iii) any alien who is the child of a United States citizen or who is seeking to enter the United States pursuant to an IR–2, IR–3, IR–4, IH–3, or IH–4 visa;

(iv) any alien seeking to enter the United States pursuant to an IR–5 visa, provided that the alien or the alien's sponsor demonstrates to the satisfaction of the consular officer that the alien's healthcare will not impose a substantial burden on the United States healthcare system;

(v) any alien seeking to enter the United States pursuant to a SB–1 visa;

(vi) any alien under the age of 18, except for any alien accompanying a parent who is also immigrating to the United States and subject to this proclamation;

(vii) any alien whose entry would further important United States law enforcement objectives, as determined by the Secretary of State or his designee based on a recommendation of the Attorney General or his designee; or

(viii) any alien whose entry would be in the national interest, as determined by the Secretary of State or his designee on a case-by-case basis.

(c) Consistent with subsection (a) of this section, this proclamation does not affect the entry of aliens entering the United States through means other than immigrant visas, including lawful permanent residents. Further, nothing in this proclamation shall be construed to affect any individual's eligibility for asylum, refugee status, withholding of removal, or protection under the Convention Against Torture and Other Cruel, Inhuman or Degrading Treatment or Punishment, consistent with the laws and regulations of the United States.

Sec. 3. *Implementation and Enforcement.* (a) An alien subject to this proclamation must establish that he or she meets its requirements, to the satisfaction of a consular officer, before the adjudication and issuance of an immigrant visa. The Secretary of State may establish standards and procedures governing such determinations.

(b) The review required by subsection (a) of this section is separate and independent from the review and determination required by other statutes, regulations, or proclamations in determining the admissibility of an alien.

(c) An alien who circumvents the application of this proclamation through fraud, willful misrepresentation of a material fact, or illegal entry shall be a priority for removal by the Department of Homeland Security.

Sec. 4. *Reports on the Financial Burdens Imposed by Immigrants on the Healthcare System.* (a) The Secretary of State, in consultation with the Secretary of Health and Human Services, the Secretary of Homeland Security, and the heads of other appropriate agencies, shall submit to the President a report regarding:

(i) the continued necessity of and any adjustments that may be warranted to the suspension and limitation on entry in section 1 of this proclamation; and

(ii) other measures that may be warranted to protect the integrity of the United States healthcare system.

(b) The report required by subsection (a) of this section shall be submitted within 180 days of the effective date of this proclamation, with subsequent reports submitted annually thereafter throughout the effective duration of the suspension and limitation on entry set forth in section 1 of this proclamation. If the Secretary of State, in consultation with the heads of other appropriate executive departments and agencies, determines that circumstances no longer warrant the continued effectiveness of the suspension or limitation on entry set forth in section 1 of this proclamation or that circumstances warrant additional measures, the Secretary shall immediately so advise the President.

(c) The Secretary of State and Secretary of Health and Human Services shall coordinate any policy recommendations associated with the reports described in subsection (a) of this section.

Sec. 5. *Severability.* It is the policy of the United States to enforce this proclamation to the maximum extent possible to advance the interests of the United States. Accordingly:

(a) if any provision of this proclamation, or the application of any provision to any person or circumstance, is held to be invalid, the remainder of the proclamation and the application of its other provisions to any other persons or circumstances shall not be affected thereby; and

(b) if any provision of this proclamation, or the application of any provision to any person or circumstance, is held to be invalid because of the failure to follow certain procedures, the relevant executive branch officials shall implement those procedural requirements to conform with existing law and with any applicable court orders.

Sec. 6. *General Provisions.* (a) Nothing in this proclamation shall be construed to impair or otherwise affect:

(i) United States Government obligations under applicable international agreements;

(ii) the authority granted by law to an executive department or agency, or the head thereof; or

(iii) the functions of the Director of the Office of Management and Budget relating to budgetary, administrative, or legislative proposals.

(b) This proclamation shall be implemented consistent with applicable law and subject to the availability of appropriations.

(c) This proclamation is not intended to, and does not, create any right or benefit, substantive or procedural, enforceable at law or in equity by any party against the United States, its departments, agencies, or entities, its officers, employees, or agents, or any other person.

Sec. 7. *Effective Date*. This proclamation is effective at 12:01 a.m. eastern daylight time on November 3, 2019.

IN WITNESS WHEREOF, I have hereunto set my hand this fourth day of October, in the year of our Lord two thousand nineteen, and of the Independence of the United States of America the two hundred and forty-fourth.

Addressing Improving Enhanced Vetting Capabilities and Processes for Detecting Attempted Entry into the United States by Terrorists or Other Public-Safety Threats, Proclamation No. 9983, 85 Fed. Reg. 6,699 (Jan. 31, 2020)

A Proclamation

In Executive Order 13780 of March 6, 2017 (Protecting the Nation from Foreign Terrorist Entry Into the United States), I temporarily suspended entry of nationals of certain specified countries and ordered a worldwide review of whether the United States would need additional information from each foreign country to assess adequately whether nationals of that foreign country seeking to enter the United States pose a security or public-safety threat to the United States, and if so, what additional information was needed. The Secretary of Homeland Security, pursuant to Executive Order 13780 and in consultation with the Secretary of State and the Director of National Intelligence, developed an assessment model using three categories of criteria to assess national security and public-safety threats: whether a foreign government engages in reliable identity-management practices and shares relevant information; whether a foreign government shares national security and public-safety information; and whether a country otherwise poses a national security or public-safety risk.

Following a comprehensive worldwide review of the performance of approximately 200 countries using these criteria, the Secretary of Homeland Security presented the results of this review, focusing in particular on those countries that were deficient or at risk of becoming deficient in their performance under the assessment criteria. After a subsequent period of diplomatic engagement on these issues by the Department of State, the Acting Secretary of Homeland Security submitted a report in September 2017, which found that eight countries were hindering the ability of the United States Government to identify threats posed by foreign nationals attempting to enter the United States. The Secretary of Homeland Security then recommended that I impose travel restrictions on certain nationals of those countries. After consultation with relevant Cabinet officials and appropriate Assistants to the President, I issued Proclamation 9645 of September 24, 2017 (Enhancing Vetting Capabilities and Processes for Detecting Attempted Entry Into the United States by Terrorists or Other Public-Safety Threats).

In Proclamation 9645, I suspended and limited the entry into the United States of certain nationals of eight countries that failed to satisfy the criteria and were unable or unwilling to improve their information sharing, or that otherwise presented serious terrorism-related risks. Those travel restrictions remain in effect today, with one exception. On April 10, 2018, I issued Proclamation 9723 (Maintaining Enhanced Vetting Capabilities and Processes for Detecting Attempted Entry Into the United States by Terrorists or Other Public-Safety Threats), removing travel restrictions on nationals of the Republic of Chad. Chad had improved its identity-management and information-sharing practices by taking steps to issue more secure passports and by increasing the integrity of how its government handles lost and stolen passports. Chad also began to share information about known or suspected terrorists in a manner that makes that information available to the United States screening and vetting programs, and it created a new, standardized process for the United States to request relevant criminal information.

Pursuant to my directives in section 4 of Proclamation 9645, the Department of Homeland Security (DHS) has continued to assess every 180 days and report to me on whether the interests of the United States require the suspension of or limitation on entry of certain classes of foreign nationals. DHS has also continued to assess ways to further improve its processes for measuring how countries perform under the assessment criteria. From July 2018 through August 2019, DHS updated its methodology to assess compliance with the assessment criteria, which has allowed for more in-depth analysis and yields even more granularity and increased accuracy regarding each country's performance under the criteria.

In this updated methodology, the general overall criteria for review have not changed. The United States Government still expects all foreign governments to share needed identity-management information, to share national security and public-safety information, and to pass a security and public-safety risk assessment. Building on experience and insight gained over the last 2 years, DHS has, however, refined and modified the specific performance metrics by which it assesses compliance with the above criteria. For example, while the prior model determined whether a country shares certain needed information, the revised model accounts for how frequently the country shares that information and the extent to which that data contributes to border and immigration screening and vetting. As another example, the prior system asked whether a country issued electronic passports at all, whereas the refined metrics assess whether a country issues electronic passports for all major classes of travel documents. Similarly, the lost and stolen passports criterion previously assessed whether a country had prior instances of reporting loss or theft to the International Criminal Police Organization (INTERPOL), whereas the revised model now assesses whether the country has reported lost or stolen passports to INTERPOL within 30 days of a report of a loss or theft.

The DHS improvements to the assessment criteria also involve additional, and more customized, data from the United States Intelligence Community. DHS's original evaluation under Executive Order 13780 relied on existing intelligence products to assess the threat from each country. With the benefit of 2 years of experience, DHS has worked closely with the Intelligence Community to define intelligence requirements and customize intelligence reporting that offers a detailed characterization of the relative risk of terrorist travel to the United States from each country in the world. This additional detail improves DHS's assessment of national security and public-safety risk.

In addition, DHS greatly increased the amount of information obtained from United States Embassies abroad, which work closely with foreign governments. United States Embassies are best positioned to understand their host countries' ability and willingness to provide information to the United States, and United States Embassies' assessments contribute to a clearer understanding of how well a foreign government satisfies the assessment criteria. DHS also consolidated statistical information on operational encounters with foreign nationals. This information speaks to the frequency with which a country's nationals commit offenses while in the United States or otherwise develop grounds for inadmissibility under the Immigration and Nationality Act (INA).

Finally, as more precise, granular data became available, it became clear that many countries were only partially implementing each criterion. The 2017 process had three basic potential compliance ratings for each criterion: in compliance, out of compliance, or unknown. The updated methodology allows the United States to account for ways in which countries partially comply with the metrics associated with each criterion. As a result, for example, countries that DHS assessed in the 2017 review have now received more nuanced, partial compliance ratings. In addition, the process now weighs each criterion and risk factor based on its degree of importance to the United States Government for conducting screening and vetting of visa applicants and other travelers to the United States.

Using this enhanced review process, DHS conducted its most recent, worldwide review pursuant to Proclamation 9645 between March 2019 and September 2019. The process began on March 11, 2019, when the United States Government formally notified all foreign governments (except for Iran, Syria, and North Korea) about the refined performance metrics for the identity-management and information-sharing criteria. After collecting information from foreign governments, multilateral organizations, United States Embassies, Federal law enforcement agencies, and the Intelligence Community, multiple subject matter experts reviewed each country's data and measured its identity-management and information-sharing practices against the criteria. DHS then applied the data to an algorithm it developed to consistently assess each country's compliance with the criteria.

DHS identified the worst-performing countries for further interagency review and for an assessment of the potential impact of visa restrictions. As in the worldwide review culminating in Proclamation 9645, the Acting Secretary of Homeland Security assessed that Iraq did not meet the baseline for compliance. As part of the interagency review process, the Acting Secretary of Homeland Security determined, however, not to recommend entry restrictions and limitations for nationals of Iraq. In his report, the Acting Secretary of Homeland Security recognized a close cooperative relationship between the United States and the democratically elected government of Iraq, the strong United States diplomatic presence in Iraq, the significant presence of United States forces in Iraq, and Iraq's commitment to combating the Islamic State of Iraq and Syria (ISIS). The Acting Secretary of Homeland Security considered another similarly situated country and determined that, for reasons similar to those present in Iraq, entry restrictions and limitations would not be appropriate.

In addition, the United States Government, led by the Department of State, continued or increased engagements with many countries about those countries' deficiencies. A number of foreign governments sent senior officials to Washington, D.C., to discuss those issues, explore potential solutions, and convey views about obstacles to improving performance. As a result of this engagement, one country made sufficient improvements in its information-sharing and identity-management practices and was removed from consideration for travel restrictions.

On September 13, 2019, the Acting Secretary of Homeland Security, after consulting with the Secretary of State, the Attorney General, the Director of National Intelligence, and the heads of other appropriate agencies, submitted a fourth report to me recommending the suspension of, or limitation on, the entry of certain classes of nationals from certain countries in order to protect United States national security, including by incentivizing those foreign governments to improve their practices. The Acting Secretary of Homeland Security recommended maintaining the current restrictions on the seven countries announced in Proclamation 9645 (apart from Chad), as well as implementing suspensions and limitations on entry for certain nationals of twelve additional countries.

Since the Acting Secretary of Homeland Security issued his report on September 13, 2019, the Secretary of State, consistent with section 4(b) of Proclamation 9645, has continued to engage many foreign governments regarding the deficiencies identified in DHS's report and has continued to consult with the Acting Secretary of Homeland Security, the Secretary of Defense, and other Cabinet-level officials about how best to protect the national interest. Based on these engagements, in January 2020, those senior officials recommended that I maintain the entry restrictions adopted in Proclamation 9645 (as modified by Proclamation 9723), and that I exercise my authority under section 212(f) of the INA to suspend entry into the United States for nationals of six new countries Burma (Myanmar), Eritrea, Kyrgyzstan, Nigeria, Sudan, and Tanzania until those countries address their identified deficiencies.

The January 2020 proposal recommended visa restrictions on fewer countries than identified by the September 2019 DHS report. For example, the January 2020 proposal recommended no entry restrictions on nationals of one country that had been recommended for restrictions in the September 2019 report. This country made exceptional progress in correcting deficiencies since the September 2019 report, such that it could no longer be characterized as a country that is among those posing the highest degree of risk. In addition, the January 2020 proposal recommended that, for five poorly performing countries, foreign policy interests warranted a different approach than recommended in the September 2019 report. Specifically, the January 2020 proposal suggested that diplomatic engagement and requests for specific improvements during a defined 180-day period would be more appropriate and more likely to result in immediate improvements in these five countries. Each of these five countries provides critical counterterrorism cooperation with the United States and therefore holds strategic importance in countering malign external actors. In several of the five countries, the United States has experienced a recent deepening of diplomatic ties that generally mark increased cooperation toward achieving key regional and global United States foreign policy goals. Importantly, all five countries have credibly communicated willingness to work directly with the United States Government to correct their outstanding deficiencies, and the United States believes progress is imminent for several countries and underway for others. For these reasons, these countries will be given an opportunity to show specific improvements in their deficiencies within the next 180 days.

Consistent with recommendations contained in the January 2020 proposal, I have decided to leave unaltered the existing entry restrictions imposed by Proclamation 9645, as amended by Proclamation 9723, and to impose tailored entry restrictions and limitations on nationals from six additional countries. I have decided not to impose any nonimmigrant visa restrictions for the newly identified countries, which substantially reduces the number of people affected by the proposed restrictions. Like the seven countries that continue to face travel restrictions pursuant to Proclamation 9645, the six additional countries recommended for restrictions in the January 2020 proposal are among the worst performing in the world. However, there are prospects for near-term improvement for these six countries. Each has a functioning government and each maintains productive relations with the United States. Most of the newly identified countries have expressed a willingness to work with the United States to address their deficiencies, although it may take some time to identify and implement specific solutions to resolve the deficiencies.

Consistent with the January 2020 proposal, I have prioritized restricting immigrant visa travel over nonimmigrant visa travel because of the challenges of removing an individual in the United States who was admitted with an immigrant visa if, after admission to the United States, the individual is discovered to have terrorist connections, criminal ties, or misrepresented information. Because each of the six additional countries identified in the January 2020 proposal has deficiencies in sharing terrorist, criminal, or identity information, there is an unacceptable likelihood that information reflecting the fact that a visa applicant is a threat to national security or public safety may not be available at the time the visa or entry is approved.

For two newly identified countries that were among the highest risk countries, but performed somewhat better than others, I have decided, consistent with the January 2020 proposal, to suspend entry only of Diversity Immigrants, as described in section 203(c) of the INA, 8 U.S.C. 1153(c). Such a suspension represents a less severe limit compared to a general restriction on immigrant visas, given the significantly fewer number of aliens affected. The Acting Secretary of Homeland Security considers foreign-government-supplied information especially important for screening and vetting the Diversity Visa population in comparison to other immigrant visa applicants, and I agree with that assessment. In many cases, the United States Government may not have the same amount of information about Diversity Visa applicants compared with other categories of immigrant visa applicants because Diversity Visa applicants, with limited exceptions, do not have the burden to show certain family ties to or employment in the United States, or particular service to the United States Government, as required for other immigrant visa categories.

Consistent with the January 2020 proposal, I have decided not to impose any restrictions on certain Special Immigrant Visas for nationals of the six newly identified countries. Applicants under Special Immigrant programs generally do not need to demonstrate the same work or familial ties as other immigrant visas, but do need to show other unique qualifications. This exception is intended to cover those Special Immigrants who have advanced United States interests (and their eligible family members), such as foreign nationals who have worked for a United States Embassy for 15 years or more and are especially deserving of a visa.

As President, I must continue to act to protect the security and interests of the United States and its people. I remain committed to our ongoing efforts to engage those countries willing to cooperate, to improve information-sharing and identity-management protocols and procedures, and to address both terrorism-related and public-safety risks. And I believe that the assessment process, including enhancements made to that process, leads to new partnerships that strengthen our immigration screening and vetting capabilities. Until the countries identified in this proclamation satisfactorily address the identified deficiencies, I have determined, on the basis of a recommendation from the Acting Secretary of Homeland Security and other members of my Cabinet, to impose certain conditional restrictions and limitations on entry into the United States of nationals of the countries identified in section 1 of this proclamation, as set forth more fully below.

NOW, THEREFORE, I, DONALD J. TRUMP, President of the United States of America, by the authority vested in me by the Constitution and the laws of the United States of America, including sections 212(f) and 215(a) of the INA, 8 U.S.C. 1182(f) and 1185(a), and section 301 of title 3, United States Code, hereby find that, absent the measures set forth in this proclamation, the immigrant entry into the United States of persons described in section 1 of this proclamation would be detrimental to the interests of the United States, and that their entry should be subject to certain restrictions, limitations, and exceptions. I therefore hereby proclaim the following:

Section 1. *Suspension of Entry for Nationals of Countries of Identified Concern.* The entry into the United States of nationals of the following countries is hereby suspended and limited, as follows, subject to section 2 of this proclamation.

(a) The entry suspensions and limitations enacted by section 2 of Proclamation 9645 are not altered by this proclamation, and they remain in force by their terms, except as modified by Proclamation 9723.

(b) Burma (Myanmar)

(i) Although Burma has begun to engage with the United States on a variety of identity-management and information-sharing issues, it does not comply with the established identity-management and information-sharing criteria assessed by the performance metrics. Burma does not issue electronic passports nor does it adequately share several types of information, including public-safety and terrorism-related information that are necessary for the protection of the national security and public safety of the United States. Burma is in the process of modernizing its domestic identity-management and criminal-records systems and has worked with the United States to develop some of those systems. It has also recognized the need to make improvements. As its capabilities improve, the prospect for further bilateral cooperation will likely also increase. Despite these encouraging prospects, Burma's identified deficiencies create vulnerabilities that terrorists, criminals, and fraudulent entrants could exploit to harm United States national security and public safety.

(ii) The entry into the United States of nationals of Burma as immigrants, except as Special Immigrants whose eligibility is based on having provided assistance to the United States Government, is hereby suspended.

(c) Eritrea

(i) Eritrea does not comply with the established identity-management and information-sharing criteria assessed by the performance metrics. Eritrea does not issue electronic passports or adequately share several types of information, including public-safety and terrorism-related information, that are necessary for the protection of the national security and public safety of the United States. Further, Eritrea is currently subject to several nonimmigrant visa restrictions. Eritrea does not accept return of its nationals subject to final orders of removal from the United States, which further magnifies the challenges of removing its nationals who have entered with immigrant visas. Eritrea has engaged with the United States about its deficiencies, but it also requires significant reforms to its border security, travel-document security, and information-sharing infrastructure. Improvements in these areas will increase its opportunities to come into compliance with the United States Government's identity-management and information-sharing criteria.

(ii) The entry into the United States of nationals of Eritrea as immigrants, except as Special Immigrants whose eligibility is based on having provided assistance to the United States Government, is hereby suspended.

(d) Kyrgyzstan

(i) Kyrgyzstan does not comply with the established identity-management and information-sharing criteria assessed by the performance metrics. Kyrgyzstan does not issue electronic passports or adequately share several types of information, including public-safety and terrorism-related information, that are necessary for the protection of the national security and public safety of the United States. Kyrgyzstan also presents an elevated risk, relative to other countries in the world, of terrorist travel to the United States, though it has been responsive to United States diplomatic engagement on the need to make improvements.

(ii) The entry into the United States of nationals of Kyrgyzstan as immigrants, except as Special Immigrants whose eligibility is based on having provided assistance to the United States Government, is hereby suspended.

(e) Nigeria

(i) Nigeria does not comply with the established identity-management and information-sharing criteria assessed by the performance metrics. Nigeria does not adequately share public-safety and terrorism-related information, which is necessary for the protection of the national security and public safety of the United States. Nigeria also presents a high risk, relative to other countries in the world, of terrorist travel to the United States. Nigeria is an important strategic partner in the global fight against terrorism, and the United States continues to engage with Nigeria on these and other issues. The Department of State has provided significant assistance to Nigeria as it modernizes its border management capabilities, and the Government of Nigeria recognizes the importance of improving its information sharing with the United States. Nevertheless, these investments have not yet resulted in sufficient improvements in Nigeria's information sharing with the United States for border and immigration screening and vetting.

(ii) The entry into the United States of nationals of Nigeria as immigrants, except as Special Immigrants whose eligibility is based on having provided assistance to the United States Government, is hereby suspended.

(f) Sudan

(i) Sudan generally does not comply with our identity-management performance metrics and presents a high risk, relative to other countries in the world, of terrorist travel to the United States. Sudan is, however, transitioning to civilian rule, a process which should improve opportunities for cooperation in the future, and it has already made progress in addressing its deficiencies in several areas. For example, Sudan now issues electronic passports and has improved its coordination with INTERPOL in several respects. Sudan has also shared exemplars of its passports with the United States and now permanently invalidates lost and stolen passports and fraudulently obtained travel documents. Because Sudan performed somewhat better than the countries listed earlier in this proclamation and is making important reforms to its system of government, different travel restrictions are warranted.

(ii) The entry into the United States of nationals of Sudan as Diversity Immigrants, as described in section 203(c) of the INA, 8 U.S.C. 1153(c), is hereby suspended.

(g) Tanzania

(i) Tanzania does not comply with the established identity-management and information-sharing criteria assessed by the performance metrics. Tanzania does not adequately share several types of information, including public-safety and terrorism-related information, that is necessary for the protection of the national security and public safety of the United States. The Government of Tanzania's significant failures to adequately share information with the United States and other countries about possible Ebola cases in its territory detract from my confidence in its ability to resolve these deficiencies. Tanzania also presents an elevated risk, relative to other countries in the world, of terrorist travel to the United States. Tanzania does, however, issue electronic passports for all major passport classes, reports lost and stolen travel documents to INTERPOL at least once a month, and has provided exemplars of its current passports to the United States. Further, Tanzania does share some information with the United States, although its processes can be slow, overly bureaucratic, and complicated by limited technical capability. In light of these considerations, different travel restrictions are warranted.

(ii) The entry into the United States of nationals of Tanzania as Diversity Immigrants, as described in section 203(c) of the INA, 8 U.S.C. 1153(c), is hereby suspended.

Sec. 2. *Scope and Implementation of Suspensions and Limitations.* (a) Subject to the exceptions set forth in section 3(b) of Proclamation 9645, any waiver under section 3(c) of Proclamation 9645, and any enforcement provision of section 6(b) through (e) of Proclamation 9645, the suspensions of and limitations on entry pursuant to section 1(b) of this proclamation shall apply to foreign nationals of the designated countries who:

(i) are outside the United States on the applicable effective date of this proclamation;

(ii) do not have a valid visa on the applicable effective date of this proclamation; and

(iii) do not qualify for a visa or other valid travel document under section 6(d) of Proclamation 9645.

(b) The Secretary of State and the Secretary of Homeland Security shall coordinate to update guidance, if necessary, to implement this proclamation as to nationals of the six countries identified in section 1(b) of this proclamation, consistent with the provisions of this section.

(c) For purposes of this proclamation, the phrase "Special Immigrants whose eligibility is based on having provided assistance to the United States Government" means those aliens described in section 101(a)(27) (D) through (G) and (K) of the INA, 8 U.S.C. 1101(a)(27)(D) through (G) and (K), any alien seeking to enter the United States pursuant to a Special Immigrant Visa in the SI or SQ classification, and any spouse and children of any such individual.

Sec. 3. *Reporting Requirements.* (a) Section 4 of Proclamation 9645 is amended to read as follows:

"Sec. 4. Adjustments to Removal of Suspensions and Limitations.

"(a) The Secretary of Homeland Security, in consultation with the Secretary of State, shall on October 1, 2020, and annually thereafter, submit to the President the results of an evaluation as to whether to continue, terminate, modify, or supplement any suspensions of, or limitations on, the entry on certain classes of nationals of countries identified in section 2 of this proclamation and section 1(b) of the Proclamation "Improving Enhanced Vetting Capabilities and Processes for Detecting Attempted Entry into the United States by Terrorists or Other Public-Safety Threats," signed on January 31, 2020.

"(b) The Secretary of Homeland Security, in consultation with the Secretary of State and the Director of National Intelligence, shall not less than every 2 years evaluate whether each country in the world sufficiently shares relevant information and maintains adequate identity-management and information-sharing practices to mitigate the risk that its citizens or residents may travel to the United States in furtherance of criminal or terrorist objectives, or otherwise seek to violate any law of the United States through travel or immigration. In doing so, the Secretary of Homeland Security shall:

"(i) in consultation with the Secretary of State, Attorney General, and the Director of National Intelligence, report to the President, through the appropriate Assistants to the President, any instance in which, based on a review conducted under subsection (b) of this section, the Secretary of Homeland Security believes it is in the interests of the United States to suspend or limit the entry of certain classes of nationals of a country; and

"(ii) in consultation with the Secretary of State and the Director of National Intelligence, regularly review and update as necessary the criteria and methodology by which such evaluations are implemented to ensure they continue to protect the national interests of the United States.

"(c) Notwithstanding the requirements set forth in subsections (a) and (b) of this section, the Secretary of Homeland Security, in consultation with the Secretary of State, Attorney General, and the Director of National Intelligence, may, at any time, recommend that the President impose, modify, or terminate a suspension or limitation on entry on certain classes of foreign nationals to protect the national interests of the United States."

(b) Section 5 of Proclamation 9645 is revoked.

Sec. 4. *Effective Date.* This proclamation is effective at 12:01 a.m. eastern standard time on February 21, 2020. With respect to the application of those provisions of Proclamation 9645 that are incorporated here through section 2 for countries designated in section 1(b), and that contained their own effective dates, those dates are correspondingly updated to be January 31, 2020, or February 21, 2020, as appropriate.

Sec. 5. *Severability.* It is the policy of the United States to enforce this proclamation to the maximum extent possible to advance the national security, foreign policy, and counterterrorism interests of the United States. Accordingly:

(a) if any provision of this proclamation, or the application of any provision to any person or circumstance, is held to be invalid, the remainder of this proclamation and the application of its other provisions to any other persons or circumstances shall not be affected thereby; and

(b) if any provision of this proclamation, or the application of any provision to any person or circumstance, is held to be invalid because of the lack of certain procedural requirements, the relevant executive branch officials shall implement those procedural requirements to conform with existing law and with any applicable court orders.

Sec. 6. *General Provisions.* (a) Nothing in this proclamation shall be construed to impair or otherwise affect:

(i) United States Government obligations under applicable international agreements;

(ii) the authority granted by law to an executive department or agency, or the head thereof; or

(iii) the functions of the Director of the Office of Management and Budget relating to budgetary, administrative, or legislative proposals.

(b) This proclamation shall be implemented consistent with applicable law and subject to the availability of appropriations.

(c) This proclamation is not intended to, and does not, create any right or benefit, substantive or procedural, enforceable at law or in equity by any party against the United States, its departments, agencies, or entities, its officers, employees, or agents, or any other person.

IN WITNESS WHEREOF, I have hereunto set my hand this thirty-first day of January, in the year of our Lord two thousand twenty, and of the Independence of the United States of America the two hundred and forty-fourth.

Addressing Suspension of Entry as Immigrants and Nonimmigrants of Certain Additional Persons Who Pose a Risk of Transmitting 2019 Novel Coronavirus, Proclamation No. 9996, 85 Fed. Reg. 15,341 (Mar. 14, 2020)

A Proclamation

On January 31, 2020, I issued Proclamation 9984 (Suspension of Entry as Immigrants and Nonimmigrants of Persons Who Pose a Risk of Transmitting 2019 Novel Coronavirus and Other Appropriate Measures To Address This Risk). I found that the potential for widespread transmission of a novel (new) coronavirus (which has since been renamed "SARS-CoV-2" and causes the disease COVID-19) ("SARS-CoV-2" or "the virus") by infected individuals seeking to enter the United States threatens the security of our transportation system and infrastructure and the national security. Because the outbreak of the virus was at the time centered in the People's Republic of China, I suspended and limited the entry of all aliens who were physically present within the People's Republic of China, excluding the Special Administrative Regions of Hong Kong and Macau, during the 14-day period preceding their entry or attempted entry into the United States, subject to certain exceptions. On February 29, 2020, in recognition of the sustained person-to-person transmission of SARS-CoV-2 in the Islamic Republic of Iran, I issued Proclamation 9992 (Suspension of Entry as Immigrants and Nonimmigrants of Certain Additional Persons Who Pose a Risk of Transmitting 2019 Novel Coronavirus), suspending and limiting the entry of all aliens who were physically present within the Islamic Republic of Iran during the 14-day period preceding their entry or attempted entry into the United States, subject to certain exceptions. And, most recently, on March 11, 2020, I issued Proclamation 9993 (Suspension of Entry as Immigrants and Nonimmigrants of Certain Additional Persons Who Pose a Risk of Transmitting 2019 Novel Coronavirus), suspending and limiting the entry of all aliens who were physically present within the Schengen Area during the 14-day period preceding their entry or attempted entry into the United States, subject to certain exceptions.

The Centers for Disease Control and Prevention (CDC), a component of the Department of Health and Human Services, has determined that the virus presents a serious public health threat, and CDC continues to take steps to prevent its spread. But CDC, along with State and local health departments, has limited resources, and the public health system could be overwhelmed if sustained human-to-human transmission of the virus occurred in the United States on a large scale. Sustained human-to-human transmission has the potential to cause cascading public health, economic, national security, and societal consequences.

CDC has determined that the United Kingdom is experiencing widespread, ongoing person-to-person transmission of SARS-CoV-2. As of March 13, 2020, the World Health Organization reported that the United Kingdom had 594 cases of COVID-19, 5 times more cases than there were 7 days prior.

The Republic of Ireland has an open border with the United Kingdom in that persons can generally move freely between the Republic of Ireland and the United Kingdom by land to and from Northern Ireland and by ferry or aircraft to and from Wales, England, and Scotland. This general ability to travel freely between the United Kingdom and the Republic of Ireland poses the same challenges that the Schengen Area posed for suspending and limiting entry to the United States by travelers who had been physically present within any of the Schengen Area countries. CDC has also determined that the Republic of Ireland is experiencing ongoing sustained person-to-person transmission of SARS-CoV-2. As of March 13, 2020, the World Health Organization reported that the Republic of Ireland had 70 cases of COVID-19, 5 times more cases than there were 7 days prior.

The United States Government is unable to effectively evaluate and monitor all of the travelers continuing to arrive from the United Kingdom and the Republic of Ireland. The potential for undetected transmission of the virus by infected individuals seeking to enter the United States from the United Kingdom and the Republic of Ireland threatens the security of our transportation system and infrastructure and the national security. Given the importance of protecting persons within the United States from the threat of this harmful communicable disease, I have determined that it is in the interests of the United States to take action to restrict and suspend the entry into the United States, as immigrants or nonimmigrants, of all aliens who were physically present within the United Kingdom, excluding overseas territories outside of Europe, or the Republic of Ireland during the 14-day period preceding their entry or attempted entry into the United States. The free flow of commerce between the United States and the United Kingdom and the Republic of Ireland remains an economic priority for the United States, and I remain committed to facilitating trade between our nations.

NOW, THEREFORE, I, DONALD J. TRUMP, President of the United States, by the authority vested in me by the Constitution and the laws of the United States of America, including sections 212(f) and 215(a) of the Immigration and Nationality Act, 8 U.S.C. 1182(f) and 1185(a), and section 301 of title 3, United States Code, hereby find that the unrestricted entry into the United States of persons described in section 1 of this proclamation would, except as provided for in section 2 of this proclamation, be detrimental to the interests of the United States, and that their entry should be subject to certain restrictions, limitations, and exceptions. I therefore hereby proclaim the following:

Section 1. *Suspension and Limitation on Entry.* The entry into the United States, as immigrants or nonimmigrants, of all aliens who were physically present within the United Kingdom, excluding overseas territories outside of Europe, or the Republic of Ireland during the 14-day period preceding their entry or attempted entry into the United States is hereby suspended and limited subject to section 2 of this proclamation.

Sec. 2. *Scope of Suspension and Limitation on Entry.*

(a) Section 1 of this proclamation shall not apply to:

(i) any lawful permanent resident of the United States;

(ii) any alien who is the spouse of a U.S. citizen or lawful permanent resident;

(iii) any alien who is the parent or legal guardian of a U.S. citizen or lawful permanent resident, provided that the U.S. citizen or lawful permanent resident is unmarried and under the age of 21;

(iv) any alien who is the sibling of a U.S. citizen or lawful permanent resident, provided that both are unmarried and under the age of 21;

(v) any alien who is the child, foster child, or ward of a U.S. citizen or lawful permanent resident, or who is a prospective adoptee seeking to enter the United States pursuant to the IR–4 or IH–4 visa classifications;

(vi) any alien traveling at the invitation of the United States Government for a purpose related to containment or mitigation of the virus;

(vii) any alien traveling as a nonimmigrant pursuant to a C–1, D, or C–1/D nonimmigrant visa as a crewmember or any alien otherwise traveling to the United States as air or sea crew;

(viii) any alien

(A) seeking entry into or transiting the United States pursuant to one of the following visas: A–1, A–2, C–2, C–3 (as a foreign government official or immediate family member of an official), E–1 (as an employee of TECRO or TECO or the employee's immediate family members), G–1, G–2, G–3, G–4, NATO–1 through NATO–4, or NATO–6 (or seeking to enter as a nonimmigrant in one of those NATO categories); or

(B) whose travel falls within the scope of section 11 of the United Nations Headquarters Agreement;

(ix) any alien whose entry would not pose a significant risk of introducing, transmitting, or spreading the virus, as determined by the Secretary of Health and Human Services, through the CDC Director or his designee;

(x) any alien whose entry would further important United States law enforcement objectives, as determined by the Secretary of State, the Secretary of Homeland Security, or their respective designees, based on a recommendation of the Attorney General or his designee;

(xi) any alien whose entry would be in the national interest, as determined by the Secretary of State, the Secretary of Homeland Security, or their designees; or

(xii) members of the U.S. Armed Forces and spouses and children of members of the U.S. Armed Forces.

(b) Nothing in this proclamation shall be construed to affect any individual's eligibility for asylum, withholding of removal, or protection under the regulations issued pursuant to the legislation implementing the Convention Against Torture and Other Cruel, Inhuman or Degrading Treatment or Punishment, consistent with the laws and regulations of the United States.

Sec. 3. *Implementation and Enforcement.* (a) The Secretary of State shall implement this proclamation as it applies to visas pursuant to such procedures as the Secretary of State, in consultation with the Secretary of Homeland Security, may establish. The Secretary of Homeland Security shall implement this proclamation as it applies to the entry of aliens pursuant to such procedures as the Secretary of Homeland Security, in consultation with the Secretary of State, may establish.

(b) Consistent with applicable law, the Secretary of State, the Secretary of Transportation, and the Secretary of Homeland Security shall ensure that any alien subject to this proclamation does not board an aircraft traveling to the United States.

(c) The Secretary of Homeland Security may establish standards and procedures to ensure the application of this proclamation at and between all United States ports of entry.

(d) An alien who circumvents the application of this proclamation through fraud, willful misrepresentation of a material fact, or illegal entry shall be a priority for removal by the Department of Homeland Security.

Sec. 4. *Termination.* This proclamation shall remain in effect until terminated by the President. The Secretary of Health and Human Services shall recommend that the President continue, modify, or terminate this proclamation as described in section 5 of Proclamation 9984, as amended.

Sec. 5. *Effective Date.* This proclamation is effective at 11:59 p.m. eastern daylight time on March 16, 2020. This proclamation does not apply to persons aboard a flight scheduled to arrive in the United States that departed prior to 11:59 p.m. eastern daylight time on March 16, 2020.

Sec. 6. *Severability.* It is the policy of the United States to enforce this proclamation to the maximum extent possible to advance the national security, public safety, and foreign policy interests of the United States. Accordingly:

(a) if any provision of this proclamation, or the application of any provision to any person or circumstance, is held to be invalid, the remainder of this proclamation and the application of its provisions to any other persons or circumstances shall not be affected thereby; and

(b) if any provision of this proclamation, or the application of any provision to any person or circumstance, is held to be invalid because of the lack of certain procedural requirements, the relevant executive branch officials shall implement those procedural requirements to conform with existing law and with any applicable court orders.

Sec. 7. *General Provisions.* (a) Nothing in this proclamation shall be construed to impair or otherwise affect:

(i) the authority granted by law to an executive department or agency, or the head thereof; or

(ii) the functions of the Director of the Office of Management and Budget relating to budgetary, administrative, or legislative proposals.

(b) This proclamation shall be implemented consistent with applicable law and subject to the availability of appropriations.

(c) This proclamation is not intended to, and does not, create any right or benefit, substantive or procedural, enforceable at law or in equity by any party against the United States, its departments, agencies, or entities, its officers, employees, or agents, or any other person.

IN WITNESS WHEREOF, I have hereunto set my hand this fourteenth day of March, in the year of our Lord two thousand twenty, and of the Independence of the United States of America the two hundred and forty-fourth.

Addressing Suspension of Entry of Immigrants Who Present a Risk to the United States Labor Market During the Economic Recovery Following the 2019 Novel Coronavirus Outbreak, Proclamation No. 10014, 85 Fed. Reg. 23441 (Apr. 22, 2020)

A Proclamation

The 2019 Novel Coronavirus (COVID-19) has significantly disrupted the livelihoods of Americans. In Proclamation 9994 of March 13, 2020 (Declaring a National Emergency Concerning the Novel Coronavirus Disease (COVID-19) Outbreak), I declared that the COVID-19 outbreak in the United States constituted a national emergency, beginning March 1, 2020. Since then, the American people have united behind a policy of mitigation strategies, including social distancing, to flatten the curve of infections and reduce the spread of SARS-CoV-2, the virus that causes COVID-19. This needed behavioral shift has taken a toll on the United States economy, with national unemployment claims reaching historic levels. In the days between the national emergency declaration and April 11, 2020, more than 22 million Americans have filed for unemployment.

In the administration of our Nation's immigration system, we must be mindful of the impact of foreign workers on the United States labor market, particularly in an environment of high domestic unemployment and depressed demand for labor. We must also conserve critical State Department resources so that consular officers may continue to provide services to United States citizens abroad. Even with their ranks diminished by staffing disruptions caused by the pandemic, consular officers continue to provide assistance to United States citizens, including through the ongoing evacuation of many Americans stranded overseas.

I have determined that, without intervention, the United States faces a potentially protracted economic recovery with persistently high unemployment if labor supply outpaces labor demand. Excess labor supply affects all workers and potential workers, but it is particularly harmful to workers at the margin between employment and unemployment, who are typically "last in" during an economic expansion and "first out" during an economic contraction. In recent years, these workers have been disproportionately represented by historically disadvantaged groups, including African Americans and other minorities, those without a college degree, and the disabled. These are the workers who, at the margin between employment and unemployment, are likely to bear the burden of excess labor supply disproportionately.

Furthermore, lawful permanent residents, once admitted, are granted "open-market" employment authorization documents, allowing them immediate eligibility to compete for almost any job, in any sector of the economy. There is no way to protect already disadvantaged and unemployed

Americans from the threat of competition for scarce jobs from new lawful permanent residents by directing those new residents to particular economic sectors with a demonstrated need not met by the existing labor supply. Existing immigrant visa processing protections are inadequate for recovery from the COVID-19 outbreak. The vast majority of immigrant visa categories do not require employers to account for displacement of United States workers. While some employment-based visas contain a labor certification requirement, because visa issuance happens substantially after the certification is completed, the labor certification process cannot adequately capture the status of the labor market today. Moreover, introducing additional permanent residents when our healthcare resources are limited puts strain on the finite limits of our healthcare system at a time when we need to prioritize Americans and the existing immigrant population. In light of the above, I have determined that the entry, during the next 60 days, of certain aliens as immigrants would be detrimental to the interests of the United States.

NOW, THEREFORE, I, DONALD J. TRUMP, President of the United States, by the authority vested in me by the Constitution and the laws of the United States of America, including sections 212(f) and 215(a) of the Immigration and Nationality Act, 8 U.S.C. 1182(f) and 1185(a), and section 301 of title 3, United States Code, hereby find that the entry into the United States of persons described in section 1 of this proclamation would, except as provided for in section 2 of this proclamation, be detrimental to the interests of the United States, and that their entry should be subject to certain restrictions, limitations, and exceptions. I therefore hereby proclaim the following:

Section 1. *Suspension and Limitation on Entry*. The entry into the United States of aliens as immigrants is hereby suspended and limited subject to section 2 of this proclamation.

Sec. 2. *Scope of Suspension and Limitation on Entry*. (a) The suspension and limitation on entry pursuant to section 1 of this proclamation shall apply only to aliens who:

(i) are outside the United States on the effective date of this proclamation;

(ii) do not have an immigrant visa that is valid on the effective date of this proclamation; and

(iii) do not have an official travel document other than a visa (such as a transportation letter, an appropriate boarding foil, or an advance parole document) that is valid on the effective date of this proclamation or issued on any date thereafter that permits him or her to travel to the United States and seek entry or admission.

(b) The suspension and limitation on entry pursuant to section 1 of this proclamation shall not apply to:

(i) any lawful permanent resident of the United States;

(ii) any alien seeking to enter the United States on an immigrant visa as a physician, nurse, or other healthcare professional; to perform medical research or other research intended to combat the spread of COVID-19; or to perform work essential to combating, recovering from, or otherwise alleviating the effects of the COVID-19 outbreak, as determined by the Secretary of State, the Secretary of Homeland Security, or their respective designees; and any spouse and unmarried children under 21 years old of any such alien who are accompanying or following to join the alien;

(iii) any alien applying for a visa to enter the United States pursuant to the EB–5 Immigrant Investor Program;

(iv) any alien who is the spouse of a United States citizen;

(v) any alien who is under 21 years old and is the child of a United States citizen, or who is a prospective adoptee seeking to enter the United States pursuant to the IR–4 or IH–4 visa classifications;

(vi) any alien whose entry would further important United States law enforcement objectives, as determined by the Secretary of State, the Secretary of Homeland Security, or their respective designees, based on a recommendation of the Attorney General or his designee;

(vii) any member of the United States Armed Forces and any spouse and children of a member of the United States Armed Forces;

(viii) any alien seeking to enter the United States pursuant to a Special Immigrant Visa in the SI or SQ classification, subject to such conditions as the Secretary of State may impose, and any spouse and children of any such individual; or

(ix) any alien whose entry would be in the national interest, as determined by the Secretary of State, the Secretary of Homeland Security, or their respective designees.

Sec. 3. *Implementation and Enforcement.* (a) The consular officer shall determine, in his or her discretion, whether an immigrant has established his or her eligibility for an exception in section 2(b) of this proclamation. The Secretary of State shall implement this proclamation as it applies to visas pursuant to such procedures as the Secretary of State, in consultation with the Secretary of Homeland Security, may establish in the Secretary of State's discretion. The Secretary of Homeland Security shall implement this proclamation as it applies to the entry of aliens pursuant to such procedures as the Secretary of Homeland Security, in consultation with the Secretary of State, may establish in the Secretary of Homeland Security's discretion.

(b) An alien who circumvents the application of this proclamation through fraud, willful misrepresentation of a material fact, or illegal entry shall be a priority for removal by the Department of Homeland Security.

(c) Nothing in this proclamation shall be construed to limit the ability of an individual to seek asylum, refugee status, withholding of removal, or protection under the Convention Against Torture and Other Cruel, Inhuman or Degrading Treatment or Punishment, consistent with the laws of the United States.

Sec. 4. *Termination.* This proclamation shall expire 60 days from its effective date and may be continued as necessary. Whenever appropriate, but no later than 50 days from the effective date of this proclamation, the Secretary of Homeland Security shall, in consultation with the Secretary of State and the Secretary of Labor, recommend whether I should continue or modify this proclamation.

Sec. 5. *Effective Date.* This proclamation is effective at 11:59 p.m. eastern daylight time on April 23, 2020.

Sec. 6. *Additional Measures.* Within 30 days of the effective date of this proclamation, the Secretary of Labor and the Secretary of Homeland Security, in consultation with the Secretary of State, shall review nonimmigrant programs and shall recommend to me other measures appropriate to stimulate the United States economy and ensure the prioritization, hiring, and employment of United States workers.

Sec. 7. *Severability.* It is the policy of the United States to enforce this proclamation to the maximum extent possible to advance the interests of the United States. Accordingly:

(a) if any provision of this proclamation, or the application of any provision to any person or circumstance, is held to be invalid, the remainder of this proclamation and the application of its provisions to any other persons or circumstances shall not be affected thereby; and

(b) if any provision of this proclamation, or the application of any provision to any person or circumstance, is held to be invalid because of the lack of certain procedural requirements, the relevant executive branch officials shall implement those procedural requirements to conform with existing law and with any applicable court orders.

Sec. 8. *General Provisions.* (a) Nothing in this proclamation shall be construed to impair or otherwise affect:

(i) the authority granted by law to an executive department or agency, or the head thereof; or,

(ii) the functions of the Director of the Office of Management and Budget relating to budgetary, administrative, or legislative proposals.

(b) This proclamation shall be implemented consistent with applicable law and subject to the availability of appropriations.

(c) This proclamation is not intended to, and does not, create any right or benefit, substantive or procedural, enforceable at law or in equity by any party against the United States, its departments, agencies, or entities, its officers, employees, or agents, or any other person.

IN WITNESS WHEREOF, I have hereunto set my hand this twenty-second day of April, in the year of our Lord two thousand twenty, and of the Independence of the United States of America the two hundred and forty-fourth.

V. TREATIES AND RELATED MATERIALS

CONVENTION RELATING TO THE STATUS OF REFUGEES

Done at Geneva, July 28, 1951

Entry into force, April 22, 1954

189 U.N.T.S. 137

PREAMBLE

THE HIGH CONTRACTING PARTIES

Considering that the Charter of the United Nations and the Universal Declaration of Human Rights approved on 10 December 1948 by the General Assembly have affirmed the principle that human beings shall enjoy fundamental rights and freedoms without discrimination,

Considering that the United Nations has, on various occasions, manifested its profound concern for refugees and endeavoured to assure refugees the widest possible exercise of these fundamental rights and freedoms,

Considering that it is desirable to revise and consolidate previous international agreements relating to the status of refugees and to extend the scope of and the protection accorded by such instruments by means of a new agreement,

Considering that the grant of asylum may place unduly heavy burdens on certain countries, and that a satisfactory solution of a problem of which the United Nations has recognized the international scope and nature cannot therefore be achieved without international co-operation,

Expressing the wish that all States, recognizing the social and humanitarian nature of the problem of refugees, will do everything within their power to prevent this problem from becoming a cause of tension between States,

Noting that the United Nations High Commissioner for Refugees is charged with the task of supervising international conventions providing for the protection of Refugees, and recognizing that the effective co-ordination of measures taken to deal with this problem will depend upon the co-operation of States with the High Commissioner,

Have agreed as follows:

CHAPTER I. GENERAL PROVISIONS

Article 1. Definition of the term "Refugee"

A. For the purposes of the present Convention, the term "refugee" shall apply to any person who:

(1) Has been considered a refugee under the Arrangements of 12 May 1926 and 30 June 1928 or under the Conventions of 28 October 1933 and 10 February 1938, the Protocol of 14 September 1939 or the Constitution of the International Refugee Organization;

Decisions of non-eligibility taken by the International Refugee Organization during the period of its activities shall not prevent the status of refugee being accorded to persons who fulfil the conditions of paragraph 2 of this section;

(2) As a result of events occurring before 1 January 1951 and owing to well-founded fear of being persecuted for reasons of race, religion, nationality, membership of a particular social group or political opinion, is outside the country of his nationality and is unable or, owing to such fear, is unwilling to avail himself of the protection of that country; or who, not having a nationality and being outside the country of his former habitual residence as a result of such events, is unable or, owing to such fear, is unwilling to return to it.

In the case of a person who has more than one nationality, the term "the country of his nationality" shall mean each of the countries of which he is a national, and a person shall not be deemed to be lacking the protection of the country of his nationality if, without any valid reason based on well-founded fear, he has not availed himself of the protection of one of the countries of which he is a national.

B. **(1)** For the purposes of this Convention, the words "events occurring before 1 January 1951" in Article 1, Section A, shall be understood to mean either:

(a) "events occurring in Europe before 1 January 1951" or

(b) "events occurring in Europe or elsewhere before 1 January 1951"

and each Contracting State shall make a declaration at the time of signature, ratification or accession, specifying which of these meanings it applies for the purpose of its obligations under this Convention.

(2) Any Contracting State which has adopted alternative *(a)* may at any time extend its obligations by adopting alternative *(b)* by means of a notification addressed to the Secretary-General of the United Nations.

C. This Convention shall cease to apply to any person falling under the terms of Section A if:

(1) He has voluntarily re-availed himself of the protection of the country of his nationality; or

(2) Having lost his nationality, he has voluntarily re-acquired it; or

(3) He has acquired a new nationality, and enjoys the protection of the country of his new nationality; or

(4) He has voluntarily re-established himself in the country which he left or outside which he remained owing to fear of persecution; or

(5) He can no longer, because the circumstances in connexion with which he has been recognized as a refugee have ceased to exist, continue to refuse to avail himself of the protection of the country of his nationality;

Provided that this paragraph shall not apply to a refugee falling under section A(1) of this Article who is able to invoke compelling reasons arising out of previous persecution for refusing to avail himself of the protection of the country of nationality;

(6) Being a person who has no nationality he is, because the circumstances in connexion with which he has been recognized as a refugee have ceased to exist, able to return to the country of his former habitual residence;

Provided that this paragraph shall not apply to a refugee falling under section A(1) of this Article who is able to invoke compelling reasons arising out of previous persecution for refusing to return to the country of his former habitual residence.

D. This Convention shall not apply to persons who are at present receiving from organs or agencies of the United Nations other than the United Nations High Commissioner for Refugees protection or assistance.

When such protection or assistance has ceased for any reason, without the position of such persons being definitively settled in accordance with the relevant resolutions adopted by the General Assembly of the United Nations, these persons shall *ipso facto* be entitled to the benefits of this Convention.

E. This Convention shall not apply to a person who is recognized by the competent authorities of the country in which he has taken residence as having the rights and obligations which are attached to the possession of the nationality of that country.

F. The provisions of this Convention shall not apply to any person with respect to whom there are serious reasons for considering that:

(a) he has committed a crime against peace, a war crime, or a crime against humanity, as defined in the international instruments drawn up to make provision in respect of such crimes;

(b) he has committed a serious non-political crime outside the country of refuge prior to his admission to that country as a refugee;

(c) he has been guilty of acts contrary to the purposes and principles of the United Nations.

Article 2. General obligations

Every refugee has duties to the country in which he finds himself, which require in particular that he conform to its laws and regulations as well as to measures taken for the maintenance of public order.

Article 3. Non-discrimination

The Contracting States shall apply the provisions of this Convention to refugees without discrimination as to race, religion or country of origin.

Article 4. Religion

The Contracting States shall accord to refugees within their territories treatment at least as favourable as that accorded to their nationals with respect to freedom to practise their religion and freedom as regards the religious education of their children.

Article 5. Rights granted apart from this Convention

Nothing in this Convention shall be deemed to impair any rights and benefits granted by a Contracting State to refugees apart from this Convention.

Article 6. The term "in the same circumstances"

For the purpose of this Convention, the term "in the same circumstances" implies that any requirements (including requirements as to length and conditions of sojourn or residence) which the particular individual would have to fulfil for the enjoyment of the right in question, if he were not a refugee, must be fulfilled by him, with the exception of requirements which by their nature a refugee is incapable of fulfilling.

Article 7. Exemption from reciprocity

1. Except where this Convention contains more favourable provisions, a Contracting State shall accord to refugees the same treatment as is accorded to aliens generally.

2. After a period of three years' residence, all refugees shall enjoy exemption from legislative reciprocity in the territory of the Contracting States.

3. Each Contracting State shall continue to accord to refugees the rights and benefits to which they were already entitled, in the absence of reciprocity, at the date of entry into force of this Convention for that State.

4. The Contracting States shall consider favourably the possibility of according to refugees, in the absence of reciprocity, rights and benefits beyond those to which they are entitled according to paragraphs 2 and 3, and to extending exemption from reciprocity to refugees who do not fulfil the conditions provided for in paragraphs 2 and 3.

5. The provisions of paragraphs 2 and 3 apply both to the rights and benefits referred to in articles 13, 18, 19, 21 and 22 of this Convention and to rights and benefits for which this Convention does not provide.

Article 8. Exemption from exceptional measures

With regard to exceptional measures which may be taken against the person, property or interests of nationals of a foreign State, the Contracting States shall not apply such measures to a refugee who is formally a national of the said State solely on account of such nationality. Contracting States which, under their legislation, are prevented from applying the general principle expressed in this article, shall, in appropriate cases, grant exemptions in favour of such refugees.

Article 9. Provisional measures

Nothing in this Convention shall prevent a Contracting State, in time of war or other grave and exceptional circumstances, from taking provisionally measures which it considers to be essential to the national security in the case of a particular person, pending a determination by the Contracting State that that person is in fact a refugee and that the continuance of such measures is necessary in his case in the interests of national security.

Article 10. Continuity of residence

1. Where a refugee has been forcibly displaced during the Second World War and removed to the territory of a Contracting State, and is resident there, the period of such enforced sojourn shall be considered to have been lawful residence within that territory.

2. Where a refugee has been forcibly displaced during the Second World War from the territory of a Contracting State and has, prior to the date of entry into force of this Convention, returned there for the purpose of taking up residence, the period of residence before and after such enforced displacement shall be regarded as one uninterrupted period for any purposes for which uninterrupted residence is required.

Article 11. Refugee seamen

In the case of refugees regularly serving as crew members on board a ship flying the flag of a Contracting State, that State shall give sympathetic consideration to their establishment on its territory and the issue of travel documents to them on their temporary admission to its territory particularly with a view to facilitating their establishment in another country.

CHAPTER II. JURIDICAL STATUS

Article 12. Personal status

1. The personal status of a refugee shall be governed by the law of the country of his domicile or, if he has no domicile, by the law of the country of his residence.

2. Rights previously acquired by a refugee and dependent on personal status, more particularly rights attaching to marriage, shall be respected by a Contracting State, subject to compliance, if this be necessary, with the formalities required by the law of that State, provided that the right in question is one which would have been recognized by the law of that State had he not become a refugee.

Article 13. Movable and immovable property

The Contracting States shall accord to a refugee treatment as favourable as possible and, in any event, not less favourable than that accorded to aliens generally in the same circumstances as regards the acquisition of movable and immovable property and other rights pertaining thereto, and to leases and other contracts relating to movable and immovable property.

Article 14. Artistic rights and industrial property

In respect of the protection of industrial property, such as inventions, designs or models, trade marks, trade names, and of rights in literary, artistic and scientific works, a refugee shall be accorded in the country in which he has his habitual residence the same protection as is accorded to nationals of that country. In the territory of any other Contracting State, he shall be accorded the same protection as is accorded in that territory to nationals of the country in which he has habitual residence.

Article 15. Right of association

As regards non-political and non-profit-making associations and trade unions the Contracting States shall accord to refugees lawfully staying in their territory the most favourable treatment accorded to nationals of a foreign country, in the same circumstances.

Article 16. Access to courts

1. A refugee shall have free access to the courts of law on the territory of all Contracting States.

2. A refugee shall enjoy in the Contracting State in which he has his habitual residence the same treatment as a national in matters pertaining to access to the Courts, including legal assistance and exemption from *cautio judicatum solvi*.

3. A refugee shall be accorded in the matters referred to in paragraph 2 in countries other than that in which he has his habitual residence the treatment granted to a national of the country of his habitual residence.

CHAPTER III. GAINFUL EMPLOYMENT

Article 17. Wage-earning employment

1. The Contracting State shall accord to refugees lawfully staying in their territory the most favourable treatment accorded to nationals of a foreign country in the same circumstances, as regards the right to engage in wage-earning employment.

2. In any case, restrictive measures imposed on aliens or the employment of aliens for the protection of the national labour market shall not be applied to a refugee who was already exempt from them at the date of entry into force of this Convention for the Contracting States concerned, or who fulfils one of the following conditions:

(a) He has completed three years' residence in the country;

(b) He has a spouse possessing the nationality of the country of residence. A refugee may not invoke the benefits of this provision if he has abandoned his spouse;

(c) He has one or more children possessing the nationality of the country of residence.

3. The Contracting States shall give sympathetic consideration to assimilating the rights of all refugees with regard to wage-earning employment to those of nationals, and in particular of those refugees who have entered their territory pursuant to programmes of labour recruitment or under immigration schemes.

Article 18. Self-employment

The Contracting States shall accord to a refugee lawfully in their territory treatment as favourable as possible and, in any event, not less favourable than that accorded to aliens generally in the same circumstances, as regards the right to engage on his own account in agriculture, industry, handicrafts and commerce and to establish commercial and industrial companies.

Article 19. Liberal professions

1. Each Contracting State shall accord to refugees lawfully staying in their territory who hold diplomas recognized by the competent authorities of that State, and who are desirous of practising a liberal profession, treatment as favourable as possible and, in any event, not less favourable than that accorded to aliens generally in the same circumstances.

2. The Contracting States shall use their best endeavours consistently with their laws and constitutions to secure the settlement of such refugees in the territories, other than the metropolitan territory, for whose international relations they are responsible.

CHAPTER IV. WELFARE

Article 20. Rationing

Where a rationing system exists, which applies to the population at large and regulates the general distribution of products in short supply, refugees shall be accorded the same treatment as nationals.

Article 21. Housing

As regards housing, the Contracting States, in so far as the matter is regulated by laws or regulations or is subject to the control of public authorities, shall accord to refugees lawfully staying in their territory treatment as favourable as possible and, in any event, not less favourable than that accorded to aliens generally in the same circumstances.

Article 22. Public education

1. The Contracting States shall accord to refugees the same treatment as is accorded to nationals with respect to elementary education.

2. The Contracting States shall accord to refugees treatment as favourable as possible, and, in any event, not less favourable than that accorded to aliens generally in the same circumstances, with respect to education other than elementary education and, in particular, as regards access to studies, the recognition of foreign school certificates, diplomas and degrees, the remission of fees and charges and the award of scholarships.

Article 23. Public relief

The Contracting States shall accord to refugees lawfully staying in their territory the same treatment with respect to public relief and assistance as is accorded to their nationals.

Article 24. Labour legislation and social security

1. The Contracting States shall accord to refugees lawfully staying in their territory the same treatment as is accorded to nationals in respect of the following matters:

(a) In so far as such matters are governed by laws or regulations or are subject to the control of administrative authorities: remuneration, including family allowances where these form part of remuneration, hours of work, overtime arrangements, holidays with pay, restrictions on home work, minimum age of employment, apprenticeship and training, women's work and the work of young persons, and the enjoyment of the benefits of collective bargaining;

(b) Social security (legal provisions in respect of employment injury, occupational diseases, maternity, sickness, disability, old age, death, unemployment, family responsibilities and any other contingency which, according to national laws or regulations, is covered by a social security scheme), subject to the following limitations:

(i) There may be appropriate arrangements for the maintenance of acquired rights and rights in course of acquisition;

(ii) National laws or regulations of the country of residence may prescribe special arrangements concerning benefits or portions of benefits which are payable wholly out of public funds, and concerning allowances paid to persons who do not fulfil the contribution conditions prescribed for the award of a normal pension.

2. The right to compensation for the death of a refugee resulting from employment injury or from occupational disease shall not be affected by the fact that the residence of the beneficiary is outside the territory of the Contracting State.

3. The Contracting States shall extend to refugees the benefits of agreements concluded between them, or which may be concluded between them in the future, concerning the maintenance of acquired rights and rights in the process of acquisition in regard to social security, subject only to the conditions which apply to nationals of the States signatory to the agreements in question.

4. The Contracting States will give sympathetic consideration to extending to refugees so far as possible the benefits of similar agreements which may at any time be in force between such Contracting States and non-contracting States.

CHAPTER V. ADMINISTRATIVE MEASURES

Article 25. Administrative assistance

1. When the exercise of a right by a refugee would normally require the assistance of authorities of a foreign country to whom he cannot have recourse, the Contracting States in whose territory he is residing shall arrange that such assistance be afforded to him by their own authorities or by an international authority.

2. The authority or authorities mentioned in paragraph 1 shall deliver or cause to be delivered under their supervision to refugees such documents or certifications as would normally be delivered to aliens by or through their national authorities.

3. Documents or certifications so delivered shall stand in the stead of the official instruments delivered to aliens by or through their national authorities, and shall be given credence in the absence of proof to the contrary.

4. Subject to such exceptional treatment as may be granted to indigent persons, fees may be charged for the services mentioned herein, but such fees shall be moderate and commensurate with those charged to nationals for similar services.

5. The provisions of this article shall be without prejudice to articles 27 and 28.

Article 26. Freedom of movement

Each Contracting State shall accord to refugees lawfully in its territory the right to choose their place of residence and to move freely within its territory, subject to any regulations applicable to aliens generally in the same circumstances.

Article 27. Identity papers

The Contracting States shall issue identity papers to any refugee in their territory who does not possess a valid travel document.

Article 28. Travel documents

1. The Contracting States shall issue to refugees lawfully staying in their territory travel documents for the purpose of travel outside their territory unless compelling reasons of national security or public order otherwise require, and the provisions of the Schedule to this Convention shall apply with respect to such documents. The Contracting States may issue such a travel document to any other refugee in their territory; they shall in particular give sympathetic consideration to the issue of such a travel document to refugees in their territory who are unable to obtain a travel document from the country of their lawful residence.

2. Travel documents issued to refugees under previous international agreements by parties thereto shall be recognized and treated by the Contracting States in the same way as if they had been issued pursuant to this article.

Article 29. Fiscal charges

1. The Contracting States shall not impose upon refugees duties, charges or taxes, of any description whatsoever, other or higher than those which are or may be levied on their nationals in similar situations.

2. Nothing in the above paragraph shall prevent the application to refugees of the laws and regulations concerning charges in respect of the issue to aliens of administrative documents including identity papers.

Article 30. Transfer of assets

1. A Contracting State shall, in conformity with its laws and regulations permit refugees to transfer assets which they have brought into its territory, to another country where they have been admitted for the purposes of resettlement.

2. A Contracting State shall give sympathetic consideration to the application of refugees for permission to transfer assets wherever they may be and which are necessary for their resettlement in another country to which they have been admitted.

Article 31. Refugees unlawfully in the country of refuge

1. The Contracting States shall not impose penalties, on account of their illegal entry or presence, on refugees who, coming directly from a

territory where their life or freedom was threatened in the sense of Article 1, enter or are present in their territory without authorization, provided they present themselves without delay to the authorities and show good cause for their illegal entry or presence.

2. The Contracting States shall not apply to the movements of such refugees restrictions other than those which are necessary and such restrictions shall only be applied until their status in the country is regularized or they obtain admission into another country. The Contracting States shall allow such refugees a reasonable period and all the necessary facilities to obtain admission into another country.

Article 32. Expulsion

1. The Contracting States shall not expel a refugee lawfully in their territory save on grounds of national security or public order.

2. The expulsion of such a refugee shall be only in pursuance of a decision reached in accordance with due process of law. Except where compelling reasons of national security otherwise require, the refugee shall be allowed to submit evidence to clear himself, and to appeal to and be represented for the purpose before competent authority or a person or persons specially designated by the competent authority.

3. The Contracting States shall allow such a refugee a reasonable period within which to seek legal admission into another country. The Contracting States reserve the right to apply during that period such internal measures as they may deem necessary.

Article 33. Prohibition of expulsion or return ("refoulement")

1. No Contracting State shall expel or return (*"refouler"*) a refugee in any manner whatsoever to the frontiers of territories where his life or freedom would be threatened on account of his race, religion, nationality, membership of a particular social group or political opinion.

2. The benefit of the present provision may not, however, be claimed by a refugee whom there are reasonable grounds for regarding as a danger to the security of the country in which he is, or who, having been convicted by a final judgement of a particularly serious crime, constitutes a danger to the community of that country.

Article 34. Naturalization

The Contracting States shall as far as possible facilitate the assimilation and naturalization of refugees. They shall in particular make every effort to expedite naturalization proceedings and to reduce as far as possible the charges and costs of such proceedings.

CHAPTER VI. EXECUTORY AND TRANSITORY PROVISIONS

Article 35. Co-operation of the national authorities with the United Nations

1. The Contracting States undertake to co-operate with the Office of the United Nations High Commissioner for Refugees, or any other agency of the United Nations which may succeed it, in the exercise of its functions, and shall in particular facilitate its duty of supervising the application of the provisions of this Convention.

2. In order to enable the Office of the High Commissioner or any other agency of the United Nations which may succeed it, to make reports to the competent organs of the United Nations, the Contracting States undertake to provide them in the appropriate form with information and and statistical data requested concerning:

(a) the condition of refugees,

(b) the implementation of this Convention, and

(c) laws, regulations and decrees which are, or may hereafter be, in force relating to refugees.

Article 36. Information on national legislation

The Contracting States shall communicate to the Secretary-General of the United Nations the laws and regulations which they may adopt to ensure the application of this Convention.

Article 37. Relation to previous conventions

Without prejudice to article 28, paragraph 2, of this Convention, this Convention replaces, as between parties to it, the Arrangements of 5 July 1922, 31 May 1924, 12 May 1926, 30 June 1928 and 30 July 1935, the Conventions of 28 October 1933 and 10 February 1938, the Protocol of 14 September 1939 and the Agreement of 15 October 1946.

CHAPTER VII. FINAL CLAUSES

Article 38. Settlement of disputes

Any dispute between parties to this Convention relating to its interpretation or application, which cannot be settled by other means, shall be referred to the International Court of Justice at the request of any one of the parties to the dispute.

Article 39. Signature, ratification and accession

1. This Convention shall be opened for signature at Geneva on 28 July 1951 and shall thereafter be deposited with the Secretary-General of the United Nations. It shall be open for signature at the European Office of the United Nations from 28 July to 31 August 1951 and shall be reopened for signature at the Headquarters of the United Nations from 17 September 1951 to 31 December 1952.

2. This Convention shall be open for signature on behalf of all States Members of the United Nations, and also on behalf of any other State invited to attend the Conference of Plenipotentiaries on the Status of Refugees and Stateless Persons or to which an invitation to sign will have been addressed by the General Assembly. It shall be ratified and the instruments of ratification shall be deposited with the Secretary-General of the United Nations.

3. This Convention shall be open from 28 July 1951 for accession by the States referred to in paragraph 2 of this Article. Accession shall be effected by the deposit of an instrument of accession with the Secretary-General of the United Nations.

Article 40. Territorial application clause

1. Any State may, at the time of signature, ratification or accession, declare that this Convention shall extend to all or any of the territories for the international relations of which it is responsible. Such a declaration shall take effect when the Convention enters into force for the States concerned.

2. At any time thereafter any such extension shall be made by notification addressed to the Secretary-General of the United Nations and shall take effect as from the ninetieth day after the day of receipt by the Secretary-General of the United Nations of this notification, or as from the date of entry into force of the Convention for the State concerned, whichever is the later.

3. With respect to those territories to which this Convention is not extended at the time of signature, ratification or accession, each State concerned shall consider the possibility of taking the necessary steps in order to extend the application of this Convention to such territories, subject where necessary for constitutional reasons, to the consent of the governments of such territories.

Article 41. Federal clause

In the case of a Federal or non-unitary State, the following provisions shall apply:

(a) With respect to those articles of this Convention that come within the legislative jurisdiction of the federal legislative authority, the obligations of the Federal Government shall to this extent be the same as those of Parties which are not Federal States,

(b) With respect to those articles of this Convention that come within the legislative jurisdiction of constituent States, provinces or cantons which are not, under the constitutional system of the federation, bound to take legislative action, the Federal Government shall bring

such articles with a favourable recommendation, to the notice of the appropriate authorities of States, provinces or cantons at the earliest possible moment.

(c) A Federal State Party to this Convention shall, at the request of any other Contracting State transmitted through the Secretary-General of the United Nations, supply a statement of the law and practice of the Federation and its constituent units in regard to any particular provision of the Convention showing the extent to which effect has been given to that provision by legislative or other action.

Article 42. Reservations

1. At the time of signature, ratification or accession, any State may make reservations to articles of the Convention other than to articles 1, 3, 4, 16(1), 33, 36 to 46 inclusive.

2. Any State making a reservation in accordance with paragraph 1 of this article may at any time withdraw the reservation by a communication to that effect addressed to the Secretary-General of the United Nations.

Article 43. Entry into force

1. This Convention shall come into force on the ninetieth day following the day of deposit of the sixth instrument of ratification or accession.

2. For each State ratifying or acceding to the Convention after the deposit of the sixth instrument of ratification or accession, the Convention shall enter into force on the ninetieth day following the day of deposit by such State of its instrument of ratification or accession.

Article 44. Denunciation

1. Any Contracting State may denounce this Convention at any time by a notification addressed to the Secretary-General of the United Nations.

2. Such denunciation shall take effect for the Contracting State concerned one year from the date upon which it is received by the Secretary-General of the United Nations.

3. Any State which has made a declaration or notification under article 40 may, at any time thereafter, by a notification to the Secretary-General of the United Nations, declare that the Convention shall cease to extend to such territory one year after the date of receipt of the notification by the Secretary-General.

Article 45. Revision

1. Any Contracting State may request revision of this Convention at any time by a notification addressed to the Secretary-General of the United Nations.

2. The General Assembly of the United Nations shall recommend the steps, if any, to be taken in respect of such request.

Article 46. Notifications by the Secretary-General of the United Nations

The Secretary-General of the United Nations shall inform all Members of the United Nations and non-member States referred to in article 39:

(a) of declarations and notifications in accordance with Section B of Article 1;

(b) of signatures, ratifications and accessions in accordance with article 39;

(c) of declarations and notifications in accordance with article 40;

(d) of reservations and withdrawals in accordance with article 42;

(e) of the date on which this Convention will come into force in accordance with article 43;

(f) of denunciations and notifications in accordance with article 44;

(g) of requests for revision in accordance with article 45.

In faith whereof the undersigned, duly authorized, have signed this Convention on behalf of their respective Governments,

Done at Geneva, this twenty-eighth day of July, one thousand nine hundred and fifty-one, in a single copy, of which the English and French texts are equally authentic and which shall remain deposited in the archives of the United Nations, and certified true copies of which shall be delivered to all Members of the United Nations and to the non-member States referred to in article 39.

Schedule

Paragraph 1

1. The travel document referred to in Article 28 of this Convention shall be similar to the specimen annexed hereto.

2. The document shall be made out in at least two languages, one of which shall be English or French.

Paragraph 2

Subject to the regulations obtaining in the country of issue, children may be included in the travel document of a parent or, in exceptional circumstances, of another adult refugee.

Paragraph 3

The fees charged for issue of the document shall not exceed the lowest scale of charges for national passports.

Paragraph 4

Save in special or exceptional cases, the document shall be made valid for the largest possible number of countries.

Paragraph 5

The document shall have a validity of either one or two years, at the discretion of the issuing authority.

Paragraph 6

1. The renewal or extension of the validity of the document is a matter for the authority which issued it, so long as the holder has not established lawful residence in another territory and resides lawfully in the territory of the said authority. The issue of a new document is, under the same conditions, a matter for the authority which issued the former document.

2. Diplomatic or consular authorities, specially authorized for the purpose, shall be empowered to extend, for a period not exceeding six months, the validity of travel documents issued by their Governments.

3. The Contracting States shall give sympathetic consideration to renewing or extending the validity of travel documents or issuing new documents to refugees no longer lawfully resident in their territory who are unable to obtain a travel document from the country of their lawful residence.

Paragraph 7

The Contracting States shall recognize the validity of the documents issued in accordance with the provisions of Article 28 of this Convention.

Paragraph 8

The competent authorities of the country to which the refugee desires to proceed shall, if they are prepared to admit him and if a visa is required, affix a visa on the document of which he is the holder.

Paragraph 9

1. The Contracting States undertake to issue transit visas to refugees who have obtained visas for a territory of Final destination.

2. The issue of such visas may be refused on grounds which would justify refusal of a visa to any alien.

Paragraph 10

The fees for the issue of exit, entry or transit visas shall not exceed the lowest scale of charges for visas on foreign passports.

Paragraph 11

When a refugee has lawfully taken up residence in the territory of another Contracting State, the responsibility for the issue of a new document, under the terms and conditions of Article 28, shall be that of the competent authority of that territory, to which the refugee shall be entitled to apply.

Paragraph 12

The authority issuing a new document shall withdraw the old document and shall return it to the country of issue, if it is stated in the document that it should be so returned; otherwise it shall withdraw and cancel the document.

Paragraph 13

1. Each Contracting State undertakes that the holder of a travel document issued by it in accordance with Article 28 of this Convention shall be re-admitted to its territory at any time during the period of its validity,

2. Subject to the provisions of the preceding sub-paragraph, a Contracting State may require the holder of the document to comply with such formalities as may be prescribed in regard to exit from or return to its territory.

3. The Contracting States reserve the right, in exceptional cases, or in cases where the refugee's stay is authorized for a specific period, when issuing the document, to limit the period during which the refugee may return to a period of not less than three months.

Paragraph 14

Subject only to the terms of paragraph 13, the provisions of this Schedule in no way affect the laws and regulations governing the conditions of admission to, transit through, residence and establishment in, and departure from, the territories of the Contracting States.

Paragraph 15

Neither the issue of the document nor the entries made thereon determine or affect the status of the holder, particularly as regards nationality.

Paragraph 16

The issue of the document does not in any way entitle the holder to the protection of the diplomatic or consular authorities of the country of issue, and does not confer on these authorities a right of protection.

CONVENTION—STATUS OF REFUGEES

ANNEX

Specimen Travel Document

The document will be in booklet form (approximately 15 x 10 centimetres).

It is recommended that it be so printed that any erasure or alteration by chemical or other means can be readily detected, and that the words "Convention of 28 July 1951" be printed in continuous repetition on each page, in the language of the issuing country.

(Cover of *booklet)*

TRAVEL DOCUMENT

(Convention of 28 July 1951)

No. _____

(1)
TRAVEL DOCUMENT
(Convention of 28 July 1951)

This document expires on ....
unless its validity is extended or renewed.

Name ....

Forename(s) ....

Accompanied by ....child (children)

1.   This document is issued solely with a view to providing the holder with a travel document which can serve in lieu of a national passport. It is without prejudice to and in no way affects the holder's nationality.

2.   The holder is authorized to return to ....
....[state here the country whose authorities are issuing the document] on or before ....unless some later date is hereafter specified.
[The period during which the holder is allowed to return must not be less than three months]

3.   Should the holder take up residence in a country other than that which issued the present document, he must, if he wishes to travel again, apply to the competent authorities of his country of residence for a new document. [The old travel document shall be withdrawn by the authority issuing the new document and returned to the authority which issued it.][1]

(This document contains .... pages, exclusive of cover.)

---

[1]The sentence in brackets to be inserted by Governments which so desire.

---

(2)

Place and date of birth ....
Occupation ....
Present residence...
*Maiden name and forename(s) of wife ....
....
*Name and forename(s) of husband..
....

Description

Height _____

Hair _____

Colour of eyes _____

Nose _____

Shape of face _____

Complexion _____

Special peculiarities _____

Children accompanying holder

Name	Forename(s)	Place and date of birth	Sex
_____	_____	_____	_____
_____	_____	_____	_____
_____	_____	_____	_____

*Strike out whichever does not apply.

(This document contains _____ pages, exclusive of cover.)

(3)

Photograph of holder and stamp of issuing authority
Finger-prints of holder (if required)

Signature of holder _____

(This document contains _____ pages, exclusive of cover.)

(4)

1. This document is valid for the following countries:

_____
_____
_____
_____

2. Document or documents on the basis of which the present document is issued:

_____
_____
_____

Issued at _____

Date _____

Signature and stamp of authority
issuing the document:

Fee paid: _____

(This document contains _____ pages, exclusive of cover.)

(5)

Extension or renewal of validity

Fee paid:

Done at _____

From _____
To _____
Date _____

Signature and stamp of authority
extending or renewing the validity
of the document:

_____

Extension or renewal of validity

Fee paid:

Done at _____

From _____
To _____
Date _____

Signature and stamp of authority
extending or renewing the validity
of the document:
(This document contains _____ pages, exclusive of cover.)

(6)

Extension or renewal of validity

Fee paid:

Done at _____

From _____
To _____
Date _____

Signature and stamp of authority
extending or renewing the validity
of the document:

_____

Extension or renewal of validity

Fee paid:

Done at _____

From _____
To _____
Date _____

Signature and stamp of authority
extending or renewing the validity
of the document:
(This document contains _____ pages, exclusive of cover.)

(7-32)

Visas

The name of the holder of the document must be repeated in each visa.
(This document contains _____ pages, exclusive of cover.

889

PROTOCOL RELATING TO THE STATUS OF REFUGEES

Done January 31, 1967

Entry into force, October 4, 1967

606 U.N.T.S. 267, 19 U.S.T. 6223, T.I.A.S. No. 6577

The States Parties to the present Protocol,

Considering that the Convention relating to the Status of Refugees done at Geneva on 28 July 1951 (hereinafter referred to as the Convention) covers only those persons who have become refugees as a result of events occurring before 1 January 1951,

Considering that new refugee situations have arisen since the Convention was adopted and that the refugees concerned may therefore not fall within the scope of the Convention,

Considering that it is desirable that equal status should be enjoyed by all refugees covered by the definition in the Convention irrespective of the dateline 1 January 1951,

Have agreed as follows:

Article I. General provision

1. The States Parties to the present Protocol undertake to apply articles 2 to 34 inclusive of the Convention to refugees as hereinafter defined.

2. For the purpose of the present Protocol, the term "refugee" shall, except as regards the application of paragraph 3 of this article, mean any person within the definition of article 1 of the Convention as if the words "As a result of events occurring before 1 January 1951 and . . ." and the words ". . . as a result of such events", in article 1A(2) were omitted.

3. The present Protocol shall be applied by the States Parties hereto without any geographic limitation, save that existing declarations made by States already Parties to the Convention in accordance with article 1B(1)*(a)* of the Convention, shall, unless extended under article 1B(2) thereof, apply also under the present Protocol.

Article II. Co-operation of the national authorities with the United Nations

1. The States Parties to the present Protocol undertake to co-operate with the Office of the United Nations High Commissioner for Refugees, or any other agency of the United Nations which may succeed it, in the exercise of its functions, and shall in particular facilitate its duty of supervising the application of the provisions of the present Protocol.

2. In order to enable the Office of the High Commissioner, or any other agency of the United Nations which may succeed it, to make reports to the competent organs of the United Nations, the States Parties to the present Protocol undertake to provide them with the information and statistical data requested, in the appropriate form, concerning:

(a) The condition of refugees;

(b) The implementation of the present Protocol;

(c) Laws, regulations and decrees which are, or may hereafter be, in force relating to refugees.

Article III. Information on national legislation

The States Parties to the present Protocol shall communicate to the Secretary-General of the United Nations the laws and regulations which they may adopt to ensure the application of the present Protocol.

Article IV. Settlement of disputes

Any dispute between States Parties to the present Protocol which relates to its interpretation or application and which cannot be settled by other means shall be referred to the International Court of Justice at the request of any one of the parties to the dispute.

Article V. Accession

The present Protocol shall be open for accession on behalf of all States Parties to the Convention and of any other State Member of the United Nations or member of any of the specialized agencies or to which an invitation to accede may have been addressed by the General Assembly of the United Nations. Accession shall be effected by the deposit of an instrument of accession with the Secretary-General of the United Nations.

Article VI. Federal clause

In the case of a Federal or non-unitary State, the following provisions shall apply:

(a) With respect to those articles of the Convention to be applied in accordance with article I, paragraph 1, of the present Protocol that come within the legislative jurisdiction of the federal legislative authority, the obligations of the Federal Government shall to this extent be the same as those of States Parties which are not Federal States;

(b) With respect to those articles of the Convention to be applied in accordance with article I, paragraph 1, of the present Protocol that come within the legislative jurisdiction of constituent States, provinces or cantons which are not, under the constitutional system of the federation, bound to take legislative action, the Federal Government shall bring such articles with a favourable recommendation to the notice of the appropriate authorities of States, provinces or cantons at the earliest possible moment;

(c) A Federal State Party to the present Protocol shall, at the request of any other State Party hereto transmitted through the Secretary-General of the United Nations, supply a statement of the law and practice

of the Federation and its constituent units in regard to any particular provision of the Convention to be applied in accordance with article I, paragraph 1, of the present Protocol, showing the extent to which effect has been given to that provision by legislative or other action.

Article VII. Reservations and Declarations

1. At the time of accession, any State may make reservations in respect of article IV of the present Protocol and in respect of the application in accordance with article I of the present Protocol of any provisions of the Convention other than those contained in articles 1, 3, 4, 16(1) and 33 thereof, provided that in the case of a State Party to the Convention reservations made under this article shall not extend to refugees in respect of whom the Convention applies.

2. Reservations made by States Parties to the Convention in accordance with article 42 thereof shall, unless withdrawn, be applicable in relation to their obligations under the present Protocol.

3. Any State making a reservation in accordance with paragraph 1 of this article may at any time withdraw such reservation by a communication to that effect addressed to the Secretary-General of the United Nations.

4. Declarations made under article 40, paragraphs 1 and 2, of the Convention by a State Party thereto which accedes to the present Protocol shall be deemed to apply in respect of the present Protocol, unless upon accession a notification to the contrary is addressed by the State Party concerned to the Secretary-General of the United Nations. The provisions of article 40, paragraphs 2 and 3, and of article 44, paragraph 3, of the Convention shall be deemed to apply *mutatis mutandis* to the present Protocol.

Article VIII. Entry into force

1. The present Protocol shall come into force on the day of deposit of the sixth instrument of accession.

2. For each State acceding to the Protocol after the deposit of the sixth instrument of accession, the Protocol shall come into force on the date of deposit by such State of its instrument of accession.

Article IX. Denunciation

1. Any State Party hereto may denounce this Protocol at any time by a notification addressed to the Secretary-General of the United Nations.

2. Such denunciation shall take effect for the State Party concerned one year from the date on which it is received by the Secretary-General of the United Nations.

Article X. Notifications by the Secretary-General of the United Nations

The Secretary-General of the United Nations shall inform the States referred to in article V above of the date of entry into force, accessions, reservations and withdrawals of reservations to and denunciations of the present Protocol, and of declarations and notifications relating hereto.

Article XI. Deposit in the Archives of the Secretariat of the United Nations

A copy of the present Protocol, of which the Chinese, English, French, Russian and Spanish texts are equally authentic, signed by the President of the General Assembly and by the Secretary-General of the United Nations, shall be deposited in the archives of the Secretariat of the United Nations. The Secretary-General will transmit certified copies thereof to all States Members of the United Nations and to the other States referred to in article V above.

CONVENTION AGAINST TORTURE AND OTHER CRUEL, INHUMAN, OR DEGRADING TREATMENT OR PUNISHMENT

Adopted and Opened for Ratification Dec. 10, 1984

Entry into force, June 26, 1987

1468 U.N.T.S. 85

The States Parties to this Convention,

Considering that, in accordance with the principles proclaimed in the Charter of the United Nations, recognition of the equal and inalienable rights of all members of the human family is the foundation of freedom, justice and peace in the world,

Recognizing that those rights derive from the inherent dignity of the human person,

Considering the obligation of States under the Charter, in particular Article 55, to promote universal respect for, and observance of, human rights and fundamental freedoms,

Having regard to article 5 of the Universal Declaration of Human Rights and article 7 of the International Covenant on Civil and Political Rights, both of which provide that no one may be subjected to torture or to cruel, inhuman or degrading treatment or punishment,

Having regard also to the Declaration on the Protection of All Persons from Being Subjected to Torture and Other Cruel, Inhuman or Degrading Treatment or Punishment, adopted by the General Assembly on 9 December 1975,

Desiring to make more effective the struggle against torture and other cruel, inhuman or degrading treatment or punishment throughout the world,

Have agreed as follows:

Part I

Article 1

1. For the purposes of this Convention, torture means any act by which severe pain or suffering, whether physical or mental, is intentionally inflicted on a person for such purposes as obtaining from him or a third person information or a confession, punishing him for an act he or a third person has committed or is suspected of having committed, or intimidating or coercing him or a third person, or for any reason based on discrimination of any kind, when such pain or suffering is inflicted by or at the instigation of or with the consent or acquiescence of a public official or other person acting in an official capacity. It does not include pain or suffering arising only from, inherent in or incidental to lawful sanctions.

2. This article is without prejudice to any international instrument or national legislation which does or may contain provisions of wider application.

Article 2

1. Each State Party shall take effective legislative, administrative, judicial or other measures to prevent acts of torture in any territory under its jurisdiction.

2. No exceptional circumstances whatsoever, whether a state of war or a threat or war, internal political instability or any other public emergency, may be invoked as a justification of torture.

3. An order from a superior officer or a public authority may not be invoked as a justification of torture.

Article 3

1. No State Party shall expel, return ("refouler") or extradite a person to another State where there are substantial grounds for believing that he would be in danger of being subjected to torture.

2. For the purpose of determining whether there are such grounds, the competent authorities shall take into account all relevant considerations including, where applicable, the existence in the State concerned of a consistent pattern of gross, flagrant or mass violations of human rights.

Article 4

1. Each State Party shall ensure that all acts of torture are offences under its criminal law. The same shall apply to an attempt to commit torture and to an act by any person which constitutes complicity or participation in torture.

2. Each State Party shall make these offences punishable by appropriate penalties which take into account their grave nature.

Article 5

1. Each State Party shall take such measures as may be necessary to establish its jurisdiction over the offences referred to in article 4 in the following cases:

(a) When the offences are committed in any territory under its jurisdiction or on board a ship or aircraft registered in that State;

(b) When the alleged offender is a national of that State;

(c) When the victim is a national of that State if that State considers it appropriate.

2. Each State Party shall likewise take such measures as may be necessary to establish its jurisdiction over such offences in cases where the alleged offender is present in any territory under its jurisdiction and it does not extradite him pursuant to article 8 to any of the States mentioned in paragraph I of this article.

3. This Convention does not exclude any criminal jurisdiction exercised in accordance with internal law.

Article 6

1. Upon being satisfied, after an examination of information available to it, that the circumstances so warrant, any State Party in whose territory a person alleged to have committed any offence referred to in article 4 is present shall take him into custody or take other legal measures to ensure his presence. The custody and other legal measures shall be as provided in the law of that State but may be continued only for such time as is necessary to enable any criminal or extradition proceedings to be instituted.

2. Such State shall immediately make a preliminary inquiry into the facts.

3. Any person in custody pursuant to paragraph I of this article shall be assisted in communicating immediately with the nearest appropriate representative of the State of which he is a national, or, if he is a stateless person, with the representative of the State where he usually resides.

4. When a State, pursuant to this article, has taken a person into custody, it shall immediately notify the States referred to in article 5, paragraph 1, of the fact that such person is in custody and of the circumstances which warrant his detention. The State which makes the preliminary inquiry contemplated in paragraph 2 of this article shall promptly report its findings to the said States and shall indicate whether it intends to exercise jurisdiction.

Article 7

1. The State Party in the territory under whose jurisdiction a person alleged to have committed any offence referred to in article 4 is found shall in the cases contemplated in article 5, if it does not extradite him, submit the case to its competent authorities for the purpose of prosecution.

2. These authorities shall take their decision in the same manner as in the case of any ordinary offence of a serious nature under the law of that State. In the cases referred to in article 5, paragraph 2, the standards of evidence required for prosecution and conviction shall in no way be less stringent than those which apply in the cases referred to in article 5, paragraph 1.

3. Any person regarding whom proceedings are brought in connection with any of the offences referred to in article 4 shall be guaranteed fair treatment at all stages of the proceedings.

Article 8

1. The offences referred to in article 4 shall be deemed to be included as extraditable offences in any extradition treaty existing between States Parties. States Parties undertake to include such offences as extraditable offences in every extradition treaty to be concluded between them.

2. If a State Party which makes extradition conditional on the existence of a treaty receives a request for extradition from another State Party with which it has no extradition treaty, it may consider this Convention as the legal basis for extradition in respect of such offences. Extradition shall be subject to the other conditions provided by the law of the requested State.

3. States Parties which do not make extradition conditional on the existence of a treaty shall recognize such offences as extraditable offences between themselves subject to the conditions provided by the law of the requested State.

4. Such offences shall be treated, for the purpose of extradition between States Parties, as if they had been committed not only in the place in which they occurred but also in the territories of the States required to establish their jurisdiction in accordance with article 5, paragraph 1.

Article 9

1. States Parties shall afford one another the greatest measure of assistance in connection with criminal proceedings brought in respect of any of the offences referred to in article 4, including the supply of all evidence at their disposal necessary for the proceedings.

2. States Parties shall carry out their obligations under paragraph I of this article in conformity with any treaties on mutual judicial assistance that may exist between them.

Article 10

1. Each State Party shall ensure that education and information regarding the prohibition against torture are fully included in the training of law enforcement personnel, civil or military, medical personnel, public officials and other persons who may be involved in the custody, interrogation or treatment of any individual subjected to any form of arrest, detention or imprisonment.

2. Each State Party shall include this prohibition in the rules or instructions issued in regard to the duties and functions of any such person.

Article 11

Each State Party shall keep under systematic review interrogation rules, instructions, methods and practices as well as arrangements for the custody and treatment of persons subjected to any form of arrest, detention or imprisonment in any territory under its jurisdiction, with a view to preventing any cases of torture.

Article 12

Each State Party shall ensure that its competent authorities proceed to a prompt and impartial investigation, wherever there is reasonable ground to believe that an act of torture has been committed in any territory under its jurisdiction.

Article 13

Each State Party shall ensure that any individual who alleges he has been subjected to torture in any territory under its jurisdiction has the right to complain to, and to have his case promptly and impartially examined by, its competent authorities. Steps shall be taken to ensure that the complainant and witnesses are protected against all ill-treatment or intimidation as a consequence of his complaint or any evidence given.

Article 14

1. Each State Party shall ensure in its legal system that the victim of an act of torture obtains redress and has an enforceable right to fair and adequate compensation, including the means for as full rehabilitation as possible. In the event of the death of the victim as a result of an act of torture, his dependants shall be entitled to compensation.

2. Nothing in this article shall affect any right of the victim or other persons to compensation which may exist under national law.

Article 15

Each State Party shall ensure that any statement which is established to have been made as a result of torture shall not be invoked as evidence in any proceedings, except against a person accused of torture as evidence that the statement was made.

Article 16

1. Each State Party shall undertake to prevent in any territory under its jurisdiction other acts of cruel, inhuman or degrading treatment or punishment which do not amount to torture as defined in article I, when such acts are committed by or at the instigation of or with the consent or acquiescence of a public official or other person acting in an official capacity. In particular, the obligations contained in articles 10, 11, 12 and 13 shall apply with the substitution for references to torture of references to other forms of cruel, inhuman or degrading treatment or punishment.

2. The provisions of this Convention are without prejudice to the provisions of any other international instrument or national law which prohibits cruel, inhuman or degrading treatment or punishment or which relates to extradition or expulsion.

* * *

CONVENTION AGAINST TORTURE—
U.S. RESOLUTION OF ADVICE AND CONSENT (WITH RESERVATIONS, UNDERSTANDINGS AND DECLARATIONS)

136 Cong. Rec. 36198–99 (1990).

Resolved (two-thirds of the Senators present concurring therein), That the Senate advise and consent to the ratification of the Convention Against Torture and Other Cruel, Inhuman or Degrading Treatment or Punishment, adopted by unanimous agreement of the United Nations General Assembly on December 10, 1984, and signed by the United States on April 18, 1988: Provided, That:

I. The Senate's advice and consent is subject to the following reservations:

(1) That the United States considers itself bound by the obligation under Article 16 to prevent "cruel, inhuman or degrading treatment or punishment," only insofar as the term "cruel, inhuman or degrading treatment or punishment" means the cruel, unusual and inhumane treatment or punishment prohibited by the Fifth, Eighth, and/or Fourteenth Amendments to the Constitution of the United States.

(2) That pursuant to Article 30(2) the United States declares that it does not consider itself bound by Article 30(1), but reserves the right specifically to agree to follow this or any other procedure for arbitration in a particular case.

II. The Senate's advice and consent is subject to the following understandings, which shall apply to the obligations of the United States under this Convention:

(1)(a) That with reference to Article 1, the United States understands that, in order to constitute torture, an act must be specifically intended to inflict severe physical or mental pain or suffering and that mental pain or suffering refers to prolonged mental harm caused by or resulting from: **(1)** the intentional infliction or threatened infliction of severe physical pain or suffering; **(2)** the administration or application, or threatened administration or application, of mind altering substances or other procedures calculated to disrupt profoundly the senses or the personality; **(3)** the threat of imminent death; or (4) the threat that another person will imminently be subjected to death, severe physical pain or suffering, or the administration or application of mind altering substances or other procedures calculated to disrupt profoundly the senses or personality.

(b) That the United States understands that the definition of torture in Article 1 is intended to apply only to acts directed against persons in the offender's custody or physical control.

(c) That with reference to Article 1 of the Convention, the United States understands that "sanctions" includes judicially imposed sanctions and other enforcement actions authorized by United States law or by judicial interpretation of such law. Nonetheless, the United States understands that a State Party could not through its domestic sanctions defeat the object and purpose of the Convention to prohibit torture.

(d) That with reference to Article 1 of the Convention, the United States understands that the term "acquiescence" requires that the public official, prior to the activity constituting torture, have awareness of such activity and thereafter breach his legal responsibility to intervene to prevent such activity.

(e) That with reference to Article 1 of the Convention, the United States understands that noncompliance with applicable legal procedural standards does not per se constitute torture.

(2) That the United States understands the phrase, "where there are substantial grounds for believing that he would be in danger of being subjected to torture," as used in Article 3 of the Convention, to mean "if it is more likely than not that he would be tortured."

(3) That it is the understanding of the United States that Article 14 requires a State Party to provide a private right of action for damages only for acts of torture committed in territory under the jurisdiction of that State Party.

(4) That the United States understands that international law does not prohibit the death penalty, and does not consider this Convention to restrict or prohibit the United States from applying the death penalty consistent with the Fifth, Eighth and/or Fourteenth Amendments to the Constitution of the United States, including any constitutional period of confinement prior to the imposition of the death penalty.

(5) That the United States understands that this Convention shall be implemented by the United States Government to the extent that it exercises legislative and judicial jurisdiction over the matters covered by the Convention and otherwise by the state and local governments. Accordingly, in implementing Articles 10–14 and 16, the United States Government shall take measures appropriate to the Federal system to the end that the competent authorities of the constituent units of the United States of America may take appropriate measures for the fulfillment of the Convention.

III. The Senate's advice and consent is subject to the following declarations:

(1) That the United States declares that the provisions of Articles 1 through 16 of the Convention are not self-executing.

(2) That the United States declares, pursuant to Article 21, paragraph 1, of the Convention, that it recognizes the competence of the

Committee against Torture to receive and consider communications to the effect that a State Party claims that another State Party is not fulfilling its obligations under the Convention. It is the understanding of the United States that, pursuant to the above mentioned article, such communications shall be accepted and processed only if they come from a State Party which has made a similar declaration.

IV.   The Senate's advice and consent is subject to the following proviso, which shall not be included in the instrument of ratification to be deposited by the President:

The President of the United States shall not deposit the instrument of ratification until such time as he has notified all present and prospective ratifying parties to this Convention that nothing in this Convention requires or authorizes legislation, or other action, by the United States of America prohibited by the Constitution of the United States as interpreted by the United States

VI. SELECTED IMMIGRATION FORMS

BASIC DOCUMENTS

Form I–94 **Arrival-departure record**

DEPARTMENT OF HOMELAND SECURITY
U.S. Customs and Border Protection

OMB No. 1651-0111

Welcome to the United States
I-94 Arrival/Departure Record
Instructions

This form must be completed by all persons except U.S. Citizens, returning resident aliens, aliens with immigrant visas, and Canadian Citizens visiting or in transit.

Type or print legibly with pen in ALL CAPITAL LETTERS. Use English. Do not write on the back of this form.

This form is in two parts. Please complete both the Arrival Record (Items 1 through 17) and the Departure Record (Items 18 through 21).

When all items are completed, present this form to the CBP Officer.

Item 9 - If you are entering the United States by land, enter LAND in this space. If you are entering the United States by ship, enter SEA in this space.

5 U.S.C. § 552a(e)(3) Privacy Act Notice: Information collected on this form is required by Title 8 of the U.S. Code, including the INA (8 U.S.C. 1103, 1187), and 8 CFR 235.1, 264, and 1235.1. The purposes for this collection are to give the terms of admission and document the arrival and departure of nonimmigrant aliens to the U.S. The information solicited on this form may be made available to other government agencies for law enforcement purposes or to assist DHS in determining your admissibility. All nonimmigrant aliens seeking admission to the U.S., unless otherwise exempted, must provide this information. Failure to provide this information may deny you entry to the United States and result in your removal.

CBP Form I-94 (05/08)

OMB No. 1651-0111

Arrival Record

Admission Number

1. Family Name
2. First (Given) Name
3. Birth Date (DD/MM/YY)
4. Country of Citizenship
5. Sex (Male or Female)
6. Passport Issue Date (DD/MM/YY)
7. Passport Expiration Date (DD/MM/YY)
8. Passport Number
9. Airline and Flight Number
10. Country Where You Live
11. Country Where You Boarded
12. City Where Visa Was Issued
13. Date Issued (DD/MM/YY)
14. Address While in the United States (Number and Street)
15. City and State
16. Telephone Number in the U.S. Where You Can be Reached
17. Email Address

CBP Form I-94 (05/08)

DEPARTMENT OF HOMELAND SECURITY
U.S. Customs and Border Protection

OMB No. 1651-0111

Departure Record

Admission Number

18. Family Name
19. First (Given) Name
20. Birth Date (DD/MM/YY)
21. Country of Citizenship

CBP Form I-94 (05/08)

See Other Side

STAPLE HERE

This Side For Government Use Only

Primary Inspection

Applicant's
Name _____

Date
Referred _____ Time _____ Insp. # _____

Reason Referred

☐ 212A ☐☐ ☐ PP ☐ Visa ☐ Parole ☐ L/O ☐ TWOV

Other _____
_____

Secondary Inspection

End Secondary
Time _____ Insp. # _____

Disposition _____
_____

22. Occupation	23. Waivers
24. CIS A Number A-	25. CIS FCO
26. Petition Number	27. Program Number
28. ☐ Bond	29. ☐ Prospective Student

30. Itinerary/Comments
_____
_____
_____
_____
_____
_____
_____

31. TWOV Ticket Number

Paperwork Reduction Act Statement: An agency may not conduct or sponsor an information collection and a person is not required to respond to this information unless it displays a current valid OMB control number. The control number for this collection is 1651-0111. The estimated average time to complete this application is 8 minutes per respondent. If you have any comments regarding the burden estimate you can write to U.S. Customs and Border Protection, Asset Management, 1300 Pennsylvania Avenue, NW, Washington DC 20229

Warning A nonimmigrant who accepts unauthorized employment is subject to deportation.
Important Retain this permit in your possession; *you must surrender it when you leave the U.S.*
Failure to do so may delay your entry into the U.S. in the future.
You are authorized to stay in the U.S. only until the date written on this form. To remain past this date, without permission from Department of Homeland Security authorities, is a violation of the law.
Surrender this permit when you leave the U.S.:
   - By sea or air, to the transportation line;
   - Across the Canadian border, to a Canadian Official;
   - Across the Mexican border, to a U.S. Official
Students planning to reenter the U.S. within 30 days to return to the same school, see "Arrival-Departure" on page 2 of Form I-20 **prior to surrendering this permit.**

Record of Changes
_____
_____
_____
_____

                                                    Departure Record
Port:
Date:
Carrier:
Flight No./ Ship Name:

Sample nonimmigrant visa

Reading a US Nonimmigrant Visa

This is a simple guide to reading the data contained in a US Nonimmigrant Visa. Data and format are identical for each version of the visa. Earlier versions have slight variations.

MRV 2000
(First issued at certain posts beginning May 2000)

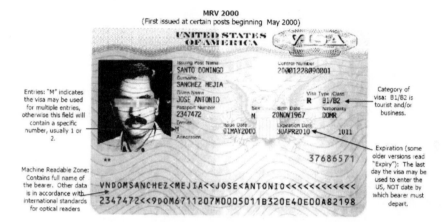

Entries: "M" indicates the visa may be used for multiple entries, otherwise this field will contain a specific number, usually 1 or 2.

Category of visa: B1/B2 is tourist and/or business.

Machine Readable Zone: Contains full name of the bearer. Other data is in accordance with international standards for optical readers

Expiration (some older versions read "Expiry"): The last day the visa may be used to enter the US, NOT date by which bearer must depart.

Lincoln Visa
(First issued at certain posts beginning February 2002)

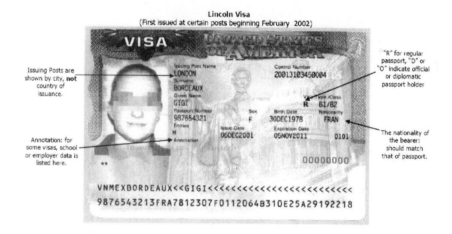

Issuing Posts are shown by city, **not** country of issuance.

"R" for regular passport, "D" or "O" indicate official or diplomatic passport holder

Annotation: for some visas, school or employer data is listed here.

The nationality of the bearer: should match that of passport.

Form I-551   Permanent resident card

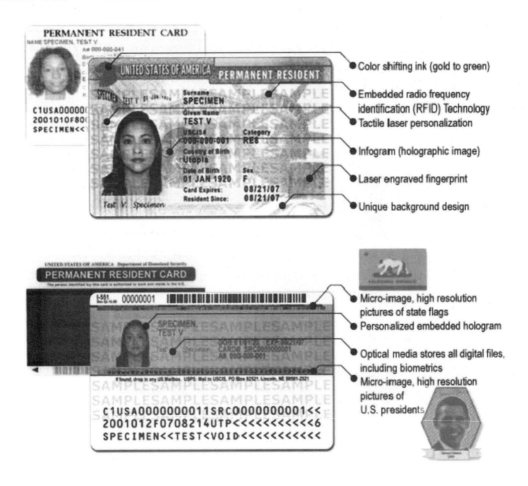

Color shifting ink (gold to green)

Embedded radio frequency identification (RFID) Technology

Tactile laser personalization

Infogram (holographic image)

Laser engraved fingerprint

Unique background design

Micro-image, high resolution pictures of state flags

Personalized embedded hologram

Optical media stores all digital files, including biometrics

Micro-image, high resolution pictures of U.S. presidents

Source:
http://www.uscis.gov/portal/site/uscis/menuitem.5af9bb95919f35e66f6141 76 543f6d1a/?vgnextoi
d=34233893c4888210VgnVCM100000082ca60aRCRD&vgnextchannel=68439c7755cb9010Vg
nVCM10000045f3d6a1RCRD

(Newer version of the card appears in the foreground.)

Form I–797A   Notice of action (sample)

Department of Homeland Security
U.S. Citizenship and Immigration Services

I-797A, Notice of Action

THE UNITED STATES OF AMERICA

RECEIPT NUMBER WAC-		CASE TYPE I129 PETITION FOR A NONIMMIGRANT WORKER
RECEIPT DATE September 8, 2008	PRIORITY DATE	PETITIONER
NOTICE DATE September 19, 2008	PAGE 1 of 1	BENEFICIARY

CHARLES MEDINA ESQ

Notice Type: Approval Notice
Class: E2
Valid from 10/01/2008 to 09/30/2010

The above petition and change of status have been approved. The status of the named foreign worker(s) in this classification is valid as indicated above. The foreign worker(s) can work for the petitioner, but only as detailed in the petition and for the period authorized. Any change in employment requires a new petition. Since this employment authorization stems from the filing of this petition, separate employment authorization documentation is not required. Please contact the IRS with any questions about tax withholding.

The petitioner should keep the upper portion of this notice. The lower portion should be given to the worker. He or she should keep the right part with his or her form I-94, *Arrival-Departure Record*. This should be turned in with the I-94 when departing the U.S. The left part is for his or her records. A person granted a change of status who leaves the U.S. must normally obtain a visa in the new classification before returning. The left part can be used in applying for the new visa. The petitioner may also file Form I-824, *Application for Action on an Approved Application or Petition*, with this office to request that we notify a consulate, post of entry, or pre-flight inspection office of this approval.

The approval of this visa petition does not in itself grant any immigration status and does not guarantee that the alien beneficiary will subsequently be found to be eligible for a visa, for admission to the United States, or for an extension, change, or adjustment of status.

THIS FORM IS NOT A VISA NOR MAY IT BE USED IN PLACE OF A VISA.

Please see the additional information on the back. You will be notified separately about any other cases you filed.
U.S. CITIZENSHIP & IMMIGRATION SVC
CALIFORNIA SERVICE CENTER
P. O. BOX 30111
LAGUNA NIGUEL CA 92607-0111
Customer Service Telephone: (800) 375-5283
Form I797A (Rev. 09/07/93)N

PLEASE TEAR OFF FORM I-94 PRINTED BELOW, AND STAPLE TO ORIGINAL I-94 IF AVAILABLE

Detach This Half for Personal Records

Receipt # WAC-
I-94#
NAME
CLASS E2
VALID FROM 10/01/2008 UNTIL 09/30/2010

PETITIONER:

Receipt Number WAC-
Immigration and
Naturalization Service

I-94
Departure Record   Petitioner:

14. Family Name		
15. First (Given) Name		16. Date of Birth
17. Country of Citizenship KOREA, SOUTH		

Form I-797A (Rev. 10/31/05) N

Form DSP–150   Border crossing card ("laser visa," as issued from 10/1/2008)

The new border crossing card being issued by the U.S. Department of State in cooperation with the Department of Homeland Security is a credit card-sized plastic card that conveys the same purpose and effect as a B1/B2 Visa foil. However, the Border Crossing Card will be issued only to Mexican nationals. The purpose of the BCC is to facilitate travel and inspection at land border crossings for Mexican nationals in general, and especially to facilitate frequent crossings for those persons living in Mexican border communities along the southwestern tier of the United States. The BCC permits the bearer to travel to the U.S. for tourism and/or business but does not authorize employment in the United States.

Like the U.S. Passport Card, the new BCC will contain a radio frequency identification chip (RFID chip) and an integrated contactless circuit (ICC) antenna, which will be recognized by DHS' PASS System and will respond with a unique 'read-only' electronic number. No BCC card recipient's personal information is written to the RFID chip itself.

For further information about visas and the regulations coming into force to facilitate and govern travel and inspection under the terms of the Western Hemisphere Travel Initiative (WHTI), please visit the Department of State's website located at www.travel.state.gov.

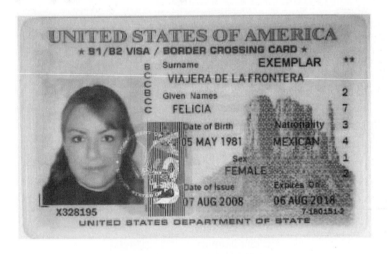

Source: http://monterrey.usconsulate.gov/press_bol100108.html

EMPLOYMENT

Form M–274   Handbook for employers (excerpts)

Handbook for Employers M-274

Guidance for Completing Form I-9 (Employment Eligibility Verification Form) | Current as of July 2017

How to Download Our Manuals in PDF (PDF)

U.S. Citizenship
and Immigration
Services

Last Reviewed/Updated: 01/11/2018

* * *

13.0 Acceptable Documents for Verifying Employment Authorization and Identity

The following documents are acceptable for Form I-9 to establish an employee's employment authorization and identity. The comprehensive Lists of Acceptable Documents can be found here and on the last page of Form I-9. Samples of many of the acceptable documents appear in Sections 13.1 – 13.3.

To establish both identity and employment authorization, a person must present to their employer a document or combination of documents from List A, which shows both identity and employment authorization; or one document from List B, which shows identity and one document from List C, which shows employment authorization.

If a person is unable to present an acceptable document from the List of Acceptable Documents within three business days of the date work for pay begins, the employer must accept an acceptable "receipt" within that time. The employee must indicate by checking an appropriate box in Section 1 that they are authorized to be employed in the United States. The employee must also present the actual document when the receipt validity period ends.

Receipts showing that a person has applied for an initial grant of employment authorization are not acceptable. Receipts are also not acceptable if employment is for fewer than three business days. For a list of acceptable receipts for Form I-9, see Table 1 in Section 4.0. For examples of acceptable employment authorization documents issued by the Department of Homeland Security (List C #7), please visit uscis.gov/i-9-central.

Note that a USCIS-issued Notice on Form I-797C acknowledging receipt of an EAD renewal application presented in combination with an expired EAD is considered an unexpired EAD under List A in certain limited circumstances. See Section 4.2 *Automatic Extensions of Employment Authorization Documents in Certain Circumstances* for more information. This document combination is a List A document and is NOT considered a "receipt" that may be presented in lieu of an acceptable List document.

Sections 13.1-13.3 show the most recent versions and representative images of some of the various acceptable documents on the list. These images can assist you in your review of the document presented to you. These pages are not, however, comprehensive. In some cases, many variations of a particular document exist and new versions may be published subsequent to the publication date of this handbook. Keep in mind that USCIS does not expect you to be a document expert. You are expected to accept documents that reasonably appear to be genuine and to relate to the person presenting them.

LIST A: Documents That Establish Both Identity and Employment Authorization

All documents must be unexpired.

1. U.S. Passport or U.S. Passport Card
2. Permanent Resident Card or Alien Registration Receipt Card (Form I-551)
3. Foreign passport that contains a temporary I-551 stamp or temporary I-551 printed notation on a machine-readable immigrant visa (MRIV)
4. Employment Authorization Document (EAD) that contains a photograph (Form I-766).Form I-766 expired on its face combined with Form I-797 based on an automatic EAD extension in certain circumstances qualifies as unexpired Form I-766; see Section 4.2 *Automatic Extensions of Employment Authorization Documents in Certain Circumstances*.
5. For a nonimmigrant alien authorized to work for a specific employer incident to status, a foreign passport with Form I-94 or Form I-94A bearing the same name as the passport and an endorsement of the alien's nonimmigrant status, as long as the period of endorsement has not yet expired and the proposed employment is not in conflict with any restrictions or limitations identified on the form
6. Passport from the Federated States of Micronesia (FSM) or the Republic of the Marshall Islands (RMI) with Form I-94 or Form I-94A indicating nonimmigrant admission under the Compact of Free Association Between the United States and the FSM or RMI

LIST B: Documents That Establish Identity

All documents must be unexpired.

For individuals 18 years of age or older:

1. Driver's license or ID card issued by a state or outlying possession of the United States, provided it contains a photograph or information such as name, date of birth, gender, height, eye color, and address
2. ID card issued by federal, state, or local government agencies or entities, provided it contains a photograph or information such as name, date of birth, gender, height, eye color, and address
3. School ID card with a photograph
4. Voter's registration card
5. U.S. military card or draft record
6. Military dependent's ID card
7. U.S. Coast Guard Merchant Mariner Card
8. Native American tribal document
9. Driver's license issued by a Canadian government authority

For persons under age 18 who are unable to present a document listed above:

1. School record or report card
2. Clinic, doctor, or hospital record
3. Day-care or nursery

LIST C: Documents That Establish Employment Authorization

All documents must be unexpired

1. A Social Security Account Number card unless the card includes one of the follwing restrictions:
   - NOT VALID FOR EMPLOYMENT
   - VALID FOR WORK ONLY WITH INS AUTHORIZATION
   - VALID FOR WORK ONLY WITH DHS AUTHORIZATION
2. Certification of report of birth issued by the U.S. Department of State (Forms DS-1350, FS-545, FS-240)
3. Original or certified copy of a birth certificate issued by a state, county, municipal authority or outlying territry of the United States bearing an official seal
4. Native American tribal document
5. U.S. Citizen Identification Card (Form I-197)
6. Identification Card for Use of Resident Citizen in the United States (Form I-179)
7. Employment authorization document issued by the Department of Homeland Security. For examples, please visit uscis.gov/i-9-central

13.1 List A Documents That Establish Identity and Employment Authorization

The illustrations provided do not necessarily reflect the actual size of the documents.

U.S. Passport

The U.S. Department of State issues the U.S. passport to U.S. citizens and noncitizen nationals. There are a small number of versions still in circulation that may differ from the main versions shown here.

Current U.S. Passport cover and open

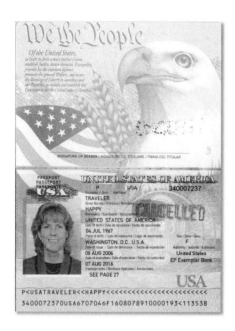

Older U.S. Passport cover and open

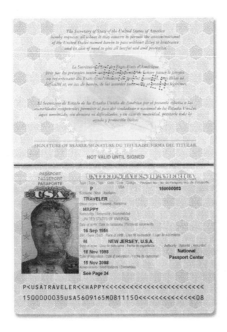

U.S. Passport Card

The U.S. Department of State began producing the passport card in July 2008. The passport card is a wallet-size card that can only be used for land and sea travel between the United States and Canada, Mexico, the Caribbean, and Bermuda.

Passport Card front and back

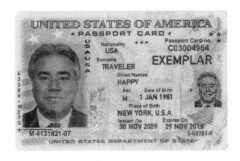

Permanent Resident Card (Form I-551)

On May 1, 2017 USCIS began issuing a redesigned Permanent Resident Card, Form I-551 (also known as the "Green Card"). The card contains the bearer's photo on the front and back, name, USCIS number, date of birth, card expiration date and laser engraved fingerprint. The new card does not have a signature or an optical stripe on the back. Some Permanent Resident Cards issued after May, 1 2017 may display the previous design format. Both the new and previous versions of the Permanent Resident Card remain valid until the expiration date shown on the card.

Current Permanent Resident Card (Form I-551) front and back

The previous version of the Permanent Resident Card was issued after April 30, 2010.This redesign changed the card color to green. The card is personalized with the bearer's photo, name, USCIS number, alien registration number, date of birth, and laser-engraved fingerprint, as well as the card expiration date. Note that on the card, shown below, the lawful permanent resident's alien registration number, commonly known as the A number, is found under the USCIS # heading. The A number is also located on the back of the card.

These cards may or may not contain a signature. A signature is not required for the card to be acceptable for Form I-9 purposes.

Previous version Permanent Resident Card (Form I-551) front and back

Another older version of the Permanent Resident Card shows the DHS seal and contains a detailed hologram on the front of the card. Each card is personalized with an etching showing the bearer's photo, name, fingerprint, date of birth, alien registration number, card expiration date, and card number.

Also in circulation are older Resident Alien cards, issued by the U.S. Department of Justice, Immigration and Naturalization Service, which do not have expiration dates and are valid indefinitely. These cards are peach in color and contain the bearer's fingerprint and photograph.

Older version Permanent Resident Card (Form I-551) front and back

Foreign Passport with I-551 Stamp or MRIV

USCIS uses either an I-551 stamp or a temporary I-551 printed notation on a machine-readable immigrant visa (MRIV) to denote temporary evidence of lawful permanent residence. Sometimes, if no foreign passport is available, USCIS will place the I-551 stamp on a Form I-94 and affix a photograph of the bearer to the form. This document is considered a receipt.

Unexpired Foreign Passport with I-551 Stamp   **I-551 Stamp**

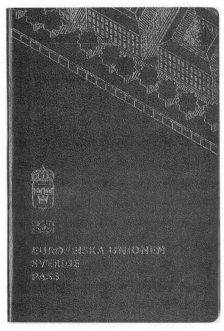

The temporary Form I-551 MRIV is evidence of permanent resident status for one year from the date of admission.

Temporary I-551 printed notation on a machine-readable immigrant visa (MRIV)

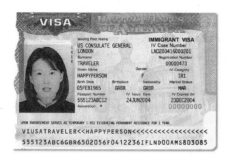

Employment Authorization Document (Form I-766)

On May 1, 2017 USCIS began issuing a redesigned Employment Authorization Document (Form I-766) EAD to certain individuals with temporary employment authorization to work in the United States. The card contains the bearer's photograph on the front and back, name, USCIS number, card number, date of birth, laser-engraved fingerprint, and the card expiration date. Cards may contain one of the following notations above the expiration date: "Not Valid for Reentry to U.S.", "Valid for Reentry to U.S." or "Serves as I-512 Parole."

Some EADs issued after May 1, 2017, may still display the previous design format. Both the existing and new EADs will remain valid until the expiration date shown on the card.

Current Employment Authorization Document (Form I-766) with notation "NOT VALID FOR REENTRY TO U.S." front and back

The older version of the Employment Authorization Document (Form I-766) contains the bearer's photograph, fingerprint, card number, Alien number, birth date, and signature, along with a holographic film and the DHS seal. The expiration date is located at the bottom of the card. Cards may contain one of the following notations above the expiration date: "Not Valid for Reentry to U.S.", "Valid for Reentry to U.S." or "Serves as I-512 Advance Parole."

Previous version Employment Authorization Document (Form I-766)

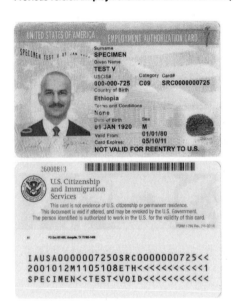

Form I-20 Accompanied by Form I-94 or Form I-94A

Form I-94 or Form I-94A for F-1 nonimmigrant students must be accompanied by a Form I-20, Certificate of Eligibility for Nonimmigrant Students, endorsed with employment authorization by the designated school official for curricular practical training. USCIS will issue an Employment Authorization Document (Form I-766) to all students (F-1 and M-1) authorized for optional practical training (OPT).

Form I-20 Accompanied by Form I-94 or Form I-94A

See Form I-94 below.

Form DS-2019 Accompanied by Form I-94 or Form I-94A

Nonimmigrant exchange visitors (J-1) must have a Form I-94 or Form I-94A accompanied by an unexpired Form DS-2019, Certificate of Eligibility for Exchange Visitor (J-1) Status, issued by the U .S. Department of State, that specifies the sponsor. J-1 exchange students also need a letter from their responsible officer authorizing their employment.

DS-2019 Accompanied by Form I-94 or Form I-94A

See Form I-94 below.

Form I-94 or Form I-94A Arrival/Departure Record

CBP and sometimes USCIS issue arrival-departure records to nonimmigrants. This document indicates the bearer's immigration status, the date that the status was granted, and when the status expires. The immigration status notation within the stamp on the card varies according to the status granted, for example, L-1, F-1, J-1. Form I-94 can contain a handwritten date and status or be computer-generated. Form I-94A has a computer- generated date and status. Both may be presented with documents that Form I-9 specifies are valid only when Form I-94 or Form I-94A also is presented, such as the foreign passport, Form DS-2019, or Form I-20.

Form I-9 provides space for you to record the document number and expiration date for both the passport and Form I-94 or Form I-94A.

Electronic Form I-94 Arrival/Departure Record

Form I-94 Arrival/Departure Record

Departure Number   OMB No. 1651-0111

000000000 00

I-94
Departure Record

F-1
DIS

14. Family Name
S T U D E N T

15. First (Given) Name   16. Birth Date (Day/Mo/Yr)
I M A   0 1 0 1 7 0

17. Country of Citizenship
A N Y   C O U N T R Y

CBP Form I-94 (10/04)

See Other Side   STAPLE HERE

Form I-94A Arrival/Departure Record

Passport of the Federated States of Micronesia and the Republic of the Marshall Islands

2003, Compacts of Free Association (CFA) between the United States and the Federated States of Micronesia (FSM) and Republic of the Marshall Islands (RMI) were amended to allow citizens of these countries to work in the United States without obtaining an Employment Authorization Document (Form I-766).

For Form I-9 purposes, citizens of these countries may present FSM or RMI passports accompanied by a Form I-94 or Form I-94A indicating nonimmigrant admission under the CFA, which are acceptable documents under List A. The exact notation on Form I-94 or Form I-94A may vary and is subject to change. The notation on Form I-94 or Form I-94A typically states "CFA/FSM" for an FSM citizen and "CFA/MIS" for an RMI citizen.

Passport of the Federated States of Micronesia and the Republic of the Marshall Islands

13.2 List B Documents That Establish Identity

The illustrations provided do not necessarily reflect the actual size of the documents.

State-issued **Driver's License**

A driver's license can be issued by any state or territory of the United States (including the District of Columbia, Puerto Rico, the U .S. Virgin Islands, Guam, American Samoa, and the Commonwealth of the Northern Mariana Islands) or by a Canadian government authority, and is acceptable if it contains a photograph or other identifying information such as name, date of birth, gender, height, eye color, and address.

Some states may place restrictive notations on their drivers' licenses. For Form I-9 purposes, these drivers' licenses may be acceptable.

Driver's License from Mississippi

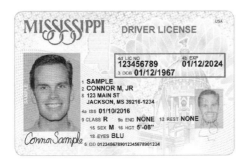

State-issued ID Card

An ID card can be issued by any state (including the District of Columbia, Puerto Rico, the U.S. Virgin Islands, Guam, American Samoa, and the Commonwealth of the Northern Mariana Islands) or local government. It is acceptable if it contains a photograph or other identifying information, such as name, date of birth, gender, height, eye color, and address.

Some states may place restrictive notations on their ID cards. For Form I-9 purposes, these cards may be acceptable.

Identification card from Mississippi

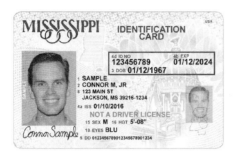

13.3 List C Documents That Establish Employment Authorization

The illustrations provided do not necessarily reflect the actual size of the documents.

U.S. Social Security Account Number Card

The U.S. Social Security account number card is issued by the Social Security Administration (older versions were issued by the U.S. Department of Health and Human Services), and can be presented as a List C document unless the card specifies that it does not authorize employment in the United States. Metal or plastic reproductions are not acceptable.

U.S. Social Security Card

Certifications of Birth Issued by the U.S. Department of State

These documents may vary in color and paper used. All will include a raised seal of the office that issued the document, and may contain a watermark and raised printing.

Certification of Birth Abroad Issued by the U.S. Department of State (FS-545)

Certification of Report of Birth Issued by the U.S. Department of State (DS-1350)

Consular Report of Birth Abroad Issued by the U.S. Department of State (FS-240)

Birth Certificate

Only an original or certified copy of a birth certificate issued by a state, county, municipal authority, or outlying possession of the United States that bears an official seal is acceptable. Versions will vary by state and year of birth.

Beginning October 31, 2010, only Puerto Rico birth certificates issued on or after July 1, 2010 are valid. Please check uscis.gov for guidance on the validity of Puerto Rico birth certificates for Form I-9 purposes.

Birth Certificate

U.S. Citizen Identification Card (Form I-197)

Form I-197 was issued by the former Immigration and Naturalization Service (INS) to naturalized U.S. citizens. Although this card is no longer issued, it is valid indefinitely.

U.S. Citizen Identification Card (Form I-197)

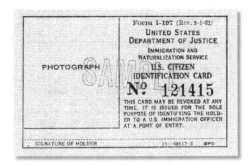

Identification Card for Use of Resident Citizen in the United States (I-179)

Form I-179 was issued by INS to U.S. citizens who are residents of the United States. Although this card is no longer issued, it is valid indefinitely.

Identification Card for Use of Resident Citizen in the United States (I-179)

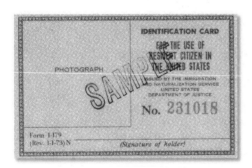

Form I–766   Employment authorization document (EAD)

DETAINERS AND RELATED DOCUMENTS

Form I–247A   Immigration detainer—notice of action [current form]

DEPARTMENT OF HOMELAND SECURITY
IMMIGRATION DETAINER - NOTICE OF ACTION

Subject ID: Event #:	File No: Date:

TO: (Name and Title of Institution - OR Any Subsequent Law Enforcement Agency)	FROM: (Department of Homeland Security Office Address)

Name of Alien: _____

Date of Birth: _____ Citizenship: _____ Sex: _____

1. DHS HAS DETERMINED THAT PROBABLE CAUSE EXISTS THAT THE SUBJECT IS A REMOVABLE ALIEN. THIS DETERMINATION IS BASED ON *(complete box 1 or 2).*

- ☐ A final order of removal against the alien;
- ☐ The pendency of ongoing removal proceedings against the alien;
- ☐ Biometric confirmation of the alien's identity and a records check of federal databases that affirmatively indicate, by themselves or in addition to other reliable information, that the alien either lacks immigration status or notwithstanding such status is removable under U.S. immigration law; and/or
- ☐ Statements made by the alien to an immigration officer and/or other reliable evidence that affirmatively indicate the alien either lacks immigration status or notwithstanding such status is removable under U.S. immigration law.

2. DHS TRANSFERRED THE ALIEN TO YOUR CUSTODY FOR A PROCEEDING OR INVESTIGATION *(complete box 1 or 2).*

- ☐ Upon completion of the proceeding or investigation for which the alien was transferred to your custody, DHS intends to resume custody of the alien to complete processing and/or make an admissibility determination.

IT IS THEREFORE REQUESTED THAT YOU:

- **Notify DHS** as early as practicable (at least 48 hours, if possible) before the alien is released from your custody. Please notify DHS by calling ☐ U.S. Immigration and Customs Enforcement (ICE) or ☐ U.S. Customs and Border Protection (CBP) at _____. If you cannot reach an official at the number(s) provided, please contact the Law Enforcement Support Center at: (802) 872-6020.
- **Maintain custody** of the alien for a period **NOT TO EXCEED 48 HOURS** beyond the time when he/she would otherwise have been released from your custody to allow DHS to assume custody. The alien **must be served with a copy of this form** for the detainer to take effect. This detainer arises from DHS authorities and should not impact decisions about the alien's bail, rehabilitation, parole, release, diversion, custody classification, work, quarter assignments, or other matters
- Relay this detainer to any other law enforcement agency to which you transfer custody of the alien.
- Notify this office in the event of the alien's death, hospitalization or transfer to another institution.

- ☐ If checked: please cancel the detainer related to this alien previously submitted to you on _____ (date).

_____   _____
(Name and title of Immigration Officer)   (Signature of Immigration Officer) (Sign in ink)

> **Notice:** If the alien may be the victim of a crime or you want the alien to remain in the United States for a law enforcement purpose, notify the ICE Law Enforcement Support Center at (802) 872-6020. You may also call this number if you have any other questions or concerns about this matter.

TO BE COMPLETED BY THE LAW ENFORCEMENT AGENCY CURRENTLY HOLDING THE ALIEN WHO IS THE SUBJECT OF THIS NOTICE:

Please provide the information below, sign, and return to DHS by mailing, emailing or faxing a copy to _____ .

Local Booking/Inmate #: _____ Estimated release date/time: _____

Date of latest criminal charge/conviction: _____ Last offense charged/conviction: _____

This form was served upon the alien on _____ , in the following manner:

☐ in person   ☐ by inmate mail delivery   ☐ other (please specify): _____

_____   _____
(Name and title of Officer)   (Signature of Officer) (Sign in ink)

DHS Form I-247A (3/17)   Page 1 of 3

NOTICE TO THE DETAINEE

The Department of Homeland Security (DHS) has placed an immigration detainer on you. An immigration detainer is a notice to a law enforcement agency that DHS intends to assume custody of you (after you otherwise would be released from custody) because there is probable cause that you are subject to removal from the United States under federal immigration law. DHS has requested that the law enforcement agency that is currently detaining you maintain custody of you for a period not to exceed 48 hours beyond the time when you would have been released based on your criminal charges or convictions. **If DHS does not take you into custody during this additional 48 hour period, you should contact your custodian** (the agency that is holding you now) to inquire about your release. **If you believe you are a United States citizen or the victim of a crime, please advise DHS by calling the ICE Law Enforcement Support Center toll free at (855) 448-6903.**

NOTIFICACIÓN A LA PERSONA DETENIDA

El Departamento de Seguridad Nacional (DHS) le ha puesto una retención de inmigración. Una retención de inmigración es un aviso a una agencia de la ley que DHS tiene la intención de asumir la custodia de usted (después de lo contrario, usted sería puesto en libertad de la custodia) porque hay causa probable que usted está sujeto a que lo expulsen de los Estados Unidos bajo la ley de inmigración federal. DHS ha solicitado que la agencia de la ley que le tiene detenido actualmente mantenga custodia de usted por un periodo de tiempo que no exceda de 48 horas más del tiempo original que habría sido puesto en libertad en base a los cargos judiciales o a sus antecedentes penales. **Si DHS no le pone en custodia durante este periodo adicional de 48 horas, usted debe de contactarse con su custodio** (la agencia que le tiene detenido en este momento) para preguntar acerca de su liberación. **Si usted cree que es un ciudadano de los Estados Unidos o la víctima de un crimen, por favor avise al DHS llamando gratuitamente al Centro de Apoyo a la Aplicación de la Ley ICE al (855) 448-6903.**

AVIS AU DETENU OU À LA DÉTENUE

Le Département de la Sécurité Intérieure (DHS) a placé un dépositaire d'immigration sur vous. Un dépositaire d'immigration est un avis à une agence de force de l'ordre que le DHS a l'intention de vous prendre en garde à vue (après cela vous pourrez par ailleurs être remis en liberté) parce qu'il y a une cause probable que vous soyez sujet à expulsion des États-Unis en vertu de la loi fédérale sur l'immigration. Le DHS a demandé que l'agence de force de l'ordre qui vous détient actuellement puisse vous maintenir en garde pendant une période ne devant pas dépasser 48 heures au-delà du temps après lequel vous auriez été libéré en se basant sur vos accusations criminelles ou condamnations. **Si le DHS ne vous prenne pas en garde à vue au cours de cette période supplémentaire de 48 heures, vous devez contacter votre gardien (ne)** (l'agence qui vous détient maintenant) pour vous renseigner sur votre libération. **Si vous croyez que vous êtes un citoyen ou une citoyenne des États-Unis ou une victime d'un crime, s'il vous plaît aviser le DHS en appelant gratuitement le centre d'assistance de force de l'ordre de l'ICE au (855) 448-6903**

NOTIFICAÇÃO AO DETENTO

O Departamento de Segurança Nacional (DHS) expediu um mandado de detenção migratória contra você. Um mandado de detenção migratória é uma notificação feita à uma agência de segurança pública que o DHS tem a intenção de assumir a sua custódia (após a qual você, caso contrário, seria liberado da custódia) porque existe causa provável que você está sujeito a ser removido dos Estados Unidos de acordo com a lei federal de imigração. ODHS solicitou à agência de segurança pública onde você está atualmente detido para manter a sua guarda por um período de no máximo 48 horas além do tempo que você teria sido liberado com base nas suas acusações ou condenações criminais. **Se o DHS não leva-lo sob custódia durante este período adicional de 48 horas, você deve entrar em contato com quem tiver a sua custódia** (a agência onde você está atualmente detido) para perguntar a respeito da sua liberação. **Se você acredita ser um cidadão dos Estados Unidos ou a vítima de um crime, por favor informe ao DHS através de uma ligação gratuita ao Centro de Suporte de Segurança Pública do Serviço de Imigração e Alfândega (ICE) pelo telefone (855) 448-6903.**

THÔNG BÁO CHO NGƯỜI BỊ GIAM

Bộ Nội An (DHS) đã ra lệnh giam giữ di trú đối với quý vị. Giam giữ di trú là một thông báo cho cơ quan công lực rằng Bộ Nội An sẽ đảm đương việc lưu giữ quý vị (sau khi quý vị được thả ra) bởi có lý do khả tín quý vị là đối tượng bị trục xuất khỏi Hoa Kỳ theo luật di trú liên bang. Sau khi quý vị đã thi hành đầy đủ thời gian của bản án dựa trên các tội phạm hay các kết án, thay vì được thả tự do, Bộ Nội An đã yêu cầu cơ quan công lực giữ quý vị lại thêm không quá 48 tiếng đồng hồ nữa. Nếu Bộ Nội An không đến bắt quý vị sau 48 tiếng đồng hồ phụ trội đó, quý vị cần liên lạc với cơ quan hiện đang giam giữ quý vị để tham khảo về việc trả tự do cho quý vị. Nếu quý vị là công dân Hoa Kỳ hay tin rằng mình là nạn nhân của một tội ác, xin vui lòng báo cho Bộ Nội An bằng cách gọi số điện thoại miễn phí 1(855) 448-6903 cho Trung Tâm Hỗ Trợ Cơ Quan Công Lực Di Trú.

被拘留者通知書

國土安全部(Department of Homeland Security，簡稱DHS)已經對你發出移民拘留令。移民拘留令為一給予執法機構的通知書，闡明DHS意欲獲取對你的羈押權(若非有此羈押權，你將會被釋放)；因為根據聯邦移民法例，並基於合理的原由，你將會被遞解離美國國境。DHS亦已要求現正拘留你的執法機構，在你因受到刑事檢控或定罪後，而在本應被釋放的程序下，繼續對你作出不超過四十八小時的監管。若你在這附加的四十八小時內，仍未及移交至**DHS**的監管下，你應當聯絡你的監管人(即現正監管你的機構)查詢有關你釋放的事宜。若你認為你是美國公民或為罪案受害者，請致電**ICE**執法部支援中心**(Law Enforcement Support Center)**知會**DHS**，免費電話號碼：**(855)448-6903**。

Form I–200   Warrant for arrest of alien [current form—must accompany detainer as of 2017]

U.S. DEPARTMENT OF HOMELAND SECURITY   Warrant for Arrest of Alien

File No. _____

Date: _____

To: Any immigration officer authorized pursuant to sections 236 and 287 of the Immigration and Nationality Act and part 287 of title 8, Code of Federal Regulations, to serve warrants of arrest for immigration violations

I have determined that there is probable cause to believe that _____ is removable from the United States. This determination is based upon:

☐ the execution of a charging document to initiate removal proceedings against the subject;

☐ the pendency of ongoing removal proceedings against the subject;

☐ the failure to establish admissibility subsequent to deferred inspection;

☐ biometric confirmation of the subject's identity and a records check of federal databases that affirmatively indicate, by themselves or in addition to other reliable information, that the subject either lacks immigration status or notwithstanding such status is removable under U.S. immigration law; and/or

☐ statements made voluntarily by the subject to an immigration officer and/or other reliable evidence that affirmatively indicate the subject either lacks immigration status or notwithstanding such status is removable under U.S. immigration law.

YOU ARE COMMANDED to arrest and take into custody for removal proceedings under the Immigration and Nationality Act, the above-named alien.

_____
(Signature of Authorized Immigration Officer)

_____
(Printed Name and Title of Authorized Immigration Officer)

Certificate of Service

I hereby certify that the Warrant for Arrest of Alien was served by me at _____
(Location)

on _____ on _____, and the contents of this
(Name of Alien)   (Date of Service)

notice were read to him or her in the _____ language.
(Language)

_____   _____
Name and Signature of Officer   Name or Number of Interpreter (if applicable)

Form I-200 (Rev. 09/16)

Form I–205　　　Warrant of removal/deportation

DEPARTMENT OF HOMELAND SECURITY
U.S. Immigration and Customs Enforcement

WARRANT OF REMOVAL/DEPORTATION

File No: _____

Date: _____

To any immigration officer of the United States Department of Homeland Security:

_____
(Full name of alien)

who entered the United States at _____ on _____
(Place of entry)　　　　　　　　　　　　　　　(Date of entry)

is subject to removal/deportation from the United States, based upon a final order by:

☐ an immigration judge in exclusion, deportation, or removal proceedings

☐ a designated official

☐ the Board of Immigration Appeals

☐ a United States District or Magistrate Court Judge

and pursuant to the following provisions of the Immigration and Nationality Act:

I, the undersigned officer of the United States, by virtue of the power and authority vested in the Secretary of Homeland Security under the laws of the United States and by his or her direction, command you to take into custody and remove from the United States the above-named alien, pursuant to law, at the expense of:

_____
(Signature of immigration officer)

_____
(Title of immigration officer)

_____
(Date and office location)

ICE Form I-205 (8/07)　　　　　　　　　　　　　　　　　　　　　　　　Page 1 of 2

To be completed by immigration officer executing the warrant: Name of alien being removed:

_____

Port, date, and manner of removal: _____

Photograph of alien
removed

Right index fingerprint
of alien removed

_____

(Signature of alien being fingerprinted)

_____

(Signature and title of immigration officer taking print)

Departure witnessed by: _____

(Signature and title of immigration officer)

If actual departure is not witnessed, fully identify source or means of verification of departure:

_____

_____

_____

_____

If self-removal (self-deportation), pursuant to 8 CFR 241.7, check here.   ☐

Departure Verified by: _____

(Signature and title of immigration officer)

Form I-138   Immigration enforcement subpoena to appear and/or produce records

<table>
<tr>
<td colspan="2">1. To (Name, Address, City, State, Zip Code)</td>
<td colspan="2">DEPARTMENT OF HOMELAND SECURITY

**IMMIGRATION ENFORCEMENT
SUBPOENA**

to Appear and/or Produce Records
8 U.S.C. § 1225(d), 8 C.F.R. § 287.4</td>
</tr>
<tr>
<td colspan="4">Subpoena Number</td>
</tr>
<tr>
<td colspan="4">2. In Reference To

_____   _____
(Title of Proceeding)   (File Number, if Applicable)</td>
</tr>
</table>

By the service of this subpoena upon you, **YOU ARE HEREBY SUMMONED AND REQUIRED TO:**

(A) ☐ **APPEAR** before the U.S. Customs and Border Protection (CBP), U.S. Immigration and Customs Enforcement (ICE), or U.S. Citizenship and Immigration Services (USCIS) Official named in Block 3 at the place, date, and time specified, to testify and give information relating to the matter indicated in Block 2.

(B) ☐ **PRODUCE** the records (books, papers, or other documents) indicated in Block 4, to the CBP, ICE, or USCIS Official named in Block 3 at the place, date, and time specified.

Your testimony and/or production of the indicated records is required in connection with an investigation or inquiry relating to the enforcement of U.S. immigration laws. Failure to comply with this subpoena may subject you to an order of contempt by a federal District Court, as provided by 8 U.S.C. § 1225(d)(4)(B).

<table>
<tr>
<td>3. (A) CBP, ICE or USCIS Official before whom you are required to appear

Name

Title

Address

Telephone Number</td>
<td>(B) Date

(C) Time   ☐ a.m. ☐ p.m.</td>
</tr>
<tr>
<td colspan="2">4. Records required to be produced for inspection

</td>
</tr>
</table>

If you have any questions regarding this subpoena, contact the CBP, ICE, or USCIS Official identified in Block 3.

5. Authorized Official

_____
(Signature) (Sign in ink)

_____
(Printed Name)

_____
(Title)

_____
(Date)

CERTIFICATE OF SERVICE AND ACKNOWLEDGMENT OF RECEIPT

A. CERTIFICATE OF SERVICE

I certify that on _____ , I served this subpoena on the witness named in Block 1 in the following manner:

(Date)

_____

(Details of how service was effected)

_____

(Signature of Official Serving Subpoena) (Sign in ink)

_____

(Printed Name of Official Serving Subpoena)

_____

(Title of Official Serving Subpoena)

B. ACKNOWLEDGMENT OF RECEIPT

I acknowledge receipt of a copy of the subpoena on the front of this form.

Signature (Sign in ink)

Title	Date	Time
		☐ a.m. ☐ p.m.

ADMINISTRATIVE REMOVAL AND REINSTATEMENT OF PRIOR ORDER

Form I-851   Notice of intent to issue administrative removal order

Notice of Intent to Issue a Final Administrative Removal Order

In removal proceedings under section 238(b) of the Immigration and Nationality Act

FIN #

Event No:

File Number _____

To: Sample Form _____

Address: _____
(Number, Street, City, State and ZIP Code)

Telephone: _____
(Area Code and Phone Number)

Pursuant to section 238(b) of the Immigration and Nationality Act (Act) as amended, 8 U.S.C. 1228(b), the Department of Homeland Security (Department) has determined that you are amenable to administrative removal proceedings. The determination is based on the following allegations:

1. You are not a citizen or national of the United States.

2. You are a native of _____ and a citizen of _____

3. You entered the United States (at)(near) _____ on or about _____

4. At that time you entered _____

5. You are not lawfully admitted for permanent residence.

6. You were, on _____, convicted in the _____Court
   _____for the offense of _____
   in violation of _____
   for which the term of imprisonment imposed was _____.

Charge:
You are deportable under section 237(a)(2)(A)(iii) of the Act, 8 U.S.C. 1227(a)(2)(A)(iii), as amended, because you have been convicted of an aggravated felony as defined in section 101(a)(43)(   ) of the Act, 8 U.S.C. 1101(a)(43)(   ).

Based upon section 238(b) of the Act, 8 U.S.C. 1228(b), the Department is serving upon you this NOTICE OF INTENT TO ISSUE A FINAL ADMINISTRATIVE REMOVAL ORDER ("Notice of Intent") without a hearing before an Immigration Judge.

Your Rights and Responsibilities:
You may be represented (at no expense to the United States government) by counsel, authorized to practice in this proceeding. If you wish legal advice and cannot afford it, you may contact legal counsel from the list of available free legal services provided to you.

You must respond to the above charges in writing to the Department address provided on the other side of this form within 10 calendar days of service of this notice (or 13 calendar days if service is by mail). **The Department must RECEIVE your response within that time period.**

In your response you may: request, for good cause, an extension of time; rebut the charges stated above (with supporting evidence); request an opportunity to review the government's evidence; admit deportability; designate the country to which you choose to be removed in the event that a final order of removal is issued (which designation the Department will honor only to the extent permitted under section 241 of the Act, 8 U.S.C. 1231); and/or, if you fear persecution in any specific country or countries on account of race, religion, nationality, membership in a particular social group, or political opinion or, if you fear torture in any specific country or countries, you may request withholding of removal under section 241(b)(3) of the Act, 8 U.S.C. 1231(b)(3), or withholding/deferral of removal under the Convention Against Torture and Other Cruel, Inhuman, or Degrading Treatment or Punishment (Convention Against Torture). A grant of withholding or deferral of removal would prohibit your return to a country or countries where you would be persecuted or tortured, but would not prevent your removal to a safe third country.

You have the right to remain in the United States for 14 calendar days so that you may file a petition for review of this order to the appropriate U.S. Circuit Court of Appeals as provided for in section 242 of the Act, 8 U.S.C. 1252. You may waive your right to remain in the United States for this 14-day period. If you do not file a petition for review within this 14-day period, you will still be allowed to file a petition from outside of the United States so long as that petition is filed with the appropriate U.S. Circuit Court of Appeals within 30 calendar days of the date of your final order of removal.

_____   _____   _____
(Signature and Title of Issuing Officer)   (City and State of Issuance)   (Date and Time)

Form I-851 (Rev. 08/01/07)

Certificate of Service

I served this Notice of Intent. I have determined that the person served with this document is the individual named on the other side of the form.

_____   _____
(Signature and Title of Officer)   (Date and Manner of Service)

☐   I explained and/or served this Notice of Intent to the alien in the _____language.

_____   _____
(Name of interpreter)   (Signature of interpreter)

Location/Employer:

I Acknowledge that I Have Received this Notice of Intent to Issue a Final Administrative Removal Order.

_____   _____
(Signature of Respondent)   (Date and Time)

☐   The alien refused to acknowledge receipt of this document.

_____   _____
(Signature and Title of Officer)   (Date and Time)

☐   **I Wish to Contest and/or to Request Withholding of Removal**

☐   I contest my deportability because: *(Attach any supporting documentation)*

     ☐   I am a citizen or national of the United States.
     ☐   I am a lawful permanent resident of the United States.
     ☐   I was not convicted of the criminal offense described in allegation number 6 above.
     ☐   I am attaching documents in support of my rebuttal and request for further review.

☐   I request withholding or deferral of removal to _____[Name of Country or Countries]:

     ☐   Under section 241(b)(3) of the Act, 8 U.S.C. 1231(b)(3), because I fear persecution on account of my race, religion, nationality, membership in a particular social group, or political opinion in that country or those countries.
     ☐   Under the Convention Against Torture, because I fear torture in that country or those countries.

_____   _____   _____
(Signature of Respondent)   (Printed Name of Respondent)   (Date and Time)

☐   **I Do Not Wish to Contest and/or to Request Withholding of Removal**

☐   I admit the allegations and charge in this Notice of Intent. I admit that I am deportable and acknowledge that I am not eligible for any form of relief from removal. I waive my right to rebut and contest the above charges. I do not wish to request withholding or deferral of removal. I wish to be removed to

_____

☐   I understand that I have the right to remain in the United States for 14 calendar days in order to apply for judicial review. I do not wish this opportunity. I waive this right.

_____   _____   _____
(Signature of Respondent)   (Printed Name of Respondent)   (Date and Time)

_____   _____   _____
(Signature of Witness)   (Printed Name of Witness)   (Date and Time)

RETURN THIS FORM TO:
Department Of Homeland Security

_____

_____

_____

ATTENTION: The Department office at the above address must <u>RECEIVE</u> your response within 10 calendar days from the date of service of this Notice of Intent (13 calendar days if service is by mail).

Form I-851 (Rev. 08/01/07)

Form I–851A   Final administrative removal order

Final Administrative Removal Order

In removal proceedings under section 238(b) of the Immigration and Nationality Act

Event No:

FIN #

File Number _____

Date ____ ___ _____

To: Sample Form _____

Address: _____

(Number, Street, City, State and ZIP Code)

Telephone: _____

(Area Code and Phone Number)

ORDER

Based upon the allegations set forth in the Notice of Intent to Issue a Final Administrative Removal Order and evidence contained in the administrative record, I, the undersigned Deciding Officer of the Department of Homeland Security, make the following findings of fact and conclusions of law. I find that you are not a citizen or national of the United States and that you are not lawfully admitted for permanent residence. I further find that you have a final conviction for an aggravated felony as defined in section 101(a)(43)( ) of the Immigration and Nationality Act (Act) as amended, 8 U.S.C. 1101(a)(43)( ), and are ineligible for any relief from removal that the Secretary of Homeland Security, may grant in an exercise of discretion. I further find that the administrative record established by clear, convincing, and unequivocal evidence that you are deportable as an alien convicted of an aggravated felony pursuant to section 237(a)(2)(A)(iii) of the Act, 8 U.S.C. 1227(a)(2)(A)(iii). By the power and authority vested in the Secretary of Homeland Security, and in me as the Secretary's delegate under the laws of the United States, I find you deportable as charged and order that you be removed from the United States to:

_____

or to any alternate country prescribed in section 241 of the Act.

_____

(Signature of Authorized Official)

_____

(Title of Official)

_____

(Date and Office Location)

Certificate of Service

I served this FINAL ADMINISTRATIVE REMOVAL ORDER upon the above named individual.

_____

(Date, Time, Place and Manner of Service)

_____

(Signature and Title of Officer)

Form I-851A (Rev. 08/01/07)

Form I–871   Notice of intent/decision to reinstate prior order

U.S. Department of Homeland Security | **Notice of Intent/Decision to Reinstate Prior Order**

File No. _____

Date: _____

Name: _____

In accordance with section 241(a)(5) of the Immigration and Nationality Act (Act) and 8 CFR 241.8, you are hereby notified that the Secretary of Homeland Security intends to reinstate the order of_____entered against you. This intent
(Deportation / exclusion / removal)
is based on the following determinations:

1. You are an alien subject to a prior order of deportation / exclusion / removal entered on _____ at
(Date)

_____.
(Location)

2. You have been identified as an alien who:

☐ was removed on _____ pursuant to an order of deportation / exclusion / removal.
(Date)

☐ departed voluntarily on _____ pursuant to an order of deportation / exclusion / removal on or
(Date)
after the date on which such order took effect (i.e., who self-deported).

3. You illegally reentered the United States on or about _____ at or near _____
(Date)   (Location)

In accordance with Section 241(a)(5) of the Act, you are removable as an alien who has illegally reentered the United States after having been previously removed or departed voluntarily while under an order of exclusion, deportation or removal and are therefore subject to removal by reinstatement of the prior order. You may contest this determination by making a written or oral statement to an immigration officer. You do not have a right to a hearing before an immigration judge.

The facts that formed the basis of this determination, and the existence of a right to make a written or oral statement contesting this determination, were communicated to the alien in the _____ language.

_____   _____
(Printed or typed name of official)   (Signature of officer)

_____
(Title of officer)

Acknowledgment and Response

I ☐ do ☐ do not wish to make a statement contesting this determination.

_____   _____
(Date)   (Signature of Alien)

Decision, Order, and Officer's Certification

Having reviewed all available evidence, the administrative file and any statements made or submitted in rebuttal, I have determined that the above-named alien is subject to removal through reinstatement of the prior order, in accordance with section 241(a)(5) of the Act.

_____   _____   _____
(Date)   (Location)   (Signature of authorized deciding official)

_____   _____
(Printed or typed name of official)   (Title)

Form I-871 (Rev. 08/01/07)

EXPEDITED REMOVAL

Form I–867AB   Record of sworn statement in proceedings under section 235(b)(1) of the Act

Record of Sworn Statement in Proceedings under Section 235(b)(1) of the Act

U.S. Department of Homeland Security

Office: _____   File No: _____

Statement by: _____

In the case of: _____

Date of Birth: _____   Gender (circle one):   Male   Female

At: _____ Date: _____

Before: _____
                                        (Name and Title)

In the _____ language. Interpreter _____ Employed by _____

I am an officer of the United States Department of Homeland Security. I am authorized to administer the immigration laws and to take sworn statements. I want to take your sworn statement regarding your application for admission to the United States. Before I take your statement, I also want to explain your rights, and the purpose and consequences of this interview.

You do not appear to be admissible or to have the required legal papers authorizing your admission to the United States. This may result in your being denied admission and immediately returned to your home country without a hearing. If a decision is made to refuse your admission into the United States, you may be immediately removed from this country, and if so, you may be barred from reentry for a period of 5 years or longer.

This may be your only opportunity to present information to me and the Department of Homeland Security to make a decision. It is very important that you tell me the truth. If you lie or give misinformation, you may be subject to criminal or civil penalties, or barred from receiving immigration benefits or relief now or in the future.

Except as I will explain to you, you are not entitled to a hearing or review.

U.S. law provides protection to certain persons who face persecution, harm or torture upon return to their home country. If you fear or have a concern about being removed from the United States or about being sent home, you should tell me so during this interview because you may not have another chance. You will have the opportunity to speak privately and confidentially to another officer about your fear or concern. That officer will determine if you should remain in the United States and not be removed because of that fear.

Until a decision is reached in your case, you will remain in the custody of the Department of Homeland Security.

Any statement you make may be used against you in this or any subsequent administrative proceeding.

Page 1 of _1_   I-867A (08/01/07)

Jurat for Record of Sworn Statement in
Proceedings under Section 235(b)(1) of the Act

U.S. Department of Homeland Security

Q: Why did you leave your home country or country of last residence?

A.

Q. Do you have any fear or concern about being returned to your home country or being removed from the United States?

A.

Q. Would you be harmed if you are returned to your home country or country of last residence?

A.

Q. Do you have any question or is there anything else you would like to add?

A.

I have read (or have had read to me) this statement, consisting of __1__ pages (including this page). I state that my answers are true and correct to the best of my knowledge and that this statement is a full, true and correct record of my interrogation on the date indicated by the above named officer of the Department of Homeland Security. I have initialed each page of this statement (and the corrections noted on page(s)_____).

Signature: _____

Sworn and subscribed to before me at _____
on _____.

_____
Signature of Immigration Officer

Witnessed by:_____

Page __1__ of __1__

I-867B (08/01/07)

Form M–444   Information about credible fear interview

U.S. Department of Homeland Security   **Information about Credible Fear Interview**

Purpose of this notice

The purpose of this notice is to explain what will happen while you are in detention, what rights you have, and what may happen to you as a result of statements you make. It is important that you understand your rights and what will happen. **PLEASE READ THIS NOTICE CAREFULLY.**

You have been detained because the U.S. Department of Homeland Security (DHS) believes that you may not have the right to stay in the United States. You have indicated an intention to apply for asylum or a fear of persecution or return to your country. You will be interviewed by a specially-trained asylum officer to determine if you have a "credible fear of persecution." You will be detained until that interview takes place. If the DHS finds that you have a credible fear of persecution, you may or may not be released.

Right to consult with other persons

Normally, the interview will not take place sooner than 48 hours after you arrive at the detention facility. You may use this time to rest and consult with family members, friends, or other representatives. In unusual circumstances, you may be given additional time to contact someone. If you need this additional time, you should inform a DHS officer. You may request that the interview take place sooner if you are prepared to discuss your fears or claim immediately.

You may consult with a person or persons of your choosing, provided that such consultation is at no expense to the government and does not delay the process. A person of your choice can be present with you at your interview. A list of representatives who may be able to speak to you free of charge is attached to this notice. You may use the telephone while you are in detention to call a representative, friend or family member in the United States, collect or at your own expense. If you wish to call someone, you should inform an DHS officer for assistance. You also may contact the United States Office of the United Nations High Commissioner for Refugees, at (202) 296-5191 from 9:00 a.m - 5:00 p.m. (eastern standard time), Monday thru Friday.

Description of credible fear interview

The purpose of the credible fear interview is to determine whether you might be eligible to apply for asylum before an immigration judge. This interview is not your formal asylum hearing. It is only to help us determine whether there is a significant possibility that you may qualify as a refugee.

At your interview, you will have the opportunity to explain to the asylum officer why you think you should not be returned to your home country. If you want to apply for asylum in the United States, or think you will be harmed, persecuted or tortured if you return to your home country, you must show an asylum officer that you have a credible fear of being harmed or persecuted because of your race, religion, nationality, membership in a particular social group or political opinion, or that it is likely that you will be tortured.

If the officer determines that you have a credible fear or persecution or that you might face torture if you are returned to your home country, you may be eligible to remain in the United States.

It is very important that you tell the officer all the reasons why you have concerns about returning to your home country or are afraid to return to your home country. There are regulations protecting the confidentiality of asylum claims.

It is also very important that you tell the truth during your interview. Although the purpose of this interview is not to gather evidence against you, failure to tell the truth could be used against you in this or any future immigration proceeding.

Form M-444 (Rev. 08/01/07)

946

Need for interpreter or special consideration

If you do not speak English well or if you prefer to be interviewed in your own language, DHS will provide an interpreter for the interview. The interpreter has been told to keep the information you discuss confidential. If the interpreter is not translating correctly or you don't feel comfortable with the interpreter, you may request another interpreter. The officer will take written notes.

If you will need to tell the asylum officer information that is very personal and very difficult to talk about, you may request a female officer and female interpreter, or a male officer and male interpreter. The DHS will provide them if they are available. You will also have the opportunity to speak with the asylum officer separately from your family if you so desire.

Consequences of failure to establish credible fear and review of determination

If the asylum officer determines that you do not have a credible fear of persecution, you may request to have that decision reviewed by an immigration judge. The immigration judge's review will be in person or by telephone or video connection. The review will happen as soon as possible, to the maximum extent practicable within 24 hours, but in no case later than 7 days from the date of the asylum officer's decision. You may consult with a person or person of your choosing before the review by the immigration judge, provided it does not cause unreasonable delay. You will be given a copy of the asylum officer's record of determination to examine prior to the review by the immigration judge. If any of the information is incorrect, you should notify the immigration judge. The immigration judge may decide that you do have a credible fear and that you are eligible for a full asylum hearing before an immigration judge. If you are ordered removed, you may be barred from reentry to the United States for a period of 5 years or longer.

Interpreter Certification

I _____ (name of interpreter) certify that I am fluent in both the _____
and English languages, that I interpreted the above information from English to _____ completely and
accurately, and that the recipient understood my interpretation.

_____
Signature of interpreter

_____
Date

Alien Acknowledgment of Receipt

I acknowledge that I have been given notice concerning my credible fear interview. I understand that I may consult with a person or persons of my choosing prior to the interview as long as it does not unreasonably delay the process and is at no expense to the Government.

_____
Alien's signature

_____
Date

Form M-444 (Rev. 08/01/07)

Form I–869 Record of negative credible fear finding and request for review by immigration judge

U. S. Department of Homeland Security
U.S. Citizenship and Immigration Services

Record of Negative Credible Fear Finding and Request For Review by Immigration Judge

Alien File Number:

1. To be explained to the alien by the asylum officer:

U.S. Citizenship and Immigration Services (USCIS) has determined that you do not have a credible fear of persecution or torture pursuant to 8 CFR 208.30 for the following reason(s):

A. ☐ You have not established a credible fear of persecution in your country of nationality, country of last habitual residence, or a country to which you have been ordered removed because:

 ☐ You have not indicated that you were harmed in the past and you have not expressed fear of future harm.

 ☐ There is no significant possibility that you could establish in a full hearing that the harm you experienced and/or the harm you fear is on account of your race, religion, nationality, political opinion, or membership in a particular social group.

 ☐ You have not indicated that you were harmed in the past, and there is no significant possibility you could establish in a full hearing that the harm you fear is well founded.

 ☐ There is no significant possibility that you could establish in a full hearing that the harm you experienced or fear was/is sufficiently serious to amount to persecution.

 ☐ There is no significant possibility that you could establish in a full hearing that the entity that harmed you or would harm you was/is an agent of the government or an entity the government was/is unable or unwilling to control.

 AND

☐ You have not established a credible fear of torture in a country to which you have been ordered removed because you have not established that there is a significant possibility that:

 ☐ You would suffer severe physical or mental pain or suffering.

 ☐ The harm you fear would be specifically intended to inflict severe physical or mental pain or suffering.

 ☐ The harm you fear would be inflicted by or at the instigation of, or with the consent or acquiescence of, a public official or other person acting in an official capacity.

 ☐ The harm you fear would be inflicted while you are in the custody or physical control of the offender.

 ☐ The harm you fear would not arise only from, would not be inherent in, and would not be incidental to, lawful sanctions.

B. ☐ Considering the totality of the circumstances and all relevant factors, you have not established that your testimony is credible.

Therefore, you are ordered removed from the United States. You may request that an Immigration Judge review this decision.

If you request that an Immigration Judge review this decision, you will remain in detention until an Immigration Judge reviews your case. That review could occur as long as 7 days after you receive this decision.

If you do not request that an Immigration Judge review the decision, you may be removed from the United States immediately.

2. To be completed by the alien:

☐ **Yes, I request Immigration Judge review** of the decision that I do not have a credible fear of persecution or torture.

☐ **No, I do not request Immigration Judge review** of the decision that I do not have a credible fear of persecution or torture.

Applicant's Last Name/ Family Name (Print)	Applicant's First Name (Print)	Applicant's Signature

Asylum Officer's Last Name (Print)	Asylum Officer's First Name, (Print)	Date

The contents of this form were read and explained to the applicant in the _____ language

Interpreter used:

By telephone (list interpreter service /ID number used _____).

In person (I, _____ , certify that I am fluent in both the _____ and English languages. I interpreted the above information completely and accurately to the alien.)

Interpreter's Signature	Date

Form I-869 (02/15/17)

Form I–863   Notice of referral to immigration judge

U.S. Department of Homeland Security

Notice of Referral to Immigration Judge

	Date
	A-File
Name	**Country of Citizenship**
Place and Manner of Arrival null	**Date of Arrival**

To immigration judge:

☐ 1. The above-named alien has been found inadmissible to the United States and ordered removed pursuant to section 235(b)(1) of the Immigration and Nationality Act (Act). A copy of the removal order is attached. The alien has requested asylum and/or protection under the Convention against Torture and the matter has been reviewed by an asylum officer who has concluded the alien does not have a credible fear of persecution or torture. The alien has requested a review of that determination in accordance with section 235(b)(1)(B)(iii)(III) of the Act and 8 CFR § 208.30(g).

☐ 2. The above-named alien arrived in the United States as a stowaway and has been ordered removed pursuant to section 235(a)(2) of the Act. The alien has requested asylum and/or withholding of removal under the Convention against Torture and the matter has been reviewed by an asylum officer who has concluded the alien does not have a credible fear of persecution or torture. The alien has requested a review of that determination in accordance with section 235(b)(1)(B)(iii)(III) of the Act.

☐ 3. The above-named alien arrived in the United States in the manner described below and has requested asylum and/or withholding of removal under the Convention against Torture. The matter is referred for a determination in accordance with 8 CFR § 208.2(c). Arrival category (check one):

   ☐ Crewmember/applicant   ☐ Crewmember/refused   ☐ Crewmember/landed

   ☐ Crewmember/violator   ☐ VWP/applicant   ☐ VWP/violator

   ☐ 235(c) order   ☐ S-visa nonimmigrant   ☐ Stowaway: credible fear determination attached

☐ 4. The above-named alien has been ordered removed by an immigration officer pursuant to section 235(b)(1) of the Act. A copy of the removal order is attached. In accordance with section 235(b)(1)(C) of the Act, the matter is referred for review of that order. The above-named alien claims to be (check one):

   ☐ a United States citizen   ☐ a lawful permanent resident alien

   ☐ an alien granted refugee status under section 207 of the Act   ☐ an alien granted asylum under section 208 of the Act.

☐ 5. The above-named alien has been ordered removed pursuant to section 238(b) of the Act, or the Department of Homeland Security (DHS) has reinstated a prior exclusion, deportation, or removal order of the above-named alien pursuant to section 241(a)(5) of the Act. A copy of the removal order and, if applicable, the notice of reinstatement, are attached. The alien has expressed fear of persecution or torture and the claim has been reviewed by an asylum officer who has concluded the alien **does not** have a reasonable fear of persecution or torture. The alien has requested a review of that determination in accordance with 8 CFR §§ 208.31(f) and (g).

☐ 6. The above-named alien has been ordered removed pursuant to section 238(b) of the Act, or the DHS has reinstated a prior exclusion, deportation, or removal order of the above-named alien pursuant to section 241(a)(5) of the Act. A copy of the removal order and, if applicable, the notice of reinstatement, are attached. The alien has expressed fear of persecution or torture and the claim has been reviewed by an asylum officer who has concluded the alien **has** a reasonable fear of persecution or torture. The matter is referred for a determination in accordance with 8 CFR § 208.31(e).

☐ 7. The Secretary of Homeland Security has determined that the release from custody of the above-named alien who is under a final order of removal would pose a special danger to the public according to the standards set in 8 CFR § 241.14(f)(1). The DHS has therefore invoked procedures to continue the alien's detention even though there is no significant likelihood that the alien will be removed from the United States in the reasonably foreseeable future. The matter is referred to the immigration judge for a review of this determination in accordance with 8 CFR § 241.14(g).

U.S. Department of Homeland Security   **Notice of Referral to Immigration Judge**

NOTICE TO APPLICANT

You are ordered to report for a hearing before an immigration judge for the reasons stated above. Your hearing is scheduled on

_____ at _____ . You are to appear at _____
      (Date)   **(Time)**

(Complete office address)

☐ You may be represented in this proceeding, at no expense to the government, by an attorney or other individual authorized and qualified to represent persons before an Immigration Court. If you wish to be so represented, your attorney or representative should appear with you at this hearing. In the event of your release from custody, you must immediately report any change of your address to the Immigration Court on Form EOIR-33, which is provided with this notice. If you fail to appear for a scheduled hearing, a decision may be rendered in your absence.

☐ You may consult with a person or persons of your own choosing prior to your appearance in Immigration Court. Such consultation is at no expense to the government and may not unreasonably delay the process.

☐ Attached is a list of recognized organizations and attorneys that provide free legal service.

_____
(Signature and title of immigration officer)

CERTIFICATE OF SERVICE

☐ The contents of this notice were read and explained to the applicant in the _____ language.

☐ The original of this notice was delivered to the above-named applicant by the undersigned on _____ and the alien has been advised of communication privileges pursuant to 8 CFR 236.1(e). Delivery was made:

    ☐ in person   ☐ by certified mail, return receipt requested   ☐ by regular mail

_____
(Signature and title of immigration officer)

Attachments to copy presented to immigration judge:

☐ Passport   ☐ Form I-860

☐ Visa   ☐ Form I-869

☐ Form I-94   ☐ Form I-898

☐ Forensic document analysis   ☐ Asylum officer's reasonable fear determination worksheet (I-899)

☐ Fingerprints and photographs   ☐ Asylum officer's credible fear determination worksheet (I-870)

☐ EOIR-33

☐ FOR 8 CFR 241.14(f) CASES ONLY: Written statement including summary of the basis for the Secretary's determination to continue the alien in detention, and description of the evidence relied on in finding the alien specially dangerous (with supporting documents attached).
☐ FOR 8 CFR 241.14(f) CASES ONLY: Written notice advising the alien of initiation of proceedings and informing alien of procedures governing the Reasonable Cause Hearing at 8 CFR 241.14(h).

☐ Other (specify): _____

Page 2 of 2   Form I-863 (Rev. 08/01/07)

Form I-860   Notice and order of expedited removal

U.S. Department of Homeland Security   **Notice and Order of Expedited Removal**

DETERMINATION OF INADMISSIBILITY

File No: _____

Date: _____

In the Matter of: _____

Pursuant to section 235(b)(1) of the Immigration and Nationality Act (Act), (8 U.S.C. 1225(b)(1)), the Department of Homeland Security has determined that you are inadmissible to the United States under section(s) 212(a) ☐ (6)(C)(i); ☐ (6)(C)(ii); ☐ (7)(A)(i)(I); ☐ (7)(A)(i)(II); ☐ (7)(B)(i)(I); and/or ☐ (7)(B)(i)(II) of the Act, as amended, and therefore are subject to removal, in that:

Name and title of immigration officer (Print)   Signature of immigration officer

ORDER OF REMOVAL
UNDER SECTION 235(b)(1) OF THE ACT

Based upon the determination set forth above and evidence presented during inspection or examination pursuant to section 235 of the Act, and by the authority contained in section 235(b)(1) of the Act, you are found to be inadmissible as charged and ordered removed from the United States.

Name and title of immigration officer (Print)   Signature of immigration officer

---
Name and title of supervisor (Print)   Signature of supervisor, if available

☐ Check here if supervisory concurrence was obtained by telephone or other means (no supervisor on duty).

CERTIFICATE OF SERVICE

I personally served the original of this notice upon the above-named person on _____
                                                                            (Date)

Signature of immigration officer

Form I-860 (Rev. 08/01/07)

IMMIGRATION COURT

Form I–862　　## Notice to appear

DEPARTMENT OF HOMELAND SECURITY
NOTICE TO APPEAR

In removal proceedings under section 240 of the Immigration and Nationality Act:

File No: _____

In the Matter of:

Respondent: _____ currently residing at:

_____

(Number, street, city, state and ZIP code)　　　　　　　(Area code and phone number)

☐ You are an arriving alien.

☐ You are an alien present in the United States who has not been admitted or paroled.

☐ You have been admitted to the United States, but are removable for the reasons stated below.

The Department of Homeland Security alleges that you:

On the basis of the foregoing, it is charged that you are subject to removal from the United States pursuant to the following provision(s) of law:

☐ This notice is being issued after an asylum officer has found that the respondent has demonstrated a credible fear of persecution or torture.

☐ Section 235(b)(1) order was vacated pursuant to:　　☐ 8CFR 208.30　　☐ 8CFR 235.3(b)(5)(iv)

YOU ARE ORDERED to appear before an immigration judge of the United States Department of Justice at:

_____

(Complete Address of Immigration Court, including Room Number, if any)

on _____ at _____ to show why you should not be removed from the United States based on the
　　(Date)　　　　　　(Time)

charge(s) set forth above.

_____

(Signature and Title of Issuing Officer) (Sign in ink)

Date: _____　　_____

(City and State)

Notice to Respondent

Warning: Any statement you make may be used against you in removal proceedings.

Alien Registration: This copy of the Notice to Appear served upon you is evidence of your alien registration while you are in removal proceedings. You are required to carry it with you at all times.

Representation: If you so choose, you may be represented in this proceeding, at no expense to the Government, by an attorney or other individual authorized and qualified to represent persons before the Executive Office for Immigration Review, pursuant to 8 CFR 1003.16. Unless you so request, no hearing will be scheduled earlier than ten days from the date of this notice, to allow you sufficient time to secure counsel. A list of qualified attorneys and organizations who may be available to represent you at no cost will be provided with this notice.

Conduct of the hearing: At the time of your hearing, you should bring with you any affidavits or other documents that you desire to have considered in connection with your case. If you wish to have the testimony of any witnesses considered, you should arrange to have such witnesses present at the hearing. At your hearing you will be given the opportunity to admit or deny any or all of the allegations in the Notice to Appear, including that you are inadmissible or removable. You will have an opportunity to present evidence on your own behalf, to examine any evidence presented by the Government, to object, on proper legal grounds, to the receipt of evidence and to cross examine any witnesses presented by the Government. At the conclusion of your hearing, you have a right to appeal an adverse decision by the immigration judge. You will be advised by the immigration judge before whom you appear of any relief from removal for which you may appear eligible including the privilege of voluntary departure. You will be given a reasonable opportunity to make any such application to the immigration judge.

One-Year Asylum Application Deadline: If you believe you may be eligible for asylum, you must file a Form I-589, Application for Asylum and for Withholding of Removal. The Form I-589, Instructions, and information on where to file the Form can be found at www.uscis.gov/i-589. Failure to file the Form I-589 within one year of arrival may bar you from eligibility to apply for asylum pursuant to section 208(a)(2)(B) of the Immigration and Nationality Act.

Failure to appear: You are required to provide the Department of Homeland Security (DHS), in writing, with your full mailing address and telephone number. You must notify the Immigration Court and the DHS immediately by using Form EOIR-33 whenever you change your address or telephone number during the course of this proceeding. You will be provided with a copy of this form. Notices of hearing will be mailed to this address. If you do not submit Form EOIR-33 and do not otherwise provide an address at which you may be reached during proceedings, then the Government shall not be required to provide you with written notice of your hearing. If you fail to attend the hearing at the time and place designated on this notice, or any date and time later directed by the Immigration Court, a removal order may be made by the immigration judge in your absence, and you may be arrested and detained by the DHS.

Mandatory Duty to Surrender for Removal: If you become subject to a final order of removal, you must surrender for removal to your local DHS office, listed on the internet at http://www.ice.gov/contact/ero, as directed by the DHS and required by statute and regulation. Immigration regulations at 8 CFR 1241.1 define when the removal order becomes administratively final. If you are granted voluntary departure and fail to depart the United States as required, fail to post a bond in connection with voluntary departure, or fail to comply with any other condition or term in connection with voluntary departure, you must surrender for removal on the next business day thereafter. If you do not surrender for removal as required, you will be ineligible for all forms of discretionary relief for as long as you remain in the United States and for ten years after your departure or removal. This means you will be ineligible for asylum, cancellation of removal, voluntary departure, adjustment of status, change of nonimmigrant status, registry, and related waivers for this period. If you do not surrender for removal as required, you may also be criminally prosecuted under section 243 of the Immigration and Nationality Act.

U.S. Citizenship Claims: If you believe you are a United States citizen, please advise the DHS by calling the ICE Law Enforcement Support Center toll free at (855) 448-6903.

Sensitive locations: To the extent that an enforcement action leading to a removal proceeding was taken against Respondent at a location described in 8 U.S.C. § 1229(e)(1), such action complied with 8 U.S.C. § 1367.

Request for Prompt Hearing

To expedite a determination in my case, I request this Notice to Appear be filed with the Executive Office for Immigration Review as soon as possible. I waive my right to a 10-day period prior to appearing before an immigration judge and request my hearing be scheduled.

Before: _____

_____
(Signature of Respondent) (Sign in ink)

Date: _____

_____
(Signature and Title of Immigration Officer) (Sign in ink)

Certificate of Service

This Notice To Appear was served on the respondent by me on _____ , in the following manner and in compliance with section 239(a)(1) of the Act.

☐ in person   ☐ by certified mail, returned receipt # _____ requested   ☐ by regular mail

☐ Attached is a credible fear worksheet.

☐ Attached is a list of organization and attorneys which provide free legal services.

The alien was provided oral notice in the _____ language of the time and place of his or her hearing and of the consequences of failure to appear as provided in section 240(b)(7) of the Act.

_____   _____
(Signature of Respondent if Personally Served) (Sign in ink)   *(Signature and Title of officer) (Sign in ink)*

Privacy Act Statement

Authority:
The Department of Homeland Security through U.S. Immigration and Customs Enforcement (ICE), U.S Customs and Border Protection (CBP), and U.S. Citizenship and Immigration Services (USCIS) are authorized to collect the information requested on this form pursuant to Sections 103, 237, 239, 240, and 290 of the Immigration and Nationality Act (INA), as amended (8 U.S.C. 1103, 1229, 1229a, and 1360), and the regulations issued pursuant thereto.

Purpose:
You are being asked to sign and date this Notice to Appear (NTA) as an acknowledgement of personal receipt of this notice. This notice, when filed with the U.S. Department of Justice's (DOJ) Executive Office for Immigration Review (EOIR), initiates removal proceedings. The NTA contains information regarding the nature of the proceedings against you, the legal authority under which proceedings are conducted, the acts or conduct alleged against you to be in violation of law, the charges against you, and the statutory provisions alleged to have been violated. The NTA also includes information about the conduct of the removal hearing, your right to representation at no expense to the government, the requirement to inform EOIR of any change in address, the consequences for failing to appear, and that generally, if you wish to apply for asylum, you must do so within one year of your arrival in the United States. If you choose to sign and date the NTA, that information will be used to confirm that you received it, and for recordkeeping.

Routine Uses:
For United States Citizens, Lawful Permanent Residents, or individuals whose records are covered by the Judicial Redress Act of 2015 (5 U.S.C. § 552a note), your information may be disclosed in accordance with the Privacy Act of 1974, 5 U.S.C. § 552a(b), including pursuant to the routine uses published in the following DHS systems of records notices (SORN): DHS/USCIS/ICE/CBP-001 Alien File, Index, and National File Tracking System of Records, DHS/USCIS-007 Benefit Information System, DHS/ICE-011 Criminal Arrest Records and Immigration Enforcement Records (CARIER), and DHS/ICE-003 General Counsel Electronic Management System (GEMS), and DHS/CBP-023 Border Patrol Enforcement Records (BPER). These SORNs can be viewed at https://www.dhs.gov/system-records-notices-sorns. When disclosed to the DOJ's EOIR for immigration proceedings, this information that is maintained and used by DOJ is covered by the following DOJ SORN: EOIR-001, Records and Management Information System, or any updated or successor SORN, which can be viewed at https://www.justice.gov/opcl/doj-systems-records. Further, your information may be disclosed pursuant to routine uses described in the abovementioned DHS SORNs or DOJ EOIR SORN to federal, state, local, tribal, territorial, and foreign law enforcement agencies for enforcement, investigatory, litigation, or other similar purposes.

For all others, as appropriate under United States law and DHS policy, the information you provide may be shared internally within DHS, as well as with federal, state, local, tribal, territorial, and foreign law enforcement; other government agencies; and other parties for enforcement, investigatory, litigation, or other similar purposes.

Disclosure:
Providing your signature and the date of your signature is voluntary. There are no effects on you for not providing your signature and date; however, removal proceedings may continue notwithstanding the failure or refusal to provide this information.

TOPICAL INDEX

CITATIONS

INA § ....Section number of the Immigration
and Nationality Act
__ USCA § ....Title and section number of the U.S. Code
__ CFR § ....Title and section number of the Code of
Federal Regulations

ADJUSTMENT

Status. Immigration, this index

ADMINISTRATION

Naturalization, INA § 332

ADMINISTRATIVE PROCEDURE ACT

Immigration, government organization and employees, APA §§ 551 et seq.

ADMINISTRATIVE REMOVAL

Forms, immigration, I–851, I–851A

ADMISSION

Aliens, this index
Immigration, record of admission for permanent residence, INA § 249
Nationality, this index
Visas, this index

AFFIDAVITS

Forms, this index

AGENCY

Defined, INA § 551

AGENTS

Powers and duties, INA § 103

AGRICULTURAL ASSOCIATIONS

Aliens, temporary H–2A workers, INA § 218

AGRICULTURAL WORKERS

Immigration, selection system, INA § 210

ALASKA

Nationality at birth and collective naturalization, INA § 304

ALIENS

Additional immigration statutory provisions, categories of aliens for purposes of refugee
determinations, Designation and Adjustment of Soviet and Indochinese Refugees § 599D

TOPICAL INDEX

TOPICAL INDEX

TOPICAL INDEX

TOPICAL INDEX

---

* Available online at: http://www.uscis.gov/forms.

TOPICAL INDEX

---

* Available online at: http://www.uscis.gov/forms.

TOPICAL INDEX

---

* Available online at: http://www.uscis.gov/forms.

TOPICAL INDEX

COMMUNICATIONS

Immigration, this index

CONDITIONS

Aliens, conditional permanent resident status for alien spouses and sons and daughters, INA § 216
Crewmen, conditional permits to land temporarily, INA § 252
Forms, petition to remove conditions on residence, I–751*
Lawful permanent residence status, conditional basis for. Nationality, this index

CONTROL

Crewmen, INA § 254
Nationality, this index

CONVENTION

Refugees, convention relating to status of, 189 U.N.T.S. 137

CONVENTION AGAINST TORTURE

Nationality, asylum and withholding of removal, CFR §§ 208.16–208.18

COPIES

Nationality, copies issued by Attorney General, INA § 343

CORPSES

Travel expenses and expense of transporting remains of officers and employees dying outside United States, INA § 283

COSTS AND EXPENSES

Immigration, this index
Nationality, this index

CREDIBLE FEAR

Expedited removal forms, I–869, M–444
Nationality, this index

CREWMEN

Aliens
    Generally, INA § 251
  Conditional permits to land temporarily, INA § 252
  Control of alien crewmen, INA § 254
  Discharge of alien crewmen, INA § 256
  Employment on passenger vessels of aliens afflicted with certain disabilities, INA § 255
  Hospital treatment of alien crewmen afflicted with certain diseases, INA § 253
  Intent to evade immigration laws, INA § 257
  Limitations on performance of longshore work by alien crewmen, INA § 258
  Penalties
    Discharge of alien crewmen, INA § 256
    Intent to evade immigration laws, INA § 257
Blank forms of manifest and crew lists, INA § 282
Conditional permits to land temporarily, INA § 252
Control of alien crewmen, INA § 254
Discharge of alien crewmen, INA § 256
Employment on passenger vessels of aliens afflicted with certain disabilities, INA § 255
Hospital treatment of alien crewmen afflicted with certain diseases, INA § 253
Intent to evade immigration laws, INA § 257
Limitations on performance of longshore work by alien crewmen, INA § 258
Penalties. Aliens, ante, this heading

---

* Available online at: http://www.uscis.gov/forms.

TOPICAL INDEX

963

TOPICAL INDEX

DIRECTOR OF OFFICE OF REFUGEE RESETTLEMENT

Appointment of, INA § 411

DISCHARGE

Crewmen, discharge of alien, INA § 256

DISCLOSURE

Nationality, disclosure to third parties, asylum and withholding of removal, CFR § 208.6

DIVERSITY IMMIGRANTS

Selection system, INA §§ 201, 203

DOMESTIC RESETTLEMENT

Refugee assistance, INA § 412

ELIGIBILITY

Qualification, this index

EMPLOYMENT

Labor and Employment, this index

ENEMIES

Nationality, INA § 331

ENGLISH LANGUAGE

Nationality, INA § 312

ENTRY

Aliens, this index
Definitions, entry through or from foreign territory and adjacent islands, INA § 233

EQUIPMENT

Naturalization statistics, payment for compilation of, INA § 347

EXAMINATION

Investigation, this index
Naturalization, examination of applicants for, INA § 335

EXCEPTIONS

Immigration, adjustment of status of certain resident aliens to nonimmigrant status, INA § 247
Nationality, this index

EXCLUSION

Aliens excludable, INA § 212
Nationality, asylum and withholding of removal, CFR § 208.22
Proclamations
    Addressing Mass Migration Through the Southern Border of the United States, Proclamation No. 9822 (Nov. 9, 2018) (IV. Other Federal Materials)
    Enhancing Vetting Capabilities and Processes for Detecting Attempted Entry into the United States by Terrorists or Other Public Safety Threats, Proclamation No. 9645 (Sept. 24, 2017) (IV. Other Federal Materials)
    Improving Enhanced Vetting Capabilities and Processes for Detecting Attempted Entry Into the United States by Terrorists or Other Public-Safety Threats, Proclamation No. 9983 (Jan. 31, 2020)
    Suspension of Entry as Immigrants and Nonimmigrants of Persons who Pose a Risk of Transmitting 2019 Novel Coronavirus, Proclamation No. 9984 (Jan. 31, 2020) (IV. Other Federal Materials)
    Suspension of Entry as Immigrants and Nonimmigrants of Certain Additional Persons Who Pose a Risk of Transmitting 2019 Novel Coronavirus, Proclamation No. 9996 (Mar. 14, 2020)

TOPICAL INDEX

---

* Available online at: http://www.uscis.gov/forms.

TOPICAL INDEX

---

* Available online at: http://www.uscis.gov/forms.

TOPICAL INDEX

---

* Available online at: http://www.uscis.gov/forms.

TOPICAL INDEX

---

* Available online at: http://www.uscis.gov/forms.

TOPICAL INDEX

IMMIGRATION

Additional immigration statutory provisions
    Adjustment of status for certain Soviet and Indochinese parolees, Designation and Adjustment of Soviet and Indochinese Refugees § 599E
    Categories of aliens for purposes of refugee determinations, Designation and Adjustment of Soviet and Indochinese Refugees § 599D
Adjustment, status
    Additional immigration statutory provisions, adjustment of status for certain Soviet and Indochinese parolees, Designation and Adjustment of Soviet and Indochinese Refugees § 599E
    Admission for permanent residence, record of, INA § 249
    Change of nonimmigrant classification, INA § 248; CFR § 248.1
    Entrants before certain date, INA § 245A
    Exceptions, adjustment of statute of certain resident aliens to nonimmigrant status, INA § 247
    Naturalized citizen, effect of rescission upon, INA § 246
    Nonimmigrants, INA §§ 245, 247, 248
    Record of admission for permanent residence, INA § 249
    Removal of aliens falling into distress, INA § 250
    Rescission, effect upon naturalized citizen, INA § 246
Administrative Procedure Act, government organization and employees, APA §§ 551 et seq.
Admission for permanent residence, record of, INA § 249
Agency defined, APA § 551
Agricultural workers, selection system, INA § 210
Aliens, this index
American Indians born in Canada, INA § 289
Applications, government organization and employees, APA § 701
Armed forces, applicability to members of, INA § 284
Asylum procedure, selection system, INA § 208
Athletes, selection system, INA § 204
Attorneys, right to counsel, INA § 292
Authority of States and political subdivisions, 8 U.S.C.A. § 1624
Blank forms of manifest and crew lists, INA § 282
Bonds, deposit of and interest on cash received to secure immigration bonds, INA § 293
Burden of proof, INA § 291
Canada, American Indians born in, INA § 289
Categories of aliens for purposes of refugee determinations, Designation and Adjustment of Soviet and Indochinese Refugees § 599D
Central file, establishment of, INA § 290
Change or modification
    Public charge, this index
    Status adjustment, change of nonimmigrant classification, INA § 248
Child soldier recruitment, §§ 212, 237
Children
    Selection system, children fathered by United States citizens, INA § 204
Collection of money, INA § 286
Corpses, travel expenses and expense of transporting remains of officers and employees dying outside United States, INA § 283
Costs and expenses
    Aliens, collection of penalties and expenses, INA § 280
    Nonimmigrant visa fees, INA § 281
    Travel expenses and expense of transporting remains of officers and employees dying outside United States, INA § 283
Court. Immigration Court, this index
Crew lists, blank forms of manifest and, INA § 282
Death, travel expenses and expense of transporting remains of officers and employees dying outside United States, INA § 283
Definitions
    Agency, INA § 551
    Government organization and employees, APA §§ 551, 701
Deposit of and interest on cash received to secure immigration bonds, INA § 293
Diversity immigrants, selection system, INA §§ 201, 203
Employment. Labor and employment, post, this heading

TOPICAL INDEX

TOPICAL INDEX

IMMIGRATION AND NATURALIZATION SERVICE

IMMIGRATION COURT

INDIANS

INDOCHINESE

INSPECTION AND EXCLUSION

INTENT

---

* Available online at: http://www.uscis.gov/forms.

TOPICAL INDEX

INTEREST ON MONEY

Immigration bonds, interest on cash received to secure, INA § 293

INTERNAL SECURITY OFFICERS

Liaison with, INA § 105

INTERVIEWS

Nationality, interview before asylum officer, CFR §§ 208.9, 208.10

INVESTIGATION

Immigration, undercover investigation authority, INA § 294
Nationality, investigation of applicants for naturalization, INA § 335

JOINT PETITION

Conditional basis for lawful permanent residence status. Nationality, this index

JUDICIAL REVIEW

Aliens, judicial review of orders of removal, INA § 242

JURISDICTION

Immigrant stations, local jurisdiction over, INA § 288
Nationality, asylum and withholding of removal, CFR § 208.2

KAMPUCHEA

Immigration, preferential treatment for children fathered by United States citizens and born in
Kampuchea, INA § 204

KOREA

Immigration, preferential treatment for children fathered by United States citizens and born in
Korea, INA § 204
Nationality, this index

LABOR AND EMPLOYMENT

Aliens, this index
Crewmen, this index
Federal government (Immigration and Naturalization Service), communication between State
and local government agencies and, Personal Responsibility and Work Opportunity
Reconciliation Act of 1996, § 434, 8 U.S.C.A. § 1644
Forms, this index
Government Organization and Employees, this index
Immigration, this index
Nationality, this index

LAND ACQUISITION AUTHORITY

Powers and duties, INA § 103

LAOS

Immigration, preferential treatment for children fathered by United States citizens and born in
Laos, INA § 204

LAW ENFORCEMENT

Attorney General Press Release & Dep't of Justice, FY 2017 Solicitation for Byrne Jag Grants (IV.
Other Federal Materials)
Enforcement of the Immigration Laws to Serve the National Interest (Feb. 20, 2017) (IV. Other
Federal Materials)
Enhancing Public Safety in the Interior of the United States, Executive Order No. 13768 (Jan. 25,
2017) (IV. Other Federal Materials)
Renewed Commitment to Criminal Immigration Enforcement (Apr. 11, 2017) (IV. Other Federal
Materials)

LIMITATIONS OR RESTRICTIONS

LOCAL JURISDICTION

LOCAL PUBLIC BENEFITS

LOSS OF NATIONALITY

MANIFEST

MODIFICATION

MONEY OR CASH

NATIONALITY

TOPICAL INDEX

TOPICAL INDEX

TOPICAL INDEX

---

* Available online at: http://www.uscis.gov/forms.

TOPICAL INDEX

TOPICAL INDEX

Status
Asylum and withholding of removal, restoration of status, CFR § 208.23
Naturalization, U.S. noncitizen national status, INA § 341
Stowaways, credible fear of persecution, CFR § 208.30
Termination
Asylum or withholding of removal or deportation, CFR § 208.24
Textbooks, publication and distribution of citizenship textbooks, INA § 346
Third parties, asylum and withholding of removal, CFR § 208.6
Torture, Convention Against Torture, CFR §§ 208.16–208.18
Totalitarian forms of government, prohibition, INA § 313
Travel outside United States, limitations on, CFR § 208.8
Treaties, application of treaties, loss of nationality, INA § 357
Vessels, constructive residence through service on certain U.S. vessels, INA § 330
Vietnam hostilities. Naturalization, ante, this heading
Virgin Islands, nationality at birth and collective naturalization, INA § 306
Voluntary action, loss of nationality, INA § 349
Withholding of removal. Asylum and withholding of removal, ante this heading
World War I. Naturalization, ante, this heading
World War II. Naturalization, ante, this heading

NATIVE-BORN CITIZEN

Nationality, loss of nationality, INA § 349

NATURALIZATION

Nationality, this index
Rescission, effect of, INA § 246

NEGATIVE CREDIBLE FEAR

Expedited removal forms, record of negative credible fear finding, I–869

NONIMMIGRANTS

Forms, this index
Immigration, this index
Qualifications for admission, INA § 214

NONPROFIT ORGANIZATIONS

Naturalization, married persons and employees of nonprofit organization, INA § 319

NOTICE

Expedited removal forms, I–860, I–862, I–863
Forms, this index

NUMBERS OR NUMBERING

Immigration, numerical limitations, selection system, INA §§ 201, 202
Nationality, INA § 333

OATHS

Expedited removal forms, record of sworn statement in proceedings under section 235(b)(1) of Act, I–867AB
Naturalization, oath of renunciation and allegiance, INA § 337

OFFICE OF REFUGEE RESETTLEMENT

Generally, INA § 411

OFFICERS AND EMPLOYEES

Immigration, this index

ORDERS

Aliens, this index

TOPICAL INDEX

TOPICAL INDEX

---

* **Available online at: http://www.uscis.gov/forms.**

TOPICAL INDEX

TOPICAL INDEX

---

* Available online at: http://www.uscis.gov/forms.

TOPICAL INDEX

---

* Available online at: http://www.uscis.gov/forms.

TOPICAL INDEX

TOTALITARIAN FORMS OF GOVERNMENT

Naturalization, prohibition, INA § 313

TRAVEL

Aliens, travel control, INA § 215
Asylum and withholding of removal, limitations on travel outside United States, CFR § 208.8
Immigration, travel expenses and expense of transporting remains of officers and employees dying outside United States, INA § 283

TREATIES

Naturalization, application of treaties, loss of nationality, INA § 357

UNDERCOVER INVESTIGATION AUTHORITY

Immigration, INA § 294

UNITED NATIONS

Refugees, cooperation of national authorities with United Nations, Protocol Relating to the Status of Refugees, Art. II, T.I.A.S. 6577, 19 U.S.T. 6223, 606 U.N.T.S. 267

VENUE

Immigration, venue of proceeding, government organization and employees, APA § 703

VERIFICATION

Forms, verification of employment eligibility, I–9*
Attorney General Press Release & Dep't of Justice, FY 2017 Solicitation for Byrne Jag Grants (IV. Other Federal Materials)

VESSELS

Naturalization, constructive residence through service on certain U.S. vessels, INA § 330

VIETNAM

Immigration, preferential treatment for children fathered by United States citizens and born in Vietnam, INA § 204
Nationality, this index

VIRGIN ISLANDS

Nationality at birth and collective naturalization, INA § 306

VISAS

Admission. Immigration, post, this heading
Forms
    Immigrant visa and alien registration application, DS–230
    Nonimmigrant visa application, DS–156
General counsel of visa office, powers and duties, INA § 104
Immigration
    Admission
        Documents, issuance of entry documents, INA §§ 221, 222, 224
        Immediate relative and special immigrant visa, issuance of entry documents, INA § 224
        Waiver of visa program for certain visitors, INA § 217
    Aliens, visa waiver program for certain visitors, INA § 217
    Nonimmigrant visa fees, INA § 281
    Selection system
        Diversity immigrants, INA § 203
        Employment-based immigrants, INA § 203
        Family-sponsored immigrants, INA § 203
        Unused immigrant visas, INA § 206
Powers and duties, visa office, INA § 104
Selection system. Immigration, ante, this heading

---

* Available online at: http://www.uscis.gov/forms.

TOPICAL INDEX

---

* **Available online at: http://www.uscis.gov/forms.**